ISBN 978-1-5279-5542-4
PIBN 10924545

1 MONTH OF
FREE
READING

at
www.ForgottenBooks.com

By purchasing this book you are eligible for one month membership to ForgottenBooks.com, giving you unlimited access to our entire collection of over 1,000,000 titles via our web site and mobile apps.

To claim your free month visit:
www.forgottenbooks.com/free924545

THE

AMERICAN DECISIONS

CASES OF GENERAL VALUE AND AUTHORITY

DECIDED IN

THE COURTS OF THE SEVERAL STATES

FROM THE EARLIEST ISSUE OF THE STATE REPORTS TO
THE YEAR 1869.

COMPILED AND ANNOTATED BY
A. C. FREEMAN,

COUNSELOR AT LAW, AND AUTHOR OF "TREATISE ON THE LAW OF JUDGMENTS,"
"CO-TENANCY AND PARTITION," "EXECUTIONS IN CIVIL CASES," ETC.

EXTRA ANNOTATED
BY THE EDITORIAL DEPARTMENT OF
THE LAWYERS CO-OPERATIVE PUBLISHING COMPANY.

·Vol. XXXIV.

BANCROFT-WHITNEY CO.   THE LAWYERS CO-OP. PUB. CO.
SAN FRANCISCO, CAL.   ROCHESTER, N. Y.
1910

AMERICAN DECISIONS.

VOL. XXXIV.

The cases re-reported in this Volume will be found originally reported in the following State Reports:

AMERICAN DECISIONS.

VOL. XXXIV.

CASES REPORTED.

CASES CITED.

AMERICAN DECISIONS.
VOL. XXXIV.

CASES

IN THE

SUPREME JUDICIAL COURT

OF

MASSACHUSETTS.

———

INHABITANTS OF LOWELL *v.* BOSTON AND LOWELL R. R. CORPORATION.

[23 PICKERING, 24.]

CORPORATIONS MUST SO EXERCISE THEIR RIGHTS as not to injure others.

RAILROAD CORPORATION REMOVING CERTAIN BARRIERS ON A HIGHWAY ARE LIABLE to a town, if the town has been subjected to a suit and recovery by a person who was injured in consequence of the removal of such barriers, the corporation having the right to remove the barriers for the purpose of constructing its road, but being guilty of negligence in not replacing them at night, and in not notifying the town of their removal.

CORPORATION IS ANSWERABLE FOR NEGLECT IN WORK DONE BY ITS AUTHORITY, though such neglect is attributable to the agents and servants of a contractor, to whom the work had been let for a stipulated sum.

FOR NEGLIGENCE OR NON-FEASANCE OF HIS SERVANTS, the principal is responsible to any person injured thereby.

IF TWO PARTIES PARTICIPATE IN A CRIMINAL ACT, neither can compel the other to indemnify him for damages suffered thereby; but if they are not equally criminal, the chief delinquent is sometimes held answerable to his less blamable coadjutor.

PARTICIPANTS IN AN OFFENSE INVOLVING MORAL TURPITUDE are all, in law, deemed equally guilty.

PARTICIPANTS IN OFFENSES NOT INVOLVING MORAL TURPITUDE are not always deemed equally in the wrong. The law will therefore consider their degrees of guilt and their relative delinquency, and administer justice between them.

CONTRIBUTIVE NEGLECT—PERSON GUILTY OF NEGLIGENCE, whereby a street is left in a dangerous condition, and the town subjected to an action and judgment for injuries suffered, can not avoid a recovery by the town on the ground that its officers and agents were also negligent in not replacing the barriers which such person had negligently failed to replace.

WHERE PARTIES ARE NOT IN PARI DELICTO, and one is compelled to pay damages, he may sue the other for contribution.

AM. DEC. VOL. XXXIV—3

TOWN SUBJECTED TO DOUBLE DAMAGES FOR NEGLIGENCE in leaving a street
in a dangerous condition can, in an action against another, by whose neg
lect the street was so left, recover single damages only, without including anything for the costs incurred by the town in the action against it.

CASE. The declaration stated that the plaintiffs were bound
to keep a certain highway in repair; that defendants entered on
such highway, removed certain barriers, required to prevent
travelers from falling into a deep cut, and neglected to replace
them; that two persons, owing to the absence of the barriers,
fell into the cut and were seriously injured; that such persons
commenced actions against plaintiffs and recovered judgment,
which, with counsel fees and costs, aggregated upwards of eight
thousand dollars. The jury gave plaintiffs a verdict for ten
thousand dollars in the present action.

Hoar and Loring, for the defendants.

Dexter, Robinson, Smith, and Ames, for the plaintiffs.

By Court, WILDE, J. Several important and interesting questions are involved in the decision of this case, which have
been ably argued by counsel, and which we have taken time to
consider with the attention and deliberation that their importance and difficulty seemed to require. Our first impressions
as to one of the questions on which the decision of the case depends, were not free from doubt. No adjudged case has been
found in all respects similar; but reasoning from analogy, taking
into consideration the principles of law, and the decided cases
which have the closest application to the question in dispute, we
have been brought to a conclusion which appears to us satisfactory, and which will enable us to administer justice between
the parties without violating any known rule of law.

The facts on which the plaintiffs rest their claim have not been
disputed except in one particular, which has been ascertained
by the jury in favor of the plaintiffs. By the report of the case
it appears, that the defendants, being authorized by law to construct a railroad from Boston to Lowell, had occasion, in so
doing, to cut across and through one of the highways situated in
Lowell, and which the plaintiffs were bound by law to keep in
repair, whereby it became necessary to place barriers across the
highway to prevent travelers from falling into the chasm or
deep cut made by the defendants. Barriers were accordingly
so placed by them. Afterwards it became necessary for the defendants to make use of the highway for the purpose of removing stone and rubbish from the deep cut, and the barriers were

removed by persons in the defendants' employ, who neglected to replace them; in consequence whereof, two persons driving along the highway, in the nighttime, were precipitated into the deep cut, and were greatly injured; and, on account thereof, recovered large damages against the plaintiffs, which the plaintiffs have been compelled to pay. The amount thus paid, they claim the right to recover of the defendants in this action, they having become liable by law to pay, and this liability having been incurred, in consequence of the negligence of the defendants' agents.

The defendants resist this claim on several grounds.

1. The principles, or most of the principles on which the defendants rely, as the first ground of defense, may well be admitted; but they furnish no criterion by which we can be guided to a legal and just decision. It is undoubtedly true, that the defendants had a right to make the excavation in the highway. And they were not bound to erect barriers across the way, provided they had given seasonable notice to the officers of the town of their intended operations. So, after barriers were erected, the defendants might take them down from time to time, if necessary, for the purpose of removing rocks and rubbish, which could not be otherwise removed. These acts the defendants were authorized to do, and can not be responsible to any one for consequential damages. But the plaintiffs' claim of indemnity is not for damages arising from these acts; they do not controvert the defendants' right to make the excavation in the highway, or to take down the barriers when necessary. The action is founded on the negligence of the defendants' agents and servants in not replacing the barriers when the works were left, the day before the accident happened. These barriers, although voluntarily erected by the defendants, were approved and adopted by the selectmen of the town; and if the defendants were under the necessity of removing them for the purpose of making use of the road, they were bound to replace them when the necessity of using the road ceased, or, at least, every evening when their agents or laborers left the works. This was imperatively required by a due regard to public safety; otherwise an accident might happen before the town had notice, actual or constructive, and no one would be responsible for the damages. It is not true, as has been contended by the defendants' counsel, that all the defendants' duties and liabilities are created and prescribed by their act of incorporation. Corporations as well as individuals, by the principles of the common law, are bound so to exer-

cise their rights as not to injure others. The principle, *sic utere tuo, ut alienum non lædas*, is of universal application.

2. But the defendants deny their responsibility for the negligence of the persons employed in the construction of that part of the railroad where the accident happened, because this section thereof had been let out to one Noonan, who had contracted to make the same for a stipulated sum, and who employed the workmen. We do not, however, think that this circumstance relieves the defendants from their responsibility. The work was done for their benefit, under their authority, and by their direction. They are therefore to be regarded as the principals, and it is immaterial, whether the work was done under contract for a stipulated sum, or by workmen employed directly by the defendants at day wages. This question was very fully discussed and settled in the case of *Bush* v. *Steinman*, 1 Bos. & Pul. 403. In that case it appeared, that the defendants had contracted with A. to repair his house for a stipulated sum. A. contracted with B. to do the work; and B. contracted with C. to furnish the materials. The servant of C. brought a quantity of lime to the house and placed it in the road, by which the plaintiff's carriage was overturned. And it was held, that the defendant was answerable for the damage. This decision is fully supported by the authorities cited and by well-established principles.

3. Another objection to the plaintiffs' claim was made in argument, which can not be sustained. It is objected that the defendants are not answerable for the tortious acts of their agents or servants. And this is true, if the acts were accompanied with force, for which an action of trespass *vi et armis* would lie, or were willfully done. But the acts complained of were not so done. The defendants' workmen had a right to remove the barriers for a necessary purpose. Their only fault was their neglect in not replacing them at night when they left their work. For this negligence or non-feasance the defendants were clearly answerable.

Thus far then the case is free from all difficulty. The defendants were answerable to the parties injured for all damages. But the doubt is, whether they are responsible to the plaintiffs.

4. It has been urged that the plaintiffs or their officers have been guilty of neglect, as well as the agents of the defendants; that it was their especial duty to see to it that their roads and streets were kept in good repair and safe for travelers; and that they, therefore, being culpable, and *participes criminis*, are not,

by the policy of the law, allowed to recover damages, as an indemnity, against their co-delinquents. This objection is certainly entitled to much consideration. The general rule of law is, that where two parties participate in the commission of a criminal act, and one party suffers damage thereby, he is not entitled to indemnity, or contribution, from the other party. So also is the rule of the civil law, *Nemo ex delicto consequi potest actionem.* The French law is more indulgent, and allows a trespasser, who has paid the whole damage, to maintain an action for contribution against his co-trespasser: Pothier on Oblig., 282. Whether the latter rule be or be not founded on a wiser policy and more equal justice, is a question which we are not called upon to decide. This case, like all others, must be decided by the law as it is, whether it be consonant with sound policy or not.

Our law, however, does not in every case disallow an action, by one wrong-doer against another, to recover damages incurred in consequence of their joint offense. The rule is, *in pari delicto potior est conditio defendentis.* If the parties are not equally criminal, the principal delinquent may be held responsible to his co-delinquent for damages incurred by their joint offense. In respect to offenses, in which is involved any moral delinquency or turpitude, all parties are deemed equally guilty, and courts will not inquire into their relative guilt. But where the offense is merely *malum prohibitum*, and is in no respect immoral, it is not against the policy of the law to inquire into the relative delinquency of the parties, and to administer justice between them, although both parties are wrong-doers. This distinction was very fully considered in a case recently decided by this court, *White* v. *Franklin Bank*, 22 Pick. 181. In that case the plaintiff had deposited in the bank a large sum of money payable at a future day, in violation of a provision in the revised statutes, which prohibits any such deposit or loan. Both parties were culpable, but as the defendants were deemed the principal offenders, it was held, that the plaintiff was entitled to recover back his deposit.

No one will question the manifest justice of that decision; and it is fully sustained by the authorities. The cases, for instance, where persons who had paid more than lawful interest on usurious contracts, have been allowed to recover back the surplus, although they were parties in illegal transactions, were decided on the same distinction. So, in *Smith* v. *Bromley*, 2 Doug. 696, which is a leading case on this point. The plaintiff, who was

the sister of a bankrupt, was persuaded to pay the defendant a
certain sum of money, which he exacted as the condition upon
which he would consent to sign the bankrupt's certificate; and
it was held, that although the transaction was illegal, the plaintiff was entitled to recover back the money paid, she not being
in pari delicto with the defendant. So money paid to a plaintiff
in a *qui tam* action, in order to compromise the action contrary
to the prohibition of the statute of 18 Eliz., c. 5, was recovered
back in the case of *Williams* v. *Hedley*, 8 East, 378. So in
Jacques v. *Golightly*, 2 W. Bl. 1073, it was held, that money
paid to a lottery-office keeper, as a premium for an illegal insurance, might be recovered back in an action for money had
and received. In all these instances, the defendants were
deemed the principal offenders, and the cases were decided on
the distinction already stated. This distinction, Chief Justice
Parker says, "is founded in sound principle, and is worthy of
adoption as a principle of common law in this country:" *Worcester* v. *Eaton*, 11 Mass. 377.

The principle established by these cases arising from illegal
contracts, has long been admitted in certain cases of torts,
where the parties were not *in pari delicto*. If a servant, in
obedience to the command of his master, commits a trespass
upon the property of another, not knowing that he is doing any
injury, he is nevertheless answerable for the tort as well as his
master, to the party injured; yet he is entitled to an action
against his master for the damages he may suffer, although the
master also was ignorant that the act commanded was unlawful;
because he is deemed the principal offender. So, if a sheriff's
deputy takes the property of A. on a writ or execution against
B., and A. recovers damages of the sheriff for the trespass, he
may maintain an action for indemnity against his deputy; and,
in a like case, if the property be taken by the command of the
plaintiff in the writ or execution against B. under a promise of
indemnity, the deputy may maintain an action against the creditor on his promise, although the deputy be himself a trespasser.
So, also, if A., with a forged warrant, should arrest B., and
command C., to whom he shows his warrant, to confine B. a
reasonable time, until he could carry him to prison, and C., being ignorant of the forgery, confines him accordingly, an action
for indemnity by C. against A. would lie, notwithstanding both
parties were trespassers: *Fletcher* v. *Harcot*, Hutt. 55; 1 Roll.
Abr. 95, 98. The distinction in all these cases is the same.

The parties are not *in pari delicto*, and the principal offender is held responsible.

This distinction is manifest in the case under consideration. The defendants' agent, who had the superintendence of their works, was the first and principal wrong-doer. It was his duty to see to it that the barriers were put up when the works were left at night; his omission to do it was gross negligence; and for this the defendants were clearly responsible to the parties injured. In this negligence of the defendants' agent, the plaintiffs had no participation. Their subsequent negligence was rather construct- ive than actual. The most that can be said of it is, that one of their selectmen confided in the promise of the defendants' agent to keep up the barriers; and by this misplaced confidence the plaintiffs have been held responsible for damages to the injured parties. If the defendants had been prosecuted instead of the town, they must have been held liable for damages, and from this liability they have been relieved by the plaintiffs. It can not therefore be controverted, that the plaintiffs' claim is founded in manifest equity. The defendants are bound in justice to indemnify them so far as they have been relieved from a legal liability; and the policy of the law does not in the present instance interfere with the claim of justice. The circumstances of the case distinguish it from those cases where both parties are *in pari delicto*, and one of them, having paid the whole dam- ages, sues the other for contribution.

From a view of the evidence reported, and the finding of the jury, we are to consider, that the defendants' agents or servants were, while employed in the construction of the railroad, the principal, if not the only, actual delinquents, and that for their delinquency the defendants are responsible to all persons suffer- ing damage thereby; and they, in their turn, may maintain an action for indemnity against their negligent agents or ser- vants. Unless, therefore, the plaintiffs are estopped by some inflexible principle of law, they are entitled to indemnity, so far as they have suffered a loss by the fault of the defendants' servants; and holding as we do, for the reasons stated, that they are not so estopped, we are of opinion, that they are entitled to recover. They are not, however, entitled to a full indemnity, but only to the extent of single damages. To this extent only were the defendants liable to the parties injured; and so far as the plaintiffs have been held liable beyond that extent, they have suffered from their own neglect; and whether it was actual or constructive, is immaterial. The damages were doubled by

reason of the neglect of the town; and although there was, in
fact, no actual negligence, yet constructive negligence was sufficient to maintain the action against them; and they must be
responsible for the increased amount of damages, and can not
throw the burden on the defendants.

The only remaining question relates to the costs of the former
action against the town. And we are of opinion, that the plaintiffs are not entitled to recover any part of those costs. The
ground of defense in that action, on the part of the town, was,
that they had no sufficient notice of the defect in the road, and
that the remedy for the injured party was against the present
defendants. The suit therefore was not defended at the request
of the defendants or for their benefit; at least, no such request
has been proved; and the ground of defense taken by the town
in the former action, is well remembered, although it does not
appear in the present report. If the claim of the injured parties had been made on the defendants, or if they had had notice
that the town defended the suit against them in behalf of the
defendants, they might have compromised the claim. But however this may be, we think there is no ground on which the defendants can be held liable for the costs and expenses of the
suit against the town.

Judgment for the plaintiffs.

———

NEGLIGENCE OF PERSON, BY WHICH A PUBLIC STREET IS LEFT IN AN UN-
SAFE AND DANGEROUS CONDITION, will, if the town be subjected to an action
and judgment for injuries resulting therefrom, enable the latter to maintain an
action against the person by whose neglect the injuries were caused. The
town and the person whose negligence was the immediate cause of the injuries complained of are not, in such case, *in pari delicto.* The principal case
is a leading authority upon this subject, and has been frequently cited and
approved in the same state. Upon the authority of the principal case, the
position has been fully sustained, that the party who placed an obstruction
in the highway can not resist the claim of the town to indemnity for damages paid, on the ground that the neglect of the town to remove the obstruction contributed to the injury: *Woburn* v. *Boston and Lowell R. R. Co.*, 109
Mass. 285; *Gray* v. *Boston Gas Light Co.*, 114 Id. 154; *West Boylston* v. *Mason*, 102 Id. 342; *Inhabitants of Milford* v. *Holbrook*, 9 Allen, 23; *Snow* v.
Housatonic R. R. Co., 8 Id. 443; *Inhabitants of Swansey* v. *Chace*, 16 Gray,
304; *Boston* v. *Worthington*, 10 Id. 499; *Lowell* v. *Short*, 4 Cush. 277; *Inhabitants of Andover* v. *Sutton*, 12 Metc. 189. The person whose neglect produced the injuries is the party upon whom the ultimate liability rests. A
payment by such person of a sum of money to the plaintiff in satisfaction of
the damage sustained by him, is a bar to a subsequent action for the same injury against the town which was bound to keep the highway in repair: *Brown*
v. *Cambridge*, 3 Allen, 474, citing the principal case. In *Campbell* v. *Somerville*, 114 Mass. 334, the plaintiff contracted with the defendant to dig trenches
in its streets for the purpose of laying down water pipe, the former agreeing

so be responsible for all damages caused by his negligence, and also that twenty per cent. of the contract price should be reserved until the work was finished, as a guaranty for its full performance, and that any damage done to persons or property should be deducted from the twenty per cent. reserved. Suit having been brought against the town for personal damage occasioned by falling into one of the trenches, and the plaintiff being notified and assisting in its defense, and a recovery being had against the town, it was held, in an action brought by the plaintiff to recover pay for digging the trenches, that the town and the plaintiff were not *in pari delicto*, and that the town could recoup in damages the amount paid in the former suit, although in excess of the stipulated twenty per cent. of the contract price reserved for the purpose of defraying such demands.

"It is too late," said Colt, J., in that case, "under the decisions of this court, to object that it is against public policy to allow the set-off claimed, or that the parties are to be treated as *in pari delicto*, so that neither is entitled to contribution or indemnity." And the principal case is relied upon to support the judgment. Where, however, a mill-owner had overflowed a public highway, and rendered it so unsafe and impassable that the town, which was legally bound to keep it in repair, was indicted for unseasonably neglecting to do so, and compelled to pay costs as well as to make the necessary repairs; in an action by the town against the mill-owner, to recover the amount expended in repairing the road and rendering it safe, the costs of the indictment were not allowed, in addition to the cost of the repairs and interest thereon from the day of demand: *Andover v. Sutton, supra.* And where the town makes the necessary repairs, and recovers judgment against the person who, as against the town, was bound to repair the highway, the latter can not recover costs against a corporation whose charter bound it to make the repairs, and which had neglected so to do, unless, in the action by the town, the suit was defended by such person, at the request of the corporation, or for its benefit, or after notice to it to appear and defend: *Locks and Canals v. Lowell Horse R. R. Co.*, 109 Mass. 221, citing the principal case. Cited and approved also in *Cheshire v. Adams and Cheshire Reservoir Co.*, 119 Id. 356.

SIMONDS, JUN., *v.* HEARD ET AL.

[23 PICKERING, 120.]

AGENT IS NOT PERSONALLY LIABLE when acting in the name of his principal and within the scope of his authority.

AGENT IS PERSONALLY RESPONSIBLE ON CONTRACTS which show an intention to bind himself personally.

AGENT ACTING IN A PUBLIC CAPACITY, and making a contract on behalf of the public, is not personally answerable thereon.

COMMITTEE OF A TOWN APPOINTED TO REBUILD A BRIDGE has authority to enter into all contracts necessary to accomplish that purpose, including the borrowing of money.

COMMITTEE OF A TOWN EXECUTING A CONTRACT IN THEIR INDIVIDUAL NAMES, therein describing themselves as a committee of the town of W., and stipulating that "said committee are to pay," etc., are personally answerable on the contract.

ASSUMPSIT against Horace Heard, Eli Sherman, and Newell Heard, by William Simonds and John Chaplin, on a writing, of which the material parts are stated in the opinion. The defendants were a committee of the town of Wayland, but the contract was signed by them individually, and they were sought to be made personally responsible. Verdict for plaintiffs

Mellen, for the defendants.

Hoar, Bigelow, and Bigelow, for the plaintiffs.

By Court, SHAW, C. J. Two points were made for the defendants in the present case; first, that the defendants, having acted as a committee of the town of Wayland, in making the contract with the plaintiffs, and that, in relation to the erection of a bridge, in which they had no personal concern, but which was the concern of the town, and being duly authorized by the town to act in their behalf, were not personally liable to an action on the contract; and secondly, that the work had not been executed according to the contract. The latter was submitted to the jury as a question of fact, who found for the plaintiffs, that the contract had been duly executed on their part. The other is a question of law and turns upon the construction of the contract, which is set forth in the case. It has been fully argued, and many authorities are cited on both sides.

The question, whether a contract made by persons acting or professing to act, as agents for others, binds their principals, or themselves, or both, is often one of great difficulty. The cases run so closely into each other, that whether a particular contract falls within one or the other of these lines, it is not easy to determine. Some rules are well settled; as, where an agent acts within the scope of his authority, and professes to act in the name and behalf of his principal, he is not personally liable. So one standing and acting in a public capacity, who makes a contract in behalf of the public, is not personally liable: *Macbeath* v. *Haldimand,* 1 T. R. 172; *Hodgson* v. *Dexter,* 1 Cranch, 345; *Freeman* v. *Otis,* 9 Mass. 271. But this rule is not applicable to the present case, it not being a contract in behalf of the public, but, at most, of a corporation capable of making contracts and liable to an action on its contracts.

It was contended, that the defendants did not act within the scope of their authority, because inasmuch as the town, by appropriating money, and empowering them to borrow money on the credit of the town, had furnished them the means of performing the duty authorized, there was no necessity for binding the town by a contract. But we are of opinion, that the votes of the town appointing them a committee to rebuild the bridge, which the town, in its corporate capacity, was under obligation to rebuild, carried with them an implied authority to make the necessary contracts for that purpose: *Damon* v. *Granby*, 2 Pick. 345. We think also that it is manifest, from the subject-matter of the contract and from their describing themselves as a committee, that they were acting under some authority from the town.

But without going into all the distinctions on this very prolific subject, there is one rule, well established by authorities, and defined with a good degree of certainty, which is applicable to this case. It is this, that although an agent is duly authorized, and although he might avoid personal liability by acting in the name and behalf of his principal, still, if by the terms of his contract he binds himself personally, and engages expressly in his own name to pay or perform other obligations, he is responsible though he describe himself as agent: *Appleton* v. *Binks*, 5 East, 148; *Tippets* v. *Walker*, 4 Mass. 595; *Duvall* v. *Craig*, 2 Wheat. 56; *Stone* v. *Wood*, 7 Cow. 453. These are cases of specialty, in which perhaps some more exactness in the mode of execution is necessary, in order to bind the principal and exempt the agent; but the same principle is held to apply in cases of simple contract when, from the relation in which the party stands, or from the terms of the contract itself, it is obvious that the agent intended to become personally responsible: *Forster* v. *Fuller*, 6 Mass. 58. Where one, as president of an incorporated company having authority to make notes, signed a promissory note by which he promised to pay, it was held that he was liable upon the personal engagement and promise to pay, though he described himself as president of such company, and that it was not the note of the company: *Barker* v. *Mechanics' Bank*, 3 Wend. 94. A known agent of a country bank drawing a bill and directing the drawees to place the amount to the account of such bank, was held personally liable: *Leadbitter* v. *Farrow*, 5 Mau. & Sel. 34. In a more recent case, where the solicitors to the assignees of a bankrupt gave an agreement to this effect, " We, as solicitors, etc., do hereby undertake to pay," it was held that they were personally bound: *Burrell* v. *Jones*, 3 Barn. & Ald. 47. In this case Mr. Justice Bayley says: " It is clear that an agent may so contract as to make himself personally liable, and I think the words here used, ' we undertake,' are sufficient to place the defendants in that situation:" *Norton* v. *Herron*, 1 Car. & P. 648; *Eaton* v. *Bell*, 5 Barn. & Ald. 34.

In examining this contract the court are of opinion, that it falls clearly within this rule. The introductory part is an agreement "between Horace Heard, Eli Sherman, and Newell Heard, committee of the town of Wayland, on the one part, and William Simonds and John Chapin, on the other part;" and after a specific description of the work to be done, the contract on the part of the defendants is this: "Said committee are to pay said Simonds and Chaplin the sum of three hundred and seventy-five dollars when said work is completed," etc.

Two things are here observable. The first is, that they do not profess to act in the name or behalf of the town, otherwise than as such an intention may be implied from describing themselves as a committee. But such description, although it may have some weight, is far from being conclusive, and in many of the cases cited, a similar designation was used, which was held to be a mere *descriptio personarum*, and designed to show for whose account the contract was made, and to whose account the amount paid under such contract should be charged. The second and more decisive circumstance respecting this contract is, that here is an express undertaking on the part of the committee to pay. "Said committee are to pay said Simonds and Chaplin," etc. Having described themselves as a committee, this undertaking is as strong and direct as if the names had been repeated, and Heard, Sherman, and Heard, had promised to pay.

The court are therefore of opinion, that by the terms of this contract, the committee intended to bind themselves, and did become personally responsible, and that the action is well brought against them. Nor is it to be considered very improbable, that they should intend thus to contract personally, if, indeed, the subject was distinctly presented to their minds. Being furnished by the town with ample means to meet any engagement they might enter into, to an amount beyond the payments to be made by this contract, such personal responsibility would be considered as subjecting them to very little risk. The subsequent vote of the town passed after this action was brought, can have no effect upon the present question, of the personal liability of the defendants upon this contract when it was made and executed. On the other point, the admissibility of the evidence tending to show that the plaintiffs considered the town as their debtors, the objection came from the plaintiffs, and therefore, as the other question is now decided, this point is immaterial. But as some argument was had on the effect of that evidence, it may be proper to make a remark respecting it.

We think the evidence was competent, being the acts and declarations of the plaintiffs, tending to show to whom the credit was given. But we think, as the case stood, it was entitled to no weight. The question was, whether, by the contract, the defendants were personally liable. The plaintiffs' admission tended to show, that the plaintiffs knew that the work was done under the authority of the town, in pursuance of a corporate duty, and that the work was ultimately to be paid for, out of the funds of the town. A desire and an attempt to get their pay directly of the town, by a purchase of town property and a set-off, proved nothing more than the same knowledge and understanding on their part. But their knowledge that the work was done for the town, and was ultimately to be paid for by them, was perfectly consistent with the fact, that they had the personal obligation of the committee to pay them for it. The same facts appeared on the contract itself. The evidence, therefore, had no tendency to explain or illustrate the contract in this particular, or to give effect or meaning to its terms. The jury, therefore, ought not to be influenced by it.

Judgment on the verdict for the plaintiffs.

———

AGENT IS PERSONALLY RESPONSIBLE, if he engages expressly in his own name to pay a sum of money, although he describes himself as agent, and is duly authorized by his principal to enter into the engagement, and although he might have avoided such liability by acting in the name of his principal: *Fiske* v. *Eldridge*, 12 Gray, 474; *Morell* v. *Codding*, 4 Allen, 403; *Guernsey* v. *Cook*, 117 Mass. 548; but whenever it appears upon the face of a simple contract made by the agent of a person named therein, and whom he can legally bind thereby, that he acts as agent and intends to bind his principal, the law will give effect to the intention in whatever form expressed: *Barlow* v. *Congregational Society*, 8 Allen, 460, in all of which the principal case is cited and approved.

AGENT DRAWING A BILL IN HIS OWN NAME is personally liable, when: *Newhall* v. *Dunlap*, 31 Am. Dec. 45, and cases cited in the note.

———

WILLIAMS v. NELSON ET AL.

[23 PICKERING, 141.]

PRESCRIPTION—KEEPING UP A DAM AND FLOWING THE LANDS of another for twenty years, without paying damages or being questioned, is evidence of the right to maintain such dam and flow such lands, and a bar to any action for damages in so doing. This is true under the statutes of this state as well as at common law.

ABANDONMENT OF A PRESCRIPTIVE RIGHT to maintain a dam and flood lands is not presumed from nine years non-user.

ACTION for flowing lands. The defendants showed that their mill was built in 1783, from which date, until 1826, they maintained their dam, operated their mill, and flooded the complainant's land. In 1826 they ceased to use the mill and removed the greater part of it. In 1835 it was rebuilt, and in the year after went into operation. They had never paid any damages to any one. The plaintiff proved that the mill was discontinued in 1826; that some of its owners stated to plaintiff that it would never again be operated; and that between 1826 and 1835 the lands had been improved and put into grass and used as a meadow. The trial court decided in favor of defendant.

Baylies and Miller, for the plaintiff.

Eddy and Coffin, for the defendants.

By Court, SHAW, C. J. This is a case upon the statute, for flowing, by the respondents' mill-dam; and the question is, whether they can defend, by showing that they have kept up their mill and flowed the land in question more than forty years, without payment or claim for damages, on the part of the present complainant, or those under whom he claims. I state the question thus, because, from the general tenor of the report, and from the course of the argument, I so understand the case; although construing the report literally, it is only, that the respondents, during the period mentioned, had paid no damages.

The court are of opinion, that where a mill-owner and his predecessors have in fact enjoyed and exercised the right of keeping up his dam and flowing the land of another, for a period of twenty years, without payment of damages, and without any demand or claim of damages, or any assertion of the right to damages, it is evidence of a right to flow without payment of damages, and will be a bar to such claim. It is very clear, that to raise a dam on one's own land, by which the water is set back on another's, without grant from the latter, would be a tort, for which case would lie. If such a dam is continued twenty years, without action, complaint, or protest, on the part of the land-owner, it is evidence of a right; and as such right may be and often is acquired by grant, it is taken to be presumptive evidence of a grant, and may be so pleaded: *Campbell* v. *Wilson*, 3 East, 294; *Tyler* v. *Wilkinson*, 4 Mason, 397. These principles are very clear and are constantly acted upon, where the rules of the common law apply. The question is, whether they are applicable to the case of flowing, as it is regulated in this commonwealth by statute.

The statute still regards the flowing of one's lands, by the mill-dam of another, as a grievance and cause of damage; but, on considerations of equity and public policy, it changes the mode of redress, by allowing the recovery of a gross sum, as a compensation for the perpetual easement, or an allowance of annual damages. The statute, strictly speaking, does not confer on the mill-owner the right to flow the land of another, it conveys no interest in the nature of a leasehold or easement, or otherwise, or any authority to make any actual use of the other's land, as a pond or reservoir. The owner may still embank against the water, if he pleases, and thus preserve his own land from being flowed. But the extent of the power conferred on the mill-owner by the statute is, to erect and maintain the dam on his own land, and keep up his head of water to his own best advantage, notwithstanding it may flow back on the land of others. And a mode of ascertaining and securing payment of the damages is provided.

But the statute clearly implies, that there may be a right on the part of mill-owners to flow the lands of others, without payment of damages, and provides for a mode of trying such right, considering it as a good bar to a complaint: Stat. 1797, c. 63, secs. 1, 2. It is treated as a substantive right, annexed to the mill, and belonging to its owners and occupants, into whose hands soever it may come. How can such a right be acquired? One mode certainly is, by a grant on the part of the owner of the lands flowed. It is a servitude or easement to which the land may be perpetually subjected by its owner as a right of way. It is equally visible and notorious and can not deceive purchasers. It may be founded on a composition, satisfaction, or release of damages. For as the right to erect the dam on one's own land is conferred by statute, and exists independently of any act or consent of the owner of the land to be flowed, the right to flow it free of claims for damages, is not such an interest in the land as must be necessarily proved by deed. The claim of the land-owner is personal and for damages only; and a satisfaction or release of those damages, would forever exempt the mill-owner from further claim. The statute power, and such satisfaction or release together, would constitute the right contemplated by the statute, to flow without payment of damages.

Perhaps such a right may be acquired in other ways. Suppose, for instance, a man owning a large tract of land, with a mill-site, should erect a mill and dam, and flow back, but wholly on his own land. Suppose he should sell the mill and mill-site, with the privileges and appurtenances, but not including all the land flowed; could he, against such a deed, claim of his grantee, damages for the flowing of the part of the land retained? We are inclined to think he could not. But if he could not, privies in estate, coming in under him, could not. The owner of such a mill would therefore enjoy the right of flowing such land, without paying damage, and might use it as a bar to any complaint. It is a general and highly salutary rule of law, that a right or easement which may be acquired by grant, may be acquired by long-continued peaceable use and enjoyment, without contest or claim on the part of those, who would have an interest in denying or contesting it. For convenience, such continued, uninterrupted, and uncontested use, is deemed evidence of a grant, from an owner of the land or person capable of granting: *Ricard* v. *Williams*, 7 Wheat. 109.

I have not used the term "adverse," because it sometimes happens, that such a right may be acquired and such a grant presumed, where there is no actual use made of the land or property of another, and where, therefore, the owner could bring no action, during the time the privilege is used, which, after a certain length of time, is taken to be evidence of a grant. Of this nature are the enjoyment of light and air, in a house. The owner does no act upon the property of another, for which an action would lie; he has a right to the light and air as they come to him over the land of another, and yet enjoyment for twenty years gives a right and raises the presumption of a grant: *Moore* v. *Rawson*, 3 Barn. & Cress. 332. The case of a land-owner against a mill-owner is in some respects similar. The former could maintain no action, simply for erecting and keeping up the dam; but he could file and prosecute his complaint for damages, or he could make his claim *in pais*, which, we think, would rebut the presumption of grant from mere use and enjoyment.

Perhaps there is another view in which the case may be considered. As these presumptions are made for the purpose of quieting titles and possessions, and preventing stale and obsolete claims, difficult of proof, the law will presume that act, whether grant, release, or otherwise, which will best give security to long-continued possessions, exemptions, and other privileges. Courts have sometimes said, that they would presume a judgment, or an act of parliament, or whatever act might be necessary, to give security to a long, uninterrupted, and undis-

puted enjoyment of a privilege.   The law will presume a release
or satisfaction of a mortgage or specialty debt, after twenty
years.   As there may in the outset, or at the first erection of a
mill-dam, have been a release or satisfaction of all damages ever
to arise from the flowing occasioned by such dam, why should
not twenty years' enjoyment of the privilege, without claim of
damage, upon the principles stated, be held to warrant a presumption of such satisfaction or release?

All those considerations of expediency and public policy, as
well as of law, on which the ordinary presumption is founded,
in favor of actual enjoyment, and on which such enjoyment is
deemed to be rightful, apply with great force and exactness to
the case of flowing, without liability for damage.   If such flowing were not originally rightful, on the mill-owner's own land
or by permission of the land-owner, it seems not easily accounted for, that such owner should acquiesce for a long series
of years, without any claim to damage.   The inference therefore
is, that his consent was given voluntarily, or purchased by some
deed or other act, which is lost by lapse of time.   There are undoubtedly many mill-dams, connected with ancient mills, which
do now, to a certain extent, flow the lands of others, but which
have been held and enjoyed without claim of damage for long
periods of years.   It would now be difficult, if not impossible,
in consequence of lapse of time, to prove the circumstances, under
which such mill-dams were erected, or to prove the actual satisfaction or release of damages, even where there is no reasonable doubt, that such satisfaction was made.   It would tend
greatly to disturb and unsettle this class of rights, if the right
to flow without claim of damages could only be proved by deed
or other formal express proof, and could not, like other rights
of the same nature, be established by proof of long and undisturbed enjoyment on the one side, without objection, notice, or
claim of damage on the part of him whose lands are affected and
incumbered by such enjoyment.

This decision is opposed by no direct authority, except a decision of the very respectable supreme court of Maine, upon
statutes nearly similar, if not precisely the same.   We feel the
highest deference for the judicial decisions of that eminent court.
But the case in question, *Tinkham* v. *Arnold*, 3 Greenl. 120, was
new, and it was contrary to what we believe has long been considered as law in this commonwealth, though never judicially
decided; and we think that the reasons given for the decision,
are not such as to render it a conclusive authority.   It goes upon

the ground, that as the erecting and keeping up the dam was
lawful and rightful, and made so by statute, neither the erecting
nor continuance of it could be considered as proof of a grant,
because they might be as well done without grant. It is true,
that there would be no proof of the grant of the right to erect
and keep up the dam. But the grant pleaded was of a grant of
the right to erect and keep up the dam, and to flow the complainant's land, free of any claim for damages. This was relied
on as a distinct, single, and substantive right. The statute of
1714 did not confer this right; but only a right or power to erect
and keep up the dam, paying damage. Therefore, the enjoyment of the right, free from all claim for damages, for forty
years, was a right beyond that conferred by statute. Then the
enjoyment of this entire right, beneficial to the mill-owner, and
onerous to the land-owner, without claim for damages, could
only be accounted for by-the presumption of a grant, or by the
satisfaction or release of damages, or other lawful act, inducing
this acquiescence on the part of the land-owner. The case in
Maine is founded on the implied admission, that the easement
had a lawful origin and a lawful continuance. The case also goes
on the supposition, that to found the presumption of a grant,
the enjoyment must be adverse, and of such a nature that, but
for the presumed grant, it would be unlawful. It may be
deemed adverse, if, in any degree, it tend to impose any servitude or burden on the estate of another. But, in many cases,
as the enjoyment of air and light by the owner of a house, the
act is not unlawful without a grant by the owner of the land
over which they come; yet the enjoyment of such privilege for
a long time, without obstruction or notice on the part of the
owner of the adjoining land, is proof of a right, and may raise
the presumption of a grant.

The case of a mill-owner is, in some degree, similar. He may,
by force of the statute, raise and maintain his dam, without
grant or license of the owner of the land flowed by it; but he
can not maintain it free from all claim for damage. If he does
maintain it, twenty years, free of all claim for damage, we think
it warrants the legal presumption of a grant or other lawful
origin, of such right, and establishes the right upon the principle of presumed grant.

On the subject of abandonment, the court are of opinion, that
the mere non-user for nine years, proved in the present case, is
not sufficient to extinguish the right which the defendants had
acquired, of flowing the plaintiff's land without being liable to

the payment of damages on that account. See *French* v. *Braintree Mfg. Co.*, 23 Pick. 216.

  Complaint dismissed.

———

EXERCISE OF RIGHT OF RAISING OR DIVERTING WATER FOR PERIOD OF TWENTY YEARS by maintaining a dam and flowing the lands of another, by a mill-owner, without objection or claim of damages, is evidence of a right to so use the water as if acquired by prescription or grant. The principal case is cited upon this proposition in *Cowell* v. *Thayer*, 5 Metc. 256; *Brace* v. *Yale*, 10 Allen, 441. So a right of way, as appurtenant to land, may be acquired by the adverse use, for twenty years together, of several persons in succession, who claim under the same title: *Leonard* v. *Leonard*, 7 Id. 277. And the right to the use of a ditch through the land of another, for the purpose of drainage, may be established by adverse use: *White* v. *Chapin*, 12 Id. 516. The owner of land bordering on a stream may lawfully dig a canal upon his own land, which will prevent it from being flowed by the erection or raising of a dam below, if he does not thereby divert the water from its natural course; and the fact that the owner below has already begun to build or raise his dam is immaterial: *Storne* v. *Manchaug* Co., 13 Id. 10. The "mill act," authorizing the maintenance of a dam to raise a head of water, although its effect will be to overflow the land of another proprietor, is not in any proper sense a taking of the property of the owner of the land flowed. It is a provision by law for regulating the rights of proprietors, on one and the same stream, from its rise to its outlet, in a manner best calculated to promote and secure their common rights in it: *Lowell* v. *Boston*, 111 Mass. 467. One who maintains a dam under the mill act has not such an easement in the flowed lands as will enable him to maintain a petition against the land-owner, under the general statutes, to compel him to try title: *Boston Mfg. Co.* v. *Burgin*, 114 Id. 340. In all of the cases cited above, the principal case is referred to.

———

PRUDEN ET AL. v. ALDEN.

[23 PICKERING, 184.]

LOST OR DESTROYED RECORD MAY BE PROVED by collateral or secondary evidence.

EVIDENCE—SHORT NOTES MADE BY THE CLERK in the minute book must stand as the record until a more complete and intelligible record is made up; and if, in the mean time, they are lost or destroyed, this constitutes a loss of the records, and secondary proof of their contents may be received.

LICENSE TO SELL LANDS WILL BE CONSIDERED PROVED when it is recited in a deed under which thirty years' undisturbed possession has been held, and the recital is corroborated by other circumstances, and the dockets of the court have been lost.

WRIT of right. Demandants were heirs of Peleg Gulliver, who died seised of the premises in 1806. Tenants claimed under conveyance made in 1807 by the administratrix of Gulliver, in which it was recited that "a license was obtained by order of the court of common pleas, begun and held at Plymouth, on the second Tuesday of August, 1807, to make a sale of the real estate of said deceased, so far as should be necessary," etc. One Delano testified to acting as agent for the administratrix, and applying for a license to sell, and, to his belief, that it was granted. It was shown to have been the practice of the judge to give the applications for licenses to sell to his clerk with directions of the court respecting them; that the clerk, from 1807 to 1810, was very inattentive to his duties, leaving most of them to be performed by his wife, who was unskillful in that kind of work; that the docket for August term, 1807, can not be found. The question was whether the jury would be authorized to find a legal license to sell.

Eddy and Baylies, for the demandants.

Warren and Beal, for the tenant.

By Court, SHAW, C. J. It being very clear that the administratrix could make no valid sale, without a license, the title of the tenant depends upon proof of such license. It is contended on the part of the demandants, that there is no legal proof of such a license having been granted. We think it may be admitted, as contended for by the demandants, that a license by the court of common pleas must be proved by its records. But the court are to take notice how the records of their own and of other courts are in fact made and kept. The clerk intrusted with the duty of keeping records, must of necessity take down the doings of the court, in short and brief notes; this he usually does in a minute-book called the docket, from which a full, extended, and intelligible record is afterwards to be made up. But until they can be made up, these short notes must stand as the record; and if, in the mean time, through the death or sickness of the clerk, or other casualty, they are lost, it must be deemed a loss of the records, and secondary proof may be offered of their contents: *Evans* v. *Thomas*, 2 Stra. 833; *Dayrell* v. *Bridge*, Id. 1264. If a record be lost or consumed by fire, it may be proved by collateral evidence: Com. Dig., Evidence, A, 3; *Thurston* v. *Slatford*, 1 Salk. 284.

In the present case, the license relied upon is supposed to have been granted at the August term, 1807; and is so recited in the deed to the tenant; and it is proved that the docket of that term is missing. The recital in the deed, corroborated by many other circumstances, together with more than thirty years' undisturbed possession by the tenant under a deed which could

only be good by force of such license, appears to the court to be
sufficient proof of the existence and loss of the record, to let in
secondary evidence. And from the evidence thus offered, the
court are satisfied, that such license was in fact granted, and
some minute of it entered by the clerk, which would have been
sufficient to warrant him in making up an extended record, according to the usual course of business in his office.

Under the agreement of the parties, the court are of opinion
that the jury would have been authorized to find that there was
a legal license to the administratrix to sell the estate, and that
the tenant took a good title under it: See *Whitney* v. *Sprague,*
23 Pick. 198.

Demandants nonsuit.

———

ADMISSIBILITY OF PAROL EVIDENCE TO PROVE THE CONTENTS OF LOST
WRITING: *Compton* v. *Mathews,* 22 Am. Dec. 167, and cases in this series
cited in the note. The principal case is cited to the point that after satisfactory evidence has been produced of the loss or destruction of a record, its
contents may be proved by parol, in *Eaton* v. *Hall,* 5 Metc. 290; and to the
point that the minutes or memoranda upon the docket of the clerk of the
court or a magistrate, are competent evidence of an order or proceeding, in
case the final or extended record has not been made up, it is cited in *Townsend* v. *Way,* 5 Allen, 426; *Waters* v. *Gilbert,* 2 Cush. 31, and *Benedict* v. *Cutting,*
13 Metc. 186.

———

SPEAR *v.* CUMMINGS.

[23 PICKERING, 224.]

BETWEEN SCHOOLMASTER IN PUBLIC SCHOOL AND THE PARENTS OF PUPILS,
  there is no privity of contract.

SCHOOLMASTER IN PUBLIC SCHOOL IS NOT RESPONSIBLE to a parent for refusing to receive and instruct his child.

CASE against the defendant, a teacher of a public district
school, for refusing to teach plaintiff's child. The trial judge
held, that the action was not sustainable.

Dexter and Churchill, jun., for the plaintiff.

Metcalf and Gourgas, for the defendant.

By Court, SHAW, C. J. This is an action of new impression,
and it is not known that a similar one has ever been brought in
this or any of the other states. It is certainly a consideration
of great weight, that no such action has ever been maintained,
but it is not decisive.

In the first place, it is manifest, that there is no privity of
contract, between the parents of pupils to be sent to school,

and the schoolmaster. The latter is employed and paid by the town; and to them only is he responsible on his contract. And, again, the master of a school is not an independent public officer, bound to exercise the functions of his office, for the benefit of individuals, under fixed and settled rules and obligations, prescribed by law, like a sheriff; nor is he to exercise his own will and judgment, in receiving or excluding pupils. The law provides, that every town shall choose a school committee, who shall have the general charge and superintendence of all the public schools in such town: Rev. Stat., c. 23, sec. 10. The general charge and superintendence, in the absence of express legal provisions, includes the power of determining what pupils shall be received and what pupils rejected. The committee may, for good cause, determine that some shall not be received, as, for instance, if infected with any contagious disease, or if the pupil or parent shall refuse to comply with regulations necessary to the discipline and good management of the school. But the plaintiff contends, and so he has averred in his declaration, that where an instructor is employed to keep a district town school, it is his imperative duty to receive all pupils between the ages of seven and sixteen years, who are sent to him by any parent residing in the district, and to instruct them; that it is the absolute and personal right of every parent, master, or guardian, residing within the district, to send children of either sex and within those ages, and that a refusal by the master to receive and instruct them, is a violation of such personal right, for which an action will lie. But conformably to the view already taken, we think that this is not the relation in which the master and parent stand to each other. It overlooks the superintending and managing power of the committee. It would compel the master, on peril of an action for damages, to take pupils, whom the committee might determine not to be proper subjects for admission.

But further, the argument assumes the principle, that whenever there is a breach of public duty by negligence or misfeasance, any party who sustains a damage by it, may have his action against the party guilty of such violation. But this position, to this extent, we think can not be maintained. It is made the duty of towns to keep roads in repair; but no action lies at common law in favor of an individual who suffers by the neglect of such duty: *Mower* v. *Leicester*, 9 Mass. 247. Such action will only lie, where an action is given by the statute. So, in case of a common nuisance, an action will not lie against the person causing it, at the suit of an individual who sustains an inconvenience from it, unless of a special nature affecting him differently from the rest of the community. The argument from inconvenience against such an action is also extremely forcible. If one member of the school district may have an action against the master, every member has the same right; if he may sue for a general refusal to receive and instruct a child, there seems to be no reason why an action will not lie in case the master does not instruct with due skill, capacity, and diligence. Such a state of things would not be likely to improve the condition of the schools, and would lead to vexatious and ruinous litigation.

But it is asked, what is the remedy of parents and guardians, whose children are refused the benefit of schools designed for the instruction of all. We think, if a child of proper age and qualifications is rejected by the master, the proper course for the parent is, to appeal to the committee. If, on their requisition, the master should refuse to accept the pupil, they would have ample means to enforce their authority, by means of their contract with the master. If they shall approve and confirm the act of the master, we are to believe that there is good and sufficient cause for the rejection of the pupil. The law will not presume that the committee, who are invested with the power of superintendence and management, will act arbitrarily and unjustly, in a matter submitted to their judgment. If, after all, there should be found practically, any danger of an encroachment upon private rights, in a matter in which the whole community have so deep an interest, it is for the legislature to provide more ample and specific security against such danger.

The plaintiff relied mainly for the support of his action, upon a class of cases in which it has been held, in this commonwealth, that a qualified voter, who has been denied the privilege of voting, may have his action for damages, against the selectmen, who have thus practically deprived him of his legal and constitutional privilege: *Gardner* v. *Ward,* 2 Mass. 244, note; *Lincoln* v. *Hapgood,* 11 Id. 350; *Bridge* v. *Lincoln,* 14 Id. 367. But the principle upon which these cases were decided, was, that this is a great personal, political, and constitutional privilege, in danger of being frequently and wantonly violated by those in the exercise of power, and that it would be difficult, in most cases, to prove actual malice; and, *ex necessitate,* the law allows such action, upon considerations of great public policy, to prevent greater mischief. This principle is not applicable to the case under consideration, and can not be relied upon, as a precedent.

The court are all of opinion, that the action can not be maintained, and that the nonsuit was right.

CHILD MAY BE EXCLUDED FROM PUBLIC SCHOOLS who is deemed to be of a licentious and immoral character, although not manifested by licentious or immoral acts within school: *Sherman* v. *Charlestown*, 8 Cush. 160.

SCHOOL COMMISSIONERS, BEING PUBLIC OFFICERS, ARE NOT HELD TO BE ACCOUNTABLE to individuals who may be aggrieved, for the manner in which they exercise their public functions: *Searock* v. *Putnam*, 111 Mass. 499; nor can a prisoner in the house of correction maintain an action against the person in charge, for neglect to provide him with sufficient food, clothing, and fires, if he is kept in the same manner as other prisoners, and there is no evidence of malice: *Williams* v. *Adams*, 3 Allen, 171; nor is a town agent liable in damages for refusing under any circumstances to sell intoxicating liquors: *Dwinnels* v. *Parsons*, 98 Mass. 470; in all of which the principal case is mentioned.

SCHOOLMASTER, NATURE AND EXTENT OF HIS LIABILITY for the manner in which his duties are discharged: *State* v. *Pendergrass*, 31 Am. Dec. 416, and note discussing this subject.

PERLEY *v.* BALCH.

[23 PICKERING, 283.]

A WARRANTY OF TITLE BUT NOT OF QUALITY is implied in every sale of chattels.

To RESCIND A CONTRACT OF PURCHASE, the vendee must return the property, unless it be entirely worthless to both parties.

PARTIAL FAILURE OF CONSIDERATION, or breach of warranty, or deception in the quality or value of goods sold, may be shown in mitigation of damages, in an action to recover the purchase price.

ASSUMPSIT on a note. The defendant offered evidence that the note was given in payment for an ox, which plaintiff warranted would fatten well; and that the ox was in fact diseased, and of no value, and that plaintiff made divers misrepresentations, etc., concerning the ox; and that the ox was worthless for any purpose. The action was brought several years after the sale. Defendant had not returned the ox, nor notified plaintiff of any dissatisfaction with the purchase. Defendant also proved that he bought the ox expressly for fattening, and so stated to plaintiff at the time. Verdict for plaintiff.

Perkins, for the defendant.

Lord, for the plaintiff.

By Court, MORTON, J. The instruction, that there was no implied warranty, is not now complained of, and is undoubtedly correct: See *Emerson* v. *Brigham*, 10 Mass. 197; *Shephead* v.

Temple, 8 N. H. 455. Every sale of chattels contains an implied warranty, that the property of them is in the vendor. But it is well settled by authority as a general rule, that no warranty of the quality is implied from the sale. The maxim, *caveat emptor*, governs: 2 Kent's Com. 478; Chit. on Con. 133; *Champion* v. *Short*, 1 Camp. 53; *Bragg* v. *Cole*, 6 Moore, 114; *Stuart* v. *Wilkins*, 1 Doug. 20; *Parkinson* v. *Lee*, 2 East, 314; *Mockbee* v. *Gardner*, 2 Har. & G. 176. But the learned justice of the common pleas further instructed the jury, that if there was a fraud in the sale, or an express warranty and a breach of it, in either case, the defendant might avoid the contract, by returning the ox within a reasonable time; or, if the ox would have been of no value to the plaintiff, then without returning him. Whether the jury found their verdict upon the ground, that no fraud or express warranty was proved, or that the ox was of no value, does not appear. If, therefore, any part of the instructions was incorrect, the defendant is entitled to a new trial.

Where the purchaser is induced, by the fraudulent misrepresentations of the seller, to make the purchase, he may, within a reasonable time, by restoring the seller to the situation he was in before the sale, rescind the contract, and recover back the consideration paid, or, if he has given a note, resist the payment of it. Here was no return of the property purchased; but if that property was of no value, whether there was any fraud or not, the note would be *nudum pactum*. The defendant's counsel, not controverting the general rule, objects to the qualification of it. He says, that the ox, though valueless to the defendant, might be of value to the plaintiff, and so the defendant would be bound by his contract, although he acquired nothing by it. But a damage to the promisee is as good a consideration as a benefit to the promisor. If a chattel be of no value to any one, it can not be the basis of a bargain; but if it be of any value to either party, it may be a good consideration for a promise. If it is beneficial to the purchaser, he certainly ought to pay for it. If it be a loss to the seller, he is entitled to remuneration for his loss.

But it is apparent that a want of consideration was not the principal ground of defense. The defendant mainly relied upon fraud or a warranty. And to render either available to avoid the note, it was indispensable that the property should be returned. He can not rescind the contract, and yet retain any portion of the consideration. The only exception is, where the property is entirely worthless to both parties. In such case the return would be a useless ceremony, which the law never re-quires. The purchaser can not derive any benefit from the pur-chase and yet rescind the contract. It must be nullified *in toto*, or not at all. It can not be enforced in part and rescinded in part. And, if the property would be of any benefit to the seller, he is equally bound to return it. He who would rescind a con-tract, must put the other party in as good a situation as he was before; otherwise he can not do it: Chit. on Con. 276; *Hunt* v. *Silk*, 5 East, 449; *Conner* v. *Henderson*, 15 Mass. 314.

The facts relied upon by the defendant to defeat the note, might, if proved, be used in mitigation of damages. If there was a partial failure of consideration, or deception in the quality and value of it, or a breach of warranty, the defendant may avail himself of it to reduce the damages to the worth of the chattels sold, and need not resort to an action for deceit, or upon the warranty: Chit. on Con. 140; *Germaine* v. *Burton*, 3 Stark. 32; *Barton* v. *Butler*, 7 East, 480; *Poulton* v. *Lattimore*, 9 Barn. & Cress. 259; Bayley on Bills, 2d Am. ed., 531, and cases cited. But he is not bound to do this. He may prefer to bring a sep-arate action, and he has an election to do so. The present judg-ment will not bar such an action. But however this may be, it does not appear that any instructions were given or refused upon this point. The value of the property to the defendant would have been the true rule of damages. And had he desired it, doubtless, such instructions would have been given. But as he did not request them, he can not complain of their omission.

Judgment of the court of common pleas affirmed.

VENDOR OF PERSONAL PROPERTY IS NOT LIABLE FOR DEFECTS in its qual-ity, without express warranty or fraud: *Hyatt* v. *Boyle*, 25 Am. Dec. 276, in the note to which the cases reported in this series upon the subject are col-lected; also *Borrekins* v. *Bevan*, 23 Id. 85, and note. No particular form of words is necessary to constitute a warranty: *Beeman* v. *Buck*, 21 Id. 571.

ACTION ON IMPLIED WARRANTY may be maintained without returning or offering to return the property to the defendant: *Borrekins* v. *Bevan*, 23 Am. Dec. 85. In case of a rescission of the contract, however, as will appear from the note to the case cited above, it is necessary that the property should first be restored to the original owner before an action for the purchase price can be maintained. The respective parties must be placed in the same situation that they were previous to the contract. The vendee must therefore return the property, unless it be entirely worthless. The principal case is relied upon to sustain this proposition in the following cases: *Bartlett* v. *Drake*, 100 Mass. 176; *Morse* v. *Brackett*, 98 Id. 210; *Kent* v. *Bornstein*, 12 Allen, 342; *Bryant* v. *Isburgh*, 13 Gray, 612; *Dorr* v. *Fisher*, 1 Cush. 274; *Thayer* v. *Turner*, 8 Metc. 552. In the note to *Hough's Adm'rs* v. *Hunt*, 15 Am. Dec. 572, the subject of the rescission of contracts is treated at length. The vendee must make the restoration within a reasonable time, or at least signify his election: *Bassett* v. *Brown*, 105 Mass. 557, citing the principal case.

VENDEE RESCINDING CONTRACT MAY SHOW IN REDUCTION OF DAMAGES a failure of consideration, or breach of warranty, or the false and fraudulent representations of the vendor. This principle is enunciated upon the authority of *Perley* v. *Balch*, in the following cases: *Burnett* v. *Smith*, 4 Gray, 51; *Carry* v. *Guillow*, 105 Mass. 20; *Dorr* v. *Fisher*, 1 Cush. 275; *Tuttle* v. *Brown*, 10 Id. 264; *Mixer* v. *Coburn*, 11 Metc. 561; *Howard* v. *Ames*, 3 Id. 311. The cases reported in this series upon this subject will be found in the note to *McAlpin* v. *Lee*, 30 Am. Dec. 611.

FABENS *v.* THE MERCANTILE BANK.

[23 PICKERING, 330.]

BANK RECEIVING NOTE FOR COLLECTION must use reasonable skill and diligence, and, therefore, must make seasonable demand of the promisor, and, in case of dishonor, give due notice to charge the indorsers.

BANK RECEIVING FOR COLLECTION A NOTE PAYABLE AT ANOTHER PLACE, or whose acceptor resides in another place, need only seasonably transmit the same to some suitable bank or agent for collection at the place of payment or of the residence of such acceptor.

BANK HOLDING NOTE AS COLLATERAL, OR FOR COLLECTION, is not answerable for the negligence of another bank in good standing, to which in the ordinary course of business the note was transmitted for collection.

CASE. Thomas Appleton gave the defendants his promissory note; and, to secure this note, plaintiff left with defendants a note made by K. F. Edgell, of Philadelphia, payable to S. D. Massey or order, indorsed in blank. Thirteen days before this last note became due, it was, by defendants, transmitted by mail to the bank of the United States, at Philadelphia, for collection. This last bank received the note in due time, but neglected to present it until twelve days after it became due. Payment was refused. This action was for damages occasioned by the delay in presenting the note. It was admitted that the bank of the United States was solvent and in good standing.

Perkins and Fabens, for the plaintiff.

Ward, for the defendants.

By Court, SHAW, C. J. The plaintiff seeks to recover damages, in an action of the case, on the ground, that the defendants are chargeable with negligence, in respect to a note which he left with them for collection.

We think this question must depend upon the general usage and custom of merchants and bankers, and the implied obligations upon the latter, resulting from their relations, as no spe-

cial contract was made, and no special instruction given in the
present case.   We think it very clear upon principle and authority, that by a general usage, now so well understood as safely to
be considered a rule of law, when a bank receives a note for collection, it is bound to use reasonable skill and diligence in making the collection, and for that purpose is bound to make a seasonable demand on the promisor, and, in case of dishonor, to
give due notice to the indorsers, so that the security of the
holder shall not be lost or essentially impaired by the discharge
of indorsers.   How far this liability may be modified by agreement or by general or special notice, is a subject of distinct consideration: *Smedes* v. *Utica Bank*, 20 Johns. 372; *Mechanics'
Bank* v. *Earp*, 4 Rawle, 384.   But it is equally well settled, that
when a note is deposited with a bank for collection, which is
payable at another place, the whole duty of the bank so receiving the note in the first instance, is seasonably to transmit the
same to a suitable bank or other agent at the place of payment.
And as a part of the same doctrine, it is well settled, that if the
acceptor of a bill or promisor of a note, has his residence in another place, it shall be presumed to have been intended and
understood between the depositor for collection and the bank,
that it was to be transmitted to the place of the residence of the
promisor, and the same rule shall then apply, as if on the face
of the note, it was payable at that place: *Bank of Washington* v.
Triplett, 1 Pet. 25; *Allen* v. *Merchants' Bank*, 15 Wend. 482;
Jackson v. *Union Bank*, 4 Har. & J. 146; *Lawrence* v. *Stonington Bank*, 6 Conn. 528.   In the present case, it was known at
the time of the indorsement of the note that the promisor lived
in Philadelphia, and of course, that the note must be sent there
for collection.   We are therefore of opinion, that the defendants had performed their duty, when they transmitted the note
to a solvent bank in good standing, and were not responsible
for the misfeasance or negligence of that bank.

We can not perceive, that it makes any difference, in respect
to the defendants' liability, that this note was received as collateral security.   The general property was still in the plaintiff.
It was to be collected for him.   It was a power coupled with
an interest, and therefore could not be revoked.   But it was
only on the contingency of being collected, that this note or its
proceeds were to be applied to the payment of Appleton's note.
Until then the whole beneficial interest was in the plaintiff.
And so the plaintiff himself understood it, by paying the fees
and taking it up.   According to the decision in *Bank of Wash-*

ington v. *Neal*, above cited, the plaintiff will have his remedy against the bank of the United States, if his loss is imputable to their negligence.

Plaintiff nonsuit.

———

BANK RECEIVING NOTE FOR COLLECTION MUST USE DUE DILIGENCE in making demand and giving notice: *Thompson* v. *Bank of South Carolina*, 30 Am. Dec. 354, and note, containing the cases hitherto reported in this series; also *Mechanics' Bank* v. *Merchants' Bank*, 6 Metc. 13, citing the principal case. In the following cases the principal case is relied upon as authority to show that when a bank receives a note for collection which requires the employment of a sub-agent, the principal agent is not responsible for the defaults of the sub-agent, provided a proper sub-agent was selected: *Warren Bank* v. *Suffolk Bank*, 10 Cush. 585; *Dorchester Bank* v. *New England Bank*, 1 Id. 186. A bank which receives from another bank a note for collection is bound to present the note to the maker for payment, and, if it is not paid, to give notice of non-payment to the bank from which the note was received, but it is not bound, unless by special agreement, to give such notice to the other parties to the note: *Phipps* v. *Millbury Bank*, 8 Metc. 79, also citing the principal case.

———

CREASE v. BABCOCK ET AL.

[23 PICKERING, 334.]

CHARTER OF INCORPORATION IS A CONTRACT between the government and the corporators; and except with reference to the implied or express reservations embraced in it, is exempt from legislative revocation or interference.

STATUTE PROVIDING THAT ACTS OF INCORPORATION SHALL BE SUBJECT to amendment, alteration, or repeal at the pleasure of the legislature, provided that no act of incorporation shall be repealed unless for some violation of its charter or other default, is constitutional. The legislature may make this reservation. And when it thereafter repeals the act, the courts are bound to presume that a contingency had arisen warranting the exercise of the power reserved.

INQUIRY BY THE LEGISLATURE TO DETERMINE whether a default had happened, upon which it reserved the right to repeal an act of incorporation, is not a judicial act which the legislature is prohibited from entering upon.

REPEAL OF ITS CHARTER DISSOLVES THE INCORPORATION and subjects the stockholders to all such remedies as the law gives against them on the expiration of the corporation.

BILL in equity. The Chelsea bank and a number of persons alleged to be its stockholders were defendants. The facts sufficiently appear in the opinion. Demurrer to the bill.

C. G. Loring, W. H. Gardiner, Rufus Choate, and *B. Sumner,* for the defendants.

B. Rand and E. H. Derby, for the complainant.

By Court, MORTON, J. This is a bill in equity by one of the creditors of the Chelsea bank against a part of the stockholders, to recover of them, individually, the amount of two bank notes of one thousand dollars each. To this bill some of the defendants have filed pleas, and others have demurred. Several questions were started in relation to the state of the pleadings, and some doubts occurred whether the bill could be maintained at all in its present form. But as these subjects were not fully discussed, we have not deemed it proper to investigate them, and not having formed a decisive opinion, we will not give any intimation in relation to them. With the aid of the great liberality always allowed in chancery proceedings, it may, even without investigation, be assumed, that any defects in form may, in the progress of the suit, be remedied. Two questions, which arise upon the demurrer, and lie at the foundation of a recovery by the creditors of the bank against its stockholders, have been fully and ably argued. And as their decision will speed the final termination of the controversy, whatever form the claim may eventually assume, we have carefully considered them and agreed upon a result, which I will state, with some of the reasons which have led us to it.

The plaintiff, in support of his bill, relies upon the thirty-first section of the thirty-sixth chapter of the revised statutes; which provides, that " the holders of stock in any bank, at the time when its charter shall expire, shall be liable, in their individual capacities, for the payment and redemption of all bills which may have been issued by said bank, and which shall remain unpaid, in proportion to the stock they may respectively hold at the dissolution of the charter." It is not necessary to stop here to remark, that this provision is extremely general, and that much is left to implication, in relation not only to its import, but especially to the mode of carrying it into execution. It is not even stated to whom the stockholders shall be liable, whether to the corporation, by assessments to raise the funds for redeeming the outstanding bills, or directly to the billholders, in a bill in their own names. And if the latter remedy be intended, it does not appear, except by inference, whether the actions are to be joint or several, in equity or at law. If the stockholders are liable to suits, it is very obvious that a bill in chancery is well adapted to the case, and will lie.

This bank was incorporated April 16, 1836, to continue till October 1, 1851, and has not expired by its own limitation: Stat. 1836, c. 274. On the nineteenth of April, 1837, the legislature passed an act repealing its charter: Stat. 1837, c. 225. This, if it has the force and operation of a law, terminated the corporate existence of the bank long before the expiration of the term for which it was granted. But the validity of this act is disputed. Its constitutionality is denied; and this raises the first and most important question which we are called upon to decide.

That a charter of incorporation is a contract between the government and the corporators, is a proposition which seems to be fully supported by the highest judicial authorities: 2 Kent's Com., 3d ed., 272, 306; *Dartmouth College* v. *Woodward*, 4 Wheat. 518; *Charles River Bridge* v. *Warren Bridge*, 7 Pick. 344. That it is exempt from the ordinary action of legislative power, beyond the reservations, express or implied, contained in it, is equally well supported. In other words, the government can rightfully do nothing inconsistent with the fair meaning of the contract which it has made. If therefore the legislature grant a charter for a definite period, they can not at their will and pleasure revoke it. This comes within the prohibition of the tenth section of the first article of the constitution of the United States. But it is not necessary further to discuss these general principles, which are not in controversy between the counsel, and which will furnish very little aid in the decision of the question under consideration. That depends upon the proper construction of the several statutes to which I am about to refer.

The Chelsea bank charter expressly entitled it " to all the powers and privileges," and subjected it " to all the duties, liabilities, and requirements contained in the thirty-sixth chapter of the revised statutes." By that chapter, and by the terms of the charters granted after the enactment of these statutes, all the banks in the commonwealth are put upon the same legal and constitutional footing. The limits of the powers and duties of all must be found in that chapter. It was intended to regulate the banking operations of the commonwealth, and virtually constitutes the charters of all the banks.

It is not disputed that the contract with the corporators of the Chelsea bank must be defined by this act. Indeed it derives all its powers from this source. The fortieth section contains very important reservations applicable to this and other bank charters, which have been relied upon by the plaintiff's counsel. It contains a reserved right to the legislature, by its committees, to examine into the doings and the vaults and books of all the banks, and for certain specified causes, to declare any of their charters forfeited. To the constitutionality of this reservation it is objected, that although a charter may be forfeited for many causes, yet the declaration of a forfeiture is a judicial act, which by the thirtieth article of the bill of rights the legislature is prohibited from exercising.

The objections of the defendants' counsel to this section, are entitled to grave consideration, and we perceive great difficulty in the proper construction of it. But we do not think it necessary, in this case, to give any opinion upon it. The second section of the thirty-sixth chapter expressly provides, that each bank shall be entitled to all the powers and privileges, and be subject to all the liabilities contained in the forty-fourth chapter. As all the revised statutes were enacted at the same time and came into existence by the same legislative fiat, by a well-known rule of construction they must all be considered together and construed as one act. And when the Chelsea bank charter is expressly made subject to the provisions of the thirty-sixth chapter, which refers to the forty-fourth, it must be taken to be subject to the same rules of construction which govern in all other cases. Nothing can be plainer than the intention of the legislature to place all the banks upon an equal footing.

The last section of the thirteenth title, upon the subject of corporations, is general, and manifestly applies to and governs all the preceding regulations upon the subject, as much as if it had been repeated at the end of each chapter. No one doubts that it applies to banks. It provides, that all acts of incorporation passed after a certain time, " shall, at all times, be subject to amendment, alteration, or repeal, at the pleasure of the legislature; provided that no act of incorporation shall be repealed, unless for some violation of its charter, or other default, when such charter shall contain an express provision limiting the duration of the same." This section constitutes a part and must govern the construction of the contract with the Chelsea bank, as much as if it had been recited *verbatim* in its charter. Upon the import of this language must depend the repealing act. Whatever may be its meaning, the corporators have directly agreed to it by accepting their charter, of which this was a constituent part. We think there can be no doubt of the right of the legislature to make such a contract. Their power to make an unlimited charter, without some such reservation, express or implied, so as to bind their own and their successors' constituents forever, we apprehend, would be more liable to be questioned. How far they might part with any portion of sovereign power, irrevocably, beyond the recovery of the people themselves, we have no occasion to inquire.

The making of grants of real and personal estate, of franchises and other rights and privileges, whether strictly speaking it may be deemed legislation or not, is undoubtedly within the competence of our legislative body. The power has always been exercised by them, and undoubtedly is more safe in their hands and falls more appropriately within their province than any other department of the government.

If they have a right to make grants, they of necessity must prescribe the terms upon which they shall be made. If they may limit their duration, they may also impose other restrictions. They may determine how much or how little, how large or how small, an estate or franchise, they will grant. They may grant absolutely or on condition; so they may grant during pleasure, or until a certain event happens. And if a grant be accepted on the terms prescribed, it becomes a compact; and the grantees can have no reason to complain of the execution of their own contract. And Chancellor Kent, though with some appearance of reluctance (2 Kent's Com. 306), says: "If a charter be granted and accepted, with that reservation, there seems to be no ground to question the validity and efficiency of the reservation:" Angell & Ames on Corp. 504.

The case of *McLaren* v. *Pennington*, 1 Paige, 107, is a strong case to this point. The legislature of New Jersey granted a bank charter, for which they received a bonus of twenty-five thousand dollars. In the act of incorporation, they reserved the power to alter, amend, or repeal it. The bank went into operation, paid its bonus, and in less than one year, a shorter time than the Chelsea bank continued, the legislature deemed it necessary to interfere and actually repealed the charter. This, upon full consideration, was adjudged to be a valid repeal. It was contended that the reservation was repugnant to the grant, and therefore void. But this ground was distinctly overruled by the chancellor; who said, this reservation "is not a condition repugnant to the grant; it is only a limitation of the grant." Had the proviso to this section been omitted, this charter might have been amended, altered, or repealed, "at the pleasure of the legislature;" but the defendants' counsel argue that the proviso not only restricts the power to repeal, but entirely takes it away, because the inquiry whether the bank has violated its charter or committed any default, is a judicial act, and therefore can not constitutionally be performed by the legislature. The effect of this argument is to raise banks above the control of the legislature, and place them and all corporations with limited charters, upon a different basis from other corporations.

All acts of incorporation are supposed to be granted with a view to the public welfare, as well as to promote private interest and individual enterprise, and therefore it is to be presumed that the legislature, when charters are holden at their pleasure, will not repeal them capriciously, nor without due inquiry into all the facts, and satisfactory evidence that they have ceased or failed to accomplish the objects for which they were established. In such case, the exercise of the reserved power to repeal could not be vitiated or invalidated, because the legislature investigated the case to see whether it was reasonable to exercise the power before they actually repealed a charter.

The true question is, whether the legislature can, in any case, repeal an act of incorporation granted for a term of years. Any charter may be forfeited by a violation or for other sufficient cause; and on a proper process, a judgment of forfeiture might be decreed. But this would be a judicial act, and might be done without the concurrence, and against the will of the legislature. It is entirely independent of and unconnected with the power to repeal.

But the legislature clearly intended to reserve the power to discontinue corporations, not only for violations of their charters, but also for other defaults; which must mean, if anything, some acts short of violations, but which were inconsistent with, if not subversive of the ends for which the corporation was established. They reserve the power to repeal at pleasure, provided that on certain charters, they will not exercise it, unless the corporations have committed some default. If a default has been committed, then, by the express terms of the compact, they have a right to exercise the power. They have exercised it, and therefore, by the courtesy and confidence, which is due from one department of the government to another, we are bound to presume that the contingency, upon which the right to exercise it depended, has happened. Nor is the objection that the legislature had no power to inquire into the existence of the contingency, valid. If any man, or body of men, is invested with power to do a certain act upon the occurrence of a certain event, when the event happens they have a right to perform the act, and the most that can be urged against it is, that if it be exercised before the event happens, it is void. And this is true, by whomsoever the fact is to be ascertained.

But we do not believe that the inquiry into the affairs or defaults of a corporation, with a view to continue or discontinue it, is a judicial act. No issue is formed. No decree or judgment is passed. No forfeiture is adjudged. No fine or punishment is imposed. But an inquiry is had in such form as is deemed most wise and expedient, with a view to ascertain facts upon which to exert legislative power; or to learn whether a contingency has happened upon which legislative action is required. This is the constant and necessary course of proceeding, not only in relation to private and special acts, but also to many public acts. In granting new charters, or enlarging, modifying, or renewing old ones, and in a large portion of ordinary legislation, it is the duty of the legislature to inquire and ascertain, whether existing facts render their action expedient or necessary. These proceedings, though they bear some resemblance to, and have in view the same general object, the ascertainment of truth, yet in no proper sense can they be called judicial acts.

It is indispensable that this inquiry should, in the first instance, be made by the legislature. No other body can do it for them. They have restricted themselves from exercising the power of repeal, until a certain event happens. This they must necessarily ascertain before they can properly exercise the power. Their decision must, *prima facie*, be presumed to be right. Whether it be conclusive or not, is a question which it is not necessary now to determine.

From a careful examination of the whole subject, my own opinion is, that the true construction of the twenty-third section is this. The legislature reserve to themselves the right to amend, alter, and repeal, at their pleasure, all acts of incorporation, passed after 1831, provided that they will not repeal any such act, granted for a term of years, without ascertaining to their satisfaction that the corporation has violated its charter or committed some other default. This restriction is imposed upon the legislative will, and the corporators confide in the wisdom and justice of the legislature not to exercise the power unless the facts clearly authorize and require them to do it. This is not an unreasonable confidence. It is to be recollected, that this restriction applies only to a total repeal, and not to an alteration or amendment, which they may exercise at pleasure in limited as well as unlimited corporations. Now if corporators are willing to accept charters with an unlimited power to amend or alter, why should they hesitate to accept them with this guarded and restricted power to repeal? In whatever light, therefore, I view the subject, I am satisfied that the legislature had the power to repeal the Chelsea bank charter, and that their act of April 19, 1837, was valid and effectual to repeal the act by which the bank was established.

We are next to inquire what consequences ensued upon this repeal of the charter. By the revised statutes, c. 44, sec. 7, it is provided that all corporations, whose charters shall expire or be annulled by forfeiture or otherwise, shall be continued bodies corporate, for certain purposes therein mentioned. The object of this section is to authorize them to collect their dues, to dispose of their property, to pay their debts, and to distribute their capital stock; but not to transact any business other than what is necessary to settle and close their concerns. It is argued for the defendants, that the stockholders are entitled to three years after the repeal, to close the affairs of the bank, before they are liable for the bills which the corporation has refused to pay. The provision in the thirty-first section is, that those who are stockholders when the charter expires, shall be liable. If the charter could not be said to expire till three years after its repeal, it would furnish the stockholders of an insolvent bank with ample opportunity to dispose of their stock to individuals wholly unable to redeem the bills, and thus avoid their responsibility and render this important safeguard for the public nugatory. The bills outstanding at the time of the dissolution, are to be paid; and the amount is to be apportioned among the stockholders according to the amount of stock held by each at the time of the dissolution.

When the charter is repealed, it has ceased to have force as a charter. It has expired. This is its dissolution. The corporation derives no power from it. It can not carry on business. It exists by virtue of the seventh section, and that gives it force only for certain, definite, specific, and limited purposes. This qualified prolongation of the existence of the corporate body, is in the nature of an administration of its estate. All rights under the defunct corporation were fixed at its dissolution. But it has a nominal existence for the purpose of closing its concerns in the most convenient manner, and especially of compelling it to execute its contracts and discharge its obligations and liabilities: *Foster et al.* v. *Essex Bank*, 16 Mass. 245.

The result to which our investigation has brought us is, that the repealing act is constitutional and valid; that by force of it the charter of the Chelsea bank expired and was dissolved on the nineteenth of April, 1837, within the meaning of the thirty-first section before cited, and the billholders and other creditors of the bank, from that time became entitled to all the remedies against the officers and stockholders, provided in the thirty-sixth chapter of the revised statutes.

CHARTER OF INCORPORATION IS A CONTRACT, and an act of the legislature impairing its obligation is void: *Regents* v. *Williams*, 31 Am. Dec. 72, in the note to which the cases in this series upon this subject are cited. The principal case is cited in *Durfee* v. *Old Colony and Fall River R. R. Co.*, 5 Allen, 246, to the point that by accepting its charter the corporation directly agrees to adopt a provision reserving to the legislature the right to amend, alter, or repeal the act of incorporation, as a constituent part of their contract. This power of repeal under the statute of Massachusetts relative to incorporations, is limited to cases in which there is either a violation of its charter by the corporation, or some act of default: *Commonwealth* v. *Essex Co.*, 13 Gray, 253, approving the principal case.

JACKSON ET AL. v. THE MASSACHUSETTS MUTUAL FIRE INSURANCE COMPANY.

[23 PICKERING, 418.]

INSURANCE BY MORTGAGOR AND MORTGAGEE SEVERALLY, may be effected without the insurance of either impairing that of the other.

INVALID INSURANCE CAN NOT OPERATE TO ANNUL PRIOR POLICY of insurance which stipulates that if the assured shall have made, or shall hereafter make any other insurance "upon said property, this policy shall be null and void." Such a policy is not avoided by taking out a second policy having the same condition; for, by the condition, the second policy never becomes operative and does not amount to "an insurance."

A PROVISION IN A POLICY AVOIDING IT IN THE CASE OF "ALIENATION by sale or otherwise," does not apply to a conveyance by way of mortgage, while the mortgagor remains in possession, and there has been no entry for foreclosure.

ASSUMPSIT on two policies of insurance. The defendants claimed that the policies had become void before the loss occurred, by reason of a reinsurance, and also of a conveyance by way of mortgage. The conditions of the policy and the rules of the company, so far as material to this action, are stated in the opinion. The second insurance was payable to the mortgagees.

Hubbard, Bartlett, and *Atwood,* for the plaintiffs.

C. P. and *B. R. Curtis,* for the defendants.

By Court, DEWEY, J. This is an action upon two policies of insurance, made by the defendants, whereby they assured to the

plaintiffs certain buildings against loss or damage by fire. The
execution of the polices and the loss of the property by fire, are
admitted; but the defendants insist, that the plaintiffs have forfeited their right to enforce the payment of the policies, by
reason of their violation of the terms and conditions annexed to
them: 1. Because subsequently to the making of the policies by
the defendants, the plaintiffs caused the same property to be insured at another office.   2. Because of the alleged alienation of
the property by the plaintiffs, after the making of the policies,
and before the loss occurred.

The first question arises upon that article in the policies made by the defendants, which provides that the policy
shall be taken subject to the conditions and limitations expressed in the rules of the company, one of which is of the following purport: "When a subsequent insurance shall be made
by another company, or by any person, on property insured in
this office, without the consent of the president in writing, and
according to the terms in such consent expressed, it shall *ipso
facto* annul the policy."

A policy of insurance was subsequently obtained at the National insurance office upon the same property, in the names of
certain mortgagees holding under a mortgage from the plaintiffs, which mortgage was executed at a period subsequent to the
policy made by the defendants.   The policy obtained at the National insurance office was for the term of one year, and was for
several successive years renewed from time to time to a period
later than that of the loss of the premises by fire, and it is this
policy which it is contended has vacated those made by the defendants.   That both mortgagor and mortgagee may severally
insure their respective interests, is well established, nor can it
be maintained that a subsequent policy effected by a mortgagee
upon his separate interest, is a violation of the condition in a
previous policy of the mortgagor, such as is stated in the rules
annexed to the policy made by the defendants: *Traders' Insurance Co.* v. *Roberts*, 9 Wend. 404.

But it is insisted in the present case that the facts show that
a double insurance has been effected at the instance and for the
benefit of the plaintiffs.   The several insurances at the National
office, it is said, although taken in the names of the mortgagees,
were taken in pursuance of a stipulation of the parties contained
in the mortgage deed, and upon the understanding and with the
object of placing the avails of those policies in the hands of the
mortgagees, for the direct benefit of the mortgagors, and in case

of payment of those policies to the mortgagees, the result will be tantamount to a payment of the same amount by the plaintiffs to their mortgagees. Whether this is the proper view of the situation of these parties in reference to the policy at the National insurance office, and whether such would be the effect, had that policy been effected under the circumstances supposed, it is unnecessary for us to decide, as we think that in no view of the case can the objection of a double insurance having been effected avail the defendants.

In the conditions and limitations annexed to the policies obtained of the National insurance company, it is provided, "if they shall have made, or shall hereafter make, any other insurance upon said property, without the knowledge and consent of said company, the policy shall be null and void." If the insurance at the National office was in truth an insurance for the plaintiffs, then by the condition of that policy, as just recited, that insurance was wholly void and inoperative, and being so, can not be set up by the defendants as evidence of the plaintiffs having procured a second insurance. An insurance that shall operate to avoid the policy of the defendants, as a violation of the tenth article of their rules, must be a valid and legal policy, and effectual and binding upon the assurers.

Assuming the second policy to have been made for the direct benefit of the plaintiffs, it was wholly nugatory and of no effect; and can not for this reason be now set up to defeat the policy made by the defendants. On the other hand, if the policy made at the National insurance office is to be considered as made at the instance and for the sole benefit of the mortgagees, then upon general principles it was a policy effected for other interests, and is no violation of the condition stipulated on the part of the plaintiffs, that they would not procure any other insurance; so that, in either aspect of the case, this ground of defense must fail. The view of the case now taken does not render nugatory and wholly ineffectual the rule restricting the party assured from making a second insurance. It will apply in its full force in all cases where a party procures a second insurance at an office, whose rules allow such double insurance. Such second insurance would annul the previous policy.

The second objection taken by the defendants, arises upon the eleventh rule of the Mutual insurance company, which is in these words: "When any mansion house or other building shall be alienated by sale or otherwise, the policy shall thereupon be *ipso facto* void; but the grantee or alienee, having the policy assigned to him by the insured, may, upon application to the secretary, within thirty days, with the consent of the president, have his policy renewed upon becoming responsible for the payment of his proportion of the conditional funds." Was this conveyance by the plaintiffs to Minot and Faulkner, by way of mortgage to secure the payment of five thousand dollars, an alienation, in the true intent and meaning of this article in the rules of the Mutual insurance company? The defendants contend that the term alienation is here used in its broadest sense, and as embracing the case of a conveyance by mortgage as well as that of an absolute transfer of the whole interest. It seems to us that this is an erroneous view of the question, and the improbability of such having been the purpose of that rule is much strengthened from the consideration of the frequency of this mode of transfer, and the numerous cases of liens of this character created for temporary purposes and to an amount very small in comparison with the value of the property mortgaged.

As has been before remarked, in the ordinary course of insurance, the interests of both mortgagor and mortgagee are distinct subjects of insurance, and each may well insure his interest in the property. A transfer by the insured by way of mortgage may create a new insurable interest in another, but this does not, under the general rules of insurance, divest the mortgagor of such an estate as is requisite to sustain his previous insurance, and the court are of opinion that this principle was not intended to be changed by the rule attached to the policies made by the defendants, and that a policy effected while the whole interest is in the insured, is not vacated by a conveyance in mortgage. It is however restricted to the case of a mortgagor still remaining in possession, and where there has been no entry for foreclosure. This limitation is necessary to give effect to the twentieth rule of the Mutual insurance company, providing "that when any estate mortgaged shall be taken possession of by the mortgagee for breach of the condition expressed in the mortgage deed or in any bond of defeasance, the policy shall thereupon be absolutely void, unless the policy shall be transferred to the mortgagee with the consent of the president." The rule last cited also strengthens in some degree our construction upon the general question we have been considering, as it assumes that the interest of a mortgagee is an insurable interest within the rules of the company. It would be quite conclusive, but for the reason that this provision may have effect if it be limited to cases of mortgages existing before the issuing the policy, and be held applicable solely to such. We think however that it may be well applied to cases of mortgages made after as well as before the making of the policy, and that upon a proper construction of the eleventh rule of the Mutual insurance company, a conveyance by mortgage does not defeat a previous policy made in favor of the mortgagor while the entire estate remained in him.

The eleventh rule may, as respects the owner in fee who has taken a policy of insurance, perhaps be considered as merely declaratory of the common law principle, that when all interest in the premises insured ceases, the policy becomes ineffectual and inoperative, and also as having been more particularly framed for the purpose of providing a mode by which the insurance made in favor of the original owner may be made to inure to the benefit of the purchaser, without the payment of any further premium, and to the amount of that premium it is a beneficial provision to the insured, as he may value his estate at so much advance, as this premium amounts to.

Judgment for the plaintiffs.

————

DOUBLE INSURANCE, WHAT CONSTITUTES: *Ætna Fire Ins. Co.* v. *Tyler*, 30 Am. Dec. 90, in the note to which the cases referring to this subject will be found. An insurance that shall operate to avoid a policy as being "another insurance," so as to violate the condition against such insurance, contained in the policy, must be a valid and legal policy, and binding upon the assurers. A second policy, taken out for the direct benefit of the person to whom a prior policy has been issued, is wholly nugatory, if it contain a like condition. It can not therefore be set up to defeat a recovery upon the first policy. The doctrine of the principal case is approved in *Clark* v. *New England Ins. Co.*, 6 Cush. 350; *Barrett* v. *Union Mutual Ins. Co.*, 7 Id. 179; *Kimball* v. *Howard Ins. Co.*, 8 Gray, 35; *Hardy* v. *Union Ins. Co.*, 4 Allen, 221; *Thomas* v. *Builders' Fire Ins. Co.*, 119 Mass. 122; execution of a mortgage is not such an alienation as will vitiate a policy containing a condition avoiding it in case of "alienation" by the assured: *Edmands* v. *Mutual Safety Ins. Co.*, 1 Allen, 311; *Rice* v. *Tower*, 1 Gray, 429, in both of which the principal case is relied upon.

CASES

IN THE

HIGH COURT OF ERRORS AND APPEALS

OF

MISSISSIPPI.

ORNE *v.* SULLIVAN.

[3 HOWARD, 161.]

ARBITRATORS TO APPRAISE IMPROVEMENTS.—Where two parties enter into
an agreement by which one is to erect improvements on the lands of the
other, the value thereof to be estimated by two disinterested persons,
one party can not defeat the right to an appraisement by refusing to appoint an arbitrator, and a refusal or failure to appoint gives the other
party an undisputed right to have the valuation made.

WHEN NO MODE OF APPOINTMENT IS AGREED UPON in such a case, the court
infers the intention to be that each party is to appoint one arbitrator.

WHAT REFUSAL SUFFICIENT TO GIVE OTHER PARTY RIGHT OF APPOINTMENT.
Where one party requests the other to appoint an appraiser, and the
latter appoints a man to survey the land, but instructs him not to appraise, as he had fixed rules for valuing improvements, this would be
a sufficient refusal to justify the first party in having the appraisement
made.

APPEAL from the circuit court of Pontotoc county. The opinion
states the case.

Gholson, for the appellant.

Miller, contra.

By Court, SHARKEY, C. J. Sullivan brought this action on
a special contract entered into between himself and Orne,
concerning improvements to be made on a tract of land which
belonged to Orne. That portion of the agreement which it is
necessary to consider in order to settle the question made for
adjudication, is in these words : "And if the said Sullivan shall
not think proper to buy said lands at such price as they may fix

thereon, then, and in that case, the said Orne agrees to pay him, the said Sullivan, so much for the improvements that he may make on said two sections of land, as two disinterested persons may value said improvements to be worth." As there was a demurrer to the evidence, it will be necessary to collect the substance of what was proved, and then make an application of the law of the contract. Watts, the agent of Sullivan, stated that improvements had been made on the land; that he called on Orne at the request of Sullivan, and stated to him that he wished to settle the matter. Orne stated to him that he had selected Pinson, on his part, to survey the land, and the witness replied that he selected Hodges. Orne then said that all they (Pinson and Hodges) would have to do would be to survey the lands; that they (meaning himself and others) have fixed rules for valuing improvements. That after a valuation had been made by Pinson and Hodges, he called on Orne with it, who objected to pay, and stated that he had only authorized Pinson to survey the land, and not to estimate the value. Pinson was then introduced, and proved that he was notified by Watts of his appointment to value the improvements. Witness and Hodges appointed a day to attend to it, and when they were about doing so the witness called on Orne to know whether he would go; he replied that it was not worth while, that all they had to do was to survey the land. Witness returned to Watts, and informed him what Orne said, and was answered that they had an agreement, which they examined, and concluded it was their duty to value the improvement, and he again informed Orne of their determination, who again stated that they were only to measure the land, and that they had a rule by which to pay for the improvements, and again said that it was not worth his while to go. The witness and Hodges then went and valued the improvements.

We must first give a fair interpretation of the contract, and see what was to be done by each party before the other could be bound. The agreement was to pay so much as two disinterested persons should say the improvements were worth. It was therefore a matter wholly immaterial whether Orne had rules for fixing the value or not. It was not the contract that his rules should govern. How were these disinterested persons to be chosen? No mode was agreed on, and it must, therefore, have been the intention that one should be chosen by each party, but Orne could not defeat the contract by failing or refusing to choose; and if he so failed, or refused on request for that pur-

pose, then Sullivan's power to have the valuation made must be
undisputed. A different construction would place it in the
power of Orne to defeat the right to recover, by refusing or failing to select an arbitrator. We have only to determine, therefore, whether he so far failed or refused, as to justify Sullivan in
having the appraisement made. No positive refusal is shown,
but still it may be implied from his acts. He was called on by
the agent of Sullivan, for the purpose of appointing an appraiser;
he promptly answered that he had selected Pinson to survey the
land. This remark was well calculated to mislead the agent of
Sullivan, because surveying the land was no part of the contract. It might, as a preliminary step, have been necessary in
order to the correct ascertainment of the value of the improvements, but it was his duty to have stated the object of the survey, and if intended merely as a preliminary measure, it was
also his duty to have selected an appraiser. His reason for not
doing so, is fully disclosed by the subsequent testimony. When
called on by Pinson to accompany the appraisers, he stated that
it was unnecessary, as they had but to survey the land, and that
he then had rules, by which the improvement was to be valued.
From this it is obvious, that he intended to value the improvement according to his own rules, and not to have it done according to the contract. His rules, however, could in no respect govern in the valuation, nor could the existence of such
rules afford any excuse for his failure to comply with the contract.
He had notice that the improvements would be appraised, and
was again called on to accompany the appraisers, and again
stated that he would not go, as they would have nothing to do
but to survey the land. He then made no objection to the appraisers, but his opposition to any appraisement was again
manifested, by his declaration that the appraisement was to be
made according to the rules which he had for that purpose.
This conduct was certainly tantamount to an express refusal to
have the land valued, and is irreconcilable with an intention to
comply with the terms of the contract. He was not only requested to make an appointment of an appraiser, but was actually
advised that they would appraise the land. If he thought Pinson
an unsuitable person for that purpose, he had an ample opportunity to select another, and why did he not do so? The reason
is manifest: he did not intend to have the improvements valued
in any other way than according to his own rules. The same
object was again manifested, when he was informed of the appraisement. He then stated that it was too high, and that he

had rules by which to regulate the appraisement. His reply to
Pinson, when informed that they had examined the contract,
and thought it their duty to appraise the improvement, was
equivalent to a direct refusal. The rules which he pretended to
insist on can afford him no shield against the force of his contract, but this was evidently his pretext for the failure. No intimation was ever given, that he intended to appoint an appraiser,
and the whole course of his conduct shows that he did not; his
object being to settle the value on his own terms. As the party
on whom the obligation of the contract rested, everything is to
be taken most strongly against him, but even on a fair interpretation, his acts amounted to a refusal to appoint an appraiser,
and justified Sullivan in having the value fixed according to the
contract; and having done all that he could, the justice of the
case is manifestly with him, and for these reasons the

Judgment must be affirmed.

WHO MAY SUBMIT TO ARBITRATION: See *Hutchings* v. *Johnson*, 30 Am.
Dec. 622, and note 626.

AWARDS, WHEN SET ASIDE: See note to *Doolittle* v. *Malcom*, 31 Am. Dec.
673.

BENNETT *v.* McGAUGHY.

[3 HOWARD, 192.]

TO TRANSFER A NOTE PAYABLE TO TWO, it must be indorsed by both payees.
AVERMENT INSUFFICIENT TO MAINTAIN TITLE OF ASSIGNEE, WHEN.—An averment that one of the payees had released his interest in the note to the
other is not a sufficient allegation to sustain a suit by the assignee of the
latter against the maker.

ERROR to the circuit court of Leak county. Debt upon a
sealed note, executed by Bennett and payable to Allensworth
and Ewing. The declaration avers a release by Ewing to Allensworth and assignment by indorsement by the latter to McGaughy.
The plaintiff in error demurred on the ground of an insufficient
allegation of title in McGaughy. The court overruled the demurrer and the defendants appealed.

Yerger, for the plaintiffs in error.

Hughes, contra.

By Court, TROTTER, J. It is well settled, that where a note
or bill is payable to two, it must be indorsed by both, in order
to transfer the entire interest in it to the indorsee: Chit. on
Bills, 67, 226. But it is urged, that the authority of Allens-

worth to assign, by his sole indorsement, the whole interest in
the note in this case, is stated and shown by the release of
Ewing's interest. The averment is not, however, sufficient for
this purpose. It is a well-established rule in pleading, that all
persons who are ostensibly interested, must join in the action,
and any private arrangement amongst themselves, will not be
noticed. Could Allensworth have maintained an action on this
note in his own name, on the averment in the declaration of the
release by Ewing? It is believed he could not. If so, his
assignee can not. The case of *Burdick* v. *Green*, 15 Johns. 249,
is a direct authority in support of these views. That was an
action on a promissory note, which was made payable to the
plaintiff, who indorsed it to one Ketchum, and the declaration
averred, that Ketchum afterwards, by his instrument in writing,
under his hand, assigned the said note to the plaintiff, by which,
the indorsement to Ketchum became canceled, and the plaintiff
restored to all his rights, as though the indorsement had not
been made. Upon demurrer, the court held, that this averment
was not sufficient to divest Ketchum of the legal title. That
the indorsement should have been canceled.

Let the judgment of the court below be reversed, and the
cause remanded, with leave to the plaintiff to amend his pleadings.   .   ——————

DICKSON *v.* PARKER.

[3 HOWARD, 219.]

DEFECTIVE INCLOSURE.—Where a party neglects to keep a sufficient inclosure,
under the act of 1822, he has no authority to take the redress into his
own hands for any injury he may have sustained in consequence of such
insufficiency.

RIGHT TO DISTRAIN CATTLE DAMAGE FEASANT does not exist unless the owner
of the cattle would be liable to an action.

TRESPASS IS THE PROPER REMEDY where there is no right to distrain, and the
seizure is illegal.

ABUSE OF LEGAL AUTHORITY OR LICENSE by one who at first acted with propriety under it, makes him a trespasser *ab initio.*

LIABILITY FOR DISTRAINING, WHEN EXISTS.—Where a mule got into the defendant's grounds, in consequence of the insufficiency of his fence, and was
destroyed by his act, he is liable to the owner for its value.

MEASURE OF DAMAGES IN SUCH A CASE is regulated by the jury.

ERROR to the circuit court of Leak county. Trespass to recover value of a mule. From the bill of exceptions it appears
that the mule had broken into the defendant's close; that he had
seized and tied it, and that it was strangled in its efforts to

escape. Verdict for plaintiff. The defendant moved for a new trial. Motion refused. Exceptions were taken, and writ of error to this court.

Hays and Yerger, for the defendant in error.

By Court, TROTTER, J. The principal error assigned is, the decision of the judge overruling the motion for a new trial, on the evidence contained in the record. If the defendants' fence had been a lawful inclosure, according to the provisions of the act of 1822, which declares what shall be deemed such, there could be no difficulty in determining this question. The inclosure, however, was not a sufficient one under the law, and the defendant had no authority to take the means of redress into his own hands, for any injury he may have sustained in consequence of such insufficiency. And yet he seeks to justify the seizure and detention of the mule in this case, under the law which allows cattle, doing damage on another's land, to be distrained by the owner. This case presents none of the features of a regular distress. It is very true that where cattle are found upon land doing an injury, the owner, under certain restrictions, is allowed to seize and detain them as a pledge or security for the payment of the damages he has sustained. But this, as a means of redress, can never be allowed unless in cases where the owner of the cattle would be liable to an action. Could the plaintiff have maintained a suit on the facts disclosed by the record in the present case? He could not. How then can he justify himself under the law of distress? It has been insisted, however, that, be this as it may, the action should have been case and not trespass. This argument is rested upon the assumption that the taking of the mule in the first place was a lawful act. But if there was no right to distrain, then the seizure was illegal, and trespass is the proper remedy: Bac. Abr., tit. Trespass, B. If, however, it had been a case in which the right contended for did exist, yet if the defendant afterwards abused or killed the animal, he would become a trespasser *ab initio*. For it is a well-settled rule, that whenever a person, who at first acted with propriety under an authority or license given him by law, afterwards abuses that authority, he becomes a trespasser *ab initio*: Id., tit. Trespass. And, therefore, says the same authority, if J. S., who has distrained a beast damage feasant, afterwards kill it, he is a trespasser. In this case it is clearly shown that the mule got into the defendant's grounds in consequence of the insufficiency of his fence, and if it was destroyed by his act, he must submit to pay the owner its value. The third section of the act of 1822, provides, that if any person injured, for want of such sufficient fence as is required by a preceding section, shall hurt, wound, lame, kill, or destroy, etc., by shooting, hunting with dogs, or otherwise, any horses, mares, mules, etc., he shall pay and satisfy to the owner of the beast so hurt, etc., double damages. This statute is quite decisive of the question of the defendant's liability, and the jury should have found a verdict for the plaintiff, for the value of the mule, as ascertained by the testimony. What the value was, it was their peculiar prerogative to decide. Some of the witnesses have stated that it was worth five dollars; others, one hundred dollars, and others that it was worth nothing. To the jury exclusively, pertained the province to compare and weigh the testimony, and pronounce the result. They have done so, and we are not inclined to disturb their verdict. The whole case was before them with all the circumstances; and although it would appear from the bill of exceptions that the preponderance of the proof was in favor of the plaintiff, yet we can not, for that reason alone, award a new trial. It is not our business to weigh the testimony. It is sufficient that we see, upon the record, proof which legally conduced to the verdict which was rendered.

Let the judgment of the court below be affirmed.

NECESSITY OF MAINTAINING FENCE—RIGHT TO DISTRAIN.—At common law tenant of a close was not bound to fence against an adjoining close except by prescription or agreement, but each proprietor was at his peril to keep his cattle on his own land: *Holladay* v. *Marsh*, 20 Am. Dec. 678; nor was any one bound to fence against cattle on the highway, the reason being they are not rightfully there: *Mills* v. *Stark*, 17 Id. 444; *Stackpole* v. *Healy*, 8 Id. 121. But against cattle lawfully grazing on common land pursuant to a town ordinance, the adjoining owner must maintain sufficient fence to protect his crops: *Holladay* v. *Marsh*, 20 Id. 678. At common law cattle doing damage on land inclosed or uninclosed might be distrained, or the owner was liable in trespass: Id. But one can not impound neat cattle taken damage feasant in his inclosure unless the fence he was bound to repair was such as the law required: *Mooney* v. *Maynard*, 18 Id. 699. To justify as for a distress damage feasant the defendant must show actual possession of the land trespassed upon: *Orser* v. *Storms*, 18 Id. 543.

ABUSE OF PROCESS IS A TRESPASS AB INITIO: See *Barrett* v. *White*, 14 Am. Dec. 352, and note 365; *Barrett* v. *Lightfoot*, 15 Id. 110. In *Baumgard* v. *Mayor*, 29 Id. 437, it was held that a seizure under a municipal ordinance becomes a trespass *ab initio*, if there has been a failure to comply with the subsequent proceedings prescribed by the ordinance. Case is the proper remedy for acts done in abuse of process: *Pierson* v. *Gale*, 30 Id. 487.

POSSESSION NECESSARY TO MAINTAIN TRESPASS: See *Orser* v. *Storms*, 18 Am. Dec. 543, and note 546.

Thompson *v.* Grand Gulf R. & B. Co.

[3 Howard, 240.]

Compensation for Property Taken in the Exercise of the Right of Eminent Domain, must be secured or made, and a statute divesting the owner's title and turning him over to obtain his compensation under judgment rendered for his damages, violates that provision of the bill of rights which declares that "no person's property shall be taken or applied to public use without just compensation first made therefor."

In Construing Constitutions, no Word is to be Rejected or disregarded which may have a material bearing on the rights of citizens, and such construction should be given as will best protect private rights.

Judgment is not Compensation, but a security for compensation or satisfaction.

Defect in Clause Providing Compensation can not be Remedied by the court's giving a different judgment from that directed by the legislature.

Appeal from the circuit court of Claiborne county. The opinion states the case. There was a motion to dismiss in this court on the grounds of want of jurisdiction and of proper parties. On this point, Trotter, J., delivered the following opinion: "The motion to dismiss this cause for want of jurisdiction in this court must be overruled. The present proceeding was authorized by the act of 1833, and the supplemental act of 1836, to incorporate the Grand Gulf Railroad and Banking company. The plaintiff in error was properly and necessarily a party to the proceeding, because his interests were involved in the suit. It was therefore a controversy between the defendants in error and the plaintiff, and an appeal lies in all such cases after final judgment."

Montgomery and Boyd, for the appellants.

Anderson, for the appellee.

By Court, Sharkey, C. J. The present controversy arose out of an application by the appellees to the circuit court of Claiborne county, to have the damages assessed to the appellee, which he might sustain by running the railroad through his land. The proceeding was instituted under the fourth section of the charter, which authorizes the company to purchase of individuals any lands, or the use and occupation of any lands which they may deem necessary; and in case they can not agree upon the terms of purchase, with the owners of land, they may petition the circuit court of Claiborne county to impanel a jury of twelve freeholders, who shall be sworn to view and value the land without favor or partiality, and report their valuation to the circuit court, and the court shall thereupon cause a conveyance

to be made to the company, and adjudge the assessed value
thereof to the owner of the land. The amendment to the
charter, passed in 1837, provides in addition, that in assessing the
damages, the jury shall take into consideration the benefits resulting to the owner of land from constructing such road, but
only towards the extinguishment of the damages, and that the
court shall grant a conveyance, and render judgment and award
execution against the company for the amount of the damages
assessed.

Several objections are made to the regularity of the proceedings of the circuit court, but it will be unnecessary to notice
them in detail, as the case must be disposed of on the grave
question of the constitutionality of the charter, taken and relied upon in the argument. That part of the charter which is
said to conflict with the constitution, is the latter clause of the
first section of the amendment. The ground taken arises under
the provision in the bill of rights, which declares that " no person's property shall be taken or applied to public use without the
consent of the legislature, and without just compensation first
made therefor."

It is insisted that the compensation should be first made, and
that a judgment is not compensation. On the other hand, it is
said that it is sufficient for the legislature to provide the means
by which compensation is to be acquired. To determine between the constitution and the legislature, is often embarrassing,
and always demands a cautious and deliberate investigation.
In the inquiry is involved the highest function of the judicial
department. The acts of the legislature should be sustained, if
possible; the constitution must be preserved inviolate. We have
approached this question under a due sense of its importance;
and have given to it such investigation as the limit of our time
would admit, and we are entirely satisfied with the correctness
of the result to which that investigation has led.

It is a sound rule in construing constitutions, that no word is
to be rejected or disregarded which may have a material bearing
on the rights of the citizen, and such construction should be
given as will best protect private rights, because constitutions
are limitations, which confine each department of the government to the exercise of such powers only as have been delegated.
The word " first," used in the bill of rights, can not be regarded
as useless; nor are we at liberty to suppose that it was inserted
without design or by accident. The sentence is perfectly intelligible as it stands, and in accordance with first principles. By

regarding the word "first" as material, there can be no difficulty
in carrying the provision into execution by proper legislation;
but by rejecting it, and assuming the position that it is sufficient
for the legislature to provide the means or the mode of obtaining
compensation, the provision might be wholly defeated, and
owners compelled to part with their property without compensation. If the law be sustainable, it must operate generally, there
is no exception to it. Suppose that a company or corporation,
to whom private property is adjudged, should be wholly irresponsible, and it is not straining too much to suppose such a
case, what compensation has the owner for his property? But
even if it should be responsible, is it fair or just to convey away
private property, and only provide the owner with a legal remedy for the value, which may easily be exhausted in the pursuit
of the remedy? These, amongst others, are evils which might
follow under an administration of the provisions of the charter,
if they are sufficient, and being evils so apparent, it is fair to
presume that the convention intended to guard against them,
and the presumption derives strength from the fact that the words
they employed, if literally construed, are of all others, best calculated to effect this object. The power in a state to appropriate
private property by virtue of its right of eminent domain, should
be exercised only in the strictest justice towards the owner of the
property. Blackstone, in his commentaries, says, "the public is
now considered as an individual, treating with an individual for an
exchange:" 1 Bl. Com. 139. If this remark be true, it is obvious
that neither party would have a right to enforce terms on the
other, which are not acceptable. We can not presume that the
convention intended that this right should be exercised unless
on terms the most favorable to individuals. Life, liberty, and
property are three great objects of governmental protection, and
we must infer that due precaution has been used for the protection of each of them. To divest the right to property without
ample compensation, would be unjust. The judgment in this
case is not compensation. A judgment is but a security for compensation or satisfaction, which may or may not prove productive. In principle there is no difference between a judgment and
a bond, except that one is a security of a higher nature than
the other. Suppose the legislature had said that the railroad
company should give bond for the payment of the damages
assessed, could it be said to be a compensation? And yet it
might be quite as available as a judgment. Angell, in a note on
this subject, says, "there can be no other just equivalent but

money:" Angell on Watercourses, 40. We must, therefore, understand that when the convention said that private property should not be taken without compensation first made, that they did not intend that a mere security should be substituted for compensation.

The authorities cited for the defendants in error, can not be considered as entirely applicable. The constitution of New York is different from ours, in not requiring that compensation shall be first made; it merely declares that private property shall not be appropriated to public purposes without just compensation. The authorities, however, do not fairly cover the point in controversy. The most recent opinion directly on the point, and the one which we rely on as an authority, is that of Chancellor Kent, in a copious note to the third edition of his commentaries. After citing many authorities in regard to the right of eminent domain, he proceeds to say: " The better opinion is, that the compensation, or offer of it, must precede or be concurrent with the seizure and entry upon private property under the authority of the state. The government is bound, in such cases, to provide some tribunal for the assessment of the compensation or indemnity, before which each party may meet and discuss their claims on equal terms; and if the government proceeds without taking these steps, their officers and agents may, and ought to be restrained by injunction:" 2 Kent, 339, note. He says further: " The settled and fundamental doctrine is, that government has no right to take private property for public purposes without giving a just compensation; and it seems to be necessarily inplied, that the indemnity should, in cases which will admit of it, be previously and equitably ascertained, and be ready for reception concurrently, in point of time with, the actual exercise of the right of eminent domain." It is worthy of remark too, that Chancellor Kent has not given the foregoing opinion in view of any constitution requiring, in direct terms, a previous indemnity, but in reference to constitutions containing nothing more than the general provision, that private property shall not be taken for public uses without full compensation being made; and in reference also to the universal principles of justice, independent of all constitutions; for in support of it, he cites Puffendorf, Grotius, and others. He also cites the civil code, and code Napoleon, as both requiring previous indemnity; and says the American constitutions being substantially the same in these provisions, though not in the same words, would seem to require the same construction; from which we may infer that under these codes, previous indemnity is required to be made. The provision in the civil code is, that "no one can be divested of his property, unless for some purpose of public utility, and on consideration of a previous and equitable indemnity, and in a manner previously prescribed by law:" Civ. Code of La., art. 489. The idea is not new, that compensation should precede, or be concurrent with the appropriation of private property, nor is the provision peculiar to our constitution. As the right to apply private property to public uses, is an incident of inherent sovereignty which might be exercised to the prejudice of individuals, it is fair to infer that the convention were not content that the restriction should rest upon the uncertain application of the general principles of justice, and therefore incorporated it into the constitution, thus placing it out of the power of the legislature to exercise the right on any other than equitable and just terms. Under this view, we think it was incompetent for the legislature to authorize the railroad company to take private property, giving the owner no other compensation than a judgment and execution.

But it is contended that an imperfect mode of compensation does not necessarily make the charter void. That is true, if it could be carried into effect. This was held to be the law in the authorities cited. An act appropriating private property without providing adequate means for making compensation, was held sufficient to protect the agents from an action of trespass. The act, it seems, is to be considered *prima facie* good, until the party be judicially prevented from acting under it. But when there is no mode prescribed for making the necessary compensation, a court of chancery would prevent the party from proceeding under it by injunction, as was done in the case of *Gardner* v. *Village of Newburg*, cited by the counsel. That is precisely the case here. The legislature have prescribed no mode of making the required compensation, or what is the same thing, have prescribed a mode which can not be constitutionally carried into effect, and the plaintiff in error refuses to give up his property, and he can not be compelled to do so. The consequence is, that that portion of the charter which authorizes the taking of private property, must be inoperative, and we do not wish to be understood as interfering with any other part of it. If there was any mode of construing the charter by which a constitutional remedy could be given, we should think it our duty to give it that construction. But the legislature has provided that the owner of land in whose favor damages are as-

sessed, shall have judgment and execution for the amount. This
is the only remedy that is given, and we say it is not sufficient;
but we can not make a remedy that is sufficient by authorizing
the court to give a different judgment from that which is
directed by the legislature. That is the business of the legislature itself, if it should be deemed necessary. If the money
had been paid on the rendition of the judgment, we should not
be prepared to say that it would not have been sufficient; but
this was not done, and the party has nothing but the judgment.
It was competent for the legislature to prescribe the mode of
assessing the damages as they did.

In support of this opinion, it may not be out of place to remark that one of the members of this court was also a member
of the convention, and recollects that the above-mentioned provision in the bill of rights was discussed, and it was framed as
it is on due deliberation, and with a view to secure to individuals a previous indemnity for property taken.

Under these views, we feel constrained to reverse the judgment, and dismiss the application.

EXERCISE OF RIGHT OF EMINENT DOMAIN—COMPENSATION: See note to
Varick v. *Smith*, 28 Am. Dec. 423; and *Bloodgood* v. *Mohawk and Hudson R.
R. Co.*, 31 Id. 313, and note 372, where the cases in this series on the subject
of eminent domain are collected.

FITCH v. SCOTT.

[3 HOWARD, 314.]

TO SUBJECT AN ATTORNEY TO AN ACTION BY HIS CLIENT, two things are
    necessary to be shown: gross or unreasonable neglect or ignorance, and a
    consequent loss to his client.
AN ATTORNEY IS PERSONALLY LIABLE FOR NEGLIGENCE, when a note al-
    ready due is placed in his hands for collection, and he permits a term to
    go by before commencing suit, and then dismisses the suit, surrenders
    the note, and accepts the transfer of a judgment against another person.
ATTORNEY IS LIABLE FOR THE WHOLE AMOUNT DUE upon the note in such
    a case.
ATTORNEY HAS NO AUTHORITY TO COMPROMISE THE CLAIM of his client,
    and if he does so, he takes upon himself the consequence of its loss, or
    the damages which he may sustain.

APPEAL from the circuit court of Yazoo county. Scott placed
in the hands of Fitch and Morgan, for collection, a note then due,
but suit was not commenced on it till the following term, when
the suit was dismissed, the note surrendered, and the transfer of
a judgment on a third person accepted. Morgan having died,

Scott instituted an action on the case against Fitch for the value
of the note. Judgment for the plaintiff. Fitch appealed.

Yerger, for the appellant.

Thompson, contra.

By Court, TROTTER, J. The law implies a promise on the part
of attorneys, that they will execute the business intrusted to
their professional management, with a reasonable degree of care,
skill, and dispatch, and they are liable to an action, if guilty of
a default in either of these duties, whereby their clients are injured: Chit. on Con. 166. There must, however, be gross negligence or ignorance, and if the attorney acts to the best of his
skill, and with a *bona fide* degree of attention, he will not be
responsible: 4 Burr. 2061. This was the rule laid down by Lord
Mansfield in the case of *Pitt* v. *Yalden*, in which he remarked
that that part of the profession which is carried on by attorneys
is liberal and reputable, as well as useful to the public, when
they conduct themselves with honor and integrity, and that they
ought to be protected when they act to the best of their knowledge and ability. These principles are recognized in the case of
Gilbert v. *Williams*, 8 Mass. 51, 59 [5 Am. Dec. 77]. In that
case the court say there can be no doubt that for any misfeasance
or unreasonable neglect of an attorney, whereby his client suffers a loss, an action may be supported. An attorney, however,
is not liable for every mistake, but shall be protected where he
acts in good faith. Two things are, therefore, to be shown in
order to subject an attorney to an action: 1. Gross or unreasonable negligence or ignorance; and 2. A consequent loss to his
client. Do the proofs exhibited in this cause make out the
points? The note in this case, was placed in the hands of the
attorney in August, 1834, in time to have commenced suit upon
it to the October term of the circuit court of that county, in the
same year. This was undoubtedly the duty of the attorney.
And in the absence of any instructions to the contrary, we are
bound to infer that such were his engagements. The note was
placed in his hands to be put in suit, and it is repugnant to the
very terms of his contract, to infer an authority to delay suit
until the second term of the court. The debtors might be entirely able to pay a judgment rendered in October, 1834, and
totally insolvent in April, 1835, and this consideration in all
probability might have influenced the creditor to place the note
in the attorney's hands for suit. Be this, however, as it may,
we think it was the duty of the defendant to have brought suit

at the first term, and that in not doing so, he was guilty of unreasonable neglect.

This was the view of the court in *Palmer's case*, commented upon by Lord Mansfield in *Pitt v. Yalden*, 4 Burr. 2061. The defendant in the suit in which Palmer had been retained, was arrested on bailable process, and by a rule of court was entitled to his discharge on filing common bail, unless declared against, before the end of the second term after his arrest. Palmer let the second term pass without declaring, and the defendant accordingly obtained his discharge. It was held to be a case of gross negligence, for which he was liable to his client. This is very similar to the case before us. The defendant not only permitted a term to pass before suit, but upon the return of the writ to the April term following, dismissed the suit, and surrendered the note to the debtors. The only excuse offered for this remissness is the reputed insolvency of the Platners. But this is no excuse. The suit should have been prosecuted to a final judgment, and then the process for obtaining satisfaction of it, strictly followed up. By doing so, the ability of the debtors to pay the claim, could have been tested by a legal and certain criterion. In the absence of any authority from their client, this was the only legal course of conduct for the attorneys to pursue. Instead of this, however, they take an assignment of a judgment, and deliver the claim to the debtors. An attorney has no authority to compromise the claim of his client, and if he does so, he takes upon himself the consequences of its loss, or the damages which he may sustain. The plaintiff in error was therefore guilty of a violation of his engagement to prosecute the claim of his client with proper diligence. It is a clear case of unreasonable neglect, and he is responsible to the extent of the loss which his client has sustained. The evidence has furnished us with no criterion of damages save the note which was surrendered. But the plaintiff in error insists that at the time it was exchanged for the judgment it was of but little value. In support of this assertion, he has furnished us with no other evidence than the mere opinions of some three or four persons. The sheriff, who was examined before the jury, states, that he made the money on all the executions which were in his hands returnable to the April term, 1835, of the Yazoo circuit court, against the Messrs. Platners, and that he had also learned that one of them had a negro, though he had not been able then to find it. How then can we say that if judgment had been obtained at October term, 1834, it might not have been satisfied as others were?

In the case before noticed, of *Gilbert* v. *Williams*, the attorney disobeyed the instructions of his client to institute suit immediately. And although he did afterwards sue out the attachment, yet the debtor's property was then covered by liens which defeated the attachment. The attorney gave the indulgence which he did on repeated promises by the debtor that the claim, which was small, should be paid, and his motive was to save the debtor from the vexation and costs of the suit. He appeared to possess ample property to pay that claim and much more. The debtor was, however, as it afterwards turned out, insolvent. Nevertheless, the court held the attorney liable for the whole debt. Because, if he had promptly obeyed the instructions of his client, the debt might have been saved by acquiring a priority of lien. So in the case before us, if the plaintiff in error had complied strictly with his engagement, and obtained a judgment in October, it is highly probable the debt would have been saved. But we are clearly of opinion, that the surrender of the note to the debtors in this case, renders the attorney responsible for the whole amount due upon it, in the absence of any certain proof, that the creditor has not by such compromise lost his whole debt. That we take to be the only legal inference from the act, and there has been no proof to destroy it. It may be proper to remark, that Mr. Fitch appears never to have had the possession or control of the claim in question, and that everything done in regard to it was transacted by his late partner. He is not, therefore, justly subject to any blame. He is in law, however, responsible for the acts of his partner. We think the verdict is sustained by the proof.

Let the judgment of the court below be affirmed, with damages and costs.

———

GENERAL RULE AS TO ATTORNEY'S LIABILITY FOR NEGLIGENCE AND WANT OF SKILL.—It is a universal rule of law that an attorney, in the management of his professional business, is bound to use only a reasonable degree of care and skill, and is liable only for gross ignorance or neglect. "The attorney is bound to execute business in his profession with a reasonable degree of care, skill, and dispatch. If the client be injured by the gross fault, negligence, or ignorance of the attorney, the attorney is liable; but if he acts with good faith, to the best of his skill, and with an ordinary degree of attention, he will not be responsible:" Per Emery, J., in *Wilson* v. *Russ*, 20 Me. 421. The rule as thus formulated is the one that has guided the courts in their decisions from the earliest cases to the present day: *Pitt* v. *Yalden*, 4 Burr. 2060; *Kemp* v. *Burt*, 4 Barn. & Ad. 424; *Godefroy* v. *Dalton*, 6 Bing. 460; *Baikie* v. *Chandless*, 3 Camp. 17; *Laidless* v. *Elliott*, 3 Barn. & Cress. 738; *Nisbet* v. *Lawson*, 1 Ga. 275; *O'Barr* v. *Alexander*, 37 Id. 195; *Cox* v. *Sullivan*, 7 Id. 144; *Holmes* v. *Peck*, 1 R. I. 242; *Gilbert* v *Williams*, 8 Mass. 51; *Caverly* v.

McOwen, 123 Id. 574; *Evans* v *Watrous*, 2 Port. 205; *Mardis* v. *Shackleford*, 4 Ala. 493; *Pennington* v. *Yell*, 6 Eng. 212; *Walker* v. *Scott*, 8 Id. 644; *Sevier* v. *Holliday*, 2 Ark. 512; *Palmer* v. *Ashley*, 3 Id. 75; *In re Spencer*, 21 Law T. (N. S.) 808; S. C., 39 L. J. Ch. 841; *Lee* v. *Dixon*, 3 Fost. & F. 744; *Parker* v. *Rolls*, 14 Com. B. 691; *Lewis* v. *Collard*, Id. 208; *Montrion* v. *Jeffery*, 2 Car. & P. 113; *Lanphier* v. *Phipos*, 8 Id. 475; *Shilcock* v. *Passman*, 7 Id. 289; *Chapman* v. *Van Toll*, 8 El. & Bl. 396; *Elkington* v. *Holland*, 9 Mee. & W. 658; *Hart* v. *Frame*, 6 Cl. & Fin. 193; *Purves* v. *Londell*, 12 Id. 91; *Gambert* v. *Hart*, 44 Cal. 542; *Stevens* v. *Walker*, 55 Ill. 151; *Chase* v. *Heaney*, 70 Id. 268; *Reilly* v. *Cavanaugh*, 29 Ind. 435; *Eggleston* v. *Boardman*, 37 Mich. 14; *Estate of A. B.*, 1 Tucker (N. Y. Surr.), 247; *Hatch* v. *Fogerty*, 33 N. Y. Sup. Ct. 166; *Bowman* v. *Tallman*, 27 How. Pr. 212; *Morrill* v. *Graham*, 27 Tex. 646; *Crosbie* v. *Murphy*, 8 Ir. C. L. 301; *Hodge* v. *Frame*, 3 Jur. 547; *Suydam* v. *Vance*, 2 McLean, 99. In *Bowman* v. *Tallman*, 27 How. Pr. at page 274; S. C., 2 Robt. 385, Robertson, C. J., uses the following language: "There is no implied agreement in the relation of counsel and client, or in the employment of the former by the latter, that the former will guarantee the success of his proceedings in a suit, or the soundness of his opinions, or that they will be ultimately sustained by a court of last resort. * * * He only undertakes to avoid errors which no member of his profession of ordinary prudence, diligence, and skill would commit. * * * It is not enough that doubts may be raised of the soundness of his opinions or correctness of his course, unless they are accompanied by the absence of all reasonable doubts of the propriety of an opposite course or opinion in the mind of every member of his profession of ordinary skill, sagacity, and prudence, caused by a decisiveness of reason and authority in its favor."

The general rule being thus firmly established, the difficulty lies in its application. What amounts to the gross negligence, such as will charge an attorney? The answer to this question is, that each case must depend upon its own particular facts, and whether these facts amount to chargeable negligence or not rests with the determination of the jury: *Evans* v. *Watrous*, 2 Port. 205; *Walker* v. *Goodman*, 21 Ala. 647; *Pennington* v. *Yell*, 6 Eng. 212; *Waldpole* v. *Carlisle*, 32 Ind. 415; *Dearborn* v. *Dearborn*, 15 Mass. 315; *Caverly* v. *McOwen*, 123 Id. 574; *Hunter* v. *Caldwell*, 10 Q. B. 69; *Brazier* v. *Bryant*, 2 Dowl. Pr. 600. In California a different rule as to the determination of the question of negligence prevails, and it was there decided that when the facts were ascertained, the question of negligence was a question of law to be decided by the court: *Gambert* v. *Hart*, 44 Cal. 542.

MISTAKES ON POINTS OF LAW AND ERRORS IN JUDGMENT.—It is not every mistake or misapprehension of an attorney that will make him liable to an action for negligence: *Shilcock* v. *Passman*, 7 Car. & P. 289. "Every man is liable to error, and I should be very sorry that it should be taken for granted that an attorney is answerable for every error or mistake, and to be punished for it by being charged with the debt which he was employed to recover for his client from the person who stands indebted to him. * * * Not only counsel but judges may differ, or doubt, or take time to consider. Therefore an attorney ought not to be liable in cases of reasonable doubt:" *Per* Mansfield, C. J., in *Pitt* v. *Yalden*, 4 Burr. 2060. For a want of proper knowledge of all matters of law in common use, or of such plain and obvious principles as every lawyer is presumed to know, an attorney is liable; but an error of judgment upon an unsettled and controverted question of law is not such gross ignorance that he will be chargeable with the damages resulting from it: *Morrill* v. *Graham*, 27 Tex. 646; nor is any error in judgment, or mistake on a point of law, actionable negligence if it be such that a cautious man would fall into: *Montrion* v. *Jefferys*, 2 Car. & P. 113; *Lewis* v. *Collard*, 23 L. J. C. P. 32. A lawyer is not liable when he accepts as a correct exposition of the law a decision of the supreme court of his state: *Hastings* v. *Halleck*, 13 Cal. 203; but the case of *Marsh* v. *Whitmore*, 21 Wall. 178, modifies this last rule to the extent that the state decision must be in advance of any decision in the United States supreme court on that point.

In the construction of statutes the same general rule prevails, and an attorney is not liable for error if the act be difficult or doubtful: *Crosbie* v. *Murphy*, 8 Ir. C. L. 301; *Elkington* v. *Holland*, 9 Mee. & W. 658; *Kemp* v. *Burt*, 1 Nev. & M. 262. But he is bound to watch the changes in the public statutes, and in the *Estate of A. B.*, 1 Tucker (N. Y. Surr.) 236, where an attorney was sued for failing to do so, the surrogate said: "It is not claimed that a person who undertakes to perform his professional business should be acquainted with the whole circle of jurisprudence, and able to apply all the multitudinous rules, principles, and distinctions with absolute accuracy. He is, however, bound to understand the leading and fundamental principles of the common law, and he can not be excused for ignorance of the public statutes of the state." In *Bulmer* v. *Gilman*, 4 Man. & Gr. 108, an attorney put a construction on an order of the house of lords which was doubtful in its terms, such construction being different from that adopted by the standing orders committee and by the house, and in consequence, a bill he was intrusted to get through had to be abandoned; on the trial it was held that he was not guilty of such gross negligence as to disentitle him to compensation.

NEGLECT IN COLLECTION OR PRESENTMENT OF CLAIMS.—"It is the duty of an attorney who undertakes the collection of a debt (without special instructions), to pursue it through all the stages, as well against the sheriff and bail as against the principal, till the object is effected; and he is justified in not prosecuting (unless expressly directed), in cases where he is influenced by a prudent regard for the interest of the creditor:" *Per* Skinner, C. J., in *Crooker* v. *Hutchinson*, 2 D. Chip. 117. But where the client places a note in the attorney's hand and instructs him to bring suit, and the attorney, under an honest impression that the client's interests would best be subserved by delaying, omits to bring suit immediately, and the claim is thereby lost, the attorney is liable: *Cox* v. *Livingston*, 2 Watts & S. 103; *Gilbert* v. *Williams*, 3 Mass. 51; S. C., 5 Am. Dec. 77. In the absence of peremptory instructions, however, the attorney is allowed a reasonable discretion as to when to sue, and what is a reasonable time is for the determination of the jury: *Rhines* v. *Evans*, 66 Pa. St. 192. Six months' delay against a failing debtor is unreasonable: *Livingston* v. *Cox*, 6 Barr. 360; and where the attorney delayed so long that the debt became barred by the statute of limitations, he is chargeable: *Oldham* v. *Sparks*, 28 Tex. 425; *Hunter* v. *Caldwell*, 10 Q. B. 69; where by his gross negligence he puts the claim in such a situation as to embarrass the creditor in obtaining payment, liability will attach, though the debtor always has been and still is able to pay: *Wilson* v. *Coffin*, 2 Cush. 316; and where he agrees to collect a judgment, he is liable for a failure to use reasonable care and skill in the collection, though he does not practice in the county where judgment was entered: *Riddle* v. *Poorman*, 3 Pa. 224. A note against notoriously insolvent debtors was placed in an attorney's hands, with instructions to "do the best he could with it," and he exchanged the note with one of the drawers, who fraudulently gave him a note which did not belong to him, but which was made by solvent parties; he was held not negligent: *Wright* v. *Ligon*, Harp. Eq. 137. An attorney must use reasonable diligence in presenting a claim against the estate of a deceased debtor; and where, on

account of a want of prosecution or an unreasonable delay in getting recognized, the time for distribution passes without a recognition of the claim and
it is thereby lost, he is responsible: *Stevens* v. *Dexter*, 55 Ill. 151; but a failure to file the claim against an insolvent's estate is not negligence, when it
appears that the debtor was living at the time the note was put in his hands,
and it is not shown that he had knowledge of the debtor's subsequent death:
Stubbs v. *Breene*, 37 Ala. 627.

ERRORS IN INSTITUTING PROCEEDINGS OR SUITS AT LAW.—An attorney is
liable for his disregard, in the bringing of a suit, of a rule which is well and
clearly defined, and which had existed and been published long enough to
justify the belief that it was known to the profession; and he can not be allowed to prove at the trial that he consulted a distinguished attorney respecting the proper course to be pursued by him: *Goodman* v. *Walker*, 30 Ala. (N.
S.) 482. And where an attorney, in making a writ, used a printed form containing the common money counts, with blank spaces for the insertion of the
sums, in which forms the word hundred, formerly printed, was omitted in the
later blanks, one of which he made use of, so that by mistake he declared for
twelve dollars, instead of for one thousand two hundred dollars, and property
of the value of one thousand two hundred dollars was attached, but lost on account of the mistake, and the demand itself was lost on account of the subsequent insolvency of the maker; the attorney was held liable: *Varnum* v. *Martin*, 15 Pick. 440. An attorney received instructions to sue for particular
average loss for goods shipped to Calcutta and there sold. Under an impression that the only defense the underwriters would set up would be a set-off
against the broker in whose name the policies were effected, he sued out writs
in the lord mayor's court, which had no power to issue a commission for the
examination of witnesses abroad; but the actions being defended, a commission became essential, and the proceedings were necessarily abandoned; for
the loss consequent the attorney became chargeable: *Cox* v. *Leech*, 1 Com. B.
(N. S.) 617. In that case, Cockburn, C. J., in the course of his opinion, said:
"If an attorney, with or without express instructions from his client, takes
out a writ, and proceeds thereon in a court of special and peculiar jurisdiction, he is bound to acquaint himself with the machinery by which the practice of that court is regulated, and to see that it is adequate to the carrying
out of the objects of the suit." So an attorney is responsible for bringing an
action within a limited jurisdiction on a cause of action arising out of such
jurisdiction: *Williams* v. *Gibbs*, 6 Nev. & M. 788; also, where, on being em
ployed by a master to take proceedings against his apprentices for misconduct, he proceeded specially on the section of the statute relating to servants
and not to apprentices: *Hart* v. *Frame*, 6 Cl. & F. 193; and for not charging a prisoner in custody in due time: *Pitt* v. *Yalden*, 4 Burr. 2060; *Russell*
v. *Stewart*, 3 Id. 1787; also where the defendant gives insufficient bail, of the
entry of which the plaintiff's attorney fails to give him (plaintiff) notice, in
consequence of which plaintiff is prevented from excepting, and a loss ensues.
McWilliams v. *Hopkins*, 4 Rawle, 382.

NEGLECT OR WANT OF SKILL IN THE CONDUCT OR MANAGEMENT OF A SUIT.
In *Godefroy* v. *Dalton*, 6 Bing. 468, Tindall, C. J., says: "He," the attorney,
"is liable generally for the consequences of ignorance of the rules of practice
of the court [where he practices], for the want of care in the preparation of
the cause for trial. or of attendance thereon with his witnesses, and for the
mismanagement of so much of the conduct of a cause as is usually and ordinarily allotted to his department of the profession." His retainer obliges
him to the right conduct of a suit, but not for the judgment of the court, for

that is beyond his control: *Gallaher* v. *Thompson*, Wright, 466; *Bowman* v. *Tallman*, 27 How. Pr. 274; S. C., 2 Robt. 385. Where an attorney suffered a case to be called on without previously ascertaining whether a material witness whom the plaintiff had undertaken to bring into court had arrived, and consequently plaintiff was nonsuited, he was held liable for negligence: *Reece* v. *Righy*, 4 Barn. & Ald. 202; and where a suit is called and tried as an undefended cause in consequence of the defendant's attorney neglecting to give his briefs to the counsel, he becomes chargeable with costs: *De Roufigny* v. *Peale*, 3 Taunt. 484. So when an attorney is employed to conduct an ejectment suit, which is referred to an arbitrator, and he fails to attend at the time appointed, he becomes responsible for the damages consequent upon such failure: *Swannel* v. *Ellis*, 1 Bing. 347. He is also responsible for an unreasonable delay in bringing a cause to trial; as where an attorney employed to recover certain land brought ejectment in 1866, and in 1870 had not brought the cause to trial nor made the necessary preparation, and no satisfactory excuse for the delay was shown: *Walsh* v. *Shumway*, 55 Ill. 471. And where a defendant, examined on oath before a master upon a reference to appoint a receiver upon a creditor's bill, refuses on the advice of his counsel to answer questions of whose propriety and pertinency there is no real doubt, and suffers damages thereby, he can hold his attorney therefor: *Gihon* v. *Shaw*, 7 Paige, 278.

An attorney has no implied power to compromise or give up any right of his client, or to consent to a judgment against his client: *Wadhams* v. *Gay*, 73 Ill. 415; *Preston* v. *Hill*, 50 Cal. 43; S. C., 19 Am. Rep. 647; nor to confess judgment, unless specially empowered: *Edwards* v. *Edwards*, 29 La. Ann. 597; though a confession with the knowledge and at the instance of the party was held sufficient without any special authorization to that effect, in *Lyon* v. *Williams*, 42 Ga. 168. And if the attorney allows judgment to go against him by default when he should have pleaded the general issue, he is liable: *Godefroy* v. *Day*, 5 Moo. & P. 284. But a client has no right to control the attorney in the due and orderly conduct of a suit, and the latter may waive a default contrary to the instructions of his client, if the case was such that there was no doubt in his mind, that according to the settled rules of procedure, the default would be opened by the court on the usual terms: *Anonymous*, 1 Wend. 108. The attorney can not settle the suit and conclude his client in relation to the subject-matter in litigation without the consent of his client: *Mandeville* v. *Reynolds*, 68 N. Y. 528. It is gross negligence to bring a suit and then dismiss it improperly: *Evans* v. *Watrous*, 2 Port. 205; or to dismiss a suit and receive in payment claims upon other parties: *Coopwood* v. *Baldwin*, 25 Miss. 129. An attorney commenced an action on a replevin bond; two years after suffered it to be dismissed; four years after recommenced action as on a lost bond, and two years after that dismissed it as to all solvent defendants, they having denied its existence under oath; and the bond being afterwards found in plaintiff's office, he was held responsible for the loss of the claim: *Waldpole* v. *Carlisle*, 32 Ind. 415. Still an attorney will be justified in ceasing to proceed with the client's cause, unless instructed to go on, whenever *bona fide* influenced to this course by a prudent regard for his client's interest: *Pennington* v. *Yell*, 6 Eng. 212; nor is he guilty of actionable negligence if he enters into a compromise without the consent of his client, provided he acts with care, skill, and good faith, and the compromise is made for the benefit of the client, and not in defiance of his express instructions: *Chown* v. *Parrot*, 14 Com. B. (N. S.) 74; *Crooker* v. *Hutchinson*, 2 D. Chip. 117. Where an attorney accepts employment in a case, the law, in the absence of a special contract to the contrary, implies an obligation on his part to attend to it until it is determined, and he can not abandon it without just cause. He may demand payment of fees already earned, and if they are not paid may withdraw from the case: *C. & St. L. R. R. Co.* v. *Koerner*, 3 Bradw. 248. But he must give reasonable notice of his withdrawal: *Harris* v. *Osbourn*, 2 Car. & M. 632; *Nichols* v. *Wilson*, 2 Dowl. 1031; *C. & St. L. R. R. Co.* v. *Koerner*, 3 Bradw. 248.

NEGLIGENCE IN PROCEEDINGS AFTER VERDICT OR JUDGMENT.—Where an attorney attempts the collection of a debt, it becomes his duty to sue out all process, mesne and final, necessary to effect that object; he should pursue bail and those who have become bound: *Pennington* v. *Yell*, 6 Eng. 212; *Crooker* v. *Hutchinson*, 1 Vt. 73; he is liable for neglecting to charge defend-ant by execution, whereby he was discharged: *Russell* v. *Palmer*, 2 Wils. 325; also if *non est inventus* be returned on the execution and he fails to sue out *scire facias* against the bail in a reasonable time: *Dearborn* v. *Dearborn*, 15 Mass. 315. But where the law allows a certain time for the performance of an act, an attorney is not liable for delay if he performs the act within that time: *Holmes* v. *Peck*, 1 R. I. 242. In that case an attorney died twelve days before the return day of an execution, without having levied the attachment, real estate having been attached by the original writ, and the attachment, not being subsequently levied, was lost; it was held that the attorney was not liable for the damages sustained, as nothing had been lost at the time of his death. Where an attorney submits a motion for a new trial before the certificate in support of it is certified, he is liable: *Gambert* v. *Hart*, 44 Cal. 542; so, also, where he obtains a new trial but conducts the proceedings in obtaining it so carelessly and negligently that the order granting the same is reversed in the supreme court; and his liability is not altered by the fact that the attorney employed other counsel in the same case: *Drais* v. *Hogan*, 50 Cal. 121; and where a jury returned a verdict in the attorney's favor, and he took the same, and by his negligence and unskillfulness altered the verdict so as to include only a worthless piece of the property sought to be recov-ered, and the jury at his request accept the same as their verdict, he must answer for the damages that result: 36 Ind. 319; so where, in drawing up a decree, the solicitor erroneously inserted the word "inquiry" for the word "sale." *In re Bolton*, 9 Beav. 272.

An attorney has no power to satisfy a judgment without payment: *Mande-ville* v. *Reynolds*, 68 N.Y. 528; nor to release the same: *Kirk's appeal*, 87 Pa. St. 243; 30 Am. Rep. 357; nor to settle the judgment by allowing the same in payment of an account against himself: *Chapman* v. *Burt*, 77 Ill. 337; nor to receive payment in depreciated money: *Trumbull* v. *Nicholson*, 27 Id. 149; nor to receive anything but money in payment: *Herriman* v. *Shomon*, 24 Kan. 387; S. C., 36 Am. Rep. 261.

LIABILITY OF ATTORNEY FOR NEGLIGENCE OF PARTNER, CLERK, OR SUB-ATTORNEY.—Lawyers practicing in partnership are equally responsible for each other's negligence or want of skill, and each individual member is liable for the misconduct of any of the other members: *Poole* v. *Gist*, 4 McCord, 259; *Dwight* v. *Dimon*, 4 La. Ann. 490; *Norton* v. *Cooper*, 3 Sm. & G. 375; *Wilkinson* v. *Griswold*, 12 Smed. & M. 669; *Livingston* v. *Cox*, 6 Pa. St. 360. He can not re-lieve himself from liability by hiring or substituting other counsel: *Smallwood* v. *Norton*, 20 Me. 83. And where he employs another person to prosecute a claim placed in his hands for collection, he is chargeable with the negligence of the person so employed, and he is not relieved from liability by the fact that such person is himself a competent attorney: *Walker* v. *Stevens*, 79 Ill. 193. So where notes were placed in his hand for collection, and the maker residing i...

a county where the attorney did not practice, he sent them to an attorney in that county, and the latter collected them and converted them to his own use, he is liable to the client for the amount: *Pollard* v. *Rowland*, 2 Blackf. 22. And where a receiver was appointed by the court upon the representation of the plaintiff's solicitor that the receiver had entered into the usual recognizances, which he had not in fact done; and a loss occurred in consequence of the receiver's liability being only in the nature of a simple contract, the solicitor was held personally responsible, though he practiced in the country and the representations were made by his London agents: *Simmons* v. *Rose*, 31 Beav. 1. An attorney must answer to the client for the negligence of his clerk as much as if it was his own immediate act: *Floyd* v. *Nangle*, 3 Atk. 568; *Birkbeck* v. *Stafford*, 14 Ab. Pr. 285, as where the employee of an attorney failed to give him notice of the trial of a cause which was consequently undefended and lost: *Collard* v. *Griffin*, Barnes, 37; also, when he collected money and gave it to a third person, from whom it was stolen, even though such third person was trustworthy: *Grayson* v. *Wilkinson*, 5 Smed. & M. 268.

MISCELLANEOUS APPLICATIONS OF THE RULE REQUIRING DILIGENCE AND SKILL.—When there is reasonable doubt whether an instrument drawn by an attorney is illegal or not on account of champerty, and there is no want of ordinary care, and the attorney consults those in whom he had confidence and acts under their advice, he is not liable if the instrument afterwards proves illegal; he does not guarantee the instrument: *Potts* v. *Sparrow*, 8 Car. & P. 749. But an attorney acting for a lender is liable if he takes insufficient security: *Donaldson* v. *Haldane*, 7 Cl. & Fin. 762; *Langdon* v. *Godfrey*, 4 Fost. & F. 445; or where he received instructions to prepare security for the payment of an annuity, and he does so by mere agreement and not under seal: *Parker* v. *Rolls*, 14 Com. B. 691; and where he lent money to A. on an agreement by which C. charged, as security, his interest in five thousand pounds consols, standing in the names of trustees in trust for him, but neglecting to give the trustees notice, a judgment creditor who subsequently obtained a charging order under statutes 1 and 2 Vic., c. 110, sec. 4, notice of which he gave to the trustees, obtained precedence, in consequence of which the debt was lost: *Watts* v. *Porter*, 3 El. & Bl. 743; S. C., 2 C. L. 1553.

An attorney employed to complete a contract for the purchase of leasehold property, must make a reasonable inquiry into the vendor's title, and he is liable if the vendee is afterwards turned out on account of a mortgage on the place and loses the purchase money: *Allen* v. *Clark*, 1 N. R. 358; so where a solicitor, in the published rental of premises advertised to be sold, misdescribed one portion, he becomes chargeable with the consequent damages: *Taylor* v. *Gorman*, 4 Ir. Eq. 550. But where an attorney employed to draw up a deed of assignment for the benefit of creditors by a person whose property he knew had been taken possession of on a petition for protection by the official assignee, is informed by the client that he believes all the creditors would sign, he (the attorney) is not bound to ascertain whether the creditors would sign, and it is not negligence in him not to do so: *Lewis* v. *Collard*, 2 Com. L. 1345; S. C., 14 Com. B. 208. An attorney may be liable for a debt lost by his negligence, but is not, of course, liable for the loss of the evidence of the debt; and in a suit brought against him for such loss, he may show that the plaintiff had another remedy for the recovery of his debt, which he has successfully pursued: *Huntington* v. *Rumnill*, 3 Day, 390.

MEASURE OF DAMAGES AGAINST AN ATTORNEY.—If a party sustains loss by the negligence or want of skill of his attorney, the latter is liable in damages, to be measured by the amount of the actual loss sustained: *Hardie* v. *Shackleford*, 4 Ala. 493; *Pennington* v. *Yell*, 6 Eng. 212; *Nisbet* v. *Lawson*, 1 Ga. 275; *Cox* v. *Sullivan*, 7 Id. 144; *Stevens* v. *Walker*, 55 Ill. 151; *Eccles* v. *Stephenson*, 3 Bibb, 517; *Grayson* v. *Wilkinson*, 5 Smed. & M. 268; *Suydam* v. *Vance*, 2 McLean, 99; *Arnold* v. *Robinson*, 3 Daly, 298; *Crooker* v. *Hutchinson*, 2 D. Chip. 117; *Rootes* v. *Stone*, 2 Leigh, 650. The nominal amount of the debt in the first suit is not the criterion: *Eccles* v. *Stephenson*, 3 Bibb, 517; *Cox* v. *Sullivan*, 7 Ga. 144; *Crooker* v. *Hutchinson*, 2 D. Chip. 117; and where the negligence complained of, in its legal effects, works no injury to the client, the attorney is not liable: *Harter* v. *Morris*, 18 Ohio St. 492. It is incumbent on the plaintiff to show that he had a valid claim which has been impaired or lost by the negligence or misconduct of the attorney: *Spiller* v. *Davidson*, 4 La. Ann. 171; for unless this be shown, he is liable only for nominal damages: *Pennington* v. *Yell*, 6 Eng. 212. The proof of actual damage may extend to facts that occur and grow out of the injury, even up to the day of the verdict: *Wilcox* v. *Plummer*, 4 Pet. 172.

As a general rule, an attorney is not liable for interest on the demand, but he is chargeable with interest where he collects money and converts it to his own use: *Chapman* v. *Burt*, 77 Ill. 337; *Waldpole* v. *Bishop*, 31 Ind. 156; *Mansfield* v. *Wilkerson*, 26 Iowa, 482; or is guilty of unreasonable delay in paying it over: *Dwight* v. *Simon*, 4 La. Ann. 490; *Chapman* v. *Burt*, 77 Ill. 337; or tenders client an insufficient amount, after deducting his fees: *Ketcham* v. *Thorp*, 91 Id. 611. In *Johnson* v. *Semple*, 31 Iowa, 49, and *Waldpole* v. *Bishop*, 31 Ind. 156, it was held that a demand must be made of the attorney to charge him with interest. The amount of the damages lies with the jury, and is determined by it: *Godefroy* v. *Jay*, 5 Moo. & P. 284; *Russell* v. *Palmer*, 3 Wils. 325; *Crooker* v. *Hutchinson*, 2 D. Chip. 117; *Eccles* v. *Stephenson*, 3 Bibb, 517.

EWING v. GLIDWELL.

[3 HOWARD, 332.]

FROM A VOLUNTARY NONSUIT, a writ of error will not lie.

COURTS DO NOT POSSESS POWER TO NONSUIT in this state, but they instruct the jury to find as in case of a nonsuit.

ERROR to the circuit court of Warren county. The opinion states the case.

Norcom and Mayson, for the plaintiffs in error.

Mayes, contra.

By Court, TROTTER, J. This was an action of assumpsit, in the Warren circuit court, upon a bill of exchange. The defendants pleaded *non assumpsit*. On the trial the plaintiffs offered to read to the jury the bill on which the suit was brought, which the court refused, on the ground of variance in the description of the bill declared on, from the one offered in evidence. The plaintiffs then suffered a nonsuit, and there was judgment against them for the costs.

In answer to the assignment of errors, it was insisted by the counsel for the defendants that this is not a proper case for a writ of error, and that error will not lie from a judgment for a voluntary nonsuit. It is very evident that the reasons in support of appeals and writs of error, can not be made to embrace the case of a voluntary default; for, in that case, though the judgment be ever so erroneous, yet being a consequence of the party's own conduct, he can not be heard to impeach it. It is a judgment sought by the party, and supposed to be rendered for his benefit. How then can he complain of it? Can it be assigned for error that the court allowed the plaintiff to take the step asked for by himself? This view of the subject has been taken by the courts in England, and also by those in this country. In the case of _Kempland_ v. _McCauley_, 4 T. R. 436, it was held by all the judges, that error would not lie on a voluntary nonsuit. They say "it is apparent that there can be no error of which the plaintiff can avail himself; for if the record were manifestly erroneous, the plaintiff, who has made default by suffering a nonsuit, can never have a judgment afterwards in his favor. "The case of _Bax_ v. _Bennet_,[1] 1 H. Bl. 432, is an authority for the same doctrine. The case of _Evans_ v. _The United States_, 5 Cranch, 280, is identical in principle with the one before us, and it was there held by the supreme court of the United States, that error could not be supported. In support of the writ of error, the counsel for the plaintiffs have relied on the case of _Smith_ v. _Lutts_,[2] 2 Johns. 9; and other cases decided by the supreme court of New York. But upon looking into these, we find that in each of them the nonsuit was compulsory, was the judgment of the court upon the motion of the defendant, and that it was resisted by the plaintiff; such was the case of _Smith_ v. _Sutts_.

In _Van De Veer_ v. _Stanton_, 1 Cow. 82, the justice before whom the cause was tried, nonsuited the plaintiff on the motion of the defendant, and gave judgment against him for the costs. The supreme court says: "The justice erred in nonsuiting the plaintiff." In _Schemerhorn_ v. _Jenkins_, 7 Johns. 373, the same principle is stated. It was an action of assault and battery by an infant. The defendant pleaded in chief. It was admitted at the trial that the plaintiff was an infant. The defendant thereupon moved for a nonsuit, unless a guardian was appointed for the plaintiff, and none being appointed, the court ordered the plaintiff to be nonsuited. In New York, the courts possess the power to nonsuit the plaintiff; and when this is done against his

---

1. _Bax_ v. _Bennett_.   2. _Smith_ v. _Sutts_.

consent, he should be allowed to impeach the decision. In this state the courts possess no such power, and never exercise it. The utmost extent to which they can go is to instruct the jury to find a verdict as in case of nonsuit, and this is often done. When erroneously done, the plaintiff has an undoubted right, upon principle and authority, to review the judgment in the court of errors. In the present case, the plaintiff voluntarily abandoned his cause, made default in the language of the books, and suffered a nonsuit. This step, on his part, may have been superinduced by an error in the court in rejecting his proof; but that can not alter the effect of the judgment. We can not look into the motives which influenced the plaintiff. It is sufficient that the record informs us that he was nonsuited by his consent, and on his own motion.

Let the cause be dismissed with costs to the defendant, etc.

———

GRANTING COMPULSORY NONSUIT: See note to *French* v. *Smith*, 24 Am. Dec. 620. Nonsuit does not bar a subsequent suit for the same cause except in some particular case: *Dana* v. *Gill*, 20 Id. 255. Appeal from an order of the circuit court, refusing to set aside a nonsuit, lies to the supreme court: *Simon's Ex'rs* v. *Gratz*, 23 Id. 33.

ERRORS IN FAVOR OF A PARTY objecting to a decree are not alone sufficient ground for revising it: *Griffith* v. *Depew*, 13 Am. Dec. 141; *Brown* v. *Caldwell*, 13 Id. 660.

———

NEWMAN *v.* FOSTER.

[3 HOWARD, 383.]

PLAINTIFF IN EJECTMENT IS ENTITLED TO RECOVER upon full proof of title and an adverse possession by the defendant at the time of the commencement of the suit.

IT IS NOT ERROR TO REFUSE INSTRUCTIONS, unless the party shows proof to which they could be applied.

BOUNDARY A QUESTION FOR THE JURY.—Whether a boundary has been so run and marked as to preclude further inquiry, is a question for the jury.

CALLS OF PATENT MAY BE CONTROLLED BY SURVEY.

ARTIFICIAL OR NATURAL BOUNDARIES PREVAIL over courses and distances.

PAROL EVIDENCE IS ADMISSIBLE TO PROVE BOUNDARY.

A MAP AND CERTIFICATE OF SURVEY ARE NOT CONCLUSIVE EVIDENCE *per se* that the lines were run as marked on them, but they are open to explanation by the surveyor.

TO BRING PLAT WITHIN RULE OF CLOSED SURVEY, the line of division must be marked on the ground.

IN EJECTMENT, EVIDENCE OF DEFENDANT'S POSSESSION at commencement of the suit is necessary.

A SPECIAL CONSENT RULE IS NECESSARY only where actual entry must be made previous to suit brought.

ERROR WILL NOT LIE for allowance of amendments.

EJECTMENT. The question arose as to the boundary line between two adjoining sections. The title to the sections themselves was not in dispute. The appellees rely upon the plat and certificate of survey made by the surveyor-general, and returned to the office of the register, containing a diagram of the sections and the established corner on the township line. A dotted line, as shown by this map, runs from this corner diagonally north-west, then turns to the north-east, and continues till it strikes the external boundary. The appellees claim the land east of this line as included in their section. The appellants claim under a map made from an actual survey after the suit was commenced. It differs from the other in no particular, except that the boundary line runs due north from the established corner. The appellant claims the land west of the line thus run. McFail, the last surveyor, states that he made diligent search for the boundary as indicated by the dotted line, but could not find it, and that no division line had ever been run and marked on the ground between the two sections, until he had run his line, as shown on his map. The appellees admit this fact, and also that this is the true line of division under the act of congress of February 11, 1805, but insist that the dotted line is a part of the plat of survey, and though made in mistake, is to be taken as the settled boundary line, and can not be corrected to the prejudice of their claim. The plaintiff moved the court to instruct the jury that if they believed the defendants, at the commencement of the suit, were in possession of the land to which they had shown title, they must find for the plaintiff; and also, that if the boundary line, as shown by the dotted line in the original survey, was not actually run and marked on the ground, that the true division line was to be ascertained by running due north from the established corner, and if the defendants are in possession west of this line, they must find for the plaintiff. The court refused to give these instructions. This refusal was assigned for error. Plaintiff also assigned for error that the court allowed the defendant to amend the consent rule.

Thrasher, for the appellant.

By Court, TROTTER, J. That the plaintiff in ejectment is entitled to recover upon full proof of title, and an adverse possession by the defendant, at the time of commencing the suit, is a legal proposition not susceptible of controversy. It is not every refusal, however, to state legal principles to a jury, however clear in themselves as abstract doctrines of the law, which will be decided to be error. It is sometimes very hazardous to lay general principles of law before the jury, where they can not be directly applied to the facts in proof. It has been uniformly decided, therefore, that it is not error in the judge to refuse instructions unless the party shows the existence of proof to which they can be fairly applied. Before we can decide that the court below was wrong in refusing this instruction, it will be necessary to examine in connection with it, the facts of the case, and this will be done in determining upon the propriety of the second instruction asked for and refused. The questions embraced in this instruction are essentially all that arise out of the whole record, and in disposing of them we shall necessarily decide this cause. The principles involved in the above charge, asked for by the plaintiff, are within the established rule upon the subject of boundary. The act of congress, of the eleventh of February, 1805, provides, that the boundary lines of sections, which shall not have been actually run and marked, as required, shall be ascertained by running straight lines from the established corners to the opposite corresponding corners, but in those portions of the fractional townships where no such opposite corresponding corners have been or can be fixed, the said boundary line shall be ascertained by running from the established corners, due north and south, or east and west lines, as the case may be, etc. If there was, then, no proof before the jury, that the division line between the sections had been actually run and marked on the ground by the original survey, the line could be ascertained in no other legal mode than that pointed out in the act of congress referred to. Whether it had been run and marked so as to close all further inquiries into the question of boundary, was certainly a question for the jury. And it might very properly have been submitted for their determination. With a view, however, to determine, fully and satisfactorily, the whole question involved in this assignment of the errors, we will consider it in connection with the decision made by the judge, upon the legal effect of the dotted line of partition in the original plat of survey. That decision was, that this line being part of the map and so appearing upon its face, could not be corrected after a sale of the land, though made in mistake.

The rule on this subject is well settled, and is uniform in all the cases which have been adjudicated where boundary was to be ascertained. The survey is to be taken as part of the patent. It is the source of title, is a matter of record, and may, therefore. be resorted to in order to control the calls of the patent.

A consequence of this principle is, that if the plat and certificate of survey show artificial or natural boundaries, though they may vary from the course or distance called for, they will nevertheless be taken as the true boundaries of the tract, if they can be well ascertained as described in the grant: 1 Marsh. 96;[1] Pirtle's Dig. 125. The reason and policy of this doctrine is well explained in the case of *Hubert and Wife* v. *Wise et al.*, 3 Call, 238.[2] Judge Pendleton says: "The marked trees upon the land remain invariable, and are to govern as to the boundary. Such lines, therefore, when proved, are never suffered to be departed from. If the true line according to course and distance, called for in the plat and certificate of survey, depart from the line proved to be actually run, and evidenced by marked trees or other natural or artificial monuments, the latter must prevail;" and he gives as the reason, the liabilities to mistakes by the surveyor, sometimes putting north for south, east for west, or in copying the descriptions into the patent. It would be highly detrimental, therefore, if a mistake in the calls of a patent might not be corrected by reference to the plat and certificate of survey. In the case of *Throop* v. *Cheeseman*, 16 Johns. 264, it is said by the court that the corner of lots as fixed by the surveyor-general can not be disregarded. In the case of *Lyon* v. *Ross and Wife*, 1 Bibb, 467, the same doctrine is fully stated and illustrated. The court say, when a line has been ascertained and marked by natural or artificial objects, it is to be considered as the proper boundary, though found to deviate from a rectilinear or mathematical line. That case was precisely analogous to the one before the court. Both parties claimed under deeds from the same grantor. The farms lay adjoining, and the question was purely one of boundary. The partition line called to run from corner to corner without any intervening object. By a plat filed in the cause, the spring which was claimed to be on the land of the defendant was represented to be one pole from a straight line according to the calls in the deed. But the proof was full that the line of partition which was run by the grantor, passed through the middle of the spring and was so run purposely to give both farms the use of the water. And on this proof the court decreed in favor of the complainants to have the quiet and undisturbed use of the spring.

The general rule is as stated and relied on by the counsel for the appellees, that the actual or visible boundary, whether natural or artificial, called for in a certificate of survey, is to pre-

1. *Francis* v. *Haslerig*, 1 A. K. Marsh, 96.
2. *Herbert et Ux.* v. *Wise et al.*, 3 Call, 239.

vail so long as it can be found or proved. The legal presumption is, that the surveyor has done his duty by marking and bounding the survey. And though this presumption can be destroyed by undoubted testimony, yet, as this was the fault of the officer of the government and not of the owner of the survey, he ought not to be injured. This being the case, the present inquiry is satisfied by determining whether the line of partition between the sections in this case, was actually run and marked by the original survey. The question of boundary is to be decided, like all others, by proof, and parol evidence is as much admissible to prove boundary as any other fact. We will, therefore, consider this subject in reference to the testimony furnished by the original plat of the survey, and by the witness who testified in regard to it. Does the map, *per se*, furnish us with conclusive evidence that the line was run? If so, the controversy is at an end, for it can not be disregarded, nor can it now be corrected. What are the indications on the plat, that this was done? The dotted line from the corner which runs north-west and intersects the Flowers tract, is the evidence relied on by the defendants. Is this to prevail in contravention of the established and admitted fact that it is a wide deviation from the true line as ascertained by actual survey? Is it to control the acknowledgments of the parties, and the proof of witnesses? It may be answered that it certainly must, and according to settled rules should do so, if it is to be considered as a part of the plat and certificate of survey. Is every trace or line upon the map to be regarded as an essential and constituent part of the survey, in the absence of any collateral or concurrent testimony of the surveyor to designate its office? Does every lineament of the plat speak a certain and well-defined language? What is spoken by the dotted line in this plat? We are not authorized to say what office it performs, because there is nothing in the certificate of the survey itself, which explains it.

But it may be said in answer to all this, that the purchaser is not to be prejudiced by difficulties of this character. That he bought on the faith of the survey, and that the line of boundary indicated on the plat is to be preserved at all events. But this would only lead us directly back to the question of the intrinsic proof furnished by such a line. Looking at it as a naked trace of the pen, one who is not conversant with the structure and figure of maps of this kind, and the uses of the various lines of the diagram, would be able to form no opinion perhaps. But if it should so attract attention as to excite a curiosity to find out its use and object, an inquiry would be very naturally made of the surveyor himself to explain it. Its meaning would, therefore, depend on his explanation. As a technical question of science, its design upon the map is to be determined by the opinion of those whose skill in the science enables them to decide. The testimony of McFail is, therefore, to be regarded on this subject. He was one of the deputy surveyors of the United States. He says that this dotted line from the corner at B. is not designed to fix the boundary. That it is no line. That the dotting of it is evidence that the partition or boundary between the two sections never was run and marked on the ground as required by law. And this is so understood, he tells us, among all surveyors. This must also have been the view taken of it by the surveyor-general, who ordered McFail to make the survey returned by him and approved by the surveyor-general. We take it, therefore, that the dotted line upon the face of the original map contains no intrinsic proof that the boundary indicated by it was ever made. Is there, then, any extrinsic proof that it was ever run? There is none furnished us. On the contrary, all the evidence on the record shows that it never was run. The surveyor, McFail, states that he searched diligently for the line but could find none, and that none had ever been run and marked on the ground by any one until he did it. This proof is fully calculated to destroy the force of the dotted line, if it did not carry its own explanation upon it face. For even in cases where the line has been run, if there were no objects on its direction to give it locality, or where those that existed have become extinct, it must then be ascertained by the course called for.

If, therefore, we adopt the interpretation of the dotted line, which is contended for by the appellees, and take it to say that the boundary was closed by the original survey, by what criterion is its identity and locality to be ascertained? Where are the natural or artificial objects by which it was ascertained and marked? By what monument can it now be traced? How is it to be fixed? Where are the marked trees to indicate its direction? McFail tells us that there are none. It is true that the line intersects the Flowers tract, but there are no monuments or objects, on any part of the boundary of that tract, by which we can fix the point of intersection. If then the line was run, we have no means of ascertaining its locality. It is, therefore, in reason, necessity, and principle, the same as if it never had been run. This distinction is fully sanctioned by the decision of the court in the case before noticed of *Lyon* v. *Ross and Wife*, 1 Bibb,

238.[1] The line of division must not only be run, but it must be marked on the ground, to bring it within the general rule of a closed survey. We are therefore clearly of the opinion that the court below erred in holding this line to be conclusive evidence of boundary, and also in refusing to give the first and second instructions asked for. This disposes of all of the errors assigned, except that which refers to the allowance of the amended consent rule. The consent rule, as it is technically termed, was adopted in the court of king's bench and common pleas in England, for the sake of convenience, and was a consequence of the fictions allowed in the action of ejectment. By its terms the defendant simply consents to waive proof of the lease, entry, and ouster, stated in the declaration, and then the cause is submitted to the jury upon the question of title. It could never work any prejudice to the party. The practice for some time varied in the two courts, the rule being special in the common pleas and general in the king's bench. The court of common pleas required the defendant to specify the particular part of the premises to which he claimed title. But at this time, the practice on this subject is the same in both courts, and it is now necessary in all cases to give evidence of the defendant's possession of the disputed premises at the time of the commencement of the suit: Tillinghast's Adams on Eject. 235; 9 Cow. 661.[2]

The only case now in which a special consent rule can be necessary is, where an actual entry is necessary to be made upon the land previous to suit brought. Thus, where an ejectment is brought by one joint tenant, tenant in common, or coparcener against his companion, as an actual ouster is necessary, the defendant may apply to the court upon affidavit for leave to file a special consent rule, to confess lease and entry, but not ouster: 9 Cow. 236. And this will always be granted: 2 Id. 442.[3] The effect of these rules of practice is to render nugatory the amendment of the consent rule in this cause. Since it can have no influence upon the rights of the parties or the quality and measure of proof required in the cause, it did not prejudice the plaintiff, and he can not, therefore, assign it for error. But, at any rate the allowance of amendments is not a matter for which error will lie: 3 Com. Dig. 566; 11 Wheat.[4]

For the reasons, however, which have been stated in relation to the other assignment of errors, the judgment of the court below must be reversed, the cause remanded, and a *venire de novo* awarded.

---

1. 1 Bibb, 466.   2. *Jackson* v. *Ives.*   3. *Jackson* v. *Lytle.*
4. *Chirac* v. *Reinicker*, 11 Wheat. 280.

BOUNDARIES, WHICH PREVAIL: See note to *Wendell* v. *Jackson*, 22 Am. Dec. 642, and *Heaton* v. *Hodges*, 30 Id. 734, citing cases in the American Decisions. Natural or artificial boundaries in the ground control the courses and distances: *Hall* v. *Powel*, 8 Id. 722; *Frost* v. *Spaulding*, 31 Id. 150, and note 154; and also have preference over marked lines and generally control them: *Hurley* v. *Morgan*, 28 Id. 579, and note 584; but the natural objects must be identified: *McCoy* v. *Galloway*, 17 Id. 591. If an established or admitted line varies from the calls of a grant, the other lines, if not marked, should be run with the same variation as the admitted line: *Sevier* v. *Wilson*, 14 Id. 741. If calls in a grant are imperative, they must be complied with and the courses and distances rejected, if they do not correspond with the calls. But if the calls are not imperative or can not be proved, the location must be according to the courses and distances: *Hammond* v. *Ridgely*, 9 Id. 522. Courses and distances will prevail in determining the *termini* of a line, over the further description of this point as being "near" to given objects: *Den* v. *Graham*, 27 Id. 226. Where a conveyance described land by courses and distances without any natural boundaries, the party in locating his lands must be confined to the courses and distances, and can not explain by parol what land was intended to be conveyed: *Hamilton* v. *Cawood*, 1 Id. 378.

CONFUSION OF BOUNDARIES, EQUITY JURISDICTION IN RELATION TO: See note to *Stuart's Heirs* v. *Coalter*, 15 Am. Dec. 745.

EVIDENCE OF BOUNDARY.—Where a covenant to convey land is silent as to quality, quantity, and boundary, parol evidence is admissible: *Cock* v. *Taylor*, 5 Am. Dec. 650. Parol evidence is admissible in relation to the boundaries of land, though such boundaries differ from the courses described in the patent: *McNeil* v. *Dixon*, 10 Id. 740. Verbal agreement of adjoining claimants and their acts in pursuance thereto in fixing upon a boundary line, is evidence that the line so agreed upon is the true line: *Nichol* v. *Lytle's Lessee*, 26 Id. 240. Declarations and admissions of a party are admissible as evidence of boundary: *Coate* v *Speer*, 15 Id. 627, and note 628; *Deming* v. *Carrington*, 30 Id. 591, and note 595. Mistakes in the calls of a patent may be corrected by reference to plat and certificate of survey: *Steele* v. *Taylor*, 13 Id. 151; but a survey is not evidence without showing an authority to make it, or proving that such authority existed and was afterwards lost: *Wilson* v. *Stoner*, 11 Id. 664. Questions in relation to boundary lines are for the determination of the jury: *Comegys* v. *Carley*, 27 Id. 356; *Hall* v. *Powel*, 8 Id. 72.

INSTRUCTIONS.—The court can not instruct the jury as to whether facts have been given in evidence, but can only instruct them as to the law upon certain facts, if they should find them well proved: *Irish* v. *Smith*, 11 Am. Dec. 648. Abstract instructions should not be given: *Porter* v. *Robinson*, 13 Id. 153.

AMENDMENTS.—Amendments are largely within the discretion of *nisi prius* courts, but this is a legal discretion, and if abused, will be corrected on appeal: *Robbins* v. *Treadway*, 19 Am. Dec. 152; *Carpenter* v. *Gookin*, 21 Id. 566. Amendments allowed in supreme court are reviewable in court of errors on a writ of error which brings up only the pleadings as amended: *Tuttle* v. *Jackson*, 21 Id. 306.

CARTER *v.* SPENCER.

[4 HOWARD, 42.]

A PATENT IS THE HIGHEST EVIDENCE OF TITLE, and can be impeached only on the ground of fraud or mistake.

APPLICATION FOR PRIVATE ENTRY WITHOUT FILING AFFIDAVIT that land was not subject to right of pre-emption, as required by an instruction of the secretary of the treasurer under act of April 5, 1832, is not of itself evidence of fraud.

WHERE SETTLER ERECTS IMPROVEMENTS AT THE CORNER OF SECTIONS, an entry of one of the sections on which the improvements were made is a bar to pre-emptive right over the other sections.

BILL to vacate patent, alleging that the complainant Carter, at the passage of the act of congress of April 5, 1832, was in the exclusive possession of the south-west quarter of section twelve, the land in controversy; that he made an application, but his entry was not received, as the defendant Spencer had previously entered the same land; that Spencer had obtained a patent for the land and brought an action of ejectment. The chancellor dismissed the bill, and Carter appealed.

Hutchinson, for the appellant.

Hughes, contra.

By Court, SHARKEY, C. J. The legal title is unquestionably with the defendant. A patent is the highest evidence of title; it is evidence that all prerequisites have been complied with, and can not be questioned either in a court of law or equity, unless it be on the ground of fraud or mistake.

The legal title being with the defendant, it devolves on the complainant to show that it was obtained in fraud of his rights. There is no proof whatever which can be deemed sufficient to establish fraud, nor was the entry such as to raise a presumption of fraud. The act under which complainant claims is very indefinite: it merely provided that actual settlers, being house-keepers, should have a right of pre-emption to enter within six months, a half quarter section, to include his improvements, under such regulations as had been or might be prescribed by the secretary of the treasury. Under this act the secretary prescribed rules and regulations by which individuals claiming under it, should be governed. The claimant was required to make proof by his own affidavit, supported by the affidavit of a disinterested person, that he was an actual housekeeper and settler on the land. Another rule was that the right conferred by the act was not to interfere with public sales or private entries. And in order to prevent confusion, an applicant for private entry was required to swear that the land designed to be entered was not subject to a right of pre-emption. In the violation of this last-mentioned rule it is said the fraud was perpetrated, but this position is not supported by proof. It is alleged in the bill, that Spencer entered without making this affidavit. This is admitted by the answer, which avers also, that no such affidavit was required of him by the register, in addition to which the entry without it, is evidence that it was dispensed with by the register. If therefore he chose to permit an entry without the affidavit, this in itself is not evidence of fraud. It was a mere instruction which required the affidavit, the law did not require it. By the general law, the land was subject to entry by any person who should apply for it, and by the second instruction given, that right was not to be interfered with. But if the instruction was violated, it was done by the register, and not by Spencer. No concealment, evasion, or trick is fixed on Spencer, and in the absence of such proof there can be no ground for the interference of a court of chancery.

But there are other considerations which must be regarded as prejudicial to the complainant. We are told in the argument that the complainant's house was placed where the lines of four different sections intersect, or in other words, over the corner. That in December, 1831, he made a private entry in section 14, and in June, 1832, after his right of pre-emption had been given, he entered in section 11, adjoining the land claimed, which last entry also covered part of his improvement. His right of pre-emption was as good to that part of section 11, as it was to section 12; perhaps it was better. There is another rule prescribed by the secretary of the treasury directly in point; it is that when a settlement was made on the corners of sections, the pre-emption should be confined to that section in which most of the improvement had been made. Carter has stated that one third of his improvement was in section 12; where was the other two thirds? It was, says the bill, on adjoining lands around him. His right of pre-emption accrued on the fifth day of April, to that eighth of land in which he had made the greatest improvement; and it was essential that this should have been made known, and yet we find that his affidavit to the register conceals it; his bill conceals it, and whether by design or accident, it gives an unfavorable aspect to the case. If the most of his improvement was in section 11, his right of pre-emption was there, and he could not transfer it by entering that eighth, and then claiming another. But when he entered, he had availed himself of all the benefit the law intended for him, for a right of pre-emption is but a right to buy.

The decree of the chancellor must be affirmed.

FRAUD IN PATENT, EFFECT OF: See *Bird* v. *Ward*, 13 Am. Dec. 506, and note; *White* v. *Jones*, 2 Id. 564, and note.

VALIDITY OF PATENT, HOW FAR IMPEACHABLE: See *Alexander* v. *Greenup*, 4 Am. Dec. 541; *Lassly* v. *Fontaine*, Id. 510; *Jackson* v. *Hart*, 7 Id. 280; *Norvell* v. *Camm*, 8 Id. 742; *Richardson* v. *Hobart*, 18 Id. 70.

KINLEY *v.* FITZPATRICK.

[4 HOWARD, 59.]

TO CONSTITUTE A WARRANTY, AN EXPRESS AFFIRMATION OF QUALITY or condition is necessary; a mere expression of opinion is not sufficient.

WHETHER AN AFFIRMATION AMOUNTS TO A WARRANTY is a question for the jury, and a bill of sale containing the alleged warranty should be submitted to the jury for determination.

ANY LANGUAGE SHOWING AN INTENTION TO WARRANT is sufficient; the word "warrant" is not necessary.

COVENANT for breach of a warranty of soundness in a bill of sale, under seal, for two negroes sold by Fitzpatrick to Kinley. One of the negroes, it appears, was diseased. In support of the breach, the plaintiff produced the following bill of sale: "Received of David Kinley the sum of two thousand two hundred dollars in full payment of two negroes, the one named Sam, aged about twenty-seven years; the other named Jim or James, aged about thirteen, sound in mind and body, and slaves for life. And I do hereby warrant the title of said negroes to David Kinley, his heirs and assigns forever. In witness whereof," etc. The defendant objected to the reading of this bill on the ground that it did not contain a warranty of soundness, and the court sustained the objection. The correctness of this ruling is the only question before the court.

Chaplain, for the plaintiff in error.

Thrasher, contra.

By Court, TROTTER, J. It is a well-settled rule that in every action on a warranty, it must be shown, that there was an express and direct affirmation of the quality or condition of the thing sold. And that a mere expression of opinion as to the soundness of the property by the vendor is not sufficient.

Whether the affirmation of the vendor amounts to a warranty or to an opinion merely is in every case a question for the jury, who are required to decide it in reference to the intention of the vendor, as it is to be inferred from all the facts connected with the contract. The court below should therefore have permitted the bill of sale to go before the jury, whose province it was to determine whether it contained an express warranty of soundness as alleged by the plaintiff. This was so ruled in the case of *Chapman* v. *Murch*, 19 Johns. 290 [10 Am. Dec. 227], and also in that of *Duffee* v. *Mason*, 8 Cow. 25. And also in 2 Id. 138;[1] 4 Id. 422.[2] But we are of opinion that the court also erred, in determining that the language of the vendor, in relation to the quality and condition of the slaves mentioned in the bill of sale, did not amount to a warranty. It is true that there must be an express affirmation by the vendor that the property is sound. But when that is shown, it would be an anomaly to require that the word warrant should be used. Such was the language of the court in the case of *Chapman* v. *Murch*, before noticed. If a man should say on the sale of a horse, "I promise you the horse is sound," it is difficult to conceive that this is not a warrant. No particular phraseology is requisite to constitute a warranty. Any affirmation by the vendor of the quality of the property, showing an intention to warrant its soundness, is sufficient: Com. on Con. 116. We have no doubt that such is a fair interpretation of the words used by Fitzpatrick in the bill of sale.

In the case of *Cramer* v. *Bradshaw*, 10 Johns. 484, the language of the vendor was very similar to that used by the defendant in this case. It was that he had granted, bargained, and sold to the plaintiff, "a negro woman named Sarah, aged about thirty years, being of sound mind and limb, and free from all disease." There then follows, as in the bill of sale in the case at bar, a formal warranty of title. The court held these not to be words of description, but to constitute an express warranty of soundness. In the case of *Gilchrist* v. *Morrow*, 2 Carolina L. 607, the negro sold, was described in the bill of sale as "about eleven years old, sound and healthy," after which there is, as in this case, a formal warranty as to the title. And this was held to be a warranty of soundness. The case of *Ditto* v. *Helm*, 2 J. J. Marsh. 129, is similar in principle. The bill of sale states that the vendor sold the negro described in it "to Ditto as a sound and healthy negro;" and these words were held to amount to a

1. *Roberts* v. *Morgan*, 2 Cow. 438.   2. *Oneida Man. Soc.* v. *Lawrence*, 4 Cow. 440.

warranty. In all these cases the words used, were held to be more than a mere affirmation. They were considered as an agreement, a stipulation that the property was sound, and as carrying with them an intention to guarantee the sound condition of the property, as much so as if more formal and technical language had been used. The only case in which similar words have received a contrary interpretation, which we have been enabled to find, is that of *Smith* v. *Miller*, 2 Bibb, 616. That case, however, is not sustained by principle or authority.

Let the judgment be reversed, and a *venire de novo* awarded.

WHAT AFFIRMATIONS AMOUNT TO A WARRANTY: See note to *Seixas* v. *Woods*, 2 Am. Dec. 220; *Erwin* v. *Maxwell*, 9 Id. 602; *Chapman* v. *Murch*, 10 Id. 227; *Sweet* v. *Colgate*, 11 Id. 266; *Hastings* v. *Lovering*, 13 Id. 420; *Osgood* v. *Lewis*, 18 Id. 317; *Beeman* v. *Buck*, 21 Id. 571; *Borrekins* v. *Bevans*, 23 Id. 85.

LEWIS *v.* WOODS.

[4 HOWARD, 86.]

SPECIFIC PERFORMANCE WILL NOT BE DECREED when the party applying has omitted to execute his part of the agreement by the time appointed, unless he can satisfactorily account for such omission, or the other party has expressly or impliedly assented to such delay.

PARTY LOSES RIGHT TO SPECIFIC PERFORMANCE, WHEN.—Where a party, by the terms of the sale, agrees to pay a certain amount in cash and give his promissory notes for the balance, and pays but a portion of the cash, and refuses for two years to pay the balance or to execute the notes, he is guilty of such negligence that he will not be decreed a specific performance.

APPEAL from the superior court of chancery. In 1835, Wailes, trustee, under a deed of trust, executed by Woods to indemnify one J. A. Foster, sold the land in question to Lewis. By the terms of the sale, Lewis was to pay one thousand two hundred dollars cash, and execute his promissory notes for the balance. But eight hundred dollars cash was paid, and the notes were not executed; Lewis took possession, though no deed of the land was executed. Afterwards Wailes, under the same deed of trust, sold the land a second time to A. G. Foster, administrator of J. A. Foster, who commenced an action of ejectment against Lewis. Lewis prays an injunction and a specific performance of his contract. The court below rendered a decree in favor of defendants.

S. S. Boyd, for the appellant.

Winchester, contra.

By Court, SHARKEY, C. J. (after stating the case). It was insisted in argument that the complainant acquired such a right by the first sale as must be enforced in chancery, and that the second sale was void, and that therefore the title under it must be set aside. If it can be found that a specific performance can not be decreed under the first sale, the validity of the second is of course a matter of no consequence, so far as the rights of the complainant are concerned.

It is a universally acknowledged rule that a court of equity will not decree a specific performance of a contract, when the party applying for it has omitted to execute his part of the agreement by the time appointed for that purpose, unless he can satisfactorily account for such omission; or unless the other party has assented expressly, or by acquiescence impliedly, to such delay. No one will be allowed the benefit of a contract which he has treated in bad faith. A party can not be permitted to violate his contract and wait until he sees that his bargain will be profitable, and then invoke the aid of a court of chancery to have it executed. There are instances, it is true, in which courts of chancery, after great delay, have decreed specific performance, but in such cases the courts act on the principle that the party has had a reasonable excuse for the delay; or that it has been sanctioned by the other party. Both time and circumstances are to be taken into consideration, for time may be of the very essence of a contract, otherwise a party might select his own time for performance. The case of *Benedict* v. *Lynch*, 1 Johns. Ch. 370 [7 Am. Dec. 484], is an authority in point. The contract was for a tract of land, to be paid for in four annual installments, and the deed to be made on the completion of the payments. The plaintiff took immediate possession and made valuable improvements, but failed to make either of the three first payments. Before the last payment fell due, he tendered all the purchase money, the defendant in the mean time having sold to another person. The court refused to decree a specific performance. There was, however, a stipulation in the contract that it should be void in case of failure to make either payment, but this circumstance seems to have had no greater weight than the laches of the vendee. The case of *Harrington* v. *Wheeler*, 4 Ves. 686, was also similar to the present. The conveyance was to be made, and the money or the residue to be paid on a future day, the plaintiff having paid part of the purchase money down. The contract was not carried into effect, and several years afterwards the plaintiff filed

his bill for a specific performance, which was refused, exclusively
on the ground of delay. The case of *Alley* v. *Deschamps*, 13
Id. 225, bears in every particular a complete analogy to the present case. The purchaser of an unexpired term agreed to pay in
two, four, and six years, with interest, and was put in immediate
possession, which was continued for three years, and one hundred pounds paid, and still a specific performance, applied for
after the time of payment had elapsed, was refused.

Now, what are the facts in this case? Lewis was to make the
balance of the cash payment, and execute the notes the next day
after the sale. Instead of doing so, he lies by nearly two years,
repeatedly refusing to fulfill his engagement; the defendants
having made frequent applications to him for that purpose, prior
to the second sale, which took place in May, 1836, sixteen months
after the first. Even after all this delay, nothing is heard from
him until it became necessary to shield himself from a recovery,
in an action of ejectment from the premises. When he is driven
to this alternative, he professes to have been always ready to
comply with his contract, and yet shows no offer to complete it
by a tender of the money. No reasonable excuse is given for
this delay, nor did the parties interested acquiesce in it, but
from time to time urged the fulfillment of the contract. Under
such circumstances, they were at liberty to consider it as abandoned. After all this even worse than negligence, his claim presents no equity.

The decree of the chancellor is affirmed.

DEFAULT OR NEGLIGENCE, WHEN GROUND FOR REFUSAL OF SPECIFIC PER-
FORMANCE: See *Bowman* v. *Irons*, 4 Am. Dec. 686; *Tyree* v. *Williams*, 6 Id.
663; *Benedict* v. *Lynch*, 7 Id. 484; *Bellas* v. *Hays*, 9 Id. 385; note to *McKean*
v. *Reed*, 12 Id. 324; *Moore* v. *Skidmore*, Id. 333; *Tiernan* v. *Beam*, 15 Id. 557;
Craig v. *Martin*, 19 Id. 157; *Craig* v. *Leiper*, 24 Id. 479; *Moore* v. *Fitz Randolph*, 29 Id. 208.

MICHIE *v.* PLANTERS' BANK.

[4 HOWARD, 130.]

WHERE TWO WRITS ARE DELIVERED TO THE SHERIFF, and he executes the
one bearing teste the last day, such execution shall not be avoided, but
the plaintiff improperly postponed shall have his remedy against the
sheriff only.

LIEN OF A JUDGMENT IS BUT A SECURITY to be pursued with diligence and
good faith; it may be lost by laches.

WHERE JUDGMENT CREDITOR SUSPENDED EXECUTION FOR TWO TERMS, a
subsequent execution, levied in the mean time, will take priority, though
by the act of 1824, a judgment is a lien from the time of its entry.

ERROR from the circuit court of Yazoo county. At the April term, 1838, Michie obtained judgment against one Mitchell. Execution issued in August, and the sheriff levied on property of Mitchell. At the November term Michie moved that the money made be applied in satisfaction of his judgment. The appellees oppose this motion on the ground that they have a prior judgment against Mitchell, recovered in 1836. On this judgment execution was levied, and a forthcoming bond taken and forfeited. *Alias* execution was put in the hands of the sheriff, but before he had levied he was ordered to suspend proceeding under it until the next term, and then he was instructed to have a new execution issued, which might be suspended, with the same consent, till the following term. In October, 1838, the orders suspending the execution were revoked, and a writ of *scire facias* was issued. It was proved that but for the suspension, the execution of the Planters' bank would have been paid long since; and that an application of the fund made to the satisfaction of the execution of the Planters' bank, would exclude the execution in favor of Michie. The court decided that the execution of the Planters' bank was entitled to priority.

G. S. Yerger, for the plaintiff in error.

Thompson, contra.

By Court, TROTTER, J. By the common law, a judgment creditor acquired a lien upon the goods of the defendant from the teste of the writ of *fieri facias*. The act of 29 Charles II. gives the lien from the time of the delivery of the writ to the sheriff. It has always been held, however, in England, that if two writs are delivered, and the sheriff shall execute the one bearing teste the last day, or the one last delivered, such execution shall not be avoided, but the plaintiff improperly postponed shall have his remedy against the sheriff only, who is bound to do his duty at his peril. The property in the goods is bound by the sale, and can not be seized by the elder execution. The reason is, that sales made by the sheriff ought not to be defeated, for if they are, no man will buy goods levied upon a writ of execution. Such was the language of Lord Holt, in the case of *Smallcomb* v. *Cross and Buckingham*, Ld. Raym. 252. The language of the statute, 29 Charles, is, that the goods of the defendant shall be "bound from the delivery of the writ to the sheriff." In the case of *Lowland* v. *Tomkins*,[1] 2 Eq. Cas. Abr. 381, Lord Hardwicke has given the same construction to

---

1. *Lowthal* v. *Tonkins*.

these words of the statute, that Lord Holt has in the case of *Smallcomb* v. *Buckingham,* just noticed. He says that neither at common law, nor since the statute, is the property of the goods altered. This doctrine is sanctioned by the court of king's bench, in the case of *Payne* v. *Drewe,* 4 East, 539, in which it is declared to be a well-settled principle, that a sale by a sheriff under a second execution, when he had a former one in his hands, is valid and vests the property in the purchaser. That though the writ is binding as against the defendant from delivery, yet it can not be regarded as self-executed by its own proper force and legal effect for all purposes. That whilst it is the duty of the sheriff as between himself and the several plaintiffs to sell under the writ first delivered, though he may have seized under the last; yet his sale under the junior writ is good. The court of appeals of Kentucky have established the same rule in the case of *Tabb* v. *Harris,* 4 Bibb, 29 [7 Am. Dec. 732], in the construction of a statute of that state, similar to the act of Charles. In that case, the money in the hands of the sheriff was levied upon Tabb's execution, though it was delivered after Harris', yet the court ordered it to be applied to Tabb's execution.

The act of 1822 of this state is exactly like the statute of Charles, and is therefore subject to the same construction. It is, therefore, beyond controversy, that the lien in favor of judgment creditors either at common law or since our act of 1822, does not bind against other judgment creditors, but may be defeated or lose its priority by a sale under a junior execution. But the act of 1824 binds the property of the defendant from the time of entering the judgment, and it is urged by the counsel for the appellees that the analogy of the decisions in relation to the English statute, does not apply to a lien by virtue of a judgment. That in consequence a sale under the junior judgment is void as against an elder one, and that the property is still subject to be seized in satisfaction of the prior judgment. Be this, however, as it may, it is very evident that the lien created by this statute is, in one respect, similar to that given by the act of 1822, it may lose its priority by the act of the creditor himself.

The lien after all is but a security, and whether that which is created by the act of 1824 binds all the world or not, it is still as a mere security, to be pursued with diligence and in good faith. When therefore the law gives to a prior judgment a right to a prior satisfaction, it intends that this favor shall be pursued with as little delay or injury to other creditors as possible. It

may be lost by laches.   Has the bank pursued its remedy in this
case with the diligence thus required by law and sound policy?
The letter of the attorney to the sheriff which was authorized by
a resolution of the directory of the bank, was an instruction to
the sheriff to stay the execution, if not for an indefinite period,
at any rate for six months.   He is directed to return the writ
then in his hands to the succeeding court, and afterwards to take
out a new one, which might be suspended in like manner until
the next court afterwards, with the same consent.   This was
not only an agreement to stay the execution then in the hands
of the officer, but is an undoubted promise to suspend the next in
the same manner.   This is surely a much stronger case than
that of *Porter's Lessee* v. *Thomas Cocke*, Peck, 30, in which the
lien of the elder judgment was postponed.   In that case the execution on the senior judgment was levied on land of the defendant.   An injunction was obtained, and after its dissolution the
plaintiff agreed with the defendant, in consideration of a partial payment of the judgment, to stay the execution six months.
In the mean time an execution on a junior judgment came to the
hands of the sheriff, under which he sold.   It was held that the
lien of the first judgment was defeated as against the other
judgment creditor, and the sale was held to be valid.

If, says the judge who delivered the opinion of the court, the
plaintiff may delay the collection of his judgment six months,
and retain his lien, to what time may he not extend it?   In the
case of *Payne* v. *Drewe*, before noticed, the court held that a
sequestration which bound the goods had lost its priority by
reason of the laches of the sequestrators in delaying to execute
the writ for eighteen months, and it was so held upon principles
of public convenience and to prevent fraud and vexatious delay.
It is again emphatically asked by the judge in that case, "If the
sequestration was not enforced within the eighteen months, at
what period was it expected that it would?"   The judgment of the
court is put upon the simple ground of delay and negligence.
The sequestration had been in the hands of the sequestrators for
the eighteen months when the writ of *fieri facias* was delivered
to the sheriff.   The intention in the delay was not made a subject of inquiry.   The writ of sequestration became dormant and
therefore lost its lien.

In the case of *Whipple* v. *Foot*, 2 Johns. 216 [3 Am. Dec. 442],
it was held that if the sheriff, by directions from the plaintiff,
suffer goods which have been levied upon, to remain in the possession of the defendant, it is a fraud upon other creditors, and

the execution becomes dormant. The same point is settled in the case of *Storm* v. *Woods*, 11 Id. 110. The same is held in several other cases in New York. If the lien created by the law in this case be merely a security, and confers no *jus ad rem*, it may be lost by any agreement or act of the judgment creditor, which would discharge the liability of a surety, under an ordinary contract. It has been decided that where the creditor, by agreement with the principal debtor, enlarges the time of payment without the consent of the surety, the latter is discharged: 3 Meriv. 278.[1] It would be repugnant to every principle of sound policy, and open the broadest avenues to fraud and injustice, to hold that the lien in favor of judgment or other creditors may be enforced at the mere option of the party, or that it may keep off other creditors equally meritorious, without any step to preserve it. We are therefore of the opinion that the agreement of the bank in this case, rendered the execution in its favor dormant, as against the claim of Michie, and that he is entitled to the money levied on his execution.

The judgment of the court below must be reversed, and judgment rendered here, that the sheriff pay the money accordingly.

PRIORITY IN CASE OF SEVERAL EXECUTIONS: See *Adams* v. *Dyer*, 5 Am. Dec. 344; *Tabb* v. *Harris*, 7 Id. 732; *Green* v. *Johnson*, 11 Id. 763; *Lynn* v. *Gridley*, 12 Id. 591, and note; *Palmer* v. *Clarke*, 21 Id. 340; *Jones* v. *Jones*, 18 Id. 327; *Johnson* v. *Ball*, 24 Id. 451, and note; *Sigourney* v. *Eaton*, 25 Id. 414; *Stebbins* v. *Walker*, 25 Id. 499; *Laflin* v. *Willard*, 26 Id. 629.

HOW LIEN MAY BE LOST OR POSTPONED: See *Locke* v. *Coleman*, 15 Am. Dec. 118; *Adair* v. *McDaniel*, 19 Id. 664, and note; *Hickok* v. *Coates*, 20 Id. 632; *Palmer* v. *Clarke*, 21 Id. 340; *Commonwealth* v. *Stremback*, 24 Id. 351; *Conway* v. *Jett*, Id. 590; *Hickman* v. *Caldwell*, 27 Id. 274.

CARPENTER *v.* STATE.

[4 HOWARD, 163.]

CONSTRUCTION OF COMMON LAW TERMS IN STATUTES.—Where terms used in the common law are contained in a statute or the constitution, without an explanation of the sense in which they are employed, they should receive that construction which has been affixed to them by the common law.

NUMBER OF THE JURY AT COMMON LAW could never be less than twelve.

WHERE AN ISSUE IS SUBMITTED TO ELEVEN PERSONS, their finding can not be considered as the verdict of a jury, upon which a court would be warranted in pronouncing judgment.

OMISSION IN THE CAPTION OF AN INDICTMENT to state the place where the court was holden, the indictment found, or that the grand jury were

---

1. *Samuell* v. *Howarth*.

drawn from the county where the offense was committed, is fatal to its validity.

WHAT CONSTITUTES PERJURY.—Where an affidavit falsely charges that a felony has been committed by some person, and was made for the purpose of obtaining a search warrant for the discovery of the property alleged to have been stolen, the affiant is guilty of perjury, though no particular individual is charged with the offense.

ERROR from the circuit court of Hancock county. Carpenter made an affidavit before a justice of the peace of Hancock county, stating that certain articles of household furniture had been stolen from his possession, and that he suspected and believed they were secreted in and about the premises of one Eldridge. Carpenter was tried and convicted of perjury. Objections were taken to the caption of the indictment and to the record; also that the crime charged did not constitute perjury. These sufficiently appear from the opinion.

Mitchell, for the plaintiff in error.

Collins, attorney-general, contra.

By Court, SMITH, J. At the August term, in the year A. D. 1838, in the circuit court of Hancock county, Samuel A. Carpenter was indicted, tried, and convicted of the crime of perjury; and having received sentence, has by writ of error removed his cause into this court, and asks a reversal of the judgment against him, for several errors and irregularities alleged to exist in the record of the proceedings and judgment of the court below. It appears by the record, that the issue in the cause was submitted to eleven persons, who were impaneled and sworn as a jury; and that as such they found the prisoner guilty of the offense charged in the indictment. In all prosecutions by indictment or information, the accused is entitled to "a speedy public trial, by an impartial jury of his country." This right, justly regarded as the palladium of the personal liberties of the citizen, is guaranteed by the fundamental law of the land, and is placed by express provision beyond the control of legislative authority. But neither by the federal constitution, nor by that of our own state, have the qualifications of a juror been defined; or the number necessary to constitute a "jury," been fixed.

It is a general rule that, where terms used in the common law are contained in a statute or the constitution, without an explanation of the sense in which they are there employed, [they] should receive that construction which has been affixed to them by the former. To ascertain then in what the right of trial by jury consists, we must necessarily recur to the provisions of the common law defining the qualifications, and ascertaining the number of which the jury shall consist; as the standard to which, doubtless, the framers of our constitution referred. At common law the number of the jury, for the trial of all issues involving the personal rights and liberties of the subject, could never be less than twelve; though there are some precedents which show that a verdict by a greater number would not on that account be void. The legislation of the state has left this particular topic untouched. It has in no instance prescribed the number of the jury, if it were at all important for it to have done so; but in all cases where the term "jury" is used in our statutes, it is regarded as one of fixed and determined meaning, ascertained by the paramount law. Our courts have also proceeded on the assumption that the constituents of the jury, at least so far as the number is involved, have been fixed by the constitution, as they existed at common law, at the time of its adoption. See *Byrd's case*, 1 How. 177.

The finding in the case before us, therefore, can not be considered as the verdict of a jury, upon which the court was warranted in pronouncing judgment. For this cause the judgment of the circuit court should be reversed and a new trial awarded; but it is insisted that other objections exist, which strike at the foundation of the indictment, and require not only a reversal of the judgment, but also a discharge of the prisoner. These objections apply to the caption of the indictment, as well as to the subject-matter charged. We do not deem it important to notice all of them in detail, but shall confine our examination to some of the most obvious.

1. It is insisted that the caption does not show a place at which the court was holden, the indictment found, or the prisoner tried.

To test the validity of this exception, we must refer to the caption as it is presented in the record. It is set out in the following words, to wit: "*The State of Mississippi* v. *Samuel A. Carpenter:* Pleas in the circuit court of Hancock county: B. Harris, judge, presiding, the term of August in the year of our Lord one thousand eight hundred and thirty-eight. Be it remembered that on the second day of the present term, being the thirtieth day of August, A. D. 1838, the grand jury of the state of Mississippi being duly impaneled, sworn, and charged; to wit: (Asa Russ, foreman), Antoine Field, etc., came into court and presented the following indictment, to wit."

The fact that the court was holden for the county of Hancock,

is stated with sufficient certainty, and also that it was held at
the time appointed by law; but does this statement in the caption necessarily include the additional fact, that it was holden
at the place in the county designated by the statute.　It is not
directly expressed, and no presumption can be indulged which
contradicts the record; nor are we warranted in the assumption
of any fact which is not necessarily included in that which is expressed.　In the case of *Woodsides* v. *The State*, the record
showed that one of the grand jurors was sworn as foreman; and
it was considered tantamount to a direct statement, that he had
been appointed as such by the court; as he could not have been
sworn in that capacity without having been appointed.　Here the
court may have been holden in Hancock county, and yet it be true
that it was not held at the court-house.　If the court was holden
at any other place in the county, other than that designated by
law, it is obvious that it could rightfully have exercised no jurisdiction in the cause, and therefore requires no argument to
show that all of its proceedings were irregular.　It is clear from
authority that it should appear not only that the court was
holden for the proper county, but that it was also holden at the
proper place within the county.　To show this fact is part of
the appropriate office of the caption: See 1 Chit. Crim. L., c. 7,
p. 327; 2 Hawk. Pl. C. c. 25, sec. 128; and 2 Hall, 166.　This
omission therefore in the caption, to state the place where the
court was holden, and the indictment found, must be considered
as a valid objection.

The omission of any material statement in the record or caption, can not be supplied by the recital in the indictment, which
becomes no part of the record until it is returned into court in
the manner prescribed by law.　The record in the case now
under investigation does not directly state that the grand jurors
who returned the bill of indictment into court, were the grand
jurors of the county where the court was holden; and this is
the ground of the second objection which we deem it necessary
to notice.　The grand jurors for any county, duly selected and
impaneled according to the directions of the law, may with
strict legal propriety, be termed the grand jurors of the state;
as it is on behalf of the state and by its authority, that they are
required to discharge the functions assigned to them.　But it is
objected that the record which describes the grand jury who
returned the bill into court, as the " grand jurors of the state
of Mississippi, duly impaneled, charged, and sworn," does not
show by that description that they were selected from the

proper county. No man can be held to answer for any criminal violation of the law, unless he shall be first charged by a grand jury of the county where the offense may have been committed. This fact must be shown by the caption of the indictment, or it will be presumed that the court has proceeded without authority. The forms of proceeding in prosecutions for public offenses, are designed to protect the life and liberty of the citizen, and are justly regarded as a valuable appendage to the right of trial by jury. Objections of a merely technical character may sometimes impede, instead of advancing the cause of justice; and although courts of justice have very properly manifested a disposition to relax the rigor of ancient forms, where no injury could result to the accused, yet there must be some limit beyond which judicial innovations should not be permitted to advance. Upon the principle of this relaxation, this court in *Byrd's case*, and subsequently in that of *Woodsides*, where the record showed that the grand jury were "sworn in and for the body of the county," held that it was equivalent to a statement that they were the grand jurors of the proper county. But it appears to me that it would be extending this principle too far to hold that the description of the grand jury in the record before us necessarily evinces the fact, that they were selected from the county where the prisoner was charged with the offense.

The other objection which we shall notice is in effect this, that the act charged does not amount, in law, to the crime of willful and corrupt perjury. The argument in support of this exception proceeded on the ground, that the affidavit of the prisoner set out in the indictment, charged no particular individual with the commission of an offense, and that, therefore, although the affidavit may have been false, it did not constitute an act of perjury. It is not denied that the magistrate before whom the affidavit was sworn to, was legally authorized to administer the oath. The affidavit charges unequivocally, that a felony had been committed by some person, and was made for the purpose of obtaining a search warrant, for the discovery of the property alleged in it to have been stolen. We can not perceive that it makes the slightest difference, that no particular person was averred to have committed the felony.

We therefore think that this objection is untenable; but for the errors before noticed, we are bound to reverse the judgment of the circuit court, and order the prisoner to be discharged.

CONSTRUCTION OF DOUBTFUL OR AMBIGUOUS STATUTES: See *Hillhouse v. Chester*, 3 Am. Dec. 265; *People* v. *Utica Ins. Co.*, 8 Id. 243; *Commonwealth* v.

PROSSER *v.* LEATHERMAN.
[4 HOWARD, 237.]

ASSIGNEE OF ADMINISTRATOR CAN NOT RECOVER, WHEN.—Where an administrator for his own private benefit transfers a note belonging to the estate of the decedent to a third person, who has full knowledge, the latter can not recover the amount of the note from the maker.

ERROR to the circuit court of Wilkinson county. The opinion states the case.

Boyd and Henderson, for the plaintiff in error.

By Court, SHARKEY, C. J. This action was brought on a promissory note made by the appellant to Ephraim Fleshman, in his life-time, on whose estate the said Leatherman is administrator *de bonis non.* The appellant pleaded that the note came to the hands of Leatherman in his capacity as administrator, and without lawful authority or right he indorsed the note to Hutchins, for whose use the suit is brought, in a trade for certain negroes, and avers a knowledge on the part of Hutchins of the fact. There was a demurrer to the plea, which was sustained, and this appeal taken.

The question presented by the plea directly involves the power of an administrator to dispose of the assets, and assign the debts due him in his representative capacity, for his own use, with knowledge of the fact on the part of the purchaser. The plea is rather loosely drawn, but I think substantially good, if the subject-matter is such as will support it. In regard to transactions of this kind, great contrariety of opinion has existed in the courts of England, of very high authority. The most of the cases on this subject are reviewed by Chancellor Kent, in the case of *Field* v. *Schieffelin,* 7 Johns. Ch. 150 [11 Am. Dec. 441]. The rule as held by Lord Hardwicke and Lord Mansfield, was, that an executor could dispose of the assets or choses in action of his intestate for a valuable consideration, and that the purchaser would hold, by good title, unless there was fraud or collusion between the executor and purchaser, or unless a contrivance appeared between them to make a devastavit. Lord Kenyon condemned the decision in one of the cases, and adopted this rule: "If upon the face of the assignment of property it appeared to have been made in satisfaction of a private debt of the executor, the sale was fraudulent against the persons interested under the will, and equity would relieve. It would be a case of implied fraud." Lord Thurlow adopted the same rule. He says that in general the purchaser has nothing to do with the application of the money; "but if one concerted with the executor to obtain the effects at a nominal price, or at a fraudulent undervalue, or in extinguishing the private debt of the executor, or in any other manner contrary to the duty of the office of executor, the purchaser or pawnee will be liable." Sir William Grant and Lord Eldon have held the same doctrine, and Chancellor Kent comes to a similar conclusion. He says, "that the purchaser is safe, if he is no party to any fraud in the executor, and has no knowledge or proof that the executor intended to misapply the proceeds, or was in fact by the very transaction applying them to the extinguishing of his own private debt: The great difficulty has been to determine how far the purchaser dealt at his peril, when he knew from the very face of the proceeding that the executor was applying the assets to his own private purposes, as the payment of his debts. The latter and the better doctrine is, that in such case he does buy at his peril."

All the cases on this subject are fully discussed by Chief Justice Savage, in the case of *Colt* v. *Lasnier*, 9 Cow. 320, where he brings the rule as settled in England and New York down to this, "that any person receiving from an executor the assets of his testator, knowing that this disposition of them is a violation of his duty, is to be adjudged as conniving with the executor; and that such person is responsible for the property thus received, either as a purchaser or a pledgee."

This rule seems to me to be entirely unobjectionable, either on the score of justice to all parties, or as resulting clearly and necessarily from the prescribed powers and duties of executors and administrators. It is the duty of an executor to collect the debts of the deceased and take care of the assets, and apply them to the proper objects, and the law gives the power to do this, but nothing more. He is to act in the capacity of a trustee for the benefit of those interested in the estate, but it is certainly not the policy or intention of the law that the debts and assets in his hands should be a fund for him to trade on at pleasure for his own emolument. The creditors have a lien created by law on all the assets, and one which they have a right to enforce in the due course of administration, and which is incompatible with an indiscriminate sale or transfer of them by the executor for his own private purposes. If there are no creditors, the legatees or distributees have a direct interest in the estate, the law having directed that it should be distributed. The executor having the rightful possession of the assets, a knowledge on the part of the purchaser of the illegal disposition, would of course be necessary.

As a legal proposition it surely can not be denied that an executor or administrator may assign a note or chose in action, which he holds in that capacity, but it must be done for a purpose which will meet the sanction of law, and not for his individual benefit. The principles as above laid down arise from cases decided in equity, and we are to consider whether the debtor may avail himself of them in an action at law. The authorities all agree that an improper transfer with the knowledge of the purchaser, imposes on him a liability in equity in favor of those interested. They evidently proceed on the ground of an express or implied fraud, which may also be inquired into at law, and courts of law will not enforce a right thus acquired. It can not be proper, therefore, to permit a recovery in this instance, when it would impose an equitable liability on the plaintiff below, and thus change the nature of the remedy in favor of creditors and distributees, and thus far sanction a transaction which was illegal.

Although the plea does not expressly aver that the trade was made for the sole benefit of Leatherman, yet the transaction is such as to leave no other conclusion. As administrator he could not purchase negroes, and the very transaction shows the illegal application of the note. In principle there can be no difference between the transfer of a note in payment of a pre-existing debt, and a transfer of property for individual benefit. The subject-matter of the plea, therefore, formed a good bar in law, and the demurrer should have been overruled and judgment of *respondeat ouster* awarded, which must be the judgment of this court.

———

RIGHTS OF PURCHASERS FROM OR ASSIGNEES OF EXECUTORS OR ADMINISTRATORS: See *Sutherland* v. *Brush*, 11 Am. Dec. 383, and note 387.

CASES

IN THE

SUPREME COURT

OF

MISSOURI.

HICKMAN *v.* GRIFFIN.

[6 MISSOURI, 37.]

ORIGINAL PAPERS IN PROCEEDING BEFORE JUSTICE OF PEACE ARE NOT ADMISSIBLE in evidence in the circuit court, without some proof of their authenticity, when there is nothing in the record to show how they became part of the case.

PROOF BY THE JUSTICE IN WHOSE COURT PROCEEDING TOOK PLACE, of the identity and authenticity of the papers, and that they had been acted upon, is sufficient.

WHETHER WARRANT RUNNING "STATE OF MISSOURI, COUNTY OF COLE, SS.' would be valid or not, *quære.*

GENERAL RULE THAT PARTY CAN NOT BE ALLOWED TO MAKE EVIDENCE in his own favor is not departed from in an action for malicious prosecution except in cases of necessity.

DEFENDANT IN ACTION FOR MALICIOUS PROSECUTION can not be allowed to prove what he swore to when there were several other witnesses present at the time.

REAL INQUIRY IN AN ACTION FOR MALICIOUS PROSECUTION is whether there was probable cause for the prosecution, not the knowledge or belief of the party prosecuting as to its existence.

ERRONEOUS INSTRUCTIONS ARE NOT CURED by the fact that correct instructions accompany them.

APPEAL from the circuit court of Cole county. The opinion states the case.

Hayden and Adams, for the appellant.

Todd and Kirtley, contra.

By Court, NAPTON, J. Griffin sued Hickman for a malicious prosecution before a justice of the peace. The declaration charged that the defendant (below) appeared before one Glaze-

brook, a justice of the peace in Cole county, and charged him
(Griffin) with petty larceny; and procured said justice to issue
his warrant; that he caused said Griffin, by virtue of said warrant, to be arrested, and recognized for appearance at the Cole
circuit court. The declaration further avers the continued prosecution of plaintiff by defendant before the grand jury, and
the refusal of said grand jury to find any indictment. The
general issue was pleaded, and the parties went to trial.

On the trial, the plaintiff offered in evidence the warrant of
the justice, without proving the handwriting of said justice,
which the defendant objected to, but the court permitted the writing to go to the jury. Plaintiff also read the
indorsement on the warrant of the return of the constable, without first proving said constable's handwriting. The plaintiff
also proved that the said constable took plaintiff in custody, and
carried him before a magistrate. Plaintiff also gave in evidence
the recognizance, which said justice caused him to enter into,
and the records of the circuit court of Cole county, reciting the
impaneling of the grand jury, their failure to find any bill
against Griffin, and the subsequent discharge of Griffin by the
court. To the introduction of all this evidence the defendant
below objected—but the objection was overruled. The plaintiff
then introduced the justice of the peace, Glazebrook, and proved
by him that the defendant appeared before him, and applied to
him for a warrant against Griffin, and that upon his (Hickman's)
application, he (Glazebrook) issued the warrant, being the writing first offered. The defendant proposed to prove, upon the
cross-examination of said justice, what the defendant swore to
before him upon his examination, but the court refused to allow the justice to state what the defendant below had sworn
to, the plaintiff having previously proved, that several other
witnesses were present at the time the alleged larceny was said
to have been committed. The plaintiff also proved by said
justice (Glazebrook) that he (Glazebrook) caused the plaintiff
Griffin to enter into a recognizance to appear at the next term
of the Cole circuit court, and both plaintiff and defendant gave
evidence conducing to show the existence or want of probable
cause and malice.

At the instance of the plaintiff, the court then gave the jury
the following instruction: "If the jury believe from the evidence
that the defendant prosecuted the plaintiff upon a charge of larceny, and the plaintiff was acquitted and discharged therefrom,

and that the defendant had no probable cause to believe him
guilty of the charge, they will find for the plaintiff."

The defendant also asked for the following instructions, which
were given by the court:

1. That to enable the plaintiff to recover in this cause, it is
necessary they should be satisfied from the evidence in the cause,
that the defendant prosecuted the plaintiff in malice, and without probable cause; 2. That if the defendant had probable cause
to institute the prosecution, that then they ought to find a verdict in his favor; 3. That it matters not how malicious the motive of Hickman was in prosecuting the plaintiff, yet if they believe from the evidence that Hickman had probable cause for
prosecuting him, they ought to find a verdict for the defendant
Hickman; 4. That the fact that the justice of the peace, Glazebrook, upon the inquiry before him, recognized the plaintiff in
a recognizance, binding him to appear at the Cole circuit court,
to answer over to the charge mentioned in the prosecution, is
evidence of there being probable cause for the prosecution, and
that the jury ought to find for the defendant on such evidence,
unless the plaintiff prove by other evidence that the prosecution
was instituted without any probable cause; 5. That it is not
necessary in this action that the defendant should show that the
plaintiff was absolutely guilty, to entitle Hickman to a verdict,
but that it is only necessary that they should believe from the
evidence that the defendant, Hickman, had probable cause to
prosecute him, Griffin; 6. That it matters not how small the
amount of money stolen from the defendant was, the defendant
stands justified in the law for prosecuting the plaintiff, if he had
probable cause for the prosecution.

The jury found for plaintiff, and defendant moved for a
new trial, on the following grounds: 1. The court permitted the
plaintiff to give improper testimony; 2. The court refused to permit the defendant to give all and every part of his testimony; 3.
The court misdirected the jury.   Which motion was overruled
by the court, and to reverse this judgment the plaintiff in error
has relied on the following points, which I will examine seriatim:
1. That the court erred in permitting the warrant of the justice, the return of the constable thereon, and the recognizance
for Griffin's appearance, to be read to the jury, without proof of
their execution; 2. That the warrant produced did not run in
the name of the state of Missouri, and consequently, the action
should have been trespass vi et armis; 3. That the court erred in·
not permitting Hickman's testimony before the magistrate to go

to the jury; 4. That the court erred in giving the instruction asked by plaintiff.

1. If the papers of the justice had been duly certified by him, and it appeared from the record that they were on file in the circuit court, there could be no question of their admissibility, without further proof. But the papers offered were original papers, and there is nothing preserved in the bill of exceptions to show how they got into the circuit court. The papers were not admissible without some proof of their authenticity. But the plaintiff, immediately after the introduction of this testimony, in his examination in chief proved by the justice of the peace, Glazebrook, the identity and authenticity of the warrant and recognizance, and the fact that the constable, whose name was indorsed on the warrant, had taken the plaintiff in custody and brought him before him (the justice) for his examination. Whatever, therefore, might have been defective in the testimony of the plaintiff when first introduced, he proceeded to supply those deficiencies by competent and full proof, and I do not see any good reason for reversing because of this irregularity. If it could be shown that defendant was anywise prejudiced by this course, it might constitute a sufficient reason with this court to set aside the judgment. But no such injustice appears.

2. It is urged that the warrant, not running in the name of the state of Missouri, was not merely voidable, but absolutely void, and that therefore this action should have been trespass. The warrant in this case ran in these words: "State of Missouri, county of Cole, ss.;" after reciting the inducement, it proceeded, "these are therefore to command you to take the body," etc. I am not prepared to say whether this would be a valid warrant or not, under the decisions of this court, but this court in the case of *Miller* v. *Brown*, 3 Mo. 130, at least declared, that such a warrant was sufficient to justify the constable, the magistrate by whom it was issued having jurisdiction over the person and subject-matter. The distinctions between case and trespass, as laid down in many of the books, are so exceedingly refined, that, like the colors of the rainbow, they run into each other, and would puzzle a man of common sense to make the discrimination. I hold that case was well brought here, and that an action of trespass could not have been sustained against the constable, merely because of this defect in the process which he served.

3. The defendant, on his cross-examination of the justice, offered to prove what he had sworn to before him, on the trial

of the accused before him (the justice). This the court very properly excluded. The general rule that a party can not be allowed to make evidence in his own favor is not departed from in an action of malicious prosecution, except upon the ground of necessity. If no other person were present when the felony was committed, the evidence, which the defendant himself gave, may be read as evidence in this action: *Johnson* v. *Browning*, 6 Mod. 216, cited in Bayard's Peake, 158–311. In that case Hale, C. J., allowed what the defendant's wife had testified at the trial of the indictment to be given in evidence on behalf of the husband, when sued for a malicious prosecution, there having been no other person present at the commission of the alleged felony. So also in an action on the statute of Winton, the party robbed was held a competent witness, and the author remarks, "these are the only cases, I believe, in the books, where parties to the cause have been permitted to give evidence for themselves; and in the latter case, it seems to have been taken for granted, that the party could not be examined, though his former evidence was admitted:" Bayard's Peake, 151, in note. The dictum in Buller cited at the bar (Bull. N. P. 14), is unsupported by authority, and is contradicted by himself on the next page, in which he lays down the rule as established in *Johnson* v. *Browning*. In the case of *Hays* v. *Waller*, 2 Mo. 222, this court perhaps extend the rule, and allow what the defendant swore to on the trial of the indictment, to be read in his defense on his trial for a malicious prosecution, where it appeared that he swore to a fact which no one who was present except himself bore witness to. Admitting this to be correct, it devolved upon defendant (plaintiff in error) to show by the bill of exceptions, that this state of facts existed. Not having done so, the judgment of the circuit court on this point must be held correct.

4. The first instruction asked by the plaintiff and given by the court, is open to criticism. Two objections were urged to it; first, that the prosecutor's belief of the existence of probable cause is made the test, instead of the existence of probable cause, whether within the knowledge of the prosecutor or not; and, second, the jury are not told of the necessity of malice as well as the want of probable cause. The instruction is certainly not sufficiently distinct on this last point, for though malice may be inferred from the want of a probable cause, it is still an essential ingredient in the guilt of the prosecutor, and his liability to the plaintiff. But the subsequent instructions are full and clear on this point, and lay down the law with such precision (so far

as this point is concerned), that I do not see how the jury could have drawn any inference from the first instruction calculated to prejudice the defendant. The instruction is, that if the jury believe from the evidence, etc., "that defendant had no probable cause to believe him guilty of the charge, they will find for plaintiff." The true question, as laid down in *Mowry* v. *Miller*, 3 Leigh, 565, is not whether the defendant had probable cause to believe the plaintiff guilty, but whether there existed a probable cause for the prosecution, no matter whether the defendant knew of its existence or not.

The second instruction given by the court, at the instance of the defendant, is liable to the same objections. "If the defendant had probable cause to institute the prosecution," is the language of this instruction also, and the words "to institute the prosecution," may well be substituted for the words "to believe him guilty." For if the defendant had probable cause to "institute the prosecution," he had probable cause to "believe him guilty," and *vice versa*, whereas the real point of inquiry for the jury was not whether the defendant had probable cause to believe the plaintiff guilty, or whether he had probable cause to institute the prosecution, but whether there was probable cause for the prosecution, thereby referring the jury to the state of facts that existed in relation to the party accused, and not to the knowledge or belief of those facts in the party prosecuting.

Where the court gives erroneous instructions, the error is not cured by the fact that correct instructions accompanied them: *Jones* v. *Talbot*, 4 Mo. 274. Mere defective instructions may be supplied, but an instruction which is erroneous in itself, may mislead the jury. For this reason, the judgment of the circuit court is reversed, and the cause is remanded.

PROCESS MUST RUN IN THE NAME OF THE COMMONWEALTH: *White* v. *Commonwealth*, 6 Am. Dec. 443; *Little* v. *Little*, 32 Id. 317.

WHAT NECESSARY TO MAINTAIN MALICIOUS PROSECUTION, AND EVIDENCE OF.—Malice and want of probable cause must concur: *Kelton* v. *Bevins*, 5 Am. Dec. 670; *Bell* v. *Graham*, 9 Id. 687; *Turner* v. *Walker*, 22 Id. 329; *Leidig* v. *Rawson*, 29 Id. 354; *Williams* v. *Hunter*, 14 Id. 597; *Stone* v. *Stevens*, 30 Id. 611. Good cause for prosecution exempts prosecutor, though his motives were malicious: *Ulmer* v. *Leland*, 10 Id. 48; *Adams* v. *Lisher*, 25 Id. 102; nor is he liable if there is an apparent guilt arising from circumstances he honestly believes: *Plummer* v. *Gheen*, 14 Id. 572; nor if defendant is guilty, though prosecutor did not know it: *Adams* v. *Lisher*, 25 Id. 102. Such conduct by the accused as warrants the inference that the prosecution was undertaken for public motives, amounts to probable cause: *French* v. *Smith*, 24 Id. 616.

The principal case is approved on the point that a party can not give in evidence what he swore to before the magistrate, in *Riney* v. *Vanlandingham*, 9 Mo. 811; but the defendant can bring in evidence of what he testified to upon the trial of the plaintiff for the purpose of showing probable cause: *McMahan* v. *Armstrong*, 23 Am. Dec. 304. And the admission of a copy of the record showing the arrest, trial, and acquittal of defendant, in a proceeding under a search warrant, in a subsequent action brought by him for malicious prosecution, is not a ground for new trial, where the same facts appear to have been proved by other evidence, not objected to by the adverse party: *Stone* v. *Stevens*, 30 Id. 611.

DICKEY v. MALECHI.

[6 Missouri, 177.]

Circuit Court has Appellate Jurisdiction in Matters of Probate over the decisions of the county court, under statute of 1825, section 10.

Recital in Petition of the Rejection of Supposed Will by the county court, with the annexation of the record of the judgment of the county court, proving that fact, is sufficient to give the circuit court appellate jurisdiction under that statute.

Will Destroyed before or after Death of Testator, without his knowledge, does not cease to be his will.

One Witness is Sufficient to prove the contents of a lost will.

Whole of Lost Will need not be Proved; so much as is proved will be admitted to probate.

Where a Demurrer to a Petition is Overruled, but not Withdrawn, a withdrawal will be implied where the parties go before the jury on an issue made up under the direction of the court; the demurrer will not remain a confession of the facts in the petition.

General and Sweeping Objections are Insufficient; the party must point out objections specifically, to authorize the appellate court to interfere.

In a Suit to Establish a Lost Will, the deposition of an heir at law, who is also a devisee under the will, is admissible in evidence.

APPEAL from the circuit court of Ste. Genevieve county. The opinion states the case.

Cole, for the appellee.

Scott and Zeigler, contra.

By Court, NAPTON, J. One Antoine Simmino of Ste. Genevieve county, about the fifth of January, 1833, made his last will and executed it according to law, in the presence of two witnesses, John Findley and John Blital Beauvais, and died about four or five days after making his said will. John Campbell and Ebenezer Dickey, who had married sisters of Simmino, were appointed executors by the will. Immediately after the execution of the will by Simmino, who was proved to have been of disposing mind at the time, he handed the will to Campbell and requested him to place it in his (Simmino's) pocket-book, and put the pocket-book in his (Simmino's) desk, which was in the room where he lay. Campbell did as he was directed: but on the morning after the death of Simmino, Campbell and Dickey, the executors named in the will, went to Simmino's house to take possession of the will, but could not find it; nor has it ever been produced since. There was proof conducing to show that the will was in existence, on the evening before the testator died, and also on the morning after, in the course of which it disappeared. It also appears from the testimony, that the provisions of the will were in accordance with the previously fixed intentions of the testator frequently expressed to various individuals.

In January, 1833, Ebenezer Dickey took out letters of administration upon the estate of Simmino, and proceeded to act under the same. About the first of March, 1834, Francis Malechi, to whom a considerable real and personal property had been left by the will, by his guardian, Ichabod Sargent, presented his petition to the county court of Ste. Genevieve county, praying that the paper writing annexed to his petition, purporting to be the substance of the will of Simmino, might be admitted to probate, and calling on the heirs at law to show cause, etc., and requiring them to answer on oath touching the premises. The cause came on to a hearing in the county court, and that court adjudged that there was no such last will and testament of Simmino as Malechi in his petition had alleged.

In June, 1836, the defendant in error, Francis Malechi, by his guardian, filed his petition in the circuit court, praying to have the will established, reciting the rejection of the same by the county court, and citing the heirs at law to appear. The heirs at law, plaintiffs in error, appeared and pleaded, first to the jurisdiction of the court, alleging substantially, that the matters in the petition had been fully adjudicated in the county court, and that that court had exclusive jurisdiction. To this the petitioner demurred, and the court sustained the demurrer. The heirs at law then demurred to the petition, which demurrer was overruled; and afterwards they put in a plea in bar grounded on the former adjudication by the county court; to which plea plaintiff in error demurred, and the demurrer was sustained. The case was then submitted to the jury, upon an issue made up by the parties under the direction of the court; and a verdict was found for the petitioner; a new trial was granted at the instance of the defendants in error, and another issue made up, and upon that issue the jury found for the petitioner the will as annexed to his petition. A motion was made by the heirs at law for another new trial, and in arrest of judgment, both of which were refused, and the heirs at law have appealed to this court. There were four bills of exceptions taken on the trial of the issues in the circuit court containing the entire testimony; which seems to have consisted altogether of depositions. These depositions were taken by consent of parties, waiving any exceptions to their formality, as to time, place, notice, etc.; but the plaintiffs in error reserving to themselves the privilege of objecting to the testimony on the trial for incompetency or irrelevancy.

The provisions of the will were established by the testimony of Joseph D. Grafton, who drew it up; neither of the subscribing witnesses being privy to its contents. The deposition of Ebenezer Dickey and John Campbell, the two executors named in the will, and who had married sisters of the deceased, were also read in evidence, together with so much of the affidavit of Ebenezer Dickey as related to his belief in the existence of a will, and that after the most diligent search it could not be found. Objections were taken to the reading of the depositions on the ground of incompetency and irrelevancy; and to the deposition of Ebenezer Dickey, because he was a party to the cause. After closing the testimony, the defendants asked the court for the following instructions to the jury:

1. That if they do not believe that the said supposed will existed at, and after the death of the said Antoine Simmino, they must find for the defendants. 2. That if they believe that the supposed will was lost, or destroyed, before the death of the said Antoine Simmino, by his consent, connivance, or direction, they must find for the defendants. 3. That unless they believe the said paper purporting to be the last will and testament of Antoine Simmino, was signed by said Antoine Simmino, with a full knowledge of all its provisions, or by some person for him by his directions, they must find for the defendants. 4. That if the said supposed will was lost, or destroyed, two witnesses who read the will prove its existence at and after the death of the testator, remember its contents, and depose to its tenor, are necessary to establish the same. 5. That in the event of the loss or destruction of said will, it will require the testimony of two witnesses to establish the contents thereof, and that one witness is not sufficient. 6. That the whole provisions of the will must be established, and not a part only, and if the

jury are satisfied that the facts proved establish a part only of
the provisions of the will, they must find for the defendants.

The court gave the second and third instructions asked, and·
refused to give the first, fourth, fifth, and sixth instructions, and
in lieu thereof instructed the jury, that one witness was sufficient to establish the contents of a will, after the execution of·
the will has been proven by two subscribing witnesses, and also·
that they might find such parts of the will as were proved without finding anything in regard to the residue, and also that it
was not necessary to prove that the will existed at, or after the
death of the testator.

Defendants excepted to the giving of the several instructions
given, and the refusal to give those asked for, and after the verdict of the jury for the petitioner, moved for a new trial, which
was refused, and afterwards in arrest of judgment, which was
also overruled.

The appellants have made various points, on which they rely
for a reversal of this judgment, but it is believed that though
couched in different terms, and presented under a variety of
aspects, they are substantially as follows: 1. That the circuit
court had no jurisdiction over the subject-matter presented in the·
petition of Francis Malechi; but that the jurisdiction was exclusively in the county court.   2. That the circuit court erred·
in giving improper instructions, and in refusing those asked for·
by defendants.   3. That the court admitted improper and incompetent testimony on the trial.

1. The petition of Malechi was founded on the tenth section.
of the act respecting wills (revised code of 1825, p. 792); this section provides that, " where any will is exhibited to be proved
(in the county court), the court or clerk may immediately receive
the proof and grant a certificate of probate; or if such will be·
rejected, a certificate of rejection. If any persons interested·
shall, within five years thereafter, appear, and by his petition to·
the circuit court of the proper county, contest the validity of
the will proved, or pray to have a will proved that has been
rejected, an issue shall be made up whether the writing produced
be the will of the testator or not, which shall be tried by the
court, or by a jury, if either party require it."

The objection urged to the exercise of jurisdiction in this case,
rests on the provision of the act of 1825, by which the courts
of probate were invested with exclusive original jurisdiction in
all cases relative to the probate of last wills and testaments, the
granting letters testamentary, and repealing the same, etc., and·

upon the act of the second of January, 1827, by which the probate court was abolished, and all its jurisdiction transferred to the county court. I do not see that the circuit court in entertaining the petition of Malechi did exercise any original jurisdiction. The respective provisions of the two acts above recited are entirely consistent with each other. The legislature may undoubtedly provide other modes besides the ordinary form of appeal, by which the controlling power of the circuit court may be exercised, and in the tenth section of the act respecting wills and testaments, they have made such a provision. The recital in the petition of the rejection of the supposed will by the county court, with the annexation of the record of the judgment of the county court proving that fact, was sufficient to give jurisdiction to the circuit court. The judgment of the county court, in which they found that no such will as the paper writing presented to them existed, was a virtual certificate of rejection, sufficient to authorize the petitioner to proceed under the thirtieth section, and demand a review of that judgment in the circuit court. The circuit court did not therefore err in overruling the demurrer to the petition, and in sustaining the demurrers to the pleas of the defendants.

2. The first instruction asked for by defendants, and refused by the court, was, that if the jury do not believe that the said supposed will existed at and after the death of the said Antoine Simmino, they must find for the defendants. This instruction was very properly refused by the court, whether the will was destroyed before, or after the death of the testator: if it was destroyed without his knowledge, or consent, it did not cease to be his will, and its contents could be established by competent proof. The cases cited at the bar in support of the principle laid down in this instruction have not been produced, but I apprehend that the courts have never gone farther than to declare that proof of the non-existence of a will before the death of the testator might be presumptive evidence of its revocation, and [to] throw the burden of proof on the party setting up the will, it required satisfactory proof of its loss or destruction. But the principle laid down in the instructions asked, would open the door to knavery and fraud, and place it in the power of the dishonest to frustrate that disposition which every man has a right to make of his own property. Here the court gave the second instruction asked, which embraced the true law, and which was much more applicable to the evidence, than the first could have been, admitting it to have been abstractly true. The testimony

of Dickey, who was named in the will as one of the executors, was that he saw the will about sunset, of the evening preceding the morning when Simmino died; that he was with Simmino from the time he last saw the will until Simmino died; and during that time, Simmino expressed no dissatisfaction with the will, indeed said nothing relating to it, and that Simmino could not have destroyed the will without his knowledge. The evidence of Findley, one of the subscribing witnesses, was that Campbell, one of the executors named in the will, in a conversation had with witness on the morning of the funeral of the deceased, informed witness, that the will was in existence; that Simmino had made no alteration in the will, but that it remained the same as it was drawn by Mr. Grafton, and witnessed by him, Findley. Dickey also testified that on the day after the funeral, when he and Campbell went to get the will, for the purpose of proceeding under it, they were unable to find it, and Campbell observed to him, "he wished he (Dickey) had come sooner, it would have saved trouble, as the will could not have been gone above half an hour." Findley also testified that he heard Bazil Simmino, a brother of the deceased, say, with an oath, that his sister, the wife of John Campbell, would give him the will, and he would destroy it; giving as a reason for its destruction, that the will was "ungrateful" towards the family of Antoine Simmino, as it gave the greater part of his property to a half negro.

Upon this state of evidence, the instruction given was surely strong enough for the defendants, "that if they believed that the supposed will was lost or destroyed before the death of Antoine Simmino by his consent, connivance, or direction, they must find for defendants."

The fourth and fifth instructions are in substance, that two witnesses are necessary to establish the contents of a lost will. This point was expressly adjudicated upon a review of the authorities by this court in the case of *Graham et al.* v. *O'Fallon, Ex'r of Mullanphy*, 4 Mo. 601. There was no error in refusing these instructions.

The next instruction, the refusal of which is complained of, was that the whole provisions of the will must be established and not a part only, and if the jury are satisfied that the facts proved establish a part only of the provisions of the will, they must find for the defendants. This point has also been settled by this court in the case of *Jackson* v. *Jackson et al.*, 4 Mo. 211, in which the court held that so much of the will as can be proved may be admitted to probate.

3. The only point remaining for consideration is relative to the admission of improper testimony. It is urged, by counsel for defendant in error, that inasmuch as the defendant below demurred to the petition, and the demurrer was overruled and never withdrawn, the demurrer remains on the record a confession of the facts of the petition, and this court is precluded from inquiring into the testimony either as to its sufficiency or legal admissibility. This was the strict rule of law in England and may be so here, but I apprehend that where the court does not give judgment on the demurrer, but proceeds to suffer the parties to go before a jury on the issues made up under the direction of the court, it amounts to an implied withdrawal of the demurrer, and it is too late now for the defendant in error to rely on the technical advantage of which he might possibly have availed himself in the circuit court. It would be allowing him to take advantage of his own laches, for had he moved for a judgment on the demurrer in the court below, the opposite party would, no doubt, have asked and obtained leave to withdraw their demurrer, such being, I believe, the uniform practice in this state, restricted only by the power of the court to impose terms on the party asking for a leave to withdraw.

It is also urged, that as there were two verdicts in this case for the petitioner, and consequently one new trial granted, the law in relation to the granting of a second new trial, by which the court is restricted to cases where the jury have misbehaved or have erred in matters of law, is applicable to the reviewing powers of this court. The statute under which this application was made is also referred to. That statute provides "that the verdict of the jury, or the judgment of the court, shall be final as to the facts, saving to the court the right of granting a new trial as in other cases, and to either party an appeal in matters of law to the supreme court, as in other cases." By this I understand that this court can not inquire into the sufficiency of the evidence to sustain the verdict of the jury, but that, as in other cases, if the court have allowed illegal testimony to go to the jury, this court has power to correct such error. The introduction of incompetent testimony is as much an error of law as the giving of wrong instructions, and it is a matter which the court will look into. The act in relation to new trials has no application, except to the objection urged in this court that the circuit court overruled this second application for a new trial. In support of which objection the plaintiff in error should have made out the existence of one of the two states of fact pointed out in the law to justify the granting of a second new trial. Nothing appears on the record to show either that there was any misbehavior of the jury, or any error of law committed by them. The jury are clearly not responsible for the correctness of the law as given by the court, but a failure to obey its instructions, or a misunderstanding of their meaning as evidenced by the facts found in their verdict, must be the error of law contemplated in this section of the statute: *Hill* v. *Wilkins*, 4 Mo. 86.

Believing, then, that this court is not precluded from examining the legality of the testimony offered on the trial, I proceed to notice the portions of the written testimony objected to. The reading of all the depositions was objected to by the defendants below upon the general charge of incompetency and irrelevancy. This court has often determined that such general and sweeping objections are insufficient. The party must point out the objections more specifically to authorize this court to interfere. I, however, see nothing illegal or irrelevant in the testimony to which these general objections were taken. But the defendants specified more particularly their objections to the admission of Dickey's deposition; to the reading of this deposition, it appears from the bill of exceptions, defendants objected "as being both irrelevant and incompetent, the said Dickey being one of the defendants in the cause." The decisions of this court would, I believe, sustain me in saying that it does not appear from this record that Dickey was in fact a defendant, and that the defendants' assertion that he was in the motion to exclude the deposition, was no proof of this fact, and the court might have overruled the motion on the ground that the facts stated in the motion were not true.

In *Davidson* v. *Peck*, 4 Mo. 438, it was held that where the circuit court overruled a motion to exclude certain depositions on account of alleged informalities in their execution, and the fact of such informalities existing is not preserved by bill of exceptions, this court can not know but that the circuit court overruled the motion because the facts stated in the motion did not exist or were falsely stated. In *Cozzens* v. *Gillespie*, Id. 82, the defendant offered to read the deposition of one Walter D. Scott, and objections were made to the same on the ground that Scott was interested, and to show the interest, it was proved that "defendant and one Walter D. Scott had once beeen partners;" it was held that the identity of witness with the person who had once been the partner of the defendant was not proved, and could not be inferred from the identity of names, and the deposition was therefore admissible. These cases seem to establish the insufficiency of the objections here taken to Dickey's testimony, but I am unwilling to rest an opinion on the technical difficulty sustained by these cases, conceiving that the facts stated in the motion in the one case and in the bill of exceptions in the other, raised a violent presumption of their truth, especially as they were uncontroverted in the circuit court.

This deposition was admissible, as I think, upon other grounds. The proceeding had in this case, though the heirs at law are made nominal parties, was in truth in the nature of an *ex parte* proceeding. It was a revival of the same proceeding in the circuit court, which had been previously had in the county court. There can be no question that in the county court the deposition or answer of Dickey, or any other heir, could have been read unless objected to on other grounds than the mere fact that he had been cited as one of the heirs at law, and consequently stood on the record as one of the defendants. In truth, the citation is for them to appear and show cause, etc., why the paper shall not be established. The same legal rules that govern the investigation in the county court must apply in the circuit court. The deposition of Dickey was nothing more nor less than his answer on oath to certain interrogatories propounded by the petitioner. Whether he could be compelled to answer or not, is no question raised by this record. No subpœna *ad testificandum* was issued. The deposition seems to have been voluntarily made, and whether admissible as evidence on the trial or not, must depend, not on the question whether he was a defendant, but whether there was no other objection to him on account of a personal disability or an interest in the event. The interest of Dickey was clearly against the party calling him—he was one of the heirs at law, and from the contents of the will as proved by Mr. Grafton, his share of the estate as heir, would have greatly exceeded the trifling legacy which had been left him in the will. The principle decided in *Graham* v. *O'Fallon, Ex'r of Mullanphy*, is therefore applicable. On the ground of interest there could be no objection to Dickey even had he been a party *de facto*. It may be questioned whether he could not have voluntarily waived the privilege which that position gave him, and his deposition be read. His admission could have been proved, and why not his voluntary admission under oath? But whether a party in interest, Dickey's testimony, whether in the shape of a deposition, in answer to interrogatories, or as an answer to the citation following the petition, was good evidence either in the county or circuit court, unless some other objection to it existed besides what is founded on the fact of his being a party.

Any other construction of the law would lead to intolerable consequences. A party seeking to establish a lost will is bound to cite the heirs at law. The relations of a testator are most likely to be the persons most conversant with his intentions, and around and about his person and house during his last illness. If the testimony of all these persons must be excluded on the ground of their being parties, and they are necessarily made parties in such proceedings, it must become exceedingly difficult in most cases, and in many cases absolutely impracticable, to establish most of the facts necessary to authorize the probate of a lost will. It places it in the power of the persons most likely to be interested in suppressing the will, to shut out all investigation and shield themselves under a rule of law from all responsibility. Such a state of things could never have been contemplated either by our statute law regulating proceedings to establish wills, or sanctioned by the common law rules of evidence.

Judgment affirmed.

McGirk, J., absent.

———

WILL MAY BE PROVED BY ONE OF THE SUBSCRIBING WITNESSES: *Jackson* v. *La Grange*, 10 Am. Dec. 237; *Lindsay* v. *McCormack*, 12 Id. 387; *Welch* v. *Welch*, 15 Id. 126; *Dan* v. *Brown*, Id. 395; *Jackson* v. *Vickory*, 19 Id. 522.

REVOCATION OF A WILL, WHAT AMOUNTS TO: See *Gains* v. *Gains*, 12 Am. Dec.. 375, and note 377, citing cases in this series; *Greer* v. *McCracken*, 14 Id. 755; *Graves* v. *Sheldon*, 15 Id. 653, and note 659; *Dan* v. *Brown*, Id. 395; *Wells* v. *Wells*, 16 Id. 150; *Hawes* v. *Humphreys*, 20 Id. 481; *Sneed* v. *Ewing*, 22 Id. 41; *Apperson* v. *Cottrell*, 29 Id. 239; *Bohanon* v. *Walcot*, 29 Id. 631.

PRINCIPAL CASE HAS BEEN CITED TO THE FOLLOWING POINTS: That objections to reading depositions must be specific, and the court will disregard general objections: *State Bank* v. *Merchants' Bank*, 10 Mo. 128; *Roussin* v. *St. Louis Perpetual Ins. Co.*, 15 Id. 247; that heirs and devisees are competent witnesses in establishing a will: *Garvin* v. *Williams*, 50 Id. 213; *Holmes* v. *Holloman*, 12 Id. 537; that a contest may be transferred from an inferior to a superior court without formal appeal: *Benoist* v. *Murrin*, 48 Id. 52; that where errors are made in the admission or exclusion of testimony, and are preserved by proper exceptions, they will be corrected on appeal: *Letton* v. *Graves*, 26 Id. 251.

CASES

IN THE

SUPERIOR COURT OF JUDICATURE

OF

NEW HAMPSHIRE.

SNOW *v.* CHANDLER.

[10 NEW HAMPSHIRE, 92.]

COVENANT NOT TO SUE ONE OF TWO JOINT TRESPASSERS, does not operate as a discharge of the other.

NOTHING SHORT OF PAYMENT OF DAMAGES by one joint trespasser, or a release under seal, can operate to discharge the other.

ANY PARTIAL PAYMENT MADE BY A CO-TRESPASSER in satisfaction of the damages sustained by reason of the joint trespass, inures to the benefit of the other, and, in an action against the latter, must be considered by the jury in determining the amount of their verdict.

TRESPASS for a joint assault and battery committed by defendant and one Holt, upon plaintiff. Prior to the commencement of this action, plaintiff had covenanted with Holt, in consideration of twenty dollars, not to sue him for the assault except upon the return of the money paid. At the time this action was brought the twenty dollars had not been refunded. Plaintiff had verdict, defendant appealed.

Mead, for the plaintiff.

Chamberlain and Vose, for the defendant.

UPHAM, J. In this case the strongest ground on which the defendant can place his defense is, that the contract with Holt, by which the twenty dollars was received, was a covenant not to sue him; and it is argued that if this agreement can have such effect, it bars the plaintiff from a suit against either trespasser. But we are not aware that this result necessarily follows. It is well settled that a covenant not to sue one of several debtors will not operate to discharge all the debtors; and the reason assigned for this, in the Massachusetts cases is, "because it can not be inferred from such a covenant that it was the intention to discharge the debt:" *Ruggles* v. *Patten*, 8 Mass. 480; *Sewell et al.* v. *Sparrow*, 16 Id. 24; *Shed* v. *Pierce et al.*, 17 Id. 623. The same is holden in *Walker* v. *McCulloch*, 4 Greenl. 421; and it is there said that "nothing short of payment by one of several joint debtors, or a release under seal, can operate to discharge the other debtors from the contract." These authorities have been fully sustained in this state, in the case of *Durell* v. *Wendell et al.*, 8 N. H. 369.

There seems to be no reason why a more favorable rule should be established as to what may constitute a release or discharge of a claim of damages in trespass, where there are joint trespassers, than a release of a debt where there are joint debtors. There can be no reason why damages for a wrong done should be more easily settled and canceled than a claim for a debt due; or that the law should favor the discharge of trespassers more than the release of debtors.

The principle of the decisions, therefore, as to what constitutes a release of a contract where there are joint debtors, is fully applicable; and we see no objection to holding, in this case, that a covenant not to sue one of two joint trespassers does not operate as a discharge of the other trespasser, for the same reason assigned in the Massachusetts cases as to joint debtors, "because it can not be inferred from such a covenant that it was the intention to discharge the claim of damage." The general rule, also, as stated in the case in Greenleaf as to joint debtors, may well be applied in case of joint trespassers, viz.: that nothing short of payment of damage by one of two joint trespassers, or a release under seal, can operate to discharge the other trespasser. If so, a covenant not to sue Holt would avail nothing in defense to this action, and nothing short of payment by him for the damage sustained can discharge this defendant.

No release of damages was here given; and the only question is, whether the sum paid was in satisfaction of the damage incurred. If it was not so received, it is clear that the claim is not discharged. The evidence is, that at the time of receiving the money from Holt, the plaintiff declared that he would not settle with Chandler for five hundred dollars. The substance of the arrangement betwixt the plaintiff and Holt seems to have been this: that the plaintiff was willing to receive a small portion of the damage from Holt, either for the reason that he conceived him to be less to blame than the defendant, or that he was less able to pay his proportion of the damage; and on condition of receiving this sum the plaintiff engaged to pursue the defendant for the remainder of his claim. It is clear that the sum paid was not received in satisfaction of the damage, but only in part satisfaction; and the fact that it was coupled with the engagement not to sue Holt does not alter the case. It is still but a partial satisfaction of the damage, and the plaintiff may sue or omit to sue whom he pleases, by contract or otherwise. The other trespasser has no equitable or legal claim to prevent such an arrangement. He remains liable for the whole damage, until satisfaction is made.

If the individual receiving the injury sees fit to visit the penalty upon any one guilty individual rather than another, such individual has no right to complain. It is part of the necessary liability that he incurs in committing the trespass, and should serve to deter him from such wrongful acts. At the same time, any partial payment by a co-trespasser avails so far for his benefit. Such was the ruling in this case. To this extent the defendant can avail himself of the plaintiff's arrangement with his co-trespasser, but there was nothing in that contract which constitutes a bar to this suit. There must, therefore, be

Judgment on the verdict against the defendant.

MEASURE OF DAMAGES IN ACTION OF TRESPASS: *Woolley* v. *Carter*, 11 Am. Dec. 484, and note. When exemplary damages are allowed: See note to *Merrells* v. *Tariff Man. Co.*, 27 Id. 684.

HURD *v.* SILSBY.

[10 NEW HAMPSHIRE, 108.]

No ASSIGNMENT FOR THE BENEFIT OF CREDITORS IS VALID, under the statute of July 5, 1834, unless it provides for an equal distribution of the debtor's estate among all his creditors, in proportion to their respective demands.

CONDITIONAL ASSIGNMENT for the benefit of creditors is invalid.

ASSIGNMENT FOR THE BENEFIT OF SUCH CREDITORS as will execute the instrument, and signify their willingness to receive the prospective dividends in full discharge of all demands, is conditional, and therefore invalid.

FOREIGN attachment brought by plaintiffs, creditors of Silsby, against the latter's assignees in insolvency, to charge them as trustees. Plaintiffs had orally assented to the assignment for the benefit of creditors. The further facts appear in the opinion.

Gilchrist, for the plaintiffs.

Hubbard, for the defendants.

PARKER, C. J.   Prior to the statute of July 5, 1834, for the equal distribution of property assigned for the benefit of creditors, this assignment would have been valid to the extent of the claims of the trustees, if any, and of the creditors who had become parties to it prior to the service of the plaintiff's writ.   By the provisions of that act, no assignment made for the benefit of creditors shall be valid, except the same shall provide for an equal distribution of all real, mixed, or personal estate, among the several creditors of the person making such assignment, in equal proportion, according to their respective demands; nor until the assignor has made oath that he has placed and assigned, and that the true intention of his assignment was to place in the hands of his assignee, all his property of every description, except such as is exempted from attachment and execution by an act for the relief of poor debtors, passed January 3, 1829, to be divided among his creditors in proportion to their respective demands.

The oath required by the statute has been taken in this case, and the question is, whether this is an assignment in favor of all the creditors, and so conformable to the provisions of the act. It is stated in the introduction to be an indenture between the debtor, the trustees, and the creditors who have executed it. The trust is declared to be, to pay the several creditors of Silsby, in equal proportion, according to their respective claims.   This last clause would seem to have been intended to be in conformity with the statute.   But another clause follows, which gives a different character to the assignment, viz.: "It being the meaning of the parties to this instrument that the creditors shall accept their several proportions, in full discharge of their respective claims."   The indenture then, in truth, conveys the property in trust to be distributed among the creditors who will execute the instrument, and thus signify their willingness to receive the dividend in full discharge of their claims.   It is apparent that this is not such an assignment as is permitted by the statute.   In *Jefts* v. *Spaulding and Trustee,* Hillsborough,[1] December term, 1837, the assignment provided that the creditors should become parties in sixty days, and it was held bad under the statute.   In that case, as in this, the assignment did not in fact provide for distribution among all the creditors.   There the

---

1. Not reported.

condition on which they were to receive a dividend was, that they should become parties in sixty days; and some of the creditors might not gain information that such assignment had been executed by the assignor, within that time, and thus be excluded.

In the present case, the distribution is to be made among those who will become parties and release their demands. It certainly does not appear that all will be willing to do this; and if they are not—if they do not execute the instrument—no provision is made for a distribution to them. An assignment under the statute, should have no conditions annexed to it. It need not even provide that the creditors should become parties by executing it. If no conditions are annexed, the assignment being for the benefit of all the creditors, the assent of all may be presumed, until the contrary appears: *Halsey* v. *Fairbanks and Whitney, Trustee,* 4 Mason, 207. But such assent can not be presumed where a condition is affixed: Id.; *Leeds* v. *Sayward,* 6 N. H. 85.

Where there is no condition, the assent of the creditors being presumed until the contrary appears, the property is well held in trust for the benefit of all the creditors, until dissent is in some way manifested. It is competent, of course, for any one to dissent, but this will not destroy the assignment. If he causes the trustees to be summoned, in such case, he can only take such surplus as may remain after paying those who do not dissent. Where an assignment is made for the benefit of all the creditors, they must be allowed a reasonable time in which to bring in their claims before final distribution; and it is not necessary that the assignment itself should contain any provision upon that subject. That the plaintiffs assented to the assignment in this case can not make any difference. Being void under the act, they could take nothing by it, other creditors having commenced suits, unless there was a surplus.

Trustees charged.

———

EFFECT OF CLAUSE IN ASSIGNMENT for the benefit of creditors, exacting a release from the creditor of all demands against the debtor, is discussed in the notes to *Lippencott* v. *Barker,* 4 Am. Dec. 433; *Bordan* v. *Sumner,* 16 Id. 338; *Atkinson* v. *Jordan,* 24 Id. 281; see also *Niolon* v. *Douglas,* 30 Id. 368; *Skipwith* v. *Cunningham,* 31 Id. 642.

NEWPORT MECHANICS MANUF'G CO. *v.* STARBIRD.

[10 NEW HAMPSHIRE, 123.]

PROMISSORY NOTE, PAYABLE TO THE "PRESIDENT, DIRECTORS, AND COMPANY OF" a certain corporation, is payable to the corporation.

PAROL EVIDENCE IS ADMISSIBLE to show who were intended as payees by a description in a promissory note.

ACTION on the following promissory note:

"Newport, May 27, 1835. For value received, I promise to pay the president, directors, and company of the Newport Mechanics manufacturing company, five hundred dollars, on demand, with interest annually. NAYLOR STARBIRD."

Defendant objected to parol testimony to prove to whom the note was intended to be given, but the objection was overruled. Plaintiff had verdict; defendant appealed.

Edes, for the plaintiffs.

Burke and Handerson, for the defendant.

UPHAM, J. The general rule as to corporations is, that each corporation shall have a name by which it is to sue and be sued, and do all legal acts: Com. Dig., tit. Franchise, F, 9; 10 Co. Lit. 29, b. The name of a corporation in this respect, designates the corporation, in the same manner that the name of an individual designates the person. There is this difference, however, that the alteration of a letter, or transposition of a word, usually makes an entirely different name of the person, while the name of a corporation frequently consists of several descriptive words, and the transposition of them, or an interpolation, or omission, or alteration of some of them, may make no essential difference in their sense. It is said in 10 Co. 135, that in all grants by or to corporations, if there is enough expressed to show that there is such an artificial being, and to distinguish it from all others, the body politic is well named, although there is a variation of words and syllables. See, also, Bac. Abr., Corporations, c. 2; Bro. Abr., Misnomer, 73; *Mayor and Burgesses of Stafford* v. *Bolton*, 1 Bos. & Pul. 40; *Mayor and Burgesses of Malden* v. *Miller*, 1 Barn. & Ald. 699; *Medway Cotton Manufactory* v. *Adams et al.*, 10 Mass. 360.

The inquiry in this case is the same as in 10 Mass. 360, "whether the name of the note sufficiently indicates the plaintiffs, and were they known by it as the promisees?" That case is far stronger than the present, and it would seem quite clear, in the absence of evidence to the contrary, that a note to the

president, directors, and company of the Newport Mechanics
manufacturing company was a note to the Newport Mechanics
manufacturing company; at least, as much so as a grant to the
mayor, burgesses, etc., of the borough town of Malden, is a
grant to the mayor, burgesses, etc., of Malden; which is the case
cited from 1 Barn. & Ald. 699. It is held that the utmost certainty
required in grants concerning the names of the parties is, "that
there be sufficient shown to ascertain the grantor and grantee,
and to distinguish them from all others:" Bac. Abr., Grant, 6;
Co. Lit. 3.

The description in the note declared on would seem clearly to
indicate the plaintiffs as the promisees, in distinction from all
others. But however this may be, as an inference from the face
of the paper, the fact is clearly so, as shown in the case. The
case finds "that the plaintiffs were the persons interested in the
note as payees, by the description in said note, and that it was
given to the plaintiffs for one tenth part of their capital stock,
being the value of five shares taken by the defendant." This
fact may be shown by extraneous evidence. It is sometimes
made a question for the jury, whether a particular corporation
was intended under some given description: *Society for Propa-
gating the Gospel* v. *Young*, 2 N. H. 310; and we have no hesitation in holding that where such fact appears, and the whole
corporate name is given, with the addition prefixed merely of
the names of the officers and company of said corporation, the
promise may be regarded as to the corporation itself, and the variance is not such as to preclude a recovery in the corporate name.

Judgment on the verdict for the plaintiffs.

SUIT BY PRINCIPAL ON NOTE TO AGENT.—The doctrine laid down in the
foregoing case is similar to that of *Arlington* v. *Hinds*, 12 Am. Dec. 704,
where it was held that a note made payable to a town treasurer may be sued
on by the town; and see also *Johnson* v. *Harris*, 26 Id. 425. In the note to
Arlington v. *Hinds, supra,* a general discussion of the right of principals to
sue on notes made to their agents, especially in the case of corporation and
public officers, may be found.

The principal case is cited in *People* v. *Sierra B. Q. M. Co.*, 39 Cal. 514,
as an authority to the point that slight discrepancies in the name of a corporation will not vitiate contracts of the corporation, and to the same point
in *Board of Education etc.* v. *Greenebaum*, 39 Ill. 614.

BURLEY *v.* RUSSELL.

[10 NEW HAMPSHIRE, 184.]

MINOR IS NOT ESTOPPED TO AVOID HIS CONTRACT on the ground of infancy,
by reason of false representations as to his age, made at the time of contracting.

INFANT IS LIABLE, IN AN ACTION ON THE CASE, for the fraudulent affirmation that he is of age, if he afterwards avoids his contract by reason of his infancy.

ASSUMPSIT on four promissory notes, executed by defendant when a minor. Plaintiff contended that defendant was estopped from proving his infancy, by reason of certain declarations made by him at the time the notes were made, to the effect that he was then of full age. Defendant had verdict. Plaintiff moved for new trial.

Bartlett and Quincy, for the plaintiff.

Rogers, for the defendant.

PARKER, C. J.   The position contended for by the counsel, that the declaration of the defendant, that he was of age, is an estoppel to him to set up his infancy, in avoidance of the contract, it is conceded is not supported by any direct authority; and our decision in *Fitts* v. *Hall*, 9 N. H. 441, does not lead to such a result. That decision is, that an infant is liable, in case, for a fraudulent affirmation that he is of age, whereby another is induced to enter into a contract with him, if he afterwards avoids the contract, by reason of his infancy. In an action of that description, he is subjected to such damages as the other party has sustained. But this may or may not be to the amount which he promised to pay by his contract. The measure of damages is by no means necessarily the same. The amount promised to be paid may be greater than the damage sustained, by reason of the inexperience of the minor, which has led him to promise a greater sum than the property received is worth. To hold him estopped might punish him, therefore, beyond his demerits.

And, besides, this would overturn much of the doctrine which has long been received in relation to the right of a minor to avoid his contracts, and introduce a new rule, which seems not to be required by the exigency of the case, or justified by principle or precedent.

Judgment on the verdict.

———

INFANTS' CONTRACTS, WHEN VOIDABLE: See the cases in this series collected in the note to *Lynde* v. *Budd*, 21 Am. Dec. 86. In *Conroe* v. *Birdsall*, 1 Id. 105, it was decided that although an infant, at the time of making a bond, fraudulently alleged that he was of full age, yet the bond was nevertheless voidable at his election; but in *Badger* v. *Phinney*, 8 Id. 105, it was held that where goods are sold to an infant upon such representations, and the infancy is pleaded to avoid payment, the vendor may reclaim the goods, as the property did not pass.

Hoit *v.* Underhill.

[10 New Hampshire, 220.]

Promise of a Person after He Arrives at Age, to pay a debt contracted during his minority, removes the bar of infancy, and authorizes a recovery on the original contract.

Ratification of a Contract Entered into during Infancy, after a minor's arrival at age, is sufficient although made to the undisclosed agent of the other contracting party.

Admissions of a Spendthrift, made while under a commission of guardianship, are competent evidence to show a contract, or a ratification of one, made prior to the guardianship.

Assumpsit for money paid. Defendant having been adjudged a spendthrift after his arrival at age, appeared by his guardian, who set up as a defense, the plea of infancy at the time the contract was made. The other facts sufficiently appear in the opinion. Plaintiff had verdict.

Pillsbury, for the plaintiff.

H. F. French, for the defendant.

Parker, C. J. It appears that the defendant, after he became of age, before this suit was commenced and before the appointment of a guardian, made a promise that he would pay the plaintiff the debt now claimed. The promise was made to a person who was in fact the agent of the plaintiff, specially authorized to call on the defendant and see what he would say, and if he would not pay what the plaintiff had paid for him. In this respect this case differs from the case before us at the last term: 9 N. H. 436.[1] It does not appear, however, that the fact that the person was agent of the plaintiff was disclosed to the defendant at the time.

Upon this evidence, it is objected, that there could be no contract, because the defendant, if he made the declaration without knowledge that the party to whom he made it was agent, could not have understood that he was making a contract, but must have made a mere declaration of intention.

This objection comes, perhaps, with a better grace from a guardian of the defendant than it would from the party himself. It may well be answered, that the promise of an infant, when he becomes of age, operates only to remove the legal bar to a recovery, on a contract made before. The suit is on the original contract. And an infant may remove this bar, without any communication with the creditor, or any agent of his. It is well

---

1. *Hoit v. Underhill.*

settled that he may ratify the contract by his act: *Aldrich* v. *Grimes*, 10 N. H. 194; *Orvis* v. *Kimball*, and authorities cited, 3 Id. 315; *Roberts* v. *Wiggin*, 1 Id. 75 [8 Am. Dec. 38]. And this not only without the presence of the creditor, or any agent of his, but without his having, at the time, either by himself, or any agent, any knowledge whatever of any such ratification. That he may ratify by acts alone, shows that the action should not be instituted on the new promise, if there is one, and that the original contract is the foundation of the suit, although it furnishes no legal cause of action until it is ratified after the party is of full age: *Merriam* v. *Wilkins*, 6 Id. 372 [25 Am. Dec. 472]; 7 Id. 372;[1] 8 Id. 432.[2] It is not necessary, therefore, that there should be a new contract, according to the technical definition of a contract. There is no need of a new bargain between the creditor and debtor. The infant may ratify after he is of age, even against the consent of the other party.

While, then, in order to guard his rights, he should not be bound by loose declarations of his intentions (3 N. H. 315), or by any mere expression of an intention to pay, made to a person having no authority whatever in the matter (9 Id. 436), it would seem to be enough, if the ratification is made by a deliberate declaration, made to a third person, who was in fact agent, on an application well calculated to lead him to presume that the party thus applying came in behalf of the creditor, without any express declaration of authority, and without any express evidence that the defendant had knowledge of the authority. And we are of opinion that this evidence is sufficient to sustain the action.

The other evidence in the case, if it stood alone, is sufficient to charge the defendant. A promise by the defendant, after he was placed under guardianship, or after suit, would be insufficient; but an admission, after suit, of a promise made before the suit, would be competent evidence where no guardianship existed; and the guardianship does not change all the ordinary rules of evidence. The defendant might be charged for any tortious acts, notwithstanding the guardianship; and those acts might be proved, we think, by his confessions; and if so, he may make declarations in relation to his previous transactions, which will be competent to be weighed by the jury. He could not make a contract after he was placed under guardianship, and the evidence was not offered to prove one. It was offered for the purpose of showing that he had

---

1. *Conn* v. *Coburn.*   2. *Merriam* v. *Wilkins.* 6 N. H. 432.

previously made such contract, or ratified one, and was in that point of view admissible, and to be weighed by the jury. Unless they believed that the promise was actually made before the guardianship, and before the suit, the evidence of the admissions would be unavailing to sustain the action; but there was no evidence tending to contradict it, and no desire to have the jury pass upon it. As the evidence was rightly admitted, there must be

Judgment on the verdict.

RATIFICATION OF INFANT'S CONTRACT, WHAT AMOUNTS TO: See *Rogers* v. *Hurd*, 4 Am. Dec. 182, and note; *Martin* v. *Mayo*, 6 Id. 103; *Whitney* v. *Dutch*, 7 Id. 229, and note; *Overbach* v. *Heermance*, 14 Id. 546; *Thompson* v. *Lay*, 16 Id. 325; *Cheshire* v. *Barrett*, 17 Id. 735; *Benham* v. *Bishop*, 23 Id. 358; *Delano* v. *Blake*, 25 Id. 617; *Wheaton* v. *East*, 26 Id. 251.

WOOD *v.* GALE.

[10 NEW HAMPSHIRE, 247.]

GUARDIAN HAS THE RIGHT TO REMOVE AN IMPROPER PERSON for his ward to associate with, from the ward's premises, using no more force, and removing such person no further than is necessary to prevent a renewal of such association.

EVIDENCE OF WANT OF CHASTITY IN THE PERSON REMOVED IS ADMISSIBLE, in an action of trespass, to show the reasons a guardian may have had to expect such person's return, and to justify the removal.

TRESPASS for an assault and imprisonment, done by defendant, the guardian of one Bartlett, in removing plaintiff from Bartlett's house, and in carrying her a considerable distance to a neighboring town. Defendant set up in justification that plaintiff was a person of ill-fame, not fit to associate with his ward, and that the removal was necessary by reason of her refusal to leave the premises. The trial court, against plaintiff's objections, admitted evidence to show plaintiff's want of chastity. Defendant had verdict; plaintiff appealed.

Tilton and Bell, for the plaintiff.

Sullivan and Bartlett, for the defendant.

UPHAM, J. It is not contended in this case that the guardian had no authority to remove an improper person for his ward to associate with, from the ward's premises; but it is alleged that no legal right exists for a removal to any greater distance.

The original act of the defendant, then, is not objected to, but that the exercise of authority, which was originally legal, was continued to such extent as to render the defendants tres-passers *ab initio.* It can hardly be contended that the right of removal would be limited to the precise line of the premises owned by the ward. This doctrine would preclude the right of removal of an improper associate, or a separation of him from the company of the ward, except on the ground of a mere right in the soil. But the guardian's right to protect his ward from the company or intrusions of improper associates, is a personal right which can not be limited in this manner. He had a clear right of removal of the plaintiff from the premises, on her refusal to retire; and, to protect his ward from a threatened return, a far-ther removal, under some circumstances, would be clearly justi-fiable. The same right would exist as in the removal of a com-mon brawler or disturber of the public peace; which, if it existed at all, would justify a removal to such extent as to obviate the nuisance.

Any exercise of authority of this kind is an exception to the general rule, and can not be too strictly limited, lest, under some pretense of the preservation of the peace, or maintenance of personal privilege, the rights of the citizen should be in-fringed. We apprehend, however, that no injury can arise in these special cases from the ruling of the court, that the party injured may remove an individual from his premises, under the circum-stances here disclosed, and keep her out, " using no more force, and removing her no further than is necessary to effect this ob-ject." The rights of the citizen will be sufficiently protected under such a limitation. The jury have found that the acts of the defendants were within the rule thus prescribed, and we think their verdict should be sustained.

It has been further contended, that evidence of the character of a party could not be offered except when it is put directly in issue. To this it is replied, that the character of the plaintiff for chastity, owing to the peculiar nature of the facts in this case, was in issue, and that the case is thus brought within the general principle laid down in Stark. Ev., pt. 4, 366. It be-came necessary to show that the plaintiff had repeatedly sought the intimacy of the defendant's ward, against the prohibition of the defendant for her to continue to associate with him or to be upon his premises; and also to put in evidence, not only the manner of her being found in company with the ward, but her character for chastity, in order to show the reasons the defend-ant had to expect her immediate return, unless he caused her to be removed to some short distance from the premises; and to justify her removal to that extent, we are of opinion the evidence submitted was admissible, as directly bearing on the ground of defense set up in justification.

Judgment on the verdict.

RIGHTS AND POWERS OF GUARDIAN.—In general, see notes to *Thompson* v. *Boardman*, 18 Am. Dec. 689; *Matter of Van Houten*, 29 Id. 712; to submit claim of ward to arbitration: *Hutchins* v. *Johnson*, 30 Id. 622, and note on page 633.

JENNESS *v.* BEAN.

[10 NEW HAMPSHIRE, 266.]

INDORSEMENT OF A PROMISSORY NOTE after maturity, given in pledge as collateral security, is not one which is protected as a commercial indorsement for value.

UPON THE INDORSEMENT OF A PROMISSORY NOTE IN PLEDGE after maturity, the general property in the note remains in the indorser, and the indorsee takes it, like a chose in action not negotiable, subject to all equities existing in favor of the maker as against the indorser, at the time when notice is given of the indorsement; and the maker may set off a debt due to himself from the indorser, at the time of the transfer, in an action by the indorsee on such note, notwithstanding the insolvency of the indorser.

ASSUMPSIT on a promissory note of defendant, payable on demand to Moore & Sargent, or order, and indorsed by plaintiff. Defendant filed the general issue, and set off claims in his favor against Moore & Sargent, existing at the time of indorsement. It appeared that the note was indorsed by Moore & Sargent, after maturity, in pledge to secure certain obligations of their own, and that they were now insolvent. Verdict for defendant. Plaintiff moved for new trial.

Cilley, for the plaintiff.

St. Clair and Bell, for the defendant.

PARKER, C. J. If the property of the note, upon which this action is founded, had been transferred absolutely and *bona fide*, to Eaton, when it was indorsed to him, no demand in favor of the maker against the payees could have been filed in set-off, notwithstanding the note might have been considered as a discredited note, from the time which had elapsed subsequent to its date: *Chandler* v. *Drew*, 6 N. H. 469 [26 Am. Dec. 704.] The defendant having by his contract made the legal title assignable, and promised to pay any one to whom the note should be duly transferred and indorsed, could not, after such a transfer, be permitted to avoid the obligation of his contract to pay the indorsee, by alleging that another distinct and separate debt was due from the payees to himself, and offering to set off the one against the other. The case before us, however, does not find a transfer of that character. The note has not, in fact, been negotiated in the usual course of business, and become absolutely the property of the indorsee. It is transferred to him, to hold merely as a collateral security for a debt due from the payees to himself. The indorsement, it is true, transferred the legal title to the indorsee, so that he could institute a suit in his own name, or, as in this instance, in the name of a third person. And the indorsee is not a mere nominal party having no interest in the matter. If no defense exists, and no rights of the maker intervene, the indorsee, as between the indorser and himself, has the right to collect the note and apply the avails to the satisfaction of his claims against the indorser.

But the question still remains, whether the right and title of the indorsee is not subject to a right in the maker, to set up any defense he could make against the payees, had the suit been by them, and to set off any demand he had against them at the time when he received notice of the indorsement.

Aside from the insolvency of the payees, which seems to have occurred since the indorsement, we think there is no reason to deny such a right. The general property of the note still remains in the payees. So far as the general property is concerned, they are the real owners of the note, and parties in interest. If the amount is recovered of the defendant it will go to discharge so much of a claim which the indorsee holds against them.

If the demand should be lost by the insolvency of the defendant, without any fault of the indorsee, the loss would not be his. If the payees were solvent, it would be wholly immaterial to the indorsee whether the defendant was solvent or insolvent, or whether he recovered judgment or not, except that a loss of cost might fall upon him. He could, in that case, collect his demands against the payees, and by that act terminate all his interest under the indorsement; and the payees, by a settlement of the demand against them, might put an end to his interest. It is true that by reason of the insolvency of Moore & Sargent, if Eaton is unable to collect the money he may sustain a loss to that amount; but we are of opinion that their insolvency can not change the principle upon which the case is to be decided. It does not change the legal relation in which the parties stand to each other. It neither transfers any new title, nor enlarges any right. The indorsee still holds the note as a security merely. His debt against the indorsers is not discharged, nor their interest in the note ended, by their insolvency. If Eaton sustains a loss, it will be upon his demand against Moore & Sargent, and not a loss of a debt due from the defendant. It will not be a loss of this demand. If the set-off is allowed he will be unable to appropriate the interest of his debtors in this demand, to the payment of his debt; but this will be because his rights were dependent upon their interest, which is thus discharged and defeated.

If the insolvency made a distinction, a question of difficult solution might arise in some cases; that is, whether the indorser was in fact insolvent, and whether therefore the right of defense existed or not. If the rights of the indorsee were enlarged by the insolvency, it might not be easy to determine at what time he commenced holding this note exonerated from any defense or set-off.

For these reasons we are of opinion that an indorsement of a note in pledge as a collateral security is not one which is protected as a commercial indorsement for value. The general property remaining in the indorser, the indorsee takes it, like a chose in action not negotiable, subject to all defenses to which it would be subject, in the hands of the indorser, at the time when notice is given of the indorsement; and the maker may set off a debt, due to himself from the indorser, at that time.

Judgment on the verdict.

———

PROPERTY IN PROMISSORY NOTE PLEDGED.—In *Garlick* v. *James*, 7 Am. Dec. 294, the general property in a promissory note, given in pledge, was held to remain in the pledgor. In the case of *Cortelyou* v. *Lansing*, 2 Cai. Cas. 200, reported in the note to *Garlick* v. *James*, the opinion of Chancellor Kent discusses, 1, the right of the pledgee to dispose of the security; 2, whether the property in the pledge becomes absolute by the death of the pledgor; 3, whether a tender is requisite before suit; and 4, whether the measure of damages is in the discretion of the jury.

SET-OFF, generally, as to what may be the subject of, see note to *Gregg* v. *James*, 12 Am. Dec. 152. Demand for unliquidated damages can not be set off against an ascertained demand: *Christian* v. *Miller*, 23 Id. 251; assignee of an account takes it subject to the debtor's right to set off a subsisting note held by him against the assignor: *Cary* v. *Bancroft*, 25 Id. 393. In *Chandler* v. *Drew*, 26 Id. 704, and note, it is held that the maker of a promissory note, although discredited, can not set off against the indorsee, demands which he may have against the indorser.

STEVENSON v. MUDGETT.

[10 NEW HAMPSHIRE, 338.]

AMENDMENTS ARE NOT ALLOWED WHICH ARE INCONSISTENT with the nature of the pleadings, or change the cause of action. Particular allegations may be changed, and others added, provided the identity of the cause of action is preserved.

DELIVERY OF A RELEASE BY A WITNESS TO AN ATTORNEY in a cause, is a delivery to the party who employed him.

RELEASE OF A WITNESS WHO APPEARS TO BE THE REAL PLAINTIFF of all interest in the suit, which he delivers to the attorney of the plaintiff of record, is a delivery to himself, and consequently unavailing.

WITNESS WHO APPEARS TO BE INTERESTED IN A SUIT can not be made competent by his own testimony.

EVIDENCE THAT AN ATTORNEY WAS EMPLOYED BY THE PLAINTIFF OF RECORD, and not by a witness, may be given after verdict.

ASSUMPSIT. The original writ contained but one count, upon a note, dated November 30, 1830, signed by defendant, to the effect that three years from date, at a certain place, for value received, he would pay to plaintiff the sum of one hundred and four dollars and sixteen cents, in young, likely neat stock. Subsequently plaintiff moved to amend by filing a new count, which set forth defendant's indebtedness, and that afterwards defendant, in consideration of plaintiff's allowing him the sum of forty dollars in part payment for a pair of steers sold to plaintiff, and in extending the time of payment one year, had promised to pay the balance of the one hundred and four dollars and sixteen cents, in like manner, at plaintiff's house. The amendment was allowed, subject to defendant's exceptions. John M. Stevenson, a witness of plaintiff, was objected to by defendant, on the ground that he was the real plaintiff in interest, and it was proved that the plaintiff of record had stated that the note belonged to witness. Stevenson then executed a release of all claim in the action, and gave it to plaintiff's attorney. Plaintiff was not present, and there was no further delivery of the release. The witness then testified that he had no interest in the claim. Plaintiff had verdict on the amended count, and defendant appealed.

Peabody, Emerson, and Bartlett, for the plaintiff.

Blazo and Christie, for the defendant.

PARKER, C. J. An amendment is not admissible which is inconsistent with the nature of the declaration, or which changes the cause of action. This is the rule laid down in *Butterfield* v. *Harvell,* 3 N. H. 201, and which has since been unifcrmly recognized as the true principle. The application of the principle, in that case, is, perhaps, somewhat questionable. It is evident that the matter of the amendment there offered might have been regarded as merely an additional particular of the contract declared on, which had been omitted in the original draft of the declaration, although it undoubtedly superadded a further item to the obligation, which the declaration alleged that the defendant had assumed by his contract. The difficulty which sometimes exists, in the application of the rule, arises from the fact that almost all amendments change, to some extent, the cause of action, as originally stated. An amendment which changes the alleged date of a contract, or the sum to be paid, or any particular of the matter to be performed, or the time or manner of performance, changes, in one sense, the cause of the action; but it is not in this sense that the rule is to be understood. Amendments of that character, so long as the identity of the matter upon which the action is founded is preserved, are admissible; the alteration being made, not to enable the plaintiff to recover for another matter than that for which he originally brought his action, but to cure an imperfect or erroneous statement of the subject-matter, upon which the action was in fact founded. So long as the form of action is not changed, and the court can see that the identity of the cause of action is preserved, the particular allegations of the declaration may be changed, and others superadded, in order to cure imperfections and mistakes in the manner of stating the plaintiff's case.

The new count, which was admitted in this case, in addition to the statement of the written contract, which was set forth in the original count, contains averments of further stipulations betwen the parties, made subsequently to that time, and which constituted, in fact, a further contract, superadded to the contract in writing. In one sense this may be regarded as another contract, made at a subsequent date, and the breach of which would furnish a different cause of action from that which would have arisen by a breach of the original agreement. But this subsequent matter was merely an extension of the original contract, with a variation of the place of performance; and according to the statement of the counsel the action was in fact founded upon the breach of the contract, as modified and varied by the subsequent agreement; the additional averments, contained in the amended count, being omitted, under a supposition that this additional matter might be offered in evidence, by way of answer to any defense which might be attempted. In that view the case is clearly one of an imperfect declaration upon the contract intended as the foundation of the action, by the omission to set out the farther matter, which modified the original contract and altered the time and place of performance. The cause of action in both counts is a contract for the delivery of certain cattle, and a breach of that contract. The particulars of time and place, set forth in the amended count, are materially different from those in the original; and the additional averments are founded upon matter superadded by a further contract between the parties, after the original agreement was entered into. But it was upon a breach of the contract as modified that the plaintiff brought his suit; and he asked, by his amendment, to perfect his declaration, so that he might be enabled to prosecute it, and recover for that breach. In this view of the case the amendment was rightly admitted. The form of the action is not changed, and the identity of the cause is preserved: It is a variation in the mode of demanding the same thing, that is, damages for the breach of the original contract for the delivery of the cattle, some of the terms of which were modified by the subsequent agreement of the parties, but the additional matter, through mistake, was not stated: *Burnham* v. *Spooner*, 10 N. H. 165; *Ball* v. *Claflin*, 5 Pick. 305 [16 Am. Dec. 407]; *Swan* v. *Nesmith*, 7 Id. 220 [19 Am. Dec. 282]; *Mixer* v. *Howarth*, 21 Id. 205.

In *Goddard* v. *Perkins*, 9 N. H. 488, the proposed amendment departed wholly from the cause of action originally stated; the declaration, as drawn in the first instance, being founded upon an unlawful conversion of the plaintiff's property, and the proposed amendment alleging a breach of duty by the defendant, as deputy sheriff, in neglecting to retain certain property, attached by him on a writ in favor of the plaintiff.

The release from the witness, as the case now stands, was not well delivered. The evidence introduced by the defendant, to exclude his testimony, went to show that the contract upon which the action was founded belonged to the witness; and if so, the inference is that the suit was in fact his own. If he is the real plaintiff, the attorney in the suit is his attorney, and the delivery of the release to his attorney is a delivery to himself. The witness, however, on being admitted, testified that he never in fact had any interest in the contract. If it had been shown that the attorney to whom the release was delivered was in fact employed by the plaintiff on the record, it would have been sufficient; but the witness can not be made competent by his own testimony.

We have no doubt that a delivery of a release, by a witness, to the attorney employed to conduct the cause, is a sufficient delivery to the party who employed him. And a delivery to a third person, who was not in fact the agent of the releasor, might, perhaps, be a good delivery; for when it appears that the release is for the benefit of the party, his assent may be presumed, until his dissent is shown.

The evidence that the attorney was in fact employed by the plaintiff of record, is evidence to the court, and not to the jury, and it is not too late now to offer it. If that fact is established, judgment may be rendered upon the verdict.

———

AMENDMENTS VARYING OR ALTERING CAUSE OF ACTION, HOW FAR ALLOWED.—The courts of this country and of England, both prior and subsequent to any of the late statutory changes in methods of procedure, have always been actuated by a greater or less degree of liberality in allowing amendments to pleadings, for the purpose of doing substantial justice between litigants, and deciding controversies upon their merits. At the present day, the subject of amendments to pleadings, and the powers of the courts to grant or refuse the same, are very generally regulated by statute. Such statutory provisions, especially those which are contained in the codes of the several states which have adopted the reformed system of procedure, although they differ somewhat in detail, are remarkably similar in their general scope and effect. They divide amendments to pleadings into two classes: *first*, those which are permitted before trial, which include amendments allowed as a matter of course, without any special application to the court, and amendments made as the result of a motion for such purpose, or which are allowed after a demurrer is sustained; and *second*, amendments made during or after trial, for the purpose of harmonizing the allegations of the pleadings with the facts proved, or offered to be proved. The granting or refusing a proposed amendment, in the latter class of cases, is a matter of discretion with the court, to be liberally exercised in furtherance of justice: *Tiernan* v. *Woodruff*, 5 McLean, 135; *Hayden* v. *Hayden*, 46 Cal. 332; and the refusal to allow an amendment will be presumed to be just unless the contrary appears in the record: *Jessup* v. *King*, 4 Id. 331. Such discretion, however, is by no means arbitrary or capricious, and if it appears to the appellate court that there has been an abuse of discretionary power, the action of the lower court will be reversed: *Cooke* v. *Spears*, 2 Id. 410; *Pierson* v. *McCahill*, 22 Id. 128; *McMinn* v. *O'Connor*, 27 Id. 239; *Lord* v. *Hopkins*, 30 Id. 76; and the same result will follow if the amendment is refused on the ground of want of power in the court to allow it, when such power does in fact exist: *Russell* v. *Conn*, 20 N. Y. 81.

In the practical application of the power of granting amendments to pleadings, the rule laid down in the principal case, that no amendments which change or alter the cause of action contained in the original pleading are allowed, has, in legal actions, been maintained by an overwhelming weight of judicial authority, and must be considered as the settled doctrine on the subject: Chit. Pl. 198; Pomeroy's Remedies, sec. 566; Bliss on Code Pl., sec. 429. Thus amendments have been refused which sought to change the cause of action from assumpsit, on the judgment of another state, to debt: *India*

Rubber Co. v. *Hoyt*, 15 Vt. 92; or from assumpsit to account rendered: *Strock* v. *Little*, 33 Pa. St. 409; or from a real action to an action of forcible entry and detainer: *Fay* v. *Taft*, 12 Cush. 448; or from trover to assumpsit: *People* v. *Circuit Judge*, 13 Mich. 206; or from debt to case; but after such amendment has been allowed, leave will be given to the plaintiff to change his action to its original form: *Houghton* v. *Stowell*, 28 Me. 215; or from an action *in rem*, to foreclose a mortgage on a vessel, to an action to recover possession thereof: *In re John Jay*, 3 Blatchf. C. C. 67. Nor in real actions will an amendment be allowed so as to embrace more or different land from that described in the complaint: *Wyman* v. *Kilgore*, 47 Me. 184; *Slater* v. *Mason*, 15 Pick. 345; but see *Russell* v. *Conn*, 20 N. Y. 81, where the refusal to allow an amendment to the description of land described as bounded on the east, etc., so as to make it read as bounded on the west, etc., was held error. Nor in an action against a stockholder, where the declaration contained allegations sufficient to bring the case within one statute, will an amendment be permitted so as to bring it within a different statute: *Mulliken* v. *Whitehouse*, 49 Me. 527. The following additional cases, upholding the general doctrine, are cited, not so much for the purpose of supporting the rule, as of illustrating some of the many instances in which it has been applied: *Casnard* v. *Eve*, Dudley, 108; *Little* v. *Morgan*, 31 N. H. 499; *Bishop* v. *Baker*, 19 Pick. 517; *Guilford* v. *Adams*, 19 Id. 376; *Ross* v. *Bates*, 2 Root, 198; *Williams* v. *Hollis*, 19 Ga. 313; *Cooper* v. *Waldron*, 50 Me. 80; *Lawrence* v. *Langley*, 14 N. H. 70; *Butterfield* v. *Harrell*, 3 Id. 201; *Edgerly* v. *Emerson*, 4 Id. 147; *Eagle* v. *Almer*, 1 Johns. Cas. 332; *Stiffy* v. *Carpenter*, 37 Pa. St. 41; *Carpenter* v. *Gookin*, 2 Vt. 495; *Sumner* v. *Brown*, 34 Id. 194. When the amendment sought to be introduced has been apparently barred by the statute of limitations, the general rule is especially applicable: *Wood* v. *Anderson*, 25 Pa. St. 407; *Wright* v. *Hart*, 44 Id. 454; and the same is true if the effect of the amendment would be to deprive defendant of his right to plead the statute of limitations: *Van Syckels* v. *Perry*, 3 Robt. 621. It follows, also, from the tenor of the adjudications, that no distinction can be drawn between a proposed amendment which is embodied in a new and independent count, provided a separate and distinct cause of action is stated therein, and an amendment of the same character to a count already contained in the original pleading: *Thompson* v. *Phelan*, 22 N. H. 339; *Wood* v. *Folsom*, 42 Id. 70; *Burt* v. *Kinne*, 47 Id. 361.

For the purpose of determining whether the new matter contained in an amendment is entirely foreign to the cause of action already set forth, the latter, as was said by the court in *Nevada etc. Canal Co.* v. *Kidd*, 28 Cal. 673, must receive a liberal construction. Thus in the case last cited, where the complaint alleged ownership of certain lands in the bed of, and near the bank of a stream, and sought to recover possession thereof from an adverse holder, an amendment, by inserting proper averments of prior appropriation of the water, and a diversion by defendant, with prayer for an injunction, was allowed. In fact it may be laid down as a general rule, that so long as the plaintiff adheres to the original instrument or contract on which his pleading is based, any alteration of the grounds of recovery on that instrument or contract, or of the modes in which the defendant has violated it, is not an alteration of the cause of action: *Yost* v. *Eby*, 23 Pa. St. 327; *Stevenson* v. *Mudgett*, 10 N. H. 338; *Church* v. *Syracuse etc. Co.*, 32 Conn. 372; *Cabarga* v. *Suget*, 17 Pa. St. 514. This latter rule, however, is subject to the limitations, that an action, in form *ex contractu*, can not be changed to an action *ex delicto*. *Sanborn* v. *Sanborn*, 9 Gray, 142; *Lane* v. *Beam*, 19 Barb. 51; *Ramirez* v.

Murray, 5 Cal. 222; nor, conversely, can an action in form *ex delicto* be amended so as to state an action *ex contractu: Whitcomb* v. *Hungerford,* 42 Barb. 177.

So, also, where an intended cause of action, although defectively set forth, can be distinguished as clearly from another cause of action as if the original pleading had been perfect, the defect may be cured without infringing against the rule prohibiting a new cause of action from being stated: *Pullen* v. *Hutchinson,* 25 Me. 249; *Kinner* v. *Grant,* 12 Vt. 456. Thus in an action of assumpsit by one town against another, for supplies furnished to a family, an amendment was allowed showing a liability of the defendants under the pauper act: *Brewer* v. *East Machias,* 27 Me. 439.

AMENDMENTS IN EQUITABLE SUITS.—The discussion of the doctrine in reference to the extent to which amendments to pleadings are allowed, which alter or vary the cause of action, has thus far been confined to legal actions. Notwithstanding the liberal tendencies of equity, its repugnance to mere form, and its continued struggle to decide controversies upon their merits, the rule was as equally well settled in equity as it was in law, that amendments which altered or varied the cause of action could not be permitted. See in support of this rule, and for illustrations of its application: *Curtis* v. *Leavitt,* 11 Paige, 386; *Dudd* v. *Astor,* 2 Barb. Ch. 395; *Darling* v. *Roarty,* 5 Gray, 71; *Hayward* v. *Hapgood,* 4 Id. 437; *Hannum* v. *Cameron,* 20 Miss. 509; *Rogers* v. *Atkinson,* 14 Ga. 320; *Larkins* v. *Biddle,* 21 Ala. 252; *Fenno* v. *Coulter,* 14 Ark. 39; *Goodyear* v. *Bourn,* 3 Blatchf. C. C. 266; *Sneed* v. *McCoull,* 12 How. 407; *Shields* v. *Barrow,* 17 Id. 130; *Verplank* v. *Mercantile Ins. Co.,* 1 Edw. Ch. 46; *Carey* v. *Smith,* 11 Ga. 539. In *Tourtelot* v. *Tourtelot,* 4 Mass. 506, however, a bill for divorce on the ground of adultery was amended by alleging a different day for the adulterous act from that originally pleaded, and in *Anderson* v. *Anderson,* 4 Me. 100, a similar bill was amended by adding a charge of extreme cruelty and praying for a limited divorce. But see *Hoffman* v. *Hoffman,* 35 How. Pr. 384, where a contrary doctrine is held.

AMENDMENTS UNDER THE CODES.—Notwithstanding the similarity of the provisions in the codes governing amendments to pleadings, a decided conflict of opinion exists between the decisions of the various states on the subject of amendments which alter or vary the cause of action. In a majority of the code states, the courts have established the doctrine, that the powers conferred upon them by their codes in this respect, are no greater than had previously existed at the common law, and that they were not authorized to grant amendments, at any stage of the proceedings, which altered or varied the cause of action: Pomeroy's Remedies, sec. 566; Bliss on Code Pl., sec. 429; *Ramirez* v. *Murray,* 5 Cal. 222; *Supervisors* v. *Decker,* 34 Wisc. 378; *Johnson* v. *Filkington,* 39 Id. 62; *Skinners* v. *Brett,* 38 Id. 648; *Rutledge* v. *Vanmeter,* 8 Bush, 354; *McGrath* v. *Balser,* 6 B. Mon. 141. Thus in *Supervisors* v. *Decker,* 34 Wisc. 378, the complaint as originally framed stated a cause of action for the conversion of money. After a demurrer thereto had been sustained, plaintiff amended by omitting the allegations, "and converted the same to his own use," etc. Upon an appeal from an order striking this amended complaint from the files, the appellate court, in affirming the action of the lower tribunal, said: "An amendment which attempts to change the nature of the action from one in tort to one in contract is properly not an amendment, but a substitution of a cause of action different in nature and substance from that originally stated. The power of amendment does not go to that extent." The correctness of this decision has been questioned by subsequent text-writers. Mr. Pomeroy, in commenting upon it, remarks: "It should be noticed that the actual substantial cause of action was unchanged; the only variation was in the manner and form of its statement:" Pomeroy's Remedies, sec. 566, n. 1. And Mr. Bliss, in his work on Code Pleading, page 520, n. 5, says: "It is believed that in most of the code states this amendment would be permitted." The same court has also held, that in an action to enforce a lien for work done and materials furnished under contract, an amendment could not be had, at the trial, for damages resulting from defendant's refusal to permit plaintiff to perform the contract: *Johnson* v. *Filkington*, 39 Wisc. 62; but in another case, an action for work and labor was allowed to be amended so as to charge a lien upon defendant's property: *Lackner* v. *Turnbull*, 7 Id. 105. Nor can an action against a sheriff to restrain him from removing and selling certain goods, be changed to one for conversion: *Skinners* v. *Brett*, 38 Id. 648. Nor in an action for overflowing land, will an amendment be allowed to charge defendant, under a statute, for appropriating the land to his own use: *Newton* v. *Allis*, 12 Id. 378. But, on the other hand, in an action against a corporation upon an express contract, which the court held to be *ultra vires*, an amendment seeking to charge defendant upon an implied contract was allowed: *North Western etc. Co.* v. *Shaw*, 37 Id. 655. Again, when a complaint was held bad on demurrer, because no cause of action was stated, an amendment was allowed which changed the cause of action from what it was originally intended or purported to be: *Vliet* v. *Shérwood*, 38 Id. 159.

In striking contrast to, and in fact in direct conflict with, the line of decisions last referred to, a few of the states have established a contrary doctrine, and allow amendments which vary or alter the cause of action as originally alleged, when upon a full consideration of the circumstances attending the application, it appears just. This liberal rule now prevails in New York, the earlier decisions to the contrary having been overruled. The courts of that state have settled the doctrine, that the right of amendment is not restricted to setting forth a cause of action of the same class as that contained in the original complaint, but that one of an entirely different class may be inserted, provided the summons continue to be appropriate: *Brown* v. *Leigh*, 12 Abb. Pr. (N. S.) 193. So, also, upon an amendment of course, a new cause of action may be inserted, the only restrictions imposed being that the amendment shall not be for purposes of delay, nor to prevent a trial at a term for which the action is or may be noticed for trial, and that the cause of action added be one that may properly be united with the one contained in the original complaint: *Mason* v. *Whitely*, 1 Abb. Pr. 85. And the same liberality of amendment is allowed, when a trial has once been had, and a new trial ordered: *Troy etc. R. R.* v. *Tibbets*, 11 How. Pr. 168. For further illustrations of the application of the rule as settled in New York, the following cases may be consulted with profit: *Brown* v. *Babcock*, 3 How. 305; *McQueen* v. *Babcock*, 13 Abb. Pr. 268; S. C., 3 Keyes, 428; *Wyman* v. *Remond*, 18 How. Pr. 272; *Prindle* v. *Aldrich*, 13 Id. 466; *Watson* v. *Rushmore*, 15 N. Y. 51. An equally liberal doctrine prevails in North Carolina. Thus, in *Robinson* v. *Willoughby*, 67 N. C. 84, an action in the form of ejectment, to recover possession of land under an absolute deed, which the court held to be a mortgage, was allowed to be amended so as to change the form of the action into a bill of foreclosure; and in *Bullard* v. *Johnson*, 65 Id. 436, a still greater freedom of amendment was allowed. This was an action brought by a lessor to recover rent. It appeared upon the trial that during the continuance of the term, the plaintiff had assigned his right in the premises. The court, however, ordered the assignee to be made a party plaintiff, dismissed the complaint as to the original plaintiff, and gave judgment in favor of the one substituted.

In Texas, also, amendments changing the cause of action are allowable, provided: 1. That the amendment does not prejudice the defendants; 2. That the plaintiff pays the costs up to the time of making such amendment; 3. That the amendment shall not relate back to the commencement of the suit, so as to interrupt the running of the statutes of limitations, but be confined, in all respects, to the time of filing: *Williams* v. *Randon*, 10 Tex. 74.

STATE *v.* KEAN.

[10 NEW HAMPSHIRE, 347.]

MARRIAGE IN A FOREIGN STATE MAY BE PROVED by the testimony of any person who was present at the ceremony, provided it is also shown to have been valid according to the laws of the country in which it was celebrated.

PROOF THAT A MARRIAGE WAS PERFORMED BY AN OFFICIATING PRIEST, and that it was understood by the parties to be the marriage ceremony, according to the customs of the foreign country, is presumptive evidence of marriage.

EVERY ORDAINED MINISTER, RESIDING IN THIS STATE, MAY SOLEMNIZE MARRIAGES, after having recorded the credentials of his ordination. Such recording will be presumed until the contrary appears.

INDICTMENT FOR BIGAMY NEED NOT ALLEGE that the same was committed "with force and arms."

ABBREVIATIONS OF THE PROPER NAMES of persons described in an indictment are allowable.

INDICTMENT WHICH CONCLUDES, "against the peace and dignity of our said state," instead of "the peace and dignity of the state," as required by the constitution, is not such a substantial variance as to vitiate the same.

INDICTMENT for bigamy. The defendant was convicted, and moved for a new trial and an arrest of judgment. The facts of the case and the grounds of the motion are stated in the opinion.

Woodman, for the state.

Christie, for the respondent.

UPHAM, J. The evidence offered to show the first marriage of the respondent was by a witness who was present at the time of the marriage, and who testified that it was solemnized at Cornish, in the state of Maine, and that the settled minister of Cornish officiated in the services on that occasion. The witness testified that the same clergyman officiated in the marriage services of the witness, and that he had also been present at several other marriages at Cornish, when the marriage ceremony was performed by him. There was farther evidence showing a cohabitation of some years subsequent to this marriage. In many cases, long-continued cohabitation as husband and wife is *prima facie* evidence of marriage: *Newburyport* v. *Boothbay*, 9 Mass. 414; *People* v. *Humphrey*, 7 Johns. 314; *Van Buskirk* v. *Claw*, 18 Id. 346. A copy of the record of the certificate, however, of the person by whom the ceremony is performed, is the evidence which is most ordinarily offered of a marriage. But this evidence is in no case indispensable. In *Commonwealth* v. *Littlejohn*, 15 Mass. 163, which was an indictment for lascivious cohabitation, it was holden that the marriage of one of the parties might be proved either by the record of the minister or magistrate who solemnized the marriage, or by the testimony of witnesses who were present; and in *Commonwealth* v. *Norcross*, 9 Id. 492, which was an indictment for adultery, it was remarked by the court that the testimony of witnesses who were present at the solemnization of the marriage is more satisfactory than a copy of the record, and is, moreover, necessary to prove the identity of the party.

In the case before us, the marriage was in another government, and the rule as settled in England in such cases is that the marriage may be proved by any person who was present at the ceremony, provided that such circumstances are also proved from which the jury may presume that it was a valid marriage according to the laws of the country in which it was celebrated. Proof that the ceremony was performed by a person appearing and officiating as a priest, and that it was understood by the parties to be the marriage ceremony, according to the rights and custom of the foreign country where they were residing at the time, is presumptive evidence of marriage: *Rex* v. *Brampton*, 10 East, 282; 2 Stark. Ev. 938. Under these authorities the evidence of the marriage offered in this case is clearly sufficient.

The objection to the evidence showing a second marriage is, that it does not appear that it was solemnized by any person authorized to do so by the laws of this state. This exception is founded on the statute of 1791 (1 Laws N. H. 172), which provided that every ordained minister of the gospel, in the county where he is settled, or hath his permanent residence, and in no other place, is empowered to solemnize marriages; but this restriction is withdrawn by the act of December 12, 1832. By that act every regular ordained minister of the gospel, residing in this state, and in regular standing with the denomination to which he belongs, is authorized and empowered to solemnize marriages in any county within the state, after having caused the credentials of his ordination to be recorded in the office of the clerk of the court of common pleas, in the county where he shall solemnize any marriage as aforesaid. The obligation of causing such record to be made is directory upon the minister, and may be presumed to be complied with, until the contrary is shown. The case is silent upon that point. As the facts now appear, the exception can not prevail. There was a marriage in fact, and that is sufficient.

Motion is also made in arrest of judgment, for the reasons that the offense is not alleged in the indictment to have been committed with force and arms; that the indictment contains characters and abbreviations instead of words; and that it does not conclude, as required by the constitution, "against the peace and dignity of the state." Courts hold to a high degree of strictness in pleadings in criminal cases; but this strictness has been much relaxed from the earlier decisions. It is very questionable, however, whether under any former decisions the exceptions here taken would prevail. Hawkins says, in his pleas of the crown, that the words *vi et armis*, are necessary in indictments for offenses which amount to an actual disturbance of the peace, as nuisances, assaults, etc., but that they were never necessary where it would be absurd to use them, as in indictments for conspiracies, slanders, cheats, escapes, and such like: 2 Hawk. P. C., c. 25, sec. 90.

The abbreviation complained of in the indictment, is the writing of the original name of the former wife, as McKusic; but this has become the more ordinary spelling, or at least writing of names with such a prefix, and custom must govern in this respect.

The indictment concludes, "against the peace and dignity of our said state," instead of " the peace and dignity of the state," as required by the constitution. It is unnecessary for us to determine here how far a departure from the precise words required by the constitution would be admissible in indictments. We are satisfied, however, that a departure to this extent from the words, "the state," to " our said state," is not such a variance from the provision of the constitution, and from a strict and rigid compliance with the same, as to vitiate an indictment.

Judgment against the respondent.

––––

FOREIGN MARRIAGES, WHEN VALID: *Midway* v. *Needham*, 8 Am. Dec. 131, and note; *West Cambridge* v. *Lexington*, 11 Id. 231; *Fornshill* v. *Murray*, 18 Id. 344, and see also cases in this series cited in note; *Sneed* v. *Ewing*, 22 Id. 41; *Harding* v. *Allen*, 23 Id. 549.

MARRIAGES, HOW PROVED.—The general subject is discussed in note to *Taylor* v. *Sweet*, 22 Am. Dec. 157; see also *Holmes* v. *Holmes*, 26 Id. 482.

WHO MAY PERFORM CEREMONY OF MARRIAGE: *Churchill* v. *Warren*, 9 Am. Dec. 73, and note.

CLARK *v.* CLARK.

[10 New Hampshire. 380.]

GENERAL LAWS PROVIDING FOR THE DISSOLUTION OF EXISTING MARRIAGES, but operating upon transactions subsequent to their passage, are not within the provision of the United States constitution, prohibiting the states from passing any laws impairing the obligations of contracts.

PETITION FOR DIVORCE has, in New Hampshire, the character of a civil judicial proceeding.

LAWS MAY BE RETROSPECTIVE, if they affect an existing cause of action, or an existing right of defense, by taking away or abrogating the same, although no suit or legal proceeding then exists.

DIVORCE MAY BE HAD ACCORDING TO THE LAW OF DOMICILE of the parties, at the time of the injury complained of, and is not confined to the *lex loci contractus.*

DESERTION, TO CONSTITUTE A GROUND OF DIVORCE, must have continued up to the time of filing the libel.

STATUTE, AUTHORIZING A DIVORCE ON ACCOUNT OF DESERTION which had occurred prior to its passage, is a retrospective law, and consequently invalid.

LIBEL for divorce, brought under the statute of July 6, 1839, on the ground of desertion, alleged to have continued since February 28, 1836. The libelee made no defense.

Tebbets, for the libelant.

PARKER, C. J. This is one among a number of applications under the statute of July 6, 1839, to regulate divorces, and providing, among other causes, that "where either of the parties shall unnecessarily, without sufficient cause, and against the consent of the other, leave the other, or has heretofore left the other, and shall unnecessarily, and without sufficient cause, refuse, or has heretofore refused, to cohabit with the other, for the space of three years together, it shall be deemed and taken to be a sufficient cause of divorce, provided such cause shall continue to exist at the time when the petition for a divorce shall be filed."

Upon the policy or impolicy of granting a divorce for mere desertion and refusal to cohabit, we have not to decide. In some governments no divorce *a vinculo* is granted for any cause. Others make adultery only an exception to that rule; but the policy of this state has never been quite so far restrictive. Cases of great hardship often exist, where wives are deserted by their husbands, and left to struggle with the difficulties and disabilities necessarily attendant upon such a situation; and cases of this character undoubtedly have appealed very strongly to the sympathies of the legislature.

This case is of a different character, but addresses itself perhaps not the less forcibly to a sense of justice.   One of the evils resulting from a dissolution of a marriage is, that it usually leaves the guilty party free to form another connection, and for that reason the guilt is sometimes deliberately contracted, with the design and purpose of producing a divorce.   If a divorce may be decreed in this instance, it will operate to release the libelee from vows and obligations which, it would seem, she has violated very lightly and recklessly; and it will empower her to contract another marriage, the duties of which may be as suddenly and as criminally discarded; but, on the other hand, there is something of humanity in discharging the libelant from his obligations to one who has proved herself so unworthy of his confidence and affection.

The language of the statute is explicit enough. It embraces cases which are past, as well as those which shall occur hereafter. In this case, the desertion has continued up to the present time; but what has occurred since the passage of the statute can make no difference, three years not having elapsed since that period. The statute has no provision that where a desertion has existed for a certain period before its passage, and shall continue for a certain time after, giving reasonable time for a return, that the whole matter shall be a cause of divorce.   It is of no consequence, therefore, that this libel was not filed until some time had elapsed after the passage of the act.   If a divorce may be granted upon this libel, one might have been granted had it been filed on the next day after the act was passed.

We come, then, to the broad question, whether the legislature can authorize this court to grant a divorce for any matter which was entirely past at the time of the passage of the act, and which did not, when it arose, furnish any ground for such a proceeding.

A perfected negotiation, or treaty, of marriage, is undoubtedly a civil contract: *Londonderry* v. *Chester*, 2 N. H. 268 [9 Am. Dec. 61].   It contains all the essential characteristics of a contract, and it has something superadded.   It has been said to be a matter of civil institution, and to be the very basis of the whole fabric of civilized society; by which, of course, is not intended that it is anyway a part of the structure of civil government, but that it is a contract, and relation, necessary to the existence of civilized society, and to be regulated accordingly—as to its continuance and obligations—not by the mere will of the parties, but by the general provisions of the municipal law.   It is a contract of a very peculiar character; and on account of the interest which society has in it, public notice that the parties intend to enter into the relation of husband and wife is required in some states, and in others a license is to be taken out. In many instances the law prescribes what persons may solemnize the marriage, or give the public sanction of the government to the agreement, and prohibits others from interfering, under penalties. But in most governments the contract is held to be valid and binding, notwithstanding it is entered into with no rites or ceremonies. It may be said that to a certain extent it has made its own law—the evil consequences of too great restriction upon it having sometimes induced the legislative authority to modify its regulations, and the judicial to admit certain exceptions in relation to it, particularly respecting the application of the *lex loci contractus*, which are not allowed in other matters of contract: *Vide* 2 Kent's Com. 77–80, lec. 26; Story's Conf. L. 116.

And the peculiarities of the contract, and of the relations and duties inseparable from its existence, have not only induced civilized governments to regulate, in a greater or less degree, the manner in which the contract is to be perfected, or celebrated; but have also required corresponding peculiarities in the remedies for enforcing its obligations, or proceeding in some cases for a breach of them. For a breach of some of the duties arising from it, no government provides a legal remedy. In other cases, proceedings may be had, in some governments, for a restitution of conjugal rights. Unlike most other contracts, damages are not deemed an appropriate remedy for a breach of the obligations arising out of it; but the suffering party, in the grosser instances of their infraction, has been relieved by a divorce from bed and board, or by an entire dissolution of the marriage, annulling all further obligation of the contract. A dissolution of a marriage, however, in the life-time of the parties, is usually attended with such injurious consequences to society, and to the offspring of the marriage, that civilized governments do not permit the parties to dissolve it at their pleasure. In England a divorce *a vinculo* is only to be obtained by special act of parliament; but a divorce *a mensa et thoro* may be sought through the action of the ecclesiastical courts.

In some states of the union, divorces are granted by the legislature alone. It was so here until the adoption of the constitution, which took effect in June, 1784. From the nature of the contract, and the manner in which the relation affects the public interest, it has been deemed competent for the government to provide for this dissolution of it, on the application of one party against the consent of the other; and a contract of marriage is understood to be subject to this power. It has been said that it " may be abrogated by the sovereign will, either with or without the consent of both parties, whenever the public good, or justice to both or either of the parties, will thereby be subserved." If by this it is intended that the sovereign power may dissolve a marriage, regularly contracted and celebrated according to law, without the consent of either of the parties, and without any breach of the contract, the proposition is not admitted.

There is no doubt that the legislative power may, by law, provide, in certain cases, for the dissolution of existing marriages. And this may be done upon facts and transactions, past at the time of the passage of the act, in those governments where divorces are obtained only by a special act of the legislature. How far the legislative power ought, in such case, to be considered as restricted, if at all; and whether a divorce can regularly be granted in such states, by the legislature, upon past transactions of a character never before deemed sufficient to justify a dissolution of the marriage, we need not inquire.

Notwithstanding marriage is a civil contract, it appears, from the nature of the obligations it imposes, from the appropriate remedies when they are violated, and from the reasons which must have actuated the framers of the constitution of the United States, that general laws, providing for the dissolution of existing marriages, but operating upon transactions subsequent to their passage, are not within that clause of the constitution, prohibiting the several states from passing any law impairing the obligation of contracts. If anything more than this is to be understood by the incidental opinions expressed in *Dartmouth College* v. *Woodward* (1 N. H. 132; 4 Wheat. 629, 695, S. C. in error), it seems only to be, that the legislature in those states where divorces are not regulated by general laws, may provide for divorces, by special acts, for causes which have been previously deemed good grounds of divorce, and perhaps for any causes within the discretion of the legislature. But it is not necessary to pursue this part of the subject.

The constitution of this state provides, that all causes of marriage, divorce, and alimony, " shall be heard and tried by the superior court, until the legislature shall by law make other provision." That the provision here intended, was a provision by ordinary legal enactment, for the action of some judicial tribunal, is not to be doubted; and this gives to a grant of a divorce, here, the character of a judicial proceeding. The legislature, it is believed, have not, since that period, passed any special law granting a divorce, nor is it supposed to be within their constitutional power so to do.

The twenty-third article of the bill of rights denounces retrospective laws as "highly injurious, oppressive, and unjust," and declares that " no such laws should be made, either for the decision of civil causes, or the punishment of offenses."

In *Woart* v. *Winnick*, 3 N. H. 481 [14 Am. Dec. 384], this court held, that this clause, so far as it applied to civil causes, "was intended to prohibit the making of any law prescribing new rules for the decision of existing causes, so as to change the ground of the action, or the nature of the defense." That was sufficient for the case then under consideration, which was in fact pending when the law then in question was passed. But the considerations there suggested evidently point to a broader application of it than one which would make it operative merely upon actions, or causes, pending in court at the time of the passage of the act. A law may be retrospective in its operation, if it affect an existing cause of action, or an existing right of defense, by taking away or abrogating a perfect existing right, although no suit or legal proceeding then exists. Of course it is not intended to deny the right of the legislature to vary the mode of enforcing a remedy; or to provide for the more effectual security of existing rights; or to pass laws which change existing rules, under which rights would be acquired by the lapse of a certain period of time, part of which has already passed. The statute of limitations may be changed by an extension of the time, or by an entire repeal, and affect existing causes of action, which by the existing law would soon be barred. In such cases the right of action is perfect, and no right of defense has accrued from the time already elapsed. But if a right has become vested, and perfect, a law which afterwards annuls or takes it away, is retrospective. Thus a law which should provide that promissory notes made payable on demand should be payable at the expiration of a year, and that no suit should be maintained upon them until the expiration of that time, if applied to existing contracts of that character, would be a retrospective law for the decision of a civil cause, not only in relation to actions then pending upon such contracts, but also as to all notes of that description then in existence. And so of any other law which impairs vested rights acquired by existing laws: *Merrill* v. *Sherburne*, 1 N. H. 213 [8

Am. Dec. 52]. To subject a party to the payment of damages, or to other loss or detriment, upon considerations entirely past, is within the principle. Thus a statute of this state, passed in 1805, made provision, that where there had been peaceable possession and actual improvement of land by virtue of a supposed legal title, under a *bona fide* purchase, for more than six years before the commencement of an action for the recovery of it, the tenant should be entitled to the increased value of the premises by virtue of buildings and improvements, if the demandant recovered. In an action brought in 1807, it was held that the act, applied to a possession existing, and to improvements made, prior to its passage, was a retrospective law, within the clause of the constitution already cited: *Society* v. *Wheeler*, 2 Gall. 105.

A statute which attempts to confer authority upon the court to grant a divorce, for matters already past, and which, at the time when they occurred, furnished no ground for a dissolution of the marriage, or for other legal proceedings, is, in our view, clearly a retrospective law, and well entitled to the epithets applied to such laws in the constitution. On the supposition that the past matter, which is thus made the ground of a divorce, was of a character inconsistent with the perfect obligations of the marriage covenant, and such, therefore, as could not be justified, or even excused, in a court of morals; still, if it was not such as subjected the party, when it took place, to any penalty or punishment; or entitled the other party to any remedy; and especially, if it was not such as then furnished any ground upon which a dissolution of those obligations could be sought or predicated; it must, by a law making it a ground for a divorce, have a different character and operation bestowed upon it. Its legal character would thereby be changed, and its effect enlarged. That which, if not of itself innocent, was not, when it occurred, such a breach of marital obligations as to warrant an interference with them, would be made operative not only to release one party from the further obligations of what is generally admitted to be a contract, but would be made the means of depriving the other party of the benefit of those obligations, and of rights of property derived from them. It would subject that party to loss and detriment for past acts, altogether by the retrospective operation of the law which authorized and gave effect to the divorce. Such a law can not enforce the obligations of the marriage, nor is it a provision relating to the remedy merely; for whatever breach may have occurred, the obligation of the contract still remains, and requires a prospective performance of marital duties. But the principle upon which the law must be founded, would, if admitted, dissolve all marriages at the will of the legislative power.

Desertion for three years, by the husband, coupled with neglect to make suitable provision for the support and maintenance of the wife, where it was in his power so to do, has, for a long period, furnished a sufficient cause for a dissolution of the marriage, in this state. But, under that statute, if the husband had not pecuniary ability, there was no cause for a divorce. The present act makes desertion alone, by either party, for the term of three years, if without sufficient cause and against the consent of the other, a substantive ground of divorce. It is, therefore, a new cause; and that part of the act which attempts to make such desertion, then past, sufficient, must, if enforced, impair vested rights, provided there are any vested rights in the existence of a marriage. We shall not add to the length of this opinion, by attempting to show that such rights exist.

But in order to bring a law within the constitutional provision we are considering, it must be a law for the decision of a civil cause, or for the punishment of an offense. All retrospective laws are not within the prohibition, notwithstanding the general terms of the first part of the article. They may be made for the mitigation of punishment: 3 N. H. 476.[1] That a retrospective law for a divorce operates oppressively and unjustly, however, tends to show that it is within the condemnation of the constitution.

"Regulations on the subject of marriage and divorce," it has been said, "are rather parts of the criminal than of the civil code:" *Barber* v. *Root*, 10 Mass. 265. And in the same opinion it is farther stated, that "a divorce, for example, in a case of public scandal and reproach, is not a vindication of the contract of marriage, or a remedy to enforce it; but a species of punishment, which the public have placed in the hands of the injured party to inflict, under the sanction, and with the aid of the competent tribunal; operating as a redress of the injury, where, the contract having been violated, the relation of the parties, and their continuance in the marriage state, has become intolerable or vexatious to them, and of evil example to others." If a proceeding for a divorce was to be regarded as a part of the criminal code, and the divorce itself as a punishment, a retrospective law for the purpose would be an *ex post facto* law, and thus clearly void.

---

1. *Woart* v. *Winnick, supra.*

We are inclined, however, to regard a petition or libel for a divorce, especially under our constitution and laws, as a proceeding in a civil cause. It may, in its result, partake, in some instances, of the character of a punishment of the offending party; but it is too true, in point of fact, that it is very often considered and felt to be otherwise. In all cases it operates upon the civil rights of the parties, and especially upon the rights of property. The husband is no longer bound to support the wife, or answerable for her acts; nor can he afterwards claim her services, or derive a title to her earnings, or to property which may descend to her. He loses the right to the income of her real estate. There is a corresponding change in the situation of the wife; and in addition to this, she may have, in some instances, a decree assigning to her a part of the property of the husband, or entitling her to a sum of money from him, which may be enforced by action, or, under our practice, by execution. This is not as damages for the past, nor as a penalty; for it is regulated more by the necessities of the wife, and the ability of the husband, than by the aggravation of the causes of divorce. If it were a penalty, that would not show that the cause was not a civil cause, for penal actions belong to the civil side of the court: 3 N. H. 481.[1] Nor is the deprivation of the society of the injured party a mere punishment of the offender, in any case. It results from the dissolution of the contract, by which it was originally secured. Where a disability to marry again, during the life of the injured party, is part of the effect of a divorce, it may perhaps be regarded as punishment; but this does not necessarily accompany a divorce, nor does it result from one, in any case in this state. Where it does, it is only a denial of a right in the party to enter into another similar contract, so long as the previous one ought to have existed. The proceeding, therefore, seems to have all the characteristics of a civil cause.

From the character of the contract, its appropriate remedies, when it is broken, may be had according to the law of the actual domicile of the parties at the time of the injury, and is not confined to the *lex loci contractus.* But this does not prove that it is a criminal proceeding. The matter is not prosecuted by the government, or for the government; and there is neither fine nor imprisonment, nor usually any incapacity or disability of any kind. Forgiveness of the wrong by the party injured, precludes any divorce, except upon some new violation of conjugal obligations: *Quincy* v. *Quincy,* 10 N. H. 272. And by the terms of

1. *Woart* v. *Winnick, supra.*

the statute upon which this application is founded, whether the desertion be one before or after the passage of the act, and however long it may have continued, no divorce is to be had unless it continues up to the time of filing the libel. And furthermore, for adultery, which constitutes one of the causes of divorce, a specific punishment is provided in the criminal code. These considerations seem to show, conclusively enough, that a divorce is not to be regarded as the punishment of the offender. If it were so, two punishments would be prescribed for the offense of adultery. And in confirmation of this view we have the express opinion of Chancellor Kent, which perhaps might well sustain the position, without any reasoning upon the subject. "The remedy by divorce," he says, "is purely a civil and private prosecution, under the control, and at the volition of the party aggrieved, and he may bar himself of the remedy by his own act:" 2 Kent's Com. 84, lec. 27.

Considering a petition for a divorce as a civil and private prosecution, so much of the statute as purports to authorize a divorce on account of desertion which had occurred prior to its passage, must be held to be a retrospective law for the decision of a civil cause, and as such within the constitutional prohibition.

That part of the act which provides for divorces on account of desertion and refusal to cohabit for three years after its passage, is not objectionable, notwithstanding it may operate upon existing marriages. Regulations intended to enforce the obligations of the contract in future, impair no vested rights. The contract of marriage, it is well understood, is subject to them, and all persons may avoid their operation by an adherence to the duties imposed by the contract itself. And we have no doubt that the legislature may so amend the act that a continuance of a prior desertion, for a period after the passage of the new statute long enough to give a reasonable time for a return, and a resumption of marital duties, shall be a good cause for a dissolution of the marriage.

Libel dismissed.

———

DIVORCE, AS IMPAIRING OBLIGATION OF CONTRACTS.—In *Tolen* v. *Tolen*, 21 Am. Dec. 742, it was held that general laws authorizing divorces are not in conflict with the constitutional provision prohibiting laws impairing the obligations of contracts, provided the legislature, in the exercise of its power, does not pass beyond the rights of its own citizens, and act upon the rights of citizens of other states.

LEX DOMICILII GOVERNS IN DIVORCE: *Tolen* v. *Tolen*, 21 Am. Dec. 742, and note: *Harteau* v. *Harteau*, 25 Id. 372.

RETROSPECTIVE LAWS AUTHORIZING DIVORCES.—The doctrine of *Clark* v.

Clark, *supra*, seems to be in conflict with that of *Jones* v. *Jones*, 5 Id. 645, which holds, that a statute declaring adultery to be a cause of divorce, and giving power to the courts to grant divorces for adultery committed before its passage, is not retrospective within the meaning of the constitutional prohibition.

BATCHELDER *v.* KELLY.

[10 NEW HAMPSHIRE, 436.]

TREBLE DAMAGES CAN BE RECOVERED FOR TRESPASS ON TIMBER LANDS, only when the act was done knowingly and willfully. If done by mistake or accident, recovery can be had only for the value of the injury actually sustained.

TREBLE DAMAGES CAN NOT BE RECOVERED FOR HAULING AWAY TIMBER cut by mistake on another's land, even if done after the mistake was discovered.

EVIDENCE IN AN ACTION FOR TRESPASS ON TIMBER LANDS, under the statute is regulated by the rules of the common law, and is not confined to the parties to the action; such latter evidence is merely cumulative.

TRESPASS, to recover the penalties under the statute for cutting and carrying away trees from the land of plaintiff. It appeared by several witnesses, not parties to the action, that the trees were cut down by mistake, by the agent of defendant, and were carried away by the latter after the mistake was discovered. Defendant objected to this testimony on the ground that the statute confined the evidence to the oath of the parties, but the objection was overruled. Verdict was given for the plaintiff, in accordance with the instructions of the court, the excepted portions of which, together with the further facts, are contained in the opinion.

Fletcher and Perley, for the plaintiff.

Pierce and Fowler, for the defendant.

UPHAM, J. This action is founded exclusively upon the statute for preventing trespasses upon timber lands. The jury have found a verdict against the defendant. Their verdict, however, follows the charge of the court rather than the declaration in the plaintiff's writ. The allegation in the plaintiff's writ is, that the defendant cut and carried away divers trees, of more than one foot in diameter, and the penal damage of forty shillings, prescribed by the statute, is claimed for each of the trees so cut, together with three times their actual value, in addition to the forty shillings. The verdict finds that the defendant is guilty of carrying away two trees belonging to the plaintiff, of more than one foot in diameter, and that the value of the trees is eighty-five cents. It admits of serious doubt whether this verdict can be sustained, as not meeting the charge in the plaintiff's declaration; but however this may be, there are exceptions taken to the charge of the court which must be fatal to the verdict taken in the case.

The charge is correct in this respect, that to subject a party to the penalty prescribed in the statute, it must appear that the act was done knowingly and willfully, and not through mistake or accident; in which latter case the party would be entitled to recover only the value of the injury he had actually sustained. The general tenor of the statute is such as wholly to preclude the idea that it was designed to apply to unintentional trespasses. This has been in previous instances holden to be the true construction of the statute, and it fully conforms to the present views of the court in relation to it.

But the charge proceeds farther. The jury were instructed, if the evidence satisfied them that, after the line was ascertained and well known to the defendant, the defendant went upon the plaintiff's land and hauled away the timber for his own use, that would in law be an affirmance of what his servant had done in cutting over the line, and render the defendant answerable for the act of the servant, in the same manner as if he had knowingly and intentionally committed the act himself. Carrying the timber away might have had some tendency to have convinced the jury that the defendant was cognizant of and approved the original cutting; but such would not have been the necessary legal effect of the evidence, as a rule of law; and most clearly an affirmance of the cutting in this manner would not have altered the original nature of the act, so as to have rendered that willful and malicious that was originally an unintentional and accidental trespass. Could it have had any bearing in this point of view, it would only have been for the consideration of the jury; but the evidence was not submitted to the jury in this manner, but was held to be conclusive against the party as a matter of law. The instruction was therefore erroneous.

The exception was taken on the trial, that the testimony offered was inadmissible, for the reason that the statute on which the action was founded confined the evidence to the oath of the parties. This exception was rightly overruled. Such a mode of trial is merely cumulative. The act provides that the oath of the parties may be admitted, for the reason, "that it is very hard and difficult to detect and convict any trespasser against the statute, in the ordinary method or course of law, because the trespasses which the act is intended to prohibit are generally committed where positive evidence can scarcely ever be had." This is a sufficient reason for the special provision as to the admission of such testimony, under circumstances where the party injured may deem it essential; but it is no good ground to prevent a trial by the rules of common law, in those cases where no such necessity exists on account of the want of the testimony ordinarily admissible. The evidence, therefore, admitted on trial, was properly received; but, for misdirection of the court in relation to its effect, the verdict must be set aside, and a

New trial granted.

———

TRESPASS BY CUTTING DOWN TREES.— In California a statute (Practice act, sec. 251), which provided that a person who cut down or injured the trees on the land of another, "without lawful authority," should be liable for treble the amount of the damages done to the owner, received a construction similar to the foregoing, in *Barnes* v. *Jones*, 51 Cal. 303. In this case, the trial court awarded the plaintiff treble damages for injury done to his trees through the defendant's mistake. In modifying this judgment, the supreme court said: "The ground chiefly relied upon for a reversal of the judgment is, that the court erred in trebling the damages; and we are of opinion that the judgment is erroneous in this particular. While the statute does not so state in terms, it is clear, we think, that it was not intended to apply to cases in which the trespass was committed through an innocent mistake as to the boundary or location of a tract of land claimed by the defendant. Similar statutes of other states have received this construction, and we are satisfied it is correct:" Citing *Batchelder* v. *Kelly*, *supra; Russell* v. *Irby*, 13 Ala. 131; *Perkins* v. *Hackelman*, 26 Miss. 41; *Whitecraft* v. *Vanderver*, 12 Ill. 235, in all of which cases, as also in *Cohn* v. *Neeves*, 40 Wisc. 401, and *Morrison* v. *Bedell*, 22 N. H. 237, a similar doctrine was laid down, and the principal case cited as an authority.

The principal case is also cited in *Thurn* v. *Alta Tel. Co.*, 15 Cal. 474, to the effect that a statute imposing a penalty should be strictly construed.

———

HALE *v.* WOODS.

[10 NEW HAMPSHIRE, 470.]

DEED BY AN ATTORNEY MUST BE EXECUTED IN THE NAME, and as the act and deed, of the principal. Whether such is the case, must be determined by a construction of the whole instrument, and not from any particular clause.

DEED, THE GRANTING CLAUSE AND COVENANTS OF WHICH ARE IN THE NAME OF THE PRINCIPAL, but signed "D. K., attorney for Z. K.," is the act of the principal, and passes his estate.

WRIT of entry. Demandant claimed title to one half the premises in controversy, under the deed referred to in the opinion, and recovered verdict. Defendant appealed.

Farley, for the demandant.

Atherton, for the defendant.

UPHAM, J. The deed of an attorney, to be valid, must be in the name, and purport to be the act and deed of the principal: *Fowler* v. *Shearer*, 7 Mass. 14 [8 Am. Dec. 126]; *Elwell* v. *Shaw*, 16 Id. 42; *Stinchfield* v. *Little*, 1 Greenl. 231 [10 Am. Dec. 65]; *Elwell* v. *Shaw*, Id. 339; *Cofran* v. *Cochran*, 5 N. H. 459; *Montgomery* v. *Dorion*, 7 Id. 484. But whether such is the purport of an instrument, must be determined from its general tenor, and not from any particular clause. Such construction must be given, in this as well as in other questions arising on conveyances, as shall make every part of the instrument operative as far as possible; and where the intention of the parties can be discovered, such intention should be carried into effect, if it can be done consistently with the rules of law: *Jackson* v. *Blodgett*, 16 Johns. 172; *Bridge* v. *Wellington*, 1 Mass. 219; *Davis* v. *Hayden*, 9 Id. 514; *Hatch* v. *Dwight*, 17 Id. 289 [9 Am. Dec. 145].

The deed which is under consideration in this case, is executed by Daniel King, for himself and for Zachariah King, a joint owner of the land. The terms of the conveyance are: "I, Daniel King, as well for myself as attorney for Zachariah King, doth for myself and the said Zachariah, remise, release, and forever quitclaim the premises described in the deed, together with all the estate, right, title, interest, use, property, claim, and demand whatsoever, of me, the said Daniel, and said Zachariah, which we now have, or heretofore had at any time, in said premises. And we, the said Daniel and Zachariah, do hereby, for ourselves, our heirs, and executors, covenant that the premises are free of all incumbrance, and that the grantee may quietly enjoy the same without any claim or hindrance from us, or any one claiming under us, or either of us. In witness whereof, we, the said Daniel for himself, and as attorney aforesaid, have hereunto set our hands and seals," etc. Signed Daniel King; and also, "Daniel King, attorney for Zachariah King, being duly authorized as appears of record," with seals affixed to each signature.

The covenants in this case in the deed are clearly the covenants of the principal; and we think, from the terms used, the grant purports to be the act of the principal. The grant is for said Daniel and Zachariah, of all the interest which we now have or have heretofore had in the premises. If these terms, together with the covenants, purport a conveyance of the interest of the principal, the execution of the deed would seem to be sufficient to effect the intent of the instrument. In *Wilks* v. *Back*, 2 East, 142, the court say: "There is no particular form of words required to be used, provided the act be in the name of the principal; for where is the difference between signing I. B., by M. W., his attorney (which must be admitted to be good), and M. W. for I. B.? In either case the act of sealing and delivery is done in the name of the principal, and by his authority. Whether the attorney put his name first or last can not affect the validity of the act done:" 2 Stark. Ev. 477, 605; see, also, *Montgomery* v. *Dorion*, 7 N. H. 484, where the principle of the case of *Wilks* v. *Back* is fully sustained.

We are of opinion that the deed as executed passed the title both of Daniel and Zachariah King. The plaintiff is, therefore, entitled to recover one half the demanded premises; and judgment will be entered on the verdict for that amount.

———

DEED BY AGENT, WHEN BINDS PRINCIPAL.—As to the manner of executing a deed by an agent, in order to bind his principal, see *Scott* v. *McAlpin*, 7 Am. Dec. 70; *Elwell* v. *Shaw*, 8 Id. 126; *Bellas* v. *Hays*, 9 Id. 385; *Stinchfield* v. *Little*, 10 Id. 65; *Locke* v. *Alexander*, 11 Id. 750; *Magill* v. *Hinsdale*, 16 Id. 70; *Garrison* v. *Combs*, 22 Id. 120. In *Magill* v. *Hinsdale*, it was held that no particular form of words is necessary for an agent to bind his principal, provided it appears from the instrument that he intended the act for the principal. Where this intent appears in the body of the instrument, signing the same "A. as agent for B.." is sufficient.

———

PEASLEE, ADM'R, v. BREED.
[10 NEW HAMPSHIRE, 489.]

RIGHT OF CONTRIBUTION EXISTS BETWEEN THE JOINT MAKERS of a promissory note, in favor of one who has paid the whole thereof, notwithstanding the remedy of the holder against the maker in default is barred by the statute of limitations.

ACTION for contribution for money paid by plaintiff, as administrator, and by his intestate, Israel Peaslee, on a promissory note, dated October 22, 1827, jointly executed by intestate and defendant, and payable on demand. The note was allowed by the commissioner of the estate, and a dividend paid thereon July 25, 1836. The principal question was, whether the joint maker was liable to contribute for such payment. Verdict was taken for the plaintiff, by consent, subject to the opinion of this court.

Farley, Sawyer, and Emerson, for the defendant.

Atherton and Brown, for the plaintiff.

PARKER, C. J.   When the intestate paid the interest, in 1831, and in 1833, the defendant was liable on the note, as well as himself, and a cause of action arose in favor of the intestate, to recover one half of those sums.   The action was commenced within six years from the time when the first of those sums was paid, and of course no question can be raised as to them.   The intestate might have maintained a suit, had he lived: *Odlin* v. *Greenleaf,* 3 N. H. 270; *Crosby* v. *Wyatt,* 10 Id. 318. The other part of the case raises the question whether, when one of two makers of a note is discharged by the statute of limitations, and the other remains liable, and pays, the latter is entitled to recover of the former a contribution.

Sibley v. *McAllaster, Ex'r,* 8 N. H. 389, was an action brought to recover money paid.   The plaintiff was surety on a note signed by the defendant's intestate.   The creditors neglected to present the note to the executor for more than two years, although its existence was mentioned within that time.   The plaintiff afterwards paid the note, and brought his action to recover the amount.   The executor contended that all proceedings to recover the note of the estate were barred by the neglect to present it—that the surety was thereby discharged, and could not make his voluntary payment a ground of action.   It was held that the omission to call upon the executor for payment, was mere neglect to proceed against the principal, which would not discharge the surety, even if it had continued so long that the remedy against the principal was barred—that the plaintiff, continuing liable, might well pay, and that he thereupon had a remedy to recover of the estate the amount he had paid.   The principal question in that case was, whether the surety was not discharged, and thus far it has no application here.   No doubt was entertained, that if the surety continued liable, he had the right to recover, notwithstanding a direct remedy, by the creditor, against the estate, was barred by the provisions of the statute that no action should be sustained against an executor or administrator, unless the demand was exhibited within two years from the original grant of administration.   Upon this latter point that case bears a strong analogy to this; and we are of opinion that the plaintiff in this case is well entitled to recover, for the amount paid by his intestate after the period when, according to the facts stated in the case, no action could have been sustained directly against the defendant, by the payee of the note.

When the plaintiff's intestate, and the defendant, signed the note to Thompson, there was an implied promise, on the part of each, to pay the other one half of any sum that the other might lawfully pay on the note. This promise was a subsisting implied promise when the estate made the payment. The liability of Peaslee, the intestate, having been continued by payments, from time to time; when he, or his estate, paid, a cause of action arose in his favor, or in favor of his administrator, against the defendant, on that promise. And this liability is in no way affected by the circumstance that Thompson could not have compelled the defendant to pay. He could have compelled both to pay when the partial payments were made by Peaslee, in 1831 and 1833; and by means of the recognition of the debt, arising out of those payments, thus made when Peaslee had no defense, and which furnished evidence to take the case out of the statute as to him, Thompson could enforce a payment of the remainder from his estate.

The cause of action which accrued to the plaintiff, as Peaslee's administrator, upon this last payment, is not affected by the question, whether Thompson could or could not, at that time, maintain an action against the defendant, upon the note. The case, in this respect, is, in principle, like that of *Crosby* v. *Wyatt*, decided in Strafford, upon the present circuit, although different in other particulars. It is immaterial whether Peaslee's liability was continued by evidence of partial payments, made at a time when he was liable to pay the whole, and accompanied with no disclaimer of further liability, or whether it was continued by a judgment. The administrator brings this action on an entire different promise of the defendant from that which he made to Thompson; one arising by operation of law from the same transaction, but not a promise between the same parties. There is nothing to bar an action on this promise. Had it appeared that Peaslee was at any time discharged by the operation of the statute of limitations, and that he, or his administrator, after that, refused to avail himself of the defense, and voluntarily paid money which he could not at the time be compelled to pay, that would have presented a very different case.

On the facts of this case, the liability of Peaslee was at all times continued, and the case, as to him, taken out of the operation of the statute of limitations; not by any new agreement, or by an assent to any new agreement, not contemplated by the original contract; but by a part performance of what was stipulated in the original contract itself. The defendant, therefore, can not object that Peaslee paid wrongfully, or that the payment does not come within the implied promise to contribute.

Judgment on the verdict.

CONTRIBUTION BETWEEN JOINT OBLIGORS, WHEN EXISTS: See the cases in this series cited in the notes to *Harrison* v. *Lane*, 27 Am. Dec. 612; *Thompson* v. *Murray*, 29 Id. 72.

CASES

IN THE

SUPREME COURT

OF

NEW JERSEY.

OBART *v.* LETSON.

[2 HARRISON, 78.]

SHERIFF HOLDING INQUEST TO TRY A CLAIM TO PROPERTY has authority to exclude illegal testimony.

RECEIPT GIVEN BY THE DEFENDANT IN ATTACHMENT TO THE CLAIMANT for the purchase price of the property is competent, and *prima facie* evidence that the property was sold to the claimant.

THE opinion states the case.

W. H. Lupp, for the plaintiff in certiorari.

J. Van Wyke, for the defendant, who was plaintiff in attachment.

By Court, DAYTON, J. A writ of attachment having issued from the Middlesex pleas, returnable December term, 1838, against one Wareham Fifield, the sheriff, by virtue thereof, attached one bay mare, which was claimed by Obart, the plaintiff in certiorari. Upon the trial of his claim, before the sheriff's inquest, Obart offered in evidence, after the same was duly proved, a receipt from Fifield for one hundred and ten dollars, for a bay mare about six years old, dated October 30, 1838. I infer from the dates and proceedings, that the receipt was prior to the execution of the attachment, and that there was no dispute as to the identity of the mare. The receipt having been overruled by the sheriff, it is agreed that the case here shall be decided on the errors assigned: 1. That the sheriff holding said inquest, had no authority to exclude testimony. 2. That the receipt which he excluded, was competent evidence.

That the legislature intended the sheriff should have authority
to exclude testimony in such a case is evident from the language
of the fifth section of the supplement to the attachment act
passed thirteenth of February, 1830, Harr. Comp. 293, which
enacts among other things, that "the sheriff or other officer
shall have power, not only to administer the usual oath or affirmations to the jurors, but to swear or affirm the witnesses offered
by either party, and admitted by him." This language most
clearly recognizes his right to admit or reject testimony. The
case of *Tillotson* v. *Cheetham*, 2 Johns. 63, cited upon the part of
the plaintiff, simply shows that the powers of the sheriff on the
ordinary inquest of damages, after a judgment by default, are
ministerial, and may be exercised by deputy; not that he may
not admit or reject evidence, which is really requisite to the performance of his ministerial act. The power to admit or reject
evidence, in such cases, is in the sheriff, not the jury: *Snowden*
v. *Johnson*, 2 Penn. 469; *Williams* v. *Cooper*, 3 Dowl. 204; 3
Chit. Pr. 48, 673.

And of course nothing is competent, except such as would be
competent upon the trial of an issue in court: 2 Saund. on Pl. and
Ev. 686. The sheriff had authority in this case, to reject illegal
evidence; but the receipt offered was not illegal evidence—it was
clearly competent. The issue was, did Fifield own the mare?
The receipt was *prima facie* evidence that he had sold her to the
claimant, and received the purchase money. It was not necessary to produce Fifield himself, even if he had been disposed to
come. If fraud or collusion were alleged, it was the duty of
Obart to prove it.

For the rejection of this evidence, the inquisition must be set
aside.

HORNBLOWER, C. J., and FORD, WHITE, and NEVIUS. JJ.. concurred.

Inquisition set aside.

———

RECEIPTS AS EVIDENCE: See *Ensign* v. *Webster*, 1 Am. Dec. 108; *Cassell*
v. *Cooke*, 11 Id. 610; *Watson* v. *Blaine*, 14 Id. 669; *Reid* v. *Reid*, 18 Id. 570;
Fuller v. *Crittenden*, 23 Id. 364.

PAROL EVIDENCE TO VARY EFFECT OF RECEIPT: See *Ensign* v. *Webster*, 1
Am. Dec. 108; *Trisler* v. *Williamson*, Id. 396; *Tobey* v. *Barber*, 4 Id. 326;
Stackpole v. *Arnold*, 6 Id. 150; *Raymond* v. *Roberts*, 16 Id. 698; *Grier* v. *Hu-
ston*, 11 Id. 627; *Bridge* v. *Gray*, 25 Id. 358.

SINNICKSON *v.* JOHNSON.

[2 HARRISON, 129.]

ACT AUTHORIZING PRIVATE PERSON TO STOP UP A NAVIGABLE CREEK upon condition that he cut a canal upon his own property at his own expense in lieu thereof, is a private act for the individual benefit of such person.

IF PRIVATE OWNER ERECTS DAM IN PURSUANCE OF SUCH ACT, and thereby injures the land lying back, he is responsible to the owners in damages.

DAMAGES. The facts sufficiently appear from the opinion.

R. P. Thompson, for the plaintiff.

W. N. Jeffers, contra.

DAYTON, J. The declaration complains of the defendants for an injury done to their meadows by reason of the erection and continuance of a dam over Salem creek. The defendants plead as a justification, that said dam was erected and continued by virtue of an act of the legislature of this state, entitled, "An act to authorize John Denn, of the county of Salem, to shorten the navigation of Salem creek, by cutting a canal," passed November 6, 1818. All which is set out with proper averments. To this plea, the plaintiff has demurred, and the defendants have filed a joinder.

The act in question (Pamph. L. of 1818, p. 5), enacts substantially as follows:

Section 1. That John Denn be authorized to cut the canal, as therein prescribed.

Sec. 2. That the canal shall be cut wholly on the land of said Denn, at least twenty-two feet broad at the top, and of sufficient width at the bottom, and depth of water for all vessels navigating said creek; and shall, when cut and opened, be at all times afterward a public highway, and be kept open at least of the depth and width aforesaid, at the sole expense of said Denn, his heirs and assigns.

Sec. 3. That when said Denn shall have completed the canal, as is directed, and obtained a certificate thereof from the chosen freeholders of the townships of Mannington and Lower Penns Neck, or a majority of them, and filed the same in the clerk's office of the county of Salem, "it shall and may be lawful for the said John Denn, his heirs and assigns, to build a bridge over the said Salem creek, for the accommodation of himself, his heirs and assigns, opposite the mansion-house of the said John Denn," provided that the land to be occupied in its construction be his own, and that he do not by its abutments, contract the creek so as to injure the navigation; and do put a draw in the-same, at least twenty-two feet wide, and that he, his heirs and assigns, maintain said bridge and · draw, at their own cost and charges.

Sec. 4. That any person who shall obstruct the digging of the canal, etc., or injure the bridge, etc., shall forfeit one hundred dollars to said Denn, his heirs and assigns.

Sec. 5. That when the canal shall have been completely finished, and made navigable for vessels as aforesaid, and shall be used and found sufficient for the space of three years after being first used, "it shall and may be lawful for the said Denn, his heirs, or assigns, to stop the creek at the place where the said bridge may have been erected;" from which time, his liability to maintain the bridge and draw shall cease.

The point presented by the demurrer, is this: Does the above act exonerate John Denn, his heirs and assigns, from the payment of damages done to individuals, by stoppage of the creek? Great care has been used by the legislature, in providing another navigable highway for the public, in lieu of that which was authorized to be stopped up. So, too, the legislature have provided against all damages (which could be anticipated) to private rights. John Denn was to use no one's land but his own, and everything was to be done at his individual expense. But although I think it plain that the legislature never intended to injure private rights, yet the unforeseen result is otherwise. The meadows in question are admitted by the state of the pleadings to have been damnified by the stoppage of this creek; and yot the statute which authorizes the act has not provided compensation for the injury. The constitutionality of the law is not now questioned; but it is insisted that the common law right of the plaintiff to recover damages, is in full force. And in this position, I think, the plaintiff is right.

It is a well-settled rule, that statutes in derogation of common law rights, are to be strictly construed; and we are not to infer that the legislature intended to alter the common law principles, otherwise than is clearly expressed: 11 Mod. 149. Chancellor Vroom, in an opinion delivered in the term of August, 1835, in reference to another branch of the same subject-matter which is now before us, laid down the position distinctly, that the act in question does not exempt him who does an injury, from damages; which opinion, thus far, the counsel contend, is not law. But the question whether a party who has acted in pursuance of a statute, is protected from damages, where the

statute itself is silent, has been before some, at least, of our
most respectable state courts. In the case of *Gardner* v. *The
Trustees of Newburgh et el.*, 2 Johns. Ch. Cas. 162 [7 Am. Dec.
526], a company had been chartered to supply the town of Newburgh with pure water, but were restrained by injunction
from diverting a water-course, as authorized by the statute,
until compensation was made to the owners of the land through
which it ran, although the act made no provision for such compensation to them; and Kent, Ch., observed, that the owner of
the lands "would be entitled to his action at law, for the interruption of his right, and all his remedies at law, and in that
court, remained equally in force."

The case of *Crittenden* v. *Wilson*, 5 Cow. 166 [15 Am. Dec.
462], is in point. In this case, the court held that the right of
the legistature to grant the privilege of making a dam over the
Otselic river, which was a public highway, was too clear to be
disputed, but the grantee took it subject to the restriction, *sic
utere tuo, ut alienum non lædas*. That if no provision for the
payment of damages done to individuals, by reason of the dam,
had been made by statute, the defendant would still be liable to
pay them. It is true that in *Rogers* v. *Bradshaw*, 20 Johns. 785,
it is intimated that an exception to this rule may exist in the
case of public commissioners acting under direction of the
statute, as the direct agents of the state in the execution of a
great public improvement, and not as volunteers for their own
benefit. In the case of *Stevens* v. *Proprietors of the Middlesex
Canal*, 12 Mass. 466, it is said that should the legislature authorize an improvement (as cutting a canal), the execution of
which would require or produce the destruction, or diminution
of private property, without at the same time giving relief, the
owner would undoubtedly have his action at common law for
damages.

These authorities would appear to cover and rule the present
case. But it was contended by counsel, that they were decided
upon their respective states' bills of rights, which declare that
private property shall not be taken for public use, without just
compensation, and that as our constitution contains no such
limit or restriction, the cases have no application, or in other
words, that the legislature of New Jersey, being unrestricted by
constitutional provisions, is omnipotent, and may take private
property for public use, without compensation, whenever it
shall will to do so.

The right to take private property for public use, does not

depend on constitutional provisions, but is one of the attributes of sovereign power; and the constitution of the United States recognizes it as such, when it says, the right shall not be exercised without just compensation. This power to take private property reaches back of all constitutional provisions; and it seems to have been considered a settled principle of universal law, that the right to compensation, is an incident to the exercise of that power: that the one is so inseparably connected with the other, that they may be said to exist not as separate and distinct principles, but as parts of one and the same principle: Puffendorf, b. 8, c. 5, p. 222; 2 Montesquieu, c. 15, p. 200; Vatt. 112, 113; 1 Bl. Com. 139; 2 Kent's Com. 339, 340; 2 Johns. Ch. Cas. 168;[1] 1 Pet. Com. 99, 111;[2] 3 Story's Com. on Constitution, 661; *Bonaparte* v. *Camden and Amboy Railroad Company*, Baldw. 220. The language of Judge Baldwin in the case last cited, is "the obligation" (to make compensation), "attaches to the exercise of the power" (to take the property), "though it is not provided for by the state constitution, or that of the United States had not enjoined it."

And Story calls the provision on this subject, in the constitution of the United States, merely "an affirmance of a great doctrine established by the common law." This principle of public law, has been made by express enactment, a part of the constitution of the United States (*vide* fifth amendment); but it has been decided that as a constitutional provision, it does not apply to the several states: *Barron* v. *Mayor of Baltimore*, 7 Pet. 247; *Livingston's Lessee* v. *Moore*, Id. 551, 552. Still, if the opinions of the above distinguished jurists be correct, it is operative as a principle of universal law; and the legislature of this state can no more take private property for public use, without just compensation, than if this restraining principle were incorporated into, and made part of its state constitution. I have felt it a duty to notice this point, thus far, because of its interest and importance in the abstract, and of the great reliance placed upon it in the argument of the counsel, though I scarcely considered it necessary for the settlement of this case, to pronounce upon it a definite opinion.

According to my understanding of the act in question, the legislature neither intended to take, nor has it taken, private property for public use, in the sense in which these terms are properly to be understood. For the accommodation of John Denn, they authorized him (if he thought proper so to do), to stop up a nav-

1. *Gardner* v. *Newburgh, supra.* 2. *Ware* v. *Hylton*, 1 Pet. Con. 99; B. C., 3 Dall. 199

igable creek, upon condition that he cut a canal at his own expense and upon his own property, as a highway for the public, in lieu of the creek. By the terms of the act, therefore, I think, the legislature has manifested a clear intent to provide against any interference with private property. It merely agreed to give up its right of passage upon the creek (or, in other words, its public property there), for another right of passage equally or more valuable, to be provided by John Denn. The damages which have accrued to the meadow owners, have not arisen from cutting the canal, which in one sense, was for the benefit of the public, but by the stoppage of the creek, which was for the individual benefit, or private emolument of John Denn.

The case therefore, is not within the principle laid down in 4 T. R. 796, and *Sutton* v. *Clarke,* 6 Taunt. 29, 41, where it was held that public officers acting under the authority of an act of parliament, in repairing public streets, were not answerable for damages, unless they were guilty of an excess of jurisdiction; that the maxim applied, " *salus populi, suprema est lex,*" and that if no satisfaction were given by the act of parliament, the party was without remedy. It is not therefore necessary to inquire whether or not these cases conflict in principle with those already cited. Gibbs, C. J., in *Sutton* v. *Clarke,* carefully distinguishes the case of a public officer, who is bound to execute a duty imposed on him by statute, from that of a mere volunteer, who acts not for public purposes, but private emolument. I think it can hardly be pretended, that John Denn stopped Salem creek for public purposes under any obligatory directions of the statute. So far from this, it is evident on the face of the act, that it was done voluntarily, and for his own accommodation. The most that can be said for him is, that by cutting the canal, he paid a consideration to the public, for the privilege of doing so.

The powers given by the act to John Denn, are such only as he would have had, if the creek in question had been his own. He can build his bridge over it, or dam it up, at his pleasure, and his bridge or dam can not be complained of by the public, as a nuisance; but if in exercising his rights, he damnifies the property of his neighbors, he is liable, like every other citizen, to respond in damages to the amount of the injury.

Judgment must be entered for the plaintiff on demurrer, with costs.

NEVIUS, J. The declaration in this case sets forth that the plaintiff was seised in fee on the first day of July, 1835, of several tracts of meadow land, containing together one hundred and thirty acres more or less, situate in the township of Lower Penns Neck in the county of Salem, adjoining an ancient stream of water called Salem creek, the water of which from time immemorial has and still ought to run in its ancient and usual channel along said lands without obstruction. That the defendants, meaning to injure the plaintiff in the enjoyment of his said lands, and to deprive him of the profits arising therefrom, on the day aforesaid, did raise and build anew, a dam across said creek, without the plaintiff's license, and below his said lands, and have continued the same, and so obstructed, heightened, and impeded the flow of said stream, that afterwards, on the day aforesaid, and on divers other days between that day and the eighteenth of June, 1836, the waters of said creek did not run off or subside low enough to let the rain-water and other water run off said lands, out of the sluices and water works of said lands, as formerly, before the said dam was erected; but by reason of said dam, the flow of the water in said creek prevented the water in the ditches and drains on said lands from running off and draining the same as before, and that by means of said dam the said lands have been and are overflowed, and the herbage and grass thereon drowned and destroyed, and rushes and worthless grasses, and noxious weeds, by reason thereof, have grown up and spread over the said lands, and the same rendered useless and unproductive, and impassable for men and cattle and teams, and the ditches and drains filled up and rendered useless, by means of which the plaintiff is injured and aggrieved, and sustained loss, in his said lands, and is deprived of the benefit and advantage he was accustomed to have from them, before the erection of said dam, and has sustained damages to the amount of five thousand dollars.

To this declaration, the substance of which is above stated, the defendants have pleaded:

1. The general issue.

2. That by an act of the legislature of New Jersey, passed the sixth day of November, 1818, entitled "an act to authorize John Denn of the county of Salem to shorten the navigation of Salem creek, by cutting a canal," it was enacted (setting forth the act in full) in substance as follows, viz.: That John Denn be and hereby is authorized to cut a canal to shorten the navigation of Salem creek, describing the course of such canal to be on the line between John Denn's land and the land of David Ware.

2. That it shall be wholly upon the land of John Denn, and twenty-two feet in width at the top, and of sufficient width at the bottom, and sufficient depth of water throughout, for the free passage of all vessels navigating the said Salem creek; and shall be a public highway and kept open of the depth and width foresaid, at the sole expense of John Denn, his heirs and assigns forever, and he and his heirs are bound accordingly.

3. When the canal is opened and completed, and John Denn has obtained a certificate of the chosen freeholders, or a majority of them of the townships of Mannington and Lower Penns Neck, that the same is completed and sufficient for the purposes aforesaid, it should be lawful for the said John Denn, his heirs and assigns, to build a bridge over Salem creek opposite his own mansion-house, for the accommodation of him, his heirs and assigns; provided it be upon his own lands, and have a sufficient draw so as not to obstruct the navigation of said creek, and that he, his heirs and assigns should always maintain said bridge at his and their own costs and charges.

4. That any person obstructing the construction of said canal, or injuring its banks, or the bridge or draw, should forfeit to the said John Denn, his heirs and assigns one hundred dollars.

5. That when the canal should be finished and made navigable and shall be used and found sufficient for the space of three years after being first used, it shall be lawful for the said John Denn, his heirs and assigns to stop the said creek at the place where the said bridge shall have been erected, and from that time, their liability to keep up said bridge and draw shall cease.

The plea then proceeds to aver that John Denn, named in the said act, cut the said canal to shorten the navigation of Salem creek, and that the same was constructed in the place and manner directed and required by said act, and has at all times since been a public highway and kept open according to the requirements of said act, at the expense of him the said John Denn and his assigns. And that having completed said canal, he obtained the required certificate, which was filed according to law, after which he erected a bridge at the place, and of the description required by said act, and for the purpose named in said act.

And it further avers that the said John Denn having finished the said canal, and made it navigable agreeably to said act, and the same having been used and found sufficient for more than three years after having been first used, he, the said John Denn, erected the said dam and stopped the creek at the place where said bridge had been erected. And it further avers that on the seventeenth of April, 1834, Isaac Johnson, one of the defendants, purchased of John Denn, all his right, title, property, claim, and demand in and unto the said lands on each side of said bridge, and in and unto the bridge, dam, stopping, and privileges as granted by the said act, by deed of conveyance (which is set out in said plea), and that on the twenty-ninth of January, 1835, Isaac Johnson conveyed the one moiety thereof to William Johnson, the other defendant; and that the said defendants being the assignees of the said John Denn, as aforesaid, entered upon and raised and new erected the said dam as lawfully they might do, and this they are ready to verify, etc.

To this plea, the plaintiff has filed a general demurrer, and insists that the same constitutes no legal answer or defense to the cause of action set forth in his declaration. The defendants by this plea do not deny the injury complained of by the plaintiff, but justify their own acts under the authority of the legislature, as contained in the act of 1818, and insist that they are not responsible for such injury. · The demurrer admits the truth of the matters alleged by the plea, and denies that they constitute a justification or defense of the acts complained of.

The character of this act of the legislature by which John Denn was authorized to construct this canal, becomes the first subject of inquiry. Is it a public act and designed exclusively to promote the interest, and convenience, and welfare of the public, and was this authority vested in John Denn as an agent on the part of New Jersey, to carry into effect an object of public interest or importance? Or is it to be considered as a mere private act, designed to secure or advance, or protect the private interest of John Denn, his heirs or assigns; or is it to be esteemed as an act designed for private purposes, whilst at the same time it might incidentally promote the public interest? A correct answer to these questions, may and will have an important bearing upon the decision of the case. If the statute is wholly of a public character, and designed exclusively for the public welfare, and John Denn is to be esteemed as the agent of the government, employed under this act to effect in the name and for the use of the state, a public improvement wholly distinct from any private interest, I can not doubt but that the plea is a complete answer to the complaint in the declaration. Where the state authorizes an act to be done exclusively for the public interest, and appoints an agent to execute that act, and such agent shall act within the scope of his authority, he can not be personally responsible to individuals for the consequences of

executing his commission. Should private property be necessarily and unavoidably injured, taken away, or destroyed by the
execution of such trust, without any compensation provided in
the act itself, the remedy can only be by contesting the constitutionality of the law, or appealing to the justice and mag-
nanimity of the legislature. But if the statute has provided a
mode of compensation in such case, the party injured must resort to that, and can not pursue his common law remedy, by
resorting to a suit at law. In support of these general positions,
I refer to the case of *Rogers* v. *Bradshaw*, 20 Johns. 735, decided
upon a very conclusive argument in the court of errors of New
York. And also, to the case of *Calking et al.* v. *Baldwin*, reported in 4 Wend. 667, and the case of *Steele* v. *Pres. etc.
Western Inland Lock Navigation Company*, 2 Johns. 283; and
also to the case reported in 4 Taunt. 44.[1]

But if on the other hand, the act of the legislature is to be
considered of a private character, designed to confer upon John
Denn exclusive privileges for his own private and individual
interest and convenience, and if the act itself in no wise violates
any constitutional provision, and does not in terms provide
compensation for private property that may be taken, injured,
or destroyed, the same not having been foreseen, John Denn
or his assigns must execute that act at their peril and must respond for all consequences that may result from it to private
property. See *Crittenden* v. *Wilson*, 5 Cow. 165 [15 Am. Dec.
462]. And why should it not be so? The legislature can not
take private property for public purposes without compensation,
much less can they take it for private purposes or take the property of one citizen and give it to another. I refer also to the opinion of Chancellor Vroom, rendered in a case between the same
parties, where this question was distinctly raised, and under-
went a full examination. In the present case, if the design of
the legislature was to confer upon John Denn, his heirs and
assigns, a personal and private privilege, for his own exclusive
use and interest, he can protect himself by virtue of such act,
only against any public complaint. It may be lawful for him
and his assignees, to execute this act, so far as the public interests, the rights of navigation, fishing, etc.. are concerned, and
he may plead, and successfully plead the act, to any indictment
for a nuisance, or against any complaint for an infringement of
a public right, but can not plead it as a justification for a private
injury, which may result from the execution of the statute. Or

---

[1]. *Sutton* v. *Clarke*, 6 Taunt. 44.

again, if it is to be esteemed an act to promote the interest of
John Denn whilst the execution of it may incidentally advance
the public interest, I apprehend the same construction is to be
given to it as in the latter case.   And the defendants are to be
answerable to the same extent for any consequences resulting
from the execution of the act as if it was wholly a private act.

Upon examining this act I can not view it in any other light
than a private act and intended for the benefit of John Denn.
He seeks the privilege of erecting a dam across a navigable
stream, and the legislature having the constitutional right to
grant such privilege (see *Willson et al.* v. *The Blackbird Creek
Marsh Company*, 2 Pet. 245), do grant it and impose upon him
certain terms, among others that he shall construct a canal to
answer the purposes of navigation.   It is to be of sufficient
depth and width to admit the passage of such vessels as were
used to navigate this creek.   It was to be constructed upon his
own land and at his own expense, and forever to be kept in repair at his own cost, to be fairly tested and tried, before the
grant to him to erect a dam, should become complete and absolute.   Nor was it made incumbent on him to construct this canal.
After the passage of the act it was entirely optional with him
whether he would construct it or not.   It was not made obligatory except he availed himself of the benefit of the grant, by
the erection of the dam.   In all these particulars, the act bears
no resemblance to a public act.   It would seem to have been induced by the application of John Denn himself, and in its passage, the legislature seem only to have been careful to protect
the public interests.   The construction of this canal was a permission and not a direction or obligation imposed upon the
grantee; it was an authority to do it, not a requirement.   Nor
does the language used in the title and in the first section of the
act "to shorten the navigation of Salem creek" at all change
its character.   It was essentially and to all intents and purposes
a private act and designed for the benefit of John Denn, and
only induced by the consideration that it might not be injurious
to public interest, but that the public interest might thereby be
incidentally promoted.

Does this act, then, confer upon John Denn and his assigns,
the right to take, injure, or destroy private property without
compensation to the owners?   If it does, it is unconstitutional
and void, and in violation of natural justice, and therefore
would not be a defense to the plaintiff's claim.   If it does not
confer such right, it constitutes no justification, and the plea

can not therefore be sustained. The legislature are to be considered as conferring nothing but what they had a constitutional right to grant. They could not grant to him the right to overflow the land of the plaintiff, or in any other way to injure or destroy it without compensation, and if no such compensation is provided for, the plaintiff has a right to seek his remedy through courts of justice by suit. It is no answer to say that the party injured must or may resort to the justice of the legislature. If such be his only remedy, it is of too vague, indefinite, and uncertain a character to be recognized by courts. The constitution and laws of this state can never leave the citizen such remedy only, for a clear infringement of his private rights. Nor is it an available argument to say that if the defendants, as the assignees of John Denn, are to respond to the plaintiff in this action for the injury to his property by reason of an act authorized by law, the consequences to them may be ruinous, and the work contemplated by the act, absolutely prevented. Suppose it to be so, may it not be answered that in accepting the grant, they acted voluntarily, and should have foreseen and provided against the consequences, and would it not be equally if not more unjust and oppressive upon the plaintiff, to ruin and destroy his property, without the slightest compensation or recompense?

I am of opinion, that the plea is no justification to the act complained of, and that the demurrer, therefore, be sustained.

HORNBLOWER, C. J., concurred in sustaining the demurrer. He had not time to prepare a written opinion. FORD, J., read an opinion sustaining the demurrer. WHITE, J., was not present at the argument, and gave no opinion.

Judgment for plaintiff, on the demurrer, with costs.

———

COMPENSATION FOR DAMAGES occasioned by an act authorized by private statute: See *Calking* v. *Baldwin*, 21 Am. Dec. 168.

CASES

IN THE

COURT OF CHANCERY

OF

NEW JERSEY.

GARWOOD v. ELDRIDGE.

[1 GREEN'S CHANCERY, 145.]

IGNORANCE OF LAW NO GROUND OF RELIEF IN EQUITY.—Where a party purchases land subject to two mortgages, and after paying them cancels them on the record, and in consequence the land is sold under the lien of a judgment subsequent to the mortgages but prior to the deed, of which he was ignorant, he will not be relieved in equity on the ground that he was ignorant of the legal effect of the cancellation.

VENDEE OF LAND, SATISFYING MORTGAGE THEREON and canceling it, will not be substituted to the place of mortgagee, where through his gross neglect he has failed to discover the existence of a prior incumbrance on the land, under which it is sold.

CANCELLATION OF RECORD WHEN THE MORTGAGE HAS BEEN REDEEMED, paid, and discharged, is an absolute bar and discharge of the same in the absence of fraud, accident, or mistake.

THE opinion states the case.

Wall, for the complainant.

Kinsey and H. W. Green, contra.

PENNINGTON, Chancellor. A short statement of facts will present everything in this case necessary for its decision. Josiah Smith, being the owner in fee of a lot of land of between nine and ten acres, in the county of Burlington, executed with his wife a mortgage on the same on the twenty-sixth of February, 1810, to the executors of John Smith, to secure a bond for three hundred and seventy dollars. Sarah Jones was also a party to this mortgage, and there was embraced in it a lot belonging to her. This bond and mortgage was assigned finally to Zebedee Wills and Isaac Haines. On the twenty-ninth of April, 1815,

Josiah Smith and his wife made a second mortgage on the same premises to Aaron Engle, to secure a bond for seven hundred and fifty dollars. These mortgages were both placed on record in the county of Burlington, shortly after their execution. On the sixth of January, 1824, the mortgaged premises were conveyed by Josiah Smith and wife, the above-stated mortgagors, to the complainant, for the consideration of five hundred dollars. This money was applied to the payment of the two mortgages on the property, on which there was then due about five hundred dollars; upon which, by the consent of all parties, they were discharged and canceled of record.

William Eldridge obtained a judgment against Josiah Smith in the inferior court of common pleas of the county of Burlington, on the thirtieth of May, 1822, and issued execution thereon to the sheriff of that county, returnable to the term of August thereafter. This judgment, although long subsequent to the date of the canceled mortgages, was prior to the complainant's deed, and therefore at law bound the property free and clear of incumbrances. By virtue of this execution the sheriff, shortly after the complainant's purchase, and on the nineteenth of April, 1824, sold and conveyed the aforesaid premises to William Eldridge, the plaintiff in the execution, for three hundred and thirty dollars. From the evidence of John Crispen, the only witness examined on this subject, it would seem that the price paid by the complainant was a full and fair consideration for the premises; and from Eldridge's lying still with his execution, from August, 1822, until after the complainant had discharged the mortgages, as well as from the price paid by him at the sheriff's sale, it is to be presumed that the property would have brought nothing beyond the incumbrances. Under these circumstances, the complainant asks the interference of this court. At law, it is quite certain, he is without remedy; for although he may have been, as he alleges, without actual notice of the Eldridge judgment at the time he purchased, yet he had constructive notice by the record, and unless the power of this court is sufficient to grant relief, the complainant will have lost the five hundred dollars with which he paid off the mortgages, and Eldridge will have received on his purchase the exclusive benefit thereof. There is then, to my mind, a natural justice in the complainant's case, to which I should be disposed to extend relief, if I could do so without disturbing well-established principles.

The first ground upon which this relief is asked, is, that the complainant canceled these mortgages unwittingly, and with-

out a knowledge of the legal effect of that act. It is not from
any mistake or want of knowledge of facts, but of the law; for
as to the existence of the judgment, he had, or might have had
full knowledge, by using the ordinary and proper precaution of
examining the public records. "*Ignorantia legis neminem ex-
cusat,*" is the general rule, as well in equity as at law. This rule
is not without its exceptions, and it would seem those exceptions are not by any means well settled. The American cases
have been strenuous in supporting the general rule, from the
great danger of opening a door for so common a pretense. It
has been decided, that a court of equity could not relieve an
obligee, when he released one joint obligor, supposing the other
to be bound. In the case of *Lyon and another* v. *Richmond et
al.*, 2 Johns. Ch. 60, the chancellor says: "The courts do
not undertake to relieve parties from their acts and deeds fairly
done on a full knowledge of facts, though under a mistake of
the law. Every man is to be charged at his peril with a knowledge of the law. There is no other principle which is safe and
practicable in the common intercourse of mankind." The same
principle is afterwards recognized in the case of *Storrs* v. *Barker*,
6 Johns. Ch. 170 [10 Am. Dec. 316]. Many of the cases in
which exceptions to this general rule have been allowed, are
those in which a mistake in the facts, as well as the law, has
taken place, or some suppression of the truth, fraud, or contrivance in the party. In such cases, there can be no doubt,
it is the peculiar province of this court to interpose. This whole
subject, with a reference to the cases, will be found ably and
fully discussed in 1 Story's Eq. 121; in which it will be found,
that able judge is tenacious of adhering to the general principle.
In the present case, I can not bring myself to believe that the
complainant acted under any misapprehension of the law. He
had purchased the property; and his plain course, believing as
he alleges he did, that the property had no other liens upon it
than the two mortgages, was to take them up and cancel them.
There is no fraud proved on the part of Eldridge, the judgment
creditor. He was not bound to give any more information of
the existence of his judgment, than the records of the court
furnish. It was the result of carelessness and neglect in the
party not to have examined at the proper office for liens on the
property. It is asking too much of the credulity of the court,
to believe that a man competent to the transaction of business,
and buying property, should not understand the law upon tear-
ing off the seals and canceling mortgages of record. It is far

more natural to suppose that the complainant, believing these
the only incumbrances, intended to relieve his property from
them by their discharge and cancellation. Upon this ground,
therefore, I must deny the complainant the relief here sought.

The remaining ground taken by the complainant is, that he
should be placed in the situation of the mortgagee; in other
words, that new life and action should be given to those instruments, so that they may stand now in the complainant's hands
as subsisting liens on the property. There are cases, undoubtedly, in which courts of equity have, after the discharge of a
bond and mortgage, substituted the person who took them up
in the place of the mortgagee, and kept them alive. This was
expressly recognized in the case of *Ex parte Coster*, 2 Johns. Ch.
503. These cases are where the bond and mortgage are discharged by a third person, and not where they are taken up by
the obligor himself. In fact, in the case just cited, the chancellor declined making any order for assigning the bond and
mortgage, because it had been paid off by the obligor himself.
In the present case the bonds and mortgages can hardly be said
to have been taken up by a stranger—they were virtually taken
up by Smith himself. This was done with the purchase money
for which he sold the land, and that money extinguished the
incumbrances. Smith's deed covenants against all incumbrances, and obliged him, therefore, to have them discharged.
In such cases, the courts have refused to interfere: *Toulmin* v.
Steere, 3 Meriv. 221; *Parry* v. *Wright et al.*,[1] 1 Cond. Ch. 188.
The complainant purchased the property, subject of course to all
incumbrances; and if by his own neglect, in examining the public records, he has found himself embarrassed by this judgment,
it is his own fault. Was it his intention to cancel the mortgages? I have no doubt it was. He meant to extinguish the
incumbrances; and should they now be reinstated, it would be
against the express intention of the parties. What right has
this court to bring to life obligations which Smith himself, the
obligor, has taken up and caused, by the understanding of all
parties, to be canceled on the public records? The complainant
purchased only the equity of redemption of Smith in these lands,
and he was as much bound to see that the judgment was removed
as the mortgages. There is nothing in the case looking like
fraud or improper concealment of the Eldridge judgment, or
mistake in canceling the papers, but a mere neglect of complainant in not examining the records. To interfere in such a

1. 1 Sim. & Stu. 369.

case, and put the complainant in the place of the mortgagees, would introduce, in my opinion, a dangerous precedent, and encourage parties in the grossest negligence. Should this course be taken, what shall be done with the purchase by Eldridge? By reason of the property being freed from all incumbrances, he paid three hundred and thirty dollars for his purchase. Is he to lose this money? Suppose another had purchased, could he be affected by it? And if not, can the plaintiff in the execution, standing as the purchaser, be any otherwise affected?

It must be borne in mind, too, that the complainant not only neglected to have an assignment of these bonds and mortgages made to him, and had the seals torn off as evidence of their being discharged, but caused them to be canceled on the public records. Our statute (Rev. L. 464) declares such cancellation of record, when the mortgage has been redeemed, paid, and discharged, to be an absolute bar and discharge of the same. I am aware that this statute has been held repeatedly not to apply to a case where such cancellation may have taken place through fraud, accident, or mistake. In the present case, the cancellation was made without either fraud, accident, or mistake, but with the consent and understanding of all the parties. After the best reflection on this part of the case, and from looking into the authorities, I am constrained to think it would be an improper exercise of the jurisdiction of the court, to grant the relief asked.

The remaining point in the case relates to the Eldridge judgment. The complainant alleges that it has been paid off. There is some evidence to that effect. It seems to have been given as an indemnity, and I am willing to have this subject more fully inquired into. I shall, therefore, direct a reference to a master to ascertain and report whether the Eldridge judgment has been paid, when, and under what circumstances. The question of costs, and all other matters, are reserved.

Order accordingly.

––––––

RELIEF AGAINST THE SATISFACTION OF A MORTGAGE was given in *Russell* v. *Mixer*, 42 Cal. 475. Russell and one Miller agreed that the former should purchase of the latter a certain mortgage made by Mixer. "Russell and Miller proceeded together to the recorder's office; when they arrived there, Miller, at the suggestion of Russell, entered satisfaction of the mortgage upon the record, both he and Russell supposing that the previous agreement to assign it would be effectuated thereby, and both being surprised when they afterwards learned that they had thereby wholly discharged the lien of the mortgage, instead of keeping it on foot in the hands of Russell, as they intended to do." Russell sued to vacate the satisfaction and foreclose the mortgage. It would seem that his difficulty arose solely from his mistaking or being ignorant of the legal effect of the satisfaction of a mortgage, and assuming that a satisfaction would, in law, operate as a transfer. His right to relief was denied on the ground that he was not entitled to relief founded on his ignorance or mistake of law. But a majority of the court held that "there is no appreciable distinction between this case, and that where a scrivener, through ignorance or inattention, fails to select or prepare such an instrument as effectuates the previous agreement of parties, and relief is always decreed in that case."

IGNORANCE OR MISTAKE OF LAW, RELIEF AGAINST IN EQUITY: See *Williams* v. *Hodgson,* 3 Am. Dec. 563; *Warder* v. *Tucker,* 5 Id. 62; *Drew* v. *Clarke,* Id. 698; *Fisher* v. *May,* Id. 626; *McKean* v. *Reed,* 12 Id. 318; *Lowndes* v. *Chisholm,* 16 Id. 667; *Lawrence* v. *Beaubien,* 23 Id. 155; *Underwood* v. *Brockman,* 29 Id. 407; *Storrs* v. *Barker,* 10 Id. 316, and note, in which the subject of ignorance of law, as a ground of equitable relief, is discussed at length.

DISCHARGE OF MORTGAGE, WHAT AMOUNTS TO: See *McEwen* v. *Wells,* } Am. Dec. 39; *Collins* v. *Torry,* 5 Id. 273; *Jackson* v. *Wood,* 7 Id. 315; *Dunham* v. *Dey,* 8 Id. 282; *Brinckerhoff* v. *Lansing,* 8 Id. 538; *Jackson* v. *Stackhouse,* 13 Id. 514; *Johnston* v. *Gray,* 16 Id. 577; *Breckenridge* v. *Ormsby,* 19 Id. 71. The principal case is cited to the effect that the cancellation of a mortgage and a discharge of record, unless effected through accident, mistake, or fraud, is an absolute bar and a discharge of the mortgage, in *Guy* v. *Du Uprey,* 16 Cal. 199, and *Bentley* v. *Whittemore,* 3 C. E. Green, 374.

SEAMAN *v.* RIGGINS.

[1 GREEN's CHANCERY, 214.]

To JUSTIFY INTERFERENCE BY THIS COURT IN SHERIFF's SALES, there must be a foundation of fraud, accident, or mistake laid, by which the rights of the parties have been affected.

MISTAKE IN NAMING PLACE OF SALE, by complainant's solicitor, and an accident happening to an agent of a party wishing to bid, by which he misses the road, form sufficient ground for the interference of this court, when the property is sold for less than its value in consequence.

DISCRETION EXERCISED BY SHERIFF IN CONDUCTING SALES, must be a legal one, and this court will not permit such an exercise of it as shall work injustice and wrong.

PETITION to avoid sheriff's sale. The opinion states the case.

A. Whitehead and Vanarsdale, for the petitioner.

Williamson and Speer, contra.

PENNINGTON, Chancellor. This is an application by John Moir, a defendant, to set aside a sale made under the execution issued in this cause, on the eighteenth of February last, by the sheriff of the county of Middlesex. By the execution, the sheriff was directed to sell the mortgaged premises, and to satisfy out of the proceeds, first, four thousand three hundred and fifty dollars due the complainant on his mortgage, with interest and costs;

and second, to satisfy John Moir, a defendant, three thousand and forty-five dollars and forty-five cents, the amount of a second mortgage, with interest and costs. The property was owned by William Riggins, the other defendant, and the amount of these two mortgages was to be raised by the sale. It is admitted by all the witnesses, by Mr. Travers, by the sheriff, and by the solicitors for both parties, that the property is worth the amount to be raised by the execution, as well that due to Mr. Moir as that due the complainant. The sale was first advertised for the fourth of February, at South Amboy, and was then adjourned to Applegate's tavern, at the mouth of Cheesequakes creek, between two and three miles south of South Amboy. Mr. Moir constituted his solicitor his agent to attend the sale, and authorized him to bid up the property to the amount due the complainant and himself. On the first day fixed for the sale, Mr. Moir's agent did not attend, having the promise of the complainant's solicitor that no sale should take place in his absence; and though a sale was then pressed, it was postponed by the firmness of the complainant's solicitor, who had given his word that none should take place in the absence of Mr. Whitehead, the agent of Mr. Moir. The complainant's solicitor, after the first day of sale, wrote Mr. Whitehead that the sale was adjourned to the eighteenth day of February, at one o'clock, at the house of Mr. Appleby, about a mile or a mile and a half from the ferry at South Amboy. On the day of sale, Mr. Whitehead, being under the impression, from inquiries made, that the place of sale was between South Amboy and New Brunswick, and having further learned that the steamboat from New York to South Amboy did not stop at Elizabeth town point, took the train of cars that pass through Newark about a quarter before ten in the morning, for New Brunswick, and from thence set out in a private conveyance to attend the sale. After pursuing his journey and making inquiries on the road, he came to a tavern-house belonging to a Mr. Appleby, though not occupied by him, between New Brunswick and South Amboy. When he arrived there, he found out by a person who happened to have been present at the time of the adjournment of the sale, that the place of sale was at William Applegate's tavern, on the other side of South Amboy, and that he had gone out of his way some five or six miles. He then went on and arrived at the place of sale at five minutes before two o'clock, and found that the property had been sold to Mr. John Travers, for and in behalf of William Riggins, the defendant, for four thousand five hundred dollars, a sum about sufficient to satisfy the complainant's mortgage, and cutting off entirely the defendant, John Moir. The sale was fixed for one o'clock, and the property struck off without any other bidder than Mr. Travers, at about half past one. Under this state of facts, John Moir applies by petition to set aside this sale, offering on his part to bid upon a resale the full amount due him and the complainant also. Burnet, the mortgagor in the mortgage of Mr. Moir, is stated to be insolvent; and unless the relief here asked is granted, the money on this second mortgage must be entirely lost. No deed has yet been executed by the sheriff to the purchaser.

The power of the court to interfere in this case is not denied. It has been frequently done in the state of New York, and in this court. No exercise of the power of the court can be plainer, than that of controlling sales by public officers on its own process: *Williamson* v. *Dale*, 3 Johns. Ch. 290; *Duncan et al.* v. *Dodd et al.*, 2 Paige, 99; *Requa* v. *Rea and Wife*, Id. 339.

In this court, the case of the *Ex'rs of Gouverneur Morris* v. *Swartwout et al.* was cited at the bar, though not reported. The cases referred to on the argument from the English courts, on the subject of the opening of biddings, though not applicable to our method of making sales, show a very strong disposition to open sales upon the single ground that more can be got for the property. They open the biddings continually, upon an offer made to bid more for the property, without any allegation of surprise or fraud. Holding a power over the subject, they do so for the interest of the estate alone. These cases do not apply to sales made with us; they have never been adopted either in the state of New York or in this state. To justify the interference of the court, there must be a foundation laid—either fraud or mistake, or some accident, by which the rights of parties have been affected. In the present case, I have no doubt either as to the power of the court, or its plain duty, to interpose and set aside this sale. The bare statement of the facts shows, that an accident on the part of the agent in missing the road, and a mistake wholly unintentional in the complainant's solicitor in naming the house at which the sale was to take place, have occasioned the whole difficulty; and it would be a reproach on the administration of justice if no remedy could be afforded. Had Mr. Moir, or his agent, neglected his business, there might have been some reason against interfering; but they both have shown diligence, and certainly did intend to be present and to bid, and would have done so but for the accidental occurrences which have been

stated. I consider the misapprehension under which the agent
labored, and honestly so, no doubt, as to the situation of the
place where the sale was to take place, and the wrong information given him by the complainant's solicitor, as a sufficient
ground for interference. Moir was not a mere stranger, who
contemplated attending the sale as a purchaser, but a party
having a deep interest, and manifesting in all his conduct a determination to be present, and to bid the amount due him. The
property was worth the amount, and his mortgagor was insolvent; he had therefore every motive for such a course.

But it is said that it is dangerous to interfere with sheriffs'
sales; that they have a right, as public officers, to exercise a discretion as to sales, and the manner of conducting them; and that,
if the court will set aside such sales, purchasers will not attend.
A sheriff is a public officer, and as such has a certain discretion,
intrusted to him by law, and with that it is not my intention or
desire to interfere; that discretion must, however, be a legal
one, and the court will not permit such an exercise of it as shall
work injustice and wrong. Thus far my opinion is formed from
reasons wholly independent of the sheriff; and without intending now to charge on that officer in this case a designed fraud,
I can never be led to think his conduct in respect to this execution was right. It may have been, and I incline to think it was,
more the result of indiscretion than design. He had a large execution in his hands; he knew that the sale, made as it was,
would cut off entirely the second mortgage, amounting to more
than three thousand dollars; he knew that it was the intention
of the person holding this second mortgage to be represented at
the sale; and he knew the property to be worth the amount of
both the mortgages. Under such circumstances, his plain duty
was, either to adjourn the sale, or to have waited until a later
hour. In the absence of this party, to strike off the property in
half an hour, when he had until five o'clock, more than three
hours, at his disposal, was unnecessary and unreasonable haste.

As to the course pursued by Mr. Travers, it is very clear his
interest and that of Mr. Riggins, the purchaser, was one in this
transaction. Mr. Riggins was his relative, and probably has
acted thoughout with a view to befriend Mr. Travers, which he
had a perfect right to do. One thing is certain; Mr. Travers
meant to get this property at as cheap a rate as possible, and
availed himself of the opportunity which he considered presented itself of defeating this second mortgage. At the first day
fixed for the sale, after learning that a sale for the amount of

the first mortgage would defeat the second entirely, he still
pressed the sale of the property, which must then have taken
place but for the commendable course pursued by Mr. Williamson. He may have excused this course to himself, upon the
ground that considerable improvements had been put on this
property by himself and Mr. Riggins, and that without such improvements the property would not have been worth the amount
of this second mortgage. This consideration, it can not be pretended, should enter into this question. Any improvements
thus made can never be set up as a reason for defeating a *bona
fide* mortgage.

The place, too, for the sale, was fixed by Mr. Travers—a place
every way unfit for such a sale, and only to be excused for the
reason that it was near the premises to be sold.

The sale made by the sheriff must be set aside, and a new sale
made, upon a readvertisement according to law. Each party to
pay their own costs on this application.

Sale set aside.

<hr/>

DISCRETION OF SHERIFF IN EXECUTION SALES: See *McLeod* v. *Pearce*,
11 Am. Dec. 742; *Kean* v. *Newell*, 14 Am. Dec. 321; *McDonald* v. *Neilson*, Id.
431, and note 457; *Gorham* v. *Gale*, 17 Id. 549; *Cain* v. *Maples*, 26 Id. 184;
Russell v. *Richards*, Id. 532; *Nesbitt* v. *Dallam*, 28 Id. 236.

SHERIFFS' SALES, WHEN SET ASIDE: See *Cresson* v. *Stout*, 8 Am. Dec.
373; *Ainsworth* v. *Greenlee*, 9 Id. 615; *Stockton* v. *Owings*, 12 Id. 392; *Mills*
v. *Rogers*, 13 Id. 263; *Patterson* v. *Carneal*, Id. 208; *Kean* v. *Newell*, 14 Id.
321; *Smith* v. *Greenlee*, 18 Id. 564; *Martin* v. *Blight*, 20 Id. 226; *Groff* v.
Jones, 22 Id. 545; *Farr* v. *Sims*, 24 Id. 396; *Reed* v. *Carter*, 26 Id. 422; *Mc-
Meekin* v. *Edmonds*, Id. 203; *Crary* v. *Sprague*, 27 Id. 110; *Nesbit* v. *Dallam*,
28 Id. 236; *Smith* v. *Tritt*, Id. 565; *Eastin* v. *Dugat*, 29 Id. 461. The principal case has been cited to the effect that a supervision of sheriffs' sales is of
common occurrence with courts of chancery, in *Marlatt* v. *Warrick*, 3 C. E.
Green, 123, and *Aldrich* v. *Wilcox*, 10 R. I. 414; and also in support of the
position that there is no doubt of a court of chancery's power to set aside
a sheriff's sale where there is gross inadequacy of price, or the party whose
interest is injured is prevented from attending, by mistake or accident, in
Wetzler v. *Schaumann*, 9 C. E. Green, 64.

<hr/>

READ v. CRAMER.

[1 GREEN'S CHANCERY, 277.]

WHERE PARTY SELLS LAND ACCORDING TO A MAP as containing "fifteen
acres, more or less," and in the deed describes the land according to the
map, but is induced by the fraudulent representations of the grantee to
alter the description so as to make it include an additional twenty-seven
acres, the grantor being ignorant of the effect produced by the alteration,
the grantee will be decreed to reconvey the portion thus fraudulently obtained.

BILL for relief.   The opinion states the case.

. *J. Wilson* and *I. H. Williamson*, for the complainants.

Vroom, contra.

PENNINGTON, Chancellor.   Samuel J. Read, in the year 1834, purchased at a sheriff's sale a farm at Little Eggharbor, in the county of Burlington.   The property formerly belonged to Samuel Loveland, and was sold under a decree of this court to satisfy certain mortgages.   After making this purchase, General Read determined to sell off the property in parcels at auction, and for that purpose he advertised it for sale in the spring of the year 1835.   Not knowing much about the premises, previous to the day of sale he sent Robert Leeds, a surveyor, to run out the land and make a map of it; this he did, and furnished the map to General Read before the time fixed for the sale.   On this map there is a tract lying south of a thoroughfare, said to contain about fifteen acres, which at the auction was sold to Charles Cramer, one of the defendants; and the controversy in this cause relates entirely to the sale of this lot.   The bill charges, that the complainant sold this lot according to the map, for a fifteen-acre tract, more or less, and with the agreement that the purchaser should pay for fifteen acres whether it turned out to be more or less.   That after the sale he made out a deed according to the map, when, by the fraud and misrepresentation of the defendants, he was induced to vary the description of the premises, and besides the fifteen acres which he really sold, he has included twenty-seven acres additional which were never sold, so that the defendant, instead of fifteen acres, has a deed for forty-two acres.   The prayer of the bill is, that the deed may be corrected, or that the defendant, Cramer, may reconvey the twenty-seven acres and account for the profits of this excess of land during the time he has possessed it.

The answer denies that any such map was exhibited at the sale, or that the defendant bought by any map, and on the contrary insists that he bought the land by certain boundaries which were publicly announced by the complainant at the time of the sale, and by which boundaries he is entitled to all the forty-two acres described in the deed.   There is a mass of evidence taken in the cause, agreeing in many particulars but widely differing in others, so that the main difficulty is to arrive at the true state of facts.   This was a public sale, and at the distance of two years and a half persons at the sale are called upon to state what took place. In such cases it will always be found, that among perfectly upright men their stories will differ, and perhaps materially. I deem it unnecessary to go over the whole evidence. I have examined it carefully, and shall now content myself with stating the conclusions to which I have come, and the principles on which the case must be decided.

In the first place, I consider it fully made out by the evidence that General Read sold by the map. The answer denies that any map of this lot was exhibited at the sale to the knowledge of the defendant who purchased, or that he heard of any; but that the map was exhibited, is stated by almost every witness, and by some of them it is said that at the time the defendants were not more than ten or twelve feet off. The defendants' own witnesses admit that the map was exhibited at the sale. It is very manifest that General Read himself, at the time of the sale, did not know the extent of the property he owned there. He thought he owned only the fifteen acres or thereabouts, south of the thoroughfare, when in truth he did own forty-two acres. He had purchased the entire farm a short time before, and without any knowledge of the metes and bounds himself, had sent a surveyor to lay off the land for sale from the best information he could derive from others. The surveyor who made the map testifies, that he only put on the map the fifteen acres which he supposed the extent of the Samuel Loveland line. And this was the extent of the line for a period of forty years, but Samuel had bought another strip of Charles Loveland, which carried his line down to Cramer's land and the ditch.

In the second place, General Read, when he made out the first deed, made it from the map, and when he made the alteration in the description in the second deed, he did so from the information alone which he derived from the defendants, and from the confidence which he reposed in them. They indeed stated to him that his description did not embrace all the land which they purchased, but they did not explain to him in an open, frank manner, as they were bound to do, the extent they claimed. He had no idea that this new starting-place in the description made the difference between fifteen and forty-two acres. Had they so explained it, his eyes would have been opened, and the deed would never have been executed as it was.

In the third place, although the evidence is contradictory on this point, yet from the fact that the defendants' witnesses swear positively to it, and among the rest the auctioneer himself, and the complainants' witnesses only speak negatively that they did not hear it, I must believe that General Read, when he was called upon for the bounds of the land at the auction, did say that it bounded on the thoroughfare, Wading river, Cramer's line, and others; and that he particularly mentioned Cramer's line. But it is equally certain that he did so without understanding where Cramer's line was, and without any intention of going beyond the fifteen acres set off in the map.

In the fourth place, as the land was sold for fifteen acres, more or less, although General Read did say they were only to pay for that quantity if the land turned out to be more or less, yet the defendants, as reasonable men, could never have supposed that he intended in a sale of fifteen acres to embrace a tract of forty-two acres. The difference was too great. They must have seen, as other witnesses swear they did, that he was laboring under a mistake when he declared he sold to Cramer's line. The expression he used was clearly intended to cover a miscalculation of a fraction, or a few acres at most: it never could have been intended to cover so large a difference as twenty-seven acres. The defendants resided in the neighborhood and knew all about the land, and General Read did not.

In the fifth place, the price at which the land sold was sufficient to have satisfied the purchaser of the mistake. The land sold was worth the price paid per acre, and could the defendants have believed they were to receive twenty-seven acres in addition, worth at least fifteen dollars per acre? This was enough, surely, to have demanded an explanation on their part.

In the sixth place, the offer made by General Read when he discovered the mistake, was a perfectly fair and reasonable one. He said in substance: By your directions I have given you a deed for more land than I intended. I supposed you to be fair, honest men. You must re-convey the land and I will return you what you have paid, and thus put an end to the whole contract, or you must pay me the same price for the additional acres that you paid for the others, or I shall seek my redress in the courts of law. The defendants refused the proposition, and it is my duty, upon this state of facts, to settle the rights of these parties according to the principles and rules of this court.

If this land was sold, as I believe it was, from the map, the twenty-seven acres were not in it at all, and therefore could not have been sold. When the deed was made, the twenty-seven acres were put in it from the representation alone of the defendants and from the confidence reposed in them, and it covers that much more land than was intended, or than would have been put in, had the grantor at the time been informed of all the circumstances attending the case. As the defendants knew the fact that the alteration in the description would take in this whole tract, they should have so explained it to the grantor.

It is among the first principles of a court of equity to correct mistakes, and to prevent parties from being injured in their property, and especially their freeholds, by any misapprehension or concealment of the true state of facts. The cases are numerous where relief has been afforded under like circumstances: *Bingham* v. *Bingham*, 1 Ves. sen. 126; *Gee* v. *Spencer*, 1 Vern. 32; *Evans* v. *Llewellyn*, 2 Bro. Ch. 151; *De Riemer* v. *De Cantillon*, 4 Johns. Ch. 88; 1 Story's Eq. 159, 160. Charles Cramer has, in my opinion, a deed for twenty-seven acres more land than he should have, and I shall decree a reconveyance from him to the heirs at law of General Read, for all the land in his deed beyond the fifteen acres described on the map under which the sale was made, or that the present deed be rectified, as may be most convenient for the parties, the result being the same in either case; and that he pay the annual value of the excess from the time he entered into possession, to be ascertained by a master. The bill as to Isaac Cramer must be dismissed, there being no ground for a decree against him.

As some reason was given by the course of General Read at the auction, for the purchaser to suppose the land sold bounded on Cramer, though not enough, in view of all the circumstances, to justify me in letting him hold to that line, I do not think he should pay costs. The decree will be without costs.

Decree accordingly.

————

Fraud in Deed, Effect of: See *Taylor* v. *King*, 8 Am. Dec. 746; *Chesterman* v. *Gardner*, 9 Id. 265; *Thomas* v. *Thomas*, 13 Id. 220; *Jackson* v. *King*, 15 Id. 354.

Relief was Asked for on the Ground of Fraud in the principal case, and was granted on the ground of the complainant's mistake as to the real amount of the land conveyed; and hence the principal case has become an authority for the position that though relief is asked for on the ground of fraud, it will be granted on the ground of mistake, and has been cited as such in *Graham* v. *Berryman*, 4 C. E. Green, 34; S. C., 6 Id. 378.

CASES

SUPREME COURT OF JUDICATURE

OF

NEW YORK.

MATTER OF GALLOWAY.
[21 WENDELL, 32.]

ADMINISTRATOR OF DECEASED TENANT IS PERSONALLY LIABLE on a covenant in the lease to pay assessments, etc., as an assignee, where he receives the rents and profits after his intestate's death, and need not be named as executor, though in certain special cases he may defend in part, as by showing that there are no assets and that the land is worth less than the sum due; but this is strictly matter of defense.

ATTACHMENT LIES AGAINST A NON-RESIDENT ADMINISTRATOR as a non-resident debtor under the statute in an action on a covenant in a lease to his intestate to pay assessments, etc., upon which he is personally liable by reason of having received the rents and profits.

CERTIORARI to the first judge of Kings county, to review proceedings relative to the issuance of an attachment against John Galloway, jun., as a non-resident debtor. From the return it appeared that letters of administration had been issued to the said Galloway, a resident of England, upon the estate of John Galloway, sen., late of Kings county; that prior to his decease the intestate had taken a lease from one Johnson for certain premises in Brooklyn for a term of years at a certain annual rent, in which lease the tenant covenanted that he, his executors or administrators or assigns would pay all "taxes, duties, and assessments" upon the premises. The administrator had received the rents and profits of the premises up to the issuance of the attachment. The proceedings were instituted to collect a certain sum which Johnson, the lessor, was compelled to pay on account of an assessment imposed upon the premises for opening a certain road. The allegation was that John Galloway,

AM. DEC. VOL. XXXIV—14

jun., was personally indebted to the attaching creditor in the
sum named.

M. T. Reynolds, for the debtor.

J. A. Lott, for the creditor.

By Court, COWEN, J.   The only objection to the proceedings
insisted on was, that this being a debt against John Galloway the
younger in his representative character, he could not be proceeded
against as an absent debtor.

The ground taken for the debtor is in general true, and indeed
always so where the debt is due by the administrator or executor, solely in his representative character: *Matter of Hurd and Sel-
den*, 9 Wend. 465.   But it is also perfectly well settled, that
where rent or money for breach of covenant falls due after the
death of the testator or intestate, and the executor or administrator enters, or which is the same thing, as here charged, receives the rents and profits, he is chargeable in the debet and
detinet, or directly on the covenant as an assignee, and need not
be named as executor or administrator.   In certain special cases
he may, it is true, defend in part, as where he has no assets and
the land is in truth worth less than the sum due.   But this is
strictly matter of defense.   *Prima facie* the land is worth more.
The authorities to these points are numerous, and are all one
way; and most of them may be seen collected in 2 Wms. Ex.
1076, 1077, Phila. ed. of 1832, where the doctrine is fully stated.

The result is, that John Galloway the younger may be pursued
in the case presented here as an absent debtor, within the statute.   The proceedings are affirmed, and must be remitted to the
first judge of the county of Kings, to be followed up in due
form of law.

LIABILITY. OF EXECUTOR OR ADMINISTRATOR ON COVENANTS in deeds of
testator or intestate: See *Booth* v. *Starr*, 5 Am. Dec. 149; *McCrady* v. *Bris-
bane*, 9 Id. 676.   The principal case is recognized as authority for the position, that an executor of a lessee is liable for the rent so far as he receives
the rents and profits, in *Miller* v. *Knox*, 48 N. Y. 236.   It is cited also as an
analogous case in discussing the liability of assignees for the benefit of creditors of an insolvent tenant, for the rent of the leased premises, in *Dennistoun*
v. *Hubbell*, 10 Bosw. 182, and *Jermain* v. *Pattison*, 46 Barb. 14.

ASSESSMENT FOR PAVING STREET IS NOT EMBRACED in "taxes and other
public dues," which a lessee undertakes to pay: *Bolling* v. *Stokes*, 21 Am.
Dec. 606.

SWART *v.* SERVICE.

[21 WENDELL, 36.]

MERE MORTGAGEE, OR THOSE CLAIMING UNDER HIM, CAN NOT RECOVER IN EJECTMENT under the revised statutes of New York.

DEED ABSOLUTE ON ITS FACE MAY BE SHOWN BY PAROL TO BE A MORTGAGE to defeat a recovery by the grantee in ejectment against a defendant in possession, though the latter shows no privity of title with the grantor. *Contra*, Bronson, J., dissenting.

LAPSE OF TIME MAY AFFORD PRESUMPTIVE EVIDENCE OF PAYMENT OF A MORTGAGE.

EJECTMENT by the children of the heir at law of Derick Swart, deceased. As evidence of title, the plaintiffs introduced a lease and release of the premises to Derick Swart, executed in 1784 by one Cuerdon, who died in possession several years before the trial. . The defendant offered to show that the lease and release constituted in fact a mortgage, which was paid by Cuerdon before his death, but the evidence was rejected because the defendant showed no privity of title with Cuerdon. The defendant also requested an instruction, that the evidence showed an adverse possession by Cuerdon, which instruction was refused. Verdict for the plaintiffs. Motion for a new trial on the above grounds, and also because the lapse of time afforded a presumption of payment of the mortgage.

M. T. Reynolds, for the defendant.

S. Stevens, for the plaintiffs.

By Court, COWEN, J. The first offer made by the defendant had no dependence on privity of title between him and Cuerdon. It was a simple offer to prove an outstanding title, by turning the conveyance by lease and release into a mortgage, and showing its extinction by payment. That would divest the title of Swart and of his grandchildren, the plaintiffs; for payment extinguishes a mortgage at law as well as in equity: *Jackson ex dem. Roosevelt* v. *Stackhouse*, 1 Cow. 122 [13 Am. Dec. 514]. But independent of that, if Swart were a mere mortgagee, neither he nor those claiming under him could recover: 2 R. S. 237, sec. 37, 2d ed. *Jackson ex dem. Titus* v. *Myers*, 11 Wend. 533, 538, 539; *Stewart* v. *Hutchins*, 13 Id. 485; *Morris* v. *Mowatt*, 2 Paige, 586 [22 Am. Dec. 661].

It has often been held in the courts of equity of this state, that a deed, though absolute on its face, may, by parol evidence, be shown to have been in fact a mortgage in the terms offered here; and the same doctrine was held by this court in

Roach v. *Cosine*, 9 Wend. 227, and *Walton* v. *Cronly's Adm'r*, 14 Id. 63, equally applicable to a court of law, and has, it seems, ceased to be the subject of contest; for no objection to the doctrine is now made. For one, I was always at a loss to see on what principle the doctrine could be rested, either at law or in equity, unless fraud or mistake were shown in obtaining an absolute deed where it should have been a mortgage. In either case, the deed might be rectified in equity; and perhaps even at law, in this state, where mortgages stand much on the same footing in both courts. Short of that, the evidence is a direct contradiction of the deed; and I am not aware that it has ever been allowed in any other courts of equity or law. But with us the doctrine is settled, and I am not disposed to examine its foundations, at least, without the advantage of discussion. It is not necessary to say whether the lapse of time might be called in as presumptive proof of payment, though that, as a general doctrine, is too clear to be disputed. If the defendant, on a new trial, shall succeed in making out a mortgage, he will be entitled to such proofs of payment as the nature of his case may afford, subject to the answering proofs of the plaintiffs, provided proof of payment shall become necessary.

It will not, however, be necessary that we see, to complete his defense here, whatever it may be on a bill filed to foreclose by the representatives of Derick Swart; for since the revised statutes, showing that the plaintiffs or those under whom they claim are mere mortgagees, proves, as we have seen, an outstanding title.

There was no evidence of adverse possession in Cuerdon. I am of opinion that a new trial should be granted, the costs to abide the event.

The chief justice concurred.

BRONSON, J. Although I seldom allow myself to depart from the decisions of those who have gone before me in this court, I can not agree with my brethren in following one or two recent cases which hold that an absolute deed can be turned into a mortgage in a court of law, by parol evidence. Where the transaction was intended as a mortgage, and through fraud or mistake the conveyance has been made absolute in its terms, a court of equity, acting upon well-established principles, can reform the deed. But this will only be done on a direct and appropriate proceeding for that purpose, and after such ample notice to all parties in interest, as will tend most effectually to guard against surprise, fraud, and false swearing. And besides, a court of equity can and will protect third persons, who may have parted with their money on the faith of the deed. But a court of law has neither power nor process to reform a deed. If parol evidence to contradict or insert a condition in the conveyance can be received at all, it must of necessity be in a collateral proceeding; and it must be received whenever either party chooses to offer it. It can be given without notice, and without the means of guarding against the obvious danger of fraud, surprise, and perjury. And beyond this: when a court of law turns an absolute deed into a mortgage, it has no power to protect a *bona fide* purchaser. Other mischiefs will be likely to result from admitting such evidence; but without attempting at this time to point them out, I shall content myself with dissenting from what I deem a new and very dangerous doctrine.

———

MORTGAGEE CAN NOT RECOVER IN EJECTMENT IN NEW YORK: See *Morris* v. *Mowatt*, 22 Am. Dec. 661. See also *Runyan* v. *Mersereau*, 6 Id. 393; *Wilson* v. *Troup*, 14 Id. 458, and *Jamieson* v. *Bruce*, 26 Id. 557, and cases cited in the note thereto as to the rule in other states.

ADMISSIBILITY OF PAROL EVIDENCE TO SHOW ABSOLUTE DEED A MORTGAGE: See *Ross* v. *Norvell*, 1 Am. Dec. 422; *Washburn* v. *Merrills*, 2 Id. 59; *Thompson* v. *Patton*, 15 Id. 44, and note; *Reading* v. *Weston*, 20 Id. 97, and note; *Hale* v. *Jewell*, 22 Id. 212. See also the note to *Chase's case*, 17 Id. 300. The case of *Swart* v. *Service* is cited on this point in *Lee* v. *Evans*, 8 Cal. 433, where, however, it was held that parol evidence was not admissible to prove a deed a mortgage, except in cases of fraud or mistake. In *Jackson* v. *Lodge*, 36 Id. 44, 65, the case is also referred to, and its doctrine adopted by the majority of the court. It is cited and commented on also in *Brainerd* v. *Brainerd*, 15 Conn. 586, and in *Fuller* v. *Parrish*, 3 Mich. 223, *per* Martin, J., dissenting. It is referred to in *Egleston* v. *Knickerbocker*, 6 Barb. 464, and *Cook* v. *Eaton*, 16 Id. 444, as overruled on this point by *Webb* v. *Rice*, 6 Hill, 219. Other references to the case on the same point are found in *Russell* v. *Kinney*, 1 Sandf. Ch. 37; *Carr* v. *Carr*, 4 Lans. 329, and *Bank of Albion* v. *Smith*, 27 Barb. 491.

PRESUMPTION OF PAYMENT OF MORTGAGE FROM LAPSE OF TIME: See *Wanmaker* v. *Van Buskirk*, 23 Am. Dec. 748, and note. As to the presumption of payment, generally, from lapse of time, see *Bailey* v. *Jackson*, 8 Id. 309; *Atkinson* v. *Dance*, 30 Id. 422, and other cases in this series cited in the note thereto.

———

SMITH v. CLARK.

[21 WENDELL, 83.]

CONTRACT TO DELIVER WHEAT TO A MILLER AND TO TAKE FLOUR THEREFOR of a specified quality, at the rate of a certain number of pounds for so many bushels of the wheat, is a sale and not a bailment, where there is no agreement to manufacture the flour from the wheat delivered; and one purchasing from the miller flour made from the wheat so delivered, is not liable in replevin to the party delivering such wheat.

PURCHASER OF GOODS FROM A BAILEE IS NOT LIABLE IN REPLEVIN to the owner, for a tortious taking, but only for the detention, and the declaration should be in the *detinet* only.

REPLEVIN for the taking and detention of certain barrels of flour. Pleas, *non cepit* and property in defendant. It appeared at the trial at the circuit, that the defendant purchased the flour from one Hubbard, a miller; that prior to the purchase, the plaintiffs had entered into an agreement with Hubbard, to deliver wheat at his mill, for which he was to deliver to the plaintiffs warranted superfine flour, at the rate of one barrel for every four bushels and fifty-five pounds of the wheat. A large quantity of wheat was delivered under the contract, and was stored by Hubbard in a large bin, with other wheat belonging to himself and others. Only part of the flour called for by the contract was delivered. The flour purchased by the defendant was made from wheat taken from the bin above referred to. The plaintiffs claimed also that Hubbard had previously delivered to them the barrels of flour purchased by the defendant. Motion for a nonsuit denied. Verdict for the plaintiffs under the direction of the court, and a motion for a new trial. Other facts appear from the opinion.

H. Welles and *S. Stevens*, for the defendant.

S. Cheever, for the plaintiffs.

By Court, BRONSON, J. The contract between the plaintiffs and Hubbard was, in effect, one of sale—not of bailment. The property in the wheat passed from the plaintiffs at the time it was delivered at the mill, and Hubbard became a debtor, and was bound to pay for the grain in flour, of the specified description and quantity. There was no agreement or understanding, that the wheat delivered by the plaintiffs should be kept separate from other grain, or that this identical wheat should be returned in the form of flour. Hubbard was only to deliver flour of a particular quality, and it was wholly unimportant whether it was manufactured from this or other grain: Jones on Bail. 102, 64. A different doctrine was laid down in *Seymour* v. *Brown*, 19 Johns. 44; but the authority of that case has often been questioned: 2 Kent, 589; Story on Bail. 193, 194, 285; *Buffum* v. *Merry*, 3 Mason, 478; and the decision was virtually overruled in *Hurd* v. *West*, 7 Cow. 752, and see 756, note. The case of *Slaughter* v. *Green*, 1 Rand. (Va.) 3 [10 Am. Dec.

488], is much like *Seymour* v. *Brown*. They were both hard
cases and have made bad precedents.

There was, I think, no evidence which would authorize the
jury to find that the flour in question had been delivered by
Hubbard to the plaintiffs. There certainly was no direct evidence of that fact, and Hubbard himself testified expressly that
there had been no delivery. The proof given by the plaintiffs
of what Hubbard had said to others about the flour in the mill,
was not necessarily inconsistent with his testimony. But if
there had been a delivery, so that the property in the flour
passed to the plaintiffs, they still labor under a difficulty in relation to the form of the remedy. Notwithstanding the transfer,
the property was left in the possession and under the care of
Hubbard. He was a bailee of the goods, and as such would
have been answerable to the plaintiffs for any loss happening
through gross negligence on his part. The defendant took the
flour on delivery from the bailee, who had a special property in
it. Such a taking is not tortious: *Marshall* v. *Davis*, 1 Wend. 109
[19 Am. Dec. 463]; *Earl* v. *Camp*, 16 Id. 570. The plaintiffs
should have counted on the detention, not on the taking of the
goods: *Randall* v. *Cook*, 17 Id. 57; 10 Id. 629.[1] There must be
a new trial.

New trial granted.

DELIVERY OF WHEAT TO MILLER, TO BE PAID FOR IN FLOUR, constitutes a
bailment and not a sale, when: See *Slaughter* v. *Green*, 10 Am. Dec. 488, and
note. The doctrine of *Smith* v. *Clark* is approved and followed in *Baker* v.
Woodruff, 2 Barb. 523, and it was there said that the two cases were not distinguishable. There the contract between the miller and the other party was
to take wheat and to give therefor one barrel of superfine flour for every four
bushels and thirty-six pounds. This was held a sale, and not a bailment.
This decision was affirmed by the court of appeals, where the principal case
was again referred to with approval. The principle of the case was approved
and applied also in *Reed* v. *Abbey*, 2 N. Y. S. C. (T. & C.) 382, where one
agreed to take a certain number of sheep from another in 1869, to be returned
in 1871, "said sheep to be returned as good and in as good condition and age
as when taken." This too was held a sale and not a bailment. The principal
case was distinguished, however, in *Mallory* v. *Willis*, where the contract
was to deliver good merchantable wheat at a mill, "to be manufactured into
flour," the defendant agreeing to deliver one hundred and ninety-six pounds
of superfine flour for every four bushels and fifteen pounds of wheat. The
defendant was to receive a certain sum per barrel, and a certain other sum
extra if the plaintiffs should make a certain profit. The plaintiffs were to have
the "offals." This was held a bailment because the flour returned was to be
ground from the identical wheat. The principal case was distinguished also
in *Pierce* v. *Schenck*, 3 Hill, 30, 31, which was a contract to deliver logs to be
made into boards, each party to have half the boards; and again in *Wescott* v.

---

1. *Nichols* v. *Nichols*.

Tilton, 1 Duer, 55, where ale was sold in barrels, the barrels to be returned, and if not returned to be charged at a certain price. In both these cases the transactions were construed to be bailments.

In *Baker* v. *Woodruff*, 2 Barb. 523, some facts are given by Welles, J., as to the subsequent history of the principal case. He says in substance that the case was taken to the court of errors and reversed, though the decision reversing it was never reported, because the principle settled by the supreme court was not intended to be disturbed. The ground of the reversal, he says, was that the judge at the circuit erred in telling the jury that there was no evidence of a delivery of the flour to the plaintiffs, when there was some evidence on that point on both sides, and also in taking from the jury the question as to what the contract in fact was between Hubbard and the plaintiffs, inasmuch as it was an oral contract. His honor concludes that the decision of the supreme court on the main point is unshaken by this reversal, and is to be "regarded as a sound exposition of the law."

DELIVERY BY BAILEE, NOT A WRONGFUL TAKING SO AS TO SUPPORT REPLEVIN: See *Marshall* v. *Davis*, 19 Am. Dec. 463, and note.

HANNA *v.* MILLS AND HOOKER.

[21 WENDELL, 90.]

EVIDENCE OF PAYMENT UNDER GENERAL ISSUE IN ASSUMPSIT is admissible.

VERDICT FOR PLAINTIFF ON ISSUE OF NON ASSUMPSIT where payment is also pleaded, without noticing the latter plea, is informal merely, and not defective in substance.

VENDOR OF GOODS TO BE PAID FOR BY NOTE PAYABLE IN FUTURO, if such note is not given, may sue immediately for a breach of the special agreement and recover the value of the goods as damages, though he can not sue for goods sold and delivered until the term of credit expires.

EVIDENCE OF A SALE OF GOODS TO BE PAID FOR BY A "SATISFACTORY NOTE" will not support a declaration on a sale for the purchaser's note "to the order of, and indorsed by, a person who should be satisfactory" to the vendor, there being no evidence of a usage attaching such meaning to the words used at the sale.

ERROR to the New York superior court in assumpsit, to which *non assumpsit* and payment were pleaded. The principal and only material count of the declaration set forth a sale of certain goods by the plaintiffs to the defendant, for which the defendant promised to pay by his promissory note, payable six months from date, " to the order of, and indorsed by, a person who should be satisfactory as such indorser to the plaintiffs," and that the goods were delivered and the note not given though demanded. The evidence was that the sale was at auction, and that the terms, stated in the sales book, were, "six months' satisfactory notes," and that the notes demanded were notes " with satisfactory indorsers." Motion for nonsuit overruled.

Verdict for plaintiffs on the plea of *non assumpsit*, assessing as damages the value of the goods, without noticing the plea of payment. Judgment for plaintiffs, and the defendant brought error.

S. Stevens, for the plaintiff in error.

M. T. Reynolds, for the defendants in error.

By Court, BRONSON, J. Several objections are taken to this judgment. 1. It is said that the jury did not pass upon the issue on the plea of payment. The verdict is only informal—not defective in substance. Payment might have been given in evidence under the general issue, as well as under the special plea; and if it was proved, the jury could not have found for the plaintiffs on *non assumpsit*. The jury have therefore in effect, though not in form, passed upon both issues: *Law* v. *Merrills*, 6 Wend. 268. This is not like the case of *Boynton* v. *Page*, 13 Id. 425, on which the plaintiff in error relies. There the jury in an action of replevin found for the plaintiff on the plea of *non cepit* without taking any notice of another plea, of property, in a third person, and justifying the taking under an attachment. This matter could not have been given in evidence under the plea of *non cepit;* and the second issue was not at all involved in the first. It might very well be that the defendant took the goods, and that he had a right to do so, because they belonged to the third person against whom he had an attachment. The verdict did not go to the question of property in the goods— neither directly, nor by necessary implication; and consequently it could not authorize a judgment for the plaintiff. But here the verdict, t$_h$oug$_h$ informal, covers the whole ground.

2. When goods are sold to be paid for by a note or bill payable at a future day, and the note or bill is not given, the vendor can not maintain assumpsit on the general count for goods sold and delivered, until the credit has expired; but he can sue immediately for a breach of the special agreement: 4 East, 147;[1] 3 Bos. & Pul. 582;[2] 9 East, 498;[3] 3 Camp. 329.[4] In such an action he will be entitled to recover as damages the whole value of the goods, unless perhaps there should be a rebate of interest during the stipulated credit. The cases referred to by the counsel for the plaintiff in error give no countenance to the argument in favor of a different rule of damages. The right of action is as perfect on a neglect or refusal to give the note or bill, as it

---

1. *Mussen* v. *Price.*
2. *Dutton* v. *Solomonson.*
3. *Hoskins* v. *Duperoy.*
4. *Hutchinson* v. *Reid.*

can be after the credit has expired. The only difference between suing at one time or the other, relates to the form of the remedy; in the one case the plaintiff must declare specially, in the other he may declare generally. The remedy itself is the same in both cases. The damages are the price of the goods. The party can not have two actions for one breach of a single contract; and the contract is no more broken after the credit expires, than it was the moment the note or bill was wrongfully withheld.

3. According to the terms of sale, the purchaser was to pay for the goods by a satisfactory note. The contract laid in the declaration is to pay for the goods by a note to be made by the purchaser, payable to the order of, and indorsed by a person who shall be satisfactory as such indorser to the vendor. It is not improbable that persons acquainted with the course of this business may have understood the terms of sale as the pleader has expounded them. But there was no proof that the words had acquired any peculiar meaning among merchants, and I am unable to say that a satisfactory note necessarily means either a note of the vendee or an indorsed note. For aught I can see, the note of a third person of undoubted solvency, or a note of the vendee with sufficient sureties, would have been a performance of the contract of sale. Much as we may regret the necessity of reversing the judgment on this narrow ground, I think the objection that the proof did not support the declaration, can not be got over. The defendant will probably gain nothing in the end by the writ of error. The costs will be ordered to abide the event, and on another trial the plaintiffs may be able to help out their case by further evidence, or the court may allow such an amendment as will avoid the question of variance.

Judgment reserved.

———

VENDOR MAY SUE IMMEDIATELY, NOTWITHSTANDING A STIPULATION FOR CREDIT, where the purchaser agrees to give his notes payable *in futuro* for the contract price, and fails to give the notes, but the action, in such a case, is not to recover the price, but damages for the breach of the contract. The doctrine of the foregoing decision on this point is approved and applied in *O'Connor* v. *Durgley*, 26 Cal. 22, and in *Lee* v. *Decker*, 3 Abb. App. Dec. 54; S. C., 6 Abb. Pr. (N. S.) 394; 43 How. Pr. 480; see, also, 3 McLean, 554.

VERDICT MUST PASS UPON ALL MATERIAL ISSUES submitted to the jury: *Jenkins* v. *Richardson*, 22 Am. Dec. 82, unless, as in the principal case, a finding upon one issue necessarily disposes of the rest. The case is cited on this point in *Van Steenburgh* v. *Hoffman*, 6 How. Pr. 492.

NEWCOMB v. RAYNOR.

[21 WENDELL, 108.]

DISCHARGE OF PRIOR INDORSER BY THE HOLDER RELEASES SUBSEQUENT INDORSERS of a promissory note.

ASSUMPSIT against defendants as indorsers of a certain promissory note. Plea *puis darrein continuance* that the plaintiff, since the commencement of the action, had, by a release under seal, discharged one Goings, the payee, and first indorser of the note, from all liability thereon. Demurrer to this plea.

B. Davis Noxen, for the plaintiff.

M. T. Reynolds, for the defendants.

By Court, NELSON, C. J. I am of opinion the plea constitutes a good bar to the action. As between the first and subsequent indorsers, the former must be regarded in the light of principal; he stands behind them upon the paper, and is bound to take it up, in case of default of the maker. A discharge of him, therefore, by the holder (regarding the relative position of the parties), on general principles, operates to release them.

It is said their rights are not prejudiced, as they may still resort to an action against him if subjected to the payment of the note, as the release leaves the implied contract existing between the first and subsequent indorsers unimpaired. Conceding this to be so, to permit a recovery against the defendants would but lead to an unnecessary circuity of action. The plea shows a discharge for a presumed good consideration (as it is under seal) of the first indorser, and it can not be doubted as the case stands, that if the defendants should be obliged to call upon him, the plaintiff would be bound to take his place. The case, therefore, comes within the familiar rule, that a release of the principal operates to discharge the surety.

It is further said, that Goings may not have been legally charged as an indorser. If this were so, the plaintiff should have replied the fact, as we will not presume it in the face of the acts of both him and the plaintiff to the contrary. The release would not have been necessary on such a supposition.

Judgment for defendants on demurrer; leave to amend on usual terms.

———

RELEASE OF FIRST INDORSER BY THE HOLDER releases subsequent indorsers: *Farmers' Bank of Amsterdam* v. *Blair*, 44 Barb. 654; *Deck* v. *Works*, 18 Hun, 272; S. C., 57 How. Pr. 308, both citing *Newcomb* v. *Raynor*.

HERKIMER COUNTY BANK v. COX.

[21 WENDELL, 119.]

CERTIFICATE OF A NOTARY WHO IS A STOCKHOLDER IN A BANK SUING the indorser on a note, is inadmissible to prove demand and notice.

ASSUMPSIT against the indorsers of a note. To prove demand, protest, and notice, the plaintiffs offered in evidence the certificate of one Story, a notary, who was at the time a stockholder and cashier of the plaintiffs' bank, which was admitted against the defendants' objection. Verdict for the plaintiffs and a motion for a new trial.

M. T. Reynolds, for the defendants.

D. Burwell, for the plaintiffs.

By Court, BRONSON, J. Although the language of the statute is general, that the certificate of a notary shall be presumptive evidence of the facts contained in it, Stat. Sess. of 1833, p. 395, sec. 8, I think it should not be so construed as to admit the certificate in a case where the notary, by reason of interest, would be an incompetent witness. The legislature did not intend to dispense with the necessity of proving a demand and notice, for the purpose of charging an indorser, but only to change the mode of proof. The statute has rendered it unnecessary to call the notary, by giving the same effect to certain facts set forth in his official certificate, as though he had appeared in court, and sworn to those facts. I can not think that the legislature intended to sanction this secondary evidence in a case where the officer was an incompetent witness at the time he made the certificate. The same question has arisen in Pennsylvania, *Bank* v. *Porter*, 2 Watts, 141, and the certificate was rejected.

New trial granted. _____

UTICA AND SCHENECTADY R. R. Co. v. BRINCKER-HOFF.

[21 WENDELL, 139.]

MUTUAL PROMISES MUST BE CONCURRENT AND OBLIGATORY AT THE SAME TIME to render either binding, and must be so stated in the declaration.

DECLARATION SETTING OUT NO PROMISE BY PLAINTIFF as consideration for the defendant's promise is fatally defective on demurrer; as where a declaration by a railroad company sets out a written agreement with the defendant, stipulating that if the company would locate their road in a certain place, the defendant, in consideration of benefits accruing to him therefrom, would pay the value of certain lands required for such location, and that afterwards, on the same day, in consideration of such agreement, and that the plaintiffs, at the defendant's request, promised to perform the agreement on their part, the defendant undertook and promised to perform it on his part, and alleges performance by the plaintiffs and non-performance by the defendant.

ASSUMPSIT. The declaration alleged an agreement in writing on a certain day between the plaintiffs and the defendant, whereby it was stipulated that if the plaintiffs would locate their road on a certain street, and should require certain lands for that purpose, the defendant, in consideration of benefits to be derived from such location, would pay the appraised value of lands taken for such purpose; and the declaration further alleged that afterwards, at the same time and place, in consideration of said agreement, and that the plaintiffs at the defendant's request had then and there promised to perform the same on their part, the defendant faithfully promised to perform the same on her part, but that, though the plaintiffs had performed the agreement by locating the road at the place mentioned, the defendant had not performed the agreement on her part. There was a second count, setting out substantially the same facts, but with greater particularity. Demurrer to both counts, assigning among other grounds that no consideration for the defendant's promise was shown.

S. Stevens, for the defendant.

M. T. Reynolds, for the plaintiffs.

By Court, NELSON, C. J. The difficulty in sustaining this action is, that no consideration appears for the undertaking of the defendant. The written instrument is but a simple proposition, and no averment that it was acceded to by the plaintiffs. The fact that they afterwards located the road agreeably to the terms of the proposition is, of itself, nothing; it should have appeared that they had agreed with the defendant, thus to locate it as a consideration for the promise. The promise of each must be concurrent and obligatory at the same time to render either binding, and should be so stated in the declaration: 1 Cai. 585;[1] 4 Johns. 235;[2] 7 Id. 87;[3] 3 T. R. 653,[4] 148;[5] 9 Wend. 336.[6]

This case is not unlike *Burnet* v. *Biscoe*, 4 Johns. 235, and *Cooke* v. *Oxley*, 3 T. R. 653. In the first, the defendant made an agreement with the plaintiff on the twentieth of February, by

1. *Livingston* v. *Rogers*.	3. *Comstock* v. *Smith*.	5. *Payne* v. *Cave*.
2. *Burnet* v. *Bisco*.	4. *Cooke* v. *Oxley*.	6. *De Zeng* v. *Bailey*.

which she agreed to give him the refusal of her farm for two years, from the first of April following, on certain terms specified. The plaintiff averred, that on the first of April he performed the agreement, etc. On demurrer, the court say, there was no consideration stated; that though the defendant agreed to give the refusal of the farm, the plaintiff did not agree to take it; that there was no promise on his part for the promise of the defendant, nor any money paid, or other valuable consideration given. The other case is, if possible, still stronger. There the defendant agreed to give the plaintiff till four o'clock P. M., to agree to the proposal, and the declaration averred that he did agree and gave notice before the hour; still the judgment was arrested. At the time of entering into the contract, the engagement was considered all on one side, and it did not appear that the parties came to any subsequent agreement.

The pleader in the cause before us, assumes that the instrument was obligatory on both parties on the fourth of August, when it was executed by the defendant, and upon the strength of the legal liability arising thereupon, alleges, as usual, mutual promises by the parties to fulfill and perform the aforesaid agreement. Where this legal liability arises from the contract as set forth, it is sufficient to state it without alleging formally that the defendant promised: 1 Chit. Pl. 299; 2 N. R. 62. And it is equally clear, if none appears, the *super se assumpsit* will not help the count. Without the legal liability, the promise fails. The radical vice in the pleading is, that the agreement, and the undertaking and promise of the plaintiffs to perform it, which they set forth as the sole consideration for the promise of the defendant, amounts to nothing, as the agreement is not binding upon them; it is an agreement only upon one side.

The other objections I am inclined to think untenable. The appraisal referred to, was to be made agreeably to the act of incorporation in such cases provided.

Judgment for defendant.

MUTUAL PROMISES AS CONSIDERATION: See *Howe* v. *O'Mally*, 3 Am. Dec. 693; *Tucker* v. *Woods*, 7 Id. 305; *Gould* v. *Banks*, 24 Id. 90. Upon the general proposition that where no promise by the plaintiff is set out as the consideration for the defendant's promise, but it is merely averred that the defendant's promise was subsequently acted on by the plaintiff, such promise can not be enforced, the principal case is cited as authority in *Boyce* v. *Brown*, 7 Barb. 90; *Barnes* v. *Perine*, 15 Id. 254; *Walker* v. *Gilbert*, 2 Daly, 84; S. C., 2 Rob. 223. The case is distinguished on the same point in *Burrell* v. *Root*, 40 N. Y. 499. See also *McConnell* v. *Brillhart*, 17 Ill. 361, referring to the case as authority on this subject.

DOWNING *v.* RUGAR.

[21 WENDELL, 178.]

PRESUMPTION IS THAT A TOWN HAS TWO OVERSEERS OF THE POOR until the contrary appears, where the statute requires each town to elect two.

WHERE PUBLIC OR PRIVATE AUTHORITY IS CONFERRED ON SEVERAL, all must confer; but if the authority be public, a majority may decide and bind the minority.

PUBLIC AUTHORITY CONFERRED UPON TWO CAN NOT BE EXERCISED BY ONE without the other's consent, because the number does not admit of a majority; but it seems that to prevent a failure of justice, where immediate action is necessary, one may act alone if the other is dead, absent, or interested.

ONE OF TWO OVERSEERS OF THE POOR MAY, BY CONSENT OF THE OTHER, ACT ALONE, as the agent or deputy of both, in applying for and executing a warrant, under the statute, against the property of one who has absconded, leaving his family chargeable to the town, and the consent of the other overseer will be presumed, if the warrant is regular on its face, and recites an application by both.

PRESUMPTION THAT AN OVERSEER OF THE POOR ACTED REGULARLY, and with the consent of his colleague, in proceeding against the property of one who has absconded leaving his family chargeable to the town, must prevail, and justify his acts until the want of such consent is affirmatively shown by the testimony of the other overseer, he being a competent witness.

RETURN IN THE NAME OF ONLY ONE OF THE OVERSEERS of the poor of a seizure of the property of one who has absconded, leaving his family chargeable to the town, is informal only, if jurisdiction has been regularly acquired, and not impeachable in an action against the overseer who made the seizure.

ISSUANCE OF A WARRANT ON INCOMPETENT TESTIMONY is merely erroneous, and does not render the proceeding void, as where the warrant is issued solely on the testimony of the wife of the person whose property is seized thereunder.

TROVER for the taking of certain chattels. Justification, that the seizure was made by the defendant as overseer of the poor of the town of Potter, in Yates county, under a warrant issued against the property of the plaintiff as having absconded, leaving his family chargeable to the public. The warrant, which was regular on its face, was introduced in evidence. The plaintiff proved, however, that the application for the warrant, the seizure, and the return were made by the defendant alone, no other overseer of the poor acting with him, and that the warrant was issued solely on the testimony of the plaintiff's wife, and insisted that the proceedings were therefore without jurisdiction, and void. The provisions of the statute and other facts are set out in the opinion. Another objection insisted on by

the plaintiff was, that the duties of the overseers of the poor of
the several towns in Yates county had been, by the supervisors,
transferred to the county superintendents of the poor, which
question was left to the jury by the judge. Verdict for the defendant. Motion for a new trial.

S. Stevens, for the plaintiff.

D. B. Prosser, for the defendant.

By Court, COWEN, J. The jury found, under the charge of
the judge, that the distinction between town and county poor
had not been abolished in the county of Yates, and the only
questions presented by this case are: 1. Whether the proceeding was void for want of action by two overseers; and if not,
then, 2. Whether it was void because the plaintiff's wife was the
sole witness before the justices.

1. The statute requires each town to elect two overseers: 1 R.
S. 332, sec. 4. I therefore think, till the contrary be shown,
we must intend there were two in the town of Potter. Besides,
it is quite doubtful whether, if there be not two, any act whatever can be done as overseer by the other. Should the town
omit to choose the requisite number, they would not pursue the
statute authority; though if one should die or be disqualified,
it would seem that the other might then act alone: 14 Vin. Abr.
Joint and Several (B), pl. 1; 45 Ass., pl. 3; Jenk. 40, case 76.
Though otherwise of judicial officers: *Auditor Curle's case*, 11
Rep. 2; Jenk. 40, case 76.

The statute under which the defendant proceeded, 1 R. S.
624, secs. 8–10, provides that when a father, etc., shall abscond,
leaving his wife and children chargeable to any town, or likely
to become so, the overseers may apply to any two justices, who,
upon due proof, may issue their warrant authorizing the overseers to seize his goods. By virtue of this warrant the overseers
may seize the goods and be vested thereby with all the owner's
right. The overseers shall make an inventory, and return it, together with their proceedings, to the next general sessions, there
to be filed; and the court may confirm the warrant and seizure,
or discharge the same. The statute in terms confers a joint authority; and containing no express provision that each of the
overseers may proceed separately, it is objected that all is void
here for want of jurisdiction, because it did not appear affirmatively that both of them actually joined in the complaint and
subsequent proceedings. The rule seems to be well established
that in the exercise of a public as well as private authority,

whether it be ministerial or judicial, all the persons to whom it is committed must confer and act together, unless there be a provision that a less number may proceed.   Where the authority is public, and the number is such as to admit of a majority, that will bind the minority, after all have duly met and conferred: *Green* v. *Miller*, 6 Johns. 39, 41 [5 Am. Dec. 184]; *Grindley* v. *Barker*, 1 Bos. & Pul. 236; 2 R. S. 458, sec. 27, 2d ed.; 3 Id. 780, note, sec. 44, referring to 6 Johns. 39; *Rex* v. *Beeston*, 3 T. R. 592, 594.   It follows, that where there are only two, nothing can be done without the consent of both.   And this has been held as a general rule where a county has two coroners or sheriffs: 6 Vin. Abr., Coroner (H), pl.; 14 Vin., *ut supra; Rex* v. *Warrington*, 1 Salk. 152.   Yet, there are authorities which hold clearly, that to prevent a failure of justice, one may act alone without consulting the other; as if one be dead, or interested, or absent where it is necessary to make an immediate arrest.   All this may be collected from Viner and Salkeld, before cited, to which may be added *Naylor* v. *Sharpless*, 2 Mod. 23; and see *Auditor Curle's case*, 11 Rep. 2, and *Rich* v. *Player*, 2 Show. 286. I should infer, from these authorities, that one overseer alone might at his pleasure make a seizure of the goods.

But admitting that it were necessary they should act jointly throughout, and that should one act without the assent of the other, all would be void, the warrant here on its face appears to be regular.   It recites the application as being made by both; and it being the duty of the acting overseer not to proceed without obtaining the other's consent, I think we are bound strongly to presume that such consent was obtained.   It can not be necessary that both should be corporally present.   The duty is strictly ministerial, and one may act alone as the agent or deputy of both, with the other's consent.   Ministerial officers may, in general, depute their powers to one another or to a third person: Toml. L. Dict., Deputy.   Can there be a doubt, that overseers of the poor, in prosecuting under the excise law, or otherwise appearing as parties, may make an attorney?   So of various other municipal officers.   This right has never been questioned, nor that they may delegate all their authority to one of their body to act as attorney.   The delegation need not be in writing; it is good, though merely oral: *Gaul* v. *Groat*, 1 Cow. 113; *Tullock* v. *Cunningham*, Id. 256.   It is very common for such officers and others, acting as commissioners under various statutes, not only to delegate in particular instances, but to agree generally, that one of the board shall act in behalf of the whole in the execution of whatever measure they may resolve on. This is convenient, and it is many times impossible that ministerial duties should be executed without the employment of agents or deputies. The law allows it in respect to such convenience, always holding the officers themselves accountable for the acts of their agents; of this, various instances are put in the *Earl of Shrewsbury's case*, 9 Rep. 48, 49. It being the duty of the overseers to act jointly, and they having power thus to act by one of their body in the mere execution of their resolves; and such too being the common course of business, which is convenient and many times absolutely necessary, a very strong intendment arises when one comes to act for all, that he has done his duty by conferring with his companions, and obtaining the requisite power.

There is also another principle on which the assent of the other overseer should be presumed. The case was a fit one for prosecution, and the suit beneficial to the town represented by the overseers. It has been often held, that any of the principles mentioned authorize a presumption that the party charged with a neglect of duty proceeded regularly. This presumption prevails till the contrary be clearly shown. One instance of presumption from official duty, is a constable being sued for making an arrest on execution without first searching for property. He shall be presumed to have made the search, and the plaintiff be put to prove the negative: *Barhydt* v. *Valk*, 12 Wend. 145, 146 [27 Am. Dec. 124]. The cases are numerous under all the heads of presumption I have mentioned, and too familiar to need citation. It was said by Bayley and Littledale, justices, in *Bailey* v. *Culverwell*, 8 Barn. & Cress. 448, that where an act is for the benefit of the party, though it be done by another without any apparent authority, a subsequent assent is sufficient, and shall be presumed. Can there be a doubt of this? Suppose one of two overseers of the poor receives money due to the poor fund, who would hesitate to presume that the other would assent to the payment?

The presumptions of which I have spoken, especially those arising from official duty, are very strong; and that the duty was not performed must be shown by calling those whose relation to the transaction can put a direct negative upon it, unless their absence be accounted for. This was distinctly held in *Williams* v. *The East India Co.*, 3 East, 192, wherein it was sought to charge the company because their officer had neglected to give notice to the plaintiff's chief mate, that certain combustibles laden by the defendants on board the plaintiff's ship were of such a character as to endanger its safety. The court presumed that the defendant's officer had given notice; and the chief mate being dead, it was held essential to produce the officer himself who delivered the materials—for want of which the plaintiff was nonsuited. Proof by the captain and second mate that they had no notice, was held to be merely circumstantial, and therefore insufficient.

In the case at bar, if the absent overseer had not given his consent and authority to proceed, he alone could say so; and I think it due to the defendant and the general safety of this kind of officers to presume they proceeded regularly, till the best sources of information are exhausted. The other overseer was a competent witness; and in his absence it was right at the circuit to regard the defendant as properly acting for both. Had the other been dead or his absence otherwise accounted for, the circumstances might have been sufficient to negative the proper authority till it was shown affirmatively. As the case stands, nothing was· shown which is necessarily inconsistent with the assent of the other overseer. The proof establishes merely that he did not appear in the matter personally. The process then must be taken to have been regularly sued out so far as authority was concerned. The seizure of the plaintiff's goods was consequently lawful, unless the proceeding be otherwise impeachable; and though the return to the general sessions should regularly have been in the name of both overseers, the omission is but an informality, which after jurisdiction properly acquired, can not be objected in this collateral action. It was but a clerical error, which might have been amended on motion so as to speak according to the legal effect of the seizure.

Next it is objected that the wife was an incompetent witness; and that the warrant was taken out on her testimony alone, there was a want of jurisdiction. But according to *Van Steenbergh* v. *Korts*, 10 Johns. 167, the admission of improper proof is a mere error of the magistrate; and can not be objected as rendering the proceeding void.

New trial denied.

———

AUTHORITY DELEGATED TO SEVERAL FOR PUBLIC OR PRIVATE PURPOSE, HOW EXERCISED: See *McCoy* v. *Curtice*, 24 Am. Dec. 113, and other cases in this series and elsewhere cited in the note to that decision. See also *Peirce* v. *N. O. Building Co.*, 29 Id. 448; *Williams* v. *School District*, 32 Id. 243, and note; and *Crocker* v. *Crane*, *post*. The general doctrine laid down in the foregoing decision, that where an authority is conferred upon several, either for a public or private purpose, and whether such power be ministerial or judicial, all must meet and confer together in order to render its exercise valid, is referred to with approval in *Schuyler* v. *Marsh*, 37 Barb. 355; *Parrott* v. *Knickerbocker Ice Co.*, 38 How. Pr. 510; S. C., 8 Abb. (N. S.) 236; *Powell* v. *Tuttle*, 3 N. Y. 401. The language of Cowen, J., on this point is said, however, in *People* v. *Walker*, 2 Abb. Pr. 427; S. C., 23 Barb. 310, to be merely dictum, not sustained by the authorities cited by him, so far as it relates to public bodies not acting judicially, and that in such cases, if a majority may decide, a majority is a quorum. In *Perry* v. *Tynen*, 22 Barb. 140, Paige, J., citing the principal case, states the rule to be, that when a public authority, judicial in its nature, is conferred on several, all must meet and consult, though a majority may decide; and that where the power is ministerial, a majority must concur in the performance of the act, but they may act separately. For the former of these two principles, *Downing* v. *Rugar* is relied on as authority in *Harris* v. *Whitney*, 6 How. Pr. 176; *Matter of Thirty-fourth Street Sewer*, 31 Id. 51; *Matter of Fourth Avenue*, 11 Abb. Pr. 200; *Keeler* v. *Frost*, 22 Barb. 401; *People* v. *Supervisors of Chenango Co.*, 11 N. Y. 571; *Johnson* v. *Dodd*, 56 Id. 79. To the point that where an act to be done by several under a public authority is performed by less than the whole number, if the proceedings are otherwise regular, it will be presumed, in the absence of proof to the contrary, that all met and consulted, the principal case is cited in *Tucker* v. *Rankin*, 15 Barb. 480; *Perry* v. *Tynen*, 22 Id. 141; *Doughty* v. *Hope*, 3 Denio, 253; *Board of Commissioners* v. *Doherty*, 16 How. Pr. 49; *Board of Excise* v. *Sackrider*, 35 N. Y. 158; *People* v. *Palmer*, 52 Id. 87.

PRESUMPTION THAT OFFICIAL DUTY WAS REGULARLY PERFORMED: See *Hartwell* v. *Root*, 10 Am. Dec. 232; *Terry* v. *Bleight*, 16 Id. 101; *Farr* v. *Sims*, 24 Id. 396. The principal case is cited as an authority on this subject in *Brick's estate*, 15 Abb. Pr. 41; *Tuthill* v. *Wheeler*, 6 Barb. 366; *Miller* v. *Lewis*, 4 N. Y. 568.

JUSTIFICATION OF OFFICERS BY THEIR PROCESS.—This subject is discussed at length in the note to *Savacool* v. *Boughton*, 21 Am. Dec. 190. See also *Carle* v. *Delesdernier*, 29 Id. 508; *Parker* v. *Walrod*, 30 Id. 124; *Pierson* v. *Gale*, Id. 487; *Lewis* v. *Avery*, Id. 469; *Haskins* v. *Young*, 31 Id. 426, and the notes to those decisions referring to other cases in this series on the same point.

CROCKER *v.* CRANE.

[21 WENDELL, 211.]

NOTARY'S CERTIFICATE IS PRIMA FACIE SUFFICIENT EVIDENCE that notice of non-payment of a check was properly directed.

SPECIAL WORDS ARE NOT ESSENTIAL TO REVIVE A STATUTE providing for the construction of a railroad, which has expired because the work has not been commenced within the time therein limited, but a statute passed after such expiration extending the time, will be a sufficient revivor.

RECEIVING SUBSCRIPTIONS OF STOCK IS A MINISTERIAL ACT under a statute authorizing commissioners to take subscriptions, and subsequently to distribute the stock, and such act may be performed by an agent or deputy, or by one without authority, whose act is afterwards ratified by the commissioners.

DISTRIBUTION OF STOCK IS A JUDICIAL ACT under a statute empowering certain commissioners to distribute the stock of a corporation among the subscribers "in such manner as they shall deem most conducive to the interests of the said corporation," and all the commissioners must be present and consult respecting such distribution, or the proceeding will be without jurisdiction and void.

Commissioners Exercising Judicial Powers under a statute must all meet and consult, though a majority may decide.

Distribution of Stock is a Condition Precedent to the existence of a corporation under a statute providing that certain parties and such other persons as shall become stockholders shall constitute the corporation.

Check Given for Stock in a Corporation which Acquires no Existence because the stock is not distributed by the number of commissioners required to constitute a legal board, is void for want of consideration.

Commissioners have no Authority to Receive Indorsed Checks in Lieu of Cash, especially where it is known that the drawers have no funds, under an act authorizing them to take subscriptions for stock in a corporation, and requiring the payment of a certain sum upon each share at the time of subscription, and a check so taken is void as against the policy of the statute.

Judge and not the Jury must Decide whether Checks are Receivable instead of cash in payment of a percentage required by statute to be paid at the time of subscribing for stock in a corporation.

Fraud Practiced by Commissioner upon his Co-commissioners as to the distribution of stock in a corporation, that being a matter in which they are acting judicially, does not render their proceedings void as respects the subscribers, if they have jurisdiction in the premises.

Misapplication of a Check Taken upon a Subscription of stock in a corporation by paying it away upon the private debt of one of the directors, will not vitiate it if otherwise valid.

Assumpsit against the defendant, as drawer of a certain check, payable to the order of one Saxton, and indorsed by him and certain other parties. The plaintiffs introduced the certificate of a notary to prove presentment and notice, from which it appeared that the notice was sent by mail to the drawer and indorsers at Fredonia, but there being no evidence offered to show that they resided at that place, the defendant moved for a nonsuit on that ground, and also on the ground of an alleged variance between the check produced in evidence and that described in the plaintiffs' bill of particulars. The motion was overruled. From the evidence offered by the defendant, it appeared that the check in question was given in payment of the percentage required by statute upon a subscription by the defendant for certain shares of stock in the Buffalo and Erie railroad company. The evidence tended further to show that the commissioners who took the subscription and received the check, knew that the defendant had no funds in the bank, and trusted entirely to the credit of the drawer and indorsers, and that it was the understanding that it was not to be presented for thirty days. The evidence as to the commissioners' practice in taking uncurrent bills and indorsed checks from other subscribers, is sufficiently stated in the opinion. It further appeared that some of the commissioners appointed by the act to receive subscriptions, were not present when the subscriptions were received, nor when the stock was distributed. This was one of the grounds relied on by the defendant as rendering the proceedings void, and his check worthless. It further appeared that one of the commissioners practiced a fraud on his colleagues by acting, without their knowledge, as the agent of a person who desired to have the road established along a certain route, and by procuring large subscriptions of stock for his benefit, in the names of other parties. The result was, that although the majority of the commissioners intended, in distributing the stock, to give a majority of it to those favoring another route, they were induced by the practices of their colleague, to distribute the majority of the stock to those subscribers who favored the route preferred by the person in whose interest such colleague was acting. It further appeared that the defendant's check was put in circulation with others, contrary to the express directions of a majority of the commissioners, made after discovering the fraud practiced on them, and it was paid away on the private debt of Van Buren, one of the directors of the corporation. The plaintiffs admitted that the check in their hands was subject to the same equities as it would be in the hands of the corporation. It further appeared that the construction of the road was not commenced until July, 1836, after the expiration of the time limited in the original act of incorporation of April 14, 1832. The plaintiffs contended, however, that the provisions of that act were revived and continued by the act of May 7, 1836, by which the time for commencing the work was extended, and the judge so charged the jury against the request of the defendant. The judge also instructed the jury, contrary to the request and prayer of the defendant, that the commissioners acted ministerially, and not judicially, in receiving subscriptions and distributing the stock, although they had a discretion as to the persons who should receive stock and the amounts, and that therefore all need not concur, but a majority could act; and that the fraudulent conduct of one of the commissioners did not invalidate the proceedings of the majority who acted in good faith, and though it might affect the title of those for whom such commissioner obtained stock, it could not affect the defendant, who had received his stock in precise accordance with his subscription and with the intention of the majority of the commissioners, and had voted upon it, and could not now object that others had been defrauded, or that he would have realized greater benefits if the majority of the stock had been issued to other parties than those who had obtained it through the fraudulent conduct of one of the commissioners. The judge also, contrary to the request of the defendant, left it to the jury to decide, as a matter of fact, whether the checks received by the commissioners were received in the ordinary course of business as cash payments, without any agreement to give credit to the subscribers, and instructed them that if they should so find, it would be a valid payment under the statute. Verdict for the plaintiffs, and a motion for a new trial, based on exceptions to the rulings of the judge at the circuit.

A. Taber and S. Stevens, for the defendant, claimed: ·1· That the nonsuit should have been allowed; first, because of the variance above referred to, and second, because there was no evidence that the notice was sent to the drawer's place of residence. 2. That the act of 1832 was not revived by the act of 1836. 3. That the acts of the commissioners in receiving subscriptions and distributing stock were void because all did not unite. 4. That the check was void; first, because taken without authority, and second, because there was no legal payee. 5. That the check was void because the commissioners could take cash only in payment. 6. That the fraud of one of the commissioners vitiated the proceedings. 7. That the misapplication of the check would bar a recovery.

M. T. Reynolds, for the plaintiffs.

By Court, COWEN, J. The first subdivision of the plaintiff's first point does not arise. The declaration and bill of particulars delivered with it are not set out in the bill of exceptions, so that we can judge whether there was a variance or not from the check given in evidence. As to the second subdivision of the first point, the notary's certificate is not set forth. *Non constat,* but it was well on its face, and sufficient to prove notice. If the objection mean that independent proof should have been given that the notice was properly directed, that is a mistake. The certificate is, *per se, prima facie* sufficient evidence that it was properly directed: 2 R. S. 212, sec. 46, 2d ed.

The second point of the defendant is not well taken. The act of 1836 does not say in terms that the first act shall be revived; but it does the same thing by implication. The first act

had expired by its own provision, because the road had not been
commenced within four years. The last act declares that the
time shall be extended, and then professes to amend the former
act and repeal parts of it. The meaning of the legislature is
perfectly plain; and apt words are not essential: Dwarris on
Statutes, 702, 703.

As to the defendant's third and fourth points, the receiving
of subscriptions was not a ministerial act. Any one had a right
to subscribe and pay in the four per cent. Such an act might
be allowed by an agent or deputy appointed by the commissioners, or by one without authority at the time; the acts being
afterwards ratified by the board. But the question is different
as to the distribution of stock. The fourth section provides
that "if more than six hundred and fifty thousand dollars shall
have been subscribed, they (the commissioners) shall distribute
the said stock among the several subscribers in such manner as
they shall deem most conducive to the interests of the said corporation:" Statutes, ses. of 1832, p. 191. Here, it appears to
me, is a judicial power vested in the commissioners; a power to
exercise a discretion founded on such considerations as may appear to them beneficial to the company's interests. These may
be various and important, while the decision is in its nature beyond the reach of appeal: *Walker* v. *Devereaux*, 4 Paige, 229.
And see *The People ex rel. Case* v. *Collins*, 19 Wend. 56, 60, etc.
Then it has long been perfectly well settled that where a statute
constitutes a board of commissioners or other officers to decide
any matter, but makes no provision that a majority shall constitute a quorum, all must be present to hear and consult, though
a majority may then decide: *Ex parte Rogers*, 7 Cow. 526, 529, 530,
and the cases there cited, and see note (a). The statute, 2 R. S.
458, sec 27, 2d ed., was passed in affirmance of this rule, which
it adopts in terms. The rule has been applied to ordinary commissioners of highways: *Babcock* v. *Lamb*, 1 Cow. 238, and a
statute was thought necessary to qualify the rule in this case,
which has been done slightly by 1 R. S. 520, sec. 129, 2d ed.

The statute in question, section 1, provides that Heman McClure,
Benjamin Walworth, John Crane, and such other persons as
shall become stockholders, shall constitute the corporation, and
if no stock was distributed, there is no corporation. The objection that there was no party payee who could legally receive the
check, is unfounded in fact. Saxton was a competent payee
But the awarding and distributing of the stock by the proper
authority was a condition precedent to the existence of the cor

poration. This is the view taken by the present chancellor in
Walker v. *Devereaux*, 4 Paige, 229, upon a statute with similar
provisions as to the mode of organization, under which the Utica
and Schenectady railroad company was constituted, and which
view I am satisfied is perfectly sound. The distribution being
conducted throughout by a number of commissioners not sufficient to constitute a legal board, was *coram non judice*, and void.
It follows that there never was any corporation. The defendant
got no stock, and all consideration for the check has failed.
See also the reasoning of Lansing, chancellor, in *Jenkins* v.
Union Turnpike Co., 1 Cai. Cas. in Err. 94, 95.

With regard to the fifth point, the commissioners, in a matter
wherein they had a right to act, received uncurrent money and
indorsed checks, instead of cash for the percentage, required
by the act to be paid at the time of the subscription. I can not
collect from the evidence that they made any serious stand on
the condition that cash should be paid. By cash I mean specie,
or its equivalent in current bills of specie-paying banks. They
received uncurrent money for a while, and at last resolved to
receive checks, lending an easy ear to the presumption urged
upon them, that a drawer of a check had current funds in place.
I can not feel a doubt on reading the evidence that the whole
was a mere evasion of the statute. In that I certainly differ
from the jury to whom the question was left. It ought not to
have been left to a jury, whether knowingly paying and receiving uncurrent money was a compliance with the mandate of the
legislature. At what discount the money stood does not appear.
It must, I think, have been wretchedly worthless to have been
uncurrent amid the inflations of 1836. The checks were received
mainly because they were preferred to this uncurrent money.
There was some question started whether the drawers had funds,
those very drawers too who had, it seems, nothing but uncurrent
money to pay. A good indorser was required; but looking at
the whole transaction, this was evidently a substitution of individual credit for cash payment. Giving time of payment was
talked of, inasmuch as the money would not be wanted for immediate use. I think the jury fell into a plain mistake when,
under the charge of the judge, they pronounced this the ordinary course of receiving checks, to effectuate a cash payment.
Why are they taken as cash in the ordinary course of business?
Because they are a mere transfer of money which a man has at
his banker's. I do not deny that receiving an occasional check
might have been a fair substitute. But checks being crowded

on the commissioners in a mass, because no subscriber had
anything but uncurrent money to pay, is another matter. The
commissioners might as well have received anything else which
an accommodating construction would call an equivalent for
cash. But the statute did not allow a mere equivalent. It would
not, for instance, have recognized a mortgage or stocks as a payment, of whatever value. The commissioners were here acting
ministerially, and if they have not pursued the purposes of the
statute, their acts can not be sustained.

I am therefore strongly inclined to the opinion that the check
in question was void, as contrary to the policy of the statute.
Nor can there be any doubt, I imagine, that the comtemplated
corporation, if I am right as to the facts, failed of going into
existence, for want of the proper payments as a condition precedent. Such is the doctrine laid down by Chancellor Lansing in
Jenkins v. *Union Turnpike Co.*, 1 Cai. Cas. in Err. 94, 95, and
recognized by this court in *Goshen Turnpike Co.* v. *Hurtin*, 9
Johns. 217 [6 Am. Dec. 273]; and see *Highland T. P. Co.* v. *Mc-
Kean*, 11 Johns. 98, and *Dutchess Cotton Manufactory* v. *Davis*,
14 Id. 238 [7 Am. Dec. 459]. These cases go farther. Each subscriber must pay as a condition to his own liability attaching.
Payment was a requisite which the commissioners could not
waive: *Starr* v. *Scott*, 8 Conn. 483.

As to the sixth point: the fraud practiced by one of the commissioners was, I think, properly treated by the judge as not
vitiating the whole proceeding, if it had been otherwise regular.
He deceived his co-commissioners, who took it upon them to distribute the stock. In this they acted judicially; and had they
been a quorum, their judgment would have been binding, notwithstanding the fraud. A judgment is sometimes void where
it is got up collusively, and with a view to cheat a third person,
who has no chance of being heard. It is then void in respect
to that person, who may impeach it in a collateral suit. But it
is never holden void as to a party who has legal notice and may
be heard to contest it, even though the judges and party complaining may be defrauded either in respect to the form of proceeding or the merits. The party injured being before the court,
must take his remedy there in the course of the suit. That a
stranger may impeach a covinous or collusive judgment, see *The
Duchess of Kingston's case, passim*, 11 St. Tr. 198, Hargr. ed.,
and especially page 262. But that a party or privy shall not,
see 1 Ph. Ev., 7th Lond. ed. 346; *Peck* v. *Woodbridge*, 3 Day, 30;
and note (c) to *Doe dem. Day* v. *Haddon*, 3 Doug. 312, 313.

Where, in a proceeding like that now in question, a quorum of commissioners assemble and the payments are regularly made, the board acquire jurisdiction, and the subscribers are to be considered as parties to the adjudication, by which the stock is distributed. The objection that the check was misapplied, being turned out by Van Buren, may be true; but it would not vitiate it, if it was valid in its concoction, or if it became valid by the due organization of the company. In such an event, it could not be material to the defendant in what name the collection was enforced. He would obtain his stock and pay the stipulated compensation; and the directors would be accountable for the amount of the check, at least Van Buren would be, if, as suggested, he was one of them. The point, however, does not appear to have been raised at the trial.

But as the corporation do not appear to have been organized, there having been no quorum to distribute the stock; and as the receiving of the uncurrent money and checks was in fraud of the statute, the check in question is void, both as wanting a consideration, and as an act which violated the policy of the law.

New trial granted; costs to abide the event.

NOTARY'S CERTIFICATE AS EVIDENCE OF NOTICE: See *Stewart* v. *Allison*, 9 Am. Dec. 433; *Browne* v. *Philadelphia Bank*, Id. 463; *Smith* v. *McManus*, 27 Id. 519; *Smith* v. *Janes*, 32 Id. 527, and cases cited in the notes thereto.

AUTHORITY DELEGATED TO SEVERAL, HOW EXECUTED: See *Downing* v. *Rugar, ante*, 223, and cases cited in the note thereto. To the point that where a public authority is conferred upon several, all must meet and consult, unless the statute makes a less number a quorum, though a majority may decide, especially where the power is judicial in its nature, the principal case is cited as authority in *Doughty* v. *Hope*, 3 Denio, 253; *Perry* v. *Tynen*, 22 Barb. 140; *Keeler* v. *Frost*, Id. 400; *Parrott* v. *Knickerbocker Ice Co.*, 38 How. Pr. 510; S. C., 8 Abb. Pr. (N. S.) 236; *Oakley* v. *Aspinwall*, 3 N. Y. 565; *People* v. *Nostrand*, 46 Id. 383; *Birge* v. *People*, 5 Park. Crim. 13; *People* v. *Coghill*, 47 Cal. 363; *Peay* v. *Schenck*, Woolw. C. C. 188. Where, however, the majority act, and the proceeding is regular, the presence and concurrence of all will be presumed, in the absence of evidence to the contrary: *Tucker* v. *Rankin*, 15 Barb. 480, also citing the principal case.

PAYMENT OF PERCENTAGE REQUIRED BY STATUTE ON SUBSCRIPTIONS OF STOCK is a condition precedent, which, if dispensed with, renders the subscription void: *Hibernia T. Corp.* v. *Henderson*, 11 Am. Dec. 593.

PAYMENT BY CHECK, WHETHER PAYMENT IN CASH.—To the general position that a payment by check is not a cash payment, particularly in cases where payment on a percentage on a subscription of stock is required, the principal case is cited in *Ogdensburgh etc. R. R. Co.* v. *Wolley*, 1 Keyes, 130, per Johnson, J., dissenting; *Syracuse etc. R. R. Co.* v. *Gere*, 4 Hun, 394; S. C., 6 N. Y. S. C. (T. & C.) 638. In *Thorp* v. *Woodhull*, 1 Sandf. Ch. 417, which, like the case last above cited, was one relating to the payment of the percentage required by statute on a subscription of stock, *Crocker* v. *Crane* was commented on, and it was held, following the intimation of Cowen, J.,. that an occasional receipt of payment by the subscriber's check would not be invalid. In the case of *Beach* v. *Smith*, 28 Barb. 261, which was also one involving the validity of a payment of the required percentage on a subscription of stock, Bacon, J., referring to Wendell's report of *Crocker* v. *Crane*, says: "The marginal note of the reporter states, as a point decided by the court, that the company was not authorized to receive checks in payment of the sum required to be paid, but that specie or its equivalent current bills of specie-paying banks must be demanded. Looking at the facts in that case, and the opinion of the court, it is manifest that they intended to hold no such broad proposition as this." His honor then goes on to show that the decision in the principal case, being limited to the facts before the court, related simply to the validity of a payment by check upon such a subscription where it was known that the drawer had no funds.

INTENTION GOVERNS IN CONSTRUING A STATUTE if such intention can be discovered, though it be apparently contrary to the letter of the statute: *People* v. *Deming*, 1 Hilt. 274; S. C., 13 How. Pr. 444, citing *Crocker* v. *Crane*. That the intention has a controlling influence in the construction of a statute, see *People* v. *Utica Ins. Co.*, 8 Am. Dec. 243; *Orndorff* v. *Turman*, 21 Id. 608; but the intention must be sought for in the statute itself: *Salling* v. *McKinney*, 19 Id. 722.

MORRIS *v.* SCOTT.

[21 WENDELL, 281.]

CASE FOR MALICIOUS PROSECUTION IN COURT WITHOUT JURISDICTION will lie if the malice and falsehood be put forward as the gravamen and the arrest as the consequence. Hence, in such an action an allegation that the court had jurisdiction is unnecessary.

ERROR from Alleghany common pleas in an action on the case for a malicious prosecution. The charge was that the defendant had maliciously and without probable cause complained to a magistrate against the plaintiff, and caused his arrest for the offense of assisting a party in removing his property to defraud his creditors, upon which charge the plaintiff was tried and acquitted. Under a plea of the general issue, evidence offered to prove the declaration was excluded, because there was no allegation that the magistrate had jurisdiction. Nonsuit, and the plaintiff brought error.

S. B. Cooley, for the plaintiff.

G. Miles, for the defendant.

By Court, COWEN, J. Authorities are cited by the counsel for the plaintiff in error, that an action on the case lies for a malicious prosecution, although the court in which it is instituted had no jurisdiction. *Goslin* v. *Wilcock*, 2 Wils. 302. In

Smith v. *Cattel*, Id. 376, it is said: "The sting of all these kinds of actions is malice and falsehood, and the injury done in pursuance thereof." The question has also been much discussed in a later case, on error: *Elsee* v. *Smith*, 1 Dow. & Ry. 97; S. C., 2 Chit. 304. A party who pursues a man by arrest in a court destitute of jurisdiction, may be sued in trespass for the false imprisonment; and the objection is, that whatever might have been his malice, and however plain the want of probable cause, the injured man can not bring an action on the case, especially if he mention and claim damages in his declaration for the arrest and imprisonment. In such case, he has committed an assault and false imprisonment, an act which, in its own nature, is a trespass *vi et armis*. But taking the authorities together, they give a decided countenance to an action on the case, though there may be a total want of jurisdiction, provided the malice and falsehood be put forward as the gravamen, and the arrest or other act of trespass be claimed as the consequence. This case, therefore, as it stood at the common law, seems properly set down by Mr. Chitty as presenting a right to elect between case and trespass: 1 Chit. Pl. 127, Phil. ed. of 1828. But, be that as it may, a clear right of election arises under the statute: 2 R. S. 456, 2d ed., sec. 16. By that section, case may now be brought for almost any trespass affecting the person or personal property. Conceding, therefore, that the declaration failed to show jurisdiction, the evidence offered should have been received.

The judgment must be reversed, and a *venire de novo* go from the court below, the costs to abide the event.

CASE WILL LIE FOR MALICIOUS PROSECUTION IN COURT HAVING NO JURISDICTION, WHEN: See *Stone* v. *Stevens*, 30 Am. Dec. 611, in the note to which the previous cases in this series respecting actions on the case for a malicious prosecution are collected. The doctrine above laid down, that case will lie for a malicious prosecution in a court having no jurisdiction, where malice and falsehood are the gravamen of the offense, is referred to with apparent approval in *Platt* v. *Niles*, 1 Edm. 232, but is held not to apply where malice and falsehood are not the gravamen. In the same case in the supreme court the principal case was again distinguished: *Rice* v. *Platt*, 3 Denio, 83. The case is also cited as somewhat analogous to the one before the court in *Dennis* v. *Ryan*, 63 Barb. 149; S. C., 5 Lans. 251; S. C. in court of appeals, 65 N. Y. 389. In that case the prosecution complained of was in a court of competent jurisdiction, but the charge on which the prosecution was instituted did not constitute a crime.

HOWARD *v.* THOMPSON.

[21 WENDELL, 819.]

ACTION FOR LIBEL LIES FOR ADDRESSING LETTERS TO PUBLIC OFFICER CHARGING SUBORDINATE, whom he is authorized to remove, with fraud and malfeasance in the execution of his trust; but to maintain the action the plaintiff must prove malice and want of probable cause, as in an action for malicious prosecution.

KNOWLEDGE OR INFORMATION OF A CONVERSION OF PUBLIC PROPERTY BY AN OFFICER to his own use, furnishes sufficient probable cause for addressing a letter to such officer's superior to procure his removal to defeat an action of libel therefor, or at least to be left to the jury, although, unknown to the defendant, such conversion was authorized, and although the defendant was actuated by ill-will.

PROBABLE CAUSE, WHERE THE FACTS ARE UNDISPUTED, is a question of law in actions for malicious prosecution or for libel in the nature of malicious prosecution.

DEFENDANT HAVING PLEADED JUSTIFICATION MAY WAIVE SUCH PLEA at the trial and rely upon proof of probable cause, in actions for malicious prosecution or *quasi* such, because probable cause is a complete bar to the action in such cases, and not merely matter of mitigation.

ACTION for libel. The case appears sufficiently from the opinion. Motion for a new trial after a verdict for the plaintiff.

D. Lord, jun., and *J. W. Gerard*, for the defendant.

H. Nicoll, for the plaintiff.

By Court, COWEN, J. This is an action in which the plaintiff, Howard, complains, that while he held the office of inspector of the customs and keeper of the public stores of the United States, the defendant falsely libeled him by addressing certain letters to the secretary of the treasury, charging and offering to prove that the plaintiff had been guilty of fraud in the execution of his trust as such keeper; specifying particularly the conversion of timber belonging to the United States in 1832. The secretary of the treasury was the officer who had legal cognizance of the complaint, and the power of removing the plaintiff on its being substantiated. For some reason, however, the investigation, which we must presume was duly made, proved so unsatisfactory to the secretary, that he thought it his duty to deliver up the letters to the plaintiff; and they were used by him as evidence to the jury. The defendant had given notice with his plea, that he would prove the truth of his charge in bar; and seems to have entertained the confidence of being able to do it, till, on the trial, he became so doubtful of success in convincing the jury, that on the plaintiff's resting, he avowedly abandoned the attempt, and staked his defense: 1. Upon the unwarrantable nature of the prosecution; and 2. On evidence that, though he might have been mistaken, yet the circumstances were such as to have afforded at least probable cause for the representations he had made. The first ground was presented in the form of a motion for a nonsuit, insisting that the plaintiff must, as in the ordinary case of a malicious prosecution, show a want of probable cause. The judge thought otherwise, holding that the proof given of the defendant's ill will towards the plaintiff was enough to carry the cause to the jury. This presents the first question which we are called upon to examine. Does a complaint addressed by a citizen to the proper tribunal against another, from motives of ill will towards the latter, subject the complainant to an action of slander, as for a libel, unless it be apparent that it was without probable cause? It may be put still more shortly; is it subject to be prosecuted as a libel? Must it not be pursued as a malicious prosecution or complaint?

This is not precisely like the case of a written communication between private persons, concerning their own affairs, nor was it addressed to a man or a set of men chosen by a voluntary society, a bishop or presbytery for example, and having, by common consent among the members, a power to redress grievances. It is therefore not necessary to inquire whether, in such instances, an action for a libel may not be brought in the common form. It has generally been so brought; and, though the communication has been deemed *prima facie* privileged, yet I believe where ill will towards the plaintiff has appeared, or motives of interest, and the defendant has failed in proving at least probable cause, the action has generally been sustained. The rule in respect to such mere private communications seems to have been laid down very sensibly by Mr. Justice J. Parke, in *Cockayne* v. *Hodgkisson*, 5 Car. & P. 543. The defendant had made representations by letter to Lord Anglesey against his gamekeeper. In an action by the latter, the defendant failed to prove the truth, relying on the good faith with which he made the communication. The judge left it to the jury, mainly on the letter itself, whether it was such as a man would write merely wishing to put Lord Anglesey on his guard, and cause him to institute an inquiry; or whether the defendant was actuated by malice, and wished to supplant the plaintiff. In the former case, he said the defendant was entitled to a verdict; in the latter, the plaintiff. This too was after very clear proof that the defendant had been told the stories which he had written to

Lord Anglesey, and seems to have had probable cause.   He had
also been requested by Lord Anglesey to give him information
of anything wrong.   The letter was put on the naked footing of
a libel; for it was said the defendant could not prove its truth
without a plea of justification; which is clearly otherwise where
an action is brought for a malicious prosecution.

The principle of the case cited and a number of others which
preceded it, is very obvious.   The private business of society
could not be conducted without the liberty of speaking and
writing in the honest pursuit of its purposes, even though,
under other circumstances, the words would be slanderous; and
though all that is said be a mistake, yet the words shall not,
for that reason alone, be actionable.   The distinction was a good
deal considered in *Bromage* v. *Prosser*, 4 Barn. & Cress. 247,
where it was allowed in a case of oral slander.   And see Holt on
Libels, 197; also *Delany* v. *Jones*, 4 Esp. 191.   But actual ill
will towards the plaintiff may raise a presumption in the mind
of the jury, that the appearance of a lawful purpose was assumed in order to injure him.   When they are brought to believe this, it is their duty to find that the defendant acted in
fraud of the law, which gives the privilege, and award damages
against him.   Whenever the communication is, for this or
any other cause, taken out of the protective rule, the law
acts upon it directly as a slander.

The rule is known to be different where the communication
made or caused is in itself the institution of a judicial inquiry.
There, if it be apparently pertinent, it is absolutely exempt from
the legal imputation of slander; and the party injured is turned
round to a different remedy, an action for malicious prosecution;
wherein he is bound to prove in the first instance, not merely
that the communication was made in bad faith; but that it was
not countenanced by probable cause.   Such is the familiar instance of a criminal complaint addressed to a judicial magistrate or a grand jury, which results in a warrant or an indictment:
1 Curzon's Hawk. 554.   The same thing may be said of any
other definite or specific step in he progress of the cause; as
the presentment of the bill in open court by the grand jury, Id.,
or the publication of it by the clerk or prosecuting attorney
upon arraignment.   And yet many things may occur incidentally
in the course of the cause, which would subject the speaker to
an action of slander.   Such are slanderous words spoken untruly and impertinently by witnesses, or by counsel: *Ring* v.
Wheeler, 7 Cow. 725.   Such words communicated in writing .

would be the subject of an action, as a libel. The ordinary prosecutor of an indictment may doubtless make himself liable in an action of slander in the same way, by what he may incidentally say of the case. Sergeant Hawkins lays down the rule of exemption, as it stands upon the cases in respect to the definite proceedings in a cause, without any qualification. But he throws out the idea upon his own authority, that a malicious prosecution may subject the guilty participators in it to an action, as for a libel: Hawk. P. C., b. 1, c. 28, sec. 8. He does not, however, pretend to be countenanced by authority; and it would be very difficult to apply the suggestion even to the prosecutor of an indictment any more than to the ministers of justice: See per Best, J., in *Fairman* v. *Ives*, 5 Barn. & Ald. 648. Sound policy would seem to exempt the prosecutor to the same extent as the grand jury. Either is liable to an action for corruptly procuring an indictment; but to treat it directly as a libel, would be quite as effectual in discouraging due inquiries concerning crime, when applied to the former, as to the latter. The law, therefore, seems to require in such case, a remedy more specific in form, and calling for more evidence to sustain it, than it receives as sufficient in an action for an ordinary libel.

Another class of writings has, in practice, been pursued as libels. These are such as contain false and scandalous matter, addressed to executive, administrative, or other officers intrusted with the power of appointment to or removal from inferior offices; and seeking either to prevent appointments or promote removals, on charges importing want of integrity, or other causes of unfitness. Such was a petition to the council of appointment, praying the removal of a district attorney: *Thorn* v. *Blanchard*, 5 Johns. 508; a deposition made with the view of presenting it to the governor of Pennsylvania, containing charges against a justice of the peace: *Gray* v. *Pentland*, 2 Serg. & R. 23; and a memorial to a board of excise, remonstrating against the granting of a tavern license: *Vanderzee* v. *McGregor*, 12 Wend. 545 [27 Am. Dec. 156]. In regard to such writings, there is certainly no authority for saying that, in form, the injured party shall be put to his action for a malicious prosecution, complaint, or remonstrance; nor would it, perhaps, be safe to interpose such a restriction. Although the reason for giving countenance to information may be of as much force as that in respect to judicial prosecutions for crime, yet the precautions against ill-founded charges and irregularities in conducting them are much less; nor is there any restraint by settled precedents and forms of proceed-

ing. To this intermediate class between judicial prosecutions
and privileged communications in regard to matters having no
immediate connection with the functions of government, the
letters in question belong. The form of the action we take to be
correct, but this is certainly not decisive of what shall be deemed
full proof to sustain it. Must the plaintiff show not only malice
but want of probable cause, the same as if the action had been
technically for a malicious prosecution? The evidence established no publication at large, none in the newspapers, no reading to the neighbors. The letters were addressed to the officer
having the power, and on whom rested the duty to remove, if
the cause assigned were found by him to be true; and they were
forwarded directly to him. Nothing impertinent can be imputed
to them. There is not the least doubt that, so far, they were for
the reasons assigned in *Thorn* v. *Blanchard*, and other cases already cited in connection with that, as much without the doctrine
of libel as an indictment. They were equally, not to say still
more so, upon the reasoning of *Fairman* v. *Ives* and other English cases hereafter to be noticed; for some of the latter, I think,
take them absolutely out of the doctrine, under any qualification.

They very nearly resemble the printed book sought to be
prosecuted in *Rex* v. *Baille*, 2 Esp. N. P. 91, Gould's ed. of
1811. It contained an account of the abuses of Greenwich hospital, treating the officers of that institution, and Lord Sand-
wich in particular, who was then first lord of the admiralty, with
much asperity; but copies were distributed among the govern-
ors of the hospital only. On motion for a criminal information, Lord Mansfield stopped the prosecution, on the point that
such a proceeding did not amount even to a publication. He
put it on the ground that the distribution had been confined to
persons who were, from their situation, called on to redress the
grievances complained of, and had, from their situation, power
to do it. If this was not a publication, certainly no private action could have been maintained as for a libel: Holt on Libels,
290, N. Y. ed. 1818. The party must have been turned over to
an action for a malicious prosecution of the complaint, in which
form he must have shown, on his own side, a want of probable
cause. It is better, perhaps, that such a form of action should
not be exacted. There is room, I think, for saying, on principle and authority, that on showing enough to take away the
privilege, that is to say, when the party has defrauded the rule
which confers it, he is a false libeler. The rule is void as to
him. What facts work a nullity? It does not follow that be-

cause we allow an action of slander, the defendant should,
therefore, be put to justify, as in the ordinary action, by proving the truth. That is not so even as to writings which concern
private matters. On its appearing that they are privileged, the
defendant is protected under the general issue, until malice is
shown. When we come to information, in which not only the
interests of the private citizen as related to the country, but
those of the nation itself are concerned, the difficulty of turning a case against him, wherein he is presented as *prima facie* in
the path of honest duty, certainly ought not to be less; and
both the prevailing opinions in *Thorn* v. *Blanchard*, which was
decided by the court of errors, required more. They held that
the action, though in form for a libel, was in the nature of a
malicious prosecution. L'Hommedieu, senator, said the council
of appointment being a court, if he might so call it, to hear all
complaints against officers, etc., there is an implied protection
for the complainants, unless it can be proved that the complaints
were malicious: 5 Johns. 527. Clinton, senator, carried these
premises out more distinctly to their consequences. He said it
was incumbent on the plaintiff to prove that the petition was
false, malicious, and groundless; and he goes into the reasons
at length, repeating and illustrating the position: Id. 529, *et seq.*

The case of *Gray* v. *Pentland*, before the supreme court of
Pennsylvania, was of the same character; and I understand all
the judges as admitting that the suit, though in form for a libel,
was in the nature of an action for a malicious prosecution;
though they do not, like the opinions in *Thorn* v. *Blanchard*,
throw, in express terms, the *onus* of showing want of probable
cause on the plaintiff. *Fairman* v. *Ives*, 5 Barn. & Ald. 642, was
an action for a libel. The paper complained of was a representation by a creditor of the plaintiff, a half-pay officer, addressed
to the secretary of war, charging him with fraudulently evading
the payment of a debt. All the court agreed that, if the representation was honestly made, that was a defense under the general issue. Holroyd, J., mentioned as an analogous case, words
spoken by a barrister in the course of a cause, in which he said,
"it may not, perhaps, be sufficient to allege and show even that
the words are false and malicious, without also alleging and
showing that they were uttered without reasonable or probable
cause." Best, J., said he did not think there was a sufficient
publication to support the action; and mentioned the case of
Greenwich Hospital; but adds, "if the communication be made
maliciously and without probable cause," an action will lie. In

Vanderzee v. *McGregor,* 12 Wend. 545 [27 Am. Dec. 156], there was a failure to prove either malice or want of probable cause; and the court said the plaintiff could not recover without proving express malice. It was unnecessary to go farther. The court professedly acted upon the authority of *Thorn* v. *Blanchard;* and they could not mean to imply that you may recover on showing malice, where there appears to have been probable cause, contrary to the strong expressions in that case, nor even to deny that the plaintiff must himself show a want of probable cause. In the principal case, there was nothing to throw a shade of suspicion upon the motive. It was the simple remonstrance of a neighbor against the licensing of a tippling shop, which is, I must say, somewhat unfortunately, still recognized as an object of legal protection, *lucri causa.* It was a call to withhold the privilege of peddling popular poison from hands which were believed to have abused that privilege. It is to be feared there are too many real not to say melancholy causes of personal offense against dealers in alcohol; cases of private suffering, which may engender hatred and malice in those who are reached by its influence; and shall their state of mind, where they act upon probable appearances, though mistaken in the fact, be imputed to them as a fraud *per se* upon the protective rule? In *Fairman* v. *Ives,* the creditor showed in his letter to the secretary of war, that he must have been greatly provoked by the apparently mean evasions which the half-pay officer had practiced, to avoid the payment of his honest debt; and though it turned out that the creditor was mistaken, the court held him protected by probable cause, without regard to his state of mind. He was there personally interested; and the supposed provocation had rankled into a sinister desire to punish the delinquent—express malice of a severe complexion; yet the protective rule was held to be unbroken. In this case, too, as we have seen, Best, J., like Lord Mansfield, in the case of *Greenwich Hospital,* denied that the paper had been so published as to make it a libel. That is clearly going farther than did Clinton, senator, in *Thorn* v. *Blanchard;* for he thus not only demands the same measure of proof, as in an action for a malicious prosecution, but the same form of action *mutatis mutandis,* while *Thorn* v. *Blanchard* is content with the proof.

If the action is to be regarded as standing on the same footing as to evidence, with one for a malicious prosecution, I need hardly go into the authorities to prove that whatever degree of malice may be shown, it is still necessary to go farther, and establish want of probable cause. The cases of *Purcel* v. *Mc-Namara*, 1 Camp. 199; *Incledon* v. *Berry*, Id. 203, note (a), with Id. 206, note (a), and the authorities there cited, are full to the point. The cases to the same point are yet more fully collected in 2 Sel. N. P., Phil. ed. 1839, p. 1079, note (2). And *vide* per Nelson, J., in *Weaver* v. *Townsend*, 14 Wend. 193. I confess I am strongly inclined to think that the same quantum of proof is necessary in actions for this class of libels, and that the plaintiff should, therefore, have been nonsuited; although I admit the judge was right in saying there was such proof as might be taken into the consideration of the jury on the question of express malice.

But admitting the *onus* to lie on the defendant, the cases cited agree most clearly, that actions for petitions or remonstrances addressed to the appointing power, being *quasi* for a malicious prosecution, will not lie where it comes out on the whole evidence, that there was probable cause. I refer particularly to *Thorn* v. *Blanchard*, and *Gray* v. *Pentland*, with the general remark that they are entirely sustained, at least in this, by the whole body of British authority. Adequate references will be found in *Thorn* v. *Blanchard*. The marginal note to *Gray* v. *Pentland*, states that such libels are "excused if they did not originate in malice and without probable cause." Tilghman, C. J., there took the view most favorable to the plaintiff, yet remarked: "Anything which satisfies the jury that the proceeding did not originate in malice and without probable cause, is sufficient to excuse him:" 2 Serg. & R. 30. At any rate, all the cases which have spoken to the point, hold that probable cause, when shown by the defendant, will make out a complete defense, or is receivable in mitigation: and so much, at least, was agreed by the learned judge, who tried the cause now before us. It was received in mitigation where the libel was published by the editor of a newspaper against an elective officer, after he had succeeded in his election: *Vide King* v. *Root*, 4 Wend. 114, 139, 143 [21 Am. Dec. 102]. Some courts have held that, even in the ordinary action of slander, the defendant may show in mitigation that a person told him what he uttered as a slander, especially where the slander, in terms, professes to be founded on a hearsay: *Kennedy* v. *Gregory*, 1 Binn. 85. It will never do to say that where there are circumstances raising strong suspicion of official misconduct, the friends of the officer, or persons indifferent alone, shall come within the protection. It is important that others more ready to complain, should be equally favored. There is no reason, if they bear actual ill will to the plaintiff, why this should remove from them what would be, of itself, a complete shield to the rest of the community.

This brings us to the only remaining question in the case. Suppose I am mistaken as to the *onus*, was there not here proof of probable cause? Or, at least, so much evidence that the judge was not warranted in withdrawing the question from the jury? The plaintiff himself admits that he took the timber intrusted to him as keeper of the public stores, and converted it to his own use, in building a dwelling-house. The defendant saw, or at any rate was informed of the fact by a neighbor, who suggested that it would be well to communicate the fact to the government. This the defendant did, at the same time drawing his own inference that the act was done fraudulently. Admitting for the present, that the plaintiff had a right thus to convert the timber, can it be said that his conduct was so entirely pure on its face, as to raise no misgivings in the minds of his neighbors? They knew him for a public trustee; and saw him converting to his own use, a portion of what he had in charge. They knew nothing of the manner in which he had acquired a title. Suppose one of them had seen a carrier start with a box of goods; and overtaking him on his way, far from the eye of his bailor, had afterwards seen him in the act of breaking bulk, and selling a part of the goods. Such a juncture of circumstances would, in a court of justice, be *prima facie* evidence of larceny; and could it be said that the spectator would be open to a malicious prosecution should he procure an indictment? If his neighbor, happening to see the same thing, should inform him of it, and urge a prosecution, this would heighten his suspicion. It would operate as an additional cause for the prosecution. Indeed, had he merely heard of the circumstance from the observer, it is by no means certain that he would not be justified in giving information to the magistrate. In *Cockayne* v. *Hodgkisson*, before stated, the judge put it to the jury to say, whether the defendant had been told by a third person what he had communicated in the libel; and whether he believed it; and we have seen that the same thing has been received as mitigating evidence in actions for common libels and slanderous words. It would not differ the case, that the carrier had secretly bought of his bailor, the articles which he took from the box, unless the defendant had been informed of the purchase. *Weaver* v. *Townsend*, 14 Wend. 192, which was a case of malicious prosecution, turned on the fact that the defendant knew the plaintiff had a *prima facie* title to the property, for stealing which the defendant had caused him to be indicted.

I do not see that the case at bar comes materially short of the supposed carrier's, except in the degree of the offense. In that the circumstances would raise a suspicion of larceny; in this a suspicion of embezzlement. That the act was done openly, is by no means conclusive to the mind, nor has it much force, unless it appear that the owner was present or known by the peculator to have means of promptly detecting and punishing him. With others it might be regarded as a mere affectation of conscious innocence. If the property taken was trifling in amount, with some that might lull suspicion, while with others it might increase it, and be considered as an index to greater spoliations. "If," says Washington, J., in *Wilmarth* v. *Mountford*, 4 Wash. C. C. 79, 84, the plaintiff, "by his folly or his fraud, exposed himself to a well-grounded suspicion, the prosecution had at least probable cause for its basis, and this is sufficient to defeat the action." It appears to me that the judge in this view of the matter was most clearly bound, at least, to have left the question to the jury. If it was to be decided as matter of law, and that is generally so with the question of probable cause where the facts are undisputed, Dallas, J., in *Hill* v. *Yates*, 2 B. Moore 80, 82; .*Pangburn* v. *Bull*, 1 Wend. 345, *Gorton* v. *De Angelis*, 6 Id. 418; then I think he should have told the jury that probable cause had been established.

But it is objected that the defendant was too late in his offer to show probable cause after he had set up on the record that he would prove the truth. It is a sufficient answer to say that the judge did not think so, and the defense proceeded on the ground that the proof was admissible. If the defendant had been denied that view, *non constat*, but he might have pursued his notice of justification by giving farther evidence of its truth. But independent of the course thus taken, we have seen enough to say that the objection is founded on a misapplication of the cases. It is indeed generally true that such a justification, where the defendant fails to prove it, may be used as evidence of express malice; and it is too late to waive it at the trial and resort to mistake: *Patty* v. *Stetson*, 15 Mass. 48;[1] Walworth, Chancellor, in *King* v. *Root*, 4 Wend. 139, 140 [21 Am. Dec. 102]; *Clinton* v. *Mitchell*, 3 Johns. 144; *Lent* v. *Butler*, 3 Cow. 370. But the rule is co-extensive with those cases only where probable cause is matter of mitigation merely. In actions for a

---

1. *Jackson* v. *Stetson.*

malicious prosecution, or *quasi* such, where it makes a bar, the reason ceases.   It was never held that because a man pleads in bar specially or gives notice of special matter, he shall be cut off from another defense which is receivable under the general issue.   The contrary has often been held: *Levy* v. *Gadsby*, 3 Cranch, 180, 186; *Smith* v. *Gregory*, 8 Cow. 114; *Fulton Bank* v. *Stafford*, 2 Wend. 483; *Bradley* v. *Field*, 3 Id. 272.

But more.   It is not quite easy to see, that on the plaintiff's own showing, his case was exempt from a still stronger view, had the defendant chosen to pursue it.   Swartwout, the collector, had given the plaintiff leave to take the timber, and the letters alluded to him as a party to the frauds which were going on. He was called as a witness, but certainly did not make the plainest case of the matter against actual embezzlement.   Admitting him to have had a right to sell the timber at auction, or otherwise, for the best price he could get; that did not authorize him to give, any more than it did the plaintiff to take it, in exchange for an article of mere luxury, or at most, convenience, viz., the bath-house which the plaintiff volunteered to build for the United States.   Nor was the manner of payment by any means the most prudent.   Telling the plaintiff to carve for himself, till he was satisfied, might certainly have been no more than was due from Mr. Swartwout to him as an honest neighbor, had the timber in question belonged to him in his own right.   Holding for the public, it at least laid the proceeding open to invidious remark; nor can I collect that Swartwout took any precaution to limit the amount within the measure of a just *quid pro quo*.   In short, a *carte blanche* was given to the plaintiff, first for himself, and secondly in favor of the poor inhabitants, for the purposes of fuel.   I repeat, that all this might have been very well as a disposition of Mr. Swartwout's own property; but that it was not technical embezzlement when applied to the public property, is by no means clear.   It might not have been morally so; but it was an instance of such gross neglect in a few things, as might well lead a citizen, jealous of the public rights, to question whether the same practices had not been extended to many things by the same men.   Though in itself a " trifle light as air," it disclosed a principle which might have operated as " confirmation strong" that more extensive peculation had been committed in secret, especially when taken in connection with the late poverty of the plaintiff, his small wages, his extravagant living, and the now splendid mansion, in the erection of which he was employing the property of the nation.   These things are asserted in the letter, and not contradicted by the proof. I admit, that in the ordinary action of slander, they would be presumed false. In this we have seen the presumption is reversed, and I therefore mention them.

Had all the circumstances of this case been disclosed to the treasury department, I can hardly believe that its upright, able, and sagacious head would have voluntarily surrendered these letters to be used as evidence. In *Gray* v. *Pentland*, the court held that they could not compel the governor to produce the paper, nor would they allow parol evidence to be given of its contents. Being a complaint properly addressed to him as a visitorial magistrate, the court held, upon the ground of policy, that they would not control the exercise of his discretion, nor would they allow its intended effect to be evaded by the introduction of secondary evidence. In this they were fully sustained by the decisions at Westminster hall, and several cases which might be cited from American books. I know that the right of remonstrance may be abused; and I can not doubt that the secretary was pressed with what the defendant's counsel admitted at the bar: the great public services and elevated character of the plaintiff. Had the defendant printed and published his remonstrance, the case would have been far different; his privilege then would have been lost. Even the privilege of parliament is forfeited by a member publishing a slanderous speech or a slanderous report. But, for aught that appears, these letters have performed no other office than furnishing a sort of information, vital, above all things, to the safe operation of the fiscal department of the government. At any rate, whatever may be the general merit of the plaintiff, and however innocent he may be in the particular matter, we can not hold the defendant criminal for thus communicating what the plaintiff has been so unfortunate as to give him probable cause for supposing to be true.

New trial granted.

———

COMMUNICATION DESIGNED TO SECURE THE REMOVAL OF AN OFFICER and addressed to the body or officer having power to remove, is libelous, when, and when not: See *Bodwell* v. *Osgood*, 15 Am. Dec. 228, and note; *State* v. *Burnham*, 31 Id. 217, and other cases cited in the note thereto. See, also, generally as to the privilege attaching to communications addressed to bodies having power to remedy an abuse complained of: *Vanderzee* v. *McGregor*, 27 Id. 156, and cases in the note. That communications made in good faith for justifiable ends to public officials having power to remedy the evils complained of, or to public or private persons having an interest in the matters concerning which the communications are made, are privileged, and that express malice must be shown to destroy this privilege, is a point to which the principal case is cited in *O'Donaghue* v. *McGovern*, 23 Wend. 31; *Lathrop* v *Hyde*, 25 Id. 449; *Hosmer* v. *Loveland*, 19 Barb. 116; *Smith* v. *Kerr*, 1 Edm. 193; *Van Wyck* v. *Aspinwall*, 17 N. Y. 193; *Ormsby* v. *Douglass*, 37 Id. 480; *Newfield* v. *Copperman*, 42 N. Y. Super. Ct. (10 Jones & S.) 306. So a written communication between private persons concerning their own private affairs: *Klinck* v. *Colby*, 46 N. Y. 433. That an action brought for a communication made concerning the plaintiff to his superior officer to procure his removal is an action for malicious prosecution though in form an action of slander is a point for which *Howard* v. *Thompson* is referred to as authority in *Streety* v. *Wood*, 15 How. Pr. 110; *Viele* v. *Gray*, 18 Id. 570. That an officer to whom letters are addressed to procure the removal of a subordinate can not be compelled to produce the letters in an action by such subordinate against the writer, is a point to which the principal case is cited in *Worthington* v. *Scribner*, 109 Mass. 491.

PROBABLE CAUSE, HOW FAR A QUESTION OF LAW OR FACT IN ACTIONS FOR MALICIOUS PROSECUTION: See *Nash* v. *Orr*, 5 Am. Dec. 547; *Ulmer* v. *Leland*, 10 Id. 48; *Plummer* v. *Gheen*, 14 Id. 572; *Miller* v. *Brown*, 23 Id. 693; *French* v. *Smith*, 24 Id. 616.

BLANCHARD *v.* ELY.

[21 WENDELL, 342.]

ASSIGNMENT OF CLAIM BY PLAINTIFF TO ONE OF DEFENDANTS before suit is no bar to such suit except where, in order to sue, the same person must appear on the record as both plaintiff and defendant.

ASSIGNMENT OF CHOSE IN ACTION BY WAY OF A PLEDGE, or even absolutely, does not transfer the assignor's legal interest.

MEASURE OF DAMAGES FOR DEFECTS IN CONSTRUCTION OF A STEAMBOAT under a contract, which may be deducted in an action to recover the contract price, is the expense necessarily incurred in making good those defects, except in case of fraud.

DAMAGES FOR LOSS OF PROFITS AND DELAYS OF VOYAGES by reason of defects in the construction of a steamboat can not be deducted, where the case is free from fraud, in an action to recover the price agreed on for the construction of such steamboat, such damages being too remote.

DISALLOWANCE BY JURY OF A DEDUCTION FOR DAMAGES FOR DEFECTS in executing a contract in an action to recover the contract price is ground for awarding a new trial, where there is a strong preponderance of evidence showing the defendant entitled to the deduction, and the disallowance is plainly inferable from the amount of the verdict.

DEBT to recover the contract price for the construction of a certain steamboat by the plaintiff for the defendants under articles of agreement entered into between them. The boat was to have been finished by May 1, 1835, but was not so finished, but accepted by the defendants on condition that she should be completed. She was finished in July, 1835. The defendants claimed a deduction for damages for certain defects in the construction of the boat respecting the shafts, wheels, guards, etc., which they, the defendants, had been compelled to remedy at considerable expense. They also claimed damages for delays occasioned by the necessity of remedying these defects, and the consequent loss of ˙ profits of a number of trips which they would have been able to make, if no repairs had been needed. The judge, however, instructed the jury that the damages for loss of voyages and of profits were too remote and could not be allowed, though they might be recovered in a cross action, and that the true measure of damages was the sum necessarily expended by the defendants in remedying the defects. The defendants also produced in evidence an assignment by the plaintiffs to one of the defendants, before suit, of the contract with the defendants, and of the sum due thereon, in which he admitted the receipt of all but four thousand five hundred and twenty-four dollars and sixty-six cents of the contract price. This assignment, the defendants insisted, was a bar to the plaintiff's recovery. The plaintiff, however, introduced a writing of the same date as the assignment, which was signed by the payee, from the tenor of which it was clear that the assignment was made not absolutely, but as security for the payment of certain advances, made by the assignee to the plaintiff. The judge decided that the assignment was no bar. Verdict for plaintiff for five thousand two hundred and forty dollars and thirty-one cents. Motion for a new trial.

S. Stevens, for the defendants.

S. P. Staples, for the plaintiff.

By Court, COWEN, J. The objection that the assignment of the articles of agreement by the plaintiff to one of the defendants should have been received as a bar, is founded on the principle that where the right of the creditor and the liability of the debtor, or any one of several debtors meet in the same person, such coincidence works a release by operation of the law. The reason is that a man can not sue himself; the action is suspended by the voluntary act of the creditor; and is gone and discharged forever: 2 Wms. Ex., Phil. ed. 1832, p. 811. It is obvious from the bare statement of the argument, that it must mean a vesting of the legal right, or, in other words, a right to sue in the creditor's own name, in the person of his debtor. Otherwise the reason fails. It will, I apprehend, be found applicable to those cases only where the same individual, in order to sue, must appear on the record both as plaintiff and defendant:

Mainwaring v. *Newman*, 2 Bos. & Pul. 120. The case of *Van Ness* v. *Forrest*, 8 Cranch, 30, will be found an authority for this distinction. Besides, it is suggested that the assignment in this case was merely by way of pledge, or security to one of the defendants for money lent; the plaintiff thus still retaining his interest as general owner. It is certainly very clear, that even if he could have divested his legal interest by an absolute assignment, that could not be done by merely pledging it; but he could not part with it in either form. This court has held that a defendant may, before suit brought, purchase a chose in action against the plaintiff, and use it as a set-off: and we have often held that the assignee is the real party, and shall be protected. But this has always been held in an equitable sense, which would rather go to favor the present action than to defeat it.

Did the judge narrow the jury too much in the rule of damages? The plaintiff had failed in some comparatively trifling respects, to make so perfect a boat as he had stipulated for. The shafts were not of adequate strength, in consequence of which the boat was interrupted in some of her trips; and the company incurred expense in procuring repairs to be done, and in towing the boat to a proper place for undergoing her repairs. All this the judge left to the jury to deduct in their discretion, from the acknowledged balance of account for building her. But he directed them not to allow for delays, and for profits which might have been made from the trips that were lost. No common law authority was cited at the bar, one way or the other, having any direct application to the measure of damages in such a case as this; nor am I aware that any exists. If there be none, it is somewhat singular, considering the many contracts for building boats and other vessels which must have been made in England and this country.

We have to regret, that the attention of the counsel seemed to have been entirely turned from the character of this claim in the abstract, by a remark of the judge implying that damages for loss of profits were admissible in a cross action, but not in mitigation. This led the counsel for the defendant to stop with citing *Reab* v. *McAllister*, 8 Wend. 115, to show that proof of any damages arising from a plaintiff's breach of the contract upon which he sues, may be received to reduce his claim. This we all understand to be clearly so. The counsel for the defendant, too, merely thought it their duty to cite cases showing that in an action on a warranty of land, the plaintiff recovers only the consideration money paid, with interest and costs, etc.; and we were reminded particularly of one reason for that rule as given by Chief Justice Savage, in *Dimmick* v. *Lockwood*, 10 Wend. 150, viz.: "That it would be ruinous and oppressive to make the seller respond in damages for any accidental rise in value of the land or the increased value in consequence of the improvements by the purchaser." He, at the same time, however, notices some technical reasons for the rule which render it less decisive in respect to executory contracts, especially those which regard personal property. The prevalence of the rule is very extensive in its application to covenants of title: *Vide* 1 Sel. N. P. 533, Phil. ed. 1839. The rule is more pertinent when applied, as it has been in several cases, to the breach by failure of title of a covenant to convey: *Baldwin* v. *Munn*, 2 Wend. 399 [20 Am. Dec. 627]. Sutherland, J., there adopts a former remark of Chief Justice Kent, importing that it must block up sales of real estate, if the vendor were to be made liable in proportion to the rise of property. It is added on the same authority, that "the safest rule is to limit the recovery as much as possible, to an indemnity for the actual injury sustained, without regard to the profits the plaintiff has failed to make:" Id. 406. This was A. D. 1829. As long ago as 1811, in *Letcher* v. *Woodson*, 1 Brock. 212, Marshall, C. J., laid down the rule of damages on a similar covenant, in nearly the same words with Mr. Justice Sutherland: *Combs* v. *Tarlton's Adm'rs*, 2 Dana, 466, 467, S. P., A. D. 1834. This rule would cut off all rise of the value intermediate the contract and time fixed for its execution. The rule on agreement to sell and deliver goods, is universally broader; giving the vendee advantage of the rise in market, and the consequent advantage of profit on any sale which he might have made at the time stipulated for delivery, or whenever it becomes due: *Smee* v. *Huddlestone*, Sayer's Dam. 49. See many other cases cited in Chief Justice Marshall's note to *Letcher* v. *Woodson*, 1 Brock. 218; *Clark* v. *Pinney*, 7 Cow. 681, 687, and the cases there cited. Nay more, under circumstances, the rise is considered even down to the time of the trial: Id.

The rule of damages in respect to contracts for the sale of chattels is the general one, and some courts have refused to depart from it, in measuring damages for breach of covenants to convey real estate: *Hopkins* v. *Lee*, 6 Wheat. 109, 117, 118; *Caniell* v. *McLean*, 6 Har. & J. 297. I do not dwell upon these cases, more of which may perhaps be found. In both classes, the courts are seeking after an indemnity; that is to say, making good to the vendee what he has paid his money for. Both

classes of cases profess to deny the allowance of damages remotely consequential, as of profits resting in speculation. The
possible or even probable use to which the vendee may put the
property, aside from a market sale, is clearly excluded. Going
upon analogy, then, suppose the owners of this boat, the defendants, had sold out; in the absence of evidence that there had
been a rise of the boat's value in market, we must take the stipulated value at which it was to be built: *Bailey* v. *Clay*, 4 Rand.
846; and then the sum which would command the materials and
work for making good the defects, would be the measure of damages in an action, or by way of recoupment in a defense. In
like manner, a contract to insure a cargo will not, in the event
of loss, carry the speculative profits of the adventure, though
these may be insured in express terms, even by an open policy:
1 Ph. Ins. 320, 325; Id. 46. Yet, insurance is called pre-emi-
nently a contract of indemnity. The damages are what will restore the value of the cargo on shipboard at the port of departure: Id. 46, *et seq.* The rule is nearly the same in respect to
damages for breach of warranty. The defect arising from the
vice warranted against, must be made good in such sense that
the article shall fetch a sound price, which *prima facie*, we have
seen is the one agreed on between warrantor and warrantee: 4
Rand., *ut supra;* 2 Leigh's N. P., Phil. ed. 1838, p. 1506. *Caveat emptor* in search of a horse: 1 Rural Lib. N. Y., No. 5, for
1837, p. 140; *Clare* v. *Maynard*, 7 Car. & P. 741; S. C., 1 Nev.
& P. 701. *Chesterman* v. *Lamb*, 4 Nev. & M. 195; S. C., 2 Ad.
& El. 129; 1 Selw. N. P., ed. before cited, p. 654, tit. Deceit, I,
1, and notes; *Bacon* v. *Brown*, 4 Bibb, 91 [4 Am. Dec. 640].
Yet, in all the cases mentioned, as in that of insurance, there is
no doubt, that by an express contract, on good consideration,
the vendor may stipulate expressly to indemnify in respect to
loss of profits arising from the defect against which he contracts.
In short, it will be seen by the cases cited and many more,
that on the subject in question, our courts are more and more
falling into the track of the civil law, the rule of which is thus
laid down by a learned writer: "In general, the parties are
deemed to have contemplated only the damages and interest which
the creditor might suffer from the non-performance of the obligation, in respect to the particular thing which is the object of it; and
not such as may have been accidentally occasioned thereby in respect to his own affairs:" 1 Ev. Poth. 91, London ed. 1806. He
illustrates the rule by the rise of value in goods which the promisor
fails to deliver. He adds, if the lessor's title to a house fail, he is

bound to pay to his lessee the expense of removal, and indemnify him against the advance of rents, but not against the loss of custom in a business he may have established while residing in the house.   He also adverts to the distinction that the vendor may, notwithstanding, incur liability for extrinsic damages of the creditor, if it appear they were stipulated for or tacitly submitted to in the contract.   One instance is that of stipulating to deliver a horse in such time that a certain advantage may be gained by reaching such a place.   There the debtor shall, on default, pay·for the loss of the advantage.   The case of tacit submission is illustrated by a case of demising premises expressly for use as an inn.   There, if the tenant be evicted, a loss of custom may be taken into the account: Id. 91, 92.   This latter rule was in some measure acted upon in the late case of *Driggs* v. *Dwight*, 17 Wend. 71 [31 Am. Dec. 283].   There was a promise to demise a tavern stand at a day certain, which was refused by the promisor, after the promisee had broken up his former residence, and proceeded with a view to take possession.   We allowed to the latter damages for removing his family and furniture; in this, following the case of *Ward* v. *Smith*, 11 Price, 19.   In *Brackett* v. *McNair*, 14 Johns. 170 [7 Am. Dec. 447], the broken contract was to transport goods from one place to another; and the increase of value in the goods at the latter place was allowed as damages; though even this principle of estimate seems to have been denied in the previous case of *Smith* v. *Richardson*, 3 Cai. 219.   In another case, the plaintiff sued for stone delivered to be used in building a church, and the defendants claimed a recoupment, because they had not been delivered at the day. They insisted, among other things, on damages, by reason of their workmen lying idle for want of the material.   The court did not deny the claim absolutely, but held that the defendants, even if the delivery had been stopped, would have been bound to use diligence in keeping their workmen employed on other materials, to be supplied as soon as they could be procured; thus avoiding all unnecessary loss, and that the deduction must be governed with a view to that principle: *Miller* v. *Mariners' Church*, 7 Greenl. 51, 55 [20 Am. Dec. 341].   The unreasonable delay of workmen stood somewhat on the footing of unreasonably delaying the boat in this case, which the judge refused to allow, though he directed that damages might be due for taking the boat to a proper place for being repaired.

But to go the length insisted upon by the defendants would, I apprehend, transgress what the law should allow, even had the

plaintiff, without fraud, tortiously broken the machinery of this
boat, as by a negligent collision, in navigating his own boat
The profits of a voyage broken up, are constantly denied consideration, even in questions relating to marine trespasses: *The
Amiable Nancy*, 3 Wheat. 546, 560, and the cases there cited;
La Amistad de Rues, 5 Id. 385, 389. Of course I lay out of
view, as do all the cases, that the transaction is accompanied with
wanton outrage, fraud, or gross negligence; the cases just cited
from Wheaton show that these are exceptions. And see *Merrils* v.
The Tariff Manufacturing Co., 10 Conn. 384 [27 Am. Dec. 682.]
The case of *De Wint* v. *Wiltse*, 9 Wend. 325, must, I think, have
been regarded by this court as a fraudulent breach of a covenant
to keep a ferry in repair, which materially benefited the plaintiff's
tavern. The defendant left it unrepaired, in order to favor his
own ferry. Therefore, damages were allowed for loss of custom
at the plaintiff's inn. Pothier, as before cited, maintains the
same distinction. In *Nurse* v. *Barns*, T. Raym. 77, the defendant, in consideration of ten pounds, promised to demise a mill
to the plaintiff, who laid in a large stock to employ it, which he
lost, because the defendant refused to let him have possession.
The jury were held properly to have assessed the damages at
five hundred pounds. Very likely it appeared that the breach
of contract was committed to favor some particular interest of
the defendant or his friend, though the case mentions a simple
refusal to perform.

The case at bar, so far as I have been enabled to discover
from the evidence, stands entirely clear of fraud. If some of
the iron used for shafts was rotten, there is nothing going
to fix knowledge, or, that I see, gross negligence, in the
plaintiff or his superintendent. The extent to which the iron
proved bad, was doubtful, though the jury were authorized to
infer it was by no means all of a good quality. There is no
proof, however, that such iron was used intentionally; and we
ought not to infer that a fraud was committed by any one.
No new trial can, therefore, be granted on any error of the
judge.

Still, we think, complete justice can not be done without the
cause being submitted to another jury; for the plain inference
is, that they totally disallowed anything whatever for defects in
the boat. The plaintiff's counsel make a computation by which
they show that sixty-two dollars deduction was made; but even
this assumes that interest ran on the balance mentioned in the
assignment, four thousand five hundred and twenty-four dollars

and sixty-six cents, from the first of May. This could not be so. All parties agreed that the boat was not finally completed until pretty well along in July, and she was accepted, subject to completion. At most, the interest ought not to run till after the job was finished. It is sufficient to say, we think there is a strong preponderance of evidence in favor of some deduction.

New trial granted on payment of costs.

SAME PARTY PLAINTIFF AND DEFENDANT: See *Livingston* v. *Livingston*, 12 Am. Dec. 684; *Pearson* v. *Nesbit*, 17 Id. 569; *King* v. *Green*, 19 Id. 46; *Allin* v. *Shadburne*, 25 Id. 121, and note.

CONSEQUENTIAL DAMAGES FOR BREACH OF CONTRACT.—Damages will not be allowed for a conjectural loss of profits: *Bond* v. *Quattlebaum*, 10 Am. Dec. 702; nor for incidental or remote injurious results: *Jackson* v. *Adams*, 6 Id. 94. But special damages may be recovered for expenses incurred in preparing to perform the contract on the plaintiff's part: *Driggs* v. *Dwight*, 31 Id. 283, and note, citing the principal case. See also *Jeffrey* v. *Bigelow*, 28 Id. 476, and the note thereto referring to other cases in this series on the subject of consequential damages. The rule laid down in the principal case that in an action for breach of contract the measure of damages is the sum necessary to make good the actual loss, and that, generally, in actions for damages, the party can recover only for the natural and proximate consequences of the act complained of, and not for remote consequences, except in case of fraud, is referred to with approval in *Green* v. *Mann*, 11 Ill. 615; *Wilbert* v. *New York etc. R. R. Co.*, 19 Barb. 48; *Vanderslice* v. *Newton*, 4 N. Y. 134; *Sharon* v. *Mosher*, 17 Barb. 522; *Allaire Works* v. *Guion*, 10 Id. 57; *Hargous* v. *Ablon*, 5 Hill, 473; S. C., in court of errors, 3 Denio, 409; *Mott* v. *Hudson River R. R. Co.*, 1 Rob. 593; *Flynn* v. *Hatton*, 43 How. Pr. 352. The case is especially cited to the point that, except when there is fraud, there can be no recovery for the loss of contingent, probable, or speculative profits or gains, in *Freeman* v. *Clute*, 3 Barb. 427; *Giles* v. *O'Toole*, 4 Id. 264; *Walrath* v. *Redfield*, 11 Id. 371; *Griffin* v. *Colver*, 22 Id. 591; S. C., 16 N. Y. 492; *Rogers* v. *Beard*, 36 Barb. 37; *Dorwin* v. *Potter*, 5 Denio, 308; *St. John* v. *Mayor etc. of New York*, 13 How. Pr. 533; S. C., 6 Duer, 321; *Devlin* v. *Mayor*, 50 How. Pr. 19; *Cassidy* v. *Le Fevre*, 45 N. Y. 567; *City of Brooklyn* v. *Brooklyn City R. R. Co.*, 47 Id. 482; *Krom* v. *Levy*, 48 Id. 680; *Wehle* v. *Haviland*, 69 Id. 451; *Mitchell* v. *Cornell*, 44 N. Y. Super. Ct. (12 Jones & S.) 404; *The Rhode Island*, 2 Blatchf. 114; S. C., 1 Abb. Ad. 103. But it is held that the plaintiff may recover for a loss of profits which is the direct and proximate result of the defendant's negligence, occasioning a collision in the highway: *Albert* v. *Bleecker St. R. R. Co.*, 2 Daly, 389, criticising the principal case. See also *Draper* v. *Sweet*, 66 Barb. 147, holding that the plaintiff may, in an action for a breach of warranty, recover for the loss, by reason of defects in the thing sold, of profits which would, in the ordinary course of things, have resulted to the purchaser, and which may be presumed to have been in the contemplation of the parties.

City Fire Ins. Co. v. Corlies.

[21 Wendell, 367.]

Destruction of Insured Building by an Explosion of Gunpowder is a loss by fire within the meaning of the policy.

Placing Gunpowder in a Building is not a "Storing" of gunpowder therein within the meaning of an exception in the policy, where the powder is placed there with a lighted match, for the purpose of an explosion.

Voluntary Destruction of Insured Building by Order of the Mayor, by blowing it up with gunpowder, for the purpose of stopping a conflagration, which in all probability would have consumed the building, renders the insurers liable, although the insured may also have a remedy against the city.

Mere Excess of Jurisdiction by Lawful Magistrate is not Usurpation of power within the meaning of a policy, exempting the insurers from liability for a loss by "usurped power."

Error from the superior court of New York city, in an action on a policy of insurance. The insured building was destroyed by order of the mayor of the city by exploding a quantity of gunpowder therein, for the purpose of arresting the spread of a conflagration which was raging in its vicinity, and which, as the evidence showed, would in all probability have consumed it if it had not been blown up. The defendants insisted that this was not a loss within the policy, and moved for a nonsuit, which was overruled. Verdict and judgment for the plaintiffs, and the defendants brought error. The points relied on sufficiently appear from the opinion.

J. W. Gerard, for the plaintiffs in error.

D. Lord, jun., for the defendants in error.

By Court, Bronson, J. 1. There has, I think, been a loss by the peril insured against, within the meaning of the policy. In *Grim* v. *The Phœnix Ins. Co.*, 13 Johns. 451, no doubt seems to have been entertained, either by the court or counsel, that a loss by the explosion of gunpowder was a loss by fire. And in *Waters* v. *The Merchants' L. Ins. Co.*, 11 Pet. 213, the point was so adjudged. The court was of opinion, that fire was the proximate cause of the loss.

2. According to the terms of the policy, if the building was used for the purpose of storing gunpowder, the contract was for the time suspended. And see *Duncan* v. *The Sun F. Ins. Co.*, 6 Wend. 488 [22 Am. Dec. 539]. But placing gunpowder with a lighted match in the building, for the express purpose of pro-

ducing an explosion, which immediately followed, was a very different thing from what the parties contemplated when they inserted this provision in the contract. Whether the insurers are liable for this voluntary destruction of the property, is a question yet to be considered. But I think it quite clear that they have not established the allegation that the building was used for the storing of gunpowder.

3. The building containing the goods was destroyed by order of the mayor of the city, for the purpose of arresting the progress of a conflagration. Are the insurers answerable for this voluntary destruction of the property? This question has been presented in a double form—the one supposing that the mayor acted with, and the other that he acted without, authority.

First. Let us first assume that the mayor acted illegally. If the fire had been kindled by an incendiary, it is not denied that the insurers would be answerable. Why are they not then answerable, if the mayor acted without authority? The act, though not done for a wicked purpose, was as illegal as though it had been the work of a felon. The answer attempted is, that although the mayor had no authority, yet as he acted *colore officii*, this is a case of loss happening by means of usurped power, which is expressly excepted by the policy.

It is impossible to maintain that a mere excess of jurisdiction by a lawful magistrate, is the exercise of an usurped power within the meaning of this contract. That is not what the insurers had in mind when they made the exception. It was an usurpation of the power of government, against which they intended to protect themselves. Such was the interpretation given to the same words in a policy as early as the year 1767: *Drinkwater* v. *The London Assur.*, 2 Wils. 363. The property insured was destroyed by a mob, which arose on account of the high price of provisions; and the insurers were held liable, notwithstanding a proviso in the policy that they would not answer for a destruction by "usurped power." Bathurst, J., said, those words, according to the true import thereof and the meaning of the parties, could only mean an invasion of the kingdom by foreign enemies to give laws and usurp the government, or an internal armed force in rebellion, assuming the power of government, by making laws, and punishing for not obeying those laws. Wilmot, C. J., said, the words meant an invasion from abroad, or an internal rebellion, when armies are employed to support it; when the laws are dormant and silent, and firing of towns is unavoidable. In *Langdale* v. *Mason*, 2 Marsh. Ins. 791, it was said by Lord Mansfield, that these words were ambiguous, but they had been the subject of judicial determination; that they must mean rebellion conducted by authority—determined rebellion, with generals who could give orders. And he added, "Usurped power takes in rebellion, acting under usurped authority." Whatever doubt there may have been originally about the meaning of the words "usurped power," in a policy, their legal power had been settled long before this contract was made; and we can not assume that these parties used the words in any other than their legal sense.

Second. But the mayor acted under lawful authority; there was no usurpation of any kind. Whether he had the concurrence of two aldermen, as the statute provides, or not, there can be no doubt of his common law power, as the chief magistrate of the city, to destroy buildings, in a case of necessity, to prevent the spreading of a fire. Indeed, the same thing may be done by any magistrate, or even by a citizen without official authority: *The Mayor of N. Y.* v. *Lord,* 17 Wend. 285.

4. If the mayor acted by lawful authority, it is then said that the property was destroyed for the benefit of the city, and that the corporation (not the insurers) must bear the loss. This case does not fall within the statute charging certain losses on the city, because it does not appear that the mayor had "the consent and concurrence of any two aldermen:" 2 R.. L. 368, sec. 81; and for the further reason that the property would have been consumed by fire, if its destruction had not been ordered by the magistrate: *The Mayor of N. Y.* v. *Lord.* 17 Wend. 285. It is said that the corporation is liable at the common law for the acts of the mayor: but no authority was cited in support of the position, and I am not prepared to say, that in a case like this, the doctrine can be maintained. The inclination of my mind is strongly the other way.

But suppose the city is liable, I do not see how that fact can affect this contract. If the insurers pay the loss, they may, perhaps, have an action against the corporation of the city, in the name of the assured, to recover back the money: *Mason* v. *Sainsbury,* 2 Marsh. Ins. 794; S. C., 3 Doug. 61. But however that may be, the fact that the assured may have a remedy against the city, can not change or qualify the undertaking of the insurers.

This leads me to notice a little more particularly the extent of the contract. The company agrees to make good unto the assured all such loss or damage to the property as shall happen by fire. Thus far, there is no limit or qualification of the undertaking. If the loss happen by fire, unless there was fraud on the part of the assured, which is not pretended in this case, it matters not how the flame was kindled. Whether it be the result of accident or design—whether the torch be applied by the honest magistrate, or the wicked incendiary—whether the purpose was to save a city, as at New York, or a country, as at Moscow—the loss is equally within the terms of the contract. That the insurers intended the general undertaking should extend to every possible loss by fire, is evident from the fact that they afterwards proceed to specify particular losses by fire for which they will not be answerable: *Columbia Ins. Co.* v. *Lawrence*, 10 Pet. 507. The exceptions are contained in the sixth condition of the proposals annexed to the policy. It is unnecessary to recite the clause, because it is not pretended that this case comes within any of the exceptions, save that relating to a loss happening by means of "usurped power," and that point has already been considered.

There has then been a loss by fire. The case falls within the general undertaking of the insurers, and is not affected by any of the exceptions which they thought proper to make to the extent of their liability. We can not add another exception. The insurers are bound by their contract.

Judgment affirmed.

————

Loss BY FIRE, WHAT IS.—The foregoing case is cited in *Pentz* v. *Receivers of Ætna Fire Ins. Co.*, 3 Edw. Ch. 343, to the point that a voluntary destruction of an insured building by an explosion of gunpowder, by municipal authorities, for the purpose of checking a fire, is a loss within the policy. That was a case of this description, but the insured first resorted to an action against the city, and the verdict was for less than the insurance and the absolute loss, and it was held that he could not recover the balance from the insurers. The principal case is cited also in *Babcock* v. *Montgomery Co. Mut. Ins. Co.*, 6 Barb. 640, to the point that any loss which is the immediate consequence of fire or burning is within the terms of a fire insurance policy. So a loss caused by water used to quench the fire, or by removal to save the insured property from the fire. In the case of *Tilton* v. *Hamilton Fire Ins. Co.*, 1 Bosw. 367, also a loss by removal was held within the policy, citing *City Fire Ins. Co.* v. *Corlies*. A loss occasioned in part by explosion and in part by combustion of gunpowder, was held in *Scripture* v. *Lowell Mut. Fire Ins. Co.*, 10 Cush. 356, to be a loss within the policy, citing the principal case.

"USURPED POWER."—What is said in the foregoing decision as to the proper construction and meaning of these terms in a policy, is commented on with approval in *Boon* v. *Ætna Ins. Co.*, 12 Blatchf. 33.

SHANNON *v.* COMSTOCK.

[21 WENDELL, 457.]

AFFIDAVIT FOR COMMENCING A SUIT BY WARRANT IN JUSTICE'S COURT that the defendants are non-residents, though sufficient to make the warrant regular in the first instance, is not conclusive, and if met by sufficient proof to the contrary, the justice should set aside the proceedings.

PLEA IN ABATEMENT THAT ONE OF SEVERAL DEFENDANTS IS A RESIDENT of the state where the suit has been commenced by warrant in a justice's court, is bad, because, though personal to only one of the defendants, it goes to the whole suit.

GENERAL ISSUE PLEADED DOES NOT WAIVE THE PROPRIETY OF AN ARREST of the defendants in a suit in a justice's court, where the objection has been taken and overruled.

MEASURE OF DAMAGES FOR BREACH OF CONTRACT TO FURNISH FREIGHT to be transported by the plaintiff for a stipulated sum is the actual loss to the plaintiff, and not the contract price, and the defendant may reduce the damages by showing that the plaintiff received freight from others, in lieu of that which the defendant failed to furnish, or by proving in any other way that the injury was less than the contract price.

TENDER OF PERFORMANCE BY PLAINTIFF IS EQUIVALENT TO PERFORMANCE of a contract only for the purpose of sustaining the action, and not for regulating the damages.

ERROR from Washington common pleas, in an action for breach of contract brought to that court on certiorari to a judgment in a justice's court in favor of the plaintiff. It appeared that the action was commenced by warrant in the justice's court, founded on an affidavit that the defendants were non-residents. The defendants, before pleading to the action, moved to quash the proceedings on the ground that they were, and had been for more than thirty days, residents of the state, which was admitted for the purpose of the motion. Motion overruled. Plea in abatement, that one of the defendants was, at and for more than thirty days before the commencement of the action, a resident of the state, adjudged bad on demurrer. The defendants then pleaded the general issue. The contract declared on was for the transportation by the plaintiffs on their boat from Whitehall to Albany, of a number of horses for the defendants for a certain sum, and the plaintiffs averred readiness and offer to perform on their part and non-performance by the defendants. It appeared that the horses were embarked on the day agreed on, but becoming restive, the defendants were compelled to take them off and abandon that method of transportation. The defendants offered evidence to show that the plaintiffs' damages did not exceed five dollars, but the justice rejected the evidence, and instructed the jury in substance that the contract price was the true measure of damages. Verdict for less than half the contract price, and judgment thereon, which was affirmed by the common pleas, whereupon the defendants brought the case here.

E. D. Culver, for the plaintiffs in error.

L. Gibbs, for the defendants in error.

By Court, COWEN, J. Upon the motion to quash the warrant, the plaintiffs before the justice admitted that the defendants were residents of Granville, in Washington county, and had been so for more than thirty days before the warrant was taken out. The justice had jurisdiction of the process, and the affidavit on which the warrant issued made it regular in the first instance. But certainly the affidavit was not conclusive. It was still open to be met by the defendants, on proof that it was made under a plain mistake. That was admitted, and the justice should, therefore, have dismissed the suit; or, to speak more technically, he should have set aside the proceedings for irregularity. I admit the plea in abatement was bad. It went to the whole suit, for a cause personal to one of the defendants only. It was therefore bad as a plea, whatever it might have been as a motion: *De Forest* v. *Jewett*, 1 Hall, 137. I am inclined to think that where two persons are arrested in a suit against both jointly upon a contract, and one is a resident of this state and has been for more than a month, he must be dischargd. But let that pass. Nor is it any answer that the defendants finally pleaded in bar. Such an answer must rest on the ground of voluntary waiver; here the propriety of the arrest was questioned at once, on admitted facts, and the defendants were compelled to plead over.

Again, the rule of damages was mistaken. The defendants were indeed bound to furnish the proposed freight in horses, and the plaintiffs were ready to take it at the fifty-five dollars agreed to be given; but it by no means follows that the latter was the sole measure of damages. The plaintiffs tendered their labor, which it was impossible for the defendants to avail themselves of. Suppose the plaintiffs had the next hour been furnished with freight entirely adequate to the voyage, at the same sum; they then would have been entitled to the damage arising from detention for that time, but no more. The authorities cited for the defendants in error are altogether misapplied. They go to show, what no one will dispute, that a tender and offer to perform is equivalent to performance. But that is merely for the purpose of sustaining an action. It is a rule of pleading in which you do not aver performance. If it were actual performance, you need not even declare specially. This shows that it is not performance, though in one respect it resembles it consequentially. In this, it is *quasi* performance; but it does not regulate the amount of damages. A man agrees to convey his farm, and the money is tendered, but he can not give a title; this is not a case for damages even for the loss of a good bargain; but the damages would be merely nominal. Yet if the tender were the same in respect to damages, as a performance, that is to say, actual payment, the vendee might keep his money and recover the value of the thing: See *Baldwin* v. *Munn*, 2 Wend. 399 [20 Am. Dec. 627]; and *per* De Grey, C. J., in *Flureau* v. *Thornhill*, 2 Bl. 1078.

Suppose the defendants below had, on the very day of the contract, given notice to the plaintiffs that they could not furnish the horses, and should not attempt to do so; it is equally well settled that the plaintiffs might have recovered damages, without any tender or offer to perform on their part. In such case, or where it becomes impossible for one party to perform, the other side is absolved from all obligation to move and may sue immediately. That too is considered equivalent to a performance by the side which is not in fault. And yet shall it be said that the whole sum to be paid for actual performance may be recovered? Suppose in the case of the covenant to convey a farm for a specified sum, and a deed tendered but refused, and the vendor sells to another, shall he yet recover the whole price of the original vendee? I admit that in some cases, where property is so tendered, and the tender is not withdrawn, the price may be recovered; but this is on the ground that the thing sold has an independent existence, and the corpus not being perishable, and having legally passed by the tender and subsequent recovery, may still be actually delivered over whenever the vendee shall demand it. That was held where a deed had been tendered in *Alna* v. *Plummer*, 4 Greenl. 258. The same rule was applied to goods, in *Bement* v. *Smith*, 15 Wend. 493. The vendor was to make a sulky, deliverable at a certain time and place to the vendee   It was finished and tendered, but refused, and the vendor told the vendee he would leave it with De Wolf, who resided in the neighborhood. The vendor was allowed to recover the price. This court held that he had his election to resell, and recover what he lost by the resale, or make the tender, and keep it good, and recover the whole original price agreed. But the distinction between that case and the one at bar is very obvious. Here we have a contract to sell labor and services. On the vendee declining them, the vendor sells them to another or converts them to his own use: in other words, he goes about his business in another direction, which fetches him the same or nearly the same, or more, perhaps, than the agreed price, which has failed. This is necessarily so unless the vendor of the labor choose to lie idle, for the supposed length of time which performance would have demanded. But that he has no right to do. The rule of this subject is well laid down by Mellen, C. J., in *Miller* v. *Mariners' Church*, 3 Greenl. 51, 55, 56.[1] "In general, the delinquent party is holden to make good the loss occasioned by the delinquency. But his liability is limited to direct damages, which, according to the nature of the subject, may be contemplated or presumed to result from his failure. The purchaser of perishable goods at auction fails to complete his contract. What shall be done? Shall the auctioneer leave the goods to perish, and throw the entire loss upon the purchaser? That would be to aggravate it unreasonably and unnecessarily. It is his duty to sell them a second time, and if they bring less, he may recover the difference, with commissions and other expenses of resale, from the purchaser. If the party entitled to the benefit of the contract can protect himself from the loss arising from a breach, at a reasonable expense, or with reasonable exertions, he fails in his social duty, if he omits to do so, regardless of the increased amount of damages for which he may intend to hold the other contracting party liable."

The reason and justice of these remarks are open to continual illustration in the affairs of men. A mason is engaged to work for a month and tenders himself and offers to perform, but his hirer declines the service. The next day the mason is employed at equal wages elsewhere for a month. Clearly his loss is but one day; and it is his duty to seek other employment. Idleness is in itself a breach of moral obligation. But if he continue idle for the purpose of charging another, he superadds a fraud which the law had rather punish than countenance. "Damages and interest," says the civil law and the continental writers, "are the loss which a person has sustained, or the gain which he has missed:" 1 Ev. Poth. 90, Lond. ed. 1806.

In the case at bar it is hardly possible that the deck of the plaintiffs' boat could have remained entirely useless and unprofitable during all the time necessary for a trip to Albany. The jury, I perceive, notwithstanding the total exclusion of evi-

---

1. 7 Greenl. 51; S. C ; 20 Am. Dec. 341.

dence and the rigor of the rule laid down by the magistrate in his charge, reduced the damages to less than one half the contract price, probably on the general knowledge which they had of the facilities for engaging freight at Whitehall, and thereby avoiding the injury arising from disappointments like that in question. Clearly the defendants should have been allowed, as they offered, to show that a farther reduction would have been just. The loss arose from their mere misfortune. If they had acted selfishly or fraudulently, this would have made a shade of difference against them. But all the witnesses concur that the failure was from causes which the defendants could not have anticipated, much less have controlled. The judgment of the court below must be reversed.

Ordered accordingly.

MEASURE OF DAMAGES FOR BREACH OF CONTRACT IS THE INJURY SUSTAINED, WHEN: See *Terry* v. *Eslava*, 27 Am. Dec. 626, and cases referred to in the note thereto. See also *Blanchard* v. *Ely*, *ante*, 250, and note. Compensation for the loss sustained is the general rule of damages: See the note to *Merrills* v. *Tariff Mfg. Co.*, 27 Id. 684. The principal case is a recognized authority on the subject of the measure of damages for the breach of a contract. It is cited in *Masterton* v. *Mayor etc. of Brooklyn*, 7 Hill, 75, and *Bagley* v. *Smith*, 10 N. Y. 497; S. C., 19 How. Pr. 5, for the general doctrine that for breach of a contract, the other party being ready to perform may recover precisely what he would have made by full performance on both sides. In the latter decision it is said that in such cases the amount of profits lost is the measure of compensation. But it is the duty of the complainant not to lie idle and trust to his action for entire remuneration. He must do what he can to lessen the damages, as in the case of a breach of a contract for employment, by endeavoring to procure employment elsewhere, or the like: *Huntington* v. *Ogdensburg etc. R. R. Co.*, 33 How. Pr. 419; *Hamilton* v. *McPherson*, 28 N. Y. 77; *Utter* v. *Chapman*, 38 Cal. 666; *Bailey* v. *Damon*, 3 Gray, 97; *Gillis* v. *Space*, 63 Barb. 182, all citing the principal case. But to mitigate the damages below the contract price, the burden is on the defendant to show that by reasonable exertions the plaintiff might have lightened his loss by procuring employment elsewhere, or otherwise, according to the nature of the case: *Gillis* v. *Space*, *supra*.

TENDER OF PERFORMANCE, HOW FAR EQUIVALENT TO PERFORMANCE OF A CONTRACT.—On this point the principal case is recognized as authority in *Richards* v. *Edick*, 17 Barb. 265; *Billings* v. *Vanderbeck*, 23 Id. 554; *Polk* v. *Daly*, 4 Daly, 414; S. C., 14 Abb. Pr. (N. S.) 159; *Hale* v. *Trout*, 38 Cal. 242.

ANSWER TO THE MERITS DOES NOT WAIVE ANY LEGAL OBJECTION insisted on in the answer: *Teague* v. *Dendy*, 16 Am. Dec. 643. Nor does an answer to the merits waive objections to fatal defects in the affidavit upon which a warrant of arrest or an attachment was sued out, the objection thereto having been duly made and overruled: *Broadhead* v. *McConnell*, 3 Barb. 190, and *Dewey* v. *Greene*, 4 Denio, 94, both citing *Shannon* v. *Comstock*.

AFFIDAVIT FOR ARREST OF DEFENDANT as a fraudulent debtor is not conclusive, but may be rebutted on motion for discharge by counter affidavits: *Johnson* v. *Florence*, 32 How. Pr. 232.

GRIFFITH v. REED AND DIXSON.

[21 WENDELL, 502.]

ADDING THE WORD "SURETY" TO THE SIGNATURE of one signing a bill with the drawer, gives notice to all to whose hands it may come that the person so signing is liable only as a surety.

PRESUMPTION FROM ACCEPTANCE OF A BILL IS THAT THE ACCEPTOR HAS FUNDS of the drawer in his hands; but, as between drawer and acceptor, this presumption may be rebutted by showing that the bill was accepted and paid for the drawer's accommodation.

ACCEPTOR PAYING A BILL FOR THE DRAWER'S ACCOMMODATION, may recover the amount from the drawer on an implied contract to indemnify him, but not on the bill, because its vitality is destroyed by payment.

SURETY IS UNDER NO IMPLIED CONTRACT TO INDEMNIFY THE DRAWEE upon the latter's paying the bill for the drawer's accommodation, having notice of the suretyship, a surety being bound only by his express contract.

SURETY'S UNDERTAKING IS THAT THE DRAWEE WILL ACCEPT and pay the bill; and when the bill is paid by the drawee, the surety's contract is at an end. He has no contract with the drawee.

ASSUMPSIT, the declaration containing the common money counts. Reed only was served. The object of the action was to recover the amount of certain bills drawn upon the plaintiffs by the defendant Dixson and by the defendant Reed, who affixed to his signature the word "surety," which bills had been paid by the plaintiffs. It appeared that the plaintiffs were commission merchants, and had been in the habit of receiving shipments of flour from Dixson and selling them, Dixson drawing bills upon them from time to time, which they paid, and charged to Dixson. They insisted that they had no funds of Dixson at the time of paying the bills now in controversy, while the defendant Reed claimed that the proceeds of certain flour, sold by the plaintiffs, should have been applied to those bills. Report by referees in favor of the plaintiffs, which the defendant now moved to set aside on grounds appearing from the opinion.

A. Worden, for the defendant.

O. Hastings and M. T. Reynolds, for the plaintiffs.

By Court, BRONSON, J. If we assume that the plaintiffs are right on all the controverted questions of fact in the case, they must still fail in their action. If they were in truth accommodation acceptors, and had no funds applicable to the payment of these bills, their remedy is against Dixson, the principal, for whose accommodation they accepted; and not against Reed the surety.

As an original question, it would, perhaps, be well that a man should never be allowed to become a party to commercial paper as a surety—or rather, that his character of surety should be wholly disregarded. But it is quite too late to agitate that question in this state. It has been long settled that a man may become a party to a promissory note or bill of exchange as a surety, and that he is entitled to all the privileges applicable to that character, as fully as though he were surety in a different form of contract: *Pain* v. *Packard*, 13 Johns. 174 [7 Am. Dec. 369]; *King* v. *Baldwin*, 17 Id. 384 [8 Am. Dec. 415]; *Manchester Iron Co.* v. *Sweeting*, 10 Wend. 162; *Huffman* v. *Hulbert*, 13 Id. 375; *Harris* v. *Warner*, Id. 401. These remarks do not apply to an indorser; for though he is in the nature of a surety, he is not for all purposes entitled to that character: *Trimble* v. *Thorne*, 16 Johns. 152 [8 Am. Dec. 302]; *Beardsley* v. *Warner*, 6 Wend. 610; S. C. in error, 8 Id. 194. When it does not appear on the face of the paper that the party is a surety, notice of the character in which he contracted must of course be brought home to the holder before he can be affected by it. In this case the character in which Reed contracted appeared on the face of the bill, and every one into whose hands it came was bound to know that Dixson was the principal, and Reed his surety. Although the relation of principal and surety between the joint drawers could not affect the ordinary rights and remedies of the holder, yet, under certain circumstances, the surety might be discharged, although the principal should remain liable. If, for example, the bill had been protested for non-payment, the holder could not safely treat with Dixson in any way which should prejudice Reed; and if the holder, after a request to enforce his remedy against the principal while he was able to pay, should neglect to do so until he became insolvent, the surety would be discharged. This doctrine will be found in the cases already cited.

To understand the effect which the relation of principal and surety between the drawers will have upon the acceptors, it will be proper to consider very briefly the nature and office of a bill of exchange. A bill of exchange imports that a debt is due from the drawee to the drawer, which is assigned to the payee of the bill; and if the drawee accepts, it is an acknowledgment on his part that he has funds of the drawer in his hands to the amount of the bill. The presumption of funds in the hands of the acceptor is conclusive as between him and every *bona fide* holder of the paper; and it is so strong in favor of the drawer, that when the bill is payable to his own order, he may, like any

other holder, maintain an action on the bill against the acceptor.
The undertaking of the drawer is, that the bill shall be accepted
and paid by the drawee, and on acceptance his undertaking becomes collateral to that of the acceptor, who is then regarded
as the principal debtor.   The primary resort for payment is to
the acceptor, and it is only on his default and after due notice
to the drawer, that the latter becomes liable to pay the holder
When the bill is paid and taken up by the drawee, it ceases to
be obligatory upon any of the parties; it has performed its office,
and is no better than a piece of blank paper, except as the
memorial of a past transaction.   These principles are so nearly
elementary, that I shall only refer to a few cases: *Cruger* v.
Armstrong, 3 Johns. Cas. 5 [2 Am. Dec. 126]; *Simmons* v. *Par-
menter*, 1 Wils. 185; *Vere* v. *Lewis*, 3 T. R. 182; *Thompson* v.
Morgan, 3 Camp. 101; *Raborg* v. *Peyton*, 2 Wheat. 385; Chit.
on Bills, Phil. ed. 1826, 1, 182; 2 Stark. Ev. 275, 302.

The presumption that the drawer has funds in the hands of
the acceptor may be rebutted.   The drawee may show that he
accepted and paid the bill for the accommodation of the drawer;
and then, in the absence of any express stipulation, the law will
imply an undertaking on the part of the drawer to indemnify
the acceptor.   On this implied obligation the acceptor may have
an action against the drawer, but not on the bill itself: *Young*
v. *Hockley*, 2 Wils. 346;[1] *Chilton* v. *Whiffin*, Id. 13;[2] Chit. on
Bills, 344, 410; Chit. jun. on Bills, 38, 40; Stark. Ev. 276.   As
between the drawer and drawee, the bill is a mere request or
direction to pay money; it never speaks, as it does between
other parties, the language of contract, or imports any obligation.   When the acceptor sues, whether he declares specially on
the implied promise to indemnify, or generally for money paid,
the bill itself is not the foundation of the action; it is but an
item of evidence.   So if one man lend his own note to another,
and is afterwards obliged to pay and take it up, the law will imply a promise on the part of the borrower to indemnify the
maker; but surely, the maker could not sue the borrower on the
note itself.   The thing is preposterous.   It would be no less
absurd to suppose that an accommodation acceptor can maintain an action against the drawer on the bill itself.   When a
note is paid by the maker, or a bill by the acceptor, its vitality
is gone.   It ceases to be a binding contract upon any one.   In
the case at bar, the plaintiffs have not thought of suing on the
bill.   They go on an implied assumpsit to refund the money,

---

1. 3 Wils. 346.   2. 3 Wils. 13.

which they say springs out of the fact that they paid the bill without having funds of the drawers in their hands.

This brings us to an insuperable difficulty in the way of maintaining this action. Reed is a surety, and the plaintiffs seek to charge him, not on the contract which he made, but on one which they say may be implied by law. No case was mentioned on the argument, nor do I know of any where the law will imply a promise or obligation against a surety. He is bound by his express contract, and by that only. Had the bill been protested for non-payment, the payee or other holder could treat him as one of the joint drawers, and have a remedy on the bill itself. His undertaking was, as we have already seen, that the bill should be accepted and paid. That was his contract, and he was bound by it. But he made no agreement whatever with the drawees of the bill: See *Douglass* v. *Reynolds*, 7 Pet. 113.

If this seems a narrow view of the question, let us see what was the fair import of the transaction. And first, what was the language of the bill to those who took it? The payee and every other holder, on observing that Reed was a surety, would at once read the bill thus: Dixson is the principal; it is a debt due to him that the bill purports to transfer; it is Dixson, and he alone, that has dealings with the drawees. But for the purpose of inducing us to discount and advance money on the bill, Reed has become the surety of Dixson, and both agree that the bill shall be accepted and paid by the drawees. If not paid, we shall have a remedy against both; but we must take care not to have any negotiations with the principal which may prejudice the surety. And here I may remark that Reed, as well as every one else, had a right to suppose that Dixson had funds in the hands of the drawees. What was the language of the bill to the drawees when it was presented to them? They could not but read it thus—Dixson is the principal—he draws on us, and Reed has lent his name as a surety. Dixson agreed with the holder that we should accept and pay, and Reed was a surety for the performance of that contract; he became such surety for the purpose of inducing the payee to discount the bill and advance the money to Dixson. The bill is not drawn on the funds of Dixson and Reed, but on the funds of Dixson, the principal. If we pay the bill, we must charge the money to his account If he has no funds with us, and does not provide them, we must look to him on the implied undertaking to refund the money. Now this is precisely the way in which the plaintiffs did read and reason upon this bill. They had dealings with Dixson—

they understood that the bill was drawn on his account, and to him they charged the money. They judged rightly in doing so. The afterthought of bringing this action was, to say the least of it, a mistake.

I have noticed the two facts that Dixson had dealings with the plaintiffs, and that they charged the money to his account, for the purpose of showing that they have not been misled. They did not pay the bill under any impression that they could resort to Reed, and compel him to refund the money. But I do not consider those facts material in making out a legal defense. When they saw on the face of the bill that one of the joint drawers was a surety for the other, they were bound to know that they accepted and paid for and on account of the principal, and him only. We were told on the argument that the original theory of a bill of exchange, which supposes funds in the hands of the drawee, is no longer true; but bills are now more commonly drawn without, than with funds; and that our adherence to the old doctrine would shake a multitude of commercial transactions. It is no doubt true that bills are now very commonly drawn for purposes quite wide of their appropriate office, and I think it equally true that this mode of creating credit has led to the most mischievous consequences. The evil began to be seen and felt many years ago. In *Pentum v. Pocock,*[1] 5 Taunt. 192, Mansfield, C. J., said, "the paying respect to accommodation bills is not what one would wish to do, seeing the mischiefs arising from them;" and Heath, J., said, "the courts had gone much too far in lending support to these mischievous instruments, the evils resulting from which we see every day." Mr. Chitty, in the sixth edition of his treatise on bills, says: "The pernicious effects of a fabricated credit by the undue use of accommodation bills of exchange, drawn out of the ordinary course of trade, have been too much felt to require any observation; the use of them where there is no real demand subsisting between the parties, is injurious to the public as well as to the parties concerned in the negotiation:" p. 4. If he were now to review this opinion, whether standing on this or the other side of the Atlantic, he would find no occasion to question the severity of the judgment which he pronounced in 1822 upon this species of paper. The portentous cloud which at this moment hangs over the whole commercial world, has gathered much of its fearful aspect from the modern practice of fabricat-

---

1. *Pentum v. Pocock.*

ing credit by means of bills drawn out of the ordinary course
of trade.

There is nothing, then, in the fact that accommodation bills
are in common use, which should induce us to give them any
new sanction. We do not deny their validity. We only adhere
to an old and well-established rule of law. Although many
bills are drawn where there is no real demand subsisting between
the parties, we can not presume that such is always the case;
and if we could, we can not impart a new quality or force to
the instrument, and make it speak the language of contract as
between the drawer and the drawee. We must go this length
before the plaintiffs can make out a cause of action against the
surety.

Report set aside.

PRESUMPTION IS THAT DRAWER HAS FUNDS in the drawee's hands until
the contrary appears: *Baxter* v. *Graves*, 12 Am. Dec. 374; especially after
acceptance by the drawee: *Kendall* v. *Galvin*, 32 Id. 141. See also *Lee Bank*
v. *Satterlee*, 17 Abb. Pr. 10; *Phœnix Bank* v. *Bank of America*, 1 Leg. Obs.
27; *Hidden* v. *Waldo*, 55 N. Y. 297, citing the principal case.

TO ENABLE THE ACCEPTOR AFTER PAYMENT TO RECOVER FROM THE DRAWER
he must overcome the presumption arising from his acceptance that he has
funds of the drawer in his hands: *Kendall* v. *Galvin*, 32 Am. Dec. 141.

ADMISSIBILITY OF EVIDENCE TO SHOW THAT DEFENDANT SIGNED A NOTE AS
SURETY: See *Harris* v. *Brooks*, 32 Am. Dec. 254; see also *Artcher* v. *Douglass*, 5 Denio, 513; *Suydam* v. *Westfall*, 4 Hill, 218; *Barry* v. *Ransom*, 12 N.
Y. 466; *Easterly* v. *Barber*, 3 N. Y. S. C. (T. & C.) 423, all citing the
principal case.

SURETY IS LIABLE TO PAYEE, NOT TO ACCEPTOR: *Wright* v. *Garlinghouse*, 27
Barb. 477, citing the principal case.

OTHER POINTS TO WHICH THE PRINCIPAL CASE IS CITED are: An indorser,
although in the nature of a surety, is not, for all purposes, entitled to the
privileges of that character: *Bradford* v. *Corey*, 5 Barb. 462; S. C., 4 How.
Pr. 162. Notice of a party's being a surety being brought home to the
holder of a note, such party is entitled to have the principles of the law of
suretyship applied in determining his rights: *Dunham* v. *Countryman*, 66
Barb. 270. The law raises an implied promise by the principal, and not by
the surety, to refund the amount of a bill to the drawee, where the latter
pays without having funds for that purpose: *Wing* v. *Terry*, 5 Hill, 162. The
law implies an obligation on the part of a drawer to indemnify the acceptor:
Pomeroy v. *Tanner*, 70 N. Y. 552. A drawee may show, after acceptance,
that he has no funds in his hands, and that he was merely an accommodation acceptor: *Easterly* v. *Barber*, 66 N. Y. 438. That a drawer is relieved
from his implied obligation to indemnify his drawees against the payment of
drafts drawn on them without funds, where there was an arrangement between such drawees and the payees, that the bills should be accepted for the
accommodation of the payees, to whose account they should be charged, and
to whom the acceptors were to look for payment: *Thurman* v. *Van Brunt*, 19
Barb. 411.

HARTFIELD v. ROPER AND NEWELL.

[21 WENDELL, 615.]

OBJECTION TO EVIDENCE NOT MADE AT THE TRIAL, can not be heard on a motion for a new trial.

ACTION FOR AN INJURY TO A CHILD LIES IN THE NAME OF THE CHILD.

NEGLIGENCE MAY BE PREDICATED OF AN INFANT.

PARENTS PERMITTING A CHILD TWO YEARS OLD TO BE IN A PUBLIC HIGHWAY unattended, are guilty of such contributory negligence as will defeat an action in the child's name for an injury done to it by a traveler in the highway, where willful fault or gross negligence is not imputable to the defendant.

OWNER OF TEAM DEMISED FOR A TERM IS NOT LIABLE FOR INJURY done by it while being driven along the highway by the tenant, though the owner was in the vehicle at the time, if there was no positive and active concurrence in the injury on his part.

CO-DEFENDANT IS NOT ENTITLED TO ACQUITTAL SO AS TO BE MADE A WITNESS for other defendants, unless there is a total failure of evidence against him.

ACTION on the case brought in the name of the plaintiff, an infant, by his next friend, for an injury caused by his being run over by a sleigh and horses by the defendants. The accident happened when the plaintiff was but two years old. He was sitting or standing in the public road at the time, and the defendant Roper was driving along the highway at a moderate pace, the defendant Newell and his daughter Mrs. Lewis being in the sleigh with him, but none of them saw the child until the injury happened. The remaining facts sufficiently appear from the opinion. Motion for a nonsuit overruled; also a motion to instruct the jury to acquit Newell, so that he might be used as witness, on the ground that nothing was proved against him. Verdict for the plaintiff under the judge's charge for five hundred dollars. Motion for a new trial.

J. A. Spencer, for the defendants.

W. Tracy and W. C. Noyes, for the plaintiff.

By Court, COWEN, J. The injury to this child was doubtless a very serious misfortune to him. But I have been utterly unable to collect, from the evidence, anything by which the jury were authorized to impute such carelessness as rendered these defendants responsible. It is true they might have seen the child from the turn of the road in descending, had they looked so far ahead; but something must be allowed for their attention to the management of the horses and their own safety in descending the hill to a bridge. So unobserving were they, in fact, that Mrs. Lewis, who sat in the rear of the sleigh, on the left side, and therefore in the best position of the three to overlook the road in its full extent, as far as the place where the child was, did not discern him. It was somewhat severe, in a case like this, to allow testimony of Newell's ability to pay, though it was not objected to. It seems to imply that he had been so brutal as silently to allow Roper's going on and endangering the child's life, after he, Newell, had discovered it to be in the road. But perhaps no objection can now be heard to that evidence having been received, because it was not made at the trial. No doubt the action was properly brought in the name of the child. Nor is there any objection to its form, since the statute, 2 R. S. 456, section 16, 2d ed. Nor could the father have brought an action for loss of service, in respect to so small a child, according to the English case of *Hall* v. *Hollander*, 4 Barn. & Cress. 660; though I should think it quite questionable whether that case can be considered as law here. If the defendants were, in truth, so reckless of the child's safety, as to run over it, in the way described, after knowing it to be in the road, the verdict is none too large. But such trifling with human life ought not to be presumed; and there was no proof of it, either direct or circumstantial. This is not a case, however, for interfering upon the ground of excessive damages.

The only question which seems to be open for our consideration is that of negligence. This respects both parties. It is quite necessary to drive at a moderate pace, and look out against accidents to children and others, in a populous village or city. See *McAllister* v. *Hammond*, 6 Cow. 342, and *per* Lawrence, J., in *Leame* v. *Bray*, 3 East, 597. But this accident happened in the country, where was a solitary house; a child belonging to it, happened to be in the road, a thing most imprudently allowed by its parents, and what could have been easily prevented by ordinary care. Travelers are not prepared for such things. They, therefore, trot their horses. They are warrantably inattentive to small objects in the road, which they may be incapable of seeing in the course of a drive for miles through the country, among a sparse population. To keep a constant lookout, would be more than a driver could do, even if he were continually standing and driving on a walk. Yet to this the matter must come, if he is to take all the responsibility. The roads would thus become of very little use in the line for which they were principally intended. It seems to me that the defendants exercised all the care which, in the nature of this case, the law required. If so, it is a case of mere unavoidable accident; for which they are not liable: *Dygert* v. *Bradley*, 8 Wend. 469, 472, 473; *Clark* v. *Foot*, 8 Johns. 421; *Penton* v. *Holland*,[1] 17 Id. 92.

Was the plaintiff guilty of negligence? His counsel seemed to think he made a complete exception to the general rule demanding care on his part, by reason of his extreme infancy. Is this indeed so? A snow path in the public highway, is among the last places in this country to which such a small child should be allowed to resort, unattended by any one of suitable age and discretion. The custody of such a child is confided by law to its parents, or to others standing in their place; and it is absurd to imagine that it could be exposed in the road, as this child was, without gross carelessness. It is the extreme of folly even to turn domestic animals upon the common highway. To allow small children to resort there alone, is a criminal neglect. It is true that this confers no right upon travelers to commit a voluntary injury upon either; nor does it warrant gross neglect; but it seems to me that, to make them liable for anything short of that, would be contrary to law. The child has a right to the road for the purposes of travel, attended by the proper escort. But at the tender age of two or three years, and even more, the infant can not personally exercise that degree of discretion, which becomes instinctive at an advanced age, and for which the law must make him responsible, through others, if the doctrine of mutual care between the parties using the road is to be enforced at all in his case.

It is perfectly well settled that, if the party injured by a collision on the highway has drawn the mischief upon himself by his own neglect, he is not entitled to an action, even though he be lawfully in the highway pursuing his travels: *Rathbun* v. *Payne*, 19 Wend. 399; *Burcle* v. *N. Y. Dry Dock Company*, 2 Hall, 151; which can scarcely be said of a toppling infant, suffered by his guardians to be there, either as a traveler or for the purpose of pursuing his sports. The application may be harsh when made to small children; as they are known to have no personal discretion, common humanity is alive to their protection; but they are not, therefore, exempt from the legal rule, when they bring an action for redress; and there is no other way of enforcing it, except by requiring due care at the hands of those to whom the law and the necessity of the case has delegated the exercise of discretion. An infant is not *sui juris*. He belongs

1. *Penton* v. *Holland;* S. C., 8 Am. Dec. 369.

to another, to whom discretion in the care of his person is exclusively confided. That person is keeper and agent for this purpose; and in respect to third persons, his act must be deemed that of the infant; his neglect, the infant's neglect. Suppose a hopeless lunatic, suffered to stray by his committee, lying in the road like a log, shall the traveler, whose sleigh unfortunately strikes him, be amenable in damages? The neglect of the committee to whom his custody is confided shall be imputed to him. It is a mistake to suppose that because the party injured is incapable of personal discretion, he is, therefore, above all law? An infant or lunatic is liable personally for wrongs which he commits against the person and property of others: *Bullock* v. *Babcock*, 3 Wend. 391, 394. And when he complains of wrongs to himself, the defendant has a right to insist that he should not have been the heedless instrument of his own injury. He can not, more than any other, make a profit of his own wrong. *Volente non fit injuria.* If his proper agent and guardian has suffered him to incur mischief, it is much more fit that he should look for redress to that guardian, than that the latter should negligently allow his ward to be in the way of travelers, and then harrass them in courts of justice, recovering heavy verdicts for his own misconduct.

The counsel for the plaintiff probably have the advantage of saying that the neglect of an infant has not, in any reported case, ever been allowed by way of defense in an action for negligently injuring him. But so far, there is an equal advantage on the other side. The defense has not been denied in any book of reports. The defendant has also another advantage. The reports expressly say that negligence may be predicated of an infant or lunatic. All the cases agree that trespass lies against an infant. That was adjudged in *Campbell* v. *Stakes*, 2 Wend. 137 [19 Am. Dec. 561], and *Bullock* v. *Babcock*, before cited. And it is equally well settled that where an injury is free from all negligence, as if it arise from inevitable accident, there trespass does not lie: *Weaver* v. *Ward*, Hob. 134; Marcy, J., in *Bullock* v. *Babcock*, 2 Wend. 393;[1] *Dygert* v. *Bradley*, before cited. The cases maintaining trespass against an infant, therefore, imply that he may be guilty of negligence. Trover will also lie for a mere non-feasance, e. g., a non-delivery of goods where they do not come to the infant's hands by contract. Lawrence, J., in *Jennings* v. *Rundall*, 8 T. R. 337; *Campbell* v. *Stakes*, 2 Wend. 143 [19 Am. Dec. 561]. The cases most favorable to

1. 2 Wend. 396.

infants, all agree in that. And so, where the contract of bailment to an infant has expired, it was agreed that on non-delivery the owner may maintain detinue, replevin, or trover: *Penrose v. Curren*, 3 Rawle, 351 [24 Am. Dec. 356]. And see *per* Rogers, J., Id. 354. It was said trespass lies against an infant though only four years of age: 25 Hen. VI., 11 b, *per* Wangford, though this is put by Brook with a *quære*: Br. Abr. Corone, pl. 6. No doubt, however, he may bring a suit at any age; and if that suit depends upon a condition on his side, he must show that it was performed. It was said in *Stowell* v. *Zouch*, Plowd Com. 364, if an infant lord, who has title to enter for mortmain, does not enter within the year, he shall be bound by his laches; "for there he had but title to a thing which never was in him." To warrant an action he must have entered within the year; and not having done so, he could have no remedy. Several like instances are put in the same page, which are also collected and arranged in 9 Vin's Abr., Enfant (B 2), pl. 7, 8, p. 376, of the octavo ed.

But it is plain in the nature of things, that if an infant insist on a right of action, he must share a compliance with the conditions on which his right is to arise and this is entirely irrespective of his age. Land descends to an infant of a year old; and he is bound to make a share of the partition fence. He neglects to do so, whereby his neighbor's cattle enter and trespass upon the land. No one would think of contending that his neighbor, must, therefore, be deprived of his defense. The infant has neglected to fulfill the condition, on which he could sue, or his guardian has done so, which is the same thing. He might as well sue because his neighbor had left a gate on his own premises open, through which the infant had crept, and fallen into a pit and hurt himself. The man has a right to keep his gate open; and the child's parents must keep him away. But one has no plainer right to walk about his own premises, and open and shut his own gates, than he has to travel in the highway with his horses. An infant creeps into the track from your field to your barn, and is injured by your driving a load of hay along the path; are you to be deprived of all excuse in an action for the injury?

The argument for this plaintiff goes quite too far and proves too much. It was said that drivers are bound to suppose that small children may be in the road, and as all the care lies on the side of the former, damages follow of course for every injury to the latter. Suppose an infant suddenly throws himself in the way of a sleigh, a wagon, or a railroad car, by which his limb is fractured; it may be said with equal force, he is incapable of neglect. So if he be allowed to travel the road alone in the dark. The answer to all this is, the law has placed infants in the hands of vigilant and generally affectionate keepers, their own parents; and if there be any legal responsibility in damages, it lies upon them. The illustration sought to be derived from the law in respect to the injury of animals turned or suffered to stray into the street, does not strike me as fortunate. If they be there without any one to attend and take care of them, that is a degree of carelessness in the owner which would preclude his recovery of damages arising from mere inattention on the side of the traveler. Indeed it could rarely be said that animals entirely unattended are lawfully in the roads or streets at all. They may be driven along the road by the owner or his servants; but if allowed to run at large for the purpose of grazing, or any other purpose, entirely unattended, and yet travelers are to be made accountable in all cases of collision, such a doctrine might supersede the use of the road, so far as comfort or expedition is concerned. The mistake lies in supposing the injury to be willful, to arise from some positive act, or to be grossly negligent. Such an injury is never tolerated, be the negligence on the side of the party injured what it may: *Clay* v. *Wood*, 5 Esp. 44; *Rathbun* v. *Payne*, before cited. But where it arises from mere inadvertence on the side of the traveler, he is always excused by the law on showing that there was equal or greater neglect on the side of his accuser. It is impossible to say, then, that the accuser was not himself the author of the injury which he seeks to father upon another. My difficulty in the case at bar is to find the least color for imputing gross negligence, or indeed any degree of negligence to the defendants. But if there were any, there was, I think, as much and more on the side of the plaintiff.

It therefore seems to me that there was a good defense established at the trial, on the ground that the defendants being free from gross neglect, and the plaintiff being guilty of great neglect on his part, indeed being unnecessarily, not to say illegally occupying the road, having no right there (for he does not appear to have been traveling, nor even on the land which belonged to his family), the injury was a consequence of his own neglect, at least such neglect as the law must impute to him through others.

Again; I collect from the evidence that Newell had demised the team for a term of two years, which was unexpired at the

time of the injury, to his son-in-law and co-defendant, Roper.
Newell then had no control of the team, and can not be made
liable without proof of positive and active concurrence in the
injury, a thing for which there is no pretense in the proof, and
which implies a barbarous temper, which the law can not presume in any one. He, at least, should have been acquitted by
the jury. He neither actually participated in the management
of the team, nor could his interference have been legally efficient to prevent mischief. He had no lawful control of the
horses. Roper was the exclusive owner *pro hac vice*. The evidence, at the time when the motion was made to allow the jury
to pass upon the case of Newell, had made out nothing actual
against him, if Roper, the driver, may be said to have been im-
plicated as a wrong-doer. But Newell might, at this stage, perhaps have been regarded by the jury as owner of the horses,
and Roper as his servant. The lease was not in proof. Constructively, his liability would follow from the neglect of his
servant; and in this view it can not be said there was no evidence
against him. It is only where the evidence totally fails as to
one whose case can be separated from the other, that he is entitled to be acquitted for the purpose of being sworn as a witness for his co-defendant.

The motion for a nonsuit, which followed, seems to have been
the more proper one; for I have been utterly unable to see that,
so far, the evidence had made out any neglect, or the semblance
of neglect, on the part of the defendants, while it had established clear neglect on the other side. But this question has
been sufficiently dwelt upon in connection with the defendant's
proofs, and that which the plaintiff adduced at the close of the
cause. It was enough, if the cause of action was then made
out, although the judge might have refused to nonsuit. It appears to me it was not.

It follows that a new trial should be granted. The costs
should, I think, abide the event; for the judge erred in omitting
to nonsuit the plaintiff. The case was certainly not made better
for the plaintiff by the subsequent evidence. It is not, therefore, merely the case of a verdict against the weight of evidence,
which calls for payment of costs.

New trial granted; costs to abide the event.

———

OBJECTION TO EVIDENCE NOT MADE AT THE TRIAL DEEMED WAIVED:
See *Snyder* v. *Laframboise*, 12 Am. Dec. 187; *Jackson* v. *Davis*, 15 Id. 451;
Wait v. *Maxwell*, 16 Id. 391. See also *Edelen* v. *Hardey's Lessee*, Id. 292;
Carlton v. *King*, 23 Id. 295.

INFANT'S LIABILITY FOR NEGLIGENCE: See *Campbell* v. *Stakes*, 19 Am. Dec. 561, and note. As to the liability of infants for torts generally, see the note to *Humphrey* v. *Douglass*, 33 Id. 179, where the subject is discussed at length. On this point the principal case is cited in *Crozier* v. *People*, 1 Park. Crim. 455.

CONTRIBUTORY NEGLIGENCE DEFEATING RECOVERY FOR INJURY: See *Smith* v. *Smith*, 13 Am. Dec. 464; *Bush* v. *Brainard*, Id. 513; *Washburn* v. *Tracy*, 15 Id. 661; and *Reed* v. *Northfield*, 23 Id. 662, and the note thereto. The principal case is frequently referred to as an authority for the general doctrine that to enable one to recover for an injury occasioned by another's negligence he must himself be free from negligence: *Brownell* v. *Flagler*, 5 Hill, 283; *Brown* v. *Maxwell*, 6 Id. 593; *Clark* v. *Syracuse etc. R. R. Co.*, 11 Barb. 116; *Spencer* v. *Utica etc. R. R. Co.*, 5 Id. 338; *Haring* v. *New York etc. R. R. Co.*, 13 Id. 15; *Center* v. *Finney*, 17 Id. 98; *Dascomb* v. *Buffalo etc. R. R. Co.*, 27 Id. 228; *Brooks* v. *Buffalo etc. R. R. Co.*, 25 Id. 602; *Bowman* v. *Troy etc. R. R. Co.*, 37 Id. 519; *Morris* v. *Phelps*, 2 Hilt. 39; *German* v. *New York etc. R/ R. Co.*, 3 Rob. 31; *Gonzales* v. *New York etc. R. R. Co.*, 39 How. Pr. 415; *Munger* v. *Tonawanda R. R. Co.*, 4 N. Y. 359; *Button* v. *Hudson River R. R. Co.*, 18 Id. 251; *Eckert* v. *Long Island R. R. Co.*, 43 Id. 507. per Allen, J., dissenting; *Barker* v. *Savage*, 45 Id. 193; *Chicago etc. R. R. Co.* v. *Patchin*, 16 Ill. 202; *Galena etc. R. R. Co.* v. *Jacobs*, 20 Id. 495; *Hull* v. *Richmond*, 2 Woodb. & M. 345. The point mentioned in the principal case, as to whether a plaintiff guilty of some negligence can recover from a defendant who has been guilty of gross negligence, is referred to but not decided in *McGrath* v. *Hudson River R. R. Co.*, 32 Barb. 155; S. C., 19 How. Pr. 224.

NEGLIGENCE OF PARENT CONTRIBUTING TO INJURY OF INFANT.—The doctrine laid down in *Hartfield* v. *Roper*, that where an infant of such tender age as to be *non sui juris* is injured by another's negligence, but there has been contributory negligence on the part of the parent or guardian in permitting such infant to wander into the highway unattended, or the like, neither such infant nor his administrator can recover for the injury, is approved and followed in a number of cases: *Lehman* v. *City of Brooklyn*, 29 Barb. 237; *Mangam* v. *Brooklyn City R. R. Co.*, 36 Id. 238; S. C., in court of appeals, 38 N. Y. 456, et seq.; *Mowrey* v. *Central City Railway*, 66 Barb. 51; *Thurber* v. *Harlem etc. R. R. Co.*, 60 N. Y. 333; *McGarry* v. *Loomis*, 63 Id. 107; *McLain* v. *Van Zandt*, 39 N. Y. Super. Ct. (7 Jones & S.) 351; *Wright* v. *Malden etc. R. R. Co.*, 4 Allen, 287. Nor can the parent recover for such injury: *Honegsberger* v. *Second Avenue R. R. Co.*, 2 Abb. App. Dec. 381; S. C., 33 How. Pr. 199; *Burke* v. *Broadway etc. R. R. Co.*, 49 Barb. 532; *Kreig* v. *Wells*, 1 E. D. Smith, 77; *Ihl* v. *Forty-second St. R. R. Co.*, 47 N. Y. 323. Hogeboom, J., in *Lannen* v. *Albany Gas Light Co.*, 46 Barb. 270, seemed not to approve the doctrine in its full extent that an infant can not recover for an injury because his parent has been guilty of contributory negligence. After citing the principal case and some others, he says: "I know of no just or legal principle, which, when the infant himself is free from negligence, imputes to him the negligence of the parent, when if he were an adult he would escape it." That was a case, however, where the child was of such an age as to have perhaps some degree of discretion. In *Thurber* v. *Harlem etc. R. R. Co.*, 60 N. Y. 333, Allen, J., refers to *Hartfield* v. *Roper* as a "leading case;" and in *Mangam* v. *Brooklyn City R. R. Co.*, 36 Barb. 239, Emott, J., says it "is and deserves to be a leading case for the very able opinion of Judge Cowen."

BANK OF UTICA v. BENDER.

[21 WENDELL, 643.]

WHAT IS REASONABLE DILIGENCE IN ASCERTAINING INDORSER'S RESIDENCE for the purpose of giving him notice of the dishonor of a bill, is a question of law, where all the facts are known.

HOLDER MAKING DILIGENT INQUIRY FOR AN INDORSER, and acting upon the best information he is able to procure in giving notice of non-payment, has used reasonable diligence, though the notice was in fact misdirected and never received.

INQUIRY AS TO ACCOMMODATION INDORSER'S RESIDENCE, MADE OF THE DRAWER, for whose accommodation the bill was indorsed and discounted, and sending notice of non-payment by mail to the place designated by him, are sufficient to charge the indorser, though he resides and receives his mail at another place.

ASSUMPSIT against the indorser of a bill drawn by one Cobb, indorsed for his accommodation by the defendant, and discounted by the plaintiffs for Cobb's benefit. The question was as to whether there was sufficient notice of non-payment. It appeared that the plaintiffs, being unacquainted with the defendant, inquired of Cobb as to his residence, and were informed that it was Chittenango, at which place the bill was dated. They accordingly sent the notice by mail to that place. The defendant had never resided there, but resided in Manlius, and received his mail at the Hartsville post-office, three miles from Chittenango. Verdict for the plaintiffs, under the direction of the court, and a motion for a new trial founded on exceptions to the opinion of the court that the defendant was liable.

J. A. Spencer, for the defendant.

W. C. Noyes, for the plaintiffs.

By Court, BRONSON, J. When the facts are all ascertained, what is reasonable diligence is a question of law. "This results," said Spencer, J., in *Bryden* v. *Bryden*, 11 Johns. 187, "from the necessity of having some fixed legal standard by which men may not only know the law, but be protected by it:" Bayley on Bills, 142, 144, and notes. The judge was not requested to submit the question of due diligence to the jury; but had it been otherwise, he was right in treating it as a question of law, there being no dispute about the facts. Was there reasonable diligence in endeavoring to ascertain the place to which the notice should be directed? Not knowing where the defendant lived, the plaintiffs inquired of the drawer, for whose accommodation the bill was discounted, and relying upon the information

given by him, they sent the notice to Chittenango, when it should
have been sent to Manlius or Hartsville. This is not like the
case of the *Catskill Bank* v. *Stall*, 15 Wend. 364; affirmed in error,
18 Id. 466; for there the person who took the note to the
bank, and gave the information on which the notice was misdirected, was the agent of the indorsers, and they had no right
to complain that credit had been given to what was, in effect,
their own representation.

But I am unable to distinguish this from the case of the *Bank
of Utica* v. *Davidson*, 5 Wend. 587. This was an action against
the indorser of a note which had been discounted for the accommodation of the maker, and the notice of protest was sent
to Bainbridge, when it should have been sent to Masonville,
where the indorser lived. The person who took the note to the
bank, and gave the information on which the plaintiffs acted,
was the agent of the maker, and it was held that there had
been due diligence, and judgment was rendered for the plaintiffs. Sutherland, justice, mentions the fact that the note was
dated at Bainbridge, where the notice was sent, and that the
indorser had but recently removed from that place; but the case
was put mainly on the ground that the plaintiffs had a right to
rely on the information given by the agent of the maker when
the note was discounted. In the case at bar, notice was directed
to the place where the bill purports to have been drawn; and
the only difference between this and the case of the *Bank of
Utica* v. *Davidson*, consists in the single fact that the indorser
of this bill had never lived at Chittenango. That does not, I
think, furnish a sufficient ground for a solid distinction between
the two cases.

How does the question stand upon principle? It is not absolutely necessary that notice should be brought home to the
indorser, nor even that it should be directed to the place of his
residence. It is enough that the holder of a bill make diligent
inquiry for the indorser, and acts upon the best information he is
able to procure. If after doing so, the notice fail to reach the
indorser, the misfortune falls on him, not on the holder. There
must be ordinary or reasonable diligence—such as men of business usually exercise when their interest depends upon obtaining
correct information. The holder must act in good faith, and
not give credit to doubtful intelligence when better could have
been obtained. Now, what was done in this case? The plaintiffs
inquired of Cobb, the drawer of the bill, who would of course
be likely to know where his accommodation indorser lived.

They saw that the defendant, by lending his name, had evinced his confidence in the integrity of the drawer; and so far as appears, nothing had then occurred which should have led the plaintiffs, or any prudent man, to distrust the accuracy of Cobb's statements concerning any matter of fact within his knowledge. He professed to be able to give the desired information, and his answer was unequivocal. If Cobb was worthy of being believed, there was no reason for doubt that the indorser resided at Chittenango. The plaintiffs confided in the information, and acted upon it.

But it is said that Cobb had an interest in giving false information for the purpose of protecting his accommodation indorser, and consequently that the plaintiffs should not have trusted to his statement. He certainly had no legal interest in the question. If the bill was not accepted and paid by the drawee, Cobb, as the drawer, was bound to pay and take it up from the holder; and if the indorser was charged, Cobb was bound to see him indemnified. In a legal point of view, it was wholly a matter of indifference to him whether notice of the dishonor of the bill should be brought home to the indorser or not. Before anything can be made out of the objection, we must say that the plaintiffs were bound to suspect that Cobb, when he presented the bill, intended to commit a fraud; that he was obtaining a discount upon a draft which he knew would not be paid, either by the drawee or by himself; that the money was to be lost to some one, and that he preferred the loss should fall on the holder rather than the indorser; and consequently, that he would give false information concerning the proper place for directing notice. It is quite evident that the plaintiffs entertained no such suspicion; for if they had, they would neither have confided in the statements of Cobb, nor would they have loaned him the money. I think they were not bound to believe that a fraud was intended. There was nothing in the circumstances of the case calculated to induce such a belief in the mind of any man of ordinary prudence and foresight. This was an every-day business transaction, where men must of necessity repose a reasonable degree of confidence in each other, and no one can be chargeable with a want of diligence for trusting to information which would usually be deemed satisfactory among business men. If there was any ground whatever for suspecting fraud on the part of Cobb, it was, to say the least, very slight, and was fully counterbalanced by the fact, that the defendant had testified his confidence in Cobb by lending his name as indorser. The plaintiffs have, I think, lost nothing by trusting to information derived from the drawer of the bill, instead of seeking it from some other individual.

The case then comes to this. The plaintiffs applied for information to a man worthy of belief, and who was likely to know where the indorser lived. They received such an answer as left no reasonable ground for doubt that Chittenango was the place to which the notice should be sent. I think they were not bound to push the inquiry further. Men of business usually act upon such information. They buy and sell, and do other things affecting their interest, upon the credit which they give to the declarations of a single individual concerning a particular fact of this kind within his knowledge. This is matter of common experience. Ordinary diligence in a case like this can mean no more than that the inquiry shall be pursued until it is satisfactorily answered. This is the only practical rule. If the holder of a bill is required to go further, it is impossible to say where he can safely stop. Would it be enough to inquire of two, three, or four individuals, or must he seek intelligence from every man in the place likely to know anything about the matter? It would be difficult, if not impossible, to answer this question.

New trial denied.

———

WHAT IS REASONABLE DEMAND AND NOTICE is a question of law where the facts are known: *Hadduck* v. *Murray*, 8 Am. Dec. 43; *Nash* v. *Harrington*, 16 Id. 672; *Thompson* v. *Bank of South Carolina*, 30 Id. 354. But it is held in *Nichol* v. *Bate*, 27 Id. 505, that the question whether a holder has used due diligence in ascertaining the indorser's place of residence for the purpose of sending him notice is for the jury. The foregoing case of *Bank of Utica* v. *Bender* is very often referred to as an authority for the doctrine that where the facts upon which the question of due diligence depends are known, it becomes purely a question of law: *Spencer* v. *Bank of Salina*, 3 Hill, 521; *Dole* v. *Gold*, 5 Barb. 491; *Strawbridge* v. *Robinson*, 5 Gilm. (Ill.) 473; *Bell* v. *Hagerstown Bank*, 7 Gill, 232; *Minor* v. *Edwards*, 12 Mo. 139; *Brighton Market Bank* v. *Philbrick*, 40 N. H. 509; *Walker* v. *Stetson*, 14 Ohio St. 96; *Rhett* v. *Poe*, 2 How. (U. S.) 481.

WHERE THE HOLDER USES DUE DILIGENCE to ascertain the residence of the indorser, and from information so received sends the notice to the wrong post-office, it is, nevertheless, sufficient; *Nichol* v. *Bate*, 27 Am. Dec. 505. See, also, *Reid* v. *Payne*, 8 Id. 311, and *Bank of Columbia* v. *McGruder*, 14 Id. 271. To the same effect, citing the principal case, are: *Branch Bank at Decatur* v. *Peirce*, 3 Ala. 324; *Garver* v. *Downie*, 33 Cal. 181; *Wood* v. *Corl*, 4 Metc. 206; *Ransom* v. *Mack*, 2 Hill, 592; *Hunt* v. *Maybee*, 7 N. Y. 271; *Gawtry* v. *Doane*, 51 Id. 93; *Requa* v. *Collins*, Id. 148; *Carroll* v. *Upton*, 2 Sandf. 176; *McVeigh* v. *Bank of Old Dominion*, 26 Gratt. 806; *Wilson* v. *Senier*, 14 Wis. 386. But the inquiry must be pursued until all sources of information are exhausted, unless satisfactory information is sooner received, and then it may stop: *Saco Nat. Bank* v. *Sanborn*, 63 Me. 343. Inquiry may, and should, indeed, be made of the maker, if the information can not be

otherwise obtained: *Lawrence* v. *Miller*, 16 N. Y. 240. Such diligence should
be used as business men usually employ when their interest depends upon
obtaining accurate information, and doubtful intelligence should not be accepted when better can be obtained: *Whitridge* v. *Rider*, 22 Md. 559; *Greenwich* v. *De Groot*, 7 Hun, 212.

NELLIS v. LATHROP.

[22 WENDELL, 121.]

SHERIFF'S DEED RELATES TO THE TIME WHEN PURCHASER WAS ENTITLED
to it as between such purchaser and the judgment debtor, or his assignee
where the delay was caused by an injunction by the debtor.

TENANT MAY ACQUIRE HIS LESSOR'S TITLE BY A PURCHASE ON EXECUTION
against the lessor, or by redeeming the premises after an execution sale,
as a judgment creditor of the lessor, and may set up his title in bar of an
action for rent subsequently accruing.

TENANT MAY SHOW THAT HE HAS BECOME OWNER OF PART of the leased
premises by a purchase or redemption under a judgment against the
lessor, to mitigate the damages in an action for rent, but not as a bar to
the action.

RENT IS APPORTIONABLE where the tenant becomes owner of part of the
premises under an execution sale against the lessor.

COVENANT for rent from October 1, 1833, to April, 1834, on a
lease made to the defendant by one Ferguson and assigned to
the plaintiff. Rent was paid to October 1, 1833, when the defendant left the premises. The defendant offered to show that
he became entitled to a sheriff's deed for part of the premises
on October 4, 1833, as a redeeming creditor, after a sale of the
reversion on an execution against the lessor, but did not obtain
his deed until February 28, 1835, owing to an injunction sued
out by the lessor. The evidence was rejected as impertinent
and constituting no defense, the judge instructing the jury that
the doctrine of relation did not apply, and therefore the defendant's title did not accrue till the deed was executed, which was
after the rent claimed became due. Verdict for the plaintiff and
motion for a new trial.

W. Tracy and W. C. Noyes, for the defendant.

C. P. Kirkland, for the plaintiff.

By Court, COWEN, J. It is clear, that as between the now
defendant and Ferguson, the lessor, the deed of February 28,
1835, related back to the fourth of October, 1833; and from that
time divested all title of Ferguson to that part of the demised
premises included in it. The plaintiff claiming under him must,
therefore, abide the legal consequences arising from Ferguson's

failure of title. The plaintiff stands in Ferguson's place, being
his assignee; and both must be to taken to have been *pro tanto*
totally destitute of title, and of all right to demise and to hold
as landlord, from the fourth of October, 1833. Here has been
no eviction of the defendant, nor any act equivalent to an eviction by the plaintiff, from the whole or any part of the demised
premises. The judge was right, therefore, in saying that no
defense arose upon that ground. But the plaintiff lost his title
subsequent to the giving of the lease, and the lessee acquired it
as to part of the demised premises. Had he a right to acquire
the title of his landlord, and set him at defiance? So long as
he is not expelled, he has, in general, no right to question his
landlord's title. He can not deny that he had a right to demise
at the time of the lease. He can not defend, on the ground
that he has acquired an outstanding title adverse to that of the
landlord. But I am not aware that the estoppel goes farther.
If the landlord part with his title pending the lease, the duty of
the tenant, including that of paying rent, is due to the assignee;
and should the tenant buy in the assignee's right, the lease
would be extinguished. So, should the landlord sell and release
to the lessee. In these cases, no action would lie for the rent.
Therefore, had there been a sheriff's sale of the whole reversion
in the demised premises, and the defendant had redeemed or
purchased under the judgment, no action could have been sustained; for a purchase or acquisition of title under a judgment
against the lessor is the same thing as if he had granted by deed.
It is, to be sure, acquiring title indirectly and by operation of
law, from the lessor; but it comes through his act and consent,
or his neglect, and is therefore the same in legal effect as if he
had granted or devised the reversion.

But the title to only a part of the demised premises passed to
the defendant. I do not say this on the ground that Ferguson's
wife who joined him as lessor must be taken to have been seised
of some portion, for her seisin must be deemed that of her husband, at least during the life of both; and during that time, her
right was subject to be sold under execution for his debts. But
the deed to the defendant covered only part of the demised
premises. His case was not, therefore, in any view, one of total
defense; and the judge was right in saying that the evidence
could not be received as a bar to the action.

But I think the judge erred in shutting out the evidence as
totally impertinent. It should have been received in mitigation
of damages. The plaintiff, or rather his assignor, who, as I re-

marked, are in this case legally identical, having after the date
of the demise, parted in effect with the reversion of a part of
the demised premises, rent should have been recovered for the
residue only.   The rent is incident to the reversion, and follows
the grant of it without express words.   So if the reversion in
part of the land be granted, a proportional part of the rent follows: Gilb. on Rents, Dubl. ed. of 1792.   In short, the evidence offered raised a case of apportionment.   It is the same as
if the lessor, or his assignee or other persons holding the reversion, should release his title in a part of the land to the lessee.
This would extinguish the rent for so much; but, being by the
act of the parties, the rent would be apportionable.   It comes,
in principle, to the case stated in Woodf. Land. and Ten. 252,
Lond. ed. of 1804, citing Vin. Abr., Apportionment, B, 5, 12.
Woodfall says: "If lessee for years of land, rendering rent,
accept a new lease from the lessor, of part of the land, which is
a surrender of this part, the rent shall be apportioned; for this
comes by the act of the parties."   The duty in question is a rent
service, of which Gilbert remarks, that if a man who has such
a rent, purchase part of the land out of which it issues, yet the
rent shall be apportioned; though otherwise of a rent charge,
which is wholly extinguished: Gilb. on Rents, 151, 2 Dubl.
ed. of 1792.   But he says in another place, even of the latter,
that a release of part of the rent to the tenant of the land shall
not extinguish the whole; but the rent shall be apportioned:
Id. 163.   Indeed, nothing is more reasonable than that, where
both landlord and tenant participate in destroying their relation as to a part of the land, the rent should continue and be apportioned on the residue.   It is the same thing if that consequence be regarded in the case at bar as arising from the
operation at law: See *per* Wilde, J., in *Montague* v. *Gay*, 19
Mass. 439, 440.   It could not have arisen without their mutual
participation.

The defendant's counsel did not characterize his evidence, on
the offer he made at the trial, by saying whether he intended it
as a bar, or in mitigation.   Had he presented it in the former
character merely, the ruling at the circuit would have been
proper.   But the evidence seems to have been offered generally
for what it was worth; and should not have been totally excluded.   The decision of the judge went to that extent, probably on the ground that, during all the time when the rent claimed
was running, the legal title to the whole was in Ferguson.   It
is in that alone we differ with him.   The defendant's right to a

deed clearly arose on the fourth of October, 1833, before either
of the two quarters' rent claimed by this action fell due. The
date of the deed of February 28, 1835, must be read as of the
day when the deed became due. The principle of relation here
is the same as if the now defendant had been the direct purchaser at a sheriff's sale before the statute. There, though the
sheriff sold at one day, and did not give a deed till afterwards,
the law antedated it by inserting the day of sale: *Jackson ex dem.
Noah v. Dickinson*, 15 Johns. 309; *Evertson v. Sawyer*, 2 Wend.
507; *Jackson ex dem. De Forest v. Ramsay*, 3 Cow. 75, and the
cases cited in this last case by Sutherland, J.

On the whole, we think there must be a new trial. And if the
rights of the parties be not changed, the question must be referred to the jury to make a just apportionment of rent upon
that part of the demised premises which lie without the sheriff's
deed: Gilb. on Rents, 189, Dubl. ed. 1792; and see the case of
Hodgskins v. Robson, 1 Vent. 276, which relates both to the principle and practice of apportionment. See also *Gillespie v. Thomas*,
15 Wend. 464, 469, and the books cited by Mr. Justice Nelson
at the latter page.

New trial granted; costs to abide the event.

SHERIFF'S DEED RELATES TO DAY OF SALE, WHEN: See *Jackson v. Dickinson*, 8 Am. Dec. 236; *Jackson v. Ramsay*, 15 Id. 242, and note. The doctrine
of *Nellis v. Lathrop* on this point is approved and applied in case of a deed
executed by a master under a decree of foreclosure in *Fuller v. Van Geesen*, 4
Hill, 174.

RENT IS INCIDENT OF THE REVERSION: See *Johnson v. Smith*, 24 Am. Dec.
339.

APPORTIONMENT OF RENT: See *Cuthbert v. Kuhn*, 31 Am. Dec. 513, and
note. As to when rent is apportionable, the principal case is recognized as
authority in *Van Rensselaer v. Jones*, 2 Barb. 662; *Van Rensselaer v. Chadwick*, 24 Id. 339; *Van Rensselaer v. Gallup*, 5 Denio, 468.

TENANT'S RIGHT TO SET UP TITLE ACQUIRED UNDER EXECUTION SALE
AGAINST LANDLORD.—To this point the principal case is cit d in *Ten Eyck v.
Craig*, 62 N. Y. 423; *Hetzel v. Barber*, 69 Id. 15. So in *harpe v. Kelley*, 5
Denio, 433, in discussing the question as to whether the tenant can set up
title acquired from a stranger. It is cited also in *Moffatt v. Strong*, 9 Bosw.
68, respecting the right of a tenant to resist payment of rent by showing an
eviction by title paramount.

CASES

COURT OF ERRORS

NEW YORK.

———

ALLEN v. MERCHANTS' BANK OF NEW YORK.

[22 WENDELL, 215.]

BANK TAKING BILL PAYABLE IN ANOTHER STATE FOR COLLECTION is liable for the neglect of its correspondent in the latter state, to whom it sends it, in failing to give due notice of non-acceptance to an indorser, whereby such indorser is discharged.

LIABILITY OF BANK TAKING BILL FOR COLLECTION MAY BE VARIED by express agreement, or by an implied agreement, arising from the common understanding of merchants and the custom of trade, so that such bank shall not be held liable for negligence of competent and responsible agents in another state whom it employs to make the collection.

OPINIONS OF MERCHANTS AS TO THE LIABILITY OF BANKS TAKING NOTES FOR COLLECTION, however general, can not vary the legal liability of such banks, but are admissible to show the common understanding as to the meaning of such contracts, and to prove a usage.

LAW OF THE STATE IN WHICH A BILL IS DRAWN AND INDORSED governs as to protest and notice to charge the indorser.

NOTICE OF NON-ACCEPTANCE OF A BILL MUST BE GIVEN, under the general commercial law, to charge an indorser, although presentment for acceptance was unnecessary.

BANK IS LIABLE FOR NEGLECT OF A NOTARY employed by it to protest a bill taken for collection with respect to giving notice of non-acceptance, that not being a strictly official act, though it may be otherwise as to acts purely official.

ERROR from the supreme court in an action of assumpsit, brought originally in the superior court of New York city, to recover the amount of a bill of exchange drawn in New York on a mercantile house in Philadelphia, payable five days after date to the drawer's order, and subsequently indorsed to the plaintiffs, who deposited the same with the defendants for collection. The ground upon which a recovery was sought was, that the amount of the bill was lost to the plaintiffs through neglect to give the indorsers notice of non-acceptance. The defendants sent the bill to a Philadelphia bank, who, on the second day after the day of its date, delivered it to their notary. It was presented on the same day for acceptance, acceptance refused and noted, but no notice thereof given to the indorsers. It was afterwards duly presented for payment, payment refused, and notices thereof sent to the defendants for the plaintiffs and for the drawer. The plaintiffs, on the next day after receiving the notice, gave notice to their indorser. In a subsequent action brought by them against him (of which the defendants were duly notified and their aid requested), there was a failure to recover, on the ground of the want of notice of non-acceptance. It further appeared that the indorser, after waiting a reasonable time for notice of non-acceptance, supposing that the bill had been accepted, surrendered certain securities for its payment, which had been deposited with them by the drawer, and that on the sixth day after the date of the bill the drawer became insolvent. The plaintiffs, to prove a usage in New York that banks were held liable for the diligence of those to whom they sent bills outside the city for collection, introduced a number of brokers and merchants, who testified that such was their understanding and opinion. A number of bank officers introduced by the defendants testified that the banks did not so understand it; but that the collection of paper outside the city was a mere matter of favor, and that the banks undertook only to transmit such paper to proper agents. The defendants also proved that the Philadelphia bank and their notary were distinguished for punctuality and diligence in such matters; and that by the law merchant of Pennsylvania, presentment for acceptance and notice of non-acceptance of such bills were unnecessary. The jury were charged by Oakley, J., that in the absence of any usage or agreement the defendants were bound only to transmit the bill in proper time to a proper agent, and were not liable for such agent's negligence. The judge left it to the jury to determine whether there was any such usage as the plaintiffs claimed, instructing them that to establish such usage it must appear that the practice of the banks had generally conformed to it so long as to make it generally known; that he did not think any such practice had been shown, but that they must determine. He further instructed them that if they should find there

was no such usage, they should inquire whether there was any
mutual understanding to the same effect between the plaintiffs
and the defendants, or between the defendants and their customers generally; that if they should find no such usage or mutual understanding, the defendants were not liable, notwithstanding any notorious understanding among business men to
the contrary. Verdict for the plaintiffs, and judgment thereon,
which was removed into the supreme court on exceptions to the
charge, and there affirmed: 15 Wend. 486. The plaintiffs
brought error.

H. E. Davies and S. A. Foot, for the plaintiffs in error.

H. P. Edwards and G. Wood, for the defendants in error.

WALWORTH, Chancellor, after some preliminary remarks, said
that it was the settled law of New York, as well as of England,
Scotland, and France, that a bill payable on a day certain need
not be presented before due, though it was the duty of an agent
holding it for negotiation to obtain acceptance of it without delay for the benefit of his principal; but that if such a bill was
actually presented for acceptance and dishonored, notice thereof
must be immediately given to the drawer and indorsers: 17
Wend. 368; 1 T. R. 712; 2 Pet. 170; Morr. Dict. of Dec. 1494,
1558; 2 Pardes, Droit Com. 417, No. 358; 3 Kent's Com. 82;
Chit. on Bills, 38, 46; Muir on Bills, 22; Bayley on Bills, 102.
He then referred to the law merchant of Pennsylvania on this
point as proved by the testimony.

On the question of usage he said that the instructions of the
court below were unquestionably right, the inquiry in such cases
being one of fact, and not as to the opinions of traders and merchants, as to the legal obligations of banks. The case of *Car-
vick* v. *Vickery,* 2 Doug. 653, n., he remarked, was unlike the
present one, because there the offer was not merely to prove an
understanding as to the necessity of all the payees indorsing a
note, but to prove the universal usage, understanding, and practice of bankers and merchants on that point. His honor conceded that the testimony of persons engaged in a particular
business was frequently admitted to prove the sense in which
certain words or terms were used in that business: *Powell* v.
Horton, 2 Hodge, 16; but this, he insisted, was not that kind of
a case. To prove such a usage as that contended for in this
case, he said, there must be shown not merely an isolated case
of an allowance of such a claim by a particular bank, but a general usage or practice of the banks to make compensation for

losses incurred through the negligence or default of their correspondents or agents in other places.

The learned chancellor, while admitting it to be a general rule of law that banks and other corporations, as well as individuals, were liable for the acts and omissions of their agents, claimed that where, as in this case, the nature of the business intrusted to the bank or corporation, forbade the employment of its ordinary officers and agents, and made it necessary to employ subagents in another place, the person intrusting the business to the bank or corporation must be intended to have authorized the employment of such subagents and to take the risk of their neglect. He admitted that if it had been the custom for banks to charge commissions beyond the difference in exchange and the actual expenses for collections in distant places, the case might be in the nature of a *del credere* commission, rendering the bank liable for the neglect of its correspondents; but he insisted that the incidental benefits of exchange and the chance of having the money on deposit for a short time, though furnishing a sufficient consideration for the undertaking by the bank to be liable for the acts of its own officers and immediate agents, as held in *Bank of Utica* v. *McKinster*, 11 Wend. 473, was not enough to support an agreement to warrant the plaintiffs against the negligence or mistakes of the Philadelphia bank or its agents.

His honor further admitted that it was probably the duty of the defendants to give their Philadelphia correspondents such instructions as to notices, etc., as would enable them to comply with the New York law, it being the duty of the Philadelphia agents to take such steps as to presentment for acceptance and payment, and protest, and notice of non-acceptance, and non-payment, as would hold the indorsers: Poth. Traité Cont. du Change, c. 4, No. 82; *Allen* v. *Suydam*, 20 Wend. 321 [32 Am. Dec. 555]; since this bill must be regarded as a foreign bill, because payable in another state, in accordance with the doctrine of *Buckner* v. *Finley*, 2 Pet. 586; *Duncan* v. *Course*, 1 Mill, 100; *Lonsdale* v. *Brown*, 4 Wash. C. C. 148, upon the same principle that a bill drawn in England, payable in Scotland, Ireland, or the colonies, is a foreign bill: *Salomans* v. *Stavely*, 3 Doug. 298; *Mahoney* v. *Ashlin*, 2 Barn. & Adol. 478; *Reynolds* v. *Syme*, Morr. Dict. of Dec. 1598; Muir on Bills, 52; 3 Kent's Com. 82. An agent, however, his honor said, contracts only "for reasonable skill and ordinary diligence in the discharge of his duties, that is, the usual skill belonging to other persons engaged in the like business, and the degree of diligence which prudent men exercise in relation to their own business. * * * But, as a general rule, an agent who conducts the business with which he is intrusted by his principal, according to the ordinary custom and usages of all other persons engaged in the like employment or business, is not answerable to his principal" for a loss, though it might have been prevented by greater diligence and by an unusual departure from ordinary practice in such matters. There being some evidence in this case, therefore, that the omission to send instructions was in accordance with the customary practice of the New York banks, it was proper, the chancellor thought, to leave it to the jury to determine whether there was any departure from the usual course, or any negligence in not sending instructions. Upon the whole case, his honor's opinion was in favor of affirming the judgment of the supreme court.

VERPLANCK, Senator. Payment of a bill of exchange was lost to the holders in consequence of the omission of giving notice of refusal to accept. Assuming for the present that such omission was a culpable and unjustifiable neglect, let us first proceed to the consideration of the chief and more important question in this cause. A bill of exchange drawn in New York upon a person resident in Philadelphia is deposited for collection in a New York bank, is received for that purpose, and duly transmitted to their correspondent and agent, a Philadelphia bank, the notary of which is guilty of a neglect, whereby on refusal to accept at Philadelphia, payment from the New York drawer or indorser is lost. Is the New York bank first receiving this paper for collection, responsible for the loss or damages arising from the default of its Philadelphia agent?

Viewing this as a question of very great importance, both in itself as relates to the responsibilities of our moneyed institutions, and the usage of commercial collections, and also as materially affecting the general law of agency and contracts, I have given the subject much consideration. The conclusions to which I have come are in opposition to the opinion of the supreme court, as well as to the charge of the eminent judge before whom the cause was tried in the court below. I have consequently hesitated in forming my judgment, and have repeatedly reviewed the question before giving this opinion.. But I can not now entertain any doubt on this subject.

It is well settled in this state that there is an implied undertaking by a bank or banker receiving negotiable paper deposited for collection, to take the necessary measures to charge the

drawer, maker, or other proper parties, upon the default or refusal to pay or accept: *Smedes* v. *Bank of Utica*, 20 Johns. 372;
and S. C., in this court, 3 Cow. 663; *McKinster* v. *Bank of Utica*,
9 Wend. 46; S. C., 11 Id. 473.   The ground of this rule is, that
the acceptance of negotiable paper thus deposited for collection,
forms an implied undertaking to make the demands and give the
notices required by law or mercantile usage for the perfect protection of the holder's rights against all previous parties; for
which undertaking the use of the funds thus temporarily obtained, or of the average balances thereof, for the purposes of
discount or exchange, forms a valuable consideration.   Had we
no express authority on this head, I should consider the acceptance by a bank of paper for collection from a customer, in the
usual course of his business, as sufficient evidence of a valuable
consideration.   The whole ordinary business of a bank with its
dealers is one of mutual profit or accommodation, and must be
taken together (unless some part is separated by express understanding), and it is not for a bank to allege, or for a court
to consider (as the chief justice seems to do) that a collection in
a particular place must be regarded as a gratuitous favor.   If
accepted at all, the general profits and advantages of the business of which this may perhaps be an unproductive part, form a
good consideration for the undertaking.   This, however, is not
an open question after the decision of this court in the two cases
against the bank of Utica.

What then is the ordinary undertaking, contract, or agreement of a bank with one of its dealers, in the case of an ordinary
deposit of a domestic note or bill, payable in the same town received for collection?   It is a contract made with a corporate
body having only a legal existence, and governed by directors,
who can act only by officers and agents; or if it be with a private
banker, he too is known to carry on his business by clerks and
agents.   The contract itself is to perform certain duties necessary for the collection of the paper and the security of the holder.
But neither legal construction nor the common understanding
of men of business can regard this contract (unless there be
some express understanding to that effect) as an appointment of
the bank as an attorney or personal representative of the owner
of the paper, authorized to select other agents for the purpose of
collecting the note and nothing more.   There is a wide difference
made as well by positive law as by the reason of the thing itself,
between a contract or undertaking to do a thing, and the delegation of an agent or attorney to procure the doing the same thing—

between a contract for building a house (for example) and the appointment of an overseer or superintendent, authorized and undertaking to act for the principal, in having a house built. The contractor is bound to answer for any negligence or default in the performance of his contract, although such negligence or default be not his own, but that of some sub-contractor, or under workman.   Not so the mere representative agent, who discharges his whole duty if he acts with good faith and ordinary diligence in the selection of his materials, the forming his contracts, and the choice of his workmen.

Now in the case of the deposit for collection of a domestic note or bill payable in the same town, no one can imagine that this instead of being a contract with the bank to use the proper means for collecting the paper, is a mere delegation of power to act as an attorney for that purpose.   If this were so, and it should happen that by the fraud, the carelessness, or the ignorance of a clerk or teller, the only responsible parties were discharged, or the note itself lost or destroyed, it would be a sufficient defense for the bank if it could show that the directors had employed ordinary care and caution in selecting their officers; or any similar defense which would be good in the mouth of an attorney in fact, or a steward acting in good faith for his principal, who had been defrauded in any transaction. If such were the understanding of this business, and the merchant had to look to the responsibility of the teller or clerk through whose hands his paper may pass, and not to that of the bank which employs them, few deposits for collection would be made, and it would soon be found expedient to deal only with banks or bankers who would guarantee their officers.   But the natural and general understanding of men of business is surely not this; it is that of an implied agreement with the bank itself, of whose officers and agents they have no knowledge, and with whom they have no privity of contract.

The decisions of our own courts, above cited, call this transaction a contract and treat it as such.   Then the law is clear, that by the employment of under agents or servants, for his own convenience or to perform part of what he has contracted to do, the employer becomes civilly responsible to those with whom he contracts or deals in his business.   The general principle of Lord Holt has always been cited with approbation, though the correctness of its application to a political office was denied, that "where a trust is put in one person, and he whose interest is intrusted is damnified by the neglect of such as that person employs in the discharge of that trust, he shall answer to the person damnified:" 12 Mod. 490. The same doctrine is thus summed up by Judge Story, from a long succession of authorities: "It is a general doctrine of law, that the principal is held liable to third persons in a civil suit for the frauds, deceits, misrepresentations, torts, negligences, and other malfeasances or misfeasances and omissions of duty of his agent in the course of his employment, although the principal did not authorize or justify, or indeed know of such misconduct, or even if he forbade them or disapproved of them:" Story on Agency, c. 17, sec. 452, and authorities cited in note 3. "The maxim is," says Lord Kenyon, "*Respondeat superior* — the principals are responsible for the acts of the servants in those things that respect their duty under them, though not answerable for things that do not respect their duty:" 8 T. R. 531. This rule sums up the doctrine with great force, clearness, and precision. Thus the carrier is liable for the negligence of his agent, by which goods committed to his care are damaged. So the ship-owner is liable to the shipper for damages caused by reason of the neglect or misconduct of the master or mate. "This liability," says Judge Story, "extends not only to the injuries and wrongs of the agent immediately employed in a particular business (as in this case to the Merchants' bank itself), but also to the injuries and wrongs done by others who are employed by that agent under him, or with whom he contracts for the performance of the business; for the liability reaches through all the stages of the service:" Story on Agency, sec. 454, and cases there cited in note. It is this distinction, on which I have already insisted as founded in the reason of contracts, between the undertaking to perform anything, and the mere receiving a delegation of authority to act for another, which reconciles many decisions evidently equally just in themselves, but apparently clashing in words and conflicting in authority. I include among these, in addition to the class of cases already cited or referred to, those in which persons dealing or contracting with an agent or contractor, and trusting to his credit, have endeavored to charge his principal, with whom, however, they themselves had no privity; see, for instance, the two cases in 6 Taunt. 147, 148. If it be not a mere representative agency, but a contract or undertaking to do the business, the original principal is answerable; and for the same reason he is to look to the immediate contractor with himself, and not to the inferior and distant under contractors or agents, for defaults injurious to his own interest.

Such then being the general law, the bank in undertaking to collect negotiable paper is answerable for the neglect of its ordinary agents. Is there anything in the mere fact of the paper being payable in another city, and therefore requiring the aid of other agents, sufficient to take that case out of the general rule? I mean irrespectively of any agreement or implied understanding as to the matter. The chief justice, in delivering the opinion of the supreme court, holds that there is, and says: "A note or bill left at a bank and received for the purpose of being sent to some distant place for collection, would seem to imply, upon a reasonable construction, no other agreement than that it should be forwarded with due diligence to some competent agent, to do what should be necessary in the premises. The language and acts of the parties fairly import so much, but nothing beyond it. The person leaving the note is aware that the bank can not personally attend to the collection, and that it must therefore be sent to some distant or foreign agent." This seems to me to assume the very question in dispute. In a deposit of a note for collection, payable in the same place, the holder is equally aware that the bank can not personally attend to the collection, and its management must be left to some one or more competent agents. But he makes an implied contract with the bank that the proper and expedient means shall be used to collect his note. So he does as to a foreign debt; and in each case he alike presumes that proper agents will be employed. In neither case has he any knowledge of the agents or privity with them. I can perceive no reason for liability or exemption from liability in either case which does not equally apply to the other. The bank, if its officers think fit, and the dealer will consent, may vary that liability in either case. It may receive the paper only for transmission to its correspondents. That would form a new and different contract, and would limit the responsibility to good faith and due discretion in the choice of an agent. But if this be not done, or unless there be some implied understanding on the subject, I see no difference between the responsibility assumed in the undertaking to collect foreign bills, and that for collecting domestic paper, payable at home. It is assumed in the same manner, in the same words, and on the same consideration.

If the reasoning of the supreme court be correct, I can not perceive how, either in the case of domestic collection, or in any

other case, the principal is to be made liable for the default of
his own agent, if, from the nature of the business, it was evident
that some under agent must be employed, and that the principal
could not do the business without aid.   On this principle, the
ship-owner would not be answerable for the negligence of the
captain, whom all the world knows he must employ.   The master
mechanic who must (as those who contract with him are well
aware) employ sub-contractors, journeymen, and laborers,
would no longer be liable for their negligence in the work he
contracts to have executed.   The same reasoning which would
here make the New York bank merely an agent " to select other
agents abroad for the party to become his agents in the collection," would equally make the ship-owner and the contracting
builder mere agents to select masters, mates, journeymen, and
laborers, for those with whom they deal.   If it be " unreasonable" to suppose, as the chief justice holds, that the bank assumed " to become responsible for the fidelity of agents abroad,"
who " all parties knew must intervene before collection," and
when the plaintiffs " knew that others must be trusted," it must
be quite as unreasonable in the case of domestic collections, and
of all other transactions, where the parties know that " agents
must intervene and others be trusted."   But in all these cases,
the parties are not governed by the mere rule of personal representative agency, but are subject to the responsibilities imposed
by the law of commercial contracts, of bailment or of shipping.
In all these cases, we are not to look to the necessity of the employment of the distant or under agents.   We are to look to the
contract itself.   *Legem enim contractus dat.*   We are to look
whether the contract be only for the immediate services of the
agent, and his acting faithfully as the representative of his
principal, doing for him, in the business confided to his care,
what the principal is not able or willing to do for himself, or
whether the contract looks mainly to the thing itself to be done,
and the undertaking be for the due use of all the proper means
for its performance.   In the one case, the responsibility ceases
with the limits of the personal services undertaken; in the other,
it extends to cover all the necessary and proper means for the
accomplishment of the object, by whomsoever used or employed.

Again: it is not true, in the usual and well-known course of
trade, that there is no other agreement implied than that deposited paper payable abroad shall be forwarded with due diligence, or as Judge Oakley charged, that " the banks are only
bound to transmit such paper in due form and in due time."

By the known ordinary usage of business, unless when altered
by some special agreement or usage, the banks undertake something more than this. This the holders of paper could do for
themselves. But the banks also undertake to receive and pay
the funds here, when collected elsewhere. The foreign bank
does not know the owner of the bill so as to open an account
with him, and to authorize him to draw upon his funds when
collected. They know only the bank from which the paper was
received, and that bank has at least undertaken to manage the
business of exchange between the places; on what ground then
is the bank receiving for collection, to be answerable only for
the first and last stages of the transaction, and to be discharged
from any liability as to all intermediate steps? Such are my
views of the general principles involved in the case. Let us now
look to the authorities bearing or supposed to bear upon it.

The chief justice relies much upon the decision of the supreme
court of the United States, in *The Bank of Washington* v. *Triplett and Neale,* 1 Pet. 25, and on the reasoning of Chief Justice
Marshall, in delivering the opinion of the court. He said, in
that case, "that the bill was not delivered to the Mechanics'
bank at Alexandria for collection, but for transmission; that the
bank in Washington became the agent of the holder; that the
bank in Alexandria performed its duty by transmitting the bill,
and the whole responsibility of the collection devolved on the
bank which received it for that purpose." Unquestionably it was
so in that case; for that was the express contract between the parties. The case does not state that the bill, payable at Washington,
was deposited for collection in the Alexandria bank, but it expressly states that " the holder of the bill placed it in the hands
of the cashier of the Alexandria bank, for the purpose of being
transmitted to the bank at Washington for collection." It nowhere appears, or is alleged, that the bank at Alexandria had
made any undertaking, express or implied, to collect the paper.
This might be from the known course of business in the district of Columbia, or it might be from the express agreement as
to this paper, or from the manner in which the bank received
the paper: that does not appear, but the fact, nevertheless, is
admitted. The Washington bank received instructions from the
holder and replied to him. Of course, there is nothing in the
views I have taken of the general question which is contradicted
by the conclusion of Chief Justice Marshall, " that the bank of
Washington, by receiving the bill for collection, and by its letter, became the plaintiff's agent, and assumed the responsibili-

ties of that character." Under these circumstances, I consider
the authority of the supreme court of the United States, in this
decision, as indirectly, at least, in opposition to the doctrine of
the supreme court of this state, and certainly as giving it no
support.

On the other hand, a recent and equally high authority goes
directly to support the doctrine I have sustained. It is the case
of *Van Wart* v. *Woolley*, 3 Barn. & Cress. 419, upon the authority
of which, another great question of the law of negotiable paper
was decided in this court, during the last year, in the case of *S.
and M. Allen* v. *Suydam and Boyd* [32 Am. Dec. 555]. In *Van Wart*
v. *Woolley*, the defendants at Birmingham received a bill upon
London to get accepted. This they forwarded to their London
banker, who did not protest the bill for non-acceptance, nor give
notice to any of the parties to the paper of the refusal to accept.
Lord Tenterden, in delivering the judgment of the court, said:
" Upon this state of facts, it is evident that the defendants, who
can not be distinguished from, but are answerable for their London correspondents, have been guilty of a neglect of the duty
they owed the plaintiff, their employer, for which they received
a pecuniary reward. The plaintiff is therefore entitled to maintain his action against them to the extent of any damage he
may have sustained by their neglect." The case embraced some
other points, but the decision of all rested upon this position.
Upon these authorities, and for these reasons, I am clear, that
by the deposit of the bill in question with the bank, and the
receiving it for collection, the bank, upon general principles of
law and independently of any custom or usage, or of any express agreement, is liable for a neglect of duty occurring in that
collection, whether from the default of its officers here, or of
their correspondents at Philadelphia, from whom (in Lord Tenterden's words), " they can not be distinguished, and for whom
they are answerable."

Can not that legal liability be varied? I can not doubt that
it may be, either by the express condition on which paper for
collection is received, or by the implied understanding of the
parties arising from the common understanding of merchants,
and the custom of trade. It was, therefore, proper to admit
the evidence of men of business to show what was the usage or
general understanding of such transactions. I agree entirely
with Judge Oakley as to the authority and object of such evidence. The opinion of merchants, however general, is no authority to show the legal liability of any party. It is the

exclusive province of the law to decide that point. But such evidence is good to show the common understanding of any contracts, the meaning of the language of such contracts in their ordinary commercial sense, to prove any custom, usage, or mode of business which may naturally and justly be presumed to enter into and form part of any transaction or agreement. It is good for the purpose of giving probable proof of the degree and kind of responsibility understood to be assumed by the party sought to be charged; but it is not good to show what the legal consequences of the assumption of any such responsibility may be. It is good for the interpretation of the contract, not for the establishment or the exposition of the law. Now, if the conclusions to which I have previously come, be sound, the direction of the judge at the trial as to this sort of evidence, though correct in his view of the weight and authority to which it was entitled, was wrong as to the point to which he directed the attention of the jury. He told them that the bank was not liable on general principles, and was not responsible, unless they were of opinion, from the evidence, that there was some agreement, express or implied, between the parties, in relation to the transmission of the bill, or unless there existed some custom or usage in the city of New York, changing the obligation imposed by the deposit, by which custom, banks receiving bills payable out of the city, are responsible for the negligence of any bank or notary, or other agent to whom such bills might be sent. According to my view of the law, the reception of the bill for collection, in the usual manner, imposed the liability for neglect or omission of the proper means, by any one employed for that purpose by the banks or by its agents; but it was open for the bank to show, and it was for the jury to decide, whether there was not some express or implied agreement, or mutual understanding between the parties, which varied that obligation and limited the bank's responsibility, as to foreign bills, to the safe transmission to a competent agent; or whether there did not exist some custom or usage in the city of New York, discharging the legal liability as to bills payable abroad, in the same manner: which usage was sufficiently general, long continued, and known to men of business, to be presumed to have entered into and formed part of the contract. This distinction is not a matter of form or theory merely. On the contrary, it might wholly change the verdict of the jury. In the case before us, though the great weight of commercial evidence appears to me to be on the side of the understood liability of the banks, there

was enough from cashiers and experienced bank officers on the
other side, to warrant the jury in finding, as they did, for the
defendants; they, in fact, finding that there was no agreement or
custom specially charging the banks with a liability which the
law would not otherwise impose. Had they been directed, as I
think they should have been, that the bank was liable unless
they thought that there was sufficient evidence of some agreement or custom discharging that responsibility, the verdict upon
such conflicting evidence might well have been found for the
plaintiffs.

In a question like this, involving principles that must govern
the law of a wide range of commercial dealings, considerations
of public policy can not well be overlooked, though they must
not be allowed to disturb the conclusions of natural justice or
well-settled positive jurisprudence. Some such considerations
have been suggested in the course of the arguments, founded
upon the great and inconvenient responsibilities which a decision,
reversing that of the courts below, would impose upon our
moneyed institutions; and their consequent withdrawal in part or
in whole, from a business so necessary to our internal exchanges.
To me the subject appears in a very different light. I can not but
think that if the law of this case were now to be settled, not
judicially, but legislatively, upon considerations of public policy
alone, the doctrine I have maintained in opposition to that of
our courts, would be found the safest and wisest. If the present
judgment be affirmed, no small doubt will be thrown upon the
responsibilities of collecting banks and bankers, even in domestic collections, for the acts of any of their officers. As in
the case of corporate banks, or those under our general law, all
the business is practically done by agents, that doubt would
cover the whole of our banking transactions. The same difficulty may arise in numerous analogous commercial affairs, the
law as well as the usage of which is now settled, unless it be
shaken by the influence and authority of decisions and reasoning
like that of the supreme court in this case.

On the other side, if we hold collecting banks and bankers to
be liable for all neglect or omission of the necessary and proper
means for the due performance of that which they have in general terms undertaken to do, whether such omission or negligence be their own or that of others in their employ—we preserve that harmony of the law which is so essential to its being
understood by those who are to regulate their dealings by it;
and unquestionably much doubt and litigation will be excluded.

If the responsibility thus imposed be onerous or inconvenient as to foreign bills, or to any especial class of transaction, it is easy for banks and bankers to avoid that inconvenience by stating the terms upon which they will receive the deposited paper. A notice to customers and dealers, or a different mode of entry in the bank books of the notes received for collection, and those for transmission only, will put an end to all future questions, and discharge any such responsibility—or, it might be assumed, if considered as a valuable though somewhat hazardous branch of business, for any reasonable and adequate compensation.

2. The second point, though essential to the decision of the cause, is of less general interest, and I shall speak of it more briefly. The bill drawn in New York upon Philadelphia was presented for acceptance and refused. The notary in Philadelphia neglected to give notice of non-acceptance, by which the drawer and a New York indorser were discharged. It is in evidence that if notice had been promptly given, the bill would have been paid out of securities belonging to the drawer, in the hands of an indorser, which were given up after waiting a sufficient time for the receipt of notice of non-acceptance. The holder also failed on the ground of want of notice, in a suit against the same indorser. It is now contended that the notary was not guilty of any negligence or misfeasance in omitting to give notice of the non-acceptance, such notice not being required by the common law, as it is interpreted in Pennsylvania. The evidence of distinguished counsel in Philadelphia shows that, according to the decisions of that state, protest for non-payment would be sufficient, and neither protest nor notice of non-acceptance was necessary to bind drawer or indorser in Pennsylvania. I can not consider this objection to the recovery as of any weight. The bill was drawn in New York, and was a foreign bill in Pennsylvania.

Those who undertake to collect foreign paper, are as much bound to inform themselves as to what is necessary to protect the holders of such paper, as if it were domestic and governed wholly by their own local law. On the contrary, the law of New York, so far as regards the New York parties, must, on the broad principles of commercial and international jurisprudence, form part of the local law itself, if the New York indorser or drawer should be accidentally sued in the courts of Pennsylvania. If this defense could be sustained, it would be fatal to the most valuable interests of our internal trade and exchanges between state and state. Besides, the law of which the defendants claim that their agent had a right to be ignorant, is a part of the more general commercial law from which the jurisprudence of Pennsylvania differs. That general law which is recognized as governing negotiable paper, is this: " If a bill be in fact presented, though unnecessarily, and acceptance be refused, notice should be immediately given to the persons to whom the holder may resort for payment, or they will be discharged from their respective liabilities." See Chit. on Bills, last ed., 354; 2 Kent's Com., lec. 44, *passim.* Then I borrow the language of Judge Story, strictly applicable to the very case before us: " By the common law, the protest is to be made at the time, in the manner, and by the persons prescribed in the place where the bill is payable. But as to the necessity of making a demand or protest, the circumstances under which a demand may be required or dispensed with, these are incidents of the original contract which are governed by the laws of the place where the bill is drawn. They constitute implied conditions upon which the liability of the drawer is to attach according to the *lex loci contractus,* and if the bill is negotiated, the responsibility attaches upon each successive indorser, according to the law of the place of his indorsement, for each indorser is a new drawer:" Story's Conf. L., sec. 360. It may be observed here, that this doctrine prevails not only in the countries and states under the authority or influence of our common law, but also in France and other countries whose jurisprudence flows from another source: Pardes. Droit Com., sec. 1497, 1499. I mention this fact, not in support of the authority of the rule, but as showing how universal it is, and that consequently, whoever undertakes in any way to collect or negotiate foreign paper, ought to be acquainted with it, or must take the risk of ignorance or negligence upon himself. If, however, this should be allowed as a good defense for the notary against those to whom he is immediately accountable, it is not so in the mouths of the present defendants. It was their duty to see the steps required by our law, and the general law merchant, taken when they became necessary, and to give instructions to their agent, unless, as is commonly very safely done, they voluntarily chose to leave the business to the discretion of some proper person; which discretion they must assume as their own.

3. There is yet one other point in this case. This, if I recollect rightly, was not pressed in the argument before us, yet when it was first suggested, it seemed to me of more force than any other in the defense. It is the fact of this negligence hav-

ing been committed by a notary, a commissioned public officer appointed by the executive authority of the state. If this laches had been committed by that officer in that part of his duty which was peculiarly official, and could only be performed by himself or some other notary, he having been requested or instructed to perform such duty, I doubt whether the collecting bank or any other institution or person employing him, would be responsible for his neglect in that which was not voluntarily confided to him, but wherein his official duties were rendered necessary by the requirements of the law; and where his employer had done all that was within his power for the performance of the original undertaking. Then it would seem that the notary would alone be responsible. This verdict might therefore stand, though upon other grounds than those upon which it was placed by the judge at trial, or by the supreme court. Further consideration has led me to think that this principle does not apply here. Notaries are commissioned public officers, whose office gives to their notarial attestation, a peculiar authority and effect according to the law of negotiable paper. This attestation it is their duty to grant when directed and required. But they are with us, also in practice, the agents of the several banks in whose employ (in the phrase used in evidence here) they may be. As such agents, it appears that business, connected with their official character, yet still not strictly official, is confided to them; such as sending of notices of non-acceptance or non-payment where no protest is required. To them the evidence shows the banks often send paper, when at maturity, to be presented for acceptance, without specific instructions, confiding wholly to them as their agents to do what may be necessary or expedient in the case. In the present instance the notary's strictly official acts were sufficiently correct. Upon refusal to accept he noted the bill for protest. This is all that the law required: "The notarial protest is a requisite step in the case of a foreign bill, and must be made promptly on refusal. It is sufficient, however, to note the protest on the day of demand, and it may be drawn up in form at a future period:" 2 Kent's Com. 93; see also Chit. on Bills.

The giving notice of non-acceptance was another and important duty, not necessarily and strictly official, which those who employed the notary thought fit for reasons of convenience to confide to him, but which might have been executed by any clerk. Again: the bill was sent without particular instructions, and left to the notary's discretion. On a similar bill of the same drawer and drawee, two days before, he had instructions to give notice, which was done, and the bill was saved. All this gives to the notary, in my view, the character of an agent, to whose discretion his employers trusted in part, and for whose neglect they should be answerable. But these are not strictly mere conclusions of law. The fact of the relation of this notary at Philadelphia to his bank, the question of the duty and usage of special instruction, the duties of the Philadelphia banks on a bill being returned by their notary merely as noted for protest, all these present mixed questions of law and fact which should have gone to the jury, under the direction of the judge. The misdirection of the judge turned the attention of the jury wholly to other points, and therefore (as is said in a recent case), "inasmuch as the verdict may have resulted from the error of the judge, a new trial ought to be granted:" 9 Cow. 674. Besides, were the probability of a different verdict far less than I think it is, I should still judge a new trial proper. The granting or refusing a new trial for misdirection is wholly within the discretion of the court above, to be so applied as to promote the substantial ends of justice. The misdirection here so completely covers the whole ground of the verdict, excluding all other points from the consideration of the jury, and its result has so important a bearing upon commercial usage and understanding, that it appears to me that the justice of the case and public policy will alike be promoted by a reversal of the judgments of the courts below. The emphatic language of Chief Justice Parsons is peculiarly applicable here. "The law is our criterion of right and wrong, in the decision of causes; and if it be mistaken by the court, whose duty it is to declare the law, the consequence of error may be extensive, reaching far beyond the action in which it was committed, and materially affecting other legal questions:" 5 Mass. 365.

On the question being put, Shall this judgment be reversed? the members of the court divided as follows:

In the affirmative: Senators FOX, HAWKINS, HUNT, HUNTINGTON, LEE, H. A. LIVINGSTON, MAYNARD, MOSELEY, NICHOLAS, PECK, SKINNER, VAN DYCK, VERPLANCK, WAGER—14.

In the negative: The chancellor, and Senators BEARDSLEY, CLARK, HULL, HUNTER, JOHNSON, JONES, PAIGE, SPRAKER, STERLING—10.

Whereupon the judgment of the supreme court was reversed, a *venire de novo* directed to be awarded, and the costs in this court and in the supreme court ordered to abide the event.

LIABILITY OF BANK AS AGENT FOR COLLECTION—PRELIMINARY OBSERVA-
TIONS.—The taking of notes and bills for collection is a regular and customary part of the banking business, requiring no special authorization in the
bank charter: *Tyson* v. *State Bank,* 6 Blackf. 225. Some, however, have
seemed to suppose that banks do not undertake such collections, as they do
other branches of their business, solely from motives of profit, but as an
accommodation of their customers; and that as they have no ownership or
interest in the paper collected, the service is in a measure gratuitous unless
extra commissions are charged. From this notion has no doubt sprung the
disposition of some courts to hold banks to a less stringent accountability
with respect to paper taken for collection than would be enforced against
agents for hire generally in the management of the business of their principals. Such a notion, however, is entirely fallacious as shown in the principal
case. Banks are not in this, any more than in any other part of their business, charity institutions. They undertake collections, not from motives of
benevolence, but because by long experience they have found it directly or
indirectly profitable to do so. If they should find it unprofitable they would
cease to perform the service, however advantageous it might be to the world at
large. The benefit derived from the use of the money collected for the time that
it may be left in their hands, the extension of their business, and the advantage of settling their accounts with distant banks, without being compelled to
send money to and fro between them, by means of collections made in the
places where such banks are situated, furnish ample consideration for the undertaking to collect: *Thompson* v. *Bank of South Carolina,* 30 Am. Dec. 354;
Reeves v. *State Bank of Ohio,* 8 Ohio St. 465; *Titus* v. *Mechanics' National
Bank,* 35 N. J. L. 588; 1 Dan. Neg. Inst., sec. 324. There is no need therefore
of any special tenderness on the part of the law, in dealing with banks when
engaged in such service.

INCEPTION OF THE AGENCY, AND EFFECT OF IN GENERAL.—The usual
mode of constituting a bank an agent for collection, is by indorsing to it the
paper to be collected: *Caldwell* v. *Evans,* 5 Bush, 380. The indorsement may
either be in blank or it may be expressly made "for collection." The latter
is, of course, the preferable mode, since it represents the real nature of the
transaction, and prevents any danger of loss to the real owner through intrusting the apparent title to the agent. Where a note is indorsed merely
"for collection," its negotiability is thereby restrained: *Sweeny* v. *Easten,* 1
Wall. 166. It does not vest title in the collecting bank, but simply constitutes it the agent of the owner: *First National Bank of Crown Point* v. *First
National Bank of Richmond,* 14 Chicago Leg. News, 114 (Indiana supreme
court). Indeed, whatever may be the form of the indorsement, if in fact it
be for collection only, the title to the paper or its proceeds certainly does not
pass as between the parties or those having notice of the facts. The title
does not pass so as to enable the bank to pay away the note or bill on its own
debt, until the bank has become absolutely liable to the owner for the amount,
which can not be before collection, except by contract expressed, or implied
from an unequivocal course of dealing: *Scott* v. *Ocean Bank,* 23 N. Y. 289;
Dickerson v. *Wason,* 47 Id. 439, reversing S. C., 54 Barb. 230. The fact
that the holder is a large depositor of notes and bills, and is in the habit of
drawing drafts against his remittances under an arrangement allowing him
interest on his average balances, and that he continues, after the failure of the
bank, so to draw on its branch office in another state, is not sufficient: *Scott*
v. *Ocean Bank,* 23 N. Y. 289. But where the owner of a bill sends it to his
correspondent to be collected and placed to his credit and draws at the same

time at sight against the fund, the title passes, so that the proceeds of the
bill can not be followed into the hands of third persons receiving the same in
good faith, although the correspondent becomes insolvent before the drafts of
the depositor are paid: *Clark* v. *Merchants' Bank*, 2 Id. 380. In that case,
however, the indorsement was in blank, and therefore the agent was the apparent owner. Merely crediting the amount of the bill, note, or other paper
to the depositor before collection is not sufficient to transfer the title so as to
make the bank liable for the money at all events, whether collected or not.
Where on receiving a check for collection the amount is credited to the depositor in his pass-book if it is not paid, the check may be returned and the
credit canceled: *National Gold Bank etc. Co.* v. *McDonald*, 51 Cal. 64; particularly where the collection is undertaken merely for accommodation and no
negligence is imputable to the bank: *Freeholders of Middlesex* v. *State Bank*,
32 N. J. Eq. 467. But if at maturity the bank, supposing the note to have
been paid, places the amount to the depositor's credit on his book, but after
wards, on discovering that it has not been paid, erases the credit, but is notified
by the depositor that he holds it responsible, and if the bank then sues the
maker or drawer and his bail, but fails to recover, it shall be deemed by so
doing to have assumed the property in the note, and will be held liable for its
payment: *Wetherill* v. *Bank of Pennsylvania*, 1 Miles, 399.

Making a note payable at a bank is not of itself sufficient to constitute
such bank an agent for its collection: *Ward* v. *Smith*, 7 Wall. 447; S. C., 8
Am. L. Reg. (N. S.) 354; *Caldwell* v. *Evans*, 5 Bush, 380; *Pease* v. *Warren*,
29 Mich. 9; *Balme* v. *Wambaugh*, 16 Minn. 116. Therefore, where the note
is made payable at a bank and the amount is deposited there by the maker
with instructions to apply it on the note, which the bank refuses to do on an
untenable ground, such deposit does not amount to a payment which discharges the note: *Pease* v. *Warren*, 29 Mich. 9. And a tender of the amount
of a note to the cashier of the bank at which it is made payable but not indorsed for collection, coupled with a demand for the return of the note, where
such tender is not kept good or renewed, is not effectual to discharge the lien
of a mortgage given to secure the note: *Balme* v. *Wambaugh*, 16 Minn. 116.
Where, however, a note is made payable at a certain bank, and is indorsed to,
or deposited with that bank for collection, the bank becomes the agent of the
payee and not of the maker: *Ward* v. *Smith*, 7 Wall. 447; S. C., 8 Am. L.
Reg. (N. S.) 354; *Smith* v. *Essex Co. Bank*, 22 Barb. 627; *Alley* v. *Rogers*, 19
Gratt. 366; 1 Dan. Neg. Inst., sec. 325. The bank, therefore, is not liable
to the maker, but to the payee, if it collects the money and fails to pay it
over: *Smith* v. *Essex Co. Bank*, 22 Barb. 627. And as the bank is the agent
of the holder, it undoubtedly remains so after the maturity of the note so long
as it remains deposited there, and the maker may safely pay to such bank
unless notified that it has no authority to receive the money: *Alley* v. *Rogers*,
19 Gratt. 366.

GENERAL RULE AS TO DUTY AND LIABILITY OF BANK is, that it must use
due diligence in taking all such steps, by presentment, demand, protest, and
notice, as are necessary to fix the liability of all the parties to whom its principal has a right to resort for payment. So far the rule as to its liability is well
settled, whatever diversity of opinion there may be as to the parties to whom
it is required to give notice: *Bank of Mobile* v. *Huggins*, 3 Ala. 206; *McKinster* v. *Bank of Utica*, 9 Wend. 46; *Montgomery County Bank* v. *Albany City
Bank*, 7 N. Y. 460; *First National Bank* v. *Fourth National Bank*, 77 Id. 320;
S. C., 33 Am. Rep. 618; *Warren Bank* v. *Suffolk Bank*, 10 Cush. 582; *Merchants'
etc. Bank* v. *Stafford Bank*, 44 Conn. 565. In the case last cited Shipman,

J., delivering the opinion, says: "The general duty of an agent, who receives for collection a bill of exchange, is to use due diligence in presenting the same for acceptance, and in presenting it for payment if it has been accepted, and to give the holder and other parties to the paper, by the next day's post, the notices of dishonor required by law in case acceptance or payment is refused, and to give to his principal any special notice which is required by the terms of the instructions to the agent, or of the contract which the agent has entered into with his principal. The agent is also required to protest, in case of non-acceptance or non-payment, if protest is not forbidden, and to send the protest to the holder: *Walker* v. *Bank of State of New York*, 9 N. Y. 582; *Hamilton* v. *Cunningham*, 2 Brock. 350." So far as notice to other parties than the holder is concerned, what is here said by Judge Shipman is, as we shall presently see, decidedly contrary to the weight of authority. Otherwise the rule which he lays down is unexceptionable. If the collecting bank fails to take the necessary measures to fix the liabilty of the parties, prior to its principal, it is liable therefor either in case or assumpsit: *McKinster* v. *Bank of Utica*, 9 Wend. 46. But although the bank may have performed its duty in such a way as to render all the parties to the bill or note chargeable, it must nevertheless be held liable if, through its negligence, the amount of the debt is actually lost: *First National Bank* v. *Fourth National Bank*, 77 N. Y. 320; S. C., 33 Am. Rep. 618; *Boddington* v. *Schlencker*, 4 Barn. & Adol. 752; S. C., 1 Nev. & M. 540. On the other hand it is laid down in *Bank of Washington* v. *Triplett*, 1 Pet. 25, and *Alexander* v. *Burchfield*, Car. & M. 75;.S. C., 3 Scott (N. R.), 555, that the collecting bank may so act as to discharge the drawer without becoming liable to the owner of the paper. It does not follow that the bank is liable because there has been a failure to recover from the indorser, for want of due demand and notice. The judgment in favor of the indorser does not estop the bank from showing that there was demand and notice: *Miranda* v. *City Bank*, 26 Am. Dec. 493. And, on the other hand, the bank is not released because not made a party to the suit in which that judgment was rendered: *Id*.

INSTRUCTIONS—USAGE.—Of course where there is a special contract between the bank and the holder, or where there are special instructions given by the holder, such contract or instructions furnish the measure of the bank's duty. If there be an instruction to "protest," it must be complied with, although protest might not otherwise be necessary: *Ayrault* v. *Pacific Bank*, 47 N. Y. 570; S. C., 7 Am. Rep. 489. And instructions given to the bank taking the note or bill for collection, must be transmitted to its correspondent, where the collection is to be made in a distant place: *Borup* v. *Nininger*, 5 Minn. 523. This is certainly true without regard to the question to be discussed elsewhere in this note, whether the correspondent is deemed the agent of the holder or of the transmitting bank: *Borup* v. *Nininger*, *supra*. The usages or by-laws of the bank with respect to making collections, if known to the holder, form part of the contract and are binding upon the holder: *Lincoln etc. Bank* v. *Page*, 6 Am. Dec. 52; *Hartford Bank* v. *Stedman*, 3 Conn. 489. Indeed, the better opinion is probably that a settled usage of the bank on this subject will bind the depositor, although he is not informed of it: *Bank of Washington* v. *Triplett*, 1 Pet. 25; for from his neglecting to make inquiry on that point he must be assumed either to know and approve the usage or to be indifferent to it: Morse on Banking, 2d ed., 398. Another ground upon which this doctrine may be explained is, that as the bank is bound only to ordinary care and diligence, if it follows its usual methods, it fulfills the measure of its duty: *Indig* v. *National City Bank*, 80

N. Y. 100; S. C., 59 How. Pr. 10. It is not required to depart from its custom in such matters because a particular depositor happens not to know what its custom is. Where a customer, having deposited a note for collection, knows the steps that have been taken to make such collection, and interposes no objection thereto, he is estopped from subsequently disavowing those steps if the note is lost thereby without the fault of the bank or its agent: *Jacobsohn* v. *Belmont*, 7 Bosw. 14.

DUTY AS TO PRESENTMENT FOR ACCEPTANCE.—Although presentment for acceptance may be ·unnecessary as between the holder and drawer and indorsers, the bank taking the bill for collection will nevertheless be liable for any damages resulting from a failure to present the bill for acceptance: *Tyson* v. *State Bank*, 6 Blackf. 225; *Allen* v. *Suydam*, 32 Am. Dec. 555; 1 Dan. Neg. Inst., sec. 330. But the bank is not liable for non-presentment where presentment would be entirely nugatory, as where a bill is drawn in payment of a pre-existing debt by an insolvent drawer upon an insolvent drawee, the payee having knowledge of the insolvency: *Mobley* v. *Clark*, 28 Barb. 390. If the bank takes anything but an explicit unequivocal acceptance without treating it as a refusal to accept and giving notice thereof, it will be liable for any loss resulting from its negligence in that particular. Thus where a bill was drawn by the Empire mills, upon E. C. Hamilton, and the drawee, upon its being presented for acceptance, wrote upon it as follows: "Accepted at Am. Ex. Bank. Empire Mills, by E. C. Hamilton, treas.," and the bank, treating this as an acceptance, omitted to give notice to the drawer or indorsers, who all failed before the bill matured, it was held liable to the holder for the amount: *Walker* v. *Bank of New York*, 9 N. Y. 582.

DUTY AS TO DEMAND OF PAYMENT.—Neglect by a bank having a note for collection to make demand of payment, whereby the indorser is discharged, renders the bank liable: *Durnford* v. *Patterson*, 12 Am. Dec. 514; *Thompson* v. *Bank of South Carolina*, 30 Id. 354; *Branch Bank* v. *Knox*, 1 Ala. 148; *Bank of Washington* v. *Triplett*, 1 Pet. 25. If the demand is prematurely made, it is as bad as if made too late or not at all. Hence, if through mistake as to the date of the note, *Bank of Delaware Co.* v. *Broomhall*, 38 Pa. St. 135, or for any other cause, demand and protest are made before the note matures, or before the expiration of the days of grace, where grace is allowed, and the indorser is thereby discharged, the bank is liable: *Ivory* v. *Bank of Missouri*, 36 Mo. 475; *American Express Co.* v. *Haire*, 21 Ind. 4; S. C., 3 Am. L. Reg. 269; *Georgia National Bank* v. *Henderson*, 46 Ga. 487; S. C., 12 Am. Rep. 590. If a note is payable at the bank to which it is indorsed for collection, no demand is necessary. "It is enough if the note be in the bank on the day appointed for its payment:" *Goodloe* v. *Godley*, 13 Smed. & M. 233. If the note is payable at another bank, sending it by mail to that bank is a sufficient presentment for payment, that being the usual mode among banks: *Indig* v. *National City Bank*, 80 N. Y. 100; S. C., 59 How. Pr. 10; reversing S. C., 16 Hun, 200, where it was held that the effect of transmitting the note to the bank at which it was payable constituted such bank the agent of the transmitting bank. In the case of checks on other banks taken for collection, presentment for payment before the close of business on the next day after receiving the check, is sufficient: *Rickford* v. *Ridge*, 2 Camp. 537; *Hare* v. *Henty*, 10 Com. B. (N. S.) 65; *Alexander* v. *Burchfield*, Car. & M. 75; S. C., 3 Scott (N. R.), 555; *First National Bank* v. *Fourth National Bank*, 77 N. Y. 320; S. C., 33 Am. Rep. 618; Morse on Banking, 2d ed., 390; 1 Dan. Neg. Inst., sec. 332. Where the check is on a bank in another town, it may be transmitted to such bank by the mail of the next day after its receipt: *Hare v. Henty*, 10 Com. B. (N. S.) 65. Where, by the custom of banks in the same city, crossed checks must, as between the collecting and the drawee bank, be presented through the clearing-house on the day of receipt, if received in time, presentment on the next day is not in season, although it is sufficient as between holder and drawer by the general law: *Boddington* v. *Schlencker*, 4 Barn. &. Adol. 752; S. C., 1 Nev. & M. 540. Otherwise in the case of banks not using the clearing-house: *Alexander* v. *Burchfield*, Car. & M. 75; S. C., 3 Scott (N. R.), 555.

DUTY AS TO NOTICE OF DISHONOR.—There is some diversity of adjudication on the point whether it is the duty of a bank, having a note or bill for collection, to give notice of its dishonor to all the prior indorsers, or only to its principal. Undoubtedly the bank must give such notice as to preserve the holder's remedy against prior parties; but is it bound to give the notice directly to the prior parties, or is it required merely to give notice to its principal in season to enable him to give notice to the prior parties? In some cases it has been expressly decided, and in others it has been said very positively, though the point did not require decision, that the collecting bank must give notice to all the indorsers: *Thompson* v. *Bank of South Carolina*, 30 Am. Dec. 354; *Smedes* v. *Bank of Utica*, 20 Johns. 372; *McKinster* v. *Bank of Utica*, 9 Wend. 46; S. C., in the court of errors, 11 Id. 473; *Downer* v. *Madison County Bank*, 6 Hill, 648; *Chapman* v. *McCrea*, 63 Ind. 360. But the decided preponderance of authority is in favor of the position that, in the absence of special instructions, notice given by the collecting bank to its principal in time to enable him to give seasonable notice to those to whom he intends to resort, is sufficient, the bank being regarded as the real holder so far as giving and receiving notice is concerned: 1 Dan. Neg. Inst., sec. 331; Morse on Banking, 2d ed., 401; *Bank of Mobile* v. *Huggins*, 3 Ala. 206; *Burnham* v. *Webster*, 19 Me. 232; *Colt* v. *Noble*, 5 Mass. 167; *Mead* v. *Engs*, 5 Cow. 303; *Howard* v. *Ives*, 1 Hill, 263; *State Bank of Troy* v. *Bank of the Capitol*, 41 Barb. 343; *Farmers' Bank* v. *Vail*, 21 N. Y. 485; *United States Bank* v. *Goddard*, 5 Mason, 366; *Bird* v. *Louisiana State Bank*, 93 U. S. 96. In the case last cited the point is not directly decided, but it is held, that where the bank fails to give notice to its principal, or to the indorser so that the latter is discharged, the bank is liable, Bradley, J., who delivered the opinion, saying that the bank's duty was to give notice "at least to its principal," so that he might do what was necessary for his protection. Mr. Chief Justice Parsons, in *Colt* v. *Noble*, 5 Mass. 167, speaking on this point, says: "A person appointed a factor to cause a bill to be presented, is intrusted with no other powers, and it is his duty to notify his principal. The factor may not know to which of the prior parties the principal intends to resort; and if he does so, he may not know their domiciles, as he has no interest in the bill or privity with the parties." The bank must give notice to its principal in the same time as if it were a party to the note, and the principal may then give notice to the indorsers, and it will be sufficient: *United States Bank* v. *Goddard*, 5 Mason, 366; *Colt* v. *Noble*, 5 Mass. 167; *Howard* v. *Ives*, 1 Hill, 263; *Farmers' Bank* v. *Vail*, 21 N. Y. 485. So where the note is transmitted by the collecting bank to another, the latter is to give notice to its principal, one day being allowed to each recipient of notice to give notice to his or its predecessor: *Prideaux* v. *Criddle*, L. R., 4 Q. B. 455. So whatever may be the number of banks through which the note passes. Even where the bank undertakes to send notice to some of the prior parties, this is not evidence of an agreement to notify all the indorsers: *State Bank of Troy* v. *Bank of the Capitol*, 41 Barb. 343. Although the bank is not required to give notice to any-

body but its immediate principal, if it in fact gives notice to the drawer in
the same time as he would have received it from the holder, it is sufficient:
Tunno v. *Lague*, 1 Am. Dec. 141. And if the collecting agent uses due diligence to ascertain the indorser's residence, and, in accordance with the information received, sends the notice to the wrong address, it is nevertheless
good, it seems, although the holder knew the indorser's residence: *Bartlett* v.
Isbell, 31 Conn. 296. If the indorser has expressly waived notice by an indorsement on the note, such waiver excuses the bank from giving him notice,
even if it would otherwise be required to do so: *Blanc* v. *Mutual National Bank*,
28 La. Ann. 921; S. C., 26 Am. Rep. 119. And generally, where notice is
not necessary to charge the indorser, the collecting bank is not liable for omitting to give him notice, as where the bill was indorsed by a partnership, all
the members of which were members of the firm that drew the bill: *West
Branch Bank* v. *Fulmer*, 3 Pa. St. 399. Failure to give notice to the drawer,
that the drawee, when called upon to accept, was not at home, is not such
negligence as will release the drawer: *Bank of Washington* v. *Triplett*, 1
Pet. 25.

BANK NOT REQUIRED TO BRING SUIT.—It is not part of the duty of a bank
taking a note or bill for collection to employ counsel and bring suit in case of
non-payment, unless there is an express stipulation to that effect in the contract by which it undertakes the collection: *Crow* v. *Mechanics' etc. Bank*,
12 La. Ann. 692. In case of non-payment after due demand, if the bank gives
due notice of the default to its principal, and thus puts him in a position to
give such notices and institute such actions as may be necessary for the protection of his rights, its duty is ended.

WHETHER BANK MAY ACCEPT ANYTHING BUT MONEY IN PAYMENT.—A bank
taking notes for collection can receive payment only in money "or in bills
which pass as money at their par value by the common consent of the community," and has no right to accept depreciated notes of state banks: *Ward* v.
Smith, 7 Wall. 447. It may take state bank bills circulating as money,
although depreciated in value, if it has given notice to that effect which is
brought home to the depositor; and if after collection and notice to the depositor it keeps the notes intact until called for, or sends them to the depositor,
it is not liable for any depreciation at the time of payment or afterwards:
Marine Bank v. *Fulton Bank*, 2 Wall. 252. But it is liable for subsequent
depreciation where it mingles the amount collected with its general funds:
Marine Bank v. *Rushmore*, 28 Ill. 463; *Marine Bank* v. *Fulton Bank*, 2 Wall.
252. A bank receiving notes for collection at a time when confederate money
was the only currency, could no doubt make collection in that currency; but
where the notes were deposited before the war in a southern bank by a non-
resident, and were protested for non-payment, but still left on deposit, the bank
had no power to bind the owner by accepting payment in confederate money:
Alley v. *Rogers*, 19 Gratt. 366. Taking payment by the acceptor's check and
surrendering the bill will not, it seems, render the bank chargeable with negligence where that is the established mode of transacting such business, even
though the check is dishonored: *Russell* v. *Hankey*, 6 T. R. 12; Morse on
Banking, 2d ed., 429; although under ordinary circumstances an agent for collection taking the debtor's check in payment is himself liable if the check is
not paid. Thus, where a collecting bank took a check in payment, but did
not present the check until the next day, and the drawer failed in the mean
time, and it appeared that the check would have been paid if presented on the
day when it was drawn, the bank was held liable: *First National Bank* v.
Fourth National Bank, 77 N. Y. 320; S. C., 33 Am. Rep. 618. See, generally,

as to the right of a collection agent to take anything but money in payment, the note to *Martin* v. *United States*, 15 Am. Dec. 129.

BANK'S LIABILITY FOR MONEY COLLECTED.—After collection the bank may, on the one hand, keep the money separate from its other funds, as a special deposit, for which it will be liable as a mere bailee, after notice to the owner: *Marine Bank* v. *Fulton Bank*, 2 Wall. 252; or, on the other hand, it may place the amount to the depositor's credit, and mingle it with its other funds, when it will be liable to the holder as a simple contract debtor: *Tinkham* v. *Heyworth*, 31 Ill. 519; *Jockusch* v. *Towsey*, 51 Tex. 129; *In re West of England Bank*, L. R., 11 Ch. Div. 772; 1 Dan. Neg. Inst., sec. 334. So although the owner does not usually deposit in that bank: *Tinkham* v. *Heyworth*, 31 Ill. 519. Of course, in such a case, if the bank subsequently fails, the depositor has no preferred lien, but must come in with the general creditors: *In re West of England Bank*, L. R., 11 Ch. Div. 772. And if there is a subsequent depreciation in the currency collected, it falls, as we have already seen, on the bank: *Marine Bank* v. *Rushmore*, 28 Ill. 463; *Cushman* v. *Carver*, 51 Id. 509. Another consequence of the relation between the bank and customer in such cases being that of debtor and creditor, is that case is not the proper remedy against the bank for a failure to pay over the money: *Tinkham* v. *Heyworth*, 31 Ill. 519. In this respect there is a very marked difference between the liability of banks and that of attorneys and other collecting agents. Other collectors can not thus appropriate the money of their principals and become mere debtors for the amount. There is an obvious reason, however, for the rule permitting collecting banks to make use of the money collected as their own. If it were not so, banks would not be willing to undertake collections without special compensation. Besides, the financial strength of banking institutions furnishes, as a rule, sufficient security to the depositor for the safety of his money. It is not so in the case of ordinary agents. Where, however, the collecting bank suspends payment before the collection is accomplished, and the money is afterwards collected either by the bank or the receiver, it is held as a trust fund for the holder of the note, and does not fall into the general assets of the bank: *Jockusch* v. *Towsey*, 51 Tex. 129; *Levi* v. *Missouri Bank*, 5 Dill. C. C. 104.

LIABILITY FOR NEGLIGENCE OF NOTARIES, CORRESPONDENTS, ETC.—There is very great conflict in the adjudged cases as to how far a bank taking notes and other negotiable paper for collection is liable for the defaults of agents employed in making the collection. Unquestionably the bank is liable for any loss occasioned by the negligence or other fault of its immediate servants in the collection of such paper. Thus where the cashier of the bank fraudulently omits to enter collection paper on the books, and holds it without collection, protest, or notice, so that the holder's remedies against indorsers and others are lost, the bank is liable: *Pahquoque Bank* v. *Bethel Bank*, 36 Conn. 325; S. C., 4 Am. Rep. 80. But where the services of a notary or of a corresponding bank in a distant city are employed in making the collection, and a loss occurs through the default of such notary or corresponding bank, there is much difference of opinion upon the point as to whether or not the bank originally taking the paper for collection is liable.

First, as to the defaults of notaries, it is held in a number of cases that where the bank having paper for collection intrusts it to a competent notary for presentment, protest, and notice, particularly where the notary is the one usually employed by such bank in collecting its own paper, it thereby discharges its duty to its customer, and is not responsible for the neglect of such notary to take the proper steps for securing the liability of the drawer and indorsers of the paper, and that the holder must look to the notary and his sureties: *Tiernan* v. *Commercial Bank*, 7 How. (Miss.) 648; *Agricultural Bank* v. *Commercial Bank*, 7 Smed. & M. 592; *Bowling* v. *Arthur*, 34 Miss. 41; *Hyde* v. *Planters' Bank*, 17 La. 560; *Baldwin* v. *Bank of Louisiana*, 1 Id. 13; *Citizens' Bank* v. *Howell*, 8 Md. 530; *Bellemire* v. *Bank of United States*, 1 Miles, 173; S. C., 4 Whart. 105; S. C., 33 Am. Dec. 46; *Warren Bank* v. *Suffolk Bank*, 10 Cush. 582; *Stacy* v. *Dane County Bank*, 12 Wis. 629. The ground upon which some of these decisions put the doctrine that the bank is not liable for the notary's default, is that he is a public officer in whose competency and integrity the bank has a right to trust: *Hyde* v. *Planters' Bank*, 17 La. 560; *Baldwin* v. *Bank of Louisiana*, 1 La. Ann. 13; *Agricultural Bank* v. *Commercial Bank*, 7 Smed. & M. 592. And it is said that the presumption that the bank has used due care in confiding the business of its customer to such an officer, is not overcome by showing the notary to be a dissipated man, unless it is shown that he was drunk at the time, or that his habits were so "universally intemperate" as to disqualify him for the discharge of an official act: *Agricultural Bank* v. *Commercial Bank*, *supra*. Chief Justice Gibson, however, lays no stress on this point, but rests the doctrine on much broader ground: *Bellemire* v. *Bank of United States*, 4 Whart. 105; 33 Am. Dec. 46.

On the other hand are cases holding that banks are liable for the omissions and mistakes of notaries employed by them in making collections, in the same way as for the acts of their immediate servants. The cases on that side are not so numerous as on the other: *Miranda* v. *City Bank*, 26 Am. Dec. 493; *Thompson* v. *Bank of South Carolina*, 30 Id. 354; *American Express Co.* v. *Haire*, 21 Ind. 4; *Gerhardt* v. *Boatman's Saving Inst.*, 38 Mo. 60; *Ayrault* v. *Pacific Bank*, 47 N. Y. 570; S. C., 7 Am. Rep. 489.

There is the same conflict of opinion concerning the liability of a bank for the negligence of its correspondents where it is required to send the paper to another city or state for collection; although some of the courts holding banks liable for the defaults of notaries employed in making collections, hold them excused from responsibility for like defaults by their correspondents. Compare *Gerhardt* v. *Boatman's Saving Inst.*, 38 Mo. 60, and *Daly* v. *Butchers' and Drovers' Bank*, 56 Id. 94. The doctrine of the principal case, that where a note payable at a distance is taken by a bank for collection and transmitted to its correspondent at the place of payment, the correspondent is the agent of the transmitting bank and not of the holder, and that the transmitting bank is therefore liable for the defaults of the correspondent, is well settled in New York: *Bank of Orleans* v. *Smith*, 3 Hill, 560; *Montgomery County Bank* v. *Albany City Bank*, 7 N. Y. 459; *Commercial Bank* v. *Union Bank*, 11 Id. 212; S. C., in supreme court, 19 Barb. 391; *Ayrault* v. *Pacific Bank*, 47 N. Y. 570; S. C., 7 Am. Rep. 489; *Indig* v. *National City Bank*, 16 Hun, 200; reversed on another point in S. C., 80 N. Y. 100. The same doctrine is adopted also by several other courts: *Titus* v. *Merchants' National Bank*, 35 N. J. L. 588; *Reeves* v. *State Bank of Ohio*, 8 Ohio St. 465; *Hyde* v. *First National Bank*, 7 Biss. 156; *Taber* v. *Perrot*, 2 Gall. 565; *Van Wart* v. *Woolley*, 3 Barn. & Cress. 439; *Mackersy* v. *Ramsay*, 9 Cl. & Fin. 818. Payment to the correspondent bank, under this rule, is payment to the transmitting bank, and if the correspondent bank afterwards fails, the loss must be borne by the transmitting bank: *Taber* v. *Perrot*, 2 Gall. 565; *Mackersy* v. *Ramsay*, 9 Cl. & Fin. 818. And in case of a default by the correspondent bank occasioning a loss, the transmitting bank may maintain an action against it immediately, without waiting until itself sued by the holder: *Commercial Bank* v. *Union Bank*, 19 Barb. 391; S. C., 11 N. Y. 203.

But even in states where the correspondent bank has been held to be the agent, not of the transmitting bank, but of the owner of the paper, if, through the correspondent's neglect to give notice of non-payment, the transmitting bank pay over the amount to the holder, supposing it to have been paid, it may, on discovering the mistake, recover the amount from the correspondent bank: *Merchants' etc. Bank* v. *Stafford Bank*, 44 Conn. 564. But in *Bank of Louisville* v. *First National Bank*, 8 Baxter (Tenn.), 101; S. C., 35 Am. Rep. 691, it is held that the transmitting bank is not responsible for a loss through the negligence of the correspondent bank, and if it pays the amount over to the payee voluntarily, it can not maintain an action against the correspondent.

The preponderance of authority is against the doctrine of the principal case, and in favor of the rule that the liability of a bank taking a note or bill for collection, which is payable at a distance, extends merely to the selection of a suitable and competent agent at the place of payment, and to the transmission of the paper to such agent with proper instructions, and that the correspondent bank is the agent, not of the transmitting bank, but of the holder, so that the transmitting bank is not liable for the defaults of the correspondent, where due care has been used in making the selection of such correspondent: *Fabens* v. *Mercantile Bank*, 23 Pick. 332; *Dorchester etc. Bank* v. *New England Bank*, 1 Cush. 177; *Jackson* v. *Union Bank*, 6 Har. & J. 146; *East Haddam Bank* v. *Scovil*, 12 Conn. 303; *Lawrence* v. *Stonington Bank*, 6 Id. 521; *Milliken* v. *Shapleigh*, 36 Mo. 596; *Daly* v. *Butchers' and Drovers' Bank*, 56 Id. 94; S. C., 17 Am. Rep. 663; *Ætna Ins. Co.* v. *Alton City Bank*, 25 Ill. 246; *Bank of Louisville* v. *First National Bank*, 8 Baxter (Tenn.), 101; S. C., 35 Am. Rep. 691; *Guelick* v. *National Bank of England*, 9 N. W. Rep. 328; S. C., 12 Rep. 237 (Iowa supreme court); *Stacy* v. *Dane County Bank*, 12 Wis. 629. If the note or bill is expressly taken for the purpose of being transmitted to the correspondent of the bank for collection, there would seem to be little question that the transmitting bank is liable only for the selection of a competent agent and for the transmission of the paper with proper instructions: *Bank of Washington* v. *Triplett*, 1 Pet. 25; *Farmers' Bank* v. *Owen*, 5 Cranch C. C. 504; *Mechanics' Bank* v. *Earp*, 4 Rawle, 384.

The grounds upon which it is held that banks are not liable in cases of this sort for the defaults of their correspondents are much the same as those upon which, as above mentioned, they have been held exempt from responsibility for like defaults of notaries. The argument on that side of the question was well stated by Chancellor Walworth in his opinion in the principal case, a synopsis of which is given above. The theory is that there is no consideration sufficient to support an undertaking by the bank to be liable for such defaults of its correspondents; that as those dealing with banks must know that the bank officers can not in person attend to collections at distant points, they are presumed to assent to the employment of such agencies as are usually made use of by the banks in such collections; and besides, that according to the usage and course of dealing of banks when they receive paper for collection at a distance, the undertaking on their part is not for the collection of the paper, but merely for the transmission of it to competent persons with proper instructions. So far as the matter of consideration is concerned, it has already been shown elsewhere in this note that the advantages of exchange between distant points furnish a sufficient inducement on the part of banking institutions to undertake such collections.

The rule laid down in the principal case is precisely the rule that is applied to attorneys, mercantile agencies, and the like. Where an attorney takes a note "for collection," and puts it into the hands of another attorney, he is liable for a loss through the latter's negligence or misconduct: *Lewis* v. *Peck*, 10 Ala. 142; *Wilkinson* v. *Griswold*, 12 Smed. & M. 669; *Cummins* v. *Heald*,

24 Kan. 600. In like manner a collection agency taking paper for collection either in the same or another state is liable for the defaults of the attorneys or other agents to whom it intrusts such collection: *Bradstreet* v. *Everson*, 72 Pa. St. 124; *Morgan* v. *Tener*, 83 Id. 305; *Hoover* v. *Wise*, 91 U. S. 308; S. C., 8 Chicago L. N. 193. In the case last cited, Hunt, J., delivering the opinion, refers to and approves the principal case, and applies the doctrine of it to the case before him. We can conceive of no valid reason why a different rule of responsibility should be applied to collections made by such agencies from that applied in cases of banks.

Mr. Morse in his work on banking law manifests a very decided preference for the doctrine of those cases holding a bank not liable for the negligence of its correspondents in making collections at a distance, and criticises the principal case at considerable length: Morse on Banking, 2d ed. 406-417. Mr. Daniel, on the other hand, approves the rule laid down in *Allen* v. *Merchants' Bank.* He says: "The cases which hold the bank absolutely liable for any laches or negligence, whereby the holder of the paper suffers loss, commend themselves to our approbation. Any other rule opens the door to carelessness in the conduct of banking business, which should be conducted with every safeguard to the customer who intrusts his interests to the keeping of such agents. If they are averse to dealing with distant and unknown parties, they should decline undertaking the collection or handling of the paper; and if they assume it, they should do so for sufficient compensation, and be held responsible. If unwilling to take charge of the collection under this implied understanding, they should insist on a special contract or refuse it. General usage might vary this liability, but the mere practice of banks for their own convenience would raise no implication of such usage:" 1 Dan. Neg. Inst., sec. 342. These observations seem to us eminently sound and just.

HOLDER'S RIGHT OF ACTION AGAINST SUBAGENT.—Although the correspondent or subagent to whom the bank intrusts the collection of paper received by it for that purpose, is the agent of such bank and not of the holder, there is no doubt that where the subagent has collected the money, the holder, upon notice to him before he has paid the amount over, may recover it from him in an action for money had and received: *Wilson* v. *Smith*, 3 How. (U. S.) 763; *Lawrence* v. *Stonington Bank*, 6 Conn. 521; *Bank of Orleans* v. *Smith*, 3 Hill, 560; *Miller* v. *Farmers' etc. Bank*, 30 Md. 392. There is nothing in this inconsistent with the principal case. Although the correspondent is not the holder's agent, the title to the paper and to its proceeds, until mingled with the general funds of the transmitting bank, remains in the holder, and he may assert it at any time if he can do so without prejudice to the rights of the correspondent.

RIGHT OF CORRESPONDENT TO RETAIN PROCEEDS ON BALANCE DUE FROM TRANSMITTING BANK.—Where a note or bill is deposited for collection indorsed in blank, thus constituting the bank the apparent owner, and the bank transmits it to its correspondent for collection, it is held by the supreme court of the United States that where there is a balance due from the transmitting bank to the correspondent, which is suffered to remain on the credit of the paper, and there is a usage between the banks to apply the proceeds of collections on the balances from time to time, the correspondent may so apply the proceeds of such note or bill: *Bank of Metropolis* v. *New England Bank*, 6 How. (U. S.) 227. See also *Wood* v. *Boylston Nat. Bank*, 129 Mass. 358; S. C., 37 Am. Rep. 366. Otherwise, where the indorsement is "for collection," thus notifying the correspondent that the bank is not the owner: *Sweeny* v. *Easter*, 1 Wall. 166; *Cecil Bank* v. *Farmers' Bank*, 22 Md. 148;

Miller v. *Farmers' etc. Bank*, 30 Id. 392.   In New York it is settled that the correspondent bank can not, even where it has no notice that the bank is not the owner, retain the proceeds of collection paper, and apply it on a balance due from the transmitting bank, because without advancing some new consideration it can not be regarded as a *bona fide* purchaser: *McBride* v. *Farmers' Bank*, 26 N. Y. 450; *Commercial Bank* v. *Marine Bank*, 3 Keyes, 337; *Van Amee* v. *Bank of Troy*, 8 Barb. 312; *West* v. *American Exchange Bank*, 44 Id. 175; *Lindauer* v. *Fourth National Bank*, 55 Id. 75; *Dod* v. *Fourth National Bank*, 59 Id. 265.

PAYMENT TO HOLDER BY MISTAKE, RECOVERY IN CASE OF.—If a bank having a note or bill for collection, supposing that the money has been collected, pays the amount over to the holder, it may, on discovery of the mistake, recover such payment, if no rights have been lost against the drawer or indorsers by reason of the mistake: *De Nayer* v. *State National Bank*, 8 Neb. 104; *East Haddam Bank* v. *Scovil*, 12 Conn. 303; *Union National Bank* v. *Sixth National Bank*, 43 N. Y. 452; S. C., 3 Am. Rep. 718.   But the bank may waive its right against the holder by endeavoring, after discovering the mistake, to recover the amount from the drawer: *Wetherill* v. *Bank of Pennsylvania*, 1 Miles, 399.   If the payment is made to the holder on the credit of the maker, a depositor in the bank, and the maker afterwards fails, leaving only a trifling balance to his credit, the payment can not be retracted on the ground of mistake: *Whiting* v. *City Bank*, 77 N. Y. 363.

MEASURE OF DAMAGES in an action against a bank for negligence in collection, whereby the holder's remedy against prior parties is lost, is the actual loss sustained: *Van Wart* v. *Woolley*, 3 Barn. & Cress. 439; *Bank of Mobile* v. *Huggins*, 3 Ala. 206; *Merchants' etc. Bank* v. *Stafford*, 44 Conn. 564; *First National Bank* v. *Fourth National Bank*, 77 N. Y. 320; S. C., 33 Am. Rep. 618; *Borup* v. *Nininger*, 5 Minn. 523.   *Prima facie* the amount of the debt is the measure of the loss: *Allen* v. *Suydam*, 32 Am. Dec. 555, and note; *Durnford* v. *Patterson*, 12 Id. 514; *Miranda* v. *City Bank*, 26 Id. 494; *Washington Bank* v. *Triplett*, 1 Pet. 25.   The bank may show, however, that the plaintiff's remedy against the drawer or indorsers is only delayed, and not lost: *Van Wart* v. *Woolley*, 3 Barn. & Cress. 439; or that, although the remedy against some of the parties is lost, there are other solvent parties still bound, from whom the debt can be collected: *First National Bank* v. *Fourth National Bank*, 77 N. Y. 320; S. C., 33 Am. Rep. 618.   Or that the note is secured in whole or in part, or that the parties against whom the holder's remedy is lost were in fact insolvent: *Borup* v. *Nininger*, 5 Minn. 523.   The costs and expenses of a suit in which it was unsuccessfully attempted to hold the indorser, can not be included in the damages: *Downer* v. *Madison County Bank*, 6 Hill, 648.

INDORSEMENT GOVERNED BY LEX LOCI: See *Aymar* v. *Sheldon*, 27 Am. Dec. 137, and note.   See, also, citing the principal case, *Hunt* v. *Standard*, 15 Ind. 35; *Huse* v. *Hamblin*, 29 Iowa, 504; *Nichols* v. *Porter*, 2 W. Va. 22.

COMMERCIAL BANK OF BUFFALO v. KORTRIGHT.

[22 WENDELL, 348.]

PRINCIPAL IS BOUND BY AGENT'S ACT IN VIOLATION OF SECRET INSTRUCTIONS in transferring stock in a corporation, where the written authority of such agent gives him full power to make such transfer.

PROVISION IN CHARTER THAT TRANSFERS OF STOCK MUST BE REGISTERED in a book kept for that purpose, to be valid, is merely for the protection of the corporation, and does not invalidate a transfer not so registered as between the former owner and a vendee or pledgee, who has done everything necessary under the rules of the corporation, to entitle him to a perfected transfer.

CORPORATION IS LIABLE FOR A WRONGFUL REFUSAL BY ITS PRESIDENT to permit a transfer of stock, without proof of a formal delegation of authority to him, where he has been in the habit of permitting transfers, or where the corporation has ratified his acts.

POWER TO TRANSFER STOCK, MADE IN BLANK, by the owner placing his name and seal, with the subscription of a witness, upon the back of the certificate, which is subsequently filled up by the party to whom the certificate is transferred, is valid.

EVIDENCE OF A CUSTOM OF TRANSFERRING STOCK BY MEANS OF BLANK POWERS indorsed on the certificates is admissible, not to vary the law, but to show the intent of a party in signing his name in blank on a certificate.

MEASURE OF DAMAGES FOR WRONGFUL REFUSAL TO PERMIT A TRANSFER of stock in an action against the corporation therefor, is the highest price of the stock between the demand for such transfer and the trial.

ACTION FOR DAMAGES FOR REFUSAL TO PERMIT A TRANSFER OF STOCK is a convenient common law remedy, and by bringing such action the plaintiff waives his right to the stock, and agrees to accept compensation.

ERROR from the supreme court in an action of assumpsit against the corporation defendant, for refusal to permit a transfer to the plaintiff upon the books of the corporation, of certain stock standing in the name of one Barker. It appeared that Barker sent the certificate of stock, with his name and seal indorsed thereon in blank, together with his note for ten thousand dollars, to one Bartow, as collateral security, for the purpose of obtaining a loan for that amount; that Bartow negotiated and delivered the certificate to the plaintiff for a loan of twenty-five thousand dollars, the plaintiff giving a receipt, stipulating to return the certificate on payment of the loan within a certain time. Bartow having absconded, the plaintiff filled up the blank transfer with an assignment to himself, and an authority to one Sherwood to do all acts necessary to perfect it. Sherwood having requested permission to transfer the stock on the books of the bank, was refused by Barker, who was then the president of the bank. Barker, it appeared, had obtained from Bartow the ten thousand dollars which he had authorized him to borrow, and offered to pay over that sum to Sherwood, which was refused. The defense here was probably made in the interest of a certain bank of which Bartow was cashier, and to which he was largely indebted. Between the time of demanding permission to make the transfer and the commencement of the suit, the stock rose to three hundred per cent. advance. There was evidence as to the customary mode of transferring stock, which is sufficiently stated in the opinion. The jury were instructed that the measure of damages in this action was the highest price of the stock between the refusal of permission to transfer the stock and the bringing of the action. Verdict for the plaintiff for thirteen thousand five hundred and thirty-six dollars and thirty-five cents. Motion for a new trial overruled, and the defendants brought error.

J. Van Buren and S. Stevens, for the plaintiffs in error.

S. Sherwood and D. B. Ogden, for the defendant in error.

WALWORTH, Chancellor, delivered an opinion in favor of reversing the judgment, the substance of which is given in the following synopsis:

The objection that the demand of permission to transfer the stock, made on Barker, who was at the same time the legal owner of the shares and the president of the bank, was not sufficient, is not well taken. A person desiring such a transfer is not bound to hunt up the directors, and have a person appointed to comply with his demand. It is sufficient for him to make his demand at the bank, during ordinary business hours, upon the officers in attendance there. In the absence of proof to the contrary, it may well be presumed that the principal officer or clerk at the bank during business hours is authorized to permit transfers of stock, that being a matter of common occurrence. If the officers in attendance have no such authority, they should either refer the party to the officer who has authority or procure his attendance. It is the duty of the directors of the bank to have an officer in attendance authorized to permit transfers to be made in the way in which the charter provides.

The transfer in this case gave the plaintiff no legal title to the stock, because not registered as required by the charter: Stat. 1834, p. 265. It merely gave an equitable lien, subject to all prior equities in favor of any other person from whom such assignment was obtained: *Stebbins v. Phœnix Fire Ins. Co.*, 3 Paige Ch. 350. To the same effect, see *Union Bank of Georgetown v. Laird*, 2 Wheat. 391; *Marlborough Mfg. Co. v. Smith*, 2 Conn. 579. Proof of a custom to make transfers otherwise than as provided by statute, can not make such transfers legal. But since a *bona fide* agreement to transfer, founded upon a consideration actually paid, or an actual hypothecation of the stock

for the payment of a specified debt, is, though not registered, a
good equitable transfer or hypothecation, and gives a good equitable title which will prevail against any one who has not a prior
equity or who has not taken the legal title without notice of an
outstanding equity, the plaintiff's case here stands thus: Bartow
having, by virtue of the indorsement and delivery of the certificate to him with Barker's note, an equitable lien to the extent of
that note, has transferred that interest to Kortright. Kortright's equitable title is better than that of any *of* the creditors
of Bartow, but the legal title is still in Barker.

But Kortright is not entitled to a transfer of the stock upon
the books, and the supreme court was wrong in holding him entitled to damages to the full value of the stock. The amount
for which the stock was pledged was the ten-thousand-dollar
note given by Barker to Bartow, and that amount was tendered
to the plaintiff's agent when he asked permission to make the
transfer. The case of *Kirton* v. *Breathwaite*, 1 Mee. & W. 310;
S. C., 2 Gale, 48, shows that if Sherwood was authorized to
demand a transfer, because the loan for which the stock was
pledged was not paid, he was also his agent to receive a tender
of the money. Although Barker was the president of the bank,
and as such refused to permit the transfer, he acted in his individual capacity in tendering the money.

The case of *Rex* v. *Bank of England*, 2 Doug. 524, is not an
authority in favor of Kortright's right to maintain assumpsit,
even though he be equitably entitled to a transfer as against
Barker. In that case the action was by the legal owners of the
stock for a refusal to permit them to transfer to another. The
case of *Gray* v. *Portland Bank*, 3 Mass. 364 [3 Am. Dec. 156],
was distinguishable also as an action of assumpsit founded
upon the duty of the bank to the plaintiff, who was legally
entitled to certain new stock which the corporation issued
to another. In *Sargent* v. *Franklin Ins. Co.*, 8 Pick. 90
[19 Am. Dec. 306]. the corporation unjustifiably attempted
to defeat a sale and transfer of stock to the plaintiffs by the
owner thereof, by attaching and selling it for its own debt, after
notice of the plaintiff's rights. Case was probably the proper
remedy there. So here, perhaps, case would lie if the corporation, having notice of the plaintiff's equitable lien, had suffered
Barker to transfer the stock to a *bona fide* purchaser, or to receive the dividends thereon, so as to prevent an enforcement of
the lien by a resort to the proper tribunal. But the plaintiff
was not entitled to a transfer to himself under any circumstances

without the consent of Barker, the pledgor, but could only have it sold if the money was not paid, and the bank was not liable for refusing to permit a transfer until the rights of the parties were settled amicably or by adjudication of the proper tribunal.

If the blank indorsement in this case had accompanied an absolute sale of the stock, no doubt it could have been filled up by the purchaser so as to secure to him a legal transfer, and to effectuate the actual intent. *Nelson* v. *Dubois*, 13 Johns. 175; *Campbell* v. *Butler*, 14 Id. 349; and *Herrick* v. *Carman*, 12 Id. 161, though relating to mere guaranties, contain the principle applicable to such a case, because a seal is unnecessary to a transfer of stock. But here the attempt was to fill up the blank contrary to the intent of the parties. Kortright knew when he took the certificate that it could only be transferred on the books of the bank, and that he only obtained an equitable pledge of Bartow's equitable interest, and therefore took subject to every equity in favor of Barker or of any other person to whom the stock had been previously assigned. Yet he filled up the blank with an absolute assignment and an authority to make a legal transfer. No doubt Kortright, as an equitable pledgee of Bartow's interest, could, in case of non-payment of Bartow's debt, upon due notice to attaching creditors of Bartow and to Barker, have sold the pledge, and out of the proceeds paid over to Barker all beyond the amount due to Bartow on Barker's note, and out of that amount retained the whole or so much as was due from Bartow to him.

But if the action had been right, the measure of damages given to the jury at the circuit was clearly wrong. The bank's refusal to permit the transfer did not impair Kortright's title, if any he had, nor can a recovery against the corporation give it any right to the stock or to the dividends. The plaintiff may still file a bill against Barker and the bank to compel a sale of the pledge and a transfer to the purchaser on the books of the bank. The bank can not become the owner of the stock, because it can not reduce its capital by purchasing its own stock, and is prohibited by law from receiving it even as security for a loan. The true rule of damages, therefore, would be the depreciation in value, since the stock and dividends would still belong to him.

VERPLANCK, Senator. Let us examine separately such of the prominent points in this cause as bear on the merits of the controversy, or the legal principle governing similar affairs.

1. Supposing the assignment and power of attorney on the stock certificate to have been legally executed, was the plaintiff

below entitled to a transfer of the stock? Bartow, as appears
in the evidence, was intrusted by Barker with the certificate
of this stock for the purpose of borrowing money on its
security. The certificate was accompanied with such an authority to transfer (now presuming that authority to be valid)
as would hold out Bartow, to any one to whom he might apply
for a loan, in the character of an agent having full right to transfer, or to substitute some other person as the attorney for that
purpose. Bartow does not appear himself the pledgee (for then
the power would have been made out to him immediately), but
as an agent empowered to obtain money on a pledge of stock.
The precise use Barton was expected to make of the stock, and
the different use he may have actually made, were nothing to
the purpose, as against those who acted upon the faith of the
general authority intrusted to the holder of the certificate and
its blank indorsements. "So far as the agent, whether general
or special, is in any case held out to the public at large or to
third persons dealing with him, as competent to contract for or
to bind the principal, the latter will be bound by the acts of the
agent, notwithstanding he may have deviated from his secret instructions, and orders, for otherwise such instructions and
orders would operate as a fraud upon the unsuspecting confidence of the other party." See Story on Agency, secs. 127, 133,
and especially the well-reasoned distinctions and explanations
in note 1, page 117, and note pages 118, 119, and authorities
there cited.

The intent of Barker and his understanding with Bartow
were, that the stock should be used as a security for a loan of
ten thousand dollars for himself. But he held out Bartow, or
whomsoever he might substitute to himself, as authorized to
make any disposition of the stock whatever. Bartow was intrusted with what Lord Ellenborough, in a well-known leading
case on the law of agency, 15 East, 44, expressly terms, "the
usual external *indicia* of the right of disposing of the property."
On the faith of these external *indicia*, Kortright lent twenty-five
thousand dollars upon the aggregate security of this and other
stocks. If the law should now hold this transaction to be void,
it would, indeed, as Judge Story says, "operate as a fraud
upon the unsuspecting confidence of the other party." If the
holder of the certificate and the power has been voluntarily exhibited to the money-dealing public, as having the competent
right of pledge, disposal, and transfer vested in him by means
of all the usual and well-known evidences of such right, the pri-

vate understanding of Barker and Bartow, and the former supposition that the stock was to be or was pledged in a manner different from that which actually took place, can not affect the rights of those who, if misled, were misled by Barker's own acts. Much stress is laid upon the enactment in the bank charter, that "no transfer shall be valid, unless such transfer shall have been registered in a book kept for that purpose by the directors." Does it then follow that Kortright had not a legal title to the stock, such as he could assert by suit, the transfer not being yet perfected, or, in the words of the charter, "valid"? This provision of the charter is evidently for the protection of the bank in the payment of dividends; for the ascertaining the legal voters at its election; and finally, as appears from the comparison of the charter with the general regulations of our moneyed corporations, for preventing, in case of corporate bankruptcy, the escape from liability to contribute for the deficiency. Such a provision does not interfere with the rights of ownership, as between the person in whose name the stock may stand, and his vendee or pledgee. The title might be perfect as between them, and yet not valid as to any other liability or right which was meant to be protected by this legal evidence of transfer on the books.

Such legal evidence, it is made the bank's duty, by operation of law as well as by its own express understanding in its certificates, to furnish to the person entitled to the possession, whenever he has complied with the conditions prescribed to show that right. The bank sets forth those conditions in its stock certificate. It there states to the world the terms upon which that valid and perfect title shall be furnished; the shares are there made transferable only " on the books of the bank by the said stockholder, or his attorney, on surrender of the certificate." When the evidence of the certificate and the power of attorney has been produced as required (and that evidence furnished by the prior stockholder himself), how can either the bank or that stockholder be at liberty to deny the legal obligation of making a formal transfer on the books? The bank was previously at liberty to require by its by-laws and certificate other evidence; it might have required that the transfer should be made only by the former owner in person, or by his oral assent. The directors have not done so; they made other conditions, and must stand by them. To restrict directly or indirectly the right of having a transfer on the books, to those who in addition to the *prima facie* proof of property can show an undisputed ownership in themselves, and not merely a qualified right or interest, would be contrary to the intent of the charter, the necessities of business, and even to reason and justice. It would cut off trustees and assignees, as well as prevent the common and very convenient practice of *bona fide* stock loans! The subsequent refusal of the stockholder, who has sold or pledged such stock and given a power of attorney to transfer, to perfect his contract, or his inhibition of the transfer, can not lessen the obligation of the bank to comply with its own rules, its express understanding, and its legal duty.

2. Barker is a party to the transaction on his own account. He is also president of the bank. Was that legal proof that he had authority to act for the bank in this behalf, there being no evidence of any formal delegation to him of authority by the vote of the directors? If he had no authority to act on behalf of the bank in relation to the transfer, then the refusal was on his own account alone, and the action against the bank must fail. This difficulty would have been formidable, it might perhaps have been insuperable, in the days of Lord Coke or of Hale. But the old law of corporate delegation has been modified by the customs and wants of modern commerce. It is in evidence from the cashier, that "the president or the cashier permitted transfers." Barker appears to have been at the banking-house as president, and to have there acted for the bank as well as on his own business. The bank, in defending this very suit, has ratified his acts, which might have been disavowed. If, as president, Barker was in the habit of permitting transfers, or if the board had ratified his acts, the directors can not now reject him as their agent and representative. "As the appointment of an agent may not always be evidenced by the written vote of the directors, it is now the settled doctrine, at least in America, that it may be inferred or implied from the adoption or recognition of the acts of the agent by the corporation or its functionaries. Thus, if a cashier of a bank should openly act as such in the common transactions of the bank, with the full knowledge and assent of the directors, his acts would be obligatory upon the bank, although there might be no written vote or record to establish his appointment:" 12 Wheat. 64, 74; Story on Agency, sec. 52.

3. The power of attorney to transfer, etc., was made in blank, by the owner placing his name and seal with the subscription of a witness upon the back of the certificate, which was sent for the purpose of having a power written above the name and seal,

to any person who might advance money on its security, to whomsoever he might direct: was that power valid when thus written? This objection, like the last, would have been more formidable in England a century or two ago, than it is now in this country. Evidence was given that this was the customary mode for years, of transferring stock in our great stock market of New York, as well as elsewhere. Such a custom certainly could not vary the settled law, if that pronounced a deed or other sealed instrument to be void when written and executed in this manner; but the evidence of custom is good not to contradict or change the law, but to explain the meaning and intent of parties in contracts: as here, to show Barker's understanding and design in regard to the authority he gave. Judge Edwards, at the trial, stated its effect with precision. He said that "the testimony was legal proof not to vary the law, but to show Barker's intention in thus executing an instrument in blank." I will not repeat what I have elsewhere said, as to my view of the nature and effect of evidence of commercial usage: See *S. and M. Allen* v. *Merchants' Bank*, 22 Wend. 215 [*ante*, 289]. But does not this custom, whatever may have been Barker's intent, vary or contradict the settled general law? It might have done so in older times when the authority of the rule in Sheppard's Touchstone, and in Perkins (as cited and relied upon in the argument), was still paramount. It was then held that if a man write his name and affix his seal to a blank paper, and give direction to another to write a deed over it, and such other write such deed, it is nevertheless no deed. I say this might then have been fatal; but at a very early day, the strong equities of special cases sometimes compelled courts to break through the rule, and as long ago as 40 Elizabeth, when in a bond given *pour le sauver harmless*, *i. e.*, for indemnity, a blank was left to insert the Christian name, which was filled up after execution by consent of parties, the bond was held good. If, however, we leave the antiquarian part of the law and come down to a state of society like our own, we shall find the more rational doctrine well established. The case of *Texira* v. *Evans*, before Lord Mansfield, was, I think, the first where the doctrine was clearly and broadly applied: 1 Anst. 229. Evans wanted to borrow four thousand pounds, or as much of it as could be raised on his security. He executed a bond with blanks for the name and sums (certainly the most material parts, thus being in blank), on which Texira lent half the desired sum, and the agent filled up the bond with his name and that amount; this bond was held to be good.

Some years after, Judge Wilson, in *Addis* v. *Baker*, 1 Anst. 229, says: "On navy bills which are not in their nature negotiable, the common practice is this: a letter of attorney to receive the money (which is a deed under seal), is made out in blank for the name. This is always sold with the navy bill, and thus they are negotiated from hand to hand, till any purchaser chooses to fill up the blank with his own name." The decision of the case was in conformity with these views.

On the foundation of these cases and the corresponding usage in this country, the courts here and in other states, have made many analogous decisions. Thus in 4 Johns. 54, it was held that a deed might be altered in a material part, by consent of parties, and more recently by our supreme court, that bonds executed in blank with parol authority to fill up and deliver them were valid: 6 Cow. 60; and 8 Id. 118. So in *Knapp* v. *Maltby*, 13 Wend. 587, the instrument was signed and sealed by the party, and the authority given, was to make certain material alterations on it: this was held valid. See also 5 Mass. 536. Those familiar with the business of our custom-houses, well know that the usage of executing bonds in blank is of daily occurrence there, and this is unquestionably done with the sanction of the legal advisers of the United States, nor has the validity of such bonds ever been questioned. Now the writing of a whole power to transfer, with verbal or implied authority to do so, above a seal and signature on the back of a stock certificate, where nothing else could with any propriety be possibly written, is a far smaller excuse for delegated authority, than where the name of a party is inserted, or still more the sum for which he is to become bound. There the responsibility that the agent may impose upon his principals is unlimited. Here it is confined to the hundred shares of stock, with the latitude of inserting one name or another as the vendee, pledgee, or the attorney.

4. Is the rule of damages applied by the jury correct? If the estimate of the rights and character of the parties to the transaction above taken be correct, then the rule of damages laid down by the chief justice appears to me to be equally so. If the bank be bound by the acts of Barker as its president; if Barker be bound by that evidence of authority to transfer his stock which he voluntarily held out to all who might deal with his agent, then the pledge to the plaintiff below of this stock with others for a larger amount than the sum intended by Barker, gave to such a pledgee a perfect right to the possession of his

security, and all the legal incidents which follow such possession. If he was prevented from realizing or securing his debt by the bank's refusal to allow the transfer, the bank must be liable for the highest price of the stock at any time after the demand and before trial. Our supreme court, in 3 Cow. 84, quoted and adopted the rule of Judge Grose in 2 East, 211; " the true measure of damages in all these cases is that which will indemnify the plaintiff for the breach." In 9 Cow. 697, Judge Sutherland, in a *per curiam* opinion, comes to the conclusion, that " if the plaintiff without unreasonable delay prosecute the suit, we think it just that the fluctuations in price be exclusively at the hazard of the defendant, the plaintiff having done everything in his power to have the contract settled, and which is prevented only by the default of the defendant. In such a case the plaintiff is entitled to the highest price between the day when the delivery should have been made and the day of trial." It is true that this rule relates primarily to express contracts of sale, but the reasons apply with equal force to, and have always governed actions in any form (trover, assumpsit, or case), where compensation in damages is claimed for refusal to deliver, or illegal conversion of anything, to the property or possession of which the plaintiff is lawfully entitled. In this case, according to Judge Grose's rule, the highest measure of damages can hardly indemnify the plaintiff below, as it seems that the whole amount of stock pledged is not sufficient to secure his loan of twenty-five thousand dollars.

The action for damages is a convenient common law remedy by a civil suit for what otherwise would have to be sought by mandamus to direct the transfer; so that the damages are the substitute for the stock itself, and should be of the value of the highest security it afforded, or at least the highest within the amount of the debt for which it was pledged: See Doug. 523. It has been argued that the plaintiff below is still the owner of the stock, and can claim no damages beyond the loss sustained by its fall in price. Not so; the bank has denied that the plaintiff is the owner. He himself, by the election of this action and the acceptance of the amount he recovers, will waive his right to the stock, and signify his assent to accept compensation or damages instead. Such recovery will be an effectual bar to any further claim to the stock itself. It is analogous to the case of a recovery in trover, where, when the suit and the damages are not for the temporary detention but for the actual conversion, the conversion is so far ratified by the judgment as to pass the right of property to whomsoever may be the holder in consequence of such tortious conversion. "Judgment in trover for a permanent conversion, say the books, changes the property unless it should be made to appear that the damages were given for a temporary conversion merely, not for the value of the thing itself:" Bull. N. P. 49; Gilb. L. of Ev. 265; Stark. Ev., pt. 4, p. 1508. Here the action and the evidence supporting it are for the value of the stock itself, and that evidence shows that Kortright's actual damages incurred by the refusal to transfer are quite equal at least to the highest value. If the bank has not been indemnified by Barker, or whoever else may have an interest in the matter, as is the ordinary course of things under such circumstances, it will, I presume, upon payment of the judgment, be entitled to receive from Barker the amount of the loss incurred by a refusal to transfer, made at his request and for his advantage. The loan was honest and friendly, and as one of the two parties Kortright or Barker, one or the other, must ultimately suffer, the true inquiry will be that which Judge Buller says "is the common question every day at Guildhall, when one or two innocent persons must suffer by the fraud or negligence of a third—which of the two gave credit?" Here Barker trusted Bartow and enabled him to gain credit from others, and whoever stands in Barker's place takes his responsibilities. On the other hand, to what did Kortright give credit? First, to the bank, its certificate and the forms of transfer there held out; second, he trusted Barker's name and seal, duly attested and signed to paper written by his authority. Who of these parties ought to suffer?

Judge Edwards' charge I think incorrect in one point only, that Barker would have a claim against Kortright for any sum recovered by him against the bank, beyond the ten thousand dollars for which the stock was meant to be pledged. I regard the pledge as good for any amount that Bartow obtained on it, so that Kortright was entitled for himself to such damages as would make him whole, within the limits of the highest market price of the stock. But this does not affect the verdict, which has rendered substantial justice, and I would not disturb it, unless the legal difficulties were far more serious than those presented here. The judgment should be affirmed.

On the question being put, Shall this judgment be reversed? the members of the court divided as follows:

In the affirmative: The chancellor, and Senators CLARK, DICKINSON, POWERS, WAGER—5.

In the negative: The president of the senate, and Senators FURMAN, HAWKINS, HULL, HUNTINGTON, JONES, H. A. LIVINGSTON, MAYNARD, NICHOLAS, PECK, SKINNER, STERLING, VERPLANCK, WORKS —14.

Whereupon the judgment of the supreme court was affirmed.

SECRET INSTRUCTIONS GIVEN TO AGENT ARE NOT BINDING ON THIRD PERSONS when in his dealings with them he acts within the scope of his apparent authority: *Blane* v. *Proudfit*, 2 Am. Dec. 546; *Munn* v. *Commission Co.*, 8 Id. 219; *Rossiter* v. *Rossiter*, 24 Id. 62; *Topham* v. *Roche*, 27 Id. 387; *Jeffrey* v. *Bigelow*, 28 Id. 476. On this point the principal case was approved in *Mallory* v. *Burrett*, 1 E. D. Smith, 243.

SHARES OF CORPORATION ARE ASSIGNABLE NOTWITHSTANDING BY-LAW limiting their transfer to the office of the company or providing that a transfer shall not be valid until registered on the books of the company: *Bank of Utica* v. *Smalley*, 14 Am. Dec. 526, and note; *Sargent* v. *Franklin Ins. Co.*, 19 Id. 306; and in support of this position the principal case is cited as authority in *Black* v. *Zacharie*, 3 How. (U. S.) 513; *Comeau* v. *Guild Farm Oil Co.*, 3 Daly, 220; *Orr* v. *Bigelow*, 14 N. Y. 560; *Leitch* v. *Wells*, 48 Id. 593; *Johnson* v. *Underhill*, 52 Id. 210; *Burrall* v. *Bushwick R. R. Co.*, 75 Id. 219; *Mechanics' Banking Ass.* v. *Mariposa Co.*, 3 Robt. 403; and approved on that point in *Mechanics' Bank* v. *N. Y. & N. H. R. R. Co.*, 13 N. Y. 624; but distinguished from that case, as there the certificate was obtained by the holder, by fraud. The principal case was referred to as an authority respecting the transfer of stock generally, in *Thorp* v. *Woodhull*, 1 Sandf. Ch. 415; and *Delafield* v. *State of Illinois*, 2 Wend. 219.

LIABILITY OF CORPORATION FOR ACTS OF ITS AGENT: See *Beatty* v. *Marine Ins. Co.*, 3 Am. Dec. 401; *White* v. *Westport Mfg. Co.*, 11 Id. 168; *Mott* v. *Hicks*, 13 Id. 550; *Lyman* v. *White River Bridge Co.*, 16 Id. 705; *Frankfort St. Co.* v. *Churchill*, 17 Id. 159; *Garrison* v. *Combs*, 22 Id. 120; *Leggett* v. *N. J. & B. Co.*, 23 Id. 728; *Rabassa* v. *Orleans Nav. Co.*, 25 Id. 200; *Pa. etc. Nav. Co.* v. *Dandridge*, 29 Id. 543; *Marlatt* v. *Levee S. C. P. Co.*, Id. 468; *Everett* v. *United States*, 30 Id. 584. The doctrine of the principal case, as to the liability of the corporation for the acts of its agents, is approved in *Bank of Vergennes* v. *Warren*, 7 Hill, 94; *Bank of Lyons* v. *Demmon*, Hill & D. 406; and *Mitchell* v. *V. C. M. Co.*, 67 N. Y. 282.

TRANSFER OF STOCK MADE IN BLANK.—On this point the principal case was cited as authority in *McNeil* v. *Tenth Nat. Bank*, 46 N. Y. 331; *Holbrook* v. *N. J. Zinc Co.*, 57 Id. 623; *Bartlett* v. *Board of Education*, 59 Ill. 371; and was approved in *Dunn* v. *Commercial Bank of Buffalo*, 11 Barb. 584, but a distinction drawn, as in that case the complainant held in his hand the naked blank assignments and the certificates, and did not prove that he owned them or had any interest in them whatever.

REFUSAL TO TRANSFER STOCK, MEASURE OF DAMAGES FOR.—As to liability of a company for refusing to transfer stock, see *Morgan* v. *Bank of N. A.*, 11 Am. Dec. 575; *Sargent* v. *Franklin Ins. Co.*, 19 Id. 306. The principal case is regarded as authority on the point that an action for damages is a proper remedy against a corporation for the refusal of its officers to transfer stock, in *People* v. *Parker Vein Coal Co.*, 1 Abb. Pr. 129; *Ramsey* v. *Erie Railway Co.*, 7 Abb. (N. S.) 183; *N. Y. & N. H. R. R. Co.* v. *Schuyler*, 38 Barb. 555; *Clark* v. *Miller*, 47 Id. 40; *Comeau* v. *Guild Farm Oil Co.*, 3 Daly, 220; *Ex parte Fire-*

men's Ins. Co., 6 Hill, 243; *People* v. *Parker Vein Coal Co.*, 10 How. Pr. 551; *Ramsey* v. *Erie Railway Co.*, 38 Id. 217; *Cushman* v. *Thayer Mfg. Jewelry Co.*, 53 Id. 61; *Smith* v. *Am. Coal Co.*, 7 Lans. 321, and also on the point that where the value of the property is fluctuating, the measure of damages is the highest market value between the time of the injury complained of and the time of trial: *Hamer* v. *Hathaway*, 33 Cal. 120; *Smith* v. *Dunlap*, 12 Ill. 192; *Scott* v. *Rogers*, 4 Abb. App. Cas. 163, n.; *Wilson* v. *Matthews*, 24 Barb. 296; *Van Allen* v. *Illinois Central R. R. Co.*, 7 Bosw. 538; *Wilson* v. *Little*, 2 N. Y. 450; *Clark* v. *Miller*, 54 Id. 535.

OTHER POINTS UPON WHICH THE PRINCIPAL CASE IS CITED, are: In support of the rule that if the owner of stock places it in the possession of another, with the usual *indicia* of ownership, he is bound by any disposition made of it by such person to one who takes it without notice for valuable consideration on the strength of such *indicia*, in *Brewster* v. *Sime*, 42 Cal. 147; *Moore* v. *Metropolitan Nat. Bank*, 55 N. Y. 46; *Muller* v. *Pondir*, Id. 335; and to the point that a party may file a bill to compel a bank to transfer stock to a purchaser, in *Cushman* v. *Thayer Jewelry Mfg. Co.*, 4 Daly, 332. The case is approved on that point, but held not to apply where the transferror was indebted to the corporation, in *Driscoll* v. *West Bradley & C. M. Co.*, 59 N. Y. 106.

HASTINGS *v.* LUSK.

[22 WENDELL, 410.]

WORDS SPOKEN BY COUNSEL OR BY A PARTY CONDUCTING HIS OWN CASE, in the course of judicial proceedings, if relevant and pertinent to the question before the court, are privileged, and not subject to an action for slander, however false, malicious, and injurious they may be.

WORDS NOT RELEVANT OR PERTINENT TO THE MATTER IN QUESTION, spoken in the course of judicial proceedings, are nevertheless privileged if spoken in good faith, under a belief that they were relevant and proper, and without actual malice, of which the jury are to judge.

PRIVILEGE WILL NOT AVAIL ON A MOTION IN ARREST OF JUDGMENT against the defendant in slander, where there are special pleas that the words were used in the course of judicial proceedings in conducting the defendant's own cause, were relevant and pertinent, and were not spoken maliciously, and those facts being put in issue are all found against the defendant.

ERROR from the supreme court in an action of slander for speaking certain words charging the plaintiff with perjury, the words having been spoken while the defendant was testifying before a magistrate on his examination on a criminal charge preferred against him by the plaintiff. Pleas, the general issue and three special pleas, the substance of which is stated in the opinion, and two replications to each special plea, the substance of which is also stated in the opinion. Verdict finding for the plaintiff on all the issues, and assessing his damages at six cents. Motion in arrest of judgment denied by the supreme court, and the defendant brought error.

M. J. Bidwell, for the plaintiff in error.

W. C. Noyes, for the defendant in error.

WALWORTH, Chancellor. The principle involved in this case is of great importance to the community, inasmuch as it involves the rights and privileges of counsel and of parties in the investigation of suits and other proceedings before our judicial tribunals; and as I believe it is the first cause of the kind which has been brought before this court of *dernier ressort*, and has been very fully and most ably argued here by the counsel upon both sides, I have considered it my duty to examine the law on the subject more fully than would be necessary or proper in an ordinary case of mere verbal slander; for it is not only right and proper that parties and their counsel should know what their privileges are, but also that the law should be deliberately and correctly settled. In applying the principles of law to the case under consideration we must, therefore, be careful on the one hand that we do not restrict counsel within such narrow limits that they will not dare to openly and fearlessly discharge their whole duty to their clients, or to themselves when they manage their own cases; and on the other hand we must not furnish them with the shield of Zeus, and thereby enable them with impunity to destroy the characters of whomsoever they please.

There are two classes of privileged communications recognized in the law in reference to actions of slander, and the privileges of counsel may sometimes fall within the one class and sometimes within the other. In one class of cases, the law protects the defendant so far as not to impute malice to him from the mere fact of his having spoken words of the plaintiff which are in themselves actionable, though he may not be able to prove the truth of his allegations. But the plaintiff will be able to sustain his action for slander, if he can satisfy the jury, by other proof, that there was actual malice on the part of the defendant, and that he uttered the words for the mere purpose of defaming the plaintiff. In the other class of cases the privilege is an effectual shield to the defendant; so that no action of slander can be sustained against him, whatever his motive may have been in using the slanderous words.

One of the earliest cases of the first class is *Parson Prit's case*, reported by Rolle: 1 Roll. Abr. 87, pl. 5. Although the report of this case is very short, it will be perfectly understood by a reference to Fox's Martyrology, where the author, in giving an account of the severe punishments inflicted by the vengeance of

heaven upon some of the persecutors of the protestants during
the reign of the bloody Mary, states that Grimwood, or Greenwood as he is called by·Rolle, one of the perjured witnesses who
was hired to swear away the life of John Cooper, an innocent
person, who was convicted and hanged, was soon after destroyed
by the terrible judgment of God; being suddenly seized while
in perfect health, so violently that his bowels gushed out. From
the report it appears the defendant, Parson Prit, having been
recently settled in the parish, and not knowing all his parish-
ioners, in preaching against the heinous sin of perjury cited this
case, from the Book of Martyrs; and, no doubt, commented
severely upon Greenwood and upon White, his forsworn companion, who, by their perjury, had caused an innocent man to
be drawn in quarters and his wife and children to be left deso-
late. It turned out, however, that Greenwood was not dead,
and that being a resident of that parish, he was present in the
church and heard the sermon, and afterwards brought a suit
against the parson for charging him with perjury. But the
court held that it was a privileged communication, and the circumstances under which the words were spoken showed there
was no actual malice towards the plaintiff. See also Cro. Jac.
91. This case has been followed by a numerous class depending upon the same principle; in which the speaking of the words
is held to be a privileged communication, the occasion of the
speaking being such, that *prima facie* there could have been no
malicious intent to defame the person of whom they were spoken,
and the interests of society requiring that the defendant
should be permitted to speak freely in the situation in which he
is placed, provided he confine himself within the bounds of what
he believes to be the truth. In cases of this kind, the defendant
may avail himself of his privilege under the plea of the general
issue, even under the new rules of pleading adopted in England.
This was so decided in the recent case of *Lillie* v. *Price*, 2
Harr. & Woll. 645, in the court of king's bench; where Lord
Denman, C. J., after taking time to consult with the judges,
and referring to the new rule which declares the defense under
the general issue in slander shall be the same as before, says:
" We are all of opinion that this defense does not require to be
pleaded specially. It goes to the very root of the action. It
shows the party not guilty of malice, and consequently it is open
to him without having pleaded it." The presumption in these
cases, that there was no malice, is not rebutted by the plaintiff's
merely showing that the charge against him was untrue in

point of fact; it must be further shown that the defendant either knew or had reason to believe it was untrue, at the time of the speaking of the words complained of: *Kine* v. *Sewell*, 1 Hom. & Hurl. 83; S. C., 3 Mee. & W. 297. Proving that the defendant knew the charge to be false, would unquestionably be evidence of express malice; and would destroy the defense in this class of cases.

As the plaintiff has a right to prove express malice in such cases, to sustain his action notwithstanding the privilege, it follows, of course, that if the defendant attempt to set up his privilege as a defense, by a special plea, he must not only plead the fact which rendered it a privileged communication, but he must deny the allegation in the declaration, that the words were maliciously spoken, to enable the plaintiff to go to the jury upon the question of actual malice, if he thinks proper to do so: *Smith* v. *Thomas*, 1 Hodges, 353; S. C., 2 Bing. (N. S.) 372. It follows, of course, upon a motion in arrest of judgment, if the charge of malice was denied in the plea, and issue taken thereon, or if the general issue only was pleaded, so that the plaintiff would be bound to prove express malice to entitle him to a verdict in this class of cases, the court must presume it was proved upon the trial; although it should appear from the declaration or other pleadings, that it was *prima facie* a privileged communication.

The second class of privileges embraces words spoken by members of parliament, or of congress, or of the state legislature, in the discharge of their official duties in the house, for which no action of slander will lie, however false and malicious may be the charge against the private reputation of an individual. To this class, also, belong complaints made to grand juries and magistrates, charging persons with crimes for which no action of slander will lie, although express malice as well as the absolute falsity of the charge can be established by proof. But the law has provided a different remedy in cases of that kind, where, in addition to what has before been stated, it can be proved that the party who made the complaint had no probable cause for believing that the charge was true. Upon a full consideration of all the authorities on the subject, I think that the privilege of counsel in advocating the causes of their clients, and of parties who are conducting their own causes, belongs to the same class where they have confined themselves to what was relevant and pertinent to the question before the court, and that the motives with which they have spoken what was relevant and pertinent to the cause they were advocating, can not be questioned in an action of slander. Thus far, it appears to be necessary to extend the privilege for the protection of the rights of parties; as those rights might sometimes be jeoparded if counsel were restrained from commenting freely upon the characters of witnesses, and the conduct of parties, when such comments were relevant, for fear of being harassed with slander suits, and attempts to prove they were actuated by malicious motives in the discharge of their duty. Such I understand also to be the conclusion at which the court of king's bench arrived in the case of the present lord chief baron of the court of exchequer: *Hodgson* v. *Scarlett*, 1 Barn. & Ald. 232; Holt's N. P. 621.

Although Mr. Holt has attempted to give a statement of what occurred *in banc*, as well as a report of the case at *nisi prius*, to understand the decision correctly it is necessary to examine the case in Barnewall & Alderson, not only as to the final opinion of the judges, but also as to what occurred in the course of the argument. There was no question as to the fact that the plaintiff was nonsuited upon the opening, by Baron Wood, who held the assizes, without permitting him to go to the jury. He, therefore, had no opportunity to prove express malice, or to have it inferred from the manner in which the charge was made. His counsel upon the argument insisted that the learned judge had stopped the cause too soon, without hearing the evidence. To this it was answered that Baron Wood had reported that the counsel at the assizes admitted that the alleged slanderous words were used by the defendant as observations in a cause, and were pertinent to the matter in issue. But as there appeared to have been a misapprehension on this point, the court heard a statement of the proceedings in the original suit from the notes of Mr. Justice Bailey, who tried the cause. The plaintiff's counsel still contended there was a question which ought to have been left to the jury, as they were to say whether there was not malice to be inferred from the facts. Upon which Lord Ellenborough immediately inquired if the words were relevant, whether they were not within the protection of the law ? And it was in answer to this part of the argument, that in delivering his final decision in the cause he said, although he admitted it might have been too much for the counsel to say that the attorney was wicked and fraudulent: "It appears to me that the words spoken were uttered in the original cause, and were relevant and pertinent to it, and consequently that this action is not maintainable."

I do not understand from this, however, that everything that in any state of facts would be relevant and pertinent to the matter in question before the court, comes within this rule of protection, where those facts which would have rendered it relevant and pertinent do not exist. Thus, if counsel, in the argument of his client's cause, should avail himself of that opportunity to say of a party, or of a witness, against whom there was nothing in the evidence to justify a suspicion of the kind, that he was a thief or a murderer, it might be a proper case for a jury to say whether the counsel was not actuated by malice, and improperly availed himself of his situation as counsel to defame the party or witness. Such appears to have been the opinion of the judges in the case of *Hodgson* v. *Scarlett*, and such also must have been the opinion of the supreme court of this state in the case of *Ring* v. *Wheeler*, 7 Cow. 725, for the language of the defendant as stated in any of the seven first counts of the declaration in that case might have been relevant and pertinent, and the words charged in the fourth and sixth counts probably were relevant to the matter before the arbitrators, if the counsel was opening his defense, and merely stating what he expected to prove, according to the case of *Moulton* or *Boulton* v. *Clapham*, 1 Roll. Abr. 87, which was so much relied upon by the counsel for the plaintiffs in error upon the argument of this cause. Upon the authority of that case, perhaps, they should have been considered as relevant and pertinent, even after verdict.

I do not, however, consider the case of *Moulton* v. *Clapham* as an authority for holding that everything which may be said to the court or jury, by a party or his counsel, in the progress of a cause, as absolutely protected, although it was not relevant or pertinent to the matter in question, so as to preclude the party injured thereby from showing to a jury that the language was used maliciously, and for the mere purpose of defaming him. Many of these old cases are very imperfectly reported, and are therefore apt to mislead us, unless they are examined with care. This case, although it is to be found in D'Anvers, Sir William Jones, March, and in Rolle's Abridgment, is not stated by either two of them in precisely the same way. As reported by Sir William Jones, it would lead us to the conclusion that the court meant to decide that anything said in court by a party in disaffirmance of what was sworn against him was absolutely protected, although found by the jury to have been said maliciously; but by referring to Rolle, it will be seen that the language used by the defendant was addressed to the court, and was a mere

statement that the affidavit was untrue, and that he would prove
to them by forty witnesses that it was so; and therefore it was
holden that the action was not maintainable, as it appeared from
the plaintiff's declaration that the answer made by the defendant
to the affidavit was spoken merely in defense of himself, and in
a legal and judicial way, "inasmuch as he said he would prove
it by forty witnesses."

Neither is the dictum of Cromwell's chief justice of the upper bench, Style, 462, to be taken as broadly as stated by the
reporter, without knowing the state of facts in reference to which
the dictum was applied. I presume he must have used this language in reference to words spoken by counsel in opening the defense of his client's cause to the jury, stating what he should
prove. For he immediately adds, "it is his duty to speak for
his client, and it shall be intended to be spoken according to
his client's instructions." But surely no one can for a moment
suppose the learned chief justice intended to say that it was the
duty of counsel to say anything that was not relevant to the
matter in question; or to go beyond the case for the purpose of
maligning a witness or the adverse party, although he might
have been instructed to do so by his client. As I understand
the case of *Brook* v. *Montague*, Cro. Jac. 90, the plea must have
alleged that the words were spoken by the counsel in relation
to the evidence which was to be given in favor of the jury
against Brook, who had attainted them. He probably was instructed by his client that Brook had been convicted of felony;
and if so, he was probably incapable of proceeding in the attaint
against the jury, as the law then stood: Co. Lit. 130, a; *Sleight*
v. *Kane*, 2 Johns. Cas. 236. The language of the reporter is,
that the counsel spoke the words in evidence. This certainly
could not be so, as there was no pretense that the counsel was a
witness on the trial. I have no doubt, therefore, that the language of the plea was that the counsel, in reference to the matters to be given in evidence, spake the words mentioned in the
plaintiff's declaration, etc., and that by a slip of the reporter's
pen, or otherwise, a part of the sentence is left out in the
printed report. The case of *Badgley* v. *Hedges*, 1 Penn. 233, is
like that of *Moulton* v. *Clapham;* for it is evident the defendant
spoke in reference to the contradictory evidence which he intended to give in the cause, or which he already had given. If
so, what he said was relevant, although perhaps not said at the
right time. I am satisfied, therefore, that there is no law, either
ancient or modern, which affords complete protection to parties

or counsel so as to bring the language used by them in the course of judicial proceedings within the second class of privileged communications which I have stated, except where the words complained of as slanderous were relevant or pertinent to the question to be determined by the court or jury.

There may be cases which properly belong to the first class of privileged communications, arising in the course of judicial proceedings. Parties and even counsel sometimes misjudge as to what is relevant and pertinent to the question before the court, and especially parties who are not much acquainted with judicial proceedings; and it may be very proper in such cases to leave it as a matter of fact for the jury to determine, whether the words were spoken in good faith, under a belief that they were relevant or proper, or whether the party using them was actuated by malice and intended to slander the plaintiff. The case of *Allen* v. *Crofoot*, 2 Wend. 516, appears to be a case of this kind, for it is evident that the words spoken were not relevant in the judicial proceeding, or pertinent to any question then before the court. But as circumstances showed that the defendant either supposed he was bound to answer the question, or that it was relevant and pertinent to the proceedings, I think the court very properly decided that it should have been left to the jury to determine whether the defendant acted in good faith supposing it was relevant and proper to answer the question put to him by the plaintiff, although he had not yet been sworn as a witness on the examination of the complaint which he had previously made on oath, or whether he was actuated by malice. In cases belonging to that class of privileged communications, malice in fact may be inferred from the language of the communication itself, as well as from extrinsic evidence: *Wright* v. *Woodgate*, 1 Gale, 329.

But though the slanderous words were spoken in the course of a judicial proceeding, and were relevant and pertinent to the matter in question, or the defendant may have used them in good faith, supposing them to be pertinent, without actual malice or any intention of slandering the plaintiff, yet if these facts do not appear from the pleadings or the finding of the jury, it will not aid the defendant upon a motion in arrest of judgment. On such motion the court can not know that the slanderous words were pertinent, or that the plaintiff did not satisfy the jury that they were not only impertinent to the matter in question before the court, but also that the defendant spoke them with a malicious intent, for the mere purpose of defaming the plaintiff and wounding his feelings. Such is the effect of the decision of the supreme court, both in the case of *McClaughry* v. *Wetmore,* 6 Johns. 82, decided nearly thirty years ago, and in the more recent case of *Ring* v. *Wheeler,* to which I have before referred.

Each of the counts in the plaintiff's declaration in this case contains more or less slanderous expressions, imputing the crime of perjury, in language which *prima facie* could not have been pertinent to any question before the court, for it does not appear to have been addressed to the court, but to the plaintiff himself, who was a witness there: and if the defendant used all the abusive language towards or in reference to the witness which is stated in either of those counts, although some of it might have been relevant to the matter in question, no jury could hesitate in coming to a correct conclusion whether that which was not pertinent was uttered in good faith or with a malicious intent to defame the plaintiff; although the defendant must have proved that he had great provocation to excuse all this harsh language, or no honest jury could have given a verdict of only six cents against him.

The defense in this case is set up by several special pleas in addition to the general issue; and the objection urged by the third point of the plaintiff in error is, that although the declaration may have been *prima facie* sufficient, the replications are bad, and sufficient is admitted upon the whole record to constitute a good defense. On the other hand it is urged, that if there are any material issues the pleas are bad, and as the defendant committed the first fault in pleading, it is not a case for a repleader. I have examined the special pleas particularly, and think either of them would have been held good upon general demurrer, if I am correct in the conclusion at which I have arrived as to the law of the case. It is expressly stated by Mr. Justice Buller, that the defendant may by way of justification plead that the words were spoken by him as counsel in a cause, and that they were pertinent to the matter in question, or he may give them in evidence under the general issue, for they prove him not to have been guilty of speaking the words maliciously: Bull. N. P. 10. See also *Lord Cromwell's case,* 4 Co. 14. The two first special pleas, therefore, showing that the slanderous words stated in the declaration were spoken by the defendant in the judicial proceeding, while conducting his own defense without counsel, and that they were pertinent to the matter in question, constituted a good bar to the action, as they brought the

case within the second class of privileged communications which.
I have noticed.   To each of these pleas there were two replications (as authorized by the revised statutes upon a special application to the court), each of which replications was a good.
answer to the plea: one replication traversed the fact that the
words spoken were either pertinent or material to the matter in
question, and the other traversed the allegation in the plea that
the words were used by the defendant in the matter in question
before the justice, while conducting his defense therein; and as
the jury found a verdict for the plaintiff on all the issues,.
neither of those pleas can aid the defendant.   In the last special
plea the defendant, in addition to the facts stated in the two
preceding pleas, also averred that the words were spoken without any malice towards the plaintiff, and therefore, if I am right
in supposing that a party is not answerable for words innocently
spoken by him in conducting his defense in a judicial proceeding, and without malice, although they may not have been
strictly pertinent, perhaps a replication merely denying the
pertinency of the words would not have been a sufficient answer
to this plea.

The first replication to this special plea does, however, in substance, put in issue the question of malicious intent as well as
the pertinency of the slanderous words, although the malice is.
only stated by way of inducement to the traverse of the malicious intent.   As that part of the replication directly nega-
tives the allegation in the plea which it was material to negative
in connection with the traverse of the pertinency of the slanderous words, its effect, after verdict, must be different from the
case of a replication which merely sets up new matter as inducement to the traverse, and then traverses an immaterial allegation in the plea, leaving that which was most material unanswered.   It is in this case at most but a misjoining of the issue,.
which is cured after verdict; and the jury have found in terms,
in reference to this issue, that the words were spoken falsely
and maliciously, and that they were not pertinent and material.
Again: the second replication to this plea is a full answer to it,
even if the first replication is stricken entirely out of the record;
and upon the last replication the jury have found that the slanderous words were not uttered by the defendant while conducting his own defense on the examination before the justice, as
alleged in his last special plea.

For these reasons I think the supreme court were right in re-

fusing to arrest the judgment, and that their decision should
be affirmed.

The court being unanimously of the same opinion, the judgment of the supreme court was accordingly affirmed.

PRIVILEGE AS TO WORDS SPOKEN IN JUDICIAL PROCEEDINGS: See *Shock*
v. *McChesney*, 2 Am. Dec. 415; *McMillan* v. *Birch*, Id. 426, and note; *Jarvis*
v. *Hatheway*, 3 Id. 473; *Bunton* v. *Worley*, 7 Id. 735; *Hardin* v. *Cumstock*, 12
Id. 427, and note; *Stackpole* v. *Hennen*, 17 Id. 187, and note; *Allen* v. *Crofoot*,
20 Id. 647; *Vausse* v. *Lee*, 26 Id. 168. The case of *Hastings* v. *Lusk* is recognized as an authority with respect to the existence and limits of this privilege, and its doctrine approved and applied in *Gilbert* v. *People*, 1 Denio, 43;
Suydam v. *Moffat*, 1 Sandf. 464; *Marsh* v. *Ellsworth*, 36 How. Pr. 535; S. C.,
50 N. Y. 312; *Perkins* v. *Mitchell*, 31 Barb. 469; *Hoar* v. *Wood*, 3 Metc. 193.
It is also cited as an authority concerning privileged communications generally, in *Streety* v. *Wood*, 15 Barb. 111; *Hosmer* v. *Loveland*, 19 Id. 116; *Klinck*
v. *Colby*, 46 N. Y. 434.

GARDNER *v.* GARDNER.

[22 WENDELL, 526.]

LOAN BY HUSBAND TO WIFE FOR THE BENEFIT OF HER SEPARATE ESTATE
is valid in equity as a charge on such estate, unless prohibited by the instrument under which she holds; and such loan, if collectible, must be
accounted for by the wife as administratrix of her husband, and the reasonable presumption is that the separate estate is sufficient to repay the
loan.

DESTROYING A BOND, WITH A DECLARED INTENT TO FORGIVE THE DEBT, is
sufficient by way of gift to release the debt.

COURT OF CHANCERY HAS POWER TO AWARD AN ISSUE TO TRY THE SANITY
of a donor of a gift in the nature of a bequest, and, in case of doubt, it
is its duty to do so.

HABITUAL DRUNKARD IS PRESUMED COMPETENT WHEN SOBER to make a
will or a valid gift, unless it appears that intemperance has produced a
settled derangement of the faculties.

GENERAL INFLUENCE OF A WIFE OVER HER HUSBAND, arising from affection produced by her kindness, does not constitute or afford an inference
of undue influence.

UNDUE INFLUENCE TO VITIATE AN ACT MUST AMOUNT TO COERCION destroying free agency, or harassing importunity producing compliance for the
sake of peace.

APPEAL from a decree of the court of chancery, 7 Paige, 512,
affirming a decree of the surrogate confirming a report of auditors charging the appellant, in her account as administratrix of
her deceased husband, with a certain sum of two thousand dollars, alleged to have been borrowed by her from her husband
for the improvement of certain separate estate of hers in Will-

iamsburgh.   The administratrix claimed that her husband before his death destroyed the bond given for said loan, and made her a gift of the money.   The evidence on that point is sufficiently stated in the opinion.   The respondents, distributees of a moiety of the estate of the deceased, insisted that he was at the time *non compos mentis*, by reason of being an habitual drunkard.   The facts relating to that matter are also stated in the opinion.   To prove the deceased's incompetence, the respondents gave evidence to show that within a few days after the alleged destruction of the bond the deceased was, by the court of chancery, removed, on the ground of insanity, from the guardianship of a certain infant's estate: *Kettletas* v. *Gardner*, 1 Paige, 488.   Other facts are stated in the opinion.

M. T. Reynolds, for the appellant.

J. Rhoades and S. Stevens, for the respondents.

Cowen, J.   The main objection here, is, that Mrs. Gardner was not chargeable with the two thousand dollars which she had borrowed from her husband.   1. It is said she was not liable, because the loan was by the husband to his wife.   It is admitted to be void at law, upon the ground that the wife can not contract a debt to any one, and especially to her husband.   This rule is universal at law, and it is the general rule of a court of chancery, which follows the law: *Simpson* v. *Simpson*, 4 Dana, 140.   Chancery, however, has raised an exception: not an exception in terms, but yet a substantial one.   If the wife holds an estate separate from and independent of her husband, as she may do in equity, chancery considers her in respect to her power over this estate a *feme-sole*: 2 Kent's Com. 164, 3d ed.; and, although she is still incapable of charging herself at law, and equally incapable in equity of charging herself personally with debts, yet I think the better opinion is that separate debts contracted by her expressly on her own account, shall in all cases, be considered an appointment or appropriation for the benefit of the creditor, as to so much of her separate estate as is sufficient to pay the debt, if she be not disabled to charge it by the terms of the donation.   Chancery, then, considers the debt as a valid charge *pro tanto*, or will at least enforce its collection specifically, by fixing it as a lien upon the separate estate: 2 Story's Eq., 627, secs. 1399 to 1401, inclusive, and the cases there cited: 2 Kent's Com. 164, 3d ed.; Id. 166.   I see no objection in this theory to a debt being contracted by the wife directly to the husband.   Such a power seems to have been recognized in *Heally* v. *Thomas*.

15 Ves. 596, wherein it appeared that the wife had given her husband a bond of indemnity. The case is equally within the principle, whether we consider her acting as *feme-sole*, or under a power of appointment in favor of her husband. In answer to this view of the question, the argument of policy is insisted on.

It is said that the principle will give an opening to the exercise of undue influence by the husband, in procuring this equitable mortgage. That may be so. Such an influence is perhaps too often exerted in various indirect legal methods of acquiring the wife's estate. But the power of restraint lies with the donor. If he give the estate to the wife unshackled as to the mode of alienation, he avows himself willing to repose upon her discretion; and run the risk of her husband's influence. If the donor be distrustful of either, his business is to interpose such guards in respect to the occasions and the forms of alienation as shall obviate the supposed danger. When the wife holds her separate estate untrammeled by any such precautionary control, it is right that such estate should be appropriated to the payment of her separate debts. And this is especially so where, as in the case at bar, they are contracted for the benefit of her separate estate. I say as in the case at bar. Such was Mrs. Gardner's object in obtaining the loan, as she admitted before the surrogate. She had, no doubt, stated the object to her husband, viz., the improving of her estate at Williamsburgh; and I, for one, can not agree with her learned counsel in saying that her declaration must be presumed to have been falsified by her conduct; that she probably deceived her husband, even admitting the truth of her declaration, is to be regarded as a matter of mere abstract moral obligation. And above all, if the counsel be correct in supposing that an application of this money to the proposed improvement were essential to secure its reimbursement, I think the chancellor was bound to presume that she had not misapplied it, at least until the contrary was shown. It was no more than saying she shall be presumed to have acted honestly. If the declaration of her purpose be considered as made to the surrogate only, a thing not very probable, it was in no way qualified with a suggestion that the purpose had not been fulfilled. I feel quite clear, therefore, that a valid loan was established by the proof, chargeable on the appellant's trust estate, which it became her duty as administratrix to account for, if it were collected or collectible intermediate her appointment as administratrix and her accounting, unless the debt was discharged by her husband.

2. It is said, that she is not to be made liable inasmuch as it was not shown that the debt had been collected or might have been collected with ordinary diligence. Direct evidence of actual collection is not pretended; and it is insisted that the debt was not even shown to have been separate. Mrs. Gardner herself admitted that the two thousand dollars was loaned with a view to employ it in the erection of buildings at Williamsburgh, on her property which lay there; and this did not constitute the whole of her separate estate. I think it is not too much to presume that the property which the two thousand dollars was destined to improve, bore such a reasonable proportion in value, as to call for the improvement; and that, in whatever mode the sum may have been invested for her use, the whole, investment and all, would form a fund perfectly adequate to the reimbursement of the money. That is but presuming an exercise of due discretion in the improvement of her estate. Ordinary prudence is to be presumed till the contrary be shown; and in this case the contrary was not even pretended. Ordinary diligence in collecting, and therefore actual collection, might also have been inferred by the auditors, and Mrs. Gardner be holden liable on that ground. At any rate, it was by no means straining a point to say, that, after a lapse of time, she ought to have collected the debt from a fund sufficient in itself; and probably, in a great measure, under her personal control. If the contrary of all this were true, why was that not shown by her? The presumption was not conclusive against her.

I have thus far gone through with several branches of the argument submitted to us by the counsel of the appellant, because I did not know how far the members of the court would agree with me in respect to another branch of it, still ranging under the main point in the cause. On that I have felt myself constrained to agree with him; and should the court think with me in the view which I have taken of it, they will perceive that the appeal is well founded.

Lastly. It was said that the testator, in his life-time, forgave Mrs. Gardner the debt in question, by procuring and burning the bond which was taken as evidence of it. The only direct proof of this fact is derived from the deposition of Mrs. Milnor, the daughter of the appellant, and the step-daughter of the testator, who, as I infer, was either a resident in the testator's family, or very often with them, from 1827, when she says the loan was made, to February or March, 1829, when she says the bond was destroyed. The testator died in July next ensuing.

She says that he at first kept the bond himself, but when he got sick he gave it to Mr. Williams, with instructions that, if anything happened to him, the testator, he, Mr. Williams, should destroy it. He afterwards told Mrs. Gardner to destroy it, if anything happened, which she declined. He then sent for the bond, and himself committed it to the fire, telling Mrs. Gardner that the money was hers.

I have not been able to read Mrs. Milnor's deposition without the impression that the chancellor appears to have entertained, viz., that the bond was in truth destroyed by the testator, with the intent to forgive this debt; nor have the collateral facts, which are supposed to furnish marks of fabrication on the part of the witness, had the effect to weaken my impression. The strongest of these facts is an alleged want of recollection by the witness, of the person by whom the testator sent to Mr. Williams for the bond; as if she might fear contradiction from risking a disclosure of the name. But besides omitting to say that she even saw the messenger, she names Mr. Williams, who might have contradicted her in several important particulars, if she spoke untruly, and whose non-production by the legatees is entirely unaccounted for. That a family transaction of this kind should have been witnessed only by the family, is of all things the most natural; and it is not surprising that the only witnesses were the mother and daughter, whose offices were at that time important about the person of the testator. He had no children of his own, and was not on the best terms with his brother, to whose children he bequeathed a portion of his estate. He appears to have entertained sentiments of great kindness for the witness, to whose son he had conveyed a small tenement; and towards his wife, the appellant, to whom he bequeathed one half of his personal estate.

His will had been made in 1825; and having, perhaps, lived in some measure upon her bounty; and at any rate been the cause of much trouble and mortification to her by his habits of intoxication, it is not strange that, in the interval of recollection which seems to have returned upon him, he should have thought the scanty provision in his will unequal to the demands upon his gratitude and his kindlier feelings. With a competency of her own, on which she might have separated from him, she had forborne to do so; and, by taking care of him, had given an earnest of disinterested affection sufficient to account for the destruction of the bond upon principles far other than those of undue influence. That he himself was childless, that his wife's daughter was a pensioner upon the bounty of her mother, and the family of his brother, the respondents, had been in some measure alienated, even if it were by his own fault, furnished perhaps an additional motive, which we have no right to question. Such a concourse of circumstances, coming in aid of Mrs. Milnor's narrative, to my mind much more than counterbalances the criticisms founded on her relationship to the respondent, or interest in adding to her mother's means of kindness to herself. As the gift of the debt was in nature a testamentary disposition, it is undoubtedly right that we should look to the motives which argue the fitness of the act, both as a test of its probability and sanity.

The chancellor seems to have entertained great doubt of the testator's sanity, and assuming that the bond was destroyed with the intent imputed, he presumed that the wife or some one else had persuaded the testator to that act, he not being at the time of sound and disposing mind and memory, or being at least open to the assaults of undue influence. I entirely agree to adopt the test proposed by the chancellor; if the testator was unfit to make a codicil, he was equally unfit to forgive the debt. The proof on that subject is, that he was an intemperate man, and had been so from 1815 to 1829, some fourteen or fifteen years, though Mrs. Milnor says he was never out of his senses till 1825. His derangement at this time could not have amounted to any very serious disqualification: for in that year he made a very judicious will, in which all parties acquiesce. In the course of the ensuing four years his fits of drunkenness became more frequent, his intemperance had grown into a confirmed habit, and his constitution was found to be gradually giving way, notwithstanding the efforts of his friends to break the habit. He was twice confined in the lunatic asylum, which I understand to have been among the expedients resorted to for the purpose of checking his career of drunkenness.

I read of no insanity among the proofs except what arose from the excessive use of ardent spirits. I lay no stress on his being removed from the office of guardian, because I think any master in chancery would report in favor of removing an intemperate man from such a place, though he were yet far short of insanity. That he had surrendered the management of his property and business to his wife, was evidence either of unusual discretion on his part, or of a salutary influence on hers. I can not deny that, in the words of the chancellor, the testator was a broken-down inebriate; nor that such a man might be entirely unqualified to make a will. Reason might have been dethroned, memory might have lost its seat, and the man have been reduced to the condition of a mere driveler; but ordinarily this is not so. To whatever extent the constitution may be physically impaired by intemperance, the mind retains sufficient strength for the purpose of transacting common business, when not clouded by actual intoxication. Cases were cited at the bar, that if general insanity be established, it will be presumed to continue, unless a lucid interval at the time of the transaction in question be clearly shown; but does proof that a man is in the habit of often getting drunk, and has even been a drunkard for years, make out a case of general insanity within the rule? The greatest drunkard is frequently sober, perhaps every day; his habit is in a degree under the control of himself and his friends; and during the few months that this man spent in the lunatic asylum, the mad-house, as it has been called by way of emphasis, he was no doubt entirely sober and therefore sane. If his unfortunate indulgence in the use of ardent spirits had resulted in a settled derangement of mind, independent of the immediate influence of drink (and if the proof comes short of this, a case of general insanity is not established), why was nothing of that kind shown or attempted to be shown at the hearing? Why was not the family physician called? General sanity is the natural and ordinary condition of the mind, and is to be presumed till the contrary is established.

But we are not left to presumption. Mrs. Milnor says that about a month before the bond was destroyed, she and her mother having received word that the testator was perfectly himself, went and brought him home from the asylum, whither he had been for the last time. He soon after told Williams to destroy the bond, and finally sent for it and destroyed it himself, being perfectly sane of mind; in the phrase of the witness, he was entirely himself; he was not very well; but only weak. I do not find a word of proof that after he returned home the last time his mind was unsettled, or that he had even relapsed into his accustomed indulgence. His whole conduct in making the gift, as sworn to, bears strong marks of deliberation; and the transaction is in its own character an argument in favor of sanity. If there were in truth the power of malign influence on the part of the wife, and a disposition to abuse the power, why was it not exerted in a total alteration of the will? Why suffer any part of the estate to pass to the respondents? They had stood in the will for half the personal estate ever since 1825;

the one half only having been bequeathed to the wife. The destruction of the bond was the addition of only one thousand dollars more; for the will already carried one half of the bond to her. What more natural, I ask, than that, in a long turn of perfect sobriety, confined by bodily weakness with his family, he should review the four years which had elapsed since his will had been made, the care, the anxiety, the shame which his unfortunate appetite had in the mean time inflicted on his wife; and see the fitness of adding at least this meager and disproportionate codicil? Is there the least difficulty in accounting for such an act without raising the hypothesis of insanity or of undue influence?

In turning over the books with a view to the form of this gift, I was struck with its similarity, in several respects, to a case which came before Lord Hardwicke in 1740: *Richards* v. *Syms*, Barnardist, Ch. 90. There the defendant borrowed three thousand pounds of the complainant's father, giving a bond and mortgage. The defendant's mother was uneasy on account of his contracting so heavy a mortgage debt; but the mortgagee told her in her son's presence, that she need not be uneasy, as it was in his power to be kind to her son. The bond and mortgage were kept for some time by a trustee; but the defendant procured them from him, and brought them in a box to the mortgagee's house, where the mother was, and requested him to take and keep them himself. Upon this, as it was sworn on the part of the defendant, the mortgagee put back the bond and mortgage with his hand; and said, " Take back your writings: I freely forgive you the debt." Turning to the mother, he said, "I always told you I would be kind to your son; now you see that I am as good as my word." But this evidence was contradicted on the part of the complainant, who was the mortgagee's son and heir. Lord Hardwicke held that, taking the case as made out on the part of the defendant, the gift discharged both the bond and mortgage. But inasmuch as the contradictory evidence left it doubtful whether the mortgagee did make the expressions imputed to him, his lordship directed an issue on that question. In the case at bar, which is an appeal from a surrogate, I am not aware of any express statute giving the chancellor power to award an issue, as is done by the revised statutes in certain cases while before the surrogate or before a circuit judge in probate cases; but the appeal is given, in the case before us, to the court of chancery, as such: 2 R. S. 506, 2d ed. And the reason why the legislature were silent, was probably, because they knew that the court of chancery has the general incidental power to award an issue in all proper cases. I have no doubt of its power in the case before us, if not expressly restrained; and I presume its jurisdiction is not, in regard to issues, narrowed anywhere in the revised statutes.

Taking the court of chancery to hold its ordinary power in this particular, and conceding, for the sake of the argument, that Mrs. Milnor's testimony was shaken, then I think much the better course would have been to award an issue. The case at bar seems more strikingly to call for such a direction previous to a decision by the chancellor, than that of *Richards* v. *Syms*, where the evidence was agreed to be contradictory. The lord chancellor would not pronounce against the gift even in such a case, till the defendant's testimony had been overruled by the verdict of a jury. In the case at bar, I have endeavored to show, that there is, at least, very great difficulty in seeing a doubt either in respect to the form and intent of the gift, or the sanity of the donor or his freedom from undue influence. Yet the court of chancery has nullified the gift, without even taking the opinion of a jury. If, as was held by Lord Hardwicke, the intent to give ought not to be negatived without an issue in *Richards* v. *Syms*, such a precaution in the case before us, even if we do not go beyond an inquiry as to what the testator said, seems to me still more proper. But when we come to doubt on the question of insanity and undue influence, such a case has always been deemed peculiarly proper for the consideration of a jury. I noticed before, that the gift was in nature of a bequest. The question is of the same character as that which frequently arises on offering a will for probate, in respect to which the legislature have made special provisions for an issue on appeal to the circuit judge: 2 R. S. 10, 505, 2d ed. It is analogous to the issue of *devisavit vel non*, so familiarly known to the profession. Mingled, as this matter was before the auditors, with the general account, and introduced by the way of supplemental charge at an advanced stage of the hearing (though I do not mean to deny the regularity of that course in strict practice), it is easy to perceive that the hearing must have been greatly wanting in that fullness of preparation, and singleness of attention, and thorough examination peculiar to the trial of a feigned issue. May I be permitted to say again that, to my mind, there was an unaccountable paucity of proof to show insanity?

In *Kettletas* v. *Gardner*, read in evidence from 1 Paige, 488, the master reported that Gardner was of sound mind when the report was made, though his bodily health was impaired and his habits of intemperance laid him open to frequent attacks of insanity. It is evident from the report that the fits of insanity spoken of were entirely voluntary; the man got drunk often and that was the amount of his insanity. The report was made in 1829, after he had come from the asylum the last time, a sober man, as Mrs. Milnor says; nor was there a particle of evidence that he was even drunk after that time. The amount of the master's report is that he was liable to become insane. That he ever became so after he left the asylum he does not say, and when he destroyed the bond he was, as Mrs. Milnor says, perfectly himself. She had been long acquainted with him, and could doubtless tell as a matter of fact at the time whether he was drunk or sober. It must have been a surprise to this widow to be told that her husband who had been in the habit of getting drunk could not, for that reason, make a codicil, or add to her legacy by way of *donatio causa mortis*, when he was perfectly sober. I feel fully authorized to believe that there was nothing in the case different from the ordinary alternations of an intemperate man. That his habit had at any time resulted in delirium tremens is nowhere said. Even that, the worst and commonly the most imbecile state of the drunkard, is often attended with turns of sobriety sometimes for weeks.

Again, I ask if there was anything more than common drunken fits, why was it not shown? Doctor Rogers had advised that he should be confined. Why was the doctor not examined? Mrs. Gardner had raised the issue. Her own witness had pronounced the man sober at the very moment of the gift; and also declared that he came from the asylum, on an invitation to fetch him as a cured man. If she was mistaken in her estimate of his condition, she might have been met by a cloud of witnesses; the physicians at the asylum, the keeper and his agents, in addition to the family physician, and the neighbors who had noticed him since his return. If his faculties had become so impaired that he was too stupid for plain business when clear of drink, surely this must have been well known, and could have been easily proved. Yet all was rested on criticising the testimony of Mrs. Milnor, and the judicial removal of the man from his office of guardian because he was intemperate. It is true that Mrs. Gardner might have called the witnesses of whom I speak; but I do not think her counsel was warranted in doubting that her case was fully made out, and must stand, till it was more seriously impeached, than it had yet been by opposing testimony.

Beck, in his treatise on medical jurisprudence, vol. 1, 376, 1st.
ed., advises that "the conduct of drunkards should be particularly noticed during the intervals of temperance. If spirituous
liquors exercise such an influence as to render us doubtful concerning the state of mind at this time, we may reasonably infer
that the alienation is becoming permanent." Why was not such
an obvious point of view resorted to? Was it enough to talk of
the mad-house? This was evidently a mere misnomer. Doctor
Rush, in treating of mental diseases, calls it a sober-house, and
advises that an hospital be established in every city and town in
the United States, for the exclusive reception of hard drinkers:
Diseases of the Mind, 267, ed. of 1812. The ground taken by
Rush is, that drunkards are mischievous. Swinburne says the
drunkard is like a mad man during the time of his drunkenness; and can not make a will when he is so excessively drunk
that he is utterly deprived of the use of reason and understanding; otherwise, "if he be not clean spent, albeit his understanding be obscured and his memory troubled:" 1 Swinb.
133, 134, ed. of 1803. Blackstone, 2 Com. 497, says, "he is
incapable when his senses are besotted with drunkenness."
Mr. Stock, in his late treatise on the law of *non compotes
mentis*, 46, 47, gives us the result of the authorities, that "proof
of drunkenness amounting to insanity will invalidate a will; but
if it be shown that the testator was not under the influence of
strong liquors at the time of the execution, the presumption
will be in favor of the will, a presumption strengthened or impaired of course by the internal evidence of the contents."
What reason, I ask, had Mrs. Gardner to suppose she did not
stand within the very terms of the rule, after proving that her
husband was perfectly sober when he destroyed the bond?
Least of all, I think, had she reason to expect the imputation
of undue influence, and feel herself called upon to repel anything
of that kind. There was not one particle of evidence that she had
ever urged her husband on the subject; and I must be permitted to deny, on authority, that her general influence could
be received as any proof against her. In *Williams* v. *Goude*, 1
Hagg. Ecc. 577, 581, 595, a like inference was sought to be
made. There the husband was a tavern-keeper; and, it seems,
not only drank, but had become a good deal stupefied under an
attack of the apoplexy. In respect to the charge of undue influence, Sir John Nicholl remarks: "There was the general influence of an active, bustling, high-spirited wife, over a good-
natured, easy husband; in consequence of his attack, it was

necessary she should take a still more decided lead in the management of the concerns of the house. It was necessary she
should, as a kind nurse and an affectionate wife naturally would,
insist on his going to bed at his regular hour; on his not in-
dulging too freely in liquor," etc.; adverting to other acts of
salutary influence. But he adds: "I can find no trace of any
unfair importunity, on the part of the wife, to induce him to
alter his will, or do any testamentary act."

The general influence arising from his affection for and deference to his wife, the learned judge refuses to admit as matter of
suspicion. He says, in another place: "Indeed, it would be
extraordinary, if the influence of affection and of warm attachment is to take away the power of benefiting the object of that
regard. The influence, to vitiate an act, must amount to force
and coercion destroying free agency, it must not be the influence
of affection and attachment, it must not be the mere desire of
gratifying the wishes of another; for that would be a very strong
ground in support of a testamentary act. Further, there must
be proof that the act was obtained by this coercion; by importunity that could not be resisted; that it was done merely for
the sake of peace, so that the motive was tantamount to force
and fear." Was there anything of all this in Mrs. Gardner's
case which it lay with her to repel? I confess myself utterly at
a loss to conjecture on what the mind can fasten itself bearing
the remotest semblance of undue influence. These probate in-
vestigations were an every-day matter with Sir John Nicholl,
who fixes the *onus* on the party charging undue influence, saying he must put his finger on the act, showing how it was
wrought. In the case at bar, the auditors say Gardner was exposed to undue influence. The surrogate adds he may perhaps
have labored under the terror of being sent back to the mad-
house; and the chancellor says, "I must presume the mother,
or some one else, had persuaded the decedent to destroy the
bond." Certainly he was exposed to influence, and so is every
man on a bed of sickness, or in the hands of his nurse, even
though she be his wife. Are we, therefore, to presume that it
was exerted? Perhaps he was afraid of being sent back—are
we therefore to presume that Mrs. Gardner shook his purpose
by threats of incarceration?

If we proceed from exposure, into the regions of conjecture,
it is difficult to conceive how a great majority of testamentary
acts are to escape the imputation of undue influence. If I could
presume that Mrs. Gardner, or some one else, persuaded her

husband to forgive her the loan, it appears to me, with great deference, to be a perfect *non sequitur.* Was there fraud? Was there terror? Was there harassing importunity, and a compliance for the sake of peace in the dying hour? Stock's Non Comp. Ment. 47, 48. Had Mrs. Gardner the least reason to suppose that her conduct was open to this harsh construction? Why did she not seize with unbecoming eagerness on the request that she herself would destroy the bond? A messenger is resorted to. The trustee gives up the bond. The testator is allowed time to pause and reflect. This is the proof. Is it not more natural to suppose that she had been slow and sorrowful, in yielding to the severe treatment of her unhappy husband? Is it possible I can be mistaken, when I suppose that no presumption ought to arise against her, because she had taken the helm from the hand of a drunken pilot, and thus saved the remnant of his fortune from shipwreck? What would otherwise have been left for him to bequeath in favor of the respondents or anybody else? We are not dealing with a needy and artful adventuress insinuating herself into a marriage with age and weakness, for the sake of a fortune. Each had a competency; and we find the testator living at Mrs. Gardner's own house in Prince street. They had doubtless contracted their union with the ordinary expectation of wealth and respectability and domestic happiness. Mrs. Gardner had lived to see all these hopes fade, without any fault of hers, and, moreover, found herself involved in the usual round of fallacious expedients to reclaim an intemperate husband. She must have been miserable; but her suffering for years does not appear to have subdued her affection, or led her to fault in the discharge of her duty. The husband seems to have become sensible of all this in his last sickness; and I have been unable to detect any other influence as leading to a destruction of the bond.

He had the undoubted legal power to forgive this debt to his wife: 2 Kent's Com. 153, 3d ed., and the cases there cited, in the form which the deposition of Mrs. Milnor represents him as having pursued: *Richards* v. *Syms,* 1 Barn. Ch. 90. And to my mind the proof is entirely clear, not only that the requisite form was complied with; but that it is free from the imputation of insanity or undue influence.

The whole, however, I think, resolves itself into a question of evidence; and I agree to the proposition of one of the counsel for the respondents in his argument, that if this court should believe there was a fair conflict of evidence before the auditors, and the law will not allow an issue, their conclusion ought not to be disturbed. I would give it the force which we allow to a verdict on a motion for a new trial, and refuse to reverse their report, except in a case where they may have concluded against the decided weight of evidence. Such I think is the case at bar. But even if there was a fair conflict of evidence, as I think there was power in chancery to award an issue, it should have been done. In either view I am for a reversal of the chancellor's decree. Should this court, however, differ with me upon the force of the evidence with regard to the destruction of the bond, then I am of opinion the decree of the chancellor should be affirmed.

The manner of introducing the charge of the two thousand dollars before the auditor, was a mere matter of practice; and the costs, though final, are not in this case the subject of appeal. Both rested in the discretion of the court below: *Rogers* v. *Holly*, 18 Wend. 350, and the cases there cited: *Rowley* v. *Van Benthuysen*, 16 Id. 369.

On the question being put, Shall this decree be reversed? twenty members of the court answered in the affirmative, and three in the negative. Whereupon so much of the decree of the chancellor as affirmed the decree of the surrogate, charging the appellant with the sum of two thousand dollars loaned to her by her husband, was reversed.

———

LIABILITY OF WIFE'S SEPARATE ESTATE FOR DEBTS contracted for its benefit: See the note to *Thomas* v. *Folwell*, 30 Am. Dec. 233, where the whole subject of a married woman's power to bind or charge her separate estate is discussed, and where the previous cases in this series on that point are referred to. See also *Dyett* v. *North American Coal Co.*, 32 Id. 598, and note, and *Dorrance* v. *Scott*, 31 Id. 509, and note. The authority of *Gardner* v. *Gardner* upon this subject is recognized in *Cheever* v. *Wilson*, 9 Wall. 119; *Miller* v. *Newton*, 23 Cal. 565; *Strong* v. *Skinner*, 4 Barb. 554; *Colvin* v. *Currier*, 22 Id. 380; *Goelet* v. *Gori*, 31 Id. 321; *Mallory* v. *Vanderheyden*, 3 Barb. Ch. 11; S. C. in court of appeals, 1 N. Y. 452; *Howland* v. *Fort Edward Paper Mill Co.*, 8 How. Pr. 507; *Chapman* v. *Lemon*, 11 Id. 238; *Cobine* v. *St. John*, 12 Id. 335; *Yale* v. *Dederer*, 17 Id. 177; S. C., 18 N. Y. 278; *Hoard* v. *Garner*, 3 Sandf. 191.

HABITUAL INTEMPERANCE of one of the parties to a contract may be a ground for denying specific performance: *Seymour* v. *Delancy*, 15 Am. Dec. 270. See generally as to contracts of intoxicated persons, *Wigglesworth* v. *Steers*, 3 Id. 602; *Wade* v. *Colvert*, 12 Id. 652, and note; *Woodson* v. *Gordon*, 14 Id. 743; *Barrett* v. *Buxton*, 16 Id. 691; *Crane* v. *Conklin*, 22 Id. 519; *Harbison* v. *Lemon*, 23 Id. 376. A drunkard is incompetent only when his mind is clouded or his reason dethroned by actual intoxication: *Van Wyck* v. *Brasher*, 81 N. Y. 262, citing *Gardner* v. *Gardner*.

GENERAL PRESUMPTION IS IN FAVOR OF SANITY till the contrary appears:
Coffey v. *Home Life Ins. Co.*, 35 N. Y. Super. Ct. (3 Jones & S.) 322; S. C.,
44 How. Pr. 483, citing the principal case.

UNDUE INFLUENCE, WHAT CONSTITUTES: See *Miller* v. *Miller*, 8 Am. Dec.
651; *McCants* v. *Bee*, 16 Id. 610; *Small* v. *Small*, 16 Id. 253, and note discussing the subject at length; *Clark* v. *Fisher*, 19 Id. 402, and note; *Davis* v. *Cal-
vert*, 25 Id. 282. The doctrine of *Gardner* v. *Gardner* on this point is approved
in *Dickie* v. *Carter*, 42 Ill. 388; *Butler* v. *Benson*, 1 Barb. 538; *Davis* v. *Culver*, 13 How. Pr. 69.

GIFT OF CHOSE IN ACTION: See the note to *Bradley* v. *Hunt*, 23 Am. Dec.
600, discussing the various phases of this subject. See also *Fink* v. *Cox*, 9
Id. 191; *Priester* v. *Priester*, 23 Id. 191; *Parish* v. *Stone*, 25 Id. 378; *Elam* v.
Keen, 26 Id. 322. The principal case is cited as an authority on this subject in
Doty v. *Wilson*, 5 Lans. 10; *Brinckerhoff* v. *Lawrence*, 2 Sandf. Ch. 413. In
the latter case it is said that the reporter's head note in *Gardner* v. *Gardner*
makes it out a case of *donatio mortis causa*, when there was nothing approaching it in the case.

POWER, DUTY, AND DISCRETION OF COURT OF CHANCERY AS TO AWARDING
ISSUE: See *Le Guen* v. *Gouverneur*, 1 Am. Dec. 121; *Pryor* v. *Adams*, Id. 533;
Hooe v. *Marquess*, 2 Id. 570; *Seymour* v. *De Lancey*, 14 Id. 552; *Reybold* v.
Dodd, 26 Id. 401. *Gardner* v. *Gardner* is cited on this point in *Patterson* v.
Gaines, 6 How. (U. S.) 584; *O'Brien* v. *Bowes*, 4 Bosw. 661, and *Brinkley* v.
Brinkley, 2 N. Y. Sup. Ct. (T. & C.) 504.

CASES

COURT OF CHANCERY

OF

NEW YORK.

HEYER v. PRUYN.

[7 PAIGE'S CHANCERY, 465.]

PURCHASERS OF MORTGAGED PREMISES ARE BOUND by an acknowledgment
of the mortgage as a valid and subsisting incumbrance made by their
grantor, a purchaser on execution against the mortgagor under a judgment subsequent to the mortgage, within twenty years before the commencement of a suit to foreclose such mortgage, and can not, therefore,
rely upon the statute of limitations as a bar.

SUFFERING A FORECLOSURE BILL TO BE TAKEN AS CONFESSED is an admission of liability on the part of the mortgagor sufficient to take the case
out of the statute of limitations where such an admission is necessary.

MORTGAGOR'S ACKNOWLEDGMENT WITHIN TWENTY YEARS IS UNNECESSARY
to continue the lien of the mortgage, where the mortgagor has ceased to
be the owner of the land.

MORTGAGE LIEN CONTINUES THOUGH THE DEBT MAY BE BARRED by the
statute of limitations, and is not to be presumed paid until the lapse of
twenty years, where the personal liability of the mortgagor has become
separated from the ownership of the land.

MORTGAGED PREMISES CONSTITUTE THE PRIMARY FUND for the payment
of the mortgage in equity, as against a purchaser of the land under an
execution against the mortgagor.

BILL filed in January, 1832, to foreclose a mortgage made by
Pruyn, defendant, to the plaintiff's testator, in 1809, to secure
payment of a certain bond, and duly proved and recorded. The
bill was taken as confessed as against Pruyn. The other defendants answered, claiming to be *bona fide* purchasers and incumbrancers without notice of the mortgage, and insisting that
as to them the mortgage was to be presumed satisfied from lapse
of time. Other facts are stated in the opinion. Decree by the
vice-chancellor in favor of the complainants, and the defendants
appealed.

K. Miller and S. Stevens, for the appellants.

W. H. Tobbey, for the respondents.

WALWORTH, Chancellor.   There is very little dispute as to
the real facts in this case.   Shaver, who purchased the mortgaged premises in October, 1813, had no notice of the existence
of this mortgage except the legal constructive notice arising
from the registry thereof.   And these defendants were equally
ignorant of the actual existence of such an incumbrance upon
the premises, at the time their several rights and interests
therein accrued.   But as this suit was commenced in January,
1832, which was but a little more than eighteen years after the
conveyance to Shaver, the defendants are not entitled to protection by lapse of time if this bond and mortgage had been recognized by Van Dyke, the former owner of the premises, as a valid
and subsisting incumbrance thereon, previous to his conveyance
to Shaver, and within twenty years before the commencement
of this suit.   Whether the payment of the five hundred dollars
by Van Dyke in May, 1814, which does not appear to have been
authorized or sanctioned either by the mortgagor or by the then
owner of the premises, would be sufficient to rebut the presumption of payment in favor of Shaver and those claiming under him,
and to preserve the lien of the mortgage for twenty years from
that time, is a question which it is not necessary to decide here.
It may be remarked, however, that at the time of that payment
Van Dyke was not a mere volunteer.   Neither was there a want
of privity between him and the owner of the land in relation to
that payment.   For by his covenants in the deed to Shaver he
was bound to pay off the mortgage, so as to protect the premises from the lien thereof.   And those covenants would run with
the land into whosesoever hands it might come by assignment
from Shaver, so as to create a similar privity between Van Dyke
and them in relation to the payment of this mortgage.

It appears by the pleadings and proofs that, subsequent to the
giving of this mortgage, Pruyn, the mortgagor, failed in business
and became insolvent, and that in September, 1812, there were
several judgments against him, and other incumbrances upon
the mortgaged premises, some of which judgments and incumbrances were older and some younger than the mortgage to
Heyer.   An arrangement was then made by H. L. Van Dyke,
who owned the junior judgment, and the other incumbrancers,
except Heyer who lived in New York and knew nothing of that
arrangement at that time, by which it was agreed that Van Dyke

should bid in the premises under the youngest judgment, subject to the prior incumbrances thereon; and that the other creditors should wait upon him five years, if necessary, for the payment of their respective claims, to enable him to sell the property and obtain the payment of the purchase money in the mean time.   This arrangement was carried into effect, by a sale of the premises by the sheriff to Van Dyke, on the twenty-eighth of September, 1812; and the appellants claim title to the premises under that sale.   At the time when that arrangement was made a statement of all the judgments and other incumbrances upon the property was made out, and Heyer's mortgage was included therein for the whole amount of principal and interest from its date, as a valid and subsisting incumbrance upon the premises. This was therefore a distinct recognition, by Van Dyke, the purchaser, of the existence of that bond and mortgage as a valid lien upon the premises in September, 1812.   And if he had continued the owner of the mortgaged premises until the commencement of this suit, in January, 1832, it is evident that he could not have set up lapse of time as a bar to the complainants' suit, even if there had been no subsequent payment on the bond and mortgage, nor any recognition of the same as a subsisting debt. The defendants, therefore, claiming through the conveyance from Van Dyke to Shaver, sit in the seat of the grantor in that conveyance, and are bound by his previous recognition of the mortgage as a subsisting incumbrance upon the premises within twenty years.   In the case of *Hughes* v. *Edwards*, 9 Wheat. 490, the supreme court of the United States held that purchasers from the mortgagor, who had either actual notice of the mortgage at the time of their purchases, or had constructive notice by means of the registry, were bound by a previous acknowledgment of the person under whom they claimed of the existence of the indebtness within twenty years.

Neither is the lien of the mortgage gone because there is no proof of an admission or recognition of Pruyn, the mortgagor, of his indebtness within twenty years.   If a formal admission of his continuing liability on the bond were necessary in this case, we have it by his suffering the bill to be taken as confessed against him; which entitles the complainants to a decree against him personally for the deficiency, if the mortgaged premises should be insufficient to pay the debt and costs.   It is not necessary, however, to show that the personal liability of the mortgagor still continues; for the lien of the mortgage would not be impaired even by an absolute discharge of the mortgagor under the insolvent act. The intimation of an opinion by Mr. Justice Sutherland in *Jackson* v. *Sackett*, 7 Wend. 94, that a mortgage to secure a simple contract debt was presumed to be paid in six years, because the statute of limitations might at the expiration of that time be pleaded to a suit on the note, certainly can not be law. At least such a principle can not apply to a case like this, where the real security upon the land is separated from the personal responsibility of the mortgagor by a sale of the equity of redemption upon execution. While the party who is personally liable for the debt continues to be the absolute owner of the equity of redemption in the mortgaged premises, a judgment in his favor which would be an absolute bar to any recovery against him for the debt, on the ground of payment or usury, etc., might also, as an estoppel, bar a suit against him to obtain satisfaction of the debt out of the mortgaged premises. But where the personal liability of the mortgagor has been separated from the ownership of the land, a recovery against the mortgagor upon his bond, after such separation, would not estop the owner of the land from showing that the mortgage was paid. And as estoppels must be mutual, a judgment in favor of the mortgagor, in a suit instituted upon his bond, after his equity of redemption in the land had been sold by the sheriff, could not be pleaded by the purchaser in bar to a bill to foreclose the mortgage. Here the mortgaged premises constituted in equity the primary fund for the payment of the debt; as the purchaser at the sheriff's sale took the land subject to the specific lien of this prior mortgage thereon: *Tice* v. *Annin*, 2 Johns. Ch. 128. The recognition of the existence of the incumbrance, therefore, by the party who was in equity bound to apply the funds in his hands to pay off the mortgage, should, as against him and those claiming under him by the subsequent conveyance, be considered of the same force as a recognition by the mortgagor himself.

There was nothing inequitable in the arrangement with Heyer, in May, 1814, by which a part of the purchase money received from Shaver was applied towards Colonel Van Vleck's judgment instead of being paid on the mortgage. As both were incumbrances upon the premises in the hands of the purchaser, it was perfectly immaterial to him which was paid first. Whether the money was applied to satisfy the judgment or the mortgage, the amount of the incumbrances on the property remaining unpaid would be precisely the same.

The note of L. Van Dyck does not appear to have been lost by any negligence on the part of Heyer. It was not indorsed

over to him, so as to enable him to collect it in his own name,
if it was not voluntarily paid. And he had no directions to sue it
in the name of Doctor Van Dyck, from whom he received it. It
was for the interest of these defendants that Heyer should retain that note, and should endeavor to get the money thereon
from the assignees and apply it in payment of the mortgage, instead of delivering the note up to H. L. Van Dyck, who might
have used the money for other purposes.

For these reasons, I do not see any ground for differing from
the vice-chancellor in the conclusion at which he arrived in this
case. And the decree appealed from must therefore be affirmed
with costs.

ACKNOWLEDGMENT TO TAKE CASE OUT OF THE STATUTE OF LIMITATIONS,
generally: See *Frey v. Kirk*, 23 Am. Dec. 581, and note, collecting the previous cases in this series on that subject; *Austin v. Bostwick*, 25 Id. 42, and
note; *Newlin v. Duncan*, Id. 66; *Conway v. Williams*, 29 Id. 466; *Johnson
v. Bonnethea*, 30 Id. 347; *Elliott v. Leake*, 32 Id. 314.

SUBSEQUENT ACKNOWLEDGMENT REBUTS PRESUMPTION OF PAYMENT arising from lapse of time: *Newlin v. Duncan*, 25 Id. 66. To the point that
where one purchases land under mortgage, he is bound by an acknowledgment of the mortgage as a subsisting lien, made by one under whom
he claims title within twenty years before commencement of a suit to foreclose the mortgage, so as to rebut the presumption of payment arising from
lapse of time, the principal case is cited in *Harrington v. Slade*, 22 Barb. 165;
New York Life Ins. Co. v. Covert, 3 Abb. App. Dec. 356; S. C., 6 Abb. Pr.
(N. S.) 166. A verbal acknowledgment was sufficient for this purpose before the revised statutes in New York: *Carll v. Hart*, 15 Barb. 567, also
citing the principal case. In *Morey v. Farmers' Loan and Trust Co.*, 18 Id.
404, the case is referred to generally as an authority as to what evidence is
sufficient to rebut the presumption of payment of a sealed instrument arising
from lapse of time.

PRESUMPTION OF PAYMENT OF MORTGAGE FROM LAPSE OF TIME: See
Swart v. Service, *ante*, 211, and note referring to other cases in this series.
That no presumption of payment of a mortgage or like lien arises from lapse of
time until the expiration of twenty years, is a point to which *Heyer v. Pruyn*
is cited in *Mayor etc. of New York v. Colgate*, 12 N. Y. 156; *Fisher v. Mayor*,
3 Hun, 652; *Gould v. Holland Purchase Ins. Co.*, 16 Id. 540.

RUNNING OF STATUTE ON NOTE SECURED BY MORTGAGE or other lien
raises no presumption of payment so as to cut off the lien: *Belknap v. Gleason*, 27 Am. Dec. 721, and note. *Heyer v. Pruyn* is recognized as an authority for this principle in *Pratt v. Huggins*, 29 Barb. 285; *New York Life Ins.
Co. v. Covert*, Id. 441; *Borst v. Corey*, 15 N. Y. 510; *Gillette v. Smith*, 18
Hun, 12; *Jones v. Merchants' Bank of Albany*, 4 Rob. 227; *Almy v. Wilbur*,
2 Woodb. & M. 404, where it is said that the better view is perhaps that the
debt is not barred if the mortgage is not.

LAND IS THE PRIMARY FUND FOR PAYMENT OF A MORTGAGE as respects
a purchaser of the equity of redemption: *Clift v. White*, 12 N. Y. 534; S. C.,
in supreme court, 15 Barb. 74; *Weaver v. Toogood*, 1 Id. 241; *Gilbert v.
Averill*, 15 Id. 23; *Woods v. Spalding*, 45 Id. 607; *Vanderkemp v. Shelton*, 11
Paige Ch. 34, all citing *Heyer v. Pruyn*.

MILLSPAUGH *v.* MCBRIDE.

[7 PAIGE'S CHANCERY, 509.]

PURCHASE OF SENIOR MORTGAGE BY A PURCHASER OF THE EQUITY OF RE-
DEMPTION to protect his title does not create a merger so as to extinguish
the lien of the mortgage in favor of an intermediate mortgagee, and on
a foreclosure by the latter the first mortgage must be first paid.

DECREE OF FORECLOSURE BY DEFAULT MAY BE OPENED even after enrollment to let in a defense that a prior mortgage, alleged in the bill to have
been paid by the defendant, was in fact purchased by him, and is entitled to priority of payment, where such defense was prevented by the
negligence or mistake of the defendant's solicitor; so, even after a sale
under the decree where the complainant is the purchaser, and has not
resold to a purchaser without notice.

ORDER to show cause why a decree of foreclosure heretofore
entered and enrolled in this cause should not be vacated and the
sale set aside to permit the defendants, Pinckney and Bertine,
to deny an allegation in the bill that a certain prior mortgage
had been paid by the defendants, and to show that they had in
fact purchased the same to protect their title as purchasers of
the equity of redemption. It appeared that the defendants permitted the bill to be taken as confessed against them by the advice of their solicitor, who neglected to look into the bill served
on him, or the decree entered, and did not, therefore, know that
it was alleged in the bill that the prior mortgage was paid by the
defendants, and that the decree made no provision for its payment. The complainant was the purchaser at the foreclosure
sale.

J. Edwards, for the complainant.

J. Rhoades, for the defendants.

WALWORTH, Chancellor. There is no doubt in this case, from
the facts as stated, that the defendants Pinckney and Bertine
were the first incumbrancers upon the mortgaged premises, and
that their mortgage, which was assigned to them for the purpose of protecting their title against the junior mortgage, was
not, as against such junior mortgage, merged in the equity of
redemption. It was, in equity, impossible for the prior mortgage, or the equitable interest of the defendants therein, to
unite with their legal title to the equity of redemption, by reason of the intermediate equity which the complainant had by
virtue of his mortgage. The establishment of a different principle would bring us back to the doctrine of tacking; or a

merger which would cut off the complainant's mortgage altogether.

That the lien of the prior mortgage still continues in such a case, as against the intermediate mortgage, is distinctly recognized by Chancellor Kent in the case of *McKinstry* v. *Mervin*, 3 Johns. Ch. 446, in a case precisely like the present in that respect: See also *Crow* v. *Tinsley*, 6 Dana, 402. If the mortgagee is considered as holding the legal estate and the mortgagor the mere equity, the effect of a merger would be to unite to their prior mortgage the equity of redemption purchased by these defendants, so as to overreach the junior incumbrance altogether, at law, and leave him to his remedy in equity only. And when he comes here to ask equity he must do equity by paying off the first incumbrance. The same result follows if a mortgagee is considered as having a mere equitable lien upon the land for the payment of his debt. In that case the second mortgagee, when he seeks the aid of this court to obtain satisfaction of his mortgage, by a foreclosure and sale of the equity of redemption, which equity of redemption in this present case belongs to the owners of the senior mortgage, must still pay off such senior mortgage which is due in equity, even if there is a legal merger. In this case, therefore, if the facts as they now appear had been truly stated in the bill, the defendants might have obtained a correction of the erroneous decree by a bill of review. But in consequence of the false allegation in the bill that the prior mortgage was paid off to the original mortgagee, instead of stating, as the fact was, that the defendants bought the mortgage and took the assignment thereof, the decree is right upon the case as made by the bill. No relief therefore can be given to the defendants unless the court has the power, in this stage of the proceedings, to open the order to take the bill as confessed, and all the subsequent proceedings, to enable them to put in an answer, denying the erroneous statement in the bill that their mortgage had been paid and was legally satisfied, upon such terms and conditions as may be just and equitable in regard to the complainant.

I think the counsel for these defendants has been successful in showing that it is within the power of the court to open a regular decree by default, even after enrollment, for the purpose of giving a defendant an opportunity to make his defense; where such defense is meritorious, and he has not been heard in relation thereto, either by mistake or accident, or by the negligence of his solicitor. The cases of *Kemp* v. *Squire*, 1 Ves. sen. 205, and

of *Robson* v. *Cranwell*, 1 Dick. 61, show that the enrollment
may be discharged when necessary, for the purpose of opening
the decree. And in *Beekman* v. *Peck*, 3 Johns. Ch. 415, Chancellor Kent set aside a regular decree by default, upon motion,
after enrollment, to let in a defense upon the merits. The case
of *Erwin* v. *Vint*, 6 Munf. 267, also shows that this is the proper
course, where the error can not be corrected by a rehearing or
upon a bill of review. The fact that there has been a sale in
this case forms no objection to the application, as the complainant himself bid in the premises, for the amount due on his mortgage with costs, and has not parted with his interest therein to
a *bona fide* purchaser, or incumbrancer. The decree may be
permitted to stand, and he may keep the premises at the price
for which he has purchased them, in case he elects to pay the
principal and interest due on the prior mortgage within twenty
days, deducting therefrom his taxable costs of opposing this application. If he does not think proper to do that, the order to
take the bill as confessed against Pinckney and Bertine, and all
subsequent proceedings, must be set aside; and the enrollment of
the decree must be discharged and the master's deed canceled,
and those defendants be let in to answer and defend the suit so
far as relates to their claim or priority under their mortgage,
upon payment of the costs of the order to take the bill as confessed and of all subsequent proceedings. The costs in that
case must be paid within twenty days after service of a copy of
the taxed bill on the defendant's solicitor, and their answer is to
be put in within the same time.

MERGER OF MORTGAGE IN EQUITY OF REDEMPTION: See *Hunt* v. *Hunt*, 25
Am. Dec. 400, and other cases and notes in this series referred to in the note
thereto. The principle enunciated in the foregoing opinion, that where a
mortgage and equity of redemption unite in the same person, they will not
merge in equity against the intention of the parties, and where it is for the
interest of the person in whom the legal and equitable titles are united that
they should be kept distinct, is referred to with approval in *Skeel* v. *Spraker*,
8 Paige, 196; *Thompson* v. *Van Vechten*, 27 N. Y. 579; S. C., 5 Abb. Pr. 464;
6 Bosw. 465; *Casey* v. *Buttolph*, 12 Barb. 639; *Warner* v. *Blakeman*, 36 Id.
524; *Schermerhorn* v. *Merrill*, 1 Id. 516; *Day* v. *Mooney*, 4 Hun, 134; *Clift*
v. *White*, 12 N. Y. 533; *Payne* v. *Wilson*, 74 Id. 354.

OPENING DECREE AFTER ENROLLMENT.—The general rule is, that a decree
regularly enrolled can not be altered, except by a bill of review: *Lilly* v.
Shaw, 59 Ill. 76. But a decree by default may without doubt be opened to
let in a defense on the merits of which a party has been deprived by the
negligence of his counsel: *Tripp* v. *Vincent*, 8 Paige Ch. 180; *Curtis* v. *Ballagh*, 4 Edw. Ch. 639; *Nash* v. *Wetmore*, 33 Barb. 159; *Thompson* v. *Goulding*,
5 Allen, 82, all referring to *Millspaugh* v. *McBride*.

NODINE *v.* GREENFIELD.

[7 PAIGE'S CHANCERY, 544.]

DEVISEES TAKE VESTED REMAINDERS IN FEE, WHEN.—Where a testator, after empowering his executors to sell his realty, etc., gives the rents and profits of such as shall remain unsold from time to time, together with the income of certain investments, to his wife for life, and devises the principal of such investments and the residue of his realty and personalty after his wife's death to the children of a certain brother, who should then be living, and to the lawful issue of those who should be deceased, *per stirpes*, the wife, at the testator's death, takes a life estate in the realty, and the children of the testator's brother then in being take vested remainders in fee as tenants in fee, subject to open and let in after-born children, and also subject to be defeated by a sale by the executors, and are necessary parties to a suit to foreclose a mortgage given by the testator on such realty.

PARTIES TO FORECLOSURE SUIT.—Persons having future contingent interests in the equity of redemption need not be made parties to a suit to foreclose a mortgage, but those *in esse* having the first vested estate of inheritance are necessary parties to make the decree a bar to their right or to that of any contingent remainder-man not made a party.

BILL for specific performance of a contract to purchase a certain lot. The purchaser refused to complete the contract because the vendor could not make a good title. A reference was directed to a master, who reported in favor of the title. It appeared that the plaintiff's title was acquired under a foreclosure sale of the said lot on a mortgage executed by one J. Ruden. After the mortgage was executed Ruden made his will, empowering his executors to sell and convey his realty, and directing them to sell his personalty and invest the proceeds in certain permanent securities. He then gave the income of those investments, with the rents and profits of the real estate remaining unsold from time to time, to his wife for life, and after her death devised the principal of the investments aforesaid, and all the lands, tenements, property, and effects then belonging to his estate, to the children of his brother, A. Ruden, who should then be living, and to the lawful issue of those who should be deceased, *per stirpes*, and in default of such children or issue, then over. At the death of the testator, his wife, his brother (who was his only heir at law), and a number of children of the latter were still living, and a number of children had been born since. The mortgage, being unpaid, was foreclosed after the mortgagor's death, the executors, the widow, and the brother only being made parties. Other facts appear from the opinion. The case came before the chancellor on exceptions to the master's report.

J. L. Mason, for the complainant.

J. W. Gerard, for the defendants.

WALWORTH, Chancellor. The objection to the title in this cause is, that the children of A. Ruden, who were in existence at the time the bill of foreclosure was filed, and who were the first devisees of the remainder in fee after the termination of the life estate of the widow, were not made parties to the suit; and that their equity of redemption was, therefore, not extinguished by the sale under the decree in that suit. This objection appears to be well taken; and the master therefore erred in reporting that the complainant could give a good title.

No estate whatever was vested in the executors in this case by the will of the testator; but they had a mere power in trust to sell and convey the estate for the purposes of the will. Neither did the legal title to the premises descend to the heir at law of the testator until the execution of such power; for by the terms of the will, the rents and profits of the real estate remaining unsold are devised to the widow for life, and the estate itself, if not sold by the executors, is devised to the children of his brother who may be living at the time of her death. Upon the death of the testator, therefore, the widow took a life estate in the premises, and the children of A. Ruden, who were then *in esse*, took vested remainders in fee, as tenants in common therein, subject to open and let in after-born children; and subject to be divested by death during the life-time of the widow, or to be defeated by the execution of the power of sale by the executors or the survivor of them: *Doe* v. *Provoost*, 4 Johns. 61 [4 Am. Dec. 249]; *Doe* v. *Martin*, 4 T. R. 39; *Osbrey* v. *Bury*, 1 Ball & Bea. 53. Where there is a contest in chancery in relation to real estate, or where a mortgagee wishes to foreclose a mortgage, in a case where there are several future and contingent interests in the equity of redemption, it is not necessary to make every person having or claiming a future and contingent interest in the premises a party to the bill, in order to bar his right or claim, by the decree in the cause; but it is sufficient, if the person who has the first vested estate of inheritance, and all other persons having or claiming prior rights or interests in the premises, are brought before the court: Story's Eq. Pl., p. 140, sec. 144; p. 182, sec. 198; 1 West, 619;[1] Ambl. 564.[2] The person having the first estate of inheritance, and who is *in esse*, appears, however, to be a necessary party to a bill of foreclosure, to make the de-

---

1. *Hopkins* v. *Hopkins*.   2. *Reynoldson* v. *Perkins*.

cree a bar either to his right, or to the right of any contingent remainder-man who is not made a party to the suit. In the case of *Gore* v. *Stackpoole*, 1 Dow, 31, in the house of lords, upon an appeal from Ireland. Lord Chancellor Eldon said, it was clear equitable law, that in order to make a foreclosure valid as against all claimants, he who had the first estate of inheritance must be brought before the court; and even then, the intermediate remainder-men for life ought to be brought before the court, to give them an opportunity to pay off the mortgage if they thought fit: See also Coote's L. of Mort. 522; *Yates* v. *Hambly*, 2 Atk. 237. In this case, the children of A. Ruden, who were *in esse* at the time of filing the bill of foreclosure, had the first estate of inheritance in the mortgaged premises, in remainder after the termination of the life estate of the widow; and not being made parties, neither they nor the children born subsequently were bound by the decree. The exception to the master's report must therefore be allowed, with costs.

It appears by the report of the master that it was proved before him that the estate of the decedent was insufficient to pay the several legacies charged thereon after satisfying the debts. If such was the fact, it was unquestionably the duty of the surviving executors to sell the equity of redemption, or to release it to the mortgagees in satisfaction of their debt if the value thereof did not exceed the amount due. And as the surviving executor has not only the power but is actually directed by the will to sell the estate and pay the debts and legacies, it is probable a perfect title may still be procured by the complainant by a conveyance of the equity of redemption by the executor; which equity is probably worth nothing beyond the amount due on the mortgage. If a perfect title to the premises can be made in that way, I will reserve the right to the complainant to make such an application on the subject as he may think proper. But as the defendants have probably sustained a serious injury by the delay, and by the inability of the complainant to give them a good title at the time when their contract of purchase should have been consummated by a conveyance, which would render it improper to compel a specific performance upon a new title now to be procured, I can not give any further directions on the subject without affording them an opportunity to be heard in relation to the right of the complainant to compel them to take the title if it can now be made perfect.

VESTED REMAINDER IN FEE, DEVISEE TAKES, WHEN: See *Doe* v. *Provoost*, 4 Am. Dec. 249; *Jackson* v. *Merrill*, 5 Id. 213. The foregoing decision is cited on this point in *Wood* v. *Mather*, 38 Barb. 477, and is commented on and distinguished in *Sohier* v. *Williams*, 1 Curt. 493, and in *Larocque* v. *Clark*, 1 Redf. 471; S. C., Tuck. 34.

Parties to Foreclosure Suit: See *John* v. *Hunt*, 12 Am. Dec. 245; *Newman* v. *Chapman*, 14 Id. 766; *Hundley* v. *Webb*, 20 Id. 189. The principal case is cited on this point in *Daly* v. *Burchell*, 13 Abb. Pr. (N. S.) 268, and *Brevoort* v. *Grace*, 53 N. Y. 254. It is cited also on an analogous question in *Mead* v. *Mitchell*, 17 N. Y. 215.

Reed *v.* Wheaton.

[7 Paige's Chancery, 663.]

To Entitle Judgment Creditor to Relief in Equity to obtain payment of his judgment, on the ground that he has exhausted his remedy at law, he must, by his bill, show affirmatively if the judgment is one upon which execution may be issued to any county in the state, that he has issued execution to the county where the defendant then resided, which execution was returned unsatisfied, or must show a legal and sufficient excuse for not doing so.

Appeal from a refusal by the vice-chancellor to dissolve an injunction. From the bill it appeared that the complainant, having a judgment against the defendant, had issued execution thereon to Genesee county, which was returned unsatisfied; but it was not averred that the defendant resided in that county at that time. The defendant averred in his answer that before the recovery of judgment he had removed to Niagara county, of which the complainant was informed when the execution was returned, and that at the date of the execution he had property in that county subject to levy sufficient to satisfy it.

N. Hill, jun., for the appellant.

W. L. F. Warren, for the respondent.

Walworth, Chancellor. It is evident in this case that the complainant has not exhausted his remedy at law on his judgment. And, if the averments in the answer are true, there has not even been a *bona fide* attempt to collect the debt out of the defendant's property. But as the allegations in the answer, that the defendant lived in Niagara county at the time of issuing the execution, and that the complainant well knew that fact at the time of filing his bill in this suit, are not responsive to anything contained in the bill, the vice-chancellor would probably have been right in disregarding them, if the bill itself had shown sufficient to have authorized the issuing of the injunction originally. The bill, however, is defective in substance in this respect; as there is no averment therein that the defendant, at the time of the issuing of the execution to the sheriff of Genesee, was a resident of that county, or that he ever had resided there. In the case of *Leggett* v. *Hopkins and Smith,* 7 Paige, 149, it was decided that where the judgment was in the common pleas, so that an' execution could not be issued to any other county than that in which the judgment was obtained, it would be sufficient to issue an execution to the sheriff of that county, although the defendant resided elsewhere. In such a case it is not necessary, in the bill, to say anything about the defendant's residence. But where the judgment is in the supreme court, so that an execution may be issued to any part of the state, or where the bill is founded upon a decree of the court of chancery, the process of which court may also be sent into any county, the complainant who comes into this court for relief upon the ground that he has exhausted his remedy by execution on the judgment or decree, must show affirmatively, by his bill, that he has issued his execution to the sheriff of the county where the defendant resided at the time such execution was issued; or he must insert some other averment showing a sufficient and legal excuse for not sending his execution to the county where the defendant resides. If the defendant has removed from the state, or if his residence, upon diligent search and inquiry, can not be found, that may be a sufficient excuse for sending the execution to the county where he resided at the time of the commencement of the original suit against him, or where his last known place of residence was. But such an excuse will not avail the complainant where it distinctly appears that previous to the filing of the bill here, he is informed that the defendant has a fixed residence in this state; in case he has visible property there subject to sale on execution, sufficient to satisfy the debt and costs. Where it is necessary to show that the complainant has exhausted his remedy, by the issuing of an execution to the county where the defendant resides, it is not sufficient merely to describe the defendant in the bill as a resident of a particular town or county; as that description of the defendant, even if it could be considered as sworn to by the complainant, merely relates to the time of filing the bill; and is not an averment of residence at the time of issuing the execution. But here the defendant is not even described as being a resident of the county to which the execution issued, either at the time of filing the complainant's bill, or at any time previous thereto. As there was nothing in the bill to show that the complainant had exhausted his remedy at law, so as to authorize him to come into this court for relief, the vice-chancellor was clearly wrong, in refusing to dissolve the injunction, which had been erroneously allowed upon the bill itself.

His decision must, therefore, be reversed, with costs; and the injunction is dissolved.

————

JUDGMENT CREDITOR MUST SHOW LEGAL REMEDIES EXHAUSTED before resorting to equity to obtain satisfaction: *Screven* v. *Bostick*, 16 Am. Dec. 664; *Candler* v. *Pettit*, 19 Id. 399; *Beck* v. *Burdett*, Id. 436; *Edmeston* v. *Lyde*, Id. 454. To the same effect is *Voorhees* v. *Howard*, 4 Keyes, 383; S. C., 4 Abb. App. Dec. 504, citing the principal case. The particular point decided above, that in cases of this kind where execution may issue to any county in the state, the creditor must show, by his bill, that execution has been issued to the county where the debtor then resided or show a legal excuse for not doing so, is approved, and the case followed in *Merchants'* etc. *Bank* v. *Griffith*, 10 Paige, 520; *Smith* v. *Fitch*, Clarke's Ch. 266; *Wheeler* v. *Heermans*, 3 Sandf Ch. 599; *Payne* v. *Sheldon*, 63 Barb. 176.

————

BRANDRETH *v.* LANCE.

[8 PAIGE'S CHANCERY, 24.]

INJUNCTION TO RESTRAIN PUBLICATION OF A LIBEL holding the complainant up to ridicule will not lie, where such publication will not be an invasion of rights of literary or other property of the complainant.

BILL for an injunction to restrain the defendants perpetually from publishing a ludicrous pretended biography of the complainant, with intent to libel him and bring him into public disgrace and contempt by attributing to him various ridiculous and disgraceful adventures. The bill set out that the complainant was the proprietor and vendor of a valuable nostrum known as "Brandreth's vegetable universal pills," which, by extensive advertising, had become the source of a comfortable income to the complainant. It also set out certain alleged facts going to show that the proposed publication originated in a desire of one of the defendants to revenge himself upon the complainant for having discharged him from his employ. There was also set out at length the first sheet of the proposed work, containing the title-page, a ludicrous preface, table of contents, etc. Demurrer to the bill.

James Smith, for the complainant.

T. W. Clarke and S. Sherwood, for the defendants.

WALWORTH, Chancellor. It is very evident that this court can not assume jurisdiction of the case presented by the complain-

ant's bill, or of any other case of the like nature, without infringing upon the liberty of the press, and attempting to exercise a
power of preventive justice which, as the legislature has decided,
can not safely be intrusted to any tribunal consistently with the
principles of a free government: 2 R. S. 737, sec. 1, and re-
visers' note. This bill presents the simple case of an application
to the court of chancery to restrain the publication of a pamphlet which purports to be a literary work, undoubtedly a tale of
fiction, on the ground that it is intended as a libel upon the
complainant. The court of star chamber in England once exercised the power of cutting off the ears, branding the foreheads,
and slitting the noses of the libelers of important personages:
Hudson's Star Chamber, 2 Collect. Jurid. 224. And, as an incident to such a jurisdiction, that court was undoubtedly in the
habit of restraining the publication of such libels by injunction.
Since that court was abolished, however, I believe there is but
one case upon record in which any court, either in this country
or in England, has attempted, by an injunction or order of the
court, to prohibit or restrain the publication of a libel, as such,
in anticipation. In the case to which I allude, the notorious
Scroggs, chief justice of the court of king's bench, and his associates, decided that they might be safely intrusted with the
power of prohibiting and suppressing such publications as they
might deem to be libelous. They accordingly made an order of
the court prohibiting any person from printing or publishing a
periodical, entitled "The Weekly Packet of Advice from Rome,
or the History of Popery." The house of commons, however,
considered this extraordinary exercise of power on the part of
Scroggs as a proper subject of impeachment: 8 Howell's State
Trials, 198. And I believe no judge or chancellor from that
time to the present has attempted to follow that precedent.
There is, indeed, in the reported case of *Du Bost* v. *Beresford*, 2
Camp. 511, which was an action of trespass against the defendant for destroying a libelous picture, a most extraordinary
declaration of Lord Ellenborough, that the lord chancellor, upon
an application to him, would have granted an injunction against
the exhibition of the libelous painting. It is said, however, in a
note to *Horne's case*, in the state trials, that this declaration of
Lord Ellenborough, in relation to the power of the lord chancellor to restrain the publication of a libel by injunction, excited great astonishment in the minds of all the practitioners in
the courts of equity: 20 Howell's St. Tr. 799. It must unquestionably be considered as a hasty declaration, made without

reflection during the progress of a trial at *nisi prius;* and as such it is not entitled to any weight whatever.

The utmost extent to which the court of chancery has ever gone in restraining any publication by injunction, has been upon the principle of protecting the rights of property. Upon this principle alone Lord Eldon placed his decision, in the case of *Gee* v. *Pritchard*, 2 Swanst. 403, continuing the injunction which restrained the defendant from publishing copies of certain letters written to him by the complainant. But it may, perhaps, be doubted whether his lordship in that case did not, to some extent, endanger the freedom of the press by assuming jurisdiction of the case as a matter of property merely, when in fact the object of the complainant's bill was not to prevent the publication of her letters on account of any supposed interest she had in them as literary property, but to restrain the publication of a private correspondence, as a matter of feeling only. His decision in that case has, however, as I see, received the unqualified approbation of the learned American commentator on equity jurisprudence: See 2 Story's Eq. 222, sec. 948.

In this case the complainant does not claim the exercise of the extraordinary jurisdiction of this court on the ground of any violation of the rights of literary property, or because a work is improperly attributed to him which will be likely to injure his reputation as an author, or even as a manufacturer of pills. For although his counsel insist that it must necessarily have the effect to injure the sale of his pills, he has not alleged in his bill that he even believes it will have any such effect. And in the absence of such an allegation, I am, as a matter of opinion, inclined to the belief that with that class of persons who would be likely to buy and take his " universal pills," as a general remedy for any and every disease to which the human body is subject, the supposition that he was the author of the publication in question, and was also the extraordinary personage which this table of the contents of the work indicates, would be very likely to induce them to purchase and use his medicine the more readily. As the publication of the work, therefore, which is sought to be restrained, can not be considered as an invasion of the rights either of literary or medical property, although it is unquestionably intended as a gross libel upon the complainant personally, this court has no jurisdiction or authority to interfere for his protection. And if the defendants persist in their intention of giving this libelous production to the public, he must seek his remedy by a civil suit in a court of

law; or by instituting a criminal prosecution, to the end that
the libelers, upon conviction, may receive their appropriate punishment, in the penitentiary or otherwise.

The demurrers must be allowed, and the complainant's bill
dismissed, as to these defendants, with costs.

INJUNCTION AGAINST PUBLICATION OF LETTER: See *Denis* v. *Leclerc*, 5 Am.
Dec. 712, and note. The principle announced by Chancellor Walworth in the
decision above reported, that chancery will not interfere to restrain any publication, except with a view to protecting the complainant's rights of literary
or other property, is approved in *Wetmore* v. *Scovell*, 3 Edw. Ch. 529; *Woolsey*
v. *Judd*, 4 Duer, 597, *per* Bosworth, J., dissenting; and in *New York Juvenile
Guardian Soc.* v. *Roosevelt*, 7 Daly, 189. See also articles in 4 Cent. L. J.
171, and 9 Id. 314.

BELL *v.* LOOKE.

[8 PAIGE'S CHANCERY, 75.]

INJUNCTION AGAINST PUBLISHING A NEWSPAPER OF THE SAME NAME as
complainant's for the fraudulent purpose of deceiving the public and depriving the complainant of the good will of his paper, will lie, but not
where the simulation is not such as is calculated to lead the public to
believe that it is in reality the same paper, so as to injure the circulation
of the complainant's paper.

ORDER to show cause why an injunction should not be granted
restraining the publication of a certain newspaper. The facts
appear from the opinion.

T. W. Tucker, for the complainant.

W. D. Craft, for the defendant.

WALWORTH, Chancellor. The allegation in the complainant's
bill is, that the defendant has assumed the name of the complainant's newspaper, for the fraudulent purpose of imposing
upon the public and supplanting him in the good will of his
established paper by simulating the name and dress thereof;
with the intent to cause it to be understood and believed by the
community that the defendant's newspaper was the same as the
complainant's, and thereby to injure the circulation of the latter.
If this were in fact so, I should have no difficulty in making
this order absolute. For although the business of publishing
newspapers ought, in a free country, to be always open to the
most unlimited competition, fraud and deception certainly are
not essential to the most perfect freedom of the press. There
is indeed no patent right in the names. Yet as the names of
party newspapers, in these days, have no necessary connection

with the principles which they advocate, and are manufactured
as readily as the new names if not the new principles of political parties, there could be very little excuse for the editor of a
new paper who should adopt the precise name and dress of an
old established paper; which would be likely to interfere with
the good will of the latter, by actually deceiving its patrons.
In the case of *Hogg* v. *Kirby*, 2 Ves. 226,[1] Lord Eldon considered the publication by the defendant, of what upon its face
purported to be a continuation of the plaintiff's magazine, to be
such a fraud upon the good will of that periodical work as to
call for the interference of the court of chancery. And in the
more recent case of *Knott* v. *Morgan*, 2 Keen, 213, Lord Langdale granted an injunction to restrain the defendant from running an omnibus, having upon it such names, words, and devices
as to form a colorable imitation of those which had previously
been placed upon the omnibuses of the plaintiff; with the evident intention of obtaining a part of the business of the latter
by deceiving the public. And this decision of the master of the
rolls was subsequently affirmed by Lord Cottenham upon appeal.

The defendant in the present case, however, expressly denies
that the new paper which he edits is published under the name
of New Era with the intention of thereby inducing the public to
suppose it is the same paper as the "Democratic Republican
New Era." Neither do I think that the defendant's paper is
such a simulation of the complainant's present publication as to
injure the circulation and patronage of the latter, by deceiving
the public and inducing a belief that it is in reality the same
paper. It is true, the two words of the title which are in Roman
capitals, are the same in both papers; except that in the defendant's publication they are printed upon a much larger type.
But surely no one can mistake the wide-spread wings and the
warlike attitude of "the bird of Jove," which occupies so large
a space in the heading of the defendant's paper, for the very
modest device which sustains the democratic republicanism of
the complainant's New Era. Besides, the defendant's paper,
upon its face, purports to be a revival of an old publication in
which he was formerly interested with the complainant; which
publication had been voluntarily discontinued by both for more
than eighteen months. The particular name, therefore, which
he has assumed had been so long derelict, except in its subsequent democratic connection, that even an opposition editor
might lawfully have seized upon it, and appropriated it to the

---

1. 8 Ves. 215.

use of his political friends; without any danger of deceiving the public, or drawing off the patronage of those who really wished to read the complainant's daily paper.

In the absence of anything which is really calculated to deceive the intelligent patrons of the complainant's Democratic Republican New Era, the decision of Chancellor Sanford in *Snowden* v. *Noah*, Hopk. 347, is an authority against this application for an injunction, to restrain the defendant from publishing his paper, entitled "New Era, revived by Richard Adams Locke, its original editor." The order to show cause is therefore discharged with costs.

———

INJUNCTION AGAINST PUBLISHING NEWSPAPER OF SIMILAR NAME with complainant's will not lie, when: See *Snowden* v. *Noah*, 14 Am. Dec. 547. The doctrine announced by the chancellor in the foregoing opinion, as to the jurisdiction of chancery to restrain a fraudulent simulation of another's trademark, or the like, has been approved and applied in a great variety of cases; such as assuming the name of the complainant's newspaper: *Matsell* v. *Flanagan*, 2 Abb. Pr. (N. S.) 462; or the name of his hotel, or other business house: *Marsh* v. *Billings*, 7 Cush. 333; *Howe* v. *Searing*, 6 Bosw. 371; S. C., 19 How. Pr. 26, *per* Moncrieff, J., dissenting; or the name of a corporation: *Ex parte Walker*, 1 Coop. Ch. (Tenn.) 100; *Newby* v. *Oregon Central R. R. Co.*, Deady, 616; or imitating a trade-mark: *Taylor* v. *Carpenter*, 2 Woodb. & M. 10; S. C., 11 Paige Ch. 297; *Coffeen* v. *Brunton*, 4 McLean, 519; *Bloss* v. *Bloomer*, 23 Barb. 609; *Corwin* v. *Daly*, 7 Bosw. 225; *Talcot* v. *Moore*, 6 Hun, 108; *Potter* v. *McPherson*, 21 Id. 564, or other like cases; *Tyack* v. *Bromley*, 4 Edw. Ch. 274; S. C., 1 Barb. Ch. 535; *Colton* v. *Thomas*, 2 Brewst. 310; S. C., 7 Phila. 259.

GOOD WILL, jurisdiction of equity over contract relating to: See *Zeigler* v. *Sentzner*, 29 Am. Dec. 534. The principal case is cited, as an authority respecting property in a good will, in *Jerome* v. *Bigelow*, 66 Ill. 455; *Moorehead* v. *Hyde*, 38 Iowa, 385; *Perkins* v. *Currier*, 3 Woodb. & M. 94.

CASES

SUPREME COURT

OF

NORTH CAROLINA.

McMORINE *v.* STOREY, EXECUTOR.

[4 DEVEREUX AND BATTLE'S LAW, 189.]

ADMINISTRATOR OF FRAUDULENT ASSIGNEE is liable as executor *de son tort* to the creditors of a deceased debtor by whom the assignment was made.

GRANT OF LETTERS OF ADMINISTRATION does not confer upon the administrator the right to the possession of property fraudulently assigned to the deceased, as against the creditors of the assignor.

EVIDENCE OF FACTS SWORN TO BY A DECEASED WITNESS in another and different suit is inadmissible.

APPEAL. David Davis made a transfer of all his slaves to his brother Joseph, alleged by the plaintiff to be fraudulent, and afterward died, being indebted to the plaintiff. Joseph died subsequently, while still in possession of the property. The defendant qualified as his administrator. Plaintiff, as a creditor of David Davis, brought this action against Storey, seeking to charge him as executor *de son tort* of David. Plaintiff, in proving the fraudulent transfer, offered a witness to prove what a witness then dead had sworn to upon a trial previously had, in an action brought by the administrator of David Davis, against Joseph, in his life-time, for the recovery of the same property. The evidence was admitted. Verdict and judgment for plaintiff. Defendant appealed.

A. Moore, for the defendant.

Kinney and J. H. Bryan, for the plaintiff.

DANIEL, J. (after stating the facts of the case). The counsel for the defendant admits that if Joseph Davis was alive, and if the present plaintiff (a creditor of David) had sued him, he could have recovered, as Joseph was an executor *de son tort* of David: *Osborne* v. *Moss*, 7 Johns. 161 [5 Am. Dec. 252]. But that as Joseph died in possession of the slaves, Storey intermeddled with them under a color of right as administrator of Joseph. He cited the case of *Turner* v. *Child*, 1 Dev. 25 [17 Am. Dec. 555]; and W. Ex. 140. We think the counsel's references are not in point for him. In the first, Samuel Child was left agent by Francis Child, to sell property at a credit of six months, and collect the proceeds of the sale. He sold, and before the credit was out, his principal died, and he, having possession of the evidences of the debts, proceeded to collect. Two of the judges of this court, against the opinions of the chief justice and the judge who tried the cause in the superior court, were of the opinion that this did not make him an executor *de son tort*. Samuel Child had been rightfully put into the possession of the property, not only as to his principal, but as to all the world. But Storey, *quoad* the claim of the present plaintiff, had no right to intermeddle with the slaves by force of the letters of administration on the estate of Joseph, granted to him. The letters granted by the court, authorized him to administer the goods and chattels that lately belonged to Joseph. As to the creditors of David, these slaves were the assets of David. Storey, not having the possession, nor any legal authority, as to the plaintiff, to take possession by force of his character of administrator of Joseph, is in law a wrong-doer or intermeddler with those assets of David which the law had appropriated to the satisfaction of the plaintiff's debt. In Williams on Executors, it is said, if the person claims a lien on the goods, though he may not be able to make out his title completely, he is not an executor *de son tort*. In the case referred to by Williams, of *Femings* v. *Jarrat*, 1 Esp. N. P. Cas. 335, the person had the possession of the goods at the time of the death of the owner. He retained and intermeddled under a colorable claim of a lien consistent with a general property in the deceased. In the case before us, Storey had not the possession. He illegally took possession of these slaves as the assets of Joseph, when, in law, they were the assets of David Davis, for the benefit of his creditors.

The defendant's counsel again contends, that a *bona fide* assignee of an executor *de son tort*, is never liable to be sued by the creditors of the deceased debtor. For this he cited Godol. Orph. Leg., pt. 2, c. 8, sec. 6; and contended that Storey, being administrator of Joseph, was, in law, the assignee of the

slaves from him, the said Joseph, the first executor *de son tort.*
Without stopping to inquire whether the law be as is stated, we
nevertheless think if the law be so, it has no applicability to
this case. The law never assigns anything to an administrator
but what may be rightfully assigned. The law declares that
these assets in the hands of Joseph, were applicable to the payment of the creditors of David. The death of Joseph could not
have the effect of making them his assets, to the detriment of
the creditors of David. The grant of administration did not
assign these assets to Storey. As to the creditors of David, he,
Storey, took the slaves without any legal assignment. He is
consequently, in our opinion, liable to the plaintiff as executor
de son tort of David. The administrator can not ever be doubly
charged, viz., to the creditors of both the brothers, if he is careful in his pleading.

2. The court admitted the evidence of what a deceased witness had sworn to in another and different suit. This was
erroneous: Stark. on Ev. 43; and for this reason, there must
be a new trial.

By COURT. Judgment reversed.

———

FRAUDULENT DONEE IS LIABLE AS EXECUTOR DE SON TORT to creditors of
his donor, for personal property taken possession of and consumed by him,
since his donor's death: *Tucker* v. *Williams,* 31 Am. Dec. 561. Executrix of
a deceased debtor is not liable to her husband's creditors as executrix *de son
tort,* when it appears that the husband died abroad, and the wife, before
hearing of his death, used the property left by him for the support of his
family and the payment of his debts: *Brown* v. *Benight,* 23 Id. 373, the note
to which contains the cases in this series relative to who is liable as executor
de son tort.

EVIDENCE OF WHAT A DECEASED WITNESS SWORE on a former trial of the
same cause, is admissible: *Watson* v. *Lisbon Bridge,* 31 Am. Dec. 49, in the
note to which the cases in this series, upon this subject, are collected.

———

ANDERS *v.* MEREDITH ET AL.

[4 DEVEREUX AND BATTLE's LAW, 199.]

TENANT IN COMMON CAN NOT MAINTAIN TRESPASS *quare clausum fregit,*
either against his co-tenant, or those who, under the direction or authority of the latter, broke and entered upon the premises.

ORDER DENYING MOTION TO BE ALLOWED TO AMEND a declaration is not
appealable.

TRESPASS *quare clausum fregit.* Pleas, general issue and *lib-
erum tenementum.* The proof showed Meredith to be a tenant

in common with the plaintiff of the premises upon which the
alleged trespass was committed; that he and the other defendants, under his direction, entered upon the land in the absence
of plaintiff, broke open the door of a house, and removed some
articles of personal property. After the evidence had closed,
and the arguments of counsel had commenced, plaintiff moved
to amend the declaration by adding a count for the trespass to
the personal property. Motion denied. The court charged
that if the plaintiff and defendant were tenants in common, the
former could not recover. Verdict and judgment for defendant.
Plaintiff appealed.

Strange, for the plaintiff.

No appearance for the defendant.

DANIEL, J. (after stating the case). We are of the opinion, that
the charge of the judge was correct. The possession of one tenant in common is the possession of the other; each has a right
to enter upon the land and enjoy it jointly with the others. If
one tenant in common destroys houses, trees, or does any act
amounting to waste or destruction in woods or other such property, the other tenant may have an action on the case against
him. But he never can, in any event, have an action of trespass
quare clausum fregit against his co-tenant: Co. Lit. 200; 1 Thom.
Co. Lit. 785; 1 Chit. Gen. Pr. 271. The other defendants were
not trespassers; as they entered and acted by the direction of
Meredith.

The rejection by the court of the plaintiff's motion to amend
the declaration, was a matter in the discretion of the judge; and
it is not a ground of appeal to this court. It may be proper to
remark, that as no objections were taken at the trial to the sufficiency of the pleas, we understand the note of the plea of *lib-
erum tenementum* (afterwards to be drawn out in full) to mean
that the *locus in quo* was the freehold of Meredith, and that
Causey entered with him and under his authority. We think
the judgment must be affirmed.

By COURT.   Judgment affirmed.

TRESPASS QUARE CLAUSUM WILL NOT LIE by a tenant in common of land
against his co-tenant: *Duncan* v. *Sylvester*, 29 Am. Dec. 512; the subject of
trespass by one co-tenant against another is discussed at length in the note to
Porter v. *Hooper*, Id. 480. The principal case is cited in *Bond* v. *Hilton*,
Busb. L. 308, to the effect that case will lie by one co-tenant against another,
where there has been some act resulting in a partial injury to the common
property; but where the injury amounts to a total destruction of it. trover
or trespass may be sustained.

HORAH v. LONG ET AL.

[4 DEVEREUX AND BATTLE'S LAW, 274.]

NEGOTIABLE PROMISSORY NOTE PAYABLE TO A PARTICULAR PERSON as cashier of a bank, vests in the person named, individually, the legal interest in the note so far as to enable him to sue for its collection in his own name.

WORD "CASHIER" IN A NEGOTIABLE PROMISSORY NOTE following the name of the person designated as payee, is merely descriptive.

RECOVERY UPON A NOTE PAYABLE TO "WILLIAM H. HORAH, CASHIER, or order," is not defeated by the expiration of the charter of the bank at which it was negotiable and payable.

SETTING ASIDE A JUDGMENT IS NOT EQUIVALENT TO A DISCONTINUANCE, where, after procuring the judgment to be set aside, the defendant appeared and pleaded to the action, and the cause was then reinstated on the trial docket, and regularly continued until verdict and final judgment were rendered.

DEBT. Action on a promissory note payable to "William H. Horah, cashier, or order," and "negotiable and payable at the branch State Bank at Salisbury." The action was commenced in the county court of Mecklenburg, and at the November term, 1834, the parties and their attorneys appeared in open court, when the following entry was made, viz.: "Judgment." At May term, 1835, the cause was, by order of court, reinstated on the trial docket, and defendants entered their pleas. The cause was tried at a subsequent term and verdict and judgment rendered in favor of plaintiff. The cause was appealed to the superior court, where, after trial, verdict was rendered for plaintiff, and defendant then moved in arrest of judgment upon the following grounds, viz.: 1. Because the charter of the State Bank had expired. 2. Because it appeared on the record certified from the county, to the superior court of Mecklenburg, that there had been a discontinuance of the suit. Motion overruled. Judgment for plaintiff. Defendant appealed.

Boyden and *A. M. Burton*, for the defendants.

D. F. Caldwell, for the plaintiff.

GASTON, J. Neither of the exceptions in arrest of judgment is good. The expiration of the charter of the bank, whereof the plaintiff was cashier at the time of the execution of the note on which he brought this action, is a circumstance which in no way affects his right to recover the debt demanded. It was due to him personally. The word "cashier," was but descriptive of the individual to whom the note was made payable. The legal interest of the debt was in the plaintiff. The action was properly brought by him, and the judgment rendered for him in his natural capacity. Whether he was a trustee for the bank or any other person, is an inquiry with which a court of law has no concern. There has been no discontinuance of the action, whereof the defendants can take advantage. A judgment had been rendered for the plaintiff, which put the defendants out of court. But they came into court, had the judgment set aside, and, at the same term, pleaded over to the action. Subsequently to this voluntary appearance on their part, the cause has been regularly continued in court until the final judgment. But if there had been a discontinuance, it is cured by the verdict under the statute 32 Henry VIII., and our act of amendment: 1 R. S., c. 3, sec. 5. The judgment is affirmed with costs.

By COURT.   Judgment affirmed.

NOTE PAYABLE TO THE CASHIER OF A BANK may be sued upon by the bank as promisee, if the consideration proceeded from the bank: *President of Com. Bank* v. *French*, 32 Am. Dec. 280, and note. In the note to *Arlington* v. *Hinds*, 12 Id. 713, the subject is reviewed at length. The principal case is cited in *White* v. *Griffin*, 2 Jones L. 3, to show that the administrator of a deceased person who was indebted to him on bills of exchange payable to the former as "cashier" of a bank, has a right to retain against creditors of the same class.

LEWIS, ADMINISTRATOR, *v.* MOBLEY.

[4 DEVEREUX AND BATTLE'S LAW, 323.]

LAW PRESUMES, AFTER SEVEN YEARS' CONTINUED ABSENCE, that a person concerning whom nothing has been heard or known during that time, is dead.

ACTION OF TROVER BY A PERSON ENTITLED TO ESTATE IN REMAINDER in a female slave, to recover for a conversion alleged to have occurred during the existence of a precedent life estate, imposes upon the plaintiff the burden of proving the slave to have been alive at the time his estate in remainder vested in possession.

TROVER CAN NOT BE MAINTAINED BY OWNERS OF ESTATE IN REMAINDER, to recover for a conversion occasioned by an absolute sale of the entire estate in the property by a purchaser from a precedent tenant for life, where such sale was made during the continuance of the particular life estate.

TROVER CAN BE SUSTAINED ONLY where the plaintiff's right of immediate possession was complete at the time of the alleged conversion.

TROVER to recover for the conversion of a female slave named Ruth. The evidence showed that Joseph Kemp died in 1805. By his will he bequeathed to his son, William Kemp, the negro

woman, Ruth, during his natural life, and at his death to his
eldest son; if he should have nò such son, then the negro and
her increase to be divided equally between David and John
Kemp, sons of testator. William Kemp, having survived both
David and John, died in 1836 without issue. The plaintiff
Lewis, upon the death of William, took out letters of administration upon the estates of David and John, and brought this
action. On the part of the defendant it was shown that in 1810
he had purchased the negro woman, Ruth, of William Kemp,
and soon after had sold her to another, since which time she had
been neither seen nor heard of. The court charged that if Ruth
died before William, the remainder to David and John never took
effect; that whether Ruth was dead or alive in 1836, when William died, was a question of fact for the jury; that the presumption is, that a person who has been neither seen nor heard of
during seven years, is dead; that there could be no conversion
unless, at the time alleged, the woman was alive; that if the jury
found the negro to have been alive, and the defendant, after
purchasing from William Kemp a life estate merely in the slave,
had sold her out and out, that is, the whole estate, to another,
in that case the facts would amount to a conversion. Verdict
and judgment for defendant. Plaintiff appealed.

Strange, for the plaintiff.

W. H. Haywood, for the defendant.

GASTON, J. Upon examining the instructions which were
given to the jury in this case, we discover no error of which the
plaintiff has cause to complain.

There is an opinion, however, expressed in these instructions,
which we apprehend to be erroneous, and which, had the verdict and judgment been in favor of the plaintiff, might have
justified a reversal of the judgment upon the appeal of the defendant. And we notice this opinion now, because we have
reason to believe from our meeting with it not only here, but in
a case tried before another learned judge, that it is of importance
to check it before it receive a too general acceptance. His
honor was of opinion, and so charged the jury, that if the defendant, having purchased William Kemp's life estate in the
negro woman Ruth, had, in 1810, sold the negro out and out,
and subsequently William Kemp had died, living the said negro, then the persons entitled in remainder might have maintained an action of trover and conversion against the defendant,
because of that conversion. We think they could not. To

maintain this action, it is indispensable that the plaintiff should show a conversion by the defendant of property whereunto the plaintiff, at the time of that conversion, had a present right of possession. It is certain that an action could not have been brought for this alleged conversion, during the life of William Kemp, because the right of possession had not then accrued to the ultimate proprietors: *Gordon* v. *Harper*, 7 T. R. 9; *Andrews* v. *Shaw*, 4 Dev. 70. And it follows as clearly, we think, that it could not lie after the death of William Kemp, when the right of possession accrued, because there was no act of conversion thereafter. Upon the death of William Kemp, the rightful proprietors, being entitled to the possession, might have demanded their property from any person having possession thereof. And a withholding of it then, would have been, on the part of such a person, an act of conversion, for which they might have brought trover. What redress they could have against the tenant for life—who by a previous alienation of the subject-matter of his and their property might have defeated the beneficial enjoyment of their right, when the time for its enjoyment arrived—is a question well worthy of consideration. But trover could not be maintained against him.

The judgment below is affirmed, with costs.

By COURT. Judgment affirmed.

———

TROVER WILL NOT LIE FOR THE CONVERSION OF A REVERSIONARY ESTATE in a chattel prior to the determination of the particular estate: *Steele* v. *Williams*, 31 Am. Dec. 546, in the note to which the cases in this series on this subject are cited.

THE PRESUMPTION AFTER PROOF OF EXISTENCE is, that the person continued to live: *Proctor* v. *McCall*, 23 Am. Dec. 135; *Nidler* v. *Bates*, 8 Id. 651, and note.

THE PRINCIPAL CASE IS CITED to the point that an action of trover will not lie by a remainder-man against one who, having purchased the life estate in a slave, during the continuance of the life estate, removed the latter to parts unknown, in *Cole* v. *Robinson*, 1 Ired. L. 541; also in *Brazier* v. *Ansley*, 11 Ired. 12, to indicate that the right of property and possession in the thing claimed must, at the time of an alleged conversion, have been vested in the plaintiff, to enable him to sustain trover. And in *Haughton* v. *Benbury*, 2 Jones' Eq. 337, to the effect that though the remainder-man is not entitled to a decree for the value of a slave sold and taken out of the state during the continuance of the life estate, nor to the purchase money less the interest during the estate of the tenant for life, still, when a slave is sold with intent to defraud the remainder-man, though the slave dies during the life of the tenant for life, the remainder-man may elect to ratify the sale, and is entitled to a decree for such part of the purchase money, with interest thereon from the day of sale, as his proportionate interest in the slave bears to the value of the whole. Cited also and approved in *Jones* v. *Baird*, 7 Jones, 152.

THROWER, ADMINISTRATOR OF THROWER, v. MC-INTIRE.

[4 DEVEREUX AND BATTLE's LAW, 359.]

ADMINISTRATOR IS NOT ENTITLED TO SUE FOR BREACH OF COVENANT to convey land to a deceased covenantee.

RIGHT OF ACTION UPON A COVENANT TO CONVEY IS IN THE HEIRS of the deceased covenantee.

COVENANT TO CONVEY LAND TO ANOTHER, WITHOUT ANY MENTION OF THE HEIRS of the covenantee, whether considered as a mere personal covenant or not, does not invest the administrator with any right of action for a breach.

COVENANT. McIntire sold certain land to Thrower, and executed the following covenant: "I bind myself to make a deed therefor to Jesse Thrower, when called for." Plaintiff sued as administrator of Jesse Thrower, alleging that after the death of his intestate, he requested defendant to execute a deed for the land in fee to the heirs, which defendant refused. Pleas, covenants performed and not broken. Judgment of nonsuit, from which plaintiff appealed.

Winston, for the plaintiff.

J. H. Haughton, for the defendant.

RUFFIN, C. J. (after stating the case). The opinion delivered by his honor is, we believe, correct. Perhaps in the events which have happened, no action at law by any person will lie; for if the covenant, by its silence as to the heirs, be for a conveyance to the covenantee personally, it is gone by his death. But we do not determine that question, because assuming the construction put on the agreement by the plaintiff to be correct, we are still of opinion against him. The legal effect imputed in the declaration to the instrument is, that the defendant obliged himself to convey to Thrower, or to his heirs, upon their respective request; and no request having been made by Thrower, the plaintiff alleges that the defendant refused to convey to the heirs when requested by them, after the death of the ancestor. It is insisted, on the part of the plaintiff, that the heirs can not have their action, because the covenant being merely an executory agreement, does not run with land and come with it to the heir; and also because the heir is not named in the instrument, and therefore can not take benefit thereby: and it is thence inferred that the present action is sustainable, since it would be unreasonable that there should be no remedy for any person. But it may well be inquired, if this agreement is by construction to be made to be an engagement to convey to the heirs of Thrower, as well as to Thrower himself, upon request, whether the same principle of construction does not make it, by implication, a covenant with the heir as well as with the ancestor; in which case, according to the old authority cited at the bar, F. N. B. 145, and Shep. Touch. 171, the heir, and not the executor, should have the action thereon. Be that, however, as it may, it is to be remembered, that the ground of the damages demanded in this declaration is, that the defendant has not conveyed to the heirs of the plaintiff's intestate. Now, the heir and administrator, as such, are strangers to each other in respect to this question; for what concern is it of the administrator whether the heir get the land or not? After the death of the intestate, the defendant was either not bound to convey to any person, or, if to any person, to the heir. If the latter, and he has failed to do so, who is injured? Clearly, not the administrator; and therefore the administrator can have no action on the covenant. Every plaintiff, in an action on this instrument, whether the heir or the administrator, must show a damage to himself, before he can recover: *Kingdom* v. *Nottle*, 1 Mau. & Sel. 355; *Chamberlain* v. *Williamson*, 2 Id. 408; *Markland* v. *Crump*, 1 Dev. & Bat. 94.

By COURT.   Judgment affirmed.

CONTRACT TO CONVEY LAND vests in the covenantee an equitable interest, and in equity he is regarded as the complete owner, and is entitled to call for a conveyance of the legal title. Upon his death intestate his equitable ownership, if the land be not conveyed, vests in his heirs at law. Nor can any arrangement between his administrator and the covenantor, whereby the bond of the latter, given to secure the conveyance, was redelivered to him upon his paying costs and a sum of money in satisfaction of the contract, defeat the right of the heirs: *Rutherford* v. *Green*, 2 Ired. Eq. 121, citing the principal case. It is cited also in *Mills* v. *Abrams*, 6 Id. 456, to the point that the right of action on a covenant to convey is in the heirs of deceased, and not in his executor.

STATE *v.* HOOVER.

[4 DEVEREUX AND BATTLE's LAW, 365.]

KILLING OF A SLAVE BY HER OWNER IS MURDER, when, from an evident malignant pleasure in inflicting pain, or insensibility to human suffering, barbarous and cruel injuries were inflicted, from which death resulted.

UNMISTAKABLE INTENT TO PRODUCE DEATH IS NOT ESSENTIAL to establish murder.

DEATH RESULTING FROM SEVERE TORTURE, wantonly inflicted with the design of producing grievous suffering, will render the perpetrator answerable as for murder.

INDICTMENT for murder. On the trial it was shown that the prisoner had inflicted upon the deceased, a slave owned by him, the most barbarous, cruel, and malignant injuries, from which death resulted. The defendant offered no testimony. Verdict of conviction. Motion 'or new trial overruled. Judgment rendered and sentence of death pronounced. Defendant appealed.

Daniel, attorney-general, for the state.

No appearance for the defendant.

RUFFIN, C. J. With deep sorrow we have perused the statement of the case as it appeared upon the evidence; and we can not surmise a ground on which the prisoner could expect a *venire de novo.* Indeed, it seems to us, that the case was left hypothetically to the jury, much more favorably for the prisoner than the circumstances authorized. A master may lawfully punish his slave; and the degree must, in general, be left to his own judgment and humanity, and can not be judicially questioned: *State* v. *Mann,* 2 Dev. 263. But the master's authority is not altogether unlimited. He must not kill. There is, at the least, this restriction upon his power: he must stop short of taking life. It has been repeatedly held, that independent of the act of 1791, the killing of a slave may amount to murder; and this rule includes a killing by the master as well as that by a stranger: *State* v. *Will,* 1 Dev. & Bat. 121. It must indeed be true, in the nature of things, that a killing by the owner may be extenuated by many circumstances, from which no palliation could be derived in favor of a stranger. But it is almost self-evident that this prisoner can claim no extenuation of his guilt below the highest grade. It is, perhaps, sufficient merely to declare that to be the opinion of the court, without undertaking the revolting task of collating and minutely commenting on the horrid enormities detailed by the witnesses. But some of the terms used in laying the case before the jury render it our duty, as we think, to notice the circumstances somewhat more particularly.

If death unhappily ensue from the master's chastisement of his slave, inflicted apparently with a good intent, for reformation or example, and with no purpose to take life, or to put it in jeopardy, the law would doubtless tenderly regard every circumstance which, judging from the conduct generally of masters towards slaves, might reasonably be supposed to have hurried the party into excess. But the acts imputed to this unhappy man do not belong to a state of civilization. They are barbarities which could only be prompted by a heart in which every humane feeling had long been stifled; and indeed there can scarcely be a savage of the wilderness so ferocious as not to shudder at the recital of them. Such acts can not be fairly attributed to an intention to correct or to chastise. They can not, therefore, have allowance, as being the exercise of an authority conferred by the law for the purposes of the correction of the slave, or of keeping the slave in due subjection.

The court is at a loss to comprehend how it could have been submitted to the jury that they might find an extenuation from provocation. There is no opening for such an hypothesis. There was no evidence of the supposed acts, which, it was thought, might be provocations. But if they had been proved, this court could not have concurred in the instructions—given, doubtless, from abundant caution and laudable tenderness of life. We could not have concurred, because however flagrant the provocation, the acts of the prisoner were not perpetrated in sudden heat of blood, but must have flowed from a settled and malignant pleasure in inflicting pain, or a settled and malignant insensibility to human suffering. There was none of that brief fury to which the law has regard, as an infirmity of our nature. On the contrary, without any consideration for the sex, health, or strength of the deceased, through a period of four months, including the latter stages of pregnancy, delivery, and recent recovery therefrom, by a series of cruelties and privations in their nature unusual, and in degree excessive beyond the capacity of a stout frame to sustain, the prisoner employed himself from day to day in practicing grievous tortures upon an enfeebled female, which finally wore out the energies of nature and destroyed life. He beat her with clubs, iron chains, and other deadly weapons, time after time; burnt her; inflicted stripes over and often, with scourges, which literally excoriated her whole body; forced her out to work in inclement seasons, without being duly clad; provided for her insufficient food; exacted labor beyond her strength, and wantonly beat her because she could not comply with his requisitions. These enormities, besides others too disgusting to be particularly designated, the prisoner, without his heart once relenting or softening, practiced from the first of December until the latter end of the ensuing March; and he did not relax even up to the last hours of his victim's existence. In such a case, surely, we do not speak of provocation; for nothing could palliate such a course of conduct. Punishment thus immoderate and unreasonable in the measure, the continuance, and the instruments, accompanied by other hard usage and painful privations of food, clothing, and rest, loses all character of correction *in foro domestico*, and denotes plainly that the prisoner must have contemplated the fatal termination, which was the natural consequence of such barbarous cruelties.

In such a case, too, we think it incorrect to say that the jury must be satisfied the prisoner intended to kill the deceased before he could be properly convicted. It is ordinarily true that an actual intent to kill is involved in the idea of murder. But it is not always so. If great bodily harm be intended, and that can be gathered from the nature of the means used or other circumstances, and death ensue, the party will be guilty of murder, although he may not have intended death. The intent, by severe and protracted cruelties and torments, to inflict grievous and dangerous suffering, or, in other words, to do great bodily harm, imports from the means and manner thereof, a disregard of consequences; and consequently the party is justly answerable for all the harm he did, although he did not specially design the whole: 1 Hale P. C. 440; Fost. 219; East P. C. 257.

In conclusion, the court is obliged to say, that whatever error crept into the trial was in favor of the prisoner; and that nothing occurred of which he can complain. It is the opinion of this court that the judgment ought not to be reversed; which will accordingly be certified to the superior court, that further proceedings may be there had for the execution of the sentence of the law on the prisoner.

By COURT. Judgment affirmed.

INTENT TO KILL IS ESSENTIAL TO CONSTITUTE MURDER: *Bower* v. *State,* 32 Am. Dec. 325; *Whiteford* v. *Commonwealth,* 18 Id. 771, in the note to which the subject is reviewed at length.

INTENT TO KILL.—Death of a slave from punishment inflicted by his master in the use of immoderate and unreasonable means, will render the latter guilty of murder. The right of the master to administer reasonable chastisement will not reduce the crime to manslaughter, when death results from acts of excessive and wanton cruelty: *State* v. *Robbins,* 3 Jones' L. 249, citing the principal case. Referred to also in *State* v. *Shirley,* 64 N. C. 610, in support of the proposition that intent to kill, or else to do great bodily harm, is necessarily involved in the idea of murder.

STATE *v.* POOR.

[4 DEVEREUX AND BATTLE'S LAW, 384.]

LEVY OF ATTACHMENT IS INCOMPLETE WITHOUT ACTUAL SEIZURE, or some-other equivalent act of universal notoriety.

LEVY UPON A GROWING CROP IS INSUFFICIENT, unless the officer took open: and notorious possession by entering the premises, and publicly announcing the seizure to answer the writ.

INDICTMENT for assault and battery. In an action before a justice of the peace against a brother of the defendant, an attachment was issued, and delivered to a constable on the twentieth of August, 1838, for service. Without going on or near the land of the defendant in that action, the constable, at twelve o'clock noon of the day on which the writ was issued, returned it with the following indorsement: "Levied on a field of growing corn of Thomas Poor." On the same day, another attachment was issued from the county court of Guilford, where these proceedings occurred, against the same party, and placed in the hands of a deputy sheriff, who, late in the evening, went upon the land, and levied upon the corn there growing. Judgment was entered up later on, in the action first mentioned, in the justice's court, and an order of sale issued, and the corn advertised. In the mean time, the constable, who pretended to hold the corn under the first attachment, authorized the defendant to go upon the land and cut it. While the defendant, under this authority, was proceeding to gather the corn, the deputy sheriff, acting under the attachment from the county court, mentioned above, also came upon the land with a wagon and necessary implements, for the same purpose. The defendant resisted, and assaulted him. The court charged that the levy made by the constable was insufficient, and that the defendant derived no authority from him to resist the deputy sheriff. Verdict of guilty. Judgment thereon, and appeal.

W. A. Graham, for the defendant.

Daniel, attorney-general, for the state.

GASTON, J. We think that it was correctly held by his honor that the constable by indorsing on the writ of attachment in the manner set forth in the case, that he had levied on the growing crop of the defendant in the attachment, did not acquire the legal possession thereof. To the levy of a writ upon personal property—whether a writ of attachment or of execution—the law requires a seizure. If, in the nature of the thing, actual seizure be impossible, then some notorious act as nearly equivalent to actual seizure as practicable, must be substituted for it. The least that can be required in the levy on a growing crop is, that the officer should go to the premises, and there announce that he seizes the same to answer to the exigency of his writ. To allow the possession and property to be transferred without a seizure—or other equivalent act—would be to violate principle and to lead in practice to mischievous results.

This decision must be certified to the superior court of law for the county of Guilford, with directions to proceed to judgment and sentence agreeably thereto, and to the laws of the state.

By COURT.   Judgment to be affirmed.

ACTUAL SEIZURE IS GENERALLY NECESSARY to constitute a valid levy, but the defendant may dispense with it for his own accommodation, and as between him and the officer it will be valid: *Trovillo* v. *Tilford*, 31 Am. Dec. 484, and cases cited in the note.

DEAVER *v.* RICE, ADMINISTRATOR.

[4 DEVEREUX AND BATTLE'S LAW, 431.]

LANDLORD HAS NO LIEN ON A TENANT'S CROP in preference to other creditors, for payment of rent, though the stipulated rent of the premises consisted of a portion of crops raised thereon.

LEASE WITH RENT RESERVED IN KIND confers upon the lessee an estate in possession in severalty, and the entire property in the whole crop raised and growing upon the land during the term is in the lessee.

COVENANT TO GIVE LESSOR A PORTION OF CROPS raised upon land, in return for its use, creates a right resting only in contract, and does not vest the lessor with any title to the crops, as against an attaching creditor of the lessee.

AGREEMENT BETWEEN LESSOR AND LESSEE that the former should take all the corn standing in a particular field for his rent, does not entitle the lessor to the crop, as against a purchaser at an execution sale of the same corn made afterwards upon a judgment against the lessee, under a writ, the teste of which preceded the date of the agreement.

TRESPASS *vi et armis.*   Plaintiff, in 1836, leased to Ruth a lot of land for the term of one year, for which the latter covenanted to give the former one third of the grain, if sowed to grain, or if not, five hundred bushels of corn. The lessee entered and raised a crop. At July term of the same year, judgment was rendered in the county court of Buncombe county against the lessee, and execution issued tested of the same term. Levy thereunder was made, and a field of corn standing on the demised premises sold, in October following, as the property of Ruth, defendant and lessee. In August, prior to the levy and sale, the lessor and lessee had agreed that the former should take the corn standing in this field for his rent. The defendant's intestate, having purchased at the execution sale, entered the field and gathered and carried away the corn. The court charged: 1. That when rent was reserved in kind, or part of a crop, the law gave the landlord a lien upon the crop in preference to all other creditors. 2. That the allotment to plaintiff of the corn in this particular field, if *bona fide*, vested the title in the plaintiff, the lessor, notwithstanding the teste of the execution was before the said agreement. Verdict and judgment for plaintiff. Defendant appealed.

Clingman, for the defendant.

No appearance for the plaintiff.

DANIEL, J. (after stating the case). As to the first branch of the judge's charge, we must confess that we are unacquainted with any law of this state which gives to the landlord a lien on the crop of his tenant, where the rent, instead of money, is agreed by the parties to be paid in kind, or in a part of the crop. The lessor, whether such an agreement is contained in or is out of the lease, stands upon no better footing than the other creditors of the lessee; he has no lien or any other particular privileges that we are aware of. The English law of distress and sale for rent by the landlord has never been in use and practice in this state. Such an agreement is but a chose in action. Secondly, we are of the opinion that Ruth, by virtue of the lease to him, had an estate in possession in severalty during the term, and the plaintiff had the reversion. The crop growing or standing on the land was entirely the lessee's property at the teste of the execution. This case is not like that of the *State* v. *Jones*, 2 Dev. & Bat. 360.[1] In that case, the owner of the land had never made a lease, and the entire property in the staves was in the owner of the land on which grew the timber, out of which the staves were made. Here, there was a lease, and the term and the entire crop on the land was in the lessee. The plaintiff's claim, either for the one third of the grain which should be made on the land, or the corn standing in the particular field, rested only in agreement or contract. There being no partition or separation of any portion to the plaintiff out of the general mass of the crop before the teste of

---

1. 2 Dev. & Bat. 544.

the execution, the whole crop belonged in law to the lessee at that period, and the execution bound the property in the hands of Ruth, and all others claiming under him, from the teste. *Den on dem. of Stamps* v. *Irwin*,[1] 2 Hawks, 232; *Gilky* v. *Dickerson*, Id. 341; *Bickerdike* v. *Arnold*,[2] 3 Id. 296. The plaintiff claims under Ruth, by an agreement made after the teste of the execution. . The plaintiff, although the landlord, was bound by the execution against his tenant.

We are of the opinion that the judge erred in his charge to the jury on both points raised in the cause. The judgment must be set aside and a new trial granted.

By COURT. Judgment reversed.

———

GROWING CROPS UPON LAND LEASED WITH STIPULATION to pay rent out of grain raised, accompany the reversion upon a sale of the land by the lessor: *Johnson* v. *Smith*, 24 Am. Dec. 339, and note citing cases in this series.

THE PRINCIPAL CASE IS CITED in *Rose* v. *Swaringer*, 9 Ired. 481, as decisive of the question that where a lease, either by parol or in writing, is executed with rent reserved to be paid in a part of the crop, the lessor has no lien on the crop, but the whole belongs to the lessee, until the portion to which the lessor is entitled has been separated and set aside. Cited to the same effect in *Harrison* v. *Ricks*, 71 N. C. 7; *Haywood* v. *Rogers*, 73 Id. 320; *Gordon* v. *Armstrong*, 5 Ired. 409. Rent reserved on a lease for years, but not due at the time, passes with the reversion to the purchaser of the lessor's interest at an execution sale, and can not be afterwards subjected to the payment of the debts of the lessor: *Kornegay* v. *Collier*, 65 N. C. 69, citing principal case. In *Biggs* v. *Ferrell*, 12 Ired. 1, the principal case is cited to show that where the owner of land to which a ferry is annexed as a franchise, leases the land together with the ferry, he is not responsible for any damage sustained by a third person from mismanagement of the ferry, while in possession of the lessee. The general doctrine of the principal case is further approved, not citing it, however, in the following cases. The interest of the lessor in the crop is not liable to levy under an execution against him before separation: *Walston* v. *Bryan*, 64 N. C. 764. Lessee who rents land on shares to farm, the lessor furnishing a horse, is a tenant for years, and not a "cropper," and may maintain trespass *quare clausum* against his landlord: *Hatchell* v. *Kimbrough*, 4 Jones' L. 163. Shortly after the decision in *Deaver* v. *Rice*, the legislature changed the rule declared in that case, by giving to the lessor, when the rent was to be paid in a portion of the crop, a lien thereon as against other creditors of the lessee: Act of 1840, c. 37.

———

HAFNER v. IRWIN ET AL.

[4 DEVEREUX AND BATTLE'S LAW, 433.]

HABENDUM OF A DEED IS VOID IF REPUGNANT TO THE ESTATE granted in the premises.

ESTATE CONVEYED IN THE PREMISES OF A DEED is not divested by the fact that another and different grantee is named in the *habendum*.

———

1. *Stamps* v. *Irvine*.   2. *Beckerditte* v. *Arnold*.

TROVER. A deed of trust in due form was produced on the trial, containing clauses as follows: "Know all men that I, Thomas Dwight, have granted, bargained, sold, and conveyed to the said Alfred Hafner, his heirs, executors, etc., the following property:" description. The deed then continued: "To have and to hold unto the said M. W. Curry, his heirs and assigns, for ever, in trust and confidence, for the purpose now mentioned." Signed and sealed by Dwight and plaintiff Hafner. Plaintiff charged a conversion by defendant of the property described. The court being of the opinion that plaintiff could not, under this deed, sustain an action in his own name, entered a nonsuit, from which plaintiff appealed.

Barringer, Boyden, and Hoke, for the plaintiff.

No counsel appeared for the defendant.

DANIEL, J. The authorities cited by the plaintiff's counsel show clearly that the judge erred, when he decided the plaintiff could not sustain an action of trover in his own name, to recover the value of the articles mentioned in the deed, if they were converted by the defendants. Dwight, in the premises of the deed, bargained and sold the property to the plaintiff, his heirs, executors, etc. However, in the same deed, the *habendum* is to M. W. Curry, his heirs and assigns in trust, etc. All the parts of a deed which precede the *habendum*, taken together, are called the premises; of which it is said, the office is rightly to name the grantor and grantee, and to comprehend the certainty of the thing granted. But though the grantee should first be named in the *habendum*, the grant to him will yet be good, provided there was not another grantee named in the premises: Co. Lit. 26, b, note; or if there were, provided the estate given by the *habendum* to the new grantee was not immediate, but by way of remainder. The *habendum* part of a deed was originally used to determine the interest granted, or to lessen, enlarge, explain, or qualify the premises. But it can not perform the office of divesting an estate already vested by the deed; for it is void if it be repugnant to the estate granted in the premises: 2 Bl. Com. 298; *Goodtitle* v. *Gibbs*, 5 Barn. &. Cress. 709; 4 Kent's Com. 468. Chancellor Kent remarks, that in modern conveyancing the *habendum* clause in deeds has degenerated into a mere useless form; for the premises contain the names of the parties and the specifiation of the thing granted, and the deed becomes effectual without any *habendum*. In the case before us, the whole interest in the property is granted and conveyed to the plaintiff

in the premises of the deed. The same interest being afterwards
limited in the *habendum* to Curry, makes that part of the deed
repugnant to the premises, and therefore void. The judgment
of nonsuit must be set aside, and a new trial granted.

By COURT. Judgment reversed.

———

THE PRINCIPAL CASE IS CITED in *Midgett* v. *Brooks*, 12 Ired. 145, to show that
no precise or technical form of language or arrangement is necessary to give
a deed validity. Any words which amount to or import an agreement, being
under seal, are sufficient to constitute a covenant.

———

JONES *v.* JUDKINS.

[4 DEVEREUX AND BATTLE'S LAW, 454.]

TITLE OF PURCHASER AT EXECUTION SALE UNDER A JUNIOR EXECUTION
is not affected by a subsequent levy under another execution against the
same defendant, bearing a prior teste, where there were two executions
issued from different courts upon the same day, one of which was tested
before the other.

TRUTH OF FACTS CERTIFIED IN A RECORD can not be collaterally impeached
by evidence *aliunde*.

TROVER for a horse. Plaintiff, as sheriff, claimed title by
virtue of a levy under three *fi. fa.'s*, issued and directed to him
on the twenty-third of January, 1839, against Thomas Christmas,
who owned the horse at that time. The writs were tested as of
the November term, 1838, returnable the following February.
Plaintiff showed the writs to have been levied on the property
of Christmas, including the horse, on the twenty-third or
twenty-fourth of January. The defendant, Judkins, claimed
title to the horse as purchaser at a constable's sale, and offered
in evidence a judgment and execution against Christmas, issued
by a justice of the peace, on the twenty-third of January, 1839,
and indorsed as levied on the same day. The sale and purchase
were also proved. The plaintiff offered to prove that the constable's indorsement on the writ was false; that he was a person
of bad character, whose veracity was not to be trusted, and that
the warrant on which the justice's judgment was rendered never
was served, nor did Christmas have notice of it. The offer was
denied. Verdict and judgment for defendant. Plaintiff appealed.

No counsel appeared for the plaintiff.

Battle, for the defendant.

DANIEL, J. At common law, the goods of the party against

whom a writ of *fieri facias* issued, were bound from the teste of the writ: by which is meant that the writ bound the property as against the party himself, and all claiming by assignment from, or by representation under, him; so that a sale by a defendant of his goods *bona fide*, excepting in market overt, did not protect them from a *fieri facias* tested before, although not issued or delivered to the sheriff until after the sale: *Payne* v. *Drewe*, 4 East, 523; Cro. Eliz. 174;[1] Cro. Jac. 451;[2] 1 Sid. 271. Subject to the foregoing restrictions, the property of the goods is not altered, but continues in the defendant till the execution is executed: *Lowthel* v. *Tomkins*, 2 Eq. Cas. Abr. 381; *Payne* v. *Drewe*, 4 East, 540. If, therefore, the property is levied on and sold under a junior execution, the vendee gets a good title; and the party having the first execution, can not seize them by virtue of his writ first tested: *Smallcomb* v. *Buckingham*, 1 Ld. Raym. 252; 1 Salk. 320;[3] Comyns, 35;[4] if he could, no person would bid at sheriffs' sales. The party who has the execution of the first teste, may have his remedy against the sheriff, whose duty it was to execute that writ first, which was first tested. If the sheriff has only levied under the younger execution, and before the sale an elder execution in point of teste comes to his hands, he may, and ought, to apply the property to the satisfaction of the execution bearing the first teste: *Green* v. *Johnson*, 2 Hawks, 309 [11 Am. Dec. 763]; *Jones* v. *Atherton*, 7 Taunt. 56. The above remarks apply to the case where several executions of different dates come to the hands of one officer. But when several executions, issuing from different competent courts, are in the hands of different officers (as in the case before us), then, to prevent conflicts, if the officer holding the junior execution seizes property by virtue of it, the property so seized is not subject to the execution in the hands of the other officer, although first tested. Lord Ellenborough, in delivering the opinion of the court in *Payne* v. *Drewe*, held that where there are several authorities equally competent to bind the goods of a party, when executed by the proper officer, that they shall be considered as effectually and for all purposes bound by the authority which first actually attaches upon them in point of execution, and under which an execution shall be first executed. We think that a levy attaches upon the goods in point of execution. The jury, under the charge of the court upon that point, found that the constable made the first levy. We are of the opinion that the sale by him gave the purchaser a good title.

---

1. *Anonymous.*   2. *Baskervile* v. *Brocket.*   3. Same case.   4. Same case.

When we say that the property of the goods, notwithstanding the teste of the execution, is not altered, but remains in the defendant until the execution executed, we are not to be understood as saying that the sheriff, after he has made a levy, has not such a special property in the goods as will enable him to maintain trespass or trover against any person who may take them out of his possession: for he may, as he is answerable to the plaintiff to the value of the goods: *Wilbraham* v. *Snow*, 2 Saund. 47; Watson on Sheriffs, 191.

We are of the opinion that the judgment on the warrant against Christmas, could not be collaterally impeached by evidence that the constable was a man of general bad character, or any other parol evidence. It is a judicial proceeding which is conclusive, unless upon some other proceeding directly to avoid it.

By COURT.   Judgment affirmed.

WRITS OF FIERI FACIAS ISSUED FROM DIFFERENT COURTS, bearing teste from the terms at which they were issued, and levied upon personal property, are entitled to be satisfied in the order of the priority of the judgments on which they were issued: *Johnson* v. *Ball*, 24 Am. Dec. 451, the note to which contains the cases in this series upon this subject.

Cited in *Alexander* v. *Springs*, 5 Ired. 475, to the effect, that where a *bona fide* conveyance of property to the plaintiff was made subject to the lien of a *fieri facias*, and after the transfer the defendant caused executions to be levied on the property from a justice's court, and the property was then sold by the sheriff and the constable jointly, the plaintiff is entitled to recover of the defendant the excess of purchase money received from the sale beyond what was sufficient to satisfy the *fieri facias*. Also in *Dobson* v. *Prather*, 6 Ired. Eq. 31, in support of the principle, that a purchaser under a junior execution, first levied, does not hold the property subject to the lien of an elder execution, whether he had notice of its existence or not. To the same point in *Watt* v. *Johnson*, 4 Jones' L. 190; *McDaniel* v. *Nethercut*, 8 Id. 97; *Phillips* v. *Johnston*, 77 N. C. 127; a purchaser at a sale under a junior execution acquires a good title as against a subsequent purchaser under a senior execution; *a fortiori*, is this rule true, as against a purchaser under an execution of equal teste: *Isler* v. *Moore*, 67 Id. 74; the provisions of the homestead and personal property exemption laws apply, so as to prevent the seizure and sale of the property of the debtor which had become subject to the lien of an execution, tested, but not levied, before the law was passed: *Horton* v. *McCall*, 66 Id. 159; the proceedings had on the return of a levy on land, including the rendition of judgment and issuance of execution, are judicial, and are conclusive until reversed: *Burke* v. *Elliot*, 4 Ired. 355, all citing the principal case upon the points decided.

TYLER *v.* MORRIS.

[4 DEVEREUX AND BATTLE's LAW, 487.]

WRIT OF ERROR CORAM NOBIS is not a writ of right, and can be granted only upon affidavit showing some error of fact.

FACT ASSIGNED AS ERROR in an application for a writ *coram nobis*, is not to be definitively decided by the court in granting the writ, but if the writ be granted, the other party being properly brought in, may plead, and the issue taken upon the fact assigned is to be tried by a jury and not by the court.

WRIT OF ERROR CORAM NOBIS is not *per se* a *supersedeas*.

REFUSAL OF LOWER COURT TO GRANT A WRIT CORAM NOBIS can not be revised on appeal.

APPEAL. Motion for a writ of error *coram nobis* was made in the superior court by the defendant, to reverse a judgment therein rendered against him in favor of the plaintiff for error in fact. The motion was made upon affidavits setting forth that the plaintiff Tyler was dead at the time the judgment was rendered. Motion also for a *supersedeas*. Counsel for plaintiff appeared and resisted the motion, denying that Tyler was dead. Motion denied. Defendant appealed.

No counsel appeared for the defendant.

Badger, for the plaintiff.

DANIEL, J. (after stating the case). A writ of error *coram nobis*, is not a writ of right. Before it is allowed, there must be an affidavit of some error in fact; by which, in case the fact to be assigned for error is true, the plaintiff's right of action will be destroyed: *Birch* v. *Triste*, 8 East, 415. The court in this case, was of the opinion that the affidavits did not lay a sufficient foundation to authorize it to grant the writ. This opinion of the court was one of discretion, upon the facts disclosed in the affidavits. As the affidavits did disclose probable grounds that Tyler was dead at the time the judgment was rendered, we think that the court might have allowed the writ of error, although it refused the *supersedeas*. For the question, whether Tyler was dead or not, at the time of the rendition of the judgment, was not one for the court to decide definitively. If the writ had been granted, upon the error assigned, the administrator of Tyler, when properly brought in, might have pleaded that Tyler was alive at the rendition of the judgment, and so have taken issue upon the fact assigned for error. This issue must have been tried by a jury, and not by the court: 1 Archb. Pr. K. B. 276–281. A writ of error *coram nobis*, is not a *supersedeas* in itself, it is or is not according to circumstances; and therefore execution can not be sued out after the allowance of the writ of error, without the leave of the court: 1 Archb. Pr. 277. And whether a *supersedeas* shall issue after the allowance of a writ of error, for error in fact, must depend on circumstances, to be adjudged of by the court. In this case, the refusal of the superior court to grant the writ, was founded in discretion arising upon the facts set forth in the affidavits. It has been repeatedly decided, that the supreme court has not power to revise such a decision. The appeal therefore, must, on this ground, be dismissed.

By COURT. Appeal dismissed.

WRIT OF ERROR CORAM NOBIS IS THE PROPER REMEDY to enable a party against whom a judgment has been taken on motion and without notice, to be relieved in the same court by showing error of fact: *Wynne* v. *Governor*, 24 Am. Dec. 448, and citations in the note thereto.

STATE *v.* HILL.

[4 DEVEREUX AND BATTLE'S LAW, 491.]

UNLAWFUL KILLING BY ONE WHO HAD ASSAULTED ANOTHER IS MURDER, where the intent to kill preceded the assault, although, from the violence with which the deceased retaliated, the act of killing by the prisoner became necessary, in order to save his own life.

RESISTANCE TO AN ASSAULT, if the latter be not commenced with intent to commit murder, where such resistance is entirely disproportionate to the violence of the original attack, essentially changes the character of the combat, and renders the assaulted party the assailant.

KILLING WITHOUT MALICE, RESULTING FROM THE TRANSPORT OF RAGE excited by the unusual violence with which the deceased returned a simple assault by the prisoner, is manslaughter.

DISTINCTION BETWEEN MURDER AND MANSLAUGHTER, in a case where the slayer originated the affray, but with no intent to kill, is based, not upon the inquiry whether the perpetrator at the moment of the fatal blow was possessed of sufficient deliberation and reflection so as to be conscious of the character of the act, but whether sufficient time had elapsed, after the deceased had commenced violently to retaliate by employing a dangerous and deadly weapon, and before the infliction of the death-blow by the prisoner, for the heat of passion thus excited to subside.

GENERAL RULE OF LAW THAT WORDS OF REPROACH and contempt are not sufficient provocation to free a party killing from the guilt of murder, does not obtain where, because of such insufficient provocation, the parties became suddenly heated, and engage in mortal combat, fighting upon equal terms.

INDICTMENT for murder. The prisoner and the deceased had long been on bad terms. Upon the day of the killing, the deceased was passing the prisoner, when the latter caught hold of him and stopped him, saying: "Let us talk it over." Deceased made no reply; upon which the prisoner struck him. Deceased then drew a knife and began stabbing the prisoner. The prisoner, eluding at last the grasp of deceased, drew a knife, and advancing several steps, delivered the fatal blow. The court charged the jury upon this evidence: 1. If the prisoner sought the provocation, by giving the first blow, in order to afford him a pretense for wreaking his vengeance, or with the design of using his knife, it is murder. 2. If the prisoner gave the first blow, and was then cut by deceased, although he may have been agitated by resentment and anger, yet if the jury collect from what he said and did, that at the time of giving the mortal wound he was possessed of deliberation and reflection, so as to be sensible of what he was about to do, and did the act intentionally, it is murder. If the jury did not find according to the above propositions, but found that the defendant acted under the influence of passion, excited by the provocation then received, it would be manslaughter. Verdict of guilty, and judgment, and sentence of death. Defendant appealed.

C. Manly, for the prisoner.

Daniel, attorney-general, for the state.

GASTON, J. From the case which has been stated by the judge who presided at the trial, and which constitutes a part of the record before us, it appears that it was not controverted but that the prisoner had committed the homicide wherewith he was charged, and that the only question was as to the degree of guilt which the law attached to the fatal deed. Upon this question the jury doubted, and asked for specific instructions; and it was to enable them to come to a correct conclusion upon this question that the specific instructions set forth in the case were given. It is not for us to determine whether the verdict was warranted by the evidence, but it is our duty to examine whether the law was correctly expounded. In the investigation of this question it was necessary that the jury should, in the first place, ascertain whether the prisoner commenced the affray with a preconceived purpose to kill the deceased, or to do him great bodily harm. For if he did, then there was nothing in the subsequent occurrences of the transaction which could free him from the guilt of murder. If the first assault was made with this purpose, the malice of that assault, notwithstanding the violence with which it was returned by the deceased, communicates its character to the last act of the prisoner. It is laid down as settled law that if a man assault another with malice prepense, even though he should be driven to the wall, and kill him there to save his own life, he is yet guilty of murder in respect of his first intent: Hawk., b. 1, c. 11, sec. 18, and c. 13, sec. 26. Of that part, therefore, of his honor's instructions which in the case is called "the first proposition," and which declared as a conclusion of law, that the prisoner was guilty of murder if the jury were satisfied from the evidence that the assault was made by him in order to have a pretense to kill the deceased, or to cut him with the knife, the prisoner has no cause to complain. Such craft, indeed, would but the more strongly indicate the heart fatally bent on mischief.

There was certainly evidence well deserving to be weighed by the jury in coming to a correct conclusion upon this inquiry. But what was that conclusion we have not the means of knowing. They might have believed, notwithstanding the testimony as to antecedent quarrels and the rencounter between the parties, and in relation to threats of vengeance by the prisoner, that the transaction which they were then examining sprang from the passions of the moment. For certainly where two persons have formerly fought on malice and are apparently reconciled, and fight again on a fresh quarrel, it shall not be intended that they were moved by the old grudge, unless it so appear from the circumstances of the affair: Hawk., b. 1, c. 13, sec. 30. If, upon consideration of all the evidence, the jury came to the conclusion that the first assault of the prisoner was not of malice prepense, then the subsequent occurrences demanded their careful consideration, because upon these the prisoner's guilt might be extenuated into manslaughter, or excused as a homicide in self-defense.

So much of the instructions given, upon this view of the case, as relates to excusable homicide, is, in our opinion, not liable to exception. Even if the prisoner had not begun the affray, but had been assaulted in the first instance, and then a combat had ensued, he could not excuse himself as for a killing in self-defense, unless he had quitted the combat before a mortal blow was given, if the fierceness of his adversary permitted, and retreated as far as he might with safety, and had then killed his adversary of necessity to save his own life. But the remaining part of the instructions, and that part which may have had a decisive influence upon the verdict, is, in our judgment, erroneous. According to this, which is laid down as "the second proposition," the jury were instructed, " that if the prisoner gave the first blow, and was then cut by the deceased, although he might have been agitated by excitement and anger, yet if they collected from what he said and did, when or just before he gave the mortal blow, that in fact he was possessed of deliberation and reflection, so as to be sensible of what he was then about to do, and did the act intentionally, it was murder." This proposition, as we understand it, and as we must believe it to have been understood by the jury, we are very confident can not be sustained.

The proposition supposes that the first assault was made by the prisoner without malice, and that the fatal wound was given while under the influence of indignation and resentment, excited by the excessive violence with which he had been in turn assailed by the deceased—but it refuses to the prisoner the indulgence which the law accords to human infirmity suddenly provoked into passion, if such passion left to him so much of deliberation and reflection as to enable him to know that he was about to take, and to intend to take, the life of his adversary. No doubt can be entertained, and it is manifest that none was entertained by his honor, but that the excessive violence of the deceased, immediately following upon the first assault, constituted what the law deems a provocation sufficient to excite furious passion in men of ordinary tempers. The case does not state that the first blow given by the prisoner was such as to endanger life or to threaten great bodily harm, nor that it was immediately followed up by further efforts or attempts to injure the deceased. It must be taken to have been a battery of no very grievous kind, and it justified the deceased in resorting to so much force on his part as was reasonably required for his defense—and in estimating the quantum of force which might be rightfully thus used the law will not be scrupulously exact. But when an assault is returned with a violence manifestly disproportionate to that of the assault, the character of the combat is essentially changed, and the assaulted becomes in his turn the assailant.

Such, according to the case, was the state of this affray, when the mortal wound was given. To avenge a blow, the deceased attacked the prisoner with a knife—made three cuts at him—and gave him a severe wound in the abdomen. If instantly thereupon, in the transport of passion thus excited, and without previous malice, the prisoner killed the deceased, it would have been a clear case of manslaughter. Not because the law supposes that this passion made him unconscious of what he was about to do, and stripped the act of killing of an intent to commit it—but because it presumes that passion disturbed the sway of reason, and made him regardless of her admonitions. It does not look upon him as temporarily deprived of intellect, and therefore not an accountable agent; but as one in whom the exercise of judgment is impeded by the violence of excitement, and accountable therefore as an infirm human being. We nowhere find that the passion which in law rebuts the imputation of malice, must be so overpowering as for the time to shut out knowledge and destroy volition. All the writers concur in representing this indulgence of the law to be a condecension to the frailty of the human frame, which, during the *furor brevis*, renders a man deaf to the voice of reason, so that although the act done was intentional of death, it was not the result of malignity of heart, but imputable to human infirmity.

The proper inquiry to have been submitted to the jury on this part of the case was, whether a sufficient time had elapsed after the prisoner was stabbed, and before he gave the mortal wound, for passion to subside and reason reassume her dominion—for it is only during the temporary dethronement of reason by passion, that this allowance is made for man's frailty. And in prosecuting this inquiry, every part of the conduct of the prisoner, as well words as acts tending to show deliberation and coolness on the one side, or continued anger and resentment on the other, was fit to be considered, in order to conduct the jury to a proper result.

The attorney-general, in his argument, referred to a class of cases which probably misled the judge in laying down the proposition before us—in which circumstances apparently unimportant, but indicative of deliberation, have been thought to establish malice and repel the plea of human infirmity. The explanation given by the text-writers will show that the doctrine in these cases, although in some respects analogous to that which obtains in a killing upon legal provocation, is not identical with it. The general rule of law is, that words of reproach or contemptuous gestures, or the like offenses against decorum, are not a sufficient provocation to free the party killing from the guilt of murder, where he useth a deadly weapon, or manifests an intention to do great bodily harm. This rule, however, does not obtain where because of such insufficient provocation, the parties become suddenly heated, and engage immediately in mortal combat, fighting upon equal terms. But deliberate dueling, if death ensue, however fairly the combat may be conducted, is, in the eye of the law, murder. The punctilios of false honor, the law regards as furnishing no excuse for homicide. He who deliberately seeketh the blood of another, in compliance with such punctilios, acts in open defiance of the laws of God and of the state, and with that wicked purpose which is termed malice aforethought. While, therefore, because of presumed heat of blood, the law extenuates into manslaughter a killing upon such sudden rencounter, although proceeding upon an insufficient provocation, it withholds this indulgence when, from the circumstances of the case, it can be collected that, not heated blood but a settled purpose to vindicate offended honor, even unto slaying in defiance of law, was the actual motive which urged on to the combat.

In the conclusion of his instructions, the judge informed the jury "that if they should believe according to the second proposition, that the prisoner was not possessed of deliberation and reflection at the time he gave the mortal blow, but acted under the influence of passion excited by the provocation then received, it would be a case of manslaughter." It is manifest that if there was error in the proposition which we have been examining, this general instruction did not correct it; for the jury were expressly referred to that proposition for the legal meaning of "deliberation and reflection;" and according to that proposition, there was deliberation and reflection, "if the prisoner was sensible of what he was about to do, and did the act intentionally."

Entertaining a full conviction that in this the jury were misdirected, we are of opinion that the verdict below ought to be set aside, and a *venire de novo* awarded. This decision must be certified to the superior court of Wake, with directions to proceed agreeably thereto and to the laws of the state.

By COURT.   Judgment to be reversed.

To CONSTITUTE MURDER IN THE FIRST DEGREE, the killing must have been done with intent to kill, and that intent must have been formed prior to the commission of the deed: *Bower* v. *State*, 32 Am. Dec. 325. Grievous injuries inflicted with the design of producing bodily suffering and torture, will, if death result, be sufficient to constitute murder: *State* v. *Hoover, ante*, 383.

MANSLAUGHTER AND MURDER, DISTINCTION: *State* v. *Ferguson*, 27 Am. Dec. 412; *Grainger* v. *State*, 26 Id. 278, and note to the last case, in which the subject of homicide in self-defense is discussed.

Cited in *State* v. *Carter*, 76 N. C. 20, to show that words, however grievous, are not sufficient provocation to reduce the crime of murder to manslaughter; also in *State* v. *Gentry*, 2 Jones' L. 406, to the point that a killing in a quarrel resulting from the heat of passion excited by a violent assault, is manslaughter and not murder.

MUNNERLIN *v.* BIRMINGHAM.

[2 DEVEREUX AND BATTLE'S EQUITY, 358.]

AGREEMENT FOR RESALE OF PROPERTY TO VENDOR does not constitute a mortgage, in the absence of any evidence to that effect.

FAILURE TO COMPLY WITH THE CONDITIONS OF AN AGREEMENT TO RESELL, within the time stipulated, will deprive the vendor of the benefits resulting from the agreement, and render the sale absolute and indefeasible.

BILL in equity filed in 1835, alleging that in December, 1822, plaintiff borrowed four hundred dollars of defendant, and to secure its repayment, executed a bill of sale of a female slave, and at the same time took from the defendant, on a separate paper, the following instrument: "On condition, at January, 1823, that Mr. Joseph Munnerlin does come forward and tender unto me, Charles Birmingham, four hundred dollars, lawful money of the state, I will give him a negro girl by the name of Tener, seventeen years old. If failing to comply on that day, this shall no longer stand good against me. December 12, 1822. Charles Birmingham." Plaintiff insisted that the above instrument constituted a mortgage, and prayed to be permitted to redeem.

Winston, for the plaintiff.

Mendenhall, for the defendant.

DANIEL, J. (after stating the case). The proof is satisfactory to us, that the defendant did execute the instrument of writing mentioned in the bill. But taking the bill of sale and the said instrument together, and all the circumstances which surround the case, and we are of the opinion that they do not constitute a mortgage. It seems to us, that the instrument executed by the defendant is but an agreement for a resale of the slave Tener for the sum of four hundred dollars, if the plaintiff tendered that sum by the month of January, 1823. There is nothing mentioned of a mortgage or money borrowed, in either the bill of sale or the paper writing. There is no proof that the girl was worth more than the money advanced by the defendant. There is no covenant in the instruments, or out of them, for the repayment of the money to the defendant, in case of the death of the slave, or any repayment; and there is no evidence that a loan was ever talked of or contemplated between the parties. The slave was immediately delivered to the defendant on the advancement of the money. And it was a long time (upwards of twelve years) which had elapsed without any mention by the plaintiff, until about two years before he filed his bill, that he had any claim to the slave, as mortgagor, or in any other way. We are induced to think, from the whole case, that the plaintiff never considered the transaction a mortgage, but only as an agreement for a resale, which he had lost the benefit of by not complying with the terms of it in time: *Vide Poindexter* v. *McCannon and Hauser*, 1 Dev. Eq. 373 [18 Am. Dec. 591]. We are of the opinion that the bill must be dismissed.

By COURT. Bill dismissed.

———

WHETHER AN INSTRUMENT IS A MORTGAGE OR A CONDITIONAL SALE depends upon the intention of the parties: *Hickman* v. *Cantrell*, 30 Am. Dec. 396, and note; *Stratton* v. *Sabin*, *post*. The principal case is mentioned with approval in *McLaurin* v. *Wright*, 2 Ired. Eq. 94, for the purpose of sustaining the general principle decided in the latter case, as follows: Notwithstanding an instrument is absolute in form, facts and circumstances *dehors* may be received to establish its character as a security merely. Among these circumstances, inadequacy of price is an important one. Gross inadequacy of price is a strong indication that a security only was intended. On the contrary, a fair price, and possession simultaneously taken and kept, and no covenant to repay the money advanced, will not authorize a court of equity to declare a deed absolute on its face to be only a mortgage, in the absence of other sufficient evidence.

———

JOHN HOUGH *v.* CHARLOTTE D. MARTIN.

[2 DEVEREUX AND BATTLE'S EQUITY, 379.]

EQUITY JURISDICTION DOES NOT EMBRACE the construction of devises of legal interests in land.

VAGUENESS AND OBSCURITY OF A WILL furnish no ground for an application to equity: for if not absolutely unintelligible, it will be valid at law as far as understood; and if it is so far devoid of meaning as not to amount to a designation of any *corpus*, it follows that there is no need of relief, for the devise is ineffectual.

BILL FOR ASCERTAINING CONFUSED BOUNDARIES will be entertained only when the boundaries, being at one time certain, were rendered otherwise by the default of the defendant, or those under whom he claims.

EQUITY JURISDICTION FOR ASCERTAINMENT OF CONFUSED BOUNDARIES is exercised only where there has been some agreement that the land of the several parties should be distinguished, or where, on account of a particular relation, a duty to preserve the landmarks is imposed upon one of them, by the fraud or neglect of whom the boundaries have become confused.

BETWEEN INDEPENDENT PROPRIETORS EQUITY WILL NOT INTERPOSE to decree a settlement of their boundaries, in the absence of fraud or neglect, or of express agreement.

BILL FOR AN INJUNCTION TO STAY WASTE, which fails to show the complainant to have a good and sufficient title to the particular land in which the waste is apprehended, is radically defective.

BILL FOR DISCOVERY OF DEEDS, which does not allege that the particular deeds claimed by complainant, and which are material to him in a pending action, are in the custody or under the control of defendants, is defective, and can not be maintained.

BILL in equity, alleging that plaintiff's brother died in 1821, leaving a will, by which, after sundry bequests to one James Martin and others, testator directed that all the remaining part of his land not·given away, should become the property of plaintiff; that the description of the lands devised to Martin and the others was so obscure, that plaintiff was unable to fix upon the residue, which, under said will, belonged to him; that Martin, taking advantage of this difficulty, had taken possession of a portion of the land, which plaintiff believed was not devised to him, nor otherwise disposed of by the will, and therefore belonged to plaintiff under ·the residuary clause; that plaintiff had previously brought an action of ejectment against said Martin, but had failed, by reason of his inability to locate his claim under the will; that Martin had since died, leaving a will, wherein he devised to Charlotte D. Martin, his wife, and their children, all of his interest in said lands, and appointing said Charlotte his executrix; that said devisees of Martin had possession of the lands, and unless restrained would diminish, waste, and reduce the same so as to destroy their value. The bill then prayed that the defendants might be required to show the particular land claimed by them under the will; that they might be restrained from committing waste thereon; that the land to which plaintiff should be declared entitled under said will be admeasured and laid off to him by metes and bounds; that the title deeds to all of testator's land be produced, and such as belonged to plaintiff delivered to him. Defendants demurred. Demurrer sustained. Plaintiff appealed.

No counsel appeared for the plaintiff.

Winston, for the defendants.

RUFFIN, C. J. No counsel has appeared before us for the plaintiff; and we can not, therefore, be sure that we correctly apprehend the ground or grounds on which relief was intended to be claimed in the bill. As far, however, as we have, unaided, been able to collect the grounds brought forward in the bill and exhibits, we are of opinion that the bill can not be supported, but was properly dismissed. From the general scope of the bill, the principal object, as stated particularly in the prayer, seems to be, to have the land devised to the plaintiff admeasured and laid off to him by metes and bounds; and as subsidiary to that relief, that the land devised to the other devisees respectively be laid off and ascertained, and to those ends, that the defendants may produce the title deeds of the testator's lands; and in the mean while, that the several defendants may be enjoined from cutting timber, or committing any other waste upon any of the lands devised in the will.

It is to be remarked, in the first place, that the court is not called to act between these parties on the idea of decreeing a partition of lands given or held jointly or in common. There is nothing of that kind in the will or bill. The devises are distinct to each devisee, and of distinct parcels; and therefore, there is no partition to be made. But although the bill admits that the devises are not of shares in a known subject, but are devises of different tracts of land to sundry persons in severalty, yet it states, as the grievance to the plaintiff, that the descriptions in the will of the several tracts given to Martin and the others are so obscure, that he can not identify those tracts; and, therefore, can not know what land is given to himself, the plaintiff. The object, then, is to obtain that knowledge by the aid of this court, as the plaintiff says he has failed in an attempt to identify his land upon the trial of an ejectment.

We are at a loss to conjecture what means a court of equity has of elucidating the point which creates the difficulty to the plaintiff, more than a court of law possesses, or of obviating the consequences of that difficulty under which the plaintiff is suffering, as he says. The construction of devises of legal interests in land is a legal question, and belongs to the tribunals of the law, and not to those of equity. The vagueness, or obscurity from any other cause, found in the terms in which the gift is expressed, can not change the jurisdiction; for this court has no peculiar principle of construction in such cases, but interprets the will as a court of law would, and both courts use the same means of identifying the thing given, namely: by resorting to documents, the testimony of witnesses, and surveys. The obscurity of the will, therefore, furnishes no sufficient reason for applying to equity; for if the obscurity be not so great as to render the disposition altogether unintelligible, it will be valid at law, as far as it can be understood; and if it sound to folly, so far as not to amount to a designation of any *corpus,* it necessarily follows that no court can help it, but that it must be ineffectual. For this reason, the bill can not assume the aspect of one for ascertaining confused boundaries; for although the court of equity has exercised the jurisdiction of settling boundaries of legal estates, yet it has been cautiously exercised, and in only a few instances, and in none in which the boundaries were not once certain, and had been rendered uncertain by the default of the defendant, or those under whom he claimed. In the case before us, the gravamen is not that a single landmark had been altered, or been permitted to perish by the act or neglect of the other parties; but that the testator was inexplicit and obscure in the language of his will.

If, however, that objection did not exist, the present case is not within the principles upon which the jurisdiction of ascertaining boundaries has hitherto proceeded. In all the cases there was either an agreement that the land of the several parties should be distinguished, as in *Norris* v. *Le Neve*, 3 Atk. 31; or some relation between the parties, which made it the duty of one of them to preserve the landmarks, and therefore the boundaries became confused by the neglect or fraud of the party charged with that duty—as a tenant: *The Duke of Leeds* v. *The Earl of Strafford*, 4 Ves. 180; *Attorney-general* v. *Fullerton*, 2 Ves. & Bea. 264; *Willis* v. *Parkinson*, 1 Swanst. 9. It is not enough that the boundary is controverted, or that it has become confused, although it was once plain; but the confusion must have arisen from the misconduct of the defendant, who is therefore equitably obliged to aid in its re-establishment: *Miller* v. *Warmington*, 1 Jac. & W. 492. Between independent proprietors, equity does not interpose, where there is no agreement, fraud, or neglect, and require either of them, against his will, to have his legal rights determined in any but the established legal method: *Atkins* v. *Hatton*, 2 Anst. 386; *Speer* v. *Crawter*, 2 Meriv. 417. Nor is it possible to uphold the bill as one for an injunction to stay waste, or for a discovery. As a bill of the former kind, it is radically defective, in not showing a title to the place wasted, or in which waste is apprehended. The court could not, therefore, act at all, without making the injunction as broad as the prayer of the bill on this head, and restraining the defendants from the ordinary acts of ownership in any of the devised lands, as well those given to the defendants as those claimed by the plaintiff, under the residuary disposition to him. The court must not deprive the defendants of the use of their own property, because, by possibility, the plaintiff's claim, now confessedly uncertain, may turn out, upon evidence hereafter to be discovered, to cover a part of the land in which it is said the waste is contemplated. That would render the preventive justice of the court, the instrument of positive oppression on the owner of probably the whole, and certainly a part, of the estate in his possession: *Davis* v. *Leo*, 6 Ves. 787. The bill ought to state a good title in the plaintiff to the specific land, else he can not have an injunction. A doubtful title will not be sufficient: *Jones* v *Jones*, 3 Meriv. 173; *Storm* v. *Mann*, 4 Johns. Ch. Cas. 21.

As to the discovery of the deeds and their production, it is sufficient, without noticing other things, to say, that the bill does not charge any deeds to have come to the hands of these defendants. It only alleges that James Martin, the executor of the testator Hough, had some deeds in his possession, though no description of them is given, and then that Martin died and made some of the defendants his executors, and devised to other of the defendants the lands given to him by the first testator. But, there is no allegation that any deeds for the land claimed by the plaintiff, or material to him in this controversy, have come into the custody or under the control of the defendants.

By COURT. Decree affirmed.

TALLY *v.* TALLY.

[2 DEVEREUX AND BATTLE's EQUITY, 385.]

GUARDIAN OF A LUNATIC CAN NOT BRING A BILL IN EQUITY AGAINST HER for a settlement of his accounts, and to obtain payment of the sum found due him; nor can he maintain an action in equity for the value of necessaries furnished the lunatic during the period of his guardianship, nor previously thereto, while she resided with him as a member of his family.

BILL. Defendant, an idiot, was a sister of plaintiff. In 1818, upon the death of their father, defendant became entitled to a share of his personal property. In 1836, plaintiff was appointed guardian of his sister's person and estate, and upon application for a settlement of his accounts, the county court appointed auditors, who made report that a balance amounting to over two thousand dollars was found to be due plaintiff. The bill prayed a settlement and decree of sale of sufficient of defendant's property to satisfy the balance found to be due. Defendant lived with plaintiff, and had been supported by him since 1818. Demurrer for want of equity. Demurrer overruled. Defendant appealed.

No appearance for the defendant.

Badger, W. H. Haywood, and Daniel, attorney-general, for the plaintiff.

RUFFIN, C. J. (after stating the case).   Upon the reading of the bill, it struck us as being liable to the objection of novelty; which is an objection in itself of no inconsiderable force.   Our attention was not called to any precedent for it, and none such is within our own remembrance.   In further considering the case, the court has come to the conclusion that the bill can derive as little support from principle as from the practice of the court.   How far a court could allow one notoriously of non-sane mind, like this party, to be charged even for proper maintenance, by even a brother, for so long a course of years, without applying for a commission and getting an order of the court confirming the custody of the person, and fixing a proper allowance, would at least be the subject of much consideration, if it were now to be determined.   But we do not found our judgment on that point; and, therefore, it may be assumed that, like that of an infant, the contract of one *non compos mentis* is not void, when for necessaries or things suitable to the person's fortune and habits of life.   Indeed, such appears now to be the doctrine of the courts of common law, where there is no fraud or undue advantage: *Baxter* v. *Earl of Portsmouth*, 5 Barn. & Cress. 170; *Brown* v. *Jodrell*, 3 Car. & P. 30.   Now, if it be admitted that the plaintiff's knowledge of his sister's condition makes no difference, and that he is entitled to a part, at least, or to the whole of his demand, as a debt for proper maintenance, yet that is a legal demand, for the recovery of which he has no right to come into this court.   It is simply a case for an action of assumpsit, if the idiot be liable at all; and there is nothing to change the jurisdiction from law to equity, whereby this proceeding, as an adversary one *inter partes*, can be sustained.

If the plaintiff were merely the creditor of his sister, such would be the law.   The relation between the parties does not affect this question.   That the plaintiff is the committee of the other party, rather increases the objection to this mode of proceeding, as it seems to us.   The court of equity may order a proper allowance to be paid out of the lunatic's estate for future maintenance; and it is not questioned that an order may also, in a proper case, be made for the satisfaction of past maintenance; and, indeed, for the payment of any debt of the lunatic.   But that is a jurisdiction arising out of the custody, by necessity, of the governing of the person and estate of the lunatic; and the corresponding obligation to maintain the lunatic, and to pay his debts as far as the estate may be available. If, indeed, a creditor can get a judgment at law, there will seldom be a ground on which the chancellor can restrain him from proceeding against the person or tangible property of the lunatic. But, if the creditor find it necessary to apply to the chancellor for payment, he owes his satisfaction partly to the grace of the sovereign, and partly to the duty of the chancellor to look to the ultimate benefit of the *non compos* and his estate. This last is so much the object, that Lord Eldon said he could not pay a lunatic's debts and leave him destitute, but must reserve a sufficient maintenance for him, although, in consequence, the creditors might put him in jail, and the court would have to support him there: *Ex parte Hastings*, 14 Ves. 182. But all these applications to the chancellor are made by petition, and the case does not assume the form of a controversy *inter partes*. Upon the petition, all necessary and proper inquiries are ordered; and in making them, the master is usually directed to procure the aid of the presumptive heir, or next of kin, by giving them notice to attend his proceedings; and, upon the report, the order is for the payment of such sum as may appear fair and right upon the whole, and considering the value of the property. So likewise is it in settling, or, as it is technically called, passing, the accounts of the committee, which is done upon petition.

That being the tried and settled method, the court would not like to allow it to be needlessly changed, although we are not very tenacious in matters of form merely, when the result is essentially the same. But there are substantial differences between applying by petition in the matter of a lunatic, and proceeding by bill praying a decree. In the first place, it is the duty of the court to have regard to the difference in expense. Then, in an adversary suit, the court is not left at large in its inquiries to ascertain the real justice of the case, but is trammeled by the pleadings, and confined to the matters therein put in issue, and to the parties on record. In the present case, for example, the statute of limitations, if duly insisted on, might probably bar much of the plaintiff's demand, which is of twenty years' standing; yet, in the answer, put in upon the overruling of the demurrer, no notice is taken of it. So that, however averse the court might be to countenance such laches, and although upon a petition an order might be refused for the payment of the stale parts of the claim, the point would yet be concluded in this suit by the frame of the pleadings. Besides, a decree goes much farther than an order. If the plaintiff were to get a decree at all in a suit, it would bind the person of the lunatic; and upon it, execution might be sued out against her property generally, instead of the party being confined to a particular and appropriate fund, applied thereto by the court in the order upon petition. Whatever may be the unavoidable operation of the judgment of a court of law, certainly a court of equity ought not so to act that a person peculiarly under the protection of that court, as a lunatic is, may be imprisoned for his maintenance as fixed by the court.

It is observable, also, that the legislature takes the same view, in the acts on this subject. It is contemplated in the acts of 1801 and 1817, 1 R. S., c. 57, that the matters and things therein authorized are to be done by force, simply, of the order of the court acting in the matter of the lunatic, upon the petition of the committee or other person interested.

It must, therefore, be certified to the court of equity of Warren, that, in the opinion of this court, the decree is erroneous, and that the same should be reversed, and the demurrer sustained, and the bill dismissed at the costs of the plaintiff.

By COURT.   Bill dismissed.

EQUITY WILL SET APART A FUND SUFFICIENT FOR THE MAINTENANCE OF A LUNATIC and his wife and infant children, if he has any, before directing that any portion of his property shall be applied to the payment of his debts, nor are advancements made for the prior maintenance of the lunatic chargeable upon this fund: *In the Matter of Latham,* 4 Ired. Eq. 231, citing the principal case; cited also in *Richardson* v. *Strohg,* 13 Ired. 106, declaring that contracts with lunatics are not absolutely void, but that such as are made with them for necessaries suitable to their habits and condition in life, will be sustained; the principal case is also quoted with approbation in *Patton* v. *Thompson,* 2 Jones' Eq. 411, as showing that the guardian of a lunatic can not, without permission of the court, exceed the annual income of the estate in expenditures for an account of his ward; and in *Dowell* v. *Jacks,* 5 Id. 417, as authority for the rule that a court of equity has no jurisdiction to make an order for an inquisition by jury, to determine the lunacy or idiocy of a party.

POLK *v.* GALLANT.

[2 DEVEREUX AND BATTLE'S EQUITY, 395.]

PURCHASER IS SUBJECT TO EQUITIES AGAINST HIS VENDOR in two cases: 1. When the purchase is of a legal title, but with notice of an equity in another. 2. When the purchase is of a mere equity only, whether with or without notice of a prior equity.

BETWEEN MERE EQUITIES the elder is the better.

SURETY OF A PURCHASER OF LAND AT A SALE on a specified credit under a decree in chancery, the title being retained until the purchase money should be paid, may charge the land for the payment of the sum for which he is liable, in the hands of an assignee of the purchaser who took it in good faith, without notice; nor is the title of the assignee benefited by the fact that he had afterwards bought in the same land at a sale under execution against his assignor, paying a valuable consideration therefor.

PURCHASER AT EXECUTION SALE SUCCEEDS TO THE TITLE of the defendant and is affected by existing equities against him.

ASSIGNOR OF LAND AFFECTED BY A TRUST IS NOT A NECESSARY PARTY to a bill against his assignee in an action by a surety of the former to charge lands in the hands of the latter for the payment of the purchase price for which the surety was bound, when the bill sets out that the defendant is the assignee of the entire interest in the land.

ACTUAL PAYMENT NEED NOT BE MADE by a surety to enable him to sustain an action.

BILL in equity. Daniel Gallant died intestate, and a sale of his lands for the purpose of partition was decreed, the sale to be made on a specified credit. John Gallant became the purchaser, with plaintiff as his surety for the payment of the purchase money, the title being retained until the money should be paid. John Gallant afterwards assigned his interest in the land to the defendant, Stephen Gallant, the former being then insolvent, and the purchase money still remaining unpaid. The answer averred that the defendant had no notice that the purchase money was unpaid; that he had agreed to give for the land the sum of four hundred and twenty dollars, its full value, and that at the time of his purchase there was a judgment and execution against John Gallant, to satisfy which the land was sold; and the defendant again became the purchaser at the price of one hundred and sixty dollars, which had been a clear loss to him. Replication. After the commencement of the action John Gallant died.

D. F. Caldwell, for the plaintiff.

Alexander and Hoke, for the defendant.

RUFFIN, C. J. The cause is brought to hearing without evidence, upon the bill, answer, and replication; and, from the pleadings, the case, is as follows (his honor here stated the case, and then proceeded). Upon the argument, the counsel for the defendants placed not much stress on the defenses brought forward in the answer; and we think very properly, as they are clearly insufficient. In the first place, the sheriff's sale is no bar, even if a legal title had been the subject of it, as the purchaser only succeeds to the defendant in the execution, and is affected by all the equities against him: *Freeman* v. *Hill,* 1 Dev. & Bat. Eq.

389. Much more must this be so, when the defendant in the
execution has himself but an equity. If it be of that kind which
is liable to be sold, the purchaser can only claim to stand in the
shoes of the debtor, and get a title only by doing those acts, on
the performance of which the debtor himself would have been
authorized to ask for a conveyance. Precisely on the same footing stands the purchase of the son from the father himself;
which was of an equity only. It is only the honest purchaser
of a legal title, whom equity will not disturb. If the purchase
be of the legal title, but with notice of an equity in another; or
if it be only an assignment of an equity, with or without notice
of a prior equity in another person: in either case, the estate
must, in the hands of the purchaser, answer all the claims to
which it would have been subject in the hands of the vendor.
Between mere equities, the elder is the better.

Against the present defendant, then, the plaintiff is entitled to
all the relief which this court would have given him against the
original purchaser, for whom he was surety. We have, during
the present term, in the case of *Green* v. *Crockett*, 2 Dev. & Bat.
Eq. 390, applied the equity between principal and surety to a state
of facts substantially the same with the present, and decreed for
the sureties; and in so doing, we have laid down no new principle, nor made a novel application of an old one. Neither
the purchaser nor his assignee could get the title, without paying the purchase money; and if the surety paid it, the vendor
ought not then to convey, but hold the title for the indemnity
of the surety, who has a right to it by substitution. But when
the principal is insolvent, the surety, although he may not have
paid the money, has an immediate equity to subject the land,
because that has then become, in fact, the only fund to which
he can have access, and as between it and the surety, is, as it
were, the principal debtor, and not simply a collateral security.
We are not speaking of the rights and duties of the creditor and
surety, as between themselves, but those which arise between
the surety and his principal, or the principal's assignee. As to
these last, there is a plain and strong equity, when it is admitted
or ascertained that the original debtor is personally disabled
from furnishing any means for the exoneration of the thing
pledged, that such pledge should forthwith be applied to the
purposes for which it was created, in discharge or diminution of
the surety's responsibility.

It was, however, insisted for the defendant, that his father
was a necessary party; and that the plaintiff can not have a de-

cree without reviving the suit against his heirs. There are two answers to this objection. The one, that the defendant is stated by both the bill and the answer to be the assignee of all the interest his father had; and, therefore, the latter is not a necessary party, as there could be no relief decreed against him; and the only effect of having him before the court would be to conclude him: *Thorpe* v. *Ricks*, 1 Dev. & Bat. Eq. 613. The second answer is, that what is required in the argument exists in fact; for the present defendant is admitted in the answer to be the son of John Gallant; and the latter is dead without, as far as appears, leaving any other child, or having made a will; and so the defendant is his only child and heir. It can not be requisite to bring him in as heir by bill of revivor, because the plaintiff does not seek to charge him as heir to any purpose whatever.

We think, therefore, that it must be referred to the master to inquire what is due for principal and interest of the debt for which the plaintiff is liable, as stated in the pleadings; and that it must be declared that the land, also mentioned in the pleadings, is liable for the sum that may thereupon be found due, and for the costs of the plaintiff in prosecuting this suit; and if the defendant shall not pay such principal, interest, and costs, within some reasonable time, it must be ordered that the clerk and master of Mecklenburg sell the land, and out of the proceeds pay, in the first place, the principal money and interest due on said debt; and in the next place, the said costs, if sufficient therefor.

By Court.   Decree accordingly.

PURCHASER OF TRUST PROPERTY AFFECTED BY NOTICE, WHEN: *Bunting* v. *Ricks*, 32 Am. Dec. 699, and note, referring to cases on this subject.

THE PURCHASER OF AN EQUITY TAKES IT SUBJECT TO PRIOR EQUITIES.—It is only the purchaser of the legal title, without notice of a prior equity, who can hold against such equity: *Winborn* v. *Yorrell*, 3 Ired. Eq. 117; *Smith* v. *Bank of Wadesborough*, 4 Jones' Eq. 303. Purchaser at an execution sale, when succeeds to such title only as the defendant then had, and subject to all the equities against it: *Ross* v. *Henderson*, 77 N. C. 170; *Walke* v. *Moody*, 65 Id. 599; *Carr* v. *Fearington*, 63 Id. 560; *Vannoy* v. *Martin*, 6 Ired. Eq. 169. The principal case is cited in each of the above to the points decided.

SURETY OF A PURCHASER HAS A RIGHT, upon the insolvency of his principal, when the title is retained until payment, to have the land sold for his reimbursement if he has paid the debt, or for his exoneration if he has not paid it, as against a purchaser from the principal, who took the title *bona fide* and with no notice of the non-payment of the purchase money. The rule of the principal case upon this subject is affirmed, citing it, in the following cases: *Shaffner* v. *Folgeman*, Winst. L. and Eq. 12; *Freeman* v. *Mebane*, 2 Jones' Eq.

44; *Egerton* v. *Alley,* 6 Ired. Eq. 188; *Smith* v. *Smith,* 5 Id. 34; *Barnes* v. *Morris,* 4 Id. 22. Distinguished in *Miller* v. *Miller,* Ph. Eq. 85. And the right of the surety to pursue the land to indemnify himself upon his obligation for the payment of the purchase money, is said, under the rule of the principal case, and of later authorities, to embrace only those cases where the title is retained. Hence, if the vendor execute a full title to the land, taking from the vendee a bond for the payment of the purchase money, the surety, after the insolvency of the vendee before payment, can not subject the land to the payment of his claim, in the hands of a purchaser who took it from the devisee of the vendee, although with notice.

ASSIGNOR NEED NOT BE MADE A PARTY to an action against the assignee when the bill and answer show the latter to have been the transferee of the entire interest: *Mullins* v. *McCandless,* 4 Jones' Eq. 425, citing the principal case. But where a petition was filed against the administrators of a decedent praying for a decree to compel them to pay over to the petitioner a distributive share of the estate, to which he claimed title by an assignment to him by one of the heirs and distributees, and the instrument on which his claim is based does not, on its face, purport to be an assignment, it was held, on the authority of the principal case, that the intestate's other heirs should be made parties: *Clark* v. *Edney,* 6 Ired. L. 50.

CASES

IN THE

SUPREME COURT

OF

OHIO.

St. Clair v. Morris.

[9 Ohio, 15.]

RENUNCIATION OF RIGHT OF DOWER in a mortgage executed by husband and wife, divests the right, so as to give the purchaser at a sale of the premises by the husband's administrator for the payment of the debts of the estate, a complete and unincumbered title.

BILL in chancery. Claiming dower in certain lands of which plaintiff's husband was seised in fee during coverture. The answer alleged that plaintiff had joined with her husband in a mortgage of the lands to secure a debt of four thousand dollars. After the death of plaintiff's husband, his administrator petitioned for leave to sell his intestate's property to pay the debts of his estate. Appraisement and assignment of dower being ordered, dower was assigned to plaintiff in all of deceased's real estate except the land in dispute. A sale was ordered, at which defendant purchased the mortgaged premises.

J. C. Wright, T. Walker, and H. Hall, for the plaintiff.

W. R. Morris, in propia persona.

By Court, GRIMKE, J. The position taken by the counsel for the plaintiff is, that when the mortgage money is paid, no matter how, the mortgage is extinguished, for the debt is the principal and the mortgage only the incident; that the effect of the sale by the administrator was to extinguish the mortgage, and by so doing to revive the right of dower. But this position can hardly be true to the extent to which it is attempted to carry it; for if a bill had been filed to foreclose this mortgage, it is very certain that the purchaser under the decree would have taken a title discharged of the incumbrance of dower. The debt would have been paid, and yet the right of dower would not have been revived, but would have been extinguished together with the debt. The language, the debt is the principal and the land only the incident, which was first attributed to Lord Mansfield in 2 Burr. 978,[1] is calculated to mislead, for it never was true in the universality with which it is thus stated. A mortgage in fee, as this is, is in reality a fee simple conditional, which is as large and ample an estate as a fee simple absolute, though it may not be so durable: Co. Lit. 18 a; and a transfer of such an estate can not be effected by the mere assignment of the debt. All the cases, when strictly examined, are reconcilable with this view. If the mortgagee's estate in the land is the same thing as the money due upon it, then the money due upon the land is the mortgagee's estate in it; and consequently there would be no difference between the mortgage of land for a term only, and a mortgage of it in fee. The land is the incident in one sense, because it is uncertain whether it will be necessary to resort to it as a fund for the discharge of the debt. If it is, then it ceases any longer to be the incident. By the same process by which the debt is discharged, the right to the land is also transferred. Mrs. St. Clair, by joining with her husband in the deed of mortgage, barred herself of dower in express terms, so far as the mortgagee and his assigns, and all persons claiming under them, are concerned. The only difference between a renunciation of dower in a deed in fee simple, and a deed of mortgage is, that in the former case the right of dower is *ipso facto* extinguished, and in the latter it is dependent upon some future event whether it shall be so or not. But that it may be, is most certain; otherwise there would be no meaning or utility in a relinquishment of dower. He who takes a conveyance in fee, in which is contained a relinquishment of dower, is a purchaser of the right of dower: and he who takes a mortgage to secure a debt, is also a purchaser of the right of dower, if it shall be necessary to the satisfaction of the debt; if it were otherwise, the mortgagee and the purchaser, under a judicial sale, would be in the same predicament as if the deed had been executed by the husband alone.

The act under which this sale was made, 2 Ch. St. 929, like the one now in force, authorizes the administrator, where the personal property is insufficient to pay the debts, to sell the

---

1. *Martin* v. *Mowlin.*

land for that purpose. But even admitting that the sale of the entire interest in the land was irregular, yet I do not see how it can be now cured. The proceedings of a court of probate are strictly *in rem* and not *in personam*. If it has jurisdiction, its acts are binding as against all the world. But there was no irregularity in this case. The proceeding was justified by the law, and was indispensable to carry out the provision regarding the estate of intestates. The thirty-fifth section of the act directs the administrator to make a deed for the land, which shall vest in the purchaser as complete a title as if the deed had been made by the intestate in his life-time. And admitting that this will have reference in this instance to some period in the lifetime of Arthur St. Clair, after he had executed the mortgage, then the deed would, at any rate, transfer the whole equity of redemption, freed from the incumbrance of dower. This is on the supposition that the administrator had no right to sell anything but the equity of redemption, and yet in that case the effect of the sale would be to extinguish the right of dower. But the power of the administrator was broader than this. A creditor, other than the mortgagee, can only sell the equity of redemption, because, as to him, it is the only interest in the land which the mortgagor has. But the mortgagee may, for the satisfaction of the mortgage debt, cause the entire interest in the land to be sold. The proceeding by foreclosure, which now exists, and that by *scire facias*, which formerly existed, shows this. Now, an administrator, acting on behalf of creditors by mortgages, may do the same. As the agent of the intestate's estate, and of all the creditors also, his power necessarily reached to the equity of redemption which belonged to the intestate, and to the mortgage estate which belongs to the mortgage creditor. In other words, the power of the probate court to direct a sale of the land was concurrent with the power of a court of equity to decree a foreclosure and sale. Very great inconvenience would be the consequence if this were not the case. The administrator is directed to settle up the estate, the personal property may be insufficient to pay the debts, the only real property which an intestate may have left may have been incumbered by a mortgage, there may be a residuum after the payment of that debt which may be wanting to pay other creditors, and the only just and regular mode of proceeding would be to sell the land and to distribute the proceeds among the creditors according to the priority of their claims. In the present instance, the proceeds were not nearly sufficient to discharge the mortgage debt.

The petitioner, therefore, has no equity, and the bill must be dismissed.

———

DOWER IS NOT BARRED IN EQUITY by a levy and sale by a creditor, who conveyed the land with warranty, and paid the excess of money received over the sum of his debt, to the widow and children of the debtor: *O'Brien* v. *Elliot*, 32 Am. Dec. 137, in the note to which the cases in this series, showing when and how dower may be barred, are cited.

It was held in *Taylor* v. *Fowler*, 18 Ohio, 567, citing the principal case, that a mortgage executed by husband and wife, did not divest the wife of her dower, as against a purchaser at a sale under a judgment against the husband, at the suit of a stranger, though the purchase money was applied in part to the payment of the mortgage debt. And again, in *Carter* v. *Goodin*, 3 Ohio St. 75, that where the vendee of real estate, in part payment of the purchase money, caused to be satisfied and discharged a mortgage executed by the vendor to the person from whom he derived title, and in which the wife of the former joined, no interest under the mortgage, or as the result of the transaction, accrued to the vendee in bar of the contingent dower estate of the wife of the vendor.

———

STRATTON *v.* SABIN.

[9 OHIO, 28.]

AGREEMENT FOR RECONVEYANCE OF PREMISES TO VENDOR, if, within two years, the latter should have a favorable opportunity of selling the same more advantageously, upon payment of the original purchase money with interest, does not amount to a mortgage.

BILL in chancery. Sabin, in 1822, conveyed fifty acres of land to McMillan. The deed contained the following clause: "And it is expressly understood, that if the said Sabin can, within two years from the date hereof, dispose of the said fifty acres hereby granted, to any better advantage to himself, he shall have the privilege of so doing, by paying the said McMillan the consideration money herein mentioned, viz., three hundred dollars and interest." In 1834 the above land was levied upon and sold under execution, against Sabin, plaintiff being the purchaser at the execution sale. After the levy, Sabin sold the land and received a deed from McMillan, and Sabin's vendee, on payment of the purchase money, took possession. Stratton claimed that the deed was in reality a mortgage, and that Sabin was only a mortgagor in possession; that the transfer by the latter was fraudulent, and prayed to be allowed to redeem.

G. Foos and *G. J. Smith*, for the plaintiff.

R. B. Harlan, for the defendant.

By Court, LANE, C. J. The question on which this case turns
is, whether the deed from Sabin, in 1822, was a mortgage, leaving in him the right of redemption. Because, if he had in him
the interest of a mortgagor in possession, his right to redeem
the mortgage passed to the purchaser at the sheriff's sale.
Other objections to the sale are raised by the parties, but it is
unnecessary to consider any other than this. The deed itself is
ambiguous. The sale is not absolute, but it does not necessarily imply any other interest in Sabin, than a right to repurchase, or an authority to sell. The possession continued vacant
until Hibben's purchase, except some slight acts of ownership
by McMillan; the taxes were paid by him. No proof is made
of any previous dealings between the parties; no note or covenant to pay money is shown. The answers both of Sabin and
McMillan, deny in the most positive terms, that the parties intended it as a mortgage, or that any debt subsisted between
them; or that they designed anything else, except to secure to
Sabin the privilege of repurchase. It is admitted, however,
that in 1831 or 1832, a sale of this land was made by McMillan
to Sabin; but the answers aver it was not under the privilege
retained in the deed, which had been abandoned long before,
but under an entirely new agreement. The consideration was
five hundred dollars, one hundred and eighty or one hundred
and eighty-five of which was paid down, and the remainder in
three annual payments, secured by notes. Hinkson proves that
that some time in 1833, as he believes, he drafted an agreement
between Sabin and McMillan, for the purchase of this land, the
terms of which he can not recollect. This repurchase is calculated to raise doubts; but the proof of the agreement of repurchase before the judgment in favor of the Urbana bank, corroborated the answer, notwithstanding the disparity in dates
between the answers and deposition. There is, it is true, much
in the case to awaken suspicion; but we nowhere find proof
enough to establish the relation of mortgagor and mortgagee
between these parties, against the direct denials of the answers.

In the late case of *Glover* v. *Paine*, 19 Wend. 518,[1] a similar
question was presented, and the court held, that the mere fact
of a conveyance of land, and an agreement for a reconveyance
at a future day, at an advanced price, at the election of the
grantor, afforded no evidence of an intention that the deed
should be considered a mortgage, though the question might
have arisen, had the deed been given for a pre-existing debt, or

---

1. *Glover* v. *Payn.*

on a loan of money, or had the grantor entered into an obligation to repay the consideration money expressed in the deed.

Bill dismissed.

———

———

FOOTE *v.* CITY OF CINCINNATI ET AL.
[9 Ohio, 31.]

TRESPASS QUARE CLAUSUM FREGIT CAN NOT BE SUSTAINED against a corporation aggregate.

GENERAL DEMURRER IN AN ACTION OF TRESPASS *vi et armis* must, if sustained, inure to the advantage of all the defendants, when the act complained of could not, either in point of fact or of law, be joint.

TRESPASS *quare clausum fregit.* General demurrer and joinder.

J. C. Wright, T. Walker, and E. Woodruff, for the defendants.

B. Storer and C. Fox, for the plaintiff.

By Court, GRIMKE, J. The plaintiff in this case declares in
trespass against the city of Cincinnati and two individuals,
charging them jointly with having broken and entered upon his
premises, and prostrated and destroyed several buildings, etc.
To this is general demurrer. This is the first instance, if we
except some very old cases which are alluded to in *Yarborough*
v. *The Bank of England,* 16 East, 6, in which this action has been
attempted to be supported against a corporation; and to be sure,
if the denial of the suit would draw after it, as a necessary consequence, the denial of any effectual remedy, that circumstance
would afford a powerful argument why it should be sustained.
But that consequence will not follow. Another remedy more
appropriate and equally effectual will lie; and the question is,
whether a form of action which presupposes the injury to have
been committed with force can be resorted to.

In *Yarborough* v. *The Bank of England,* it was held that trover
would lie against a corporation: and certainly it is not true, as
has sometimes been said, that no suit at common law can be
sustained against a corporation for a tort. The case of *Argent*
v. *Dean etc. of St. Paul's,* cited in 16 East, 8, note, was against
a corporation for a false return to a writ of mandamus, and no
objection was made, that the action would not lie. Indeed, instances are numerous of like suits without objection: *Riddle* v.
Proprietors of the Locks etc. on the Merrimack River, 7 Mass.

186 [5 Am. Dec. 35], was trespass on the case against a corporation. There it was contended that trespass would lie against a corporation, and that trespass on the case in its origin was merely an extension of the action of trespass *vi et armis;* the old writ of trespass being applicable only in a few instances, it was attempted to enlarge its scope so as to adapt it to every new case. But, notwithstanding in ancient times, the action of trespass on the case, as well as trespass proper, was laid *vi et armis,* as well as *contra pacem*, it is never so laid now. No two actions are kept more separate and distinct from each other, and therefore it was determined in the Massachusetts case, that an action on the case would lie against a corporation. The case of *The Chestnut Hill etc. Turnpike Company* v. *Rutter*, 4 Serg. & R. 6 [8 Am. Dec. 675], was also an action on the case, and the judge who delivered the opinion, after reviewing all the authorities, decided that the action was maintainable. Thus, trover, case, and an action for a false return, have all been decided fit remedies against a corporation; but no instance is found, since case and trespass have ceased to be confounded with each other, of trespass *vi et armis* against a corporation aggregate. In *Orr* v. *The Bank of the United States et al.*, 1 Ohio, 37 [13 Am. Dec. 588], this court decided that trespass for assault and battery would not lie against a corporation; and it is difficult to perceive any material distinction between the two cases. The whole reasoning proceeds upon the inconsistency of suing a corporation in a form of action which presupposes the injury to have been committed with force and arms, and is, therefore, equally applicable to trespass upon the person and upon realty. It is true, the objection may be denominated a technical one; but even a technical rule, after it has become a general one, should for that reason alone be preserved, unless manifest inconvenience would be the consequence. But here none such can result. The individual members of the corporation would be liable in their personal capacity, if the circumstances of the case would warrant it.

The only remaining question is, whether, as Mason and Griffin are joined in the suit, they may take advantage of the demurrer. The rule is, that if several persons be made defendants jointly, where the tort could not, in point of law, be joint, they may demur. And it is only where, in point of fact and of law, several persons might have been guilty of the same offense, that the joinder of more persons than were liable, in a personal or mixed action, offers no objection to a partial recovery: 1 Chit.

Pl. 99. Here the tort complained of could not, in point of law, be joint, and the demurrer must, therefore, be sustained in favor of all the defendants.

TRESPASS MAY BE MAINTAINED AGAINST A CORPORATION AGGREGATE: *Riddle* v. *Proprietors*, 5 Am. Dec. 42, and note. A further discussion of this subject will be found in the note to *Orr* v. *Bank of United States*, 13 Id. 596.

TOWN OF LEBANON *v.* COM'RS OF WARREN COUNTY.

[9 OHIO, 80.]

DEDICATION OF CERTAIN TOWN LOTS AS PUBLIC GROUND by recording the official town plat in which they are designated as such, is construed to intend, in the absence of other evidence, that they shall be taken for a public square for the use of the town.

DEDICATION TO PUBLIC USE IS A TRUST which takes effect from the registry of the official town plat, and neither the trust nor the title is affected by a subsequent conveyance by the proprietors.

LOCATION OF COURT-HOUSE AND JAIL on ground dedicated to the use of a town, and its subsequent occupation by the county, is an easement only, not inconsistent with the use of the premises by the town, upon the termination of which the town may reclaim its rights.

BILL in chancery. The town of Lebanon was surveyed in 1802. Four lots were designated on the registered plat thereafter filed, as "public ground." In 1805 Lebanon became the county seat of Warren county. The county commissioners, with the consent of the town, erected a court-house and jail on the lots, and continued to use and occupy them for that purpose until 1834, when having erected a new court-house and jail in another part of the town, the former buildings were abandoned. The county commissioners now proposed to lease the site of the old court-house for twenty years. This action is brought to restrain their proceeding, to secure the ground to the town, and to quiet title. The proprietors executed deeds to the commissioners in 1809.

A. H. Dunlevy and T. Corwin, for the plaintiff.

G. J. Smith and J. Probasco, for the defendants.

By Court, LANE, C. J. The object of the bill is to prevent the commissioners of the county from selling or leasing certain lots in Lebanon, claimed to have been dedicated to the town, by its original proprietors, as a public square, and to secure them to their public use. The town of Lebanon was laid out by Corwin, Hathaway, and Hurin, in 1802, but the record of that plat was not made until 1803. On the plat the lots in question are designated as "public ground." The registration of the plat by the operation of the statute of 1800, 2 Ch. St. 291, vests the fee of the land set apart for public uses, in the county, to hold upon the uses intended by the donor. The commissioners claim to hold the lots free from the trust as the property of the county, because they were conveyed to them by a deed of the proprietors in 1809, and because they have been occupied by the county ever since, in the erection and use of a court-house and jail, and because, as they say, the lots were originally designed for this purpose.

The dedicating act in this case was the registry of the town plat in 1803. The use was limited and took effect then; and a subsequent conveyance of the donors affects neither the trust nor the title. The words expressed in the act of dedication were "public ground;" a phrase which, in reference to a lot in a town, of shape, dimensions, and position suitable for this purpose, naturally, though not necessarily, means a public square: 6 Ohio, 298;[1] 7 Id. 221.[2] Where the words of dedication are ambiguous, the contemporaneous acts and declarations of the donors, and usage, may be adverted to, to explain them: 6 Id. 298; 7 Id. 88, 221. The testimony taken in this case, does not show with any certainty, that these words ought to bear a different interpretation. The subscriptions for the erection of a court-house, made in 1805, but not paid until 1809, and the erection of the court-house in that year, are probably too long after the grant, to be employed to explain its meaning. The actual occupation of the lots by a court-house and jail, is not inconsistent with the use of the property in the town; for the location of a court-house and jail on a public square, transfers no property, but is an easement only, and the town may reclaim its rights, when the county occupation shall cease.

Remanded to the county for final decree, with leave to either party to take further proof.

———

NO PARTICULAR FORM OF DEDICATION TO PUBLIC USE IS NECESSARY; the assent of the owner and user by the public are all that are required: *Vick* v. *Vicksburg*, 31 Am. Dec. 167, and note, in which the cases in this series upon this subject are collected. The principal case is cited in *Huber* v. *Gazley*, 18 Ohio, 24, to the effect that a tract of land, designated in the town plat as a public square, was thereby dedicated to the use of the town, and that such use was not affected by a subsequent disposition of it by the original proprietor.

1. *Brown* v. *Manning*; S. C., 27 Am. Dec. 255.
2. *Le Clercq* v. *Gallipolis*; S. C., 28 Am. Dec. 641.

HALL'S LESSEE v. ASHBY.

[9 OHIO, 96.]

DEED OF RELEASE IS A SUBSTANTIVE MODE OF CONVEYANCE, and transfers title, although at the time of its execution the premises were in the adverse possession of another.

CONVEYANCE OF LANDS IN THE ADVERSE POSSESSION of another is valid.

TITLE OF DEVISEE UNDER FOREIGN WILL takes effect at the death of testator, and no subsequent registry in this state is necessary to perfect it.

EJECTMENT. Plaintiffs claimed under a deed of release from F. L. Henop to Hall, executed to the latter while the defendants were in adverse possession of the premises. F. L. Henop derived his title under a will by Mary Henop, dated October, 1820, and admitted to probate in Virginia. Defendants claimed as the grantees of one Cope. Cope purchased the lands at a sale under execution on a judgment obtained by him against Mary and John and Philip Henop, her heirs at law, and obtained a sheriff's deed therefor. Verdict for plaintiff. Motion for a new trial.

C. B. Goddard and *C. C. Convers*, for the motion.

H. Stanberry, contra.

By Court, GRIMKE, J. The questions arising in this case are: 1. Is the deed from F. L. Henop to Hall, a valid conveyance of the land? and 2. Is the title derived through the will of Mary Henop, superior to that of the purchaser at sheriff's sale, the will not having been recorded in Ohio until 1838?

With regard to the first point, it has been argued that inasmuch as the deed from F. L. Henop is a deed of release, which presupposes the possession of the releasee, it was intrinsically ineffectual to transfer the title; and this is true if that mode of conveyance is governed by the same rules which are applied to it in England. There, in order to give effect to the deed of release, it is first necessary to execute a lease (or bargain and sale for a year), which by force of the statute of uses puts the lessee or bargainee in possession, and being thus in possession, although by a mere fiction, the release operating by way of enlargement of the estate, is effectual to transfer the entire title. So artificial a machinery for the purpose of effecting an object so very simple, we have always considered unnecessary in this state. The release is regarded here as a substantive mode of conveyance, and equally with the deed of quitclaim, is adopted where it is intended to convey the land without warranting the title. But even if the deed in this instance could not operate as a release, it might have such construction put upon it that it should operate in some other way. Thus a deed intended as a bargain and sale has been construed to be a covenant to stand seised, and a covenant to stand seised has been construed to be a bargain and sale.

But it is argued, in the second place, that a conveyance to the plaintiffs, while the defendant was in the adverse possession of the land, was a void act, and that no title could be derived under the deed. But we have no statute against champerty in Ohio. All the English statutes have grown out of peculiar exigencies, which are almost entirely foreign to our condition and habits. Sometimes they were passed at the close of a signal revolution, when the property of the kingdom having to a great extent changed hands, it became the interest of those who succeeded to power, to place every possible obstacle in the way of the former proprietors recovering possession. After the introduction of uses, buying what were called pretended rights and titles became very common, and this gave rise to one of the last statutes on the subject, that of 32 Hen. VIII., which prohibited the practice under the penalty of forfeiting the whole value of the land. Both of these classes of laws were adapted to a state of society very different from what prevails here. So far from opposing obstacles to the transmission of land, we have endeavored to render it as free as possible. The simple prohibition of selling land where the vendor has not a title to it, 29 Ohio L. 142, has set bounds to the only real inconvenience and mischief which has sprung from the practice of champerty.

The remaining question is more difficult than the two preceding ones; but it will admit of but one answer. We have no law which, properly speaking, requires the registry of wills. The probate and the order admitting the will to record, are judicial acts, and are neither of them intended to give notice to persons who may claim title adverse to the will. In England, the registration of wills is required whenever they happen to affect personal estate, but never if they relate to real property only. The reason of this is, that it is impossible to fix an express period for registering them, in consequence of the absence, legal incapacity, or future interest of the devisee. The utmost that has been attempted to be done, is to declare that a registry should be made before any action should be brought by the devisee.

No one supposes that in the case of a will made in Ohio, the title of the devisee takes its inception in any case from the period that the will is recorded: but it is argued that such must be the case of a foreign will. The difficulty, however, which exists in creating a registry of domestic wills, is even increased in the case of foreign ones, and no good reason can be assigned why, at any rate, the same rule in this respect should not be applied to both. The law requires the probate and record of a domestic will, 8 Ohio, 18,[1] but the record of the foreign will is not intended to give publicity to the proof of it, nor to give notice of the title acquired under it. It is to permit a certified copy to be given in evidence, when it would be difficult or impossible to produce the original. In England, a will on a trial concerning real property devised by it, is required to be proved precisely like a deed. The probate there has no relation to the realty, but only to the personal estate. In Ohio, it has relation to both, and the record which is consequent upon the probate, and which is very different from a registry in England, or of deeds, enables a copy to be given in evidence whenever a controversy arises concerning the property devised. It is evident that it is impossible to carry the provisions of the law any farther. A deed is committed to the custody of the grantee, who may record it whenever he chooses; but a will is placed in the hands of the executor, who may have no interest, or at any rate a very remote one, in the real property devised. This alone renders it absolutely impracticable to establish a registry of wills similar to one of deeds.

On the whole, we are of opinion that the deed to the plaintiffs, notwithstanding its form, and although the defendants were at the time in possession of the land, was effectual to transfer the title, and that this admission of the will to record was not necessary to perfect the title of the devisee: that his title commenced at the death of the devisor, and avoids the title under which the defendants claim.

Judgment for plaintiffs.

———

DEED BY GRANTOR OUT OF POSSESSION: *Conn* v. *Manifee*, 12 Am. Dec. 417, and note.

The principal case is cited in *Cressinger* v. *Lessee of Welch*, 15 Ohio, 190, to prove that the rule which prevails in the state of Ohio is, that a conveyance of land by a grantor who is out of possession is valid; and also in *Borland* v. *Marshall*, 2 Ohio St. 314, to the same point. Referred to moreover in *Jones* v. *Robinson*, 17 Id. 180, and approved, upon the point that the probate and record of a will when complete relate back and take effect from the death of the testator; and in *Morningstar* v. *Selby*, 15 Ohio, 364, to show that jurisdiction to determine the validity of a will is in the probate courts of common pleas.

———

1. *Swasey's Heirs* v. *Blackman.*

LESSEE OF PILLSBURY AND SARGEANT v. DUGAN'S ADMINISTRATOR.

[9 OHIO, 117.]

MISTAKE IN SPELLING NAME OF A PARTY IN AN INSTRUMENT will not invalidate it if the person can be identified.

PROCEEDING FOR PARTITION IS ANALOGOUS to a proceeding *in rem.*

CO-TENANT AGAINST WHOM PARTITION IS DEMANDED is not strictly a party to the proceeding.

DECREE IN PARTITION BINDS CO-TENANT who is beyond the jurisdiction of the court, if notice be given him of the pendency of the proceeding.

HUSBAND NEED NOT BE JOINED IN PROCEEDING FOR PARTITION OF WIFE'S LAND in order to bind her interest.

POWER OF AN ATTORNEY IN FACT to act as such is presumed to have been established by satisfactory proof, and though in a matter before a court of general jurisdiction which is required to exercise its powers upon a given state of facts to be proved before it, no authority appears upon the record, it can not be afterwards collaterally impeached.

EJECTMENT. Plaintiff shows title in his lessors by deed conveying to them under the names of Abigail and Mary Cutter. The former was married to Pillsbury and the latter to Sargeant, but prior to this action both husbands died. In August, 1805, the following petition was filed in the court of common pleas.

"The petition of the subscribers respectfully shows, that John Cutter, late of Cincinnati, died seised of certain lots in the town of Cincinnati held by purchase from the proprietors of the town (description). In which William Woodward is entitled to three eighths; Abigail, wife of said William, to one eighth; Hepsibeth Foster and Seth Cutter to one eighth each; Abigail Pillsby and Mary Cutter, both of Massachusetts, are entitled to one eighth part, for which petitioners ask partition, etc. William Woodward, Abigail Woodward, Samuel Foster, Hepsibeth Foster, Samuel Cutter, attorney for Mary Cutter."

The question was whether Abigail and Mary were parties, so as to bind their respective shares.

V. Worthington, J. C. Wright, and *T. Walker,* for the plaintiffs.

D. Van Matre, B. Storer, and *C. Fox,* for the defendants.

By Court, LANE, C. J. In adjudicating upon transactions occurring in the early settlement of our state, we must never forget the absence of precedents and system, the different usages introduced by people emigrating from every part of the country, the want of knowledge or neglect of technical learning, and the risk of loss of evidence from the lapse of time. Hence errors

of form have always been overlooked where the acts of a court
are manifest, and its jurisdiction established: 3 Ohio, 273;[1] 6 Id.
255.[2]

The petition in partition is very loosely drafted. The land is
well described, but the name Pillsbury is spelled Pillsby, and
no notice is taken of her husband, although then alive. The
non-joinder of the husband, who then held a freehold in the
wife's land for their joint lives, and a contingent tenancy by
curtesy, left his rights unimpaired. By his decease, this estate
is ended, and the wife is bound by a decree against her, until
reversed, because a judgment or decree against a *feme-covert* is
voidable only on error. It is not every mistake in names which
will invalidate an instrument or proceeding. This effect will
follow where the person can not be identified, or where the error
is such as to describe another. But words are intended to be
spoken; and where the sound is substantially preserved, bad
spelling will not vitiate. I remember a case where a lessor in
ejectment recovered in the name of Puthuff, under a deed to his
ancestor in the name of Biddulph, by proving that Biddulph,
Bottolph, Potherf, and Puthuff, were different modes of spelling
the name of the same person. In the case before us, Pillsby
and Pillbury differ little in sound, in familiar conversation, especially when pronounced with the rapidity of utterance usual
among the people with whom she then lived. In the statute
proceedings for partition, which only define existing rights
without creating new ones, and are not regarded adversary,
but analogous to proceedings *in rem*, 6 Ohio, 269,[3] the co-tenant
against whom partition is demanded, is not strictly a party.
Where he lives beyond the jurisdiction of the court, the publication of notice of the pendency and objects of the petition is all
which is required. We find, in the case before us, sufficient evidence of notice that a petition was pending to divide lot 92,
and out-lot 20, in Cincinnati, belonging to the late John Cutter,
of Cincinnati, of which Abigail Pillsby, of Massachusetts, was
entitled to one eighth. Enough is shown to apprise her of her
rights, and to bind her by the decree of partition.

The objection to the operation of the decree upon Mrs. Sargeant's eighth is, that no authority appears on the record for
Samuel Foster to institute these proceedings as her attorney in
fact. The authority of an attorney at law is presumed: 3 Ohio,
521.[4] The power of an attorney in fact, should be shown by

---

1. *Matthews* v. *Thompson.*
2. *Glover's Heirs* v. *Ruffin.*
3. *Glover's Heirs* v. *Ruffin.*
4. *Critchfield* v. *Porter.*

proof, but where a court of general jurisdiction is required to exercise its powers upon a state of facts to be proved before it, the requisite proof is presumed to have been made, and the existence of the fact can not be afterwards collaterally questioned: 2 Pet. 163,[1] 449;[2] 3 Ohio, 257,[3] 560;[4] 6 Id. 255;[5] 7 Id. 259;[6] 8 Id. 87.[7]

The defendants may take judgment.

MISTAKE IN A DEED OR WRITTEN CONTRACT will not be relieved against unless express proof be adduced of the intention of the parties: *Moore* v. *Vick*, 32 Am. Dec. 301. Chancery will correct a mistake in a deed by which words of limitation were omitted: *Chamberlain* v. *Thompson*, 26 Id. 390, and cases to that effect cited in note.

PARTITION AMONG COPARCENERS without legal notice to all interested is invalid: *Newby* v. *Perkins*, 25 Am. Dec. 160. Mortgagees of a co-tenant are not bound by a decree of partition against him unless they are parties to the suit: *Colton* v. *Smith*, 22 Id. 375. Cited in *Smith* v. *Pratt*, 13 Ohio, 550, to the point that a proceeding for partition is in no just sense an adversary proceeding, but is analogous to a proceeding *in rem.* Cited also in *Maxsom* v. *Sawyer*, 12 Id. 209, and in *Adams* v *Jeffries*, Id. 272, to show that the truth of facts averred in a record can not be collaterally impeached by evidence of matters *dehors.* Cited and approved also in *Wade* v. *Pettibone*, 11 Id. 60.

DENNISON *v.* FOSTER ET AL.

[9 OHIO, 126.]

PURCHASER FROM TENANT IN COMMON can not impose upon later purchasers of other portions of the common property, the burden of satisfying the claim of the owner of a paramount title to an undivided interest therein.

TENANT IN COMMON CAN NOT WORK A DIVISION of the common property by conveyance of his share by a deed defining its limits by metes and bounds.

DEED OF TENANT IN COMMON conveys the proportional interest only of the grantor to the portion of the common property described.

THE EQUITIES BETWEEN EARLIER AND LATER PURCHASERS of portions of common property are equal, and the former can not impose upon the latter the entire burden of a paramount title.

HEIRS OF TENANT IN COMMON ARE BOUND BY A CONVEYANCE by their ancestor, especially if it be by warranty.

BILL in equity, to quiet plaintiff's title to lot 92, in Cincinnati, and for partition of that lot from others, which, together with it, lately belonged to the heirs of Cutter. Plaintiff claims by purchase from Woodward and Foster, under deed by them to McClelland, in 1808, at which time Woodward and Foster

---

1. *Thompson* v. *Tolmie.*	4. *Ludlow* v. *Johnson ;* 8. C., 17 Am. Dec. 609.
2. *Weston* v. *Charleston.*	5. *Glover* v. *Ruffin.*
3. *Ludlow's Heirs* v. *McBride.*	6. *Mitchell* v. *Eyster.*　　　7. *Foster* v. *Dugan.*

had title to six eighths in fee, and estates for life in the remaining two eighths, of lots 92 and 20. J. C. Foster has since recovered an undivided fourth in both lots. Plaintiff demands such partition as will leave his lot 92 entire, by casting upon more recent purchasers the burden of J. C. Foster's title.

B. Storer, C. Fox, D. Van Matre, and *N. Wright,* for the plaintiff.

V. Worthington, J. C. Wright, and *T. Walker,* for the defendants.

By Court, LANE, C. J. Since the cases heretofore decided upon the interests of these parties, there remains nothing to be settled in this suit, except the claim set up by Dennison, that the first purchaser of a specific defined tract, from a tenant in common, may require from the co-tenant to apart his share from that part of the whole tract last sold by his ·grantor. That as Woodward and Samuel Foster, who claimed the whole of lots 92 and 20, first sold 92 to McClelland, under whom the plaintiff takes title, and as Joseph C. Foster has recovered an undivided fourth in both lots by these suits, the plaintiff asserts a right to set off the undivided share thus recovered, in that part of the land remaining with Woodward and Samuel Foster, after their sale to McClelland, and now held by later purchasers. It is argued, that as between tenants in common all rights are equal; that a partition giving to Joseph C. Foster his proportional value in lot 20, is as just as any for him, and more equitable to the, plaintiff, in consequence of his improvements; and that the other parties have no reason to complain, because their titles are later than, and taken with a knowledge of his.

One tenant in common can not work a division of the common property, by conveying his share, in a deed, defining its limits by metes and bounds. As between the co-tenants and the purchaser, all the effect of such a deed is to give to such purchaser, the proportional interest of his grantor, in that part of the common property described in the deed: 2 Ohio, 113;[1] 6 Id. 398.[2] The tenant making this separation of interest, and his heirs, are bound by it, especially if the deed contains a warranty, and it may be accepted and ratified by the co-tenants: 5 Id. 244;[3] Wright, 713.[4] But there seem no such relations between earlier and later purchasers, as authorize the former to impose any such obligations upon the latter. The rights and equities of each are equally ample and perfect. The loss which they suffer in this instance, is not from an incumbrance, which

---

1. *White* v. *Sayre.*   2. *Treon* v. *Emerick.*   3. *Piatt* v. *Hubbel.*   4. *Cummins* v. *Nutt.*

may be extinguished, either by the appropriation of the land left with the heirs, or by a contribution among themselves; but is a full and paramount right over a proportion of the land of each. As respects heirs, we would endeavor to mold their rights, so as to protect the alienee of their ancestor, but we find no authority to apply any such principles between purchasers, and we must leave each to sustain his share of the burden.

The right to relief, therefore, in the point of view contemplated by the bill, is not sustained. There is, however, a fact disclosed by the evidence, and in some degree touched upon by the argument, which is deserving fuller investigation. Mrs. Woodward, before her sale to Joseph C. Foster, covenanted with the executors of Woodward to release to them all claims arising from or under the conveyances of Woodward. How far this extends, how fully it precludes those who hold her estate from asserting a right which may ultimately fall upon the estate of Woodward, is a grave question. It will require a change of pleading to present it. The present suit is so complicated with other matters and other parties, that we believe it had better be dismissed, reserving the right to pursue this inquiry in a new bill.

———

TENANT IN COMMON CAN NOT CONVEY BY METES AND BOUNDS; the conveyance should be of an aliquot portion of his entire interest: *Smith* v. *Benson*, 31 Am. Dec. 614; the note to this case contains citations to this point. Tenant in common may convey his interest in a separate part of the common land: *Matter of Prentiss*, 30 Id. 203.

PARTITION BY TENANT FOR LIFE IS NOT BINDING on remainder-man: *Boo* v. *Mix*, 31 Am. Dec. 285.

PURCHASE OF SUPERIOR OUTSTANDING TITLE by tenant in common will not enable him to employ it to expel his co-tenant: *Venable* v. *Beauchamp*, 28 Am. Dec. 74, and note.

The principal case is distinguished in *Dawson* v. *Lawrence*, 13 Ohio 543, as follows: In that case two tenants in common made partition of their land in severalty, and each sold to other purchasers. The title of one of the original tenants afterward failed on account of a defect therein, by which a third person became entitled to a portion of the whole tract and the partition became void. It was held, that the rights of the purchasers from the tenant whose title had failed were subordinate to such equities as the purchasers from the holder of the valid title might exact, and that the entire burden resulting from the recovery on the outstanding title might be imposed upon their portion. The court said the principal case only placed on the same footing earlier and later purchasers from the same grantor, but did not apply to a case where the relation of the parties were those of purchasers from different vendors.

BRIGHT *v.* CARPENTER AND SCHUER.

[9 OHIO, 139.]

PARTY WHO INDORSES NOTE IN BLANK at the time of its execution may be sued as an original maker.

PAROL EVIDENCE IS ADMISSIBLE TO SHOW THE INTENTION of the parties regarding the indorser's liability.

ASSUMPSIT. The following note was offered in evidence:

" $290.   Lancaster, Ohio, July 27, 1838.   Ninety days after date I promise to pay to the order of E. Bright, at the bank of Cleveland, Ohio, two hundred and ninety dollars, value received.

"G. CARPENTER."

On the back of the note the name of Schuer was indorsed in blank. Plaintiff offered to prove that Schuer, when asked how his name came to be on the note, stated that Carpenter brought the note to him, and that he had put his name on the back of it at Carpenter's request, upon the latter's assurance that it would be soon paid. The evidence was excluded.

Hart and Borland, for the plaintiff.

H. H. Hunter, for the defendants.

By Court, LANE, C. J. The plaintiff can not recover under this form of declaration, except by showing that Carpenter and Schuer are joint makers of the note given in evidence. He insists that proof of this fact is presumed by the form in which they became a party, especially when accompanied with the proposed testimony, showing that Schuer intended to become a surety, and repelling the presumption of his being an indorser.

The defendants rely upon the form of the paper as constituting a guaranty or collateral undertaking by Schuer; which being in writing or implied by law, can not be altered by parol. This form of mercantile paper is not unusual in business, and it seems strange that the precise character of the signer on the back of the note, has not been long since established with certainty. The cases cited by the diligent counsel in this case do not so settle the question. Those from Massachusetts determine that where a person, not a party to the note originally, signs his name upon it in blank at the time of its execution, he becomes by relation a party, and may be proceeded against as maker, and that the note itself furnishes presumptive evidence of this relation by the application of the rule, that a contract is construed most strongly against the person bound: 3 Mass. 274;[1] 5 Id. 358,

---

1. *Josselyn* v. *Ames,* 3 Mass. 274.   2. *Hunt* v. *Adams;* S. C., 4 Am. Dec. 68.

546;[1] 7 Id. 58;[2] 14 Id. 116;[3] 8 Pick. 122.[4] In a late case, *Dean
v. Hall*, 17 Wend. 214, it was held that where an indorser of a
promissory note payable to bearer, was privy to the consideration, he may be charged directly as maker or as indorser, and
that a *bona fide* holder of such a note, indorsed in blank, may
fill up the indorsement in any form consistent with the intent of
the parties, and numerous authorities are there cited to support
the decision. The indorsement in the case before us being in
blank, may be looked upon as filled up to conform to the plaintiff's declaration, or may be in fact now so filled up.

We believe the principle running through these cases entirely
conformable to the law merchant, and calculated to secure the
legitimate rights of all parties. If a person, not a party, give
his name to a note already existing, his engagement is collateral
only, and he is to be held as guarantor; but if such a person sign
his name to such paper at the time of its execution, without prescribing the limits of his responsibility, he authorizes the holder
to treat him as a maker, and is as much bound as if his name
was written under that of the principal. In the case before us,
Schuer need not be treated as a guarantor: he is only entitled
to the privileges of a surety. In adopting this rule, we contravene no decision made in our own state. *Green v. Dodge and
Cogswell*, 2 Ohio, 498,[5] is in no way impugned. In that case,
either the holder or the person bound, had set out the terms of
the indorser's liability by filling the blank, and the law decided
relates only to a case where the character as guarantor is ascertained. The case of *Stone v. Vance et al.*, 6 Id. 246, turned upon
a peculiar state of facts which repelled the presumption of any
joint undertaking between the second and third defendants.

The parol evidence offered by the plaintiff is unnecessary for
his recovery. But in cases of bank signatures of this kind, such
testimony is admissible, because it is consistent with the contract either to show the intention of the parties as to the extent
of the liability, or to repel the ordinary presumption against such
indorser.

Judgment for plaintiff.

———

INDORSEMENT OF NOTE IN BLANK does not make indorser a joint maker:
Perkins v. Catlin, 29 Am. Dec. 282, and note, in which the authorities relative to this subject are cited and reviewed.

PAROL EVIDENCE IS ADMISSIBLE TO VARY THE EFFECT of an indorsement
in blank: Id.

1. *Carver v. Warren.*   3. *Stanton v. Blossom;* S. C., 7 Am. Dec. 196.
2. *Hemmenway v. Stone;* S. C., 5 Am. Dec. 27. 4. *Baker v. Briggs;* S. C., 20 Am. Dec. 311.
                            5. 2 Ohio, 430.

The principal case is cited to the point that one who places his name to a note at the time of its execution, on whatever part of the instrument the name is written, may be treated as a maker, in *Stage* v. *Olds*, 12 Ohio, 168; *Gale's Adm'r* v. *Van Arman*, 18 Id. 336. To the point that the presumption created that by an indorsement at the time of the execution of a note, the person so doing authorized the holder to regard him as a maker, may be rebutted by parol proof, showing a different intention, the principal case is cited in *Seymour* v. *Mickey*, 15 Ohio St. 515.

PENDLETON v. GALLOWAY ET AL.

[9 Ohio, 178.]

BILL IN EQUITY TO IMPEACH A JUDGMENT or decree for fraud, must set forth specifically and particularly the facts constituting the fraud.

DECREE CAN NOT BE IMPEACHED FOR FRAUD after twenty-five years' acquiescence by the plaintiff.

BILL in chancery. In 1808, John Campbell, being indebted to the plaintiff, executed a deed, conveying to the latter all his interest as heir at law in certain surveys, held under warrants issued to Campbell's father for military services. In 1800, Richard Campbell, brother of John, and also entitled to inherit as heir at law in the same surveys, had conveyed all the lands included in the surveys to Baker, who soon after died. The conveyance to Baker was intended to be a mortgage, and was executed to secure a debt. The bill in the present action alleged, that the heirs and devisees of Baker, in 1813, had filed a bill against John Campbell and others, setting forth the conveyance to Baker, and falsely and fraudulently representing it as the absolute deed of Richard Campbell, and that he was authorized by the other heirs to execute it, and that the conveyance had been lost. The bill further alleged that John Campbell had no notice of the action; that the allegations of the bill in that action were false and fraudulent, and that the conveyance by Richard was conditional and not absolute, as alleged. Complaint prayed that the decree obtained against John Campbell be set aside as false and fraudulent, and that the land be subjected to his debt in the hands of the defendants, who had purchased with notice. The complainant had, in 1835, obtained a judgment against John Campbell, for the amount of his debt.

Wm. Ellsberry, for the complainant.

Odlin, Schenck, and G. J. Smith, for the defendants.

By Court, WOOD, J. Two questions are made in this case: 1. Is the fraud set up in the bill of the kind required to impeach a decree; and, if so, is it sufficiently set forth? 2. Can a decree be impeached for fraud after the lapse of more than twenty-five years?

The first proposition, in our view, is of no importance in deciding this case, because the second is decisive of it. It is, however, a rule applicable as well to decrees in equity as to judgments at law, that when a bill is filed to impeach either on the ground of fraud, the particular and precise circumstances which constitute the fraud, must be stated: the acts done, or the words spoken, which constitute the fraud, must be set forth. *Expressio falsi vel suppressio veri*, or some fault, design, or wicked and evil intention, must be clearly set out in the bill, to which the defendant is called to answer; it will not do to impute mere laches to impeach a solemn adjudication of a court of justice: 4 Ohio, 492;[1] Coop. Eq. 217; 1 Johns. Ch. 194.[2] The only charge in this bill is, that Baker's heirs, in their suit against Campbell and others, to quiet their title, did not set out a collateral writing given to Richard Campbell, showing his deed intended as a mortgage, without charging their knowledge that such writing was within their control. If such writing existed, it was matter of defense, and should have come from the other side.

2. The decree sought to be impeached was rendered more than twenty-five years since, and the long acquiescence of the complainants, and the too obvious staleness of the claim, should not call into activity the energies of a court of equity for its relief. Lord Camden, in *Smith* v. *Clay*, 3 Bro. Ch. 640, said a court of equity is never active to relieve, when a party has slept on his rights, and acquiesced for a great length of time. Where reasonable diligence is wanting, this court is passive, and does nothing. Laches and negligence are always discountenanced, and therefore, from the beginning there was always a limitation to suits in this court. Lord North, in *Fitler* v. *Lord Macclesfield*, declared, that though there was no limitation to a bill of review, yet after twenty-two years he would not review a decree; that interest *rei publicæ ut sit finis litium*, was a maxim that had always prevailed in equity, without an act of parliament. A court of equity is governed by the circumstances of the case before it: 2 Story's Eq. 739. We think the circumstances disclosed in this case, require of us to sustain the demurrer to the bill.

Bill dismissed.

———

FRAUD, PLEADING: *Saunders* v. *Stotts*, 27 Am. Dec. 263, and cases cited in the note.

---

1. *Lisby* v. *Ludlow*.   2. *Gelston* v. *Codwise*.

TRUSTEES OF McINTIRE v. ZANESVILLE CANAL & MANUFACTURING Co

[9 Ohio, 203.]

BEQUEST TO A CORPORATION IN TRUST FOR CHARITABLE USES, though at testator's death the corporation had no legal capacity to take, may take effect as an executory devise, whenever, by subsequent incorporation, capacity is acquired.

CORPORATION MAY BE DISSOLVED: 1. By death of its members; 2. Surrender of its franchises; 3. Judgment of forfeiture for non-user or abuse.

CORPORATION FORMED FOR CONSTRUCTION OF A CANAL to be completed within a definite time, is not dissolved by failure to accomplish the work within the time specified, in the absence of any judgment declaring a forfeiture.

STATUTE RECITING THAT A CORPORATION HAD LOST ITS RIGHTS by failure to exercise them within the time required by the act creating it, and authorizing a purchase of the real estate it had acquired up to that time, is a recognition of its existence, and power to contract as a corporation.

BILL in chancery. Plaintiffs, claiming to be the lawful trustees of a charitable fund, created by the will of John McIntire, bring this bill against the Zanesville Canal and Manufacturing Co., the executors of McIntire, and his widow, for an accounting. In 1812 an act was passed by the legislature to enable John McIntire and his associates to construct a canal and collect tolls thereon. In 1824, the Zanesville canal and manufacturing company was organized, under the foregoing act. By the act of incorporation, the work was to be completed by February 11, 1835, and upon their failure within this period to finish the work, the Muskingum navigation company were authorized to take possession of and complete it. On the nineteenth of February, 1835, a law was passed, authorizing the canal commissioners to take possession of the property for the use of the state. After reciting that the Zanesville canal and manufacturing company had lost its rights to construct the canal and locks, by non-execution within time, it provides for the purchase from them of the real estate necessary to carry on and maintain the dam and canal. In 1836, the McIntire poor school was incorporated by the legislature. The act recited that property had been devised for this purpose to be managed by the Zanesville canal and manufacturing company, as trustees, and that it had been represented that said company had ceased to exist, so that there was no person competent to carry the trust into execution; and the act then proceeded to create a corporation of five trustees, who were clothed with the powers necessary to carry the devise into effect. The Zanesville canal and manufacturing company, organized in 1812, did not obtain its charter until 1816. Demurrer and answer.

C. B. Goddard and C. C. Convers, for the Zanesville Canal and Manufacturing Company.

T. Ewing and R. Stillwell, for Young and wife.

H. Stanbery and G. Swan, for the complainants.

By Court, LANE, C. J. The plaintiffs' right to relief in the present case depends upon their successfully maintaining the two following propositions, to wit: that the will of McIntire created a charitable trust, which this court can enforce, and that they are the lawful trustees. The first of these arises upon the plea of the heirs; the second is presented by the demurrers and answers of the other defendants. We have entered upon the examination of this case with much solicitude; for the great value of the property, the very talented efforts of counsel, and the consideration that this is the first proper charity which has fallen under the action of this court, all unite to magnify its importance. The positions taken by the heirs to show the bequest void, are: 1. That the objects of the testator's bounty are uncertain, and that the trustees had no capacity to take, because the Zanesville canal and manufacturing company had no existence as a corporation at the time of making and probate of the will; 2. That its corporate powers have been so forfeited as to terminate its existence; 3. That the bequest to the officers of the company, vests the estate in them, in that character, since they hold by an annual tenure, and are liable to be changed at each successive election.

It is admitted, that such a bequest as this would be sustained in England. However uncertain the object, whether the person to take be *in esse* or not, whether the bequest can be carried into exact execution or not, whether the general charitable intention is clearly manifested, a court of equity will sustain the legacy and give effect to it in some form upon principles of its own. But it is asserted by the counsel for the heirs, that this lax and wide-reaching jurisdiction in charities is peculiar to England, and depends on the statute of Elizabeth only. We would not unnecessarily enter into the much disputed and greatly perplexed inquiry of the extent of chancery jurisdiction over charities, independent of the statute. But one of the earliest elements of every social community upon its law-givers, at the dawn of its civilization, is adequate protection to its property and institutions, which subserve public uses, or are devoted to its elevation, or consecrated to its religious culture, and its sepulchers: and in a proper case, the courts of our state might be driven into the recognition of some principle analogous to that contained in the statute of Elizabeth, as a necessary element of our jurisprudence: 2 Story, 389; 17 Serg. & R. 88;[1] 9 Cow. 437.[2] But without reference to these considerations, where a trust is plainly defined, and a trustee exist, capable of holding the property and executing the trust, it has never been doubted that chancery has jurisdiction over it, by its own inherent authority, not derived from the statute, nor resulting from its functions as *parens patriæ*.

The property devised in this case, consisted of land, personalty, and stock in the Zanesville manufacturing company; the legal ownership of this was either in McIntire's executor or heir. The condition on which the devise over took effect, was the death of the daughter without issue. The objects of the testator's bounty, were the poor children of Zanesville, and the benefit intended was their education. There is no doubt that a trust attached to the property, whoever might hold it; "for whenever a person by will gives property, and points out the object, the property, and the way it should go, a trust is created." And a bequest of land to A., to construct an asylum for aged sailors, although inefficacious to pass the legal title, sufficiently defines the trust, and charges the heir with its performance: 3 Pet. 119, 152;[3] 1 Story's Eq. 415; 4 Wheat., appendix. The position, therefore, taken by the heirs in the plea, that the land descended to them, on the death of the daughter, absolved from the trust, is not supported, but overruled.

The interests of the heirs are, nevertheless, involved in the case, for the next question arising is, whether the trusts which we have thus found to exist, shall be executed by the plaintiffs, who are the trustees under the act of 1836, or the Zanesville canal and manufacturing company, who are the trustees designed by the testator, or upon the heirs upon whom the law throws the duty, if there are no other trustees. In the statement and arguments made by counsel, it seems to be assumed, that the Zanesville canal and manufacturing company had no legal existence until 1816. I am not certain this conclusion is just. In 1812, a statute enabled McIntire and his associates to build a dam across the Muskingum, and cut a canal around the falls. The objects expressed in the preamble are the advantages

---

1. *Witman* v. *Lex.*   2. *McCartee* v. *Orphan Asylum.*   3. *Inglis* v. *Trustees.*

of water-works, and the improvement of the navigation. It authorizes them to acquire lands, for the purpose of making a canal, "or the better to answer the objects of this act," and it gives the right of suit to any person injured by their neglect. The statute, therefore, imposes a common liability, and it implies the possession of common property, and the duty of accounting for profits. The organization of the Zanesville canal and manufacturing company was had in 1814, in the form of a corporation. Now, the bare grant "to hold *gildam mercatoriam*," a mercantile meeting, has been taken to carry corporate power, on account of common expenditures: 10 Co. 30;[1] 1 Roll. Abr. 513; so a grant of land, to a town on rent, and other similar cases: Ang. & Ames on Corp. 45. So the grant to a part of an ecclesiastical society, to repair their meeting-house, confers corporate powers: 2 Day (Conn.) 259.[2] It might, therefore, perhaps, be plausibly contended, that it was a legal existing corporation, before the date of the will, and the objection of their want of capacity to execute trusts might receive its answer, by the notification arising from the subsequent act of the legislature.

We do not, however, intend to place our decision upon this basis. The actual situation of the company in 1815, was that of a corporation *de facto*, with officers, and a capital stock of two hundred and fifty thousand dollars, held in the form of shares. It was in reference to this condition, that McIntire made a disposition of its property. We have seen that it consisted of his mansion-house, lands, personalty, and stock. It passed to the company for the purposes of this trust, not by the death of McIntire, but by a contingency which happened in 1820, and after the statute of 1816, which imposed upon them the most ample capacity for holding it. The bequest upon this trust, can take effect upon the very common ground as a remainder, contingent upon the death of McIntire, because limited to a person not in being, but becoming vested by the capacity acquired by the corporation, before the determination of the particular estate. And we should be justified in taking still stronger ground by the authority of a majority of the judges in the *Sailor's Snug Harbor*, 8 Pet. 99, in holding that a bequest upon charitable uses may take effect, as an executory devise, to a corporation subsequently acquiring the capacity to hold. It is, therefore, without difficulty we conclude, that on the decease of the daughter, the property of McIntire passed

---

1. *Sutton's Case.*   2. *Tilden v. Metcalf.*

to the Zanesville canal and manufacturing company upon these trusts.

It only remains to inquire if their right to it has been lost, either by their own neglect, or by subsequent legislation. The act of 1836 was passed upon the supposed case that this company had become extinct. It carefully saves the rights of all persons in the property, consequently the company lost none of its interests, if it then had a legal existence. If the corporation has been dissolved, it is not through judicial action, but by the bare and naked effect of the statute limiting the time for the completion of the dam and canal. It must be observed that it is not the fifteenth section of the statute of 1816, which works this forfeiture, since the time there given is extended in January, 1817, for one year: 15 Ohio L. 35; and in December, 1817, until December, 1818: 21 Id. 53; and in 1828 is enlarged until the eleventh of February, 1835. The last act, 26 Id. 57, 5, 26, 27, instead of declaring all rights, privileges, and immunities determined in case of failure, like the statute of 1816, only provides that the Muskingum navigation company may finish the canal and hold it, until their expenditures are reimbursed. There is no forfeiture attached to the last enlarging statute, except what arises from mere lapse of time. No further legislative act works a forfeiture, except that resulting from the act of 1835, which recites that the Zanesville canal and manufacturing company have lost "its right to construct the work," and authorizes the canal commissioners to purchase from them. Now the modes by which a private corporation in our country is dissolved, are: 1. By the death of its members; 2. Surrender of its franchises; 3. A judgment of forfeiture for non-user or abuse. But the Zanesville canal and manufacturing company has continued an organized and existing body until the present day: there has been no judicial act declaring a forfeiture, and the legislature by the act of the nineteenth of February, 1835, after the time of its supposed dissolution, recognized it as a person capable of contracting by authorizing a purchase from it: 33 Id. 90. It seems, then, plain to us, that at the time of the passage of the statute of 1836, the Zanesville canal and manufacturing company had not "ceased to exist," and that their corporate rights to execute the will of McIntire, through their officers according to his true meaning, was not affected nor impaired; consequently, the incorporation of the new board of trustees was void by the terms of the act.

The suggestion that the bill may be sustained at the suit of these plaintiffs, as the representatives of *cestui que trust*, can not be supported. This court would entertain a suit for mismanagement brought by the prosecuting attorney: 36 Ohio L. 35, sec. 43, or upon the relation of a party in interest; but such a proceeding would require a bill of a structure altogether different from this.

Bill dismissed.

———

DISSOLUTION OF CORPORATION: See cases from this series cited in note to *Rider* v. *Union Factory*, 30 Am. Dec. 497.

BEQUESTS TO CHARITABLE USES: *Burr* v. *Smith*, 29 Am. Dec. 154, the note to which refers to other cases in this series upon the subject; also *Moore's Heirs* v. *Moore's Devisees*, Id. 417, and note; also *Sanderson* v. *White*, Id. 591, and note thereto, containing numerous citations and references relative to the validity of bequests for charitable uses.

CASES

IN THE

SUPREME COURT

OF

PENNSYLVANIA.

HANNAH *v.* SWARNER.

[8 WATTS, 9.]

DEED DELIVERED TO ONE OF TWO GRANTEES NAMED THEREIN, without saying anything of the other, is void as to the latter.

WHETHER DEED HAS BEEN DELIVERED OR NOT, is a question of fact for the jury to determine.

ERROR to the common pleas of Perry county. Ejectment for a tract of land. The jury found a special verdict, upon which the parties agreed that the court should render judgment, with leave to the other party to sue out a writ of error without oath or bail. The following are such of the facts found by the special verdict, as are essential to an understanding of the opinion of the court: Joseph Smith died, leaving a will, by which he directed his executor to sell all his estate, real and personal, and out of the proceeds to pay certain legacies to his five children and one grandchild. The legatees under the will agreed to divide the real estate of the deceased among themselves in parts proportioned to the amount of the legacies bequeathed to them. After this agreement was executed, they found that the part allotted to John Smith, Sarah Hannah, and Jesse Miller was worth sixty-six dollars and sixty-seven cents more than the part allotted to Elizabeth, Mary, and Joseph; and John Smith, John Hannah, and Jesse Miller gave a note to Joseph Smith, Elizabeth Smith, and John White, for that sum. The executors of Joseph Smith, deceased, then executed a deed of conveyance to John Smith, John Hannah, and Jesse Miller for the part of the land allotted to them by the agreement. This deed was delivered to Jesse

Miller, and remained in his possession; and whether the execution and delivery thereof were assented to or not by the said John Hannah and his wife, or either of them, is not proved; and whether this amounts to a delivery of the deed and transfer of the estate to John Hannah, so as to divest the estate of his wife, the jury are ignorant, and refer it to the court. The grantees above named afterwards divided the land conveyed to them by said deed, and a judgment was obtained against Hannah, in his life-time, and an execution issued thereon, under which his portion was sold to one Gordon, who dispossessed said Hannah, and afterwards conveyed to the present defendant. John Hannah afterwards died, and his widow, Sarah Hannah, is the present plaintiff. On this verdict the court below rendered judgment for the defendant.

Watts, for the plaintiff in error.

Penrose, for the defendant in error.

By Court, GIBSON, C. J. No such facts are found as amount to a delivery in law. It is said in Viner's Abridgment, Faits, I, 7: "If a man make an obligation to two, and deliver it to one of them only, and say nothing of the other on the livery, the deed is void as to him;" for which he cites the year book, 3 Hen. VI., 19. So in *Hungate's case,* 5 Rep. 103, an action was not maintained on a bond to perform an award if made and delivered to the defendants by such a day, on proof that it was delivered to one of them and not to the other. In the verdict before us no more is found than that the deed was delivered to one of the grantees; for the jury explicitly say that they are ignorant whether the delivery to him was assented to by the others. In the *Bank of Washington* v. *Smith,*[1] 5 Serg. & R. 318, the assent of an absent grantee was presumed; but there was an actual delivery to a third person, and to the grantee's present use—a circumstance which is wanting here, and which is a distinguishing one, perhaps, in all the cases. In *Taw* v. *Bury,* 2 Dyer, 167 b, A. delivered his bond to B. to deliver it to the obligee as his deed; the obligee refused to receive it, whereupon B. left it; but the obligee afterwards sued and recovered on it, because, by the first delivery it was A.'s deed without delivery over, though, had it been given to be delivered over on the performance of a condition, it would have been otherwise. But if the writing be given to a stranger without any intimation or declaration of intention, it remains inoperative; "for the bare

---

1. *Smith* v. *Bank of Washington.*

act of delivery to him without words, worketh nothing:" Co. Lit. 36 a. The rule to be extracted from all this is, that a delivery to a third person for the present use of the grantee, makes the instrument a present deed; but that a delivery to his use when he shall perform a condition, makes not a present deed, and the grant may be frustrated by his refusal to perform it; and that a bare delivery to a stranger without words of direction to deliver over to the grantee, either absolutely or conditionally, is merely void.

Now the most favorable construction that can be made for the defendant, is to say that, for the purpose of receiving a deed, each of the grantees must be considered as standing in the relation of a stranger to the rest, else a delivery to the one, without direction to deliver it to the others, would perfect the deed as to all, which we have seen is not so; and here it is not found that there was any direction to the grantee who received the deed, it being nakedly affirmed that it was delivered to him and kept in his possession. Had it been given to him for delivery to the others also, it would have presently vested the estate in them without their consent; insomuch that they could not, on the principle of *Butler and Baker's case,* 3 Rep. 25, have divested it by a subsequent expression of oral dissent. But no such fact is found; and we are unable to pronounce on the premises, that there was a delivery in law. The difficulty is to say whether enough is found to enable us to give judgment for any one. The jury have set forth an instrument in the form of a deed, and it was their business to find a delivery in fact, or circumstances constituting a delivery in law; or to find that it was not delivered at all. The case, then, being insufficiently found, is remitted to another jury, to say either that the deed was, in fact, delivered to the grantees, if the evidence shall warrant it, or that it was delivered to one of them, and not to the rest. Other principles may be involved in the cause, which can not be settled before the facts are ascertained.

Record remitted.

———

DELIVERY OF DEED, WHAT IS: See note to *Chess* v. *Chess,* 21 Am. Dec. 361, and cases there cited and referred to. The principal case is cited in *Hastings* v. *Vaughn,* 5 Cal. 318, to the point that the fact of delivery is a question of fact for the jury.

COMMONWEALTH FOR THE USE OF HAHN *v.* McCOY.

[8 WATTS, 153.]

PLAINTIFF IN SUIT AGAINST SURETIES OF SHERIFF MUST SHOW DAMAGE sustained by him through the sheriff's neglect or failure in the performance of his duty.

SHERIFF, IN EXECUTING FIERI FACIAS, MUST BE GOVERNED BY THE SUM INDORSED on the back of the writ, and not by that contained in the body of the writ. The indorsement on the writ is the official act of the prothonotary, and is presumed to be right until the contrary is shown.

FEES OF OFFICERS ARE NOT RECOVERABLE in action against sureties of sheriff to recover money collected by him on an execution, except where such fees were previously advanced by the plaintiff.

SHERIFF IS PRESUMED TO HAVE COLLECTED AMOUNT OF FIERI FACIAS, which he has held in his hands for several years without returning, and the burden of proving that he did not collect it, is upon him or his sureties.

ERROR to the common pleas of Mifflin county. Debt upon the official recognizance of Sheriff Stuart, against the defendant, who, was one of his sureties. The plaintiff gave in evidence the record of a suit against John Hahn, in which a judgment was rendered for the defendant, and a *fi. fa.* against the plaintiff for costs, which went into the hands of Sheriff Stuart, but was never returned. The other facts are stated in the opinion.

J. A. Fisher, for the plaintiff in error.

Hale, for the defendant in error.

By Court, SERGEANT, J. By the act of assembly of the twenty-eighth of March, 1803, the condition of the sheriff's recognizance is, well and truly to serve all writs and process, and, on request, to pay over moneys coming to his hands, and well and faithfully to perform all the trusts and duties of the office. By the fourth section, authority to institute actions of debt, or of *scire facias*, is given to the commonwealth or individuals who shall be aggrieved by the misconduct of the sheriff, and upon such writs it shall be proved what damage hath been sustained, and a verdict, judgment, and execution are to be given for so much, with costs: which suits may be instituted, and the like proceedings be thereupon had, as often as such damage shall be sustained. It is necessary, therefore, under this act, for any person suing upon a sheriff's recognizance, to show that he is aggrieved by the misconduct of the sheriff, and that he has sustained damage by reason thereof, before he can recover. This official security, like other official bonds and securities required

of officers under our laws, was intended, so far as respects individuals, for their indemnity. It is not sufficient to entitle an
individual to recover upon it, that he shows a misconduct in the
officer, a violation or omission of his general duty as sheriff,
such as not returning a *fieri facias*. He can not, for that alone,
recover nominal damages in this suit. The sheriff can only be
proceeded against for it by the commonwealth, either by indictment (Dalt., Sheriff, 493), or by the courts where he is in contempt, by attachment. To sustain a civil action, the party suing
must show some loss or damage which he sustained by the acts
or omissions of the sheriff in the performance of his duty.

The question then arises, in this case, whether the plaintiff
below showed that he had sustained loss or damage under this
act by the neglect of Sheriff Stuart to return the two writs of
fieri facias put into his hands. Those writs were issued, one in
1832, and the other in 1833, and had never been returned at the
trial of this suit in the court of common pleas, but were produced by the present defendant at the trial on notice.

Regularly, it is the bounden duty of the sheriff to return all
writs to him directed, at the time and place commanded in
the body of the writ. This return is his answer to the writ:
and it is highly important, for his own protection and that of
his sureties, as well for the interest and security of the commonwealth and of suitors, that sheriffs should, in all cases, strictly
comply with this duty. By the ancient oath, at the common
law, the sheriff, amongst other things, swore well and truly to
serve and return the writs directed to him: and we see many
mischiefs and inconveniences daily grow from a neglect of this
duty, on the part of sheriffs, to themselves and others. At the
common law, the remedy seems to have been to amerce the sheriff for his neglect in this particular: for it is said that when a
writ is delivered to the sheriff to execute, he ought to receive it,
and not deliver it to the party that delivered it to him, back
again, but must execute it, and then return it into court, for so
he is commanded by the writ; and if he doth not so, upon complaint made thereof, the court will set a fine upon him: Dalt.,
Sheriff, 102. And now on the return day of a *fieri facias*, the
sheriff may be called on by rule to return the writ, and if he
neglect to do so, or to offer a reasonable excuse, the court will
grant an attachment against him: 1 H. Bl. 543;[1] Bing. Ex.
258. It would seem, however, to be held, that for merely not
returning a *fieri facias*, an action does not lie against the sheriff

---

1. *King* v. *Baker.*

at common law: Id. 251; Wats., Sheriff, 82; but the party ought to proceed by rule and attachment.

There are some authorities that look the other way, cited Dalt., Sheriff, 493. Lord Coke, in 2 Inst. 452, comments on the statute of 2 Westminster, which enacts that if any man doth fear the malice, indirect dealing, or negligence of the sheriff, in the execution of any writ, he may deliver it in open court, or may take of the sheriff a bill containing the names of the demandants and tenants, and require the sheriff to put his seal to it, and if he refuses, others present may put their seals as witnesses to it, and if the sheriff or under sheriff make not a due return of the writs delivered or offered unto him, upon complaint to the justices of the one bench or the other, they are to make a judicial writ to the justices of assize, to inquire thereof, by virtue whereof the justices of assize shall have power to inquire thereof, by those that were present when the writ was delivered; and if the sheriff be found in fault, then upon return thereof into the bench, etc., he shall be punished and yield damages, etc. In this special case, says Lord Coke, the demandant or plaintiff shall have an action against the sheriff for not returning the writ, whereas, regularly, for not returning of a writ, the sheriff shall be amerced *quousque*, but for a false return, or for embezzling of a writ, an action doth lie at the common law against the sheriff.

However this may be, if any damage has been here sustained by the omission of the sheriff to return a writ, the case falls within the provisions of the act of 1803, whether the remedy in other cases be by rule and attachment, or by indictment, or by action at common law; for the act gives a new and specific remedy in that case. Then had the present plaintiff any interest in the execution of these writs, and if he had, has he been damaged by the neglect of the sheriff to return them? The court below charged that the sheriff could only levy on writ No. 40, to August term, 1832, the sum of eleven dollars seventy-eight and one half cents, being the officers' costs, and the sum contained in the body of the writ, notwithstanding there was indorsed on the writ a further sum of seven dollars and thirty cents, the defendant's bill of costs at May term, 1830. But we think it is the duty of the sheriff, in executing a writ of *fieri facias*, to be governed in the amount to be levied by the sum indorsed on the back of the writ, and that he is not to follow that which is contained in the body; such has been the constant practice. The sum mentioned in the body is often nominal; the indorsement states the credits, the items of costs and charges, the dates of interest, and contains the real demand of the plaintiff, and has been considered as the statement of the sum really due, and the exact specification of the amount the defendant is to pay. Where they vary, the indorsement is the guide; the sheriff would be justified in receiving that, and is bound by it in collecting by sale. The court below seem to have thought that because no evidence was given when this part of the indorsement was made, the sheriff could not levy it. But it is not incumbent on the plaintiff to show this by extrinsic evidence. The writ and the indorsement are all the official acts of the prothonotary, and must be taken to be right and proper, at least till the contrary is shown. *Omnia presumuntur rite esse acta*, in the case of process issued by the proper officer. The indorsement being a matter *in pais*, the defendant might show that it was not the act of the proper officer, or that it was improperly made. But until that is done, it must be presumed to be right; and the sheriff was bound to obey the writ, and would be justified by so doing in all cases. It does not lie in his mouth to dispute or question the writ as he receives it. And here he produced these writs on notice, and there is no evidence that any addition was improperly made.

As to the fees of the officers, the charge of the court was correct. It was decided by this court last term, in *Beale* v. *The Commonwealth*, 7 Watts, 186, that in an action by the plaintiff against the sureties of the sheriff, to recover the money collected by the sheriff on an execution, the fees of the officers are not recoverable, except where they have been previously advanced by the plaintiff. The present plaintiff then had an interest in the collection of the bill of costs; and if the plaintiff in the writ No. 40, which was nonsuited, had goods or property sufficient to pay them, the sheriff was bound to levy on his property and collect them. But several years had elapsed, the sheriff had long since gone out of office, this writ remained unreturned, and was produced by the sheriff on the trial. If he has levied and collected these costs, and never paid them to the defendant, or if it was in his power to do it and he has neglected his duty, in either case the present plaintiff has sustained damage by his misconduct.

What then is the presumption that must arise where a sheriff has had a writ of execution in his hands and suffered this state of things to exist, permitted several years to pass by, had quitted the office, and had never given any answer by returning the writ as he was commanded to do, but kept it in his private custody? It appears to me that, until some evidence is given by the sheriff either of the payment of the money to the plaintiff, or of his inability to serve the process, the presumption must be that he has served it. We can not presume that he neglected his duty, or in the absence of any, even the slightest proof, that the plaintiffs were without means of payment. The difficulty has arisen from the sheriff's own neglect. If the plaintiff had no property, it was easy to return *nulla bona*, or show, now, some evidence of the fact: and that burden, we think, lies on the sheriff to make out, either by such return or by some evidence. To make a return, as has been before shown, is his bounden duty in all cases. He is to return *nil habet* or *non est inventus*, directly, and not so far as appeared to him, or by indirect reference: Dalt. 163. If he makes a return it is evidence in his own favor, and throws the burden of proof on the plaintiff. If he does not, it is right he should show why he did not collect the debt.

On the naked evidence of the delivery of the writ, and its never being returned, the case thereof, as to this bill of costs, is against the sheriff: the presumption is that he has collected the costs, and has not paid them to the party. But he may on another trial show that he never collected these costs, and that he had a good excuse for not collecting them, or that he has collected and paid them: and these will be the questions to be decided, in order to ascertain whether the present plaintiff has been aggrieved, and has sustained damage by the misconduct of the sheriff.

Judgment reversed, and *venire facias de novo* awarded.

Approved in *Commonwealth* v. *Contner*, 21 Pa. St. 274, on the point that in an action on the recognizance of a sheriff, the plaintiff can not recover, unless he has been actually aggrieved.

MILLER *v.* GETTYSBURG BANK.

[8 WATTS, 192.]

CREDITOR TO WHOM CLAIMS ARE TRANSFERRED AS COLLATERAL SECURITY, is bound to use ordinary diligence in collecting them, and is liable for loss resulting from his failure to do so; but if the transfer merely authorizes such creditor to receive the proceeds of the claims when collected, and apply them to the payment of his debt, he is not bound to prosecute their collection.

ERROR to the common pleas of Adams county. Action on the case. The plaintiff, being indebted to the defendant on two

promissory notes, confessed judgments to the sureties on said
notes, which judgments were marked for the use of the bank,
and the following paper was also executed and delivered to the
bank:

"SAMPSON S. KING, Esq. Sir: You will proceed without
delay with the collection of the accounts I left with you for that
purpose, and as the money is received, pay it over to the bank
of Gettysburg, to be credited on the debt due by William Miller
and James Reid, which they became liable for as my indorsers,
for which purpose the said accounts are hereby transferred to
the bank of Gettysburg; and as soon as these claims are satisfied this transfer to be void.   JAMES H. MILLER."

The declaration alleged that there was a transfer of the claims
therein mentioned to the bank for collection, and the bank had
neglected to prosecute them, whereby they were lost by the insolvency of the debtors and otherwise. The plaintiff on the
trial offered evidence to prove these allegations, but the judge,
being of opinion that the legal interpretation of the paper was
not such as to impose on the bank any responsibility for the
prosecution or collection of the claims, rejected all the evidence
tending to show negligence on the part of the bank. This ruling was assigned for error.

Cooper and Alexander, for the plaintiff in error.

Smyser and Stevens, for the defendant in error.

By Court, SERGEANT, J. This case depends on the construction of the instrument of the second of March, 1822. On the
part of the plaintiff it is contended that it was a transfer to the
bank of the accounts then in the hands of Sampson S. King,
Esq., justice of the peace, as a collateral security for the debt
of Miller to the bank, and that the bank was bound to use due
diligence to collect these accounts, and is responsible to the
plaintiff for their neglect in that respect, by which several of
them were lost. If the instrument were clearly such a transfer,
it became the duty of the bank to use ordinary diligence in re
alizing these accounts, and they would be responsible for loss
occasioned by any omission to do so: *Beale* v. *The Bank*, 5 Watts,
529. The instrument, however, seems to be drawn in terms
which will not admit of this interpretation. The accounts,
which were very numerous, and many of them consisting of
small items, had been previously placed by the plaintiff in the
hands of the magistrate for collection. The plaintiff, then, by

this order, directs the magistrate to proceed without delay in the collection.   In that respect, no discretion or authority is given to the defendant to interfere or control the magistrate: his course is marked out.   Then, as the money is received, he is to pay it over to the bank, for which purpose the accounts are transferred to the bank.   This seems to convey no general control or power to the bank over these accounts, but merely an authority to receive the money when collected by the magistrate, under the instructions thus given to him by the plaintiff.   The magistrate was to collect and pay over: the bank to receive and give an acquittance: and for that purpose only were the accounts transferred.   When the debt of the bank was paid, the transfer was to terminate: for it proceeds to say, that as soon as the claims of the bank are satisfied (which might be either out of these funds or in any other way), then the transfer is to be void.

According to the best construction, therefore, which I am able to give to this instrument, I am of opinion that it is not an absolute transfer of these accounts to the bank, but passes merely a qualified and restricted interest in the proceeds when collected, agreeably to the directions given by the plaintiff; that this order bound the claims when given, and continued to operate and bind them throughout; that after this order had been given, the interest of both parties in the accounts continued to such an extent (until the defendants were paid), that neither of them separately could give any new order to the magistrate varying the former, but if that were deemed necessary, the consent of both must have been obtained, and that under this instrument it was not incumbent on the defendant to prosecute the collection of the claims in the hands of the magistrate, or to do more than simply receive the money when paid over to them, and give an acquittance.   The parties must take the agreement such as they have chosen to make it—peculiar in its structure and phraseology, and of course in the duties it creates.

The determination of this point disposes of the bills of exception to evidence: for if the plaintiff's cause of action failed, the evidence to show the liability of the bank for the acts of its president was immaterial.

Judgment affirmed.

DILIGENCE WHICH HOLDER OF NEGOTIABLE PAPER AS COLLATERAL SECURITY MUST EXERCISE FOR ITS COLLECTION.—Where a creditor takes a negotiable instrument from his debtor, as collateral security for the payment of his debt, and holds it until it becomes due, it is his duty to present it for payment at maturity, and, if it is dishonored, to give notice to the parties entitled thereto, in the same manner as if he were the absolute owner of the instrument: *Peacock* v. *Pursell*, 32 L. J., C. P. (N. S.) 266; S. C., 14 C. B. (N. S.) 728; Byles on Bills, 381; 1 Dan. Neg. Inst. 677, 684; *Betterton* v. *Roope*, 3 Lea, 215; S. C., 31 Am. Rep. 633; *Smith* v. *Miller*, 43 N. Y. 171; S. C., 3 Am. Rep. 690; *Alexandria etc. R. R. Co.* v. *Burke*, 22 Gratt. 254, 262; *Sellers* v. *Jones*, 22 Pa. St. 423, 427; *Muirhead* v. *Kirkpatrick*, 21 Id. 237; *Russell* v. *Hester*, 10 Ala. 535; Schoul. Bail. 193, 213; *Wheeler* v. *Newbould*, 16 N. Y. 392; *Reeves* v. *Plough*, 41 Ind. 204; *Foote* v. *Brown*, 2 McLean, 369. But, in the performance of this duty, ordinary diligence and skill are the measure of the pledgee's responsibility: *Reeves* v. *Plough*, 41 Ind. 204; *Lee* v. *Baldwin*, 10 Ga. 208; Schoul. Bail. 193; *Goodall* v. *Richardson*, 14 N. H. 567.

FAILURE TO MAKE PRESENTMENT AND GIVE NOTICE, EFFECT OF.—If the person with whom negotiable paper is left as collateral security neglects to make presentment thereof when due, or fails to give due notice to bind the parties to it, or does not use due diligence in making the collection, so that by reason of his neglect the paper becomes worthless, he will be liable for the loss to the pledgor. The laches of the pledgee makes the instrument deposited equivalent to payment, and the debt for which it was held as collateral security becomes thereby extinguished: *Peacock* v. *Pursell*, 32 L. J., C. P. (N. S.) 266; S. C., 14 C. B. (N. S.) 728; *Hanna* v. *Holton*, 78 Pa. St. 334; S. C., 21 Am. Rep. 20; *Betterton* v. *Roope*, 3 Lea, 215; S. C., 31 Am. Rep. 633; *Smith* v. *Miller*, 43 N. Y. 171; S. C., 3 Am. Rep. 690; *Whitten* v. *Wright*, 34 Mich. 92; *Reeves* v. *Plough*, 41 Ind. 204; Byles on Bills, 381; *Wakeman* v. *Gowdy*, 10 Bosw. 208; *Word* v. *Morgan*, 5 Sneed, 79. In the case of *Peacock* v. *Pursell*, *supra*, the defendant had indorsed to the plaintiffs a bill of which he was indorsee, as collateral security for a debt of larger amount then due, the balance of which he had paid in cash. The plaintiffs failed to make presentment or to give notice, and it was decided that they had, by their laches, lost recourse against the defendant, both upon the bill and upon the original debt. Byles, J., in delivering his opinion in that case said: "It is quite clear that, as depositees of the bill, as they had the rights so they had the duties of holders. No one else could present the bill; and as they failed in that duty, they discharged the defendant." This doctrine seems to be approved by Mr. Daniel in his work on negotiable instruments: See vol. 1, page 677.

The learned American editors of White and Tudor's Leading Cases in Equity, vol. 2, pt. 2, p. 1903, say that "the American courts do not carry the duty of the creditor to take active measures to make the collateral securities for the debt available as far as the English." Whatever may have been the case formerly, it seems to us, after a careful examination of the more recent American cases, which are cited above, that our courts are now inclined to hold the pledgees or depositees of negotiable paper held as collateral security, to as strict an accountability as do the English courts. In the case of *Hanna* v. *Holton*, 78 Pa. St. 334; 21 Am. Rep. 20, Agnew, J., delivering the opinion of the court, says: "It is therefore settled in this state, that where the collateral is lost, by the insolvency of the debtor, in the collateral instrument, through the supine negligence of the creditor, he must account for the loss to his own debtor, who invested him with its entire control." In support of this view the learned judge cites the principal case, and a number of other Pennsylvania decisions. See also *Word* v. *Morgan*, 5 Sneed, 79; *Smith* v. *Miller*, 43 N. Y. 171; S. C., 3 Am. Rep. 690; *Wakeman* v. *Gowdy*, 10 Bosw. 208; *Whitten* v. *Wright*, 34 Mich. 92; *May* v. *Sharp*, 49 Ala. 140; *Lamberton* v. *Windom*, 12 Minn. 232.

HAY *v.* MAYER.

[8 WATTS, 203.]

WHERE ONE WHO HAS A POWER TO SELL and an interest in land, executes a conveyance thereof, without referring to the power, the land shall pass by virtue of his ownership, even though his ownership be of a part only, while his power is over the whole.

WHERE TESTATOR DEVISES LANDS TO HIS DAUGHTER IN FEE TAIL, directing that, in case she shall die without issue, his executors shall sell the lands and divide the proceeds among other legatees named in the will, and the daughter dies, leaving a husband who is entitled to a life estate therein, as tenant by the curtesy, such lands can not be sold by the executors until after the determination of the life estate of the husband.

POWER OF ATTORNEY IN THESE TERMS DOES NOT CONFER POWER TO CONVEY REAL ESTATE: To ask, demand, recover, or receive the maker's lawful part of a decedent's estate, giving and granting thereby to his said attorney his sole and full power and authority to take, pursue, and follow such legal course for the recovery, receiving, and obtaining the same, as he himself might or could do were he personally present; and upon the receipt thereof, acquittances, and other sufficient discharges for him, and in his name, to sign, seal, and deliver.

ERROR to the common pleas of Dauphin county. Ejectment brought by Andrew S. Morrison, administrator *de bonis non cum testamento annexo* of Hugh Hay, deceased, against Mayer and others, tenants in possession, for the purpose of enforcing the payment of a legacy under the will of said Hugh Hay, deceased. The following facts were found as a special verdict: Hugh Hay died seised of the land in question, in the year 1777, leaving a will by which he bequeathed to his daughter Margaret all his real estate, to her, to her heirs and assigns forever, and directing that in case his said daughter should die without issue, his executors should sell all his estate, and after satisfying themselves for their trouble, divide the proceeds, after the death of his widow, among the sons of his brother and sisters, share and share alike. The deceased left surviving him, his wife Mary Hay, his daughter Margaret Hay, his brother Patrick Hay, and his sisters Rebecca Buchanan and Margaret Morrison. Patrick Hay had two sons, William and Hugh; Rebecca Buchanan had one son, James; and Margaret Morrison had four sons, Hugh, Andrew, William, and Patrick. The executors named in the will renounced, and letters of administration with the will annexed were granted to said Mary Hay and Archibald McAllister. Archibald McAllister married said Margaret Hay, after the death of her father. She died the following year, having had issue born alive, who died in the life-time of the said Margaret. Said Archibald McAllister.

lived until February, 1831. The said Mary Hay afterwards married William McAlevy and died in 1793. The defendants produced a patent from the commonwealth to Hugh Hay, dated August 12, 1743, for the land in question, and the following deeds and instruments, all of which were recorded: A deed from Patrick Hay to James Buchanan; a deed from William Hay to James Buchanan; a deed from Hugh Hay (son of Patrick Hay) to James Buchanan; a deed from Hugh, Andrew, and William Morrison to James Buchanan; power of attorney from Patrick Morrison to James Buchanan; a deed of release from William McAlevy and wife to Archibald McAllister; a deed from James Buchanan to John Duffee Hay for the moiety of said land; a letter of attorney from said John Duffee Hay to William Hay; a deed from said John Duffee Hay, by his attorney in fact William Hay, to Peter Gloninger; a deed from said Gloninger to William Coleman for the same moiety; a deed from James Buchanan to Archibald McAllister for the other moiety of said land; a deed from said McAllister to Robert Coleman. The title of said Robert and William Coleman passed to the defendants by various mesne conveyances. Archibald McAllister held possession of the land in question from the death of his wife, in 1778, to the tenth day of April, 1805, when he delivered the possession to Robert Coleman, with his deed above mentioned. Letters of administration, with the will annexed, *de bonis non*, were issued to the plaintiff in 1836. The verdict concludes in these words: "If, in the opinion of the court, on the foregoing case, the plaintiff shall be entitled to recover, judgment shall be entered for him, to be released on payment, by defendants, of three thousand one hundred and seventy dollars, with or without interest on the same, from the death of Archibald McAllister, or on payment of any less sum, rating the land at sixty-five dollars per acre, with or without interest, as aforesaid, as the court shall determine; and, if judgment shall be rendered for plaintiff, he shall execute and deliver a deed of release to defendants for said land on the payment of said money." The court below rendered a judgment for one half of Patrick Morrison's legacy, one thousand five hundred and eighty-five dollars, with interest from the twelfth of May, 1832. Each party sued out a writ of error.

Roberts and Forster, for the plaintiffs below.

McCormick and Weidman, for the defendants.

By Court, KENNEDY, J. The first question arising out of this case, as stated, is whether the deed of conveyance from Archibald McAllister to Robert Coleman, bearing date the tenth of April, 1805, can be considered a good execution of the power contained in the will of Hugh Hay, dated the twenty-fourth of May, 1777, authorizing his executors, in case his daughter Margaret, to whom he had devised, by a previous clause of his will, the land mentioned and transferred by the said conveyance, " to her, her heirs and assigns forever," should die without issue, to sell the whole of his estate, of which the land formed a part; and that the money arising therefrom should, after the decease of his widow, his executors being first satisfied for their trouble, be equally divided among his brother Patrick's and his sisters Buchanan and Morrison's sons, share and share alike. Various objections seem to present themselves to the deed of conveyance being held an execution of the power: First, because, although Archibald McAllister was, at the time of his executing the deed, administrator *cum testamento annexo* of the testator, yet it appears very clearly from the face of the deed that it was not his intention, by means of it, to execute the power to sell under the will. By his having become the husband of Margaret, the devisee of the land, and having had by her issue capable of inheriting it, he upon his wife's death, notwithstanding the previous death of her issue, became tenant for life of the land by courtesy. His life estate thus acquired, which extended to the whole of the land, after reciting the manner in which he had become invested with it, he conveys distinctly and expressly by the deed as an interest which he had in himself without referring to the power; so that upon the ground of intention, as clearly expressed as it was possible on his part, as well as the principle which is uncontrovertibly settled, that where a man has both a power and an interest, and does an act even generally, and not specially, as it would seem to have been done in this case, as owner of the land, without reference to his power, the land shall pass by virtue of his ownership: 1 Sugden on Powers, 430; 15 Law Lib. 229. Then by the same duty, after showing by a recital therein, that he had also become, as he conceived, the owner of the remainder in fee of an undivided moiety of the land, he thereby conveys it also without referring to the power, and in terms which seem very clearly to exclude it.

It is plain that Archibald McAllister, at the time of executing the deed of conveyance to Robert Coleman, conceived himself invested with the absolute and indefeasible right to the remainder in fee of an undivided moiety of the land, by means of the deed of conveyance made to him by James Buchanan, on

the seventeenth of December, 1804, and the deeds of conveyance made previously to Buchanan by the sons of the testator's brother, Patrick Hay, and by his two sisters, Rebecca
Buchanan, wife of the said James Buchanan, and Margaret
Morrison, with the exception of Patrick Morrison, one of
the sons of Margaret Morrison, who never parted with his
right in any way, as will be shown in the sequel, to the money
arising from the sale of the land, to be made under the will, in
the event of the testator's daughter, Margaret, dying without
issue.   But then it is more than probable that McAllister was
made to believe, when he received the deed of conveyance to
himself from Buchanan, that the three sons therein named of
Margaret Morrison, were all that she ever had or that were then
living, because they are mentioned in such way as to raise that
belief.   And for the same reason that McAllister considered himself entitled to the remainder in fee of an undivided moiety of
the land at the time he sold and conveyed it to Coleman, he must
have believed that Peter Gloninger was the owner of the other
moiety, who derived his claim or title to it in like manner from
James Buchanan.   The conveyances from the nephews of the
testator to Buchanan, already alluded to, embraced all the land,
and were made with a view, no doubt, to invest him with a right
to the remainder in fee in the whole of it.   Mr. Sugden, in his
treatise on powers, vol. 1, p. 440, says: "It is intention then,
that in these cases governs; therefore, where it can be inferred
that the power was not meant to be exercised, the court can not
consider it as executed."

Here then it is almost morally impossible to infer that Mc-
Allister, supposing him to have been capable of exercising the
power in the will at the time, intended to do so; because, under
the power, his authority to sell extended to the remainder in
fee in the whole of the land, but his conveyance is limited to an
undivided moiety thereof, which he undertakes to show by a recital in the deed, he had become the absolute owner of, and as
such, and in fact not otherwise, he thereby intended to convey
it.   But it may perhaps be said, that intention is made the test,
only where the grantor has such estate or interest as he undertakes to convey, and, at the same time, also a power to convey
the same; and not to the case where he mistakenly supposes
himself to have such interest; because, having shown clearly, as
it may be argued, by his deed that it was his intention to transfer such interest at all events, and therefore by any means within
his power, the conveyance will be referred to the power so as

to render it effectual. Admitting this, then, to be the rule, a second objection arises, that it was not competent for him to exercise the power without relinquishing all his right in the land and giving the whole proceeds of the sale to the nephews. By the will it is clear that the testator gave his daughter an estate tail in the land, and as long as that estate endured, it is also equally clear that he did not intend the land should be sold; but upon the determination of that estate, from a failure of issue upon her part, it would seem to have been his wish that the fee simple estate in the land should then be sold, and the money arising therefrom distributed among his nephews. But before the arrival of the time when the nephews should become entitled to receive the money in possession, there is no reason to believe that it was the intention of the testator that a sale should be made. It is perfectly manifest that it was not to be sold, at any time, for the benefit of his daughter, her issue, or that of any other, who might acquire an interest in it by marriage with her. It was directed to be sold for the exclusive purpose of giving to his nephews the immediate benefit of the money arising from the sale; and, when sold for that purpose, it can not be doubted but it was his desire that it should be sold for the highest and best price that could be obtained for it. Then, in order to meet the intention of the testator, and fulfill his wishes in this respect, it is clear that a sale, under the power contained in the will, could not be effected until after the death of McAllister; because, until his life estate was determined, the full value or price of the fee simple estate in possession in it, could neither have been ascertained nor had for it. And even if it could, unless it had been paid over to them immediately, it might have been dissipated and lost to them, contrary to the design of the testator, as they could not have demanded or compelled the payment of it during the life of McAllister, the tenant for life.

This view of the question here derives support from a late decision of the court of exchequer in *Meyrick* v. *Coutts*, 1 Sug. Pow. 349, 350, where the devise was to A., the testator's wife, for life, and after her death, a power to trustees to sell and pay the money amongst the children of B., who had an infant child then living, the court held that the sale could not be made till after the widow's decease. It is also sustained, I believe, by the common course and practice of mankind, so far as we have evidence of it. In *Lee* v. *Vincent*, Cro. Eliz. 26; Co. Lit. 113 a, a case pretty much like the one under consideration, where

John Lee devised land to his son William in tail, and, if he
died without issue, directed that his sons-in-law (having then
five) should sell the land; after the death of the testator, one of
the sons-in-law died, and then William died, leaving issue a
daughter, who died afterwards without issue; then the four
sons-in-law sold the land, and never thought or supposed that
they could have done it before. Two questions were made:
1. Whether, as the son died leaving issue, though that issue
died afterwards without issue, the sale was good; and 2.
Whether, one of the sons-in-law having died, the sale could be
made by the four surviving: and both questions were decided
in the affirmative.

The next question which presents itself is, did the letter of
attorney, from Patrick Morrison to James Buchanan, bearing
date the twenty-first of June, 1780, authorize the latter to convey or transfer any interest which the former had in the land or
right to the money which should arise from the sale thereof,
made under the will of the testator? It is very clear that the
letter of attorney, according to the terms of it, has no application whatever to lands or real estate of any kind, and therefore
confers no authority to sell or dispose of such estate. It is " to
ask, demand, recover, or receive his lawful part of the estate of
Hugh Hay (meaning the testator), deceased, of the county of
Lancaster, etc., giving and granting thereby to his said attorney,
his sole and full power and authority to take, pursue, and follow such legal course for the recovery, receiving, and obtaining
the same, as he himself might or could do were he personally
present; and upon the receipt thereof, acquittances and other
sufficient discharges for him, and in his name, to sign, seal, and
deliver," etc. Now nothing can be more plain than that the
authority, given by the letter of attorney, extends merely to
such portions of the personal estate of the testator as might be
coming to the constituent. And besides, the letter of attorney
contains no authority to sell or dispose of the constituent's interest in the personal estate, but to demand and receive it, and
to do in his name whatever may be lawful and necessary to obtain and recover it. The deeds, therefore, of James Buchanan,
the first bearing date the twenty-fifth of February, 1793, to John
Duffee Hay, and the second bearing date the seventeenth of
December, 1804, to Robert Coleman, had no effect whatever
upon the right or interest which Patrick Morrison had either in
the real or personal estate of the testator. And even if the
letter of attorney had authorized James Buchanan to have sold

and assigned the interest of Patrick Morrison in the estate of
the testator, neither of the deeds purports to have been executed
by Buchanan for Morrison. It is perfectly obvious that they
are both executed for and in behalf of himself alone.

Patrick Morrison would, therefore, seem to have a right to
demand and receive one seventh part of the money arising from
a sale to be made of the land, as directed by the will. It
certainly has not been shown that he has ever released or parted
with it. The conveyances of the other nephews to James
Buchanan, may be sufficient to preclude them from ever setting
up any claim to have the land sold on their account under the
will; though it would seem from their deeds that they misap-
prehended very much the nature of their claim to, or interest in
the estate. They, in fact, had no interest in the land; each had
a right merely to receive a certain proportion of the money that
should arise from the sale thereof, when made according to the
provisions and directions of the will. Their claims, however,
may be considered as assignable in equity for a valuable consideration; and their deeds as sufficient to bind and divest
them, in equity at least, of their rights to any money that could
be raised from a sale of the land under this power. That they
had no right or interest in the land to convey and transfer, is
established not only authoritatively, but satisfactorily, by the
cases of *Allison* v. *Wilson's Ex'rs*, 13 Serg. & R. 330; and
Morrow v. *Brenizer*, 2 Rawle, 188; and more especially by the
clear and conclusive reasoning of the chief justice in the latter
case.

We therefore think that the court below were right in rendering a judgment for the plaintiff, but that they erred in directing
it to be released on the payment of one thousand five hundred
and eighty-five dollars, with interest thereon from the twelfth day
of May, 1832. We think the plaintiff, upon the case as stated,
entitled to receive the sum of three thousand one hundred and
seventy dollars, with interest thereon from the time the judgment was rendered in the court below; and accordingly direct
that the judgment be released on the payment of this sum to
the plaintiff, and the costs of the action in the court below, together with the costs which have accrued on the writ of error
in this court.

Judgment accordingly.

GENERAL CLAUSE IN POWER OF ATTORNEY GIVEN FOR SPECIFIC PUR-
POSE, authorizing the agent to do "any and every act" in the principal's
name, which he could do in person, must be construed to relate to the specific

purpose, and does not constitute such agent a general agent: *Rossiter* v. *Rossiter*, 24 Am. Dec. 62, note 65. See also *Ashley* v. *Bird*, 14 Id. 313.

The principal case is cited in *Gast* v. *Porter*, 13 Pa. St. 536, to the point that where a testator devises real estate to executors to sell, on a contingency, if the sale is made before the contingency happens the sale will be void; and in *Jones* v. *Wood*, 16 Id. 42, to the point that when the donee of a power to sell land possesses also an interest in the subject of the power, a conveyance by him without actual reference to the power, will not be deemed an execution of it, except there be evidence of an intention to execute it, or at least in the face of evidence disproving such an intention; but where the donee has no estate in the premises, and his conveyance can only be made operative by treating it as an execution of the power to sell, it will be so considered.

SHERBAN *v.* COMMONWEALTH.

[8 WATTS, 212.]

INDICTMENTS REQUIRE ONLY THE SAME CERTAINTY AS DECLARATIONS, that is, certainty to a common intent in general, and not certainty in every particular, and they need not aver that which is apparent to the court and appears from a necessary implication. It is sufficient if the indictment states the charge with sufficient certainty to inform the defendant what he is called upon to answer, and over-nice exceptions are not to be encouraged, especially in cases which do not touch the life of the defendant.

ERROR to the quarter sessions of Cumberland county. Indictment for betting on an election. The offense was laid as follows: "The grand inquest of the commonwealth of Pennsylvania, inquiring in and for the county of Cumberland, on their oaths and affirmations respectively, do present: That Daniel Sherban, late, etc., on the twenty-eighth of September, 1828, in the county aforesaid, and within the jurisdiction of this court, did lay a wager and bet with a certain Jacob Clark, and that the said Daniel Sherban did then and there lay a wager and bet of fifty dollars with the said Jacob Clark, that a certain Joseph Ritner would be elected governor of the commonwealth of Pennsylvania at an election to be held in said commonwealth, under the constitution and laws of said commonwealth, on the ninth day of October, in the year 1838, the said Joseph Ritner then and there being a candidate nominated for public office, to wit, for the office of governor of said commonwealth, contrary to the act of assembly in such case made and provided, and against the peace and dignity of the commonwealth of Pennsylvania." The defendant demurred generally, but the court overruled the demurrer, and passed sentence upon the defendant.

Watts, for the plaintiff in error.

Graham, attorney-general, contra.

By Court, SERGEANT, J.   It is a general rule that, in all indictments, the charge must be positively averred; but in what cases it is or is not sufficiently averred, is not ascertained with precision, and must be left, in a great measure, to the legal discretion of the court: 2 Hawk. P. C. 228.   Indictments require only the same certainty as declarations, namely, certainty to a common intent in general, and not certainty in every particular, as is required in pleading an estoppel: Co. Lit. 303; 2 Stra. 904;[1] 1 Chit. Crim. L. 169.   It is a rule that that which is apparent to the court, and appears from a necessary implication, need not be averred: 4 Bac. Abr. 322.   It is sufficient in indictments, that the charge be stated with so much certainty that the defendant may know what he is called on to answer, and that the court may know how to render the proper judgment thereon. Over-nice exceptions are not to be encouraged, especially in cases which do not touch the life of the defendant: 1 Chit. Crim. L. 170, 221; 2 Hale, 178.   The objection is, that the indictment does not aver that there was an election for governor about to be held in October, 1838; but it avers that the defendant made a bet dependent on an election for governor, to be held in October, 1838.   We think the fair implication is, not only that such bet was made, but that the election was to be held at that time, and that the commonwealth would be bound in this charge to prove both these facts.

Judgment affirmed.

INDICTMENT, CERTAINTY REQUIRED IN: See *State* v. *Crank*, 23 Am. Dec. 117; *State* v. *Brown*, 17 Id. 562.

CRONISTER *v.* WEISE.

[8 WATTS, 215.]

SHERIFF'S SALE UPON A JUDGMENT ON A MORTGAGE BOND DIVESTS LIEN of the mortgage at law, as to all other bonds secured by the mortgage.

PART OWNER OF MORTGAGE IS LIABLE to the other part owner thereof for positive misfeasance only.

BONA FIDE ASSERTION OF RIGHT, WHICH DETERS BIDDERS at a judicial sale, although the right turns out to be unfounded, does not estop the person who asserted it from afterwards claiming under the sale.

ERROR to the common pleas of Cumberland county. *Scire facias sur mortgage*, by Michael Weise, for the use of J. B. McLanahan, against Abraham Cronister, administrator of Jacob

---

1. *Rex* v. *Lawley.*

Cronister, with notice to James Clark, the tenant in possession. The plaintiff gave in evidence a mortgage of Jacob Cronister to Weise to secure the payment of eight bonds, payable in eight successive years after the first of April, 1817. And of these he gave in evidence the bond due April 1, 1820, of which said McLanahan was the holder, and which he claimed to recover in this suit. He also proved that Clark was in possession of the land mortgaged. The defendant gave in evidence the record of a suit and judgment—Weise for the use of one Leeper, against Jacob Cronister's administrator, founded upon a bond secured by the aforesaid mortgage, and payable April 1, 1821; the execution on said judgment, and the sale of the mortgaged premises to said Leeper, and a deed from Leeper to said Clark. In rebuttal, the plaintiff proved that at the time the sheriff sold to Leeper, said Clark was present, and gave notice " that whoever would buy, would buy a lawsuit; that he had a mortgage on the land, and he would push it or claim it." That in consequence of this notice a bidder withdrew a bid of three hundred dollars, and the land was struck down to said Leeper for one hundred and twenty-five dollars, and that it was worth two thousand dollars. The defendant excepted to the opinion of the court below, which was in favor of the plaintiff, and assigned it for error.

Biddle and *Watts*, for the plaintiff in error.

Alexander, contra.

By Court, GIBSON, C. J. The sheriff's sale certainly discharged the mortgage at law; and if Clark, then a part owner of it, but now a terre-tenant defendant at the suit of the other part owner, is to be precluded from insisting on the discharge, his purchase from the sheriff's vendor must be treated as a trust. But a misfeasance, to make him a trustee *ex maleficio*, must be such as would subject him to an action at law; and it is settled that an action on the case lies not for an act which, though it be to the damage of the party, is not prohibited by the law. Thus it was in *Semayne's case*, 5 Co. 91, where the defendant had shut the door of his house against the sheriff coming to do execution of the goods of another in it; or as it was in the *Countess of Salop* v. *Crampton*, Cro. Eliz. 784, where a lessee at will had negligently burned his house; or as it is said in F. Moore, 420, 453, where a man builds a dove-cote or coney-warren on his land, and the doves or conies hurt the neighbors—in these, and a countless number of other instances, there is *damnum absque injuria.*

The sum of the maxim *sic utere tuo* is, that you so use your own as to do no wanton damage to another; in consonance with which is *Townsend* v. *Wathen*, 9 East, 277, where the defendant, having set traps for dogs, with an intent to allure them into his grounds by the scent of bait prepared for the purpose, was held to be liable only because the purpose was malicious and unlawful. But the *bona fide* exercise of a right, how prejudicial soever its consequences to another, is followed by no such liability. Thus, an arrest for a debt mistakenly supposed due, though ruinous to the party, is justifiable as a fair use of a legal remedy. And the principle is decisive in its application to the duties of part owners, the rule being that a tenant in common is answerable to his fellow only for a voluntary destruction or abuse of the thing.

In *Martyn* v. *Knowllys*, 9 T. R. 146,[1] it was ruled that the one could not maintain an action against the other for cutting down trees of a proper age and growth, else an obstinate co-tenant might hinder the others from taking the fair profits of their estates. For the same reason, it was held in *Fennings* v. *Lord Grenville*, Taunt. 241,[2] that the conversion of a chattel to its general and profitable application, even by changing the form of its substance, is not a destruction of the thing to give an action for it betwixt tenants in common, because each has an equal right to take it and use it in its altered state. Nor do I apprehend that an accidental diminution of its value by the process, would have made a difference; for joint owners, having equal right to manage the property for the advantage of their respective interests, are answerable to each other for nothing but positive misfeasance. In the application of this principle to the matter in hand, it is to be borne in mind that there was no officious intermeddling with the plaintiff's interest; for Clark professed not to act farther than to the extent of his ownership, or for any one but himself. It had not been settled that a sale on a judgment discharged a mortgage; the current of popular opinion was that it did not, and indeed such was the advice of counsel in the particular instance. Clark, the present terre-tenant, then being a part owner of the mortgage which stood as a security for bonds separately assigned to the plaintiff and himself, and the land being put up for sale on the judgment of another, warned the bidders of the existence of the mortgage, and desired them to take notice that he meant to enforce it against the land, which consequently sold for about a twentieth of its value, and the mortgage creditors got nothing from the purchase money.

1. 8 T. R. 146.   2. 1 Taunt. 241.

Now, though it was, in any event, unnecessary to give verbal notice of a registered mortgage, the warning was, nevertheless, an act of good faith; nor could its tendency to remove misconception be deemed a legal injury to the plaintiff. On the contrary, it might well have been thought a service to him, as it would preclude an imputation of concealment by him. It was, in truth, no more than a repetition of the notice afforded by the register. Thus it stood at the sale; and it will not be said that Clark had not a right to take measures for the protection of his own interest without the consent of one whose interest was involved with it. To that other, the loss which ensued, was *damnum absque injuria;* while to Clark it was enough that he himself was equally a sufferer, especially as the connection was not of his seeking. And the principle is founded in justice and reason. Parties who have coincident but separate interests, may abridge the freedom of their action in respect to them, by agreeing to make common cause in the prosecution of them; but pursuing them separately, they are not reciprocally answerable for acts which occasioned no wanton sacrifice. Why, then, ought Clark to have been diverted from the prosecution of a promising measure, by the risk of its consequences to another? He surely had a right to act for his own preservation, without consulting one whom accident had embarked in the same bottom with him. In the unsettled state of the law at the time, notice of an intended prosecution of the mortgage might have proved to be indispensable to the safety of all parties; but as it could have given Clark no claim on the plaintiff for a benefit, it shall not subject him to his action for a loss. Even partners in a voluntary association share the losses which are occasioned by the acts of each other; and there is, to say the least, no room for the application of a severer rule to the mischances of joint owners.

There was nothing in the original transaction, therefore, to affect the terre-tenant's conscience, and it is unimportant whether in analogy to the doctrine of notice, he stands as a purchaser of the imputed innocence of the sheriff's vendee. The court put the cause on the doctrine of estoppel, according to which, it was said, a party who has affirmed a fact in a judicial proceeding, by which he gained an advantage over another, may not gain a farther advantage over him by disaffirming it. Thus it was assumed that Clark's act was adverse to the plaintiff's right; and that he had gained, while the other had lost by it, neither of which is accurately predicable. It was destined, for good or for evil, to have the same effect on the interest of each; and the loss occasioned by it was mutual. Moreover, the parties stood in no such relation of privity or mutuality as is essential to an estoppel, which binds both or neither. The proceeding was not betwixt themselves, for as joint owners they had no antagonist rights; and for that reason, also, it was impossible for the one to gain at the other's expense. But, though their interests were coincident, they might take opposite courses in the pursuit of them, for there was nothing to hinder the plaintiff from encouraging the bidders, by denying the legality of Clark's pretensions; and had he done so, instead of acquiescing in it, the act would not have precluded him from resorting to the land had his own position been found a false one; for a bidder proceeds on his own judgment of the law. A collusive misrepresentation of legal consequences to frighten bidders, might make a different case; but collusion could not be imputed to Clark without imputing to him a design to counteract his obvious interest, unless he were a secret purchaser, which has not been insinuated. Acting in good faith, therefore, his assertion that the sale would not discharge the mortgage, drew after it no legal or equitable responsibility.

Judgment reversed, and a *venire de novo* awarded.

SALE ON SECOND INSTALLMENT DUE ON MORTGAGE transfers title, free of the lien of a prior installment on the same mortgage: *Parkins* v. *Campbell*, 16 Am. Dec. 188.

JUDICIAL SALE, FAIRLY MADE, DIVESTS ALL LIENS, subject to certain exceptions founded on peculiar circumstances: *Luce* v. *Snively*, 28 Am. Dec. 725, note 728, and cases there cited. The principal case is cited as authority on this point in *Clarke* v. *Stanley*, 10 Pa. St. 479.

FORSYTHE v. PRICE.

[8 WATTS, 282.]

TENANT IS ENTITLED TO WAY-GOING CROP, and may maintain trespass *quare clausum fregit* against his landlord for an injury done thereto, after the expiration of his lease, and his removal from the premises.

TRESPASS LIES AGAINST THE OWNER OF CATTLE which escape into the lands of another, even though against the will of such owner.

ERROR to the common pleas of Mifflin county. The opinion states the case.

J. Fisher, for the plaintiff in error.

Candor, for the defendant in error.

By Court, KENNEDY, J. This was an action of trespass *quare clausum fregit*, brought originally before a justice of the peace, by the defendant in error, against the plaintiff in error, and thence by appeal into the court below. The plaintiff had been the tenant of a farm, including the *locus in quo*, belonging to the defendant below, under a lease from the latter for a term of two years, commencing on the first of April, 1834. In the autumn of 1835, the plaintiff below sowed two of the fields on the farm with wheat, which was growing thereon in the spring of 1836, when his lease expired, and he removed from the farm, giving up the possession thereof to the defendant below. The trespass complained of is, that the defendant below, after the expiration of the lease, and before the wheat had ripened, either willfully conducted his horses into the fields of wheat, or permitted them to break into the same, and there to consume and destroy the wheat of the plaintiff below, then growing, by eating and treading down the same.

That the plaintiff below was entitled to the wheat as his way-going crop, has not been denied; nor could his right thereto have been contested with any possible chance of success, after its having been settled and recognized repeatedly, by the decisions of this, as well as of every other court in the state, for half a century and more, last past, that the tenant in such case is entitled to the way-going crop. It is the settled law of the state, founded upon a custom that has prevailed and been general, at least, if not universal, throughout the same: See *Diffadorffer* v. *Jones*, decided in 1782, and cited in 5 Binn. 289, and 2 Id. 487;[1] *Stults* v. *Dickey*, 5 Id. 285 [6 Am. Dec. 411]; *Biggs* v. *Brown*, 2 Serg. & R. 14. But it was contended by the counsel for the defendant, on the trial of the cause below, and has been so argued here, that the plaintiff below could not maintain trespass *quare clausum fregit*, after the expiration of the lease and his surrender of the possession to the defendant, for throwing down the fences around the wheat, whereby cattle and horses of the defendant below were let in to eat and tread it down, and thus consume and destroy it. The last two cases, however, referred to above, establish fully and most clearly that the tenant, notwithstanding the expiration of the lease, and his having surrendered and given up the possession of the leased premises generally to the lessor, still retained such an interest in that part of the land, whereon the wheat was growing, and right to the possession thereof, as would enable him to maintain trespass,

---

1. *Carson* v. *Blazer*; S. C., 4 Am. Dec. 463.

quare clausum fregit, against the lessor or any other person who should enter thereon, and take or destroy the grain so growing, or do anything to the prejudice of the tenant's rights therein.

This is also in accordance with, and supported by, the principles of the common law as laid down and settled in Co. Lit. 4 b; Dyer, 285, pl. 40; *Arnold* v. *Skeale*, Noy, 149; and see, also, *Perrot* v. *Bridges*, 1 Vent. 221, 222; Bac. Abr. (by Wilson), tit. Trespass, 591. Indeed, it would be strange if the law of the state, after having invested the tenant with the right to the way-going crop in such case, should not protect him completely in the enjoyment of it, to its fullest extent, and when violated, no matter by whom, should not also give him ample and adequate redress, as well as the means of securing and obtaining the benefit of it: *quando lex aliquid concedit, concedere videtur et id per quod devenitur.* But the right of the tenant to the way-going crop being indisputably established in this state, the common law, as we have it from England, will enable him to maintain trespass *quare clausum fregit*, if his right in this respect be improperly interfered with; as where the reversioner, after the death of the *cestui que vie*, permits his cattle to trespass on the corn of the tenant for life; or even when the cattle trespass on the corn against the will of their owner, it has been held that trespass will lie against him: 2 Roll. Abr. 568, l. 15; Com. Dig., tit. Trespass (C. 1). This authority also meets another objection, that was raised on the trial below, and made the ground of exception here to the charge of the court. The objection is, that unless the defendant below willfully put his horses or cattle on the wheat of the plaintiff, this action can not be maintained; and the defendant below farther claiming that no evidence had been given tending to show that the defendant had done so, therefore requested the court to charge the jury that the plaintiff could not recover.

If the law were, in regard to this point, as the counsel for the defendant below contended, the evidence seems to go much farther than he appears to think it does. Indeed, some of it tends strongly to prove, that if the defendant did not willfully put his horses on the wheat of the plaintiff, he at least threw down the fences around it, so that his horses might go into it, and destroy it by eating and treading it down. But it was sufficient to make him a trespasser, if his horses broke into the wheat even against his will, and destroyed it, because it was his duty to take care of his horses, and to restrain them from committing such trespass. Mr. Chitty, in his treatise on civil pleading, vol. 1, 70, 2d London ed., speaking of trespass committed by means of "animals *mansuetæ naturæ*, as cows and sheep, says, as their propensity to rove is notorious, the owner is bound, at all events, to confine them on his own land, and if they escape, and commit a trespass on the land of another, unless through the defect of fences which the latter ought to repair, the owner is liable to an action of trespass, though he had no notice, in fact, of such propensity;" for which he cites a great many authorities in the margin. What is said in regard to cows and sheep, is equally applicable to horses, for cows and sheep are only mentioned by way of example, or illustration. In short, the law is well settled on this point, by authorities which have never been contradicted, or even called in question, that if a man's cattle escape into the lands of another, though against his will, trespass will lie. See, in addition to the authorities cited by Mr. Chitty, *Pitts* v. *Collinbeane*, 2 Roll. Abr. 568; Com. Dig., tit. Trespass (C. 1). So if B. undertake to pasture the beast of A., or has the custody of it, and it trespasses upon the close of C., while in the charge of B., C. may have trespass against B.: *Bateman's case*, Clay. 33; Bac. Abr. 593 (by Wilson); 2 Roll. Abr. 546, 1. 20; Com. Dig., tit. Trespass (C. 1).

From the authorities, therefore, on this subject, as well as the reason and fitness of the thing, the plaintiff in error has no good ground to complain of the charge of the court below. In truth, it would seem to have been more favorable to him than he had any right to claim; for, from the language of the court, in their direction to the jury, on this point, the jury might readily have apprehended the court as instructing them, that the injury complained of by the plaintiff below, must have been wantonly, that is, as the jury might well have understood it, willfully committed by the defendant, in order to entitle the plaintiff to recover. The words of the court are: "Does the evidence satisfy you that Forsythe was a wrong-doer, and did wanton injury to the crop of the plaintiff, either by his trespassing upon it, and throwing down the fences, or otherwise? If it does, the plaintiff is entitled to a verdict."

Judgment affirmed.

_____

RIGHT OF TENANT TO WAY-GOING CROPS: See *Van Doren* v. *Everitt*, 8 Am. Dec. 615, note 618. Tenant is not entitled to way-going crops where the land is leased for a certain and determinate period: *Harris* v. *Carson*, 30 Id. 510.

TRESPASS WITHOUT INTENTION: See *Guille* v. *Swan*, 10 Am. Dec. 234, note 237.

GILCHRIST *v.* BALE.

[8 WATTS, 355.]

DECLARATIONS OF WIFE OF HER HUSBAND'S ILL-TREATMENT OF HER, made at and immediately before the time of her leaving him, are admissible in evidence in an action on the case for enticing away the plaintiff's wife.

FORMER RECOVERY, RELEASE, OR SATISFACTION NEED NOT BE PLEADED, in an action on the case, but may be given in evidence under the general issue.

FORMER RECOVERY IS A BAR TO AN ACTION FOR THE SAME INJURY, although the form of action may be different in the two cases. And therefore, a recovery in an action of trespass for carrying away the plaintiff's wife, is a bar to an action on the case for enticing her away.

REQUEST TO DELIVER UP PLAINTIFF'S WIFE, and refusal by the defendant, need not be alleged in the declaration in an action on the case for enticing away the wife.

ERROR to the common pleas of Dauphin county. Trespass on the case for persuading, procuring, and enticing away the plaintiff's wife, for the purpose of affording to defendant Gilchrist a more convenient opportunity to continue an unlawful criminal intercourse with the said wife of the plaintiff. After the plaintiff had proved his case, the defendant offered to prove that about ten days before Mrs. Bale left her husband she complained to Doctor Houtze, her attending physician, that her husband had treated her badly; had beaten her, and she showed marks on her arms which she had received from his beating; that she asked him what she should do, and he told her to leave her husband and go to her father's. The plaintiff objected that the declarations of the wife were not competent evidence. The court sustained the objection. The defendant offered in evidence the record of an action of trespass by William Bale against Robert Gilchrist, founded upon the same transaction. The plaintiff objected to this evidence as irrelevant, and the court rejected it. The court sealed bills of exception at the instance of the defendant.

J. A. Fisher, for the plaintiff in error.

Rawn, for the defendant in error.

By Court, ROGERS. The gravamen of the action is the enticing away the plaintiff's wife. There was no direct and positive proof of any combination between the defendants for the purpose, but the jury was asked to infer their participation in her abduction, from their acts, declarations, and conduct before, at the time, and after her departure from the dwelling of her husband. To disprove the allegation in the declaration, that the wife deserted her husband by the advice and at the procurement and solicitation of the defendants, they offered to prove by her attending physician, that about ten days before Mrs. Bale left her husband, she complained that he had treated her badly; that she showed marks on her arms which she said she had received from his beating her, and asked him what she should do; that he advised her to go to her father's and leave her husband. This evidence was offered in connection with proof that Bale treated her kindly as long as he thought he could, by that means, prevail upon her to deliver up a certain bond for one thousand dollars, which the defendant Gilchrist had given her.

The evidence was very pertinent; for if Mrs. Bale left her husband in consequence of ill treatment, it was an answer to the plaintiff's action. The material part of the testimony was the advice of the witness that she should leave her husband. The residue of the offer explains the reasons which induced him to give this advice, and were evidence in explanation. The witness saw the marks on her arm, and was informed by her, at the time, that they arose from the ill treatment of her husband. If I am correct, the latter part of the offer was unconnected with information derived from Mrs. Bale, and in that view was undoubtedly evidence, as it tended to show the motives which governed the wife in leaving the protection of her husband. It is said that this may have been a contrivance between the wife and the defendants, and it may have been so; but the court would not be justified in excluding testimony from a jury, on the ground of suspicion that there may have been unfair and improper conduct. Of this, the jury are the best judges; such matters go to the credit rather than the competency of testimony. It is a general rule, that the declarations of a husband or a wife can not be received in evidence against each other, either civilly or criminally. But this rule can not be extended to all possible cases; for where no confidence has been violated, the law has admitted of some exceptions.

Thus in *Aveson* v. *Lord Kennard*, 6 East, 188, in an action by the husband on a policy of insurance on the life of his wife, declarations by the wife, made by her when lying in bed, apparently ill, stating the bad state of her health, etc., and her apprehensions that she could not live ten days longer, by which time the policy was to be returned, are admissible in evidence to show her own opinion of the ill state of her health at the time of effecting the policy. In the argument, it was stated by the counsel, that the declarations by the wife upon her elopement from her husband, accusing him of misconduct, could not be given in evidence against him in an action against the adulterer. To this Lord Ellenborough replied: "It is not so clear that her declarations, made at the time, would not be evidence under any circumstances. If she declared at the time that she fled from immediate terror of personal violence from her husband, I should admit the evidence, though not if it were a collateral declaration of some matter which happened at another time." For the same case, in illustration, his lordship referred to *Thompson and wife* v. *Freeman*,[1] Skin. 402, where, in an action by the husband and wife for wounding the wife, Lord Chief Justice Holt allowed what the wife said immediately upon the injury received, and before she had time to devise anything for her own advantage, to be given in evidence as part of the *res gestæ*. The motives which induced Mrs. Bale to desert her husband, are the matters in controversy; and his conduct about that time has a material bearing on the issue. The defendants allege that she left him, not for the cause assigned in the declaration, but because of his wicked and brutal conduct. This, in most cases, can not be shown, except by her declarations made at the time to her relations and friends. Few persons are so lost to every sense of propriety as to act thus in public. The treatment of which she has most reason to complain, is usually acted in secret, and can only be known from her complaints, or, as here, from marks of violence on her person.

When an act is done to which it is necessary to ascribe a motive, it is always considered that what is said at the time, from whence the motive may be collected, is part of the *res gestæ*. It was necessary to explain the reason the witness advised her to leave her husband, and for this purpose her complaints of ill treatment, with the marks of violence on her person, were competent testimony. When the conduct of the wife is in question, her declarations have been held admissible for her husband in an action against him. Thus in an action for necessaries supplied to the wife, the defense being that her husband had turned her out of doors for adultery, her declarations as to her adultery, made previously to her expulsion, were admitted: Abb. C. J., 1 Car. & P. 621.[2]

The defendants also complain of the rejection of the record of the action of trespass, *vi et armis*, for criminal connection with the plaintiff's wife. This is an action on the case, and a

<hr>

1. *Thompson et Ux.* v. *Trevanion.*   2. *Walton* v. *Green.*

difference is taken between such actions and actions in tort, which are *stricti juris*. A former recovery, release, or satisfaction can not be given in evidence in an action for tort, on the general issue, but must be pleaded; but an action on the case is founded on the mere justice and conscience of the plaintiff's case, and is in the nature of a bill in equity, and therefore a former recovery, release, or satisfaction need not be pleaded, but may be given in evidence under the general issue. For whatever will, in equity and conscience, according to the circumstances of the case, bar the plaintiff's recovery, may, in this action, be given in evidence by the defendant: because the plaintiff must recover upon the justice and conscience of his case, and upon that only: *Bird* v. *Randall*, 3 Burr. 1353; 1 Wils. 45;[1] *Thilhaffer* v. *Herr*,[2] 17 Serg. & R. 319. There is, therefore, no reasonable doubt, on authority, that the evidence was admissible on the pleading, if in other respects unexceptionable. The actions were brought on the same day, covered the same space of time, and the question is, whether they are not, in substance, for the same injury. A former recovery is no bar, unless it be for the same injury, but where the plaintiff has received a full satisfaction, for the same cause, he can not recover a second time. And this does not depend on the form of the suit; for the inquiry in every case is, whether the former recovery or satisfaction was for the same thing, or whether the grounds of controversy in the two actions are the same. Thus when a person takes the personal property of another, and sells it, the owner may elect either of four remedies, trespass, replevin, trover, or an action on the case, for money had and received, but a recovery in one, may be pleaded in bar to another action, although differing in form, for the same injury. When A. enters the close of B., cuts down his timber, and takes and carries it away, as in *Cochran and Wife* v. *Castlere*, Co. E. 96, the plaintiff may bring trespass *quare clausum fregit*, and recover for the trespass in entering the close, and also for the value of the timber under improvement. But such a recovery would be a bar to an action of replevin, trover, and to an action on the case, for the value of the timber. No person can recover a double satisfaction for the same injury, and *nemo debet bis vexari pro eadem causa*. Whether a recovery for the value of articles would be a bar to an action for breaking the close merely, it is not necessary to decide, and is not so clear.

For what injury did the plaintiff recover, in the action of tres-

---

1. *Barker* v. *Dixon*.   2. *Kilhaffer* v. *Herr*; S. C., 17 Am. Dec. 658.

pass? or, what is the same thing, as was ruled in *Hess* v. *Hall*, 6 Serg. & R.,[1] what might he have recovered? In the first action the plaintiff does not declare for the criminal conversation alone, but he also demands damages for depriving him of the comfort and society of his wife, during the whole time laid in the present action. He elects to consider the whole as one offense, and it can not be questioned that he did or might have recovered, in the first suit, for all the injury he received from the defendant, including not only the criminal intercourse with her, but also compensation for her desertion at the solicitation of the defendant, and thereby depriving him, in the language of the declaration, of her aid, comfort, and assistance. *Gavin* v. *Dawson*, 13 Serg. & R. 246,[2] was decided on this principle. Gavin brought two suits against Dawson, one on the act of the twenty-first of March, 1772, to recover double the value of his goods wrongfully distrained by the defendant, and the other, an action on the case at common law, for the same cause, and alleging his complaint in the same words. The defendant arbitrated both, and report was made in both, that the plaintiff had no cause of action. The plaintiff appealed from the decision in the case to recover double damages on the statute, but did not appeal from the action at common law, where judgment remained in full force. The court held that the plaintiff was barred, and a plea *puis darrein continuance* was held good. In the case at bar, for the same thing, the plaintiff will recover a double satisfaction for the same injury, and the defendant will be punished twice for the same offense. There was error in rejecting the record of the former recovery.

But it is said the declaration is bad, because no request by the plaintiff to the defendant, to deliver up the wife, and refusal by the defendant, are laid. This objection is made on the authority of a dictum of Chief Justice Wilmot, in *Winsmore* v. *Greenland*,[3] 1 Willes, 582. But the remark is made in reference to the third count of the declaration, but does not touch the count for enticing her away. "It is not necessary," says the chief justice, "to determine, in this case, whether a request and refusal are necessary, because both are expressly laid here; but according to my present thoughts, in the case of a detainer, I think them necessary." But however this may be restricted to a suit for detaining the wife, yet it does not apply to an action for enticing her away; for if it is necessary to aver a request and refusal, it would be necessary to prove them. But it will hardly

---

1. *Hess* v. *Hooble*, 6 Serg. & R. 57.   2. *Gavin* v. *Dawson*.   3. *Winsmore* v. *Greenbank*.

be pretended that a person could screen himself from punishment for such a wrong, by consenting (after the injury, which consists of the illegal and improper act of inducing her to desert her duty) to deliver up the wife on request. But this would be the consequence of holding that a request and refusal were necessary. In other respects we perceive no error in the record.

Judgment reversed, and a *venire facias de novo* awarded.

———

FORMER JUDGMENT, WHEN A BAR AND WHEN NOT: See note to *Eastman* v. *Cooper*, 26 Am. Dec. 609, where other cases in this series are collected.

FORMER RECOVERY AS EVIDENCE UNDER GENERAL ISSUE: See note to *Eastman* v. *Cooper*, 26 Am. Dec. 610.

THE PRINCIPAL CASE IS CITED in *Palmer* v. *Cook*, 7 Gray, 420, and in *Coleman* v. *White*, 43 Ind. 430, to the point that declarations of a wife, of her ill treatment by her husband, prior to her alleged seduction, are admissible, as evidence in an action by the husband against her seducer.

———

PATTERSON v. MARTZ.

[8 WATTS, 374.]

SPECIFIC PERFORMANCE OF CONTRACT WHICH ORIGINATED IN BREACH OF FAITH will not be decreed.

UNEXPLAINED DELAY OF VENDOR FOR SEVEN YEARS, and great rise in value of the lands forming the subject-matter of the contract, constitute an insuperable objection to the granting of a decree for the specific performance of a contract for the sale of lands.

FACTS SHOWING ABANDONMENT OF A CONTRACT BY THE PLAINTIFF furnish a decisive answer to his prayer for a specific performance thereof.

ERROR to the common pleas of Northumberland county. Ejectment for a tract of land. Peter Dimmich, being the owner of a tract of land, on the first of November, 1829, made a parol contract with Samuel J. Packer to sell it to him for eight hundred dollars, if Packer would comply by the first of December, 1829. On the sixteenth of November, 1829, Dimmich entered into a written contract with George Patterson, the plaintiff, to sell the same land to him for one thousand four hundred dollars, fifty dollars of which was paid down, and the residue of the one half of the purchase money was to be paid on January 1, 1830. On the twenty-third of November, 1829, Packer went to Dimmich and insisted upon the execution of the parol contract between them. After some hesitation, Dimmich finally executed to Packer a conveyance of the land for the sum of one thousand four hundred and twenty dollars. Soon after Dimmich sent his son to Patterson with the fifty dollars which he had received from him; but not finding him at home, he left the money with his brother's wife. Patterson's brother testified that he told his brother that the money had been returned. That he objected to his having received it; but as the money had been borrowed from him to pay to Dimmich in the first place, he retained it. It appeared from the contract between Dimmich and Patterson, that one Peter Wary was a tenant on the land, whose lease would not expire for two years, and that Patterson purchased subject to this lease. In 1831 Patterson brought ejectment for the land against Packer, Dimmich, and Wary, which was discontinued on September 28, 1832, on the ground that the plaintiff supposed he could not recover because Wary's term had not expired when the suit was brought. There was also evidence that the land had risen in value between 1829 and 1837. The instructions of the court below were, on the whole, favorable to the defendant, and the plaintiff assigned numerous alleged errors in the charge, and for the court's refusal to charge as requested by the plaintiff.

Hepburn, for the plaintiff in error.

Donnel and Greenough, contra.

By Court, GIBSON, C. J. If, as the evidence seems to show, Dimmich had previously agreed to convey to Packer, at a day still to come, a chancellor would refuse to execute the plaintiff's intermediate purchase, for the reason that no assistance is ever given to one who claims by a contract which originated in a breach of faith. In *Cooth* v. *Jackson,* 6 Ves. 17, the agreement grew out of improper disclosures of the contents of depositions taken by commissioners; and Lord Eldon dismissed the bill, though the blame was not imputable to the plaintiff. On the same ground, he refused in *Mortlock* v. *Buller,* 10 Id. 292, to execute a purchase from an agent of trustees at a price so reduced as to involve a breach of the trust. In these instances, he was actuated by considerations of public policy. For a similar reason, specific performance of a contract made with a man when he was intoxicated, was refused in *Cragg* v. *Holme,* cited in *Cook* v. *Clayworth,* 18 Id. 14, though the plaintiff had neither contributed to make him drunk, nor taken advantage of his situation when he was so. In *Campbell* v. *Spencer,* 2 Binn. 133, this court went, perhaps, still farther; and I by no means think it went too far. There was no proof that the defendant was even drunk; but the bargain, which was a very improvident one, was made at early dawn in a course of dram-drinking, at a tavern to which he had been brought. It is true, the chief justice said he would have felt great difficulty had the case come before him as a chancellor; but that the verdict had strengthened it very much. Now it was actually before him as a chancellor; and that he felt it to be so is evident, from the principles which he propounded in relation to it, and which he stated with the precision of a chancellor. In the progress of equitable administration since that decision, the time has gone by for a party to intrench himself behind what was formerly thought to be the equitable discretion of a jury, or to call it in aid of the supposed feebler power of the court; and there is little doubt that the chief justice would have ruled the cause for the defendant by a positive direction in the first instance. Rules of equity are not less precise and peremptory than rules of law, nor less a subject of exclusive administration by the court; and a verdict can no more strengthen an equity on an appeal by a motion for a new trial, than can a decree by a master of the rolls on an appeal to the chancellor. Yet the position taken by the court ought not to be regarded as a timid one for the time. It only shows from what small beginnings, and with what cautiousness we have wended our way towards a systematic administration of equity. The principle enforced in that case, by whatever means, is identical with the principle of the cases precedently quoted; and I take the opinion of Chief Justice Tilghman to be an authority in point, that a contract to entitle itself to the assistance of a chancellor, must have come from an immaculate source. Now, the plaintiff's purchase was subsequent to the oral contract with Packer, which, though it could not be specifically enforced by reason of the statute of frauds, was neither illegal nor void, inasmuch as it would have been a sufficient foundation for an action at law to recover damages for a breach of it; and it is decisive against the plaintiff's title that his purchase was founded, though innocently on his part, in a disregard of it. He was bound to relinquish it the instant he discovered the fact; and to insist on it now, is as bad as to have made it with a knowledge of the circumstances. Even on the broad ground of public policy it ought not to be decreed. From equity he can ask nothing but to be left to his remedy at law; for against a prior bargainee who did no more than pursue a conscionable and lawful contract to its legal consummation, he has no equity whatever.

The court, however, put the defense mainly on the ground of delay; and it certainly was an impregnable one. During the five years which elapsed betwixt the expiration of the lease to

Dimmich's tenant and the organization of the present suit, the plaintiff was quiescent, while the land rose rapidly in value; and of this quiescence no explanation is given, no excuse for it offered.   Nor did the existence of the outstanding lease justify the discontinuance of the suit brought within the two years it had to run.   An action of ejectment employed as a substitute for a bill in equity, as that was, lies whenever a bill would lie, and with the same direct or incidental effect.   Such an action has, indeed, the integuments of an action, but it has also the bones and articulations of a bill; and a recovery by it has the substantive and essential qualities of a decree.   The lease, therefore, would not have been an obstacle to the prosecution of the first ejectment brought, as it was, to assert the plaintiff's equity while the transaction was fresh; for the court might have protected the lessee's possession and exemption from costs, by its power over the execution.   There was, then, an unanswered delay of seven years, during which Packer's partners in the purchase were paying their contributions to the price.   Nor is that all.   The plaintiff's retention of his deposit, left for him by the vendor at his brother's house, was equivalent to a recovery of it back, and an unqualified act of rescission; for had he not acquiesced in the restoration of it, he ought instantly to have tendered the money again to the vendor.   These circumstances show not only backwardness and trifling, but a positive abandonment of the contract; either of which furnishes a decisive answer to a prayer for specific performance.

Judgment affirmed.

SPECIFIC PERFORMANCE NOT DECREED WHERE THERE IS FRAUD: See *Seymour v. Delancy*, 15 Am. Dec. 270; *Edwards v. Handley*, 3 Id. 745; *Meaux v. Helm*, 2 Id. 716.

EVANS *v.* COMMONWEALTH.

[8 WATTS, 398.]

JUDGMENT OBTAINED IN SUIT AGAINST CONSTABLE FOR OFFICIAL MISCONDUCT or neglect of duty is conclusive evidence of the liability of the sureties upon his official bond, in an action brought against them to recover the amount of such judgment.

TO RECOVER AGAINST SURETIES OF CONSTABLE, it is sufficient to show that he was insolvent in fact when the action was commenced.

ERROR to the common pleas of Luzerne county.   Action on the official bond of Evans, who had been a constable.   Carver, for whose use this action was brought, had previously recovered a judgment against Evans alone; and when this action was commenced, Evans had applied for the benefit of the insolvent laws, but had not obtained his discharge. Parol proof of his actual insolvency at the time the suit was brought, was given. The court below ruled in favor of the plaintiff and verdict and judgment were rendered accordingly.

Maxwell and Kidder, for the plaintiff in error.

Woodward, contra.

By Court, KENNEDY, J. The principle of _Masser_ v. _Strickland,_ 17 Serg. & R. 354 [17 Am. Dec. 668], as settled by a majority of this court, would seem to rule this case. There it was held that a judgment against the constable was not only conclusive against his sureties as to the misconduct or neglect of duty on the part of the constable, which was made the ground of action whereon the judgment was obtained against him, but likewise as to the amount of damages actually sustained by the plaintiff. According to the principle thus established, the judgment obtained by the plaintiff below in the suit against Evans alone, as a compensation for the damages which the former sustained by reason of the official neglect of duty or misconduct by the latter being conclusive upon his sureties, who were joint defendants in this action with him in the court below, and the plaintiffs in error here, precluded all inquiry into the matters contained in the first and second points of the plaintiffs in error, which were submitted by them to the court below for their instruction on them to the jury. It was not competent for the plaintiffs in error to go behind that judgment, and set up any matter in this action which might have been objected to the recovery therein. As the answers, therefore, of the court below ought to have been against the plaintiffs in error directly upon their first two points, they can not be injured thereby; so that, even if the answers of the court were erroneous, they have no right to assign them for error, or claim a reversal of the judgment upon that account. And, notwithstanding, it may be that the case of _Masser_ v. _Strickland_ was decided against the authority of the rule of analogy, which might have been very fairly extracted from the principles of the common law, yet as many cogent reasons exist for making such case as that and the present, an exception to the general rule on the subject; and, as it has, no doubt, been looked upon as such ever since it was so determined in that case, we all now agree that no change should be made. Seeing then that it has become the settled rule of the law in regard to the

sureties in a constable's bond, that a judgment obtained in a
suit brought against the constable alone for official misconduct
or neglect of duty, will bind and be conclusive upon them,
though not notified of the suit, they must be presumed to have
known that such was the law, when they entered into the bond;
and it must, therefore, be taken as a part of their obligation or
agreement, that they were willing to be so bound and concluded,
as often as judgment should be so obtained against their principal; and hence, those who have become sureties for constables,
since the establishment of the rule, in this respect, can have no
reason to complain of it.   Under this view then, it would seem
that the objection originally made to the establishment and application of such rule to the sureties of a constable has lost its
force; and the tendency of the rule, in its operation, being to
prevent creditors from being vexatiously and unreasonably delayed in having or obtaining execution of their judgments,
which, it is said, is the life of the law, strongly recommends it
on the ground of expediency and public policy.

The only question remaining to be decided, arises out of the
third error assigned; which is an exception to the answer given
by the court to the third point submitted by the counsel of the
defendants below.   By this point the counsel of the defendants
below requested the court to instruct the jury that the plaintiff
there could not recover, because the constable had not taken the
benefit of, and been finally discharged under, the insolvent laws,
before the commencement of this action.   This instruction was
claimed under the nineteenth section of the act of the twentieth
of March, 1810, amending and consolidating the acts of assembly giving justices of the peace jurisdiction over debts not exceeding one hundred dollars, which enacts that "any constable
who has or may thereafter give security agreeably to law for the
faithful performance of the duties of his office, and afterwards,
on neglecting or refusing to perform such duties, shall have
judgment rendered against him for such neglect or refusal; and
on being prosecuted for the recovery of such judgment, becomes
insolvent, abandons his country, or from any other reason it
becomes impracticable for such judgment or judgments to be
recovered from such constable, as aforesaid, etc., then, and in
such cases only, the justice before whom the judgment or judgments stand unpaid, shall be and he is hereby authorized
and empowered to issue a *scire facias*, and proceed against such
bail for the recovery of judgments had as aforesaid, in the same
manner that constables are now suable," etc.   This action hav-

ing been commenced in the court of common pleas, and not
before a justice of the peace, it might possibly admit of a question, whether the section of the act, just read, be applicable to
it or not.   Be this, however, as it may, we think the court below
were not bound to give the instruction required by the counsel
of the defendants below.   If the evidence given showed clearly
beyond all doubt that the constable was insolvent at the time
this action was commenced, and therefore it had become impracticable to recover from him the judgment obtained against
him in favor of the plaintiff below, his bail, according to the
plain and natural import and meaning of the nineteenth section
of the act of 1810, were liable to be sued for it upon their bond.
The insolvency of the constable here was proved on the trial
most clearly, and not attempted, as it would seem, to be controverted.   Before the commencement of the action he had
applied for the benefit of the insolvent laws, but did not obtain
a final order of relief and discharge until some time afterwards.

Judgment affirmed.

—

The proposition stated in the first sentence of the syllabus of the principal
case is cited with approval in the following cases: *Snapp* v. *Commonwealth*, 2
Pa. St. 49; *Garber* v. *Commonwealth*, 7 Id. 266; *Lloyd* v. *Barr*, 11 Id. 52;
Tracy v. *Goodwin*, 5 Metc. (Mass.) 411.

NERHOOTH *v.* ALTHOUSE.

[8 WATTS, 427.]

DEFENDANT IN EJECTMENT MAY SET UP TITLE ADVERSE to that of a person
with whom he had previously entered into a contract for the title, if, before he took possession, he gave notice to such person that he would
not take possession under him.

ERROR to the common pleas of Union county.   Ejectment for
a tract of land.   The opinion states the case.

Merrill, for the plaintiff in error.

Miller, for the defendant in error.

By Court, KENNEDY, J   This cause is presented now under
an entirely different aspect from what it was when here before,
upon a former writ of error.   It appeared from the paper-book,
which we had then of the case, that Nerhooth had taken possession of the land, under an agreement made previously with
Althouse, and without contesting that fact, offered to show that
he held the land under a right or claim altogether adverse to

that of Althouse, which the court below, as it appeared, permitted him to do. In this we thought there was error, and therefore reversed the judgment. It may be, however, that, from want of care and proper attention in making the paper-book at that time, the case was not presented to us under the same view in which the court below had it before them; and as no written opinion of this court seems to have been given, it is also most likely that on the late trial of the cause, some misapprehension existed in regard to the question which we had decided. I am the more inclined to think that some mistake must have been committed, in stating the case, because the court below, on the late trial, seems to have applied our decision to a case that never was before us. According to the statement of the case, however, as we have it now, the defendant below, who is the plaintiff in error here, not only denied his having gone into possession under Althouse, the plaintiff below, but offered to prove that his possession was adverse to Althouse from its first commencement; and that although he had entered into a written agreement, bearing date the twenty-fifth day of August, 1834, with Althouse, for the purchase of the land, under which he was to have the possession of it delivered to him by Althouse, on the first day of November then following, yet that he gave Althouse some two or three weeks after the date of the agreement, while Althouse was still in possession of the land, notice that he, Nerhooth, would not go into the possession under Althouse: that he afterwards, on the twentieth of January, 1835, entered into a written agreement with George Weirick, agreeing to unite with this last-named person in procuring a title to the land, as vacant, from the commonwealth; that in February, 1835, he took possession of the land under this agreement with Weirick, and on the twenty-third of February, 1836, obtained a warrant for it from the commonwealth, had a survey made, in pursuance thereof, on the fourth of May in the same year; and moreover offered to prove that Weirick had a written agreement with Althouse, dated March 5, 1831, by which it was agreed between Weirick and Althouse, that as the land in question was believed to be vacant, the latter should enter and make a settlement thereon with his family, as soon as it could conveniently be done, for their joint benefit; and at their equal and joint expense, afterwards procure a perfect title for the land from the commonwealth.

This evidence, however, was objected to by the counsel for the plaintiff below, and the court below being given, as would seem,

to understand somehow that our decision in the case, when here
before, rendered the evidence thus offered inadmissible, rejected
it. The defendant below having disclaimed taking possession
under the agreement with the plaintiff below, and still refusing
to fulfill or abide by it, the latter declared his determination to
ʼake the defendant at his word, and consider the agreement made
between them no longer binding on him, declared on the trial
that he brought this action to recover the possession of the land
as the absolute owner of the whole of it, seeing Weirick, as well
as the defendant below, had forfeited all right or claim to it by
their having combined together, and having taken from the state
a warrant for the land, leaving the improvement and settlement,
made by the plaintiff below, altogether out of view, for the purpose of defrauding him of his right to it. Now it may be that
Nerhooth and Weirick have acted in such a manner towards Althouse, as to preclude themselves, or either of them, from claiming an interest in the land under the agreements which they
severally made with him; but the counsel for the plaintiff below
was mistaken, if he supposed that he could have such question
decided in favor of his client by objecting to and excluding the
evidence offered, which, as it appears to me, could not have operated unfavorably to him, unless the defendant below had gone
farther, and proved a relinquishment of all claim, on the part
of the plaintiff below, to the land. Or if the counsel for the
plaintiff below conceived that he was entitled to recover back
the possession of the land, because the defendant below had
taken possession under an executory contract for the purchase
of it, and had, after obtaining the possession, disclaimed holding under such contract, he might have been right in thinking
so, but then, although he had given evidence tending to prove
that the fact was so, still that was no reason why the defendant
below should be precluded from giving evidence going to disprove the fact of his having taken the possession of the land under such agreement with the plaintiff below, by showing, as he
proposed to do, that he had given the plaintiff notice before the
plaintiff left the possession, that he would not take the land at
all under the agreement which he had made with the plaintiff;
and that, when he did go into possession, afterwards, it was under the agreement which he made with Weirick. And very possibly it might have been requisite to have gone still farther, in
order to have satisfied the jury that he had not deceived the
plaintiff below about taking possession, and for this purpose, to
have shown that he also gave the plaintiff below previous notice

of his intention to take the possession of the land, at the time he did, under Weirick.

It is clear, however, that all the evidence in relation to this question ought to have gone to the jury, as it was a question of fact, and therefore proper to be decided by them alone, after they had heard all the evidence on the part of the defendant below as well as the plaintiff. And supposing the defendant below had been permitted to give all his evidence, and he had satisfied the jury that he did not take possession of the land under the plaintiff; then the plaintiff might have shown and relied on his prior right to recover the possession of the land arising from his settlement and improvements made upon it long before the commencement of the title under which the defendant professed to claim.

Judgment reversed, and a *venire de novo* awarded.

BIRD *v.* SMITH.

[8 WATTS, 434.]

EXCLUSIVE RIGHT TO NAVIGATE WATERS OF PUBLIC RIVER can only be acquired by a grant from the public. A grant of such a right can never be presumed from length of time.

OWNERS OF SHORES OF NAVIGABLE RIVERS HAVE POWER TO CONTROL RIGHT of embarkation and landing, even at the terminus of a public road.

EXCLUSIVE RIGHT TO LAND FERRY AT POINT on bank of navigable river may be presumed from exclusive enjoyment of such right for a long period of time. And the jury ought to presume the right to be exclusive whenever its value would be lessened in the least degree by participation.

USE OF AN EASEMENT NEED NOT BE ABSOLUTELY CONTINUOUS in order to affect a purchaser with notice of its existence; it is sufficient that there is something in the aspect of the premises to put the purchaser on his guard.

EASEMENT IN LAND HELD BY A CONNECTICUT TITLE is not affected by a grant of that title from Pennsylvania, where the latter grant confirmed the Connecticut title.

ADMISSIONS OF GRANTOR OF LAND, MADE WHILE HE OWNED IT, are competent evidence against one claiming under him.

LESSOR OF EASEMENT IS COMPETENT WITNESS FOR LESSEE in an action by the latter for a disturbance thereof.

ERROR to the common pleas of Luzerne county. Action on the case to recover damages for disturbing the plaintiff's right uninterruptedly to navigate across the Susquehanna river at his ancient ferry. The plaintiff was lessee from Lucy Jenkins, and on the trial the lessor was offered as a witness by the plaintiff, and received against the objection of the defendant. The only controversy respected the right to land on the west side of the river. It appeared from the evidence that forty-six years ago Stephen and Thomas Jenkins settled upon land on the west side of the river, and about the same time Thomas Jenkins established a ferry. In an ordinary pitch of water the landing was upon the road which he had opened upon his own land between him and his brother Stephen. Thomas did all the ferrying for some time, landing at low water and sometimes at very high water upon Stephen's land. Prior to 1806 or 1807, Stephen had, at times, claimed to have a right to ferry across the river, but about that time a reference of this claim was had between the brothers, and from that time Stephen ceased to make any claim to the ferry. Thomas occupied the ferry until he died in 1812, when he devised the profits of the ferry to his wife Lucy, during her widowhood, and she continued to occupy it until March, 1837, when she leased it to the plaintiff. Prior to the commencement of this suit, the defendant appears to have used the ferry in transporting one man and a horse across. Until this act of the defendant no one attempted to interrupt the enjoyment of the ferry for about forty-six years. The defendant claims the right to have a ferry on the ground that he is the tenant of Elam Stockbridge, who owns the land on the west side of the river by virtue of a conveyance from Peter Polen, who acquired the right and title of Stephen Jenkins. It also appeared in evidence that both Thomas and Stephen Jenkins held their lands under Connecticut titles, and that in 1808 a certificate was granted to Stephen for the land where the boats were accustomed to land. The other facts sufficiently appear from the opinion.

Woodward, for the plaintiff in error.

Wright and Maxwell, contra.

By Court, GIBSON, C. J. Some of the points presented are comparatively unimportant; and as it is intimated that the cause has not been brought here merely for reversal, we have turned our attention particularly to those which involve principles of right.

Over the surface of a public river, riparian owners have no peculiar right. Such is the principle of *Carson* v. *Blazer*,[1] and *Shrunk* v. *The Schuylkill Navigation Company*,[2] which seem to have put the public rights of navigation and fishery on the same footing. The right of navigation, transverse or otherwise, being

---

1. 2 Binn. 475; S. C., 4 Am. Dec. 463.   2. 14 Serg. & R. 71.

enjoyed in common, is susceptible of exclusive appropriation
only by grant from the public, to whom it belongs; and we have,
consequently, no such thing as a ferry by prescriptive right, or
presumptive grant of exclusive navigation from length of time.
The doctrine of *nullum tempus* alone, would prevent a title
drawn from a source so like the statute of limitations, from being set up against the commonwealth or her grantee. The
foundation, however, of what is nearly as effective, is the power
which the owners of the shores have to control the subservient
and indispensable right of embarkation and landing. The existence of such a power over even the terminus of a public road, is
established by *Chambers* v. *Fury*[1] and *Cooper* v. *Smith*,[2] cited in the
argument, as well as by *Chess* v. *Manown*, 3 Watts, 219. The presumptive grant of an incorporeal right, sustained as it is by analogy
to the statute of limitations, is founded in an adverse assertion
of right, and can have no place in respect to a thing of which
there can not be an adverse use; consequently, it can have no
place in respect to a river which is navigated by general license,
pursuant to which the individual does nothing to challenge the
general right. The principle of these presumptive grants has
been carried farther, in some respects, than the admitted foundation of it would seem to warrant; as in the case of ancient
lights, which happen not to be an annoyance to the premises
they serve to overlook, and which would rather encourage a supposition of indifference on the part of the owner than a want of
right to obstruct them, inasmuch as no man is bound to inclose
his ground to prevent his neighbor from looking at it. Even as
regards acts of apparent usurpation, the rule is that they must
be such as in their nature carry with them an assertion of right.
Thus, in *Doe* v. *Reed*, 5 Barn. & Ald. 232, the jury were not
allowed to presume a conveyance after a possession of fifty
years, as a creditor under a judgment; and Chief Justice Abbot
added, that these presumptions had been carried too far.
Doubtless they have, where the possession or use bore nothing
on its face like a pretension of title. In point of reason, no
lapse of time, bearing any proportion to the period of the statute, ought to require an exertion of a man's right merely to show
that he had not parted with it, when there was nothing in the
situation or possession of the property to indicate that he had;
and such is the principle which ruled the case of *Buts* v. *Ihrie*,
2 Rawle, 218,[3] where it was held that the reservation of a right

---

1. *Chambers* v. *Fury*, 1 Yeates, 167.   2. 9 Serg. & R. 26; S. C., 11 Am. Dec. 658.
3. 1 Rawle, 218.

to swell water on the land of an adjoining owner was not lost merely because it had not been exerted for thirty-two years. Yet a window, which enables the occupant of it to pry into the domestic economy of his neighbor, is a nuisance whose continuance can be explained only by a want of right to abate it. Perhaps the apparent difficulty of reducing all the decisions on this head to principles of reason, arises from a tendency in the judicial mind to generalize, without stopping to dispose of specific differences. The rights of the parties here, however, are determinable by the plaintiff's occupancy, not of the stream, but of the shore.

Had the judge therefore charged, as it is imputed to him, that an exclusive right might be gained by an exclusive occupancy betwixt the shores, he would have been in error; but he pointedly said that no other advantage could be had on the water than was had from the ownership of the land. But the wrong charged in the declaration is a disturbance, not of the plaintiff's easement in the landing, but of an alleged right to the ancient ferry; and hence it is argued, the evidence did not support the count. Had there been a prayer for direction to that effect, it must have prevailed, for the variance would have been fatal; but nothing like it is perceptible on the record: and, indeed, to have defeated the plaintiff on that ground, would only have protracted the contest, by reserving the determination of the right for another lawsuit. In starting the point here, the defendant has slipped his time.

The title to the *locus in quo* is in the defendant's lessor, and a material question was whether the plaintiff had not acquired an exclusive right to use it, by a presumptive grant of one of the lessor's predecessors; as to which, the judge charged that a grant presumed from exclusive enjoyment is also exclusive. The extent of the right is doubtless determinable by the nature of the use; and the principle admits of a ready application to positive enjoyment, in order to carry the right to the extent of it, the difficulty being to know whether it may not be carried even farther by a want of actual participation on the other side. There is a plain implication of exclusive right, where the full benefit of the supposed grant could not be had from a concurrent enjoyment of it; as in the case of a pew barely sufficient to accommodate the occupant's family. In the case of a way, the right is not necessarily exclusive, as was admitted in *Kirkham* v. *Sharp*, 1 Whart. 333 [29 Am. Dec. 57]. The rule seems to be, that the grant shall not be extended beyond the purpose to be

answered by it; nor ought it in reason to be. The
being that there was an actual grant, there is in reason...
pose the grantee paid for, or the grantor parted with more
than was adequate to the purpose. According...
Goble, 2 Camp. 322,[1] a plaintiff who prescribed...
which admitted more light than was necessary, if the...
of a malthouse, of which it was part, was not allowed...
tain an action for the erection of a wall which...
excess. The proper inquiry below, then, was whether...
lege to land passengers on the defendant's soil was...
been curtailed by a concurrent use of it and I presume...
question of fact, which was, perhaps, not if every...
place was used only at high, or very low water...
times of the day. A common landing must...
without collision, by boats plying...
and even that is barely possible; but the...
mountable where, as on our fresh-water rivers...
plies whenever a passenger presents himself...
the jury ought to presume the right to be...
its value would be lessened in the least...
In addition to the presumption from the...
at least some parol evidence of an...
also for the consideration of the jury.

Another material question was whether the...
ment had been so notorious as to give notice...
purchasers. At common law an...
title took it clear of trusts and...
veyances, whether known to him or...
which designed to make all conveyances...
put even legal conveyances on the...
conveyance of a title to an easement...
of registration, but a conjectural...
necessity to affect a purchaser of the...
through some other channel...
lington v. *Welsh*,[2] it was settled...
effect, must be several, distinct...
eye. It was not said that it must...
nor could the enjoyment be...
it could not be kept so...
notoriety of it without...
to require it, would...
the first purchaser.

---

1. 1 Camp.

as not to allow those ordinary intermissions that are incident to the business to which the easement is subservient. Moreover, it is sufficient, where it exists, that there is something in the aspect of the premises to put a purchaser on his guard. In *Alexander* v. *Kerr*, 2 Rawle, 83 [19 Am. Dec. 616], a question was made, whether the purchaser of a mill was bound to take notice that the dam sometimes flooded the land of an adjoining proprietor; and, as the probability of the fact was apparent to the eye, it was held that there was enough to lead him to an inquiry. In like manner, was there not enough to lead the defendant's lessor and his predecessor to the fact that the land below was occasionally used for the purposes of this ferry, when it is considered that the upper landing, with its road, was but a few yards above the plaintiff's boundary? that it was obvious a boat could not reach it at high water? and that to meet such a contingency, there was a visible landing-place, with a road to it, at the *locus in quo*, the object of which must have been suggested by the aspect of the premises?

It is argued, however, that the certificate of the commissioners in 1808 was the origin of a new grant which, supplanting the Connecticut title, purged the land of its incumbrances; and that it consequently extinguished any grant of the easement in question, which existed at the time. The act of 1799 and its supplements, however, were passed, not to extinguish, but to confirm the Connecticut title within a particular district. The primary one was treated as confirmatory in *Avery* v. *Dailey*, 4 Serg. & R. 281;[1] and that it was not styled so in the act itself, is probably because an obnoxious act bearing that name had just been repealed. Its provisions, however, were confirmatory. Its declared object was to ascertain the settler's rights for confirmation by a patent, and it would have been strange had not their accessories also been confirmed. It is certainly true, that a conveyance on the basis of a Connecticut right, was declared to be illegal by the act of 1802, and it must be admitted that scruples were felt by some of us on that head in *Barney* v. *Sutton*,[2] which was consequently ruled on another point; but from the operation of that act were expressly excluded all the lands in the seventeen townships which were, or should be, submitted to the commissioners under the act of 1799. Even had the assertion of such a title been previously unlawful on grounds of general policy, the proviso would have implicitly legitimated it in the excepted instances. But it was prospectively legitimated

---

1. *Dailey* v. *Avery*.   2. 2 Watts, 31.

by the act of 1799 itself, which it was not the purpose of the
act of 1802, in the least, to repeal or disturb; for the rights of
the settlers could not be ascertained without receiving and acting on their conveyances as they might stand at the time.   The
evidences of their title were to be delivered up and deposited in
the land office, but not canceled; for a certified copy of one of
them was allowed to be competent evidence in *Carkhuff* v. *Anderson*,[1] a case which is decisive of the present; for it is impossible to understand why an incumbrance by grant shall be void,
while an incumbrance by judgment shall be valid.

It is scarce necessary to add that the admissions by a grantor
of the land, while he owned it, were competent evidence against
the defendant claiming under him; or that the widow, from whom
the plaintiff derives title, was a disinterested witness.   She had
conveyed her whole estate in the premises without warranty or covenant, and though there was a parol agreement by the plaintiff
to pay her a yearly stipend, its continuance was not dependent
on the enjoyment of the easement.   The bills of exceptions are
therefore groundless.

Judgment affirmed.

NAVIGABLE STREAMS, LAW RELATING TO: See *Lansing* v. *Smith*, 21 Am.
Dec. 89, note 101; *Attorney-general* v. *Stevens*, 22 Id. 526.

DECLARATIONS OF FORMER OWNER AS TO TITLE, WHEN ADMISSIBLE: See
Deming v. *Carrington*, 30 Am. Dec. 591, note 595, where the other cases in
this series are collected.

HOOD v. FAHNESTOCK.

[8 WATTS, 489.]

WHERE ONE ACTING AS ATTORNEY FOR ANOTHER OBTAINS KNOWLEDGE
from which a trust would arise, and afterwards becomes the attorney of
a subsequent purchaser in an independent and unconnected transaction,
his previous knowledge is not notice to such other person for whom he
acts.

BONA FIDE PURCHASER FOR VALUABLE CONSIDERATION IS PROTECTED under the statutes 13 and 27 Eliz., as adopted in this country, whether he
purchases from a fraudulent grantor or a fraudulent grantee, and there is
no difference in this respect between a deed to defraud subsequent creditors and one to defraud subsequent purchasers.

ERROR to the common pleas of Mercer county.   Ejectment for
a house and lot.   In the court below, the plaintiff, Fahnestock,
gave in evidence the record of a judgment recovered by him
against Jacob and James Henington; execution and sale there-

---

1. 3 Binn. 4.

on in August, 1834, to the plaintiff, and a sheriff's deed for the
house and lot in question. Also the deposition of Scott, showing that in 1820, deponent sold the lot to Jacob Henington;
that two years after, and after the house was built by Jacob, he
came to deponent, said that James had worked a good deal for
him, and asked deponent to lift the deed made, and make a deed
to James Henington; that deponent made the deed some time
after; that this deed was brought to deponent for execution by
Messrs. Bank, Foster, and Jacob Henington; that James paid
deponent nothing for it, and had no means to do so. The defendant gave in evidence a deed from Scott to James Henington, dated June, 1822; a judgment, in *Hood* v. *James Henington*,
dated June, 1823; execution and sale in 1824, to A. McGill.
The bond on which judgment was entered was dated June 29,
1823, in the handwriting of Jacob Henington. Also the deposition of A. McGill, showing that he was the bail of Jacob and
James; that James offered his own judgment to deponent, who
refused to take it unless he brought a written statement from
Jacob that he did not claim the house in dispute; that he brought
the writing, and he sold the lot at sheriff's sale, and became the
purchaser, and afterwards conveyed to Hood for the same price
that he gave for it; Mr. Banks drew the deed from deponent to
Hood; deponent purchased to indemnify himself as bail, and
sold to Hood to release him from his responsibility; he believed
at the time that the house was Jacob's, and that was his reason
for requiring the writing, and a subsequent verbal disclaimer of
ownership. There was proof that Jacob built and paid for the
house; that he rented it, and received the rent for it, or occupied it himself, ever since it was built. Also the record of a
judgment in favor of the plaintiff against Jacob Henington, of
June term, 1823, for six hundred and forty-two dollars, with interest from April, 1822; and judgments in Mercer county against
Jacob Henington, before the date of the deed from Scott to
James Henington, amounting to ten thousand six hundred and
seventy-one dollars and nineteen cents. There was also read in
evidence a settlement between Jacob and James, dated January,
1821. The following errors were assigned: 1. The court erred
in charging the jury " that if the defendant had notice of the
transaction between Scott, Jacob, and James, the plaintiff would
be entitled to recover." 2. In charging the jury that the disclaimer of title made by Jacob, in writing and by parol, was not
to operate in favor of defendant. 3. In answering in the negative the following point of the defendant, viz., that the employ-

ment of Banks by Hamilton and Hood, to draw a deed from
McGill to them, when, at the time, he knew of a trust arising
out of the land from having drawn the deed from Scott to Henington, is not legal notice of said trust to said Hamilton and
Hood.

Holstein, for the plaintiff in error.

Pearson and Forward, for the defendant in error.

By Court, SERGEANT, J.   The first and second errors are unsupported; but in the matter assigned as the third error, the
court answered the defendant's point incorrectly.   It is now
well settled that if one in the course of his business as agent,
attorney, or counsel for another, obtain knowledge from which
a trust would arise, and afterwards become the agent, attorney,
or counsel of a subsequent purchaser in an independent and unconnected transaction, his previous knowledge is not notice to
such other person for whom he acts.   The reason is, that no
man can be supposed always to carry in his mind the recollection of former occurrences; and, moreover, in the case of the attorney or counsel, it might be contrary to his duty to reveal the
confidential communications of his client.   To visit the principal with constructive notice, it is necessary that the knowledge of the agent or attorney should be gained in the course of
the same transaction in which he is employed by his client.   The
court, therefore, we think, erred in the answer to the defendant's third point, which is, in substance, the same as their
answer to the plaintiff's sixth point.

Another ground has been taken by the plaintiff, in the argument here, that the deed from James Henington was void by
13 Eliz., even though Hood, the defendant, was a *bona fide* purchaser for a valuable consideration—that statute protecting only
the *bona fide* purchaser from the fraudulent grantor, and not
from the fraudulent grantee.   The current of authorities, however, in this country, is to the contrary.   It is now the settled
American doctrine, that a *bona fide* purchaser for a valuable consideration is protected under the statutes of 13 and 27 Eliz., as
adopted in this country, whether he purchases from a fraudulent grantor or fraudulent grantee, and that there is no difference in this respect between a deed to defraud subsequent creditors and one to defraud subsequent purchasers: 18 Johns. 515;[1]
2 Mason, 252;[2] 14 Mass. 245;[3] 2 Pick. 184;[4] 1 Ashm. 129.[5]

Judgment reversed, and a *venire facias de novo* awarded.

1. *Anderson* v. *Roberts*, 9 Am. Dec. 235.   3. *Bridge* v. *Eggleston*, 7 Am. Dec. 299.
2. *Bean* v. *Smith*.   4. *Somes* v. *Brewer*, 13 Am. Dec. 406.
                              5. *Thompson* v. *McKean*.

NOTICE TO COUNSEL, IN THE SAME TRANSACTION, is notice to his client:
Barnes v. *McClinton*, 23 Am. Dec. 62.

AGENT'S KNOWLEDGE OF MATTERS within scope of his employment, is the
knowledge of his principal: See note to *Jeffrey* v. *Bigelow*, 28 Am. Dec. 481,
and cases there cited.

BONA FIDE PURCHASER FROM FRAUDULENT PURCHASER gets a good title:
See note to *Price* v. *Junkin*, 28 Am. Dec. 688, and the cases there collected.

THE PRINCIPAL CASE IS CITED in *Knouff* v. *Thompson*, 16 Pa. St. 364, to the
point that whatever puts a party on inquiry amounts to notice, provided the
inquiry would lead to the knowledge of the requisite fact, by the exercise of
ordinary diligence and understanding.

ABBOTT *v.* COMMONWEALTH.

[8 WATTS, 517.]

REPEAL OF STATUTE WHILE PROSECUTION UNDER IT IS PENDING, puts an
end to such prosecution, unless there is a saving clause in the repealing
act. And this is the case, not only where the latter act expressly repeals
the former, but also where its provisions are inconsistent with the former, although there be no annulling words or repealing clause therein.

ERROR to the quarter sessions of Westmoreland county. The
opinion states the case.

Beaver, for the plaintiff in error.

Foster, for the defendant in error.

By Court, ROGERS, J. A proceeding which is imperfect when
a law under which it was begun expires, can not be perfected;
what is done afterwards is void: *Steaver* v. *Immell*,[1] 1 Watts,
258. No proceeding can be pursued under a repealed statute,
though begun before the repeal, unless by a special clause in
the repealing act: 4 Yates, 392; *United States* v. *Passmore*, 4
Dall. 373. When an act of assembly directed that from and after
the passing of the act, no person should be subject to prosecution by indictment for a particular offense, at common law, it
was held that it put an end to a prosecution for that offense,
commenced and carried to conviction before the passing of the
act, but in which no judgment had been pronounced: *Commonwealth* v. *Duane*, 1 Binn. 601 [2 Am. Dec. 497]. And this is the
case not only where the latter act expressly repeals the former,
but where its provisions are inconsistent with the former, though
there be no annulling words or repealing clause; so every affirmative statute is a repeal, by implication, of a precedent one, so
far as it is contrary thereto, although there be no negative

---

1. *Stoever* v. *Immell.*

words: 14 Serg. & R. 420, and the authorities there cited. This was an indictment under the act of the twenty-fourth of March, 1817—an act to prevent the practice of wagering or betting on elections. The indictment was found to May sessions, 1839, and sentence was passed the nineteenth of August following, but in the intermediate time, viz., on the second of July, 1839, the legislature passed the act relating to elections; and this act, it is contended, repeals, or is inconsistent with and annuls the act on which the indictment was found. If this be so, then, on the authorities cited, the court of quarter sessions had no power to pass sentence, as there is no special clause which excepts this proceeding from its operation. In the seventeenth section the legislature, after enumerating the acts which they expressly repeal, add these words: ."And all other laws which are hereby altered or supplied by, or are inconsistent with this act, be and the same are hereby repealed." And the question is, whether the one hundred and fifteenth section does not alter and supply, and is not inconsistent with the act of the twenty-fourth of March, 1817; and of this there can be no doubt. It not only alters the phraseology of the act, but it changes the punishment of the offense from a "fine in a sum not exceeding the whole amount of the sum bet, nor less than twenty dollars," to a "fine of three times the amount bet or offered to be bet." It makes the offer to bet an offense—a provision not contained in the original act. In the one, the prosecution is limited to six months; in the other, it is extended to one year. The latter act, in this particular, is a substitute for the former. It can not be pretended that a person could now be indicted and convicted on the former act, which would in effect be holding that the last act was cumulative only.

Judgment reversed.

———

REPEAL OF STATUTE, EFFECT OF: See *Dixon* v. *Dixon*, 23 Am. Dec. 478; *Valsain* v. *Cloutier*, 22 Id. 179; *McCartee* v. *Orphan Asylum Society*, 18 Id. 516, note 542; *Roby* v. *West*, 17 Id. 423; *Saul* v. *His Creditors*, 16 Id. 212; *Miller* v. *Mercier*, 15 Id. 156.

WHEN ENACTMENT OF SUBSEQUENT STATUTE OPERATES AS A REPEAL of a former statute: *Saul* v. *His Creditors*, 16 Am. Dec. 212; *Towle* v. *Marrett*, 14 Id. 206, note 209; *Bartlett* v. *King*, 7 Id. 99, note 106.

THE PRINCIPAL CASE IS CITED in *Hickory Tree Road*, 43 Pa. St. 143, to the point that, in criminal cases, the repeal of a law under which the proceeding is pending, takes away the right to proceed further; and in *Butler* v. *Palmer*, 1 Hill (N. Y.), 330, to the point that the penalty is gone, though the repeal takes place while the prosecution is pending.

ALTEMAS *v.* CAMPBELL.

[9 WATTS, 28.]

ENTRY ON LAND AVOIDS OPERATION OF STATUTE OF LIMITATIONS as effectually as an action, but to have that effect the entry must bear on its face
an unequivocal intent to resume the actual possession.

ERROR to a special court of Indiana county. Ejectment for a
tract of land for which the plaintiff gave in evidence a regular
chain of title from the commonwealth down to himself. The
defendants relied on the statute of limitations, and proved a
possession of more than thirty years. To rebut this defense the
plaintiff showed that in 1818 the persons who then held the
legal title gave their power of attorney to Mr. Stannard, who
was called as a witness, and testified as stated in the opinion.
The court below charged the jury that if the possession was adverse, such an entry as that proved would not prevent the operation of the statute of limitations. That the act required a suit
or action.

Buffington, for the plaintiff in error.

H. D. Foster and *J. B. Alexander, contra.*

By Court, GIBSON, C. J. If the judge intended to charge, as
he probably did, that entry without action does not avoid the
statute of limitations, he fell into an inaccuracy. In our act of
1785, is comprised the substance of 21 Jac. 1, c. 16, under
which an entry has always had its common law properties; and
these have been attributed to it, under our own statute, by the
ablest men in the profession. In 1803, when the statute was
about to close its bar on rights of entry in existence at its enactment, the agent of the Penn family, under the direction of the
late Edward Tilghman, caused entries to be made into the mes-
suages and lots in York and Carlisle, for the preservation of the
proprietary quitrents. Indeed the statute expressly recognizes
the conservative properties of an entry alone, by treating it as
an alternative for an action. These properties, however, are
purely technical, and not to be favored. An entry puts the
owner, for a time, in actual possession; and as that, in the case
of a mixed occupancy, is referable to him exclusively who has
the right, it gives him momentarily the advantages of actual enjoyment; and momentarily displacing the adverse possession of
the occupant, it instantly undoes all that his intrusion had done
towards the accomplishment of a title. Yet it must be perceived
that this effect is subversive of the purpose of the statute, which

is to compel parties to settle their controversies while the evidence of their rights is attainable, and to put a reasonable period to the evils of a contested ownership. By repeated entries within periods of twenty-one years, a contest might be kept on foot interminably, or till the occupant's proofs had perished with those who could establish them; when, having been deterred from cultivating and improving the land, he might, at last, be left defenseless by the lapse of time, which, instead of having fortified his title as it ought, would be found to have destroyed it. Such might be the magic of a possession gained by an entry into an obscure corner of the land, which the law would not otherwise protect, and which it would not suffer the party to maintain. Such an entry, however, we are compelled by the terms of the statute to say, is as effective as an action; but we are at liberty, and policy requires us, to hold the plaintiff to strict proof of a formal observance of the ceremony. What, then, is an entry at the common law?

In *Dunning* v. *Carothers*, 3 Serg. & R. 385, I was of opinion that claim of title made upon the land, might be left to the jury as evidence of a formal entry—an opinion which I unreservedly retract, substituting, for it, the opinion expressed by Mr. Justice Washington, in the fourth volume of his reports, page 369, when the cause was brought before him by a new ejectment in the circuit court of the United States. The office of an entry is not to claim title, but to regain a pedal possession; and it has been said that to make it good, the former possessor and his servants must be removed from the land—an assertion qualified by Lord Holt in an anonymous case in 1 Salkeld, 246, who says that an entry without expulsion, makes such a seisin only, that the law will adjudge him in possession who has the right; but that it will not work a disseisin or abatement. The first bears a resemblance to livery of seisin, the difference being, that the party is invested by his own act in the one case, and by the act of the occupant in the other. Hence it is, that Lord Coke says: "By the entry of the lessee, he is in actual possession, and then the livery can not be made to him that is in possession; for *quod semel meum est, amplius meum esse non potest:*" Co. Lit. 49 b. The effect of an entry, it is agreed, depends on the intent of it, expressed by words, or intimated by an act equally significant. I would say, in a few words, that there must be an explicit declaration, or an act of notorious dominion, by which the claimant challenges the right of the occupant; or it can not perhaps be better defined than by saying that the entry must

bear, on the face of it, an unequivocal intent to resume the
actual possession. Let us turn then to the testimony of the
plaintiff's agent, to see whether his presence on the land was for
that purpose. The defendant called on him, in pursuance of a
message, to accept a lease, but no lease was executed. "It was
then arranged," said the witness, "that I should go to the
house and see it. I did so; and again told him about his taking
a lease. No agreement was entered into at that time or any
other. I did not ask him to leave the place." It is plain from
this, that the object of the visit was a compromise which was
not effected. He met the defendant on the land by appointment; and not to take or receive the possession of it from him,
but to make an arrangement that would settle him in it. Now,
what says Lord Coke to such a case? "If the bastard invite
the mulier to his house, to see pictures, or to dine with him, or
to hawk, hunt, or sport with him, or such like, upon the land
descended; and the mulier cometh upon the land accordingly;
this is no interruption, because he came by the consent of the
bastard, and therefore the coming upon the land can be no trespass; but if the mulier cometh upon the ground of his own
read, or cutteth a tree, or diggeth the soil, or take any profit,
these shall be interruptions; for rather than the bastard shall
punish him in an action of trespass, the act shall amount in law
to an entry, because he hath a right of entry:" Co. Lit. 245
b. And again: "If the tenant in an assize of an house, desire
the plaintiff to dine with him in the house, which the plaintiff
doth accordingly, and so they be both in the house; and in
truth one pretendeth one title, and the other another title; yet
the law, in this case, shall not adjudge the possession in him
that right hath:" Id. 268 a. In the case before us, the agent
came to the defendant's house by invitation—certainly by pre-
concert—the object being a visit—of business probably—but
still a visit, and not an intrusion; and though he unsuccessfully
importuned the defendant to become a lessee, the case was precisely that put by Lord Coke—where one pretendeth one title,
and the other another—as one which gives not the possession to
him who has the right. However, then, we may differ from the
judge in regard to the effect of a formal entry, we entirely concur with him, that there was no evidence of it to be left to the
jury.

Judgment affirmed.

———

ENTRY TO STOP RUNNING OF STATUTE OF LIMITATIONS.—If a tract of land
lies partly in two counties, and is held adversely to the owner, his entry on

the part in one county does not stop the running of the statute as to the part in the other county: *Hord* v. *Walker*, 15 Am. Dec. 39. See also note to *Trotter* v. *Cassady*, 13 Id. 185.

ENTRY PUTS THE OWNER FOR A TIME IN THE ACTUAL POSSESSION: *Elliott* v. *Powell*, 10 Watts, 454; *Bradley* v. *West*, 60 Mo. 42, both citing the principal case.

ENTRY ON LAND AVOIDS OPERATION OF STATUTE OF LIMITATIONS, if it is accompanied by an explicit declaration, or an act of notorious dominion, by which the claimant challenges the right of the occupant: *Hooper* v. *Garver*, 15 Pa. St. 525; *Hole* v. *Rittenhouse*, 19 Id. 309, both citing the principal case.

THE PRINCIPAL CASE IS ALSO CITED in *Smith* v. *Steele*, 17 Pa. St. 37, to the point that an entry is operative; although, at the moment, there exists in fact a mixed possession, it is yet legally regarded as residing exclusively in the true owner by virtue of his superior right; and in *Douglass* v. *Lucas*, 63 Id. 12, to the point that the law recognizes an entry alone as an alternative for an action; in *Byers* v. *Danley*, 27 Ark. 93, to the point that an entry to divest possession, is a going upon the land with palpable intent to claim the possession as the party's own; and in *City of Pella* v. *Scholte*, 24 Iowa, 296, as defining what an entry is.

McFARLAND v. NEWMAN.

[9 WATTS, 55.]

IMPLIED WARRANTY IN SALE OF CHATTEL does not arise from affirmation of soundness, which proves to be unfounded.

CONSTRUCTION OF AN ORAL AGREEMENT BELONGS TO THE JURY and not to the court.

NAKED AVERMENT OF A FACT IS NEITHER A WARRANTY ITSELF, nor evidence of one. It may, with other circumstances, be taken into consideration, but the jury must be satisfied from the whole, that the vendor actually, and not constructively, consented to be bound for the truth of his representation.

ERROR to the common pleas of Fayette county. Assumpsit against McFarland on an alleged warranty of a horse passed to the plaintiff as sound in all respects except the colt distemper. The evidence showed that the horse had a running from the nose at the time of the bargain, which, however, the defendant represented to have been of only a few days' continuance. But other testimony showed that the animal had been suffering with the disease all the time McFarland had him, a period of ten or eleven months; and the evidence was very strong that he had the glanders. Other witnesses testified that the person who sold the horse to McFarland, sold him as a glandered horse, that another person had told him that the horse had the glanders, and that he had himself said that he feared he had something worse than the distemper. The judge charged that "a positive averment, made by the defendant at the time of the contract, of a material fact, is a warranty; that it is part or parcel of the contract." The jury found for the plaintiff, and the defendant excepted.

Howel and Dawson, for the plaintiff in error.

Veech, for the defendant in error.

By Court, Gibson, C. J. On no subject have the decisions been so anomalous, as on warranty of chattels; and an attempt to arrive at a satisfactory conclusion about any principle supposed to be settled by them, would be hopeless, if not absurd. Of such jarring materials have they been compounded, that it is impossible to extract from them any principle of general application, and we are left by them in the predicament of mariners compelled to correct their dead reckoning by an observation. The civil law maxim is, doubtless, that a sound article is warranted by a sound price; but the common law courts started with the doctrine that though the sale of a chattel is followed by an implied warranty of title, and a right of action *ex delicto* for willful misrepresentation of the quality; yet that the maxim *caveat emptor*, disposes of all beside. Thus was the common law originally settled; and the current of decision ran smooth and clear in the channel thus marked out for it, from the days of the year books, till within a few years past, when it suddenly became turbid and agitated: and, as in the case of promises conjured up to elude the statute of limitations, it finally ran wild. The judges, in pursuit of a phantom in the guise of a principle of impracticable policy and questionable morality, broke away from the common law, not, however, by adopting the civil law principle of implied warranty as to soundness, but by laying hold on the vendor's commendation of his commodity, and not at first as absolutely constituting an express warranty, but as evidence of it. I say the policy of this principle is impracticable, because the operations of commerce are such as to require that the rules for its regulation admit of as few occasions for reclamation as possible; and I say its morality is questionable, because I am unable to discern anything immoral in the *bona fide* sale of an article represented to be exactly that as which the vendor had purchased it. It is to be remembered that I am speaking of the sale of a thing accepted by the vendee after opportunity had to inspect and test it, and not of a sale in which he was necessarily compelled by the circumstances to deal on the faith of the vendor's description; nor yet of a sale on the concoction of which he was overreached by misrepresentation or trick. For the latter, he doubtless has his remedy; but not by an action *ex contractu;* and I therefore lay the vendor's motive out of the case as one that can have no legitimate influence on the question of warranty. But a positive assertion of what he knew not to be either true or false, is as unconscionable, and might be as injurious, as an intentional falsehood; and what is the vendee's remedy for it where the *scienter* can not be proved? The fallacy of the question is, in assuming that he ought to have any remedy at all.

The relation of buyer and seller, unlike that of *cestui que trust,* attorney and client, or guardian and ward, is not a confidential one; and if the buyer, instead of exacting an explicit warranty, chooses to rely on the bare opinion of one who knows no more about the matter than he does himself, he has himself to blame for it. If he will buy on the seller's responsibility, let him evince it by demanding the proper security; else let him be taken to have bought on his own. He who is so simple as to contract without a specification of the terms, is not a fit subject of judicial guardianship. Reposing no confidence in each other, and dealing at arm's length, no more should be required of parties to a sale, than to use no falsehood; and to require more of them, would put a stop to commerce itself in driving every one out of it by the terror of endless litigation. Yet such would be the tendency of the civil law scion which the judges have been laboring to engraft on the common law stock. It would be curious but unprofitable to trace their advances towards the object by their footsteps in the cases. In none of them have I discovered any principle so plausible as that assumed by the judge who tried the present cause, that an averment of a material fact is part of the contract—a position, however, that will not bear a moment's examination. A sale is a contract executed, on which, of course, no action can be directly founded; but an action may be founded directly on a warranty, and it was doubted in *Stuart* v. *Wilkins*, Doug. 18, whether an action could be maintained for a breach of it in any other way; consequently, though it is a concomitant, it is also a collateral, self-existent contract; and no more a part of the sale, than a covenant of warranty in a deed is part of the conveyance. It is not easy to say what notions had previously been entertained; but for a short time after the new doctrine had been broached, the distinction between representation and warranty was ostensibly observed. But in *Wood* v. *Smith*, 4 Car. & P. 45, it was resolved "that whatever a person represents is a warranty;" and thus the previous distinction, flimsy and inoperative as it had become in practice, was formally laid aside. And that the court went even further, is manifest from a glance at the circumstances. The plaintiff, chaffering for a mare, had said interrogatively, "She is sound, of course," and the defendant had replied, "Yes, to the best of my knowledge;" but to the direct question, "Will you warrant her?" he answered: "I never warrant, I would not even warrant myself." Yet in the teeth of this peremptory refusal, it was adjudged that he had actually entered into an express warranty, and that the plaintiff had purchased on the faith of it. This conclusion is so forced, unnatural, and opposed to the very declared understanding and intent, that one is tempted to think the court had so far lost sight of the nature of a warranty as to have forgotten that it is a contract; "that the assent to every contract must be mutual; that every agreement must be so certain and complete that each party may have an action on it: and that it would be incomplete if either party withheld his assent to its terms." I quote these commonplace principles from Mr. Chitty's treatise on contracts, because I happen to have the book at hand. It is true, he says, that in many cases the law implies the party's assent to a promise; but, he also says, that such a contract is an implied one, and our business, at present, is with the elements of an express warranty.

Now, it is not, and can not be, a wholesome interpretation which involves a party in engagements he never dreamed of contracting, or to which he expressly refused to assent. If it is true, as it is said to be, that the plain, ordinary, and popular sense of words shall prevail, in preference to their strict grammatical sense, the decision in *Wood* v. *Smith* is more than questionable; for that the parties themselves put no such meaning on their discourse, as did the court, is evident from the plaintiff's request that the defendant would annex a warranty to his representation, and from the defendant's refusal to do so. After that, it is hard to see what room there was for interpretation. Even the civil law implication of warranty, if it were inadmissible on no other ground, would be repressed by it, on the foot of the maxim, *expressum facit cessare tacitum.* It may be said in extenuation, that the court did not hold the defendant to a warranty of the mare's soundness, but only to a warranty of soundness to the best of his knowledge. So much the worse. He had refused to enter into any warranty whatever, and it would have required no greater stretch to hold that he had en-

tered into a general warranty of soundness, than to hold that
he had entered into a special warranty of what he thought or
knew. It would, too, have relieved the court from the awkward-
ness of resting the recovery on the collateral warranty of an immaterial fact which, assigned as a breach, would not have entitled the plaintiff even to nominal damages. And what makes
the judicious grieve, is that all this violence to the ancient principles of the law was gratuitous; for, as in *Chandler* v. *Lopus*,[1]
as well as in the case before us, the plaintiff had a remedy as
efficacious by an action for the deceit. It will be perceived that
these remarks do not touch the case of *Borrekins* v. *Bevan*, 3
Rawle, 23 [23 Am. Dec. 385], in which it was held that an implied warranty arises, that the article is specifically that as which
it is sold.

The essential error of the present case, however, is that the
judge put a legal interpretation on oral words, and made it
matter of positive direction. In the British courts, revision on
writ of error is unfrequent; and points like the present are usually determined on motions for new trials, in which the judges
review not only the law, but the evidence in relation to its capacity to sustain the verdict. Hence, they began imperceptibly
to deal indiscriminately with matter of fact and matter of law
as equally within their province, without troubling themselves
with distinctions as to what more properly belongs to the jury.
In our own state, where abstract principles are settled by the
court of the last resort on bills of exceptions, the functions of
the judge and those of the jury are more carefully separated and
particularly defined. Now it is obvious that the sense of words
used in conversation, and what the parties meant to express by
them, is for the jury to determine, and not for the court. It is
the conceded province of the court to expound the meaning of
an instrument; but that it extends not to words uttered, of which
there can be no tenor, is evident from the uniformity with which
it is spoken of in reference to the interpretation of writings.
The same thing is evident also from the nature of the judicial
function, which is exercised only on facts supposed to be established. The terms of assent, where proof of the contract depends upon testimony, necessarily present a question of fact,
while words embodied in an instrument readily admit of interpretation. Hence, it was said by Chief Justice Abbot, 2 Barn.
& Cress. 634,[2] " that where the whole matter passes in parol, all
that passes may sometimes be taken together; but not always,

---

because matters talked of at the commencement of a bargain
may be excluded by the language used at its termination: but if
the contract be in the end reduced to writing, nothing which is
not found in the writing, can be considered as a part of the
writing." The distinction is more pointedly indicated in the
American cases. "The counsel of the plaintiff," said Chief Justice Marshall in *Levy* v. *Gadsby*, 3 Cranch, 186, "has also contended that although the paper writing produced, would, on the
face of it, import a usurious contract, yet that the jury might
possibly have inferred from it certain intrinsic facts which would
have shown the contract not to have been within the act. But
in this case, the question arises on a written instrument; and no
question is more clearly settled than that the construction of
written evidence is with the court." The converse was asserted
in *Sidwell* v. *Evans*, 1 Penn. 383 [21 Am. Dec. 387], where it
was ruled that a judge can not be required to give a legal construction to the words of a witness. That the construction of
an oral agreement belongs to the jury, and that parol evidence
connected with a writing draws the whole from the court, is so
often repeated in our own reports, that I forbear to enumerate
the cases; and I particularly advert only to *Harper* v. *Kean*, 11
Serg. & R. 280, in which the expression of an opinion on the
meaning of letters in connection with verbal communications
was held not to be erroneous, only because the jury were directed
to judge of the contract themselves.

As the cause goes back to another jury, it is proper to intimate
the principle on which a correct decision of it must depend.
Though to constitute a warranty requires no particular form of
words, the naked averment of a fact is neither a warranty itself,
nor evidence of it. In connection with other circumstances, it
certainly may be taken into consideration; but the jury must be
satisfied from the whole, that the vendor actually, and not constructively, consented to be bound for the truth of his representation. Should he have used expressions fairly importing a
willingness to be thus bound, it would furnish a reason to infer
that he had intentionally induced the vendee to treat on that
basis; but a naked affirmation is not to be dealt with as a warranty, merely because the vendee had gratuitously relied on it;
for not to have exacted a direct engagement, had he desired to
buy on the vendor's judgment, must be accounted an instance
of folly. Testing the vendor's responsibility by these principles,
justice will be done without driving him into the toils of an
imaginary contract.

Judgment reversed, and a *venire de novo* awarded.

IMPLIED WARRANTY IN SALE OF CHATTELS: See *Borrekins* v. *Bevan*, 23 Am. Dec. 85, and note 101, where the other cases in this series are collected. The principal case is cited in *Price* v. *Lewis*, 17 Pa. St. 52, and in *Smith* v. *Smith*, 21 Id. 372, to the point that for a deceitful representation on the sale of a chattel, the remedy is by an action *ex delicto*.

CONSTRUCTION OF PAROL EVIDENCE IS FOR THE JURY: See *Sidwell* v. *Evans*, 21 Am. Dec. 387, note 394.

REPRESENTATIONS OF VENDOR, EFFECT OF: See *West* v. *Anderson*, 21 Am. Dec. 737, note 741; *Williams* v. *Hicks*, 19 Id. 693, note 697; *Moore* v. *Turbeville*, 5 Id. 642.

ATWOOD v. RELIANCE TRANSPORTATION COMPANY.

[9 WATTS, 87.]

COMMON CARRIER MAY, BY SPECIAL ACCEPTANCE, LIMIT HIS COMMON LAW LIABILITY; but the terms of this acceptance operate as exceptions which leave the common law rule in force as to all beside.

DANGERS OF NAVIGATION MEAN THOSE PERILS THAT ARE INCIDENT to it in a lawful course of it, but not those that arise from pursuing an unlawful course therein.

PARTIES CAN NOT BE AFFECTED BY USAGES IN DEROGATION OF LAWS that bind them.

PRECISE RISK ONLY, WHICH INSURER CONTEMPLATED, can be introduced into contract of marine insurance, and this principle applies to contracts of inland navigation.

ERROR to the district court of Allegheny county. Action against the defendants as common carriers on the Pennsylvania canal, for damages done to goods of the plaintiff on board the defendants' boat. The goods were to be delivered "in good order, the dangers of the navigation, fire, leakage, and all other unavoidable accidents, excepted." At Harrisburg the vessel was detained while a breach in one of the locks was being repaired. The water was, in consequence of the repairs being made, rapidly subsiding in the level where she lay. The lock-keeper, in obedience to rules established by the canal commissioners, refused to let her lie in the chamber of the lower lock, and pointed out a place where she could lie in safety. Notwithstanding this, she went into the lock, where she bilged in the night, by reason of which the goods were damaged. The defendants gave evidence to show that the boat's entrance was not forbidden by the lock-keeper; that she was tight, stanch, and strong; that she was well manned and commanded; that the locks were generally safer in cases of grounding by settling than the bed of the canal; and that boat masters usually sought them as preferable berths when grounding was apprehended. The judge charged that "a common carrier may limit his re-

sponsibility by notices or agreements; and that if the captain was
not culpably ignorant of any fact in regard to the lock; not deficient in prudence, care, and judgment; not warned of his
danger; the case might be considered to come fairly within the
exceptions named in the contract." Verdict for the defendants.

Findley, for the plaintiff in error.

Forward, contra.

By Court, GIBSON, C. J. The maxim that any one may dispense
with a rule provided for its exclusive benefit, is not without its
exceptions; and notwithstanding the unfortunate direction given
to the decisions at an early day, it is still almost susceptible of
a doubt whether an agreement to lessen the common law measure of a carrier's responsibility, like an agreement to forego a
fee-simple tenant's right of alienation, or a mortgagor's right of
redemption, is not void by the policy of the law. That the
bailor is left as much at another's mercy, by an agreement like
the present, as a borrower would be by an agreement to turn his
mortgage into a conditional sale, is entirely evident from the fact
that the carrier has the exclusive custody of the goods; and that
to convict him of negligence in his function would be as impracticable as to convict him of connivance at robbery, against which
the common law rule of his responsibility was intended more
especially to guard. From his servants, who are usually the only
persons that can speak of the matter, it would be idle to expect
testimony to implicate themselves; and the owner can seldom
have any other account of his property than what they may
choose to give him. Such a state of things is not to be encouraged; and though it is perhaps too late to say that a carrier may
not accept his charge in special terms, it is not too late to say
that the policy which dictated the rule of the common law requires that exceptions to it be strictly interpreted, and that it is
his duty to bring his case strictly within them. What, then, is
the effect of an acceptance on terms of safe delivery, the dangers of the navigation, fire, leakage, and all other unavoidable
accidents, excepted? The goods were damaged by bilging in a
lock; and the question is, whether a loss incurred by resting in
a prohibited place is a loss from an excepted peril of the navigation.

Every contract is supposed to be framed on the basis of the
laws; and they are therefore left to regulate those matters for
which the parties have not specially provided. Thus a lender
implicitly stipulates for legal interest when less is not expressly

reserved; and the measure of the defendant's responsibility
would have been exactly that which the common law prescribes,
.had it not been narrowed by a special acceptance. But the
terms of this acceptance operate, as I have said, as exceptions
which leave the common law rule in force as to all beside. By
the terms dangers of the navigation, therefore, the parties meant.
to mark those perils that are incident to it in a lawful course of
it. Holding the carrier to an observance of the laws prescribed
for its regulation, the owner has a basis for an estimate of the
risk which he is to take upon himself; but the enhancement of
it from a license to transcend them, would be inappreciable, and,
in the absence of express stipulation, such a license is not to be
intended. For damage occasioned by inattention to those precautions which are enjoined to prevent collision in passing, the
carrier would obviously be liable, though he had substituted
others apparently as efficient; and why not for damage by bilging, which would have been avoided had the boat been where it.
ought, by the law of the canal, to have been? That a man will
do what the law commands, is surely a presumption on which a
party may reckon in laying the foundations of his contract.
Now by declining to assume the risks of the navigation, the carrier
compelled the owner of the goods to be his own insurer; but an
insurer is not liable to bear a loss from a deviation or change of
the risk, and there certainly is a change of it when the transit.
is not made in subordination to the laws of the navigation. Nor
is the consequence of the principle to be evaded by bringing
into view the illegal practices of other boatmen. Parties are
not to be affected by usages in derogation of laws which bind
them; and if the owner of the goods had reason to suppose the law
would not be violated, in this instance, by using the locks for a
prohibited purpose, why should he bear a risk which was out of
the prescribed course of the navigation, even though it might
not have been so great as those he would have had to bear
within it? The principles of marine insurance, founded as they
are in abstract reason and exact justice, may sometimes be fitly
applied to a fresh-water contract; and I recur to a case of it to
show that he who contracts to bear a risk may insist on having
the benefit of all his chances, however remote or inconsiderable.
Upon the principle that the voyage must be prosecuted conformably to the implied terms of the policy, it was held in *Middle-
wood* v. *Blakes*, 7 T. R. 162, that the pursuit of a particular,
though customary track by direction of the owners, was a deviation, because the insured was tacitly entitled to the benefit of

the captain's choice at the usual point of divergence; and yet the owners may have been, in fact, more competent to choose than he.

It is an implied but cardinal condition of marine insurance, therefore, that no risk be introduced but precisely that which the insurer contemplated; and that it has a place in contracts of inland navigation, is shown by *Hand* v. *Baynes*, 4 Whart. 204 [33 Am. Dec. 54]. In that case, the hides had been received at Philadelphia, as it was expressed in the bill of lading, "on board Hand's line via the Chesapeake and Delaware canal," to be delivered to the consignee in Baltimore, "the dangers of the navigation, fire, leakage, and breakage excepted." The sloop was not permitted to pass through the canal, which chanced to be shut when she arrived at the entrance of it; and the captain, being told that the repairs then in progress would not be finished for a month, proceeded to make the voyage coastwise, and lost his vessel with her cargo in a gale at sea, for which his owners were held liable on the ground that it was his duty to lie by or return, and that the goods, therefore, were not lost in the navigation contemplated by the contract. Yet the sloop, like the towboat in this instance, was tight, stanch, and competent to the voyage attempted. What avails it, then, that in a scarcity of water, the chamber of a lock may ordinarily be a safer berth than the bed of the canal, or that boat masters may have surreptitiously used it as such; or that so to have used it, in this instance, evinced no want of prudence or skill? The master was incompetent to choose it, because the owner of the goods had chosen differently. Nor is it material to inquire whether the boat had been warned off by the lock-keeper. The use of the lock for the purpose to which the master applied it, was interdicted by the law, of which he was bound to take notice; and in these respects the direction was erroneous

Judgment reversed, and a *venire de novo* awarded.

<hr />

COMMON CARRIER'S RIGHT TO LIMIT HIS LIABILITY: See *Cole* v. *Goodwin*, 32 Am. Dec. 470, and note 495.

COMMON CARRIER MAY BY SPECIAL CONTRACT LIMIT HIS COMMON LAW LIABILITY: *Bingham* v. *Rogers*, 6 Watts & S. 500; *Laing* v. *Colder*, 8 Pa. St. 484; *Leonard* v. *Hendrickson*, 18 Id. 43; *Mercantile M. I. Co.* v. *Chase*, 1 E. D. Smith, 139, all citing the principal case.

EXCEPTIONS TO LIABILITY OF COMMON CARRIER ARE STRICTLY CONSTRUED by the courts on ground of public policy: *Steele* v. *Townsend*, 37 Ala. 255; *Levering* v. *Union T. & I. Co.*, 42 Mo. 93; *N. J. S. N. Co.* v. *Merchants' Bank*, 6 How. (U. S.) 419, all citing the principal case. The principal case is also cited in *Fish* v. *Chapman*, 2 Ga. 360, to the point that a common carrier can not, by general notice or special acceptance, limit his common law liability.

Bell *v.* McClintock.

[9 Watts, 119.]

Owner of Dam on Stream is Liable for Damages Caused thereby to private property on such stream, by the ordinary and expected floods of the season, but not for those occasioned by extraordinary and unexpected floods. This principle applied in the case of a stream made navigable by law.

Error to the common pleas of Venango county. Action on the case for a nuisance. The defendant erected a dam across Oil creek, below the lands of the plaintiff, and upon the breaking up of the ice in the stream the dam held it back and forced it out upon the plaintiff's lands, which were covered with driftwood and ice, to his injury. The court charged, that if this injury was occasioned by the defendant's dam under ordinary circumstances, such as he might have anticipated when he erected it, he would be liable in this action, but if the injury proceeded from an extraordinary flood, or an act of Providence, such as could not have been foreseen, the plaintiff could not recover. Verdict for the plaintiff.

Riddle, for the plaintiff in error.

Pearson and Galbreath, contra.

By Court, Rogers, J. The general rule of law is, that every man has a right to have the advantage of the flow of water, in its natural channel, in his own land. But in using it, the owner must so apply the water as to work no material injury or annoyance to his neighbor either above or below him. The maxim *sic utere tuo ut alienum non lædas*, applies with peculiar propriety to this class of cases. By the act of the twenty-third of March, 1808, Oil creek is declared a public highway. The owners of the land adjoining the stream are authorized to erect dams for mills, and other water works, and to keep the same in good repair, provided, that in erecting said dams and keeping them in repair, they shall not disturb the navigation; and provided, also, that they shall not infringe the rights or privileges of the owners or possessors of any private property on such stream. The act in these provisions incorporates the principles of the common law, and the only difficulty arises from the application of well-settled principles to the facts of this case. The injuries of which the plaintiffs complain are of two descriptions, those which arose from the ordinary freshets, and which are of common and periodical occurrence, and those which arose from the extraordinary floods of the years 1834 and 1835. The court ruled that the defendant was liable for all damage from the ordinary, common, and expected floods of the season, but not for those occasioned by the uncommon, unexpected, and extraordinary floods. In these positions the court is sustained by principle and authority. Streams of water are intended for the common use and benefit of mankind, but they must be so used as to work no material injury to the rights of others. When the plaintiff erected his dam he was bound to notice, not only its effect at the time, but its effect at all seasons of the year. In this stream, as well as all other large streams which fall into the Allegheny river, there are regular freshets or floods, which swell the volume of water, and thereby enable the inhabitants to raft down the river the various products of the country. They are expected, with considerable certainty, at fixed times and seasons. It was the duty of the plaintiff, with reference to this, which is at least of yearly occurrence, to calculate the immediate probable effects the dam would have at all seasons of the year on the property of his neighbor, above as well as below his erection. A neglect to use the necessary precaution or a miscalculation of its effects, where it works an injury to another, may be compensated in damages. But where the injury arises from some cause out of the ordinary course, from some unusual cause, as for instance, from a flood or freshet such as has been described by the witnesses, the owner of the dam is not liable to damages. It is *damnum absque injuria*. They are not such accidents as ordinary foresight or prudence can guard against, and for this reason a distinction has been taken as to the liability of the party.

In the case of *The Lehigh Bridge Company* v. *The Lehigh Navigation Company*, 4 Rawle, 9 [26 Am. Dec. 11], it is said that if chargeable with no want of attention to its probable effects, a person is not answerable for consequences which it was impossible to foresee and prevent. When a loss happens exclusively from an act of Providence, it will not be pretended that it ought to be borne by him whose superstructure was made the immediate instrument of it. The concurrence of negligence with the act of Providence, when the mischief is done by flood or storm, is necessary to fix the defendant with liability. When, however, the injury arises from causes which might have been foreseen and avoided, as in the cases of ordinary periodical freshets, it is but right that he whose superstructure is the immediate cause of the mischief should bear the loss. In that case there is the concurrence of negligence with the act of Providence, which, as it is seen, is the criterion of liability. We are of the opinion that the court was right, in the principles of law given in charge to the jury, and that there was no error in the application of the principles to the points of the case.

Judgment affirmed.

———

Cited in *McCoy* v. *Danley*, 20 Pa. St. 89, to the point that one who erects a dam on a stream is liable for all the injuries caused by it in times of usual, ordinary, and expected freshets.

———

DAY v. SHARP.

[4 WHARTON, 339.]

COURT CAN NOT REJECT PROOF OF A FACT AS IMMATERIAL, if the question as to whether it is immaterial or not depends upon proof of another fact. The proper course in such a case is to submit the proof of both facts to the jury.

VOID PROCESS MUST BE SET ASIDE OR VACATED before trespass can be maintained against the party who caused it to issue, for acts done thereunder.

PROCESS MERELY VOIDABLE AFFORDS JUSTIFICATION for acts that have been done thereunder.

EXECUTION ISSUED AFTER DEATH OF THE PLAINTIFF, without a revival of the judgment by *scire facias*, is but voidable, not void, if it issued at the instance of the party who was entitled to collect the money under the judgment.

TRESPASS *de bonis asportatis*. Plaintiff in error, defendant below, justified the taking of the goods under a *pluries* writ of execution, issued on the judgment in the action of *Gaylord* v. *Sharp*. That action was upon a promissory note executed by Day, Sharp, and Stanton. Day executed the note as surety for Sharp. Day paid the judgment in that action. The trial court heard evidence to the point that before the *pluries* writ was issued, under which defendant Day justified, Gaylord, the plaintiff in the judgment upon which it issued, died, and after such evidence refused to allow proof of the writ. Verdict and judgment having gone for plaintiff below, defendant took a writ of error.

E. Wheeler, for the plaintiff in error.

Mallery, contra.

By Court, SERGEANT, J. In this case, the court below fell into the error which was censured by this court in *Fisher* v. *Kean*, 1 Watts, 278, and has been repeatedly the cause of the reversal of judgments. The defendant after proving a judgment before a magistrate against the plaintiff, and several successive executions thereon, offered in evidence a second *pluries* execution on the same judgment. The plaintiff objected to it, and offered evidence to prove the death of the plaintiff in the execution, which the court permitted, notwithstanding the defendant's objection to it. The necessary effect of such a course on the part of the court, is to withdraw from the jury, the decision of the facts, and to assume it by the court alone, without their participation; whereas in the present case, the *pluries* execution should have been received in evidence, as the process issued in the case; and when the counter evidence should have been given in its regular order, the fact in question would be for the jury to decide, and the questions of law arising thereon for the court to instruct the jury upon. It is matter of regret to find a principle disregarded, which is so important to the due administration of justice, and has so often been the subject of notice by this court. The reason which has been given, would compel the court to reverse this judgment, but as the case will go back again for trial, it is necessary to notice the second error assigned, presenting the points which would have arisen on the merits of the case, supposing the evidence offered had been regularly before the court below. After the court had permitted the plaintiff to show the death of Gaylord, before the issuing of the second *pluries* execution, the defendant offered to show, that it was issued at the instance, and for the use of Day, one of the defendants in the judgment, proposing further to prove that Day stood in the relation of surety to Sharp, and that Day paid the judgment at or before the assignment of the judgment to him by Gaylord, and before the issuing of the execution. The plaintiff met this offer by objecting: 1. That Gaylord was dead prior to the issuing of the execution; 2. That the judgment was previously satisfied; 3. That it should have appeared on the record before the issuing of the execution, that Day was surety as set forth in the offer. On these objections, the court rejected the *pluries* execution offered by the defendant.

This was an action of trespass *de bonis asportatis*, in which the defendant justified under a judgment and execution at the suit of Gaylord against Sharp (the plaintiff), Day (the defendant), and Stanton. He proved the judgment duly rendered before the justice on the thirty-first of July, 1827, execution issued by the plaintiff thereon, on the twenty-ninth of May, 1828, an alias execution, June 14, 1828, and a *pluries*, September 10, 1830.

Another *pluries* was issued on the tenth of June, 1835, previous
to which the plaintiff Gaylord was dead; and the question is,
whether an execution issued and levied in the name of a plaintiff, who is dead, without issuing a *scire facias*, and under the
other circumstances stated, is a justification to the party who
issued it.

A distinction has long existed between process, which is
absolutely null and void, and affords no justification whatever
to the party issuing it, in an action of trespass, and process
which is voidable merely. When the process is altogether irregular and defective, it is considered as null and void; and if it be
vacated or set aside by the court, the party who acted under it,
becomes a trespasser from the beginning, though the officer may
be justified by the command of the writ; not being bound to look
into it. Even there, however, before the party can be sued in
trespass, the process must first be set aside or vacated; for if it
still subsist in full force and vigor at the time of the action
brought, the party may justify under it. Where, however, the
process is not totally defective and irregular, but merely erroneous, and liable to be reversed on error, it is not void, but voidable, and does not make the party issuing it, a trespasser. In
the case of a plaintiff's death, no doubt it is the duty of the party
who issues process of execution, to substitute the names of his
executors or administrators; and·as there is a new party, to
issue a *scire facias*. But the not issuing of a *scire facias*, where
the law requires it, has not *per se* been considered as making an
execution void, or the party issuing it a trespasser. In *Jackson*
v. *Bartlett*, 8 Johns. 361, it was held, that if an execution issues
after a year and a day, without a revival of the judgment by a
scire facias, it is only voidable at the instance of the party, and
not void. So in *Patrick* v. *Johnson*, 3 Lev. 404, cited 4 Watts,
373,[1] a *fieri facias* sued out after a year and a day from the
judgment, is not void, but merely voidable by writ of error.
In *Howard* v. *Pitt*, 1 Salk. 261, the plaintiff sued out a *ca. sa.*
from the king's bench, while the record of the judgment was removed from thence to the exchequer chamber, where it was
abated by the death of one of the plaintiffs in error, but no re-
mittitur was entered, and therefore the writ of error was still
pending there—held to be erroneous, but not void, and the
case in 4 Leon. 197,[2] to the contrary was denied. In *Jeanes* v.
Wilkins, 1 Ves. 195, after the body of the defendant had been
taken in execution, the plaintiff issued a *fieri facias*, and sold a

---

1. *Speer* v. *Sample.*   2. *Russel's cases.*

leasehold of the defendant: Lord Hardwicke said, that by law, during the existence of the *capias* and the person in custody, a *fieri facias* ought not to be taken out, and the court would set it aside on motion, but yet the *fi. fa.* was not void. The line of distinction has not been accurately drawn, as to all the cases where the process is merely erroneous, and those where it is an absolute nullity; and perhaps each case must depend, in some measure, on its own circumstances: but as the issuing of the execution, if done by a party entitled to collect the money upon it, is rather a defect in the formal mode of proceeding, that is to say, a use of the name of a deceased plaintiff, instead of substituting executors or administrators, and issuing a *scire facias*, than a substantial defect, it seems to me on the authorities, that it must in such case be considered as an erroneous proceeding, not an irregular and void one. If, however, the plaintiff had no right to issue the execution, if being a mere stranger, he interposed and set the constable on to do execution, against one no longer liable, it would be otherwise: 3 Wils. 376.[1] But even then, it would be necessary for the party grieved to have the execution first set aside or vacated by a direct proceeding; and then he might have restitution of the money, or recover his damages in trespass, but he can not question it collaterally, while the judgment and execution are in full force. In the case before us, so far as appears, nothing of that kind was done. The writ remained in full force and virtue, at the time this action was brought, and the plaintiff acquiesced in it; and, therefore, whether it was duly issued by the defendant as surety or not, whether it was merely erroneous or absolutely void, in the legal sense of those terms, it was a justification for him in this action, as well as for the officer, or other person assisting in the execution of it.

In the case of *Priggs* v. *Adams*, Carth. 274; S. C., Salk. 674, in an action of false imprisonment, the defendant pleaded a judgment in the town court, in Bristol, obtained against Prigg, and that he was arrested and imprisoned by virtue of an execution thereon, etc. The plaintiff replied, and set forth a private act of parliament lately made, by which a court of conscience was erected in that city to have the sole conusance in the several actions therein expressed, concerning all matters under forty shillings, to be brought against any poor inhabitant of that city, and that all judgments elsewhere for such matters should be merely void, and that he was a poor inhabitant, etc.; after argu-

---

1. *Barker* v. *Braham.*

ment it was resolved by the court, that this judgment was not
absolutely void, and the officers (who served the execution) trespassers; and that the regular way to take the benefit of the act
was, for the defendant below to have pleaded this matter, and
so to have entitled himself to such benefit; that since the judgment was not absolutely void, and though Prigg had neglected
to plead the statute to the jurisdiction of the court below, yet
he was not without remedy, for he might come in upon the return of the ca. sa. in custody below, and then plead the statute,
with the necessary averments in discharge of the execution. As
upon the statute of additions (1 Hen. V., c. 5), which hath the same
words, viz., that the outlawry shall be void if there is no addition,
yet in that case it has been always held, that the person so outlawed must either reverse it, or plead it, ut supra; and Turner's
case, 2 Sid. 125; Raym. 73, 74, was cited and allowed for law.
For an irregular judgment is no judgment, and that was vacated
before the action brought, so that the plaintiff might have replied nul tiel record to the defendant's pleading the judgment;
and judgment was given for the defendant quod quer. nil capiat,
etc.   The same principles will be found recognized in the cases
reported: 1 Lev. 95;[1] 12 Mod. 178;[2] 3 Wils. 142,[3] 376;[4] T. Raym.
73;[5] 1 Stra. 509;[6] T. Jones, 215;[7] B. N. P. 83; Allison v. Rheam,
3 Serg. & R. 142 [8 Am. Dec. 644]; Berry v. Hamill, 12 Id. 210.
In the two latter cases, it is to be observed that the issuing of a
ca. sa. without calling on the defendant to show whether he
had property, was expressly prohibited by act of assembly; and
in Allison v. Rheam the writ had been previously set aside by
the court from which it issued, and I infer, from the opinion of
Judge Duncan, that it was the same in Berry v. Hamill.

Judgment reversed, and a venire facias de novo awarded.

Cited in Lloyd v. Barr, 11 Pa. St. 48, to the point that a surety paying the
judgment obtained against himself and his principal, is entitled as against
the latter to the benefit of the judgment.

EXECUTION ISSUED AFTER THE DEATH OF DEFENDANT was held in Collings-
worth v. Horn, 24 Am. Dec. 753, to be merely voidable, not void. On this
subject see Freeman on Executions, sec. 35.

1. Turner v. Folgate.   2. Britton v. Cole.   3. Parsons v. Loyd, 3 Wils. 342.
4. Barker v. Braham.   5. Turner v. Folgate.   6. Phillips v. Biron.   7. Ollet v. Bessey.
AM. DEC. VOL. XXXIV—33

MEECH v. ROBINSON.

[4 Wharton, 360.]

General Average—Stranding of a Vessel whose loss is at all events inevitable in order to save the endangered lives of the crew, will not constitute a case of general average, requiring the cargo saved to contribute, though the stranding tended to and resulted in the saving of a larger proportion of the cargo than would otherwise have been saved.

Assumpsit. On the seventeenth of September, 1838, the brig Tallahassee, then off Tampico bar, was struck by a violent gale, which drifted her, notwithstanding all efforts, towards the shore. The loss of the vessel at last came to be recognized as inevitable. In this situation the master, as stated in his deposition, "found it necessary for the preservation of the lives of the crew (as the loss of the vessel was now beyond doubt, being in four fathoms of water and the land within a mile of the brig) to run the vessel ashore." The vessel was accordingly run ashore. The wreck of the vessel and the cargo saved were subsequently sold and the proceeds paid over to defendant, a part owner of the cargo. This action was to recover plaintiffs' ratable proportion of these proceeds as owners of the brig. By the verdict of the jury it was found that if on the facts stated in their special verdict the case was one of general average, plaintiffs were entitled to seven hundred and twenty dollars; if not, then to one hundred and eighty-six dollars and thirty-one cents. The facts stated in the special verdict besides those set out above, appear from the opinion.

H. M. Phillips, for the plaintiffs.

McCall, contra.

By Court, Kennedy, J. The case before us does not seem to come within the principle of any of the cases cited by the counsel for the plaintiffs. *Sims v. Gurney*, 4 Binn. 513, has been relied on. It would be sufficient, however, to say that that case was not one where the ship was wrecked, or any apprehension entertained that she was in danger of being so, but a case merely where she, as it was firmly believed, about to be unavoidably driven on shore, without the least risk of being wrecked by it, was, for the purpose of conducting her to a place where the crew and cargo alone, not the vessel, might be saved with greater certainty, voluntarily stripped of her masts, together with the sails and rigging appertaining thereto. It may also be observed, that the correctness of the decision in

this case has been questioned; and the authority of it, though
no ways applicable to the present case, shaken at least, if not
overruled, by *Walker* v. *United States Ins. Co.*, 11 Serg. & R. 60
[14 Am. Dec. 610]. The sacrifice of the masts, sails, and
rigging of the vessel, being voluntary, and determined on with a
view to save the cargo, as well as the lives of the crew, may
perhaps have been the subject of general contribution, but beyond this, the principle of the case may well be doubted. *Gray*
v. *Waln*, 2 Id. 229 [7 Am. Dec. 642], has also been cited by the
counsel for the plaintiff. The only matter, however, settled in
it was, that a voluntary stranding of a ship for the purpose of
preserving the ship and cargo, the greater part of the cargo
being thereby saved, but the vessel wholly lost, entitled the
owners thereof to general average for this loss. The case of *Case*
v. *Reilly*, 3 Wash. C. C. 298, which is to the same effect, and was
decided before *Gray* v. *Waln*, was also adduced in support of the
plaintiffs' claim. But the stranding of the vessel in each of
these two last cases, being considered as clearly voluntary, presents at once an obvious difference beween them and the present.
In the former, for aught that appears, the vessel might have
been kept out at sea, and have weathered the storm, so that the
act of running them ashore was purely one of free agency on
the part of the masters, the agents of the owners thereof, and
done for the common benefit of all concerned; thus bringing
these cases within the reason of the rule, which lies at the
foundation of every case of general average.

The principle of general contribution, in this respect, is derived from the ancient law of Rhodes, relative to jettison, which
it is said, was formed and promulgated nine hundred years before the Christian era, and afterwards adopted by Justinian into
his digest, with an express recognition of its true origin: "*Lege
Rhodia cavetur, ut, si levanda navis gratia jactus mercium factus
sit, omnium contributione sarciatur, quod pro omnibus datum
est:*" Dig., lib. 14, tit. 2, 1. Besides, where the property of one
of the parties concerned in the adventure, is deliberately sacrificed for the benefit of the others, so that thereby his loss is
made directly to promote their gain, he becomes entitled to
claim restitution, according to the equitable maxim of the civil
law, *Nemo debet locupletari aliena jactura*. And doubtless it is a
general rule, constituting a part of the law of every commercial
country, which has been acknowledged and acted upon from
time immemorial, that if a part of the ship or cargo is voluntarily sacrificed to save the remainder from some impending dan-

ger, the owners of what is saved must contribute for the loss: 1 Ph. Ins. 334. To this rule, however, there are some exceptions, as where goods, for instance, on deck, are thrown over, it is held in general, that no contribution can be claimed: Id. 332. But it is clear that the case in hand does not fall within either the terms or the reason of the rule. The running of the vessel ashore here, can with no propriety be said to have been voluntary. Nor can it indeed, be well said, that the loss of the vessel was occasioned thereby. For according to the evidence of the master, which is all that we have, and all that the plaintiffs rely on to establish their claim, the vessel being on a lee shore, where she could not carry sail, they found it necessary for the preservation of the lives of the crew, as the loss of the vessel was then certain beyond a doubt, being in four fathoms water, and the land within a mile of her, to run her ashore; and accordingly they slipped the best bower chain, put the vessel before the wind, and in a short time struck the land. In his cross-examination he further states, that her situation was most desperate; that she would have gone to the shore at all events; but the mode in which the witness ran her on shore saved the lives of the crew, and tended to save a greater proportion of the cargo. From this it is perfectly manifest, that the loss of the vessel had become inevitable, as the consequence of the peril then present; and in such case says Mr. Phillips, in his treatise on insurance, vol. 1, 339, when the acts of the crew are intended to alleviate, instead of avoiding such consequence, it seems hardly to be voluntarily incurring a loss.

But Mr. Benecke, in his work on insurance, c. 5, p. 219, in which, says Chief Justice Abbot, in his publication on shipping, 343, there is much learning combined with practical experience, meets the present case in so many words, and declares, that "if the situation of the vessel were such as to admit of no alternative, so that without running her ashore, she would have been unavoidably lost, and that measure were resorted to for the purpose of saving the lives or liberty of the crew, no contribution can take place, because nothing in fact was sacrificed." So here the plaintiffs sacrificed nothing; their vessel was doomed to inevitable destruction by the peril of the sea which surrounded her. It was, in reality, the case of a wreck, where as Emerigon, tom. 1, p. 612, says, " the owner of the ship wrecked, and the owner of the merchandise lost in the shipwreck, have no right of contribution from those who have the good fortune to save their effects; because the losses that the one or the other has sustained, has not procured the common safety. The rule of the civil law is the same. *Amissa navis damnum, callationis consortio non sortitur per eos qui merces suas naufragio liberaverunt ; nam hujus equitatem tunc admitti placuit, cum jactus remedio, cœteris in communi periculo, salva navi, consultum est :* Lib. 5, de Leg. Rhod. It is the same as the case of fire. He who saves his own, saves for himself alone. *Cum depressa navis aut dejecta est, quod quisque ex ea suum servassat, sibi servare respondit, tanquam ex incendio :* L. 7, ff. cod." So Cleirac, page 51, note 9, says: " After shipwreck, there is no contribution between the merchandise recovered and fished up, and those lost; but save who can." So Casaregis says, Disc. 121, note 17: " He who saves, saves; he who loses, loses:" See Mr. Justice Story, note 1 to Abbot on Shipping, 349. The loss of the ship in question, appearing then to be inevitable, must therefore be borne by the plaintiffs, who were owners of her. This, says Mr. Stevens, the Digest and all authors are agreed on; for you can not in equity convert a loss, which is inevitable, into a claim, for the preservation of property: Stevens & Benecke, by Phillips, on Average, 84.

The judgment, therefore, according to the agreement of the parties, must be for the less sum in favor of the plaintiffs, that is, one hundred and eighty-six dollars and thirty-one cents.

Judgment accordingly.

————

The doctrine of the principal case seems opposed to that which has been adopted by the national tribunals: *Barnard* v. *Adams*, 10 How. 271, and cases cited in the note to *Gray* v. *Waln*, 7 Am. Dec. 651.

————

VAN AMRINGE v. MORTON.

[4 WHARTON, 382.]

DELIVERY IS ESSENTIAL to the validity of a deed.

BONA FIDE PURCHASER CLAIMING UNDER A DEED NEVER DELIVERED, but which was surreptitiously and fraudulently obtained from the possession of the grantor, while no name of a grantee had yet been inserted, such insertion being subsequently made, acquires no title.

UNAUTHORIZED DELIVERY OF A DEED may be ratified by the grantor, as by an acceptance of the consideration money from the grantee.

POSSESSION WILL PUT A SUBSEQUENT PURCHASER UPON INQUIRY as to the title of him in possession.

EJECTMENT. Plaintiff's paper title consisted in part of a deed from defendant to Thomas Glenn. Defendant denied the delivery of the deed to Glenn. Prior to the execution thereof defendant had entered into an arrangement for the sale of this property with Daniel T. Glenn. During the treaty of sale defendant executed and acknowledged a deed for the property, wherein the name of the grantee was left in blank. After the execution of the deed, Daniel T. Glenn undertaking to pay the consideration, defendant left the key of the desk in which the deed lay, with his brother, Isaac Morton, then in the company of Daniel Glenn, and left to get William Patrick to come and fill in the blank with Glenn's name. After defendant's departure Daniel Glenn induced Isaac Morton to get the deed from the desk and to fill in the blank left for the name of a grantee with the name of Thomas Glenn, his father. As an inducement to Isaac Morton to do this, he represented to him that he would obtain the remaining consideration of the purchase, two notes upon which the defendant was indorser, and return with them, or else, failing in this, that he would return the deed. Daniel Glenn neither returned with the deed nor with the notes. The other facts of the case appear from the opinion. Defendant had verdict and judgment below.

Hirst, for the plaintiff in error.

Holcomb and Meredith, contra.

By Court, ROGERS, J.   It is one of the essential requisites of a good deed, that it be delivered by the party himself, or his certain attorney. A deed takes effect from this tradition or delivery; and if it wants delivery, it is void *ab initio:* 2 Bl. Com. 308; 1 Shep. Touch. 57. The evidence tended to show, that the deed of Morton to Glenn, under which the plaintiff claimed title, was never delivered either by Morton or his authorized attorney. "Delivery is either actual, *i. e.,* by doing something and saying nothing; or, also verbal, *i. e.,* by saying something and doing nothing; or it may be by both: and either of them may make a good delivery, and a perfect deed. But by one or both these means, it must be made; for otherwise, albeit it be never so well sealed and written, yet is the deed of no force. And though the party to whom it is made, take it to himself, or happen to get it into his hands, yet it will do him no good, nor him that made it, any hurt, until it be delivered. And as proof of the delivery is a matter *in pais,* so parol evidence is properly admissible to show that the deed is wanting in that essential requisite:" 1 Shep. Touch. 57.

The court in that part of the charge which has been made the subject of exception, ruled that if the deed was never delivered, no title passed to the plaintiff, although he may have been a purchaser for a valuable consideration, without notice. The facts given in evidence, proved that the deed was never delivered, either by Morton or his attorney; that the possession of it was surreptitiously and fraudulently obtained by Glenn; if so, according to the authorities above cited, the deed was void *ab initio;* of no force and effect whatever. But this is on the supposition that the grantor has done no act ratifying the delivery; for a deed may be delivered by the party himself or by his appointment or authority precedent, or assent or agreement, subsequent; for *omnis ratihabitio mandato equiparatur.* If, therefore, the plaintiff could have proved that the grantor, as he suggests, had received the purchase money for the property, it would have amounted to an assent to the delivery of the deed to Glenn. But this was a matter for the jury; and does not enter into the exception to the charge as presented by the record. Unless there was a subsequent recognition of the delivery, or there was something done by the grantor, which enabled the grantee to deceive the purchaser, no title passed any more than in the case of a deed that was forged. But the jury have negatived every allegation of that kind. They have found, that the grantor retained the possession of the property as before the pretended sale; which was of itself notice to the purchaser so as to put him on inquiry as to the title. A *bona fide* purchaser, for a valuable consideration from a fraudulent grantor, is protected by the statute of frauds. But that is, because such fraudulent conveyances are not absolutely void, but are voidable only, at the instance of the party aggrieved. The legal title passes to the purchaser; for although void as to creditors, it is good as to the grantor: it therefore comes within a well-known principle, that where the equities are equal, the legal title shall prevail. A *bona fide* purchaser is as much a favorite of the law as creditors, and perhaps, ought to be more so; as he looks to the property itself specifically, whereas creditors look to the general funds.

On this principle, the court ruled *Price* v. *Junkin,* 4 Watts, 85 [28 Am. Dec. 685.] That was the case of the sale of land by an executor, in pursuance of a power contained in a will. It was held, that the title, though fraudulent and void as against the purchaser from the trustee, because of his having been a party to the fraud, yet, as respects a subsequent and innocent purchaser from him, the title was good. As between the original parties, the conveyance is good, although subject to be defeated, in the one case by the children, and in the other by the creditors; but inasmuch as the legal title passed, it, together with an equal equity, gave preference to the subsequent and innocent purchaser. In *Price* v. *Junkin*, Justice Sergeant says: "If a loss is to happen by the exercise of that power, it should be by those representing the testator, who created it, and thereby enabled the executor to transfer the legal estate; not by the person who trusted to a title derived under that power, and on its face, fair and legal." But this principle can not apply, when the deed was not delivered, and when the party is in no default.

We do not perceive the force of the objection to the evidence of the conversation between Giles Love and Daniel T. Glenn. The witness, at the time he saw the deed from Morton to Glenn, told Glenn he had no authority to take the house for the debt, and suggested that he should put in the name of Thomas Glenn, which was afterwards done. The evidence was pertinent, as it tended to show, that at the time witness saw the deed, it was unexecuted. Nor is it any objection, that this was a conversation between Daniel T. Glenn and the witness, because, as appeared from the testimony, the whole matter resulted from a contrivance of Glenn for his especial benefit, and took place before he surreptitiously obtained the possession of the deed, upon a false suggestion from Isaac Morton. Upon the same principle, that it is a part of the *res gestæ*, the declarations of William Morton to Isaac Morton were properly admitted in evidence.

Judgment affirmed.

————

Cited to the effect, that though a *bona fide* purchaser under a voidable deed will be protected; yet if the title which he claims originated in a void deed, his good faith will avail nothing: *Blight* v. *Schenck*, 10 Pa. St. 295; *Arrison* v. *Harmstead*, 2 Id. 197.

DELIVERY OF A DEED IS ESSENTIAL to its validity: *Church* v. *Gilman*, 30 Am. Dec. 82, and cases cited in note. The subsequent cases in this series relating to delivery are *Foley* v. *Cowgill*, 32 Id. 49, holding that a delivery can not be made to an obligee, to operate as an escrow; that if such an attempt is made, the condition is void and the delivery absolute; and *Gilmore* v. *Whitesides*, 31 Id. 563, holding that there can be no delivery of a deed subsequent to the death of the grantor.

WATKINSON v. BANK OF PENNSYLVANIA.

[4 WHARTON, 482.]

NOTICE OF DISSOLUTION OF PARTNERSHIP IS SUFFICIENT as to strangers, if the notice is published in a newspaper printed in the place where the partnership business is carried on; but it is requisite to show that actual notice was conveyed to customers of the firm.

CUSTOMER TAKING A NEWSPAPER IN WHICH NOTICE of the dissolution is printed is not affected with knowledge of such notice.

COURT CAN NOT DETERMINE WHO IS A CUSTOMER, and can not reject proof of notice published in a newspaper because the party sought to be affected is a customer; the determination of that question is within the province of the jury.

ASSUMPSIT. The action was upon a promissory note indorsed by defendants to plaintiff. This indorsement was made subsequently to the dissolution of the partnership existing between the defendants. The question was, whether or not the plaintiff had received proper notice of the dissolution. Plaintiff's evidence tended to show that prior to the dissolution of the partnership the plaintiff's bank was the one employed by defendants in the transaction of their firm business. Defendant, Richard Watkinson, to affect plaintiff with notice of the dissolution of the firm, offered to show that notice thereof had been duly published in a newspaper printed in Philadelphia, the place of business of the firm, and that this newspaper was taken by plaintiff. The evidence was excluded, on objection. Plaintiff recovered judgment.

H. M. Phillips, for the plaintiffs in error.

Chester, contra.

By Court, SERGEANT, J. The question presents itself in this case, what is sufficient notice of the dissolution of a partnership, so as to discharge a partner from debts subsequently contracted in the name of the firm, without his participation or assent? The rule seems to be, that notice of the dissolution of the partnership given in a newspaper printed in the city or county where the partnership business is carried on, is of itself notice to all persons who have had no previous dealing with the partnership. But as to persons who have had such previous dealing with the partnership, it is not sufficient. It must be shown that actual notice of the dissolution was communicated to the party in some way or other: 2 Johns. 300;[1] 7 Serg. & R. 504;[2] 3 Day, 353;[3] 6 Johns. 147;[4] 6 Cow. 16;[5] 17 Wend. 526.[6]

1. *Lansing* v. *Gaine*, 3 Am. Dec. 422.   2. *Shaffer* v. *Snyder*.
3. *Mowatt* v. *Howland*.   4. *Ketcham* v. *Clark*, 5 Am. Dec. 197.
5. *Graves* v. *Merry*, 6 Cow. 701; S. C. 16 Am Dec. 471.   6. *Vernon* v. *Manhattan Co*.

A notice in a newspaper is at the best but an uncertain method of communicating the knowledge of a fact, since the party to be affected may never see the paper, or if he does, may not read all the advertisements; but still it is sometimes the only practical mode, and is therefore either allowed by the principles of the common law, or directed by act of assembly in particular instances. But where a firm has had previous dealings with others, it can know such persons, and may send them specific notice, which is the best and most certain mode. This, I presume, is the reason of the distinction. No particular mode, however, is prescribed by law for communicating notice, even to persons having previous dealings; it is sufficient if in any way actual knowledge is traced home to the party. Merely taking a newspaper in which such advertisement is contained, is not sufficient. It is very possible, perhaps nothing is more common, than for persons to take newspapers, without reading all the advertisements they contain, even if they peruse their other contents. Our newspapers are not of any accredited character, universally recognized as the authentic depository of occurrences, in commercial or other affairs; they are a medley of news, politics, literature, trade, notices, and various other matters, which some peruse for one purpose and some for another; and it would be going a great way, to say that every one who takes a newspaper, should be visited with the knowledge of the contents of all the notices contained in it from day to day. The case of *Vernon* v. *The Manhattan Co.*, 17 Wend. 526, was very like the present. The notice was published in two of the newspapers printed in the city of New York, one of which was regularly delivered at the banking house of the plaintiffs, yet it was held not to be sufficient evidence of the dissolution of the firm to which the defendant had belonged, and with which the plaintiffs had had previous dealing. The court say that if actual notice reached them in any form, it would be sufficient, but the mere taking of a newspaper filled with notices, will not make a case for the jury.

But though this is the rule of law, and on the evidence in this cause, if heard as offered, it would have been the duty of the jury to render a verdict for the plaintiffs, yet we are of opinion that the evidence offered by the defendants ought to have been admitted, and that it was not for the court to decide that there had been previous dealing, and on that ground reject the evidence. This was matter of fact for the jury. The evidence ought to have been received and left to the jury, under the instruction that if the evidence established a previous dealing, then in point of law there should have been actual notice, and merely taking in the paper at the bank was not proof of such actual notice, without anything further. *Non constat*, but the defendant might have controverted the fact of previous dealing, or given evidence in relation to it, or if he did not, yet it was the province of the jury to determine that fact, as well as all others. For this reason the judgment must be reversed.

Judgment reversed, and a *venire facias de novo* awarded.

———

Cited to show what notice of dissolution of partnership is required: *Brown* v. *Clark*, 14 Pa. St. 476.

NOTICE OF DISSOLUTION OF PARTNERSHIP.—The same rule as that laid down in the principal case is announced in *Nott* v. *Downing*, 26 Am. Dec. 491. See also note to *Prentiss* v. *Sinclair*, Id. 290.

———

PEARCE *v.* AUSTIN.

[4 WHARTON, 489.]

WANT OF PROTEST WILL NOT WARRANT THE INFERENCE in favor of the maker of a negotiable promissory note, that the transfer of the note from the payee was after it fell due.

AGENT MAY SUE IN HIS OWN NAME upon negotiable paper indorsed in blank.

ASSUMPSIT. The suit was against the maker of a promissory note payable to the order of John Houghtin. Defendant below, plaintiff in error, contended that from the want of protest of the note, it must be inferred that it was acquired by the present holder after maturity, and that defendant should therefore be admitted to any defense that he might have against Houghtin; and thereupon pleaded part payment. The other facts relied upon by defendant in his affidavit of defense appear in the opinion. Judgment was rendered for plaintiff for the failure of the affidavit to disclose a sufficient defense.

Hopkins, for the plaintiff in error.

C. Ingersoll, contra.

By Court, ROGERS, J. A protest, not being necessary in a suit against the drawer, no legal inference can be drawn from an omission to do what the law does not require. There is nothing, therefore, in the first objection. The suit was brought to recover the amount due on a promissory note, drawn by John Pearce, the defendant, payable sixty days after date, to the order of John Houghtin. It was indorsed in blank to Charles B. Austin, agent of the Union glass works, transferred by him to T. W. Dyott, and the suit is brought in the name of Charles B. Austin, agent of the Union glass works, who is holder of the bill. The question is, can an agent bring a suit on a promissory note in his own name? This is a question which depends altogether on authority. A holder of negotiable paper can maintain an action on it in his own name, without showing title to it. The court will not inquire into his right to the paper, or his right to maintain a suit upon it, unless circumstances appear, showing his possession to be *mala fide: Dean* v. *Hewett,* 5 Wend. 257; *Talman* v. *Gibson,* 1 Hall, 308; *Livingston* v. *Gibson,*[1] 3 Johns. Cas. 263.

In *Ogilby* v. *Wallace,* 2 Hall, 553, the right to sue even by a fictitious person, when the name of the real party was disclosed, unless some question arose as to the *mala fide* possession, was asserted. The court nonsuited the plaintiff, on the ground that he was a fictitious person, but on an appeal the nonsuit was set aside, that the question of fact, connected with the possession and presentation of the note, should be submitted to a jury. This principle applies to a note payable to bearer, or indorsed in blank; for in either case an action can be maintained in the name of any person, without the plaintiff being required to show that he has any interest in it, unless he came into the possession of the note under suspicious circumstances. Here there is no allegation of *mala fides,* so that the case stands clear of that objection. The suit is brought by Austin, who is a trustee or agent for the company. He has the legal title to the bill, and the suit is brought in the name of the legal owner. Stating that he is the agent of the Union glass works, is equivalent to saying that the suit is for their use. This brings it within the principle of the cases cited. But *Mauran* v. *Lamb,* 7 Cow. 174, is still nearer the point. It is there held, that one holding a check or note payable to bearer as a mere agent, may sue on it in his own name, and that it does not lie with the opposite party to assert the plaintiff's want of interest. It can certainly make no difference whether the note is payable to bearer, or indorsed in blank, and in the possession of a *bona fide* holder.

Judgment affirmed.

AGENT MAY SUE IN HIS OWN NAME, WHEN: *Clap* v. *Day,* 11 Am. Dec. 99, and note 100.

---

1. *Livingston* v. *Clinton,* cited in *Conroy* v. *Warren,* 3 Johns. Cas. 262.

KNOWLES v. LORD.

[4 WHARTON, 500.]

SHERIFF'S RETURN IS CONCLUSIVE as to the facts therein set forth, upon
the parties, as far as the particular action is concerned. Thus, if the return state that property replevied was surrendered to the defendant
upon his giving bond, the latter may not show that less property was
replevied from him than appeared from the return.

GIVING BOND CONDITIONED TO RETURN PROPERTY REPLEVIED will preclude defendant from asserting that less property was replevied than is
described in the bond.

FRAUDULENT PURCHASER ACQUIRES NO TITLE to the goods as against the
party defrauded.

FRAUDULENT PURCHASER, ASSIGNING for the benefit of his creditors, passes
no title to his assignees to the goods obtained by fraud, though the
assignment require releases from certain of the creditors, which are given
by them.

REPLEVIN. The plaintiffs below, defendants in error, sought
to recover six cases of prints. These prints had been sold by
plaintiffs to Knowles, Schroeder, and McCalla, but the declaration alleged that the latter did not intend to pay at the time
that they bought. Shortly after their purchase, they assigned
in trust for their creditors. The assignment specified certain
preferred creditors, and directed that the residue of the fund
secured be divided ratably amongst such other creditors as
should within a designated time execute releases. In this action
the property was duly replevied, but was subsequently surrendered to defendants upon their executing the proper bond.
Defendants attempted to show on the trial, both by the sheriff
and by other evidence, that the property actually replevied was
not as much as that described in the return. No evidence however was allowed on this point. Certain releases, executed by
creditors as required by the deed of assignment, were shown.
The jury was instructed that the assignees were in no better
position with regard to the title to this property than were their
assignors. This instruction and the rejection of the evidence
previously mentioned were the grounds relied upon by plaintiffs
in error.

McCall and *J. R. Ingersoll*, for the plaintiffs in error.

Randall and *Scott*, contra.

By Court, SERGEANT, J. It is contended that the court below
erred in rejecting the evidence offered by the defendants, to

show that the number of pieces of goods actually replevied was
less than that mentioned in the writ of replevin, and also to
show the sale of divers pieces of goods mentioned in the writ of
replevin, before the issuing of the writ. We are of opinion,
however, that this evidence was properly rejected. It went to
contradict the sheriff's return to the writ of replevin. The writ
was for four cases of prints, containing each fifty pieces; one
case of prints containing forty-three pieces; one case of furniture
prints, containing sixty-five pieces; value eighteen hundred dollars, or thereabouts. The sheriff's return was " replevied, summoned, and afterwards claim property bond given." It is a well-
settled principle, applicable to every case, that credence is to be
given to the sheriff's return; so much so, that there can be no
averment against it in the same action: Dalt. 189–191; Rolle's
Abr., Return, O. Wats. Sheriff, 72. A party may make an averment consistent with the sheriff's return, or explanatory of its
legal bearing and effect, where the return is at large: 7 Hen.
VIII., pl. 14; 5 Ed. III., pl. 1; 19 Vin. 198; *Dolan v. Briggs*, 4
Binn. 496, but he can not aver a matter directly at variance
with the facts stated in return, and contradictory to it, and
showing it to be false. If a party be injured by the false
return of the sheriff, his remedy is by action on the case against
the sheriff who makes it. Thus if the sheriff returns, that the
goods are eloigned, the plaintiff may have a withernam, and
the defendant can not plead, either that he did not eloign, or
that the beasts were dead in the pound, for that is contrary to
the elongata returned by the sheriff, and not to be denied: Gilb.
Replev. 98; 1 Dall. 439.[1] The evidence offered, went not only
to contradict the sheriff's return, but also the act of the defendants, in conformity with it, of claiming the property in the
goods mentioned in the writ of replevin, and giving bond to
deliver up these goods, if the property in them should be adjudged not to be in the defendants. This was an unequivocal
admission that they had the goods, and that the sheriff either had
replevied, or would replevy them, and deliver them over to the
plaintiffs, but for this claim and bond. The defendants can not
in one breath prevent the sheriff from replevying the goods
mentioned in the writ, by claiming them as theirs, and giving a
property bond, and in the next deny that they had the goods.
I do not say that in all cases, the mere pleas of *non cepit* and
property are inconsistent, and can not be pleaded together under the statute of Anne, giving leave to the defendant to file

---

1. *Phillips v. Hyde.*

several pleas, but it would be more consistent if the defendant
meant to contend that part of the goods mentioned in the writ,
were not in his possession to claim as his property and give bond
only for those that were, and to rely on his plea of *non cepit* as to
the rest.   For the latter, the sheriff might then return elongata,
with which the plea of *non cepit* is consistent: 1 Ld. Raym. 613;
S. C., Salk. 581.[1]   But the claim of property is not; for by it
the taking is admitted: 1 Ld. Raym. 615.   And this must needs
be so, for if the plaintiff recovers damages, the goods claimed
become the property of the defendant, and such recovery is a
bar to trespass, or any other action to recover the value of
the same goods, afterwards brought by the plaintiff: Id. 614.
The action of replevin in Pennsylvania, is well known to be different from that in England.   There it is used in cases of distress (though some authorities say it lies for all goods and
chattels unlawfully taken), and the goods are actually taken by
the defendant from the plaintiff, and are always delivered up
to the plaintiff, by the sheriff, on executing the replevin, the
plaintiff giving bond to restore if he fails in the action.   The
defendant can not retain them by giving bond on a claim of
property.   Where the defendant means to deny having the goods
at all, the plea of *non cepit* is then strictly appropriate.   But in
Pennsylvania replevin lies, under our ancient act of assembly,
wherever one man claims chattels in the possession of another,
whether the defendant took them from the plaintiff or not; and
of that kind was the present replevin.   In such case the plea of
non cepit can only mean that the defendant had them not in his
possession; the mere taking or not being immaterial.   If he had
them not in his possession, the sheriff could not replevy them
so as to deliver them to the plaintiff, and the defendant has nothing to do but to rely on the plea of *non cepit*.   But if he has the
goods, and the sheriff can take them, the defendant must either
surrender them, or if he chooses he may claim property, and retain them in his custody, giving bond to the sheriff for delivering them up, in case the property shall not be found in him: 1
Dall. 156.[2]   The making such claim and giving bond, is a distinct admission that he has all the goods contained in the writ,
and mentioned in his claim and bond, and the return of the
sheriff; and these acts preclude the defendant from giving evidence to the contrary.

Nor is the second error sustained, for we think it clear that
there is nothing in the case which places the assignees in a bet-

---

1. *Moor* v. *Watts.*   2. *Weaver* v. *Lawrence.*

ter situation in respect to these goods, than their assignors. The doctrine relating to bills of exchange and promissory notes or other negotiable instruments transferred in the course of business for a valuable consideration and without notice, does not apply to this case; because the goods obtained by the assignors from the plaintiffs, and alleged to have been afterwards transferred by the assignment among various other effects of the assignors, were not negotiable instruments. They stand on the common footing of goods transferred by one having no title, in which case ordinarily no title passes to the grantee. Even the doctrine of the sale of chattels in market overt, which in England sometimes sanctions a transfer by one having no title, has no existence in Pennsylvania, and if it had, would not apply to this case. The assignors are ascertained to have had no title to these five cases of prints; the pretended purchase they made was a fraud, and the goods, so far as respected them, still belonged to the plaintiffs. There may possibly be cases, in which a party may transfer a good title, although he has none himself, in consequence of the fraud existing in the procurement of them. Judge Washington, in *Copland* v. *Bousquet*, 4 Wash. C. C. 594, went to the full extent of the law, when he says, that if the possession be delivered by the real owner, together with the usual *indicia* of property, or under circumstances which may enable the vendor to impose himself upon the world as the real owner, this might be a case of constructive fraud, which would postpone even at law the right of the real owner in favor of a fair purchaser without notice, and for a valuable consideration. But no such case exists here. The defendants are not purchasers either in their own right, or as representing creditors, who may release their debts on the strength of the assignment; so that it is unnecessary to examine the much-litigated question, on which the courts in New York and Connecticut are at variance, whether an antecedent debt be equally operative as a consideration, with the payment of money. Neither the assignees nor creditors in any sense of the word purchased these goods. They never applied to buy, or made any contract of sale, or, so far as appears, ever saw them before the assignment. They were assigned in common with all the estate of the assignors, real, personal, and mixed, whatsoever; the assignors alone prescribing the terms of the assignment, the methods of appropriation, the subsequent sale of the property by the assignees to raise the funds, and the persons who were to participate in them, as well as the order and conditions according to which

they were to be distributed; and the assignees agreed to take
the estate as the assignors offered it, without any previous dealing, bargain, contract, or even knowledge, for aught that appears. It would be a solecism to call such a transaction a sale,
or such a grantee a purchaser, or to apply these terms to the
creditors, who accept the conditions and release their claims
upon the grantor. In addition to which, all the creditors are
not required even to release; large preferences were given which
might exhaust the whole fund, and as to them the case would
be of a simple voluntary conveyance by an insolvent debtor of
property to the use of his existing creditors. Such a conveyance can not be called a sale, or such creditor a purchaser. To
do so would confound the most important legal distinctions,
and introduce a novelty fraught with the most mischievous consequences. It would tempt an insolvent debtor to defraud his
neighbors by fraudulent purchases of goods, in order that he
might pass them over for the use of favored creditors, if by his
assignment he could purge the fraud and place such creditors
in the highly favored situation of *bona fide* purchasers for a valuable consideration. A real purchaser, giving value for property
in the course of business innocently, and acting on the faith of possession and other apparent marks of ownership, is favored for
the support of trade and encouragement of fair dealing, and
may sometimes obtain a better title than his vendor. But a
voluntary assignment by a debtor has never been considered as
placing the assignee in any other situation in point of equity
than the assignor himself was; he takes the estate subject to all
outstanding equities, liens, incumbrances, and dealings between the assignor and others; and such has been the uniform construction put on assignments of this description.

Haggerty v. *Palmer*, 6 Johns. Ch. 437, is not a case unlike the
present. Goods were sold at auction in the city of New York,
to be paid for in approved indorsed notes, at four and six
months, and it is the usage in that city, where goods are so
sold, to deliver them to the buyer when called for, and for the
vendors afterwards to send for the notes. The vendee, after he
had received the goods, before he was called on for the notes,
according to the terms of sale, stopped payment, and assigned
over the goods with other property, in trust to pay certain
favored creditors; and it was held that the delivery of the goods
by the vendors, was conditional, and the vendee a trustee for
them until the notes were delivered; and that the assignment by
the vendee was voluntary and fraudulent, and did not defeat the

equitable lien of the vendors; there being no intervening purchaser for a valuable consideration without notice.

Judgment affirmed.

———

FRAUDULENT PURCHASER ACQUIRES NO TITLE as against the party defrauded: *Root* v. *French*, 28 Am. Dec. 482, and note.

SHERIFF'S RETURN IS CONCLUSIVE upon the parties to the suit: *Diller* v. *Roberts*, 15 Am. Dec. 578, and *Mentz* v. *Hamman*, *post*.

———

SMITH v. PLUMMER.

[5 WHARTON, 89.]

UNDISCLOSED PRINCIPAL is liable on the contracts of his agent, though the agency was not known to the other party at the time of the contract.

THIRD PARTY MAY CLAIM THE ENFORCEMENT OF AN AGREEMENT if the consideration moved from him. Thus, if A. delivers to B., upon the latter's sole credit, goods purchased by him for C., a subsequent agreement between A. and C. that C. shall allow the bill drawn on him by B., for the purchase price, to be protested, and shall hold himself liable to A., the bill being afterwards allowed to go to protest in pursuance of the agreement, may be recognized by B. as a contract of novation which exonerates him from liability to A., by substituting in his place C. as the latter's debtor.

ASSUMPSIT on a promissory note. The note was executed by Smith and Brown, defendants below, in favor of plaintiff Plummer. The note represented the price of certain merchandise sold by plaintiff to defendant, who purchased it for one Blake, a resident of Ohio. Some time after the purchase, Blake visited Philadelphia, and while there was informed by plaintiff that the merchandise had been purchased from him, and was requested to hold himself liable for its price to plaintiff, and to allow the bill drawn upon him by defendant, for its purchase price, to go to protest. Blake acceded to the proposal, and did subsequently allow the bill to be protested, and in his deposition used upon the trial recognized his liability to plaintiff. The jury was instructed in substance, that if at the time the goods were sold to defendants, plaintiff did not know that Blake was their principal, proof of the above state of facts would constitute a defense; but if at the time of the sale plaintiff did know of the agency, then that these facts would not afford a defense. Verdict went for plaintiff.

Scott, for the plaintiff in error.

Hanna and Clarkson, contra.

By Court, GIBSON, C. J. If the plaintiff below, apprised

that the shoes were ordered by the defendants for Blake, delivered them on their credit, he would be concluded by his election; and, without more, he could not turn round to any one else. But might he not subsequently release the defendants by accepting Blake as their substitute; as he might have done had he not known him to be the actual purchaser. It is conceded, as it must be, that ignorance of Blake's connection with the purchase, would have authorized a pursuit of him as the actual debtor, and a consequent abandonment of the credit given to the defendants; and there is no reason why the same result might not be effected with the assent of Blake, who is the only person that could object to a change of the original credit in any circumstances. At the plaintiff's instance and request, he promised to pay the debt, in consideration that the plaintiff would accept him as the debtor: and this consideration would undoubtedly sustain an action on the promise. If, then, Blake became liable, the defendants were released; for that was an implied condition of Blake's promise, which, as it did not benefit him, and would not else have prejudiced the plaintiff, would have been without consideration. What, then, is there to prevent the defendants from taking advantage of the condition? Nothing but an alleged want of privity. But their assent might perhaps be presumed on the principle of *Smith* v. *The Bank of Washington*, 5 Serg. & R. 318. There is another principle, however, which entitles them to the benefit of it. It was a part of the agreement—and one which has been executed—that Blake should suffer the plaintiff's bill drawn for funds to meet this very debt, to be protested; and would it be competent to the plaintiff afterwards to disaffirm the contract for the residue, even with Blake's consent? His agreement to accept Blake as the debtor, was in discharge of the defendants' liability; and though made to another, yet if a consideration for it moved from them, it may entitle them to the benefit of it on the principle of *Dutton* v. *Poole*, 1 Vent. 318, expanded by this court in *Hassinger* v. *Solms*, 5 Serg. & R. 8; and it can not be doubted that the injury sustained by the protest of their bill, was a consideration. In *Hassinger* v. *Solms*, a promise to indemnify the guarantor of a note who had renewed his guaranty contrary to the defendant's direction, was held to bind him, on the ground of *ratihabitio*, though made to a third person; because the defendant had benefited by a payment of a part in case of his original liability—a measure which had been exacted as a condition of the renewal.

Now to constitute a consideration, gain by the promisor, and loss by promisee, are equally efficacious; and it is indisputable, not only that the defendants have lost by the dishonor of their bill, but they stand in as much privity to the promisor, as the plaintiff did in *Hassinger* v. *Solms*. That the sacrifice of a party's resources for payment, is an injury which the law regards, was determined in *Harper* v. *Kean*, 11 Serg. & R. 280, in which a sacrifice of leather put into the creditor's hand to raise funds, was allowed to be made matter of defense; and what·is there to differ that case from this? Nothing but that the defendant's bill was not put under the plaintiff's control. But he assumed a control over it, and, it would seem, with their acquiescence; for though it was drawn six years ago, there was no evidence that they had taken any step to recover the amount of it from Blake, and they have released him by their defense here. In *Sanderson* v. *Lamberton*, 6 Binn. 129, where a carrier had, without the merchant's privity, delivered goods to a second carrier, who had in like manner delivered them to a third, it was held that the merchant had made himself a party to the last contract of bailment by suing on it, and that he had thereby released the liability of the preceding carriers. According to that case, the defendants in this had a right to become party to the subsequent arrangement; and they released Blake when they took defense on the basis of it. The plaintiff alone could not disaffirm it; and Blake swears that he still holds himself liable to the plaintiff under it. To allow the plaintiff to recover, therefore, would be a fraud on him as a third person; which is another ground to resist the enforcement of a contract. But neither could the plaintiff and Blake together get rid of it, having dishonored the defendants' bill. Such an interference, were there no remedy for it at law, would be a ground to enjoin the plaintiff in equity; but equitable relief is always accessible to a defendant in an action of assumpsit; and every principle of honor and justice calls on the plaintiff to execute the residue of the agreement.

Judgment reversed, and a *venire de novo* awarded.

———

AN UNDISCLOSED PRINCIPAL IS LIABLE for the acts of his agent: *Episcopal Church* v. *Wiley*, 30 Am. Dec. 386, and note 389.

ROMIG *v.* ERDMAN.

[5 WHARTON, 112.]

EXECUTOR, SURETY OF A LEGATEE, MAY RETAIN AGAINST AN ASSIGNEE OF THE LATTER, claiming under an assignment subsequent in date to the executor's becoming surety, the amounts that he has been obliged to pay because of his character of surety.

ERROR to Lehigh county. In 1797, Adam Romig died, leaving a will, in which provision was made for the support of his wife. By a subsequent family arrangement, the sum of two thousand dollars was set off in lieu thereof, to be put out by the executors at interest, the interest to be paid to the widow, and the principal to be divided at her death amongst the other legatees under the will. Daniel Romig, one of these legatees, in 1821, assigned to Jacob Erdman all his share in this fund. Prior to this assignment, in 1816, John Romig, one of the executors, became surety to Daniel Romig on a bond for sixty-six dollars and twenty cents. This bond he was, in 1823 and in 1824, obliged to discharge. Mrs. Romig died in 1838, and this suit was instituted by Erdman to recover from John Romig, the surviving executor, the amount to which he was entitled under the assignment. Romig claimed, whilst Erdman denied, the right to deduct from the amounts in his, Romig's, hands, the sum which he had been obliged to pay as Daniel Romig's surety. A case was stated setting forth the above facts. The court below decided against Romig's claim.

T. I. Wharton, for the plaintiff in error.

Brooke, contra.

By Court, SERGEANT, J. The principle determined in *Darroch's Executors* v. *Hay*,[1] and in *Potter* v. *Burd*, 4 Watts, 15, that an executor or administrator can not purchase in a claim against the estate he represents, and set it off in a suit against him for a claim upon his testator or intestate, is certainly a correct one; but the present case does not seem to be one in which it is applicable. The executor here has not purchased in any outstanding claim by a third person against the estate which he now attempts to set off against the legacy demanded. The ground he takes is, that while the money bequeathed was in his hands, *debitum in præsenti* to the legatee, though *solvendum in futuro*, he, at the instance of the legatee himself, became his surety in a bond to a third person, which bond he subsequently paid as such surety; the time of becoming surety being previous

---

1. 2 Yeates, 206.

to the assignment by the legatee to the plaintiff, though the payment was subsequent. And the question is, whether this is not such an equitable payment as enables him to defalk the amount from the legacy demanded; not, in the words of Chief Justice Gibson, in *Krause* v. *Beitel*, 3 Rawle, 204 [23 Am. Dec. 113], as a set-off, but as a defense that would be made available by a chancellor. And I am of opinion that it is. In *Krause* v. *Beitel*, exactly the same thing was done. One of the defendants had paid a debt for the insolvent before his discharge, and was sued for another debt which he afterwards was compelled to pay; and in a suit by the insolvent's assignees he was allowed to defalk them. In *Baughman* v. *Divler*, 3 Yeates, 9, a legatee purchased goods of the executors, and afterwards assigned his legacy; and they insisted on retaining the amount of the sale, against the assignee; and it was held that if credit was given him on that ground and was so understood, the amount of the goods would be an actual payment *pro tanto*. A surety is more favored in equity than a vendor. A surety is considered as having a right to all securities and means of payment in the power of his principal; and it would be presumed that the executor became surety on the faith of money in his hands, and is therefore entitled to retain it against the legatee himself, or one taking it by assignment from him; for such person takes it as an ordinary chose in action, not negotiable, and therefore liable to all equities existing at the time of the assignment.

I am therefore of opinion that the court below erred in holding that the defendant's claim as surety could not be admitted as evidence of a defense that might be available in the suit. But the plaintiff has objected here, that even if the defendant's payments are admissible as a defalcation, yet his claim is barred by the statute of limitations, because they were made more than six years before the institution of this suit. It is, however, answered, and I think satisfactorily, that the defendant claims by way of retainer, as executor of moneys in his own hands, which he might apply to the payment of himself at the time the transaction occurred, without being under the necessity of instituting a suit against the legatee for money paid and expended to his use as surety in the bond. This application he would not be compellable to make; but he certainly might elect to do it; and in the absence of evidence to the contrary, the defendant ought to be considered as having done so, if he insists on it, at the first opportunity presented of making his election.

Judgment reversed, and judgment for the defendant, on the case stated.

YARDLEY *v.* RAUB.

[5 WHARTON, 117.]

ARTICLES PURCHASED WITH THE CONSENT OF A WIFE by trustees of money settled to her separate use, become part of her separate property.

THE RIGHTS OF A HUSBAND'S CREDITORS will not extend over household goods and furniture, which have been purchased with the wife's consent in their own name by the trustees of money settled to her separate use, and placed by them in a tavern conducted by the husband, to be there used alike by the family and by the guests.

TROVER. In 1821, Sarah Woolston, in contemplation of marriage with George Atherton, settled her personal property upon Yardley and Raub, trustees, in trust, amongst other things, that after the marriage they should "pay the rents, issues, profits, and proceeds of the same to the said Sarah, to her sole and separate use during coverture." The marriage duly took place. In 1830, Atherton took the lease of a tavern in Northampton county. At that time, the wife's trustees purchased in their own names, with the wife's separate property, furniture, household goods, etc., for the tavern, and placed these articles therein. In 1835, this furniture was seized under execution issued against Atherton, and was afterwards sold under the execution. The present action was to recover the value of these goods from the sheriff who sold, and the attorney who directed the sale. The charge of the court below was to the effect that the furniture was liable to the husband's debts. Defendants had verdict.

Hepburn and Mallery, for the plaintiffs in error.

Brodhead and Brown, contra.

By Court, SERGEANT, J. It is far from being clear, that the trustees were guilty of any departure from the trust, in purchasing in their own name and with the trust moneys, at the instance of the wife, furniture to be placed in a tavern in the possession of the husband and wife, and to be there used and employed by them for the purpose of gaining their common livelihood, and maintaining their family. The wife is by the settlement the owner of the estate to every purpose, except that it is to be separate, and of course to be exempt from the control or liability of the husband. The whole issues and proceeds are to be paid over to her during her husband's life, and if she survived, to be hers absolutely: if not, to go according to her appointment. If the trustees converted the moneys into property with the view of benefiting the *cestui que trust*, and at her instance, and placed it in her possession as her separate estate, it still continues so. Neither a court of law nor of equity would, in such case, forfeit the property, but on the contrary would guard the rights of the wife, by following it in its converted shape and holding it to continue trust property. At law if the trust property be money and it be converted into any other chattel, that chattel or the produce will belong to the *cestui que trust*; and the same rule is said to prevail in equity: Willis on Trusts, 87; 2 Madd. Ch. 149, and cases referred to; but in such case it is presumed the party so entitled has his election either to take the chattel or make the trustee personally responsible for the fund with which the chattel has been purchased: Id. Trust money may be followed into land when it is clearly shown to have been invested in a purchase of that kind; and parol evidence is admissible to prove that fact, though express proof must be given to show that the land was bought with the trust money: 1 Hov. on Frauds, 468, 471. The wife, with the consent of the trustees, may allow her husband to use her separate property; she may give him the income as it is received; and here she does no more than allow him through the medium of the trustees, to use her furniture for their common benefit. To say this was a departure from the trust, is a *petitio principii*. It might be, if the property were thereby lost: but that is a matter between her and the trustees: and between them it is material that it was done at her request, and that she was the owner in equity: 3 Atk. 444. But whether the property lost, remains to be determined by the other question, what were the rights of the creditors against property thus situated: whether it still remained the separate estate of the wife, under the control of the trustees, or was divested by the execution and sale.

The principle is said to be, that the wife's separate estate placed in the possession of the husband, is protected against his creditors, except where he carries on trade with the goods belonging to his wife, or his possession is inconsistent with the deed. See cases collected: 1 Wats. Sheriff, 183. Assuming this for the present to be the correct doctrine, the furniture here was not conveyed to the husband, but placed in the tavern as the separate property of the wife, to be there kept and used by the family and guests, as it would be in a private family: it was bought with the wife's money, by the concurrence and in the name of the trustees, and continued under their power and control: and they might at any time have seized and removed it, if circumstances had rendered that course proper to be taken, accounting, of course, to the *cestui que trust* for their acts. It was constructively in their possession. I see no intention to give the husband the property; he was not authorized to sell or to traffic with it, or make title to it directly or indirectly, or render it liable to his creditors; nor does the nature of the property or business, raise an inference that he was authorized to carry on any trade in respect to the property.

As to inconsistency with the deed, it was an appropriation of the proceeds to her use in a different form from money. If the trustees thought proper to do this, and she preferred it, it was because they deemed it a more beneficial mode of enjoying the proceeds; and it was one which they had a right, under the settlement, to adopt without thereby divesting her title, if they saw proper to take the responsibility of employing the fund in this manner.

Judgment reversed and *venire facias de novo* awarded.

———

As to Wife's Power of Disposition over her Separate Estate: See *Dyett* v. *Coal Co.*, 32 Am. Dec. 598; *Thomas* v. *Folwell*, 30 Id. 233, and note.

———

BROTZMAN *v.* BUNNELL.

[5 WHARTON, 128.]

AN INFANT THOUGH UNDER SEVEN YEARS MAY BIND HIMSELF as apprentice, with the assent of his parent, guardian, or next friend.

DEBT to recover the penalty given by statute for harboring, concealing, and entertaining an apprentice. The jury was instructed that if, from the evidence, they believed that at the time the contract of apprenticeship was entered into, the apprentice was less than seven years of age, the contract was invalid, and they should find for defendants. The contract was with the assent of the mother of the infant. The jury found for defendants.

Ihrie, for the plaintiffs in error.

Brodhead, contra.

By Court, SERGEANT, J. No limitation of time being prescribed by the act of assembly of the twenty-ninth of September, 1770, within which an infant is incapable of binding himself by indenture of apprenticeship, I do not perceive how the courts can interpose it, without assuming legislative power. The period of seven years, under which an infant is at common law considered as not having discretion, applies only to criminal cases. It has no connection with his ability to bind himself under the statute to learn a trade. In regard to the choice of an occupation, or the judicious selection of a master, he has probably as little capacity at eight years of age as he has at six. In these matters, in truth, no reliance is placed on the judgment of the infant; they are left to the determination of the parent, or guardian, or next friend, whose assent is made indispensable to the validity of the binding. It is of importance to the interests of the community as well as of the infant, that this power of binding should be exercised; and of the time when it is proper to exercise it, others must judge for the infant, as he is incapable of deciding for himself. Cases may occur, in which it may be expedient that an infant under seven years of age should be provided for by being bound an apprentice, and it may be manifestly to his advantage to be so. We are of opinion, that the court below erred in their charge to the jury, that if the apprentice was less than seven years of age when bound, the plaintiff could not recover.

Judgment reversed, and *venire facias de novo* awarded.

POWER OF INFANT TO BIND HIMSELF AS APPRENTICE.—A contract of apprenticeship is considered at common law a contract beneficial to the infant, and one that he may for that reason enter into, without the necessity of the assent of either parent or guardian: *Kingwood* v. *Bethlehem*, 13 N. J. L. 227; *Gilbert* v. *Fletcher*, Cro. Car. 179; *King* v. *Arundel*, 5 Mau. & Sel. 259; *Woodruff* v. *Logan*, 6 Ark. 276. But the effect of such contract upon his part would at the most be to subject him to the control and discipline of his master, and to the statutory penalties prescribed for the misconduct of apprentices. In no event could he be held upon the convenants contained in the articles: *Gilbert* v. *Fletcher*, Cro. Car. 179; *Brock* v. *Parker*, 5 Ind. 538; *McKnight* v. *Hogg*, 1 Const. (S. C.) 117.

The case of *Woodruff* v. *Logan*, 6 Ark. 276, indeed holds differently, but it stands alone. The court there said: "The contract of an infant in binding himself an apprentice, being an act manifestly for his benefit, is binding in law; and when bound he can not dissolve the relation: 2 Kent, 241. If such contract is binding, a right of action necessarily results to the injured party for a breach thereof; for it is difficult to conceive a binding contract, the breach of which will not give to the injured party a right of action." As we have said, however, the prevailing doctrine is otherwise. The father or guardian of an infant was obtained to join in the articles to obviate this inconvenience, and it was determined that he was liable for the breach of the articles by the infant, though by the form of indenture each party bound himself to the other for the performance of all the covenants in the indenture; a form which would appear to bind the master to the father for the performance by the apprentice of his duties, as well as it would bind the father to the master: *Hughes* v. *Humphreys*, 6 Barn. & Cress. 687; *Branch* v *Ewington*, 2 Doug. 518.

It is well settled, that a contract of apprenticeship is not binding unless the infant is a party thereto; his father or guardian can not bind him out of their own right: *Commonwealth* v. *Moore*, 1 Ashm. 123; *Pierce* v. *Massenburg*, 4 Leigh, 495; S. C., 26 Am. Dec. 333; *Stringfield* v. *Heiskell*, 2 Yerg. 546; *Ivins* v. *Norcross*, 3 N. J. L. 977; *Matter of McDowles*, 8 Johns. 328; *Balch* v. *Smith*, 2 N. H. 437; *King* v. *Arnesby*, 3 Barn. & Ald. 584. The effect of any such covenant on the part of the father will be that of a covenant by A. that B. shall perform certain services for C. If B. do perform the services, A. is entitled to the compensation stipulated for; while if B. should refuse, A. would be liable to C. for the breach of his covenant. In the same way the father could recover if his son actually performed the contract: *Day* v. *Everett*, 7 Mass. 145; *Stewart* v. *Ricketts*, 2 Hump. 153; *Balch* v. *Smith*, 12 N. H. 437. And if the infant do perform the services, in pursuance of the contract of one who was entitled to his services, he can not recover from his master the value of his services: *Id.*, *supra*.

A Legal Contract of Apprenticeship can not be entered into without writing: *Peters* v. *Lord*, 18 Conn. 337; *Squire* v. *Whipple*, 1 Vt. 69.

The cases have sometimes considered the question as to what operation an imperfect contract of apprenticeship might have. In *Harney* v. *Owen*, 4 Blackf. 337, the articles were held not binding upon the minor because not approved by a parent or guardian as was required by statute. The minor, having rescinded the contract, sought to recover the value of the services rendered by him prior to the rescission. The court refused to entertain the action, because it was founded upon his rescission of a fair and equitable contract. *Page* v. *Marsh*, 36 N. H. 305, holds that if the articles are vacated by the minor, the father can not recover from the master the value of the services performed by his son. *Maltby* v. *Harwood*, 12 Barb. 473, goes much further, and holds that even if the apprentice be discharged by the master, upon the latter's discovering that the articles are not binding, no promise will be implied upon his part to pay the value of the services performed by the minor. The best rule probably is that of *Harney* v. *Owen*, *supra*. Statutory provisions in all or most all of the states regulate the matter of binding out infant apprentices. If these requirements be not complied with, the indentures constitute a contract for labor and service: *Bolton* v. *Smith*, 6 Ind. 264; *Page* v. *Marsh*, *supra*. Such a contract would be governed by the ordinary rules applicable to the contracts of minors; that is, it would be avoidable at the instance of the minor, but not of the master. This view is opposed by *Maltby* v. *Harwood*, *supra*, which holds that the master may avoid the articles upon discovering that they do not comply with the statute, in that they have not been executed by the minor's father, and yet refuse to pay for the minor's services.

Agnew v. Dorr.

[5 Wharton, 131.]

Stipulation in an Assignment for a release by the creditors means a technical release under seal.

Release of a Right even in a chattel is inoperative, unless by deed.

Assignment Requiring "Full and Sufficient Release" from those who wish to benefit by its provisions, will not be answered by a release conditioned on the assets realizing a certain percentage on the claim.

ASSUMPSIT. The action was upon a promissory note. Prior to this action the defendants assigned their property in trust, amongst others, for such of their creditors as might by a certain day execute a " full and sufficient release and discharge" of their claims. Upon this day, plaintiffs, who were partners, wrote to the assignees, informing them that no release had been presented them for signature, and that therefore " we now and by this writing agree to become a party to the assignment and release left in, your hands, dated August 2, 1832, on condition of the same paying twenty-five per cent. dividend on our claim, and this shall be a full and free discharge from all claims we may have against the firm of Brown & Agnew" (the defendants), " the same as if we had signed the release in your hands." The firm name was signed to this communication by one of the partners. There was no seal to the writing. Prior to the institution of this suit, the twenty-five per cent. of the amount of the note was tendered plaintiffs on the part of defendants and their assignees, but the receipt thereof was refused. The foregoing facts were disclosed by affidavit of defense; but judgment was rendered against defendants, notwithstanding, upon the ground that said affidavit was insufficient.

F. W. Hubbell, for the plaintiffs in error, defendants below.

Gerhard, contra.

By Court, GIBSON, C. J. Were not this the case of a trust, the meaning which we would be bound to assign to the technical word release, would be decisive. But even interpreting the deed like a will, which according to the rule of Lord Somers, in *Sheldon* v. *Dormer*, 2 Vern. 311, we are bound to do, we must say that the assignor stipulated for a legal, and not an equitable release. In popular as well as in technical apprehension, the release of a debt is a discharge of it by writing under seal; and the assignor must be taken, at the utmost, to have used the word as it is used in common parlance. But there are considerations peculiar to this species of trust, which require that the trustees be not left to grope their way through doubts and difficulties in the execution of it. The office is sufficiently perilous, without involving them in uncertainties which might lead to mispayments; and they are to be protected where they have followed the plain and obvious directions of the assignor. If the paper in question, then, is not a release to have brought them within the benefits of the trust, it is not a release to bring them within its disabilities; and what effect might the trustees

safely have given it on an application to them for a dividend?
It will not be pretended that they might safely have treated it
as performance of the condition. Objection could not be made
that it was executed only by one of the partners; but it is
not a deed, nor does it contain the operative words of a release.
Those, according to Littleton, section 445, are remise, release,
and quitclaim; to which Lord Coke has added renounce and acquit, intimating at the same time that some others may have the
same effect, as where the lessor grants to the lessee for life, that
he shall be discharged of the rent: 1 Inst. 264. Perhaps at this
day any words distinctly evincive of a present purpose to remit,
would be as operative. In the paper before us, however, nothing
is signified but an agreement to become party to an instrument
which was then a hundred miles distant; and surely that is not
to be taken as an equivalent for an execution of it. It is true,
that a verbal promise is susceptible of a verbal discharge before
breach of it, as it is said in Co. Lit. 246 b; but that there can
be no release of a right in a chattel without deed, appears in
Jennor and Hardy's case, 1 Leon. 283. In its frame and execution, therefore, the paper is deficient.

But independent of that, it contains a condition which would
mar it were it ever so unexceptionable in other respects. The
assignment was for the benefit of those who should execute "a
full and sufficient release;" and the plaintiffs released only on
condition that the fund should yield them at least twenty-five
per cent. How could its capacity to do so, be ascertained in
the first instance? Yet they might be called on for *pro rata*
dividends before all the assets were collected. Besides, a full
release was intended to be an absolute one. If these conditional
discharges were admissible, the trustees might be involved in
an inextricable labyrinth of discordant conditions for payment,
in every proportion which the calculation or caprice of the creditors might dictate. But it is suggested on the authority of *Coe
v. Hutton,*[1] that the debt may be gone, though the creditor may
not have entitled himself to come upon the fund. It is certain
that a technical release will discharge a duty at law, without
consideration for it, and that chancery will not relieve against
it where the releasor has acted with full knowledge of all necessary circumstances. Not such the effect of a naked agreement
which is executory, and whose force depends on the consideration which is to support it. To be let into a participation of
the fund, was a consideration for which the plaintiffs stipulated

---

1. 1 Serg. & R. 398.

as a condition precedent to parting with their debt; and their agreement could not be enforced in equity or at law, without a performance of it. Judgment therefore was rightly given in their favor for want of a sufficient affidavit of defense.

Judgment affirmed.

WHERE AN ASSIGNMENT REQUIRES A RELEASE FROM CREDITORS, a condition appended to the signature of a creditor to a release under seal, that it shall be inoperative unless he receive twenty-five per cent. on his claim, is void, and the release will be absolute. The condition will be considered inoperative because of its repugnancy to the assignment, in pursuance of which it is executed, and because of its impossibility; since as the fund realized by the assignment could be divided amongst those only of the creditors who executed absolute releases, no part thereof could be possibly distributed to a conditional releasor, and therefore, if the condition were of any effect, it must operate to defeat the release *in toto*. Also because, as the release was absolute in terms, it must operate to suspend the right of action of the releasor, and a right of action once suspended can not be revived. In other words, a release can not be executed to be void on a condition: *Tyson* v. *Dorr*, 6 Whart. 262. This case distinguishes the principal case, by showing that the latter but presented an agreement for a release, while the release then under consideration had been executed.

AN ASSIGNOR MAY PRESCRIBE the terms upon which a creditor shall be entitled to the benefit of the assignment: *Trustees' Bank*, 2 Pars. 136, citing the principal case.

ESTATE OF HINDS.

[5 WHARTON, 138.]

REDUCTION INTO POSSESSION OF THE WIFE'S CHOSES IN ACTION by the husband, is but evidence of a conversion to his use, and not in itself a conversion, and therefore may be so qualified that the property in the proceeds remains in the wife.

STEAM ENGINE ERECTED BY TENANT FOR LIFE for the purpose of carrying on a trade may be removed after his death by his representative.

APPEAL from an order of the orphans' court of Northampton county, settling the accounts of Elizabeth Hinds, administratrix of the estate of Benjamin Hinds, deceased. The administratrix was the widow of the intestate. Some time after their marriage the intestate obtained from his wife, or, as it would appear from the opinion, from an executor holding funds belonging to the wife, the sum of three hundred dollars, and at the same time delivered to the wife a written certificate to the effect that he had borrowed the money from her, and that he would pay her interest thereon. Later, Mrs. Weygandt, the mother of the administratrix, died, leaving the latter six shares of Easton bank stock. These shares were delivered to the intestate upon his executing a bond to the executor of Mrs. Weygandt that his wife would return whatever amount thereof might be required in the payment of the debts of the Weygandt estate. Mrs. Hinds, at the time of her marriage with the intestate, was possessed of some real estate, then but slightly improved. The intestate, during coverture, improved this estate and built upon it, amongst other buildings, several for his use in the course of his business of carding and of manufacturing carding machines, and in the basement of one of these buildings he placed a steam engine, with the necessary bricking, for the purpose of propelling the machinery used by him in his business. After the intestate's death the administratrix sold the engine. In her account she claimed a credit for the three hundred dollars first above mentioned, together with interest thereon, from the date upon which it was obtained from her; also for the value of six shares of Easton bank stock. These credits were disputed by appellants, who also insisted that she should be charged with the value of the engine, which she had sold, and of the buildings erected by the intestate for carrying on his trade. These claims were disallowed, while those of the administratrix were allowed.

Brodhead, for the appellants.

Maxwell and A. E. Brown, contra.

By Court, Gibson, C. J. Much of the confusion to be found in the books on the subject of a husband's power over his wife's choses in action, has arisen from viewing reduction into possession as identical with conversion to his use, and not as evidence of it. That it is evidence of it, and exceedingly powerful, must be admitted; yet it is no more. Were it very conversion, it could not be qualified; but it is well settled that the effect of it depends on the intent with which it is accompanied: and that it operates a conversion, or not, as it happens or not, to be an exercise of the wife's original dominion, of which the husband is the instrument, for the purpose of taking the property to himself. I have expressed my opinion on this subject in *Siter's case,* 4 Rawle, 475, and I will not repeat it. It must be admitted, however, that reduction to possession is in all cases *prima facie* evidence of conversion, because it is accompanied in a vast majority of cases, with that intent; but that presumption of intent, like every other which is founded on experience of the current of human transactions, may be repelled by disproof of the fact in the particular instance: consequently the question here depends on the rebutting evidence of intention. In *Wall* v. *Tomlinson,* 16 Ves.

413, a transfer, to a husband, of his wife's East India stock on
an unwritten agreement that he should hold it in trust for her
separate use, was deemed insufficient to give him such possession of it as would entitle his representative, because, as it was
significantly said, it had been made *diverso intuito*. In that case,
a verbal agreement was made before the transfer, and the evidence of it was clear; here the verbal evidence of trust consists
of subsequent declarations; which, did the case depend on them,
would be of little avail, for the reason that a man often promises, for the sake of domestic repose, what he has no intention
to perform. But these declarations that the bank shares were
still the wife's are corroborated by the refunding bond given to
the executor, and produced to him by the husband, as testified
by the niece, in proof of his assertion. The condition of it is
restitution by the wife and not by the husband—an act that
could not be performed by her if the shares belonged to him.
Restitution by any one, would questionless answer the purposes
of the executor; but the designation of the wife as the person
to make it, is a designation of her as the person in whom the
beneficial ownership was to reside, and satisfactory proof that
he received it as her representative and trustee.

The next exception stands on the same principle. As evidence
of a contract, the husband's certificate of loan by his wife, would
be destitute of force; but as evidence of his determination not
to assert a title to the money actually reduced to his possession
by the transaction—it assumes a character of decisive effect.
Can not a husband, so far as his own interest is concerned, use
his wife's money, for a limited purpose, without impairing her
right to it; or does the law impregnate it with his title by the
touch, and cast the ownership of it on him against his will?
Had the husband put the memorandum into the shape of a certificate of loan by the executor in whose hands the money stood,
the transaction would not have borne a question; but in an inquiry after actual intention, we are to look at the substance of
it without giving way to accidental circumstances of form produced by the ignorance of the parties. The object intended,
was the use of the wife's money in consistence with her ownership of it; and as there are no technical words of stubborn import in the paper, it is our business to interpret it so as to produce the results which the parties intended; and it is enough to
preclude the husband's ownership, that he intended to receive
the money from the executor as his wife's trustee; of which the
paper furnishes abundant evidence. Being void as a contract,

however, it can give her no claim to the produce of the money as interest.

The remaining exception is better founded. The steam engine put up by the husband to drive his carding and spinning mill, was clearly within the protection of that principle which obviates the conversion into realty, of fixtures for carrying on a trade; and though it was not such as might be removed by a tenant for years after the expiration of the term, as was asserted on good authority in *White* v. *Arndt*,[1] it certainly might, in analogy to the doctrine of emblements, be removed, as against the remainder-man, by the representative of a tenant for life or in tail after the expiration of the particular estate; as was held in the two leading cases of *Lawton* v. *Lawton*,[2] and *Dudley* v. *Warde*.[3] Why then should not a husband, or his representative, remove such a fixture as against the wife, after the termination of his seisin in her right, when there was the same uncertainty of its duration, and the same encouragement given to trade by the erection? I know of no case in point, but the principle of those cited is applicable to the question in all its force. The auditor's report, therefore, is to be corrected by charging the accountant with the price of the engine and bricks sold by him; and the decree is affirmed for the residue.

Decree accordingly.

———

THE EFFECT OF THE HUSBAND'S REDUCTION INTO POSSESSION of the choses in action of his wife depends upon the intention with which it is made; if he intends that the property in the proceeds shall remain in his wife, the law will not cast the ownership upon him perforce: *McDowell* v. *Potter*, 8 Pa. St. 192; *Goodyear* v. *Rumbaugh*, 13 Id. 481; *Gochenaur's estate*, 23 Id. 463; *Smethhurst* v. *Thurston*, Bright, 129. In *Timbers* v. *Kratz*, 6 Watts & S. 298, the question was between the representatives of the creditors of an insolvent husband and a daughter, to whom the wife had delivered the proceeds derived from choses in action reduced to the husband's possession subsequently to the marriage; but the court refused to consider the ownership of the proceeds to have been in the husband, the evidence being clear that he intended that the property therein should remain with his wife. *Prima facie*, however, obtaining possession of the proceeds of his wife's choses in action will amount to a conversion thereof by the husband to his own use; thus, if a husband obtain possession, as it falls due, of an annuity payable to his wife, his neglect to pay it over to her will raise the presumption that he intended to treat it as his own: *Boose's appeal*, 18 Pa. St. 394. If a debt due by the husband is bequeathed to the wife, but not to her separate use, he may treat the debt as extinguished: *Coale* v. *Smith*, 4 Id. 389.

Though it may be shown by the husband's admissions, subsequent to his reduction in possession, that at the time he intended that the property should remain in his wife, yet such admissions will not lightly be given effect to,

1. 1 Whart. 91.   2. 3 Atk. 13.   3. Amb. 113.

and must be clear and unequivocal: *Gray's estate*, 1 Id. 328, citing the principal case.

The principal case is also cited in *Johnston* v. *Johnston*, 31 Pa. St. 453; S. C., 1 Grant, 471, to the point that husband and wife can not contract with each other.

MENTZ *v.* HAMMAN.

[5 WHARTON, 150.]

DIRECTION OF AN EXECUTION CREDITOR TO THE SHERIFF TO STAY PROCEEDINGS on his execution, will postpone him to a subsequent execution creditor whose execution comes to the sheriff's hands during the stay.

SHERIFF'S RETURN THAT AN EXECUTION WAS STAYED BY PLAINTIFF'S ATTORNEY IS CONCLUSIVE upon the latter in a dispute between him and a subsequent execution creditor.

SHERIFF'S RETURN THAT EXECUTION WAS STAYED BY PLAINTIFF'S ATTORNEYS IS NOT VITIATED by the qualification which he adds that it was stayed as "I understood from J. K. Heckman." These latter words may be rejected as surplusage.

APPEAL from a decree of the court of common pleas of Northampton county, concerning the distribution of money realized under executions issued against defendant Hamman. The disputing execution creditors were Mentz & Son on the one side, and Kay & Brother on the other. The claim of the latter, who were subsequent execution creditors, was founded on an alleged stay of proceedings on the execution of the former. The sheriff paid the money in court. It was afterwards awarded to Kay & Brother. The other facts appear in the opinion.

McCartney and Browne, for the appellants.

Patrick and Hepburn, contra.

By Court, ROGERS, J. In all cases of sale upon execution, where there is a dispute concerning the distribution of the money, the court from which the execution issues, has power to determine the same, according to law and equity: Act of sixteenth of June, 1836. The money in this case was brought into court, under the authority of that act, and the question is, to whom it rightfully belongs. It has been repeatedly ruled, that an order given by an execution creditor to the sheriff, to stay all further proceedings on his execution, until further directions, is a waiver of his priority in favor of a second execution received by the sheriff during the continuance of the stay: *Eberle* v. *Mayer*, 1 Rawle, 366. This principle bears directly on the point here, which depends entirely on the fact, whether Mentz & Son,

by their attorney, gave an order to stay proceedings on their execution. And of this, as between these parties, there can be no
doubt. To the execution of Mentz & Son, the sheriff made the
following return: "To the judges within named, I do certify
and return, that the within writ came to my hands on the day
indorsed on the inner margin, and that nothing was done in
pursuance thereof, by the directions of the plaintiffs' attorney,
as I understood from J. K. Heckman, in whose hands the writ
was deposited, until the fifteenth of June last, when a *testatum
fi. fa.* issued out of the district court of the city and county of
Philadelphia, at the suit of Kay and Kay, was placed in my
hands, with directions to proceed forthwith, whereupon I levied
both writs on the personal property of the defendant, and exposed the same to sale; which sale yielded the sum of nine hundred and thirty-three dollars and twenty-six cents; which amount,
after payment of costs, is claimed by both execution creditors,
and which I have paid into court, under the authority of the
act of assembly."

On the return of the sheriff, which is conclusive evidence of
the facts contained in it, it is very clear, that the money was
properly adjudged to the younger execution creditor, Mentz &
Son having voluntarily waived in favor of that execution, all
priority arising from the fact, that their execution was first
put in the hands of the sheriff. Although it is not so formal as
it might be, yet the sheriff has substantially returned, that the
first execution was stayed by order of the plaintiffs' attorney;
and it is no manner of consequence on whose information he
chooses to rely for the truth of his return. That is a matter
which does not concern the second execution creditor: it would
not excuse the sheriff in an action for a false return, that he was
misled, either by the mistake or willful misrepresentation of his
deputy. If that be so, the deputy is liable over to him. The
words, " as I understood from J. K. Heckman," may be rejected
as surplusage, and then it stands as a return that the proceedings were stayed by order of the plaintiffs' attorney; and this
on the authority of *Eberle* v. *Mayer*, postpones him in favor of
the second execution. The subsequent levy and sale on both
executions, can not change the relative situation of the parties;
as by the order to the sheriff the first execution is irrevocably
postponed. The return of the sheriff must be certain, or it is
bad; but there is nothing in which this return is uncertain. The
material fact, that the proceedings on the first execution were
stayed by the order of the plaintiffs' attorney, is distinctly

stated; nor is there less certainty in the other parts of the return. The additional words may be stricken out without altering the sense, and can not affect its validity. *Utile per inutile non vitiatur.* The most that can be said, in objection to the return, is, that it is defective in form; but this may be amended by leave of the court. The sheriff is not obliged, unless ruled so to do, to make a return to a writ of *fieri facias;* but when he makes a return to the writ, it is conclusive between other parties, and can be impeached only in an action against the sheriff.

If the return of the sheriff be false, or there be any neglect of duty by the undersheriff or bailiff, the sheriff is alone responsible to the party injured. As between conflicting execution creditors, it can not be gainsaid; the injured party having an adequate remedy against him. This principle, if it need the aid of authority, was ruled in *Debler* v. *Roberts,*[1] 13 Serg. & R. 64, and *Blythe* v. *Richards,* 10 Id. 266 [13 Am. Dec. 672]. The parol evidence was given to contradict the sheriff's return, and for that purpose was clearly inadmissible, and must be altogether disregarded. It is a singular feature in this case, that the sheriff and his deputy were examined to the truth of the return; and this, of itself, shows the wisdom of the rule, as heretofore established. If they could be examined for, they may be examined against the return; and in this manner escape from the consequences of official misconduct. In an action against the sheriff, the truth of the return may be inquired into; and for that purpose parol evidence will be competent: this can not be as the case now stands, as the younger execution creditor can rely on the return as conclusive of his right to the money raised by the sale. The act of assembly to which reference has been made, does not dispense with, nor in any manner alter the well-established rules of evidence, nor does it in the least change the responsibility of the sheriff. It may, indeed, be doubted, whether it makes any alteration in the practice, except in the section which gives an appeal to the supreme court. There is certainly nothing in the circumstance, that the money awaits the distribution of the court, which impairs the conclusive force which the law gives to a sheriff's return. Before return made by the sheriff, the courts have always interposed to prevent injustice, but they can not alter the effect of a return; although in a proper case they may enlarge the time for making it, or may grant leave to amend it. The court is always anxious to protect the officer in the discharge of his duty; but at the

---

1. *Diller* v. *Roberts;* 16 Am. Dec. 578.

same time, we must be careful not to screen him from the necessary responsibility to suitors. It is difficult to calculate the mischief which may arise, from relaxing those wholesome restrictions on the exercise of executive authority. Nor must we for one moment give countenance to the practice of introducing parol testimony to control the sheriff's return, except in an action against him for official misconduct.

Decree of the court of common pleas affirmed.

THE SHERIFF'S RETURN IS CONCLUSIVE UPON EXECUTION CREDITORS in a contest between them as to the right of priority: *Flick* v. *Troxxell*, 7 Watts & S. 67. The return of the sheriff that a summons in an action to which a county was a party was served on A. and B., said to be "commissioners," is equivalent to a return of service on "A. and B., commissioners," as the words "said to be" may be struck out as surplusage: *Kleckner* v. *County of Lehigh*, 6 Whart. 70. As to the nature of the evidence afforded by a sheriff's return, see *Mitchell* v. *Lipe*, 29 Am. Dec. 116, and note 121, where the prior cases in this series are collected; see likewise *Knowles* v. *Lord, ante*, 525.

A DIRECTION TO THE SHERIFF TO STAY PROCEEDINGS, levy to "remain," under an execution upon personalty, postpones the execution plaintiff to a subsequent purchaser or execution creditor: *Commonwealth* v. *Strembach*, 24 Am. Dec. 351

ROBERTS *v.* WILLIAMS.

[5 WHARTON, 170.]

MORTGAGE IS EXTINGUISHED BY SALE UNDER EXECUTION of the mortgaged premises, though the execution issues on a judgment subsequent in date to the mortgage. In such case the money realized on the sale is substituted for the land.

EQUITABLE MORTGAGE DOES NOT AFFECT WHOM.—A parol agreement between a mortgagee and an execution vendee, to excuse the payment of the mortgage money to the sheriff by the latter, and that the mortgage shall remain in force as security for the payment of the money, will not affect the mortgagor nor subsequent purchasers from the execution vendee, without notice thereof.

TO AFFECT PURCHASER WITH NOTICE OF AGREEMENT TO KEEP ALIVE A MORTGAGE under such circumstances, it must be shown affirmatively that at the time of his purchase he had knowledge of the agreement.

EACH ONE OF SEVERAL DEFENDANTS IS ENTITLED to present his defense in the form of a special plea, and can not be compelled to adopt the plea of the other defendants.

THE REPRESENTATIVE OF THE MORTGAGOR IS AN INDISPENSABLE PARTY to a *scire facias* on a mortgage; without him the action can not proceed against the terre-tenants; if he make default, it is requisite, before proceeding against the latter, that judgment by default be taken against him.

SCIRE FACIAS on a mortgage executed by Richard Roberts, deceased, to John Williams. The writ ran against George S.

Roberts, administrator of the estate of said Roberts, and against the terre-tenants. The return made thereon by the sheriff appears from the opinion. Jacob Freedley, a terre-tenant not served, obtained leave to defend; he then offered to file a special plea, in which it was set forth that subsequently to the mortgage the premises were sold under an execution issued on a judgment obtained subsequently to the date of the mortgage. That at this sale the premises were bid in by Thomas Lowry for an amount greater than the mortgage debt, whereby the mortgage was discharged. That the title of Thomas Lowry to the demanded premises had since come to him by regular mesne conveyances. This plea was rejected. The plea of the other terre-tenants was payment. Some of them, however, subsequently to the filing of that plea, offered special pleas, in which the same matters of defense were relied on as appear in that of Jacob Freedley noticed above. These pleas were rejected. The other facts of the case appear from the opinion. Plaintiff did not show affirmatively on the trial any knowledge by the terre-tenants, at the time of their purchases of the agreement entered into between himself and Lowry, that the mortgage should continue to subsist, notwithstanding the sale as security for the mortgage money. The jury found for plaintiff.

Broom and Tilghman, for the plaintiff in error.

Potts and Mallery, contra.

By Court, ROGERS, J. It sometimes happens in our mixed jurisprudence of law and equity, that we are greatly embarrassed in affording that equitable relief to which a party may be justly entitled. The plaintiff's case would be one of equitable cognizance; but for want of a court of chancery, we are obliged to mold our common law forms to reach the substantial justice of the case. Richard Roberts mortgaged the land which is now in controversy to the plaintiff, John Williams. The executors of Joseph Williams obtained a judgment against Richard Roberts, in his life-time, conditioned for the payment of two thousand six hundred and eighty dollars. To a writ of *venditioni*, which was issued on this judgment, the sheriff returned, "land sold to Thomas Lowry, for the sum of twelve thousand nine hundred dollars, which money I have ready, before the judges within named, as within I am commanded." The mortgage is prior in the date to the judgment, and consequently, according to the case of *Willard* v. *Norris*, 2 Rawle, 56, and *The Corporation* v. *Wallace*, 3 Id. 109, the purchaser at the sheriff's sale takes the land, discharged of the lien of the mortgage. The money in the hand of the sheriff is substituted for the land; and the remedy by the mortgagee on this return, is against the sheriff. As respects the mortgagee, or his personal representatives, the money received by the sale being more than sufficient to discharge the amount due, the mortgagee can be compelled to enter satisfation; for it would be unjust that the debtor should be deprived of his land, by a judicial sale, and at the same time remain liable for the debt. This is so obvious as not to admit of question; but it is alleged by the plaintiff, that there was an agreement between him and the vendee, that the lien of the mortgage should remain, notwithstanding the sale. The agree-. ment was made for the convenience of the purchaser, who was unable, at that time, to pay the purchase money; and as between these parties, such a contract would raise an equity. A court of chancery would compel the purchaser to execute a mortgage, or would consider the agreement in the nature of an equitable mortgage, or would decree him to be a trustee for the mortgagee, until the debt was paid. A refusal on the part of the purchaser to perform the contract, would be a fraud—a principal ground of equitable jurisdiction, and against which a chancellor would grant relief by a special decree.

Thus the case would stand between the original parties, but as against the representative of the mortgagor, there is no equity whatever. On the contrary, as he was no party to the agreement, he has a right to complain that the mortgage has been kept on foot by a secret agreement to his manifest injury. By the sale the debt is paid, and in a suit on the bond on proof of the facts the administrator would be entitled to a verdict. This is not like the case of a sale subject to the mortgage, as in *Stackpole* v. *Glassford*, 16 Serg. & R. 166. It is not disputed, that all the purchaser would have to pay for the property, was the amount of his bid. The agreement was made to supersede the necessity of paying the money to the sheriff—an agreement which the mortgagee had the right to make, but by which he exonerated the sheriff from liability for the money raised by the sale, and at once discharged the lien of the mortgage. And whether the sheriff was privy to, or assented to the agreement, or not, can make no difference, as the question may affect the plaintiff and the vendee of the sheriff. It is also equally clear, that a *bona fide* purchaser for a valuable consideration, stands in a different position from the original purchaser. A subsequent purchaser takes the land, discharged from the equity, unless the plaintiff brings some notice to him of the agreement. Thus it will be seen, that to affect mortgaged premises in the hands of a third person with this secret equity, it will be necessary, not only to prove the contract, but in addition, that the terre-tenant had notice of the agreement.

This was a *scire facias* on the mortgage. The suit is brought against the administrator and terre-tenants. The sheriff returns "*nihil*," as to George S. Roberts and "made known" to John Freedley, James Freedley, James Wells, Thomas Lowry, and James Steel, terre-tenants. The terre-tenants who were summoned pleaded payment with leave; and as to them issue was regularly joined. Afterwards Jacob Freedley was permitted by the court to come in and take defense in the suit, and to plead in the same manner as if the original *scire facias* was served on him. Freedley then offered a special plea, which was overruled by the court; but for what reason, has not been clearly explained. If the plea was defective in form or substance, it was open to the plaintiff to demur; and if taken by surprise, the court, on motion, would have continued the cause. He had a right of which he could not be deprived, to bring his case before the court, either in the form of a special plea, or to take defense under the plea of payment. So far, then, as respects this defendant, the cause was not at issue; for it is idle to say that he adopted the pleas of the other defendants. The case of *Britton* v. *Mitchell*,[1] 5 Watts, 69, is full to the point. A party can not be compelled to try until the cause is put into legal form, by an issue properly found, between all the parties on the record.

The *scire facias* is brought against the administrator and terre-tenants; and it would be error to try the suit in a different manner. Where a *scire facias* was brought upon a recognizance in the orphans' court against the cognizor and terre-tenants, and the cognizor died before judgment, it was held, in *Reigart* v. *Ellmaker*, 6 Serg. & R. 44, and *Keen* v. *Same*, 8 Id. 4,[2] to be error to proceed to trial against the terre-tenant alone, where the administrator, upon being duly served with a *scire facias*, has neglected to come in and be made a party to the record. The proper course is, when the personal representative does not appear and take defense, to sign judgment by default, *de bonis testatoris;* and the terre-tenants will be permitted to defend *pro interesse suo.* These principles are applicable to this case. It is proper that the administrator of the mortgagor, who is the

---

1. *Bratton* v. *Mitchell.*   2. *Keen* v. *Ellmaker*, 7 Serg. & R. 1.

principal debtor, should be made a party, in order that he may have the opportunity to prove the payment of the debt. And this is necessary also for the security of the terre-tenants, who can not be presumed to be acquainted with the state of the account, between the mortgagor and mortgagee. Here the plaintiff has not thought proper to pursue this course before proceeding against the terre-tenants; and this, according to the cases cited, is clearly erroneous. The plaintiff seems to have been sensible of this error; for on the same day on which the judgment was given, the court rendered judgment against the administrator for the amount ascertained by the verdict against the terre-tenants. But a slip of this kind can not be thus noticed; for as the mortgagor is the party against whom suit is to be brought, until he is in court, the cause can not proceed, for want of parties. If he does not appear, the plaintiff must proceed, for want of appearance, to judgment by default; and having thus disposed of the legal party, he may pursue the land in the possession of the terre-tenants. Rendering judgment against the administrator is not a formal, but it is a substantial objection to the proceeding. If the judgment be permitted to stand, and hereafter the mortgaged premises should prove inadequate to pay the amount of the verdict, the estate of the deceased, or the administrator personally, must make good the deficiency. In a suit on the bond which accompanies the mortgage, the verdict on the *scire facias* would be conclusive as to the amount due. It would not be open to the administrator to insist on payment by the judicial sale; as the same subject-matter having once been tried, could not be renewed in a suit between the same parties. And yet it is too clear for argument, as has been before shown, that so far as respects the administrator, the debt has been paid.

We are further of the opinion that the court erred in omitting to swear the jury as to James Wells and Thomas Lowry. The *scire facias* was in the most approved form, against the administrator and terre-tenants. The sheriff having summoned them as terre-tenants, they are as much parties on the record, as if named in the writ. Lowry and Wells, in the first instance, asked leave to file special pleas; which was overruled by the court. Afterwards they filed disclaimers; but in filing disclaimers they do not cease to be parties. This is ruled in *Bratton* v. *Mitchell*, 5 Watts, 67, where the course to be pursued is plainly pointed out. The court may compel a party who disclaims to give judgment, which will secure costs and damages;

or they may order him to plead instanter; on which the parties may go to trial. In *Morris* v. *Morris*, Id.,[1] it is decided, that a plaintiff having issued a *scire facias*, with notice, to several terre-tenants, can not enter a *nolle prosequi* as to some of them, and proceed against the others. After having placed parties on the record, it is not in the election of the plaintiff, and one of several terre-tenants, to treat them as if they had never been summoned. It may be of the utmost importance to the defendant, that all who have once been parties, should remain so, as they may be liable for contribution, and for the costs. The court orders the jury to be sworn as to the other defendants, omitting two who had been summoned; and, what is not the least objectionable feature in the case, Lowry, one of them, is examined as a witness to prove the agreement, which is the foundation of the plaintiff's action.

We would not wish to be understood as expressing a decided opinion whether the equity of the plaintiff's case can be reached in this form of suit. Perhaps justice may be done by a replication to the defendant's plea, setting forth the agreement, and averring that the terre-tenants had notice of the agreement. Whether Lowry was a competent witness, does not seem to have been made a point at the trial. It may, however, be well worthy of serious consideration, whether, independently of his position as a party, he has not such an interest as renders him incompetent. In the view which we have taken of the case, it is immaterial to the case whether the court erred in rejecting the evidence contained in the bill of exceptions. Nor is it necessary to notice the exceptions to the charge, except, as has already been done, in the preceding remarks.

Judgment reversed, and a *venire de novo* awarded.

THE RIGHT TO SET UP A DEFENSE in the form of a special plea is not taken away by the fact that it might be proved under the general issue: *Johns* v. *Bolton*, 12 Pa. St. 342, citing the principal case.

SHARP *v.* EMMET.

[5 WHARTON, 288.]

INDORSEMENT BY A FACTOR OF A BILL OF EXCHANGE remitted to his principal in payment of goods sold on the latter's account, raises no liability on his part towards the latter, unless it may be shown that at the time of his indorsement he intended to assume a personal liability.

---

1. *Maus* v. *Maus*, 5 Watts, 315.

CONTRACT BY A FACTOR TO GUARANTEE his sale for a premium beyond the usual rate, is a contract of guaranty of the solvency of his vendees, and not of the worth of the bills purchased by him and remitted in payment.

WHETHER A WITNESS MAY BE CONTRADICTED without having been first given an opportunity to explain the evidence which is relied on for that purpose, is a question which is left to the discretion of the trial courts.

INTERPRETATION OF A CONTRACT BY ONE OF THE PARTIES can not be aided by showing his letters to one not a party to the suit, in which appears the construction that he has placed upon a similar contract with that third party.

ASSUMPSIT.   The action was upon a bill of exchange drawn by J. Thompson, of New York, on Rathbone & Co., of Liverpool, and indorsed by Thompson to Sharp, and by Sharp to Emmet. The bill was dishonored; whereupon due steps were taken to fix the liability of the indorsers, and this action was brought.   The relationship of factor and principal existed between Sharp and Emmet.   The bill was forwarded by the former in payment of goods of the latter consigned to and sold by him.   In the account of sales made by Sharp, Emmet was charged with "commission and guarany five per cent."   The construction put upon the phrase by the defendant was attempted to be aided by reading in evidence certain letters of his to Halliday, Son & Brooks, in explanation of similar account sales.   The evidence was admitted over defendant's objection.   Proof was also introduced by both parties as to the commercial standing of J. Thompson.   The other facts of the case appear from the opinion.   It was admitted by both parties that Sharp was to be held to a due exercise of discretion and judgment in his purchase of bills for remittance to his principal.   The questions in dispute were as to the effect of defendant's indorsement and of the alleged contract of guaranty.   The jury was charged that defendant's indorsement rendered him *prima facie* liable, though the indorsement was open to explanation.   The effect of the contract of guaranty was left to the jury.   The jury found for the plaintiff.

Scott and Ingersoll, for the plaintiff in error.

Cadwalader, contra.

By Court, SERGEANT, J.   Although the decision in *The Mechanics Bank* v. *Earp*, 4 Rawle, 389, is distinguishable from the present—that being the case of a mere agent for transmission, who indorsed the note, this, of a factor who remitted a bill to his principal in payment—yet the principles settled there, rule the present case.   Formerly there seems to have been in the law

merchant a severe and inflexible rule applied, that whenever an
agent or factor indorsed a bill, he was liable on his indorsement,
unless he took care at the time to limit his responsibility, stating that it was "*sans recours*," or by procuration, or some similar mode. The authorities cited by Mr. Justice Rogers, in *The
Mechanics Bank* v. *Earp*, and those referred to in the argument
here, sufficiently show this. But it is equally certain, that in
more modern times the severity of this rule has been relaxed;
and it is now held, that between the agent and the principal,
the agent remitting a bill for payment with his indorsement, is
not obliged, in order to exempt himself, to do so in express
terms on the face of the indorsement. Such a restriction is
objectionable in many instances, as calculated to throw a doubt
over the responsibility of the prior parties, and to discredit them
with those who may see the indorsement. The rule is, that
the indorsement of the factor must be construed by the circumstances under which it is made; and unless there be something
to show that in indorsing he intended to render himself personally liable, or that he was bound to do so, it ought not to be so
intended. A factor remitting a bill to his principal in payment
of goods sold on his account, and receiving no consideration
for guaranteeing the bill, nor undertaking to do so, is not personally responsible merely on his indorsement.

But it is contended, that here the factor received five per cent.
for commissions and guaranty, which included a guaranty of the
remittance. This is a question of intention on the evidence.
The general rule was very carefully considered by the supreme
court of New York, in *Leverick* v. *Meigs*, 1 Cow. 664, and it was
decided, that under a contract by a factor to guarantee his
sales, on a certain premium beyond the usual commission, the
guaranty is only of the solvency of the purchaser, and not of
the validity of the bill purchased in the usual course of business,
and remitted on account of the principal.

Two bills of exception were taken to the evidence.

1. Mr. Spackman was called and examined by the defendant.
On his cross-examination by the plaintiff, he stated that during
the period in which he was selling certain bills drawn by Thompson, he heard that he was buying cotton in New York at higher
prices than some others; but he never heard any suspicions or
doubts of the goodness of his bills, before the news from Liverpool. His brother-in-law, Mr. Wilson, did not state any doubt
on his mind about the goodness of the bills. The plaintiff in
reply called Joseph R. Evans, and offered to prove by him a

conversation which had occurred between him and Mr. Spackman, in which Spackman, before the news from Liverpool, had heard doubt and suspicion of the goodness of Thompson's bills. The defendant objected. The plaintiff, referring to the above evidence, urged that the evidence was offered to contradict that part of Mr. Spackman's testimony. The court admitted the evidence, and the defendant excepted.

The rule now relied on by the defendant is that which was established in *The Queen's case*,[1] that before giving such evidence to contradict a witness, he must be first asked particularly as to the conversation concerning which he is to be contradicted. That seems to have been considered in *The Queen's case*, as a rule of practice previously established in England. Here, it is believed, it has not been; and though there are many cases in which it would be fair and proper, that a witness should have an opportunity of refreshing his memory, by being directed particularly to the subject, before he is contradicted, yet there are other cases in which it would be inconvenient to lay it down as an uniform rule of practice. The witness may have gone away, out of the jurisdiction of the court: and in the case of a deposition, the course would be impracticable. In Massachusetts, the question was very carefully considered in their supreme court, and in a learned and able opinion they dissented from the rule *in toto*. We are disposed to leave it in Pennsylvania, as a matter for the discretion of the courts on the trial, as we believe it has, generally speaking, hitherto been.

As to the second exception, we think the transactions of the defendant with Halliday, Jones, and Brooks, were not evidence in this cause, being *res inter alios acta*.

Judgment reversed, and *venire facias de novo* awarded.

WHETHER EVIDENCE OF CONTRADICTORY STATEMENTS made by a witness shall be admitted without first interrogating the witness in regard thereto, is a question left to the sound discretion of the trial court: *McKee* v. *Jones*, 6 Pa. St. 429; *Stearns* v. *Merchants' Bank*, 53 Id. 498, citing the principal case. As to impeachment of witnesses generally, see *Chess* v. *Chess*, 21 Am. Dec. 351; *People* v. *Mather*, Id. 122, and cases cited in the note to the latter of these cases.

----

1. 2 Brod. & B. 284.

FREVALL v. FITCH.

[5 WHARTON, 325.]

SEALED INSTRUMENT, THOUGH IN FORM A PROMISSORY NOTE, is nevertheless a specialty, and no liability arises from an indorsement thereon.

BROKER IS THE GENERAL AGENT OF A PRINCIPAL who has intrusted him with the disposition of a security, and may bind him by an express guaranty that the security shall be paid by the maker.

AGREEMENT FOUNDED IN A MISCONCEPTION caused by the misrepresentation of one of the parties may be avoided, though the misrepresentation was not fraudulent.

THOUGH A MISCONCEPTION BE ONE OF LAW, the contract may be avoided on account thereof. Thus if a broker persuade a purchaser that his principal's indorsement on a sealed instrument is equivalent to an indorsement on a promissory note, the purchase may be avoided.

ASSUMPSIT. The gist of the action was defendant's indorsement on the following sealed instrument:

"5,000.   BANK OF NEW BRUNSWICK,

[SEAL.]   December 16, 1833.

"Four months after date, the president and directors of the bank of New Brunswick, promise to pay, to order Thomas Fitch, five thousand dollars, without defalcation or discount, for value received.   J. C. VANDYKE,

"F. RICHMOND, Cashier.   President."

Payment of this instrument was refused on the day of its maturity; whereupon notice was given to Fitch, and subsequently this action was begun, it being insisted that under the charter of the bank, this sealed instrument amounted but to a promissory note, and that defendant's liability was that of an indorser on negotiable paper. The provision of the charter relied upon was to the effect that "the corporation shall not directly or indirectly deal or trade, in anything except bills of exchange, promissory notes, gold or silver bullion, or in the sale of goods which shall be the produce of its lands; nor shall the said corporation take more than at the rate of seven per cent. per annum for or upon its loans or discounts." Besides the counts charging defendant as indorser of negotiable paper, the declaration contained the common money counts. The manner in which the instrument came into plaintiff's hands appears from the opinion. A nonsuit was granted in the court below.

C. Ingersoll, for the plaintiff in error.

Chester, contra.

By Court, GIBSON, C. J. It is clear, that recourse to the

defendant can not be had on his indorsement. Bearing the corporate seal of the bank on its face, though framed in other respects as a promissory note, the instrument is a specialty; and no obligation arose from the indorsement of it, either by the statute or the custom of merchants. But under the circumstances of the transfer, may not the money paid for it be recovered back on the money counts?

The defendant must abide by the representation of the broker who represented him. The note, as it is called, with the defendant's indorsement of it, was handed by him to his partner, to raise money on it on the best terms that could be had; and there was consequently no limitation of his authority. The partner put it into the hands of his broker, without instructing him that there was to be no recourse to the defendant, and without restriction as to conditions. Thus the broker became the defendant's general agent to dispose of the particular security; and nothing is better established than that, even in the absence of express restriction, the defendant would have been bound by an express guaranty, had the broker entered into one. In *Fenn v. Harrison*, 4 T. R. 177, it was settled that the guaranty of an agent employed by indorsees of a bill to get it discounted binds the employers to refund in case it be dishonored. But there was no formal guaranty; and as the law of warranty arising on a sale of chattels, is inapplicable to the transfer of a chose in action, the case could not be brought within the principle of those modern decisions, even did we approve of them, which have, in England and some of the American states, turned every representation into a warranty, in derogation of the actual meaning and intent. Still if this note was purchased under an erroneous impression received from even an innocent misrepresentation of the seller, it will not be said that the bargain may not be treated as a nullity, and the price be recovered back as so much paid without consideration, and consequently to the plaintiff's use. It is an elementary principle, that an agreement founded in a false conception, is a nullity in respect to the party who misconceived, because he assented to it, not absolutely, but on a condition not verified by the event: 2 Powell on Contracts, 196. What are the facts here? Mr. Curcier, the plaintiff's agent for investment, tells a broker of whom he is inquiring for an eligible fund, that the rate of interest is a secondary consideration, but that the security must, in his own phrase, be first-chop: on which the broker produces the note in question, and points to the name of his principal as a guaranty. The next day he repeats what he had said, and adds an assurance of the defendant's sufficiency.

Now it is fallacious to say that any part of this was not within the scope of his authority. If the defendant did not intend that the note should be negotiated on the responsibility of his name, why did he indorse it? To hold out his indorsement as a bait, knowing the paper not to be negotiable, would be to meditate a fraud which would make short work with any bargain made on the faith of it; and the most favorable construction that can be made of his conduct, is to assume that he actually intended to incur the responsibility of an indorser. The presumption is that every man who puts his name on paper thrown upon the market, does so to add to its credit; and the defendant either meant to sell on the faith of his indorsement, or he intended to commit a fraud. It is not to be doubted, then, that in the apprehension of the plaintiff's agent, the bargain rested on an assumption of the defendant's responsibilty; and, that the indorsement failing, the bargain goes with it. It is insisted, however, that a bargain can be set aside only for a misconception of fact, and not of law with which every one is bound to be acquainted. That position is disproved by *Lansdown* v. *Lansdown*, Moseley, 364; in which a deed executed on the mistaken advice of a school-master in regard to a point of law, was set aside and the party ordered to convey. This principle is not peculiar to equity; for being of the essence of every contract, it is equally enforced at law whenever the court can look at the consideration, and when a chancellor has not exclusive jurisdiction. How the cause may appear at a second trial, it is impossible to say; but as it appears in our paper book, it presents no obstacle to a recovery. It has been objected that the money was paid to the use of the partners for whom it was raised; but it was paid to the defendant's agent in the first instance, and, by consequence, to the defendant himself, with whom alone the plaintiff stood in privity; and his subsequent advancement of it to the firm, can not discharge his obligation to refund. The cause is therefore sent to another jury.

Judgment reversed, and a *venire de novo* awarded.

AN INSTRUMENT IN FORM A PROMISSORY NOTE, if under seal, will not be negotiable paper, nor governed by the rules of commercial law; therefore the defense of want of consideration may be made in an action brought thereon, even as against an innocent holder: *Hopkins* v. *Railroad Company*, 3 Watts & S. 411.

AN INDORSEMENT ON AN INSTRUMENT REQUESTING the payment of money, by the person upon whom the request is made, will not amount to an acceptance if the instrument be not negotiable: *Gillespie* v. *Mather*, 10 Pa. St..31, citing the principal case.

The cases upon the debatable question whether a mistake of law will be relieved against, reported in this series, are collected in the note to *Norton* v. *Marden*, 32 Am. Dec. 132.

BENSELL *v.* CHANCELLOR.

[5 WHARTON, 371.]

DECLARATIONS OF AN AGENT IMPUGNING HIS AUTHORITY are inadmissible against parties whose rights depend upon the existence of that authority. Thus declarations of an agent showing his belief in the insanity of his principal can not be shown against a purchaser to whom he has conveyed.

RUNNING OF THE STATUTE OF LIMITATIONS IS NOT SUSPENDED by a disability which occurs subsequently to the time that the right of action accrued.

LUNATIC MAY AVOID HIS DEED made during insanity.

EJECTMENT. Engle Bensell died in 1805, leaving a will in which he devised a life estate in the land in question to his brother, George Bensell, remainder to such of the children of the latter as might be living at the time of his death. Plaintiffs were these children; their father, George Bensell, having died in 1827. In 1803, that is, prior to the death of Engle Bensell, George Bensell, acting as his attorney in fact, executed to defendant's predecessor a deed of this land. Plaintiffs sought to avoid this deed by proof that Engle Bensell was insane at the time of its execution. In support of this branch of their case they introduced evidence of the declarations of George Bensell, about the time of his execution of the deed in 1803, which would show that he knew at the time of his brother's insanity. The evidence was rejected. Defendant relied on the statute of limitations. The jury was instructed that if the deed of 1803 was taken in good faith by the purchaser, his possession at once became adverse, and that the statute would not be interrupted because of the minority of plaintiffs at the time of the death of Engle Bensell in 1805.

Meredith, for the plaintiffs.

Cadwalader, contra.

By Court, GIBSON, C. J. The petition of Dr. Bensell to have his principal removed for mental incapacity, his agreement to pay for his maintenance as an insane patient in the Pennsylvania hospital, his memoranda of a conversation with the deputy

register, and his unfinished draught of a letter, are all evincive
of an opinion that his principal was insane. But what has his
opinion to do with the question whether he was actually so?
We know that admissions by an agent in the course of the
business, are evidence to charge the principal, because, in contemplation of law, they are the admissions of the principal; but
we know not on what grounds they can be received to affect one
who has done nothing to make them his own. To suffer an
agent's by-play to impugn his acts, would open a wide field to
collusion with his principal. Without, then, a ground laid by
evidence of conspiracy with the party to be affected, no trace of
which is discoverable in this record, an agent's surmise that his
principal was mad, is incompetent to prove him so.

Of the remaining point, little more need be said, than that it
is ruled by *Thompson* v. *Smith*, 7 Serg. & R. 209 [10 Am. Dec.
453], in which a title that had accrued during infancy, was
barred at the expiration of the indulgence allowed to that disability, though coverture had intervened and continued, without intermission, till suit brought. The principle of that case
arises directly out of the words of the statute. "If any person,"
it is said in the proviso, "having such right or title, shall be,
at the time such title first descended or accrued, within the age
of twenty-one years, *feme-covert, non compos mentis,* imprisoned,
or beyond sea, and without the United States," such person
shall have ten years to bring suit after coming of age, etc.
Thus, disabilities subsequently accruing, are not provided for;
and for that reason, the statute, having once started, runs over
every obstacle: which accords with the construction made by
the British courts of the proviso in the statute 21 Jac. 1, of
which ours is a transcript, as in *Cotterell* v. *Dutton,* 4 Taunt.
825, and *Duroure* v. *Jones,* 4 T. R. 410.[1] Were it not for this,
a play of alternate disabilities might keep a right of entry afoot
indefinitely. If, then, there was such a right in Engle Bensell,
who, though to be taken for a lunatic, was not an infant, the
plaintiffs who represent him can not call their infancy in aid of
his disability; for though they may have been infants when the
land was conveyed by his agent, it was not their infancy which
prevented him from contesting the validity of the deed by an
action.

It is said that being insane, and consequently incompetent
as it is supposed, to stultify himself, he had not a right of entry, because he could not prosecute it by action. If that were

_____
1. 4 T. R. 300.

so, the saving, in cases like the present, would be unnecessary; for the heir or alienee would have a longer period of indulgence without it.   To give him ten years from the cessation of the disability, did the statute only then begin to run, would be absurd. But that a lunatic would have right of entry, notwithstanding a well-founded personal incapacity to prosecute it by action, especially when he might prosecute it by entry, is evident from the admitted capacity of a committee to prosecute it on his title; for it can not be pretended that such a right, when founded on the invalidity of a lunatic's act, arises, for the first time, at the finding of an office.   In that respect, he might, were it necessary, be put in the predicament of an alien enemy, whose personal incapacity to sue is independent of his cause of action. But no rule founded on so absurd a supposition as that a man can not tell whether he was out of his senses at a particular period, or what he did when he was so, can hold its ground; and the wonder is, that it has been endured so long by the British courts.   Who, that has conversed with an insane man, has not heard him speak of past transactions with entire accuracy; and is it creditable that restoration to reason has the effect of effacing past impressions?   That memory is often more intense in madness than in health, that a maniac can frequently trace the disordered action of his mind through all its wanderings in the wildest delirium, and that he is, at the time, often semi-conscious of the fallacy of his illusion, is shown in a recent narrative of his own case, by an unfortunate son of the unfortunate premier, Mr. Percival—a narrative which, by its minute delineation of the morbid sensibilities and distempered, but preternaturally acute, perceptions of a religious madman, has, it is conceded, added more to the stock of professional knowledge in regard to the moral treatment proper for an insane patient, than all that had preceded it thrice told.   But of what importance are his perceptions or his reminiscences?   The question has regard, upon principle, not to what he can recollect, but what he can prove. How, then, does it stand on authority?   That one who has been insane shall not be received to allege his own infirmity, or to blemish himself, as it is sometimes improperly called, is by no means settled in England at this day.   Till the reign of Henry VI., it is admitted on all hands, the law was held that he might; and Mr. Powell, in his treatise on contracts, page 19, admits, that if the reason of the thing coincided with it, the weight of authority might be admitted to be that way; but he thinks it decisive that, unlike infancy, to which it has been compared,

this particular disability may be feigned, and that the law therefore must necessarily preclude the possibility of fraud from it
by precluding an allegation of the fact from which it might
spring.

Now to say nothing of the impossibility of suppressing all
transactions that may be infected with fraud, or of the inconsistency of precluding the lunatic himself from alleging his infirmity,
in order to be secure against imposition, and yet allowing his
committee to do it for him, it may be remarked, that the assertion of dissimilitude is unfounded in fact, as very clear proofs
of infancy may be counterfeited; and I have known a party, on
the other hand, overreached by an assumed capacity to convey.
On the other side of the question stands the name of Mr. Fonblanque (b. 1, c. 2, sec. 1, note f), who thinks that Fitzherbert's
doctrine, in opposition to that which is supposed to be currently
received, is sustained, as well by his reasons as his authorities.
Sir William Blackstone speaks of the notion that a man shall
not be admitted to plead his insanity, with evident disparagement. It is however but a question of pleading, after all; for
no one has ventured to question the decision in *Yates* v. *Boen*, 2
Stra. 1104, in which lunacy was given in evidence under *non est*
factum. Indeed, that precedent was followed in *Foulder* v. *Silk*,
3 Camp. 126, and even so late as *Bagster* v. *Portsmouth*, 7 Dow.
& Ry. 614, Mr. Justice Littledale went the whole length of affirming that a deed might be avoided by a plea of lunacy; though in
Brown v. *Jodrell*, 3 Car. & P. 30, Lord Tenterden intimated that
a lunatic might not allege his incapacity, unless he had been
imposed on in consequence of it. That, however, was said in
reference to a contract for work and labor done; which, if not
otherwise unfair, can not be avoided by the lunatic, or any one
else. Finally, in *Turner* v. *Meyers*, 1 Hagg. Cons. 414, it was
held by Sir William Scott, for clear law, that a party who was
deranged at the time of his marriage, may come into the ecclesiastical court to maintain his own past insanity; and that a defect of capacity from that cause invalidates the contract of marriage as well as any other. Thus stands the controversy in
England. In the United States, we have an explicit opinion by
the distinguished author of the commentaries on American law,
2 Kent, 451, that the doctrine of Littleton and Coke is manifestly unjust, absurd, and actually exploded; in which he is
sustained by *Webster* v. *Woodford*, 3 Day, 90; *Grant* v. *Thomp*
son, 3 Conn. 203;[1] *Mitchell* v. *Kingman*, 5 Pick. 431; and *Rice* v.
Peet, 5 Johns. 503.[2] Whatever, then, may be the rule in Eng-

---

1. 4 Conn. 203; S. C. 10 Am. Dec ___   2. 15 Johns. 503.

land, I take it to be settled in America, that the party himself
may avoid his acts, except those of record and contracts for
necessaries and services rendered by allegation and proof of insanity.   As then Engle Bensell had a right of entry on which he
was competent to maintain an action, the bar was complete at
the expiration of twenty-one years from the conveyance; for the
statute, beginning its course by reason of his capacity to regain
the possession, ran over the intermediate freehold of Dr. Bensell
under the will, and overreached the ten years allowed for the
particular disability.

Judgment affirmed.

A GRANTOR IS ALLOWED TO SHOW HIS INSANITY at the time of the execution of a deed, for the purpose of avoiding it: *Rogers* v. *Walker*, 6 Pa. St.
374.   It does not matter that the insanity was the result of intoxication, or
at least in this case he will be allowed to avoid the deed by such proof, where
no rights of *bona fide* purchasers have intervened: *Clifton* v. *Davis*, 1 Pars.
33, citing the principal case.   The principal case is also cited in *Henry* v.
Carson, 59 Pa. St. 305.   The manner in which insanity affects the right to
contract is treated of at length in the note to *Jackson* v. *King*, 15 Am. Dec. 361.

CHAPMAN *v.* COMMONWEALTH.

[5 WHARTON, 427.]

WORD "MALICIOUSLY" IS AN EQUIVALENT FOR THE WORD "WILLFULLY"
in an indictment.

INDICTMENT FOR A STATUTORY OFFENSE must conclude "*contra formam
statuti.*"

INDICTMENT for arson.   The indictment was as follows: "The
grand inquest, etc., do present that Henry Chapman, late of the
said county, laborer, on the thirteenth day of January, in the
year of our Lord 1839, with force and arms, at etc., feloniously,
unlawfully, and maliciously did set fire to a certain barrack of
Abraham Brown, there situate, with intent to destroy the same,
to the great damage of the said Abraham Brown, contrary to the
form of the act of general assembly in such case made and provided, and against the peace and dignity of the commonwealth
of Pennsylvania.   And the grand inquest, etc., do further present that the said Henry Chapman, at etc., with force and arms,
feloniously, willfully, and maliciously did set fire to and burn
a certain stable of the aforesaid Abraham Brown, there situate,
to the evil example of all others in like case offending, and
against the peace and dignity of the commonwealth of Pennsylvania."   The prisoner was convicted.   Motions were made in
arrest of judgment, upon grounds which sufficiently appear from
the opinion.

Ross, for the plaintiff in error.

Wright, contra.

By COURT. The word " maliciously," in the first count, may pass as an equivalent for the word " willfully;" but the words " barrack, rick, or stack of hay, grain, or bark," as much import a barrack of hay or grain as they do a rick or stack of hay or grain. They were used elliptically in the context to avoid repetition. The statute is an amplification of the act of 1767, under a mitigated punishment; and it is to be remarked, that it was not indictable on that act, though it is so now, to burn a barn, " unless it had hay or corn therein." It is not credible, therefore, that the legislature did not formerly extend as much protection to a barn as they subsequently intended to extend to a barrack, which, in Pennsylvania, is an erection of upright posts supporting a sliding roof, usually of thatch; for of all the buildings on a farm, it is the cheapest, and that which, independently of the property housed by it, offers the least incitement to malicious mischief. It is not generally, if at all, used by the tanner to cover his bark; but containing that material, its contents would be within the words of the statute, and the protection intended to be given by it.

The second count is for feloniously burning a stable, which is undoubtedly a subject of the statutory offense, independent of its contents; but as it does not conclude against the form of the statute, and there is no such felony at the common law, there is no count in the indictment on which the judgment can be rested.

Judgment reversed.

HEIDLEBERG *v.* LYNN.

[5 WHARTON, 430.]

SERVICE BY A PAUPER UNDER CONTRACT FOR THE SPACE OF A YEAR gains a settlement, whether all performed under one contract or whether performed under several distinct contracts.

CONTRACT OF HIRING IS BY THE YEAR where the duration of the hire is not limited, and it is provided that it can be terminated but upon three months' notice.

CONTRACT OF SERVICE IS NOT INTERRUPTED BY TEMPORARY ABSENCES where the absence is with the consent of the master and does not prevent the discharge of the servant's duties; in such cases, the servant is, during his absence. in the constructive service of the master.

APPEAL from an order of the quarter sessions quashing an order of justices directing a pauper's removal from the town-

ship of Lynn to that of Heidleberg. The question was as to
settlement. In January, 1838, Nathan Lynn, the pauper, removed from the township of Heidelberg to that of Lynn. In
that month he engaged himself to Mr. Eisenhart to work in the
latter's powder-mill for seventy-five cents a hundred. No limit
as to time was placed upon the hire, but it was provided that
the contract should not be terminated otherwise than upon
three months' notice by either party. Lynn continued to work
under the contract until in March, 1839, when he and the mill
were blown up; he died in a few months afterwards. During
the period, from January, 1838, to March, 1839, the powder-
mill was occasionally closed, and during such periods Lynn
would be sometimes employed around the mill in drying and
packing powder, and would sometimes have his time at his own
disposal; during these latter periods he either worked for Mr.
Eisenhart, went to school, or did work for the neighbors in
harvesting, etc.; and once worked, in harvesting, a few days for
his father, in Heidleberg township.

Mallery, for the appellants.

Gibons, contra.

By Court, GIBSON, C. J. As our system of poor laws had its
origin in that of England, and as many of her statutory provisions were re-enacted here, we must turn to some of them to have
a view of the whole ground in contest. By 3 and 4 William &
Mary, c. 11, "If any unmarried person, not having a child or
children, shall be lawfully hired into any parish or town for one
year, such service shall be judged a good settlement therein."
The insufficiency of this was that it went no further than 5
Eliz., c. 4, which also prohibited a retainer for less than a year;
and the insolence of servants, it is said in *Dunsfold* v. *Ridgwick*,
2 Salk. 535, gaining a settlement, as they did by 12 Car. II.,
led the way to 8 and 9 Wm. III., c. 30, by which it was enacted,
"that no person so hired as aforesaid, shall be adjudged or
deemed to have a good settlement in any parish or township,
unless such person shall continue or abide in the same service
during the space of a whole year." Hence, it became indispensable to a settlement, that there should have been both a
hiring and service for a year. Our law seems to consider service alone as a meritorious cause, and to require that there should
have been a contract for it, only as a proof that it was valuable,
and distinguishable, in that respect, from those feeble and trifling acts which are sometimes performed in requital of a gratu-

itous maintenance; in other words, to show that, instead of having been a benefit to the township as a producer, the pauper had been a burden to it as a consumer, from the beginning. In the ninth section of the statute of 1836, it is enacted, that a settlement may be gained " by any unmarried person, not having a child, who shall be lawfully bound or hired as a servant within such district, and shall continue in such service during a year." It is scarce necessary to remark on this, that time is predicated of the service, and not of the contract; and consequently that what is required, seems to be no more than a continuance in hired service during the period. It is therefore enough for the purpose, that the pauper has been in uninterrupted employment, whether under one contract or any number of contracts. Now the reason why service under a hiring to do job or piece-work, gains no settlement by the British statutes, is not that the service, but that the contract, does not come up to the exigence; and *The King* v. *The Inhabitants of St. Peters in Dorchester*, 2 Bott's Poor Laws, 197, was decided expressly on that ground. But though the contract need not be continuous, yet where there is an apparent gap in the service by temporary cessation from active duty, the terms of the hiring may be consulted to ascertain whether the pauper was not in the constructive service of an employer; and on such an inquiry, decisions on 8 and 9 Wm. III. may afford very valuable assistance. The leading principle of these is, that temporary absence from actual service, if it discharge not the contract, breaks not the relation of master and servant, it being sufficient that the pauper did all that was required of him. In the case before us, as payment in proportion to the product was stipulated to fix the rate of wages, it might easily be maintained that the hiring was not by the piece, but for an indefinite time. Was there, then, an existing contract at those intervals when he was absent on leave? The hiring was general, and on terms which forbade either party to put an end to it without three months notice; which, according to *Rex* v. *Wincaunton*, 2 Bott's Poor Laws, 195, is, by implication, a hiring for a year. Notice of dissolution had not been given; and the relation of master and servant consequently existed at the periods of absence. It seems, therefore, that the pauper had gained a settlement in the township of Lynn.

Order of the sessions affirmed.

SERVICE IF NOT UNDER CONTRACT will not gain a settlement, even though it be continued for more than a year; it is not necessary, however, that the service be all performed under the same contract, in order that a settlement be gained: *Lewiston* v. *Granville*, 5 Pa. St. 284, citing the principal case.

STEM'S APPEAL.

[5 WHARTON, 472.]

GUARDIAN IS NOT BOUND TO SUE IMMEDIATELY upon an unsecured liability which has come to his hands as part of his ward's estate.

GUARDIAN MAY RECEIVE AN UNSECURED PROMISSORY NOTE as part of his ward's estate, instead of the cash which he would have received had he insisted upon it, provided that at the time that he received the note he had never had control of the fund which it represented. Thus he may receive from administrators a note executed by a debtor of the estate, to himself as guardian.

GUARDIAN WHO FAILS TO COLLECT INTEREST on a note as it falls due, is liable for its ultimate loss.

APPEAL from an order of the orphans' court, confirming the accounts of appellant's guardian, John D. Bauman. In 1832, Bauman received from the administrators of the estate of appellant's father a promissory note, executed by D. Heimbach to himself, which he indorsed as having been received on behalf of his wards. This note was payable within six months from date, and was given in renewal of an old note, payable to the intestate. No attempt was made to collect the note at maturity, nor at any time before Heimbach's death, in 1837. After the latter's death his estate was discovered to be insolvent, and but thirty-three per cent. was paid on the amount of the note. No interest was collected by the guardian on the note, from the time that it was given, to Heimbach's death. When the guardian received the note from the administrators, the latter offered to collect the money, if he objected to the note. There was much evidence introduced as to the financial standing and reputation Heimbach enjoyed during life. The evidence was to the effect that such reputation, at all events at the time that the note was received, was excellent. The ward attempted in this proceeding to charge Bauman with the loss incurred on the note, and also with the interest which he had failed to collect; failing therein in the lower court, he took this appeal.

A. E. Browne, for the appellant.

Maxwell and Hepburn, contra.

By Court, SERGEANT, J. This does not seem to be distinguished from *Konigmacher's appeal*, 1 Penn. 207.[1] There the duty and liability of a guardian as to the investment of the money of his ward was carefully considered by this court; and the rule is stated to be, that if a guardian has on hand money of

---

1. *Konigmacher v. Kimmel*, 21 Am. Dec. 374.

his ward, and puts it out, he will generally be liable, unless he takes a surety in the note. Wherever he has the fund and disposes of it to another, he must do it with strict and proper caution, as a prudent man would, and is seldom safe unless he takes security. But where the fund never comes into the hands of a guardian, all the cases make a difference: he is not bound instantly to sue in all directions. In that case the guardian, on the settlement of the administrator's account, received part in money, and took the administrator's bond for the residue, and part of it was lost. Yet he was not held to be thereby chargeable, as having been guilty of negligence. In the present case, likewise, the money never actually came to the hands of the guardian. He received from the administrators, on his ward's account, a new note of a former debtor in lieu of the old note, payable to himself, and indorsed as received on his ward's account. It is true he was told by the administrators that he might take that, or if he did not choose to do so, they would go and collect the moneys; and there is reason to think they might have collected it. But still the case is not the same as that of money actually put into the guardian's hands, of which he makes a new investment. For in *Konigmacher's case*, the guardian received the bond of the administrator, a new security, instead of the money which the administrator was liable to pay, and for aught that appears, might have been compelled to pay. I do not see any principle applicable here that did not apply in that case. At the same time I would not be willing to extend the decision further; and wherever the money came into the guardian's hands, or immediate control, would hold him strictly to the rule that requires him to take security. And even in cases of a continuing or renewed security, he may, under the particular circumstances, make himself responsible for laches in receiving it, or not collecting it in due season.

On the whole, we think the decree of the orphans' court must be affirmed, with the exception of the interest on this money down to Heimbach's death, which the guardian ought to have collected, and for which therefore he is chargeable.

Decree accordingly.

AN INVESTMENT BY A GUARDIAN of the ward's funds must in general be upon security, or otherwise the guardian will be liable for any loss that may ensue: *Lovell* v. *Minot*, 32 Am. Dec. 206, and note.

MILLER *v.* BANK OF NEW ORLEANS.

[5 WHARTON, 503.]

DEPOSIT OF FUNDS IN BANK TO MEET THE PAYMENT of a bill of exchange payable there, amounts to a tender, and will prevent interest accruing on the bill; but a withdrawal of the fund will cause the bill to draw interest from that time.

ASSUMPSIT. A case was stated for the opinion of the court in the nature of a special verdict. In February, 1837, a bill of exchange drawn upon defendants was accepted by them. The bill was "payable at the bank of North America." Defendants deposited in the bank funds sufficient for the discharge of the bill, and left them there until February, 1838, when they were withdrawn. In July, 1839, the bill was presented for payment at the bank, and payment not having been made, was protested. The question for determination was, whether the bill bore interest from February, 1838, when the funds were withdrawn from the bank, or from July, 1839, when the bill was protested for non-payment. The judgment below established that the bill bore interest from the time that the funds were withdrawn.

Emlen, for the plaintiffs in error.

Bayard, contra.

By COURT. While the defendant kept funds in the bank to meet the particular demand, he prevented interest, the deposit being equivalent to a tender. But when it was withdrawn and used by him, a case arose which very much resembles *The Commonwealth* v. *Crevor,* 3 Binn. 121; in which a sheriff who had deposited money in contest, pursuant to an agreement betwixt the claimants, but had subsequently withdrawn and used it, was held liable to the successful party for interest from the time it was taken out of bank. Even tendered money, subsequently used, bears interest; for a plea of tender without "always ready," and a profert of the money in court, is bad. It is a rule, with scarce an exception, that he who has derived a benefit from the use of another's money, shall pay for it; and such seems to be the principle of *Fasholt* v. *Reed,* 16 Serg. & R. 266.

Judgment affirmed.

———

WHERE A CORPORATION HOLDS ITSELF PREPARED TO MEET ALL ITS INDEBTEDNESS from the time that it falls due, and keeps under control funds sufficient to meet the debt from the time that it falls due to the time that payment is demanded, it is excused from the payment of interest during such intervening period, even though no funds were placed on deposit to the credit of that particular debt: *Emlen* v. *Lehigh Co.,* 47 Pa. St. 83, citing the principal case.

Ex Parte Elliott.

[5 Wharton, 524.]

Bequest of an Annuity Payable out of Lands, gives the executor a power to dispose of the lands by sale or otherwise, adequate to the performance of the bequest.

Power to Dispose of Lands is exhausted by a disposition of the lands in consideration of ground rent, and the right to release the rent is in him in whom the estate therein is vested, not in the person who executed the power.

Petition seeking the extinguishment of certain ground rents under the act of 1821. In 1825, Andrew Hamilton died in England leaving a will, of which it is unnecessary to notice more than the following clause: "To my beloved wife, Eliza Hamilton, I bequeath the sum of twelve hundred and fifty pounds a year, payable out of my estates in Pennsylvania in America; and after her decease to my only daughter Mary Ann Hamilton, together with all and every property belonging to me, wheresoever it exists." The wife was appointed executrix. The lot of ground from which the ground rent, now sought to be extinguished, issued, was part of Mr. Hamilton's estate, and was, under certain proceedings in partition taking place after his death, set apart to his daughter. In 1828 a private act of the legislature was passed authorizing the sale of the real estate of Mr. Hamilton, situated in the county of Philadelphia, by the executrix, either in person or by attorney, the disposition whereof was allowed by the will; the money realized from the sales to be applied to the trusts raised by the will. In 1830 the attorney of the executrix conveyed the lot of land now in controversy, by deed reciting the will and the act of assemby detailed above. The consideration of the conveyance was an annual ground rent of twenty-five dollars and sixty cents, to be paid to Eliza Hamilton, the widow of the testator, her heirs and assigns; the rent to be extinguished at the option of the vendees by their payment, at any time within ten years, of the sum of four hundred and twenty-six dollars and sixty-seven cents to Mrs. Hamilton, her heirs or assigns. Prior to the filing of the petition Mrs. Hamilton died, and Mr. Cadwalader was appointed administrator *de bonis non*. The petitioner in the present proceeding was the assignee of the lot whose sale is described above. In the petition it was asserted that Cadwalader, as administrator *de bonis non*, possessed no authority to extinguish the ground rent. The petition asked the direction of the court as to whom the money to extinguish the ground

rent should be paid, and asked that such person upon payment made should execute a sufficient release thereof.   Cadwalader demurred to the petition because of its denial of his
right to receive the money in extinguishment of the rent.

Cadwalader, for the demurrer.

T. I. Wharton, contra.

By Court, GIBSON, C. J   Originally, there seems to have been
a doubt whether a testamentary power to raise portions from
profits at an indefinite time, includes a power to sell; or whether
the amount should be raised by gradual accumulation.   But the
existence of an ancillary power to sell for payment of legacies and
debts, has never been questioned.   Subsequently, when not restrained by particular expressions, the courts have implied it in
all cases without regard to the purpose; on the ground that a
devise of profits is equivalent to a devise of the land; and such
is the law at this day.   Here, however, there is a direction to
raise the widow's annuity, not out of profits at all, but out
of the land itself; and even were there a distinction betwixt
profits and the land, the power of the executrix to sell would
still be a clear one.   Deriving this power from the will, the administrator succeeds by force of the act of 1836, only to so
much of it as remains to be executed; so that the question here
is whether it has not been exhausted.

We have but few reported cases on this head.   It is an undoubted principle that execution of a power can not be repeated;
but it may be entered upon by parcels and at different times,
yet all the parts, though existing separately, must make together
no more than one entire execution.   It can not be said that the
part of the power which regards the land out of which issues
the ground rent in question, was not intended to be executed to
the utmost, though the residue of the power might be subsequently used to dispose of other lands.   The disposition made
of the property, was an ordinary sale or exchange for a ground
rent—a disposition entirely within the scope of the power,
which was not barely to sell, but to dispose of the land in any
way to raise the amount required—and the will certainly gave
the executrix no power to sell a thing to be taken in exchange.
The purpose was answered by the conveyance, and nothing
more remained to be done.   For the purpose of extinguishment,
a power under the will was unnecessary; and the act belonged
not to the executrix, but to the person in whom the estate in the
rent was executed by the statute of uses.   This is not like the

case of a mortgage, which, in equity, is not an execution of a power to revoke, though it is so at law; because a mortgage being looked on by a chancellor, not as a conveyance further than is necessary to enforce it as a security, works no alteration in the condition of the title; nor is it like a conveyance to a trustee to pay debts, with an ultimate trust for the settlor: such acts are consistent with a reservation of so much of the estate as may be left, for a final execution of the power in respect of it. In the case of the mortgage, the estate is not supposed to have passed out of the mortgagor at all; and in that of the conveyance to pay debts, the trust is a resulting one, which changes not the character of the interest retained by means of it. Here, however, every portion of the title was parted with; and it is of no account that the ground rent taken in exchange for it, has been substituted as its proper equivalent by a private act of assembly. As the administrator succeeds to no power uncreated by the will, it is requisite that he have an authority by it independent of everything else. The legal estate in this ground rent, is vested by the terms of the conveyance, in the testator's daughter, who is still in her minority; and thus one of the cases provided for by the legislature has arisen. We are therefore of opinion, that we have jurisdiction of it; that the demurrer be overruled; and that the prayer of the petitioner be granted.

Demurrer overruled.

———

POWER TO DISPOSE OF LANDS, WHEN VESTED IN EXECUTOR: See note to *Lockwood* v. *Stradley*, 12 Am. Dec. 102.

———

ESTATE OF DAVIS AND DESAUQUE.

[5 WHARTON, 530.]

TAKING NOTE FOR PRE-EXISTING DEBT does not discharge the debt, unless it is specially agreed that the note is taken in payment.

WHERE THE SEPARATE NOTE OF ONE JOINT DEBTOR IS TAKEN, the *onus* is on the other debtors to show that it was taken with the intention of extinguishing the joint debt.

PARTNER INTRUSTED WITH THE SETTLEMENT OF A DISSOLVED PARTNERSHIP, may bind the partnership by borrowing money to meet its accruing liabilities, and by actually applying the money borrowed in discharge of such liabilities.

MONEY BORROWED BY A PARTNER will be presumed to have been borrowed for the partnership, which will be liable therefor, if it has been applied to its use. The principle applies as well after a partnership has been dissolved as before.

LIABILITY OF ASSIGNEES FOR BENEFIT OF CREDITORS ON SALE OF GOODS.
Where assignees of this character deliver goods sold at cash sale, without exacting immediate payment, they are *prima facie* liable for the loss
that may be occasioned by the vendee's subsequent failure to pay, and
can only excuse themselves by showing that the vendee's credit was so
good that a prudent person would have intrusted him with the goods
without first exacting payment.

APPEAL from an order approving of the accounts of the assignees of the estate of Davis and Desauque. Davis and Desauque were partners, engaged in the wine business. Their firm
was dissolved by mutual consent on the sixteenth of October,
1830. The matter of attending to the settlement of the partnership business was left to Desauque. Desauque, besides undertaking the settlement of the business, attempted to continue
it on his own account, until the sixteenth of November, 1830,
when, in conjunction with his former partner, Davis, he made
an assignment of the partnership property, and individually an
assignment of his separate property. This assignment preferred the claims of the assignees to those of the other creditors. The partnership was dissolved on the sixteenth of October,
1830, and the assignment was made on the sixteenth of November of the same year. During this intervening month several
notes given by the partnership to L. Desauque, one of the assignees and the father of Mr. Desauque of Davis & Desauque,
fell due, and were met by Mr. F. Desauque, the partner, giving
his notes for the same amounts; as the claims of L. Desauque,
represented by these notes, were preferred by the assignment, a
question arose between the creditors of the firm and L. Desauque as to whether these claims were not extinguished by the
notes of F. Desauque. It also appeared that subsequently to
the dissolution of the partnership, F. Desauque borrowed from
L. Desauque certain sums of money, which he applied in discharge of the partnership debts. For one of these sums he
gave a note signed with the firm name, and dated back as of the
time while the partnership existed. For the other sums he
gave no evidence of indebtedness. The creditors claimed that
these amounts could not be preferred by the assignment of the
firm property, being but the private liabilities of F. Desauque.
The accounts of the assignees, giving themselves credit for these
various claims, and others in the same predicament, were approved in the court below. The other facts appear from the
opinion.

Randall, for the appellants.

Keemlé and J. R. Ingersoll. contra

By Court, Rogers, J. It is generally true, that the giving a
note for a pre-existing debt, does not discharge the original
cause of action, unless it is agreed that the note shall be taken
in payment: 12 Pet. 59;[1] 6 Cranch, 264.[2] And although it is
decided in *Evans* v. *Drummond*, 4 Esp. 90, that taking a security from one of several partners, joint makers of a promissory
note or acceptors of a bill, will discharge the other copartners,
yet in a subsequent case, *Bedford* v. *Deakin*, 2 Barn. & Ald. 210,
it is held, that where one of three partners, after a dissolution
of partnership, undertook to pay a particular partnership debt,
on two bills of exchange, and that was communicated to the
holder, who consented to take the separate notes of one partner for the amount, strictly reserving his right against all three,
and retained possession of the original bill, the separate notes
having proved unproductive, he might resort to his remedy
against the other partners; and that the taking under these circumstances, the separate notes, and even afterwards renewing
them several times successively, did not amount to a satisfaction
of the joint debt. In *Evans* v. *Drummond*, it does not appear
whether the joint bill of exchange was given up; but in *Bedford*
v. *Deakin* the fact is stated, and is one of the grounds of the
decision. Whether taking the separate note of one of the partners amounts to an extinguishment or satisfaction of a joint
debt, depends upon the intention of the parties; and in the absence of all proof of a special contract, the giving up or the retention of the original security, will in general be a decisive
circumstance; for it is difficult to account for the fact, except on
the supposition that in the one case it was intended, in case of
need, to enforce the joint liability; or, in the other, to depend
altogether upon the responsibility of one of the joint debtors.
Where a joint debtor insists that the separate note is substituted,
and is in satisfaction of the joint debt, the *onus* is thrown upon
him; and to discharge himself from liability, it will be necessary to show a special contract to that effect; or that in addition to a separate note being taken for the amount of the debt,
the original bills were given up, and even when that is the case,
it may be rebutted by countervailing proof that it was otherwise
intended. The auditors have reported that the counter notes
or memorandums were retained by the creditors; and they were
warranted in coming to this conclusion, as the presumption was,
that they were in the possession of Lewis Desauque, the payee
of the bills, and that they did not come into his possession as

---

1. *Bank of United States* v. *Daniel*, 12 Pet. 57.　　　2. *Sheehy* v. *Mandeville*.

the assignee of Davis & Desauque. If the latter was so, it was incumbent on the appellants to prove it; which might have been readily done by the testimony of F. Desauque.

A partnership may be dissolved by the act of God, by the act of the party, and by the act and operation of law. This partnership was dissolved by an agreement, the particulars of which are not stated; Davis quitting the concern, leaving Desauque in possession of the store and stock, with a general authority to wind up the business of the firm. As a general principle, when a partnership is ended in any of the modes mentioned, no one of the partners can make use of the partnership estate, in a manner inconsistent with the settlement of the joint estate. The object of the association having terminated, it follows that one of the partners can not create any new obligation binding the firm; for after a dissolution, nothing remains to be done, except to arrange the affairs of the partnership; but until they are finally arranged, the connection between the parties subsists; and for this purpose, and until a settlement takes place, the partnership continues.

There are various ways of dissolving a partnership: affluxion of time; the death of one partner; the bankruptcy of one, which operates like death; or a dry naked agreement that the partnership shall be dissolved. In no one of these cases can it be said that to all intents and purposes the partnership is dissolved; for the connection still remains until the affairs are wound up. The representatives of a deceased partner, or the assignees of a bankrupt partner, are not strictly partners, with the survivor or the solvent partner; but still, in either of these cases, that community of interest remains, that is necessary until the affairs are settled: *Peacock* v. *Peacock*, 16 Ves. 57.

When a partnership is dissolved by agreement, the partner to whom is committed the power to settle the estate, may be limited, or the most full and ample authority may be given to him; but the question here is, as to the extent of the authority of the acting partner, in relation to the assets, in the absence of all express limitations or restrictions. In general to him is given all power which may be necessary for the final settlement of the concerns. He can not enter into any new obligation, but his authority extends only to those contracts which may be consistent with the trust. Is, then, the borrowing of money, for the express purpose of paying the debts of the firm, and the application of it to that purpose, within the scope of the implied power of the acting partner? And we are of the opinion, that where the credit is given in good faith to the firm, although the partnership may have been dissolved, and where the proceeds are faithfully applied to the liquidation of the joint debts, the creditor has a claim against the firm, and is not to be considered a creditor, merely, of the partner who negotiates the loan for the benefit of the estate. And to this implied power I perceive no plausible objection. Cases may be readily supposed, where the exercise of such an authority may be highly expedient —nay, absolutely necessary—for the preservation of the rights of the creditors, and of the partners themselves; as where money is borrowed to relieve the estate from the pressing demands of a creditor who may urge the sale of the assets, to the injury or the absolute destruction of the estate. It may very well happen that money may be raised by a pledge of the partnership credit, which could not be obtained on the credit of the acting partner. He may pay the debt out of his own private funds, if he choses; but when he has not means, why may he not avail himself of the aid of others, or obtain an extension of credit by a renewal of the note?

The case of *Abel* v. *Sutton*, 3 Esp. 108, is cited in opposition to this. If that case is to be understood as ruling the general principles, that after a dissolution of the partnership, the person who has authority to settle the partnership affairs can not enter into any new obligation, or create any new debt or liability, there can be no objection to it. But here there is no new debt or obligation created. The responsibility of the firm is precisely the same; and the only alteration is, as to the person of the creditor. With every respect to the opinion of the learned judge who decided that cause, I do not see the force of the reasons on which that case was ruled. Lord Kenyon says: "That it never could be allowed that any one might make another his debtor against his will; by that means a man's greatest enemy, by paying his debt, might make himself his creditor." But this is a misapplication of a principle, which, to say the least of it, is itself of doubtful weight; for it is difficult to perceive the mischievous and distressing consequences which would ensue from permitting the acting partner to change the creditor of the firm, without altering, in the slightest degree, their responsibility. In truth, there is but little in the rule which prohibits a person from making himself the creditor of another, by payment of his debt. The time has gone by, even if it ever existed, when this power could be made an instrument of oppression. Besides, debts may be purchased without the assent of a

debtor; and to all practical purposes the rule is of little value.
I do not, however, intend by these remarks, to impinge the rule,
but to object to its application. It is a fair inference from the
whole of this transaction, that the loan was made and the money
advanced on the credit of the partnership. In the absence of
express proof of a separate contract, the application to partnership uses of money borrowed by one partner, is evidence to
show that the debt is joint. And the principle applies, as well
after, as before the dissolution of the partnership: *Ex parte
Bonbonus*, 8 Ves. 540. There is so much justice in making the
firm which receives the money pay the creditor, *qui sentit com-
modum sentire debit et onus*, that we feel disposed to seize hold,
even of slight circumstances, in addition to the receipt of the
money, to raise the implied contract, and to infer that the loan
was made to the firm, and not on the credit of the individual
partner.

But conceding that the acting partner had not power to borrow money on the credit of the firm, yet, inasmuch as all the
money that was raised, went to the payment of the debts of the
firm, a subsequent recognition of the act is equivalent to a previous authority: *Duncan* v. *Lowndes*, 3 Camp. 478; *Vere* v. *Ashby*,
10 Barn. & Cress. 288. In the assignment, Davis expressly recognizes these as partnership debts, and provides for their payment; and this is nothing more than in justice he is bound to
do. Nor does it follow, even admitting that the debts were the
private debts of one of the partners, that they can not provide
for the payment, out of their joint estate, to the extent of his
interest in the assets, to the exclusion of joint creditors. The
doctrine of marshaling assets applies where property is seized
on an execution, or in cases of insolvency or bankruptcy, but
not to a case like the present.

It only remains to consider the first exception. The sale to
Stork was a cash sale, and if the assignees chose to deliver the
goods without exacting payment, it was on their own responsibility. When the debtor fails to pay, the assignees are *prima
facie* chargeable with the debt, and can only discharge themselves from liability, by showing that the loss arose from circumstances over which they had no control; or by proof that the
purchaser was of such undoubted credit, that no prudent person
would have hesitated in trusting him with the possession without requiring payment previous to the delivery of the goods.
Here the whole matter seems to have been referred to the discretion of the clerk, and no extenuating facts are proved which

can exempt them from responsibility. Stork was in such doubtful credit, that Davis & Desauque refused to trust him before the assignment.

The decree of the court, so far as it allows the assignees two hundred and ninety-two dollars and fifty cents, the value of the goods delivered to Stork, is reversed, and confirmed as to the residue.

Decree accordingly.

———

MONEY BORROWED BY A PARTNER ON HIS SEPARATE CREDIT is not chargeable to the partnership: *Willis* v. *Hill*, 31 Am. Dec. 412. But payment by one partner after the firm is dissolved, of the debts, with money held by him as agent, makes all the members of the partnership liable to his principal for the amount so laid out: *Brown* v. *Higginbotham*, 27 Id. 618.

NOTE, WHEN OPERATES AS PAYMENT OF A PRECEDENT DEBT: *Hutchins* v. *Olcutt*, 24 Am. Dec. 634, and note.

CASES

IN THE

COURT OF APPEALS

OF

SOUTH CAROLINA.

SIMS *v.* DAVIS AND TYGART.

[CHEVES' LAW, 1.]

PRESCRIPTIVE RIGHT OF WAY OVER UNINCLOSED LANDS can not be acquired by mere use thereof.

ASSERTION OF OWNERSHIP BY THE CLAIMANT of a right of way, or some implied admission by the owner of the soil that the right exists, is essential to create a right of way by prescription over uninclosed lands.

RIGHT OF WAY BY PRESCRIPTION CAN NOT ARISE unless there is evidence that the use was adverse to that of the owner of the soil.

ACTION for obstructing plaintiff's right of way. The way claimed was through the uninclosed ground of Davis, who caused Tygart to inclose the land. Verdict for plaintiff. Defendant appealed. The other facts are stated in the opinion.

Herndon, for the defendant.

By Court, EVANS, J. The plaintiff claimed a right of way over the defendant's land, along an old road which had existed for many years. The road was called the Vincent road, but when, or by whom, it was laid out, or how it originated, did not appear. It was proved that the plaintiff, in common with his neighbors, had traveled along this road for a period exceeding twenty years, and that the plaintiff also used it as a mill road, but not always for that purpose, as he frequently sent to mill in other directions. There was no proof that the plaintiff had opened the road, or that he had worked on it, or exercised any dominion or control over it, except as above stated; or that Davis, or those from whom he derived his title, had ever acquiesced in or done any act which could be construed into an

admission of the plaintiff's right of way over the land, except that
no objection ever was made previous to the obstruction for which
this action was brought. Under these circumstances we are to decide whether the plaintiff has acquired a right of way over the
defendant's land. If he has, then the verdict is right; if he has
not, then it is wrong, and must be set aside. I need not here
repeat what is so familiar to every lawyer; that, after a possession of land for twenty years, a deed or grant will be presumed;
and also that where a man has enjoyed and used a way over another's land for the same period, it will be presumed that he had
originally a right to do so, the evidence of which has been lost
by lapse of time. In matters of antiquity, the law substitutes
the possession, in the case of land, and the use, in the case of a
way, for the deed or grant; the nature and extent of which, in
both cases, will depend on the nature of the possession and use.
To confer a title in either case, all the authorities, both English
and American, concur that the possession and the use must be .
adverse to him who was the owner. This term, adverse, as applied to ways, according to our decisions in analogous cases,
means such use as men make of their own property; and must
be accompanied by such facts and circumstances as show that it
is claimed as a right exercised without the consent, and in opposition to the rights, of the owner of the soil.

It will be perceived from this, that I am not disposed to
adopt the opinion intimated in *Rowland* v. *Wolfe*, 1 Bailey, 56,[1] and
in *McKee* v. *Garrett*, Id. 341, that in no case can a prescriptive
right of way be acquired over the uninclosed land of another.
Those cases were, doubtless, decided right upon their own facts,
but the dictum above stated, in the broad terms in which it
is laid down, was never satisfactory to the profession, and may
be considered as modified by the subsequent case of *Smith* v.
Kinard, 2 Hill, 642, n. Since this case was argued, we have
carefully considered and examined it; and we all concur in the
opinion that a right of way may exist by prescription over the
uninclosed woodlands of another, subject to the qualifications
and limitations hereinafter stated. As a general rule, I would
say that the use of every such way is permissive, or held at sufferance, where the claimant has done no act showing that he
claimed the right adversely, and the allowance of the use by the
owner of the soil has been unaccompanied by any act which
shows a recognition, on his part, of the right of the claimant to
use the road without his permission. Most of the old roads

---

1. S. C., 19 Am. Dec. 651.

which, like this, lead from one public road to another, or from neighborhood to neighborhood, sprung up from accident. In the early settlement of the country, paths through the woods were made by repeated traveling along the same track. In process of time, by continued use, these tracks were enlarged into cart and wagon ways. They were convenient to the proprietor's neighbors and did not interfere with his dominion over the land. In the beginning, therefore, they may be said to have originated in the tacit permission of the owner. The use continued in the same way, no one ever supposing that a use thus commencing could ever ripen into a right. An adverse use must be something for which the owner may sue: it must be something hostile to his entire dominion over his property. In England lands are, generally, if not altogether, inclosed, and to enter on a man's land, is, literally, to break his close; but in this country, the fact is otherwise. Most of the land is uninclosed, and I can scarcely conceive it possible that the riding over such lands, and, especially, along a road which has originated in the implied assent of the owner, can be even a technical trespass, until the implied permission has been revoked. We feel the difficulty of laying down general rules to govern all cases, and it is not intended to do it on this occasion; but we think we may venture to say that no right of way can arise from merely riding or walking over a man's uninclosed woodland, unless there be some assertion of ownership by the claimant, or some act of the owner of the soil showing an admission that the claimant had a right. Thus, if the claimant laid out the road and used it for twenty years; or if he worked on, enlarged, or kept it in repair; or if the owner of the soil cleared the land and left a lane for the claimant's use; these, with acts of the like kind, would seem to amount to an assertion of a right on the one part, and an admission of it on the other.

The plaintiff's case presents no evidence of an adverse use, or of any admission of his right by the defendant; and it is the unanimous opinion of this court that the verdict should be set aside, and the motion for a nonsuit granted; and it is ordered accordingly.

————

PRESUMPTION OF RIGHT OF WAY OVER UNINCLOSED LANDS arises from twenty-one years' uninterrupted enjoyment: *Worrall v. Rhoads*, 30 Am. Dec. 274, and note containing citations of numerous authorities.

DAVIS *v.* RUFF.

[CHEVES' LAW, 17.]

WORDS IMPUGNING THE SOLVENCY OF A PERSON and affecting his credit are actionable, though not spoken in relation to his particular trade or business.

SLANDERING A PARTNER BY DECLARING HIM TO BE INSOLVENT, is no slander of the firm of which he is a member.

COPARTNERS NEED NOT JOIN IN AN ACTION OF SLANDER for words affecting the mercantile character, credit, or solvency of one of them.

MEASURE OF DAMAGES IN AN ACTION OF SLANDER is a question for the jury to consider relatively with that of malice.

VERDICT IN AN ACTION OF SLANDER WILL NOT BE DISTURBED, because the damages awarded were in excess of what the court in its discretion might have thought proper.

SLANDER. The words were charged in the first count to have been spoken of plaintiff as a merchant. The second count alleged that plaintiff was a merchant, and that the words were spoken of him without adding "as a merchant." The declaration averred special damage. The words proved were: "He is broke and can not pay more than fifty cents on the dollar, probably not more than ten cents. His note will not do; he is broke; I have known that for some time. He is regarded or reported as being insolvent." Defendant also had repeatedly stated that Davis had made an assignment to his father to the amount of seventy-two thousand dollars. Plaintiff was a planter, and was connected with the mercantile firm of W. B. Thompson & Co. Verdict for plaintiff for three thousand five hundred dollars. Defendant moved for a nonsuit, because the averment in the first count that the words were spoken of plaintiff in his capacity as a merchant was not sustained by proof, and because the second count did not contain this averment, which was essential. Defendant also moved for a new trial: 1. Because the words did not relate to the plaintiff in his character of merchant, and were therefore not actionable. 2. If plaintiff was a merchant, and the words were spoken of him as such, the action should have been in the name of the partners. 3. Because the damages were excessive.

Clark and McCall, for the motion.

Gregg and Player, contra.

By Court, O'NEALL, J. The general rule is, as stated in 1 Saund. 242, a,[1] note 3, that where the words are only actionable because

---

1. *Craft* v. *Botts.*

they are spoken of a tradesman, the plaintiff must aver and prove that the words were spoken in relation to his trade. But to this rule, there is one plain and well-recognized exception: that where the words are such as affect a man's credit, then it is neither necessary to aver, nor to prove that they were spoken in reference to the particular trade or business which the party was pursuing. The reason assigned by Starkie, Stark. on Sland. 184, is that of common sense: "A general charge, of a want of credit, necessarily includes the particular one, and is equally pernicious with a more precise allegation." Nor is there any artificial rule which prevents us from adopting this reasonable view. Indeed, all the authorities acknowledge and sustain it, with the exception of the dicta in Sergeant Williams' notes to 1 Saund. 242, a,[1] 3, and 2 Id. 307.[2] In these, it is manifest that the learned, and, in general, very accurate editor, did not advert to the distinction which Mr. Starkie has pointed out, and which seems to be well supported by very ancient decisions. In *Read* v. *Hudson*, Ld. Raym. 610, the plaintiff declared in one count that he was a laceman, and that the defendant, speaking of his trade, said, etc.: in another count he says that the defendant, *ex ulteriori malitia sua, de statu* of the plaintiff *colloquium habens*, said these words, "You are a rascal; you are a pitiful, sorry rascal; you are next door to breaking." The question arose on this last count. The court, in the absence of Holt, C. J., gave judgment for the plaintiff, declaring that he was a tradesman, and that, where the words were spoken *de statu suo*, it is equivalent to *arte sua* and to be intended of his trade. The words in that case imported a want of credit, they affected his condition, and hence applied to him in his trade as well as any other capacity in which he stood. So in *Stanton* v. *Smith*, Ld. Raym. 1480, it was held to be actionable to say of a tradesman, "He is a sorry, pitiful fellow, and a rogue; he compounded his debts at five shillings in the pound," though there is no colloquium of his trade. That would seem to be in point to this case upon the second count, in which, as in that, there is no colloquium about his trade. In *Cawdrey* v. *Highly*, Cro. Car. 270, these words, "Thou art a drunken fool and an ass, thou wert never a scholar, and art not worthy to speak to a scholar, and that I will prove and justify," spoken to a physician, were held to be actionable without any colloquium concerning his profession. The fact, that the words were in that case addressed to the physician, can not of itself dispense with the colloquium. The same words

1. *Craft* v. *Butts.*   2. *Todd* v. *Hastings.*

spoken of him would have had the same effect. They imputed a want of knowledge, which, like a want of credit, attached to the person and went with him in every business and affected him therein. After these authorities, it can not be necessary to pursue further the defendant's grounds for nonsuit: they can not avail him.

As to the grounds for new trial; the court held that, on the first, which was a question of fact, the jury had been properly charged, and their decision was final: and that, as to the second, it was no slander of a firm to say that one of the partners was broke. Such words went, not to the particular business, but to the general merchantile character of the individual. In regard to the damages, the court adhered to the opinion of the judge below, that, although they were much larger than, according to his view of the case, he would have found, yet if there was deliberate malice then the verdict was none too high; and that was a question for the jury, which should not be disturbed on a mere difference of opinion.

Motion dismissed.

RICHARDSON, EVANS, and EARLE, JJ., concurring. GANTT and BUTLER, JJ., dissented.

———

SLANDEROUS WORDS AFFECTING ONE'S BUSINESS CHARACTER: *Hoyle* v. *Young*, 1 Am. Dec. 446, and note, in which citations and references on this subject are made at length. See also *Lewis* v. *Hawley*, 2 Id. 121; *Elliot* v. *Ailsberry*, 5 Id. 631; *Burtch* v. *Nickerson*, 8 Id. 390.

———

EXECUTORS OF THOMAS *v.* ERVIN'S EXECUTORS.
[CHEVES' LAW, 22.]

STATUTE OF LIMITATIONS OPERATES UPON A CAUSE OF ACTION against an attorney at law for negligence in not procuring judgment to be entered, and execution issued, in an action, from the time when, through the failing circumstances of the debtor rendering a loss probable and calling for diligent action, the actual neglect in forbearing to cause judgment to be entered and execution issued occurred.

ACTION AGAINST AN ATTORNEY AT LAW FOR NEGLIGENCE is barred by statute of limitations, although commenced as soon as plaintiff ascertained definitely that the consequence of the neglect was a loss of his debt, if the negligence itself, which was the incidental cause of the loss, had not happened within four years previous.

DAMAGES DEVELOPING SUBSEQUENTLY TO THE ACT OF NEGLIGENCE complained of, do not constitute a new cause of action.

APPEAL. Ervin, as an attorney at law, received a bond from Thomas in 1819, executed to the latter by Wiggin, and brought an action for its collection. The case appeared on the docket for the term of court held in the fall of 1820. The docket contained a note of "judgment final," but no judgment was entered nor execution issued. Thomas soon after died. In 1829 Ervin again brought suit, caused judgment to be entered and execution to be issued, and made every possible effort to procure payment of the debt. But Wiggin had made an assignment a year previously, and upon a bill by the assignees a decree in equity was entered in 1836, ordering Wiggins' debts to be paid, in a certain order, and the plaintiff's claim, being only a debt in bond at the time of the assignment, was postponed to others and thereby lost. It did not appear that the executors of Thomas were aware, prior to the decree, that no judgment had been entered up previous to the date of the assignment. Plea, statute of limitations. The court charged that plaintiff's right of action was barred. Verdict for defendants. Plaintiff moved for new trial.

Law, for the motion.

By Court, EVANS, J. There are four periods in the history of this case, at one of which the statute must have commenced to run: 1. When Ervin neglected to enter up judgment in 1821; 2. When Wiggins assigned his property in 1828; 3. When Ervin sued Wiggins in 1829, in the name of Thomas, who had been eight years dead; 4. When it was fully ascertained, by the decree of the court of equity in 1836, that the debt was lost. The three first of these periods are more than four years from the commencement of this action in 1838, so the question is reduced to the inquiry, whether the statute commenced to run before the effect of Ervin's negligence was fully ascertained by the final decree of the court of equity in 1836. In the consideration of the case we must carefully distinguish between the act from which the plaintiffs' loss arose, and the effect which resulted from that act. The plaintiffs' complaint is that Ervin, as their attorney, so negligently managed their case, that they have lost their debt. It is the negligence, then, of which they complain. The loss of the debt is a consequence of the negligence, and these stand towards each other in the relation of cause and effect. If Ervin had entered up judgment and issued execution, the subsequent assignment of Wiggins, the suit of 1829, and the final decree, would have been wholly immaterial to the plaintiffs. They would have had a lien on Wiggins' estate, which nothing afterwards occurring could defeat. I think therefore we may safely conclude that the plaintiffs' cause of action was the negligence of the attorney, and that what occurred afterwards was but the consequence of that neglect.

If this case be considered in reference to authorities, the same conclusion will follow. I am not aware that the question has been settled in our own courts, but it has often been decided in England and in the other states of our confederacy. Thus in *Miller* v. *Adams*, 16 Mass. 456, which was an action against a sheriff for negligently making an insufficient return. The return was in 1808, and judgment the same year: in 1814 the judgment was reversed by writ of error on account of the insufficiency of the return. The question was, at what time did the action accrue of the plaintiff? The court say, " We are all of opinion the action accrued on the return of the writ into the clerk's office." So also, in *Short* v. *McCarthy*, 3 Barn. & Ald. 626, the attorney, who had been employed for the purpose, neglected to examine whether certain stock which the plaintiff was about to purchase, stood in the seller's name on the books of the bank of England. The attorney reported that it did, and, upon the faith of this, the plaintiff purchased. More than six years afterwards it was ascertained that the report made by the attorney was untrue, and the plaintiff consequently lost the benefit of his purchase. The court held that the statute began to run from the time of the attorney's neglect. The same principle was decided in New York in the case of *Troup* v. *Executors of Smith*, 20 Johns. 33. But the case which most nearly resembles this in every particular is that of *Wilcox* v. *Executors of Plummer*, 4 Pet. 172. A note of one Banks, indorsed by Hawkins, was placed in the hands of Plummer, an attorney, on the twenty-eighth of January, 1820. Judgment was recovered against Banks on the twentieth of August, 1820, but he proved insolvent. In February, 1821, the attorney sued Hawkins in the name of wrong plaintiffs, and was nonsuited in 1824. In the mean time the note, as to Hawkins, was barred by the statute of limitations, the action which had been brought being a mere nullity. Thereupon the plaintiffs sued Plummer in the circuit court of the United States for the district of North Carolina. The case turned upon the question whether the statute of limitations began to run from the time of the attorney's neglect to sue Hawkins, within a reasonable period after receiving the note, or at the time when the effect of this negligence was manifested by the nonsuit of the plaintiffs. The supreme court decided that the statute commenced at the time of the negligence. Between that case and this, there is a remarkable similitude in every particular. In both, the relation of client and attorney continued to exist until the debts were finally ascertained to be lost, and the negligence of Plummer was as continuous as that of Ervin.

By our statute of limitations, an action must be brought within four years after the cause of it has accrued; so that the question always is, when could the plaintiff have had his action? The answer is, whenever the contract has been violated, if it be on a contract, or if it be for a tort, then when the act was done from which the injury to the plaintiff arose. It may be, that the full extent of the injury is not developed, but that can not vary the case. Can it be doubted that the plaintiffs could have sued Ervin after he had neglected to enter up judgment, so as to create a lien on Wiggins' property, or that the jury might have given damages for the injury they had sustained? In the case of *Russel* v. *Palmer*, 2 Wils. 328, one Steward had been sued and held to bail. He was afterwards surrendered by his bail; but the attorney neglected to charge him in execution; in consequence of which neglect, Steward was discharged. Lord Camden directed the jury to find against the attorney for the whole debt, three thousand pounds. A new trial was granted, because, the action being for damages, the jury should have been left to find what damages they thought fit. On the next trial, they gave five hundred pounds, Steward not appearing to be insolvent, or unable to pay the debt.

From all the cases, I think it manifest that the plaintiffs' action accrued from Ervin's neglect to enter up judgment and issue execution against Wiggins. If the damage was the cause of action, then it would follow that a new action might be brought for every new development of damage; and the plaintiffs might have sued Ervin for the negligence in 1821, and again when the debt was jeoparded by Wiggins' assignment; and if in these two actions they did not recover the whole debt, they might sue again for the balance after the final decree. But the reverse of this has been decided in *Fetter* v. *Beale*, 1 Salk. 11.

Upon the whole, we are all of opinion that the plaintiffs' action was barred by the statute of limitations; so the motion for a new trial is refused.

———

MERE IGNORANCE OF EXISTENCE OF CAUSE OF ACTION does not affect its operation: *Smith* v. *Bishop*, 31 Am. Dec. 607, and note.

ONE ACTION ONLY MAY BE MAINTAINED FOR DAMAGES developing from a single wrong, although they may have arisen at different times: *Bendernagle* v. *Cocks*, 32 Am. Dec. 448, and note.

STUCKY *v.* CLYBURN.

[CHEVES' LAW, 186.]

EXPRESS WARRANTY INCLUDES ALL DEFECTS embraced within the language of the warranty, although of a nature so obvious to the senses, that the buyer might have informed himself of their existence by examination.

PURCHASER'S KNOWLEDGE OF EXISTENCE OF A DEFECT does not exempt the seller from liability upon his express warranty of the soundness of a chattel.

ASSUMPSIT on a warranty of a male negro sold by defendant to plaintiff. The consideration was seven hundred dollars. The bill described the negro as being forty years of age, and warranted him sound in body and mind. Evidence was offered, but not admitted, to show that at the time of the sale, the negro was over sixty years of age. It appeared that the negro was also ruptured when the sale took place, and was worth only from two to four hundred dollars, and that he died about a year after. The jury were instructed that if the rupture was so apparent that it must have been seen and known by the plaintiff, it was not included in the warranty, and the defendant was entitled to a verdict. Verdict for plaintiff for twelve dollars. Defendant moved for a new trial.

Withers, for the motion.

J. M. De Saussure, contra.

By Court, EVANS, J. On the first ground, I agree with the presiding judge, that the age of the negro, as set forth in the bill of sale, is mere description. It is not unsoundness; and the warranty that the negro was sound in body and mind, precluded the implication that anything else was intended to be warranted: Chit. on Con. 359; 1 Bing. 344.[1] The rule in relation to implied warranties is, that they do not extend to defects known to the buyer, and that no implication of warranty can arise where the defect was obvious to the senses; because such defects were, or should have been, known to him. A different rule, however, must govern in relation to express warranties, and especially those that are written; because the contract is to be construed most strongly against the warrantor, and because, for anything we can know, the warranty was given expressly to cover the existing known unsoundness. Besides, a written contract can neither be enlarged, nor limited by parol; and to admit evidence that the disease was obvious to the senses, and

---

1. *Richardson* v. *Brown.*

from hence to infer that the buyer knew of its existence, and consequently, that it is not included in the warranty as understood by the parties at the time, is in no respect different from the admission of parol evidence of an agreement between the parties, that the seller was not to warrant against the defect complained of.   In the one case, the general words of the warranty are limited by an inference from the facts; in the other, they are controlled by the parol agreement of the parties; and in both cases, the contract is altered, and effect given to it different from its obvious meaning on its face.   There are cases in which the facts and circumstances connected with the contract at its creation may be resorted to as a means of interpretation. But they are those, where, without it, the contract would be wholly inoperative, because it was unintelligible.   Of this description is the case of *Collins* v. *Lemasters and Lee*, 2 Bailey, 141. The general rule is, that a contract in writing is to be interpreted by itself, and especially if it has, on the face of it, a plain and intelligible meaning.

I have thought it necessary to say this much on the subject of express written warranty, because, it seems from the report, the presiding judge charged the jury that, if the rupture was so apparent that it must have been seen and known by the plaintiff, then the warranty did not cover it.   It seems to have been supposed that this case came within the reasons of the principles stated in *Wallace* v. *Frazier*, 2 Nott & M. 517.   The rule, as stated in that case (and the same is to be found in Chitty on Contracts), is, that a general warranty " will not extend to guard against defects that are plain and obvious to the senses of the purchaser, and require no skill to detect them;" and the cases stated are the loss of an arm, a leg, or an eye.   It does not seem to me that the fact of the buyer's knowledge does, *per se,* exclude the case from the warranty; for in the case of *Wallace* v. *Frazier* it was clear, the disease was known to the purchaser when he bought, and yet the court held the vendor bound by the warranty.   I should rather conclude that the defects mentioned are exempted from the warranty, not because they are obvious to the purchaser's senses, but because they are not cases of unsoundness.   We do not understand, either in legal, or common parlance, that a negro is unsound because he wants a leg, or an arm, or a horse because he wants a tail; although the capacity of the negro for work, and the beauty of the horse are both greatly diminished by the deficiency.   But, whatever may be the reasons for excluding these cases from the warranty, they do not apply to a clear case of disease.

It is said in Chitty on Contracts, 368, that unsoundness in a horse is any "organic defect, any infirmity which renders it unfit for use and convenience;" and the same definition, as to physical unsoundness, will apply as well to a negro as to a horse. The disease alleged in this case, was a rupture, or what is called hernia. It is frequently very obvious, but its effects on the value of the negro, it requires skill and knowledge to ascertain. Sometimes it is of no little injury to him, in other cases he is rendered wholly worthless. It is not a defect that it requires "no skill to detect." In many cases no skill or science can ascertain its effects fully; they are developed by time alone. It seems to me that this case is unlike the loss of a leg or arm, and that it can not be excluded from the general warranty against unsoundness, unless we adopt the broad principle that the purchaser's knowledge of the existence of the defect, shall, in all cases, exempt the seller from liability on his warranty in cases of express, as well as of implied warranty. For such a principle there is neither argument, nor authority.

For these reasons, it would seem that that part of the charge hereinbefore quoted was error, and, if the jury had found for the defendant, I should think a new trial should be ordered. But, as the jury found for the plaintiff, the error could not have had any influence on their verdict.

The contract of warranty is an undertaking to indemnify for any injury sustained by the breach of it. What. the damages were, it is not easy to gather from the testimony. None of the witnesses express any opinion of the extent to which the value of the negro was diminished by the disease. They say the price was much beyond his value; and it probably was so, even if he had been sound. Diminution of value by reason of a disease is, at best, but opinion, and with all the facts before them, the jury were as competent to form an opinion as the witnesses. We can not, therefore, say that the jury have found less than the injury sustained by the plaintiff.

Motion dismissed; RICHARDSON, EARLE, and BUTLER, JJ., concurring.

———

IN CASE OF WARRANTY OF SOUNDNESS, THE SCIENTER NEED NOT BE PROVED: *Beeman* v. *Buck*, 21 Am. Dec. 571, and note.

STATE *v.* CHAMBLYSS.

[CHEVES' LAW, 220.]

TAVERN IS A HOUSE LICENSED TO SELL LIQUORS in small quantities, to be drunk on the spot.

LICENSE TO KEEP A TAVERN INCLUDES THE PRIVILEGE of retailing spirituous liquors.

INDICTMENT for unlawfully retailing spirituous liquors. The defendant was a tavern-keeper, and had a license as such. Verdict of guilty. Motion for new trial.

By Court, EVANS, J. The ground assumed in the notice of appeal, asserts, in substance, that the defendant, under his tavern license, had a general right to sell spirits in small quantities to travelers, guests, and other persons. I will not stop to inquire whether he who abides an hour at a tavern is not as much a guest as he who remains a day, or a week; nor whether there be any distinction between furnishing spirits to a guest, as a part of his entertainment (and increasing the charge so as to cover the expense), and furnishing it to him separate and distinct from any other entertainment. The view which we take of the subject, renders such inquiries unnecessary and unprofitable. What, then, is a tavern; and what are the rights which a license to keep a tavern confers as to the vending of spirituous liquors? Johnson, in his dictionary, says, "a tavern is a place where wine is sold and drinkers are entertained; and Webster says, a tavern is "a house licensed to sell liquor in small quantities, to be drunk on the spot, and, in some of the United States, it is synonymous with inn, or hotel, and denotes a house for the entertainment of travelers, as well as for the sale of liquors." Johnson, for his definition, gives Shakespeare's authority. It is clear, from the writings of that poet, that such was the popular sense of the word in the time of Elizabeth, and Johnson's adoption of it, shows that its meaning was unchanged when he published his dictionary, in the reign of George II. The popular sense, in America, is clearly shown by Webster's definition. It will not be questioned that, if a word, having a clear and definite meaning in common parlance, be adopted into the law, it shall be construed according to its usual meaning; unless it appear by the lawgiver in a different sense. Let us, then, inquire whether the word tavern is used in our law in a different sense, or in a more restricted one than its popular meaning as above stated. I begin by saying what will not be controverted, that, at common law, the vending of spirituous liquors was not a franchise, and therefore required no license; and, as a corollary to this proposition, that until the statutes 5 and 6 Ed. VI., c. 25, the vending of wines and other liquors was as lawful as the selling of meats or grain, or any other article of traffic. That it is within the power of the legislature of this state to control, to regulate, and even to prohibit both the sale and the use of intoxicating drinks, it is not intended here to question. All that is meant to be asserted, is, that prior to that statute, there was nothing in the law which laid any restraint upon such traffic, and that it may still be carried on in all cases and under all circumstances that are not in violation of that, or of the subsequent statutes passed upon the subject.

At a very early period of the history of man, houses were set up for the purpose of vending wines and other liquors. These had, originally, their appropriate names, as inns, taverns, ale-houses, punch-houses, victualing-houses, porter-houses, etc. I should infer, from what is said in Viner (14 Vin. 439), under the head of "Tavern," that the original employment of the keeper of a tavern was to sell wine alone; but, in process of time, these originally distinct employments became confounded. The seller of wines began to supply food and lodging for the wayfaring man; and, hence, the word tavern, came to mean pretty much the same as inn, at a period certainly as far back as the days of Elizabeth. Be that as it may, in our acts of the legislature, the word inn, has been mostly disused. It is to be found only in the act of 1784, where it is manifestly used as synonymous with tavern. In the subsequent legislation on the subject, all other descriptive terms are discontinued, and all who are required to take a license are classed under the two heads of tavern-keepers and retailers of spirituous liquors. I have gone through the legislation on the subject, in order to show that inns and taverns are synonymous, or nearly so; and I now proceed to show that all legislation upon the subject has proceeded on the ground that a tavern, or an inn, was a house where, according to Johnson, "wine was sold and drinkers entertained."

The oldest legislation upon this subject, as I have before said, is the statute 5 and 6 Ed. VI., c. 25, by which the keepers of ale-houses and tippling-houses are prohibited from carrying on their business, unless permitted by the sessions, or by two justices, who are required to take recognizance against gaming and for good order. The statute 1 Jac. I., c. 19, recites "that the ancient, true, and principal use of inns, ale-houses, and victualing-houses, was for the receipt, relief, and lodging of wayfar-

ing people, traveling from place to place," and not "meant for
harboring lewd and idle persons," to " spend and consume their
money and time in a lewd and idle manner." This statute, following up the preamble, prohibits the inhabitants of the place
where such houses are situated, from resorting to, or "haunt-
ing" them, as it is expressed. The statute 4 Jac. I., c. 5, for
repressing "the odious and loathsome vice of drunkenness," is
to the same effect. The statute 1 Car. I., c. 4, prohibits the
keepers of inns, ale and victualing houses from suffering any
one to tipple in their houses; and the second clause extends the
previous acts of James I., to keepers of taverns and such as sell
wines and keep wine and victuals in their houses. It is obvious,
from the reading of these statutes, that an innkeeper was one
whose business consisted, in part, in vending spirituous liquors,
as well to the inhabitants of his town, or village, as to the traveler and wayfaring man; and, although the statute 1 Jac. I., c.
19, recites, that the ancient, true, and principal business of inns
and ale-houses was for " the receipt, relief, and lodging of wayfaring people," yet it is obvious, from the act itself, that, at that
time, a part at least, if not the "principal" part of their business, was to supply the traveler, as well as the inhabitants of
their town, with the means of "spending their money and time
in idleness and drunkenness."

The first statute passed upon this subject, after the settlement
of Carolina, was in 1694: 2 Stat. S. C. 85. It recites that the
"unlimited number of taverns, tapp-houses, and punch-houses,
and the want of sobriety, honesty, and discretion, in the owners
and masters of such houses, have and will encourage all such
vices as usually are the productions of drunkenness." It then
goes on to enact that no person "shall sell any wine, sider,
beere, brandy, rum, punch, or any strong drink under the quantity of three gallons, until he shall have obtained a license," etc.
In the next year, the same, in almost the precise words, was re-
enacted (Id. 113), with an additional clause fixing the price at
which wines and other liquors should be sold. It was again re-
enacted, in 1703 (Id. 198) and 1709 (Id. 336), and made perpetual in 1711: Id. 362. This closes the legislation of the lords
proprietors. One general remark applies to all these statutes.
They declare it unlawful to sell wines and other liquors without;
but leave it, as it was before, lawful to sell them with a license.
The inference is clear and unquestionable, that a tavern was
then understood, by the lawmakers, to be a place where wines
and other liquors were sold. The only legislation of the regal

government are the acts of 1740 and 1741–2. By the first, every keeper of a " tavern" or punch-house is prohibited from giving, or selling any spirituous liquors to a slave. The act of 1741–2, requires the justices of the peace to meet in their respective parishes twice a year, to inquire into the qualifications of " such persons as shall desire licenses to retail strong liquors," and to " grant certificates, or orders to the public treasurer for granting licenses as aforesaid."

The next clause prohibits the public treasurer, or receiver, from granting " licenses to sell spirituous liquors, or strong drink, or to keep a billiard-table without an order for that purpose, signed and subscribed by the justices so assembled, and being and residing in the parish where the person, or persons so licensed shall or propose to keep a tavern, or punch-house, or billiard-table." By another clause of the same act, the street, lane, alley, road, bridge, ferry, village, town, or other place, where the " tavern" or punch-house, or billiard-table is to be kept, shall be particularly mentioned and specified, both in the order and the license. Can there be a doubt that, in these statutes, taverns are spoken of as places where " strong drink" and " spirituous liquors" are sold?

The first act on this subject, after the revolution, is that of 1784. It provides that (except in the parishes of St. Philips and St. Michaels), " two or more magistrates for the respective districts of this state shall be authorized and empowered, on every Easter Monday, and the first Monday in August, to grant certificates to any person or persons in their respective districts, who may apply for the same, if in their judgments, they shall think such person or persons fit and qualified to keep a tavern, inn, ordinary, punch, ale-house, or billiard-table, or to retail strong liquors as aforesaid; and the person or persons to whom such certificate shall be by them granted, shall produce the same to the clerk of the court of the district in which he or she shall reside;" and the clerk is required " to grant a license under his hand and seal, agreeable to the purport of the said certificate, to such person or persons, who are to pay to the clerk one dollar for his trouble, and also the sum of three pounds for every license to retail liquors, and the sum of fifty pounds for every license to keep a billiard table." On this statute, I would observe that the certificate is to be, that the applicant is a fit and proper person to keep a tavern, inn, ordinary, punch, ale-house, or billiard-table, or to retail strong liquors, and the license is to be agreeable to the purport of the

certificate; so that he who applies to keep a tavern, shall have
a license for that purpose, and so of the rest.   But, in the subsequent part, where the amount to be paid is fixed, all these
various licenses are included under two classes, viz.: to retail
strong liquors, and to keep a billiard-table.   Now this must
mean that the keepers of taverns, inns, and ordinaries, are to
pay nothing for their licenses, or that they are included in the
general "license to retail strong liquors."   The latter, it seems
to me, is the obvious meaning, and is in conformity with the previous legislation on the subject.   The county court act, 1 Brev.
Dig. 418, gives to the justices of that court power to grant
licenses to keep taverns and public houses, and the justices are
required to cause a fair rate of meat, drink, and lodging, and
provender for horses, to be made and ascertained, and the
tavern-keeper is required to affix the same in the most con-
spicuous part of his most public room, for the inspection of
"all persons calling at the said tavern."   He is also required
to give bond to keep clean and wholesome meat, drink, and
lodging for travelers, and the usual provender for horses.   The
act of 1788 extends the jurisdiction of the county court, over
taverns, to all persons who shall retail any brandy, rum, etc.
Here, for the first time, those who are required to take out
licenses are divided into two general classes: 1. Those who keep
taverns; and 2. Those who retail any wine, rum, brandy, etc.
The act of 1781 makes no alteration in the existing law, except
to authorize the county court to grant licenses at any court held
in the year.

On the abolition of the county courts, their power was transferred to the commissioners of roads.   By the act of 1801 (1 Brev.
Dig. 420), they are required, at any stated meeting, to hear all
applications for licenses to keep taverns and retail spirituous
liquors, and are authorized to reject such application, or grant
such license, as to them shall seem proper.   Every retailer of
spirituous liquor shall give bond according to law, and every
person who shall obtain a tavern license, shall give bond with
security, to keep clean and wholesome meat, drink, and lodging
for travelers, etc.   In another clause, it is said that "all licensed
retailers who do not keep, also, taverns and entertainment for
travelers, shall pay fifteen dollars for their license, and shall not
retail less than one quart."   To me, the obvious meaning of
this is, that there are two classes of retailers, one who do not
keep taverns and entertainment, and another who do keep taverns, and are required by law to give bond and security to keep

clean and wholesome meat, drink, etc.; for the words "all licensed retailers who do not keep taverns," imply that there are other licensed retailers who do. The first class is limited to the sale of one quart; the other, left unrestrained in quantity, as all retailers had been before that time.

From a careful review of all these statutes, I think the conclusion is, that a "tavern is a house licensed to sell liquors in small quantities, to be drunk on the spot," and "denotes a house for the entertainment of travelers, as well as for the sale of liquors." This is the American sense in which the word is used, according to Webster; and, in looking into 2 Kent's Com. 595, it will be found that the distinction between tavern-keepers and retailers of spirituous liquors, as is herein stated, is in conformity with the laws of New York, and of most of the states of the union.

I have before said that, independently of the statutes which have been passed on the subject, a man might lawfully set up an inn, tavern, or ale-house, without a license. That is distinctly stated in 1 Burn's Justice, 22, and 14 Vin. Abr. 436; and I think it is very clear, both from the English statutes made of force, and from our own, that the sole object of bringing these establishments under the supervision of the civil authority, was to limit and repress, as far as practicable, the evils resulting from the use of intoxicating liquors. I do not understand that a boarding-house, such as is found in any town or village, or that the houses on all the great highways, where travelers are entertained with meat, drink, and lodging, are required to be licensed: 12 Mod. 254. These are, in some senses, inns and taverns, and the owners are entitled to some of the privileges, and subject to some of the liabilities, of such employment; but they are not the kind of inns and taverns that come within the spirit and purview of the license law. Such, I believe to have been the universal understanding of the law upon this subject; and in no instance that I have known, or heard of, has a license been taken out for any house of entertainment, except those in which wines and liquers were sold independent of, and unconnected with eating and lodging. The construction here put on our license law is in perfect consistency with the act of 1816, "the more effectually to prevent the pernicious practice of gaming," and the act of 1835, to "amend the law in relation to granting licenses to retail spirituous liquors;" and, so far as I can learn, it has been the uniform construction of the boards of commissioners of roads. They have always granted but two kinds of licenses, one called a retailer's, and the other, a tavern license.

Until within a few years, the commissioners generally granted tav-ern licenses to every shop-keeper who would give the bond required by law, to keep clean and wholesome meat, drink, and lodging for travelers; and this pernicious practice, in some of the districts, is continued up to this time, although there is no pretense that such persons keep a tavern in the proper sense of the term.

From what has been already said, we may fairly infer: 1. That to keep a house for the entertainment of travelers, or boarders, requires no license; 2. That if, to such entertainment be added the vending of spirits in small quantities, as is usually done at the bar of a tavern, then a license is necessary; 3. That a licensed retailer, who does not keep a tavern, can not sell under a quart; and, 4. That tavern licenses are as much under the control of the commissioners of roads as the licenses to retail. Contrary to my usual habit, I have gone into much detail in the examination of this case. I have done so, not because there is any intrinsic difficulty in the subject, but because of the deep and exciting interest of the questions supposed to be connected with it. As a judge, it is my duty to expound, not to make, the law, *dicere et non facere legem;* but, on this occasion, I have the consolation to know that there is nothing new in this opinion, nor anything which will interfere with that great reformation in the habits of our people which has already taken place.

It is the opinion of this court, that there was error in the charge of the circuit court, and a new trial is, therefore, ordered.

RICHARDSON, EARLE, and BUTLER, JJ., concurred.

O'NEALL and GANTT, JJ., dissented.

For note on what is a tavern, see *Gray* v. *Commonwealth*, 35 Am. Dec.

BENTHAM *v.* SMITH ET AL.

[CHEVES' EQUITY, 33.]

CONVEYANCE TO GRANTEE FOR LIFE WITH REMAINDER to such persons as he might by will appoint, or, in default of any appointment, to the heirs of the grantee, vests the title in the heirs of the latter, as against a purchaser at a sale of the premises under a foreclosure of a mortgage, executed by the grantee during his life-time.

POWER OF APPOINTMENT BY WILL given to the grantee in a conveyance for life, is not deemed to be executed by a mortgage by the latter to creditors, followed by foreclosure and sale.

POWER OF DISPOSITION BY WILL can not be executed by a conveyance of the premises by deed.

BILL in equity. Josiah Smith conveyed to W. S. Smith cer-

tain premises to be held during his natural life, and after his
death to such person as the latter might by will appoint, or, in
default of such appointment, to the children of the grantee.
W. S. Smith, being indebted to plaintiff, executed a mortgage
of the premises to secure the debt. The plaintiff purchased the
premises at a sale under a foreclosure of the mortgage, and received a deed therefor from the sheriff in fee simple. W. S.
Smith died intestate. The complainant insisted that the mortgage was equivalent to an execution of the power. Defendant,
who was the wife of W. S. Smith, claimed to hold in right of
herself and children, under the conveyance to her husband.

DUNKIN, Chancellor. This case is presented under two aspects. The interest of the defendants under the deed of Josiah
Smith, was, it is said, during the life-time of their father, a contingent remainder, which he might have barred by feoffment and
livery of seisin. It is then urged, that if the mortgage, foreclosure, and judicial sale are not equivalent to a deed of feoffment, yet that the defendants ought not, as against creditors, to
be allowed to avail themselves of this defect, but should be enjoined from setting up the deed of Josiah Smith, and be decreed
to join in confirming the title of the complainant. The application to this court supposes and admits, that the complainant has
no remedy at law. Will this court aid a purchaser from the
tenant for life, who has made an ineffectual attempt to destroy
the contingent remainders, as against the remainder-men? In
Dehon v. *Redfern*, Dudley's Eq. 123, this court refused to compel a purchaser from the tenant for life, to receive a title, admitted to be perfect, but which was intended to defeat the remainders. In the case under consideration, the defendants take
nothing by or through their father, the tenant for life, but are
purchasers under the deed of the grantor. It is not perceived
that any difference exists between their condition and that of
strangers who were remainder-men, and whose title this court
would lend no aid in disturbing: 1 Fonbl., b. 1, c. 187, n. (w).
But on the death of the tenant for life, the estate is limited to
the use of such persons, and for such purposes as the said William S. Smith, by any writing, in nature of his last will, executed, in the presence of three credible witnesses, might appoint.
Having the power to appoint to whom he pleased, it is insisted by
the complainants that he was bound to appoint the same for the
payment of his debts; and that the deeds are an equitable execution of the power of appointment, which this court will perfect in favor of creditors. Several cases were cited, in which a

party having a general power of appointment, was treated, in
this court, as the owner of the estate. And in *Townsend* v. *Med-
ham*, 2 Ves. 1, where the power was executed in favor of a child,
it was considered as a voluntary gift, and set aside in favor of
creditors. "Where," says Lord Hardwicke, in that case,
"there is a general power of appointment of a sum of money,
which it is absolutely in the pleasure of the party to execute or
not, he may do it for any purpose whatever, and appoint the
money to be paid to himself, or his executors, if he pleases. If
he execute it voluntarily, without consideration, for the benefit
of a third person, this shall be considered as part of his assets,
and his creditors have the benefit of it." And so in *Pack* v.
Bathurst, 3 Atk. 290.[1] But in all the cases the power of appointment is general by deed or will.

There was certainly something in what was said for the complainant, that he was entitled to every security which Smith
might have given him. But this assumes that the premises belonged to W. S. Smith. Now, originally, the fee was in Josiah
Smith. By his grant, W. S. Smith had an estate for life, with
a power of disposing of the inheritance. As is said in *Tomlinson* v. *Dighton*, 1 P. Wms. 271, "the estate limited being express and certain, the power is a distinct gift, and comes in by
way of addition. In *Reid* v. *Shergold*, 10 Ves. 379, Lord Eldon
holds the rule to be well settled, that where there is an express
limitation for life, with power to dispose by will, the interest is
equivalent only to an estate for life; and the power is to be executed *prima facie*, at least, by will." He adds, "he studiously
confines her power of giving the premises to a power of giving
by will, in its nature revocable in every period of life; the
power was given in that way, to protect her against her own
act; she had nothing therefore in interest, but for her life. In
point of authority, she might, by her will, have made a disposition, to take effect after her death." The lord chancellor concludes with some remarks which may not be inapplicable to the
argument in this case. "It is then said, if the sale is not good
as a sale, it shall be taken to be either something in the nature
of a contract, with reference to which a purchaser for valuable
consideration is to be aided; or an attempt, an act done, in or
towards the execution, in respect of which this court will aid
him. I do not stay to determine, whether it appears that she
meant to execute the power," etc. "The testator did not mean
that she should so execute her power. He intended that she

---

1. 3 Atk. 269.

should give by will, or not all; and it is impossible to hold
that the execution of an instrument or deed, which, if it
availed to any purpose, must avail to the destruction of that
power, the testator meant to remain capable of execution to the
moment of her death, can be considered, in equity, an attempt
in or towards the execution of the power." On the authority of
this, and some other cases, Mr. Justice Story states the rule,
" that if the power ought to be executed by deed, but it is executed by a will, the defective execution will be aided. But if
the power ought to be executed by a will, and the donee should
execute a conveyance of the estate by a deed, it will be invalid:" 1 Story's Eq. 185.

Upon the whole, I am of opinion, that it is a case in which
the court can not interfere, for the relief of the complainant;
and the bill must be dismissed. The complainant appealed, on
the ground that the mortgage by a party who was in possession
and able to make a good title, is a contract for assuring the
premises to the mortgagee, which the heirs of the mortgagor
should be compelled to perform.

The court unanimously concurred with the chancellor, for the
reason stated in the decree.

PALMER *v.* MILLER'S LEGATEES.

[CHEVES' EQUITY, 62.]

EXECUTOR IS ENTITLED TO RECOVER OF A RESIDUARY LEGATEE, remuneration for expenditures made by the former, without any order or direction
of court, for the benefit and improvement of the estate, although before
the interest of the residuary legatee vested in possession, the improvements, from unforeseen accident, were destroyed.

EXECUTOR IS ENTITLED TO RECOVER THE VALUE OF IMPROVEMENTS at the
time when the estate left his charge.

BILL in equity. Samuel Miller died testate. His will directed
that his whole estate should be kept together for the maintenance of his wife and children until his eldest child should come
of age. Then he devised a certain vacant lot in the city of
Charleston to his wife for life, with remainder to his surviving
children or their issue. Palmer was appointed his executor.
Palmer soon after married testator's widow, and, out of his own
funds, without any order of court, he erected certain buildings
on the lot, and had possession for over thirty years, when his
wife died. The residuary legatees claimed the lot, but Palmer
first claimed the value of his improvements. Pending the contro-

versy the buildings were destroyed by fire. Decree in favor of complainant. Defendants appealed.

Hunt, for the defendant.

By Court, HARPER, Chancellor. There are some facts connected with the proceedings in the cause which were not brought to the view of the court below. It appears that, after the filing of the petition of complainant to be reimbursed the expenses of the buildings, a suit, for partition of the estate of Samuel Miller, was brought by Ann E. Thompson against the complainant and the other defendants to the present suit. A writ of partition was ordered, and the commissioner recommended a sale of the real estate. In June, 1834, a sale was made, and the house and lot in question were bid off by the present defendants, at the price of three thousand four hundred and fifty dollars, who gave their bond to the master with a mortgage of the premises, to secure the purchase money. In May, 1835, an order was made by Chancellor De Saussure, that the proceeds of the sale of the house and lot then in the hands of the master of this court, should remain with him subject to the future order of this court. Some years after the sale, the house, in the possession of the defendants, was consumed by fire. The decree of the appeal court, of 1835, determined that the complainant was entitled to be reimbursed the expenses of the improvements, so far as they added to the present value of the estate, and that decree is conclusive upon the parties and upon the court. The decree still seems to us to be sufficiently supported by authorities, and founded upon the plainest principles of equity. At that time, the defendants were suing at law to recover possession of the property. By resisting the complainant's demand, their claim was to put into their own pockets so much of the complainant's money, as the improvements added to the value of the lot; thus gaining an inequitable advantage, against which the courts of law would afford no remedy.

There are cases in which an executor would be allowed the entire amount of his expenditures in improvements, although from some unforeseen cause, they should turn out to be of little or no value. As in the case put, of his having money in his hands, and real estate entirely unproductive. If, to all human reason, they were judicious and advantageous to the estate at the time, there is no reason why he should bear the loss, although, from unforeseen casualty, they should afterwards become deteriorated in value. But perhaps it is proper that, when the executor borrows or advances money for the purpose of making the improvements, and this has been done without the previous sanction of the court, the court should do what has been done in this case, and restrict his reimbursements to the amount which the improvements added to the actual value of the property, at the time the legatee is entitled to possession. Otherwise, the objection might be made, that the legatees might be brought in debt beyond the value of the estate they receive. Yet this is but hard measure to a trustee, who has acted judiciously and faithfully, where the devisee takes from his ancestor or testator, an estate which, altogether, is much more than sufficient to reimburse him. But when he is restricted to the actual value, it should seem impossible that the objection could apply. If the entire value of the property, and the relative value of the land and of the improvements, be truly fixed, there is nothing to do, but to sell the property and to divide the proceeds according to the rights of the parties.

It is urged that the estimate of witnesses is an imperfect method of fixing the valuation of property. It might be said, that if the evidence of value on one side is imperfect, it is the business of the other party to produce the proper evidence. In some cases, however, it might be proper to bring the matter to the test of experiment, to direct a sale, and then to divide the proceeds according to the best evidence of the relative value. The court can not do so now, in this case. The property has been sold, and bid off by the defendants, at a price within a trifle of the value fixed by the witnesses. This strongly confirms the judgment of the witnesses. I must suppose that they bid so much more on account of the improvements. Is it not plain then, if they are allowed to keep the entire property and pay nothing, they put into their pockets so much money of the complainant, to which they have no shadow of a claim? But the house has been burnt down. But it was burnt after the entire property had become theirs, not only by the will of the testator, but by their own voluntary act. Men must bear their own misfortunes. If there was any neglect, in failing to insure, it was that of the defendants. It would be as reasonable, if they had purchased the property of another, to claim to be relieved from the payment of their bond, on the ground that the property had been destroyed in their possession, as to claim a similar exemption in this case. The decree is affirmed.

JOHNSON, DUNKIN, and JOHNSTON, chancellors, concurred.

DUNCAN, EXECUTOR, *v.* TOBIN.
[CHEVES' EQUITY, 143.]

EXECUTOR IS CHARGEABLE WITH INTEREST ON THE ANNUAL BALANCE only of his accounts, when the form of his final account is such that payments on account of principal and those on account of interest are distinguished and separately stated, but if the form of the account be such that the executor has charged himself with the gross sum received as the proceeds of sales, not distinguishing between principal and interest, he is to be charged with the entire amount of sales with interest thereon annually, and the balance is to be obtained by setting off the interest so computed, against the annual disbursements of the current year.

EXECUTOR IS ENTITLED PRO TANTO TO THE BENEFIT of such of his accounts as are accurate and satisfactory.

MOTION for new trial. The opinion states the facts.

Glover, for the motion.

Patterson, contra.

By Court, JOHNSON, Chancellor. This bill was filed to settle the claims of the defendants (the legatees) under the will of complainant's testator; and, in the progress of the cause, the complainant was ordered to account for his administration of the estate. In stating the accounts, the commissioner charged the claimant with the amount of sales, with interest upon it annually, and made up the annual balances by setting off the interest, in the first place, against the annual disbursements of the current year. The complainant excepted to the report, on several grounds, and among others, "for that the complainant having passed his accounts with the estate annually before the ordinary, he is only chargeable with the final balance due on such accounts and with the interest on the annual balance. The circuit court referred the accounts back to the commissioner, with directions as to this exception, that if, as it assumes, the complainant can exhibit a regular account of the interest received, to charge him with it at the time it was received, and carry it into the account current of the year. If not, that the account should be made up on the principle adopted in the report. The defendants appeal from this order on the grounds: 1. That there is no full and satisfactory return of interest; and, in the absence of this, the mode adopted by the commissioner, is the proper and legal one; 2. Because the defendant can elect which mode he will adopt, and interest on annual balances has received the sanction of the commissioner.

The whole of the testator's personal, and I believe some, or

all of his real estate had been sold, and the complainant had
taken bonds, or notes, from the purchasers, and in his annual
returns to the ordinary, he charged himself with the gross sum
received, without distinguishing between what was received on
account of principal and what on account of interest, so that it
was impossible, without traveling through all the items and entering into minute calculation, to ascertain whether the interest
account had been accurately stated; and this was rendered almost impracticable by the number and complexity of the accounts.   This is the state of things to which the complainant's
exception to the report of the commissioner, on the grounds of
this appeal refer, and but for the necessity of referring the accounts back to the commissioner, on other grounds, I should not
have subjected the defendants to further delay; but would, in
this respect, have confirmed the report.   The uncertainty, too,
whether a correct mode of stating the account, which the solicitor
for complainant thought practicable, would not result favorably
for the defendants, was another motive, and I felt less reluctance, because, at the same time, a large proportion of what,
under any circumstances, can remain due to the defendants, was
decreed to be paid.

Parties interested in an estate have the right to know of what
it consisted, and how it has been used and disposed of.   For
this purpose, executors are required by law to make an inventory of all goods, chattels, rights, and credits of the deceased.
If sales had been made, they are required to return an account
thereof to the ordinary; and, from year to year, to render to
him an account of all their receipts and disbursements, which
ought to exhibit the time when, the person to or from whom,
and the account on which they were received or paid out, distinguishing between principal and interest; the correctness of
which could be at once tested by a comparison with an inventory
and account of sales.   And the same particularity, for the same
reasons, ought to be observed in accounting to this court.
The duties of one standing in the relation of executor or administrator, and the consequences of their neglect, are so clearly
summed up in the well-considered opinion of Mr. Justice Evans
in *Dickson, Administrator,* v. *The Heirs of Hunter,* delivered in
Columbia, at December term, 1836, that little remains to be
said on the subject.   "If," says he, "an administrator acts
fairly—if he renders his accounts according to law, to the ordinary, and exhibits by his returns a full and satisfactory account
of his transactions of the trust, showing when the funds were

received and how they were disbursed, and that they had not
been suffered to remain in his hands unnecessarily and unproductive, he has done all that the law requires of him; but if he
has neglected to keep it, and is unable to render a full, fair,
and just account of his administration, he must be charged
with interest on all the funds in his hands, including all that
were, or might, with ordinary diligence, have been rendered
productive."

The account stated by the complainant falls very short of the
particularity required by these principles, and although it may be
possible to test their correctness by a reference to the account of
sales, yet, from my own observation, such is the confusion in
which they are involved, and their extent, that even a dexterous
accountant, who was a stranger to the circumstances, could not
reduce them to order in a week, perhaps a month, and but for
the reasons before stated, and the belief that it might subserve
the purpose of justice, I should have sustained the commissioner's report. The complainant's exception to the commissioner's report, before stated, seems to have been founded on a
supposition that the complainant's returns to the ordinary,
were, in themselves, evidence on the reference before the commissioner. They are *prima facie* evidence as to the receipts,
for he can produce no other than that furnished by the inventory, the bill of sales, and the amount of moneys received, which
the opposite party would, of course, be entitled to surcharge
and falsify; but not so with regard to the disbursements; that
is susceptible of other proof, and must be established and
vouched according to the general rules of evidence.

The want of uniformity and frequent irregularity in the manner of stating and vouching accounts before the commissioner,
has suggested this, as a fit occasion to refer to some of the rules
by which these matters are regulated. According to the practice of the English courts, all parties accounting before the
master, are required to bring in their accounts in the form of
debtor and creditor, accompanied by an affidavit containing a
verification of the accuracy of the schedules in which are contained the details of the account; and if any of the parties are
dissatisfied with it, they may examine the accounting parties on
interrogatories. If the party asking the account sets up a
charge not admitted in the account, nor on the examination of
the accounting party, he must substantiate it by evidence;
when that is done, either by admissions or proof, the accounting
party must discharge himself by the production of receipts. or

other competent evidence: Smith's Pr. 111–114; and proper attention to these rules would relieve the court from much embarrassment in the examination of the accounts taken before the commissioner.

The appeal must be dismissed; but it may be proper to remark that, the order of the circuit court must be carried into effect, according to the principles before stated. If the complainant is able to exhibit a sworn account in such form as will enable the defendant readily to test its correctness by the inventory and account of sales, distinguishing between the sums received on account of principal and interest, then, and to that extent, the interest is to be set down to the account of the year in which it was received, and interest computed on the annual balance; if not, the account must be made up on the principles adopted in the report. It may happen that the complainant may be able, in some instances, to state the account fully and not in others; in that event, the rules laid down, must be applied to their appropriate classes of the items in the account—the first to those where the account is clearly and fully settled, and the last to such as are not made up in that manner.

DUNKIN, Chancellor, concurred.

Chancellor JOHNSTON had left the court before this opinion was prepared, and his signature does not, therefore, appear. He was understood, however, to concur.

PRICE *v.* PRICE.

[CHEVES' EQUITY, 167.]

SON MAY RECOVER FROM HIS FATHER'S ESTATE an amount equal to the value of personal services rendered in the life-time of his parent as overseer upon his plantation, when it appears that there was an understanding that the services were not to be gratuitous, and there was no provision made for the son in his father's will.

NEGLECT TO SUE UNTIL AFTER THE DEATH OF A PARENT, by a son who had rendered certain services in the life-time of the former, in expectation that provision would be made for him in the parent's will, by way of reward, is not such neglect as will bring the demand within the statute of limitations, so as to bar an action for its recovery.

BILL against Price, as executor of his father's estate, to compel a distribution. The defendant claimed two hundred dollars a year for eight years' personal service upon testator's plantation as overseer. The testimony showed that defendant went to live with testator, and to act as overseer of his plantation, at his instance and request. There was no stipulation as to compensation. The claim was referred to a commissioner, who reported in favor of defendant on the claim for fifty dollars per annum. Both parties excepted to the report; defendant, because the amount was less than he was entitled to; complainant, because the claim was barred by the statute of limitations. Dunkin, chancellor, rendered the following opinion:

The only question submitted to the consideration of the court is, the amount of compensation to be allowed to the defendant for services rendered to the testator. The defendant insists that the annual allowance reported by the commissioner is too small; and the complainants interpose the plea of the statute of limitations to any account or demand beyond four years prior to the testator's death. Cuthbert Price, sen., the testator, and father of the defendant, made his will in July, 1826. At that time his wife was alive, and all his children were settled off; the defendant, who was the last, having married in the December previous, and shortly afterwards removed about one and a half miles from the testator's place. It appears from the testimony, that the decedent was far advanced in years; and in a conversation with one of the witnesses, John Price, the old man said "he wanted Bird (the defendant) back, and he could hardly do without him." To another witness, Tobias Phillips, he said "he must have him (defendant) back to live with him, that his negroes were neglecting their business, and that he was too old and infirm to attend to the negroes and horses, and that he must have him, let it cost him ever so much." In three or four months after the defendant's removal, the testator moved him back; "and the defendant and his negroes, and the testator and his negroes, all worked on the old man's plantation together." At first, the defendant and his wife resided in a house about one hundred yards from the testator. In September, 1826, Mrs. Price, the wife of testator, died. Some time after her death, the defendant removed into the house with his father, and so continued to reside with him until the testator's death, in 1834. The defendant's wife died in September, 1828, and he again married in the fall of 1832. In a former report, the commissioner had rejected altogether, the claim of the defendant to compensation for the services of himself and his wife. On exceptions filed, the chancellor, at June term, 1837, reversed the decision of the commissioner, in respect to the allowance of compensation for the services of the defendant, and directed the report to be recommitted. The commissioner, in his last report, recommended an annual allowance of fifty dollars, and the defendant has excepted to this, as manifestly inadequate according to the testimony submitted.

A very careful review of the testimony has left on my mind an impression, the same as seems to have influenced the chancellor who pronounced the previous decree. It is a misapprehension that this is an attempt to convert into a charge what was originally intended as a gratuity. When Cuthbert Price, the younger, at the request of his father, gave up his own establishment and returned to take charge of the testator's business, it was evidently not the understanding of either party that his service was to be gratuitous. The uniform declarations of the testator show his consciousness of what was due to his son; his recognition of the understanding between them, and that he intended to provide liberally for him, as a compensation for his acquiescence in his wishes, and his conduct in his employment. It is not less clear, from the testimony, that this was the expectation of the son. If the son was content to wait for his remuneration until the decease of his father, and from any cause, the testator failed to fulfill his promise, I think, in the language of the chancellor, that so far from relieving his estate, "the failure of the father to perform his contract lays the strongest foundation for the interposition of the court, to remunerate the son." I think the testimony, too, well warrants the presumption of an agreement that, in consideration of the services to be rendered by the defendant, the testator would, at his death, provide for him at least as much as the management of his business was reasonably worth. Nor do I think that this view does full justice to either party. The son was married and had commenced life on his own account. The father's declarations to Phillips, show that he did not expect him to sacrifice either his plans or his independence for a trifle. Neither party believed that the son was to be placed on the footing of a common hireling, or to be paid as such.

It is admitted that the ordinary wages of an overseer for such an establishment, is about two hundred dollars per annum. As far as I can gather from the testimony, the defendant appears to have been well occupied, not only in the ordinary duties of an overseer, but in attending to other matters which are said not properly to belong to this station. But, it is said, the crops prove that he is not entitled to the wages of a competent and faithful overseer. This is not always an infallible criterion; nor, does it seem to me, strictly applicable to this case. No person was so

well qualified, or had so good a right to judge of the competency
of his overseer, or of the manner in which his affairs should be
conducted, as the testator himself.   His lands were much worn
—he had many small negroes—he was, himself, much advanced
in life, yet frequently attending to plantation affairs, and the son
went with his cotton to Columbia, or was engaged in wagoning
on his father's account, or in settling his other business.   Under
these circumstances, it may readily be conceived that large crops
would not be made, and were not expected; and yet that the
services of the son were quite as important and useful to the
father, as those of the most exacting overseer.   It may be remarked, also, that the affairs of the testator continued to improve.   He added another tract of land to his farm, and paid
for a family of negroes which he had purchased.   When it is
considered that the defendant had abandoned his own arrangements, and devoted to the service of his father eight of the best
years of his life, I think it is in fulfillment of the uniform understanding, that a liberal remuneration should be allowed.   Some
of the witnesses, who had frequent opportunities of observing
the conduct of the defendant, estimated the value of his services
during the several years at from two hundred to three hundred
dollars.   All the witnesses except one, I think, agreed that the
ordinary wages to an overseer of such a force as that of the testator, is two hundred dollars.   It has been seen that the duties
and the services of the son were not confined to the employment
of an ordinary overseer.

When, in 1834, the defendant expressed a desire to remove to
the west, he was dissuaded by the testator, who then repeated
the assurances of full satisfaction for his services.   On the whole,
I think, that these engagements of the testator are fulfilled in
moderate measure, when his estate pays to the defendant no more
than he would himself have been compelled to pay to an overseer, who had faithfully superintended his plantation.   The view
I have taken, disposes of the statute of limitations.   It was not
the understanding of the parties, that the defendant should be
compensated until the death of the testator, and the right did
not accrue until that event.

It is ordered and decreed that the case be recommitted to the
commissioner, with instructions to reform his report by allowing
to the defendant credit as of the date of the sales bill, for the
sum due for his services while in the employment of the testator,
estimating the same at the rate of two hundred dollars per
annum.

From the decree made in accordance with this opinion, an appeal was taken to this court, where the opinion of the court as follows was pronounced by

. DUNKIN, Chancellor.   The court sees no cause to revise either of the decrees which are the subject-matter of appeal. Nor is it perceived that the supposed discrepancy exists.   The decree of June, 1838, merely fixes the amount at which the defendant's services should be estimated.   If the testator furnished any supplies to the defendant, not usually allowed to an overseer, or paid his accounts, there is nothing in the decree of June, 1838, which would prevent the commissioner, in making up the account, from discounting (in the language of the former decree), such advances from the annual sum at which the services are directed to be estimated.

The decrees are affirmed, and the appeal dismissed.

JOHNSON, HARPER, and JOHNSTON, chancellors, concurred.

CASES

IN THE

SUPREME COURT

OF

TENNESSEE.

CROSTHWAIT *v.* ROSS.

[1 HUMPHREYS, 23.]

POWER OF A COPARTNER TO BIND HIS ASSOCIATES extends to such matters only as, in the ordinary course of dealing, have reference to the business in which the firm is engaged.

PRESUMPTION REGARDING ONE WHO DEALS WITH A PARTNER in a matter not within the scope of the partnership is, that such person dealt with the partner on the latter's private and individual account, notwithstanding the partnership name was used.

PARTNERSHIP FOR THE PRACTICE OF MEDICINE does not authorize one of the partners to bind the firm by a note given in the name of the partnership for money borrowed for the private and individual use of the partner by whom the note was given.

ERROR. Hartwell and Crosthwait formed a copartnership for the purpose of practicing medicine. It was agreed that the partnership should be entirely equal, the profits of the business to be equally shared, and its expenses and debts equally borne. After the business had continued in this manner for over a year, Hartwell executed the following note:

"$350. Four months after date we promise to pay to William W. Ross or order, three hundred and fifty dollars, at the Planters' bank of Tennesse, value received. Witness our hands this fourteenth day of May, 1835.

"HARTWELL & CROSTHWAIT."

The note was indorsed by Ross. The opinion states the facts. Verdict and judgment for plaintiff.

Edwin A. Keeble and *James W. Campbell,* for the plaintiff in error.

Charles Ready, for the defendant.

By Court, TURLEY, J.   This is an action brought by the defendant in error to recover judgment against the plaintiff upon a note for the sum of three hundred and fifty dollars.   This note was executed by one Alfred Hartwell, who was a partner in the practice of physic with George D. Crosthwait, the plaintiff in error; it was an accommodation note for his own benefit, and not for the use of the firm.   The note was discounted in bank upon the indorsement of Ross, the defendant, and the proceeds applied by Hartwell to his own use.   The indorser took up the note at maturity, and has brought this suit to charge Crosthwait as maker, to which he pleaded *non est factum*, which, under the charge of the court below, was found against him, upon which the writ of error is prosecuted.   Several questions are presented for the consideration of the court, only one of which we think necessary to examine, as upon that the responsibility of the plaintiff in error rests, and that is as to the powers of Hartwell to make his copartner, Crosthwait, liable upon a promissory note for money received by himself and made for his own accommodation.

This question necessarily involves the power of partners to bind each other, and the extent to which it may be carried. Without entering into the question of what constitutes limited and general partnership, and what is the distinction between them as to the liabilities of the partners, which, as we think, has nothing to do with the case under consideration, we proceed to investigate the subject upon the grounds upon which we think it rests.   For this purpose, we think partners may be classed: 1. Partners in trade.   2. Partners in occupation or employment. Chancellor Kent, in the third volume of his commentaries, page 28, says: "It is not essential to a legal partnership that it be confined to a commercial business.   It may exist between attorneys, conveyancers, mechanics, artisans, or farmers, as well as between merchants or bankers."   Now the question is, how far one partner has the right, by his individual contract, to bind his copartner?   We think that when the question is properly understood there is no conflict whatever between the authorities as applicable to partners in trade and partners in occupation or employment.   A partner in either case can bind his copartner in a matter which, according to the usual course of dealing, has reference to business transacted by the firm: See 3 Kent, 41, and the numerous cases there cited in support of this proposition.   But, on the contrary, if a person deals with a partner in a matter not within the scope of the partnership, the intend-

ment of the law will be that he deals with him on his private
account, notwithstanding the partnership name be used: 3 Kent,
45; 4 Johns. 277, 278;[1] 16 Id. 38;[2] 19 Id. 154;[3] 6 Wend. 529;[4]
5 Mason, 157.[5] Therefore it is that partners in trade, whose
business is buying and selling, or of whose business this constitutes an important item, may make, draw, and indorse promissory notes and bills of exchange, and although one of the firm
may abuse his trust for his individual benefit, yet the copartner
shall be bound, unless the person contracted with knew at the
time that it was not done in good faith; and this, because in
such a business the use of such securities is not only considered
necessary, but is well sanctioned by commercial usage.

But the question recurs, what kind of contract is in the usual
course of dealing, and within the scope of the partnership? It
is not necessary, nor do we design to argue or determine this
question except in relation to the case now under consideration,
which is a case of partners in occupation. In the case of *Liv-*
ingston v. *Rosewell,* 4 Johns. 251[6] [4 Am. Dec. 273], it is held
that where there are partners engaged in a sugar refinery, if one
purchase a lot of brandy and executes a note for the payment
thereof in the name of the firm, it is not obligatory upon the
firm because not in the usual course of trade of the firm. In
the case of *Dickinson* v. *Valpray,* 21 Eng. Com. L. 41,[7] it is held
that in the case of an ordinary trading partnership the law implies the power of one partner to bind another by drawing and
accepting bills, because the drawing and accepting bills is necessary for the purpose of carrying on a trading partnership, but
that it is not generally necessary for a mining company, and
that therefore in such a case the law will not imply the power of
one of the company to bind the others by such contracts.

Now to apply these principles to the case under consideration.
Crosthwait and Hartwell were partners in the practice of physic;
this is an occupation, and they may mutually bind each other
for all things properly belonging or necessary to be used by
them in this vocation, such as medicines, surgical instruments,
et ejusdem generis; but the drawing of bills or the making of
notes is no more within the scope of their partnership, in fact
not so much so, as was the buying of the brandy by the partner
in the sugar refinery, or the drawing of the bills in the mining
company. If the note in this case had been executed for any-

---

1. *Livingston* v. *Roosevelt;* S. C., 4 Am. Dec. 273.   4. *Vallett* v. *Parker,* 6 Wend. 615.
2. *Dob* v. *Halsey;* S. C., 8 Am. Dec. 293.   5. *Osborne* v. *Benson.*
3. *Foote* v. *Sabin;* S. C., 10 Am. Dec. 208.   6. *Livingston* v. *Roosevelt,* 4 Johns. 251.
7. *Dickinson* v. *Valpy,* 21 Eng. Com. L. 128.

thing for which a firm of physicians had use, as such the firm would have been bound though the member who drew it had designed at the time to appropriate it to his own use and did so, unless the person contracted with knew of his intention at the time. But money is not an article for which such a firm has use directly, though it may indirectly, but if it has it must be raised by the individuals comprising the firm, and not by one member thereof, unless he be authorized by the others so to do independent of any right arising from the partnership.

We therefore think the judgment of the circuit court is erroneous, and must be reversed, and the cause remanded for a new trial.

———

UNAUTHORIZED ACTS OF A COPARTNER will not bind the firm unless there is evidence of assent; and such evidence must be more than slight and inconclusive: *Wilson* v. *Williams*, 28 Am. Dec. 518, and note.

CITED AND AFFIRMED upon the point that a partner has no power to bind the partnership by a contract not made for its benefit, and not legitimately within the scope of its usual and ordinary business, in *Whaley* v. *Moody*, 2 Humph. 495; *Ferguson* v. *Shepherd*, 1 Sneed, 254; *Venable* v. *Lavick*, 2 Head, 351.

———

ELLEDGE *v.* TODD.

[1 HUMPHREYS, 43.]

VERDICT IS VOID FOR IRREGULARITY where the jury, being unable to agree as to the amount for which the verdict should be returned, proceeded to allow each juror to write down an amount according to his judgment, and returned a verdict for one twelfth of the sum of the amounts so written.

AFFIDAVIT OF JUROR IS ADMISSIBLE TO IMPEACH a verdict obtained by a resort to unjust or unreasonable methods.

ERROR. The action was trover for a horse and wagon. Verdict for plaintiff. Defendant moved for a new trial, and in support thereof produced the affidavit of one of the jurors who had been sworn in the case, in which it was stated that upon retiring to consider their verdict, it was found that the jury were divided and no agreement could be had; that in order to obtain a verdict, each juror wrote down such amount as he thought proper, and by general agreement the verdict was returned for a sum represented by the aggregate of the several amounts divided by twelve. It was previously understood that this amount, whatever it should be, would constitute the sum for which the verdict should be rendered. Affiant deposed that no verdict could have been obtained in any other manner. The court refused to set aside the verdict. Defendant appealed.

Ready, for the plaintiff in error.

H. M. Burton, for the defendant.

By Court, TURLEY, J.   The question in this case is presented
upon the correctness of the opinion of the court below in dis-
allowing a new trial upon the affidavit of a juror stating in substance, that the jury, for the purpose of ascertaining what should
be the amount of damages assessed, agreed among themselves
that each member of their body should set down a sum, according with his own judgment, and that the aggregate amount
should be divided by twelve and the result returned as their
verdict, which was done. This affidavit was admissible, its
truth is not contradicted, and we think that it furnishes a legal
ground upon which a new trial should have been granted. In
the case of *John Baker* v. *Thomas Bennett,*[1] determined by this
court at Knoxville, in July, 1839, it is held " that a jury shall
not agree among themselves that each shall specify the amount
for which he is willing to find a verdict, divide the whole by
twelve, and return the sum thus produced as the amount of their
deliberations, because it is in the nature of gambling for a verdict, and places it in the power of one juror to make the amount
unreasonably great or small." This case is in point, although
in it the new trial was refused, because it was thought that no
such agreement had been made by the jury.

Reverse the cause, and let it be remanded for a new trial.

AFFIDAVIT OF JUROR TO IMPEACH VERDICT: See *Crawford* v. *State,* 24 Am.
Dec. 467, and note, in which this question is discussed. An examination of
Bennett v. *Baker,* reported *post,* will show the restriction which has been
affixed to the rule declared in the principal case, in the same state. In that
case a juror, without the knowledge of others on the jury, took the different
amounts suggested, and having added them together, and ascertained the
amount of one twelfth of their sum, proposed that the verdict should be returned for that sum, which was agreed to. The affidavit of a juror was held
not admissible to impeach the verdict. The distinction drawn between that
and the principal case, is very clearly set forth in the opinion. The cases
form an interesting comparison. Cited and distinguished for the same reasons stated above, in *Johnson* v. *Perry,* 2 Humph. 574; *Harvey* v. *Jones,* 3
Id. 157. Cited also in *Memphis and Charleston R. R. Co.* v. *Pillow,* 9 Heisk.
254, to show that it is error for a jury to allow three of their number to fix
the amount of the verdict, and that a verdict so obtained is void. Upon the
second point the principal case is cited as authority in *Norris* v. *State,* 3
Humph. 332, deciding that a new trial can not be granted on the affidavit of
jurors that they misunderstood the charge of the court.

---

1. S. C., *post,* 655.

WILKS v. FITZPATRICK.

[1 HUMPHREYS, 54.]

CHANCERY WILL MAKE PROVISION FOR THE WIFE OUT OF A LEGACY or distributive share of an estate to which she is entitled, before allowing her husband to reduce it to possession.

EQUITY OF THE WIFE IS NOT EXTINGUISHED BY AN ASSIGNMENT OF HER LEGACY, in which she joins her husband.

WIFE IS NOT BOUND BY HER TRANSFER OF A LEGACY due her, unless she be privily examined in court touching her consent.

WIFE MAY SET UP HER EQUITY TO DEFEAT A TRANSFER of her legacy by herself and husband.

APPEAL. The facts are stated in the opinion.

Frierson, for the complainant.

Cahal and Pillow, for the defendant.

By Court, GREEN, J. This bill is filed by one of the executors of John Wilks, deceased, against his co-executor and the legatees, for a settlement and final adjustment of the estate of his testator, according to the rights of the parties. Morgan Fitzpatrick, who is made defendant, claims the legacy of Polly Dearin (who, together with her husband, John Dearin, are also defendants), by virtue of a sale and transfer to him signed and sealed by John Dearin and his wife, Polly, on the twentieth of February, 1836. Polly Dearin insists that she can not be prejudiced by the execution of the transfer to Fitzpatrick, and that she is in equity entitled to a settlement, for her use, of the legacy due from her father's estate. The court decreed the portion of Polly Dearin to her, disregarding the transfer to Fitzpatrick. Fitzpatrick alone appealed to this court. It is well settled, that if a husband, or any person claiming in his right, seeks to reduce into his possession the wife's legacy or distributive share, a court of chancery will make a provision out of it for her: Clancy on Rights, 441, *et seq.;* Meigs, 559;[1] 2 Story's Eq. 1403, *et seq.* But it is said that in this case the wife has assigned away her interest. The assignment produced can have no obligatory force upon the wife, as it was made without those solemnities courts of equity require in such cases. In order to bind a wife by a transfer of a legacy due her she must be privily examined in court touching her consent to such transfer: Clancy on Rights, 444; 4 Hayw. 19;[2] 3 Cow. 599;[3] 3 Ves. 469;[4] 4 Id. 18.[5] It is insisted she was guilty of a fraud in joining

---

1. *Dearin v. Fitzpatrick.*   2. *McElhatton v. Howell.*   3. *Udall v. Kenney.*
4. *Langham v. Nenny.*   5. *Macaulay v. Philips.*

her husband in the transfer and then setting up her equity against it. If this were so, the wife never could be protected in her rights; and all her deeds, while covert, though void in law, would be set up against her on the ground of fraud. But there is no pretense for the charge of fraud; no misrepresentation was made to Fitzpatrick by her, and he was bound to know what legal rights he acquired by the transfer, and what were the rights the law permitted him to set up against it. The decree will be affirmed, with the exception that the share of Mrs. Dearin must be paid to a trustee for her use. The costs will be paid as directed in the decree below, and the defendant, Fitzpatrick, will pay the costs of this court.

WIFE'S EQUITY: In *Duvall* v. *Farmers' Bank*, 23 Am. Dec. 558, and the note thereto, this subject is fully discussed and numerous authorities cited.

THE PRINCIPAL CASE IS CITED and approved in the following cases: Upon the general principle decided, that the husband can not bar the wife's equity by an assignment of her legacy or of a chattel in which she is entitled to an estate in remainder: *Farnsworth* v. *Lemons*, 11 Humph. 140; but the proceedings to avoid the assignment and enforce the right of the wife in equity to a settlement, must be commenced in her life-time: *McCaleb* v. *Critchfield*, 5 Heisk. 288. Valid assignment of her interest, divested of her equity, may be made by the wife through a privy examination before the court or its commissioner: *Coppedge* v. *Threadgill*, 3 Sneed, 577. A wife who has suffered her personalty to be taken and invested by her husband, with no stipulation as to the use to be made of it, has no claim to land purchased with the fund by the husband in his own name: *Jennings* v. *Jennings*, 2 Heisk. 283.

PARKER AND COLLIER *v.* SWAN.

[1 HUMPHREYS, 80.]

JUSTICE'S JUDGMENT IN AN ACTION IN WHICH THERE WERE SEVERAL DEFENDANTS, is valid as a judgment against them all, though the indorsement upon the warrant indicated merely that the judgment was "in favor of plaintiff," without specifying whether it was against all the defendants, or only a portion of them.

DESCRIPTION OF LAND IN A LEVY IS SUFFICIENT, if it describe the land in general language, so that by reasonable intendment, it may be identified and connected with the sale and deed.

TITLE OF PURCHASER AT A SALE UNDER EXECUTION, upon a justice's judgment, relates to the date of the levy.

EJECTMENT. The facts are stated in the opinion.

Ready, for the plaintiffs in error.

Keeble, for the defendant.

By Court, GREEN, J. This action of ejectment was brought by the defendant in error to recover a tract of land which he claims by virtue of sheriff's deed, reciting that the same had been levied on and sold as the property of John Doak. The record of the judgment under which the sale was made shows, that on the sixth of May, 1830, two suits were commenced by warrant before a justice of the peace, wherein Moses Swan was plaintiff, and William Blakely, Moses Ashbrooks, and John Doak were defendants. The warrants were executed and returned to the justice of the peace, who rendered judgment for the plaintiffs, indorsing it on the warrants in the following words: "May 7, 1830: Judgment in favor of the plaintiff for sixty-one dollars and eighty-three cents and costs;" execution was issued by the justice and was levied on the land in dispute the twelfth of May, 1830, and at May term of the county court of Rutherford an order of sale was made, a *venditioni exponas* issued, the seventy-acre tract of land was sold to Swan, and a deed, dated the fifth of April, 1831, was executed to him by the sheriff, which was duly acknowledged, and on the twenty-first of April, 1831, was registered according to law. The indorsement of the levy of the justice's execution upon this tract of land is in these words: "Levied on the right, title, claim, and interest that John Doak has in and to seventy acres of land lying on the waters of the west fork of Stone's river; no personal property to be found." The defendants claimed title by virtue of a deed from Doak to Isaac Killough for one hundred and forty-eight acres, and by mesne conveyance from him. The deed from Doak to Killough is dated fifth May, 1830, and registered fifteenth July, 1830.

1. It is contended, in the first place, that the justice's judgment is void for uncertainty. The words written on the warrant, "Judgment in favor of the plaintiff for sixty-one dollars and eighty-three cents and costs," constitute certainly a very brief record of the determination of the case. But the plain meaning is that the judgment is rendered against all the defendants. If it had been against one only, and in favor of the rest, it would not have been true that judgment had been given in favor of the plaintiff in the whole case, for it would have been in part against him. We think there is reasonable certainty in the judgment; and to require more of these inferior tribunals would be to defeat entirely their jurisdiction.

2. It is next insisted that the levy contains no sufficient description of the land, and that the sale therefore was without

authority and void. It is certainly true that the description given in the levy is somewhat vague; it is only described as "John Doak's seventy acres of land, on the waters of the west fork of Stone's river." In the case of *Vance* v. *McNairy*, 3 Yerg. 177,[1] however, the levy was not more certain, and the court held it to be sufficient. The title does not rest upon the description in the levy, but the deed follows and defines its locality with sufficient precision. All that is necessary in the levy is some general description that will, by reasonable intendment, connect it with the sale and deed, so that a tract of land different from the one levied on may not be sold and conveyed. This, we think, is given in the levy before us.

3. It is contended the court erred in telling the jury that the plaintiff's title related to the levy by the constable upon the land, and was not limited to the date of the deed or to the order of sale by the court. The case of *Lash* v. *Gibson*, 1 Murph. 266, and *Ellar* v. *Ray*, 2 Hawks, 568, sustain the opinion of the court below, and we think proper to follow those cases.

Let the judgment be affirmed.

JUSTICE'S EXECUTION BINDS PROPERTY FROM THE LEVY: See *Metts* v. *Bright*, 32 Am. Dec. 683.

SUFFICIENT ENTRY OF JUDGMENT BY JUSTICE OF THE PEACE: See *Titus* v. *Whitney*, 31 Am. Dec. 228.

DESCRIPTION OF PROPERTY SOLD UNDER EXECUTION.—Every reasonable intendment is to be made in favor of purchasers at judicial sales: *Marshall* v. *Greenfield*, 29 Am. Dec. 559. In *Jackson* v. *Delancy*, 7 Id. 403, it was held that the land sold must be described with reasonable certainty or nothing would pass. Every intendment is to be made in favor of proceedings before a justice of the peace; if it may be determined with reasonable certainty from the form in which the judgment is entered, what was indeed meant, the validity of the entry will be sustained: *Anderson* v. *Kimbrough*, 5 Coldw. 262, in which the principal case is relied upon; see also *Glass* v. *Stovall*, 10 Humph. 452. To the point that a description of land levied upon under execution is sufficient if it be such as will, by reasonable intendment, connect it with the subsequent sale and deed, the principal case is cited in *Brigance* v. *Erwin's Lessee*, 1 Swan, 378; *Trotter* v. *Nelson*, Id. 12; *Cohen* v. *Woollard*, 2 Tenn. Ch. 692; in *Gibbs* v. *Thompson*, 7 Humph. 181, the court, citing the principal case, in conjunction with others in the same state, said: "There are two principles upon which the cases taken together rest: 1. That purchasers must have the means of knowing what land is to be sold, so as to form some estimate of its value. 2. That there must be such ascertainment, by description of identity, as shall prevent one piece of land from being sold and a distinct piece conveyed." In the following cases the description in the levy was held insufficient: "On a tract of land adjoining the lands of James McDondel, Thomas Cannon, and others, containing one hundred and sixty acres:" *Helms* v. *Alexander*, 10 Humph. 44; "Levied on lot No. —, in the town of Green-

ville, with its improvements:" *Brown* v. *Dickson*, 2 Id. 394, in which it was
held that a sale and deed by virtue of such a levy conveyed no title to the
vendee; referring to the principal case, the court declared that the doctrine
laid down in that case was in no manner in conflict with the cases above cited.
The title of a purchaser at a sheriff's sale relates to the date of the levy: *Kea-
ton* v. *Thomasson's Lessee*, 2 Swan, 137; *Knight* v. *Ogden*, 2 Tenn. Ch. 476,.
both citing the principal case.

TURBEVILLE AND DARDEN *v.* RYAN.

[1 HUMPHREYS, 113.]

AUTHORITY UNDER SEAL IS NECESSARY TO ENABLE ONE COPARTNER TO
BIND THE OTHER by a note under seal in the name of the partnership.

PREVIOUS PAROL ASSENT OR SUBSEQUENT ADOPTION will not render the unauthorized bond of a copartner binding as to the other.

ERROR.   The opinion states the facts.

George Boyd, for the plaintiffs in error.

H. S. Kemble, for the defendant.

By Court, GREEN, J.   This is an action of debt, brought by
Ryan, as assignee of Reuben Bartlett, upon a bill single, purporting to have been executed by Turbeville & Darden to the
said Bartlett for two thousand three hundred and twelve dollars
and seventy-five cents.   Darden, one of the defendants, pleaded
non est factum to the action, and on the trial proved that himself and Turbeville were partners in trade, and that the bond
upon which this suit was brought was executed by Turbeville
in the partnership name, and that it was not signed or sealed
by him or in his presence.   The plaintiff proved that on the
day of the execution of the bond, or the next day, Darden
called upon the payee of the note and told him that he was
then ready to close the contract and then give his notes for the
amount.   Bartlett then informed Darden that his partner, Turbeville, had given notes signed Turbeville & Darden, with which
he expressed himself satisfied; but the bond was not shown to
him, nor was he informed that obligations under seal had been
executed.   The plaintiff further proved that at the time the
bond in the pleadings mentioned was executed, the said Turbeville executed one or more similar bonds in the name of Turbeville & Darden, which were paid, both the defendants at different
times during the partnership paying money on said bond.   The
plaintiff proved by another witness that the bond in the pleadings mentioned was placed in his hands for collection; that he

called upon Darden and told him he wanted him to pay the
said note. He said he knew he was bound for said note, but
that they had dissolved partnership, and that Turbeville was to
pay the debts. Witness did not show the bond to Darden, nor
does he know Darden ever saw it; in speaking of the claim he
called it a note, and he did not inform Darden that it was under seal. Several credits were indorsed upon the bond, expressing in general terms, that the sums credited were paid by
Turbeville & Darden. The .court charged the jury "that one
partner had not, by virtue of the partnership, power to bind his
copartner by bond, unless such partner had authority under
seal to do so; but if they believed from the testimony that defendant, Darden, had paid notes under seal executed at the
same time and upon the same consideration to the same parties,
and that he had subsequently admitted that he was bound by
the note sued on, the court would leave it to the jury to determine the facts, whether any authority under seal had been given
by Darden to Turbeville to bind him by bond at the time of the
execution of the specialty sued on; that unless they had positive proof of the existence of such authority at the time of the
execution of the bond, or were satisfied from all the facts and
circumstances that such authority did then exist, their verdict
should be for the defendant, Darden; but if they believed that
such authority did at the time of the execution of the bond exist,
their verdict should be for the plaintiff." The jury found a
verdict for the plaintiff, and the defendants moved for a new
trial, which motion was overruled by the court and judgment
rendered upon this verdict, from which this appeal in error is
prosecuted.

No objection is made by the plaintiffs in error to the general
doctrine stated by the court in the charge to the jury; but it is
insisted his honor erred in assuming "that if Darden had paid
notes under seal, executed at the same time, and upon the same
consideration to the same parties, and had subsequently admitted that he was bound by the note sued on," these facts
would be evidence from which the jury would be authorized to
infer that Turbeville had authority from Darden under seal to
bind him at the time the bond sued on was executed. We do not
think the facts thus stated by the courts authorize the inference which it was indicated the jury might make. None of the
cases go so far as to assume that subsequent acts of ratification
constitute evidence that the deed was executed by virtue of a
written authority under seal existing at the time. If the exist-

ence of such authority be necessary, its production could not be
dispensed with unless it were shown to have been lost or destroyed, or otherwise beyond the power and control of the party
desiring to prove its contents: 1 Stark. 436. There can be no
reason why this general rule of evidence in relation to written
instruments should be dispensed with in this case. Parol proof,
therefore, that Turbeville had authority under seal to bind his
copartner would have been inadmissible, much less could evidence of the manner in which Darden had acted in reference to
other contracts of a similar character establish the existence
of such authority. But it is insisted, that although a party may
not have a written authority under seal to bind his copartner by
deed, yet, if such copartner subsequently assent to the contract,
he is bound, and that the circumstances enumerated by the
court to the jury were competent evidence to prove such subsequent assent. If it were admitted that such subsequent assent would bind a party, still the question whether there was
such subsequent assent was not propounded to this jury, nor
did they consider of the testimony in reference to such question.
It could not, therefore, be said that they had found the fact
that Darden had so assented. They were told that it must be
proved that Turbeville acted under an authority by deed. This
inquiry was as to the existence of such authority; and they were
told they might find, and they did find, from the facts and circumstances enumerated, that such authority did exist. This
being illegal, the verdict can not be supported, even though we
should think the evidence might have sustained a finding upon
the principle which it is insisted on should have been stated by
the court, because that principle not having been stated, the
evidence was not considered in reference to it.

2. But we can not adopt the principle contended for by the
counsel for the defendant in error. The two cases upon which
they rely, *Cody* v. *Shepherd*,[1] 11 Pick. 400, and *Grann* v. *Seton
and Bunker*, 1 Hall, 262, seem to us virtually to have abandoned
the doctrine that one partner can not bind another by deed unless
expressly authorized to do so by an instrument of equal dignity.
For they hold that a previous parol assent, or a subsequent
adoption, will bind the party though no written authority under
seal existed. To assume this position in one sentence, and in
the next to adopt the doctrine laid down by Lord Kenyon in
Harrison v. *Jackson*, 7 T. R. 207, seems to us contradictory and
absurd; for if a previous assent or subsequent parol adoption

---

will do to bind the party, certainly there is no necessity for a written authority under seal to do it.

But upon this question our own court has made two concurrent decisions, which we are not at liberty to disregard.   In the case of *Nunnely* v. *Doherty*, 1 Yerg. 26, the court say " that no authority is given a partner by the law merchant to bind his copartner by deed, nor does the fact that the articles of copartnership were under seal give him such authority merely from the circumstance of their being sealed; to have this effect a special power or authority must be contained in the articles."   This case was followed by the case of *Waugh and Finley* v. *Carriger*, Id. 31, and by many other cases which have not been reported, so that at this time we feel bound by their authority; and although the doctrine is no favorite with us, yet if we adhere to it at all, we feel bound to maintain it in good faith.   Certainly the alarm which Lord Kenyon in *Harrison* v. *Jackson* supposes the mercantile world would feel, however justly it may have been apprehended in England, could not be felt here if it were determined that one partner might bind the other by a contract for the payment of money though made under seal.   But the contrary doctrine is too firmly established to be shaken by the courts, and if changed at all it must be done by the legislature.

Reverse the judgment.

<hr>

AUTHORITY TO BIND COPARTNER BY CONTRACT UNDER SEAL.—A partner present and assenting to the execution of a sealed instrument by his copartner in the firm name is bound thereby; and such presence and assent may be proved by the admissions of the party: *Fichthorn* v. *Boyer*, 30 Am. Dec. 300, the note to which case contains the authorities on this subject.

THE PRINCIPAL CASE IS CITED and affirmed to the effect that one partner has no power to bind his copartner by deed, unless he be expressly empowered by deed to do so, and that this power can not be proven by parol, in the following cases: *Napier* v. *Catron*, 2 Humph. 536; *Boyd* v. *Dodson*, 5 Id. 37; *Smith* v. *Dickinson*, 6 Id. 262; *Mosby* v. *State of Arkansas*, 4 Sneed, 327; *McNutt* v. *McMahan*, 1 Head, 98; *Cain* v. *Heard*, 1 Coldw. 166.   Cited also in *Hackett* v. *Brown*, 2 Heisk. 264, to show that the court must charge the jury, not in remote and impalpable generalities, but as applicable to the facts, so as to aid the jury in arriving at a correct conclusion.

<hr>

ROBINSON *v.* MAYOR AND ALDERMEN OF FRANKLIN.
[1 HUMPHREYS. 156.]

BY-LAW OF A TOWN NOT CONSISTENT WITH THE GENERAL LAWS of the state is void.

BY-LAW PROHIBITING SALE OF INTOXICATING LIQUORS by persons within the limits of the town, when, by a general law, the sale of liquors is licensed, is in conflict with the latter, and therefore void.

PENALTY FOR VIOLATION OF A MUNICIPAL BY-LAW, void as prohibiting a traffic which is licensed by a state law, can not be enforced against a person, though the latter was not in possession of a license from the state.

ERROR. The opinion states the facts.

Meigs and Marshall, for the plaintiff in error.

Alexander, for the defendants.

By Court, GREEN, J. This is an action of debt to recover from the plaintiff in error two hundred and fifty dollars, the penalty imposed by said corporation for a breach of its by-laws. The by-law in question was passed the nineteenth day of August, 1833, and is as follows:

"Be it enacted by the mayor and aldermen of the town of Franklin: That it shall be the duty of the owner of each tavern, grocery, confectionery, or other house, or any person or persons whatever, intending to retail spirituous liquors within the limits of said corporation, before he, she, or they proceed to retail spirituous liquors within the limits of said corporation as aforesaid, to apply to the recorder and obtain license from the said corporation for the term of one year, and pay to said recorder, for the use of said corporation, a tax of one hundred dollars, and the further sum of fifty cents for granting such license, which sum of one hundred dollars is hereby declared to be the tax on each retailer of spirituous liquors within the limits of said corporation for each and every year; and if any person or persons shall proceed to retail spirituous liquors without first having obtained a license therefor, as aforesaid, such person or persons so offending shall forfeit and pay the sum of two hundred and fifty dollars, to be recovered before any jurisdiction having cognizance thereof, in the name of the mayor and aldermen of said corporation, for the use of said corporation."

There was a verdict and judgment for the plaintiffs in the circuit court of Williamson county, and a motion in arrest of judgment, which was overruled. The defendant appealed in error to this court. The question for consideration now is as to the validity of the by-law of the corporation. A corporation can pass no by-law inconsistent with the constitution and laws of the state: Ang. & Ames on Corp. 182, 188; 2 Bac. Abr. 9.

At the time this ordinance passed, and up to the period of its violation by the plaintiff in error, the laws of the state permitted persons who might obtain license as prescribed by those laws to retail spirituous liquors. Consequently individuals who had obtained a license to retail spirituous liquors under the state law could not, by an act of the corporate authorities of Franklin, be prohibited from retailing those liquors within the limits of that town. But this by-law expressly prohibits a party from retailing spirituous liquors within the corporation under a heavy penalty, unless a license be first obtained from the corporation. It comes, therefore, in direct conflict with the law of the state, and hence is void. It makes no difference that Robinson had no license under the state laws. In that case the corporate license could not have conferred upon him the right to sell, in violation of the state law; and they had no power to impose a penalty upon a man for not obtaining a license to do that which it would have been illegal for him to do if he had obtained said license. This is not an ordinance imposing a fine for retailing without a license. Such a by-law would have been valid; it would not have contradicted, but would have been in accordance with the state law. This law imposes a penalty for selling without a corporation license; a thing they had no right to grant. If he had a license under the state law their license would confer no additional privilege, and if he had not, theirs would confer no privilege at all. These views do not at all interfere with the right to tax, or to regulate and restrain tippling-houses. Although a party may have a license under the state laws to sell, and therefore the act of selling is not a nuisance, yet he may be restrained and regulated in the exercise of this privilege so as to mitigate the evils of his trade.

We think there is error in the judgment, and therefore order that it be reversed and the judgment be arrested.

———

GENERAL LIMITATIONS ON THE POWER OF MUNICIPAL CORPORATIONS TO PASS ORDINANCES.—Municipal corporations can exercise the following powers, and no others: 1. Those granted in express words. 2. Those necessarily or fairly implied, or incident to the powers expressly granted. 3. Those that are indispensable to the declared objects and purposes of the corporation with which it is of necessity invested, from its very nature and constitution. The charter of a municipal corporation is its organic law. From its charter its powers are originally derived, and to its charter every attempted exercise of power must be ultimately referred. As the powers of the corporation are conferred by its charter, so are they necessarily limited by it. As it is permitted to exercise the powers which its charter authorizes, so it is prohibited from exercising those which are not authorized. Any act or attempted exercise of power which transcends the limits expressed or necessarily inferred from the language of the instrument by which its powers are conferred, is beyond the authority of a municipal corporation, and is therefore null and void: Dill. on Munic. Corp., sec. 89; Smith v. Newbern, 70 N. C. 14; S. C., 16 Am. Rep. 766; Cook County v. McCrea, 93 Ill. 236; McCann v. Otoe County, 9 Neb. 324; S. C. & P. R. R. Co. v. Washington, 3 Id. 30; Somerville v. Dickerman, 127 Mass. 272; Bryan v. Page, 51 Tex. 532;

Francis v. *Troy*, 74 N. Y. 338; *State* v. *Passaic*, 41 N. J. L. 90; *Carron v. Martin*, 2 Dutch. 594; *Smith* v. *Newburgh*, 77 N. Y. 130; *Allen* v. *Galveston*, 51 Tex. 302; *Dore* v. *Milwaukee*, 42 Wis. 108; *Butler* v. *Nevin*, 88 Ill. 575; *Kansas* v. *Flanagan*, 69 Mo. 22; *Bentley* v. *Chicago*, 25 Minn. 259; *Indianapolis* v. *Gas Light Co.*, 66 Ind. 402; *Vance* v. *Little Rock*, 30 Ark. 435; *Ex parte Burnett*, 30 Ala. 461; *Greenough* v. *Wakefield*, 127 Mass. 275; *Memphis* v. *Water Co.*, 8 Baxter, 587; *Orphan Asylum* v. *Troy*, 76 N. Y. 108; *Petersburg* v. *Metzker*, 21 Ill. 206; *New London* v. *Brainard*, 22 Conn. 552.

MUNICIPAL ORDINANCES MUST BE CONSISTENT WITH THE CONSTITUTION and general laws of the land. All laws are subject to the limitations imposed by the constitution. Between a general law or statute enacted by the legislature, and a municipal ordinance, substantially the same relation exists, as that which is recognized between the constitution and the general laws enacted by the legislature thereunder. General laws are paramount in authority to those which are passed by municipal bodies for the purpose of local government. An ordinance which is repugnant either to the constitution or general laws is *ipso facto* void: *Burlington* v. *Kellar*, 18 Iowa, 65; *Mayor* v. *Vickers*, 3 Coldw. 205; *Indianapolis* v. *Gas Co.*, 66 Ind. 396; *Hospital* v. *Luzerne*, 84 Pa. St. 59; *Livingston* v. *Albany*, 41 Ga. 22; *Wood* v. *Brooklyn*, 14 Barb. 425; *State* v. *Hardy*, 7 Neb. 377; *Cullinan* v. *New Orleans*, 28 La. Ann. 102; *Illinois Central R. R. Co.* v. *Bloomington*, 76 Ill. 447; *Shreveport* v. *Levy*, 26 La. Ann. 671; S. C., 21 Am. Rep. 553; *Judson* v. *Reardon*, 16 Minn. 435; *New Orleans* v. *Savings Bank*, 31 La. Ann. 637; *Walker* v. *New Orleans*, Id. 828; *Vance* v. *Little Rock*, 30 Ark. 435; *Mayor* v. *Hussey*, 21 Ga. 80; *Haywood* v. *Mayor*, 12 Id. 404; *State* v. *Caldwell*, 3 La. Ann. 435. This proposition is elementary, and it is not necessary that the authorities in support of it should be multiplied. Whatever restrictions the constitution of the United States, or of the state itself, have imposed upon the state legislature, rest equally upon the instruments of government which the state by its authority has created. A municipal ordinance which impairs the obligation of a contract, or has an *ex post facto* operation, or takes private property without due compensation, or imposes upon personal liberty any restraints not authorized by the constitution, is void. The limitations to which the state in its sovereign capacity is subject, apply as well to local governments acting under the state with delegated authority. And an ordinance conflicting with a statute of the state must yield to the latter.

LIMITATIONS IMPLIED FROM FORM OF CHARTER.—It is scarcely possible, within the limits of this note, to notice the numerous instances in which particular provisions of municipal charters have been construed. It will not be attempted to accomplish more than to state some of the general canons of construction which have been adopted, and to indicate their application in a few important cases. The powers conferred by a municipal charter are express or implied. The corporation may exercise such powers as are granted to it expressly, and such incidental powers as are necessary or appropriate to the exercise and enjoyment of those expressly conferred. Corporate powers are strictly construed. The corporation is not permitted to exercise any powers not necessarily or fairly within the scope and import of those delegated in its charter; *Minturn* v. *Larue*, 23 How. (U. S.) 437; *Thomas* v. *Richmond*, 12 Wall. 349; *Leonard* v. *Canton*, 35 Miss. 189; *Nichol* v. *Nashville*, 9 Humph. 252; *Douglas* v. *Placerville*, 18 Cal. 643; *Memphis* v. *Adams*, 9 Heisk. 518; S. C., 24 Am. Rep. 331; *Henderson* v. *Covington*, 14 Bush (Ky.), 312; *State* v. *Maysville*, 12 S. C. 82; *Plaquemine* v. *Ruff*, 30 La. Ann. 497; *Caldwater* v. *Tucker*, 36 Mich. 478; S. C., 24 Am. Rep. 601; *Alton* v. *Ætna*

Ins. Co., 82 Ill. 46; *Wilson* v. *Shreveport*, 29 La. Ann. 673; *Shackelton* v. *Gut-tenberg*, 39 N. J. L. 660; *Pye* v. *Peterson*, 45 Tex. 312; *Logan* v. *Pyne*, 43 Iowa, 524; S. C., 22 Am. Rep. 261; *Keokuk* v. *Scroggs*, 39 Iowa, 447; *Johnston* v. *Louisville*, 11 Bush (Ky.), 527; *Winooski* v. *Gokey*, 49 Vt. 282; *Field* v. *Des Moines*, 39 Iowa, 575; *Carr* v. *Dooley*, 122 Mass. 257; *Latham* v. *Richards*, 19 N. Y. S. C. 362. Though the general rule is to give to the chartered powers a strict rather than a liberal construction, it is not intended to exclude any powers which are reasonably incident to those expressly delegated. The fair intention of the legislature, as evidenced in the language, intent, and purpose of the grant, is the criterion by which the scope of municipal authority may be best discovered. The doctrine of strict construction, while it is in many cases declared to be the rule, is nowhere enforced to the extent of unreasonably defeating the purpose of the legislature, as it appears upon the entire charter or enactment. If there be a fair, reasonable, and substantial doubt, whether the legislature intended to convey a particular authority, especially if the authority be one the exercise of which imposes a burden, tax, or assessment, or abridges personal liberty, or has the effect of divesting property rights, the doubt will be resolved against the corporation and in favor of the citizen: *Logan* v. *Pyne*, 43 Iowa, 524; S. C., 22 Am. Rep. 261; *Merriam* v. *Moody*, 25 Id. 170; *Minturn* v. *Larue*, 23 How. (U. S.) 437; *Chicago* v. *Rumpf*, 45 Ill. 90. Thus a writ of mandamus will not be issued to compel a municipal corporation to levy a tax if the power to levy it be at all doubtful: *Shackelton* v. *Guttenberg*, 39 N. J. L. 660.

THE POWER OF PASSING BY-LAWS for the government of a corporation is an incident inseparable from its corporate existence. A municipal corporation may exercise the power of passing ordinances and by-laws, though its charter is silent in reference to the subject. Usually the power is conferred. In many cases the charter confers the power to enact ordinances in certain particular instances and for specified purposes. Following the clause in which the particular cases in which ordinances may be passed are expressly enumerated, a grant is often inserted, in general language, authorizing the corporation to pass all ordinances and by-laws, not in conflict with the constitution or general laws, that the welfare, peace, and good order of the municipality may render necessary. Here is an express authority given to pass ordinances in a particular class of cases, followed by a general authority to pass all necessary laws. The express authority is held to be a limitation upon the general power, so far as it relates to matters which belong to the class of those expressly enumerated, but which are not, in terms, included. A general power granted to the corporation to pass all ordinances necessary for the welfare of the corporation, is qualified and restricted by those other clauses and provisions of the charter which specify particular purposes for which ordinances may be passed. Otherwise the general clause would confer authority to abrogate the limitations implied from the express provisions. This subject is very ably discussed in the case of *State* v. *Ferguson*, 33 N. H. 426, decided in 1856. The defendant in that case had been convicted and sentenced to pay a fine for a violation of an ordinance designed to prohibit the sale of liquors within the limits of the city of Concord, without a license from the mayor and aldermen. The charter conferred upon the council power to pass ordinances in relation to the sale of liquors in the following cases: 1. To prohibit the selling or giving away of any ardent spirits by any storekeeper, trader, or grocer, to be drunk. 2. To forbid the sale of intoxicating liquors to Indians and minors. Following this specific enumeration of the particular purposes for which ordinances and by-laws might be passed, was a

general provision authorizing the council to make such other regulations as
might be required for the well-being of the city, provided they were not repugnant to the constitution or laws of the state. The ordinance in question
being a general, universal prohibition against the sale of intoxicating liquors,
was in excess of the authority conferred by either of the express provisions,
and an endeavor was made to support it under the general power to pass such
laws as the welfare of the city required. Upon this subject, the court said:
"If this general provision confers the power to enact the ordinance, it is clear
that the clauses which expressly give the power to regulate sales by storekeepers, and to Indians and children, are unmeaning and useless. For, if
the general clause authorizes this ordinance, then it equally authorizes one in
the precise terms of either or both of the special clauses to regulate such
sales. To enact the latter is no greater exercise of power than the former.
Indeed, it would be a power of the same nature, and exercised in the same
direction, though narrowed in its operation. To hold, then, that the general
clause confers the power, is in effect to expunge these special provisions from
the charter. And not only these, but all the numerous clauses which go to
limit and define the precise boundaries of the power to be exercised by the
city in the various cases specified for the enactment of by-laws and ordinances.
The express grant, then, of the power of legislation upon a particular subject,
limited by the terms of the grant in respect to its extent or objects and purposes, or in reference to the mode in which it is to be exercised, may be held,
unless the contrary manifestly appears to be the intention of the legislature,
upon a view of the entire act, to exclude all authority to legislate upon that
subject beyond the prescribed limits, and in the absence of any further authority expressly granted upon every other subject:" *Tuck* v. *Waldron*, 31
Ark. 465; *Grand Rapids* v. *Hughes*, 15 Mich. 54; *Collins* v. *Hatch*, 18 Ohio,
524; *Keokuk* v. *Scroggs*, 39 Iowa, 447. A grant by the legislature to a municipal corporation, of power to legislate by ordinance on enumerated subjects
connected with its municipal affairs, is an addition to its general power of
making by-laws as an incident to its creation: *State* v. *Morristown*, 33 N. J.
L. 57.

The power of passing ordinances and by-laws does not include the power
to legislate upon general subjects. "Wherever," says Mr. Cooley, "the
municipality shall attempt to exercise powers not within the province of local
self-government, whether the right to do so be claimed under express legislative grant, or by implication from the charter, the act must be considered
as altogether *ultra vires*, and therefore void:" Const. Lim. 211. There is a
wide distinction between the power to pass ordinances or by-laws and the
power of passing general laws. The distinction rests altogether in the subject of the enactment, independent of the authority under which it is ordained. The general power of legislation is primary, while that exercised
by a municipal corporation is derivative. There are many matters, the regulation of which is peculiarly incident to the former, which the latter is not
competent to exercise, because of their being entirely foreign to its objects
and purposes. The power to pass general laws is an incident of sovereignty,
and contemplates a general power to pass laws relative to a wide variety of
subjects, dictated by considerations of interest or of policy to the collective
body composing the state, in whom all power is inherent, and whose authority
is supreme. The power to pass ordinances and by-laws is used to designate
those rules and regulations only as have especial reference to the purposes for
which municipal corporations are formed. The power to pass ordinances and
by-laws does not therefore include the power to regulate matters which are
properly an exclusive subject of control by general laws: *Commonwealth* v.

Turner, 1 Cush. 493; *Horn* v. *People*, 26 Mich. 222; *Philadelphia and Reading R. R. Co.* v. *Ervine*, 89 Pa. St. 76; *Williams* v. *Davidson*, 43 Tex. 35.

BY-LAWS, ORDINANCES, RESOLUTIONS, AND REGULATIONS DISCRIMINATED.—
The term ordinance, as applied to enactments of the law-making power of a municipality, is analogous, if not entirely identical with by-law. Chief Justice Shaw, in the case of *Commonwealth* v. *Turner*, 1 Cush. 493, denying to towns in the state of Massachusetts the authority, under the statute, to regulate the sale of intoxicating liquors within their limits, observed that the term by-law was one of peculiar and limited signification. It was employed to designate the orders and regulations which a corporation, as one of its legal incidents, has power to make, and which is usually exercised in the regulation of its internal concerns, and the reciprocal rights and duties of its members. No sensible distinction can be imagined between ordinances and by-laws. Their legal character is the same. The former may, perhaps, be usually employed with especial reference to the lawful enactments of municipal corporations, while the latter may comprehend such rules only as are adopted by corporations of a private character. No necessity seems ever to have arisen which made it desirable that any distinction affecting their legal signification should be made. An act of incorporation which in one section provided that by-laws, ordinances, resolutions, and regulations might be enacted by the council of a city, and in a following section required by-laws and ordinances to be submitted to the mayor for his approval, was held not to intend that by-laws and ordinances should receive such approval, and resolutions and regulations should not. There was nothing in the act indicating a design to make any distinction, and, save the slight distinction made in ordinary usage, none existed, either in principle or practice. The opinion of the court thus compared these terms: "Regulation is the most general of them all, meaning any rule for the ordering of affairs, public or private, and it thus becomes the generic term from which all the others are defined, specified, and differentiated. Ordinance is the next most general term, including all forms of regulation by civil authority, even acts of parliament. With us its meaning is usually confined to corporation regulations. Ordinances are all sorts of rules and by-laws of municipal corporations. Resolution is only a less solemn or less usual form of an ordinance. It is an ordinance still, if it is anything intended to regulate the affairs of the corporation. If the word ordinances does not include resolutions, the law that requires ordinances to be submitted to the mayor for his approval, is of no force at all, because it allows its substantial purpose to be defeated, by giving to ordinances the form of resolutions:" *Kepner* v. *Commonwealth*, 40 Pa. St. 130.

It has been sought to establish and maintain a distinction between ordinances and by-laws and resolutions. The signature of the presiding officer of the council is not necessary to authenticate a resolution, although required by the statute to be affixed to ordinances. If the act be one of a temporary character, such as levying a tax, and is not an order prescribing a permanent rule of government, a resolution regularly passed, though clothed with the forms of an ordinance, will be valid without the signature of the presiding officer: *Blanchard* v. *Bissell*, 11 Ohio St. 103. A by-law may be in the form of a resolution, and yet a resolution is not necessarily a by-law, though the same forms and solemnities are required in order to enact it: *Drake* v. *Hudson River R. R. Co.*, 7 Barb. 539. The passage of a resolution as well as the enactment of an ordinance, is a legislative act, and the former, if adopted with all the solemnities required by the charter, will have, ordinarily, the same force and effect as the latter: *Somer* v. *Philadelphia*, 35 Pa. St. 236; *Gus*

Company v. *San Francisco*. 6 Cal. 191. Where the charter invests the city council with a power of decision, but is silent upon the manner in which it shall be expressed, it may be accomplished by resolution as well as by ordinance. And if a general power to enact ordinances be given, and no particular form of enactment is prescribed in the charter or by statute, it is no objection to the validity of an ordinance that it purports to be a resolution: *First Municipality* v. *Cutting*, 4 La. Ann. 336; *State* v. *Jersey City*, 3 Dutch. 498; *Green* v. *Cape May*, 41 N. J. L. 46; *City of Quincy* v. *C. B. & Q. R. R. Co.*, 92 Ill. 23.

POWER OF LEGISLATURE TO DELEGATE AUTHORITY TO MUNICIPAL CORPORATION.—An ordinance or municipal by-law is an order or regulation adopted in due form by the law-making power in a municipality, in pursuance of lawful authority; and, as it has the force of law over the community in which it is adopted, its enactment is essentially an exercise of legislative power. The validity of an ordinance, if enacted in due form, depends upon whether it is within the powers vested in the corporation. This question involves, primarily, another, viz., whether the legislature was authorized to make a delegation of its own power, such as the corporation claims. Although as a general proposition it is true, that the legislature is alone competent to ordain laws, yet it is well settled that the legislature may delegate to municipal corporations the power to enact regulations, which, limited in their operation by appropriate sanctions, will have the force and effect of general laws within the territory or over the community for whose government they are adopted. Discretionary powers granted to a municipal corporation, to be exercised according to its judgment as to the necessity or expediency of a given measure, vests the corporation, within the sphere of the powers delegated, with a control as absolute as the legislature would have possessed if it had never delegated the powers, and the discretion of the municipality in respect to the exercise of the powers granted, is as wide as that possessed by the government of the state: *Gas Co.* v. *Des Moines*, 44 Iowa, 509; S. C., 24 Am. Rep. 56; Dill. on Munic. Corp., sec. 308, 3d ed.; *Ex parte Burnett*, 30 Ala. 469: *Osborne* v. *Mayor*, 44 Id. 498; *Ex parte Wall*, 48 Cal. 321; S. C., 17 Am. Rep. 425; *Covington* v. *East St. Louis*, 78 Ill. 550; *Indianapolis* v. *Gas Light and Coke Co.*, 66 Ind. 402; *Perdue* v. *Ellis*, 18 Ga. 591; *Kniper* v. *Louisville*, 7 Bush (Ky.), 601; *Mayor* v. *Morgan*, 7 Mart. 5; S. C., 18 Am. Dec. 234; *Portland* v. *Water Co.*, 67 Me. 137; *Heland* v. *Lowell*, 5 Allen, 109; *State* v. *Dwyer*, 21 Minn. 513; *St. Paul* v. *Coulter*, 12 Id. 46; *Taylor* v. *Carondelet*, 22 Mo. 110; *Metcalf* v. *St. Louis*, 11 Id. 103; *State* v. *Noyes*, 30 N. H. 288; *Howe* v. *Plainfield*, 37 N. J. L. 146; *Presb. Church* v. *New York*, 5 Cow. 541; *Markle* v. *Akron*, 14 Ohio, 590; *Respub.* v. *Duquet*, 2 Yeates, 500; *State* v. *Williams*, 11 S. C. 291; *Trigally* v. *Memphis*, 6 Coldw. 389; *Milne* v. *Davidson*, 5 Mart. 409; S. C., 16 Am. Dec. 189, and note.

The class of powers which it is competent for the legislature to delegate to a municipal corporation is limited to such as have reference to matters which form appropriate subjects of municipal regulation. The power granted must be one which relates to legitimate and proper municipal purposes. It must be local in its general character as well as in its operation. In *Howe* v. *Plainfield*, 37 N. J. L. 146, sustaining the power of a town under its charter to license the sale of intoxicating liquors, and to enforce a penalty for violation of its ordinances, Dalrimple, J., remarked that while the sale of intoxicating liquors was not included in the category of offenses which the legislature could not delegate to municipal corporations power to control, yet there were undoubtedly many criminal offenses, the prohibition and punishment of which could not be constitutionally delegated to a municipality as offenses cognizable by it under the power of police. Subject to this general restriction, if the legislature may constitutionally delegate its power at all, it may confer upon a municipal board or council, the power to pass such orders as the legislature itself might have enacted in the form of a statute in the first instance: *Ex parte Shrader*, 33 Cal. 279; *Johnson* v. *Simonton*, 43 Id. 242.

MUNICIPAL ORDINANCES THAT ARE UNREASONABLE OR OPPRESSIVE ARE VOID.—By-laws passed under the incidental powers of a municipality are required to be fair, reasonable, and impartial in their operation. Whenever a by-law appears to be unreasonable or oppressive, it will be declared void: Cooley Const. Lim., 4th ed., 243; Dill. Munic. Corp., 3d ed., 319. The application of this general rule in particular cases calls for the exercise of judicial discretion, depending upon circumstances. In the following instances by-laws have been held unreasonable and void: Requiring the police to arrest all free negroes found on the street after 10 o'clock at night, and place them in confinement until morning: *Mayor* v. *Winfield*, 8 Humph. 707; levying tax for a sidewalk in an uninhabited portion of the city, disconnected with any other street or sidewalk: *Corrigan* v. *Gage*, 68 Mo. 541; prohibiting licensed retailers of spirituous liquors from selling between six o'clock P. M. and six o'clock A. M.; *Ward* v. *Greenville*, 8 Baxter, 228; S. C., 35 Am. Rep. 700; compelling the removal from within city limits of a steam-engine, which is not in itself a nuisance: *Baltimore* v. *Radecke*, 49 Md. 217; S. C., 33 Am. Rep. 239; requiring railroad company to keep a flagman by day and a red lantern by night at a particular street crossing, which was not unusually dangerous: *T. W. & W. R. W. Co.* v. *Jacksonville*, 67 Ill. 38; S. C., 16 Am. Rep. 611; prohibiting sale without license at temporary stands in the public street, of lemonade, ice-cream, cake, cheese, nuts, pies, and fruits: *Burling* v. *West*, 29 Wis. 307; S. C., 9 Am. Rep. 576; requiring a druggist, under a heavy penalty, to furnish quarterly statement, verified by affidavit, of kind and quantity of spirituous liquor sold: *Clinton* v. *Phillips*, 58 Ill. 102; S. C., 11 Am. Rep. 52; imposing fee of five cents on every sale of hay or produce: *Kip* v. *Patterson*, 2 Dutch. 298; prohibiting gas company from opening paved street in order to connect a main pipe with the opposite side of the street: *Commissioners* v. *Gas Co.*, 12 Pa. St. 318; requiring owners and exhibitors at theaters to pay city constable a fee for his attendance at the exhibition: *Waters* v. *Leech*, 3 Ark. 110; prohibiting producer from vending vegetables upon public street, without first procuring license at an annual expense of twenty-five dollars: *St. Paul* v. *Traeger*, 25 Minn. 248; S. C., 33 Am. Rep. 462; forbidding sale of goods by storekeepers on Sunday, and exempting Jews from its provisions: *Shreveport* v. *Levy*, 26 La. Ann. 671; S. C., 21 Am. Rep. 553; imposing license fee on hucksters: *Dunham* v. *Trustees*, 5 Cow. 462; forbidding porters, hackmen, and hotel runners from approaching within twenty feet of depot, unless so requested by a passenger, the regulation being in contravention of arrangements made by the railroad company for the delivery of baggage: *Napman* v. *People*, 19 Mich. 352; refusing to supply water to premises on application of owner, on the ground that the tenant was in arrears for water furnished him while occupying premises of another landlord: *Dayton* v. *Quigley*, 29 N. J. Eq. 77; excluding applicant from entering high school, who had passed a satisfactory examination in every study except grammar, it appearing that the parent did not desire that his child should pursue that study: *Trustees* v. *People*, 87 Ill. 303; expelling child from school for declining, under direction of her parents, to study bookkeeping: *Rulison* v. *Post*, 79 Id. 567; prohibiting auctioneers from selling, except to highest bidder: *In re Martin*, 27 Ark. 467; prohibiting one person from carrying on dangerous business, and permitting another to do so: *Mayor v. Thorne*, 7 Paige, 261; prohibiting use of Babcock fire-extinguishers under any and all circumstances at fires, and providing that the chief engineer shall send persons found working them to jail: *Teutonia Ins. Co.* v. *O'Connor*, 27 La. Ann. 371; prohibiting slaughtering of animals upon one's premises, unless the building was devoted to that purpose: *Wreford v. People*, 14 Mich. 41; providing that city sexton, whose fees are paid out of the estates of deceased persons, should expend five hundred dollars on the public burying-grounds, and bury paupers free of charge: *Beroujohn v. Mobile*, 27 Ala. 58; compelling owner to destroy or remove property not shown to be a nuisance: *Pieri v. Mayor*, 42 Miss. 493; prescribing penalty of not less than one dollar nor more than five dollars for every hour that a person should keep his wagon within the limits of the market: *Commonwealth v. Wilkins*, 121 Mass. 356.

In the following instances by-laws were held to be lawful, reasonable, and valid: Imposing annual license of five hundred dollars on express company whose business extended beyond the limits of the state, and one hundred dollars on company whose business did not: *Southern Express Co.* v. *Mobile*, 49 Ala. 404; prohibiting railroad train from standing across public street for longer than two minutes at a time: *State* v. *Jersey City*, 37 N. J. L. 348; forbidding wagon loaded with perishable produce to stand in market-place for longer time than twenty minutes between certain hours: *Commonwealth v. Brooks*, 109 Mass. 355; prohibiting persons from driving wagons and carts on a trot or gallop in the streets: *Commonwealth* v. *Worcester*, 3 Pick. 461; providing that person, not being a lessee of a butcher's stall, should not offer for sale fresh meat in less quantities than one quarter: *St. Louis* v. *Weber*, 44 Mo. 547; prohibiting owner of lot on lake shore from removing sand therefrom: *Clason v. Milwaukee*, 30 Wis. 316; prohibiting building of awning: *Pedrick* v. *Bailey*, 12 Gray, 161; prohibiting restaurant from being kept open after ten o'clock P. M.: *State* v. *Freeman*, 38 N. H. 426; providing that owner of ferocious dog, which should bite any person, should be subject to fine of one hundred dollars: *Commonwealth* v. *Steffee*, 7 Bush (Ky.), 161; prohibiting driver of hackney coach from standing his carriage within thirty-five feet of front door of place of public amusement: *Commonwealth* v. *Robertson*, 5 Cush. 438; fixing price at which private person should be permitted to tap sewer: *Fisher* v. *Harrisburg*, 2 Grant's Cas. 291; providing that owner of hackney carriage should not receive more than specified fare for given distance: *Commonwealth* v. *Gage*, 114 Mass. 328; fixing market hours at from dawn to nine o'clock A. M., and providing that fresh beef should not be sold at any other than the market-place, during market hours, less than by the quarter: *Bowling Green* v. *Carson*, 10 Bush (Ky.), 164; requiring railroad to station flagman at street crossing, and to use lighted lantern at night: *Delaware, L. & W. R. R. Co.* v. *East Orange*, 41 N. J. L. 127; prohibition against allowing cattle to run at large: *Commonwealth* v. *Bean*, 14 Gray, 52; prohibiting keeping of swine within city limits: *Commonwealth* v. *Patch*, 97 Mass. 221; levying tax of one hundred and fifty dollars on every retailer of spirituous liquors: *Mayor* v. *Beasly*, 1 Humph. 426; S. C., *post*, 646; compelling boats with vegetables or putrid substances, coming from a place infected with malignant or contagious disease, to anchor in the river until examined by the city physician: *Dubois* v. *Augusta*, Dudley (Ga.), 30; forbidding keeping of gunpowder except in certain quantities, and providing that it should be kept in copper canister, and imposing fine of not less than fifty nor more than five hundred dollars for each offense: *Williams* v. *Augusta*, 4 Ga. 509; requiring license fee of five hundred dollars from retailer of ardent spirits: *Perdue* v. *Ellis*, 18

Ga. 586; punishing vagrants: *St. Louis* v. *Bentz*, 11 Mo. 61; forbidding sale
of merchandise after nine o'clock A. M. on Sunday: *St. Louis* v. *Cafferata*, 24
Id. 94; requiring saloons to close at nine o'clock P. M.: *Mayor* v. *Smith*, 3
Head. 245; imposing penalty on retail grocers for having spirituous liquors on
their premises without a license: *Council* v. *Ahrens*, 4 Strobh. L. 241;
authorizing mayor to grant license to sell and deliver milk, and declaring the
act of selling milk without such license a misdemeanor: *People* v. *Mulholland*,
82 N. Y. 324; to prevent establishment of new burial-grounds within the city:
Charleston v. *Baptist Church*, 4 Strobh. L. 306; ordering that all places where
intoxicating liquors were sold should be closed at half-past ten o'clock P. M.:
State v. *Welch*, 36 Conn. 215; authorizing commissioners to vacate or discontinue leasing or hiring of market stalls: *Charleston* v. *Goldsmith*, 2 Speer, 428;
prescribing streets as routes of travel for omnibuses, and providing for their
exclusion from other streets: *Commonwealth* v. *Stodder*, 2 Cush. 562; requiring drawbridges crossing river to be closed every ten minutes for passage of
persons and vehicles, and making it unlawful for navigators to attempt to
pass after signal had been displayed that bridge was being closed: *Chicago* v.
McGinn, 51 Ill. 266; providing that any person who shall unnecessarily obstruct or impede the running of street cars, by standing his team across the
track, or otherwise, shall be liable to a fine: *State* v. *Foley*, 31 Iowa, 527; S.
C., 7 Am. Rep. 166; requiring hackman standing at or near a railroad depot
or station to obey directions of police officer: *St. Paul* v. *Smith*, 27 Minn.
364; prohibiting person without a license from carrying offal or house dirt
through any of the streets: *Vandine, Petitioner*, 6 Pick. 187; S. C., 17 Am. Dec.
351.

To be reasonable, a by-law should be certain; certain in its definition of
the offense, and certain in the penalty inflicted by it. Thus a by-law imposing a penalty for driving any "drove" or "droves" of horned cattle
through the streets was held void, for vagueness and uncertainty in the thing
forbidden: *McConvill* v. *Jersey City*, 39 N. J. L. 42. Ordinarily the question of the reasonableness of a by-law is one of law for the court; but if the
necessity and reasonableness of the ordinance depend upon the existence of
particular facts, of which the court has no judicial knowledge, it must be
left to the jury: *Clason* v. *Milwaukee*, 30 Wis. 316; see, however, *Peoria* v.
Calhoun, 29 Ill. 317. And a clear case should be made out to authorize an
interference by them on the ground of unreasonableness: *St. Louis* v. *Weber*,
44 Mo. 547. A by-law is not void for uncertainty because the amount of the
penalty imposed for its violation is left discretionary, within fixed limits:
Huntsville v. *Phelps*, 27 Ala. 55. It was held in *Goldsmith* v. *New Orleans*,
31 La. Ann. 646, that the imposition of a license tax by the authorities of a
city was one of expediency and police regulation, of which the city authorities were the sole judges, and that the judicial tribunals had no power to
control them in the exercise of this discretion. An injunction to restrain the
collection of a tax fixed at two thousand five hundred dollars a year, on persons carrying on the business of coffee-house or saloon, with theatrical performance attached, was denied. So long as a municipality keeps within its
lawful power to tax, the courts are not authorized to restrain its exercise of
that power on the ground that it may operate to create a local prohibition of
a lawful pursuit: *Ex parte Schmidt*, 2 Tex. App. 196. Where a charter authorized the common council to license the retailing of spirituous liquors, it
was held that an ordinance prohibiting, under a penalty, the sale of spirituous
liquors in less quantities than twenty gallons, was unauthorized and void:
Harris v. *Intendant*, 28 Ala. 577. The general rule in regard to the reasonableness of by-laws is stated by Mr. Dillon, in his excellent treatise on mu-

nicipal corporations, as follows: "Where the legislature in terms confers upon a municipal corporation the power to pass ordinances of a specified and defined character, if the power thus delegated be not in conflict with the constitution, an ordinance passed in pursuance thereto can not be impeached as invalid, because it would have been regarded as unreasonable if it had been passed under the incidental power of the corporation, or under a grant of power general in its nature:" Sec. 328. The supreme court of California, sustaining a conviction under an ordinance punishing persons visiting places for the purpose of gambling, adopted the language quoted above with approval: *Ex parte Chin Yan,* February 4, 1882.

ORDINANCES IN CONTRAVENTION OF COMMON OR PRIVATE RIGHTS ARE VOID. As a natural corollary of the requirement of reasonableness, it follows, that municipal by-laws which are in contravention of common rights are unauthorized and invalid. This was held of a by-law prohibiting all persons except the inhabitants of a town from taking fish from a navigable river within its limits: *Hayden* v. *Noyes,* 5 Conn. 391; *Willard* v. *Killingworth,* 8 Id. 247; and where a city had granted to a street railway a franchise to operate a road, using a double track, it can not, after the company has proceeded and expended money, afterward restrict them to a single track by an amendment to the ordinance conferring the franchise: *Burlington* v. *Street Railway Co.,* 49 Iowa, 144; nor can an ordinance confer a right to obstruct the highway or the approaches to a bridge so as to interfere with and impede public travel: *Stack* v. *St. Louis,* 85 Ill. 377; *Pettis* v. *Johnson,* 56 Ind. 139; under a power to regulate wharves, a municipality can not define the line of high-water mark, and declare the erection of buildings below said line a nuisance: *Evansville* v. *Martin,* 41 Id. 145; a municipal corporation can not pass ordinances authorizing the sale, without notice to the owner, of property left on the levee beyond a certain time: *Lanfear* v. *Mayor,* 4 La. 97; S. C., 23 Am. Dec. 477; an ordinance imposing a tax on wagons of outside residents engaged in hauling into and out of the city is void: *St. Charles* v. *Nolle,* 51 Mo. 122; this principle does not apply to persons whose business or manufactory is outside of the city limits, and who employs wagons in delivering his wares therein: *Memphis* v. *Battaile,* 8 Heisk. 524; *Edenton* v. *Capeheart,* 71 N. C. 156; municipal ordinances are not permitted to include the regulation or prohibition of burying-grounds outside of the corporate limits: *Bergin* v. *Anderson,* 28 Ind. 79; but within the limits of the corporation, the burial and interment of the dead is an appropriate subject of regulation by ordinance: *Council* v. *Baptist Church,* 4 Strobh. L. 306; *Coates* v. *Mayor,* 7 Cow. 585; *Commonwealth* v. *Fahey,* 5 Cush. 408; *Bogert* v. *Indianapolis,* 13 Ind. 134; *New Orleans* v. *St. Louis Church,* 11 La. Ann. 244; *Presbyterian Church* v. *Mayor of New York,* 5 Cow. 538; *Commonwealth* v. *Goodrich,* 13 Allen, 546; *Mosgrove* v. *Catholic Church,* 10 La. Ann. 431; but, in *Charlestown* v. *Murray,* 16 Pick. 121, it was expressly held that such restraints must be reasonable, and that, save so far as it related to populous sections of the city, an ordinance forbidding burials within its corporate limits was void; the erection of a private hospital within the limits of a city was declared, in *Milne* v. *Davidson,* 5 Mart. 409; S. C., 16 Am. Dec. 189, to be within the purview of municipal authority, so far as to enable a by-law to be passed imposing upon such institutions an entire and total prohibition. An ordinance authorizing an arrest without a warrant is in contravention of the general law of the land, and is therefore void: *Knoxville* v. *Vickers,* 3 Coldw. 205; *Judson* v. *Reardon,* 16 Minn. 431. How far by-laws contravene common rights so as to enable the courts to declare them void, is a principle which naturally will not admit of any uniform and uni-

versal rule. The police powers of municipal corporations are both extensive
and indefinite. It seems that by-laws which are lawful, reasonable, uniform,
fair, and impartial, and which are passed in the exercise of the proper police
powers of the corporation, will be sustained, although they prohibit that
which might be otherwise lawfully done. This was substantially the language of the court, in *State* v. *Fisher*, 52 Mo. 177, sustaining the power of a
municipality to forbid the purchase of the carcasses of dead animals for the
purpose of boiling, steaming, and rendering them, and prohibiting them from
being boiled, steamed, and rendered, within certain limits.

MUNICIPAL ORDINANCES MAY REGULATE BUT NOT RESTRAIN TRADE.—Ordinances in restraint of trade will be declared void: *St. Paul* v. *Traeger*, 25 Minn.
248; *State* v. *Fisher*, 52 Mo. 174; *Burling* v. *West*, *supra*; *St. Louis* v. *Grone*, 46
Mo. 574; *Hayes* v. *Appleton*, 24 Wis. 543. In *Ex parte Frank*, 52 Cal. 606, declaring an ordinance void, which exacted a license for selling goods, and fixed
one rate of license for selling goods within the corporate limits, or *in transitu*
to the city, and another and much larger license for selling goods not within
the city, or *in transitu* to it, the court said: "The ordinance in question is
flagrantly unjust, unequal, and partial. It discriminates between merchants
of the same place, dealing in the same kind of merchandise, for no better
reason than that one deals in goods, either actually in the corporate limits or *in
transitu*, under a bill of lading, while the other deals in goods outside the corporate limits, and not *in transitu*, under a bill of lading. If this kind of discrimination be legitimate and valid, there is no reason why a merchant having
his goods in a warehouse on a particular street might not be required to pay
a license fee of ten thousand dollars, while another merchant doing the same
kind of business, in the same city and with his goods stored in another street,
would be required to pay only ten dollars. It also contravenes the public
policy of the state, in that it obstructs commercial intercourse between the
principal seaport city of the state and the interior; the policy being to foster
and encourage commercial intercourse and a free interchange of commodities
between the several sections. It is in restraint of trade, in that it exacts a
heavy tribute from the owner of goods outside the corporate limits and not *in
transitu*, as a condition on which he shall be allowed to offer them for sale in
the principal city and seaport of the state." The principle of this case was
also declared in *Nashville* v. *Althrop*, 5 Coldw. 554, in which an ordinance imposing a license fee and discriminating between merchants and manufacturers
residing outside the limits of the city, and other persons of the same class residing within, was held to be beyond the authority of the council. An ordinance restraining a merchant or dealer in family groceries from selling vegetables at his place of business during market hours, was held to be in restraint
of trade and unauthorized: *Caldwell* v. *Alton*, 33 Ill. 416; but an ordinance
requiring the taking out of a license by persons engaged in transporting coal
in wagons from point to point within a city is not so: *Gartside* v. *East St.
Louis*, 43 Id. 547; nor an ordinance prohibiting all hawking and peddling
about the streets of meat, game, and poultry: *Shelton* v. *Mobile*, 30 Ala. 540;
nor one providing that no person should keep a butcher's stall or vend fresh
meats, in less quantities than the quarter, without license taxed at two hundred dollars: *St. Paul* v. *Coulter*, 12 Minn. 41; and the keeping of markets
within certain prescribed limits may be forbidden: *State* v. *Gisch*, 31 La. Ann.
544.

Ordinances creating a monopoly, or vesting in particular persons the sole
and exclusive right to carry on a business, are void: *Gale* v. *Kalamazoo*, 23
Mich. 344; S. C., 9 Am. Rep. 80; *Logan* v. *Pyne*, 43 Iowa, 524; S. C., 22

Am. Rep. 261; *Chicago* v. *Rumpf*, 45 Ill. 90; *Tugman* v. *Chicago*, 78 Id. 405.
This principle is admitted where the power to grant licenses is conferred; but
it is said that the power to grant or refuse licenses will enable the corporation
to grant an exclusive license: *Burlington Ferry* v. *Davis*, 48 Iowa, 133; see
Norwich Gas Light Co. v. *Norwich City Gas Co.*, 25 Conn. 19. The power to
establish and keep up a market will enable the corporation to prohibit the
sale of marketable articles elsewhere during market hours. Regulations of
this character are, if reasonable, an exercise of the proper police powers of
the corporation, and are not in restraint of trade: *Buffalo* v. *Webster*, 10 Wend.
100; *Bush* v. *Seabury*, 8 Johns. 418; *Dunham* v. *Rochester*, 5 Cow. 462; *Bowling
Green* v. *Carson*, 10 Bush (Ky.), 64; *St. Louis* v. *Jackson*, 25 Mo. 37; *St. Louis*
v. *Weber*, 44 Mo. 547; *Le Claire* v. *Davenport*, 13 Iowa, 210; *Davenport* v. *Kelley*, 7 Id. 102. This power has not been admitted in all cases. The decisions
are not uniform. It was denied in the following cases, that the power to regulate markets included the power to prohibit sales elsewhere. *Caldwell* v.
Alton, supra; Bloomington v. *Wall*, 46 Ill. 489; *Bethune* v. *Hughes*, 28 Ga.
560. In the case of *In re Nightingale*, 11 Pick. 107, a by-law providing that
no inhabitant of the city or vicinity, not offering for sale the produce of his
own farm, should be allowed to occupy any stand in certain streets designated
as a market, for the purpose of vending commodities, was held to be a reasonable regulation and not in restraint of trade. So also in *Commonwealth* v.
Rice, 9 Metc. 263, a similar ordinance providing that no person should be allowed to occupy a stand in the market without permission, and requiring the
clerk who issued permits to be first satisfied that the articles were the produce of the applicant's farm, was held valid; and a violation of its provisions by a citizen of the town was held to sustain conviction and fine.

LICENSING AND REGULATION OF TRADES, OCCUPATIONS, EMPLOYMENTS, AND
AMUSEMENTS.—The power to license does not involve authority to prohibit-
Dill. on Munic. Corp., 3d ed., 357; *Hill* v. *Decatur*, 22 Ga. 203; *Sweet* v
Wabash, 41 Ind. 7. That is, that so far as useful trades and employments
are concerned, the power to license them means a power of regulation merely,
and not a power to use the license as a mode of taxation for the purposes of
revenue: *Youngblood* v. *Sexton*, 32 Mich. 406; S. C., 20 Am. Rep. 654; *Kip* v.
Patterson, 2 Dutch. 298; *Leavenworth* v. *Booth*, 15 Kan. 627; *St. Louis* v.
Wehrung, 46 Ill. 392; *Addison* v. *Saulnier*, 19 Cal. 82; *Carter* v. *Dow*, 16
Wis. 298; *Welch* v. *Hotchkiss*, 39 Conn. 140; S. C., 12 Am. Rep. 383; *State*
v. *Hoboken*, 33 N. J. L. 280; *North Hudson R. R. Co.* v. *Hoboken*, 41 Id. 71;
Johnston v. *Macon*, 62 Ga. 645; *Johnson* v. *Philadelphia*, 60 Pa. St. 445;
Goshen v. *Kern*, 63 Ind. 468; *Ash* v. *People*, 11 Mich. 347; *Chilvers* v. *People*,
Id. 43; *People* v. *Mayor*, 7 How. Pr. 81; *St. Louis* v. *Bircher*, 7 Mo. App. 169;
St. Louis v. *Boatmen's Ins. Co.*, 47 Mo. 150; *St. Louis* v. *Marine Ins Co.*, Id.
163; *New York* v. *Second Avenue R. R. Co.*, 32 N. Y. 261. Special consti-
tutional provisions concerning taxes have been held to have no application
to licenses: *Leavenworth* v. *Booth*, 15 Kan. 627; *Washington* v. *State*, 13 Ark.
752; *Holberg* v. *Macon*, 55 Miss. 112; *Johnston* v. *Macon, supra; Bright* v.
McCullough, 27 Ind. 223: *People* v. *Coleman*, 4 Cal. 46; *New Orleans* v. *La.
Savings Bank*, 31 La. Ann. 637.

The power to license must be plainly conferred or it will not be held to
exist. The general power to pass such by-laws as the welfare of the community may require, not inconsistent with general laws, will not confer
authority to license: Dill. on Munic. Corp., 3d ed., 361; *Dunham* v. *Rochester*, 5 Cow. 462; *Plaquemine* v. *Roth*, 29 La. Ann. 261. Under authority to
license, taxes can not be imposed, and the power to tax does not confer the

authority to license, the objects to be attained in the exercise of these powers not being the same. The power to regulate does not confer authority to license: *Burlington* v. *Bumgardner*, 42 Iowa, 673. A power to suppress and restrain includes the power to license: *Burlington* v. *Lawrence*, Id. 681; *Smith* v. *Madison*, 7 Ind. 86; *Winooski* v. *Gokey*, 49 Vt. 282. On the contrary, in Mississippi the power to tax and suppress does not include the power to license: *Leonard* v. *Canton*, 35 Miss. 189. When the power is conferred on a municipal corporation to license and regulate occupations, the whole charter and the general legislation of the state pertinent to the subject must be consulted, in order to determine whether the power to license and regulate includes the power to tax occupations for revenue purposes: *San Jose* v. *S. J. & S. C. R. R. Co.*, 53 Cal. 475.

Regarding public amusements, a distinction is manifested between them and ordinary trades, occupations, and employments. "The power to license, regulate, and restrain amusements," says Mr. Dillon, "it is admitted, will authorize an ordinance taxing, or requiring exhibitors to pay a specific sum for the privilege, this being considered as a means of regulating and restraining them. So a grant of power to a city or town to license exhibitions" on "such terms and conditions as to it may seem just and reasonable, "authorizes it to exact money for the license; it is not confined to regulating time and place, establishing police regulations, etc:" Munic. Corp., 3d ed., 360; *Hodges* v. *Mayor*, 2 Humph. 61; *Boston* v. *Schaffer*, 9 Pick. 415. The importance and force of the principle that the power to license does not include the power to tax for revenue, rests upon the fact that the power to tax must be conferred expressly. Depue, J., in *North Hudson* v. *Hoboken*, *supra*, remarked: "The distinction between the power to license, as a police regulation, and the same power when conferred for revenue purposes, is of the utmost importance. If the power be granted with a view to revenue, the amount of the tax, if not limited by the charter, is left to the discretion and judgment of the municipal authorities; but if it be given as a police power for regulation merely, a much narrower construction is adopted: the power must then be exercised as a means of regulation, and can not be used as a source of revenue."

Where the power to tax occupations is conferred, it is to be exercised in conformity with constitutional restrictions. A license tax on business callings need not embrace all classes of business. It is essential only that all persons pursuing the same occupation shall be taxed in the same ratio. So a license tax graduated according to the monthly sales of a merchant or of an establishment is not unequal: *Sacramento* v. *Crocker*, 16 Cal. 19; *American Union Express Co.* v. *St. Joseph*, 66 Mo. 675; nor imposing on life insurance companies an amount different from that imposed upon fire insurance companies: *Home Ins. Co.* v. *Augusta*, 50 Ga. 530. So a license tax on members of the bar is not open to the objection of inequality because it requires every lawyer to pay the same amount without reference to the amount of his income: *St. Louis* v. *Stanberry*, 69 Mo. 289; *Savannah* v. *Hines*, 53 Ga. 616; nor is such a tax unequal which taxes each member of a firm separately: *Lanier* v. *Macon*, 59 Id. 187.

The subject of licensing the sale of intoxicating liquors has been chiefly one of statutory regulation. The decisions have, therefore, but little more than a local application. The principal limitation to which municipalities are subject in this matter arises in determining how far a municipal corporation may issue a license when there is a general state law in reference to the subject. It is held that a municipal corporation may require a license to retail spirituous liquors within its limits from a person who had already procured a state license to retail within the county: *West* v. *Greenville*, 39 Ala. 69; *Pekin* v. *Smelzee*, 21 Ill. 464; *State* v. *Plunkett*, 3 Harr. (N. J.) 5; *Benefield* v. *Hines*, 13 La. Ann. 420; *Louisville* v. *McKean*, 18 B. Mon. 9; *Burckhalter* v. *Mc- Connellsville*, 20 Ohio St. 308; *Wright* v. *Mayor*, 54 Ga. 645; *Ex parte Seiben- hauer*, 14 Nev. 365. Where no express power to license is granted, licenses are subject to regulation by general law only, if any exist. But whenever the power is expressly granted, then the right to exact a fee under the gen- eral law is excluded: *Ordinary* v. *Retailers*, 42 Ga. 325. When the munici- pality is invested with a general power to license, regulate, or entirely pro- hibit the sale of spirituous liquors, it is wholly discretionary with the muni- cipality to license and regulate, or partially or entirely prohibit the traffic: *Gunnarssohn* v. *Sterling*, 92 Ill. 569; *Kettering* v. *Jacksonville*, 50 Id. 39; *Martin* v. *People*, 88 Id. 390. Where there is no express authority given to cities and towns organized under general laws to regulate or license the sale of intoxicating liquors, no such license can be required: *Cowley* v. *Rushville*, 60 Ind. 327; *Walter* v. *Columbia City*, 61 Id. 24; *McFee* v. *Greenfield*, 62 Id. 21.

FINES, PENALTIES, AND FORFEITURES IMPOSED BY ORDINANCE.—The right to make by-laws includes without further express grant, the incidental right to enforce them by pecuniary penalties: Dill. Munic. Corp. 338. Penalties must be reasonable. What is reasonable depends on the nature of the offense: *Mobile* v. *Yuille*, 3 Ala. 137. Where the charter prescribes the manner in which by-laws are to be enforced, it operates as a negative on any other man- ner of enforcing them or inflicting any other punishment. Thus a corporation having authority to impose a penalty for violation of its by-laws can not pass a by-law subjecting property to seizure and sale or declaring a forfeiture: *Hart* v. *Albany*, 9 Wend. 471; S. C., 24 Am. Dec. 165; *Miles* v. *Chamberlain*, 17 Wis. 446. Municipal ordinances can not declare a forfeiture of property unless that power is granted in express terms: *White* v. *Tallman*, 2 Dutch. 67; *Phillips* v. *Allen*, 41 Pa. St. 481; *Donovan* v. *Vicksburg*, 29 Miss. 247. An ordinance authorizing the arrest and punishment of persons keeping or visit- ing establishments for the purpose of gambling, does not authorize the seizure, detention, or destruction of the instruments used for gaming: *Ridgeway* v. *West*, 60 Ind. 371. The amount of the penalty imposed may be left discre- tionary within fixed limits, as a sum not exceeding a certain amount: *Hunts- ville* v. *Phelps*, 27 Ala. 55; Dill. Munic. Corp. 341. In *State* v. *Zeigler*, 32 N. J. L. 262, it was held that an ordinance prescribing a penalty "not ex- ceeding fifty dollars" for an offense, was void for uncertainty. This was the English rule, but Mr. Dillon does not regard it as being sound in principle.

Ordinances relative to seizure and impounding of animals should require notice to be given to the owner, or else some judicial proceeding prior to for- feiture and sale. In *Donovan* v. *Vicksburg*, *supra*, holding an ordinance directing a seizure and sale of hogs found running at large within the city limits, void because no such power was conferred, the court said: "The or- dinance deprives the citizen of his property without notice or trial, and with- out the opportunity to protect his rights, and of course without due course of law. If such a power had been expressly conferred by the act of the legisla- ture incorporating the city, it would have been obnoxious to the provisions of the constitution and void: and much less can it be justified under any general powers conferred upon the corporation by their charter." This principle is followed in *Daist* v. *People*, 51 Ill. 286; *Poppen* v. *Holmes*, 44 Id. 362; *Willis* v. *Legris*, 45 Id. 289. It has been held that ordinarily there need be no ju- dicial condemnation of the property. Previous notice to the owner is suffi- cient: *Whitfield* v. *Longest*, 6 Ired. 286; *Gassellink* v. *Campbell*, 4 Iowa, 296.

But in *Rost* v. *Mayor*, 15 La. 129, an ordinance enforcing a penalty by forfeiture and sale without a trial in due course of law, was held to be in contravention of the constitution.   The power to enforce penalties by imprisonment does not exist unless authority is expressly given, and then before it can be exercised there must be a judicial ascertainment by a competent tribunal or magistrate of the guilt of the party: Dill. Munic. Corp., 3d ed., 353; *Brieswick* v. *Brunswick*, 51 Ga. 639; S. C., 21 Am. Rep. 240.

ORDINANCES DEFINING AND PUNISHING PUBLIC OFFENSES.—Municipal corporations may declare certain acts to be unlawful. The extent of the authority to exercise this power depends upon the form and language of its charter. There are, however, some general restrictions attached to this power, the principle of which arises from the relation of municipal ordinances to general laws. The question, whether the same act can be punished, once under a general law forbidding it, and also under a municipal ordinance relating to the same offense, has given rise to some difference of opinion. The cases on this subject can scarcely be reconciled. Referring to this topic, Mr. Dillon says: "In view of the somewhat strict construction of grants of corporate powers, and of the subordinate nature and purposes of by-laws, the following rules, although seeming to rest on sound principles, are, in view of the decisions, stated with some distrust of their entire correctness: 1. A general grant of power, such as mere authority to make by-laws, or authority to make by-laws for the good government of the place, and the like, should not be held to confer authority upon the corporation to make an ordinance punishing an act—for example, an assault and battery—which is made punishable as a criminal offense by the laws of the state. The intention of the state, that the general laws shall not extend to the inhabitants of municipal corporations, or that these corporations shall have the power, by ordinance, to supersede the state law, will not be inferred from grants of power, general in their character; nor will such authority in the corporation be held to exist as an implied or incidental right. 2. Where the act is, in its nature, one which constitutes two offenses, one against the state and one against the municipal government, the latter may be constitutionally authorized to punish it, though it be also an offense under the state law; but the legislative intention that this may be done should be manifest and unmistakable, or the power in the corporation should be held not to exist. 3. Where the act or matter covered by the charter or ordinance, and by the state law, is not essentially criminal in its nature, and is one which is generally confided to the supervision and control of the local government of cities and towns, but is also of a nature to require general legislation, the intention that the municipal government should have power to make new, further, and more definite regulations, and enforce them by appropriate penalties, will be inferred from language which would not be sufficient were the matter one not specially relating to corporate duties, and fully provided for by the general laws." Also, Cooley Const. Lim. 198.

In Georgia, there being a general law against harboring seamen, the city of Savannah enacted an ordinance defining the same offense, and prescribing a punishment. The court in holding this ordinance to be void said, *per* Lumpkin, J.: "Under the general grant of power delegated, the city authorities may cover all cases not provided for by the paramount authorities of the state. All their ordinances regulating cemeteries, commons, markets, vehicles, fines, exhibitions, lamps, licenses, water works, watch, police, city taxes, city officers, health, nuisances, are legitimate and proper. Nay, I might go further, and concede that where a state law defines an offense generally, and prescribes

a punishment without reference to the place where it is committed, in town
or country, and the act, when committed in the streets and public places o.'
the city, would be attended with circumstances of aggravation, such as an
affray, for instance, the corporate authorities, with a view to suppress this
special mischief, might probably provide against it by ordinance. But this is
going quite far enough:" *Savannah* v. *Hussey*, 21 Ga. 80. And in the same
state, in *Vason* v. *Augusta*, 38 Id. 542, the question was presented, whether
the city could fine a citizen for refusing to abate a nuisance, which was also
made penal by the state laws. It was held that the authority of the city
council could not extend further than to bind the offender over to answer in
a court having jurisdiction of the offense. This doctrine is followed in *Reich*
v. *Georgia*, 53 Id. 73. Keno, being a game punishable by general law, can not
be made so by ordinance: *New Orleans* v. *Miller*, 7 La. Ann. 651; same as to
willful injuries to property: *Washington* v. *Hammond*, 76 N. C. 33. A by-law
is abrogated by a general law subsequently passed relative to the same offense,
and a prosecution under it can not be maintained: *Southport* v. *Ogden*, 23
Conn. 128. License from city will not protect the holder from indictment by
the state for same act prohibited by state law: *Davis* v. *State*, 4 Stew. & P. 83.

The weight of authority is contrary to the view of the learned judge in the
Georgia case. There is no doubt that an act made punishable by state law
may be forbidden by ordinance, and penalties inflicted for its violation. And
it seems that the court that shall first obtain jurisdiction may punish to the
extent of its power: *Rice* v. *State*, 3 Kan. 141. New and additional penalties
may be imposed upon acts already penal by state laws: *State* v. *Ludwig*, 21
Minn. 202; nor is the corporation limited or restricted to the same penalties
imposed by the general law: *Baldwin* v. *Murphy*, 82 Ill. 485. Ordinances are
not void or inoperative because the acts forbidden by them are also forbidden
by a general law applicable to the whole state: *Palinsky* v. *People*, 18 N. Y.
S. C. 390; *State* v. *Plunkett*, 3 Harr. (N. J.) 5; *United States* v. *Holly*, 3 Cranch
C. C. 656; *McLaughlin* v. *Stephens*, 2 Id. 148; *Brooklyn* v. *Lounbee*, 31 Barb.
282; *Zimmerman* v. *Owens*, 24 Mo. 94; *State* v. *Pollard*, 6 R. I. 290; *Brown-
ville* v. *Cook*, 4 Neb. 101; *Rogers* v. *Jones*, 1 Wend. 237; S. C., 19 Am. Dec.
493; *Howe* v. *Plainfield*, 37 N J. L. 145. Under the power to pass by-laws
for the enforcement of good order, a town may impose a fine for assault and
battery, although the offense is also a crime against the laws of the state;
nor will judgment of conviction in the state courts bar another prosecution
before those of the corporation: *Mayor* v. *Allaire*, 14 Ala. 400; *Amboy* v.
Sleeper, 31 Ill. 499. Although general law requires procedure by indictment,
municipal ordinance may provide that prosecution may be made by information. A general law and an ordinance may have a concurrent operation, but
if an offender be first proceeded against by the municipality, a subsequent prosecution by the state is barred: *State* v. *Cowan*, 29 Mo. 330. The minimum
penalty provided by general law can not be increased by ordinance: *Petersburg* v. *Metzker*, 21 Ill. 205. Power to pass laws concurrently with state legislature concerning public offenses can not arise by mere implication: *March*
v. *Commonwealth*, 12 B. Mon. 25. An act violating both a state law and a
municipal police regulation is punishable under either or both, and conviction
under one does not bar prosecution under the other: *Hamilton* v. *State*, 3 Tex.
Ct. App. 643. A municipal corporation, under the power to prohibit practices against good morals or public decency, may declare the utterance of pro-
fane language to be a public offense, whether uttered frequently or only once
by the same person: *Ex parte Delaney*, 43 Cal. 478. The fact that violation
of an ordinance involves a common law offense, does not render it invalid:
State v. *Williams*, 11 S. C. 288.

It was remarked by the court in *State* v. *Gordon*, 60 Mo. 585, referring to the question how far an act might be made punishable both by state law and ordinance: "The legislature has an undoubted right, in reference to statutory misdemeanors, to say in what particular jurisdiction they shall be tried, and to make that jurisdiction exclusive of all others. When the power to hear and determine these minor offenses is given to a municipal corporation, but no words of exclusion or restriction are used, the remedies between the state and the corporation will be construed to be concurrent; but where the manifest intention is that the prosecution shall be limited exclusively to one jurisdiction, that intention must prevail." See also *State* v. *Crummey*, 17 Minn. 72; *Mobile* v. *Rouse*, 8 Ala. 515; *Mayor* v. *Mullins*, 13 Id. 341; *Shaper* v. *Mumma*, 17 Md. 331.

When an act is permitted by state law it can not be prohibited by ordinance. The municipality can not prohibit that which the state has licensed. The decision in the principal case proceeded upon this ground, and it is supported elsewhere. In *Wood* v. *Brooklyn*, 14 Barb. 425, the validity of an ordinance passed by a municipal corporation forbidding the sale of spirituous liquors on Sunday under a penalty, was called in question by an attempt to enforce it against keepers of inns and taverns, licensed by the state. The court said: "Licensed innkeepers are authorized to sell strong and spirituous liquors, to be drank in their houses, without restriction, on week days, and to lodgers and lawful travelers on the Sabbath. Had the revised statutes simply prohibited the sale of spirituous liquors on Sunday to any but lodgers and law-lawful travelers, it might possibly have been competent for the common council, under their general power to make police regulations, to extend the prohibition so as to make it total on that day. At any rate there would not have been a direct conflict. But the revised statutes in this particular are not simply prohibitory; they are also expressly permissive. They authorise the vendition on Sunday to certain lodgers and travelers. It needs no reasoning to show that two provisions, one permitting and the other prohibiting the same act, are in direct conflict with each other." Also *Mayor* v. *Nichols*, 4 Hill, 209.

THE PRINCIPAL CASE IS CITED in *Smith* v. *Knoxville*, 3 Head, 245, for the purpose of determining that a corporation can not pass by-laws inconsistent with the constitution and laws of the state, and that by-laws must be reasonable and not oppressive, but that subject to these restrictions, the power to pass by-laws, and to enforce them by penalties, exists in all municipal corporations. This principle was applied in this case to sustain the power of the municipality to require all houses kept for the retailing of spirituous liquors, to be closed at nine o'clock P. M. See also *Hodges* v. *Mayor of Nashville*, 2 Humph. 61, deciding that the corporate power to license is not affected by a general law making exemptions from the classes of business subject to state taxation.

NOTES AND CASES IN THIS SERIES.—Power of municipal corporation to declare nuisance by ordinance: *Milne* v. *Davidson*, 16 Am. Dec. 192; and see *People* v. *Albany*, 27 Id. 95, the note to which embraces a number of cases relative to the general powers of municipal corporations; ordinances regulating and providing for expense of sidewalks: *Goddard, Petitioner*, 23 Id. 264, and cases cited in the note on this subject.

LAWRENCE *v.* STATE.

[1 HUMPHREYS, 228.]

CHARGE OF LARCENY MAY BE SUSTAINED by showing the stolen property to have been in the constructive possession of the owner.

PROPERTY PLACED IN A PARTICULAR PLACE AND INADVERTENTLY FORGOTTEN by the owner, is constructively in his possession, so as to enable a charge of larceny to be sustained against one who, under such circumstances, appropriated it.

ERROR. The opinion states the facts.

R. M. Burton, for the plaintiff.

Humphreys, attorney-general, for the state.

By Court, REESE, J. This is an indictment for grand larceny. The plaintiff in error was a barber, and had a shop in the town of Lebanon. Muirhead, the prosecutor, went to the shop of Lawrence late in the evening for the purpose of having his hair trimmed. This operation having been performed, prosecutor took out his pocket-book in order to pay the plaintiff in error, and gave him a one-dollar bill, but the latter not having the change, left the shop for the purpose of procuring it, and prosecutor remained. When the prosecutor took out his pocket-book, which contained four hundred and eighty dollars, he laid it upon a table in the shop. On the return of the plaintiff, prosecutor met him without the door, received his change, and departed. On retiring to bed that night, at nine or ten o'clock, he missed his pocket-book, and remembered that he had left it on the table in the shop. He then went to the shop, where he found the plaintiff, who denied all knowledge of the pocket-book. The foregoing is a sufficient statement of the evidence with reference to the question discussed before us. Upon this part of the testimony, his honor, the circuit judge, charged the jury, that if the prosecutor took out his pocket-book in the shop of the defendant and laid it upon the table, and the defendant took it, unknown to the prosecutor, with the intention of converting it to his own use, against the will and knowledge of the prosecutor, and whilst the prosecutor was in the shop, that he would be guilty of larceny. The court further charged, that if the prosecutor had taken out his pocket-book, and laid it upon the table at defendant's shop, and left it there and went away out of the house, it would still be a sufficient constructive possession in the prosecutor to make the taking and converting it to defendant's use a larceny, if such taking was accompanied with the intention of appropriating the bank notes to his own use without the knowledge, consent, or will of the prosecutor. The defendant having been convicted by the verdict of the jury, and having moved the court for a new trial, which was refused, he brings his writ of error before this court; and here it has been argued with much zeal and ingenuity by his counsel upon the authority of *Long's case*, 1 Hayw. 157, note; *State* v. *Braden*, 2 Tenn. 68; *State* v. *Wright*, 5 Yerg. 155, and *Felter* v. *State*, 9 Id. 397, that to constitute larceny, there must be at least a constructive possession in the owner of the goods and a trespass in the taking; and this is certainly so upon the authority of the cases referred to. But the question before us is, had not the prosecutor, under the circumstances proved, a constructive possession, so as to make a taking, with the intention to appropriate, a trespass, and therefore a larceny? The defendant's counsel answers the question in the negative, and strenuously contends that the prosecutor, having gone away from the shop without remembering that he had left his pocket-book behind him, the same, during the time his mind remained in that state, may be said to have been lost; and that it has been determined in the case of *Porter* v. *The State*, Mart. & Y. 226, that the fraudulent appropriation of lost goods, even where the finder knows the owner, is not larceny. We answer that the pocket-book, under the circumstances proved, was not lost, nor could the defendant be called a finder. The pocket-book was left, not lost.

The loss of goods, in legal and common intendment, depends upon something more than the knowledge or ignorance, the memory or want of memory, of the owner, as to their locality at any given moment. If I place my watch or pocket-book under my pillow in a bed-chamber, or upon a table or bureau, I may leave them behind me indeed, but if that be all, I can not be said with propriety to have lost them. To lose is not to place or put anything carefully and voluntarily in the place you intend and then forget it, it is casually and involuntarily to part from the possession; and the thing is then usually found in a place or under circumstances to prove to the finder that the owner's will was not employed in placing it there. To place a pocket-book, therefore, upon a table, and to omit or forget to take it away, is not to lose it in the sense in which the authorities referred to speak of lost property; and we are of opinion, therefore, that there was no error in the charge of the court in reference to the facts in this case, and we affirm the judgment.

TAKING OF LOST GOODS BY FINDER IS NOT LARCENY, if without felonious
intent, though followed by a felonious asportation: *State* v. *Roper*, 24 Am.
Dec. 268; to the same point see *People* v. *Anderson*, 7 Id. 462; *Tyler* v. *People*,
12 Id. 176; in the note to the former the authorities are cited and reviewed.
Cited, in *Pritchett* v. *State*, 2 Sneed, 288, to indicate that to constitute larceny,
the goods taken, must at the time be in the actual or constructive possession
of some other person.

MAYOR *v.* BEASLY.

[1 HUMPHREYS, 292.]

MUNICIPAL CORPORATION, IF AUTHORIZED BY CHARTER, MAY IMPOSE A TAX
on the privilege of selling ardent spirits, for the purposes of revenue.

TAXATION OF SALE OF LIQUORS BY MUNICIPALITY, is valid against an individual engaged therein under a license from the state.

TAX IMPOSED BY MUNICIPALITY IS NOT VOID as oppressive and unreasonable,
unless it be shown that the amount imposed is comparatively in excess
of that which the necessities or interests of the corporation require.

PLEA WHICH AVERS THAT A TAX IS OPPRESSIVE AND UNEQUAL is insufficient,
unless it set forth other facts, from which it may be determined that the
tax is oppressive, and therefore void.

ERROR. The opinion states the facts.

W. A. Cook, for the plaintiffs in error.

Cahal, for the defendant.

By Court, GREEN, J. This is an action of debt to recover
one hundred and fifty dollars, the tax assessed by the corporation aforesaid for the year 1837, upon the defendant, as the
keeper of a grocery for the retail of spirituous liquors in the
town of Columbia. The ordinance laying the tax, was passed
the nineteenth of April, 1837, and is as follows: "Be it ordained by the authority aforesaid, that a tax of one hundred
and fifty dollars be and the same is hereby levied upon each and
every grocery, confectionery, or coffee-house within the limits
of this corporation that may be opened at this time, or that may
at any time hereafter be opened during the present corporate year
for the purpose of retailing spirituous liquors by measure, drink,
or otherwise, to be paid in cash for the use and benefit of this
corporation." The defendant pleaded, first, *nil debet*, to which
there was an issue; secondly, that he sold liquors by virtue of
an authority and license under the laws of this state. To this
plea the plaintiff demurred. The third plea alleges that the tax
of one hundred and fifty dollars is oppressive and unequal. To
this plea there is a demurrer. The fourth plea alleges that the
mayor and aldermen, in imposing the tax, regarded the privilege

of selling liquor not as a lawful trade but as a vice. To this plea there was a demurrer. The fifth plea alleges that the tax was imposed with a view to prohibit the defendant from pursuing a lawful occupation, and not for the purpose of raising a revenue. To this plea there is a demurrer. The sixth plea alleges that the tax was not laid to carry any necessary measure into operation; and the seventh plea says the corporation had no power to pass the ordinance; to each of which there are demurrers. The court gave judgment upon the demurrer for the defendant on the ground that the declaration does not set out a good cause of action. From this judgment the plaintiff appealed to this court.

The charter of the corporation of Columbia, October, 1817, c. 143, sec. 2, expressly confers the power of the corporation to lay and collect taxes. The constitution, article 2, section 28, empowers the legislature to tax privileges in such manner as they from time to time may direct. By the act of 1835, c. 13, sec. 4, retailing spirituous liquors is made a "privilege," and taxed as such.

There is no question then but that the corporation had the right to tax tippling-houses to some extent. The power to lay this tax, if it exist at all, must be drawn from the direct taxing power conferred in the charter. It can not be derived from the power to regulate and restrain tippling-houses. That must be done by such ordinances as will prevent these houses from becoming disorderly, and imposing penalties, for the infraction of such laws. The taxing power could only have been exercised in reference to this trade as a lawful occupation, affording to the persons who follow it a profit, which would make it proper they should pay a tax for the privilege. By the twenty-eighth section of the second article of the constitution it is provided that all property shall be taxed according to its value, and that no one species of property from which a tax may be collected shall be taxed higher than any other species of property of equal value; but the legislature may tax privileges as they may from time to time direct. The twenty-ninth section of the same article provides that counties and corporations "shall tax property according to its value, upon the principles established in regard to state taxation." Nothing is said in this section in regard to privileges, and therefore they are left, in regard to them, to the exercise of a sound discretion. It would be safe to conform the exercise of this power to the principles established in regard to state taxation, and to tax privileges in the proportion they pay to the state. But a want of exact conformity in this respect would not make the tax void, for the legislature may tax privileges in what proportion they choose, and so may corporations, provided the inequality be not such as to make it oppressive on a particular class of the community. A by-law for oppression is void: Ang. & Ames, 184.

If, in this case, it were shown by the pleadings what amount of revenue was needed in Columbia for carrying necessary measures into operation for the benefit of the town, and what tax was paid for property, and what for other privileges, and thus it were made to appear that the taxes were so unequal as to make this an oppressive tax, we should have no difficulty in declaring the ordinance by which it is levied void. But this is not the case, and we can not act upon what we may suppose the fact to be. For aught we know, expensive improvements are in progress, and other privileges are also paying high taxes. The general statement, in the third plea, that the tax is oppressive and unequal, is not an allegation of facts from which the court can say it is oppressive and void. The other pleas, to which there are demurrers, are manifestly bad. We think, therefore, that the declaration contains the statement of a good course of action, and that no one of the pleas to which the plaintiff demurred constitutes a good defense to it, and therefore the court erred in giving judgment for the defendant.

Reverse the judgment and remand the cause to be proceeded in.

———

See *Robinson* v. *Mayor, ante,* 625, and note.

THE PRINCIPAL CASE IS CITED in *Mayor* v. *Allthrop,* 5 Coldw. 554, deciding that a municipality has no power to discriminate between merchants and manufacturers and other dealers residing without the limits of the city, and members of the same class residing within; and also in *Smith* v. *Knoxville,* 3 Head, 248, to the point that a by-law must be reasonable, and not oppressive; cited, too, in *Adams* v. *Somerville,* 2 Id. 363, in support of the principle laid down by the court in that case, that where a discretionary power is conferred upon a municipal corporation, it is no valid objection that in its exercise the municipality proceeded upon a different principle or in a different mode from that adopted by the legislature in respect to state taxation.

———

JENKINS *v.* ATKINS.

[1 HUMPHREYS, 294.]

AUTHORITY OF AN ATTORNEY IN FACT CEASES upon the death of his principal.

CONTRACT FOR SALE OF LANDS WITH AN ATTORNEY IN FACT, which was not consummated until after the death of his principal, can not be enforced, though the parties contracted in ignorance of the principal's death.

ATTORNEY IN FACT CAN NOT RECOVER THE AGREED PURCHASE PRICE in
such case, notwithstanding he has since obtained the title, and is willing
to convey.

BILL in equity. Philpot constituted Jenkins his attorney in
fact for the sale of certain lands. In pursuance of the power,
the land was sold to Atkins on October 3, 1831. Philpot died
on October 2, 1831. At the time of the agreement and sale,
both the contracting parties were ignorant of the fact of Philpot's death. Jenkins afterwards obtained the title to the land
and brings this suit to compel Atkins to accept the land and pay
over the purchase money. Bill dismissed. Complainant appealed.

A. W. O. Totten, for the complainant.

J. Dunlap, for the defendant.

By Court, GREEN, J. It has been insisted for the defendant
in this case that there was no mutuality in the agreement set up
in the bill, and that therefore he is not bound to perform it;
while the complainant's counsel contends that Jenkins was personally bound by the contract he made in the name of Philpot,
because of his want of authority to make that contract, and
therefore the defendant is liable to him, and hence the agreement creates a mutual obligation.

It is true that in some cases a party who assumes to make a
contract in the name of another, without authority to do so, is
liable personally to fulfill the obligation entered into by him: 13
Johns. 307;[1] 3 Johns. Cas. 10.[2] But such is not the case here.
The contract was made in good faith upon the supposition that
the party making it had ample authority. But the fact turned
out that his authority had recently, and without the knowledge
of the parties, ceased to exist by the death of the principal, so
that no right was communicated to the thing agreed to be sold,
and consequently there could be no obligation in Jenkins to
make a title. It is not like the case where one makes a bond for
money in the name of another without authority. In such case
he can fulfill the contract himself, and is bound to do it. But
when one undertakes, as attorney in fact for another, to sell an
article, the property of that other, he communicates to the purchaser no right to the thing sold unless he had authority to sell
it. The purchaser could not in such case maintain a bill to enforce a title either against the owner or the pretended agent.
The only remedy would be at law for damages. But these

1. White v. Skinner; S. C., 7 Am. Dec. 341.   2 Foster v. Hoyt, 3 Johns. Cas. 510.

questions can never arise except where a remedy is sought against a party thus assuming to contract for another. In this case they have no application. The defendant did not contract with Jenkins; he intended to contract with Philpot, but as he was dead the whole agreement was void. The bond of the defendant for the money was made payable to Philpot, and if he is bound to take the land the other is bound to pay the money. But to whom is he bound to pay it? Not to Jenkins certainly. As the contract was to pay it to Philpot, it must be paid to him or to some one having a legal or equitable right derived from him. But Jenkins had no such right, and there is no principle upon which a court of equity can decree the money to him. As, therefore, the complainant has no right, legal or equitable, to demand the money that Atkins agreed to pay Philpot for the land, arising either from his connection with the contract as the attorney in fact of Philpot or from the fact that he has subsequently become owner of the land and is willing to convey it, there is no equity in the bill, and it must therefore be dismissed with costs.

Affirm the decree.

CITED IN *Pipkin* v. *James*, 1 Humph. 325; S. C., *post*, 652, to show that upon an executory contract for the sale of land, where the vendor had no title at the time of the contract, or at the time of the commencement of a suit by the vendee for the recovery of the purchase money, the vendee may maintain such action, and recover the money, and equity will not oblige him to take the land, though the title be offered to him.

TUCKER v. ATKINSON.

[1 HUMPHREYS, 300.]

SURPLUS MONEYS IN THE HANDS OF A SHERIFF after satisfaction of an execution, are subject to attachment by a creditor of the execution debtor.

ERROR. Defendant, as sheriff, on December 14, 1838, by virtue of an execution, levied upon and sold two tracts of land owned by Rawlings, to satisfy a judgment against the latter. After payment of the judgment and costs, the sum of three hundred and eighty-one dollars and ninety-one cents still remained in the hands of the sheriff. Tucker now commenced an action by attachment against Rawlings. A judgment being thereupon rendered against Atkinson as garnishee, the latter appealed.

Humphreys, for the plaintiff in error.

H. G. Smith, for the defendant.

By Court, GREEN, J. The question for decision in this case is, can surplus moneys in the hands of a sheriff be attached by a creditor of the execution debtor? The act of 1817, c. 54, sec. 1, provides, whenever any sheriff, etc., shall sell property by virtue of an execution for more than sufficient to satisfy said execution it shall be his duty to pay over such surplus money to the owner of the property so sold. The moment, therefore, that the sheriff receives a larger amount of money for property sold under execution than is required for its satisfaction he is bound to pay it over to the party whose property was sold. The reasons that have been advanced in support of the adjudications which protect moneys a sheriff may have collected by virtue of an execution do not apply to the present case. These are: first, that the process of the courts would be obstructed, and their judgments rendered ineffectual; and secondly, that the money is in the custody of the law, and is not goods and effects of the judgment creditor: 3 Mass. 294, 295.[1] But in the case under consideration the process of the courts can not be obstructed by allowing the surplus money, after the satisfaction of an execution, to be attached. The sheriff retains an amount sufficient to satisfy the process in his hands, and it can not be affected by the disposition which may be made of the surplus. The other reason that money collected by execution is in the custody of the law has as little application to this case as the one already noticed. The act before referred to requires the sheriff to pay it over to the party whose property was sold. He is not required by the process to make such surplus money, but it comes into his custody incidentally, and is not held by him by virtue of an execution; nor is the sheriff required to return such surplus money into court; but the moment he receives it he is debtor to the party whose property was sold, and therefore it can in no sense be said to be in the custody of the law.

The act of 1794, c. 1, sec. 19, authorizes an attachment against the estate of an absconding debtor, "wherever the same may be found, or in the hands of any person indebted to or having any of the effects of the defendant." The sheriff being debtor to the party whose property has been sold by virtue of an execution against him for the surplus money, after satisfying such execution, and such surplus constituting effects of the debtor in

---

1. *Wilder v. Bailey.*

his hands, such money may, according to the express words of the statute, he attached in his hands.

Let the judgment be affirmed.

———

CITED AND APPROVED in *Drane* v. *McGavock,* 7 Humph. 132, and distinguished for the purpose of showing that the clerk of a court is not liable to garnishment upon an execution for moneys in his hands as clerk, and which he holds subject to the order of court, in respect to the person to whom he shall pay it. The situation of a sheriff having in his hands an overplus above what is necessary to satisfy an execution, and that of a clerk of court who receives money by virtue of his office, the court in this case says are not the same.

———

PIPKIN *v.* JAMES.

[1 HUMPHREYS, 325.]

MEMORANDUM OF CONTRACT FOR SALE OF AN INTEREST IN LANDS which consisted merely of an invoice commencing with the words, "Invoice of articles purchased by S. Pipkin and R. Oliver of Wm. R. James, this twenty-ninth August, 1836," and, after specifying numerous articles, concluding with the words, "One ice-house and lot, one hundred and forty dollars," is not a sufficient memorandum, within the statute of frauds, to bind the purchaser in respect to the real property, and he may recover the purchase money paid thereon.

MONEY PAID ON AN EXECUTORY CONTRACT to convey lands to which the defendant had no title, may be recovered in assumpsit.

ASSUMPSIT. The opinion states the facts.

W. C. Dunlap, for the plaintiff.

D. Fentress, for the defendant.

By Court, TURLEY, J. This is an action brought by the plaintiff to recover a sum of money paid as the consideration of the purchase of an ice-house and lot, upon two grounds: 1. That the contract is void by the operation of the statute of frauds and perjuries. 2. That the defendant had not, at the time of the sale, nor yet has, any title to the property sold. It appears from the proof that the plaintiff and one R. Oliver had purchased from the defendant a quantity of groceries and an ice-house and lot, and that R. P. Neily, at the request of both parties, made out an invoice or memorandum of the different articles, which was headed with the following words: "Invoice of articles purchased by S. Pipkin and R. Oliver of Wm. R. James, this twenty-ninth August, 1836." After enumerating a variety of articles, the concluding item in the invoice is in the words and figures following: "One ice-house and lot, one hundred and forty dollars." This is the only note or memorandum of the contract signed, either by the parties or any other person authorized by them. A few days after this contract was made R. Oliver became dissatisfied with it, and Isaiah Flinn agreed to take his place, and the notes of Pipkin and Flinn were executed to the defendant for the purchase money, which were paid before the commencement of this action. It also appears from the proof that the defendant had not at the time of the contract, or at the commencement of this suit, any title whatever to the lot of ground upon which the ice-house was built, and had refused to give any bond binding himself to convey the same to the plaintiff. Upon this state of facts, the two questions are presented for the consideration of the court: 1. Is the contract for the purchase of the ice-house and lot void by the operation of the statute of frauds and perjuries? We think it is. The statute provides that no action shall be brought upon any contract for the sale of lands, tenements, or hereditaments, or in the making any lease thereof for a longer term than one year, unless the promise or agreement upon which said action shall be brought, or some memorandum or note thereof, shall be in writing and signed by the party to be charged therewith or some other person by him thereunto lawfully authorized. It is contended for the defendant, that the entry made at the request of the parties in the inventory of articles bought by the plaintiff is such a note or memorandum of the contract as is required by the statute. We do not think so; because, in the first place, it is proven that the inventory was not intended by the parties as a note or memorandum of the contract, but merely as a statement of the amount of the different articles purchased, with the view of ascertaining the aggregate sum for which the notes were to be executed; and because, secondly, if it were intended as a note or memorandum of the contract it is void for uncertainty, both as to the terms of the contract and the description of the property. "The note or writing must specify the terms of the agreement, for otherwise all the danger of perjury which the statute intended to guard against would be let in:" Sug. Ven. 89.

A writing acknowledging the reception of a sum of money, being the cash part of the consideration on a sale of land to the plaintiff, without saying more, is not such memorandum as will take the case out of the statute of frauds and perjuries: 4 Bibb, 566.[1] "A memorandum of the sale of lands to be effectual must

---

1. *Ellis* v. *Deadman's Heirs,* 4 Bibb, 466.

not only be signed by the party to be charged, but must contain the substantial terms of the contract in itself, or in some other writing to which it refers:" Johns. Ch. 273;[1] 14 Johns. 15;[2] 2 Wheat. 336–341.[3] An entry by an auctioneer in his books, stating the name of the owner, the person to whom the estate is sold, and the price it sold for, is a sufficient memorandum of an agreement to satisfy the statute, provided it contains the conditions of the sale and the particulars of the property, or refers to them so as to enable the court to look at them; otherwise clearly not: Sug. Vend. 95; 7 East, 558;[4] 2 Barn. & Cress. 845.[5] The authorities are conclusive upon the question. The terms of the entry in the inventory in this case are: "Bought of Wm. R. James an ice-house and lot, one hundred and forty dollars." Here is nothing with regard to the condition of the sale, the particulars of the property, nor any such description of it as would authorize a resort to parol proof for its identification. The contract then would be void for uncertainty in its terms and in the description of the property sold even if the entry in the inventory could be considered as a note or memorandum thereof within the operation of the statute of frauds and perjuries.

2. Is the plaintiff entitled to maintain this action because the defendant has no title to the premises intended to be sold? We think he is. It is unnecessary to enter into an investigation of the principles upon which the truth of this proposition depends. They are too obvious to require examination. Sugden, in his treatise on vendors, page 287, says: "When a person sells an interest, and it appears that the interest which he pretends to sell was not the true one, as, for example, if it was for a less number of years than he had contracted to sell, the purchaser may consider the contract at an end and bring an action for money had and received to recover any sum of money which he may have paid in part performance of the agreement for sale;" for which he cites the cases of *Turner* v. *Nightingale*, 2 Esp. Cas. 639;[6] *Hearn* v. *Tomlin*, Peake's Cas. 192; *Thompson* v. *Miles*, 1 Esp. Cas. 184, and others. If this may be done in cases where the vendor has a title, but not such an one as he contracted to sell, *a fortiori*, may it be done where he has no title at all. In the case of *Dearen* v. *Bartley*, 1 Cai. 47,[7] it was held that the purchaser might maintain assumpsit to recover back the purchase money, although the contract was under seal. Upon this subject

---

1. *Parkhurst* v. *Van Cortlandt*, 1 Johns. Ch. 273.
2. S. C., 7 Am. Dec. 427.   3. *Colson* v. *Thompson*.   4. *Hinds* v. *Whitehouse*.
5. *Phillips* v. *Bistolli*, 2 Barn. & Cress. 511.
6. *Farrer* v. *Nightingale*.   7. *Weaver* v. *Bentley*.

see also 1 Dall. 228;[1] 5 Johns. 85;[2] 11 Id. 527;[3] 12 Id. 274;[4] 10 Id. 73;[5] 4 Conn. 330.[6] In the case of *Tendring* v. *London*, 2 Eq. Cas. Ab. 680, it is held, that where a person takes upon himself to contract for the sale of an estate, and is not absolute owner of it, nor has it in his power by the ordinary course of law or equity to make himself so, though the owner offer to make the seller a title, yet equity will not force the buyer to take; for any seller ought to be a *bona fide* contractor, and it would lead to infinite mischief if an owner were permitted to speculate upon the sale of another's estate. To the same purpose is 10 Ves. 315,[7] and 1 Jac. & W. 431.[8] Besides, as is observed by Sugden, 208, in his treatise on vendors, the remedy is not mutual, which is, of itself, a sufficient objection in a case of this nature, as has been held by this court at its present term in the case of *Jenkins* v. *Atkins* [*ante*, 648].

Then upon both points the court below erred. The case will therefore be reversed and remanded for further proceedings.

NOTE OR MEMORANDUM OF SALE REQUIRED BY STATUTE OF FRAUDS need not give all details, but must express the substance of the contract with reasonable certainty: *Atwood* v. *Cobb*, 26 Am. Dec. 657, and note, in which this subject is reviewed at length. It was held in *Sheid* v. *Stamps*, 2 Sneed, 172, citing the principal case, that a memorandum of the sale of lands to be effectual under the statute of frauds, must not only be signed by the party to be charged, but must contain in itself, or in some other writing to which it refers, the substantial terms of the contract. The sale, its terms, the designation of the parties, and the land sold must be stated with reasonable certainty. No particular form of words or artificial arrangement of them is necessary, provided these facts substantially appear. The same principle in substance is decided upon the authority of the principal case in *Grudger* v. *Barnes*, 4 Heisk. 584; *McCarty* v. *Kyle*, 4 Coldw. 356; *Johnson* v. *Kellogg*, 7 Heisk. 264; *Seifred* v. *People's Bank*, 2 Tenn. Ch. 23; cited also in *McClure* v. *Harris*, 7 Heisk. 385, to the point that if the vendor is not able to make a good title to land sold, where the contract is executory, the vendee will not be compelled to pay the money and accept a conveyance.

BENNETT *v.* BAKER.

[1 HUMPHREYS, 399.]

VERDICT OF A JURY IS NOT VITIATED where one juror, without any knowledge of the others, took the different amounts suggested by his fellow-jurors, and having ascertained the result of one twelfth of the aggregate sum, proposed that the verdict should be for that amount, which was then assented to by the others.

1. *January* v. *Goodman*, 1 Dall. 208.

2. *Gillet* v. *Maynard*; S. C., 4 Am. Dec. 329.

3. *Judson* v. *Wass*; S. C., 6 Am. Dec. 392.

4. *Raymond* v. *Bearnard*; S. C., 7 Am. Dec. 317.

5. *Linningdale* v. *Livingston*, 10 Johns. 37.

6. Miscited.

7. *Mortlock* v. *Buller*.

8. *Boehm* v. *Wood*, 1 Jac. & W. 419.

AFFIDAVIT OF A JUROR THAT HE DID NOT AGREE TO THE VERDICT, but
was deceived, is inadmissible to impeach a verdict.

ERROR.   The opinion states the case.

Hynds, for the plaintiff in error.

Peck, for the defendant.

By Court, TURLEY, J.   In this cause the plaintiff in error
moved the court below for a new trial upon the affidavit of one
of the jurors, who swears that the jury differed as to the amount
for which a verdict should be returned; that one of the jurors
divided the amount proposed by each juror, which resulted in .
the amount of damages returned, and that he did not agree to
the calculation and verdict, and was deceived in the same.   The
circuit court refused to grant a new trial upon this affidavit, and
we think correctly.   In the case of *Hudson* v. *The State*, 9 Yerg.
403, this court held that though the affidavits of jurors may be
made the foundation for motions for new trials, yet it is a dangerous practice, and not to be extended beyond the point to
which it had been already carried.   To grant a new trial upon
the affidavit in this case would be, as we think, to go further
than any case has yet gone upon this subject.   The principle, as
settled by the authorities, is, that a jury shall not agree among
themselves that each shall specify the amount for which he is
willing to find a verdict, divide the whole by twelve, and return
the sum thus produced as the result of their deliberation; because it is in the nature of gambling for a verdict, and places it
in the power of one juror to make the amount unreasonably
great or small, as he may think proper.   But such a case is not
made out by this affidavit; it does not appear that the jury
agreed to resort to this mode of ascertaining their verdict, but
that one of the jury, of his own accord and without consulting
his fellows, adopted it and proposed the result as the amount of
the verdict, to which they assented.   This is very different from
the case in which the jury agree in the first instance to abide by
this mode of finding a verdict.   Here they knew the amount
proposed before they agreed to find it, and it thereby became
the result of their judgment; there they agreed to find a sum
to be ascertained in a particular way, not having any idea what
the amount may be.   We consider this as nothing more than a
proposition by the juror to return the verdict for the specified
sum, which was done: *Dana* v. *Tucker*, 4 Johns. 487; *Grenell* v.
Philips, 1 Mass. 561;[1] Graham on N. T. 106.   As to that portion

1. *Grinnell* v. *Phillips*, 1 Mass. 580.

of the affidavit in which the juror says that he did not agree to
the calculation and verdict, but was deceived, all that is necessary to be observed is, that he, together with his fellow-jurors,
returned the verdict in open court, and he shall not now be
heard to allege anything to the contrary. The practice would
be exceedingly dangerous, necessarily tending in its consequences to corruption and perjury.

The judgment will therefore be affirmed.

———

AFFIDAVIT OF JUROR TO IMPEACH VERDICT: See *Elledge* v. *Todd, ante,* 616.
The principal case is cited in *Memphis and Charleston R. R. Co.* v. *Pillow,* 9
Heisk. 254; *Harvey* v. *Jones,* 3 Humph. 160, and in *Elledge* v. *Todd,* 1 Id. 44;
S. C., *ante,* 616. These cases are examined to some extent in the note to the
last case.

———

HUMES AND WILLIAMS *v.* MAYOR AND ALDERMEN
OF KNOXVILLE.

[1 HUMPHREYS, 403.]

MUNICIPAL CORPORATION MAY EXERCISE OVER ITS STREETS the rights of a
   proprietor of the soil.

INJURY TO LAND SITUATED ON A PUBLIC STREET, resulting from excavations
   made by the corporation designed to improve and grade the street, unless the work was conducted in a wanton or negligent manner, is *damnum
   absque injuria.*

ERROR. Plaintiffs were the owners of a lot in Knoxville. An
order for the grading and improvement of the street in front of
plaintiffs' lot was passed by the mayor and aldermen, and in
making necessary excavations, the stable of plaintiffs was materially injured by the caving of its foundations. Defendants
pleaded the right to open the street by virtue of their powers as
officers of the corporation. Verdict and judgment for defendants. Plaintiffs appealed.

Crozier and Jarnagin, for the plaintiffs in error.

Swan and Alexander, for the defendants.

By Court, TURLEY, J. The principle both of the civil and
common law applicable to the case under consideration is,
" that if a man does what he has a right to do upon his own
land, without trespassing upon any law or custom or the title
or possession of another, he is not liable to damage for injurious
consequences, unless he does it, not for his own advantage, but
maliciously; and the damage shall be considered a casualty for
which he is not censurable:" Case of *Thurston* v. *Hancock et al.,*

12 Mass. 226 [7 Am. Dec. 57]. This principle is recognized by
the supreme court of New York in the case of *Patton* v. *Holland*,
17 Johns. 92,[1] where it is said that a person about to erect a
house contiguous to another may lawfully sink the foundation
of it below that of his neighbor's house, and is not liable for the
damages which his neighbor may sustain in consequence of it,
provided it was unintentional, and he had used reasonable care
and diligence in digging on his own ground to prevent any injury
to his neighbor. In Rolle's Abr. 965, it is said that " if A., seised
in fee of copy-hold estate next adjoining the land of B., erects a
new house upon his copy-hold, and a part is built upon the confines next adjoining the land of B., and B. afterwards digs his
land so near the house of A. (but on no part of his land) that the
foundation of the house, and even the house itself, fall, yet no
action lies for A. against B., because it was the folly of A. that
he built his house so near the land of B., for by his own act he
shall not hinder B. from the best use of his own land that he
can." From these authorities the necessary conclusion is, that
every proprietor of land, where not restrained by covenant or
custom, has the entire dominion of the soil and the space above
and below to any extent he may choose to occupy it, and in this
occupation he may use his land according to his own judgment,
without being answerable for the consequences to an adjoining
owner, unless by such occupation he either intentionally or for
want of reasonable care and diligence inflicts upon him an injury.

To apply this principle to the case under discussion: The
corporation of Knoxville is the proprietor of the public streets
of the town, which are held in trust as easements for the convenience of the citizens. As such proprietor the corporation has
the power to grade, macadamize, or do anything else for the improvement of the streets, whereby they may be made to answer
the end for which they were designed; and if, in the exercise of
this power, the property of any individual shall be rendered less
valuable, either by being elevated above or depressed below the
common level, it is *damnum asbque injuria*, a casualty to which
his property is necessarily subject, and for which the corporation
is not responsible unless the injury has been inflicted either
wantonly or from neglecting to use reasonable diligence and
care. Neither of these cases is made out by the proof. The
improvement of the street is shown to be highly necessary to the
comfort and prosperity of the town, and therefore a duty imposed upon the corporation; the work is proved to have been

---

1. *Panton* v. *Holland;* S. C., 6 Am. Dec. 369.

executed with all care for the rights of the plaintiffs, and as little injury done them as from the nature of the excavation required was practicable.

We are therefore of the opinion that there is no error in the judgment of the court below, and direct its affirmance.

——

MUNICIPAL CORPORATION MAY REGRADE STREET whenever it may deem such an improvement useful to the local public: *Keasy* v. *Louisville*, 29 Am. Dec. 395, and note.

MUNICIPAL CORPORATION IS THE PROPRIETOR OF PUBLIC STREETS, and holds them as easements, in trust, for the benefit of the corporation, and it has the power to grade, pave, or otherwise improve them. The doctrine of the principal case upon this point is approved in *Memphis* v. *Lasser*, 9 Humph. 760; *Crawford* v. *Maxwell*, 3 Id. 477; *Nashville* v. *Brown*, 9 Heisk. 6; cited also in *Tennessee and Alabama R. R. Co.* v. *Adams*, 3 Head, 600, to show that a railroad company authorized by charter to locate their road upon a street or alley of a town, can not, so long as they keep within their charter, be sued at common law for injuries resulting from its construction, unless inflicted, either wantonly, or from neglect to use reasonable diligence and care.

——————

WALLACE *v.* HANNUM.

[1 HUMPHREYS, 443.]

SEVEN YEARS' ADVERSE POSSESSION DOES NOT CREATE A TITLE in the holder in fee simple which may be seized and sold under a *fi. fa.*, so as to vest in a purchaser at the execution sale, a better title than that of a grantee of the adverse claimant, holding by an unregistered conveyance executed prior to the levy.

ERROR. A *fi. fa.* being issued on a judgment against Berry, the land in dispute was seized and sold to Wallace. The latter then brought ejectment against Hannum, tenant in possession, to recover the possession of the premises. Plea of not guilty. The defendant claimed under one White, a grantee of Berry by a deed which was executed two years before the levy and sale above mentioned, at which plaintiff became the purchaser. The deed was unregistered. It was shown that Berry took possession in 1823, and thereafter continued in possession until the deed to White. The only title shown was that founded on this possession. The court charged that if Berry had been in possession of the lots in dispute, holding them adversely for the space of seven years, he had acquired thereby a title in fee simple which would be liable to seizure and sale by a *fieri facias*, although he had, before such seizure and sale, conveyed the lots to White and surrendered possession to the latter; White's deed from Berry not having been registered, and being therefore

void as to creditors and subsequent purchasers. Verdict for the
plaintiff. Motion for new trial, and appeal.

Jarnagin, for the plaintiff in error.

Hynds, for the defendant.

By Court, GREEN, J. In this case the question is presented
whether, under and by virtue of the provisions of the second
section of the act of limitations of 1819, a complete title is acquired by the possessor who has been in possession without interruption for seven years. This court decided, in the case of
Dyche v. *Gass*, 3 Yerg. 397, and in several subsequent cases, that
a naked trespasser, who may have taken and held possession of
the land of another for seven years without any color or pretense of right, is protected in that possession by the second section of the act of 1819. It is now insisted, and the circuit court
so decided, that such possessor is not only protected in the possession, but that he has acquired a complete legal title to the
land. We can not safely rely for the exposition of this statute
upon the decisions in England upon statutes in which language
similar to that employed in this second section is used. Although by the statute 21 Jas. I., c. 16, a possession of land for
twenty years took away the right of entry of the true owner, it
did not destroy his title nor vest in the possessor a fee simple.
He might still assert his claim by bringing a writ of right. It
is true that one who had been in possession for twenty years
might have been permitted to assert his right of possession, even
against the true owner, in an action of ejectment, because such
possession is like a descent which tolls entry and gives a right
of possession, which is sufficient to maintain ejectment: Salk.
421;[1] 1 Ld. Raym. 741;[2] Ang. on Lim. 40. But it does not follow that such a consequence could result in this state from a
seven years' naked possession, because the analogy is not complete. The writ of right is not in use in this country; so that if
the true owner were turned out by an action of ejectment it
must be because his title is extinguished by force of the seven
years' possession, and by the operation of the second section of
the act of 1819 is transferred to and vested absolutely in the
possessor. This would be giving to this second section of our
act a potency far beyond that which has ever been ascribed to
the statute of James I. But if this were not so we could not
safely ascribe to our legislature the meaning, although their
language is similar, which the English courts understood to be

---

1. *Stokes* v. *Berry.*   2. Same case.

that of the British parliament.   Our legislature had before them
the history of the statute of limitations in North Carolina and in
this state.   They knew what construction had been put by the
courts upon the acts of 1715 and 1797, and the struggles which
had been made at the bar and on the bench to establish other
views than those that had prevailed.   With all these facts before them the first section of the act of 1819 was framed, and
then the section under consideration was enacted.

With all these facts before us, surely nothing could be more
delusive than to adopt the construction which was put on the
statute of James as our guide, nor more absurd than to abandon
the clearer lights which are afforded by the history of our own
legislature.   Although the act of 1715 did not by its language
require a possessor to hold by any paper title in order to his protection, yet as the legislature (act of 1715, c. 38) had declared
that no conveyance for land should be good in law unless proved
and registered, and that all deeds so done should be valid to pass
estates in land without livery of seisin, attornment, or other ceremony in the law, the courts refused to extend the benefits of
the statute of limitations to any person except such as held possession under some paper title, constituting what was called
" color of title."

Much debate and difficulty arose in the courts as to what would
be sufficient to constitute color of title.   To remove all doubt
upon this subject the legislature passed the act of 1797, in which
they declared that a party who should hold possession of land
for seven years by virtue of a grant or deed of conveyance
founded on a grant, should be entitled to hold the same against
all persons whatsoever.   A dispute arose in the construction of
this act as to the meaning of the words " deed of conveyance
founded upon a grant."   This produced the act of 1819, c. 28.
The first section of this act declares that a party who may have
had seven years' possession of land which has been granted,
" claiming the same by virtue of a deed, devise, grant, or other
assurance purporting to convey an estate in fee simple, shall be
entitled to hold the same against all other persons," and should
" have a good and indefeasible title in fee simple in such lands."
This section is drawn with much precision and care.   In order
that a party shall be protected who has held possession of land
for seven years, he must claim the same by some assurance which
purports to convey an estate in fee simple.   In such case it not
only protects his possession, but in express words it confers on
him the title.   " He shall have a good and indefeasible title in

fee simple." Now can it be believed that the eminent lawyer who drew this act would have been so precise in his language as to the character of the estate under which a party must hold, or that he would have used express words to confer the title on the possessor, if he had intended that the same consequence should result from the provisions of the second section? or can we, without charging the legislature with folly, suppose that they intended these two sections should mean the same thing?

In construing an act of the legislature we must, arrive, if we can, at the meaning of those who made it. The particular meaning of the words as used in a given case is very often to be ascertained by reference to the connection in which they are used; and taking the second section of this act in connection with the first, there can be no doubt but that the framers of it intended to give to a possession, by virtue of an assurance purporting to convey an estate in fee simple, a benefit which was not conferred upon a naked trespasser. But the natural import of the language of the second section simply bars the remedy, but does not take away the right. It enacts that "no person or persons, or their heirs, shall have, sue, or maintain any action or suit, either in law or equity, for any lands, tenements, or hereditaments, but within seven years next after his, her, or their right to commence, have, or maintain such suit shall have come, fallen, or accrued." But there are no words that take away the right or confer the title on the possessor; nor does such consequence result necessarily from the prohibition to sue. If such effect be given to the second section it must be by construction, and not because it is the natural import of the language. But we can not so construe it, because we are expressly told in the preceding section that this effect is to be given to a particular class of cases there enumerated. Certainly, therefore, when in relation to other cases language wholly different is used, we are not to understand it as meaning the same thing.

To effect the intention of the legislature courts sometimes construe the language of a statute to mean a very different thing from that which it naturally imports; but here the legislature evidently intended that which the words naturally mean: for if the argument for the defendant in error be correct there is certainly nothing in the first section which is not embraced in the second. But to assume this is to charge the legislature with folly; with the double folly of embracing in the second section all the provisions of the first, and still retaining in the act that useless section; and this too, by the use of far less appropriate language than that they had previously employed. The second section of this act, in other respects, is very broad in its provisions; and if the construction contended for was put upon it it would be most mischievous in its consequences. We think, therefore, that to extend its provisions beyond their plain import would be alike destructive of the interests of the country and subversive of the intention of the framers.

The charge of the court, therefore, that "if Berry was in possession seven years of the lots in dispute, holding adversely and for himself, he gained a fee simple," is erroneous. A party who has thus held possession, has acquired a right of possession, but not the title. We do not say an execution may not be levied on land thus held. But in this case Berry had abandoned the possession, and the land was occupied by another before this judgment was obtained. Berry had only a right of possession, which he had transferred to White before the judgment in the record was obtained, so as to create a lien upon his right, if indeed a lien would exist in such case. It is therefore not like the case of *Rochell* v. *Benson*, Meigs, 3. In that case, the land was transferred and the possession was changed after the lien of the judgment had attached.

Let the judgment be reversed, and the cause remanded for another trial.

SEVEN YEARS' POSSESSION OF LAND UNDER A BOND FOR TITLE does not vest such a title in the purchaser as can be taken in execution: *Norris* v. *Ellis*, 7 Humph. 462. The second section of the statute of limitations of Tennessee, providing that no action for the recovery of land shall be maintained, unless commenced within seven years after the cause of action shall have arisen, bars the remedy only, but does not divest the right, nor confer a title upon the adverse holder: *Hopkins' Heirs* v. *Calloway*, 7 Coldw. 37; but the first section, providing that persons in possession of lands granted by the state, who shall have been in possession for seven years, claiming and holding under a deed, grant, devise, or other assurance of title purporting to convey an estate in fee simple, are protected in such possession, and all persons who have any claim or title to such lands, who shall, for the space of seven years, fail to enforce their claims by suit at law or in equity, shall be forever barred, not only bars the remedy, but extinguishes the right, and vests in the adverse holder an indefeasible title in fee simple: *McLain* v. *Ferrell*, 1 Swan, 53. In *Marr* v. *Gilliam*, 1 Coldw. 509, the court declared as a general principle, that by adverse possession for a time, a right was created which was transferable by deed as well as by descent, and that, if the possession of the person who originally occupied the land in that manner and others claiming under him, added together, amounted to the time limited in the statute, and was adverse to the owner of the legal title, it was a bar to a recovery. The opinion reviews the authorities at length. As the principal case is referred to and commented upon, among others, the principle is deemed sufficiently important to justify an extract from the opinion. The court said:

"Whatever may be the dicta in our own reports, we know of no adjudged case which contravenes the principle hereinbefore stated. *Wallace* v. *Hannum*, 1 Humph. 443, raised the question, whether a possession for seven years, under the second section of the act of 1819, gave a title to the land, so that a purchaser at a marshal's sale, under a judgment and execution against the tenant, could maintain ejectment against the assignee of the tenant, who had become possessed of the land under an unregistered deed after the expiration of the seven years, but prior to the rendition of the judgment. The court decided that a party who had thus held possession had acquired a right of possession, but not the title, and expressly refused to say that an execution might not be levied on the land so held; but put the case upon the ground, that Berry, the debtor, who had only a right of possession, had abandoned it, and transferred it to White, who occupied the land before the judgment was obtained against Berry, so that no lien was created upon his right, if, indeed, a lien could exist in such a case. *Norris* v. *Ellis*, 7 Humph. 463, is no more than *Wallace* v. *Hannum*, with the addition, that seven years' possession, under the second section of the act of 1819, does not make a title which is subject to execution sale; and that in a suit by the purchaser against the tenant he must fail, as he acquired nothing by the purchase. And to the same effect is *Crutinger* v. *Catron*, 10 Humph. 24, which was ejectment by the owner against the purchaser, under a *fi. fa.*, against one who had held possession for more than seven years, under the second section of the act. Such possession, say the courts, constitutes a mere defense against a possessory action, which is lost the moment the possession is abandoned. No title is acquired to lands so held, but a mere right of possession, which is not alienable nor descendible, and of course is not liable to the payment of debts, because it is no interest or estate in lands. The meaning of which is, as we take it, that if the possession be abandoned or lost, it can not be regained against the rightful owner, either by the tenant himself or his heir, or any purchaser under him, whether by execution or otherwise, such a possession being a mere matter of defense; and that in a contest between the owner and a purchaser at an execution sale, the former will prevail. But did the court mean to say that such a possession or estate, so to speak, with the legal rights and incidents attending it, could not be transmitted by devise, descent, or voluntary transfer, when it was not abandoned, but continued without interruption, in the devisee, heir, or purchaser, and sought to be used merely as a defense against the action of the owner? If so, the case did not call for it, and, as we have seen, it is not supported by authority. Such a possession or estate might very well be the subject of alienation or descent, and yet the purchaser under a *fi. fa.* could acquire no interest or right which would avail him either as plaintiff or defendant, or put him in privity, in any way, with the tenant, whose interest had been attempted to be subjected."

SMITHEAL *v.* GRAY ET AL.

[1 HUMPHREYS, 491.]

EXECUTION—RESULTING TRUST FROM PURCHASE OF LAND MAY BE SHOWN by parol, and is subject to execution against the beneficiary.

PURCHASE OF LAND AND PAYMENT OF CONSIDERATION by one who procured the deed therefor to be made out to his brother, creates a resulting trust.

in favor of the purchaser, and a levy thereon by execution is constructive notice to subsequent purchasers from the trustee.

SUBSEQUENT PURCHASER OF TRUST PROPERTY CAN NOT BE PROTECTED as an innocent purchaser, unless his plea or answer contain explicit averments that he purchased for a valuable consideration, without notice, and that he has taken a conveyance of the legal title.

BILL in equity.   The opinion states the facts.

G. D. Searcy, for the plaintiff in error.

Strother, for the defendants.

By Court, TURLEY, J.   This is a bill filed by the complainant to have his rights to a lot of ground in Portersville, in the county of Tipton, declared, upon the following facts: Ephraim Gray purchased the lot from James Hodges and paid the consideration, and on the seventeenth day of January, 1832, caused a deed of conveyance therefor to be executed by him to his brother, Harvy Gray, in trust for himself. This trust is not expressed in the deed but is raised by parol proof. On the fourteenth day of July, 1832, complainant recovered a judgment before a justice of the peace in Tipton county against Ephraim Gray, upon which a *fieri facias* was issued, which was, for want of personal property, levied on the twelfth of July, 1833, upon the lot in dispute. The execution and levy were returned to the county court of Tipton, and a regular condemnation pronounced thereon on the sixth of September, 1833, upon which a *venditioni exponas* was issued and the lot sold on the first of March, 1834, to complainant, he being the highest bidder. In the mean time, on the tenth of September, 1833, Harvy Gray sold and conveyed the lot to M. T. Martin and Robert J. Clow, who, on the fifth of May, 1834, reconveyed the same to James Hodges, who, on the thirtieth of January, 1835, sold and conveyed to John Polk, from whom Murdoch Murchison purchased on the — day of April, 1835, taking a bond with covenant for conveyance.

Upon this state of facts two questions are presented for the consideration of the court: 1. Had Ephraim Gray such interest in the lot as was by law subject to execution on the first of March, 1834, the date of the sale and purchase under the *venditioni exponas* issued against him from the county court of Tipton? and 2. If he had, do the defendants stand in such a position as to protect themselves against the complainant's rights acquired by said sale and purchase, and as subsequent purchasers for a valuable consideration without notice? The first proposition involves the question as to whether a resulting trust can be raised by parol proof, and whether it is subject to execution from a court of law. Upon this proposition we are not left to argumentative induction; the question is settled by authority both in England and the United States, so conclusively that it is no longer debatable; and however we may regret that trusts which carry an estate from the entire evidence of title have to be sustained by the courts, yet *sic ita lex scripta est*, and if it be desirable to have it changed, it must be done by the legislative department of the state: 1 Johns. Ch. 582;[1] 2 Id. 405;[2] 11 Johns. 91;[3] Vern. 367;[4] 2 Atk. 159;[5] 4 Cru. 58, 59. And finally and more conclusively upon us, because they are the decisions of our own courts, the cases of *Russell and Vance* v. *Stinson*, 3 Hayw. 5; *Shute* v. *Harder*, 1 Yerg. 9. Then Ephraim Gray had such interest as was subject to execution; and the complainant is entitled to his relief unless the defendants are protected from his claim as subsequent purchasers without notice.

Upon this proposition it is to be observed: 1. No person is protected as a subsequent purchaser unless either by his plea or answer he shows himself to be such by an explicit averment that he purchased for a valuable consideration, which he had paid without notice, and that he has taken a conveyance of the legal title. See the case of *High and Wife* v. *Battle and Bradley*, 10 Yerg. 335. This is not done in this case. And 2. There is no pretense that the defendants or any of them are such purchasers. The complainant's execution was levied on the lot on the twenty-sixth of July, 1833. Harvy Gray, the trustee, sold and conveyed to Martin and Clow on the tenth of September, 1833, before the purchase under the *venditioni exponas.* They therefore had a constructive notice of complainant's claim. They conveyed to Hodges on the fifth of May, 1834. But the bill expressly charges that he was cognizant of all the facts and a party to the fraudulent transaction, which by his neglect to answer he had admitted. He conveyed to Polk on the thirtieth of January, 1835, who, in his answer, admits that he had heard of the proceedings under the judgment in favor of the complainant. He sold it to Murchison, but has never conveyed the title, having only executed a bond for that purpose. We are therefore of opinion that the complainant purchased the legal title to the premises in dispute, and declare his rights accordingly. But inasmuch as he had no deed from the sheriff of Tipton conveying

---

1. *Boyd* v. *McLean.* 2. *Botsford* v. *Burr.* 3. *Jackson* v. *Matsdorf; S. C.,* 6 Am. Dec. 356. 4. *Gascoigne* v. *Thwing.* 5. *Waite* v. *Whorwood.*

the title, we leave him to prosecute his remedy for the possession at law when he shall have obtained the conveyance.

———

RESULTING TRUST, WHEN RAISED: *Depeyster* v. *Gould*, 29 Am. Dec. 723, and note.

INTEREST OF CESTUI QUE TRUST MAY BE TAKEN IN EXECUTION: *Pritchard* v. *Brown*, 17 Am. Dec. 431, and note; but the interest of a vendee of land under a contract to sell and convey, who pays part of the purchase money and enters into possession, but neglects to pay the residue, is not such an interest as may be taken in execution: *Bogert* v. *Perry*, 8 Id. 411.

To THE POINT that a resulting trust is such an interest as may be taken in execution, the principal case is cited in *Thomas* v. *Walker*, 6 Humph. 95; *Butler* v. *Rutledge*, 2 Coldw. 12.

CASES

SUPREME COURT

OF

VERMONT.

HUMPHREY *v.* DOUGLASS.

ONE MAY LAWFULLY TURN INTO THE HIGHWAY HORSES FOUND TRESPASS-
ING in his inclosure, although their getting into the inclosure was due
to the insufficiency of a division fence which he and the owner of the
horses were equally bound to maintain.

MOTIVE WITH WHICH A LAWFUL ACT IS DONE can never alter the character of such act.

TRESPASS on the case. The facts are sufficiently stated in the
opinion.

W. P. Briggs, for the plaintiff.

Maeck and Smalley, and F. G. Hill, for the defendant.

By Court, COLLAMER, J. At the last term it was decided that
the defendant, having found the horses in his meadow, lawfully
turned them out; and the plaintiff could not recover, as the
damage, if any, was owing to his own neglect, in not restraining his horses within his own inclosures. Let us now inquire
whether the case was essentially changed by the proof on the
last trial. It was shown that the fence, through which the
horses escaped into the meadow of the defendant's father, was
a partition fence, which it was as much the duty of the plaintiff
as the other party to repair. The horses, then, escaped by the
plaintiff's fault, as it was not the exclusive duty of the other
party to maintain the fence. Horses are not commonable beasts,
and to them, in this state, the common law applies—that is, the
owner must fence them in, others are not bound to fence them

out. The plaintiff's testimony tended to prove that the defendant acted with improper motives. This can never alter the character of a lawful act. Whatever a man has a legal right to do, he may do with impunity, regardless of his motive. It seems the defendant started the horses off north. It is difficult to see, as the court have decided that he had a right to turn off the horses, why he must not turn them off in some direction, and it certainly would not do to hold that the issue should be made to turn on the point, that if he does not turn them in that direction of compass, least likely to injure the owner, it renders the whole unlawful. There was nothing in the nature of this act which amounted to a conversion of the property, or came within this action. It was but a part of the testimony which tended to show the defendant's motive, and falls with that.

Judgment affirmed.

<hr>

ONE MAY LAWFULLY TURN OUT CATTLE found trespassing on his land if he use only the necessary force in doing so, but if he inflicts unnecessary injury upon them he will be liable therefor: *Richardson* v. *Carr*, 25 Am. Dec. 65. For a former decision of the court in this case, see 33 Am. Dec. 177.

<hr>

NIMS v. ROOD.

[11 VERMONT, 96.]

CLAIM AGAINST INSOLVENT ESTATE OF DECEDENT MAY BE OFFSET in chancery against one in favor of the estate, although the claimant, owing to an agreement of the administrator to allow it, neglected to present his claim to the commissioners on the estate.

UNLIQUIDATED CLAIM CAN NOT BE OFFSET IN CHANCERY; but a decree may be deferred to enable the claimant to have it liquidated.

BILL in chancery, alleging that the orators, being partners under the firm name of Lapham & Co., executed to Levi Rood their promissory note for fifty-four dollars and eighty-four cents, and that said Rood died before the note became due, having, before his death, become indebted to the orators for medical services rendered by Doctor Nims, one of the orators, in his last sickness, in the sum of ten dollars and fifty cents; that a few hours after said Rood's death, the orators, without knowledge of his death, purchased three notes signed by him, one for thirty-four dollars, one for thirty dollars, both payable to one McCandless, and one of two dollars, payable to one Cady; that defendant, Thomas D. Rood, was appointed administrator of the estate of said Levi Rood, and as such administrator, promised

orators to apply the whole of said account for medical attendance, and also as much of the notes purchased by them as aforesaid, as should be their share, upon orators' note above mentioned;
that in violation of said agreement he had had said note sued upon,
a judgment thereon obtained, and an execution issued. The
bill prayed for discovery and relief, and for an injunction against
the execution, which injunction was granted by the chancellor
issuing the subpœna. Defendant Rood filed an answer, the purport of which is stated in the opinion. The orators proved that
Doctor Nims attended the intestate in his last sickness, but they
offered no proof of the agreement alleged in their bill.

W. P. Briggs, for the orators.

H. Leavenworth, for the defendants.

By Court, WILLIAMS, Chancellor. The orators offer no proof
of the agreement stated in their bill; it must, therefore, be taken
as admitted in the answer. If the answer is not entitled to
credit, as the orators claim in their argument, the bill is without
any evidence to support it. With respect to the note executed by
the deceased to Cady, there is no proof in relation to it, and it is
wholly denied in the answer that there was any agreement about
it. This note must be laid out of the question. It is admitted
there was some agreement in relation to the notes given to Mc-
Candless; and, although they were purchased by the orators
after the decease of Root, and can not be set off to the full
amount against the claims which the deceased held against the
present orators, yet, inasmuch as the orators may have relied on
the agreement of the administrator, and, on that account, neglected to present them to the commissioners on the estate of the
deceased, the orators are entitled to a dividend on those two
notes, to be applied to the judgment which the defendants held
against them. The dividend, it appears, was sixty-nine cents on
the dollar.

With respect to the account against the estate for the attendance of Dr. Nims during the last sickness, it appears the orators
have a just claim against the estate for the amount which may
be found due. It is proved that Dr. Nims attended him in his
last sickness; but, as the account is unliquidated, and is denied
in the answer, as well as all agreements in relation to it, the
orators can not have a decree therefor, at this time. A final decree will not now be made in the case, that the orators may
have that claim liquidated by a suit at law, inasmuch as it will
probably never be recovered unless it is allowed as an offset to

the judgment of the defendants against the orators. The orators may take a decree for the amount of the dividend on the McCandless notes, but without cost, as the defendant had a right to sue the orators, as he did, on the note mentioned in the bill, and, moreover, in that suit the present orators claimed to have the whole of the McCandless notes applied in set-off to the defendants' notes, which claim was not allowed in their suit, and is unsupported by evidence.

N. B.   The defendants consented to the allowance of the account for last sickness, and the orator took a decree for that sum as well as for the dividend before mentioned.

SET-OFF, WHAT CAN AND WHAT CAN NOT BE MADE SUBJECT OF: See *Dugan* v. *Cureton*, 31 Am. Dec. 727, note 737; *Jenkins* v. *Richardson*, 22 Id. 89, note 84. The principal case is cited in *Smith* v. *Wainwright*, 24 Vt. 105, to the point that courts of equity will, under circumstances of peculiar equity, entertain a bill for an offset, and liquidate the matter, or allow the party to proceed at law, and obtain a liquidation, and then decree an offset.

TOWN OF MILTON *v.* STORY.

[11 VERMONT, 101.]

TOWN LIABLE TO SUPPORT OF POOR MAN CAN NOT MAINTAIN ACTION against him by whose fraudulent act he was reduced to poverty. Only the party defrauded is entitled to an action, either at law or in chancery.

BILL in chancery, which alleged that the defendant agreed with one Beeman, in consideration of the conveyance of certain lands, to support him and his wife during life; that Beeman executed the deed to the defendant, but the latter fraudulently denies the contract; and that Beeman has become chargeable to the town of Milton. Defendant answered, denying the allegations of the bill. There was testimony taken, the effect of which is stated in the opinion.

Whittemore, for the orators.

Maeck and Smalley, for the defendant.

By Court, COLLAMER, Chancellor. We have examined this bill and answer, and the testimony, and we do not find the answer, which is an entire denial of the matters stated in the bill, to be disproved, except by the testimony of one witness. The circumstances, when fully considered on both sides, rather tend to sustain than contradict the answer. (Here the chancellor proceeded fully to consider the testimony.)

But it is said, in argument, that as the defendant took the conveyance in order to enable Beeman fraudulently to obtain a pension from government, as a reduced soldier of the revolution, it is not to be expected, that the proof would be very full and explicit. We find it difficult to see, even if this were true, or in any other view we can take of this case, how the orators are entitled to any relief. If any contract for support exists between Beeman and Story, binding upon Story in law or in chancery, the only privity is between these persons; and Beeman, and he alone, is entitled to an action, either in law or chancery. If that contract was made to defraud the government, or any third persons, it was still good and binding on the parties, and only void as to those who were intended to be defrauded, but that was not the town of Milton. If the contract were executory, and made in bad faith, and *contra bonos mores*, so that a court would not enforce it between the parties, still, that creates no privity between the parties to this action. The whole contract alleged, or attempted to be proved, is a personal contract, to which the town is no party. The town may support Beeman or refuse it, if he has a support secured by contract from the defendant; but because a man has refused to fulfill his contract to another, whereby the other is reduced to poverty, this does not subject him to an action, either in law or chancery, in favor of the town or parish, liable to such poor man's support. As well might his relatives, who are compelled to yield him support, or his creditors, who are unable to collect their debts, have an action. It is only the parties to the contract, or the persons intended to be affected by a fraud, who can have an action. The town was no party to this contract, and there is no pretense that any contract was made or conveyance executed with intent to injure or defraud the town.

Bill dismissed.

STATE *v.* PHELPS.

[11 Vermont, 116.]

Forgery, at Common Law, is the False Making of any Written Instrument, for the purpose of fraud or deceit. And the offense is sufficiently alleged, in an indictment, when the forgery and the allegation of fraudulent intent fully appear, though no person is set forth as the one intended to be defrauded.

In Prosecution for Forgery, under the Statute, "The President, Directors & Co." is a good description of an artificial person.

Person whose Name is Forged is a Competent Witness for the state, in a prosecution for forgery.

CONFESSIONS MADE UNDER ENCOURAGEMENT to expect favor in the prosecution, are not admissible in criminal cases.

INFORMATION, in five counts, for the forgery of a written instrument in these words:

"No.   St. Albans, February 18, 1836.   Cashier of the bank of St. Albans, pay James Wilson, or bearer, seven hundred dollars. $700.   N. W. KINGMAN."

In all the counts the intent was alleged to be to defraud the president, directors, and company of the bank of St. Albans; and they all concluded, "contrary to the form, force, and effect of the statute in such case made and provided, and against," etc. On the trial N. W. Kingman was called as a witness for the prosecution. It did not appear either that he had been discharged from any liability on the check alleged to be forged, or that the bank claimed that he was liable on it. It did appear that he had never paid it. He was objected to, but the objection was overruled. Abel Houghton was also called by the state to prove confessions made to him by the defendant. The evidence given by this witness, so far as it is material, is stated in the opinion.

H. R. Beardsley, for the respondent.

J. J. Beardsley, state's attorney, for the prosecution.

By Court, COLLAMER, J. In an indictment for forgery, the person or persons, intended to be defrauded, may be alleged in general words, as " Drummond & Co." This has been holden sufficient as to natural persons, and " the president, directors, & Co.," is a good description of an artificial person. Forgery, at common law, is the false making of any written instrument, for the purpose of fraud or deceit; and the offense is sufficiently alleged, when the forgery and the allegation of fraudulent intent fully appear, though no person is set forth as the one intended to be defrauded. This is a misdemeanor. Therefore, if a bank or corporation is a person, within the meaning of our statute, then this information sufficiently describes an offense against our statute. If a bank or a corporation is not a person, within our statute, then this information describes a common law misdemeanor. In such a case, neither a demurrer nor motion in arrest can be sustained: *State* v. *McLeran*, 2 Aik. 311;[1] *Commonwealth* v. *Boynton*, 2 Mass. 77.

In relation to the admission of Kingman, as a witness; one, who is interested in the event of a suit, can not be a witness;

---

1. 1 Aik. 311.

and one rule for settling that question is this; could the judgment in this case be given in evidence in another action, in relation to the same subject, in which the witness may be a party? However it may have formerly been holden, it is now fully settled that the judgment in a criminal prosecution can never be given in evidence in any civil proceeding: 4 Burr. 2251.[1] Kingman had, therefore, no interest in the event of the prosecution, and, on general principles, was an admissible witness. In England, it has always been holden, that a person, who would be bound by a paper, if genuine, can not be admitted as a witness of its forgery. This has been attempted to be sustained on a variety of grounds, to us all unsatisfactory or inapplicable to our circumstances. In some cases, it is said that the paper is forfeited to the crown, with the other effects of the felon, on his conviction; and that the crown would never pursue the signer. We have no such forfeiture. Again it is said that the court impounds the paper, and so its enforcement, afterwards, is much embarrassed or impracticable. This is unsatisfactory, and the English courts have long viewed the rejection of such witness as an anomaly in the law: *Rex* v. *Boston*, 4 East, 582. Probably, this anomaly was long retained *in favorem vitœ;* as forgery was then a capital felony and its penalty seldom remitted. But now, in England, by statute 9 Geo. IV., c. 32, such witness is admissible. Here, forgery is not capital and there is no reason for preserving this anomaly. It has been discarded in New Hampshire, Massachusetts, New York, and Pennsylvania, and we can not recognize it as law.

After all the experience which has been had in criminal jurisprudence, it undoubtedly becomes courts to be cautious in admitting the confessions and admissions of the accused. Even in our own state, the Bourns were convicted of murder, on full confession, when no one had been killed. "A confession must never be received in evidence, where the defendant has been influenced by any threat or promise." "The law can not measure the force of the influence used, or decide upon its effect upon the mind of the prisoner, and therefore excludes the declaration, if any degree of influence is used:" 2 Stark. Ev. 49. In relation to the admissions of Phelps, in this case, we have had some difficulty. On the one side it appears that the interview with Houghton was of Phelps' seeking; that no admissions were sought or expected by Houghton, and no direct assurances of favor were given to procure them. On the other

---

1. *Abrahams* v. *Bunn.*

hand, "upon the trial of Hall for burglary, proof was offered that the prisoner had desired Last to apply to the justice to admit him as a witness for the crown; but the evidence of such request was rejected, on the ground that it had been made under the hope of being admitted king's evidence, and could not be considered voluntary:" Id. That case goes the whole length of holding that whenever he entertains a hope of advantage, though such hope is of his own creating, his confessions are inadmissible. We do not consider it necessary to go that length. But in this case, the prisoner proposed to assist the bank in procuring security for the debt, and expressed the expectation of favor in this prosecution, if he did so. In this he was encouraged by Houghton, who said that he and the bank would give all the favor they properly could. He then proceeded to make the statements. Did he not then act under the expectation of favor, and was not this expectation countenanced by Houghton? We think it safest to err on the side of humanity and exclude such confessions.

New trial granted.

———

FORGERY, WHAT IS, AND INDICTMENT FOR: See *Hill* v. *State*, 24 Am. Dec. 441, note 443; *Arnold* v. *Cost*, 22 Id. 302, note 306, where the whole subject is fully discussed; *Hess* v. *State*, Id. 767, note 776, where other cases in this series are collected.

WITNESS, PARTY TO INSTRUMENT FORGED, WHEN IS AND WHEN IS NOT COMPETENT: *Hess* v. *State*, 22 Am. Dec. 767, note 776, where the cases in this series are collected.

CONFESSIONS, WHEN ADMISSIBLE IN EVIDENCE, AND WHEN NOT: See *State* v. *Crank*, 23 Am. Dec. 117, note 128; *Hector* v. *State*, 22 Id. 454, note 456, where the other cases on this subject, contained in these reports, are collected. The principal case is cited and affirmed in *State* v. *Walker*, 34 Vt. 301, to the point that a confession must never be received in evidence when the respondent has been influenced by any threat or promise.

———

SEWELL v. HARRINGTON.

[11 VERMONT, 141.]

OFFICER HAVING POSSESSION OF PROPERTY BY VIRTUE OF WRIT OF EXECUTION may maintain trespass against any one who takes it out of his possession. And it is no defense to such action that the writ has not been returned, when the property was taken from his possession before the return day.

WRIT OF EXECUTION IS VOIDABLE ONLY, NOT VOID, where it issues on a judgment which was obtained in an action where the writ of attachment was made out by the officer.

TRESPASS for taking a wagon. Plea, not guilty, with notice of special matter. On the trial the plaintiff offered in evidence an execution issued on a judgment in the case of Miller against Clark, and also evidence that he had seized the wagon by virtue of the execution, and left it in the possession of a man who lived about a mile from his house, where it remained until it was taken by the defendant. There was no return on the writ. Defendant hereupon moved for a nonsuit, which was denied. The defendant then offered in evidence a writ of attachment in the case of Leffingwell against Clark, by virtue of which he took the wagon, and sold it in satisfaction thereof. He also proved that the original writ in the case of Miller against Clark was drawn and filled up by the plaintiff, who was then a deputy sheriff; and that Clark had brought a writ of review, and recovered judgment of nonsuit, because the writ was drawn and filled up by the plaintiff while deputy sheriff. It was shown in evidence that the wagon was the property of Clark. The court rendered judgment for the plaintiff, for nominal damages and costs, and the defendant excepted.

G. Harrington, pro se.

S. S. Brown and F. Hazen, for the plaintiff.

By Court, WILLIAMS, C. J. The case, as drawn up, presents but two questions: 1. Whether the plaintiff had the wagon in his possession by virtue of the execution issued on the judgment in favor of Miller against Clark; and, 2. Whether the execution was so far void that the defendant was justified in taking the property in question from the plaintiff's possession by virtue of the execution in favor of Leffingwell against Clark. On the first question, it may be remarked, that as the trial of the issue was by the court, it is to be inferred that the fact of possession was found by them, unless it should appear that the evidence was insufficient, in law, to establish the fact. The party excepting must always have enough stated to show that error has intervened. In the case before us, in stating the evidence, it is not very explicitly set forth that the plaintiff took the wagon by virtue of Miller's execution. It might, however, be inferred that such was the case. It appears that the plaintiff was a deputy sheriff; that he had the execution in his possession to serve and return, and further, that the county court who tried the issue, found that he had the wagon by virtue of an execution. We can see nothing, therefore, to induce us to disturb the judgment of the county court on this point, as we can not say the evidence was legally insufficient to prove that he took and held the wagon, as deputy sheriff, by virtue of the execution in favor of Miller. Nor was it any objection to the right of the plaintiff, in this case, that the execution was not returned. The writ of execution was a final process, and, moreover, before he could legally complete his service thereon, it was taken from his possession by the defendant.

On the other point in the case, it may be remarked, that the execution issued upon a judgment of a court of competent jurisdiction, having jurisdiction of the parties to that judgment, and also of the controversy between them. It can not, therefore, be considered as void, but voidable only. It was optional with Clark, the debtor, whether the judgment should remain good or be set aside, and if he had not thought proper to bring his writ of review, the judgment would have remained in force, notwithstanding the writ was drawn up by the plaintiff, who was a deputy sheriff. It is true, the statute declares that no sheriff, deputy sheriff, etc., be allowed to make any process, or fill up any writ, declaration, or complaint, and further declares, that all such acts, done by either of them, shall be void; and that such process, writ, declaration, etc., shall be dismissed, the plaintiff become nonsuit, and the defendant recover his costs; but the terms made use of show that it is voidable, and remains good until avoided by plea or motion, and not so absolutely void from the beginning as that no one is bound by it.

The case of *Prigg* v. *Adams et al.*, 2 Salk. 674, is very decisive of the case before us, on this point, where it was held, that although an act of parliament declared that a judgment entered for under forty shillings, in certain cases there mentioned, should be void; yet the judgment was not so far void that the party could take advantage of it in a collateral action, but it was voidable only by plea or upon error. The plaintiff therefore, at the time the property was taken by the defendant, had the custody of it, by virtue of an execution apparently good, until it was set aside on the writ of review brought by Clark against Miller. In consequence of the judgment Miller against Clark being set aside, the plaintiff was not entitled to recover of the defendant, who took the property by virtue of the execution Leffingwell against Clark, the whole value of the property, but he was entitled to the nominal damages, which were awarded to him by the county court.

The judgment of the county court is, therefore, affirmed.

OFFICER HOLDING PROPERTY UNDER WRIT MAY MAINTAIN TRESPASS for
the taking or other injury of such property: See note to *Orser* v. *Storms*, 18
Am. Dec. 550.

EXECUTION, VOID OR VOIDABLE, WHEN: See *Hoffman* v. *Strohecker*, 32 Am.
Dec. 740, note 745; *Doe* v. *Snyder*, Id. 311, note 313; *Harris* v. *Alcock*, Id.
158, note 167; *Boren* v. *McGehee*, 31 Id. 695; *Coltraine* v. *McCaine*, 24 Id. 256,
note 263; *Graham* v. *Price*, 13 Id. 199.

PELTON v. MOTT.

[11 VERMONT, 148.]

REGULAR DISMISSAL ON THE MERITS OF BILL IN CHANCERY IS A BAR to another suit on the same matters, when the matters of the bill have been
passed upon.

DISMISSAL ENTERED UPON THE MERITS BY CONSENT OF THE PARTIES is as
conclusive upon them, as if the judgment were rendered in the ordinary
course of proceeding.

ASSUMPSIT on a promissory note. Plea, *non assumpsit.* On
the trial the plaintiff gave in evidence a note signed by the defendants. The defendants offered to prove, that when the note
was signed there was pending in chancery a suit in favor of E.
Pelton against the defendants and others; that the plaintiff pretended to own and have the control of said Pelton's interest in
that suit, and in the premises in dispute therein; and for the
purpose of purchasing said interest in the suit and premises
mentioned, the defendants signed the note and put it into their
agent's hands to be delivered to the plaintiff upon condition that
E. Pelton's right and title to the premises, mentioned in the
chancery suit, should be extinguished or barred; that defendant's said agent, and attorney, entered into a written agreement
with the plaintiff's counsel that a decree of dismissal on the
merits should be drawn up, entered, and recorded in said suit at
the next term; whereupon defendants' counsel delivered the note
to plaintiff's counsel on the condition that it should not be delivered over to the plaintiff until such decree should be entered
in said suit, as would extinguish and bar E. Pelton's interest in
the said premises. The plaintiff objected to this evidence, but
the court admitted it. The defendants then gave in evidence a
decree in said suit in which said suit was dismissed upon the
merits, by consent of the parties thereto. The defendants insisted that this decree did not bar E. Pelton's interest in said
premises, but the court thought otherwise and directed a verdict
for the plaintiff. The defendants excepted.

Smalley and Adams, for the defendants.

S. S. Brown, for the plaintiff.

By Court, BENNETT, J. The only question in this case, which can be raised, is whether the conditions, upon which the note was to become operative, had been complied with; and of that we think there can be no doubt. It is settled law that when a bill in chancery is regularly dismissed upon the merits, and the matters of the bill have been passed upon, it is a bar to a second suit for the same matters, unless the first bill is dismissed without prejudice: *Perine* v. *Dunn*, 4 Johns. Ch. 140; *Prettyman* v. *Prettyman*, 1 Vern. 310; Mitf. Pl., 3d Am. ed., 299. To render this principle applicable, there must be *res adjudicata*, a passing upon the very matters of the bill; and it is contended in argument that in the present case there was not such a passing upon the matters of the first bill as to constitute a bar to a second bill for the same matter, and we are referred to the case of *Rosse et al.* v. *Rust*, 4 Johns. Ch. 300. But that case is not in point. The bill there was dismissed, because no person appeared on the part of the orator to prosecute; and, though the second bill was for the same matter contained in the first, yet the merits of the former were not discussed or passed upon by the court, and the decree of dismissal was equivalent to a judgment of nonsuit at law. Though, in point of fact, the court may not have passed upon the matters of the bill, yet by the consent and agreement of the orator the decree of dismissal was entered upon the merits, and there can be no doubt, that a judgment entered up by the court, upon the agreement of parties, is, to say the least, as conclusive upon them as if judgment were rendered in the ordinary course of proceeding. We are, then, satisfied that the decree in question would be a bar to a second bill for the same cause, and must operate to bar the equity of redemption in the orator to the premises; and that, consequently, the note now in suit is operative, and the judgment of the court below must be affirmed.

———

DISMISSAL OF BILL, WHEN A BAR: See *Neafie* v. *Neafie*, 11 Am. Dec. 380.
WHEN NOT A BAR: See *Chase's case*, 17 Am. Dec. 277. The principal case is cited in *Low* v. *Mussey*, 41 Vt. 396, to the point that the determination of a court of equity having jurisdiction, and when the parties have been heard, determines their equitable rights.

BOOTH *v.* ADAMS.

[11 VERMONT, 156.]

DIVISION IN FACT OF LAND AMONG PROPRIETORS OF TOWN, however informal, if acquiesced in for fifteen years, is equivalent to a legal division thereof.

ONE TENANT IN COMMON CAN NOT MAINTAIN TRESPASS against his co-tenant, unless he is expelled from the common estate or deprived of the common enjoyment.

TRESPASS for cutting down and carrying away the plaintiff's grass and rails. On the trial the plaintiff introduced testimony tending to prove, that at the time of the alleged trespass he was in possession of a lot of land in the town of Addison, on which were the grass and rails in question; that he had for five or six years occupied said lot, claiming it as his own, having inclosed it and run a division fence across it; he also offered evidence of the alleged trespass by the defendants. The defendants then introduced testimony to show that in cutting and taking away the grass and rails as alleged, they were acting as the hired men of Friend Adams, and did it by his direction, and showed that said Adams was the owner of the undivided lands in Addison, which belonged to the original proprietary share of one Blanchard. The court decided that Adams being a tenant in common with the proprietors of the undivided lands in Addison, the plaintiff could not maintain his action without showing that he was the owner of the lot in question, or that it was separated from the common and undivided land by some previous division. The plaintiff then showed title in S. B. Booth, under whom plaintiff claimed, to the right of one Spencer, an original proprietor in said town. The plaintiff next offered to show, by the proprietors' record, a division made by the proprietors in 1784. The court decided that this division was not in conformity with law, and could not be admitted as a legal division. The plaintiff then offered the records as evidence of a division in fact, and also further testimony to show, that the town had been settled, and the lands held under this division, and that these records of the proceedings of the proprietors were the only evidence of such division, and had always been referred to by the land owners as evidence of the location of their respective lots. This testimony the court rejected. The court then decided that if the jury should find from the evidence before them, that the plaintiff and the defendants were tenants in common of undivided lands in Addison, of which the premises in controversy were a part, the plaintiff could not recover in this action. A verdict for the defendants was taken by consent. The plaintiff excepted.

H. Seymour and P. C. Tucker, for the plaintiff.

S. S. Phelps and E. D. Woodbridge, for the defendants.

By Court, REDFIELD, J. A division of common land among the proprietors, however informal, if acquiesced in for fifteen years, has always been considered, in this state, equivalent to a legal division. But this must be a division in fact of the land, either by visible lines and monuments, or by possession under a claim of distinct and clearly defined parcels. No length of time of acquiescence, in an agreement to hold in a certain manner, has yet been holden binding upon the proprietors, unless there had, in fact, been a division of the land. Hence, the severance to all the rights in the town of Addison, which was, in fact, made at the early date named in the bill of exceptions, has been so long acquiesced in that it is now binding upon all concerned. But the severance, which the plaintiff undertook to make to the right of Isaac Spencer, not being made in the manner required by law, and of so recent a date, can have no effect. If the plaintiff recover, it must be by virtue of his possession and right, as tenant in common with the defendant. There does not seem to have been any agreement, on the part of the other tenants, to permit the plaintiff to occupy the premises in controversy. If there had been, he might maintain trespass against them for the same acts, which would constitute trespass in a stranger: *Keay v. Goodwin*, 16 Mass. 1.

But one tenant in common of land can not maintain trespass against his co-tenant, unless he is expelled from the common estate or deprived of the common enjoyment. When ejectment has been brought and sustained, trespass will lie for mesne profits: 3 Wils. 118.[1] But for a mere entry upon the land, without an ouster, trespass will not lie: Co. Lit. 323; 1 Salk. 4;[2] Co. Lit. 189. In short, any act of the co-tenant, which might be referred to his right, as gathering in crops, cutting trees fit to cut, or removing fences, as in the present case, is not the ground of such action, even on the part of him who sowed the crop or erected the fence. Perhaps the actual destruction of permanent erections might merit a different consideration: *Martin v. Knowllys*, 8 T. R. 145; *Waterman v. Soper*, 1 Ld. Raym. 737. If one tenant in common of lands hinder the other from

---

1. *Goodtitle* v. *Tombs.*   2. *Haywood* v. *Davies.*

entering to erect hurdles, it is said the other may bring trespass: Co. Lit. 200. There being nothing in this case amounting to an expulsion or hindering of plaintiff in his possession,

Judgment is affirmed.

<hr>

DIVISION IN FACT ACCOMPANIED BY LONG POSSESSION, WHEN EQUIVALENT TO PARTITION: See *Hardy* v. *Summers*, 32 Am. Dec. 167; *Compton* v. *Mathews*, 22 Id. 167, note 179, where the other cases on this subject are collected.

TRESPASS BY ONE CO-TENANT AGAINST ANOTHER: See *Odiorne* v. *Lyford*, 32 Am. Dec. 387, note 392, where other cases in this series are collected.

<hr>

HOUGH AND WOOD v. BIRGE.

[11 VERMONT, 190.]

ACTION FOR USE AND OCCUPATION OF LAND CAN NOT BE MAINTAINED against one who held the same under a contract of purchase which fell through owing to failure of title on the part of the plaintiff, without any fault on the part of the defendant.

ASSUMPSIT for use and occupation. Plea *non assumpsit*, and issue to the court. The defendant took possession of a house and lot of the plaintiff, Wood, under a contract, signed by Wood only, for the sale thereof. After he took possession the house and lot were attached by creditors of Hough and Wood, and afterwards sold under execution, to the defendant. This suit was brought to recover for the use and occupation of the premises between the time when the defendant took possession and the date of the levy thereon by the creditors of Hough and Wood. The court rendered judgment for the defendants, and the plaintiff excepted.

Briggs and Barber, for the plaintiff.

C. Linsley, for the defendants.

By Court, REDFIELD, J. The contract entered into between the defendant and Wood in relation to the purchase of this house and lot, must be considered as binding upon the plantiffs until rescinded by the defendant, which he did not do until his purchase of the lot of the creditors, and which he might well do, after all title had gone from the plaintiffs. The statute of frauds does not make contracts, not reduced to writing, for the sale of land, void; but it provides that "no action shall be maintained thereon." This contract was reduced to writing and signed by one of the parties. Not being signed by the defendant, the plaintiffs could maintain no action thereon against defendant. Some of the cases go so far as to say that, on that account, the plaintiffs might have rescinded it. But, until the contract was rescinded by one of the parties, it remained in force as a ground of defense in all things done under it. And it is unnecessary to say, that the law will imply no contract where the parties have made an express stipulation. *Expressum facit cessare tacitum.*

The case, then, presents the single question, whether this contract of sale having failed to be carried into effect in consequence of defect or loss of title in the plaintiffs, they can now recover of defendant for use and occupation, while he was in possession of the premises under the contract of purchase. It is very obvious to the court, that no such action can be maintained in the present case. The case of *Hearn et al.* v. *Tomlin*, Peake's Cas. 192, was correctly decided, no doubt. The plaintiff failed to recover, as he should have done. But the reason assigned by the learned judge, who tried the case, seems to have been intended rather to pacify the plaintiff than to justify the decision to the profession. If the defendant had derived no benefit, he could not be made liable in any event. But where he had derived benefit, he could not, on the most favorable view, be made liable, unless he had himself been in fault, as was holden in *Hull* v. *Vaughan*, 6 Price, 157. Such seems to have been the doctrine held in *Kirtland* v. *Pounsett*, 2 Taunt. 145; *Vandenheuvel* v. *Storrs*, 3 Conn. 203; 2 Greenl. 337;[1] 13 Johns. 489.[2] Although the law will, in many cases, imply a contract to pay for use and occupation of land enjoyed by the defendant, and which rightfully belonged to plaintiff, yet, in the absence of all evidence of such occupation being by plaintiff's permission even, no case has been presented in the argument, which would justify a recovery in the present case. From the great diligence in preparation, manifested on the part of the plaintiff, we are satisfied no such case exists. And we are the more satisfied in this conclusion from our utter inability to conjecture any good basis upon which such a decision could rest.

Judgment affirmed.

———

USE AND OCCUPATION, ACTION FOR AGAINST VENDEE: See *Little* v. *Pearson*, 19 Am. Dec. 289, note 290; *Richardson* v. *McKinson*, 12 Id. 308, note 312.

THE PRINCIPAL CASE IS CITED and approved in *Way* v. *Raymond*, 16 Vt. 376; *Chamberlin* v. *Donahue*, 44 Id. 59; *Dwight* v. *Cutler*, 3 Mich. 573; and in *McNair* v. *Schwartz*, 16 Ill. 25.

---

1. *Wyman* v. *Hook.*   2. *Bancroft* v *Wardwell;* S. C., 7 Am. Dec. 395.

STRONG *v.* BARNES.

[11 VERMONT, 221.]

DECISION OF TRIAL COURT ON QUESTIONS OF FACT IS FINAL, and can not be examined into on exceptions.

ONE WHO SELLS PERSONAL PROPERTY THAT HE DOES NOT OWN, is liable in assumpsit on his warranty.

DIFFERENT WRITINGS ON SAME SUBJECT EXECUTED AT SAME TIME must be treated as one instrument and construed together.

ASSUMPSIT. Plea, *non assumpsit*, and issue to the court. The plaintiff, to support his declaration, offered two papers, of which the following are copies:

"Addison, March 1, 1832. In consideration of one hundred dollars received of Moses M. Strong, of Rutland, I do hereby sell and transfer to the said Moses M. all my right, title, interest, property, claim, and demand of, in, and unto a certain carding-machine in Bristol, in the state of Connecticut, which is in the possession of Miles Lewis, it being the same machine which I used and occupied at said Bristol, and also all apparatus and appendages belonging to said carding-machine. Asahel Barnes."

"Messrs. Miles Lewis and Charles G. Gray: I have this day sold to Moses M. Strong the carding-machine which I own in Bristol, in the care of Mr. Lewis, and I wish you would deliver said machine to him or his order, and render him such assistance towards selling or otherwise disposing of said machine as you may have it in your power to do. Asahel Barnes."

The plaintiff also offered evidence tending to show that at the time of the contract the defendant had no carding-machine in the hands of said Lewis. The defendant insisted that the order was no part of the contract. But the court decided that the order was to be used in construing the contract, and that the bill of sale amounted to a warranty that the defendant was owner of a machine mentioned in the contract, and rendered judgment for the plaintiff. The defendant excepted. The other facts are stated in the opinion.

C. Linsley, for the defendant.

E. L. Ormsbee, for the plaintiff.

By Court, WILLIAMS, C. J. There does not appear to be any question of law of any importance presented in this case. The questions were principally those of fact, and, as such, the decision of the county court upon them was final. Under the declaration, all which the plaintiff was bound to show, was that the defendant sold or attempted to sell a carding-machine, when, in point of fact, he had none. If he affirmed that he had an interest in a carding-machine, and released that interest, when, in fact, he had none, he was liable to the plaintiff on his warranty, whether he sold the machine itself, or his interest, right, or title in said machine. The county court found, as a matter of fact, that the defendant was not the owner of any machine, but he affirmed that he was, and how then can it be that he said he sold any one in particular, when he did not own any one, nor can it be ascertained, nor is it of any consequence which of the three machines, about which testimony was taken, was in his mind at the time. As to the admission of the order, the county court were right. It was decided in the case of *Raymond* v. *Roberts*, 2 Aik. 204 [16 Am. Dec. 698], that different writings, upon the same subject, executed at the same time, are to be treated as one instrument, and construed together. If the order was material to a right understanding of the contract, it should have been received for that purpose. If it was not material, the admission of it would not afford any room for disturbing the judgment.

The judgment of the county court, on all the questions of law presented, was correct and must be affirmed.

———

WRIT OF ERROR DOES NOT LIE TO AN INFERIOR COURT to review its decision upon matters of fact: *People* v. *Haynes*, 28 Am. Dec. 530.

DIFFERENT INSTRUMENTS EXECUTED AT SAME TIME, between the same parties, and relating to the same subject-matter, are to be taken as one, and construed together: *Hills* v. *Miller*, 24 Am. Dec. 218, note 222; *Isham* v. *Morgan*, 23 Id. 361; *Jackson* v. *McKenny*, 20 Id. 690, note 692; *Raymond* v. *Roberts*, 16 Id. 698; *Clap* v. *Draper*, 3 Id. 215, note 217; *Rogers* v. *Bancroft*, 20 Vt. 256, citing the principal case.

———

TOWN OF MOUNTHOLLY *v.* TOWN OF ANDOVER.

[11 VERMONT, 226.]

MARRIAGE CELEBRATED BY JUSTICE OF PEACE WITHOUT CONSENT OF THE PARTIES is void, and can not change the settlement of the woman.

VOID MARRIAGE MAY BE IMPEACHED in all cases where it comes in controversy collaterally, between those not parties to the contract.

TOWN CAN NOT INSTITUTE PROCEEDINGS TO ANNUL VOID MARRIAGE.—A decree of divorce can only be obtained at the suit of the parties to the marriage.

APPEAL from an order of removal of Abigail Warner and her two children from the town of Mountholly to the town of

Andover. The defendants pleaded that the paupers were unduly removed. It was admitted that Pierce Warner had had his last legal settlement in the town of Andover. The plaintiffs introduced in evidence, without objection, the record of a certificate of marriage of the said Abigail with the said Pierce, by a justice of the peace of Rutland county. It was admitted that the children were born since the date of said marriage. The defendants offered evidence tending to show that the ceremony of marriage was had and celebrated before said justice without the consent of the parties thereto. The plaintiffs objected to this evidence, but their objection was overruled. The court instructed the jury that the marriage would be void in law, if the ceremony was had without the consent of the parties thereto. The jury returned a verdict for the defendants, and the plaintiffs excepted. .

Merrill and Ormsbee, for the plaintiffs.

S. Foot, for the defendants.

By Court, REDFIELD, J. In this case the question of the legality of the marriage of the pauper arises upon the trial of the question of her legal settlement. The case found by the jury is, that the ceremony of marriage was had before the justice, without the consent of the parties. It was a marriage by force and duress. Is such a marriage sufficient to change the settlement of the female?

Such a marriage has always been held void. Marriage is a contract, and requires the *concensus animorum* as much as any other contract. It was considered exclusively a civil contract throughout all Christendom until the time of Pope Innocent III. In the tide of usurpation of temporal power by the bishop of Rome, that of celebrating marriages would not be considered unimportant. That pope accordingly declared it to be exclusively a religious sacrament. In most Catholic countries marriage has since that period been regarded as a sacrament, and, as such, to belong to the spiritual courts. In England, too, all matrimonial cases belong exclusively to the ecclesiastical jurisdiction. With us marriage is but a civil contract, required to be celebrated in some public manner before a civil magistrate or minister of the gospel. When the relation is once created, it becomes of perpetual obligation, unless dissolved by competent authority. It is admitted on all hands, that the mere fact of marriage without the consent of parties, is of no validity. It is merely and absolutely void. It is the same as the marriage of an idiot or lunatic: 1 Russ. on Crimes, 206; 1 Bl. Com. 438, 439; 2 Stark. Ev. 937. In all cases where the marriage is void, and comes in controversy collaterally between those not parties to the contract, as in the present case, it may be impeached: *Middleborough* v. *Rochester*, 12 Mass. 363.

But, perhaps, even a void marriage, where the parties to the contract are concerned, would not be allowed to be attacked in this collateral manner. The case of *Wightman* v. *Wightman*, 4 Johns. Ch. Cas. 343, is certainly a highly respectable authority to that effect. Some of the earlier authorities consider the marriage of a lunatic or idiot, even, as binding, until dissolved by a decree to that effect: *Manby* v. *Scott*, 1 Lev. 4, 5; S. C., 1 Sid. 109; Bac. Abr., Baron and Feme, H; 1 Roll. Abr. 357. Judge Reeve and Chancellor Kent seem to consider this the settled rule upon the subject.

I should very much hesitate to differ from so respectable authority, but must say I can see no good foundation for the rule. If the ceremony is a mere form, had without the consent of the parties, it no more constitutes a marriage than if it were had without the knowledge of the parties. And it would be monstrous to suppose, that if a justice of the peace should presume to record the marriage of two parties competent to contract, but without consulting the parties, it would be necessary for them to resort to a decree of divorce, in order to avoid the effect of the record. It is difficult to perceive why a marriage, had without the consent of the parties, should be of any more validity than if one of the parties had, at the time, a former husband or wife living. In the latter case, no decree of divorce is ever required. Indeed, the court would not pass a decree in such case. We always require evidence of a marriage before we proceed to decree a divorce. The very word divorce, *ex vi termini*, imports a marriage. At all events, it could not be required that the town of Andover, in order to avoid the effect of the marriage, should institute any proceeding to annul what is, in itself, void. In short, no such proceeding could be instituted by them. A decree of divorce could only be obtained at the suit of the parties to the marriage.

Judgment affirmed.

———

MARRIAGE IS INVALIDATED BY WANT OF CONSENT: See *Fornshill* v. *Murray*, 18 Am. Dec. 344; *Ferlat* v. *Gojon*, 14 Id. 554; *Clark* v. *Field*, 13 Vt. 467, citing the principal case. The principal case is distinguished in *Wiser* v. *Lockwood's estate*, 42 Id. 725.

STATE *v.* BENEDICT.

[11 VERMONT, 236.]

THREAT TO DO GRIEVOUS BODILY HARM, ACCOMPANIED BY ACTS showing a formed intent to carry such threats into execution, if intended to produce fear of bodily harm in the mind of the person threatened, and calculated to produce that effect on the mind of a person of ordinary firmness, constitutes a breach of the peace, indictable under the statute of this state.

INFORMATION in three counts, the last of which was in these words: "And the state's attorney aforesaid, on his oath aforesaid, further gives said court to understand and be informed, that Henry Benedict, of Rutland, in said county of Rutland, on the first day of December, 1837, and on divers other days and times between that date and the time of this presentment, with force and arms, at Rutland aforesaid, did greatly disturb and break the peace by tumultuous and offensive carriage, and by threatening, quarreling, and challenging, and by lying in wait for one Sally Benedict, and by threatening to kill the said Sally Benedict, to the great disquiet, terror, and alarm of the said Sally Benedict and other good citizens of this state, and other wrongs then and there did, to the evil example of others in like case offending, contrary to the form," etc. The evidence given under this count showed that at the various times and places named therein, the defendant with many awful imprecations threatened to take the life of Mrs. Benedict, who was his wife. The court charged the jury that if they believed the threats were made with intent to put her in fear of her life or other bodily harm, and that they were calculated to produce such effect upon a person of ordinary sagacity and forecast, and that they did produce this effect, they would be warranted in finding a verdict against the defendant, notwithstanding the threats were not made in the presence of Mrs. Benedict, or under such circumstances as to induce a fear of immediate personal violence. The jury found the defendant guilty, and he excepted to the instructions of the court.

R. R. Thrall, for the defendant.

S. Foot, state's attorney, for the prosecution.

By Court, REDFIELD, J. Whatever was once thought upon the subject, it is now well settled that mere threats, in words not written, is not an indictable offense at common law. It is said, in many of the books, that it was formerly indictable. This might have been, and probably was the case at the time the statute, in this state, in relation to the subject was passed. It is there said "if any person shall, in any manner, disturb or break the peace, by tumultuous and offensive carriage, by threatening, quarreling, challenging, assaulting, beating, or striking any other person," he shall be liable, on conviction, to pay such fine as "the court taking into consideration the situation of the party smiting or being smitten, the instrument and danger of the assault, the time, place, and provocation, according to the nature of the offense, shall adjudge." The phraseology of this statute would seem to indicate, with sufficient distinctness, that threatening was one of the modes of disturbing the public peace, which was intended to be punished criminally. Seven modes of disturbing the public peace are enumerated, for any one of which it is provided the offender shall pay such fine as the court shall adjudge. Had the statute left the matter here, no doubt could have arisen in relation to its import. It is absurd to suppose that any court, in assessing a fine, should not regard the enormity of the offense in all its essential circumstances. But out of over-caution it seems that is made an express requisition of the statute. And to prevent all misapprehension, the circumstances of aggravation or excuse are enumerated. And it is said, these circumstances do not include threatening or any of its forms, but exclude it. It will not so appear on close examination. The subdivisions of the offense begin with the least considerable "tumultuous and offensive carriage," and go forward throughout the chain in a direct climax. Whereas, in enumerating the peculiar characteristics of enormity or excuse attending the several subdivisions of the offenses, the statute begins with the highest grade, *i. e.*, "smiting," etc., and proceeds throughout the degrees in an anti-climax. In this enumeration of the circumstances to be considered by the court in fixing the extent of the fine, only battery and assault are specifically named. The statute then concludes in general terms, "the time, place, and provocation," which must, of course, refer to each of the seven species of offense defined in the enacting clause; and last of all, "according to the nature of the offense shall be adjudged." What offense? Why, surely, a breach of the public peace in any one of the modes named.

It is not necessary to inquire how far threats were punishable at common law, for the offense is here defined by statute. Any threats, which disturb the public peace, are made an offense. But what is the public peace? Almost every one has some more or less certain notion of the public peace, and still it may not be very easy to define it in words. It is, so to speak, that invisible sense of security, which every man feels so necessary to his comfort, and for which all governments are instituted. A threat, in order to violate this sense of security, must be of some grievous bodily harm, must be put forth in a desperate and reckless manner, accompanied by acts showing a formed intent to execute them, must be intended to put the person threatened in fear of bodily harm, and must produce that effect, and must be of a character calculated to produce that effect upon a person of ordinary firmness. Threats of this character were no doubt intended to be made an offense, and it would do manifest violence to the statute not so to decide. The mere fact that such threats are not now considered an indictable offense at common law, can have but little weight in the argument. At the time the statute was passed this was considered doubtful, and the statute was made thus specific to relieve that doubt.

There is another reason why here, more than at common law, mere threats should be considered an offense punishable by indictment. At common law the person threatened can swear the peace against the offender, and obtain redress in that way, by obtaining security against the commission of the offense threatened. This mode of preventive justice has not been much resorted to, if, indeed, it exists in this state. It is believed the legislature intended the remedy here given to supersede its necessity. The sending of threatening letters is an offense of a different character.

Judgment, that the respondent take nothing by his exceptions, and that he pay a fine of ten dollars, to the treasurer of the state, and costs of prosecution, etc.

BENNETT, J., dissenting.

THOMAS *v.* DIKE.

[11 VERMONT, 273.]

INFANT MAY SUE BY PROCHEIN AMI, in this state, notwithstanding he may have a guardian.

WHERE INFANT MAKES CONTRACT TO SERVE ANOTHER, AND AFTERWARDS AVOIDS IT, he may recover what his services are reasonably worth, taking into account any injury the other party sustains by the avoiding of the contract. And, if such injury be equal to the value of the services rendered, he can recover nothing.

ACTION on book account. The plaintiff, an infant, sued by

prochein ami. The defendant pleaded in abatement, that the suit ought to have been brought in the name of the guardian. The county court adjudged the plea insufficient, and the defendant excepted. After judgment to account, the auditors reported that the plaintiff, who had agreed to work for the defendant for a year, left him without just cause before the expiration of the year, and that the damages to the defendant by reason of the plaintiff's leaving him, exceeded the balance claimed by the plaintiff for his labor. They therefore reported nothing due from the defendant to the plaintiff. The court accepted the report, and gave judgment for the defendant to recover his costs. The plaintiff excepted.

S. Foot, for the plaintiff.

P. Smith, for the defendant.

By Court, WILLIAMS, C. J. On the plea in abatement it is sufficient to remark, that the right of an infant to sue by *prochein ami,* although first given by statute, seems to have been recognized as a part of the common law in most of the states. In this state it has never been doubted that he may sue by *prochein ami.* It is sufficient that the guardian does not dissent, and although he may dissent, yet if it is necessary, and for the benefit of the infant, he may sue by *prochein ami,* notwithstanding such dissent. The decision of the county court on this point was correct.

On the other question it is contended that there were two separate contracts. If so, the argument of the counsel for the plaintiff is irresistible, that what was earned under the first contract could not be merged in damages for failing to perform the second. A minor would not be liable for damages in such a case. We think, however, there was but one contract or undertaking, and what is called the second contract was only making an election agreeably to the terms of the contract, and giving up the right of determining the time of service at pleasure. The question then arises, what is the effect of the contract, and the consequences of its being abandoned in the manner stated? If the plaintiff was of full age there could be no doubt. But inasmuch as the plaintiff was an infant, not bound by his contracts, but at liberty to rescind them, except in certain cases, it presents a very serious question whether he should not recover a compensation for his services without any regard to his contract. This can not be considered a contract for necessaries and therefore binding, as an infant can not judge for himself as to the value of his services, the time suitable to bind himself, or the nature of the employment. An express contract to pay for necessaries to be thereafter furnished for a length of time would not be valid. Nor can the contract be considered as binding, as contended for in the argument, because he might be compelled to go out to work by his guardian or the overseer of the poor. The infant could not have been compelled to make a contract of this nature. The infant was not bound by this contract so as to be liable to damages for the non-performance of it, but was entitled to recover what he reasonably deserved to have for his services. In a similar case in the state of Massachusetts it was held that a minor could recover no more than, under all the circumstances, the services were worth, taking into consideration any disappointment, amounting to an injury, which the other party would sustain by the avoiding of the contract: *Moses* v. *Stevens*, 2 Pick. 322.[1] The court are inclined to adopt this rule, and although I have great doubt whether it is not infringing the general rule of law on the subject of contracts with infants, yet I more readily yield my assent to this course, on principles of policy, when I reflect that so many minors are emancipated by their parents by giving them their time, as it is called—a practice which, though sanctioned by judicial decisions, I regret has prevailed—and become adults for the purpose of making contracts, and remain infants to avoid them. It would be unsafe for community, unless some such principle were adopted. The case under consideration must be decided on this ground. The plaintiff made a contract for service and avoided it. It is found that his services were of no value, and many such cases will happen when a person abandons his contract, so that the other party is injured more than the services were worth. He ought not, therefore, to recover anything.

The judgment of the county court, which was in favor of the defendant, must be affirmed.

PROCHEIN AMI SUING FOR INFANT: See *Miles* v. *Kaigler*, 30 Am. Dec. 425; *Fulton* v. *Rosevelt*, 19 Id. 409; *Apthorp* v. *Backus*, 1 Id. 26.

INFANT MAY RECOVER ON A QUANTUM MERUIT THE VALUE OF SERVICES performed by him under a contract of service which he afterwards avoids before the entire performance of it, deducting any loss the employer may sustain by the infant's failure to fully perform: *Hoxie* v. *Lincoln*, 25 Vt. 210; *Patrick* v. *Putnam*, 27 Id. 761; *Meeker* v. *Hurd*, 31 Id. 642, all citing the principal case.

1. 2 Pick. 322.

SWIFT *v.* DEAN.

[11 VERMONT, 323.]

LEVY OF EXECUTION ON EQUITY OF REDEMPTION IN MORTGAGED PREMISES IS VOID if made upon a part thereof described by metes and bounds. A levy upon any part less than the whole, must be upon some aliquot portion of the whole.

TENANT MAY DISPUTE HIS LANDLORD'S TITLE by showing that he was led to acknowledge the tenancy under a misapprehension as to such title, and that he was, at the time of his acknowledgment of said title, actually in possession as tenant of another.

EJECTMENT. Plea, the general issue. The plaintiff claimed title to the premises by virtue of a deed from one Smith, who derived his title under a levy of an execution in his favor against Dunton and Fenton. In this levy the premises were described as incumbered by four several mortgages, and a part of the whole mortgaged premises were appraised and set off by metes and bounds, subject to the mortgages. The defendants were in possession at the date of the plaintiff's writ. The plaintiff offered the said levy in evidence, but the defendants objected thereto, and the court rejected it. The plaintiff also offered testimony tending to prove that defendant Dean occupied the premises as plaintiff's tenant, and that the other defendants occupied under Dean. The defendants offered in evidence a mortgage of the premises from said Dunton and Fenton to Underhill, Sutherland, Bloomer, Vanderlip, and Petty, together with a lease from three of said mortgagees, authorizing said Dean to take and keep possession of the mortgaged premises. The plaintiff objected to the introduction of this evidence, but the court admitted it. There was also evidence tending to show that said lease was made in pursuance of an agreement by Dunton, Smith, and the mortgagees, and that Dean took possession under it with the consent of Dunton and Smith. The jury found for the defendants, and the plaintiff excepted.

S. Swift, pro se.

Sargeant and Miner, for the defendants

By Court, REDFIELD, J. In this case the plaintiff relied upon the levy of an execution in favor of *Noah Smith* v. *Dunton and Fenton* as the basis of his title to the premises sued for. That levy was, by the court below, decided to be wholly void, and there is no doubt the decision was sound. The levy of an execution upon the equity of redemption in mortgaged premises, if upon any portion less than the whole, must be upon an aliquot proportion of the whole, and not upon a part described by metes and bounds: *Collins* v. *Gibson*, 5 Vt. 243; *Smith* v. *Benson*, 9 Id. 138 [31 Am. Dec. 614]. Such levy is absolutely void. It is questionable whether such a defect would be cured by either of the statutes in this state in relation to defective levies upon real estate. It is quite certain that neither of these statutes can affect the present case. The statute of 1835 cures defects in those cases only where the creditor is in possession of the land levied upon, which is not the present case, and that of 1837 will not aid the plaintiff, because the term of two years from the passing of the act had not expired at the time of the trial in the court below. The same is true of the other objection to this levy. The amount of the mortgages is nowhere stated in the levy. This is expressly required by statute, and would seem to be an indispensable prerequisite to the passing of the title.

The levy being rejected, the other testimony by which the plaintiff attempted to show that the defendants had acknowledged themselves tenants under him, as it had express reference to his title under the levy, should also have been rejected. For it will hardly be allowed, when the debtor has a tenant in possession of land upon which his creditor levies, and the tenant promises to pay rent to the creditor upon condition of his having obtained the title to the land, that, when the levy proves void, the creditor may still put out the tenant of the debtor upon the force of this acknowledgment of tenancy. This would be extending the doctrine of tenants' estoppel from denying the landlord's title to a fraudulent, and almost to a ludicrous extent. It has long been settled, that where the landlord's title has expired, the tenant may, on that ground, defend in ejectment. I take it the reason of that rule is, that the tenant's obligation is thereby transferred to the real owner of the land, and it becomes indispensable to the right, of all concerned, that the former landlord should not interpose between the tenant and his rightful landlord. The same reason applies with greater force to the present case: 2 Stark. Ev. 533, and notes; *England* v. *Slade*, 6 T. R. 682;[1] *Doe ex dem. Jackson* v. *Ramsbotham*, 3 Mau. & Sel. 516, reported in 12 Petersdorff, 37.

The case is still stronger where the tenancy has been acknowledged, or rent paid under mutual misapprehension, or, what is sometimes the case, misrepresentation of the landlord's title. In such cases, it has been decided that the tenant is not estop-

---

1. 4 T. R. 682.

ped to show the facts in his defense: *Rogers* v. *Pitcher*, 1 Marsh.
541, abridged in 12 Petersdorff, 38, reported also in 1 Com. L.
355.[1] The last case was very similar to the one under consider-.
ation. The plaintiff, then, made out no case against the defendants, and the county court should have directed a verdict against
him. It therefore becomes unnecessary to consider the other
parts of the case.

Judgment affirmed.

———

CONVEYANCE BY METES AND BOUNDS by one co-tenant of a portion of the
common estate, is void; the conveyance should be of some aliquot portion of
the tenant's entire estate: See *Smith* v. *Benson*, 31 Am. Dec. 614, note 616.

WHEN TENANT NOT ESTOPPED FROM DISPUTING LANDLORD'S TITLE: See
Hall v. *Benner*, 21 Am. Dec. 394, note 404.

————————

EMERSON *v.* WILSON.

[11 VERMONT, 357.]

ALLOWING AMENDMENT WHICH ESSENTIALLY CHANGE THE PARTIES to an
action, is error, if such change has the effect of introducing a new cause
of action, not contained in the original declaration.

WHERE SUCH AN AMENDMENT WAS ALLOWED BY A JUSTICE OF THE PEACE,
the county court, on an appeal thereto, must dismiss the action, and can
not restore the declaration and cause of action to what it was before the
amendment.

ASSUMPSIT. Suit was commenced in a justice's court in the
name of "Emerson & Godfrey," as partners in trade. The
declaration was upon a note payable to "Emerson & Godfrey in
Co." The writ and declaration were, on motion, amended by
the order of the justice, by inserting "John" before Emerson,
and striking out the name of Godfrey. On the writ and declaration thus amended judgment was rendered in favor of Emerson and against the defendant. The defendant appealed to the
county court, where, on his motion, the cause was dismissed.
The plaintiff excepted.

R. M. Field, for the plaintiff.

O. Hutchinson, for the defendant.

WILLIAMS, C. J. It is first objected that the proceedings of
the county court, in dismissing the action, were erroneous, and
that, if the amendment was improper, they could do no more
than restore the suit to its former state, and the case of *Baker*
v. *Ripley*, 1 Aik. 84, is relied on. It is doubtless true, that, in

———

1. 1 Com. L. 577.

general, when an amendment has been improperly made by an inferior court, and that is disallowed or set aside, the case stands as though never amended, and this rule would apply to all amended declarations. If the amended declaration is rejected, the original one stands. In the present case, the only judgment, which the county court could render, was to dismiss. If Godfrey was ever a party, he ceased to be such when the amendment was made, and could not, by the county court, be brought back to the suit. The appeal was taken from a judgment rendered in favor of Emerson against the present defendant, on a note made payable to him. The defendant could not, in the county court, be compelled to answer to a suit on a different cause of action, to different parties, and if Emerson was, in point of fact, the sole party, he could not proceed with a suit declaring on a contract with another and different party.

The question then arises, whether the amendment, allowed in this case by the magistrate, was one which could be made according to established principles. Amendments are usually within the discretion of the court, and the granting or refusing them can not be questioned in any other tribunal. But when an amendment is made and the court had no power to grant it, the party affected may be entitled to relief. And although the improper exercise of a discretionary power may be without remedy, the exercise of a power where there is and can be no such discretion, is erroneous. Thus, allowing an amendment which changes entirely the form of action, and introduces a new count for a new course of action, not contained in the original declaration, has been adjudged to be such an error that the judgment of the court, making the amendment, was reversed: *Carpenter* v. *Gookin*, 2 Vt. 495 [21 Am. Dec. 566]. An amendment, essentially changing the parties, would be liable to the same objection, if the change of parties would have the effect to introduce a new cause of action, not contained in the original declaration. The amendment here allowed was of this character. It changed the parties. John Emerson might or might not have been of the firm of Emerson & Godfrey, and if he was, a suit in the name of one of the members of a firm, or for a cause of action accruing to him alone, is entirely different from a suit in the name of the firm. A note, payable to John Emerson, would not support a count on a note, payable to Emerson & Godfrey.

The authorities, which have been relied on in support of the amendment, we think, do not warrant the proceedings of the justice. A writ of error has been amended in England, by changing the parties, to make it conformable to the original record. The statute of 5 Geo. I., c. 13, permits an amendment to be made where there is a variance from the original record, and where the record is sent up to the court of error, that court, having it before them, are required to make such amendments as will make the writ conformable to the record. This was the true ground on which the amendment was allowed in the case in Cowper, 425,[1] although it was said the statute was sufficiently broad to have allowed the amendment on another ground. A new count may be added in England, and the name of the defendant may be altered. The courts have gone great lengths in amending the *capias*, and the reason given for it is, that it never appears on record: 1 Bos. & Pul. 342.[2] In the case of *Tabrum* v. *Tenant*, Id. 481, the consent of the defendant was required to an amendment of the *capias* by inserting the name of Lightfoot as a plaintiff, and the reason was, that the defendant would be in no worse situation than he then was. The plaintiff might declare against him at the suit of Tabrum, and immediately after file a declaration, by the by, at the suit of Tabrum and Lightfoot. When a defendant is arrested on a *capias*, in the courts in England, he is considered as in custody, and the plaintiff must file a declaration in chief, that is, for the cause for which the writ was prayed out, and may then file a declaration, by the by, as it is termed, for a different cause of action, and I can see no good reason why, under this practice, the amendment should not have been allowed, without the consent of the defendant. But when the writ and declaration go out together, as they do in this state, the party should be confined to the cause of action contained in his declaration, and should not be permitted, by an amendment, to introduce new parties, or a new cause of action.

We are satisfied that the magistrate permitted an amendment which was not authorized by law. The declaration and cause of action could not be restored in the county court to what it was before the amendment, and the judgment of the county court, dismissing the action, must be affirmed.

AMENDMENT WILL NOT BE ALLOWED, WHICH CHANGES WHOLE CHARACTER OF LITIGATION: See *Lloyd* v. *Brewster*, 27 Am. Dec. 88; *Ball* v. *Claflin*, 16 Id. 407, note 409; *Shock* v. *McChesney*, 2 Id. 415, note 417.

----

1. *Verelst* v. *Rafael.*   2. *Davis* v. *Owen.*

FLETCHER *v.* AUSTIN ET AL.

[11 VERMONT, 447.]

WHERE BOND, IN OBLIGATORY PART, CONTAINS NAMES OF SEVERAL PER-
SONS as sureties, if a part of them sign with an understanding, and on
the condition, that it is not to be delivered to the obligee until signed
by the others, it will not be effectual as to those who do sign, until the
condition is complied with. Nor will they be made liable by the others
signing it a long time after default in the performance of the condition of
the bond, unless they then consent to the signing and delivery thereof.

WHERE BOND IS DELIVERED WITHOUT SIGNATURES OF ALL THE OBLIGORS
named therein, the obligee is bound to inquire whether those who have
signed consent to its being delivered without the signatures of the others.

DEBT on a bond, given to the plaintiff as sheriff of Windsor
county, to save him harmless from any loss or liability, in consequence of any neglect or misconduct of one Parkhurst, who
had been appointed a deputy sheriff for the ensuing year. Three
of the defendants pleaded the general issue. The other defendants made no answer. There was a verdict for the defendants,
and the plaintiff excepted. The other facts sufficiently appear
from the opinion.

Marsh and Swan, and A. Tracy, for the plaintiff.

J. Converse and T. Hutchinson, for the defendants.

By Court, WILLIAMS, C. J. This action is defended by three
of the defendants only, and the question is, whether the bond
has ever been so delivered as to be obligatory on them. On
the case as presented, the question as to a second delivery does
not arise. There was not, as to all the signers, an inchoate or
imperfect delivery in the first place, when the bond passed from
the obligors to the obligee, to be absolute on the happening of
a certain event. If the bond was delivered so as to be effectual
against all, there was but one delivery. A deed takes effect
only from the delivery, and our attention is drawn to the inquiry whether this bond was delivered. In the first place, as to
those who first signed, viz., Austin and May, it is evident that
it never was delivered with their consent. They might require
such terms and conditions to be complied with as they thought
proper before the deed should take effect as their deed. Where
a bond contains, in the obligatory part, the names of several
persons, as sureties, if a part sign with an understanding and
on the condition that it is not to be delivered to the obligee
until signed by the others, it is not effectual as to those who do
sign, until the condition is complied with. Whether it is

necessary, to make this defense available, that the obligee should know of this condition, it is not necessary to decide.   If the bond contains the names of other obligors, and is delivered without the signature of all, the obligee must inquire whether those who have signed consent to its being delivered without the signatures of the others.   The case of *Pawling et al.* v. *The United States*, 4 Cranch, 219; *United States* v. *Lefflers*, 11 Pet. 66; *Johnson* v. *Baker*, 4 Barn. & Ald. 440, are authorities that this defense will avail those who thus sign a bond if the other signatures are not procured.

The bond was given over to the plaintiff in this situation, with the signatures of only two of the obligors, and so remained during the year that Parkhurst, the principal, was deputy sheriff, and when all the acts and neglects of Parkhurst were done or suffered, which would occasion a liability on the bond.   Austin and May were not then liable therefor, as their contemplated obligation had not taken effect, and if they knew of the default of Parkhurst they must also have known that they were not liable therefor, unless the other persons who were to be sureties with them were also liable.

If after the default of Parkhurst this bond had been executed and delivered by all who now appear as signers, it is not doubted but that all would be liable.   A bond of indemnity may as well be taken to secure for defaults previous to the delivery as for those which may be subsequent.   But it should appear that the obligors so intended at the time of the delivery, and to bring this principle to aid the plaintiff's case, it should be shown that the first signers assented to a delivery and perfecting of the bond after the defaults had happened.   This has not been shown in the case before us.   The signatures which were obtained after the year and after the bond had been sued, can not give effect to the bond not only against themselves but against those who were not liable for the acts of Parkhurst as deputy sheriff.

It was argued at the bar, and truly, that the first signers contemplated a delay in obtaining the signatures of the others. They never contemplated, however, or assented that the bond should go out of the possession of Parkhurst before the others had signed, nor could they have contemplated that a liability should be created against them at any subsequent period by the act of others against their will and without their consent.   Possibly, if the others had signed within a reasonable time, although the bond had been handed over to the plaintiff by Park-

hurst, they might have been liable. But it would not be a
reasonable time to do this after the year had expired and after
Parkhurst had ceased to be a deputy sheriff, so that the bond,
when it was delivered, should be delivered as a forfeited bond.
The conclusion is, that as to some of the defendants, they never
agreed to become sureties for the acts of the principal, unless
others should become jointly sureties with them. They never
consented to become liable for the past defaults of Parkhurst,
and therefore the bond declared on was not the joint bond of
the defendants.

The judgment of the county court is, therefore, affirmed.

———

BOND NOT SIGNED BY ALL PARTIES NAMED THEREIN, VALIDITY OF: See
Sharp v. *United States*, 28 Am. Dec. 676, note 679, where this subject is discussed at length; also *City of Sacramento* v. *Dunlap*, 14 Cal. 423, and *People*
v. *Hartley*, 21 Id. 589, citing the principal case. The principal case is distinguished in *Passumpsic Bank* v. *Goss*, 31 Vt. 318.

———

GILMAN *v.* HALL.
[11 VERMONT, 510.]

ONE MAY RECOVER ON QUANTUM MERUIT FOR WORK DONE UNDER A CON-
TRACT, although it was not performed according to such contract, if the
work is beneficial to him for whom it has been done, and the parties can
not, on a rescission of the contract, be placed *in statu quo.*

ONE WHO PROMISES TO PAY FOR WORK WHEN DONE, OR GIVE HIS NOTE
therefor payable in a year, is, on his refusal to give his note, immediately
liable to an action for the amount due for such work.

ACTION on book account. There was a judgment to account,
and an auditor appointed, who reported the accounts of the
parties. He found that, if the court should decide that the
plaintiffs were entitled immediately to recover from the defendant the whole sum due to them, owing to his refusal to give
his note, there was due to them the sum of seventeen dollars
and fifty-four cents; but if the court should decide that the
plaintiffs were not entitled to recover the balance due for building the wall, until the expiration of the year, that there was due
to them the sum of one dollar and fifty-nine cents only. The
county court decided that the plaintiffs were entitled to the latter sum only, and to this decision they excepted. The other
facts appear from the opinion.

J. A. Wing, for the plaintiffs.

O. H. Smith. for the defendant.

By Court, BENNETT, J.   Two questions are raised in the argument of this case: are the plaintiffs entitled to maintain an action for the balance due them? and, if so, can such action be brought before the expiration of the year? It is urged, that the plaintiffs, having failed to build a part of the whole wall quite four and a half feet high, as they had contracted to do, have forfeited the right to recover. It will be seen from the report, that the auditor finds that the plaintiffs have built sixty dollars' worth of wall, at the prices stipulated, though a part of the whole wall was not quite as high as the contract required. Though the plaintiffs might not be able to recover on the special contract, not having specifically performed it on their part, still we think, according to the current of authorities, they may recover on a *quantum meruit*. It does not appear that the plaintiffs' failure to build some portion of the wall quite four and a half feet high was from design. The defendant has the full benefit of their labor, and principles of common justice require that he should render an equivalent for the benefit received. The labor of the plaintiffs must, from the very nature of the case, be for the permanent benefit of the lands of the defendant, and can not in any way be made productive to the plaintiffs by a rescinding of the contract. The parties can not be placed in *statu quo*. The case of *Dyer* v. *Jones*, 8 Vt. 205, is an authority for this part of the case.

The auditor finds that the plaintiffs have received forty-five dollars, and that, as to the balance, the defendant, by the agreement, was to pay it when the wall was finished, or give his note payable in one year from that time, at his election. The plaintiffs made application to him, and he refused to give his note for any sum whatever. The effect of such refusal is to prevent the defendant from claiming any benefit from the alternative of the contract, extending the time of payment, and he becomes immediately liable upon such refusal. We think, therefore, that the judgment below should be reversed, and judgment entered on the report for the plaintiffs to recover the sum of seventeen dollars and fifty-four cents, as reported by the auditor.

————

QUANTUM MERUIT ON SPECIAL CONTRACT: See *Merrill* v. *Ithaca & O. R. R. Co.*, 30 Am. Dec. 130, and note 142, where the other cases in this series on this subject are referred to. See also *Booth* v. *Tyson*, 15 Vt. 518, citing the principal case.

GILMAN v. PECK.

[11 VERMONT, 516.]

PAYMENT IN WORTHLESS OR BADLY DEPRECIATED BANK BILLS is not a valid payment. And a person receiving such bills, without fault or negligence on his part, in payment of a pre-existing debt, may treat the payment as void and resort to his original cause of action.

ACTION ON BOOK ACCOUNT MAY BE MAINTAINED in such a case.

ACTION on book account. Judgment to account having been rendered and an auditor having been appointed, he reported that the defendant in paying the plaintiff for certain goods which he had bought from him, gave to the plaintiff, among other money, a five-dollar bill of the Franklin bank, in Boston; that at the time of said payment, the defendant warranted the bill, and said that if it was not good he would make it good; that said bank had stopped payment several months previously, and that this fact was, at the time of the payment, known to the defendant, but was not known to the plaintiff; and that the bill at the time of the payment was not worth more than twenty or twenty-five cents. The county court rendered judgment on the report in favor of the plaintiff for five dollars and twenty-five cents, and the defendant excepted.

Miller and Heaton, for the defendant.

G. B. Manser, for the plaintiff.

By Court, REDFIELD, J. Notwithstanding it is said in *Wade's case*, 5 Co. 114, in regard to the payment of money, " If there be any counterfeit money in the same, yet, if the party then accept the same, he can not compel the party to change it; or if it be rent, yet the once acceptance is good, and the lessor may not re-enter;" and notwithstanding the doubts which have been intimated in the intermediate cases by eminent judges, it is at present, I apprehend, well settled, both in England and in most of the American states, that a payment in base coin, or counterfeit, or worthless bank paper is no valid payment. This is said by Abbott, C. J., in *Wilkinson* v. *Johnson*, 8 Barn. & Cress. 428; S. C., 10 Com. L. 140,[1] to be the clear and undisputed general rule of law. The following, among other cases, fully sustain this principle: *Jones* v. *Ryde*, 5 Taunt. 488; *Markle* v. *Hatfield*, 2 Johns. 455 [3 Am. Dec. 446]; *Young* v. *Adams*, 6 Mass. 182.

There is one important exception to the general rule above stated, in regard to bills or checks, *i. e.*, where the forged in-

----
1. 10 Com. L. 198.

strument bears, or purports to bear, the signature of the person
accepting the same, or of his correspondents, and he is guilty of
negligence in accepting a forged paper when he had superior
means at hand to determine its genuineness, which were not in
the power of the other party.   This exception is, no doubt, well
founded, and is sustained by numerous adjudged cases of high
authority: *Bank of the United States* v. *Bank of Georgia*, 10
Wheat. 338; *Gloucester Bank* v. *Salem Bank*, 17 Mass. 33; *Price* v.
Neal, 3 Burr. 1354; *Smith* v. *Mercer*, 6 Taunt. 76; *Bank of St.
Albans* v. *Farmers and Mechanics Bank*, 10 Vt. 141 [33 Am. Dec.
188.]   In many of the above cases the general rule above stated
is fully and distinctly recognized.   In the case of the *Bank of
the United States* v. *Bank of Georgia*, Justice Story says: "The
modern authorities certainly do, in a strong manner, assert,
that a payment received in forged paper, or any base coin, is
not good, and if there be no negligence in the party, he may recover back the consideration paid for them, or sue upon his
original demand."   Of the same import are the cases of *Jones* v.
Ryde, and *Markle* v. *Hatfield*.   In 10 Vt. 145, Judge Phelps says:
"It seems now well settled, that a person giving a security in
payment, vouches for its genuineness."   In most of the more
recent cases it is expressly held, that the party receiving such
forged or worthless paper, without fault, may, when he pays
money for it, maintain an action for money had and received, or
if he receive it in payment of a pre-existing debt, resort to his
original cause of action.   In addition to the above cases, this
point is expressly decided in the case of *Manufacturers and Mechanics Bank* v. *Gore et al.*, 15 Mass. 75 [8 Am. Dec. 83].   In
the last case, Chief Justice Parker says, "that when goods are
purchased upon credit, or money borrowed, and the security
agreed upon by the parties turns out to be of no value, and different from what it was represented by the debtor, it may be
treated as a nullity, and an action will lie immediately for the
sum it was intended to secure."   This was the point then distinctly in judgment.

And, although in the present case the plaintiff might, probably, upon the facts found, have brought a special action, in case,
against the defendant, yet he was not bound so to do.   He
might resort to his original demand.   And in doing so, it is not
very easy to perceive any good reason why he is not entitled to
the same remedy, which he would have been entitled to if no
payment had been attempted.   The facts reported in the present case, show distinctly that it was only by the false and fraud-

ulent representation of the defendant that the plaintiff was induced to take the bill. If, then, the plaintiff may sue upon his
original demand, it comes with a very ill grace from the defendant
to insist that he shall be deprived of his remedy on book, in consequence of the acknowledged fraud of the defendant. For, without that, these articles would have been charged on book in the
ordinary course of business. But as it has been long-settled
law, that a charge on book is not essential to the right to maintain the action, no case occurs to me where the plaintiff may
maintain a general action of assumpsit, for goods sold and delivered, and can not equally maintain this form of action. We
think the plaintiff should be allowed the present remedy.

Judgment affirmed.

———

PAYMENT IN NOTES OF INSOLVENT BANK, EFFECT OF: See *Corbit* v. *Bank
of Smyrna,* 3 Am. Dec. 635, note 652, where other cases are collected. See
also *Torrey* v. *Baxter,* 13 Vt. 458, and *Goodrich* v. *Tracy,* 43 Id. 319, both
citing the principal case. The principal case is distinguished in *Hall* v.
Eaton, 12 Vt. 512.

———

MOWER *v.* WATSON.

[11 VERMONT, 536.]

NEITHER PARTIES NOR THEIR COUNSEL ARE LIABLE TO AN ACTION OF
SLANDER for words spoken *bona fide* in the ordinary course of judicial
proceedings; but a party claiming this protection must have spoken the
words in the reasonable and necessary defense or pursuit of his rights,
and words spoken by counsel, to be privileged, must have been spoken in
the discharge of his duty to his client, and must have been pertinent to
the matter in question.

PRIVILEGE OF COUNSEL AND CLIENT IN THIS RESPECT ARE CO-EXTENSIVE.

WORDS "THAT IS A LIE" SPOKEN TO A WITNESS WHILE TESTIFYING to a
material point in a cause then on trial, are actionable, if spoken by a
party maliciously, and with intent to defame such witness.

ACTION on the case for slanderous words. The words alleged
to have been spoken by the defendant, of and concerning the
plaintiff, were: "That is a lie. I do intend to charge him with
telling a lie under oath." And these words were alleged to
have been spoken with reference to testimony which the plaintiff
was, at the time of the speaking, giving in a court of justice, in
the trial of a cause there pending, and upon a material point.
The testimony in the county court tended to prove that the defendant spoke to the plaintiff in this action while testifying in a
cause on trial in a court of justice, the words "That is a lie,"
and spoke the other words charged in the declaration, in answer

to a question of the counsel for the defendant in that cause. The court charged the jury, that if the defendant left the examination of the witness, and, instead of addressing himself to the court or to his own counsel, entered into an altercation with the witness, now plaintiff, and stated to others, about the room, the words complained of, with a view to insult and outrage the plaintiff's feelings and defame his character, the defendant was liable in damages, notwithstanding he might have supposed such a course would incidentally aid him in the result of his suit. The jury found for the plaintiff, and the defendant excepted.

L. B. Peck, for the defendant.

W. Upham and A. Spalding, for the plaintiff.

By Court, REDFIELD, J. The question raised by the bill of exceptions in this case is one of very considerable practical importance, and no little difficulty. It is believed, however, that the principle upon which this case must be decided, is distinctly settled in *Torry* v. *Field*, 10 Vt. 353. It is there considered that the privilege of all, whose duty or interest calls them to participate in the proceedings of courts of justice, is not to be made liable to an action of slander or libel, for anything spoken or written therein, provided it be in the ordinary course of proceedings, or *bona fide*. This privilege extends to court, jury, witnesses, parties, and their counsel. I am not inclined to believe that there is any good ground of distinction, as to the extent of this privilege, between counsel and client. Principle and authority seem to concur in requiring, that the privilege of the one should be co-extensive with that of the other. The counsel is but the agent of the client, and in that capacity, only, could claim any protection. We incline, then, to consider, that this privilege, as to parties in courts of justice, is correctly laid down in that case, where it is said, "that the party claiming the protection, must have spoken the words, in the reasonable and necessary defense or pursuit of his rights," in a suit either then pending or about to be instituted. And words spoken by counsel, to be privileged, "must have been spoken in the course of the discharge of his duty to his client, and must have been pertinent to the matter in question." I apprehend this is the general principle to be deduced from the cases upon this subject, and is carrying the privilege as far as reason or propriety would warrant. I do not, however, wish to be understood, that there may not be found cases carrying the rule much further;

but such cases have not been generally regarded as authority. In the case of *Hodgson* v. *Scarlett*, 1 Holt, 621, Mr. Baron Wood says: "I have always considered it to be an established principle in law, that for imputed slander, originating in judicial proceedings in court, no action will lie;" thus most obviously extending the privilege to every word spoken "in court," whether pertinent to the issue or not. This was at the *nisi prius* trial of the case. The words charged to have been spoken by defendant, Sir James Scarlett, were spoken by him in summing up to the jury, in a case tried at the Gloucester assizes, and seemed to have been admitted, on all hands, to have been pertinent. The rule thus laid down by the learned judge was much broader than the case required. The case was discussed before the full bench, C. P., and is reported in 3 Com. L. 204,[1] in note, and in 1 Barn. & Ald. 232. The judges delivered their opinions *seriatim*, confirming the nonsuit which was ordered at *nisi prius*. But each judge puts much stress upon the point of the words having been pertinent to the matter in question. Lord Ellenborough says, "it was clearly proved, that the words were relevant to the matter in issue." Bayley, J., says: "They, the words, were no more than the counsel was privileged in using, as pertinent to the matter in issue." Abbot, J., says: "Here the pertinency of the expressions was manifest." Holroyd, J., says: "His opinion in this case was governed first on the ground of the pertinency of the words to the matter in issue, and secondly, that no malice was proved."

In *Sir Richard Buckley and Wood's case*, 4 Co. 14, it is said, the defendant is not justified in preferring matter in the star chamber, which was only pertinent to a trial by indictment, because that court had no cognizance of such matters, and because "the bill hath not appearance of any ordinary course of justice." Chief Justice Swift, 1 Swift's Dig. 645, says, the defendant is justified, "if the words were spoken by him as counsel, and were pertinent to the matter in question;" and on page 488, "this must be understood where the words are pertinent to the issue." Mr. Starkie, in the recent and greatly improved edition of his treatise on evidence, lays down the rule thus: "But the defense would fail, if it appeared that the mode or the extent of the publication, was not warranted by the usual course of proceedings in such cases:" 2 Stark. Ev. 467, 468. In note 3, it is said, "great allowance is to be made for what a man says, when attending his own cause. He has a right to the utmost freedom in com-

_____

1. 3 Com. L. 243.

municating his sentiments to his counsel or the court; but he may not make this privilege a cover for malicious slander;" citing 1 Bro. 40,[1] and 4 Yeates, 322.[2] To say to a witness, who had just finished his testimony, "You have sworn to a manifest lie," is actionable: *Kean* v. *McLaughlin*, 2 Serg. & R. 469. To say to a witness while giving his testimony to a material point in the case, "That is false," is actionable, if spoken maliciously: *McClaughry* v. *Wetmore*, 6 Johns. 82 [5 Am. Dec. 194]. From the foregoing cases the true ground of the privilege is readily deduced. *Prima facie*, the party or his counsel is privileged for everything spoken in court. If any one considers himself aggrieved, in order to sustain an action for slander, he must show that the words spoken were not pertinent to the matter then in progress, and that they were spoken maliciously, and with a view to defame him. So that if the words spoken were pertinent to the matter in hand, the party and counsel may claim full immunity from an action of slander, however malicious might have been his motive in speaking them. So, too, if the words were not pertinent to the matter in issue, yet, if the party spoke them *bona fide*, believing them to be pertinent, no action of slander will lie. So that the plaintiff, in order to maintain this action, must prove, first, that the words spoken were not pertinent to the matter then in hand, and secondly, that they were not spoken *bona fide*. This was the view taken by the county court, and that judgment must be affirmed. The rule here laid down is fully sustained by the case of *Torry* v. *Field*, and numerous cases there cited, to which case I beg leave to refer, as containing my own views upon the propriety of the rule, more at length than it is deemed suitable here to repeat.

LIABILITY OF COUNSEL FOR WORDS SPOKEN AT TRIAL: See *Stackpole* v. *Hennen*, 17 Am. Dec. 187, and note 194.

WORDS IMPUTING PERJURY ARE ACTIONABLE: See *Commons* v. *Walters*, 27 Am. Dec. 635; *Thompson* v. *Lusk*, 26 Id. 91, note 95; *Gilman* v. *Lowell*, 24 Id. 96, note 104, where the other cases in this series are collected.

WAINWRIGHT *v.* WEBSTER.

[11 VERMONT, 576.]

PAYMENT BY BILLS OF BANK THAT HAD STOPPED PAYMENT, at the time it was made, does not extinguish the debt, although both the person who paid and the person who took the bills were then ignorant of the failure of the bank.

---

1. *Vigours* v. *Palmer*, P. A. Brown.   2. *Swearingen* v. *Birch*.

OFFICER RECEIVING WRIT FOR SERVICE, IS NOT THEREBY MADE AGENT OF THE PLAINTIFF for collecting the demand; and if he receives payment from the debtor he holds it as agent of the latter until he actually pays it to the creditor.

DEPOSITION TAKEN UPON NOTICE TO ADVERSE PARTY IS ADMISSIBLE, although it was taken in a case where an *ex parte* deposition might have been taken.

ASSUMPSIT on a promissory note. Plea, *non assumpsit.* The plaintiff proved the execution of the note, and rested. The defendant then introduced testimony tending to show that the plaintiff left the note with an attorney for collection; that the attorney made a writ upon it and gave it to an officer to serve; that the officer went to serve the writ, but not finding the defendant at home, he took payment from the defendant's father in two bills of the bank of Windsor, and promised to pay and take up the note. On the twenty-ninth of March, 1838, the officer gave these bills to the plaintiff's attorney, and took up the note. Nothing was known at this time by any of the parties of the failure of the bank of Windsor. A few days after, the plaintiff's attorney notified the officer that the bills were not good, and the officer then offered them to the defendant's father, but he refused to take them. The plaintiff offered evidence tending to prove that the bank of Windsor had wholly stopped payment before the twenty-ninth of March, 1838. The plaintiff offered a deposition, to which the defendant objected, because it was taken *ex parte,* more than thirty miles from the adverse party's place of residence, and was not filed with the clerk of the court thirty days before the commencement of the term of the court for which it was taken. The objection was overruled. There was a verdict for the plaintiff, and the defendant excepted.

Carpenter, Buck, and L. B. Peck, for the defendant.

O. H. Smith, for the plaintiff.

By Court, BENNETT, J. It is a principle of law, too well established to need authority, that where a bill of exchange, or note of a third person, is received in payment of a precedent debt, the risk of the insolvency of the maker is upon the party from whom the bill or note is received, unless there is an express agreement between the parties that the risk of the paper in this respect is to be the receiver's, or one is to be implied from the facts and circumstances of the case; and the great question is, whether this principle is applicable to paper issued by an incorporated bank. If it is true, that upon the payment of a bank bill in satisfaction of a precedent debt, in the absence of

all other facts, there is an implied agreement that the insolvency
of the bank is at the risk of the party receiving the bill; then it
follows that the authorities applicable to bills of exchange and
promissory notes do not apply to the case under consideration.
It is true, that by common consent, bank bills have, for the
purposes of business, been treated as money; but this is a conventional regulation for the convenience of business, and not a
legal one.   No state is authorized to coin money or pass any
law whereby anything but gold and silver shall be made a legal
tender in payment of a debt.   It was decided at the last term of
this court in Rutland county, that a note payable in bank bills
was not negotiable: 11 Vt. 268.[1]   They can not be recognized
in the legal acceptation of the term as money, but it is wholly
conventional.   This conventional understanding that bank bills
are to pass as money, is founded upon the solvency of the bank
and upon the supposition that the bills are equivalent in value
to specie, and are at any time convertible into specie, at the option of the holder.   Upon no other ground do bank bills, by
common consent, pass as money; and hence, there is an implied
agreement of the parties, at the time the bills are passed, that
they are equivalent to money; and they are paid by the one
party and received by the other on that supposition; and unless
this is the case, the one party does not pay what he supposes
he pays, nor the other receive what he intends to receive.
From this principle of common consent, that bank bills should
pass as money, it is the implied understanding of the parties
that the receiver should take upon himself the risk of all after
failures of the bank; but this principle can not be carried any
farther than this conventional regulation extends, and that is,
to treat them as money only so long as the bank which issues
them continues to redeem them in specie, or at least in other
bills equally acceptable as specie to the bill-holder.

When, therefore, a bank stops payment, the bills thereof cease,
by this conventional arrangement, to be the representative of
money; whether the particular bill-holder is apprised of that
fact or not; and from that time, the bills of such bank resume
their legal character of promissory notes and mere securities
for the payment of money.   If they are afterwards passed off to
a person equally ignorant of the failure of the bank, there can
be no implied agreement from this conventional arrangement to
treat them as money, so long as they are convertible into specie,
that the receiver shall sustain the loss which had then already

---

1. *Collins v. Lincoln.*

accrued to the bill-holder. It is difficult to see why there should be a distinction between bank bills, after they cease to be, by any conventional arrangement, the representative of money, and other promissory notes. The law is well settled in this and other states, that the payment of a debt in a forged or counterfeit bank bill, is not a satisfaction, though both parties are equally ignorant of the fact: See *Markle* v. *Hatfield*, 2 Johns. 458 [3 Am. Dec. 446], where Chancellor Kent reviews the authorities with much ability. The party paying must sustain the loss, or rather is not permitted to shift it upon the other party. The parties, in such case, act upon a mistake; the thing paid by the one, and received by the other, is not what they suppose it to be; and it would, indeed, be highly inequitable, that by this mistake the loss should be shifted from him, who had already sustained it, upon the other who was equally ignorant of the fact. In the case now before the court, there was a mutual mistake. The parties supposed the bills, when paid, were then convertible into specie, and equivalent to money; and both acted upon this supposition. Common justice then forbids that this loss, already sustained, should by this mutual mistake, be shifted from the defendant to the plaintiff.

In the state of Alabama, in the case of *Lowrey* v. *Murrill*, 2 Port. 280 [27 Am. Dec. 651]. a different doctrine is said to be established, though I have only seen a note of the case. In the case of *Young* v. *Adams*, 6 Mass. 182, a different doctrine is also incidentally thrown out; but the same question has been before the supreme court, and also the court of errors in the state of New York, in the case of *Lightbody* v. *Ontario Bank*, 11 Wend. 9, and 13 Id. 101 [27 Am. Dec. 179], where the decision was in conformity with the views of this court, and we think this the better opinion, and well sustained on principle, and calculated to do the most equal justice.

It is not the business of the officer, who receives a writ for service, to receive pay on the demand. He is only to serve the writ, and if the debtor pays the demand to the officer, he holds it as agent of the debtor, till he pays it to the creditor. The money in this case being paid to the creditor on the twenty-ninth of March, and after the bank had ceased to redeem its bills, is the same as if it had been then paid by the debtor.

The statute requires notice to be given of the taking of a deposition, to the adverse party, if living within thirty miles of the place of caption. If he lives more than thirty miles therefrom, and has notice, though the deposition might have been taken *ex parte*, still this could be no objection to its admissibility. The third section of the statute which requires *ex parte* depositions to be filed with the clerk of the court, thirty days before the session of the court in which the trial is to be had, can not restrain the admissibility of a deposition taken with notice, though taken in a case where the deposition might have been taken *ex parte*.

We discover no error in the proceedings of the court below, and the judgment is therefore affirmed.

PAYMENT IN BILLS OF INSOLVENT BANK, EFFECT OF: See note to *Gilman* v. *Peck, ante,* 702.

IN EJECTMENT, DEPOSITIONS TAKEN WITHOUT NOTICE to the warrantor, are not admissible in evidence: *Woodard* v. *Spiller,* 25 Am. Dec. 139.

DEPOSITIONS TAKEN UPON NOTICE TO SOME but not to all the adverse parties, may be used against those who had notice: *Hanly* v. *Blackford,* 25 Am. Dec. 114; *Jones* v. *Pitcher,* 24 Id. 716.

EDWARDS v. EDWARDS.

[11 VERMONT, 587.]

TRESPASS MAY BE MAINTAINED BY OWNER OF PERSONAL PROPERTY for conversion thereof, although he was not in the actual possession of it.

TRESPASS for a hog. Plea, the general issue. The plaintiffs gave in evidence a bill of sale to them of the hog in question, signed by the defendant. It was admitted that this bill of sale was executed upon sufficient consideration, and that the defendant was at the time of the sale the owner of the hog; but he had never delivered him to the plaintiffs, and soon after he had killed him and converted him to his own use. The county court gave judgment for the plaintiffs, and the defendant excepted.

C. Davis, for the defendant.

J. Bell and B. N. Davis, for the plaintiffs.

By Court, WILLIAMS, C. J. The owner of personal property is considered in law, as in possession. To maintain the action of trespass, it is sufficient if a plaintiff shows himself to be owner, or, against a wrong-doer, that he is in actual possession. By the bill of sale, the plaintiff in this case became the owner of the property sold, and as there was no agreement that he should not take possession, he could maintain an action of trespass against any one who destroyed or converted it.

The judgment of the county court is affirmed.

OWNER OF CHATTEL HAS SUFFICIENT CONSTRUCTIVE POSSESSION to maintain trespass: See *Root* v. *Chandler,* 25 Am. Dec. 546, note 548, where the other cases are collected.

WOODRUFF *v.* HINMAN.

[11 VERMONT, 592.]

CONTRACT IS WHOLLY VOID if any part of the consideration thereof is the suppressing of a criminal prosecution.

ACTION on a promissory note. Plea, the general issue. The facts are sufficiently stated in the opinion.

M. Hale, for the plaintiff.

C. Davis and N. H. Joy, for the defendant.

REDFIELD, J. In the present case, the principal consideration of the note sued being the costs and expenses of a criminal prosecution and the discontinuing the same, which the plaintiff had no right to do, the counsel for the plaintiff do not even argue that the consideration is valid to the full extent of the contract. But as there was included in the note ten dollars which the plaintiff was entitled to receive of the defendant, he claims that the contract shall be held good to that amount.

There can be little doubt, I apprehend, at the present day, that a consideration of the character set forth in the bill of exceptions is against law and void: *Hinesburg* v. *Sumner et al.,* 9 Vt. 23; *Armstrong* v. *Tobler,* 11 Wheat. 258, and cases cited in note; *Dixon* v. *Olmstead,* 9 Vt. 310 [31 Am. Dec. 629], and the case of *Swasey* v. *Mead and Chase,* there referred to. If a part of the consideration be invalid simply, and not unlawful, the contract is binding: *Pikard* v. *Cottels,* Yelv. 56; 1 Com on Con. 26; 8 Mass. 51,[1] by Sedgwick, J. But it is fully settled, that when any portion of the entire consideration of a contract is against law, that the whole contract is illegal and void, and can not be enforced: Cases cited above. If part of the consideration of a bill of exchange be the sale of spirituous liquors contrary to law, though the other part be money lent, the entire contract is void, and no part of it can be enforced: *Scott* v. *Gilman,*[2] 3 Taunt. 226; *Frotherston* v. *Hutchinson,*[3] Cro. Eliz. 199; *Crawford* v. *Morrell,* 8 Johns. 253. The court have not been able to perceive any ground upon which the plaintiff can be permitted to recover upon this note even to the amount of what was justly due him. This is but a reasonable punishment for including with his just due that which he had no right to take.

CONTRACTS, ANY PART OF WHOSE CONSIDERATION IS THE SUPPRESSING of a criminal prosecution, are void: See *Shaw* v. *Spooner,* 32 Am. Dec. 348, note 350, where the other cases on this subject are collected.

1. *Bliss* v. *Negus.*   2. *Scott* v. *Gillmore.*   3. *Featherston* v. *Hutchinson.*

FOSTER *v.* McGREGOR.

[11 VERMONT, 595.]

SALE OF PERSONAL PROPERTY EXEMPT FROM EXECUTION IS VALID as against creditors of the vendor, without any change in the possession.

TROVER for a cow. Plea, the general issue. The jury, under the instructions of the court, returned a verdict for the plaintiff, and the defendants excepted. The other facts sufficiently appear from the opinion.

B. N. Davis, for the defendants.

J. R. Skinner, for the plaintiff.

By Court, BENNETT, J. It has long been the law in this state, and has been most undeviatingly adhered to, that upon the sale of personal property, there must be a delivery, and a substantial and visible change in the possession, or the sale is fraudulent and void against creditors. The principle is, that the continuance of the vendor in the possession of the property after the sale, tends to give him a false credit, and enables him to impose upon third persons; and the rule of law requiring a change of possession is well calculated to prevent fraudulent sales, and is founded upon the soundest policy. No matter how honest the transaction may be, in point of fact, the law, from principles of policy, pronounces it fraudulent *per se*, and void. But the case now under consideration is one where the property sold was not liable to attachment, or execution, at the suit of any of the creditors of Bean, and there is no reason why a change in the possession should be indispensable to a valid sale as against creditors, any more than as between the parties. Creditors could have no claim upon this cow, as a means of satisfying their debts, and it is idle to talk about acquiring a false credit from the possession of property which is exempt from attachment and execution. No principle of policy requires a change in the possession of such property. It must be as valid against creditors, as against the parties themselves without such change.

It has been said, in the argument, that the statute exemption of this cow from legal process, is a personal privilege, and that no one can avail himself of it but Bean himself. But this case does not depend upon the question, whether, where property is taken on execution which is exempt therefrom, any one but the debtor can avail himself of such exemption; but, upon what is the effect of leaving such property in the possession of the debtor after sale. Does it enable the debtor to acquire a false credit?

And is it against sound policy as opening the door to fraud?
We think not, and that this case should furnish an exception to
the general rule on this subject.

The judgment below is, therefore, affirmed.

GILMAN *v.* THOMPSON.

[11 VERMONT, 643.]

COURTS OBTAIN JURISDICTION OF DEFENDANTS BY SERVICE OF PROCESS,
either on their persons, or on their property within the jurisdiction of
the court.

WHERE OFFICER ATTACHES REAL ESTATE AND LEAVES A COPY of the writ
with the town clerk, the court thereby acquires jurisdiction of the party.

ATTACHMENT OF PROPERTY AND NOTICE TO THE PARTY ARE DIFFERENT
THINGS; and the circumstance that the officer is, in this state, by the
same process commanded to attach and to give notice does not alter
this fact.

WHERE RETURN OF ATTACHMENT DOES NOT SHOW PERSONAL SERVICE, the
court may order notice to be given in any manner recognized by law, since
it already has jurisdiction, and a judgment rendered by it after notice
given by publication is not void.

UNAUTHORIZED ALTERATION OF RETURN ON ORIGINAL WRIT does not affect
the title of a purchaser at an execution sale, where such alteration was
not in a part of the return that gave jurisdiction to the court, but only in
that which related to notice.

FACT THAT ONE HAS RESIDED SEVERAL YEARS IN CANADA does not of itself
justify the inference that he is an alien.

OFFICER IS EXCUSED FROM CALLING ON DEBTOR TO CHOOSE APPRAISERS,
where the record shows that such debtor resides without the state, and
that there is no attorney.

DESCRIPTION OF LAND IN LEVY OF AN EXECUTION is sufficiently certain, if
it can be made so by reference to a record.

EJECTMENT. Plea, the general issue. The plaintiff claimed
title to the land by virtue of an attachment on mesne process
and a levy of an execution in his favor against Moses Norris,
Mesheck Norris, and David Norris. For the purpose of showing
the source of the title claimed by the defendant, the plaintiff
gave in evidence a copy of a deed from said Moses Norris to the
defendant, conveying the land in controversy. He also offered
in evidence the copy of the original writ in the above-named
suit and the officer's return thereon, and the record of a judgment in that suit, rendered against said defendants by default,
and without any other notice than the publication of the
usual order in cases where the defendant is out of the state. It
appeared from the testimony that after the judgment and levy,

and the first trial of this action, the plaintiff's attorney, without
leave of the court, but openly and in presence of the officer
who served the writ, altered the word defendant to defendants
in the return of the officer on the writ, and at the end of the
original return added: "The defendants having removed without this state, and having no known agent or attorney within the
same." The jury returned a verdict for the plaintiff. The other
facts are sufficiently stated in the opinion.

E. Paddock, for the defendant.

Maeck and Smalley, and E. G. Johnson, for the plaintiff.

By Court, COLLAMER, J. The first question is, was the judgment, which the plaintiff recovered against Norris, void, when
rendered? To render the proceedings of a court void (not erroneous, or voidable), the court must be without jurisdiction,
either of the subject-matter or the parties; and, in such case,
the court, the officer issuing execution, and the sheriff who serves
it, are all trespassers, and no subsequent proceedings can cure
the evil. Even the appearance of the parties and submitting to
the court will not confer jurisdiction. That the court had jurisdiction of the subject-matter of that judgment, that is, of such
a debt to such an amount, there is no doubt. Had they jurisdiction of the defendants in that suit? Courts obtain jurisdiction over the persons of defendants, who have no personal exemptions, by the service of process either on their bodies or
property, within the jurisdiction of the court. The attachment
of property is one thing, the notice to the party is another.
They are different commands, and the officer has distinct duties
to perform for these purposes. The circumstance that both
commands are, in this state, contained in the same process, does
not alter the case. If the officer take personal property and
return that he has so done, or attach real estate and leave a copy
with the town clerk, he has made an attachment, and the court
has jurisdiction of the party. If the return also shows notice, it
is well; but if his return shows the officer has not done what
the law requires he should do, for that purpose, it is merely
cause of abatement. If the defendant does not appear, and the
return does not show personal service, the court may permit
amendment of the return, suffer personal notice to be otherwise
shown, order personal notice or publication, or take any other
course for notice, recognized by law, the court having, already,
jurisdiction. This principle is fully recognized in *Newton* v.
Adams and Shepherd, 4 Vt. 444.

In this case, the return stated that the officer had attached

certain lands, as the property of the defendant, and left a copy
in the town clerk's office. This gave the court jurisdiction of
the defendant party. All the rest is matter of notice, and there
is nothing tending to show that the land was not the property
of the defendants. The court published notice and gave judgment, which judgment is not void. After the plaintiff had recovered a judgment and taken execution thereon, and levied the
same on the land of one of the defendants, and commenced ejectment therefor, his attorney altered the return on the original
writ. The alterations were in no part of the return which made
the attachment and gave jurisdiction to the court, but only in
that which related to notice. This was unauthorized, but what
was its effect? The judgment and levy gave the plaintiff a title
to the land. This title can not be vacated and he divested of
his freehold by an alteration or destruction of the original writ,
any more than a man could lose his farm because his attorney
had, unauthorizedly, burnt up his deed. The writ was no part
of the record, nor was its production necessary to show the
plaintiff's title. When a judgment is recorded, a copy of that
judgment is all that need be produced.

An alien may purchase land and hold the same as against the
grantor, who is estopped by his deed; and, if a forfeiture or es-
cheat is produced, it is to the state, and for the state alone to
assert. But whether an alien can acquire any right by mere operation of law, without a deed from the grantor, is another question. But even this question does not properly arise in this case.
All the evidence was, that the plaintiff had, for many years, resided in Canada. Now, this was as entirely consistent with his
being a citizen of this state as otherwise, and, therefore, could
not justify the jury in finding him an alien. When the record
shows, as in this case, that the debtor resides without the state,
and shows no attorney, the officer is, of course, excused from
calling on him to choose appraisers: 3 Vt. 394.[1]

The degree of certainty, in the description of land in the levy
of an execution, has been frequently considered. It needs to
be no more than certainty to a common intent, and the return
should be read in the exercise of ordinary discernment, and with
reference to this rule of certainty. In this return, "running
west parallel with said lot line" means parallel with that line of
said lot which runs in a westwardly direction. After running
round a tract, it excepts about one acre and a half, sold to Abel
Wilder. This must, *prima facie*, mean sold by deed. And, as
all deeds are here recorded, that is sufficiently certain which may

---

1. *Galusha v. Sinclear.*

be so made by record. This is sufficient, until it be shown that a reference to the record still leaves it uncertain: *Maeck* v. *Sinclair*, 10 Vt. 103; 11 Mass. 517.[1]

Judgment affirmed.

JURISDICTION OF A CAUSE UPON ATTACHMENT in a justice's court depends upon its being made to appear that the defendant is concealed within the county with the intent mentioned in the statute, or has departed, or is about to depart, from the county with like intent: *Adkins* v. *Brewer*, 15 Am. Dec. 264.

DISTRESS OF DEBTOR'S PROPERTY IS INDISPENSABLE IN ATTACHMENT SUITS, in order to constitute the cause in court: *Skinner* v. *Moore*, 30 Am. Dec. 155.

DESCRIPTION OF PROPERTY SOLD BY SHERIFF, WHAT SUFFICIENT: See *Marshall's Lessee* v. *Greenfield*, 29 Am. Dec. 559, note 561.

LYNDE *v.* MELVIN.

[11 VERMONT, 683.]

CHATTEL IS NOT LIABLE TO ATTACHMENT BY CREDITORS OF VENDOR THEREOF, where it was, at the time of the sale, in the possession of a bailee who declined to deliver it to the purchaser until the time expired for which the bailment was made, although it was allowed by the bailee, before the expiration of the bailment, to go back into the possession of the vendor, but without the vendee's knowledge or consent.

TROVER for a cow. Plea, the general issue. There was a verdict for the plaintiffs, and the defendant excepted. The other facts are sufficiently stated in the opinion.

J. Sawyer, and *Maeck and Smalley*, for the defendant.

L. B. Vilas, for the plaintiffs.

By Court, BENNETT, J. The general rule that, upon the sale of personal property, the vendee must take possession, and that the change in the possession must be substantial and visible, or otherwise it will be fraudulent, *per se*, and void against creditors, is not to be questioned. This rule is founded upon the soundest policy, the object of which is the prevention of fraud, but the reason of the rule does not extend to a case where the vendor, at the time of sale, had but a constructive possession of the chattel, or to a case where it is exempt from attachment and execution. At the time this cow was transferred from Kidder to the plaintiffs, she was in the possession of Hall, under a previous contract with Kidder, and Hall had the right of possession till the first of December. The plaintiffs, upon the purchase being made, gave Hall notice of it, and requested him to keep

---
1. *Boylston* v. *Carver.*

the cow for them, to which Hall assented, but declined to give
up the cow before the time was out, when he was to return her,
and until he had received back from Kidder his own cow.
Though Hall returned the cow in question to Kidder on the first
or second day of November, and received back his own, yet it
was without the knowledge or consent of the plaintiffs.

There was no evidence that the plaintiffs knew the cow had
gone back into the possession of Kidder, or had been attached
as his property, until after the first of December, and on the
third or fourth, the plaintiffs made demand of her. Upon the
sale the plaintiffs succeeded to all the rights that Kidder then
had, but neither Kidder nor the plaintiffs had the right of actual
possession, until the first of December. It is urged in this case,
that because Hall permitted the cow to go back into the possession of Kidder prior to the first of December, though without the knowledge or consent of the plaintiffs, still that while
in his possession she was liable to attachment by the creditors of
Kidder, and it is said, this case falls within the principles of the
case of *Morris et al.* v. *Hyde*, 8 Vt. 352 [30 Am. Dec. 475]. There
is, we think, a marked distinction in the cases. In this, the cow,
at the time of sale, was in the possession of the bailee of Kidder,
for a time limited, the plaintiffs had no right of immediate possession, and could not select an agent to take or keep possession
for them, and they in fact took, at the time of the sale, all the
possession within their power. They notified the bailee of the
sale, and requested him to keep the cow for them. In the
case in 8 Vermont, the purchasers took the immediate possession of the horse and put him into the hands of their agent
to keep for them, and this agent, though without the knowledge
or consent of the vendees, shortly after, suffered the horse to go
back into the possession of the vendor. The court say: "Where
an act is necessary to consummate or perfect the right or title
of a party, and such act is omitted through the neglect or dis-
obedience of an agent, the party, who commits his rights to the
fidelity of such agent, must bear the consequences." In the
case now before the court, Hall, the bailee of Kidder, was not,
during the bailment, the agent of the plaintiffs to keep the cow,
and to say that Hall's permitting her to go back into the possession of Kidder, before the determination of his right, is to
have the effect to avoid the sale to the plaintiffs, would indeed
be to open the door for fraud and collusion.

We think the court below were correct, in holding that the
principles of a fraudulent sale, *per se*, do not apply to the facts
in this case, and the judgment of the county court is affirmed.

CASES

IN THE

COURT OF APPEALS AND IN THE GENERAL COURT

OF

VIRGINIA.

COLLINS *v.* LOFFTUS.

[10 LEIGH, 5.]

RIGHTS OF A CESTUI QUE TRUST CAN NOT BE CUT OFF BY A DECREE in equity, rendered in a proceeding to which he is not a party.

PAROL GIFT BY A FATHER TO HIS DAUGHTER can be established only by clear and convincing evidence.

RESUMPTION OF POSSESSION BY LENDER, or conveyance of the property loaned to another, within five years, is sufficient to determine the loan.

INJUNCTION. One Moses Hughes devised certain slaves to his son-in-law, Samuel Collins, in trust for his daughter, Polly Collins, the above complainant. Defendants, judgment creditors of S. Collins, brought their bill against him and the executors of Hughes, in which they alleged that said slaves were the property of Collins, and liable for his debts, by reason of his having been in possession thereof for seven years. Decree was rendered in their favor, which was about to be enforced. Complainant thereupon filed her bill, praying for an injunction against the execution of said decree. Injunction was denied. Complainant appealed. The further facts appear in the opinion.

Stanard, for the appellant.

Johnson, for the appellee.

TUCKER, P. I am far from thinking that the injunction in this case was improvidently awarded by a judge of this court. The property of the *feme-covert* settled upon her by her father's will had been decreed to be sold to satisfy her husband's debts, in a cause to which she was not a party, her trustees alone being the defendants. In the estimate of a court of equity, they were unsubstantial shadows. That court could not pronounce upon the rights of the parties really interested, without having them before it. At law, indeed, the trustee is the proper party defendant; but in equity no decree can be rendered affecting the rights of the *cestui que trust*, unless he is a party; for it is a fundamental principle of the court that all parties, however remotely concerned in interest, must be before it, or no decree can be made to bind them: Mitf. Pl. 144; 3 Munf. 376;[1] and 2 Madd. Ch. Pr. 142. This is particularly the case as to *cestui que trust*, since the trustee is a mere nominal party, and the real beneficial interest is in the *cestuis que trust*: 2 Johns. Ch. 238;[2] 1 Ball & Bea. 181, 184.[3] The exceptions to the rule it is unnecessary to state, as they would have no application here. I think the injunction was properly awarded, and that the only question in the cause is upon the merits. As to the merits, I am satisfied that the weight of the evidence is decidedly against the allegation that any of the slaves were given to Mrs. Collins. I have in other cases declared that I deemed it necessary, in order to sustain an alleged parol gift by a father to his daughter on her marriage, that the evidence of such gift should be clear and cogent; and in that opinion I understood my brethren to concur: *Brown* v. *Handley*, 7 Leigh, 119; *Mahon* v. *Johnston*, Id. 317. In this case, to say the least, the testimony is very meager. I think it altogether insufficient.

Then as to the alleged loan. It will be unnecessary to say anything upon the legal question spoken to in the cause. It has been long settled in this court, that according to the true construction of the loan act, a resumption of possession by the lender, or recording a deed or will granting away the property to another, within the five years, avoids the operation of the act, and puts an end to the loan: *Beasley* v. *Owen*, 3 Hen. & M. 449. The evidence of a loan in this case is itself equivocal. Hughes, having married his daughter to Collins, puts him upon one of his plantations to manage it for him, and sends with him various slaves, some to work in the field, and Dicey as a house-servant. She was therefore still as much in his service as any of the rest, and the evidence clearly proves that they were not loaned. On the whole of them, including Dicey, he always paid the taxes, and listed them with the commissioner of the revenue in his own

---

1. *Mayo* v. *Murchie.*   2. *Malin* v. *Malin.*   3. *Adams* v. *St. Leger.*

name. What more can the owner of slaves do, who places them in the hands of a manager to do service on his estate? How can a creditor complain of being deceived, who advances goods to my manager, not for my use, upon the credit of property held by him upon my own estate, worked by my own slaves, which slaves are listed in my name on the commissioner's books, and the taxes on them paid by me?. If he uses ordinary diligence, or if he does not wink hard that he may not see, he must learn that he should not give the credit. In this case, if he had gone to the farm, he would have found it was Hughes'; if he had applied to Collins, he would have learned that the property was not his; and if (as was most natural) he had gone to the commissioner's books, which furnish a record of the property of individuals, he would have there seen that Hughes claimed to be the owner of the slaves, and paid taxes on them as such. In no other way can the owner of property under the management of another, better manifest his own rights, and negative a pretension on the part of creditors to charge his estate with the debts of that other. Therefore, even if there was no further proof, I should be of opinion to reverse the decree.

But it is proved that in four years after the marriage, Hughes himself went and lived on the place which Collins lived on, and continued to live there till his death. It was managed for him by Collins, and he received the crops, allowing Collins a part of them for his services. He lived in the house where Dicey was house-servant, and even if she had not before that time been in his possession, yet from that time she must be construed to have been so. The possession must be construed to be with the property, unless the contrary be actually proved; and that has not been done here, as Dicey was a menial in a household where a father and his daughter and son-in-law appear to have resided together, all having the services of the slave; the father having (as one of the witnesses testifies) "gone to live with them that the daughter might be better provided for." Upon the whole, I am of opinion that this is one of the numerous instances afforded by our courts, of an attempt to make one man pay another's debts.

I am of opinion to reverse the decree, reinstate the injunction, and send the cause back for further proceedings.

The other judges concurring, decree reversed, injunction reinstated, and cause remanded for further proceedings.

PARKER, J., absent.

JUDGMENTS AGAINST TRUSTEE, WHEN BIND CESTUI QUE TRUST.—The general rule laid down in the principal case, that in all proceedings affecting the trust estate, whether brought by or against third persons, the *cestuis que trust* must be made parties in order to bind them by the judgment and decree rendered therein, has, with a few exceptions, to be hereinafter noted, been universally received as the just and correct doctrine on this subject: Perry on Trusts, sec. 873; Freeman on Judgments, secs. 157, 173; Coop. Eq. Pl. 35; Mitf. Eq. Pl. 176; Story's Eq. Pl. 187; Hill on Trustees, 543, 545; *Piatt v. Oliver,* 2 McLean, 269; *Helm v. Hardin,* 2 B. Mon. 231; *Caldwell v. Taggart,* 4 Pet. 202; *Sprague v. Tyson,* 44 Ala. 338; *Harris v. McBane,* 66 N. C. 334; *White v. Haynes,* 33 Ind. 540; *Dunn v. Seymour,* 3 Stockt. 220; *Fish v. Howland,* 1 Paige, 20; *Schenck v. Ellingwood,* 3 Edw. Ch. 175; *Stillwell v. McNeely,* 1 Green's Ch. 305; *Willink v. Morris Canal,* 3 Id. 377; *Whelan v. Whelan,* 3 Cow. 537; *Bifield v. Taylor,* 1 Mol. 198; *Adams v. St. Leger,* 1 Ball & Bea. 184; *Kirk v. Clark,* Prec. Ch. 275; *Malin v. Malin,* J. C. 238; *Douglas v. Horsfal,* 2 Sim. & Stu. 184; *Morse v. Sadler,* 1 Cox, 352; *Calverley v. Phelp,* 6 Madd. 332; and when the *cestuis que trust* are infants, the general rule is said to be especially applicable: *Orrok v. Binney,* Jac. 523. Thus in a suit brought for the purpose of obtaining relief against a mortgage, held by a trustee, all the *cestuis que trust* should be joined: *Clemous v. Elder,* 9 Iowa, 273; so, also, if a claim for necessaries furnished is sought to be enforced against the trust estate: *Prewett v. Laud,* 36 Miss. 494; or in a suit against a trustee to have a purchase made him declared to be for the benefit of the trust estate: *Campbell v. Johnston,* 1 Sandf. Ch. 148. If, on the other hand, the suit is brought by the trustee, in order to clear the trust property from an adverse claim, the *cestuis que trust* are equally necessary parties: *Blake v. Allman,* 5 Jones' Eq. 407; *Reed v. Reed,* 16 N. J. Eq. 248. So, likewise, in suits to foreclose or redeem mortgages of the trust estate, all the *cestuis que trust* must be joined either as plaintiffs or defendants: *Martin v. Reed,* 30 Ind. 218; *Henley v. Stone,* 3 Beav. 355; *Lowe v. Morgan,* 1 Bro. Ch. 368; *Palmer v. Carlisle,* 1 Sim. & Stu. 423; *Drew v. Harman,* 5 Price, 319; *Calverley v. Phelp,* 6 Madd. 229; *Wilton v. Jones,* 2 You. & Coll. Ch. 224; *Osbourn v. Fallows,* 1 Ry. & M. 741; *Yates v. Hambly,* 2 Atk. 237; *Thomas v. Dunning,* 5 De G. & Sm. 618. But see contra, *Johnson v. Robertson,* 31 Md. 476; *N. J. F. Co. v. Ames,* 1 Beas. Ch. 506. And the same reasons apply for having all the parties before the court, when the suit is brought by a *cestui que trust,* against a trustee, as exist when the proceedings are instituted by a stranger: Perry on Trusts, sec. 875.

The foregoing rule, however, is by no means arbitrarily enforced, but is controlled by convenience and necessity, with a just regard to the peculiar circumstances of each case: Freeman on Judgments, sec. 173. But if no such considerations exist, and the relaxation of the rule is not conducive to convenience, or required by necessity, the want of the *cestuis que trust,* as parties to a suit in relation to the trust property, unless the trustee is expressly authorized to represent his *cestuis que trust* by statute or otherwise, prevents the judgment and decree from binding or affecting their interests: *Piatt v. Oliver,* 2 McLean, 308. Thus, where there is a definite and fixed trust fund, in which each of the *cestuis que trust* is entitled to a certain and aliquot part, distinct from the others, so that there is no common interest in the object of the bill, all the *cestuis que trust* need not be joined in a suit by one for his individual share: Perry on Trusts, sec. 882; Hill on Trustees, 546; *Caldwell v. Taggart,* 4 Pet. 202; *Smith v. Snow,* 3 Madd. 10; *Hutchinson v. Townsend,* 2 Keen, 675; *Perry v. Knott,* 5 Beav. 293; *Hughson v. Cookson,* 3 You. & Coll. 378; *Hunt v. Peacock,* 11 Jur. 555; *Sandford v. Jodrell,* 2 Sim. & Gif. 176; *Piatt v. Oli-*

ver, 2 McLean, 307; *Montgomerie* v. *Bath*, 3 Ves. 560. This exception has, however, been criticised, and the practice condemned; nor will it be recognized when the fund is uncertain and an accounting is necessary: *Alexander* v. *Mullins*, 2 Ry. & M. 568; *Lenaghan* v. *Smith*, 2 Phil. 301; or if an assignment has been made by a *cestui que trust* of his interest, he need not be made a party: *Goodson* v. *Ellison*, 3 Russ. 583; or if the demand upon the trust property existed before the creation of the trust, no necessity exists of joining the *cestui que trust* in a suit against the trustee to enforce the same: Story Eq. Pl 191; *Piatt* v. *Oliver*, 2 McLean, 307. So also trustees for the payment of debts and legacies under a will, may sustain a suit without bringing the beneficiaries before the court: *Miles* v. *Davis*, 19 Mo. 408; as where a bill is filed by an executor, or trustee of a fund for the payment of creditors, for the purpose of obtaining directions in reference to the execution and management of the trust: *Coe* v. *Beckwith*, 31 Barb. 339; *Beal* v. *Crafton*, 5 Ga. 301. In *Wakeman* v. *Grover*, 4 Paige, 23, a suit by a creditor against his debtor and an assignee, to set aside the assignment on the ground of fraud, without the *cestuis que trust* being joined, was sustained, and a similar proceeding was upheld in *Willett* v. *Struger*, 17 Abb. Pr. 152. But see *contra*, *Stout* v. *Higbee*, 4 J. J. Marsh. 632. So likewise a judgment against the assignee of an insolvent debtor is conclusive on the *cestuis que trust*, unless it can be impeached for fraud or collusion: *Field* v. *Flanders*, 40 Ill. 470. And where a guardian contracts to pay the mother of his wards a certain sum for their support, in a suit by the mother to set off the sum against a judgment held by the guardian, it was held that the wards were not necessary parties: *Lindsey* v. *Stevens*, 5 Dana, 104. Under the codes of procedure, which severally require that all actions should be prosecuted in the name of the real party in interest, it has been decided by an overwhelming weight of authority, that an assignment of a chose in action, absolute in its terms, so that the legal title vests in the assignee, although accompanied by a collateral agreement, by virtue of which the assignee is to receive only part of the proceeds of the suit, "and is to account to the assignor or other person for the residue, or even when he is to thus account for the whole proceeds; or by virtue of which the absolute transfer is made conditional upon the fact of recovery, or by which his title is in any other similar manner partial or conditional," entitles the assignee to sue in his own name; that the judgment rendered in such action is binding on the assignor, so that the debtor can not be exposed to a second action brought by any of the parties to whom the assignee is bound to account: Pomeroy's Remedies. sec. 132; *Wetmore* v. *San Francisco*, 44 Cal. 294; *Gradwohl* v. *Harris*, 29 Id. 150; *Castner* v. *Sumner*, 2 Minn. 44; *Williams* v. *Norton*, 3 Kans. 295; *Cottle* v. *Cole*, 20 Iowa, 481; *Curtis* v. *Mohr*, 18 Wis. 615; *Hilton* v. *Waring*, 7 Id. 492; *Wilson* v. *Clark*, 11 Ind. 385; *Allen* v. *Brown*, 44 N. Y. 228; *Meeker* v. *Claghorn*, 44 Id. 349; *Sheridan* v. *Mayor*, 68 Id. 30; and the same doctrines prevail in several of the states which have not adopted the codes: *Boynton* v. *Willard*, 10 Pick. 166; *Curtis* v. *Cesna's Adm'r*, 1 Hamm. 432; *Rogers* v. *Haines*, 3 Greenl. 362.

WHEN THE CESTUIS QUE TRUST ARE NUMEROUS.—The principal exception to the general rule requiring all *cestuis que trust* to be made parties in any proceeding affecting their interest in order to bind them by the judgment therein, arises when the *cestuis que trust* are very numerous, and it would be impossible or impracticable to bring them all before the court. This exception, and the reasons for the same, were well stated by the court in *Piatt* v. *Oliver*, 2 McLean, 307, as follows: "Where there is a general trust for creditors, or others, whose demands are not specified in the creation of the trust, as their number, or the difficulty of ascertaining who may answer, etc., it is not necessary to make all the creditors parties. The bill should state, in such case, that it is filed in behalf of all interested. And it is upon this ground of numerous parties, as well as upon the ground of "irtual representation, and the general nature of the trust, that trustees of real estate, for payment of debts, may ordinarily maintain a suit either as plaintiffs or defendants, without bringing before the court the creditors or legatees for whom they are trustees, which, in many cases, would be almost impossible." The case of *Kerr* v. *Blodgett*, 48 N. Y. 62, is an instructive illustration of this doctrine. In that case, an insolvent partnership had made an assignment for the benefit of its creditors. One of the creditors brought an action in his own behalf, and that of others who should come in and claim the benefit thereof, against the assignee, for an accounting and distribution of the trust fund. An order was made appointing a referee to take and state the account of the assignee, and to report the amount due such creditors as should come in and seek the benefit of the action. Notice was given to the creditors by publication, directing them to exhibit their demands. The court held such a proceeding to be sanctioned by the doctrines of equity as indispensable to the distribution of trust funds and the settlement of trust estates, and that in the absence of fraud, all the creditors of the assignor were bound by the decree, whether they came in and proved their claims or not, and that a creditor who failed to do this was barred, although he had no notice of the action, and knew nothing of it until after the distribution of the trust fund. See also *Thompson* v. *Brown*, 4 Johns. Ch. 619; *Wilder* v. *Keeler*, 23 Am. Dec. 781; 3 Paige, 164; *Egberts* v. *Wood*, 24 Am. Dec. 236; 3 Paige, 518; *Brooks* v. *Gibbons*, 4 Id. 374; *McKenzie* v. *L'Amoureux*, 11 Barb. 516; *Shaw* v. *R. R. Co.*, 5 Gray, 170; *Willink* v. *Canal Co.*, 3 Green's Ch. 377; *N. J. Franklinite Co.* v. *Ames*, 1 Breas. 507; Perry on Trusts, sec. 885; Pomeroy's Remedies, 432, and cases cited. For similar reasons, an action was sustained foreclosing a mortgage of real estate vested in trustees for the benefit of two hundred and fifty subscribers, without making the latter parties: *Van Vechten* v. *Terry*, 2 Johns. Ch. 197; and a like proceeding was permitted against the trustee for the holder of three hundred and twenty railroad bonds, sued for the purpose of foreclosing a prior mortgage: *Board of Supervisors* v. *M. P. R. R. Co.*, 24 Wis. 127. It is said, however, that the beneficial interests of the *cestuis que trust* must be the same, in order that a few may represent a larger number, and that where this is not the case, they must all be brought before the court. *Evans* v. *Stokes*, 1 Keen, 24; *Newton* v. *Egmont*, 4 Sim. 574; *Richardson* v. *Larpent*, 2 You. & Coll. Ch. 507; *Long* v. *Younge*, 2 Sim. 385; *Bainbrigge* v. *Burton*, 2 Beav. 539; *Gray* v. *Shaplin*, 2 Sim. & Stu. 267; *Attorney-general* v. *Heelis*, Id. 76, and cases cited. What number of *cestui que trust* will be considered so great as to permit the presence of all of them to be dispensed with on the grounds of necessity and convenience, has never been judicially decided. It is inferred that each case must depend mainly upon its own peculiar circumstances. In *Harrison* v. *Stevardson*, 2 Hare, 533, twenty-one *cestui que trust* were required to be joined. In other cases, where suits were brought nearly twenty years after the creation of the trust, and the *cestuis que trust* numbered twenty-six in one and twenty-seven in another, a few were permitted to sue in behalf of all, for the purpose of obtaining an execution of the trusts: *Smart* v. *Bradstock*, 7 Beav. 500; *Bateman* v. *Margerison*, 6 Hare, 496.

STATUTE OF LIMITATIONS AGAINST TRUSTEES, WHEN BARS CESTUIS QUE TRUST.—A difference of opinion existed at an early day, in reference to the effects upon the rights of a *cestui que trust*, after the running of the statute of limitations has completely barred the legal estate of the trustee. In the important case of *Lechmere* v. *Earl of Carlisle*, 3 P. Wms. 215, Jekyll, M. R., said: " The forbearance of the trustees, in not doing what it was their office to have done, should in no sort prejudice the *cestuis que trust*;" and Lord Macclesfield once overruled the plea of the statute of limitations, on the ground that the legal estate was in trustees: *Lawley* v. *Lawley*, 9 Mod. 32. Lord Hardwicke, on the contrary, in a very carefully considered opinion, said: " The rule that the statute of limitations does not bar a trust estate holds only between *cestui que trust* and the trustee, not as between *cestui que trust* and the trustee on the one side, and strangers on the other; for that would make the statute of no force at all, because there is hardly any estate of consequence without such trust, and so the act would never take place. Therefore, where the *cestui que trust* and his trustee are both out of possession for the time limited, the party in possession has a good bar against them both:" *Llewellin* v. *Mackworth*, 3 Eq. Cas. Abr. 579; and this is now the generally accepted doctrine both in England and the United States: *Crowther* v. *Crowther*, 23 Beav. 305; *Hovenden* v. *Annesley*, 2 Sch. & Lef. 629; *Pentland* v. *Stokes*, 2 B. & B. 75; *Allen* v. *Sayer*, 2 Vern. 368; *Wych* v. *East India Co.*, 3 P. Wms. 309; *Thomas* v. *Thomas*, 2 Kay & J. 79; *Cholmondeley* v. *Clinton*, 2 Jac. & W. 191; *Herndon* v. *Pratt*, 6 Jones' Eq. 327; *Fleming* v. *Gilmer*, 35 Ala. 62; *Mason* v. *Mason*, 33 Ga. 435; *Watkins* v. *Specht*, 7 Coldw. 585; *Crook* v. *Glen*, 30 Md. 55; *Bryan* v. *Weems*, 29 Ala. 423; *Coleman* v. *Walker*, 3 Metc. (Ky.) 65; *Smilie* v. *Biffle*, 2 Barr, 152; *Elmendorf* v. *Taylor*, 10 Wheat. 152; *Williams* v. *Otey*, 8 Humph. 563; *Wooldridge* v. *Planters' Bank*, 1 Smed. 297; *Worthy* v. *Johnson*, 10 Ga. 358; *Long* v. *Cason*, 4 Rich. Eq. 60; *Henson* v. *Kinard*, 3 Strobh. Eq. 371; *Pledger* v. *Easterling*, 4 Rich. 101; and the fact that the *cestui qui trust* is an infant will not change the rule: *Wooldridge* v. *Planters' Bank*, 1 Smed. 297; *Pendergast* v. *Foley*, 8 Ga. 1; *Williams* v. *Otey*, 8 Humph. 563; *Goss* v. *Singleton*, 2 Head, 67; *Worthy* v. *Johnson*, 10 Ga. 358; *Long* v. *Cason*, 4 Rich. Eq. 60; although this latter doctrine admits of some doubt in England: Hill on Trustees, 268. This rule applies, however, only where the trustee can sue, but fails to do so. If the trustee is estopped from suing by a sale of the property, thus uniting with the purchaser in a breach of trust, the wrong is to the beneficiaries, not to him. He can not sue, and the beneficiaries, if under disability, are not affected by the statute: *Parker* v. *Hall*, 2 Head, 641.

Pownal *v.* Taylor.

[10 Leigh, 172.]

Provision in a Deed, Declaring that the Property Conveyed should be subject to the maintenance of the grantor, is not a condition upon the breaking of which the grantor may re-enter, but is simply a charge upon the land, enforceable in equity.

Date of Recording a Deed may be Ascertained from the clerk's official certificate of the fact and time of recording. But whether it will be presumed that the recording took place before the subsequent deed was executed, in a case in which the antagonist title depends on a subsequent conveyance from the same grantor, and a special verdict finds that the deed was duly recorded, *quære.*

ADVERSE POSSESSION BY A DEFENDANT RESIDING ON THE LAND, will not be presumed, without some tortious act on his part, so as to defeat a conveyance by the owner not in the actual occupancy of the land.

COURTS WILL NOT INFER ADVERSE POSSESSION in the absence of a special finding thereof.

EJECTMENT. The jury, in a special verdict, found substantially, that John Pownal, sen., owner of the premises in dispute, conveyed the same, on March 7, 1817, to John Pownal, jun., of George. Both parties resided on the land. This deed, which was found *in hœc verba*, contained the provision, that in consideration of the same the grantee would support and maintain the grantor and his sister during their natural lives, and that the property should be bound therefor into whosesoever hands it might come. On October 4, 1825, John Pownal of George, while residing on the land, conveyed the same to Asa Everett, in trust to secure the payment of a debt then owing by him to Taylor. This deed the jury found to have been duly recorded, and set forth the same *in hœc verba*. Indorsed on the back of the deed was the clerk's certificate of recording on the fourth of October, 1825. The deed contained a power of sale upon the failure to satisfy the obligation to Taylor. On December 16, 1825, John Pownal of George reconveyed the premises to John Pownal, sen., the deed reciting the fact that the grantor was no longer able to furnish the support and maintenance agreed upon by the deed of March 7, 1817. John Pownal, sen., on the same day, by a deed substantially the same as that of March 7, 1817, conveyed the land to the defendant, who immediately removed upon the land, and has resided there ever since. On June 6, 1826, John Pownal, sen., in consideration of one hundred and twenty-five dollars, conveyed the same land, in absolute fee, to defendant. All these deeds were found to have been duly recorded. Everett, the trustee, the conditions of the deed of trust not being complied with, sold the land to Thomas Taylor on March 9, 1831. Everett had no further possession of the land, except that which arose from going thereon at the time of sale. It was also found that John Pownal of George had failed to furnish the support and maintenance stipulated for by the deed of March 7, 1817. Upon the foregoing verdict judgment was given for the plaintiff, to which a *supersedeas* was allowed.

Johnson, for the plaintiff in error.

Leigh, for the defendant in error.

STANARD, J. The deed from John Pownal, senior, to his

nephew John, conveyed the land therein mentioned to the grantee, and the provision of that deed by which it is declared that the property thereby conveyed should be subject nevertheless to the maintenance of the grantor and his sister Elizabeth, did not operate as a condition under which the grantor could, on the failure of the grantee to furnish the maintenance which he had stipulated to furnish to the grantor and his sister, lawfully re-enter on the land and revest in himself the legal title therein. This and other provisions of the deed import no more than that the property should be and remain charged as a security for the due performance of the grantee's covenant to furnish maintenance. Such is the only rational interpretation of the provision that the property should be subject to the maintenance and support, and bound, therefore, into whosesoever hands it might come. Such language imports a lien on property in the hands of the grantee and his assigns, not a condition by which the title to that property is to be extinguished, and with it the lien thereon.

The special verdict finds that the deed of trust of the fourth of October, 1825, from John Pownal, junior, to Everett, was duly recorded, but does not specify the time of recording; and it is objected that as the statute does not prescribe any time for the recording of such instruments, but deprives them of efficacy against creditors and subsequent purchasers without notice until recorded, no sufficient title is shown under that deed to overreach the rights derived under the subsequent deeds of John Pownal, junior, and John Pownal, senior. The jury having found that the deed was duly recorded, in a case in which the antagonist title depends on a subsequent conveyance from the same grantor, the argument is very strong to support the proposition that the necessary intendment from such a finding, or rather that the only interpretation of such a finding, is that the recording took place before the subsequent deed was executed; that the recording found by the jury of this deed must be considered as found in relation to the hostile claim asserted under the subsequent deed, and that the only sense in which it could be duly recorded in respect to the subsequent conveyance is, that it has all the efficacy in respect to the subsequent conveyance that could be derived from recording it. I however give no final opinion on this point. The most that could be made out of the objection would be to render the verdict in this respect ambiguous, and a *venire de novo* necessary. But this result ought not to take place here. The jury find the deed *in hæc verba*, and it appears that the deed so found, and in evidence before the jury, has on it the clerk's official certificate of the fact and time of recording. I see no valid objection to a reference by the court below, or by this court, to that certificate, to ascertain the date of the recording of the deed, for the purpose of removing the ambiguity, if any, which the finding that the deed was duly recorded leaves in respect to the date of the recording.

It is objected, that the conveyance made by Everett to the purchaser at the sale under the deed of trust is nugatory, because the land at the date of the conveyance was in the possession of the grantee of John Pownal, senior, and such possession, it is contended, was adverse, and disabled the party out of possession from conveying. The effect of this objection, if available, is not to protect any right shown to be in the objector, but to disable the party having the title from conveying it. It should therefore distinctly appear to be warranted by the finding of the jury. It is a sufficient answer to this objection to say that the verdict does not find that the possession of the plaintiff in error was an adverse possession. His possession simply is found, and it is not fit that he should be allowed to say that the act, which may be rightful, and is not found to be otherwise by the verdict of the jury, is tortious, for the purpose of frustrating the otherwise effectual conveyance of the party having title. The most that can be said is, that on the facts found, the jury might have found the possession to be adverse. This, however, has not been done, and it is at least problematical whether it ought to have been done. The possession of John Pownal, junior, after the deed of trust was not tortious, nor could he have alleged it to be so, to disqualify the trustee from conveying. He was tenant at sufferance, and his possession was consistent with the right conveyed by the deed of trust. The possession of those coming in under him with notice of the deed of trust, was impressed with the same attributes, and had the jury been asked to find expressly that their possession was adverse, it would have been indispensable to show that that possession was obtained without notice of the deed of trust: *Newman* v. *Chapman*, 2 Rand. 93 [14 Am. Dec. 766]. Even this fact of want of notice is not found, if it could properly have been found in the face of the fact that the deed of trust had been duly recorded some weeks before the subsequent conveyances were executed. The entry of Everett to make the sale does not appear by the verdict to have been opposed, nor his title to make it controverted, by the occupants of the land, and their possession thereof is not found to be adverse, or in hostility to the right so asserted and exercised by him. There is no doubt of the correctness of the proposition that though the occupant trace his title to the grantor under whom the plaintiff in ejectment claims, he may show that his possession is adverse, so as to enable him to take the benefit of the statute of limitations, and, under particular circumstances, to disable the party evicted from conveying. But no such case is found by this verdict, and I am therefore of opinion that the objection to the efficacy of the conveyance from Everett is not well founded.

On the whole, I am of opinion to affirm the judgment of the circuit superior court, with costs.

CABELL, J., concurred in the opinion that the judgment should be affirmed.

TUCKER, P. The omission in the special verdict to find expressly on what day the deed of trust was recorded being obviated by the certificate of the clerk indorsed on the deed, which shows that it was recorded on the day of its date, all other difficulties in the case are easily got over. Thus, there is nothing, I think, in the position that the provision for support and maintenance constituted a condition, for the breach of which the grantor might re-enter. It was a charge, not a condition. It was a declaration of a beneficial interest or a trust, which might be enforced in equity, but which was perfectly consistent with the existence of the fee in the grantee. The distinction is well understood between a declaration of use and a condition. A feoffment, *ea intentione*, does not make a condition, unless an express re-entry be limited. It creates a trust or confidence, which may be enforced in equity: 1 Bac. Abr. 631. If it were a condition, the re-entry for breach of it would defeat the estate, and with it the charge or beneficial interest. Thus, in the case before us, the land is made subject to the support of the grantor and his sister. She, accordingly, instantly acquired a beneficial interest, which she might have enforced by bill in equity. But if the provision is a condition, then, for the breach, the grantor might re-enter, defeat the estate, reinvest himself with his original title, and annihilate the vested interest which had been by his own solemn act conferred upon Elizabeth, his sister. This can not be, unless the grantor had expressly reserved the right to re-enter upon failure of the grantee to fulfill the purposes of the grant.

The second position of the counsel is not more tenable. The deed of trust was no violation of the provisions of the grant. It

was in subordination to them, and the creditor, and all persons
claiming under his deed of trust, took subject to the charge or
incumbrance created for the support of the grantor and his
sister. And even were it otherwise, the legal title passed by the
deed, and the remedy was only in equity: *Taylor* v. *King*, 6
Munf. 358 [8 Am. Dec. 746]; *Harris* v. *Harris*, Id. 367.

The next objection is that the deed of Asa Everett the
trustee was inoperative, by reason of the adverse possession of
the defendant. The fallacy of this position is obvious. John
Pownal, senior, had conveyed to his nephew, subject to a charge
declared upon the face of the deed. The nephew, thus invested
with the fee, incumbers it with a deed of trust, which is, of
course, subordinate to the prior charge. He then reconveys to
John Pownal, senior, who, having constructive notice of the
trust, takes subject to it. He then conveys the estate, thus subject to the trust, to John J. Pownal, the defendant, who in like
manner, takes subject to the trust. The trustee entered and
sold without objection, and when he so entered, the possession
must be adjudged to have been in him: Hob. 322; Litt., sec. 701.
The possession of the defendant could not be adverse. He was
but the purchaser of the equity of redemption. He had purchased with notice of the trust, and therefore subject to it.
The possession of his grantor was the possession of the trustee,
as they stood in the relation of mortgagor and mortgagee. He
must therefore be taken to hold the possession, as his grantor
held it, for the mortgagee. Having but an equity, he will not
be taken to hold adversely without some tortious act, and none
such appears. His possession was consistent with the creditors'
title. I am aware of no case in which it has been held that the
right of a creditor by deed of trust to enforce his lien by sale,
has been defeated by a conveyance to a purchaser of the equity
of redemption, with full notice of the previous trust. On this
ground, I am of opinion that the deed of the trustee was operative and valid; and I prefer to rest the case on this principle,
without resorting to others upon which it might be sustained.
It may be remarked, however, that as the jury have not expressly found an adverse possession, the court can not infer it:
Taylor v. *Horde*, 1 Burr. 113; *Hall* v. *Hall*, 3 Munf. 536. To
presume it, would be to presume without evidence, that the defendant had committed a wrong; and this, too, for the purpose
of defeating a legitimate exercise by the lawful owner, of that
most essential right of property, the power of alienation. The
utmost strictness in the finding should always be required of

him who desires to defeat his adversary's just rights merely by
proof of his own tort: See Wheaton's Sel. N. P. 553. I am
of opinion to affirm the judgment.

Judgment affirmed.

Parker and Brooke, JJ., absent.

———

Personal Charge in Deed.—In *Taylor* v. *Lanier*, 9 Am. Dec. 599, a
clause in a deed "that the grantee is to provide for, maintain," etc., the
grantor's daughter during her life, was construed to be a personal charge on
the grantee, and not a charge upon the property conveyed. In *Jackson* v.
Topping, 19 Id. 515, a covenant on the part of the grantee to maintain the
grantor and pay his debts, and if he fails to do so the grantor may re-enter,
was construed to amount to a condition.

The principal case is cited in *Campan* v. *Chene*, 1 Mich. 415, to the point
that a provision in a deed, that the grantee shall support and maintain the
grantor, is a personal covenant only, and not a condition.

———

Moss v. Green.

[10 Leigh, 251.]

Contract for the Transfer of Property, by the terms of which the
purchaser advances a part of the purchase money, and the seller reserves
the right to abrogate the contract by returning the money so advanced,
with interest, at a particular time; and if not so abrogated, the contract
to be executed by the purchaser paying the residue of the purchase
money, and the seller surrendering the possession of the property, is a
conditional sale and not a mortgage. Tucker, P., and Brooke, J.,
dissenting.

Retention of Possession by a Vendor will not Change the nature of
a conditional sale, so as to render the same a mortgage.

Where a Plaintiff in a Suit to Redeem a Mortgage Fails by reason
of the court holding the transaction sued on to be a conditional sale,
equity, to prevent further litigation, will order a decree in favor of the
plaintiff for the balance of the purchase price, with interest, but without
costs.

Bill to redeem certain slaves alleged to have been mortgaged.
Plaintiff had judgment. Defendant appealed. The facts sufficiently appear in the opinion of Parker, J.

Shands, for the appellant.

Leigh, for the appellee.

Stanard, J. A careful examination of the record has resulted
in the conviction that the transaction between these parties which
the appellee insists was, and the court below has adjudged to be,
a loan secured by mortgage, was a conditional sale and pur-

chase. This to me is made manifest by the terms of the bill of
sale, coupled with the evidence of Parham and Myrick. The
real contract, as understood by both parties and the witnesses,
was a sale of the slaves at a price fairly fixed to the satisfaction of
both parties; the one intending to buy, and the other being willing
to sell; the purchaser advancing a part of the purchase money;
the seller reserving the right to abrogate the contract of sale by
returning the money so advanced, with interest, at or before a
particular time; and if not so abrogated, the contract to be completely executed, by the purchaser paying the residue of the purchase money, and the seller surrendering the possession of the
slaves. To give the relief sought by the appellee, would be to
give the active assistance of a court of equity to a party seeking
to absolve himself from a fair contract. This ought not to be
done.

My opinion therefore is, that the decree of the court of chancery is erroneous and ought to be reversed: and as the appellant
avows his willingness to pay the balance of the purchase money;
and as, from delay by reason of the pursuit of a supposed right
of redemption, and the sanction of that claim by the court below, and the possession by the appellant of the slaves, there may
be some difficulty in the recovery of it by a suit at law, which in
strictness was the proper remedy—therefore, to prevent the occasion of future litigation between the parties, I think it fit that a
decree should be rendered in favor of the appellee for the balance
of the purchase money and interest, but without costs.

PARKER, J. The bill was filed in this case to redeem certain
slaves alleged to have been conveyed to the defendant as a security for the repayment of a loan of three hundred and ninety-
three dollars and eighty-nine cents. The answer, which is
responsive to the bill, denies that the deed for the slaves was intended merely as a security for money loaned. It avers that the
respondent refused to advance his money on the terms proposed
by Green of pledging a slave for the repayment; but that the
proposition made and accepted was, that if Green would sell
him a negro woman named Creasy (whose husband he owned),
with her two children, for a price ascertained, he would advance
the sum then required by Green, in part payment, and Green
should be at liberty to return it on or before the twenty-fifth of the
ensuing December, and avoid the contract; but if not, that he
would pay the balance, and take the slaves in possession. The
depositions of Parham and Myrick go far to verify this statement. Green had applied to Parham to get from Moss the

money he wanted, and said he would give a bill of sale for a negro woman, to secure the repayment with interest, at the following Christmas, and that if the money was not paid at that time, Moss should have the negro. When Parham made this proposition known to Moss, he at first refused to have anything to do with Green, but after some conversation said, if Green would let him have Creasy and her two children, he would advance the money he wanted, upon condition that he would let him have them at a fair value. That value was then agreed on between Parham, the agent of Green, and Moss, at six hundred dollars, and it was arranged that Moss should, if Green approved it, advance the sum then required by Green, and take a conveyance of the slaves, with a stipulation that if the sum so advanced was returned by Christmas, with interest, Moss would release the slaves, but if the money was not then returned, he would make up the sum of six hundred dollars, and keep them. Parham informed Green of this proposition and valuation, who said he was willing to comply with it; that Creasy was the negro woman he preferred to sell, and that he thought six hundred dollars a fair price for her and her children. After this, Parham took no further part in the transaction, except, as he says, to write a letter to Moss (which it does not appear that he received), informing him of Green's acceptance of his terms.

The bill of sale was written and attested by Howell Myrick. He proves, that he was requested by Moss and Green to write a conditional bill of sale for Creasy and her two children; that Moss had previously bought, at a sheriff's sale made by Myrick, a negro woman belonging to Green, named Rhoda; and it was agreed on the occasion referred to that the price paid for Rhoda was to be a part of the consideration money for Creasy and her children, and that the balance of the consideration money in the conditional bill of sale mentioned should be paid, as it was in fact paid, to Myrick. The bill of sale expresses the consideration to be three hundred and ninety-three dollars and eighty-nine cents, and is in the common form of such instruments, but reserving liberty to Green to repay the said sum of three hundred and ninety-three dollars and eighty-nine cents, with interest, on the twenty-fifth of the ensuing December, in which event the sale was to be void. If, however, Green neglected or refused to do so, then he bound himself, upon Moss' paying him the additional sum of two hundred and six dollars and eleven cents (to make up the price agreed on of six hundred dollars) to deliver Creasy and her children to Moss, and to make him a complete title therefor. No time is fixed for this additional payment, but it must necessarily have been after the twenty-fifth of December, because, until that day expired, it could not be known whether Green would pay the three hundred and ninety-three dollars and eighty-nine cents or not. Green failed to pay or tender the money at the time stipulated, but on the twenty-seventh of December, merely said to Moss he was ready to settle with him, if he would pay him for his board; which it seems had been due, if due at all, some eight or nine years before. Moss got possession of the slaves, and on the same twenty-seventh of December, offered to pay the additional two hundred and six dollars and eleven cents; which Green refused, and in 1821 brought this suit.

Upon this state of facts, the question propounded to the court is, whether this transaction between Green and Moss was a mere mortgage or a conditional sale? If it was in its inception a mortgage, I agree that the court will not permit it to be converted into an absolute purchase, for the default in the payment of the mortgage money at the appointed time. The rule is, once a mortgage always a mortgage, to which the right of redemption is inseparably incident, and can not be restrained by any clause or agreement whatever, made at the time of the loan: *Willett* v. *Winnell*, 1 Vern. 488 (which, by the very terms of the statement, was admitted to be a borrowing of money and a mortgage to secure it). But if the intention of the parties is to do something more than provide a security for money loaned or advanced, and to make a conditional sale if a further sum is advanced or the first sum is not repaid, there is certainly no rule of law which authorizes a court to control that intention. Thus, in the case of *Newcomb* v. *Bonham*, Id. 8, 214, 232, where A. made an absolute conveyance for a sum of money paid, and by another deed of equal date the lands were made redeemable at any time during the life of the grantor, the final decision of the court of chancery, affirmed in the house of lords, was that the estate was absolute in the grantee after the death of the grantor; there being proof that such was the intent of the parties and their understanding at the time. So in the case of *Chapman's Adm'x* v. *Turner*, 1 Call, 280 [1 Am. Dec. 514], an instrument in the following words was held to be a conditional sale, irredeemable after the day fixed for the payment of the money loaned: "I this day received of Mr. Jno. Turner the sum of thirty pounds, and put a negro woman named Hannah in his hands as security, and if the said thirty pounds is not paid at or before next July Hanover court, the said Turner is to have the said negro for the said thirty pounds. (Signed) Richard Chapman." The words "and put a negro, etc., in his hands as security," were considered to have effect by construing the sale as defeasible till July Hanover court (during which time the negro would be only a security), and afterwards absolute: whereas the other words of the agreement, "and if the said thirty pounds is not paid at, etc., Turner is to have the said negro for the said thirty pounds," would have no effect (Judge Roane said), without decreeing the sale absolute after default in non-payment. It was also said in that case, that no loan was contemplated between the parties, as Turner had refused to lend, wishing to invest his money in property.

That case is stronger against the construction placed on it by the court than the one at bar, because the thirty pounds was not proved to have been the value of the negro, agreed on between Turner and Chapman, or to have been a fair value; although, as Judge Roane said, it did not fall short of the general estimate of the witnesses "in any excessive degree." Here, it is proved that the six hundred dollars was the full value of the slaves, and that Green was willing to sell them at that price, subject to his right to return the portion of the money paid, within a stipulated time. In the other circumstances the cases are alike. The sale was defeasible until Christmas, and until that period the slaves would be considered as a security; but if, after that, it is not deemed to be absolute, we shall have to reject the subsequent words of the agreement, and plainly violate the intention of the parties. In this case, too, Moss refused to lend money and take a bare security. His object was to buy the wife of a slave he owned, but to give time to Green to return the money advanced. That object was well known to Green, who consented to sell on the terms proposed. Thus the cases are similar in every circumstance relied on by the judges in *Chapman's Adm'x* v. *Turner*, to sustain their opinions that the transaction in that case was a conditional sale; and there are in the case at bar facts proved which tend to strengthen such a conclusion. Besides the fact, already alluded to, of the value of the slaves being arranged and settled with an express reference to a sale, the parties applied to Myrick to write a conditional bill of sale *eo nomine;* and it must be intended that they understood the difference between such an instrument and a mere security for money lent.

Another case in this court, confirmatory of this view of the case before us, is that of *Roberts' Adm'r* v. *Cocke, Ex'r, etc.*, 1 Rand. 121. It was a loan of money—a pledge for its repayment by a given day, with interest—and a stipulation that if not repaid at the day, Roberts should have the negro. It appearing that the one hundred pounds mentioned in the bill of sale was probably the agreed price of the negro, as evidenced by the subsequent acts of the parties, no redemption was permitted. To the same effect is the case of *Leavell* v. *Robinson*, 2 Leigh, 161.

In the case of *Robertson* v. *Campbell and Wheeler*, 2 Call, 421, Judge Pendleton observed that it was often a nice and difficult question to draw the line between mortgages and conditional sales. "The great desideratum," says he, "which this court has made the ground of their decision, is whether the purpose of the parties was to treat of a purchase, the value of the commodity contemplated and the price fixed; or whether the object was a loan of money, and a security or pledge for the repayment intended." Tried by these criteria, or by the authorities I have cited, I think the transaction between Moss and Green amounted to a conditional sale. The object of the security was not merely to compel repayment, but a sale and purchase was evidently intended, subject to the right of the vendor to defeat it.

That the agreement was executory does not render it the less binding: nor does the fact that the possession was for a time retained by Green (which, by the way, was the reason why interest was to be allowed if the money advanced was returned) change the nature of the transaction; for when Moss asked or obtained possession of the slaves, he was bound to pay the additional sum; while Green was not bound to return any part of the three hundred and ninety-three dollars and eighty-nine cents if he did not choose to do so, and although the slaves had died subsequent to the twenty-fifth of December, he would still have been entitled to the additional sum, and the loss would have fallen on Moss.

I am therefore of opinion to reverse the decree, and enter one for the balance only of the purchase money, with interest.

Cabell, J., concurred.

Decree reversed with costs. And this court proceeding, etc., it is further decreed and ordered that the appellant do pay unto the appellee the sum of two hundred and six dollars and eleven cents, with interest at the rate of six per centum per annum from the twenty-fifth of December, 1819, till payment.

BROOKE, J., and TUCKER, P., each of whom wrote a separate opinion, dissented from the views expressed by the majority of the court, and were for affirming the decree of the lower court, on the ground, that the contract was to be interpreted as a mortgage, and not as a conditional sale. Although they admitted that the line of discrimination between mortgages and conditional sales is confessedly indistinct, and that each case must depend upon its own particular circumstances, yet they thought that the facts that the slave was retained by Green as his property, and that the money was to be repaid with interest, both of which were circumstances characteristic of a mortgage, were sufficient to decide the nature of the transaction.

WHETHER TRANSACTION A CONDITIONAL SALE OR MORTGAGE: See *Chapman* v. *Turner*, 1 Am. Dec. 514, and note; *Edrington* v. *Harper*, 20 Id. 145; *Bennet* v. *Holt*, 24 Id. 455; *Hickman* v. *Cantrell*, 30 Id. 396, and cases cited in note; *Lane* v. *Borland*, 31 Id. 33.

TAYLOR *v.* COOPER.

[10 LEIGH, 317.]

SALE UNDER A DECREE IS NOT CONCLUSIVE UNTIL CONFIRMED, and if, before confirmation, the property increases in value, a resale will be ordered, unless the purchaser makes compensation; on the contrary, if the property depreciates, he is allowed a deduction.

CONFIRMATION OF A SALE UNDER A DECREE RELATES BACK to the time of sale, and entitles the purchaser to all rights which he would have had under a conveyance contemporaneous with the sale.

CONFIRMATION OF A SALE BY WHICH A CREDIT IS GIVEN to the purchaser, entitles the latter to the rents becoming due after such confirmation; and he may maintain an action for money had and received therefor against the administrator of the former owner who has wrongfully received them.

ASSUMPSIT for money had and received, brought by Jacob Cooper against John Taylor, administrator of the estate of Peter Dyerle. The jury specially found, that by a decree made October 30, 1834, certain lands belonging to Dyerle were ordered to be sold, on a credit of six, twelve, and eighteen months; that on January 10, 1835, the land was sold under the decree to Cooper, who gave his bond for the purchase money. At the time of the sale the land was rented, and the tenant paid the rent, amounting to two hundred and ten dollars, to the administrator, notwithstanding Cooper had notified him not to pay it. The sale of the land to Cooper was afterwards confirmed. Cooper having sued for the amount of the rent paid to the administrator, judgment was given in his favor, to which a *supersedeas* was allowed.

Baxter, attorney-general, and *Preston*, for the plaintiff in error.

Edward Johnston, for the defendant in error.

TUCKER, P.   I have had not the slightest doubt of the

right of Cooper the purchaser to the rent in question. The principles of the court, according to the English practice, I take to be clearly these:

1. Where there is a sale by the master, and the property appreciates by the accidental falling in of lives or by other means, the court will only confirm the sale upon the terms of the purchaser's making compensation: *Davy* v. *Barber*, 2 Atk. 490; *Blount* v. *Blount*, 3 Id. 638. And in doing this, it but acts within the scope of its rights and powers; for the sale is not conclusive until confirmed, and justice to the owner of the estate demands that where there has been a material appreciation before confirmation, a resale should be directed unless the purchaser will make compensation.

2. Where, after the sale and before confirmation, as in the cases of *Ex parte Minor*, 11 Ves. 559; and *Heywood* v. *Covington's Heirs*, 4 Leigh, 373, the property is destroyed or materially injured by flood or fire, the loss must fall on the vendor; for as, in the case of appreciation, the vendee will be charged with compensation, so, in the case of depreciation by destruction of part of the estate, he has a fair claim to a deduction. Until the sale is confirmed, he is considered in England as having no fixed interest in the subject of purchase: 11 Ves. 559. Before it is confirmed, he is always liable there to have the biddings opened, and therefore *non constat* that he is a purchaser: *Anonymous*, 2 Ves. jun. 336. In case of loss he is therefore allowed a deduction. The practice with us has gradually departed from that of the English courts in some respects which it is not necessary here to set forth.

3. But, thirdly, where the sale is confirmed, that is, where both contracting parties (the purchaser and the court) concur in ratifying the inchoate purchase, the confirmation relates back to the sale, and the purchaser is entitled to everything he would have been entitled to if the confirmation and conveyance of title had been contemporaneous with the sale: *Anson* v. *Towgood*, 1 Jac. & W. 617.[1] In this manner I think the several authorities are easily reconciled; and if this be so in England, I think it may be safely affirmed to be yet more unquestionable under our practice.

Taking these principles as fixed, the present case will be found to come within the last. In this case Cooper purchased under a decree giving a credit of six, twelve, and eighteen months. His bonds are given payable in six, twelve, and eighteen months

---

1. 1 Jac. & W. 637.

from the day of sale. If he does not receive this rent, he will have no enjoyment of the estate until nearly twelve months after the sale, so that he will have to pay his first bond several months in advance of his perception of the profits, and his twelve-months bond will be a cash payment. This is neither just nor equal. The report having been confirmed, he must be considered complete owner from the date of the sale, and of course entitled to the rent becoming due after it. I have had much doubt, however, whether the remedy of Cooper was in the court of chancery, or at law. But upon much reflection, I think the action at law is maintainable. Before confirmation of the report, indeed, and while the cause is yet pending in the court of chancery, I am of opinion that to that tribunal alone can the purchaser resort for the adjustment of his rights and the enforcement of his claim. Such was the case of *Crews* v. *Pendleton etc.*, 1 Leigh, 297 [19 Am. Dec. 750]; and *Heywood* v. *Covington's Heirs*, 4 Id. 373. But where the chancery cause is ended, or where at least, by the confirmation of the report and the execution of the deed to him, the transactions with the purchaser in that court are closed and at an end, I apprehend it is competent to him to assert in this equitable action his title to the rent paid over wrongfully to the defendant. I am therefore of opinion to affirm the judgment.

The other judges concurring, judgment affirmed.

Brooke, J., absent.

McClung v. Beirne.

[10 Leigh, 394.]

Surety on an Appeal Bond Who is Compelled to Pay the judgment is entitled to be subrogated to all the rights of the judgment creditor.

Lien of a Judgment Extends to all the Land Owned by the judgment debtor at the date thereof, or which may have been afterwards acquired.

Judgment Lien Includes not only the Amount of the original judgment, but also the damages and costs in the court of appeals.

Lands Subject to a Judgment Lien, Parts of which have been Aliened at different times, are liable to the satisfaction of the lien in the inverse order of their alienation.

Failure by a Defendant to Demand an Inquiry whether the rents and profits of the land would not satisfy the judgment within a reasonable time, raises a presumption that such right is waived.

Surety on an Appeal Bond Who has been Compelled to Pay the Judgment can recover interest on the amount of the original judgment, but not on the damages and costs of appeal.

EQUITY OF REDEMPTION IN LAND CONVEYED IN TRUST by a judgment debtor must first be sold to satisfy a judgment before recourse can be had to aliened lands.

SUIT to enforce a judgment lien. On the eighth of May, 1828, James Callison obtained a judgment against John Mays for one hundred and forty-eight dollars and sixty-three cents, with interest from September 7, 1825. Mays then took an appeal, and plaintiff, Patrick Beirne, became his surety on the appeal bond. The judgment of the lower court was affirmed on appeal on April 3, 1835, and an execution having been issued for the amount of the original judgment and for the damages and costs of appeal, amounting in all to three hundred and sixty-two dollars and sixty-four cents, and the same being returned unsatisfied, Patrick Beirne was compelled to satisfy the judgment. Mays having taken the oath of an insolvent debtor, Beirne filed his bill to be substituted to the rights of the judgment debtor, and to have the judgment satisfied out of lands aliened by Mays subsequently to the date of the original judgment. It appeared from the evidence and the allegation of the pleadings, that on January 22, 1835, Mays had conveyed certain lands in trust to secure a debt owed by him to one Withrow; that prior and subsequent to that date he had conveyed other lands to the various defendants at different times, the last of which conveyances was made to McClung on January 27, 1835. Upon the foregoing facts the lower court decreed that the lands conveyed should be sold to satisfy the amount of the judgment paid by complainant, together with interest thereon, in the inverse order of their alienation. No direction was made as to the sale of the equity of redemption remaining in Mays under the deed of trust to Withrow, nor was any inquiry asked for, to ascertain the value of the rents and profits of the lands embraced in the several deeds. McClung appealed from the decree.

Samuel Price, for the appellant.

William Smith, for the appellee.

TUCKER, P. I am of opinion that there is no error in the decree in substituting the appellee to all the rights and remedies of Callison under his original judgment. To the benefit of it he had the clearest right, upon the ordinary and well-established principles of the court; nor was it necessary to entitle him to it that he should have been a party to that judgment. It is enough that having paid off the amount of it to Callison, to whom he was bound by the appeal bond, he had a right to demand a cession of every remedy Callison had for the recovery of his demand from his debtor. Among these was the execution by *elegit*, which reached all the lands of which Mays was seised at the date of that judgment, or at any time afterwards. The decree was therefore right in giving him the benefit of it. Nor do I think there was any error in charging upon the real estate bound by the original judgment, the damages and costs in the court of appeals. Had an execution by *elegit* been sued out, it must have included those damages and costs, and must have directed the levy of them, as well as of the amount of the original judgment, by extent of the lands whereof the defendant was seised at its date. They are but emanations of that judgment, which opens to receive them, in like manner as the interest of the debt, and the fee for issuing an execution, though accruing subsequent to the judgment, are considered and taken to be part of it or appendages to it. In England, upon a writ of error in the exchequer chamber or in parliament, to a judgment in the king's bench, the damages are certified to that court, for the purpose of being included in the execution, which can only issue from it, as the record itself still remains there: Tidd's Pr. 1244; Tidd's Pr. Forms, 539; 14 Vin. Abr. 614; 2 Wms. Saund. 101,[1] z; 2 Lilly's Entries, 571. So here, the affirmance and the award of damages are certified to the court below, whose clerk is directed to calculate the amount, and the execution issues including it accordingly. The damages and costs in the appellate court thus become appendages to the original judgment; for the judgment of affirmance is no new judgment. It is but a ratification of the original judgment.

Passing over the objections to the shortness of the credit allowed and the supposed rigor of the terms of sale, which I think are without foundation, these being matters of sound discretion, and there being nothing in the record to show it was exercised improperly (see *Perine* v. *Dunn*, 4 Johns. Ch. 140, and the act of assembly, 1 Rev. Code, c. 66, sec. 41, p. 20, which authorizes a sale for cash or upon credit), I proceed to consider whether the appellant had a right to demand that the other vendees and incumbrancers should contribute ratably. In this case it is clear that had Callison the creditor issued his *elegit*, it must at law have comprehended the whole of the lands in the hands of all the defendants, and a moiety of the whole, without distinction, would have been extended for the payment of his demand. The plaintiff, who seeks in equity to be subrogated to his rights, can

---

1. *Jaques* v. *Cesar*.

not fairly be shorn of any portion of the remedy by the necessity of coming into equity. He is therefore clearly entitled to charge the whole. But it is no invasion of his rights, to provide that the respective parties should be chargeable as equity would direct, provided he is neither delayed nor deprived of any portion of his security. Of this he does not complain; and indeed, as I understand the decree, he is not delayed; for the whole of the lands are, I take it, to be advertised together, and then sold in immediate succession, until enough is raised to pay the debt. The question then is, whether, as between the defendants, either is entitled to preference, and what should be the order of liability if they are not to be charged *pro rata*.

In the case of *Conrad* v. *Harrison et al.*, 3 Leigh, 532, Sisson mortgaged three hundred and sixty acres of land to Brock. He then mortgaged two hundred and eighty-five acres of the same land to Harrison, retaining seventy-five acres: and he afterwards again mortgaged the whole, including the seventy-five acres, to Conrad. In this state of the incumbrances, it was decided that as, after the mortgage to Harrison, he had a right to demand that the seventy-five acres reserved in the hands of Sisson should be first charged by Brock's mortgage, so, after the mortgage to Conrad, he had a right still to insist on subjecting the same seventy-five acres to the discharge of the prior mortgage as far as it would go, for his indemnification. This decision rested upon the plain and equitable principle, that if there be a mortgage on two acres, and the mortgagor sells one of them, the vendee has a right to demand that the other lot retained by his vendor shall be first sold to satisfy the debt; and as this right at once attaches, it can not be lost by a sale of the other lot to a third person, but he must sit in the seat of his vendor, and be first liable. This principle had been repeatedly acted upon by Chancellor Kent, and is also recognized and approved by the whole court in *Nailer* v. *Stanley*, 10 Serg. & R. 450–455 [13 Am. Dec. 691]. By the unanimous judgment of this court, it was approved in the above mentioned case of *Conrad* v. *Harrison et al.*

In the case of *Beverley* v. *Brooke et al.*, 2 Leigh, 425, it had, however, been decided that where a judgment is obtained against a debtor, who afterwards aliens his lands to divers alienees by divers conveyances, all the lands in the hands of the several alienees are alike liable to the judgment creditor, and must contribute *pro rata*. This case is different from that of *Conrad* v. *Harrison et al.*, as it is the case of a judgment; and that difference was adverted to by the judges in the decision of

Conrad v. *Harrison*, as important. It was not expressly overruled, and it can not be distinguished, I think, from the case at bar. We must therefore either overrule it, or, in deferring to it, we must say that the decree in this case is, upon this point, erroneous. My own opinion is that that case should be reviewed, as one of the most distinguished judges who decided it, expressly renounced it in *Conrad* v. *Harrison*, and as it appears that the point was not fully discussed, nor were the respectable authorities produced which have since been brought before the court: 10 Serg. & R. 450; *Clowes* v. *Dickenson*, 5 Johns. Ch. 235. The case was decided by only three judges, one of whom having since distinctly declared that he could not distinguish it from *Conrad* v. *Harrison et al.*, which he yet decided the other way, it stands now as the decision of only two judges, and so is no longer an authority binding upon us.

Upon reviewing this case, and revolving the principles decided in *Clowes* v. *Dickenson* and *Conrad* v. *Harrison et al.*, I am compelled to say that I think those principles should govern it. The case put by Chancellor Kent, of a judgment binding lands, is precisely the case of *Beverley* v. *Brooke et al.*, and its naked statement exhibits the truth and applicability of the principle laid down by him. The case put by Judge Carr, in 3 Leigh, 539, 540, is apt and forcible for its illustration. The argument seems to me unanswerable, that the right of the prior vendee to demand that his vendor's land should, for his relief, be first charged under an *elegit*, can not be taken away without his consent. The consequences of the contrary doctrine are also worthy of the gravest consideration. A debtor who, after judgment, has sold part of his lands, has every temptation to defraud his grantee of his right to resort to the residue for his relief. He has every inducement to sell that residue and pocket the price, the purchaser holding it free from more than a *pro rata* charge. It is worth nothing in his own hands, but by selling it to another, it brings profit to himself.

It is said, indeed, that the law has settled the rights of the alienees. It has declared that all are *in æquali jure*, and that equity can not control the law. I do not think so. Admit that all are upon equal footing at law, the question still recurs whether one may not have superior equity to another. This is admitted as it respects the vendor himself. If the *elegit* takes (as in strictness it must take, and as in fact it usually does take) all the lands, as well the alienee's as the debtor's, the alienee has no relief at law, but yet he may have relief in equity against the debtor himself. Why? Because he has superior equity. So if all are alienees, they are all *in æquali jure* at law, but the prior has superior equity over the latter. He had, before the last alienation, an equitable right to charge the land so aliened. Has he lost that right by the last alienation? Does not the last alienee take subject to that equity? Assuredly, if he purchased with notice of it. He had notice of the jugdment, and that it bound his land. If he had notice that there were other lands which were bound by it, and which were previously aliened, he had notice that what he was buying was, in his vendor's hands, bound for their indemnity. If he did not know this, he must protect himself, if at all, by a plea of his purchase without notice of the equitable rights of prior alienees. This has not been done in the present case. If therefore it be admitted that the last alienee can protect himself at all, it is not upon the principle that he is, in equity, *in æquali jure*, but upon the ground that he purchased without notice of the equity, and is therefore not affected by it. It is possible that this might protect him: but as to this, I do not think it necessary now to give an opinion. It is enough here to say, that where the last alienee can not so protect himself, he must be the first to suffer in equity.

The next error assigned is the failure to ascertain whether the rents and profits would not pay the debt in a reasonable time. To this it may be answered: 1. That the defendant, not having asked the inquiry, is presumed to have waived it: *Manns* v. *Flinn's Adm'r*, 10 Leigh, 93. 2. That the price of the property (two hundred dollars) is a sufficient assurance that the rents of half of it would be inadequate even to pay the interest.

Thus far I have been able to discover no error in the decree. But I am of opinion that in some other points it is clearly erroneous. First, the decree is for interest on the aggregate sum of three hundred and sixty-two dollars and sixty-four cents, instead of the original sum of one hundred and forty-eight dollars and sixty-three cents. Secondly, the equity of redemption in the land conveyed in trust for Withrow should have been first sold out and out—not a moiety only, but the whole: *Haleys* v. *Williams*, 1 Leigh, 140 [19 Am. Dec. 743]. 3. If that fell short of satisfying the demand, then the tract conveyed to the apppellant should have been next sold, and so in succession, until the debt should be satisfied, or one half in value of the whole lands should be sold. For had the *elegit* been executed, one half of each tract would not be extended, but one half of the whole lands, and that half which was last sold should bear the burden: See *Harvey* v. *Woodhouse*, Kel. 3.

STANARD, J., dissented from the opinion that the lien existed from the date of the original judgment, for the damages and costs to which the creditor became entitled by the judgment of affirmance; and also from the opinion that a court of equity should not compel the alienees to contribute *pro rata*, considering that on this point, and those flowing from it, the decision ought to conform to that in *Beverley* v. *Brooke et al.* But

PARKER, J., concurring with the president, the decree was merely reversed in those things wherein it was declared to be erroneous in the opinion of the president, and in all other things was affirmed. The cause was sent back, that the decree might be reformed, and the case proceeded in according to the principles declared by the majority of the court.

BROOKE and CABELL, JJ., absent.

————

PRIORITY OF LIENS BETWEEN SUCCESSIVE LIENORS.—In *Jones* v. *Phelan*, 20 Gratt. 229, the doctrine of the principal case was approved and applied to the satisfaction of a lessor's lien for rent out of personal property belonging to the lessee, which the latter had incumbered by two deeds of trust, the first of which was a lien on a portion of the property, and the second of which embraced the whole. Upon a sale of the whole property, the court held that the lien of the lessor must first be satisfied, after which, whatever balance remained from the sale of the property embraced in the first deed of trust should be applied to the extinguishment of the debt secured thereby. In commenting on the principal case, the court said: "In the latter cases decided by this court on the subject, *McClung* v. *Beirne* has been followed, and *Beverley* v. *Brooke* has been considered as overruled," citing *Rodgers* v. *McCluer's Adm'r*, 4 Gratt. 81; *Henkle's Ex'r* v. *Allstadt*, Id. 284; *Alley* v. *Rogers*, 19 Id. 366.

————

HAXALL'S EXECUTORS v. SHIPPEN.

[10 LEIGH, 536.]

TENANT FOR LIFE IN A BUILDING WHICH IS DESTROYED BY FIRE, has a right to the use and possession of the insurance money, but can not deprive the husband of one entitled to the remainder of his interest therein, or of his right to sue therefor, by converting the same into realty.

DAMAGES RECOVERED ON A POLICY OF FIRE INSURANCE are not part of the inheritance; they are personal estate, belonging to the owners of the building according to their respective rights.

NO EQUITY ATTACHES TO DAMAGES RECOVERED on a policy of fire insurance, which authorizes the same to be used in replacing the buildings for the loss of which they were recovered.

INJUNCTION. Thomas Shore, having insured his house against fire, in favor of himself, his heirs and assigns, died, leaving the same, and the land on which it was situated, to his wife, Jane, for life, remainder to his daughters, Jane, Elizabeth, and Louisa. The widow soon after married Henry Haxall. The house having been destroyed by fire, the Mutual assurance society, by which it had been insured, refused to pay over the principal, amounting to seven thousand eight hundred and thirty-three dollars, to the tenants for life, but directed that interest thereon be paid them during the continuance of the life estate. Haxall and wife thereupon brought suit against the society, and the devisees in remainder, for the recovery of the insurance money, which was decreed to be paid them, upon their executing a bond for the repayment of the same to the devisees in remainder, upon the termination of the life estate. Such bond having been executed, the money was paid, and used in replacing the house which had been destroyed. Upon the death of the life tenant, the land and house thereon devolved to the devisees in remainder, Louisa, now the wife of William Shippen, and Elizabeth, now the wife of John Gilliam. The devisees having brought action on the bond, and recovered judgment thereon against William Haxall, the only surviving obligor, the latter filed this bill in equity, reciting the above facts, and praying for an injunction against the enforcement of the judgment. Haxall died pending the suit, and the same was revived in the name of his executors. The preliminary injunction having been dissolved, complainants appealed.

Leigh, for the appellants.

Rhodes and *Macfarland*, for the appellees.

TUCKER, P. Upon mature consideration of this case, and of the very able argument on both sides, I regret to be compelled to give my judgment in favor of the appellees: I regret it because it is certainly a case of some hardship on the appellants, and those for whom their testator was the surety, since the appellees, by this decision, will get both the newly erected building and the whole of the insurance money which was paid for that which was consumed.

At the very first step in this investigation, we are met by the decree of June, 1814. That decree I consider as conclusive of the rights of the parties to it, and, whether right or wrong, decisive of the questions now again brought before the court. The bill filed by Haxall and wife sets forth the burning of the

mansion-house, their purpose to rebuild it with the insurance
money, and the refusal of the mutual assurance society to pay
it to them, and prays a decree that the money should be paid to
them for that purpose.   The decree simply orders a payment of
the whole insurance money to the plaintiffs, declaring Mrs. Haxall's right " to the use of the money in like manner as she would
have been entitled to the use of the house itself;" that is, to the
uncontrolled use of it (the money) during her life, but to be
paid over to those in remainder at her death.   It gave no authority to rebuild at the charge of the daughters, nor did it
limit the life-owner in the manner of using the fund.   She had
the absolute use of it during her life, and was not bound or required to use it in rebuilding.   It might have been employed in
trade or speculation, and the parties in remainder could not,
after that decree, have arrested such an employment of the capital.   All their right was to have it returned at the expiration of
the life estate.   Such was obviously the effect of the decree;
and, accordingly, the plaintiffs were required to give bond, before they should have the benefit of it, to the two daughters for
the payment of the principal money immediately upon the death
of the mother.   The plaintiffs seem to have hesitated.   The
court had disapproved the idea of the assurers, which confined
Mrs. Haxall to the interest, since in that mode she did not enjoy
the money as she was entitled to enjoy the house.   The use of
the money was not necessarily measured by the interest, and,
therefore, the money itself was decreed to her and her husband
for her life, the repayment being secured by bond; and thus she
would truly enjoy the money as she would have enjoyed the use
of the house.   Yet for nearly two years the plaintiffs delayed
giving the bond.   At length, they did give it, conformably to
the decree, which after such a lapse of time must have been well
understood, and by entering into the obligation under it, they
assented to, ratified, and confirmed it, and made themselves absolutely debtors to the devisees in remainder for the whole
insurance money at the mother's death.

Had the chancellor designed to sanction the rebuilding at the
children's expense, the decree and the bond would have been in
the alternative, either to rebuild, or, on failure to do so, then
to refund.   But the decree is absolute, that they shall have the
use of the money for life, and that the daughters shall have the
money at the mother's death.   This decree is unassailable.   The
plaintiffs, having acquiesced in it, and indeed acted under it, can
not gainsay it, or vacate, or modify, the bond given under it.

To say that the daughters shall not have the money, but shall have the buildings in satisfaction of it, is to contradict the bond. To contradict the bond, which follows the decree, is to controvert the decree; and this can not now be done even by appeal, and much less when thus assailed collaterally only. That decree, therefore, I conceive, is conclusive upon the question of the plaintiff's claim to have the money for the purpose of rebuilding at the joint charge of the life owner and those in remainder.

I am, however, clearly of opinion, that that decree was right. Conceding that the covenant of assurance, being with the covenantee, his heirs and assigns, inured to the benefit of all who had any title in the premises, in proportion to their respective interests; conceding that the tenant for life is not chargeable for waste and for the value of the building, according to the doctrines anterior to the statute 6 Anne, c. 31; 1 Wms. Saund. 323 b;[1] 7 Bac. Abr., Waste, C, 256, and waiving the question how their respective proportions are to be ascertained; still it is obvious, that the tenant for life could have no superior right over those in remainder, to the disposition of the insurance money. Unless there was an equity, as is contended, that the money paid for the building that was burned should go to rebuild it, as that was the purpose for which it was destined (a question to be presently examined), it seems undeniable, that Mrs. Haxall could have no right to insist that a fund in which her daughters were equally interested, should be invested in any manner without their assent or against their wishes. Being entitled to its use for life, indeed, she might have used it during life as she pleased, but she could have no right so to use it as to affect or impair their right to the use of the money itself after her death. Unless all, therefore, concurred in this conversion of personalty into realty, neither could so convert it.

There was, then, no power in Haxall and wife to make the conversion without the assent of the daughters. But they were infants and could not assent. Moreover, Shippen's marriage, at least, was prior to the rebuilding. Immediately upon his marriage, his marital rights to a moiety of this fund as money attached. It was, indeed, but a chose in action; but still it would become his upon his reducing it into possession, and it has now become absolutely his by the judgment upon the bond, which he may enforce in his own right, and not as administrator of his wife. What right, then, had the tenant for life, without

---

1. *Pomfret v. Ricrost.*

his assent, to convert this money, which would belong to him
as personalty, into real estate to which he would have no title
whatever, unless he had a child, and then only the title of a
tenant by the curtesy? The law recognizes no such power in
one person, to dispose of and change and annihilate the rights
of others. And here, if the fund continues money, Shippen is
entitled to four or five thousand dollars; but if the conversion
of money into land is recognized, he may not have title to anything; for *non constat* that he would be even tenant by the
curtesy.

That I have not assumed too much in asserting the husband's
right to the insurance money, may be safely affirmed. Though
it be a covenant real for upholding the estate, yet if the insurers refuse payment, the action against them is for damages, and
damages only can be recovered. It is truly said by Vice-chancellor Leach, in *Noble* v. *Cass*,[1] that with respect to injuries to
land, for which damages are to be recovered in a personal action,
the person who brings the action is entitled to the damages;
and, accordingly, he held that the damages recovered for a
breach of a covenant running with the land, belonged to the
person who recovered them, and are not to be considered as
part of the inheritance. Now on this covenant of insurance,
the wife could not sue alone. Her husband must join, even in
actions relating to her real property: 1 Bac. Abr., Baron and
Feme, K, 499; 1 Chit. Pl. 17; and if he recovers damages,
they at once become his absolutely; he puts them in his own
pocket without accountability to any.

This occurs in various instances, seemingly of the greatest
hardship. It happens even in those cases where the damages
which thus become his, are retribution for realty which never
could have become his, and where the apparent relation between
the damages and the reparation of the estate would seem plain and
palpable. Thus, if he sues upon a covenant of seisin, in which
the value of the estate may be the measure of damages, those
damages are not applied to purchase a new estate for the wife,
but they become his own. The wife loses her real estate, and
the husband pockets its value. So in an action on a covenant
for quiet enjoyment, or of warranty, or for renewal of a lease,
the wife's retribution for her real estate goes into her husband's
hands. So in action on a covenant to repair or to rebuild,
the damages assessed must be adequate to repairing or rebuilding the premises: *Shortridge* v. *Lamplugh*, Ld. Raym. 798, yet

---

1. 2 Sim. 343.

these damages the husband recovers, and there is no equity to compel him to lay out the money in repairing or rebuilding his wife's houses. "A court of equity," says the vice-chancellor, in *Noble* v *Cass,* "never holds that damages are anything but the personal estate of the person who recovers them, and I should be introducing a new equity if I were to hold the damages recovered for breach of covenant running with the land, to be a part of the inheritance."

Upon these principles then, this court must consider the money due by the insurance society, for which the decree was rendered in June, 1814, as a chose in action, which Shippen became entitled to on his marriage, and which upon the death of the widow he would have been entitled to demand by suit, if its payment had not been secured by bond. Upon these principles too, the court in 1814 was right in considering this money as personal estate of the infants, and to be secured to them as such. The bond by which it was secured became, as to a moiety, the property of Shippen, as soon as he married, and he has since made it absolutely his own by recovering a judgment upon it. The other moiety, in like manner, belonged to Gilliam. In this view of the case, it is manifest that the tenant for life could not lawfully deprive the appellee Shippen of his marital right to sue for this money (to which, when recovered, he would have absolute right) by converting it into realty to which he would have no title. And this furnishes a sufficient answer to the idea, that the case resembles the payment of a debt by a gift or legacy: for, in those cases, the gift or legacy may not only be rejected by the party, but it goes to him who is in fact the creditor. But here the supposed gift of the buildings is to the owners of the realty instead of the husbands who are entitled to the money. The gift, therefore, does not inure to the owners of the debt.

Unless, therefore, it can be shown that the insurance money ought to be applied to the purpose for which it is said to be destined, there would seem to be little foundation for the pretensions of the appellees. Let us then inquire how stands the law in this regard. The position seems to me to be a misapprehension of the law of insurances against fire. In the case of *Vivian* v. *Champion,* 1 Salk. 141; 2 Ld. Raym. 1125, Lord Holt indeed observed, in relation to damages recovered from a tenant for ninety-nine years on a covenant to repair, that the damages should be sufficient to put the premises in repair, and the plaintiff ought, in justice, to apply them to that purpose. How he was to be compelled to do so, and whether the obligation was to be held to be perfect or imperfect, does not appear. But admitting it to be perfect, there are strong reasons for compelling such an application of the money in the case of a tenant who is bound for rent to his landlord, and who seems therefore equitably entitled to have the benefit of the damages to put the property in the stipulated state of repair. But as to policies of insurance, they are considered as distinct, independent contracts between the insurers and the insured. If the covenant does not name the heirs, the executors of the insured, and not the heirs, will be entitled to the proceeds of the policy, and those proceeds will go to pay debts, instead of being applied to rebuild houses: Ellis on Insurance, 84, 85. "As a general rule," says Mr. Hovenden in his note on *Mildmay* v. *Folgham*, 1 Hov. Supp. 305, "policies of insurance are not attached to the realty, nor do they in any manner go with the same as incident thereto, by any conveyance or assignment;" citing *Lynch* v. *Dalzell*, 4 Bro. P. C. 431. Accordingly, in the case of *Mildmay* v. *Folgham*, 3 Ves. 471, where the policy was made payable to the insured, her executors, administrators, and assigns, the lord chancellor refused to make the executor a trustee for the heir. Where, however, as in our insurances, the policy binds the insurers to pay to the insured, his heirs, etc., the policy must be considered, I conceive, as a covenant real of which the heir, and not the executor, must have the benefit. Still it does not follow, that when the money is paid to the heir, he is bound to lay it out in rebuilding: and if, as usually happens, there are several heirs, it is not perceived that either has a right to insist that the others shall unite with him in rebuilding the premises. The insurance is a compensation for a loss, and when that compensation is paid, it is money in the hands of the assured, of which they may dispose at pleasure.

The law of contribution has no application to the case. That law has strict application, indeed, where property held in common needs repair: for there, it is in existence, and each has a right to keep it in existence, and to make all essential repairs at the joint expense of all. But where the buildings on an estate are destroyed, the question is one, not of repair of what exists and is held in common, but of building out and out. And as one tenant in common can not compel another to build on their vacant lot, however it may be to their advantage, so one heir can not compel the others to rebuild a house that has been destroyed. Still less can the tenant for life; for between him and the remainderman there is no community of

interest. On the contrary, their interests are conflicting; for
if the remainder-man is compelled to spend his money in rebuilding, peradventure the life owner may live till it falls into
decay and becomes useless; or it may again be consumed by
fire, and then he will have no retribution. Accordingly, as
between tenant and landlord, the landlord who receives insurance money can not be compelled to rebuild, nor indeed is he
even compellable to repair, but that duty, to a certain extent,
rests upon the tenant. See Ellis on Ins. 82; *Leeds* v. *Cheetham,*
1 Sim. 146. In the case at bar, it must be conceded, that however ruinous the buildings might have become, the tenant for
life could have demanded no aid for repairs, but would have
been bound at her own expense to keep the property in repair.
By what right, then, could she demand that the devisees in remainder should expend their funds in rebuilding the premises
out and out? And *a fortiori,* by what right could she demand,
after the marital rights attached, that the husband should expend
what had become his funds, in rebuilding a house which never
might become his?

Much reliance was placed on the case of *Norris* v. *Harrison,*
2 Madd. Ch. 268. The various reasons for that decision are so
thrown together by Vice-chancellor Plumer, that it is difficult
to extract any distinct principle applicable to this case from his
opinion. There are some expressions which seem to indicate
the idea, that the insurance money ought of right to be employed
in rebuilding, and the court repelled the claim of the remainder-man to that portion of it which had been so employed, since
it had been "laid out on the estate for the very purpose to which
it was originally destined." Yet in deciding upon the right to
the unexpended balance of the insurance fund, he rests so
strongly on the intention of the testator, W. Bell's will, as to
induce the belief that upon that intention depended the character of the fund, as real or personal. I think, however, upon
the whole, that there is sufficient evidence that the vice-chancellor did look upon the fund as one properly devoted to rebuilding the premises, or to the erection of some other equivalent
building on the estate. But in the subsequent case of *Noble* v.
Cass, Vice-chancellor Leach did not consider his predecessor as
settling any such general principle, but as deciding the case
upon the acts of the party, and the particular expressions in the
will. If the case of *Norris* v. *Harrison* does determine that the
insurance money must be applied to rebuilding the premises,
then I can only say that I can not acquiesce in any such opinion.

The covenant does indeed run with the land, and inure to the benefit of all who have title to the estate, according to their respective interests. But the damages (or insurance money) when recovered, are not to be considered as part of the inheritance. They are a sum in gross, belonging to the parties according to their respective interests. There is no authority for the principle, that an equity attaches to the damages recovered at law, to give them the particular destination of rebuilding the premises for the loss of which they were recovered. Such a doctrine would be unreasonable and difficult of execution; unreasonable, because it might well be to the interest of the reversioner that the houses should not be rebuilt, either because of the depreciation of the property or for other causes; difficult of execution, because one party might oppose a rebuilding according to the former fashion, and the other insist upon it, and, in case of difference, the court must interfere to settle and adjust these vexatious disputes, involving petty details, embarrassing and unworthy of the tribunals of justice.

The notion, indeed, of an equity attaching to the insurance money, is wholly without foundation. There is no covenant even of the society to rebuild: it has no right to rebuild: it must pay the amount of the policy: and when so paid to the insured himself, he may do as he pleases with the money. There is nothing to bind him to rebuild. And if he gives the property to A. for life, remainder to B., he does not give to either any right to demand the concurrence of the other in rebuilding the premises. As assignees, each has a right to benefit in the covenant proportioned to his interest, and each has his distinct action at law: *Attersoll* v. *Stevens*, 1 Taunt. 183. Perhaps there is no method better adapted to effect the ends of justice, than, through a court of equity, to decree the whole money to the tenant for life for his use during life, taking care to secure repayment to the remainder-man upon the tenant's death. This is the course which the chancellor pursued in 1814, and which, upon the whole, I think is to be approved.

It remains but to say, that I think the tenants for life can not be sustained in their gratuitous act, by the allegation that the parties stood by and did not warn them against proceeding. It has been well said, that the decree itself was a warning; the bond was a warning; and *non constat*, that notice was ever given to those in remainder, that an attempt would be made to charge them. They had no right or reason to suppose, after that decree, and while they held the absolute bond for repayment, that the tenants for life were building at their charge. They had therefore no reason for interfering with the proceeding; for if the tenants chose to rebuild at their own expense, there was no one who could gainsay it.

BROOKE and CABELL, JJ., concurred.

STANARD, J., said, he entirely concurred with the president, in the general principles stated in his opinion, but he doubted, whether, considering the circumstances of the particular case, the actual value of the new house put on the premises, as it stood at the time of Mrs. Haxall's death, ought not to be allowed to the appellants, and set off against the debt. He inclined to the opinion, that, to this extent, the appellants were entitled to relief.

Decree affirmed.

PARKER, J., absent.   ____

APPLICATION OF INSURANCE MONEY BETWEEN TENANT AND REVERSIONER.—In *Brough* v. *Higgins*, 2 Gratt. 408, the court drew a distinction between a partial and a total destruction of an insured building, in which there was a life and a reversionary interest, by holding that in the former case both the tenant for life and the reversioner were entitled to have the amount recovered under the policy of insurance applied to the repair of the building, and that such application by the tenant would protect him from any future claims therefor on the part of the reversioner.

CASES

IN THE

SUPREME COURT

OF

ALABAMA.

HERBERT v. HUIE.

[1 ALABAMA, 18.]

NOTE SIGNED IN BLANK, and intrusted to another in the confidence that
it will be filled with a particular amount, is valid in the hands of a *bona
fide* holder, notwithstanding this confidence is violated by the insertion of
a greater amount.

HOLDER WHO HAS ADVANCED MONEY UPON A SIGNED BLANK, in good
faith and without knowledge of any fact which would put him upon an
inquiry which would disclose that the authority to insert an amount
therein was restricted, may fill in the amount which he has advanced,
and hold the signors responsible therefor.

THAT THE CHARGE OF THE COURT DID NOT TOUCH UPON A MATERIAL
POINT in the case is not error, if no request was made to charge thereon.

ACTION upon a promissory note. The plaintiff in error had
delivered to John G. Porter a signed blank, which he authorized the latter to fill in with a note for one thousand dollars,
payable to some bank in Mobile. Porter & Ryan indorsed
the blank and delivered it to Ross & Ford, to be filled by them
as a note to be used in bank for the benefit of the former. Ross
& Ford filled in the blank with a note for five thousand two
hundred and sixty-eight dollars and thirty-five cents, for which
amount they gave credit to Porter & Ryan, the latter being
largely indebted to them. Ross & Ford afterwards passed the
note to defendant in error as collateral security for a debt which
they owed to him. Plaintiff in error, defendant below, denied
that the filling in of the note, under such circumstances, could
be treated as authorized by him. The other facts of the case appear from the opinion.

Hopkins and Dargan, for the plaintiffs in error.

J. L. Martin, contra.

ORMOND, J.   The law is well established, and is admitted by the counsel for the plaintiff in error, that if a note is signed in blank and intrusted to another, in the confidence that it shall be filled up for a particular amount, or used in a particular mode, and that confidence is abused by the insertion of a larger amount, or by making an improper use of the instrument, that the instrument will, notwithstanding, be valid, in the hands of a *bona fide* holder for a valuable consideration.   But it is insisted that the present case is distinguishable from that, because in this instance, the note was not filled up by Porter, to whom the blank was delivered, and in whom the confidence was reposed. The argument is, that the authority to fill up the note is given to Porter alone, and that the power can not be delegated.   It is true, that when a blank note is signed and delivered to another, for the purpose of being filled up, authority must of necessity be conferred to do the act, without which the note could be of no value; but to deduce from this presumption an argument that the note when filled up and in the hands of a *bona fide* holder, can be sustained alone on this ground, is not correct. The rule by which a recovery in such a case is allowed, stands on a much broader ground—and may be thus stated.   That where one of two innocent persons must sustain a loss, he must bear it who is most in fault.   If, by misplaced confidence, one enables another to commit a fraud, it is but just he should pay the penalty of his own indiscretion: and that the loss should not be visited on another who has vested his money on the faith of the genuineness of his signature, without the means of ascertaining the fraud which had been committed.

These being the principles which govern the case, it follows that, the implied authority is given to the holder to fill up the note, with any amount which he may have advanced on it, in good faith, and without the knowledge of any fact which might lead to an inquiry and expose the fraud.   This principle as has been stated is well settled, and to permit it now to be questioned, would be of most mischievous consequence: See *Brahan and Atwood* v. *Ragland*, 3 Stew. 247; *Putnam* v. *Sullivan*, 4 Mass. 45 [3 Am. Dec. 206]; *Violett* v. *Patton*, 5 Cranch, 142; *Russell* v. *Lanstuffer*,[1] Doug. 496; and *Roberts* v. *Adams*, 8 Port. 297, and cases there cited [33 Am. Dec. 291].

It is also maintained, that as the defendant in error received the note, as collateral security for the payment of an existing

---

1. *Russel* v. *Langstaffe*, Doug. 514.

debt due from Ross & Ford to him and gave no other consideration for it, that he can not be considered a *bona fide* holder for a valuable consideration. This is an objection entitled to great weight, and would, perhaps, be decisive of this question, if the predicament·of the record was such as to permit it now to be made. Neither of the charges moved for by the plaintiff in error raised this question before the jury, they are both predicated on the idea that the note was void, because not filled by Porter, to whom the blank was intrusted, and therefore properly refused. But it is supposed that the charge given by the court authorizes this point to be made here. The charge of the court merely states the law as laid down in this opinion. It is true, the court say, that to enable the plaintiff to recover, he must be a *bona fide* holder for a valuable consideration, but whether the facts, if true, would constitute him a *bona fide* holder for a valuable consideration, was a question not raised before the court, or argued to the jury, so far as we can judge, from anything appearing on the record.

If the court refuse to give a charge, improperly asked for, and then charge the jury wrong in point of law, the case must be reversed. But that is not the fact; here the charge is right, and the objection, in effect, is that the court did not inform the jury of its own mere motion what constituted a *bona fide* purchase or holder for a valuable consideration. This the court was under no obligation to do. The consideration of that matter, as would appear from the record, was waived by the party interested in its ascertainment. The verdict of the jury has ascertained that the defendant in error was a *bona fide* holder of the note, for a valuable consideration, and it is not the province or duty of this court to examine the facts set out in the record, and revise their decision.

There is no error in the record, and the judgment must be affirmed.

SIGNING AND DELIVERING BLANK NOTE gives unlimited authority to insert any sum; and a plea that the blank was filled in with a greater sum than was authorized, is bad: *Hall* v. *Bank of Commonwealth*, 30 Am. Dec. 685; *Roberts* v. *Adams*, 33 Id. 291.

CULLUM v. EMANUEL AND GAINES.

[1 ALABAMA, 23.]

WHERE THERE IS A SURETY FOR A DEBT SECURED BY MORTGAGE, the creditor has an election, of which he can not be deprived, whether he shall proceed in equity upon his mortgage, or at law against the debtor or surety.

SURETY WHO HAS PAID HIS PRINCIPAL'S DEBT IS ENTITLED TO ALL SECURITIES held or acquired by the creditor.

CREDITOR WHO PARTS WITH OR RENDERS UNAVAILABLE SECURITIES OR a fund which he would be entitled to apply in discharge of his debt, as a general rule exonerates a surety for the debt to the extent of the value of such securities or fund.

CREDITOR WHO HAS DISABLED HIMSELF from surrendering to the surety the means of reimbursement which he once possessed, is not to be injured thereby, if he acted without a knowledge of the rights of other persons and with good faith and just intentions.

PURCHASE BY MORTGAGEE OF THE EQUITY OF REDEMPTION DOES NOT EX-TINGUISH the mortgage so as to release a surety for the mortgage debt, where the creditor disavows that it was his intention to extinguish the mortgage, and avows that he will apply the rents and profits of the land in extinguishment of the mortgage debt.

BILL in equity. The case made by the bill was this. In 1834, the defendants below sold to Stephen Schuyler certain real estate situate in the city of Mobile. At the same time they took from him ten promissory notes, payable in one, two, three, etc., years to represent the purchase money. Complainant became indorser on the four notes first falling due; this indorsement was for the accommodation of Schuyler, as was well known to defendants. Defendants likewise took from Schuyler a mortgage on the property sold, to secure the notes indorsed and unindorsed. The note that fell due first was paid. Schuyler then became insolvent and no other notes were paid. The defendants obtained judgment against complainant on one of the notes indorsed by him, and threatened to issue execution, and also to bring suit upon another of the indorsed notes. The bill alleged that the mortgaged property was sufficient for the discharge of all the notes given for the purchase money; that the mortgage security was applicable to the discharge of the notes in the order in which they fell due; that if the defendant should collect the amount of the indorsed notes from complainant, the latter would be entitled to the benefit of the mortgage, and thereby a circuity of action would be occasioned, which would be avoided if defendants were compelled to proceed in the first instance on the mortgage. Complainant therefore prayed an injunction against any proceedings by defendants in aid of their judgment against him. In further support of this relief, the bill alleged that the equity of redemption in the mortgaged land had been purchased by defendants, and that the mortgage had been thereby destroyed, and that the defendants by thus destroying the security for the debt had released complainant from his liability as surety. An answer was put in, the nature of which sufficiently appears from the opinion. A preliminary injunction granted on the filing of the bill was thereafter dissolved on motion.

J. A. Campbell, for the appellant.

Stewart, contra.

COLLIER, C. J. In the argument of this cause two points have been made for the plaintiff: 1. That the mortgage operates in equity as a lien upon the property embraced by it for the payment of all the notes made by Schuyler and Roberts—that the notes are entitled to priority of satisfaction from this security in the order in which they fall due. And that, inasmuch as the plaintiff upon payment of either of the notes in which he may be a surety, might resort to the mortgage for indemnification, equity will dispense with this circuity by requiring Emanuel & Gaines to seek a satisfaction from that source in the first instance; 2. That a surety is entitled to all the securities or means of payment to which the creditor was entitled, and if a creditor has destroyed or impaired these, the surety is *pro tanto* discharged. The defendants, Emanuel & Gaines, having purchased Schuyler's interest in the equity of redemption, extinguished the mortgage (which was an ample security for the notes of which the plaintiff was the indorser), and thus released the plaintiff from his liability.

1. It is clearly competent for a creditor to secure himself both by a lien on property and the engagement of a third person undertaking for the payment by the debtor. And the creditor is not obliged to proceed in equity upon his mortgage, but has the election either to seek a foreclosure, or to prosecute an action at law upon the promise of the debtor and his surety: *Tice* v. *Annin*, 2 Johns. Ch. 125; *Dunkley* v. *Van Buren et al.*, 3 Id. 330. The mortgage is a mere security for the debt, and is regarded as an incident to the legal contract to pay, which remains in full force, and on this ground rests the principle which permits the mortgagee to elect his remedy.

To sustain the argument for the plaintiff on this point, we have been referred to the case of *Gwathmeys* v. *Ragland*, 1 Rand. 466. The facts of that case, so far as they need be noticed, are these: "A deed of trust was executed by William and Francis Sutton, to trustees to secure the payment of three notes to a certain Anderson Barrett. The first note was paid; the second transferred, by indorsement, to Nathaniel Ragland, without any assignment to him of the deed of trust; the third note was indorsed to Robert and Temple Gwathmey, who took an assignment of the deed of trust for their security." The trustees having advertised for sale the property embraced by the deed, to satisfy the note held by Ragland, the Gwathmeys filed a' bill to enjoin the sale of the trust property to satisfy Ragland's claim, insisting that as they had taken an assignment of the deed of trust, and Ragland had not, their lien was to be preferred to his. The court of appeals held that the deed of trust was an additional security for the payment of the notes to Barrett or his assigns, in the order in which they fell due, it follows the notes into the hands of their several holders, and it was not competent for Barrett, by an assignment of the deed to the Gwathmeys, to deprive Ragland of his priority of right to demand a sale of the trust property, if necessary to the payment of his claim. There was no fraud or misrepresentation imputed to Ragland, and the assignment of the deed to the Gwathmeys gave them full notice of the order in which the notes were to have been paid, and should have put them upon inquiry whether the first and second had been paid, when they took an assignment of the third note.

This case decides: 1. That where property is conveyed to secure the payment of notes to fall due at different periods, and a controversy arises between the assignees of the notes, the holder of the one first maturing is entitled to a priority of payment from the property conveyed. 2. That the assignment of the notes carries to their assignees the interest in the security furnished by the deed, without any written declaration to that effect, by the assignor. Neither of these points is applicable to the case at bar. There is no controversy between assignees as to the right of preference; but the argument assumes that the plaintiff can not be charged upon his undertaking to Emanuel & Gaines, because the mortgaged property is of greater value than the amount of the notes indorsed by himself and Roberts. This argument we have already said can not be maintained.

2. It is a well-ascertained principle, that the surety who has paid the debt of the principal, is entitled to stand in the place of the creditor as to all securities for the debt, held or acquired by the creditor, and to have the same benefit from them as the creditor might have had. This doctrine is very clearly stated by Lord Eldon in *Craythorne* v. *Swinburne*, 14 Ves. 162. The Lord Chancellor says: "A surety is entitled to every remedy which the creditor has against the principal debtor, to enforce every security and all means of payment; to stand in the place of the creditor, not only through the medium of contract, but even by

means of securities entered into without his knowledge, having a right to have those securities transferred to him, though there was no stipulation for it; and to avail himself of all those securities against the debtor." And Chancellor Kent, in *Cheeseborough* v. *Millard*, 1 Johns. Ch. 409 [7 Am. Dec. 494], has shown that this doctrine of substitution is equally well known to the civil law and in the English chancery. See also *Parsons* v. *Briddock*, 2 Vern. 608; *Wright* v. *Morley*, 11 Ves. 12; *Harrison* v. *Glossop*,[1] 3 Ves. & Bea. 185; *Hayes* v. *Ward et al.*, 4 Johns. Ch. 123 [8 Am. Dec. 554]; 1 Story's Eq. 477. If the creditor parts with or renders unavailable securities, or any fund which he would be entitled to apply in discharge of his debt, the security becomes exonerated to the extent of the value of such securities; because securities which the creditor is entitled to apply in discharge of his debt, he is bound to apply, or to hold them as a trustee ready to be applied for the benefit of the surety: *Mayhew* v. *Crickett*, 2 Swanst. 185; *Law* v. *The East India Co.*, 4 Ves. 824; *Cheeseborough* v. *Millard*, 1 Johns. Ch. 409 [7 Am. Dec. 494]; *Capel* v. *Butler*, 2 Sim. & Stu. 457; *Hayes* v. *Ward et al.*, 4 Johns. Ch. 123 [8 Am. Dec 554]; 1 Story's Eq. 480, 481. But as the doctrine of substitution rests on the basis of mere equity and benevolence, the creditor who has disabled himself, from yielding up to the surety the means of reimbursement which he had, is not to be injured thereby; provided he acted without a knowledge of the rights of others and with good faith and just intentions, which is all that equity requires: *Cheeseborough* v. *Millard*, 1 Johns. Ch. 409 [7 Am. Dec. 494]; 1 Story's Eq. 471–483.

Ordinarily the purchase of the equity of redemption, does not operate in extinguishment of the mortgage, but the purchaser takes it charged with the lien, having acquired only the right to complete his title, by the payment of the mortgage debt. Whether the purchase by a mortgagee will have the effect to destroy the equitable right of a surety (situated as the plaintiff) to substitution, we need not determine, as the case may be disposed of on another ground. The defendants, Emanuel & Gaines, explicitly state, that they considered the equity of redemption of no value, inasmuch as the mortgaged property was of less value than the incumbrances upon it—that the purchase of Schuyler's interest was made for the purpose of avoiding controversy which might have arisen, if another person had purchased. That they were aware of the existence of the mortgage to the bank, at the

---

1. *Glossop v. Harrison.*

time of the sheriff's sale, and that it was, and still is their intention to apply the rents and profits as received, to the extinguishment of their debt and interest. Here is a direct disavowal of an intention to extinguish the mortgage, and a statement of facts showing that Emanuel & Gaines in purchasing the equity of redemption of Schuyler, acted in good faith and with just intentions. The plaintiff instead of being prejudiced by that act, is likely to be benefited, as the respondents declare that it is their intention to appropriate the rents and profits to the payment of the debt and interest due them. Even if it were conceded that the mortgaged property, without reference to the extent of its value, should be disposed of for the payment of the notes in the order in which they fall due, yet it can not be maintained that the plaintiff is released from his suretyship on the ground that the mortgage is extinguished. The disclaimer and concessions made in the answer of the respondents are sufficient to prevent such a result, whatever might be the conclusion of law apart from these. Without examining further, the arguments on this point, we are of opinion that the case made by the bill and answer, does not show an extinguishment of the mortgage, to the prejudice of the rights of the plaintiff. His interest in equity is unaffected by the purchase of Schuyler's interest by the respondents.

The result is, that the decree of the circuit court is affirmed.

THAT THE SURETY MAY IN EQUITY COMPEL THE CREDITOR to proceed against his principal, see *King* v. *Baldwin*, 8 Am. Dec. 415; *Hayes* v. *Ward*, Id. 554; *Cope* v. *Smith*, 11 Id. 582, and note 589; and note to *State* v. *Boyd*, 29 Id. 225, wherein are collected the cases to the point that the neglect of the creditor to sue the debtor at the request of the surety will release the latter in the case of any accruing loss, and those that, in consonance with the principal case, adopt the opposite view.

SURETY UPON PAYING THE DEBT is subrogated to the rights of the creditor as to all collateral securities, means, and remedies held by the latter for the enforcement of his debt: *Bank of Montpelier* v. *Dixon*, 24 Id. 640; *Hayes* v. *Ward*, 8 Id. 554; *Lowndes* v. *Chisholm*, 16 Id. 667; *Smith* v. *Tunno*, Id. 617; *Bunting* v. *Ricks*, 32 Id. 699.

BOYD v. BARCLAY.

[1 ALABAMA, 34.]

ONE OF THE PARTIES TO A CONSPIRACY TO DEFRAUD THE GOVERNMENT can not recover from the others the money realized as the fruits of the conspiracy.

ASSUMPSIT. Boyd, the defendant below, was the captain of a

volunteer company engaged in the Creek war. The government furnished neither wagons nor provisions. The company, prior to disbanding, determined to charge the government with a wagon and team, and to divide any proceeds that they might realize. Barclay consented that the members of the company might put in the account against the government in his name, and they accordingly did put in an account in which the government was charged with services of a wagon and team furnished by Barclay, although Barclay was not a member of the company, and had not rendered such service. Six hundred and six dollars were finally allowed on the claim by the government, and Boyd, as captain of the company, was appointed to receive the money. The first instruction asked by Boyd, was that if the money was obtained from the government by fraudulently representing that services had been performed by Barclay that were not performed, then Boyd held the money to the use of the government, and not to that of Barclay. The instruction was refused. Plaintiff below had verdict.

Dargan, for the plaintiff in error.

No appearance for the defendant.

GOLDTHWAITE, J. The facts of this case disclose a transaction by which the United States were defrauded of a sum of money; and one of the parties to the fraudulent transaction seeks to recover from another, the amount received from the United States, on the pretense that it was paid to the defendant as agent for the plaintiff, for a demand made out and allowed in his name. If Barclay's name had been used without his knowledge or consent, to carry into effect the illegal object to be attained, his right to recover the money received could not be disputed, unless Boyd had been notified by the United States, to retain the money. The sole object of Barclay in seeking a recovery, might be to return the money. If innocent of fraud, this would seem to be the legal as well as the charitable conclusion; and Boyd would not be permitted to disavow the agency assumed by him, or to allege his own turpitude to avoid the payment. But no such inference can be drawn in favor of the plaintiff in this action; for the evidence shows that he assented to the use of his name with a full knowledge of the falsity of his claim, and of the object to be attained. It can not be reasonably expected from one who has thus lent his name and connected himself with a deliberate fraud, to pursue a remedy against a coadjutor, for the purpose of rendering justice to the

injured party. The sole object of a suit by one thus circum-
stanced, must be to obtain the whole or a portion of the illegal
plunder to subserve his own interest. No court of justice can
rightfully lend its aid to assist him in such an attempt, not that
the condition of the defendant is more creditable than his own,
but because justice will not undertake to determine to whom the
reward of successful fraud is due.

If Boyd, throughout this transaction, had acted as the mere
agent of Barclay, and in this character had received the money,
it might be difficult to distinguish this case from those of
Tenant v. *Elliot*, 1 Bos. & Pul. 3, and *Farnur* v. *Russel*, Id. 295;[1]
in the former of which it was decided, that a broker who had
effected an illegal policy of insurance, could not retain the
money received by him from the underwriter, against his principal; and in the latter case, a carrier who had received the
payment for some counterfeit farthings sent by him to a purchaser, was held accountable for the money so received, to the
seller of the counterfeit farthings. These decisions go very far
to sustain the position, that if the person receiving money paid
on account of a fraudulent or illegal transaction, is the mere
agent for another, he will not be permitted to go into evidence
of the illegal transaction, unless it is necessarily connected with
the implied contract on which the action to compel the payment
of the money is founded.

But we think it is clear from the statement of the evidence,
that Boyd's agency in this transaction was a mere pretense, used
for the attainment of the money pretended to be due to Barclay
for services never rendered. When collected, the money was
not to be paid to him, but, by the terms of the conspiracy, was
to be paid, by Boyd, to the members of the company. There
was then, nothing real in the relation of Barclay and Boyd as
principal and agent; and moreover, the former had no claim
whatever to the money obtained; for, according to the stipulations amongst his own confederates, the money was to come to
them and not to him. To use the words of Chief Justice Wilmot, in *Collins* v. *Blantern*, 2 Wils. 347, "the manner of the
transaction was to gild and conceal the truth, and whenever
courts of law see such attempts made to conceal wicked deeds,
they will brush away the cobweb varnish and show the transactions in their true light."

In this view of the merits of this case, it is clear that the first
charge asked for by the defendant's counsel ought to have been

---

1. *Farmer* v. *Russell*, 1 Bos. & Pul. 296.

given. The second and third charges requested, do not seem to be very explicit, and do not call for a particular examination, as we conceive that the opinion we have expressed will sufficiently indicate the rules which must govern this case.

Let the judgment be reversed, and the cause remanded.

RIGHTS OF PARTIES TO ILLEGAL OR FRAUDULENT TRANSACTIONS.—In dealing with these transactions, the main motive that actuates a court is a desire to discourage them. Lord Thurlow was of opinion that the most efficient means of attaining this object was to place the parties to these contracts *in statu quo,* and thus, by unraveling all that had been done, at the instance of either party, to remove all hope of gain from their minds: *Neville* v. *Wilkinson,* 1 Bro. Ch. 544. But it is very doubtful whether the knowledge by a party to a fraud, that if his confederate break faith with him, he may have recourse to the law, and by it be replaced in his original position, would have a very deterrent influence. The more common-sense view has been adopted, that these parties should have no standing in court; that the sole reliance of the one must be the confidence reposed that the other shall fulfill his part of the corrupt agreement. In consonance with this, cases of this description are generally decided by an application of the maxim *in pari delicto potior est conditio defendentis.* Therefore if a fraudulent or illegal contract is executory, a court will refuse to enforce it; if executed, it will refuse to divest the rights that have accrued thereby.

The most familiar instance of this rule that rights vested under a fraudulent executed contract will not be defeated, is afforded by that class of cases which hold that a conveyance executed with intent to defraud creditors, though open to attack by them, will not be set aside at the instance of the grantor: *Osborne* v. *Moss,* 5 Am. Dec. 252; *Jackson* v. *Marshall,* 3 Id. 695; *Reichart* v. *Castator,* 6 Id. 402; *Peaslee* v. *Barney,* Id. 743; *Terrel* v. *Cropper,* 13 Id. 309; *Jenkins* v. *Clement,* 14 Id. 703; *Sickman* v. *Lapsley,* 15 Id. 596; *Stewart* v. *Kearney,* 31 Id. 482; *James* v. *Bird,* Id. 668; *Stewart* v. *Iglehart,* 25 Id. 206; *George* v. *Williamson,* 26 Mo. 190; *Ellis* v. *Higgins,* 32 Me. 34; *Cushwa* v. *Cushwa,* 5 Md. 45; *Broughton* v. *Broughton,* 4 Rich. 491; *Murphy* v. *Hubert,* 16 Pa. St. 57; *Huey's appeal,* 29 Id. 220; *Hendricks* v. *Mount,* 2 South. 738; *Evans* v. *Herring,* 3 Dutch. 243; *Nichols* v. *Patten,* 18 Me. 231. If the consideration of the deed is illegal, the consequence is the same; thus a grantor can not avoid his deed upon the ground that its consideration was the composition of a felony: *Worcester* v. *Eaton,* 11 Mass. 378. And so will it be if the consideration of the deed is immoral: *White* v. *Hunter,* 3 Fost. 128. And if money has been paid in furtherance of an illegal undertaking, which is in part executed, leaving part of the money unexpended, no action can be maintained to recover it: *Perkins* v. *Savage,* 15 Wend. 412. To the same effect that no relief will be granted to either party where an illegal contract has been fully consummated, are *Greene* v. *Godfrey,* 44 Me. 25; *White* v. *Crew,* 16 Ga. 420; *Walton* v. *Tusten,* 49 Miss. 569; *Dixon* v. *Olmstead,* 31 Am. Dec. 629, and *Black* v. *Oliver,* 35 Id. But where the contract is executory the court will not enforce it. Thus, if a mortgage is given with the intention of preventing the enforcement by creditors of their claims, the mortgagee will not be allowed to enforce it; and to attain this object with the more certainty, the mortgagor will be allowed to plead his own fraud in defense of the action: *Norris* v. *Norris,* 9 T. R. 317; *Miller* v. *Marckle,* 21 Ill. 152; *Westfall* v. *Jones,* 23 Barb. 9. And the maker of a note may defeat an action thereon by showing that it was executed with a fraudulent intent: *Walker* v. *McConnico,* 10 Yerg. 228; *De Merrett* v. *Miles,* 22 N. H. 526. And so it may be shown that the consideration of a note was illegal: *Wheeler* v. *Russell,* 17 Mass. 258; *Hoover* v. *Peirce,* 27 Miss. 627; *McKinnell* v. *Robinson,* 3 Mee. & W. 435; and so of a bond: *Collins* v. *Blantern,* 2 Wils. 347. So far have the courts gone in allowing a defendant to plead his own fraud in which the plaintiff has participated, to defeat the enforcement of the contract, that where an estate had been conveyed with intent to defraud creditors the vendor will not be allowed to recover the unpaid purchase money, though the fraud does not appear from the *prima facie* case made by the plaintiff: *Nellis* v. *Clark,* 20 Wend. 24. There is a dictum to the contrary, however, in *James* v. *Bird,* 31 Am. Dec. 668. And so where the action is to recover the price of goods furnished under a fraudulent agreement, in which vendor and vendee participated, the fraud may be pleaded: *Smith* v. *Hubbs,* 10 Me. 71.

The case is so much the plainer if the fraud or illegality must appear from the case made by the plaintiff himself. Thus no recovery can be had upon an agreement to lobby, which has been performed by the lobbyist: *Powers* v. *Skinner,* 34 Vt. 274; *Clippinger* v. *Hepbaugh,* 5 Watts & S. 315; *Ross* v. *Truax,* 21 Barb. 361. To the same point that the compensation provided for by an illegal contract can not be recovered, are *Badgley* v. *Beale,* 3 Watts, 263; *Dexter* v. *Snow,* 12 Cush. 594, and *Fuller* v. *Dame,* 18 Pick. 472. The rule, as established in Pennsylvania, is not quite so broad; there, though it is admitted that a fraudulent contract can not be enforced, a defendant will not be allowed to plead his own fraud; it follows, then, that unless the fraud appears from the case made by the plaintiff, the contract will be enforced. Thus, if the consideration of a bond is a fraud, and the defendant attempt to show it, he will be held not protected by the maxim *in pari delicto potior est conditio defendentis,* for by his attempt to protect himself under the fraud, he bases a claim for relief thereon which really makes of him an actor: *Hendrickson* v. *Evans,* 25 Pa. St. 441; *Evans* v. *Dravo,* 24 Id. 62; see, also, *Sickman* v. *Lapsley,* 13 Serg. & R. 225; *Stewart* v. *Kearney,* 31 Am. Dec. 482. In *Swann* v. *Scott,* 11 Serg. & R. 155, the same test was applied to the right of recovery where the defense was founded upon the illegality of the contract, it being there declared that the test whether a demand connected with an illegal transaction can be enforced at law is whether the plaintiff requires the aid of the illegal transaction to establish his case. Thus, if the action is on a bond in the ordinary form, the defendant can not show that it was given upon an illegal consideration. The correctness of this latter doctrine appears very doubtful.

The principal exception to the rule that equity will not interfere in favor of either party to an illegal or fraudulent contract arises in cases where the parties, though both in fault, are not *in pari delicto.* Wherever the position of one party is such that he is in a condition to use oppression towards the other, and he obtains from that other a contract beneficial to himself and in fraud of the rights of third persons, the former party will be allowed to rescind the contract and recover whatever he may have paid over. An instance which has arisen is the case where a creditor has refused to sign his debtor's certificate of bankruptcy, unless the latter secure to him in addition to the proportion to which he was entitled from the estate, a further sum. There, if the creditor is paid such sum, it may be recovered back from him by his debtor in an action of assumpsit: *Smith* v. *Bromley,* Doug. 696. And so where, upon signing a composition deed, the creditor enters into a secret agreement with his debtor, under which he receives the latter's promissory

note for the balance of his debt unsecured by the deed, the debtor may re
cover from him whatever he may have been obliged to pay on the note to an
indorsee thereof: *Horton* v. *Riley*, 11 Mee. & W. 492; *Smith* v. *Cuff*, 6 Mau.
& Sel. 160.

In like manner, if a conveyance with intent to defraud creditors is obtained
from an aged mother by her son, in whom she has implicit confidence, working upon her credulity and weakness, the conveyance will be set aside: *Pinck-
ston* v. *Brown*, 3 Jones' Eq. 494. And if a husband obtain such a conveyance
from his wife, the existence of the marital relation will be sufficient reason to
invalidate the conveyance at the instance of the wife: *Boyd* v. *Montagnie*, 73
N. Y. 498. In the same way the conveyance of a client to an attorney, though
with intent to defraud creditors, will be set aside in favor of the client: *Ford*
v. *Harrington*, 16 Id. 285. And where a creditor has availed himself of his
power over his debtor, and has by misrepresentation induced him to make a
fraudulent conveyance to himself, the debtor will be aided in equity, notwithstanding his fraud: *Austin* v. *Winston*, 3 Am. Dec. 583, and note 601, in
which other cases on the subject are cited. For further instances in which
relief was granted, notwithstanding that both parties were acting fraudulently, because not *in pari delicto*, see *Barnes* v. *Brown*, 32 Mich. 146; *Osborne*
v. *Williams*, 18 Ves. 381; *Cook* v. *Colyer*, 23 Mon. 71; *Freelove* v. *Cole*, 41
Barb. 318, affirmed in error, 41 N. Y. 619.

Relief will also sometimes be given where the provisions of a statute, which
prohibits something, not of itself *malum in se*, are violated; for, in these
cases, where the prohibition of the statute is directed against one of the parties alone, and upon him is affixed the penalty for a violation thereof, the
other will not in general be denied all relief. Thus, if a statute prohibit
banks from making contracts for the payment of money at a future day certain, and a depositor receives a promise that his deposit shall be repaid on a
day certain, though he may not recover on the express contract, because it is
one forbidden by law, he may recover in an assumpsit: *White* v. *Franklin
Bank*, 22 Pick. 181. And if an unauthorized note be taken from a bank on
the sale of certain stocks, the vendor may, notwithstanding, recover the value
of the stocks: *Tracy* v. *Talmage*, 14 N. Y. 162. Then, too, there may be a
violation of the statutes described by Lord Mansfield in *Smith* v. *Bromley*,
Doug. 696: "There are other laws which are calculated for the protection of
the subject against oppression, extortion, deceit, etc. If such laws are violated, and the defendant takes advantage of the plaintiff's condition or situation, there the plaintiff shall recover." Of this character are the usury laws,
and therefore the party who has paid usurious interest may recover the amount:
Wheaton v. *Hubbard*, 20 Johns. 290; *Browning* v. *Morris*, Cowp. 790.

Where money has been paid to one for the use of another, he will not be
allowed to set up in defense to an action for an accounting, that the money
was paid on an illegal contract. Thus, where defendant and plaintiff had
won money at cards, and defendant received from the maker a note for the
money, which was subsequently paid, the defendant can not resist contribution: *Owen* v. *Davis*, 1 Bailey, 315; *Gilliam* v. *Brown*, 43 Miss. 642; *Brooks*
v. *Martin*, 2 Wall. 79; *Farmer* v. *Russell*, 1 Bos. & Pul. 296; *Tenant* v. *Elliott*,
Id. 3; *Sharp* v. *Taylor*, 2 Ph. Ch. 801, in which the cases are gone over
very carefully.

WINSTON v. EWING.

[1 ALABAMA, 129.]

INTEREST IN PARTNERSHIP PROPERTY LIABLE TO THE SATISFACTION OF THE SEPARATE DEBTS of each partner, is the interest of each in the property as it stands after the partnership accounts have been settled, and the demands of the partnership creditors provided for.

DEBTOR OF A PARTNERSHIP CAN NOT BE GARNISHED in an action brought to recover the separate debt of one of its members.

ERROR. Plaintiff in error was garnished in the court below as a debtor of Alexander Bell. In answer to the summons, plaintiff admitted that he owed the firm of A. & J. R. Bell the sum of eighty dollars. The court based upon this return an order that the garnishee pay over to the garnishor the sum of forty-five dollars and thirty-two cents, as being the interest of Alexander Bell in the firm debt.

Graham, for the plaintiff.

Murphy and Jones, contra.

COLLIER, C. J. Several questions were made at the argument of this cause; but we propose only to inquire, whether an undivided interest of a partner in a debt due the copartnership can be subjected by attachment to the payment of a separate debt of one of the partners.

It may be regarded as a well-established principle of the common law, that the creditor of any one partner may execute and sell that partner's interest in all the tangible property of the partnership: 3 Bos. & Pul. 289.[1] In *Heydon* v. *Heydon*, 1 Salk. 392, it was held by Lord Holt, that in an action against one of two partners, the sheriff must seize all the goods, because the moieties are undivided; for if he seize but a moiety and sell that, the other partner will be entitled to a moiety of that moiety, but he must seize the whole, and sell a moiety thereof undivided. And in *Shaver* v. *White*, 6 Munf. 113 [8 Am. Dec. 730], the court considered the law to be, that on an attachment for the separate debt of one partner, the sheriff must seize all the partnership effects, and sell an undivided moiety, and the vendee will be a tenant in common with the other partner. It has even been held that as soon as the execution is levied, the partnership quoad, the goods seized, is at an end, and the creditor becomes tenant in common with the other partner; while the sheriff has a special property in the goods, and may be regarded as a legal agent for the sale. After the sale has been

---

1. *Chapman* v. *Koops.*

made, the vendee will be tenant in common with the other partner: 2 Swanst. 587;[1] 3 Bos. & Pul. 289; 3 Car. & P. 309;[2] 1 Salk.
392.[3] In *Skipp* v. *Harwood*, Cowp. 451, it was laid down, that
as a creditor of one partner who has the partnership effects
levied on, can only have the undivided interest of his debtor, he
must take it in the same manner as the debtor himself had it,
and subject to the rights of the other partner. And in *Ex parte
Smith*, 16 Johns. 106, the court said where an execution issues
for the separate debt of one partner, it has been the constant
practice to take the share which such partner has in the partnership property; but it has been settled, at least since the case
of *Fox* v. *Hanbury*, Cowp. 445, that the sheriff can sell only the
actual interest, which such partner has in the partnership property, after the accounts are settled; or subject to the partnership debts. The separate creditor takes it in the same manner
as the debtor himself had it, and subject to the rights of the
other partner: See also *Moody* v. *Payne*, 2 Johns. Ch. 548; *Wilson and Gibbs* v. *Conine*, 2 Johns. 280; *Ridgeley* v. *Carey*, 4 Har.
& M. 167.

The supreme court of Massachusetts in *Pierce* v. *Jackson*, 6
Mass. 242, held that an attachment of partnership goods in a
suit against one partner for his separate debt, will not prevail
against a subsequent attachment of the same goods in a suit
against the partnership. And in *Tappan* v. *Blaisdell*, 5 N. H.
190, it was decided that goods belonging to a firm can not be
held by attachment upon a writ, or by a seizure upon an execution against an individual partner, for his separate debt, so long
as any debt remains due from the company. All that can be
taken, is the interest of the debtor in the firm; not the partnership effects themselves, but the right of the partner to a share
of the surplus that may remain after all the debts are paid. To
the same effect see *Knox* v. *Summers*, 4 Yeates, 477; *Doner* v.
Stauffer, 1 Penn. 198 [21 Am. Dec. 370]; *Church* v. *Knox*, 2
Conn. 514; *Brewster* v. *Hammett*, 4 Id. 540; *Barber* v. *Hartford
Bank*, 9 Id. 407. And it has been expressly adjudged that the
interest of one partner in a debt due to the partnership can not
be subjected, by process of attachment, to the satisfaction of the
separate debt of that partner, without showing from the state of
the partnership accounts, as between the partners, and with
reference to the indebtedness of the partnership, what the right
or interest claimed amounts to: *Fisk* v. *Herrick*, 6 Mass. 271;

---

1. *Skipp* v. *Harwood*.   2. *Burton* v. *Green*.   3. 2 Swanst. 587.

Lyndon v. *Gorham*, 1 Gall. 367; *Church* v. *Knox*, 2 Conn. 514; *Brewster* v. *Hammett*, 4 Id. 540.

Thus we discover that the property of a partnership may be levied on, by execution against one of the partners, and the interest of that partner sold to satisfy it. Yet the law cautiously protects the interests of the copartners and the creditors of the firm, by restraining the vendee under execution from appropriating the property purchased to his own separate use, until the partnership accounts are adjusted, and the demands of the joint creditors either paid or provided for. It is but sheer justice that the estate of a debtor should be held liable to the payment of his debts, no matter how it may be situated, giving, however, a preference to creditors who have the highest claim upon it. It would be unjust if an individual could, by investing his estate in a partnership concern, defeat his separate creditors in the collection of their debts; and it would work quite as great injustice, if the copartner, who had acquired an interest in that estate by the connection in business, could be deprived of his lien upon it for balances due, or to pay debts. The law as we have stated it, secures the rights of all, and is established most firmly upon authority as we have already shown.

But the right to attach a debt due the partnership, to pay the separate debt of a partner, rests upon different reasoning than that which applies to the execution and sale of the joint property. In the latter case, the property is not removed and can not be appropriated till all liens upon it, growing out of or relating to the partnership, are discharged—while, in the former case, the judgment against the garnishee, if acquiesced in, changes the right of property and divests the copartner's title to the property attached. This, we have seen, can not be done so long as the partnership accounts remain unsettled, or its debts unpaid. In the case at bar no inquiry seems to have been made into the affairs of A. & J. R. Bell, so that for anything appearing to the contrary, the debt due by the plaintiff in error, may have been required to pay balances due J. R. Bell, or to enable him to discharge the liabilities of the firm.

It remains but to add, that the judgment of the circuit court is reversed and the case remanded.

EXECUTION CREDITOR OF A PARTNER sells not the partnership chattels, but the partner's interest incumbered with joint debts: *Doner* v. *Stauffer*. 21 Am. Dec. 370; and therefore, because the specific chattels are not liable to the satisfaction of the private debt of a partner, neither are they liable to attachment for such debt: *Morrison* v. *Blodgett*, 29 Id. 653, and note.

FUQUA *v.* HUNT.

[1 ALABAMA, 197.]

A GUARDIAN MAY SUE IN HIS OWN NAME for an injury done to the property of the ward in his possession.

TROVER for a slave. The declaration was demurred to upon grounds that appear in the opinion. The demurrer was sustained in the court below.

McClung, for the plaintiff in error.

Hopkins, contra.

ORMOND, J. We understand the declaration to assert that the plaintiff was in possession of the slave, sued for as guardian, and that he was deprived of that possession by the defendant. These facts are admitted by the demurrer, and it is now insisted by the counsel for the defendant in error that they authorized the judgment of the court below, on the authority of the case of *Goff* v. *Sutherland,* 5 Port. 508.[1] In that case it was decided, that "the guardian must sue in his own name, when he has a right to the possession, or when an injury is done to the possession; but when the matter lies in action, the suit must be in the name of the ward." Now, as the declaration in this case affirms, that the slave sued for, was taken from the possession of the plaintiff as guardian, that case is a direct authority to show his right to maintain the action, if he sustains the allegations of the declaration by proof. In *Sutherland* v. *Goff,* the court held the guardian could not recover because he sued, not for a slave taken from his possession, but for his value as assessed by a third person, which the court (whether correctly or not) considered a mere chose in action. The case, however, distinctly admits, that for an injury to his possession, the guardian could maintain the action. We have no intention of abandoning the principle, which governs the case of *Sutherland* v. *Goff,* but as the point was one purely technical, we feel no disposition to extend the principle to cases not clearly within the reason of that decision.

Let the judgment be reversed and the case remanded.

SUIT BROUGHT IN THE NAME OF GUARDIAN, although he describes himself as guardian, is his suit and not that of the ward: *Dowd* v. *Wadsworth,* 18 Am. Dec. 567. The action, which was trover, was therefore defeated. The case is exactly similar to the principal case, and the decision the exact reverse. It is possible that the case may be explained in some degree by remembering that in North Carolina, the jurisdiction in which *Dowd* v. *Wade-*

1. *Sutherland* v. *Goff.*

worth was decided, the courts have asserted that to maintain trover, there must have been at the time of the conversion not only a possessory right, but also a right of property: *Hostler* v. *Skull*, 1 Id. 583; while the general rule is that possession will be sufficient to entitle one to maintain the action against a wrong-doer: note to same case.

RHEA *v.* HUGHES.

[1 ALABAMA, 219.]

OCCUPATION AND IMPROVEMENT OF THE PUBLIC LANDS do not create an interest subject to sale under execution. A mere permissive occupation is never subject to such sale.

MOTION for a judgment against defendant as sheriff of Cherokee county, because of his failure to make the money on an execution intrusted to him, in favor of plaintiffs and against Robert Bell. On the trial of an issue framed under the directions of the court, it appeared that Bell, at the time the execution issued, was, and for several years had been, in the occupation of a tract of land, parcel of the public domain; that he had improved the tract, cleared about ninety acres, built a house thereon, etc. The value of these improvements was estimated at four or five hundred dollars. The jury was instructed that such improvements were not the subject of sale on execution.

J. L. Martin, for the plaintiff in error.

Hopkins, contra.

GOLDTHWAITE, J. The facts of the case present a question entirely novel; and no authorities bearing directly on it, have met our views. It can not be denied, that the possession, or rather occupation, by Bell, of the public land, in the manner shown by the records, is, to some extent, beneficial to him, and we are fully aware that an interest of this description is frequently the subject of purchase and sale. But, it is not such an interest as is capable of being sold by an execution. It is neither an estate by sufferance, at will, or for years, nor can the continued occupation of the land ever operate, so as to create a legal title. The settler has no permission from the government to enter on the lands; and any improvement made by him may inure to the benefit of another, and must, if any other person than himself purchases the land from the United States. It is true, he has hitherto been permitted to remain, unmolested, in his occupation; nay, further, by the enactment of the pre-emption acts of congress, he is the only person permitted to purchase the land during a limited period; but this right, or rather privilege, he can not transfer to another, and it ceases to himself, whenever he parts from the occupation by any agreement in any way or manner whatsoever: Pre-emption act of 1838. His interest, then, in the land is a mere permission to occupy it, personal to himself and not capable of transfer, so as to give any legal right to any other person. As well might an individual who is permitted by charity to occupy a room, or a house, be said to have a possession capable of being sold under execution.

The value which is attached, in common estimation, to an improvement of the description stated, arises solely from the knowledge of the liberality which has hitherto been exercised by the government to this class of settlers; but, though a mere expectation of a benefit, may be the subject of sale by him who looks forward to the event; such an expectation has never been supposed to be the subject of execution at law.

The only doubt which has arisen on this case, grows out of the fact, that we have heretofore held, that an occupation of this description, could be protected by the action of trespass, but this doubt vanishes when we consider, that many legal estates in possession are not the subject of sale. Such for example, are the possessions of lands by executors and guardians. And it is conceived, that no case of mere permissive occupation, when the same can not ripen into a legal estate, will create such an interest as can be sold under execution. We are not unaware of the decisions in the courts of a sister state, in which it has been held, that possession is an interest in land which is bound by a judgment, and may be sold under execution: *Jackson* v. *Parker*, 9 Cow. 73, and cases there cited; but, we consider that principle as not reaching the present case, or any other, within the rule just laid down—that a mere permissive occupation is not the subject of sale by execution. We arrive, then, at the conclusion, that the charge asked ought not to have been given, and that the instructions to the jury are free from error.

Let the judgment be affirmed.

PRINCE v. COMMERCIAL BANK OF COLUMBUS.

[1 ALABAMA, 241.]

CORPORATION IS NOT REQUIRED TO PROVE ITS INCORPORATION under the plea of the general issue.

ASSUMPSIT. *Non assumpsit* pleaded. The court below held that the plaintiff, defendant in error, was not held to proof of its corporate character.

Dunn, for the plaintiff in error.

Campbell, contra.

Ormond, J. There has been great contrariety of decision on the point presented in this case, and names of equal weight, appear to be arrayed on both sides of the question. We must, therefore, decide the question on principle. Applying the well-established rules of pleading to the question, there would not appear to be much difficulty in it. There is no rule of pleading more universal, than that, by pleading to the merits, the defendant admits the capacity of the plaintiff to sue; and no reason is perceived why a corporation should be placed on a different footing in this particular, from a natural person. The most ancient authorities of the common law do not appear to recognize any distinction. Thus, in the case of *The Mayor and Burgesses of Stafford* v. *Bolton,* 1 Bos. & Pul. 40: where, on a trial, on the plea of not guilty, the court had directed a nonsuit, because there was a variance between the style of the corporation, in the declaration, and the charter which was produced, on the trial: on a motion for a new trial, the court of common pleas set aside the nonsuit, on the authority of Broke, and the year books. Chief Justice Eyre says: "If it can not be denied, that this variance might have been pleaded in abatement, it decides this question. The arguments on the part of the defendant, go to show that it ought to be in bar. A corporation is a mere creature of the crown, having no existence, but what is derived from its name. On strict reasoning, therefore, I should be inclined to think, that, if a corporation sued by a name which did not belong to it, it would be as nothing. In the case of a mistake in the name or description of an existing person, having a right to sue, it may be pleaded in abatement. But the case in Broke, Misnomer, 93, seems to put a corporation in the same situation with a natural person, as to pleas in abatement, where it is said, in an action by a corporation, or a natural body, misnomer of one or the other, goes only to the writ: but to say that there is no such person in *rerum natura,* or no such body politic, this is in bar; for if he be misnamed, he may have a new writ by the right name; but if there be no such body politic, or such person, then he can not have an action: 22d ed., 4th C. 34. Here, there was a corporation of nearly the same name, and I think, therefore, on authorities, that the nonsuit was erroneous." Rooke, J., said, "I think we ought not to be more strict, than they were in the days of the year books." See also, the notes of Sergeant Williams, to the case of *Miller* v. *Spateman*, 1 Saund. 517.[1] From this authority, therefore, it would seem that if there be no such corporation, the defendant should plead in bar, *nul tiel corporation;* or if there be a variance between the true name of the corporation, and the one in which the suit is brought, that advantage must be taken, by plea in abatement.

The authorities referred to by the plaintiff, rest for support principally on the case of *Henriques* v. *The Dutch West India Company*, 2 Ld. Raym. 1532; but an examination of that case will show, that the point was not decided. It was a writ of error from the common pleas. Two errors were relied on: that there was no sufficient warrant of attorney, to execute a bail bond, upon which judgment had been entered, in the common pleas; and that costs were improperly rendered. The court reversed the judgment as to the costs, and affirmed it as to the residue. From this judgment a writ of error was prosecuted to the house of lords, where, in addition to the errors assigned in the king's bench, it was insisted that no recognizance in England, could be given to the Dutch West India company; for, that the law of England would not take notice of any foreign corporation: nor could they maintain an action at common law, in their corporate name; but must sue, if at all, in the name of the persons comprising the company. To this, it was answered, by counsel, that the plaintiffs were estopped by their recognizance, to say there was no such company; and where an action is brought by a corporation, they need not show how they were incorporated. But upon the general issue pleaded by the defendants, the plaintiffs must prove they are a corporation. In a note to the case, the reporter says: "And upon the trial, Lord Chancellor King told me, he made the plaintiffs give in evidence the proper instruments whereby, by the law of Holland, they were effectually created a corporation there." The judgment of the king's bench was affirmed.

It is very certain that the point under discussion did not, and could not, arise in judgment, either in the king's bench or house of lords. And this case is no authority in support of the position that the plaintiffs, under the general issue, must prove their corporate character, unless it can be considered that the statements of counsel, *arguendo*, or the loose note of the reporter, as to what Lord King told him took place on the trial, in the common pleas, can be so considered.

On reference to the report of the same case in the common

---

1. *Mellor* v. *Spateman*, 1 Saund. 339.

pleas, 1 Stra. 612, it does not appear that the point arose in the case. We are not informed what the defendants' pleas were. The action was on a covenant to pay money borrowed of the company; and the report says, that upon the trial it appeared, the money was borrowed at Amsterdam, in Holland, and by the covenant, was to be paid in bank there, and that this company had never sued by this name before, or even had any particular name given them by any act of the states; but upon the dissolution of an old West India company it was declared, that there should be still a general West India company, the members of which should be privileged to trade to the West Indies, and that all others should be prohibited. Two points were made: 1. Whether these articles could be sued in England; 2. Whether this was a good name for the company to sue by; and the court decided in favor of the plaintiff on both points. We are not informed who offered the testimony: whether the plaintiff, in support, or the defendant, to defeat the action. And it is most certain, that the case does not show that the point arose in judgment. Neither are the authorities of those courts who have held such proof necessary, always consistent with each other. In 8 Johns. 373,[1] the court, in a brief note, say "the rule seems to be, that when a corporation sues, they must, at the trial under the general issue, prove that they are a corporation." Yet we find that in the case of *The Overseers of the Poor* v. *Whitman*, 15 Id. 208, the same court held, that "the objection, that the plaintiffs had not proved that they were overseers, was properly overruled. They sue in that capacity, and are described as such in the proceedings; and this was admitted by the plea of the general issue." And in the case of the *Bank of Auburn* v. *Aikin*, 18 Id. 137, it was held, that *nul tiel corporation* was a good plea in bar. And again, in a case between the same parties, 19 Id. 300, the court held, it was not a good plea, on the ground, that matter could not be pleaded, which the plaintiff, under the general issue, was bound to prove.

It may be added, that all the analogies in similar cases, are in favor of the view taken by the counsel for the defendant in error. Thus, an administrator is not required, under the plea of *non assumpsit*, to prove his authority to sue: *Worsham* v. *Greer, Adm'r*,[2] 4 Port. 441; Wms. Ex. 1192; 11 Mass. 313.[3] So the right to sue in the courts of the United States, is admitted by a plea to the merits: 1 Pet. 498.[4] And upon the whole, .

---

1. *Jackson* v. *Plumbe*, 8 Johns. 378.

2. *Worsham* v. *Goar.*   3. *Langdon* v. *Potter.*   4. *D'Wolf* v. *Rabaud.*

we are of opinion, that although some courts of the highest authority in this country have held the doctrine contended for by the plaintiff in error, the converse of the proposition is the better law; better sustained by authority; more consonant to the philosophy of pleading, and upheld by analogous principles. In the case of *Lucas* v. *The Bank of Georgia,* 2 Stew. 150, this court remarked, "it was certainly a part of the proof of the plaintiff below, to make out his right to sue, by adducing evidence as to a corporate character;" but the question before the court was not, whether the plaintiff must make such proof; but whether the proof in the cause was sufficient to establish the corporate character of the plaintiff; and as the court held it to be sufficient, the other question, as it was not made in the court below, and not presented on the record, did not arise. We do not, therefore, consider the opinion then expressed, to be the judgment of the court; and binding as a precedent.

Our conclusion is, that there is no error in the judgment of the court below, and it is therefore affirmed.

McRae *v.* Kennon.

[1 Alabama, 295.]

Acknowledgment of Indebtedness Made to a Former Indorsee of a note by the maker thereof will inure to the benefit of the present holder. Such acknowledgment would be available though made to a stranger.

Action on a promissory note by the last indorsee against the maker. The plaintiff introduced evidence to show that subsequently to the indorsement of the note to him, the defendant had acknowledged his liability thereon to one Fuller, a former indorsee of the note. Plaintiff asked the court to instruct the jury that proof of such acknowledgment would entitle plaintiff to its verdict. The court refused to so instruct, but charged that an acknowledgment to a holder of negotiable paper by its maker would inure to the benefit of any subsequent holder. The other facts appear from the opinion.

Peck and Clark, for the plaintiff in error.

Porter, contra.

Ormond, J. The charge asked for, should have been given by the court, as it is fully within the reason, if not the letter of the decision of this court, when the case was last here. The auknowledgment supposed to be made by the defendant in error, to the witness Fuller, who had once held the note by indorsement, must inure to, and is in effect, an acknowledgment in favor of the plaintiff in error, who, by the indorsement of Fuller, had become invested with all the interest of Fuller in the note. This very question was endeavored to be anticipated by this court, when the case was last here. Thus it is said: "It was not objected in the county court, that an acknowledgment made to Fuller would not inure to the defendant in error; yet, as it is possible the question may be made upon another trial, it may be proper to remark that, if a promise or acknowledgment is made to the holder of indorsed paper, any party to it, who may afterwards take it up, may avail himself of such acknowledgment or promise, and maintain an action against the party making it."

The only difference between the facts here supposed, and the facts as they were shown to exist, at the last trial, is, that when the acknowledgment was made by the defendant to Fuller, he was not the actual holder of the paper. But how can this affect the question—the admission was of the existence of a fact, which would have been evidence against him, if made to a stranger, and certainly can lose none of its force, by being made to one, to whom he might be responsible. An acknowledgment of liability to pay the note, must be, to pay it to whoever is entitled to receive it.

It is to be lamented that a case of such small importance as this, should have been productive of so much litigation—so much expense to the parties—vexation, and delay. Great as our desire is to avoid such consequences, we can go no further than to decide the precise question before us. We can not anticipate the future aspect of the case and provide for it in advance. We hope, however, that the case is now at rest.

Let the judgment of the court below be reversed and the cause be remanded for another trial, in conformity with this and the previous opinions expressed in this cause.

INDEX TO THE NOTES.

INDEX.

ADMISSIONS.

See EVIDENCE, 12; INFANCY, 8.

ADVERSE POSSESSION.

1. SEVEN YEARS' ADVERSE POSSESSION DOES NOT CREATE A TITLE in the holder in fee simple which may be seized and sold under a *fi. fa.*, so as to vest in a purchaser at the execution sale, a better title than that of a grantee of the adverse claimant, holding by an unregistered conveyance executed prior to the levy. *Wallace* v. *Hannum*, 659.

2. ADVERSE POSSESSION BY A DEFENDANT RESIDING ON THE LAND, will not be presumed, without some tortious act on his part, so as to defeat a conveyance by the owner not in the actual occupancy of the land. *Pownal* v. *Taylor*, 725.

3. COURTS WILL NOT INFER ADVERSE POSSESSION in the absence of a special finding thereof. *Id.*

See DEEDS, 10; VENDOR AND VENDEE, 2.

AGENCY.

1. BROKER IS THE GENERAL AGENT OF A PRINCIPAL who has intrusted him with the disposition of a security, and may bind him by an express guaranty that the security shall be paid by the maker. *Prevall* v. *Fitch*, 558.

2. CONTRACT BY A FACTOR TO GUARANTEE his sale for a premium beyond the usual rate, is a contract of guaranty of the solvency of his vendees, and not of the worth of the bills purchased by him and remitted in payment. *Sharp* v. *Emmet*, 554.

3. AGENT IS NOT PERSONALLY LIABLE when acting in the name of his principal and within the scope of his authority. *Simonds* v. *Heard*, 41.

4. AGENT IS PERSONALLY RESPONSIBLE ON CONTRACTS which show an intention to bind himself personally. *Id.*

5. AGENT ACTING IN A PUBLIC CAPACITY, and making a contract on behalf of the public, is not personally answerable thereon. *Id.*

6. PRINCIPAL IS BOUND BY AGENT'S ACT IN VIOLATION OF SECRET INSTRUCTIONS in transferring stock in a corporation, where the written authority of such agent gives him full power to make such transfer. *Commercial Bank* v. *Kortright*, 317.

7. UNDISCLOSED PRINCIPAL is liable on the contracts of his agent, though the agency was not known to the other party at the time of the contract. *Smith* v. *Plummer*, 530.

8. POWER OF ATTORNEY IN THESE TERMS DOES NOT CONFER POWER TO CONVEY REAL ESTATE: To ask, demand, recover, or receive the maker's law-

ful part of a decedent's estate, giving and granting thereby to his said
attorney his sole and full power and authority to take, pursue, and follow
such legal course for the recovery, receiving, and obtaining the same, as
he himself might or could do were he personally present; and upon the
receipt thereof, acquittances, and other sufficient discharges for him, and
in his name, to sign, seal, and deliver. *Hay* v. *Mayer*, 453.

9. DECLARATIONS OF AN AGENT IMPUGNING HIS AUTHORITY are inadmissible
against parties whose rights depend upon the existence of that authority.
Thus declarations of an agent showing his belief in the insanity of his
principal can not be shown against a purchaser to whom he has conveyed.
Bensell v. *Chancellor*, 561.

10. WHERE PUBLIC OR PRIVATE AUTHORITY IS CONFERRED ON SEVERAL, all
must confer; but if the authority be public, a majority may decide and
bind the minority. *Downing* v. *Rugar*, 223.

11. PUBLIC AUTHORITY CONFERRED UPON TWO CAN NOT BE EXERCISED BY ONE
without the other's consent, because the number does not admit of a
majority; but it seems that to prevent a failure of justice, where immediate action is necessary, one may act alone if the other is dead, absent, or interested. *Id.*

12. AUTHORITY OF AN ATTORNEY IN FACT CEASES upon the death of his
principal. *Jenkins* v. *Atkins*, 648.

13. CONTRACT FOR SALE OF LANDS WITH AN ATTORNEY IN FACT, which was
not consummated until after the death of his principal, can not be enforced, though the parties contracted in ignorance of the principal's death.
Id.

14. ATTORNEY IN FACT CAN NOT RECOVER THE AGREED PURCHASE PRICE in
such case, notwithstanding he has since obtained the title, and is willing
to convey. *Id.*

15. POWER OF AN ATTORNEY IN FACT to act as such is presumed to have been
established by satisfactory proof, and though in a matter before a court
of general jurisdiction which is required to exercise its powers upon a
given state of facts to be proved before it, no authority appears upon the
record, it can not be afterwards collaterally impeached. *Pillsbury* v.
Dugan, 427.

See MASTER AND SERVANT, 3; NEGOTIABLE INSTRUMENTS, 21.

ALIENS.

FACT THAT ONE HAS RESIDED SEVERAL YEARS IN CANADA does not of itself
justify the inference that he is an alien. *Gilman* v. *Thompson*, 714.

AMENDMENTS.

See PLEADING AND PRACTICE, 11, 12, 20, 27, 28.

ANNUITIES.

See EXECUTORS AND ADMINISTRATORS, 4.

APPRENTICESHIP.

See INFANCY, 1.

ARBITRATION AND AWARD.

1. ARBITRATORS TO APPRAISE IMPROVEMENTS.—Where two parties enter into an agreement by which one is to erect improvements on the lands of the other, the value thereof to be estimated by two disinterested persons, one party can not defeat the right to an appraisement by refusing to appoint an arbitrator, and a refusal or failure to appoint gives the other party an undisputed right to have the valuation made. *Orne* v. *Sullivan*, 74.

2. WHEN NO MODE OF APPOINTMENT IS AGREED UPON in such a case, the court infers the intention to be that each party is to appoint one arbitrator. *Id.*

3. WHAT REFUSAL SUFFICIENT TO GIVE OTHER PARTY RIGHT OF APPOINTMENT. Where one party requests the other to appoint an appraiser, and the latter appoints a man to survey the land, but instructs him not to appraise, as he had fixed rules for valuing improvements, this would be a sufficient refusal to justify the first party in having the appraisement made. *Id.*

ASSIGNMENTS FOR BENEFIT OF CREDITORS.

1. NO ASSIGNMENT FOR THE BENEFIT OF CREDITORS IS VALID, under the statute of July 5, 1834, of New Hampshire, unless it provides for an equal distribution of the debtor's estate among all his creditors, in proportion to their respective demands. *Hurd* v. *Silsby*, 142.

2. CONDITIONAL ASSIGNMENT for the benefit of creditors is invalid. *Id.*

3. ASSIGNMENT FOR THE BENEFIT OF SUCH CREDITORS as will execute the instrument, and signify their willingness to receive the prospective dividends in full discharge of all demands, is conditional, and therefore invalid. *Id.*

4. STIPULATION IN AN ASSIGNMENT for a release by the creditors means a technical release under seal. *Agnew* v. *Dorr*, 539.

5. RELEASE OF A RIGHT even in a chattel is inoperative, unless by deed. *Id.*

6. ASSIGNMENT REQUIRING "FULL AND SUFFICIENT RELEASE" from those who wish to benefit by its provisions, will not be answered by a release conditioned on the assets realizing a certain percentage on the claim. *Id.*

7. LIABILITY OF ASSIGNEES FOR BENEFIT OF CREDITORS ON SALE OF GOODS. Where assignees of this character deliver goods sold at cash sale, without exacting immediate payment, they are *prima facie* liable for the loss that may be occasioned by the vendee's subsequent failure to pay, and can only excuse themselves by showing that the vendee's credit was so good that a prudent person would have intrusted him with the goods without first exacting payment. *Estate of Davis*, 574.

ASSIGNMENT OF CONTRACTS.

1. ASSIGNMENT OF CLAIM BY PLAINTIFF TO ONE OF DEFENDANTS before suit is no bar to such suit except where, in order to sue, the same person must appear on the record as both plaintiff and defendant. *Blanchard* v. *Ely*, 250.

2. ASSIGNMENT OF CHOSE IN ACTION BY WAY OF A PLEDGE, or even absolutely, does not transfer the assignor's legal interest. *Id.*

3. FRAUDULENT PURCHASER, ASSIGNING for the benefit of his creditors, passes no title to his assignees to the goods obtained by fraud, though the assignment require releases from certain of the creditors, which are given by them. *Knowles v. Lord*, 525.

ASSUMPSIT.

MONEY PAID ON AN EXECUTORY CONTRACT to convey lands to which the defendant had no title, may be recovered in assumpsit. *Pipkin v. James.* 652.

See SALES, 9.

ATTACHMENTS.

1. LEVY OF ATTACHMENT IS INCOMPLETE WITHOUT ACTUAL SEIZURE, or some other equivalent act of universal notoriety. *State v. Poor*, 387.

2. LEVY UPON A GROWING CROP IS INSUFFICIENT, unless the officer took open and notorious possession by entering the premises, and publicly announcing the seizure to answer the writ. *Id.*

3. CHATTEL IS NOT LIABLE TO ATTACHMENT BY CREDITORS OF VENDOR THEREOF, where it was, at the time of the sale, in the possession of a bailee who declined to deliver it to the purchaser until the time expired for which the bailment was made, although it was allowed by the bailee, before the expiration of the bailment, to go back into the possession of the vendor, but without the vendee's knowledge or consent. *Lynde v. Melvin*, 717.

4. ATTACHMENT OF PROPERTY AND NOTICE TO THE PARTY ARE DIFFERENT THINGS; and the circumstance that the officer is, in this state, by the same process commanded to attach and to give notice does not alter this fact. *Gilman v. Thompson*, 714.

5. WHERE RETURN OF ATTACHMENT DOES NOT SHOW PERSONAL SERVICE, the court may order notice to be given in any manner recognized by law, since it already has jurisdiction, and a judgment rendered by it after notice given by publication is not void. *Id.*

6. SURPLUS MONEYS IN THE HANDS OF A SHERIFF after satisfaction of an execution, are subject to attachment by a creditor of the execution debtor. *Tucker v. Atkinson*, 650.

See EXECUTORS AND ADMINISTRATORS, 10.

ATTORNEY AND CLIENT.

1. TO SUBJECT AN ATTORNEY TO AN ACTION BY HIS CLIENT, two things are necessary to be shown: gross or unreasonable neglect or ignorance, and a consequent loss to his client. *Fitch v. Scott*, 86.

2. AN ATTORNEY IS PERSONALLY LIABLE FOR NEGLIGENCE, when a note already due is placed in his hands for collection, and he permits a term to go by before commencing suit, and then dismisses the suit, surrenders the note, and accepts the transfer of a judgment against another person. *Id.*

3. ATTORNEY IS LIABLE FOR THE WHOLE AMOUNT DUE upon the note in such a case. *Id.*

4. ATTORNEY HAS NO AUTHORITY TO COMPROMISE THE CLAIM of his client, and if he does so, he takes upon himself the consequence of its loss, or the damages which he may sustain. *Id.*

See BONA FIDE PURCHASERS, 1; STATUTE OF LIMITATIONS, 3, 4; WITNESSES, 2-4.

BAILMENTS.

PURCHASER OF GOODS FROM A BAILEE IS NOT LIABLE IN REPLEVIN to the owner, for a tortious taking, but only for the detention, and the declaration should be in the *detinet* only. *Smith* v. *Clark*, 213.

See ASSIGNMENT OF CONTRACTS, 2; SALES, 1.

BANKS AND BANKING.

1. BANK RECEIVING NOTE FOR COLLECTION must use reasonable skill and diligence, and, therefore, must make seasonable demand of the promisor, and, in case of dishonor, give due notice to charge the indorsers. *Fabens* v. *Mercantile Bank*, 59.

2. BANK RECEIVING FOR COLLECTION A NOTE PAYABLE AT ANOTHER PLACE, or whose acceptor resides in another place, need only seasonably transmit the same to some suitable bank or agent for collection at the place of payment or of the residence of such acceptor. *Id.*

3. BANK HOLDING NOTE AS COLLATERAL, OR FOR COLLECTION, is not answerable for the negligence of another bank in good standing, to which in the ordinary course of business the note was transmitted for collection. *Id.*

4. BANK TAKING BILL PAYABLE IN ANOTHER STATE FOR COLLECTION is liable for the neglect of its correspondent in the latter state, to whom it sends it, in failing to give due notice of non-acceptance to an indorser, whereby such indorser is discharged. *Allen* v. *Merchants' Bank of N. Y.*, 289.

5. LIABILITY OF BANK TAKING BILL FOR COLLECTION MAY BE VARIED by express agreement, or by an implied agreement, arising from the common understanding of merchants and the custom of trade, so that such bank shall not be held liable for negligence of competent and responsible agents in another state whom it employs to make the collection. *Id.*

6. BANK IS LIABLE FOR NEGLECT OF A NOTARY employed by it to protest a bill taken for collection with respect to giving notice of non-acceptance, that not being a strictly official act, though it may be otherwise as to acts purely official. *Id.*

7. CREDITOR TO WHOM CLAIMS ARE TRANSFERRED AS COLLATERAL SECURITY, is bound to use ordinary diligence in collecting them, and is liable for loss resulting from his failure to do so; but if the transfer merely authorizes such creditor to receive the proceeds of the claims when collected, and apply them to the payment of his debt, he is not bound to prosecute their collection. *Miller* v. *Gettysburg Bank*, 449.

See BANKS AND BANKING, 13; PAYMENT, 1, 3.

BONA FIDE PURCHASERS.

1. WHERE ONE ACTING AS ATTORNEY FOR ANOTHER OBTAINS KNOWLEDGE from which a trust would arise, and afterwards becomes the attorney of a subsequent purchaser in an independent and unconnected transaction, his previous knowledge is not notice to such other person for whom he acts. *Hood* v. *Fahnestock*, 489.

2. BONA FIDE PURCHASER FOR VALUABLE CONSIDERATION IS PROTECTED under the statutes 13 and 27 Eliz., as adopted in this country, whether he purchases from a fraudulent grantor or a fraudulent grantee, and there is no difference in this respect between a deed to defraud subsequent creditors and one to defraud subsequent purchasers. *Id.*

BONDS.

BOUNDARIES.

BRIDGES.

BY-LAWS.

CASE.

CHARITABLE USES.

CHOSES IN ACTION.

COMMISSIONERS.

1. RECEIVING SUBSCRIPTIONS OF STOCK IS A MINISTERIAL ACT under a statute authorizing commissioners to take subscriptions, and subsequently to distribute the stock, and such act may be performed by an agent or deputy, or by one without authority, whose act is afterwards ratified by the commissioners. *Crocker v. Crane*, 228.

2. DISTRIBUTION OF STOCK IS A JUDICIAL ACT under a statute empowering certain commissioners to distribute the stock of a corporation among the subscribers "in such manner as they shall deem most conducive to the interests of the said corporation," and all the commissioners must be present and consult respecting such distribution, or the proceeding will be without jurisdiction and void. *Id.*

3. COMMISSIONERS EXERCISING JUDICIAL POWERS under a statute must all meet and consult, though a majority may decide. *Id.*

4. COMMISSIONERS HAVE NO AUTHORITY TO RECEIVE INDORSED CHECKS IN LIEU OF CASH, especially where it is known that the drawers have no funds, under an act authorizing them to take subscriptions for stock in a corporation, and requiring the payment of a certain sum upon each share at the time of subscription, and a check so taken is void as against the policy of the statute. *Id.*

5. JUDGE AND NOT THE JURY MUST DECIDE WHETHER CHECKS ARE RECEIVABLE instead of cash in payment of a percentage required by statute to be paid at the time of subscribing for stock in a corporation. *Id.*

6. FRAUD PRACTICED BY COMMISSIONER UPON HIS CO-COMMISSIONERS as to the distribution of stock in a corporation, that being a matter in which they are acting judicially, does not render their proceedings void as respects the subscribers, if they have jurisdiction in the premises. *Id.*

COMMON CARRIERS.

COMMON CARRIER MAY, BY SPECIAL ACCEPTANCE, LIMIT HIS COMMON LAW LIABILITY; but the terms of this acceptance operate as exceptions which leave the common law rule in force as to all beside. *Atwood v. Reliance Trans. Co.*, 503.

CONDITIONS.

See BONDS, 1.

CONFESSIONS.

See EVIDENCE, 16.

CONFLICT OF LAWS.

1. LAW OF THE STATE IN WHICH A BILL IS DRAWN AND INDORSED governs as to protest and notice to charge the indorser. *Allen v. Merchants' Bank,* 289.

2. DIVORCE MAY BE HAD ACCORDING TO THE LAW OF DOMICILE of the parties, at the time of the injury complained of, and is not confined to the *lex loci contractus. Clark v. Clark,* 165.

CONSPIRACY.

ONE OF THE PARTIES TO A CONSPIRACY TO DEFRAUD THE GOVERNMENT can not recover from the others the money realised as the fruits of the conspiracy. *Boyd v. Barclay,* 762.

CONSTITUTIONAL LAW.

1. STATUTE, AUTHORIZING A DIVORCE ON ACCOUNT OF DESERTION which had occurred prior to its passage, is a retrospective law, and consequently invalid. *Clark* v. *Clark*, 165.

2. GENERAL LAWS PROVIDING FOR THE DISSOLUTION OF EXISTING MARRIAGES, but operating upon transactions subsequent to their passage, are not within the provision of the United States constitution, prohibiting the states from passing any laws impairing the obligation of contracts. *Id.*

3. LAWS MAY BE RETROSPECTIVE, if they effect an existing cause of action, or an existing right of defense, by taking away or abrogating the same, although no suit or legal proceeding then exists. *Id.*
See CORPORATIONS, 5, 6.

CONSTRUCTION.

See CONTRACTS, 3, 4; EMINENT DOMAIN, 2; EQUITY, 4; JURY AND JURORS, 1; NEGOTIABLE INSTRUMENTS, 2, 4; STATUTES, 2.

CONTRACTS.

1. AGREEMENT FOUNDED IN A MISCONCEPTION caused by the misrepresentation of one of the parties may be avoided, though the misrepresentation was not fraudulent. *Prevall* v. *Fitch*, 558.

2. THOUGH A MISCONCEPTION BE ONE OF LAW, the contract may be avoided on account thereof. Thus if a broker persuade a purchaser that his principal's indorsement on a sealed instrument is equivalent to an indorsement on a promissory note, the purchase may be avoided. *Id.*

3. INTERPRETATION OF A CONTRACT BY ONE OF THE PARTIES can not be aided by showing his letters to one not a party to the suit, in which appears the construction that he has placed upon a similar contract with that third party. *Sharp* v. *Emmet*, 554.

4. DIFFERENT WRITINGS ON SAME SUBJECT EXECUTED AT SAME TIME must be treated as one instrument and construed together. *Strong* v. *Barnes*, 684.

5. CONTRACT IS WHOLLY VOID if any part of the consideration thereof is the suppressing of a criminal prosecution. *Woodruff* v. *Hinman*, 712.

6. THIRD PARTY MAY CLAIM THE ENFORCEMENT OF AN AGREEMENT if the consideration moved from him. Thus, if A. delivers to B., upon the latter's sole credit, goods purchased by him for C., a subsequent agreement between A. and C. that C. shall allow the bill drawn on him by B., for the purchase price, to be protested, and shall hold himself liable to A., the bill being afterwards allowed to go to protest in pursuance of the agreement, may be recognized by B. as a contract of novation which exonerates him from liability to A., by substituting in his place C. as the latter's debtor. *Smith* v. *Plummer*, 530.

See ASSIGNMENT OF CONTRACTS; ASSUMPSIT; MASTER AND SERVANT, 1, 2; MUNICIPAL CORPORATIONS, 8; QUANTUM MERUIT, 1; SALES, 4, 5, 6; SPECIFIC PERFORMANCE; STATUTE OF FRAUDS.

CONTRIBUTION.

1. RIGHT OF CONTRIBUTION EXISTS BETWEEN THE JOINT MAKERS of a promissory note, in favor of one who has paid the whole thereof, notwithstand-

ing the remedy of the holder against the maker in default is barred by the statute of limitations. *Peaslee* v. *Breed*, 178.

2. WHERE PARTIES ARE NOT IN PARI DELICTO, and one is compelled to pay damages, he may sue the other for contribution. *Lowell* v. *B. & L. R. R. Co.*, 33.

CONVERSION.

See HUSBAND AND WIFE, 1; TRESPASS, 18.

CORPORATIONS.

1. CORPORATIONS MUST SO EXERCISE THEIR RIGHTS as not to injure others. *Lowell* v. *B. & L. R. R. Co.*, 33.

2. RAILROAD CORPORATION REMOVING CERTAIN BARRIERS ON A HIGHWAY ARE LIABLE to a town, if the town has been subjected to a suit and recovery by a person who was injured in consequence of the removal of such barriers, the corporation having the right to remove the barriers for the purpose of constructing its road, but being guilty of negligence in not replacing them at night, and in not notifying the town of their removal. *Id.*

3. CORPORATION IS ANSWERABLE FOR NEGLECT IN WORK DONE BY ITS AUTHORITY, though such neglect is attributable to the agents and servants of a contractor, to whom the work had been let for a stipulated sum. *Id.*

4. CHARTER OF INCORPORATION IS A CONTRACT between the government and the corporators; and except with reference to the implied or express reservations embraced in it, is exempt from legislative revocation or interference. *Crease* v. *Babcock*, 61.

5. STATUTE PROVIDING THAT ACTS OF INCORPORATION SHALL BE SUBJECT TO amendment, alteration, or repeal at the pleasure of the legislature, provided that no act of incorporation shall be repealed unless for some violation of its charter or other default, is constitutional. The legislature may make this reservation. And when it thereafter repeals the act, the courts are bound to presume that a contingency had arisen warranting the exercise of the power reserved. *Id.*

6. INQUIRY BY THE LEGISLATURE TO DETERMINE whether a default had happened, upon which it reserved the right to repeal an act of incorporation, is not a judicial act which the legislature is prohibited from entering upon. *Id.*

7. REPEAL OF ITS CHARTER DISSOLVES THE INCORPORATION and subjects the stockholders to all such remedies as the law gives against them on the expiration of the corporation. *Id.*

8. BEQUEST TO A CORPORATION IN TRUST FOR CHARITABLE USES, though at testator's death the corporation had no legal capacity to take, may take effect as an executory devise, whenever, by subsequent incorporation, capacity is acquired. *McIntire* v. *Zanesville Canal and Mfg. Co.*, 436.

9. CORPORATION MAY BE DISSOLVED: 1. By death of its members; 2. Surrender of its franchises; 3. Judgment of forfeiture for non-user or abuse. *Id.*

10. CORPORATION FORMED FOR CONSTRUCTION OF A CANAL to be completed within a definite time, is not dissolved by failure to accomplish the work within the time specified, in the absence of any judgment declaring a forfeiture. *Id.*

CO-TENANCY.

chasers of other portions of the common property, the burden of satisfying the claim of the owner of a paramount title to an undivided interest therein. *Dennison* v. *Foster*, 429.

3. TENANT IN COMMON CAN NOT WORK A DIVISION of the common property by conveyance of his share by a deed defining its limits by metes and bounds. *Id.*

4. DEED OF TENANT IN COMMON conveys the proportional interest only of the grantor to the portion of the common property described. *Id.*

5. THE EQUITIES BETWEEN EARLIER AND LATER PURCHASERS of portions of common property are equal, and the former can not impose upon the latter the entire burden of a paramount title. *Id.*

6. HEIRS OF TENANT IN COMMON ARE BOUND BY A CONVEYANCE by their ancestor, especially if it be by warranty. *Id.*

7. PROCEEDING FOR PARTITION IS ANALOGOUS to a proceeding *in rem*. *Pillsbury* v. *Dugan*, 427.

8. CO-TENANT AGAINST WHOM PARTITION IS DEMANDED is not strictly a party to the proceeding. *Id.*

9. DECREE IN PARTITION BINDS CO-TENANT who is beyond the jurisdiction of the court, if notice be given him of the pendency of the proceeding. *Id.*

10. HUSBAND NEED NOT BE JOINED IN PROCEEDING FOR PARTITION OF WIFE'S LAND in order to bind her interest. *Id.*

11. DIVISION IN FACT OF LAND AMONG PROPRIETORS OF TOWN, however informal, if acquiesced in for fifteen years, is equivalent to a legal division thereof. *Booth* v. *Adams*, 680.

12. ONE TENANT IN COMMON CAN NOT MAINTAIN TRESPASS against his co-tenant, unless he is expelled from the common estate or deprived of the common enjoyment. *Id.*

COVENANTS.

See EXECUTORS AND ADMINISTRATORS, 1–3, 9; LANDLORD AND TENANT, 3; TRESPASS, 13.

CRIMINAL LAW.

1. INDICTMENTS REQUIRE ONLY THE SAME CERTAINTY AS DECLARATIONS, that is, certainty to a common intent in general, and not certainty in every particular, and they need not aver that which is apparent to the court and appears from a necessary implication. It is sufficient if the indictment states the charge with sufficient certainty to inform the defendant what he is called upon to answer, and over-nice exceptions are not to be encouraged, especially in cases which do not touch the life of the defendant. *Sherban* v. *Commonwealth*, 460.

2. INDICTMENT FOR BIGAMY NEED NOT ALLEGE that the same was committed "with force and arms." *State* v. *Kean*, 162.

3. ABBREVIATIONS OF THE PROPER NAMES of persons described in an indictment are allowable. *Id.*

4. INDICTMENT WHICH CONCLUDES, "against the peace and dignity of our said state," instead of "the peace and dignity of the state," as required by the constitution, is not such a substantial variance as to vitiate the same. *Id.*

5. OMISSION IN THE CAPTION OF AN INDICTMENT to state the place where

DAMAGES.

for awarding a new trial, where there is a strong preponderance of evidence showing the defendant entitled to the deduction, and the disallowance is plainly inferable from the amount of the verdict. *Id.*

See ATTORNEY AND CLIENT, 3; CORPORATIONS, 16, 17; EMINENT DOMAIN, 1, 3, 4; INSURANCE—FIRE, 9, 10; MUNICIPAL CORPORATIONS, 10; SALES, 5; SLANDER, 4; STATUTE OF LIMITATIONS, 5; TRESPASS, 3, 4, 11; WATER-COURSES, 6.

DAMS.

See WATERCOURSES, 2–4, 6.

DECLARATIONS.

See AGENCY, 9; EVIDENCE, 14.

DEDICATION.

1. DEDICATION OF CERTAIN TOWN LOTS AS PUBLIC GROUND by recording the official town plat in which they are designated as such, is construed to intend, in the absence of other evidence, that they shall be taken for a public square for the use of the town. *Lebanon* v. *Com'rs of Warren Co.*, 422.

2. DEDICATION TO PUBLIC USE IS A TRUST which takes effect from the registry of the official town plat, and neither the trust nor the title is affected by a subsequent conveyance by the proprietors. *Id.*

3. LOCATION OF COURT-HOUSE AND JAIL on ground dedicated to the use of a town, and its subsequent occupation by the county, is an easement only, not inconsistent with the use of the premises by the town, upon the termination of which the town may reclaim its rights. *Id.*

DEEDS.

1. DELIVERY IS ESSENTIAL to the validity of a deed. *Van Amringe* v. *Morton*, 517.

2. UNAUTHORIZED DELIVERY OF A DEED may be ratified by the grantor, as by an acceptance of the consideration money from the grantee. *Id.*

3. DEED DELIVERED TO ONE OF TWO GRANTEES NAMED THEREIN, without saying anything of the other, is void as to the latter. *Hannah* v. *Swarner*, 442.

4. WHETHER DEED HAS BEEN DELIVERED OR NOT, is a question of fact for the jury to determine. *Id.*

5. WHERE PARTY SELLS LAND ACCORDING TO A MAP as containing "fifteen acres, more or less," and in the deed describes the land according to the map, but is induced by the fraudulent representations of the grantee to alter the description so as to make it include an additional twenty-seven acres, the grantor being ignorant of the effect produced by the alteration, the grantee will be decreed to reconvey the portion thus fraudulently obtained. *Read* v. *Cramer*, 204.

6. DEED BY AN ATTORNEY MUST BE EXECUTED IN THE NAME, and as the act and deed, of the principal. Whether such is the case, must be determined by a construction of the whole instrument, and not from any particular clause. *Hale* v. *Woods*, 176.

7. DEED, THE GRANTING CLAUSE AND COVENANTS OF WHICH ARE IN THE NAME OF THE PRINCIPAL, but signed "D. K., attorney for Z. K.," is the act of the principal, and passes his estate. *Id.*

2. ASSERTION OF OWNERSHIP BY THE CLAIMANT of a right of way, or some implied admission by the owner of the soil that the right exists, is essential to create a right of way by prescription over uninclosed lands. *Id.*

3. RIGHT OF WAY BY PRESCRIPTION CAN NOT ARISE unless there is evidence that the use was adverse to that of the owner of the soil. *Id.*

4. USE OF AN EASEMENT NEED NOT BE ABSOLUTELY CONTINUOUS in order to affect a purchaser with notice of its existence; it is sufficient that there is something in the aspect of the premises to put the purchaser on his guard. *Bird* v. *Smith*, 483.

5. EASEMENT IN LAND HELD BY A CONNECTICUT TITLE is not affected by a grant of that title from Pennsylvania, where the latter grant confirmed the Connecticut title. *Id.*

6. EXCLUSIVE RIGHT TO NAVIGATE WATERS OF PUBLIC RIVER can only be acquired by a grant from the public. A grant of such a right can never be presumed from length of time. *Id.*

7. EXCLUSIVE RIGHT TO LAND FERRY AT POINT on bank of navigable river may be presumed from exclusive enjoyment of such right for a long period of time. And the jury ought to presume the right to be exclusive whenever its value would be lessened in the least degree by participation. *Id.*

8. LESSOR OF EASEMENT IS COMPETENT WITNESS FOR LESSEE in an action by the latter for a disturbance thereof. *Id.*

See DEDICATION, 3.

EJECTMENT.

1. DEFENDANT IN EJECTMENT MAY SET UP TITLE ADVERSE to that of a person with whom he had previously entered into a contract for the title, if, before he took possession, he gave notice to such person that he would not take possession under him. *Nerhooth* v. *Althouse*, 480.

2. IN EJECTMENT, EVIDENCE OF DEFENDANT'S POSSESSION at commencement of the suit is necessary. *Newman* v. *Foster*, 98.

3. A SPECIAL CONSENT RULE IS NECESSARY only where actual entry must be made previous to suit brought. *Id.*

4. PLAINTIFF IN EJECTMENT IS ENTITLED TO RECOVER upon full proof of title and an adverse possession by the defendant at the time of the commencement of the suit. *Id.*

See MORTGAGES, 9.

EMINENT DOMAIN.

1. COMPENSATION FOR PROPERTY TAKEN IN THE EXERCISE OF THE RIGHT OF EMINENT DOMAIN, must be secured or made, and a statute divesting the owner's title and turning him over to obtain his compensation under judgment rendered for his damages, violates that provision of the bill of rights which declares that "no person's property shall be taken or applied to public use without just compensation first made therefor." *Thompson* v. *Grand Gulf R. & B. Co.*, 81.

2. IN CONSTRUING CONSTITUTIONS, NO WORD IS TO BE REJECTED or disregarded which may have a material bearing on the rights of citizens, and such construction should be given as will best protect private rights. *Id.*

3. JUDGMENT IS NOT COMPENSATION, but a security for compensation or satisfaction. *Id.*

4. DEFECT IN CLAUSE PROVIDING COMPENSATION CAN NOT BE REMEDIED by the court's giving a different judgment from that directed by the legislature. *Id.*

EQUITY.

1. BILL IN EQUITY TO IMPEACH A JUDGMENT or decree for fraud, must set forth specifically and particularly the facts constituting the fraud. *Pendleton v. Galloway*, 434.

2. DECREE CAN NOT BE IMPEACHED FOR FRAUD after twenty-five years' acquiescence by the plaintiff. *Id.*

3. TO ENTITLE JUDGMENT CREDITOR TO RELIEF IN EQUITY to obtain payment of his judgment, on the ground that he has exhausted his remedy at law, he must, by his bill, show affirmatively, if the judgment is one upon which execution may be issued to any county in the state, that he has issued execution to the county where the defendant then resided, which execution was returned unsatisfied, or must show a legal and sufficient excuse for not doing so. *Reed v. Wheaton*, 366.

4. EQUITY JURISDICTION DOES NOT EMBRACE the construction of devises of legal interests in land. *Hough v. Martin*, 403.

5. VAGUENESS AND OBSCURITY OF A WILL furnish no ground for an application to equity: for if not absolutely unintelligible, it will be valid at law as far as understood; and if it is so far devoid of meaning as not to amount to a designation of any *corpus*, it follows that there is no need of relief, for the devise is ineffectual. *Id.*

6. BILL FOR ASCERTAINING CONFUSED BOUNDARIES will be entertained only when the boundaries, being at one time certain, were rendered otherwise by the default of the defendant, or those under whom he claims. *Id.*

7. EQUITY JURISDICTION FOR ASCERTAINMENT OF CONFUSED BOUNDARIES is exercised only where there has been some agreement that the land of the several parties should be distinguished, or where, on account of a particular relation, a duty to preserve the landmarks is imposed upon one of them, by the fraud or neglect of whom the boundaries have become confused. *Id.*

8. BETWEEN INDEPENDENT PROPRIETORS EQUITY WILL NOT INTERPOSE to decree a settlement of their boundaries, in the absence of fraud or neglect, or of express agreement. *Id.*

9. BILL FOR AN INJUNCTION TO STAY WASTE, which fails to show the complainant to have a good and sufficient title to the particular land in which the waste is apprehended, is radically defective. *Id.*

10. BILL FOR DISCOVERY OF DEEDS, which does not allege that the particular deeds claimed by complainant, and which are material to him in a pending action, are in the custody or under the control of defendants, is defective, and can not be maintained. *Id.*

11. CHANCERY WILL MAKE PROVISION FOR THE WIFE OUT OF A LEGACY or distributive share of an estate to which she is entitled, before allowing her husband to reduce it to possession. *Wilks v. Fitzpatrick*, 618.

12. EQUITY OF THE WIFE IS NOT EXTINGUISHED BY AN ASSIGNMENT OF HER LEGACY, in which she joins her husband. *Id.*

13. WIFE IS NOT BOUND BY HER TRANSFER OF A LEGACY due her, unless she be privily examined in court touching her consent. *Id.*

14. WIFE MAY SET UP HER EQUITY TO DEFEAT A TRANSFER of her legacy by herself and husband. *Id.*

15. REGULAR DISMISSAL ON THE MERITS OF BILL IN CHANCERY IS A BAR to another suit on the same matters, when the matters of the bill have been passed upon. *Pelton* v. *Mott*, 678.

16. DISMISSAL ENTERED UPON THE MERITS BY CONSENT OF THE PARTIES is as conclusive upon them, as if the judgment were rendered in the ordinary course of proceeding. *Id.*

17. BETWEEN MERE EQUITIES the elder is the better. *Polk* v. *Gallant*, 410.

18. COURT OF CHANCERY HAS POWER TO AWARD AN ISSUE TO TRY THE SANITY of a donor of a gift in the nature of a bequest, and, in case of doubt, it is its duty to do so. *Gardner* v. *Gardner*, 340.

See CO-TENANCY, 5; EXECUTIONS, 11–13; MORTGAGES, 5, 6, 7, 21; SET-OFF, 2.

ERROR.

See PLEADING AND PRACTICE, 19–28.

ESTATES OF DECEASED PERSONS.

See SET-OFF, 1.

EVIDENCE.

1. LOST OR DESTROYED RECORD MAY BE PROVED by collateral or secondary evidence. *Prudent* v. *Alden*, 51.

2. EVIDENCE—SHORT NOTES MADE BY THE CLERK in the minute book must stand as the record until a more complete and intelligible record is made up; and if, in the mean time, they are lost or destroyed, this constitutes a loss of the records, and secondary proof of their contents may be received. *Id.*

3. LICENSE TO SELL LANDS WILL BE CONSIDERED PROVED when it is recited in a deed under which thirty years' undisturbed possession has been held, and the recital is corroborated by other circumstances, and the dockets of the court have been lost. *Id.*

4. TRUTH OF FACTS CERTIFIED IN A RECORD can not be collaterally impeached by evidence *aliunde*. *Jones* v. *Judkins*, 392.

5. ORIGINAL PAPERS IN PROCEEDING BEFORE JUSTICE OF PEACE ARE NOT ADMISSIBLE in evidence in the circuit court, without some proof of their authenticity, when there is nothing in the record to show how they became part of the case. *Hickman* v. *Griffin*, 124.

6. PROOF BY THE JUSTICE IN WHOSE COURT PROCEEDING TOOK PLACE, of the identity and authenticity of the papers, and that they had been acted upon, is sufficient. *Id.*

7. CERTIFICATE OF A NOTARY WHO IS A STOCKHOLDER IN A BANK SUING the indorser on a note, is inadmissible to prove demand and notice. *Herkimer Co. Bank* v. *Cox*, 220.

8. NOTARY'S CERTIFICATE IS PRIMA FACIE SUFFICIENT EVIDENCE that notice of non-payment of a check was properly directed. *Crocker* v. *Crane*, 228.

9. LAW PRESUMES, AFTER SEVEN YEARS' CONTINUED ABSENCE, that a person concerning whom nothing has been heard or known during that time, is dead. *Lewis* v. *Mobley*, 379.

10. EVIDENCE OF FACTS SWORN TO BY A DECEASED WITNESS in another and different suit is inadmissible. *McMorine* v. *Storey*, 374.

EXECUTIONS.

EXECUTORS AND ADMINISTRATORS.

1. ADMINISTRATOR IS NOT ENTITLED TO SUE FOR BREACH OF COVENANT to convey land to a deceased covenantee. *Thrower v. McIntire*, 382.

2. RIGHT OF ACTION UPON A COVENANT TO CONVEY IS IN THE HEIRS of the deceased covenantee. *Id.*

3. COVENANT TO CONVEY LAND TO ANOTHER, WITHOUT ANY MENTION OF THE HEIRS of the covenantee, whether considered as a mere personal covenant or not, does not invest the administrator with any right of action for a breach. *Id.*

4. BEQUEST OF AN ANNUITY PAYABLE OUT OF LANDS, gives the executor a power to dispose of the lands by sale or otherwise, adequate to the performance of the bequest. *Ex parte Elliott*, 572.

5. POWER TO DISPOSE OF LANDS is exhausted by a disposition of the lands in consideration of ground rent, and the right to release the rent is in him in whom the estate therein is vested, not in the person who executed the power. *Id.*

6. EXECUTOR, SURETY OF A LEGATEE, MAY RETAIN AGAINST AN ASSIGNEE OF THE LATTER, claiming under an assignment subsequent in date to the executor's becoming surety, the amounts that he has been obliged to pay because of his character of surety. *Romig v. Erdman*, 533.

7. EXECUTOR IS ENTITLED TO RECOVER OF A RESIDUARY LEGATEE, remuneration for expenditures made by the former, without any order or direction of court, for the benefit and improvement of the estate, although before the interest of the residuary legatee vested in possession, the improvements, from unforeseen accident, were destroyed. *Palmer v. Miller*, 602.

8. EXECUTOR IS ENTITLED TO RECOVER THE VALUE OF IMPROVEMENTS at the time when the estate left his charge. *Id.*

9. ADMINISTRATOR OF DECEASED TENANT IS PERSONALLY LIABLE on a covenant in the lease to pay assessments, etc., as an assignee, where he receives the rents and profits after his intestate's death, and need not be named as executor, though in certain special cases he may defend in part, as by showing that there are no assets and that the land is worth less than the sum due; but this is strictly matter of defense. *Matter of Galloway*, 209.

10. ATTACHMENT LIES AGAINST A NON-RESIDENT ADMINISTRATOR as a non-resident debtor under the statute in an action on a covenant in a lease to his intestate to pay assessments, etc., upon which he is personally liable by reason of having received the rents and profits. *Id.*

11. ASSIGNEE OF ADMINISTRATOR CAN NOT RECOVER, WHEN.—Where an administrator for his own private benefit transfers a note belonging to the estate of the decedent to a third person, who has full knowledge, the latter can not recover the amount of the note from the maker. *Prosser v. Leatherman*, 121.

12. ADMINISTRATOR OF FRAUDULENT ASSIGNEE is liable as executor *de son tort* to the creditors of a deceased debtor by whom the assignment was made. *McMorine v. Storey*, 374.

13. GRANT OF LETTERS OF ADMINISTRATION does not confer upon the administrator the right to the possession of property fraudulently assigned to the deceased, as against the creditors of the assignor. *Id.*

14. EXECUTOR IS CHARGEABLE WITH INTEREST ON THE ANNUAL BALANCE only of his accounts, when the form of his final account is such that payments

on account of principal and those on account of interest are distinguished and separately stated, but if the form of the account be such that the executor has charged himself with the gross sum received as the proceeds of sales, not distinguishing between principal and interest, he is to be charged with the entire amount of sales with interest thereon annually, and the balance is to be obtained by setting off the interest so computed, against the annual disbursements of the current year. *Duncan* v. *Tobin*, 605.

15. EXECUTOR IS ENTITLED PRO TANTO TO THE BENEFIT of such of his accounts as are accurate and satisfactory. *Id.*

See FIXTURES.

FENCES.
See TRESPASS, 6, 10, 16.

FERRIES.
See EASEMENTS, 7.

FIXTURES.
STEAM ENGINE ERECTED BY TENANT FOR LIFE for the purpose of carrying on a trade may be removed after his death by his representative. *Estate of Hinds*, 542.

FORGERY.
See CRIMINAL LAW, 22-24.

FRAUD.

1. GENERAL INFLUENCE OF A WIFE OVER HER HUSBAND, arising from affection produced by her kindness, does not constitute or afford an inference of undue influence. *Gardner* v. *Gardner*, 340.

2. UNDUE INFLUENCE TO VITIATE AN ACT MUST AMOUNT TO COERCION destroying free agency, or harassing importunity producing compliance for the sake of peace. *Id.*

3. FRAUDULENT PURCHASER ACQUIRES NO TITLE to the goods as against the party defrauded. *Knowles* v. *Lord*, 525.

See BONA FIDE PURCHASERS, 3; COMMISSIONERS, 6; DEEDS, 5; INFANCY, 4, 5.

FRAUDULENT CONVEYANCES.

SALE OF PERSONAL PROPERTY EXEMPT FROM EXECUTION IS VALID as against creditors of the vendor, without any change in the possession. *Foster* v. *McGregor*, 713.

See SALES, 7.

GARNISHMENT.
See PARTNERSHIP, 12.

GENERAL AVERAGE.
See INSURANCE—MARINE, 1.

GIFTS.

1. PAROL GIFT BY A FATHER TO HIS DAUGHTER can be established only by clear and convincing evidence. *Collins* v. *Loftus*, 719.

2. RESUMPTION OF POSSESSION BY LENDER, or conveyance of the property loaned to another, within five years, is sufficient to determine the loan. *Id.*

See INTOXICATION.

GRANT.

1. A PATENT IS THE HIGHEST EVIDENCE OF TITLE, and can be impeached only on the ground of fraud or mistake. *Carter v. Spencer*, 106.

2. APPLICATION FOR PRIVATE ENTRY WITHOUT FILING AFFIDAVIT that land was not subject to right of pre-emption, as required by an instruction of the secretary of the treasurer under act of April 5, 1832, is not of itself evidence of fraud. *Id.*

3. WHERE SETTLER ERECTS IMPROVEMENTS AT THE CORNER OF SECTIONS, an entry of one of the sections on which the improvements were made is a bar to pre-emptive right over the other sections. *Id.*

See BOUNDARIES, 2; EASEMENTS, 5, 7; SURVEY.

GUARANTY.

See AGENCY, 1, 2.

GUARDIAN AND WARD.

1. GUARDIAN IS NOT BOUND TO SUE IMMEDIATELY upon an unsecured liability which has come to his hands as part of his ward's estate. *Stem's Appeal*, 569.

2. GUARDIAN MAY RECEIVE AN UNSECURED PROMISSORY NOTE as part of his ward's estate, instead of the cash which he would have received had he insisted upon it, provided that at the time that he received the note he had never had control of the fund which it represented. Thus he may receive from administrators a note executed by a debtor of the estate, to himself as guardian. *Id.*

3. GUARDIAN WHO FAILS TO COLLECT INTEREST on a note as it falls due, is liable for its ultimate loss. *Id.*

4. GUARDIAN OF A LUNATIC CAN NOT BRING A BILL IN EQUITY AGAINST HER for a settlement of his accounts, and to obtain payment of the sum found due him; nor can he maintain an action in equity for the value of necessaries furnished the lunatic during the period of his guardianship, nor previously thereto, while she resided with him as a member of his family. *Tally v. Tally*, 407.

5. GUARDIAN HAS THE RIGHT TO REMOVE AN IMPROPER PERSON for his ward to associate with, from the ward's premises, using no more force, and removing such person no further than is necessary to prevent a renewal of such association. *Wood v. Gale*, 150.

6. EVIDENCE OF WANT OF CHASTITY IN THE PERSON REMOVED IS ADMISSIBLE, in an action of trespass, to show the reasons a guardian may have had to expect such person's return, and to justify the removal. *Id.*

7. A GUARDIAN MAY SUE IN HIS OWN NAME for an injury done to the property of the ward in his possession. *Fuqua v. Hunt*, 771.

See INFANCY, 8.

HIGHWAYS.

See CORPORATIONS, 2; NEGLIGENCE, 2; TRESPASS, 16.

HUSBAND AND WIFE.

1. REDUCTION INTO POSSESSION OF THE WIFE'S CHOSES IN ACTION by the husband, is but evidence of a conversion to his use, and not in itself a conversion, and therefore may be so qualified that the property in the proceeds remains in the wife. *Estate of Hinds,* 542.
2. ARTICLES PURCHASED WITH THE CONSENT OF A WIFE by trustees of money settled to her separate use, become part of her separate property. *Yardley* v. *Raub,* 535.
3. THE RIGHTS OF A HUSBAND'S CREDITORS will not extend over household goods and furniture, which have been purchased with the wife's consent in their own name by the trustees of money settled to her separate use, and placed by them in a tavern conducted by the husband, to be there used alike by the family and by the guests. *Id.*
4. LOAN BY HUSBAND TO WIFE FOR THE BENEFIT OF HER SEPARATE ESTATE is valid in equity as a charge on such estate, unless prohibited by the instrument under which she holds; and such loan, if collectible, must be accounted for by the wife as administratrix of her husband, and the reasonable presumption is that the separate estate is sufficient to repay the loan. *Gardner* v. *Gardner,* 340.
5. DESTROYING A BOND, WITH A DECLARED INTENT TO FORGIVE THE DEBT, is sufficient by way of gift to release the debt. *Id.*

See DOWER; EQUITY, 11-14; FRAUD, 1.

IMPROVEMENTS.

See ARBITRATION AND AWARD, 1; EXECUTIONS, 15; EXECUTORS AND ADMINISTRATORS, 8; GRANTS, 3.

INDICTMENTS.

See CRIMINAL LAW, 1-7.

INDORSEMENT.

See NEGOTIABLE INSTRUMENTS.

INFANCY.

1. AN INFANT THOUGH UNDER SEVEN YEARS MAY BIND HIMSELF as apprentice, with the assent of his parent, guardian, or next friend. *Brotzman* v. *Bunnell,* 537.
2. ACTION FOR AN INJURY TO A CHILD LIES IN THE NAME OF THE CHILD. *Hartfield* v. *Roper,* 273.
3. NEGLIGENCE MAY BE PREDICATED OF AN INFANT. *Id.*
4. MINOR IS NOT ESTOPPED TO AVOID HIS CONTRACT on the ground of infancy, by reason of false representations as to his age, made at the time of contracting. *Burley* v. *Russell,* 146.
5. INFANT IS LIABLE, IN AN ACTION ON THE CASE, for the fraudulent affirmation that he is of age, if he afterwards avoids his contract by reason of his infancy. *Id.*
6. PROMISE OF A PERSON AFTER HE ARRIVES AT AGE, to pay a debt contracted during his minority, removes the bar of infancy, and authorizes a recovery on the original contract. *Hoit* v. *Underhill,* 148.

7. RATIFICATION OF A CONTRACT ENTERED INTO DURING INFANCY, after a minor's arrival at age, is sufficient although made to the undisclosed agent of the other contracting party. *Id.*

8. ADMISSIONS OF A SPENDTHRIFT, made while under a commission of guardianship, are competent evidence to show a contract, or a ratification of one, made prior to the guardianship. *Id.*

9. INFANT MAY SUE BY PROCHEIN AMI, in Vermont, notwithstanding he may have a guardian. *Thomas* v. *Dike*, 690.

10. WHERE INFANT MAKES CONTRACT TO SERVE ANOTHER, AND AFTERWARDS AVOIDS IT, he may recover what his services are reasonably worth, taking into account any injury the other party sustains by the avoiding of the contract. And, if such injury be equal to the value of the services rendered, he can recover nothing. *Id.*

INJUNCTIONS.

1. INJUNCTION AGAINST PUBLISHING A NEWSPAPER OF THE SAME NAME as complainant's for the fraudulent purpose of deceiving the public and depriving the complainant of the good will of his paper, will lie, but not where the simulation is not such as is calculated to lead the public to believe that it is in reality the same paper, so as to injure the circulation of the complainant's paper. *Bell* v. *Locke*, 371.

2. INJUNCTION TO RESTRAIN PUBLICATION OF A LIBEL holding the complainant up to ridicule will not lie, where such publication will not be an invasion of rights of literary or other property of the complainant. *Brandreth* v. *Lance*, 368.

See EQUITY, 9.

INNS.

1. TAVERN IS A HOUSE LICENSED TO SELL LIQUORS in small quantities, to be drunk on the spot. *State* v. *Chamblyss*, 593.

2. LICENSE TO KEEP A TAVERN INCLUDES THE PRIVILEGE of retailing spirituous liquors. *Id.*

INSANITY.

1. LUNATIC MAY AVOID HIS DEED made during insanity. *Bensell* v. *Chancellor*, 561.

See EQUITY, 18; GUARDIAN AND WARD, 4.

INSTRUCTIONS.

See PLEADING AND PRACTICE, 15, 16.

INSURANCE—FIRE.

1. DESTRUCTION OF INSURED BUILDING BY AN EXPLOSION OF GUNPOWDER is a loss by fire within the meaning of the policy. *City Fire Ins. Co.* v. *Corlies*, 258.

2. PLACING GUNPOWDER IN A BUILDING IS NOT A "STORING" of gunpowder therein within the meaning of an exception in the policy, where the powder is placed there with a lighted match, for the purpose of an explosion. *Id.*

3. VOLUNTARY DESTRUCTION OF INSURED BUILDING BY ORDER OF THE MAYOR, by blowing it up with gunpowder, for the purpose of stopping a

conflagration, which in all probability would have consumed the building, renders the insurers liable, although the insured may also have a remedy against the city. *Id.*

4. MERE EXCESS OF JURISDICTION BY LAWFUL MAGISTRATE IS NOT USURPATION of power within the meaning of a policy, exempting the insurers from liability for a loss by "usurped power." *Id.*

5. INSURANCE BY MORTGAGOR AND MORTGAGEE SEVERALLY, may be effected without the insurance of either impairing that of the other. *Jackson v. Mass. Mut. F. Ins. Co.,* 69.

6. INVALID INSURANCE CAN NOT OPERATE TO ANNUL PRIOR POLICY of insurance which stipulates that if the assured shall have made, or shall hereafter make any other insurance "upon said property, this policy shall be null and void." Such a policy is not avoided by taking out a second policy having the same condition; for, by the condition, the second policy never becomes operative and does not amount to "an insurance." *Id.*

7. A PROVISION IN A POLICY AVOIDING IT IN THE CASE OF "ALIENATION by sale or otherwise," does not apply to a conveyance by way of mortgage, while the mortgagor remains in possession, and there has been no entry for foreclosure. *Id.*

8. TENANT FOR LIFE IN A BUILDING WHICH IS DESTROYED BY FIRE, has a right to the use and possession of the insurance money, but can not deprive the husband of one entitled to the remainder of his interest therein, or of his right to sue therefor, by converting the same into realty. *Haxall v. Shippen,* 745.

9. DAMAGES RECOVERED ON A POLICY OF FIRE INSURANCE are not part of the inheritance; they are personal estate, belonging to the owners of the building according to their respective rights. *Id.*

10. No EQUITY ATTACHES TO DAMAGES RECOVERED on a policy of fire insurance, which authorizes the same to be used in replacing the buildings for the loss of which they were recovered. *Id.*

INSURANCE—MARINE.

1. GENERAL AVERAGE—STRANDING OF A VESSEL whose loss is at all events inevitable in order to save the endangered lives of the crew, will not constitute a case of general average, requiring the cargo saved to contribute, though the stranding tended to and resulted in the saving of a larger proportion of the cargo than would otherwise have been saved. *Meech v. Robinson,* 514.

2. PRECISE RISK ONLY, WHICH INSURER CONTEMPLATED, can be introduced into contract of marine insurance, and this principle applies to contracts of inland navigation. *Atwood v. Reliance Trans. Co.,* 503.

3. DANGERS OF NAVIGATION MEAN THOSE PERILS THAT ARE INCIDENT to it in a lawful course of it, but not those that arise from pursuing an unlawful course therein. *Id.*

INTEREST.

See EXECUTORS AND ADMINISTRATORS, 14; GUARDIAN AND WARD, 2.

INTOXICATION.

HABITUAL DRUNKARD IS PRESUMED COMPETENT WHEN SOBER to make a will or a valid gift, unless it appears that intemperance has produced a settled derangement of the faculties. *Gardner v. Gardner,* 340.

JUDGMENTS.

equity, rendered in a proceeding to which he is not a party. *Collins v. Loftus*, 719.

See CO-TENANCY, 9; EQUITY, 1, 2; JUDGMENTS, 13.

JUDICIAL SALES.

BONA FIDE ASSERTION OF RIGHT, WHICH DETERS BIDDERS at a judicial sale, although the right turns out to be unfounded, does not estop the person who asserted it from afterwards claiming under the sale. *Cronister v. Weise*, 461.

JURISDICTION.

1. CIRCUIT COURT HAS APPELLATE JURISDICTION IN MATTERS OF PROBATE over the decisions of the county court, under statute of 1825, section 10, of Missouri. *Dickey v. Malechi*, 130.

2. RECITAL IN PETITION OF THE REJECTION OF SUPPOSED WILL by the county court, with the annexation of the record of the judgment of the county court, proving that fact, is sufficient to give the circuit court appellate jurisdiction under that statute. *Id.*

3. COURTS OBTAIN JURISDICTION OF DEFENDANTS BY SERVICE OF PROCESS, either on their persons, or on their property within the jurisdiction of the court. *Gilman v. Thompson*, 714.

4. WHERE OFFICER ATTACHES REAL ESTATE AND LEAVES A COPY of the writ with the town clerk, the court thereby acquires jurisdiction of the party. *Id.*

JURY AND JURORS.

1. CONSTRUCTION OF AN ORAL AGREEMENT BELONGS TO THE JURY and not to the court. *McFarland v. Newman*, 497.

2. NUMBER OF THE JURY AT COMMON LAW could never be less than twelve. *Carpenter v. State*, 116.

3. WHERE AN ISSUE IS SUBMITTED TO ELEVEN PERSONS, their finding can not be considered as the verdict of a jury, upon which a court would be warranted in pronouncing judgment. *Id.*

4. VERDICT IS VOID FOR IRREGULARITY where the jury, being unable to agree as to the amount for which the verdict should be returned, proceeded to allow each juror to write down an amount according to his judgment, and returned a verdict for one twelfth of the sum of the amounts so written. *Elledge v. Todd*, 616.

5. AFFIDAVIT OF JUROR IS ADMISSIBLE TO IMPEACH a verdict obtained by a resort to unjust or unreasonable methods. *Id.*

6. VERDICT OF A JURY IS NOT VITIATED where one juror, without any knowledge of the others, took the different amounts suggested by his fellow-jurors, and having ascertained the result of one twelfth of the aggregate sum, proposed that the verdict should be for that amount, which was then assented to by the others. *Bennett v. Baker*, 655.

7. AFFIDAVIT OF A JUROR THAT HE DID NOT AGREE TO THE VERDICT, but was deceived, is inadmissible to impeach a verdict. *Id.*

See BOUNDARIES, 1; SLANDER, 4; WARRANTY, 2, 5.

LANDLORD AND TENANT.

1. LANDLORD HAS NO LIEN ON A TENANT'S CROP in preference to other creditors, for payment of rent, though the stipulated rent of the premises consisted of a portion of crops raised thereon. *Deaver v. Rice*, 388.

2. LEASE WITH RENT RESERVED IN KIND confers upon the lessee an estate in possession in severalty, and the entire property in the whole crop raised and growing upon the land during the term is in the lessee. *Id.*

3. COVENANT TO GIVE LESSOR A PORTION OF CROPS raised upon land, in return for its use, creates a right resting only in contract, and does not vest the lessor with any title to the crops, as against an attaching creditor of the lessee. *Id.*

4. AGREEMENT BETWEEN LESSOR AND LESSEE that the former should take all the corn standing in a particular field for his rent, does not entitle the lessor to the crop, as against a purchaser at an execution sale of the same corn made afterwards upon a judgment against the lessee, under a writ, the teste of which preceded the date of the agreement. *Id.*

5. TENANT IS ENTITLED TO WAY-GOING CROP, and may maintain trespass *quare clausum fregit* against his landlord for an injury done thereto, after the expiration of his lease, and his removal from the premises. *Forsythe* v. *Price*, 465.

6. TENANT MAY ACQUIRE HIS LESSOR'S TITLE BY A PURCHASE ON EXECUTION against the lessor, or by redeeming the premises after an execution sale, as a judgment creditor of the lessor, and may set up his title in bar of an action for rent subsequently accruing. *Nellis* v. *Lathrop*, 285.

7. TENANT MAY SHOW THAT HE HAS BECOME OWNER OF PART of the leased premises by a purchase or redemption under a judgment against the lessor, to mitigate the damages in an action for rent, but not as a bar to the action. *Id.*

8. RENT IS APPORTIONABLE where the tenant becomes owner of part of the premises under an execution sale against the lessor. *Id.*

9. TENANT MAY DISPUTE HIS LANDLORD'S TITLE by showing that he was led to acknowledge the tenancy under a misapprehension as to such title, and that he was, at the time of his acknowledgment of said title, actually in possession as tenant of another. *Swift* v. *Dean* 693.

See NEGLIGENCE, 1.

LARCENY.

See CRIMINAL LAW, 20, 21.

LIBEL.

1. ACTION FOR LIBEL LIES FOR ADDRESSING LETTERS TO PUBLIC OFFICER CHARGING SUBORDINATE, whom he is authorized to remove, with fraud and malfeasance in the execution of his trust; but to maintain the action the plaintiff must prove malice and want of probable cause, as in an action for malicious prosecution. *Howard* v. *Thompson*, 238.

2. KNOWLEDGE OR INFORMATION OF A CONVERSION OF PUBLIC PROPERTY BY AN OFFICER to his own use, furnishes sufficient probable cause for addressing a letter to such officer's superior to procure his removal to defeat an action of libel therefor, or at least to be left to the jury, although, unknown to the defendant, such conversion was authorized, and although the defendant was actuated by ill-will. *Id.*

3. PROBABLE CAUSE, WHERE THE FACTS ARE UNDISPUTED, is a question of law in actions for malicious prosecution or for libel in the nature of malicious prosecution. *Id.*

4. DEFENDANT HAVING PLEADED JUSTIFICATION MAY WAIVE SUCH PLEA at the trial and rely upon proof of probable cause, in actions for malicious prosecution or *quasi* such, because probable cause is a complete bar to the action in such cases, and not merely matter of mitigation. *Id.*

See INJUNCTIONS, 2.

LICENSE.

See EVIDENCE, 3; TAVERNS, 2.

LIENS.

See JUDGMENTS, 4, 6–8; LANDLORD AND TENANT, 1; MORTGAGES, 3, 4, 12, 17.

LUNACY.

See INSANITY.

MALICIOUS PROSECUTION.

1. DEFENDANT IN ACTION FOR MALICIOUS PROSECUTION can not be allowed to prove what he swore to when there were several other witnesses present at the time. *Hickman* v. *Griffin*, 124.

2. REAL INQUIRY IN AN ACTION FOR MALICIOUS PROSECUTION is whether there was probable cause for the prosecution, not the knowledge or belief of the party prosecuting as to its existence. *Id.*

3. GENERAL RULE THAT PARTY CAN NOT BE ALLOWED TO MAKE EVIDENCE in his own favor is not departed from in an action for malicious prosecution except in cases of necessity. *Id.*

4. CASE FOR MALICIOUS PROSECUTION IN COURT WITHOUT JURISDICTION will lie if the malice and falsehood be put forward as the gravamen and the arrest as the consequence. Hence, in such an action an allegation that the court had jurisdiction is unnecessary. *Morris* v. *Scott*, 236.

MARRIAGE AND DIVORCE.

1. MARRIAGE IN A FOREIGN STATE MAY BE PROVED by the testimony of any person who was present at the ceremony, provided it is also shown to have been valid according to the laws of the country in which it was celebrated. *State* v. *Kean*, 162.

2. PROOF THAT A MARRIAGE WAS PERFORMED BY AN OFFICIATING PRIEST, and that t was understood by the parties to be the marriage ceremony, according to the customs of the foreign country, is presumptive evidence of marriage. *Id.*

3. EVERY ORDAINED MINISTER, RESIDING IN THIS STATE, MAY SOLEMNIZE MARRIAGES, after having recorded the credentials of his ordination. Such recording will be presumed until the contrary appears. *Id.*

4. DESERTION, TO CONSTITUTE A GROUND OF DIVORCE, must have continued up to the time of filing the libel. *Clark* v. *Clark*, 165.

5. PETITION FOR DIVORCE has, in New Hampshire, the character of a civil judicial proceeding. *Id.*

6. MARRIAGE CELEBRATED BY JUSTICE OF PEACE WITHOUT CONSENT OF THE PARTIES is void, and can not change the settlement of the woman. *Mountholly* v. *Andover*, 685.

1. VOID MARRIAGE MAY BE IMPEACHED in all cases where it comes in controversy collaterally, between those not parties to the contract. *Id.*

8. TOWN CAN NOT INSTITUTE PROCEEDINGS TO ANNUL VOID MARRIAGE.—A decree of divorce can only be obtained at the suit of the parties to the marriage. *Id.*

See CONFLICT OF LAWS, 2; CONSTITUTIONAL LAW, 1, 2.

MARRIED WOMEN.

See CO-TENANCY, 3; HUSBAND AND WIFE, 2–5.

MASTER AND SERVANT.

1. CONTRACT OF HIRING IS BY THE YEAR where the duration of the hire is not limited, and it is provided that it can be terminated but upon three months' notice. *Heidleberg v. Lynn,* 566.

8. CONTRACT OF SERVICE IS NOT INTERRUPTED BY TEMPORARY ABSENCES where the absence is with the consent of the master and does not prevent the discharge of the servant's duties; in such cases, the servant is, during his absence, in the constructive service of the master. *Id.*

8. FOR NEGLIGENCE OR NON-FEASANCE OF HIS SERVANTS, the principal is responsible to any person injured thereby. *Lowell v. B. & L. R. R. Co.,* 33.

MEMORANDUM.

See STATUTE OF FRAUDS.

MISTAKE.

MISTAKE IN SPELLING NAME OF A PARTY IN AN INSTRUMENT will not invalidate it if the person can be identified. *Pillsbury v. Dugan,* 427.

See CONTRACTS, 1, 2; EXECUTIONS, 12.

MORTGAGES.

1. PURCHASERS OF MORTGAGED PREMISES ARE BOUND by an acknowledgment of the mortgage as a valid and subsisting incumbrance made by their grantor, a purchaser on execution against the mortgagor under a judgment subsequent to the mortgage, within twenty years before the commencement of a suit to foreclose such mortgage, and can not, therefore, rely upon the statute of limitations as a bar. *Heyer v. Pruyn,* 355.

2. SUFFERING A FORECLOSURE BILL TO BE TAKEN AS CONFESSED is an admission of liability on the part of the mortgagor sufficient to take the case out of the statute of limitations where such an admission is necessary. *Id.*

8. MORTGAGOR'S ACKNOWLEDGMENT WITHIN TWENTY YEARS IS UNNECESSARY to continue the lien of the mortgage, where the mortgagor has ceased to be the owner of the land. *Id.*

4. MORTGAGE LIEN CONTINUES THOUGH THE DEBT MAY BE BARRED by the statute of limitations, and is not to be presumed paid until the lapse of twenty years, where the personal liability of the mortgagor has become separated from the ownership of the land. *Id.*

5. MORTGAGED PREMISES CONSTITUTE THE PRIMARY FUND for the payment of the mortgage in equity, as against a purchaser of the land under an execution against the mortgagor. *Id.*

MUNICIPAL CORPORATIONS.

and stipulating that "said committee are to pay," etc., are personally answerable on the contract. *Id.*

9. TOWN SUBJECTED TO DOUBLE DAMAGES FOR NEGLIGENCE in leaving a street in a dangerous condition can, in an action against another, by whose neglect the street was so left, recover single damages only, without including anything for the costs incurred by the town in the action against it. *Lowell* v. *B. & L. R. R. Co.*, 33.

10. CONTRIBUTIVE NEGLECT—PERSON GUILTY OF NEGLIGENCE, whereby a street is left in a dangerous condition, and the town subjected to an action and judgment for injuries suffered, can not avoid a recovery by the town on the ground that its officers and agents were also negligent in not replacing the barriers which such person had negligently failed to replace. *Id.*

See DEDICATION, 1, 2, 3; INSURANCE—FIRE, 3, 4; MARRIAGE AND DIVORCE, 8; POOR LAWS, 2–5; TAXATION.

MURDER.

See CRIMINAL LAW, 9–16.

NAVIGABLE RIVERS.

See EASEMENTS, 6, 7; WATERCOURSES.

NEGLIGENCE.

1. OWNER OF TEAM DEMISED FOR A TERM IS NOT LIABLE FOR INJURY done by it while being driven along the highway by the tenant, though the owner was in the vehicle at the time, if there was no positive and active concurrence in the injury on his part. *Hartfield* v. *Roper*, 273.

2. PARENTS PERMITTING A CHILD TWO YEARS OLD TO BE IN A PUBLIC HIGHWAY unattended, are guilty of such contributory negligence as will defeat an action in the child's name for an injury done to it by a traveler in the highway, where willful fault or gross negligence is not imputable to the defendant. *Id.*

See ATTORNEY AND CLIENT, 1, 2; BANKS AND BANKING, 3, 4, 5, 6; CORPORATIONS, 3; INFANCY, 3; MUNICIPAL CORPORATIONS, 9, 10; PARENT AND CHILD, 2; STATUTE OF LIMITATIONS, 3–5.

NEGOTIABLE INSTRUMENTS.

1. NEGOTIABLE PROMISSORY NOTE PAYABLE TO A PARTICULAR PERSON as cashier of a bank, vests in the person named, individually, the legal interest in the note so far as to enable him to sue for its collection in his own name. *Horah* v. *Long*, 378.

2. WORD "CASHIER" IN A NEGOTIABLE PROMISSORY NOTE following the name of the person designated as payee, is merely descriptive. *Id.*

3. RECOVERY UPON A NOTE PAYABLE TO "WILLIAM H. HORAH, CASHIER, or order," is not defeated by the expiration of the charter of the bank at which it was negotiable and payable. *Id.*

4. PROMISSORY NOTE, PAYABLE TO THE "PRESIDENT, DIRECTORS, AND COMPANY OF" a certain corporation, is payable to the corporation. *Newport Mech. Mfg. Co.* v. *Starbird*, 145.

him, are sufficient to charge the indorser, though he resides and receives his mail at another place. *Id.*

20. WANT OF PROTEST WILL NOT WARRANT THE INFERENCE in favor of the maker of a negotiable promissory note, that the transfer of the note from the payee was after it fell due. *Pearce v. Austin*, 523.

21. AGENT MAY SUE IN HIS OWN NAME upon negotiable paper indorsed in blank. *Id.*

22. DEPOSIT OF FUNDS IN BANK TO MEET THE PAYMENT of a bill of exchange payable there, amounts to a tender, and will prevent interest accruing on the bill; but a withdrawal of the fund will cause the bill to draw interest from that time. *Miller v. Bank of New Orleans*, 571.

23. TAKING NOTE FOR PRE-EXISTING DEBT does not discharge the debt, unless it is specially agreed that the note is taken in payment. *Estate of Davis*, 574.

24. WHERE THE SEPARATE NOTE OF ONE JOINT DEBTOR IS TAKEN, the onus is on the other debtors to show that it was taken with the intention of extinguishing the joint debt. *Id.*

25. NOTE SIGNED IN BLANK, and intrusted to another in the confidence that it will be filled with a particular amount, is valid in the hands of a *bona fide* holder, notwithstanding this confidence is violated by the insertion of a greater amount. *Herbert v. Huie*, 755.

26 HOLDER WHO HAS ADVANCED MONEY UPON A SIGNED BLANK, in good faith and without knowledge of any fact which would put him upon an inquiry which would disclose that the authority to insert an amount therein was restricted, may fill in the amount which he has advanced, and hold the signors responsible therefor. *Id.*

27. THAT THE CHARGE OF THE COURT DID NOT TOUCH UPON A MATERIAL POINT in the case is not error, if no request was made to charge thereon. *Id.*

28 ACKNOWLEDGMENT OF INDEBTEDNESS MADE TO A FORMER INDORSEE of a note by the maker thereof will inure to the benefit of the present holder. Such acknowledgment would be available though made to a stranger. *McRae v. Kennon*, 777.

29. SEALED INSTRUMENT, THOUGH IN FORM A PROMISSORY NOTE, is nevertheless a specialty, and no liability arises from an indorsement thereon. *Frevall v. Fitch*, 558.

See BANKS AND BANKING; CONFLICT OF LAWS, 1; CONTRIBUTION, 1; CORPORATIONS, 19, 20; EVIDENCE, 8; GUARDIAN AND WARD, 2, 3; PAYMENT, 1, 3; SURETYSHIP, 1–3.

NEWSPAPERS.

See INJUNCTIONS, 1; PARTNERSHIP, 7.

NEW TRIAL.

See DAMAGES, 5; PLEADING AND PRACTICE, 18.

NONSUIT.

See PLEADING AND PRACTICE, 20, 21.

NOTARIES.

See BANKS AND BANKING, 6; EVIDENCE, 7.

NOTICE.

See BONA FIDE PURCHASERS, 1; EASEMENTS, 4; PARTNERSHIP, 6, 7, 8; TRUSTS AND TRUSTEES, 2.

NOVATION.

See CONTRACTS, 6.

OFFICES AND OFFICERS.

1. OFFICER RECEIVING WRIT FOR SERVICE, IS NOT THEREBY MADE AGENT OF THE PLAINTIFF for collecting the demand; and if he receives payment from the debtor he holds it as agent of the latter until he actually pays it to the creditor. *Wainwright* v. *Webster*, 707.
2. OFFICER IS EXCUSED FROM CALLING ON DEBTOR TO CHOOSE APPRAISERS, where the record shows that such debtor resides without the state, and that there is no attorney. *Gilman* v. *Thompson*, 714.

PARENT AND CHILD.

1. SON MAY RECOVER FROM HIS FATHER'S ESTATE an amount equal to the value of personal services rendered in the life-time of his parent as over-seer upon his plantation, when it appears that there was an understand-ing that the services were not to be gratuitous, and there was no provis-ion made for the son in his father's will. *Price* v. *Price*, 608.
2. NEGLECT TO SUE UNTIL AFTER THE DEATH OF A PARENT, by a son who had rendered certain services in the life-time of the former, in expectation that provision would be made for him in the parent's will, by way of re-ward, is not such neglect as will bring the demand within the statute of limitations, so as to bar an action for its recovery. *Id.*

See GIFTS, 1; NEGLIGENCE, 2.

PARTITION.

See CO-TENANCY, 3, 9, 10, 11.

PARTNERSHIP.

1. POWER OF A COPARTNER TO BIND HIS ASSOCIATES extends to such matters only as, in the ordinary course of dealing, have reference to the business in which the firm is engaged. *Crosthwait* v. *Ross*, 613.
2. PRESUMPTION REGARDING ONE WHO DEALS WITH A PARTNER in a matter not within the scope of the partnership is, that such person dealt with the partner on the latter's private and individual account, notwith-standing the partnership name was used. *Id.*
3. PARTNERSHIP FOR THE PRACTICE OF MEDICINE does not authorize one of the partners to bind the firm by a note given in the name of the partner-ship for money borrowed for the private and individual use of the partner by whom the note was given. *Id.*
4. AUTHORITY UNDER SEAL IS NECESSARY TO ENABLE ONE COPARTNER TO BIND THE OTHER by a note under seal in the name of the partnership. *Turbeville* v. *Ryan*, 622.
5. PREVIOUS PAROL ASSENT OR SUBSEQUENT ADOPTION will not render the unauthorized bond of a copartner binding as to the other. *Id.*

6. NOTICE OF DISSOLUTION OF PARTNERSHIP IS SUFFICIENT as to strangers, if the notice is published in a newspaper printed in the place where the partnership business is carried on; but it is requisite to show that actual notice was conveyed to customers of the firm. *Watkinson v. Bank of Pa.*, 521.

7. CUSTOMER TAKING A NEWSPAPER IN WHICH NOTICE of the dissolution is printed is not affected with knowledge of such notice. *Id.*

8. COURT CAN NOT DETERMINE WHO IS A CUSTOMER, and can not reject proof of notice published in a newspaper because the party sought to be affected is a customer; the determination of that question is within the province of the jury. *Id.*

9. PARTNER INTRUSTED WITH THE SETTLEMENT OF A DISSOLVED PARTNERSHIP, may bind the partnership by borrowing money to meet its accruing liabilities, and by actually applying the money borrowed in discharge of such liabilities. *Estate of Davis*, 574.

10. MONEY BORROWED BY A PARTNER will be presumed to have been borrowed for the partnership, which will be liable therefor, if it has been applied to its use. The principle applies as well after a partnership has been dissolved as before. *Id.*

11. INTEREST IN PARTNERSHIP PROPERTY LIABLE TO THE SATISFACTION OF THE SEPARATE DEBTS of each partner, is the interest of each in the property as it stands after the partnership accounts have been settled, and the demands of the partnership creditors provided for. *Winston v. Ewing*, 768.

12. DEBTOR OF A PARTNERSHIP CAN NOT BE GARNISHED in an action brought to recover the separate debt of one of its members. *Id.*

See SLANDER, 2, 3.

PATENTS.

See GRANTS, 1; SURVEY, 1, 2.

PAUPERS.

See POOR LAWS, 1.

PAYMENT.

1. PAYMENT IN WORTHLESS OR BADLY DEPRECIATED BANK BILLS is not a valid payment. And a person receiving such bills, without fault or negligence on his part, in payment of a pre-existing debt, may treat the payment as void and resort to his original cause of action. *Gilman v. Peck*, 702.

2. ACTION ON BOOK ACCOUNT MAY BE MAINTAINED in such a case. *Id.*

3. PAYMENT BY BILLS OF BANK THAT HAD STOPPED PAYMENT, at the time it was made, does not extinguish the debt, although both the person who paid and the person who took the bills were then ignorant of the failure of the bank. *Wainwright v. Webster*, 707.

See NEGOTIABLE INSTRUMENTS, 23.

PERJURY.

See CRIMINAL LAW, 8.

PLEADING AND PRACTICE.

1. AFFIDAVIT FOR COMMENCING A SUIT BY WARRANT IN JUSTICE'S COURT that the defendants are non-residents, though sufficient to make the warrant regular in the first instance, is not conclusive, and if met by sufficient proof to the contrary, the justice should set aside the proceedings. *Shannon* v. *Comstock*, 262.

2. PLEA IN ABATEMENT THAT ONE OF SEVERAL DEFENDANTS IS A RESIDENT of the state where the suit has been commenced by warrant in a justice's court, is bad, because, though personal to only one of the defendants, it goes to the whole suit. *Id.*

3. GENERAL ISSUE PLEADED DOES NOT WAIVE THE PROPRIETY OF AN ARREST of the defendants in a suit in a justice's court, where the objection has been taken and overruled. *Id.*

4. REQUEST TO DELIVER UP PLAINTIFF'S WIFE, and refusal by the defendant, need not be alleged in the declaration in an action on the case for enticing away the wife. *Gilchrist* v. *Bale*, 469.

5. FORMER RECOVERY, RELEASE, OR SATISFACTION NEED NOT BE PLEADED, in an action on the case, but may be given in evidence under the general issue. *Id.*

6. MUTUAL PROMISES MUST BE CONCURRENT AND OBLIGATORY AT THE SAME TIME to render either binding. and must be so stated in the declaration. *Utica & S. R. R. Co.* v. *Brinckerhoff*, 220.

7. DECLARATION SETTING OUT NO PROMISE BY PLAINTIFF as consideration for the defendant's promise is fatally defective on demurrer; as where a declaration by a railroad company sets out a written agreement with the defendant, stipulating that if the company would locate their road in a certain place, the defendant, in consideration of benefits accruing to him therefrom, would pay the value of certain lands required for such location, and that afterwards, on the same day, in consideration of such agreement, and that the plaintiffs, at the defendant's request, promised to perform the agreement on their part, the defendant undertook and promised to perform it on his part, and alleges performance by the plaintiffs and non-performance by the defendant. *Id.*

8. EACH ONE OF SEVERAL DEFENDANTS IS ENTITLED to present his defense in the form of a special plea, and can not be compelled to adopt the plea of the other defendants. *Roberts* v. *Williams*, 549.

9. WHERE A DEMURRER TO A PETITION IS OVERRULED, BUT NOT WITHDRAWN, a withdrawal will be implied where the parties go before the jury on an issue made up under the direction of the court; the demurrer will not remain a confession of the facts in the petition. *Dickey* v. *Malechi*, 130.

10. GENERAL AND SWEEPING OBJECTIONS ARE INSUFFICIENT; the party must point out objections specifically, to authorize the appellate court to interfere. *Id.*

11. AMENDMENTS ARE NOT ALLOWED WHICH ARE INCONSISTENT with the nature of the pleadings, or change the cause of action. Particular allegations may be changed, and others added, provided the identity of the cause of action is preserved. *Stevenson* v. *Mudgett*, 155.

12. ERROR WILL NOT LIE for allowance of amendments. *Newman* v. *Foster*, 98.

POOR LAWS.

1. SERVICE BY A PAUPER UNDER CONTRACT FOR THE SPACE OF A YEAR gains a settlement, whether all performed under one contract or whether performed under several distinct contracts. *Heidleberg* v. *Lynn*, 566.

2. PRESUMPTION IS THAT A TOWN HAS TWO OVERSEERS OF THE POOR until the contrary appears, where the statute requires each town to elect two. *Downing* v. *Rugar*, 223.

3. ONE OF TWO OVERSEERS OF THE POOR MAY, BY CONSENT OF THE OTHER, ACT ALONE, as the agent or deputy of both, in applying for and executing a warrant, under the statute, against the property of one who has absconded, leaving his family chargeable to the town, and the consent of the other overseer will be presumed, if the warrant is regular on its face, and recites an application by both. *Id.*

4. PRESUMPTION THAT AN OVERSEER OF THE POOR ACTED REGULARLY, and with the consent of his colleague, in proceeding against the property of one who has absconded leaving his family chargeable to the town, must prevail, and justify his acts until the want of such consent is affirmatively shown by the testimony of the other overseer, he being a competent witness. *Id.*

5. RETURN IN THE NAME OF ONLY ONE OF THE OVERSEERS of the poor of a seizure of the property of one who has absconded, leaving his family chargeable to the town, is informal only, if jurisdiction has been regularly acquired, and not impeachable in an action against the overseer who made the seizure. *Id.*

POSSESSION.
See BONA FIDE PURCHASERS, 4.

POWER OF ATTORNEY.
See AGENCY, 8.

PRE-EMPTION.
See GRANTS, 2, 3.

PRESCRIPTION.
See EASEMENTS, 1–3, 6, 7; WATERCOURSES, 3, 4.

PRESUMPTIONS.
See ADVERSE POSSESSION, 2; AGENCY, 15; EVIDENCE, 9; NEGOTIABLE INSTRUMENTS, 6; PARTNERSHIP, 2, 10; POOR LAWS, 2, 4.

PRINCIPAL AND AGENT.
See AGENCY.

PRIVILEGED COMMUNICATIONS.
See SLANDER, 6–11.

PROBABLE CAUSE.
See LIBEL, 2, 3.

PROCESS.

1. **SHERIFF'S RETURN IS CONCLUSIVE** as to the facts therein set forth, upon the parties, as far as the particular action is concerned. Thus, if the return state that property replevied was surrendered to the defendant upon his giving bond, the latter may not show that less property was replevied from him than appeared from the return. *Knowles* v. *Lord*, 525.

2. **GIVING BOND CONDITIONED TO RETURN PROPERTY REPLEVIED** will preclude defendant from asserting that less property was replevied than is described in the bond. *Id.*

3. **VOID PROCESS MUST BE SET ASIDE OR VACATED** before trespass can be maintained against the party who caused it to issue, for acts done thereunder. *Day* v. *Sharp*, 509.

4. **PROCESS MERELY VOIDABLE AFFORDS JUSTIFICATION** for acts that have been done thereunder. *Id.*

5. **WHETHER WARRANT RUNNING "STATE OF MISSOURI, COUNTY OF COLE, ss."** would be valid or not, *quære*. *Hickman* v. *Griffin*, 124.

6. **ISSUANCE OF A WARRANT ON INCOMPETENT TESTIMONY** is merely erroneous, and does not render the proceeding void, as where the warrant is issued solely on the testimony of the wife of the person whose property is seized thereunder. *Downing* v. *Rugar*, 223.

PROCHEIN AMI.

See INFANCY, 9.

PROTEST.

See NEGOTIABLE INSTRUMENTS, 20.

PUBLIC LANDS.

See EXECUTIONS, 15; GRANTS.

QUANTUM MERUIT.

1. **ONE MAY RECOVER ON QUANTUM MERUIT FOR WORK DONE UNDER A CONTRACT,** although it was not performed according to such contract, if the work is beneficial to him for whom it has been done, and the parties can not, on a rescission of the contract, be placed *in statu quo*. *Gilman* v. *Hall*, 700.

2. **ONE WHO PROMISES TO PAY FOR WORK WHEN DONE, OR GIVE HIS NOTE** therefor payable in a year, is, on his refusal to give his note, immediately liable to an action for the amount due for such work. *Id.*

See INFANCY, 10.

RATIFICATION.

See INFANCY, 7.

RECORDS.

See EVIDENCE, 1, 2, 4-6.

REMAINDERS.

CONVEYANCE TO GRANTEE FOR LIFE WITH REMAINDER to such persons as he might by will appoint, or, in default of any appointment, to the heirs of the grantee, vests the title in the heirs of the latter, as against a purchaser at a sale of the premises under a foreclosure of a mortgage, executed by the grantee during his life-time. *Bentham* v. *Smith*, 599.

See TROVER, 1, 2; WILLS, 6.

RENT.
See LANDLORD AND TENANT, 2–4, 8.

REPEAL.
See STATUTES, 1.

REPLEVIN.
See BAILMENTS.

RESCISSION OF CONTRACTS.
See SALES, 4, 5.

RETURN.
See EXECUTIONS, 9, 10, 17.

SALES.

1. CONTRACT TO DELIVER WHEAT TO A MILLER AND TO TAKE FLOUR THERE-FOR of a specified quality, at the rate of a certain number of pounds for so many bushels of the wheat, is a sale and not a bailment, where there is no agreement to manufacture the flour from the wheat delivered; and one purchasing from the miller flour made from the wheat so delivered, is not liable in replevin to the party delivering such wheat. *Smith* v. *Clark*, 213.

2. VENDOR OF GOODS TO BE PAID FOR BY NOTE PAYABLE IN FUTURO, if such note is not given, may sue immediately for a breach of the special agreement and recover the value of the goods as damages, though he can not sue for goods sold and delivered until the term of credit expires. *Hanna* v. *Mills*, 216.

3. EVIDENCE OF A SALE OF GOODS TO BE PAID FOR BY A "SATISFACTORY NOTE" will not support a declaration on a sale for the purchaser's note "to the order of, and indorsed by, a person who should be satisfactory" to the vendor, there being no evidence of a usage attaching such meaning to the words used at the sale. *Id.*

4. To RESCIND A CONTRACT OF PURCHASE, the vendee must return the property, unless it be entirely worthless to both parties. *Perley* v. *Balch*, 56.

5. PARTIAL FAILURE OF CONSIDERATION, or breach of warranty, or deception in the quality or value of goods sold, may be shown in mitigation of damages, in an action to recover the purchase price. *Id.*

6. CONTRACT FOR THE TRANSFER OF PROPERTY, by the terms of which the purchaser advances a part of the purchase money, and the seller reserves the right to abrogate the contract by returning the money so advanced, with interest, at a particular time; and if not so abrogated, the contract to be executed by the purchaser paying the residue of the purchase money, and the seller surrendering the possession of the property, is a conditional sale and not a mortgage. TUCKER, P., and BROOKE, J., dissenting. *Moss* v. *Green*, 731.

7. RETENTION OF POSSESSION BY A VENDOR WILL NOT CHANGE the nature of a conditional sale, so as to render the same a mortgage. *Id.*

8. WHERE A PLAINTIFF IN A SUIT TO REDEEM A MORTGAGE FAILS by reason of the court holding the transaction sued on to be a conditional sale, equity, to prevent further litigation, will order a decree in favor of the plaintiff for the balance of the purchase price, with interest, but without costs. *Id.*

9. ONE WHO SELLS PERSONAL PROPERTY THAT HE DOES NOT OWN, is liable in assumpsit on his warranty. *Strong* v. *Barnes,* 684.

See FRAUD, 3; FRAUDULENT CONVEYANCES; WARRANTY.

SCHOOLS.

1. BETWEEN SCHOOLMASTER IN PUBLIC SCHOOL AND THE PARENTS OF PUPILS, there is no privity of contract. *Spear* v. *Cummings,* 53.

2. SCHOOLMASTER IN PUBLIC SCHOOL IS NOT RESPONSIBLE to a parent for refusing to receive and instruct his child. *Id.*

SET-OFF.

1. CLAIM AGAINST INSOLVENT ESTATE OF DECEDENT MAY BE OFFSET in chancery against one in favor of the estate, although the claimant, owing to an agreement of the administrator to allow it, neglected to present his claim to the commissioners on the estate. *Nims* v. *Rood,* 669.

2. UNLIQUIDATED CLAIM CAN NOT BE OFFSET IN CHANCERY; but a decree may be deferred to enable the claimant to have it liquidated. *Id.*

SHERIFFS.

1. SHERIFF HOLDING INQUEST TO TRY A CLAIM TO PROPERTY has authority to exclude illegal testimony. *Obart* v. *Letson,* 182.

2. RECEIPT GIVEN BY THE DEFENDANT IN ATTACHMENT TO THE CLAIMANT for the purchase price of the property is competent, and *prima facie* evidence that the property was sold to the claimant. *Id.*

See EXECUTIONS, 1, 2, 10–13; PROCESS, 1; SURETYSHIP, 4–7.

SLANDER.

1. WORDS IMPUGNING THE SOLVENCY OF A PERSON and affecting his credit are actionable, though not spoken in relation to his particular trade or business. *Davis* v. *Ruff,* 584.

2. SLANDERING A PARTNER BY DECLARING HIM TO BE INSOLVENT, is no slander of the firm of which he is a member. *Id.*

3. COPARTNERS NEED NOT JOIN IN AN ACTION OF SLANDER for words affecting the mercantile character, credit, or solvency of one of them. *Id.*

4. MEASURE OF DAMAGES IN AN ACTION OF SLANDER is a question for the jury to consider relatively with that of malice. *Id.*

5. VERDICT IN AN ACTION OF SLANDER WILL NOT BE DISTURBED, because the damages awarded were in excess of what the court in its discretion might have thought proper. *Id.*

6. WORDS SPOKEN BY COUNSEL OR BY A PARTY CONDUCTING HIS OWN CASE, in the course of judicial proceedings, if relevant and pertinent to the question before the court, are privileged, and not subject to an action for

slander, however false, malicious, and injurious they may be. *Hastings* v. *Lusk*, 330.

7. WORDS NOT RELEVANT OR PERTINENT TO THE MATTER IN QUESTION, spoken in the course of judicial proceedings, are nevertheless privileged if spoken in good faith, under a belief that they were relevant and proper, and without actual malice, of which the jury are to judge. *Id.*

8. PRIVILEGE WILL NOT AVAIL ON A MOTION IN ARREST OF JUDGMENT against the defendant in slander, where there are special pleas that the words were used in the course of judicial proceedings in conducting the defendant's own cause, were relevant and pertinent, and were not spoken maliciously, and those facts being put in issue are all found against the defendant. *Id.*

9. NEITHER PARTIES NOR THEIR COUNSEL ARE LIABLE TO AN ACTION OF SLANDER for words spoken *bona fide* in the ordinary course of judicial proceedings; but a party claiming this protection must have spoken the words in the reasonable and necessary defense or pursuit of his rights, and words spoken by counsel, to be privileged, must have been spoken in the discharge of his duty to his client, and must have been pertinent to the matter in question. *Mower* v. *Watson*, 704.

10. PRIVILEGE OF COUNSEL AND CLIENT IN THIS RESPECT ARE CO-EXTENSIVE. *Id.*

11. WORDS "THAT IS A LIE" SPOKEN TO A WITNESS WHILE TESTIFYING to a material point in a cause then on trial, are actionable, if spoken by a party maliciously, and with intent to defame such witness. *Id.*

SPECIFIC PERFORMANCE.

1. SPECIFIC PERFORMANCE WILL NOT BE DECREED when the party applying has omitted to execute his part of the agreement by the time appointed, unless he can satisfactorily account for such omission, or the other party has expressly or impliedly assented to such delay. *Lewis* v. *Woods*, 110.

2. PARTY LOSES RIGHT TO SPECIFIC PERFORMANCE, WHEN.—Where a party, by the terms of the sale, agrees to pay a certain amount in cash and give his promissory notes for the balance, and pays but a portion of the cash, and refuses for two years to pay the balance or to execute the notes, he is guilty of such negligence that he will not be decreed a specific performance. *Id.*

3. SPECIFIC PERFORMANCE OF CONTRACT WHICH ORIGINATED IN BREACH OF FAITH will not be decreed. *Patterson* v. *Martz*, 474.

4. UNEXPLAINED DELAY OF VENDOR FOR SEVEN YEARS, and great rise in value of the lands forming the subject-matter of the contract, constitute an insuperable objection to the granting of a decree for the specific performance of a contract for the sale of lands. *Id.*

5. FACTS SHOWING ABANDONMENT OF A CONTRACT BY THE PLAINTIFF furnish a decisive answer to his prayer for a specific performance thereof. *Id.*

STATUTE OF FRAUDS.

MEMORANDUM OF CONTRACT FOR SALE OF AN INTEREST IN LANDS which consisted merely of an invoice commencing with the words, "Invoice of articles purchased by S. Pipkin and R. Oliver of Wm. R. James, this twenty-ninth August, 1836," and, after specifying numerous articles, concluding with the words, "One ice-house and lot, one hundred and forty dollars," is not a sufficient memorandum, within the statute of frauds, to bind the purchaser in respect to the real property, and he may recover the purchase money paid thereon. *Pipkin* v. *James*, 652.

STATUTE OF LIMITATIONS.

1. ENTRY ON LAND AVOIDS OPERATION OF STATUTE OF LIMITATIONS as effectually as an action, but to have that effect the entry must bear on its face an unequivocal intent to resume the actual possession. *Altemas* v. *Campbell*, 494.

2. RUNNING OF THE STATUTE OF LIMITATIONS IS NOT SUSPENDED by a disability which occurs subsequently to the time that the right of action accrued. *Bensell* v. *Chancellor*, 561.

3. STATUTE OF LIMITATIONS OPERATES UPON A CAUSE OF ACTION against an attorney at law for negligence in not procuring judgment to be entered, and execution issued, in an action, from the time when, through the failing circumstances of the debtor rendering a loss probable and calling for diligent action, the actual neglect in forbearing to cause judgment to be entered and execution issued occurred. *Thomas* v. *Ervin*, 586.

4. ACTION AGAINST AN ATTORNEY AT LAW FOR NEGLIGENCE is barred by statute of limitations, although commenced as soon as plaintiff ascertained definitely that the consequence of the neglect was a loss of his debt, if the negligence itself, which was the incidental cause of the loss, had not happened within four years previous. *Id.*

5. DAMAGES DEVELOPING SUBSEQUENTLY TO THE ACT OF NEGLIGENCE complained of, do not constitute a new cause of action. *Id.*

See CONTRIBUTION, 1; MORTGAGES, 1, 2; PARENT AND CHILD, 2.

STATUTES.

1. REPEAL OF STATUTE WHILE PROSECUTION UNDER IT IS PENDING, puts an end to such prosecution, unless there is a saving clause in the repealing act. And this is the case, not only where the latter act expressly repeals the former, but also where its provisions are inconsistent with the former, although there be no annulling words or repealing clause therein. *Abbott* v. *Commonwealth*, 492.

2. CONSTRUCTION OF COMMON LAW TERMS IN STATUTES.—Where terms used in the common law are contained in a statute or the constitution, without an explanation of the sense in which they are employed, they should receive that construction which has been affixed to them by the common law. *Carpenter* v. *State*, 116.

3. SPECIAL WORDS ARE NOT ESSENTIAL TO REVIVE A STATUTE providing for the construction of a railroad, which has expired because the work has not been commenced within the time therein limited, but a statute passed after such expiration extending the time, will be a sufficient revivor. *Crocker* v. *Crane*, 228.

See CORPORATIONS, 11; WATERCOURSES, 5.

STREETS.

See MUNICIPAL CORPORATIONS, 6, 9, 10.

SUBROGATION.

See SURETYSHIP, 10, 17.

SURETYSHIP.

1. SURETY IS UNDER NO IMPLIED CONTRACT TO INDEMNIFY THE DRAWER upon the latter's paying the bill for the drawer's accommodation, having notice of the suretyship, a surety being bound only by his express contract. *Griffith* v. *Reed*, 267.

2. SURETY'S UNDERTAKING IS THAT THE DRAWEE WILL ACCEPT and pay the bill; and when the bill is paid by the drawee, the surety's contract is at an end. He has no contract with the drawee. *Id.*

3. ADDING THE WORD "SURETY" TO THE SIGNATURE of one signing a bill with the drawer, gives notice to all to whose hands it may come that the person so signing is liable only as a surety. *Id.*

4. PLAINTIFF IN SUIT AGAINST SURETIES OF SHERIFF MUST SHOW DAMAGE sustained by him through the sheriff's neglect or failure in the performance of his duty. *Commonwealth* v. *McCoy*, 445.

5. SHERIFF, IN EXECUTING FIERI FACIAS, MUST BE GOVERNED BY THE SUM INDORSED on the back of the writ, and not by that contained in the body of the writ. The indorsement on the writ is the official act of the prothonotary, and is presumed to be right until the contrary is shown. *Id.*

6. FEES OF OFFICERS ARE NOT RECOVERABLE in action against sureties of sheriff to recover money collected by him on an execution, except where such fees were previously advanced by the plaintiff. *Id.*

7. SHERIFF IS PRESUMED TO HAVE COLLECTED AMOUNT OF FIERI FACIAS, which he has held in his hands for several years without returning, and the burden of proving that he did not collect it, is upon him or his sureties. *Id.*

8. TO RECOVER AGAINST SURETIES OF CONSTABLE, it is sufficient to show that he was insolvent in fact when the action was commenced. *Evans* v. *Commonwealth*, 477.

9. WHERE THERE IS A SURETY FOR A DEBT SECURED BY MORTGAGE, the creditor has an election, of which he can not be deprived, whether he shall proceed in equity upon his mortgage, or at law against the debtor or surety. *Cullum* v. *Gaines*, 757.

10. SURETY WHO HAS PAID HIS PRINCIPAL'S DEBT IS ENTITLED TO ALL SECURITIES held or acquired by the creditor. *Id.*

11. CREDITOR WHO PARTS WITH OR RENDERS UNAVAILABLE SECURITIES or a fund which he would be entitled to apply in discharge of his debt, as a general rule exonerates a surety for the debt to the extent of the value of such securities or fund. *Id.*

12. CREDITOR WHO HAS DISABLED HIMSELF from surrendering to the surety the means of reimbursement which he once possessed, is not to be injured thereby, if he acted without a knowledge of the rights of other persons and with good faith and just intentions. *Id.*

13. PURCHASE BY MORTGAGEE OF THE EQUITY OF REDEMPTION DOES NOT EXTINGUISH the mortgage so as to release a surety for the mortgage debt, where the creditor disavows that it was his intention to extinguish the mortgage, and avows that he will apply the rents and profits of the land in extinguishment of the mortgage debt. *Id.*

14. SURETY OF A PURCHASER OF LAND AT A SALE on a specified credit under a decree in chancery, the title being retained until the purchase money should be paid, may charge the land for the payment of the sum for which he is liable, in the hands of an assignee of the purchaser who took it in good faith, without notice; nor is the title of the assignee benefited by the fact that he had afterwards bought in the same land at a sale under execution against his assignor, paying a valuable consideration therefor. *Polk* v. *Gallant*, 410.

15. ASSIGNOR OF LAND AFFECTED BY A TRUST IS NOT A NECESSARY PARTY to a bill against his assignee in an action by a surety of the former to charge lands in the hands of the latter for the payment of the purchase price for which the surety was bound, when the bill sets out that the defendant is the assignee of the entire interest in the land. *Id.*

16. ACTUAL PAYMENT NEED NOT BE MADE by a surety to enable him to sustain an action. *Id.*

17. SURETY ON AN APPEAL BOND WHO IS COMPELLED TO PAY the judgment is entitled to be subrogated to all the rights of the judgment creditor. *McClung* v. *Beirne*, 739.

18. SURETY ON AN APPEAL BOND WHO HAS BEEN COMPELLED TO PAY THE JUDGMENT can recover interest on the amount of the original judgment, but not on the damages and costs of appeal. *Id.*

See EXECUTORS AND ADMINISTRATORS, 6; JUDGMENTS, 2.

SURVEY.

1. TO BRING PLAT WITHIN RULE OF CLOSED SURVEY, the line of division must be marked on the ground. *Newman* v. *Foster*, 98.

2. A MAP AND CERTIFICATE OF SURVEY ARE NOT CONCLUSIVE EVIDENCE *per se* that the lines were run as marked on them, but they are open to explanation by the surveyor. *Id.*

See BOUNDARIES, 2; GRANTS.

TAVERNS.

See INNS, 1, 2.

TAXATION.

1. MUNICIPAL CORPORATION, IF AUTHORIZED BY CHARTER, MAY IMPOSE A TAX on the privilege of selling ardent spirits, for the purposes of revenue. *Mayor* v. *Beasly*, 646.

2. TAXATION OF SALE OF LIQUORS BY MUNICIPALITY is valid against an individual engaged therein under a license from the state. *Id.*

3. TAX IMPOSED BY MUNICIPALITY IS NOT VOID as oppressive and unreasonable, unless it be shown that the amount imposed is comparatively in excess of that which the necessities or interests of the corporation require. *Id.*

4. PLEA WHICH AVERS THAT A TAX IS OPPRESSIVE AND UNEQUAL is insufficient, unless it set forth other facts, from which it may be determined that the tax is oppressive, and therefore void. *Id.*

TENANTS IN COMMON.

See CO-TENANCY.

TENDER.

See DAMAGES, 2; NEGOTIABLE INSTRUMENTS, 22.

TRESPASS.

1. TRESPASS QUARE CLAUSUM FREGIT CAN NOT BE SUSTAINED against a corporation aggregate. *Foote* v. *Cincinnati*, 420.

2. GENERAL DEMURRER IN AN ACTION OF TRESPASS *vi et armis* must, if sustained, inure to the advantage of all the defendants, when the act complained of could not, either in point of fact or of law, be joint. *Id.*

3. TREBLE DAMAGES CAN BE RECOVERED FOR TRESPASS ON TIMBER LANDS, only when the act was done knowingly and willfully. If done by mistake or accident, recovery can be had only for the value of the injury actually sustained. *Batchelder* v. *Kelly*, 174.

4. TREBLE DAMAGES CAN NOT BE RECOVERED FOR HAULING AWAY TIMBER cut by mistake on another's land, even if done after the mistake was discovered. *Id.*

5. EVIDENCE IN AN ACTION FOR TRESPASS ON TIMBER LANDS, under the statute, is regulated by the rules of the common law, and is not confined to the parties to the action; such latter evidence is merely cumulative. *Id.*

6. DEFECTIVE INCLOSURE.—Where a party neglects to keep a sufficient inclosure, under the act of 1822, of Mississippi, he has no authority to take the redress into his own hands for any injury he may have sustained in consequence of such insufficiency. *Dickson* v. *Parker*, 78.

7. RIGHT TO DISTRAIN CATTLE DAMAGE FEASANT does not exist unless the owner of the cattle would be liable to an action. *Id.*

8. TRESPASS IS THE PROPER REMEDY where there is no right to distrain and the seizure is illegal.

9. ABUSE OF LEGAL AUTHORITY OR LICENSE by one who at first acted with propriety under it, makes him a trespasser *ab initio*. *Id.*

10. LIABILITY FOR DISTRAINING, WHEN EXISTS.—Where a mule got into the defendant's grounds, in consequence of the insufficiency of his fence, and was destroyed by his act, he is liable to the owner for its value. *Id.*

11. MEASURE OF DAMAGES IN SUCH A CASE is regulated by the jury. *Id.*

12. TRESPASS LIES AGAINST THE OWNER OF CATTLE which escape into the lands of another, even though against the will of such owner. *Forsythe* v. *Price*, 465.

13. COVENANT NOT TO SUE ONE OF TWO JOINT TRESPASSERS, does not operate as a discharge of the other. *Snow* v. *Chandler*, 140.

14. NOTHING SHORT OF PAYMENT OF DAMAGES by one joint trespasser, or a release under seal, can operate to discharge the other. *Id.*

15. ANY PARTIAL PAYMENT MADE BY A CO-TRESPASSER in satisfaction of the damages sustained by reason of the joint trespass, inures to the benefit of the other, and, in an action against the latter, must be considered by the jury in determining the amount of their verdict. *Id.*

16. ONE MAY LAWFULLY TURN INTO THE HIGHWAY HORSES FOUND TRESPASSING in his inclosure, although their getting into the inclosure was due to the insufficiency of a division fence which he and the owner of the horses were equally bound to maintain. *Humphrey* v. *Douglass*, 668.

17. MOTIVE WITH WHICH A LAWFUL ACT IS DONE can never alter the character of such act. *Id.*

2. OWNER OF DAM ON STREAM IS LIABLE FOR DAMAGES CAUSED THEREBY to private property on such stream, by the ordinary and expected floods of the season, but not for those occasioned by extraordinary and unexpected floods. This principle applied in the case of a stream made navigable by law. *Bell* v. *McClintock*, 507.

3. PRESCRIPTION—KEEPING UP A DAM AND FLOWING THE LANDS of another for twenty years, without paying damages or being questioned, is evidence of the right to maintain such dam and flow such lands, and a bar to any action for damages in so doing. This is true under the statutes of this state as well as at common law. *Williams* v. *Nelson*, 45.

4. ABANDONMENT OF A PRESCRIPTIVE RIGHT to maintain a dam and flood lands is not presumed from nine years non-user. *Id.*

5. ACT AUTHORIZING PRIVATE PERSON TO STOP UP A NAVIGABLE CREEK upon condition that he cut a canal upon his own property at his own expense in lieu thereof, is a private act for the individual benefit of such person. *Sinnickson* v. *Johnson*, 184.

6. IF PRIVATE OWNER ERECTS DAM IN PURSUANCE OF SUCH ACT, and thereby injures the land lying back, he is responsible to the owners in damages. *Id.*

See EASEMENTS, 6, 7.

WIFE'S EQUITY.

See EQUITY, 11-14.

WILLS.

1. WILL DESTROYED BEFORE OR AFTER DEATH OF TESTATOR, without his knowledge, does not cease to be his will. *Dickey* v. *Malechi*, 130.

2. ONE WITNESS IS SUFFICIENT to prove the contents of a lost will. *Id.*

3. WHOLE OF LOST WILL NEED NOT BE PROVED; so much as is proved will be admitted to probate. *Id.*

4. TITLE OF DEVISEE UNDER FOREIGN WILL takes effect at the death of testator, and no subsequent registry in this state is necessary to perfect it. *Hall* v. *Ashby*, 424.

5. WHERE TESTATOR DEVISES LANDS TO HIS DAUGHTER IN FEE TAIL, directing that, in case she shall die without issue, his executors shall sell the lands and divide the proceeds among other legatees named in the will, and the daughter dies, leaving a husband who is entitled to a life estate therein, as tenant by the curtesy, such lands can not be sold by the executors until after the determination of the life estate of the husband. *Hay* v. *Mayer*, 453.

6. DEVISEES TAKE VESTED REMAINDERS IN FEE, WHEN.—Where a testator, after empowering his executors to sell his realty, etc., gives the rents and profits of such as shall remain unsold from time to time, together with the income of certain investments, to his wife for life, and devises the principal of such investments and the residue of his realty and personalty after his wife's death to the children of a certain brother, who should then be living, and to the lawful issue of those who should be deceased, *per stirpes*, the wife, at the testator's death, takes a life estate in the realty, and the children of the testator's brother then in being take vested remainders in fee as tenants in fee, subject to open and let in after-born children, and also subject to be defeated by a sale by the executors, and

are necessary parties to a suit to foreclose a mortgage given by the testator on such realty. *Nodine v. Greenfield*, 363.

1. POWER OF APPOINTMENT BY WILL given to the grantee in a conveyance for life, is not deemed to be executed by a mortgage by the latter to creditors, followed by foreclosure and sale. *Bentham v. Smith*, 599.

8. POWER OF DISPOSITION BY WILL can not be executed by a conveyance of the premises by deed. *Id.*

See EQUITY, 4, 5; EVIDENCE, 11; INTOXICATION.

WITNESSES.

1. WHETHER A WITNESS MAY BE CONTRADICTED without having been first given an opportunity to explain the evidence which is relied on for that purpose, is a question which is left to the discretion of the trial courts. *Sharp v. Emmet*, 554.

2. DELIVERY OF A RELEASE BY A WITNESS TO AN ATTORNEY in a cause, is a delivery to the party who employed him. *Stevenson v. Mudgett*, 155.

3. RELEASE OF A WITNESS WHO APPEARS TO BE THE REAL PLAINTIFF of all interest in the suit, which he delivers to the attorney of the plaintiff of record, is a delivery to himself, and consequently unavailing. *Id.*

4. WITNESS WHO APPEARS TO BE INTERESTED IN A SUIT can not be made competent by his own testimony. *Id.*

5. EVIDENCE THAT AN ATTORNEY WAS EMPLOYED BY THE PLAINTIFF OF RECORD, and not by a witness, may be given after verdict. *Id.*

See CRIMINAL LAW, 24; EASEMENTS, 8; PLEADING AND PRACTICE, 18.

WRIT OF ERROR.

See PLEADING AND PRACTICE, 23-28.

---

84 AM. DEC. 83, LOWELL v. BOSTON & L. R. CORP. 23 PICK. 24.

Liability of corporations.

Cited in Hooker v. New Haven & N. Co. 15 Conn. 312, holding corporations bound to use their rights so as not to injure individuals.

Cited in reference notes in 94 A. D. 106, on duty of corporation so to exercise its rights as not to injure another; 72 A. D. 363, on corporation's exercising rights so as not to injure others.

Obstructions in highway.

Cited in Snow v. Housatonic R. Co. 8 Allen, 441, 85 A. D. 720, holding every one who creates obstruction to travel in public way, guilty of creating nuisance; Wickwire v. Angola, 4 Ind. App. 253, 30 N. E. 917, holding one who places dangerous obstruction in street liable for damages for creating nuisance.

Cited in reference note in 78 A. S. R. 840, on liability for defective streets and sidewalks.

— Railroads on or across highway.

Cited in Matthews v. Missouri P. R. Co. 26 Mo. App. 75, holding that railroad which obstructs public highway must protect travelers from danger; New York C. & H. R. R. Co. v. Cambridge, 186 Mass. 249, 71 N. E. 557, holding that railroad company has right to make excavations in highway to build road; Cooke v. Boston & L. R. Corp. 133 Mass. 185, holding railroad company bound to construct road so as not to impede highway; Lackland v. North Missouri R. Co. 31 Mo. 180, on power of legislature to authorize building of railroad on street.

Liability of lot owner for nonrepair of street.

Cited in reference note in 20 A. S. R. 770, on liability of lot owner for non-repair of streets.

Duty of municipal corporations as to safety of streets.

Cited in Detroit v. Corey, 9 Mich. 165, 80 A. D. 78, holding that city cannot delegate liability to keep streets in safe condition; Wolf v. American Tract.

Soc. (Wolf v. Downey), 164 N. Y. 30, 51 L.R.A. 241, 58 N. E. 31 (dissent opinion), on duty of municipality to keep its streets in safe condition.

Cited in reference note in 61 A. D. 705, on municipal liability for defec streets.

Who are principals in crime.

Cited in reference notes in 11 A. S. R. 673, on who are principals in mission of crime; 100 A. D. 297, on criminal responsibility of persons en in commission of unlawful act for consequences flowing from it.

Liability for acts of independent contractor.

Cited in Knoop v. Alter, 47 La. Ann. 570, 17 So. 139, holding owner of wa being repaired by insurance company, liable for injuries caused by its fal Davie v. Levy, 39 La. Ann. 551, 4 A. S. R. 225, 2 So. 395, holding one w permits establishment of public nuisance upon property under his control lia for injuries; Wilbur v. White, 98 Me. 191, 56 Atl. 657, holding that o discharging public duty cannot, by subletting work, be freed from duty protect public; Clark v. Fry, 8 Ohio St. 358, 72 A. D. 590, holding employ who has no control over work not liable for negligence of those performing i Loth v. Columbia Theater Co. 197 Mo. 328, 94 S. W. 847, holding contrac and owner equally liable, when injuries result from work contractor agrees a is authorized to do; Robbins v. Chicago, 4 Wall. 657, 18 L. ed. 427; St. Pa Water Co. v. Ware, 16 Wall. 566, 21 L. ed. 485; Whitney v. Clifford, 46 W 138, 32 A. R. 703, 19 N. W. 835,—holding employer responsible for thing do by contractor which he is employed to do; Engel v. Eureka Club, 137 N. 100, 33 A. S. R. 692, 32 N. E. 1052, holding owner not liable for injuries ca by negligence of independent contractor.

Cited in notes in 14 L.R.A. 832, on employer's liability for breach of imposed duty by independent contractor; 37 L.R.A. 81, on responsibility master for injuries resulting from works of construction by independent co tractor; 9 L.R.A. 604, on railroad's liability for independent contractor's neg gence; 19 E. R. C. 186, on liability of owner for negligence of independe contractor; 65 L.R.A. 628, 629, on distinction between real and personal proper in reference to employer's liability for torts of independent contractors.

Distinguished in Hilliard v. Richardson, 3 Gray, 349, 63 A. D. 743, holdi employer not liable for negligence of carpenter employed to make alteratio whereby third party was injured; Carter v. Berlin Mills Co. 58 N. H. 52, A. R. 572, holding employer not liable for negligence of independent contrac over whom he has no control; Wright v. Holbrook, 52 N. H. 120, 13 A. R. 1 holding committee appointed by town to clear land not liable for negligen of subcontractor in burning brush; Omaha Bridge & Terminal R. Co. Hargadine, 5 Neb. (Unof.) 418, 98 N. W. 1071, holding railroad compan not liable to servant of contractor injured while using unsafe tool.

Disapproved in Morgan v. Bowman, 22 Mo. 538, on liability of owner f injuries caused by contractor; Meany v. Abbott, 6 Phila. 256, 24 Phila. Le Int. 389, holding landlord not liable for damages from defective work plumber.

—For acts of servants of independent contractor.

Distinguished in Clark v. Hannibal & St. J. R. Co. 36 Mo. 202, holding rai road not liable for injuries occasioned by trespasses of servants of contracto building road; Eaton v. European & N. A. R. Co. 59 Me. 520, 8 A. R. 43

holding railroad company not liable for injuries caused by negligence of co tractor's employees.

Disapproved in Wright v. Holbrook, 52 N. H. 120, 13 A. R. 12, holdin principal contractor not liable for negligent conduct of servants of subcontracto employed in prosecution of work.

— Liability of municipality.

Cited in Williams v. Tripp, 11 R. I. 447, holding that city cannot, by contrac for own benefit, relax statutory obligation of keeping streets safe; Wille v. Portsmouth, 35 N. H. 303, holding towns liable for defects in roads whe erected or made by others.

Distinguished in Barry v. St. Louis, 17 Mo. 121, holding municipal corpora tions not liable for damages occasioned by negligence of contractors.

— Acts in construction or operation of railroad.

Cited in Smith v. Atchison, T. & S. F. R. Co. 25 Kan. 738, holding tha railroad company cannot escape performance of duty under charter or gener laws by surrendering control of road to others; Stone v. Cheshire R. Corp. 1 N. H. 427, 51 A. D. 192, holding railroad corporation liable for injuries cause by negligent blasting by contractors; McCafferty v. Spuyten Duyvil & P. M. R Co. 61 N. Y. 178, 19 A. R.,267 (dissenting opinion), on liability of railroad for in juries caused by negligence of its contractor.

— Unguarded excavations or crossing in streets.

Cited in Wilson v. Wheeling, 19 W. Va. 323, 42 A. R. 780, holding municip corporation liable for injuries caused by excavation negligently left unguard by sewer contractor; Chicago, K. & W. R. Co. v. Hutchinson, 45 Kan. 186, 2 Pac. 576, holding railroad liable where duty of erecting cattle guards was lef to contractor; Brown v. Cambridge, 3 Allen, 474, holding payment by corporatio for injuries caused by trench in street, bar to action against city.

Cited in reference note in 86 A. D. 346, on liability of contractor for leavin street excavations unguarded.

Disapproved in Independence v. Slack, 134 Mo. 66, 34 S. W. 1094, holdin that owner owed no duty to public to safeguard obstructions placed in stree by his independent contractor.

Liability for acts of servants.

Cited in Boswell v. Laird, 8 Cal. 469, 68 A. D. 345, on liability of master fo negligence of servant; Perkins v. Eastern R. Co. 29 Me. 307, 50 A. D. 589, holdin railroad company liable for all damages arising through negligence of thei agents.

Cited in reference notes in 72 A. D. 479, on liability of railroad for inju caused by negligence of its servants; 63 A. D. 589, on railroad's liability fo injury by negligence of servants; 67 A. D. 685, on liability of corporation fo agent's fraud or tort; 91 A. D. 428, on master's liability for servant's negligenc or misconduct within scope of employment; 49 A. D. 421, on liability of cor poration for malfeasance or neglect of agent within scope of employment.

Distinguished in Gilbert v. Beach, 4 Duer, 423; McGuire v. Grant, 25 N. J L. 356, 67 A. D. 49,—holding responsibility of master for tortious acts o servants measured by control over them.

Liability of railroad for obstructing street or the like.

Cited in Philadelphia & H. de G. Steam Towboat Co. v. Philadelphia, W. & B

R. Co. Fed. Cas. No. 11,085, holding railroad company liable for damages caus
by negligence of its engineers in leaving pile in stream.

— Unguarded excavations.

Cited in Veazie v. Penobscot R. Co. 49 Me. 119, holding railroad compa
liable for injuries arising from neglect to guard road being excavated.

Contribution between joint tort feasors.

Cited in Carkins v. Anderson, 21 Neb. 364, 32 N. W. 155; Bateman v. Robi
son, 12 Neb. 508, 11 N. W. 736; Central Branch Union P. R. Co. v. Weste
U. Teleg. Co. 1 McCrary, 551, 3 Fed. 417,—on right of courts to administ
justice where acts of parties are *mala prohibita;* Paige v. Hieronymus, 1
Ill. 637, 54 N. E. 583, holding that equity will aid more innocent of parties
illegal contract when they are not *in pari delicto;* Chicago & N. W. R.
v. Dunn, 59 Iowa, 619, 13 N. W. 722, allowing contribution between joint wron
doers not *in pari delicto;* Johnson v. Torpy, 35 Neb. 604, 37 A. S. R. 447,
N. W. 575, holding joint tort feasor who knew act committed was wrong n
entitled to contribution; Tracy v. Talmage, 14 N. Y. 162, 67 A. D. 132, holdi
that courts may afford relief to less guilty party where transaction is n
malum in se; Gates v. Pennsylvania R. Co. 150 Pa. 50, 16 L.R.A. 554, 24 A
638, 30 W. N. C. 329, 23 Pittsb. L. J. N. S. 30, holding that injured party m
elect to sue wrongdoer ultimately liable; Bond v. Montgomery, 56 Ark. 5(
35 A. S. R. 119, 20 S. W. 525, holding that assumpsit will lie to recover mon
advanced upon contract prohibited by statute; Simpson v. Mercer, 144 Ma
413, 11 N. E. 720, on actual participation in wrong as bar to contribution.

Cited in notes in 12 A. S. R. 560; 1 L.R.A. 313,—on contribution betw
wrongdoers; 73 A. D. 148, on contribution between cotrespassers.

Distinguished in Cincinnati R. Co. v. Louisville & R. Co. 97 Ky. 128, 30 S.
408, holding that contribution will lie between tort feasors who are actu
participants in wrong.

Defense of pari delicto.

Cited in Congress & E. Spring Co. v. Knowlton, 103 U. S. 49, 26 L. ed. 34
holding that money paid in illegal executory contract may be recovered in actio
founded on disaffirmance; Smart v. White, 73 Me. 332, 40 A. R. 356, holdin
that money in excess of statutory allowance may be recovered from tak
by pensioner, as parties are not *in pari delicto;* Schermerhorn v. Talman, :
N. Y. 93, on doctrine of *pari delicto* as applied to usurious transaction
Phoenix Bridge Co. v. Creem, 102 App. Div. 354, 92 N. Y. Supp. 855, holdi
contractor not *in pari delicto* with subcontractor whose negligence caused inju
to pedestrian; Gray v. Boston Gaslight Co. 114 Mass. 149, 19 A. R. 324, holdi
doctrine of *pari delicto* not applicable, where one party does not join in nuisan
but is exposed to liability.

Cited in notes in 75 A. S. R. 778, on application of maxim *In pari delicto;*
L.R.A. 113, 115, on equitable relief to less guilty party to illegal contract.

Distinguished in Martin v. Wade, 37 Cal. 168, holding both parties to contra
malum in se are *in pari delicto.*

— As between municipality and tort feasor on street.

Cited in Lowell v. Glidden, 159 Mass. 317, 34 N. E. 459, holding city not
pari delicto with one who causes injury by creating nuisance in street; W
Boylston v. Mason, 102 Mass. 341, holding town not *in pari delicto* with one w
put pile of earth in highway; Milford v. Holbrook, 9 Allen, 17, 85 A. D. 73
holding town not *in pari delicto* with owner, who caused injury by defectiv

awning; Washington Gaslight Co. v. District of Columbia, 161 U. S. 316, 40 L. ed. 712, 16 Sup. Ct. Rep. 564, holding district not *in pari delicto* with company, which caused injury to pedestrian by negligence; Ft. Worth v. Allen, 10 Tex. Civ. App. 488, 31 S. W. 235, holding city not *in pari delicto* with railroad company, which injured pedestrian by negligence; Corsicana v. Tobin, 23 Tex. Civ. App. 492, 57 S. W. 319, holding same where sewer contractor failed to properly guard ditch, whether dug with or without express consent; Brooklyn v. Brooklyn City R. Co. 47 N. Y. 475, 7 A. R. 469; Independence v. Missouri P. R. Co. 86 Mo. App. 585,—holding doctrine of *pari delicto* not applicable to action by city for damages paid for negligence of another; Chesapeake & O. Canal Co. v. Allegany County, 57 Md. 201, 40 A. R. 430, holding defense of *pari delicto* not applicable to action by county to be indemnified for damages paid for injuries by negligence of canal company; Campbell v. Somerville, 114 Mass. 334; Portland v. Richardson, 54 Me. 46,—holding party who made excavation in street and city sued for injuries arising thereby not *in pari delicto*.

Distinguished in Geneva v. Brush Electric Co. 50 Hun, 581, 3 N. Y. Supp. 595, holding city which assented to location of pole which caused injury *in pari delicto* with electric company.

Right to indemnity from primary tort feasor.

Cited in Boston & M. R. Co. v. Sargent, 72 N. H. 455, 57 Atl. 688, holding that implied obligation rests upon principal to indemnify innocent agent for obeying his orders; Oceanic Steam Nav. Co. v. Compania Transatlantica Espanola, 29 Abb. N. C. 238, holding that company which paid damages for injuries caused by negligence of subletting company could enforce indemnity; Consolidated Hand-Method Lasting Mach. Co. v. Bradley, 171 Mass. 127, 68 A. S. R. 409, 50 N. E. 464, on liability of person to one against whom judgment has been recovered.

Cited in reference note in 30 A. S. R. 692, on right to indemnity of party paying damages for negligence of another.

Cited in note in 16 A. S. R. 255, on agent's right to indemnity from principal.

— Contributory negligence as between joint tort feasors.

Cited in Swansey v. Chace, 16 Gray, 303, holding contributory negligence not a defense in action by town for indemnity for damages paid to one injured by obstruction in street.

Right of municipality to indemnity from liability for defective streets.

Cited in Lowell v. Short, 4 Cush. 275, as being conclusive of right of town to be indemnified; Anderson v. Fleming, 160 Ind. 597, 66 L.R.A. 119, 67 N. E. 443; Indianapolis v. Lawyer, 38 Ind. 348,—holding that action for indemnity will lie by city compelled to pay damages for negligence of another; Aston Twp. v. Chester Creek R. Co. 2 Del. Co. Rep. 9, holding railroad company rendering highway unsafe liable to town compelled to pay damages to person injured; Rochester v. Campbell, 123 N. Y. 405, 20 A. S. R. 760, 10 L.R.A. 393, 25 N. E. 937, holding municipality subrogated to rights which party injured on defective sidewalk lead; Boston v. Coon, 175 Mass. 283, 56 N. E. 287; Holyoke v. Hadley Water Power Co. 174 Mass. 424, 54 N. E. 889; Fisher v. Cushing, 134 Mass. 374,—on liability to city of one whose negligence caused injury to pedestrian; Cheshire v. Adams & C. Reservoir Co. 119 Mass. 356, on right of town to recover from one who caused defect in highway; Sioux City v. Weare, 59 Iowa, 95, 12 N. W. 786, holding that one who placed obstruction in street must indemnify city for injuries caused thereby; Norwich v. Breed, 30 Conn. 535, holding abutter who removed fence along street bound to indemnify city for damages paid pedestrian who fell into excavation; Woburn v. Boston & L. R. Corp. 109 Mass. 283; Hamden v. New Haven & N. Co. 27 Conn. 158,—holding railroad company whose negligence made highway dangerous, bound to indemnify town for damages caused thereby; Portland v. Atlantic & St. L. R. Co. 66 Me. 485, holding railroad company liable to city for damages city pays for defect in street caused by negligence of railroad; Willard v. Newbury, 22 Vt. 458, on right of town to indemnity against railroad for judgment paid for injuries received through railroad's negligence; Boston v. Worthington, 10 Gray, 496, 71 A. D. 678, holding landlord whose negligence caused injury to pedestrian, liable over to city for damages paid; Andover v. Sutton, 12 Met. 182, holding town entitled to indemnity for repairing road overflowed by mill owner; New York v. Dimick, 49 Hun, 241, 2 N. Y. Supp. 46; Rochester v. Montgomery, 9 Hun, 394; Seneca Falls v. Zalinski, 8 Hun, 571,—holding that city had action against party to recover judgment paid person injured by failure of party to guard obstruction; Littleton v. Richardson, 32 N. H. 59, holding city entitled to indemnity for damages paid for injuries resulting from negligence of another though street was defective.

Cited in notes in 50 A. D. 776, on recovery by municipality of single damages from one leaving street unsafe where double damages have been recovered against it; 12 L.R.A.(N.S.) 953, on right of municipality which has been held liable for injuries from unsafe condition of street to recover over against owner or occupant of abutting property.

Distinguished in Hartford v. Talcott, 48 Conn. 525, 40 A. R. 189, holding that abutter need not indemnify city for damages paid person injured on icy sidewalk: Keokuk v. Independent Dist. 53 Iowa, 352, 36 A. R. 226, 5 N. W. 503, holding abutting owner not liable for injuries caused by defective sidewalk in front of his premises; Brooklyn v. Brooklyn City R. Co. 47 N. Y. 475, 7 A. R. 469, holding that right of municipal corporation to be indemnified, in absence of contract, rested upon negligence; Buffalo v. Holloway, 14 Barb. 101, holding contractor who had proceeded in accordance with instructions received from city, not liable for judgment recovered against city.

Amount of indemnity from joint tort feasor.

Cited in Locks & Canals v. Lowell Horse R. Corp. 109 Mass. 221, holding party entitled to indemnity for damages paid for injuries through negligence of another, not allowed costs of first action; Butler v. Barnes, 61 Conn. 399, 24 Atl. 328, holding grantee sued for trespass not entitled to recover in later suit against grantor expenses of first suit; Andover v. Sutton, 12 Met. 182, holding town not entitled to costs in former suit, when suing mill owner for indemnity for injuring road; Duxbury v. Vermont C. R. Co. 26 Vt. 751, holding that city might recover costs and expenses of defending such a suit; Westfield v. Mayo, 122 Mass. 100, 23 A. R. 292, holding municipality compelled to pay damages for injuries caused by negligence of others entitled to indemnity including expenses.

Recovery against one as conclusive on other primary tort feasor.

Distinguished in Schaefer v. Fond du Lac, 99 Wis. 333, 41 L.R.A. 287, 74 N. W. 810, holding recovery against primary party not binding upon other tort feasor in suit by stranger.

34 AM. DEC. 41, SIMONDS v. HEARD, 23 PICK. 120.

Liability of agent.

Cited in Triplett v. Jackson, 130 Iowa, 408, 106 N. W. 954, holding that agent may contract to bind himself in own name to perform obligations;

Millet v. Stoneham, 26 Me. 78, holding collector personally liable for expenses of advertising unpaid taxes, incurred by him; **Hodges v. Green,** 28 Vt. 358, holding party not contracting in name of church society for purchase of pew, personally liable for price agreed to be paid therefor.

Cited in reference notes in 62 A. S. R. 110, as to when agent is personally liable; 43 A. D. 684, on effect of contract made by agent in his own name; 70 A. D. 610, on personal liability of agent on contract made by him as agent; 89 A. D. 69, on agent's liability on contracts which show an intention to bind him; 11 A. S. R. 234, on remedy against agent acting without authority; 50 A. D. 793, on personal liability of agent on contract executed without authority; 55 A. D. 692, on liability of public agents on contracts made for public; 32 A. S. R. 434, on personal liability of public agents acting in public capacity on contracts made in behalf of public.

Cited in notes in 2 L.R.A. 812, on personal liability of agent; 22 A. S. R. 511, as to whether agent failing to bind principal binds himself; 48 A. S. R. 917, on personal liability to third persons of agent assuming without authority to make contract for corporations; 15 L.R.A. 512, on liability of public officers on contracts made for the public; 22 A. S. R. 510, on personal liability of public agent disclosing authority.

— Descriptio personæ.

Cited in **Hall v. Cockrell,** 28 Ala. 507, holding individuals, signing instrument as such, personally liable thereunder, although described in body thereof as "intendant and council of town;" **Morell v. Codding,** 4 Allen, 403, holding parties signing note in individual names liable personally thereunder, although describing themselves in note as "prudential committee;" **Fullam v. West Brookfield,** 9 Allen, 1, holding contract signed by individuals, adding, "committee for the town," liable personally thereunder; **Fiske v. Eldridge,** 12 Gray, 474, holding "trustee" placed after name of signer of note, *descriptio personæ,* not operating to make signer liable other than personally; **Guernsey v. Cook,** 117 Mass. 548, holding party personally liable on contract executed in his name, although described in agreement as representing specified company; **Brown v. Bradlee,** 156 Mass. 28, 32 A. S. R. 430, 15 L.R.A. 509, 30 N. E. 85, holding selectmen personally liable on agreement signed by them, although having words, "selectmen of Milton," added; **Frazer v. Shelley,** 6 Phila. 429, Phila. Leg. Int. 204, holding parties signing note in their own names, liable personally thereunder, although describing themselves in body of note as "building committee;" **Providence v. Miller,** 11 R. I. 272, 23 A. R. 453, holding party signing contract in his name, individually liable thereunder, although contract purports to be made "in behalf of city," etc.

Distinguished in **Cutler v. Ashland,** 121 Mass. 588, holding assignment signed by parties, "Commissioners of Ashland," contract of town; **Goodenough v. Thayer,** 132 Mass. 152, holding agreement made by parties, "agents" of specified company, and signed by them, "agents," agreement of company.

Authority of agent.

Cited in **Boston Electric Co. v. Cambridge,** 163 Mass. 64, 39 N. E. 787, holding authority of committee, authorized to contract for erection of schoolhouse, exhausted by making contract with contractor for that purpose; **Metropolitan Coal Co. v. Boutell Transp. & Towing Co.** 196 Mass. 72, 81 N. E. 645, holding contract made by agent with intent to bind principal, and within ostensible authority, valid; dissenting opinion in **Jones v. Williams,** 139 Mo. 1, 61 A. S. R. 436, 37

L.R.A. 682, 39 S. W. 486, holding corporation bound by contract made by one wi
authority, although authority is not recited in contract.

Cited in reference note in 59 A. D. 231, on effect of agent accepting bill
own name on liability of principal.

Right of agent on contract made for principal.

Cited in Buffington v. McNally, 192 Mass. 198, 78 N. E. 309, holding
agent may sue on contract made in own name for undisclosed principal.

34 AM. DEC. 45, WILLIAMS v. NELSON, 23 PICK. 141.

Right of flowage by prescription or limitation.

Cited in Cowell v. Thayer, 5 Met. 253, 38 A. D. 400; Augusta v. Moulton,
Me. 284,—holding that prescriptive right to flow lands may be acquired
flowage with damage for twenty years; Nelson v. Butterfield, 21 Me. 2
holding that prescriptive right to flow land may be acquired where there
been damages by the flowing; Yankee Jim's Union Water Co. v. Crary,
Cal. 504, 85 A. D. 145, holding that law will presume grant of water righ
held during period of limitations; Ludlow Mfg. Co. v. Indian Orchard Co. 1
Mass. 61, 58 N. E. 181, holding right to maintain flashboards on dam acquir
by prescription; Trambley v. Luterman, 6 N. M. 15, 27 Pac. 312, holding th
adverse continuous use of water for milling purposes for period of limitati
created easement; Cornett v. Rhudy, 80 Va. 710,—holding that right to wat
may be acquired by adverse, exclusive possession for twenty years; Roge
v. Shepherd, 33 W. Va. 307, 10 S. E. 632, holding use of easement for twen
years unexplained presumed to be under claim of right; Ruehl v. Voight,
Wis. 153, holding that, under statute, flowage of land for ten years, witho
claim for damages bars action therefor; Leonard v. Leonard, 7 Allen, 277, holdi
term requisite for prescription deemed uninterrupted when continued fro
ancestor to heir or from seller to buyer.

Cited in reference notes in 93 A. D. 674, on prescriptive right to overfl
lands; 73 A. D. 473; 82 A. D. 735,—on prescriptive right to maintain d
causing overflow of another's land; 69 A. D. 94, on effect of twenty yea
undisturbed use of water as giving right thereto; 65 A. D. 254, on right
prior occupancy or· prescription to maintenance of dams.

Cited in notes in 43 A. D. 269, on acquisition of right to maintain dam flo
another's land; 57 A. D. 688, 689, on prescriptive right to overflow or r
water upon upper mill owner; 38 A. D. 403, on prescriptive right to main
dam causing overflow of another's land.

What constitutes adverse possession.

Cited in notes in 4 L.R.A. 322, as to what constitutes adverse possessio
40 L. ed. U. S. 215, on what constitutes such adverse possession as will give titl

Easement by adverse user.

Cited in Brace v. Yale, 10 Allen, 441, holding that right to water in strea
may be lost or acquired by sufficient adverse user; White v. Chapin, 12 All
516, holding that right to use drainage ditch may be established by adverse u
Sherlock v. Louisville, N. A. & C. R. Co. 115 Ind. 22, 17 N. E. 171, holding th
right of way may be acquired by open and adverse use during period
limitation.

Cited in reference notes in 57 A. D. 299, on presumption of grant from owne
of land from long use of road by public; 82 A. D. 498, as to what must be sho
to establish presumption of right of way.

Cited in note in 10 E. R. C. 95, on acquisition of easement by prescription.

— Loss of right by nonuser.

Cited in Jones v. Van Bochove, 103 Mich. 98, 61 N. W. 342, holding that non-user, with acts indicating intent to abandon, will result in abandonment; Blackwell v. Phinney, 126 Mass. 458, holding that damages would not lie for land overflowed by dam, when there has been express abandonment of right; Kammerling v. Grover, 9 Ind. App. 628, 36 N. E. 922, holding easement created by grant not lost by neglect of enjoyment or nonuser; Pillsbury v. Moore, 44 Me. 154, 69 A. D. 91, holding that nonuser of mill privilege for less than twenty years does not impair title thereto.

Cited in reference note in 69 A. D. 94, on effect upon owner's right of nonuser of water privilege.

Cited in notes in 18 L.R.A. 537, on effect of nonuser to extinguish easement; 40 A. D. 467, 468, on abandonment of easements and other interests in land; 59 L.R.A. 845, on prevention and loss of prescriptive right to dam back water of stream; 2 L.R.A.(N.S.) 832, as to whether failure to maintain easement raises presumption as to abandonment.

Liability for flowing land.

Cited in Pixley v. Clark, 35 N. Y. 520, 91 A. D. 72, holding that action would lie against riparian owner for overflowing lands of another by interference with stream.

Cited in reference note in 37 A. D. 238, on liability for damages by overflowing land.

Milldam rights under statute.

Cited in Boston Mfg. Co. v. Burgin, 114 Mass. 340; Turner v. Nye, 154 Mass. 579, 14 L.R.A. 487, 28 N. E. 1048; Storm v. Manchaug Co. 13 Allen, 10,— holding that right to flow land under statute gave no easement directly in land flowed; Brookville & M. Hydraulic Co. v. Butler, 91 Ind. 134, 46 A. R. 580, holding that right to back water on land of another gives no right to land itself; Isele v. Arlington Five Cent Sav. Bank, 135 Mass. 142, holding that right of flowage does not give authority to make actual use of another's land; Lowell v. Boston, 111 Mass. 454, 15 A. R. 39, holding that mill acts do not take private property for private or public use; Head v. Amoskeag Mfg. Co. 113 U. S. 9, 28 L. ed. 889, 5 Sup. Ct. Rep. 441, holding constitutional a statute authorizing lands to be flowed by milldam; Vickery v. Providence, 17 R. I. 651, 24 Atl. 148, holding dam used in connection with mills not presumed to have been built under mill act.

Cited in note in 14 L.R.A. 488, on purposes for which flowage of land may be authorized by statute.

34 AM. DEC. 51, PRUDEN v. ALDEN, 23 PICK. 184.

Evidence of contents of lost instruments.

Cited in Eaton v. Hall, 5 Met. 287, holding secondary evidence admissible to prove contents of agreement shown to have been lost.

Cited in reference notes in 45 A. S. R. 793, on secondary evidence of lost instruments; 42 A. D. 642, on parol proof of lost or destroyed record; 57 A. D. 634, on recitals in deeds as evidence; 78 A. D. 552, on admissibility of secondary evidence; 57 A. D. 300, on secondary evidence of writing; 48 A. D. 771, on parol proof of lost record; 68 A. D. 459, on requisites of secondary evidence to render it admissible; 24 A. S. R. 822, on secondary evidence of contents of writing; 37 A. D. 144; 54 A. D. 217, 458,—on parol evidence to prove contents of lost writing.

— Lost records or judicial papers.

Followed in Whitney v. Sprague, 23 Pick. 198, on same facts as applied to guardian's sale.

Cited in Rhodus v. Heffernan, 47 Fla. 206, 36 So. 572, holding that lost schedule of debts, filed with court by administrator, might be shown by parol; Tillotson v. Warner, 3 Gray, 574, holding testimony by justice of former existence of complaint and warrant sufficient to warrant parol evidence of contents; Dailey v. Coleman, 122 Mass. 64, holding secondary evidence admissible to prove contents of execution proven lost.

Cited in reference notes in 36 A. D. 145, on parol proof of lost judicial record; 56 A. D. 107, on parol evidence of lost or destroyed record; 73 A. D. 210; 77 A. D. 658.—on proof of lost or destroyed record by secondary evidence.

Distinguished in Wing v. Abbott, 28 Me. 367, holding that all sources of information must be exhausted before other evidence of lost record could be admitted.

Minute entry in docket as record.

Cited in Easdale v. Reynolds, 143 Mass. 126, 9 N. E. 13; Benedict v. Cutting, 13 Met. 181; Leathers v. Cooley, 49 Me. 337; Longley v. Vose, 27 Me. 179.— holding minutes of clerk upon docket stand as record until more extended record made up; Jay v. East Livermore, 56 Me. 107, holding that judgment for divorce might be shown by certified copy of docket entry; State v. Cox. 69 N. H. 246, 41 Atl. 862; State v. Neagle, 65 Me. 468,—holding that docket entry of previous conviction might be read to jury, where no more extended record had been made; Townsend v. Way, 5 Allen, 426, holding magistrate's minutes competent evidence that recognizance had been taken orally; Good v. French, 115 Mass. 201, holding proceedings in municipal court sufficiently proved by docket; Grosvenor v. Tarbox, 39 Me. 129, holding minutes upon justice's docket sufficient to sustain suit.

Clerk's minutes as record.

Cited in Board of Education v. Moore, 17 Minn. 412, Gil. 391, holding record made up by secretary of board, and not minutes taken in meeting, original record; Waters v. Gilbert, 2 Cush. 27, holding minutes of clerk of religious society evidence in nature of record.

34 AM. DEC. 53, SPEAR v. CUMMINGS, 23 PICK. 224.

Status of teacher.

Cited in Com. v. Frank, 4 Pa. Co. Ct. 619, holding teacher of common school not officer of township.

Exclusion of pupils.

Cited in notes in 65 A. S. R. 339, on grounds for exclusion from public schools; 41 L.R.A. 605, on pleadings and practice as to right to exclude, suspend, or expel pupils from school for misconduct of pupil or parent; 41 L.R.A. 594, on right to exclude, suspend, or expel pupils from school for misconduct of parent affecting child.

Remedy for expulsion.

Cited in Morrison v. Lawrence, 181 Mass. 127, 63 N. E. 400, on person suable for expulsion from public schools: Learock v. Putnam, 111 Mass. 499, holding remedy of child for expulsion from public school action under statute against municipality; Bissell v. Davidson, 65 Conn. 183, 29 L.R.A. 251, 32 Atl. 348, holding that right to attend public school should be vindicated in proceeding by one on behalf of minor; Davis v. Boston, 133 Mass. 103, holding that parent must appeal to school committee from action of teacher expelling child; Donahue v. Richards, 38 Me. 379, 61 A. D. 256; Donahue v. Richards, 38 Me. 376,—holding that parent of child expelled from public school had no action therefor against school committee; Sorrels v. Matthews, 129 Ga. 319, 13 L.R.A.(N.S.) 357, 58 S. E. 819, holding that father of minor child had no action against teacher for expelling child from school.

Power of school officers.

Cited in Ferriter v. Tyler, 48 Vt. 444, 21 A. R. 133, on discretion left with school committee as to management of schools; Watson v. Cambridge, 157 Mass. 561, 32 N. E. 864, holding that decision of school committee as to rights of pupils to enjoy privileges of schools, when made in good faith, is final; State ex rel. Stallard v. White, 82 Ind. 278, 42 A. R. 496, holding that trustees of university had complete power to prohibit students from attending secret societies; Board of Education v. Purse, 101 Ga. 422, 65 A. S. R. 312, 41 L.R.A. 593, 28 S. E. 896, holding that children whose parents disturbed school might be suspended by school board.

Cited in notes in 76 A. D. 166, on authority, duties, and powers of school-teachers; 6 L.R.A. 534, on right of teacher in public schools to enforce discipline.

Liability of school officers.

Cited in Dritt v. Snodgrass, 66 Mo. 286, 27 A. R. 343, holding school directors not liable in damages for enforcing rule of discipline honestly made.

Cited in note in 15 E. R. C. 53, on civil liability of schoolteacher for act in official capacity.

Liability of public officers generally.

Cited in Hanlon v. Partridge, 69 N. H. 88, 44 Atl. 807, holding supervisors of check list liable for wilful, corrupt, or malicious abuse of authority; O'Hare v. Jones, 161 Mass. 391, 37 N. E. 371, holding officers of house of correction not liable for injuries received by prisoner in planing machine; Williams v. Adams, 3 Allen, 171, holding master of house of correction not liable for failure to furnish food and warmth to prisoner; Sanders v. Getchell, 76 Me. 158, 49 A. R. 606, holding selectmen not liable for refusing to receive vote of qualified voter; Kennedy v. Ray, 22 Barb. 511, holding librarian not liable to inhabitant of school district for refusing access to library and books; McKennan v. Bodine, 6 Phila. 582, 25 Phila. Leg. Int. 109, holding inspector of flour not liable in damage for honest mistake of judgment; Dwinnels v. Parsons, 98 Mass. 470, holding town agent not liable to any person for refusing under any circumstances to sell intoxicants; Williams v. Adams, 3 Allen, 171, holding rule not universal that party suffering from breach of public duty may have action against party guilty.

34 AM. DEC. 56, PERLEY v. BALCH, 23 PICK. 283.

Implied warranty on sale of chattels.

Cited in reference notes in 39 A. D. 500, on implied warranty in sale of chattels; 54 A. D. 505; 58 A. D. 767,—on warranty of title implied in sale of chattel.

Cited in notes in 62 A. D. 464, on implied warranty of title on sale of chattel; 54 A. D. 145, on implied warranty of quality in sale of goods; 43 A. D. 680, on implication of warranty from sound price paid for goods.

Right to rescind.

Cited in Harding Whitman & Co. v. York Knitting Mills, 142 Fed. 228, holding that vendee who has accepted and retained goods with knowledge of defects may not rescind; Daniel v. Learned, 188 Mass. 294, 74 N. E. 322, holding that maker of note cannot rescind when he has enjoyed advantages of delay.

Cited in reference note in 42 A. D. 182, on rescission of contracts.

Fraud as ground for rescission.

Cited in Collins v. Townsend, 58 Cal. 608 (dissenting opinion), on rescission of sale of chattels for fraud; Gifford v. Garvill, 29 Cal. 589, holding that payment of note given upon fraudulent sale of stock may be resisted if seller is put *in statu quo.*

Breach of warranty as grounds for rescission.

Cited in Warder v. Fisher, 48 Wis. 338, 4 N. W. 470; Boothby v. Scales, 27 Wis. 626,—holding that vendee may rescind contract for breach of warranty by returning goods; Whalen v. Gordon, 37 C. C. A. 70, 95 Fed. 305; Getty v. Rountree, 2 Pinney (Wis.) 379, 54 A. D. 138, 2 Chand. (Wis.) 28; Butler v. Northumberland, 50 N. H. 33; Sloan Commission Co. v. Fry, 4 Neb. (Unof.) 647, 95 N. W. 862,—on rights of vendee upon breach of warranty of goods sold and delivered; Bryant v. Isburgh, 13 Gray, 607, 74 A. D. 655, holding vendee of horse might rescind sale for breach of warranty as to soundness.

Cited in note in 54 A. D. 146, on vendee's remedies for breach of warranty of equity.

Disapproved in Matteson v. Holt, 45 Vt. 336, holding that breach of express warranty does not entitle purchaser to rescind contract of sale.

Return of consideration upon rescission.

Cited in Desha v. Robinson, 17 Ark. 228; Crossen v. Murphy, 31 Or. 114, 49 Pac. 858; Johnson v. Burnside, 3 S. D. 230, 52 N. W. 1057; Dorr v. Fisher, 1 Cush. 271; Thayer v. Turner, 8 Met. 550; Henry v. Allen, 93 Ala. 197, 9 So. 579,—holding that party complaining of fraud or deceit in sale of chattels must put adversary *in statu quo;* Pearsoll v. Chapin, 44 Pa. 9, holding that vendee who would rescind sale of land must tender reconveyance; Reddington v. Henry, 48 N. H. 273, holding that worthless evidence of title need not be returned; Christy v. Cummins, 3 McLean, 386, Fed. Cas. No. 2,708, holding that vendee of chattel cannot rescind sale without offering to return, unless article is worthless; Bishop v. Stewart, 13 Nev. 25, holding that contract must be rescinded *in toto* or not at all; Tower v. Pauly, 51 Mo. App. 75, holding that contract could not be rescinded where vendee had disabled himself from returning consideration; The Ernst M. Munn, 13 C. C. A. 370, 26 U. S. App. 592, 66 Fed. 356, holding that party who had accepted money as settlement for salvage could not repudiate settlement without returning money; Moody v. Drown, 58 N. H. 45; Lyon v. Bertram, 20 How. 149, 15 L. ed. 847,—holding that purchaser cannot rescind contract and retain any portion of consideration; Waterbury v. Andrews, 67 Mich. 281, 34 N. W. 575, holding that no rescission of void contract by which party receives nothing is necessary; Brewster v. Burnett, 125 Mass. 68, 28 A. R. 203, holding return of counterfeit bonds not necessary before bringing action for consideration; Bassett v. Brown, 105 Mass. 551, holding that one who elects to rescind contract must return consideration, if it is of any value; Snow v. Alley, 144 Mass. 546, 59 A. R. 119, 11 N. E. 764; Sanborn v. Osgood, 16 N. H. 112; Bartlett v. Drake, 100 Mass. 174, 97 A. D. 92, 1 A. R. 101,—holding same where deed was executed through fraud; Morse v. Brackett, 98

Mass. 205, holding that he who would rescind contract must put other party where he was before; Kent v. Bornstein, 12 Allen, 342, holding offer to return counterfeit bill not necessary before bringing action to recover money exchanged for same.

Cited in reference notes in 73 A. D. 268; 100 A. S. R. 705; 103 A. S. R. 59,—on return of property as prerequisite to vendor's rescission of contract.

Cited in notes in 74 A. D. 661, on rule that party rescinding contract must do equity; 43 A. D. 654, on prerequisites to rescission for fraud of sale of property.

Failure of consideration as defense to payment.

Cited in Johnson v. Titus, 2 Hill, 606, holding article of slightest value to vendor or vendee sufficient consideration for promise to pay agreed price; Johnston v. Smith, 86 N. C. 498, holding that failure of consideration means intrinsic worthlessness; Brown v. Weldon, 27 Mo. App. 251, on what constitutes total failure of consideration; Peterson v. Johnson, 22 Wis. 21, 94 A. D. 581, holding partial failure of consideration for note good defense *pro tanto* to action on it; Myers v. Conway, 62 Ind. 474, holding defense to payment of note that article for which note was given was of no value, insufficient without proof of fraud; Mooklar v. Lewis, 40 Ind. 1, holding total failure of consideration defense to payment of note; Packwood v. Clark, 2 Sawy. 546, Fed. Cas. No. 10,656, holding that fact that but one of two certificates of sale for which note was given was assigned does not amount to total failure of consideration; McIntyre v. Robinson. 8 Ill. App. 115, holding that inadequacy of consideration will not be inquired into where there was no fraud; Wheat v. Dotson, 12 Ark. 699, holding total or partial failure of consideration a good defense to a note.

Cited in reference notes in 80 A. D. 683, on right of vendee to show that article is of no value in action for price; 45 A. D. 273, on partial failure of consideration or breach of warranty, etc., as mitigation of damages in action for purchase price.

Recovery of money paid on voidable contract.

Cited in First Nat. Bank v. Peck, 8 Kan. 660, holding rescission unnecessary where there was no consideration for contract; Gassett v. Glazier, 165 Mass. 473, 43 N. E. 193, holding action to recover purchase money upon rescission one for money had and received.

Recoupment.

Cited in Strang v. Murphy, 1 Colo. App. 357, 29 Pac. 298, on right of recoupment; Hill v. Southwick, 9 R. I. 299, 11 A. R. 250, holding recoupment properly allowed for failure to carry out agreement which was consideration for note; Hatchett v. Gibson, 13 Ala. 587, holding that recoupment might be had in action for advances made on cotton for destruction of same.

Cited in note in 40 A. D. 330, as to whether goods must be returned or tendered to obtain right to recoup on action for price.

— For breach of warranty.

Cited in Florence Oil & Ref. Co. v. Farrar, 48 C. C. A. 345, 109 Fed. 254, holding defendant entitled to show, by way of reduction to price, defective workmanship and materials; Dorr v. Fisher, 1 Cush. 271; Mixer v. Coburn, 11 Met. 559, 45 A. D. 230,—holding that vendee of personal property may show, in reduction of damages, deceit or breach of warranty; Tuttle v. Brown, 10 Cush. 262, holding that breach of warranty for goods sold may be shown in reduction of damages.

Cited in reference notes in 60 A. S. R. 504, on breach of warranty in mitigation of damages in suit for purchase price; 45 A. D. 233, on admissibility as mitigating damages in action for price of goods of evidence of breach of warranty.

— For fraud.

Cited in Howard v. Ames, 3 Met. 308, holding that fraud in sale may be given in evidence in reduction of damages without rescinding contract; Carey v. Guillow, 105 Mass. 18, 7 A. R. 494, holding defendant might recoup for fraudulent representations concerning sale of horse; Ladd v. Putnam, 79 Me. 568, 12 Atl. 628, holding exclusion of evidence on misrepresentation in sale of farm. in action on mortgage for price, error; Burnett v. Smith, 4 Gray, 50, holding that fraud in sale of goods may be shown in reduction of damages in action on note given for same.

Cited in note in 40 A. D. 329, on right to recoupment for fraud or breach of contract on sale of chattel.

Election of remedies on voidable contract.

Cited in Hallidie v. Sutter Street R. Co. 63 Cal. 575, holding that, upon breach of warranty, defendant could return goods or sue on breach for damages; Bassett v. Brown, 105 Mass. 551, holding that grantee of voidable conveyance must elect whether to affirm or avoid within reasonable time; Morse v. Moore, 83 Me. 473, 23 A. S. R. 783, 13 L.R.A. 224, 22 Atl. 362, holding that acceptance has no greater effect as estoppel in executory than in executed sales.

34 AM. DEC. 59, FABENS v. MERCANTILE BANK, 23 PICK. 330.

Duty of bank receiving paper for collection.

Cited in Diamond Mill Co. v. Groesbeck Nat. Bank, 9 Tex. Civ. App. 31, 29 S. W. 169; Manhattan L. Ins. Co. v. First Nat. Bank, 20 Colo. App. 529, 80 Pac. 467,—holding that bank which receives paper for collection impliedly contracts to use reasonable skill and diligence; Bank of Orleans v. Smith, 3 Hill, 560, holding that bank must use due care in collecting through agent.

Cited in notes in 77 A. S. R. 616, on duty of bank acting as collection agent; 77 A. S. R. 618, 619, on duty of collecting banks as to demand and protest; 77 A. S. R. 620, on duty of collecting banks as to notice of dishonor; 77 A. S. R. 623, on duty of collecting banks as to transmitting to distant places.

Liability of bank receiving paper for collection.

Cited in Tyson v. State Bank, 6 Blackf. 225, 38 A. D. 139, holding bank failing to present and protest draft liable for loss sustained by owner; Bank of Lindsborg v. Ober, 31 Kan. 599, 3 Pac. 324, holding bank receiving, as agent of owner, note from another bank for collection liable to owner for loss due to improper demand and protest; Mechanics' Bank v. Merchants' Bank, 6 Met. 13, holding collecting bank not liable for loss due to premature protest of note through mistake as to doubtful matter of law; Commercial Bank v. Union Bank, 19 Barb. 391 (dissenting opinion), on liability of bank receiving draft for collection, from bank discounting it, to latter for negligent failure to collect or protest draft; Naser v. First Nat. Bak, 36 Hun, 343, holding bank collecting draft transmitted for collection by another bank liable for proceeds in attachment to creditor of drawer; Reeves v. State Bank, 8 Ohio St. 465 (dissenting opinion), on right of owner of draft sent to bank for collection and forwarded to its correspondent, which collected it, to recover against latter; Merchants' Nat. Bank v. Goodman, 109 Pa. 428, 58 A. R. 728, 2 Atl. 687, 43 Phila. Leg. Int. 28 (affirming 17 Phila. 38, 41 Phila. Leg. Int. 272, 14 W. N. C. 531), holding bank receiving check for collection liable to payee when it forwards check to bank, upon which it is drawn, and latter charges it to drawer and remits by worthless draft.

Cited in reference notes in 38 A. D. 141, on liability of bank taking note for collection; 13 A. S. R. 253, on liability of banks in making collections for their own negligence.

Cited in note in 8 L. R. A. 43, on liability of bank to which paper is indorsed for collection for neglect to give notice.

— **For acts of correspondents and agents.**

Cited in Ætna Ins. Co. v. Alton City Bank, 25 Ill. 243, 79 A. D. 328, holding bank forwarding draft, received for collection, with proper instructions, to competent reliable bank at drawee's residence not liable for latter's negligence; Waterloo Mill. Co. v. Kuenster, 158 Ill. 259, 49 A. S. R. 156, 29 L.R.A. 794, 41 N. E. 906 (affirming 58 Ill. App. 61); Irwin v. Reeves Pulley Co. 20 Ind. App. 115, 48 N. E. 601; Guelich v. National State Bank, 56 Iowa, 434, 41 A. R. 110, 9 N. W. 328; Beach v. Moser, 4 Kan. App. 66, 46 Pac. 202,—holding bank forwarding draft received for collection to reputable bank, at place of payment, not liable for latter's negligence and default; Citizens' Bank v. Howell, 8 Md. 30, 63 A. D. 714, holding bank receiving note for collecting, using due care in selection of notary, not liable for his negligence in not protesting it; Lee v. First Nat. Bank, 1 Chester Co. Rep. 109, holding bank receiving coupons to be transmitted for collection at distant point, and forwarding them to reputable bank at place of payment, not liable for latter's negligence or failure; Plymouth County Bank v. Gilman, 9 S. D. 278, 62 A. S. R. 868, 68 N. W. 735, holding bank placing notes and mortgages, received as collateral security, with reputable attorneys, at distant point, for collection, not liable for latter's negligence or default; Dorchester & M. Bank v. New England Bank, 1 Cush. 177; Stacy v. Dane County Bank, 12 Wis. 629,—holding bank forwarding note received for collection to competent agent at maker's residence, not liable for agent's negligence.

Cited in reference note in 13 A. S. R. 253, on liability of banks in making collections for acts of correspondent banks.

Cited in notes in 38 A. S. R. 777, on liability of bank for its correspondents and other subagents; 7 L.R.A. 857, on liability of indorsee bank for collection for neglect and default of correspondents and agents; 34 A. D. 315, on liability of collecting bank for negligence of notaries, correspondents, etc; 3 E. R. C. 777, on liability of bank for negligence of its correspondent bank in making collections at distant place; 35 A. R. 695, on liability of bank employed to collect paper payable at distance, for negligence of correspondent.

Distinguished in Kent v. Dawson Bank, 13 Blatchf. 237, Fed. Cas. No. 7,714, holding bank forwarding draft received for collection to bank at drawee's residence, liable for latter's default; First Nat. Bank v. Sprague, 34 Neb. 318, 33 A. S. R. 644, 15 L.R.A. 498, 51 N. W. 846, holding bank transmitting draft, received for collection, to competent reliable bank at place of payment, not liable for latter's negligence or default; Montgomery County Bank v. Albany City Bank, 7 N. Y. 459, holding bank receiving draft for collection liable to owner for negligence of bank to which it is forwarded at drawee's residence.

Disapproved in effect in Power v. First Nat. Bank, 6 Mont. 251, 12 Pac. 597, holding bank receiving draft for collection liable for negligence or default of its agents, in absence of special contract as to liability; Titus v. Mechanics' Nat.

Bank, 35 N. J. L. 588, holding bank forwarding checks received for collecti
to bank at place of payment, liable for negligence or default of latter bank.

Right of action for failure to protest.

Cited in Phipps v. Millbury Bank, 8 Met. 79, assuming direct action ma
tainable by payee against bank receiving note for collection from forwardi
bank, but failing to protest it.

Agency of collecting bank.

Cited in Lord v. Hingham Nat. Bank, 186 Mass. 161, 71 N. E. 312, holdi
bank which receives negotiable paper for collection, agent of owner of pape
Echarte v. Clark, 2 Edm. Sel. Cas. 445, holding that bank to which draft
transmitted for collection by another bank is agent for owner of paper; Smi
v. Essex County Bank, 22 Barb. 627, holding collecting bank at which n
indorsed by payee is payable, is agent of payee, and payment by maker to ba
cancels debt.

Cited in note in 2 L.R.A. 492, on bank as collecting agent.

Liability of mercantile agency for acts of subagent.

Cited in Dun v. City Nat. Bank, 23 L.R.A. 687, 7 C. C. A. 152, 14 U. S. A
695, 58 Fed. 174, holding mercantile agency, using due care in selection of s
agents, not liable to subscriber under subscription agreement because of f
information procured throughout such subagent at distant point.

Liability of gratuitous bailee.

Cited in Jones v. Parish, 1 Pinney (Wis.) 494, holding one liable for lo
of money received by him to take to bank, and have credited on note whe
he had intrusted it to another.

34 AM. DEC. 61, CREASE v. BABCOCK, 23 PICK. 334.

Charter as giving vested contract rights.

Cited in Pearsall v. Great Northern R. Co. 73 Fed. 933, holding right of ra
road corporation to consolidate with another, vested right after acceptance
grants.

Cited in reference notes in 47 A D. 478; 73 A. D. 707,—on charter as contrac
41 A. D. 120, on statute granting corporate powers as a contract after acceptan

Reserved power of legislature over corporate charter.

Cited in Greenwood v. Union Freight R. Co. 105 U. S. 13, 26 L. ed. 9(
holding charter subject to amendment, alteration, or repeal, at pleasure
legislature; Durfee v. Old Colony & F. River R. Co. 5 Allen, 230, holding t
incorporators agree to provision reserving right to repeal and amend by accepti
charter; Anderson v. Com. 18 Gratt. 295, holding that charter in which rig
to amend was reserved might be amended to make stockholders personally liabl
State ex rel. Curtis v. Brown & S. Mfg. Co. 18 R. I. 16, 17 L.R.A. 856, 25 A
246, holding that charter of corporation might be amended by subsequent a
where such right was reserved; Shields v. Ohio, 95 U. S. 319, 24 L. ed. 3(
holding constitutional an act prescribing passenger rates for railroad compa
under charter alterable at will of assembly; Mobile & O. R. Co. v. State, 29 A
573, holding that statute which declares forfeiture with consent of compa
does not impair obligation of contract.

Cited in reference notes in 84 A. D. 141, on legislative reservation of right
alter or repeal corporate charter; 73 A. D. 707, on power to destroy righ
vested in private corporation without its consent; 86 A. D. 193, as to who sh

judge when contingency occurs, when corporate charter is conferred subject to repeal on certain contingency.

Cited in note in 43 A. D. 120, on legislative power to repeal corporate franchise under conditional reservation.

Legislative repeal or forfeiture of charter.

Cited in Miner's Bank v. United States, 1 G. Greene, 553, holding that legislature may repeal charter of bank upon default, when right to repeal was reserved; Erie & N. E. R. Co. v. Casey, 1 Grant, Cas. 274, holding that, when power to repeal charter is reserved unconditionally, there can be no objection to its exercise; State v. Morris, 77 N. C. 512, on power of assembly to repeal or modify charters; State v. Hamilton, 47 Ohio St. 52, 23 N. E. 935 (dissenting opinion), on limitations and qualifications in power of repeal by legislatures; Com. v. Essex Co. 13 Gray, 239, holding power of repeal of acts of incorporation limited and qualified.

Cited in reference notes in 69 A. D. 580, on right of legislature to alter charter of private corporation; 90 A. D. 630, as to power of legislature to repeal or alter corporate charter; 86 A. D. 193, on power of legislature to alter or repeal charter of public or private corporation.

— Power to determine facts of default or forfeiture.

Cited in Re Bunkers, 1 Cal. App. 61, 81 Pac. 748, on power of legislature to investigate business and affairs of corporations; Norwalk Street R. Co's Appeal, 69 Conn. 576, 39 L.R.A. 794, 37 Atl. 1080, on power of legislature to find facts showing charter should be repealed; Com. ex rel. Atty. Gen. v. Lykens Water Co. 110 Pa. 391, 2 Atl. 63, 16 Pittsb. L. J. N. S. 459, 43 Phila. Leg. Int. 184, holding that legislature which has reserved right of repeal upon certain event might repeal charter without judicial determination; Myrick v. Brawley, 33 Minn. 377, 23 N. W. 549, holding that legislature may repeal franchise without previous judicial determination that grantee has failed in duties; Lathrop v. Stedman, 13 Blatchf. 134, Fed. Cas. No. 8,519, holding resolution of repeal of charter of corporation not judicial act; Ex parte Wells, 21 Fla. 280; Lathrop v. Stedman, 42 Conn. 583,—holding inquiry by legislature into affairs of corporation not judicial act; Com. ex rel. Atty. Gen. v. Pittsburg & C. R. Co. 58 Pa. 26, holding legislature not final judge of whether default for which charter may be repealed has accrued.

Disapproved in Flint & F. Pl. Road Co. v. Woodhull, 25 Mich. 99, 12 A. R. 233, holding determination whether corporation has violated charter judicial in nature.

Effect of repeal of charter.

Cited in Nevitt v. Bank of Port Gibson, 6 Smedes & M. 513, on dissolution of corporation upon taking away by law of power of perpetual succession; Hewett v. Adams, 54 Me. 206, holding charter of bank regarded as having expired when act of incorporation is repealed; Morley v. Thayer, 3 Fed. 737, holding that charter rights of corporation cease to exist when charter is legally repealed.

Cited in reference note in 50 A. D. 652, on dissolution of corporation by repeal of charter.

Closing up affairs of corporation.

Cited in Muscatine Turn Verein v. Funck, 18 Iowa, 469, holding that dissolution of corporation by act of stockholders does not take away power to wind up affairs; Muir v. Citizens Nat. Bank, 39 Wash. 57, 80 Pac. 1007, holding rights and liabilities of stockholders of bank determined at date of liquidation of bank; Richards v. Attleborough Nat. Bank, 148 Mass. 187, 1 L.R.A. 781, 19 N. E. 353, holding that right to manage affairs of closed bank belongs to bank through stockholders.

Constitutionality of laws.

Cited in Erie & N. E. R. Co. *t*. Casey, 26 Pa. 287, holding law passed by legislature presumed to be constitutional until clearly shown to be otherwise.

34 AM. DEC. 69, JACKSON v. MASSACHUSETTS MUT. F. INS. CO. 23 PICK. 418.

Insurable interest of mortgagee.

Cited in reference notes in 54 A. D. 693; 55 A. D. 549; 9 A. S. R. 620,—on mortgagee's insurable interest in mortgaged property.

Defense of "other insurance."

Cited in Dahlberg v. St. Louis Mut. F. & M. Ins. Co. 6 Mo. App. 121, holding question when defense of "other insurance" is set up is whether "other insurance" is valid; Turner v. Meriden F. Ins. Co. 16 Fed. 454, holding that provision in policy rendering it void if other insurance should be made, allowed company to avoid it when other insurance discovered; Hayes v. Milford Mut. F. Ins. Co. 170 Mass. 492, 49 N. E. 754, holding subsequent policies forbidden by prior policy no defense to action on prior policy; Schenck v. Mercer County Mut. F. Ins. Co. 24 N. J. L. 447, holding that failure to give notice of prior insurance rendered subsequent policy void; Gee v. Cheshire County Mut. F. Ins. Co. 55 N. H. 65, 20 A. R. 171, holding that provision against prior insurance in second policy made it void.

Cited in reference note in 2 A. S. R. 225, on effect of separate insurance by mortgagor and mortgagee.

Cited in notes in 43 A. R. 221, on what constitutes other insurance within condition in insurance policy; 20 A. R. 319, on effect of condition against double insurance as invalidating both policies.

— Other invalid policies.

Cited in Wolpert v. Northern Assur. Co. 44 W. Va. 734, 29 S. E. 1024, holding that prior invalid policy does not avoid subsequent policy containing clause against prior insurance.

Cited in note in 28 A. D. 125, on subsequent invalid policy as breach of condition against other insurance.

— Subsequent policy.

Cited in Bigler v. New York Cent. Ins. Co. 22 N. Y. 402, holding first policy avoided by second policy not invalid on its face; Lindley v. Union Farmers' Mut. F. Ins. Co. 65 Me. 368, 20 A. R. 701; Sweeting v. Mutual F. Ins. Co. 83 Md. 63, 32 L.R.A. 570, 34 Atl. 826; Clark v. New England Mut. F. Ins. Co. 6 Cush. 342, 53 A. D. 44; Kimball v. Howard F. Ins. Co. 8 Gray, 33; Obermeyer v. Globe Mut. Ins. Co. 43 Mo. 573; Gale v. Belknap County Ins. Co. 41 N. H. 170; Jersey City Ins. Co. v. Nichol, 35 N. J. Eq. 291, 40 A. R. 625; Fireman's Ins. Co. v. Holt, 35 Ohio St. 89, 35 A. R. 601; Stacey v. Franklin F. Ins. Co. 2 Watts & S. 506; Woolpert v. Franklin Ins. Co. 42 W. Va. 647, 20 S. E. 521; Rising Sun Ins. Co. v. Slaughter, 20 Ind. 520,—holding same, subsequent policy being void because company had not complied with statutes; Wheeler v. Watertown F. Ins. Co. 131 Mass. 1, holding same for failure to state in second policy interest of insured in property; Thomas v. Builders' Mut. F. Ins. Co. 119 Mass. 121, holding same, when second policy invalid for failure to obtain assent to additional insurance; Hardy v. Union Mut. F. Ins. Co. 4 Allen, 217, holding same, when second policy was invalid for failure to disclose essential facts; Hubbard v. Hartford F. Ins. Co. 33 Iowa. 325, 11 A. R. 125, holding that subsequent insurance obtained in violation of prior policy does not avoid prior policy if invalid; Sutherland v. Old Dominion Ins. Co. 31 Gratt. 176, holding that subsequent insurance to avoid prior policy must be valid.

Cited in reference note in 53 A. D. 53, as to when subsequent insurance taken on same property avoids policy.

Distinguished in Wilson v. Ætna Ins. Co. 12 Tex. Civ. App. 512, 33 S. W. 1085, holding policy containing clause avoiding it by procurance of other insurance "whether valid or not," invalidated by subsequent policy.

Disapproved in Bigler v. New York Cent. Ins. Co. 20 Barb. 635, holding that subsequent insurance, contrary to agreement of which validity is affirmed, avoided first policy; American Ins. Co. v. Replogle, 114 Ind. 1, 15 N. E. 810, holding that property owner who obtains second policy without notice thereby voids first; Lackey v. Georgia Home Ins. Co. 42 Ga. 456, holding that second insurance on same property without consent of insurer voids policy.

Nondisclosure of prior existing insurance.

Cited in David v. Hartford Ins. Co. 13 Iowa, 69; Barrett v. Union Mut. F. Ins. Co. 7 Cush. 175,—holding policy not expressing existence of prior insurance, as required by by-laws of company, void.

Assent to other or prior insurance.

Cited in First Baptist Soc. v. Hillsborough Mut. F. Ins. Co. 19 N. H. 580, holding recital in policy of prior insurance and amount sufficient compliance with charter.

Distinguished in Atlantic Ins. Co. v. Goodall, 35 N. H. 328, holding policy not wholly void for want of indorsement of directors consenting to other insurance.

Alienation of property as avoiding insurance.

Cited in Masters v. Madison County Mut. Ins. Co. 11 Barb. 624, holding contract to convey property insured not such alienation; Hammel v. Queen's Ins. Co. 54 Wis. 72, 41 A. R. 1, 11 N. W. 349, holding same of execution sale; Tittemore v. Vermont Mut. F. Ins. Co. 20 Vt. 546, holding same of deed conditioned on payment at option of grantee.

Cited in reference notes in 36 A. D. 667, on provision against alienation in insurance policy; 39 A. D. 549, on effect of alienation of insured property; 72 A. D. 708, on alienation of insured premises and effect upon policy; 81 A. D. 530, on alienaton of insured property as avoiding policy.

Cited in notes in 59 A. D. 307, on effect of condition in insurance policy restraining alienation; 4 L.R.A. 540, as to what constitutes a sale or transfer within meaning of clause avoiding insurance policy in case of sale or transfer.

— Mortgage.

Cited in Pollard v. Somerset Mut. F. Ins. Co. 42 Me. 221; Woodward v. Republic F. Ins. Co. 32 Hun, 365; Fuller v. Hunt, 48 Iowa, 163,—holding execution of mortgage on land not an alienation; Quarrier v. Peabody Ins. Co. 10 W. Va. 507, 27 A. R. 582, holding same of deed of trust, before foreclosure; Carson v. Jersey City Ins. Co. 43 N. J. L. 300, 39 A. R. 584; Judge v. Connecticut F. Ins. Co. 132 Mass. 521,—holding policy not avoided by mortgage on property by assured; Dolliver v. St. Joseph F. & M. Ins. Co. 128

Mass. 315, 35 A. R. 378, holding policy not avoided by a lease and mo
upon it; Harral v. Leverty, 50 Conn. 46, 47 A. R. 608, holding mortgage
insured property not "alienation" within provision of policy; Ethington
Dwelling House Ins. Co. 55 Mo. App. 129, holding mortgagor had not lost
interest in property because he had not paid debt as agreed; Springfield F.
M. Ins. Co. v. Allen, 43 N. Y. 389, 3 A. R. 711, 28 Phila. Leg. Int. 333, ho
ing policy, to be void upon "any change in title of property insured," forfei
by transfer of premises; Edmands v. Mutual Safety F. Ins. Co. 1 Allen, 3
79 A. D. 746, holding mortgage material alteration in ownership of proper
insured; Rice v. Tower, 1 Gray, 426, holding mortgage of personal proper
without transfer of possession not alienation.

Cited in note in 38 L.R.A. 564, on mortgage as sale of insured property.

34 AM. DEC. 74, ORNE v. SULLIVAN, 3 HOW. (MISS.) 161.

Effect of submission to appraisers.

Cited in Guild v. Atchison, T. & S. F. R. Co. 57 Kan. 70, 57 A. S. R. 3
33 L.R.A. 77, 45 Pac. 82, holding that appointment of appraisers to fix val
of land, under written contract for sale, could not be revoked at pleasure
one of parties.

Liability of party preventing appraisal under contract.

Cited in Lingeman y. Shirk, 15 Ind. App. 432, 43 N. E. 33, holding that p
ty could not be discharged because his appraiser refused to act and ascerta
what land was to pass.

34 AM. DEC. 77, BENNETT v. McGAUGHY, 3 HOW. (MISS.) 192.

Indorsement necessary to transfer note payable to two.

Cited in Allen v. Corn Exchange Bank, 87 App. Div. 335, 84 N. Y. Su
1001, holding that draft payable to two parties, not partners, must be
dorsed by both; Haydon v. Nicoletti, 18 Nev. 290, 3 Pac. 473, holding n
payable to two or more persons jointly, indorsed by only one of payees, s
ject to any equities in favor of maker as though not indorsed by either.

Cited in reference note in 123 A. S. R. 262, on authority of one of two jo
payees to indorse copayee's name.

Cited in note in 18 L.R.A.(N.S.) 631, on indorsement by one of two jo
payees or indorsees of a bill or note.

34 AM. DEC. 78, DICKSON v. PARKER, 3 HOW. (MISS.) 219.

Duty as to maintaining fence.

Cited in reference notes in 50 A. D. 588, on fencing against cattle; 71 A.
727, on duty as to fencing against cattle on highway; 72 A. D. 335, on du
to maintain, and liabilites as to partition fence; 92 A. D. 405, on duties
parties to maintain partition fences and liabilities as to them.

Liability for injury to animals unlawfully distrained.

Cited in Wilhite v. Speakman, 79 Ala. 400, holding party catching and
taining horse running in his field not inclosed with lawful fence liable for
value of the horse, where it was choked to death while so kept up.

Liability for injury to trespassing animals.

Cited in note in 49 A. D. 259, on liability for injury to trespassing an
while removing them.

Liability for injuries to animals straying upon uninclosed land.

Cited in Vicksburg & J. R. Co. v. Patton, 31 Miss. 156, 66 A. D. 552, hol
ing railroad company liable for value of horse killed while straying up
uninclosed right of way, when defendants' agents failed to take due care
prevent accident.

Trespass for damages by animals.

Cited in reference note in 42 A. D. 249, as to when trespass lies for d
ages done by animals.

Measure of damages for trespass.

Cited in reference note in 48 A. D. 530, on measure of damages in action f
trespass.

Officer as trespasser ab initio.

Cited in reference notes in 35 A. S. R. 385, on officer as trespasser
initio; 73 A. D. 318, as to when officer is a trespasser *ab initio;* 47 A. D. 6
on abuse of process as trespass *ab initio;* 84 A. D. 92, on abuse of leg
process as making one trespasser *ab initio.*

Verdict against evidence as ground for new trial.

Cited in Mann v. Manning, 12 Smedes & M. 615, holding that new tri
would not be granted on conflicting evidence, unless preponderance be great
against verdict; Humphreys v. Wilson, 43 Miss. 328; Cicely v. State,
Smedes & M. 202, 1 Morr. St. Cas. (Miss.) 435,—holding that verdict wou
not be disturbed unless opposed by decided preponderance of evidence, or ba
on no evidence whatever; Carter v. Carter, 5 Tex. 93, holding that verd
would not be set aside merely because court might, from examination of e
dence, have arrived at different conclusion; Drake v. Surget, 36 Miss. 46
on verdict against evidence as grounds for new trial.

**34 AM. DEC. 81, THOMPSON v. GRAND GULF R. & BKG. CO. 3 HO
(MISS.) 240.**

**Necessity of making compensation for property taken under eminent d
main.**

Cited in Stewart v. Raymond R. Co. 7 Smedes & M. 568, holding that ra
road company could not enjoin defendant from preventing their trains runni
over his land, they having failed to pay the compensation agreed on; Pears
v. Johnson, 54 Miss. 259, holding statute providing for seizure of private pro
erty for public use without any provison for compensation first made, unco
stitutional; Gould v. Glass, 19 Barb. 179, holding act providing for laying o
of highways through wild land without providing for compensation of ow
ers, unconstitutional; Parham v. Inferior Ct. Justices, 9 Ga. 341, holding th
compensation for property taken for public use must precede, or be concurre
with, the seizure and entry upon the land; Bensley v. Mountain Lake Wat
Co. 13 Cal. 306, 73 A. D. 575, enjoining defendants from going upon land
plaintiffs to construct reservoirs under public right until compensation fir
made; Anderson v. Turbeville, 6 Coldw. 150, holding that chancery may e
join taking of property for public use, or declare taking void, if compens
tion is not paid; Lake Erie & W. R. Co. v. Kinsey, 87 Ind. 514, affirming rig
of party to eject railroad from right of way over his land, on failure to ma
compensation; McElroy v. Kansas, 21 Fed. 257, holding compensation nece
sary precedent to lowering grade of street which damaged property of priva

owner; Sadler v. Langham, 34 Fla. 311, on whether compensation must p
cede right to take private property for public use; Isom v. Mississippi C.
Co. 36 Miss. 300, holding that compensation for private property appropri
ed for right of way for railroad must be made in money, notwithstandi
legislative provision to contrary.

Cited in reference notes in 36 A. D. 210, on compensation for land taken
eminent domain; 58 A. D. 332, on constitutional right to compensation
private property taken for public use; 61 A. D. 283, on invalidity of stat
devesting individual of his property without compensation.

Cited in notes in 42 L. ed. U. S. 273, on compensation for laying out hi
way; 31 A. D. 375, on nature of compensation for property taken for pul
use.

Distinguished in White v. Nashville & N. R. Co. 7 Heisk. 518, holding t
while private property may be taken without compensation first being ma
compensation must be provided for.

Disapproved in Cushman v. Smith, 34 Me. 247, holding that trespass wo
lie for damages for the occupation of land, when compensation had n
been made within a reasonable time after commencement of occupancy.

Judgment as compensation for property taken.

Cited in Moody v. Jacksonville, T. & K. W. R. Co. 20 Fla. 597, holdi
award of damages for taking of property not a compensation for it; Walth
v. Warner, 25 Mo. 277, holding judgment rendered against railroad compa
for damages for land taken for right of way not sufficient, actual paym
being necessary to vest title.

Cited in reference note in 86 A. D. 754, on nature of judgment.

Construction of statutes.

Cited in reference notes in 49 A. D. 705, on construction of words in s
utes or constitutions; 61 A. D. 283, on strictly construing statutes authori
ing exercise of right of eminent domain.

Determination of constitutionality of statutes.

Cited in Adams v. Capital State Bank, 74 Miss. 307, 20 So. 881, on dete
mination of the constitutionality of legislative acts.

Disability of courts to remedy defects in legislative acts.

Cited in Houston v. Royston, 7 How. (Miss.) 543, holding that courts wou
not supply deficiency in act which failed to provide for election of certa
officer.

Partial invalidity of statute.

Cited in Campbell v. Mississippi Union Bank, 6 How. (Miss.) 625, holdi
that invalidity of section of bank charter relating to pledging of faith of sta
does not invalidate balance of charter.

Appropriation of private property to public use without due process.

Cited in Griffin v. Mixon, 38 Miss. 424, holding statute providing for fo
feiture of lands to state on nonpayment of taxes null and void.

34 AM. DEC. 86, FITCH v. SCOTT, 3 HOW. (MISS.) 314.

Liability of attorney for loss to his client.

Cited in Chapman v. Cowles, 41 Fla. 103, 91 A. D. 508, holding attorn
taking depreciated paper currency in payment of a judgment liable to clie
for damages; Hill v. Mynatt (Tenn.) 52 L.R.A. 883, 59 S. W. 163, holdi

attorney not liable to client for error of judgment upon a doubtful question of law.

Cited in reference note in 38 A. D. 566, on liability of attorney.

Cited in note in 52 L.R.A. 884, on liability of attorney to client for mistake.

— Negligence rendering attorney liable.

Cited in Pennington v. Yell, 11 Ark. 212, 52 A. D. 262, on negligence necessary to render attorney liable to client.

Cited in reference notes in 35 A. D. 250; 37 A. D. 490; 50 A. D. 389,—on attorney's liability for negligence; 37 A. D. 42; 51 A. D. 497; 52 A. D. 274; 68 A. D. 142; 76 A. D. 265,—on attorney's liability for negligence and want of skill.

Cited in note in 24 E. R. C. 666, on liability of solicitor to client for negligence.

Authority of attorneys.

Cited in reference note in 83 A. D. 204, on termination of authority of attorney.

Cited in note in 30 A. R. 360, on authority of attorney at law to bind client.

— To compromise claims.

Cited in Preston v. Hill, 50 Cal. 43, 19 A. R. 647, holding that attorney had no power because of his retainer to compromise case and consent to entry of stipulated judgment, when client, with knowledge of adverse attorney, objects to it before judgment entered; Smith v. Dixon, 3 Met. (Ky.) 438, holding that judgment might be set aside which was entered against party without his authority upon a compromise by his attorney; Fleishman v. Meyer, 46 Or. 267, 80 Pac. 209, refusing to recognize a compromise made by attorney for his clients without their knowledge or consent, there being no litgation pending; Eaton v. Knowles, 61 Mich. 625, 28 N. W. 740, holding that authority of attorney to receive payment of a claim did not imply authority to compromise and settle the demand; Clark v. Kingsland, 1 Smedes & M. 248, holding attorney given claim for collection, without power to accept from debtor assignment of security.

Cited in reference notes in 44 A. D. 483, on attorney's right to compromise claim; 50 A. D. 510; 63 A. D. 704,—on attorney's power to compromise suit or claim.

Cited in note in 76 A. D. 261, on attorney's authority to compromise.

Limited in Levy v. Brown, 56 Miss. 83, holding that compromise with garnishee after judgment against him had been enjoined, and delay encountered, was binding on client.

34 AM. DEC. 96, EWING v. GLIDWELL, 3 HOW. (MISS.) 332.

Right to appeal from voluntary nonsuit.

Cited in Dannelly v. Speer, 7 Ga. 227, holding that error would not lie where party voluntarily dismissed his case subsequent to making of decisions complained of; Schulte v. Kelly, 124 Mich. 330, 83 N. W. 405, holding that party nonsuited for failing to appear on the day case was adjourned to would not be allowed to appeal from such nonsuit; Copeland v. Mears, 2 Smedes & M. 519, holding that plaintiff suffering a voluntary nonsuit could not prosecute writ of error, though the decisions of the court occasioning the nonsuit were wrong.

Cited in reference note in 10 A. S. R. 349, as to when appeal may be tak
from an order of court.

Disapproved in Gulf, C. & S. F. R. Co. v. Ft. Worth & N. O. R. Co. 68 T
98, 3 S. W. 564, on right to appeal from voluntary nonsuit.

When nonsuit will be granted.

Cited in Hudson v. Strickland, 49 Miss. 591, holding it error to nons
party for illegality of contract sued on, he being entitled under practice
trial by court and jury.

Cited in reference notes in 39 A. D. 586, as to when nonsuit shall be gra
ed or denied; 39 A. D. 368; 52 A. D. 312,—on granting compulsory nonsui
64 A. D. 631, on courts of Mississippi not possessing power to nonsuit;
A. D. 464, on nonsuit for insufficiency of evidence.

34 AM. DEC. 98, NEWMAN v. FOSTER, 3 HOW. (MISS.) 383.

Title and possession requisite to support ejectment.

Cited in reference note in 50 A. D. 232, on title necessary or sufficient
support ejectment.

Cited in note in 116 A. S. R. 570, on necessity of plaintiff's being out
possession at time action of ejectment is commenced.

Proof of possession in ejectment.

Cited in reference notes in 42 A. D. 537, on proof of defendant's possession
maintain ejectment; 43 A. D. 528; 57 A. D. 203,—on necessity and sufficiency
proof of defendant's possession in ejectment.

Duty to give requested instructions.

Cited in Wiggins v. McGimpsey, 21 Miss. 532, on right of court to refu
instructions stating correct principles of law.

Cited in reference notes in 36 A. D. 144, on duty of court to charge in absen
of evidence; 62 A. D. 688, as to whether correct but abstract and irreleva
instructions may be given; 39 A. D. 639, on abstract instructions upon pro
tions upon which there is no evidence.

Parol evidence to explain deed.

Cited in Doe ex dem. Morton v. Jackson, 1 Smedes & M. 494, 40 A. D. 10
holding parol evidence admissible to show what was meant by "swamp lan
when the map designated in deed as showing land as marked "swamp lan
contained no such description.

Jurisdiction of boundary dispute.

Cited in reference note in 67 A. D. 621, on jurisdiction of equity over boun
ary disputes.

Settling boundary by parol agreement.

Cited in reference note in 60 A. D. 732, on settling disputed boundary by pa
agreements and by possession in accordance therewith.

What controls in fixing boundary.

Cited in reference notes in 47 A. D. 327, on boundaries; 42 A. D. 550; 43 A.
339,—on boundaries which prevail; 60 A. D. 731, on what controls in determin'
boundary; 37 A. D. 562; on natural objects controlling course in deed;
A. D. 417, on control of monuments over boundaries, course, and distances;
A. D. 688, as to whether calls of patent can be controlled by survey; 65 A.
341, on artificial or natural boundaries and monuments controlling course a
distance; 88 A. D. 701, on monuments or natural objects as controlling cou

distances, quantity and description; 67 A. D. 620, on marked trees on line actually run and marked controlling line which courses and distances indicate; 88 A. D. 66, as to when river as boundary will prevail over marked lines; 37 A. D. 547, on effect of conveyance describing boundary as following body of water.

Cited in note in 4 L.R.A. 426, on courses and distances yielding to monuments in case of conflict.

Evidence as to boundary.

Cited in Schlosser v. Cruickshank, 96 Iowa, 414, 65 N. W. 344, denying admissibility of evidence *aliunde* as to whether meander line is boundary line.

Cited in reference notes in 42 A. D. 550, 50 A. D. 405, on evidence of boundaries; 37 A. D. 547; 98 A. D. 534,—on parol evidence to prove boundary; 67 A. D. 621, on declarations and hearsay evidence to prove boundaries; 40 A. D. 416, on confusion of, and evidence as to, boundaries.

Map and survey as evidence.

Cited in reference notes in 88 A. D. 66, on conclusiveness of map and survey; 88 A. D. 701, on map and certificate of survey as evidence.

Allowance of amendments.

Cited in Henderson v. Hamer, 5 How. (Miss.) 525, holding allowance of amendatory pleas after pleadings had been made, discretionary with court and not grounds for error.

Cited in reference notes in 65 A. D. 73, on amendments; 64 A. D. 64, on allowance of amendments within discretion of courts; 77 A. D. 152, as to whether error will lie for allowance of amendments.

34 AM. DEC. 106, CARTER v. SPENCER, 4 HOW. (MISS.) 42.

Patent as evidence of title.

Cited in Sweatt v. Corcoran, 37 Miss. 513, holding patent for public land conclusive evidence of title without proof of recitals contained therein.

Cited in reference note in 39 A. D. 686, on patent as highest evidence of title.

Impeachment of patent to land.

Cited in reference notes in 39 A. D. 516, on effect of patent and how impeachable; 86 A. D. 491, as to how a patent may be impeached; 61 A. D. 597, on right collaterally to impeach patent regular on its face; 38 A. S. R. 614, on impeachment of patent to public lands for fraud or illegality; 62 A. D. 701, as to when equity will relieve against decision of land officer or patent obtained by fraud.

34 AM. DEC. 108, KINLEY v. FITZPATRICK, 4 HOW. (MISS.) 59.

What is necessary to create warranty.

Cited in Carley v. Wilkins, 6 Barb. 557, holding representation by vendor that flour was of extra fine quality, and that vendee might rely on such representation, was a warranty; Otts v. Alderson, 10 Smedes & M. 476, on representations necessary to create warranty.

Cited in reference notes in 55 A. D. 725, on warranties upon sale of chattels; 59 A. D. 743, on representations as warranties; 16 A. S. R. 758, on express warranties on sale of personalty; 67 A. D. 730, on language necessary to show warranty; 11 A. S. R. 879, on sufficiency of words to constitute warranty in contract of sale; 64 A. D. 83, on what constitutes valid warranty on sale of chattels; 58 A. D. 152, on warranty constituted by express affirmation of fact; 73 A. D. 181, on necessity of particular form of words to constitute warranty.

Warranty as court or jury question.

Cited in Anderson v. Barnett, 5 How. (Miss.) 165, 35 A. D. 425, holding that whether printed representations amounted to warranty or an opinion merely, question for jury.

Cited in reference note in 64 A. D. 83, as to whether seller's statement establishes warranty as question for jury.

34 AM. DEC. 110, LEWIS v. WOODS, 4 HOW. (MISS.) 86.

Right to specific performance.

Cited in reference notes in 37 A. D. 633, on specific performance of contracts; 63 A. D. 486, as to when laches may be imputed to party seeking specific performance.

— Necessity of performance by party seeking.

Cited in Atkins v. Tutwiler, 98 Ala. 129, 11 So. 640, holding foreclosure purchaser failing to pay balance of purchase price at time specified, not entitled to enforce his purchase against subsequent purchaser of interest of mortgagor and mortgagees; Younger v. Welch, 22 Tex. 417; Findley v. Koch, 126 Iowa, 131, 101 N. W. 766,—denying specific performance of contract, when the party seeking had by his delay rendered the performance inequitable or unjust to the seller; Bird v. McLaurin, 4 Smedes & M. 50, holding that party giving notes for payment of purchase price of land, and taking bond for title, could not in equity ask for title or rescission without having paid or offered to pay purchase money; Rutland Marble Co. v. Ripley, 10 Wall. 339, 19 L. ed. 955, refusing to compel specific performance, where party seeking has disregarded his own reciprocal obligations; Miller v. Cameron, 45 N. J. Eq. 95, 1 L.R.A. 554, 15 Atl. 842, on necessity of party's showing that he had performed his part or reasons for not so doing; Anderson v. Frye, 18 Ill. 94, holding that party seeking to enjoin recovery back of purchase price of land must show offer to perform according to terms of contract or excuse for failure to do so.

Cited in reference notes in 63 A. D. 486, on effect of failure to perform on part of party seeking specific performance; 54 A. D. 496, on necessity of averment of performance or offer thereof in bill for specific performance.

Cited in reference note in 52 A. D. 295, on necessity that party seeking specific performance show performance on his part.

Time as of essence of contract.

Cited in reference notes in 70 A. D. 739, on time as essence of contract to convey land; 43 A. D. 58, as to when time is of essence of contract in equity and when not.

34 AM. DEC. 112, MICHIE v. PLANTERS' BANK, 4 HOW. (MISS.) 130.

Priority between executions.

Cited in reference note in 36 A. D. 583, on priority in case of several executions against same debtor.

Postponement of prior judgment lien.

Cited in First Nat. Bank v. Hendricks, 134 Ind. 361, 33 N. E. 110, holding that consent to decree of sale and causing order of sale to issue for payment of tax lien subordinated judgment lien to junior mortgage lien; Talbert v. Melton, 9

Smedes & M. 9, holding that no indulgence of sheriff or negligence without a
of plaintiffs would render execution dormant as to subsequent execution
Andrews v. Doe, 6 How. 554, 38 A. D. 450, on postponement of prior lien by a
of party.

Cited in reference notes in 43 A. D. 527, on postponement of judgment lien
subsequent lien; 39 A. D. 307, on how lien may be lost or postponed by lache
52 A. D. 442, on loss of lien of senior judgment by sale under junior judgme
and execution.

Distinguished in Grand Gulf Bank v. Henderson, 5 How. (Miss.) 292, holdi
subsequent judgment execution levied at same time as prior judgment executi
not entitled to be satisfied before the latter, when ordinary diligence had be
observed in keeping execution renewed; Foute use of Ball v. Campbell, 7 Ho
377, holding that stay of execution which expired before the recovery of a su
sequent judgment against same defendant did not affect lien of elder judgmen
Wood v. Gary, 5 Ala. 43, holding that return of writ of fieri facias before retu
day by order of plaintiff did not render it dormant as against execution of juni
judgment creditor subsequently issued when return might not have be
satisfied.

Effect of suspension of execution on rights of judgment creditors.

Cited in Virden v. Robinson, 59 Miss. 28, holding that junior judgment wou
take proceeds of goods seized and sold thereunder pending stay of executi
which attended one of prior date.

Cited in notes in 58 A. D. 359, on release of levy on personalty being sati
faction as to third persons generally; 27 L.R.A. 380, on loss of priority
execution by creditor's contract to suspend execution.

Effect of release of judgment against principal on liability of surety.

Cited in Anthony v. Capel, 53 Miss. 350, holding that release of princip
against whom with surety a joint judgment had been obtained operated as
release of the surety.

**34 AM. DEC. 116, CARPENTER v. STATE, 4 HOW. (MISS.) 163,
MORRIS ST. CAS. (MISS.) 126.**

Adoption of common law.

Cited in note in 22 L.R.A. 502, on adoption of common law in United Stat

Construction of statutes.

Cited in reference notes in 41 A. D. 109, on construction of words used
statute; 62 A. D. 406, as to how words in statute are construed; 49 A. D. 70
on construction of words in statutes or constitutions; 55 A. D. 384, on mode
construing words in statutes; 38 A. D. 328, on construction of statute accordi
to natural and obvious meaning; 69 A. D. 232, on construction of penal statu

— Construction of common-law terms in statutes.

Cited in Meadowcroft v. Winnebago County, 181 Ill. 504, 54 N. E. 949, holdi
terms used in statute without explanation given their common-law meanin
Mackey v. Enzensperger, 11 Utah, 154, 39 Pac. 541 (dissenting opinion),
construction of common-law terms in statutes.

Cited in note in 46 A. D. 587, on construction of common-law terms in statut

Number of jurors necessary in trial of criminal case.

Cited in Territory v. Ah Wah, 4 Mont. 149, 47 A. R. 341, 1 Pac. 732; Hu
v. State, 61 Miss. 577,—reversing judgment when record showed a trial by on
eleven men; State v. Simons, 61 Kan. 752, 60 Pac. 1052, granting new tri

where trial was by jury of eleven, though with consent of defendant; State
Wilcox, 104 N. C. 847, 10 S. E. 453, on necessity of jury in criminal case bein
composed of at least twelve men.

Cited in reference notes in 43 A. D. 521, on common-law rule as to number
jurors; 59 A. D. 677, on number of jurors in common-law jury; 1 A. S. R. 52
on necessity of having twelve jurors in jury.

Cited in notes in 43 L.R.A. 35, on number and agreement of jurors necessa
to constitute valid verdict; 43 L.R.A. 75, on validity of verdict by jury of mo
than twelve; 43 L.R.A. 62, on consent and waiver as to number and agreeme
of jurors in felony cases; 43 L.R.A. 57, on power of legislature as to numb
and agreement of jurors necessary to constitute valid verdict; 43 L.R.A. 37, ?
43, on construction of constitutional provisions as to number and agreement
jurors necessary to constitute valid verdict; 43 L.R.A. 48, on meaning of ter
"jury" and "jury trial" in constitutional provisions.

Right of trial by jury.

Cited in Nelson v. State, 47 Miss. 621, on right of trial by jury.

Cited in note in 3 L.R.A. 211, on power to waive right to jury trial.

Sufficiency of caption of indictment.

Cited in Sam v. State, 13 Smedes & M. 189, holding indictment invalid wh
its caption stated that the court was held at a certain place in county, whi
was not the proper place for court to be held; Lusk v. State, 64 Miss. 845,
So. 256, holding indictment bad when caption thereof failed to show where cou
was held.

Cited in reference notes in 54 A. D. 151, on requisites of caption of indictmen
46 A. D. 138, on effect of defect in caption of indictment.

Distinguished in Seal v. State, 13 Smedes & M. 286, 1 Morris St. Cas. 47
holding indictment sufficient though it did not recite that the jurors we
drawn from the proper county.

Requisites of indictment for perjury.

Cited in reference note in 48 A. D. 703, on what indictment for perjury mu
state.

What constitutes perjury.

Cited in reference note in 48 A. D. 703, on what constitutes perjury.

Cited in note in 85 A. D. 491, on perjury by false swearing in proceedin
authorized by law.

Place for meeting of grand jury.

Cited in Com. v. Tortman, 33 Pa. Co. Ct. 219, quashing indictment when t
grand jury met at a hotel instead of meeting at the proper place in coun
seat.

Locality from which grand jurors may be drawn.

Cited in note in 28 L.R.A. 198, on necessity that grand jurors be from part
ular county.

Sufficiency of record of proceedings in criminal case.

Cited in Mulligan v. State, 47 Miss. 304, reversing judgment of conviction
robbery, because the record failed to show time and place of holding of cou
name of judge, organization of grand jury, or proper return of indictment.

Distinguished in Com. v. Carney, 152 Mass. 566, 26 N. E. 94, holding th
record of conviction need not show place where court was held, when stat
prescribed place.

34 AM. DEC. 121, PROSSER v. LEATHERMAN, 4 HOW. (MISS.) 237.

Rights of assignee of administrator or guardian.

Cited in Thomasson v. Brown, 43 Ind. 203; Krutz v. Stewart, 76 Ind. 9; Booyer v. Hodges, 45 Miss. 78; Miller v. Helm, 2 Smedes & M. 687,—holding that negotiable note might be recovered in the hands of a transferee from administrator of estate on payment of individual debt, the taker being aware of capacity in which administrator held note; Scott v. Searles, 7 Smedes & M. 498, 45 A. D. 317, holding that subsequent administrator might enjoin collection of note given by former administrator in payment of personal debt, which note belonged to estate, of which fact assignee had notice; Pressly v. Ellis, 48 Miss. 574, on effect of assignment of assets of estate by administrator in satisfaction of individual debt; Cotton v. Parker, Smedes & M. Ch. 191, on right to recover on note belonging to estate, given by administrator in satisfaction of personal debt, when made payable to administrator; Mathis v. Barnes, 1 Ind. App. 164, 27 N. E. 308, holding that maker may resist collection of note given by guardian to pay personal debt.

Distinguished in Searles v. Scott, 14 Smedes & M. 94, holding that administrator *de bonis non* could not maintain action against former administrator and one to whom he had assigned note belonging to estate, it appearing that administrator had been duly discharged and note accounted for.

Rights of administrator de bonis non.

Cited in notes in 40 L.R.A. 50, on what assets pass to administrator *de bonis non* where sales or transfers are void; 40 L.R.A. 72, on right of administrator *de bonis non* to avoid sales or transfers made by predecessor.

Right to relief against improper transfer of assets of estate.

Cited in Buie v. Pollock, 55 Miss. 309, holding that creditors might pursue assets of estate improperly transferred by executor to legatees before settlement of claims of creditors of estate; Grant v. Lloyd, 12 Smedes & M. 191, holding that equity will relieve heirs of estate against sale of property to a purchaser who, by misrepresentation and act of executor, induced others not to bid, and purchased property at less than real value; Baughn v. Shackleford, 48 Miss. 255, holding that securities for debt due ward were not discharged by crediting a debt due by guardian to ward's debtors against the debt; Isom v. First Nat. Bank, 52 Miss. 902, holding that auditor's warrants deposited in bank as security for personal debt of party who as agent of county treasurer obtained them as interest due county on school funds belonged to county; Forniquet v. Forstall, 34 Miss. 87, on right of administrator *de bonis non* to interfere with assets of estate wrongly disposed of; Stagg v. Linnenfelser, 59 Mo. 336, holding widow, ignorant of English, indorsing note belonging to estate of husband, as sole legatee, to purchaser who relied on own judgment, not estopped to deny any title to note.

Authority of executor to bind estate.

Cited in Briscoe v. Thompson, Freem. Ch. (Miss.) 155, holding that recovery might be had by estate of note, or proceeds thereof, which an administrator sold for slaves without an order of probate court; Parham v. Stith, 56 Miss. 465, holding unauthorized acceptance by executor of bill of exchange in payment of debt due estate not binding when debtor solvent.

34 AM. DEC. 124, HICKMAN v. GRIFFIN, 6 MO. 37.

Admissibility of records of courts in evidence.

Cited in note in 46 A. D. 380, on admissibility of original papers in pro
ings before justice of peace in circuit court.

Distinguished in Carp v. Queen Ins. Co. 203 Mo. 295, 101 S. W 78, hold
records of court admissible in evidence, although not properly authentica
when identified by witnesses.

When action for malicious prosecution lies.

Cited in reference notes in 41 A. D. 649, on malicious prosecution; 44 A.
126, as to when action for malicious prosecution lies.

Probable cause in malicious prosecution.

Cited in Long v. Rodgers, 19 Ala. 321 (dissenting opinion); Sparling
Conway, 6 Mo. App. 283,—on insufficiency of mere belief; Vinal v. Core,
W. Va. 1, on probable cause necessary to justify prosecution alleged to
malicious.

Cited in reference note in 40 A. D. 527, as to what is, and evidence of, pr
able cause in action for malicious prosecution.

Disapproved in Staley v. Turner, 21 Mo. App. 244, holding reasonable bel
of probable cause sufficient; Chandler v. McPherson, 11 Ala. 916, holding th
no recovery could be had against party who, before acting, submitted facts
attorney, who advised him of the sufficiency of his charges to sustain i
dictment.

Overruled in Vansickle v. Brown, 68 Mo. 627, holding that no recovery cou
be had when defendant, at time of prosecution, had reasonable grounds for
lieving plaintiff guilty; Sparling v. Conway, 75 Mo. 510, on same point.

— Inferable malice or probable cause.

Cited in Stubbs v. Mulholland, 168 Mo. 47, 67 S. W. 650; Christian v. Ha
na, 58 Mo. App. 37,—holding that malice in a prosecution may be inferr
from want of probable cause; Casperson v. Sproule, 39 Mo. 39, holding th
want of probable cause could not be inferred from proof of malice.

Admissibility of testimony by defendant in malicious prosecution.

Cited in Riney v. Vanlandingham, 9 Mo. 816, holding defendant could n
introduce testimony given before magistrate, there being other witnesses as
what he said.

Curing error by instructions.

Cited in note in 55 A. D. 376, as to whether error in admitting evidence
cured by instruction to jury to disregard it or by ruling it out.

— Error in other instructions.

Cited in State v. Pacquett, 75 Mo. 330, holding instruction authorizing ju
to find murder in first degree without requiring them to find malice and d
liberation, not cured by another instruction correctly defining the offen
Imhoff v. Chicago & M. R Co. 20 Wis. 344; Sullivan v. Hannibal & St. J.
Co. 88 Mo. 169,—holding erroneous instruction as to contributory negligen
not cured by another instruction correctly stating the rule; Fugate v. Mill
109 Mo. 281, 19 S. W. 71, holding as to when erroneous instructions a
ground for reversal.

Cited in reference notes in 90 A. D. 344, on conflicting instructions;   70
D. 384, on instructions erroneous in one point but collectively correct
ground for reversal; 83 A. D. 572, on effect on erroneous instructions of the

being accompanied by correct ones; 41 A. D. 649; 71 A. D. 622,—on curing erroneous instruments by correct accompanying ones.

34 AM. DEC. 130, DICKEY v. MALECHI, 6 MO. 177.

General jurisdiction as to wills and probates.

Cited in Benoist v. Murrin, 48 Mo. 48, holding jurisdiction of circuit court in a proceeding to contest the validity of a will, appellate in nature; Oakley v. Taylor, 64 Fed. 245, holding that Federal courts had no jurisdiction of a direct action to cancel a will; State ex rel. Hamilton v. Guinotte, 156 Mo. 513, 50 L.R.A. 787, 57 S. W. 281, on nature of jurisdiction of circuit court in case contesting validity of will; Teckenbrock v. McLaughlin, 209 Mo. 533, 108 S. W. 46, on nature of proceeding to contest will.

Cited in reference note in 54 A. D. 457, on equity jurisdiction in case of lost or destroyed instruments.

— Jurisdictional allegations in petition for contest.

Cited in Hughes v. Burriss, 85 Mo. 660, holding jurisdiction of circuit court to determine validity of will, derived from contestants' petition to contest validity.

Destruction or revocation of will.

Cited in reference notes in 51 A. D. 386, on revocation of wills; 40 A. D. 411, on effect of destruction of will without testator's knowledge.

Cited in note in 110 A. S. R. 449, on distinction between loss or destruction of will before and after testator's death.

Right to prove lost or destroyed will.

Cited in Varnon v. Varnon, 67 Mo. App. 534, holding that evidence might be introduced to prove the contents of a page of a will which had been destroyed; Re Foster, 13 Phila. 567, 34 Phila. Leg. Int. 222, admitting a copy of a last will to probate where execution and delivery of the will were proved.

Cited in reference note in 84 A. S. R. 267, on proof of lost will.

Cited in note in 84 A. D. 630, on probate of lost or destroyed wills.

Evidence sufficient to prove contents of lost will.

Cited in Skeggs v. Horton, 82 Ala. 352, 2 So. 110; Re Page, 118 Ill. 576, 59 A. R. 395, 8 N. E. 852; Jaques v. Horton, 76 Ala. 238,—holding that lost will may be proved by one witness who has read it and remembered contents; Wyckoff v. Wyckoff, 16 N. J. Eq. 401, on sufficiency of proof by one party of contents of will.

Cited in reference notes in 47 A. S. R. 284, on sufficiency of proof of contents of lost will; 52 A. D. 687, on sufficiency of one witness to prove contents of lost will.

Cited in notes in 38 L.R.A. 450, on number of witnesses as to contents of lost or destroyed will; 110 A. S. R. 460, on effect of number of witnesses testifying to execution or contents of lost or destroyed will.

Evidence admissible to establish lost will.

Cited in Odenwailder v. Schorr, 8 Mo. App. 458; Tarbell v. Forbes, 177 Mass. 238, 58 N. E. 873,—on how contents of lost will may be proved; Colligan v. McKernan, 2 Dem. 421, 5 N. Y. Civ. Proc. Rep. 198, on right to establish lost will by single witness.

Cited in reference notes in 35 A. S. R. 868, on proof of execution of will; 99 A. D. 455, on proof of will lost or destroyed against or without testator's knowledge or consent; 45 A. D. 443, on sufficiency of one subscribing witness to prove will.

Cited in notes in 77 A. S. R. 471, on number of witnesses required for proof of will; 11 E. R. C. 507, on parol evidence to prove lost will; 56 A. R. 527, on applicability of provision against one party testifying, when other party is dead, to probate of will.

Effect of partial proof of will lost or destroyed.

Cited in Jones v. Casler, 139 Ind. 382, 47 A. S. R. 274, 38 N. E. 812, holding that part of provisions of will proved would be given effect as against fraudulent destroyer of will; Skeggs v. Horton, 82 Ala. 352, 2 So. 110, holding that will, the contents of which were only partially proved, would to that extent be admitted to probate.

Cited in reference note in 47 A. S. R. 285, on probate of portion of lost will.

Cited in notes in 38 L.R.A. 453, on proof of part of contents of lost or destroyed will; 110 A. S. R. 466, on how much of lost or destroyed will must be proved.

Sufficiency of objections to evidence.

Cited in Fields v. Hunter, 8 Mo. 128; Houston v. Perry, 5 Tex. 462; Clark v. People's Collateral Loan Co. 46 Mo. App. 248,—holding that objection, in order to be reviewable on motion for new trial, must be specific, calling court's attention to specific ground thereof; Bank of Missouri v. Merchants' Bank, 10 Mo. 123, holding that court would not look into validity of objections made in lower court, the grounds of objection not being specified; Roussin v. St. Louis Perpetual Ins. Co. 15 Mo. 244, refusing to notice objections to reading of depositions, the bill of exceptions failing to show specific objections made in lower court; Wayne County v. St. Louis & I. M. R. Co. 66 Mo. 77; Burleson v. Hancock, 28 Tex. 81; Letton v. Graves, 26 Mo. 250,—on necessity of proper exceptions to obtain review as to errors in admission or exclusion of evidence.

Cited in reference notes in 67 A. D. 131, on sufficiency of general and sweeping objections; 74 A. D. 368, on sufficiency of general objections to evidence; 64 A. D. 254, on necessity of objection to evidence stating grounds; 99 A. D. 135, on sufficiency of general exception to whole charge.

Cited in notes in 58 A. D. 553, on necessity that objections to evidence be specific; 99 A. D. 135, on necessity for specific request or exception to raise question of correctness of instructions.

Competent witnesses to establish lost will.

Cited in Hays v. Ernest, 32 Fla. 18, 13 So. 451, holding executor who is also a devisee competent to give evidence to establish will; Holmes v. Holdoman, 12 Mo. 535, holding heirs of law of testator competent witnesses to establish will; Garvin v. Williams, 50 Mo. 206, holding beneficiaries competent witnesses in proceedings to contest validity of a will; Mann v. Balfour, 187 Mo. 290, 86 S. W. 103, holding legatee interested in establishment of will competent witness on her own behalf; Inlow v. Hughes, 38 Ind. App. 375, 76 N. E. 763, holding, in suit to establish will, attorney who drew it competent party to testify as to its provisions; Vaile v. Sprague, 179 Mo. 393, 78 S. W. 609, on competent witnesses in suit to establish will.

Burden of proof in proceedings to establish will.

Cited in Harris v. Hays, 53 Mo. 90, on burden of proof in proceedings to establish a will.

Right to second new trial.

Cited in Hill v. Deaver, 7 Mo. 57, holding that second new trial would not be granted on grounds of misconception of instructions by jury, when evidence was conflicting and facts found were supported by evidence; Kreis v. Missouri P. R. Co. 131 Mo. 533, 33 S. W. 1150 (dissenting opinion), on granting of second new trials.

34 AM. DEC. 140, SNOW v. CHANDLER, 10 N. H. 92.

Covenant not to sue one of joint tort feasors as discharge of others.

Cited in Chicago v. Babcock, 143 Ill. 358, 32 N. E. 271; Arnett v. Missouri P. R. Co. 64 Mo. App. 368; Bloss v. Plymale, 3 W. Va. 393, 100 A. D. 752; Chicago v. Smith, 95 Ill. App. 335,—holding that a covenant not to sue one of joint tort feasors did not bar an action against the others; Benton v. Mullen, 61 N. H. 125, holding that covenant to save one of joint debtors from further liability on the debt did not discharge other debtors from liability.

Cited in notes in 92 A. S. R. 882, on effect of covenant not to sue one joint tort feasor on liability of others; 58 L.R.A. 300, on construing covenants not to sue and release of one joint tort feasor as covenants.

Release of one of joint wrongdoers as discharge of others.

Cited in Missouri, K. & T. R. Co. v. McWherter, 59 Kan. 345, 53 Pac. 135, holding that release of one alleged wrongdoer, not in fact guilty, did not operate as release of another, who was real wrongdoer.

Cited in notes in 73 A. D. 140, on release of one cotrespasser or satisfaction by one as release of all; 11 A. S. R. 908, on effect of release given to, or satisfaction accepted from, one of several joint wrongdoers.

Distinguished in Abb v. Northern P. R. Co. 28 Wash. 428, 92 A. S. R. 864, 58 L.R.A. 293, 68 Pac. 954, holding that release of one joint tort feasor upon payment of a sum of money, though with stipulation that it should not operate as discharge of others, released others.

Effect of partial satisfaction by one joint wrongdoer on liability of others.

Cited in Smith v. Gayle, 58 Ala. 600; Ellis v. Esson, 50 Wis. 138, 36 A. R. 830, 6 N. W. 518; Louisville & E. Mail Co. v. Barnes, 117 Ky. 860, 111 A. S. R. 273, 64 L.R.A. 574, 79 S. W. 261,—holding that payment of a sum of money by one of joint tort feasors as partial satisfaction, and as a release of party making payment, did not preclude recovery against the other; Turner v. Hitchcock, 20 Iowa, 310, on operation of partial satisfaction by one joint wrongdoer as a discharge *pro tanto* of the others.

Cited in notes in 92 A. S. R. 875, on effect of partial satisfaction by one joint tort feasor; 58 L.R.A. 302, on effect of partial satisfaction by one joint tort feasor on liability of the other.

Distinguished in Bell v. Perry, 43 Iowa, 368, holding that payment of sum in settlement of costs of one action and acknowledgment of satisfaction as against one of joint wrongdoers did not operate as satisfaction either in whole or in part of judgment rendered against other wrongdoer.

Judgment against joint wrongdoer as discharge of others.

Cited in Fowler v. Owen, 68 N. H. 270, 73 A. S. R. 588, 39 Atl. 329, holding unsatisfied judgment against one of joint debtors no bar; Jones v. Lowell, 35 Me. 538, on recovery against one joint wrongdoer as discharge of others.

Effect of satisfaction by one of several jointly liable.

Cited in Muench v. Globe F. Ins. Co. 8 Misc. 328, 28 N. Y. Supp. 509, holding that payment of appraiser's compensation by one of insurance companies represented by him in making appraisement inured to benefit of all.

34 AM. DEC. 142, HURD v. SILSBY, 10 N. H. 108.

Validity of assignment for benefit of creditors.

Cited in Derry Bank v. Davis, 44 N. H. 548, holding assignment by firm for benefit of creditors not valid where it operated as assignment of joint estate only; Spinney v. Portsmouth Hosiery Co. 25 N. H. 9, holding assignment containing stipulation prejudicial to creditor's interest not good as against attaching creditor beyond amount of claims of creditors assenting to it.

Cited in reference notes in 42 A. D. 592, as to when assignment for creditors is void; 38 A. D. 61, on effect of assignments intended to withdraw property from creditors; 38 A. D. 263, on retention by assignor of consumable property as fraud.

— Of conditional assignment.

Cited in Fellows v. Greenleaf, 43 N. H. 421, holding that assignment for benefit of creditors containing conditions unfavorable to creditors may be avoided by them; First Nat. Bank v. Newman, 62 N. H. 410; Derry Bank v. Webster, 44 N. H. 264,—on validity of conditional assignment for creditors; Albert v. Winn, 7 Gill, 446 (dissenting opinion), on validity of assignment for benefit of creditors, stipulating for release of whole debt.

Cited in reference note in 72 A. D. 415, on assignment for benefit of creditors being conditional.

Cited in note in 58 A. S. R. 83, on invalidity of conditional assignments for creditors.

— Effect of requiring releases from creditors.

Cited in reference notes in 45 A. D. 709, on effect of requiring release in assignments for benefit of creditors; 77 A. D. 515, on effect of release by creditor in assignment for benefit of creditors.

Cited in note in 16 A. D. 340, on invalidity of assignment requiring release from creditors.

— Effect of preferences.

Cited in Sanderson v. Bradford, 10 N. H. 260, on validity of assignment preferring certain creditors.

Cited in reference notes in 65 A. D. 473, on right of debtor to prefer one creditor over another; 30 A. S. R. 817, as to what preferences in assignment for creditors are void.

Presumption of assent.

Cited in Frazier v. Perkins, 62 N. H. 69, holding that acceptance of a beneficial gift is presumed; Weston v. Nevers, 72 N. H. 65, 54 Atl. 703, holding assent of creditors not assumed when assignment is made upon conditions prejudicial to their rights.

Cited in notes in 24 L.R.A. 370, on presumption of assent to assignment or deed of trust for creditors; 24 L.R.A. 373, on statutory presumption of acceptance of assignment or deed of trust for creditors; 24 L.R.A. 376, on necessity of express assent to assignment or deed of trust for creditors; 24 L.R.A. 375, on rebuttal of presumption of acceptance of assignment or deed of trust for creditors where there is a condition imposing a release.

Title to property under assignment contrary to law.

Cited in Corning v. Records, 69 N. H. 390, 76 A. S. R. 178, 46 Atl. 462, on title to property when assignment contrary to law.

34 AM. DEC. 145, NEWPORT MECHANICS MFG. CO. v. STARBIRD, 10 N. H. 123.

Effect of misnomer of society or corporation.

Cited in People v. Sierra Buttes Quartz Min. Co. 39 Cal. 511, holding assessment roll not invalid because corporation was misnamed, when the name given sufficiently described corporation; Burdine v. Grand Lodge, 37 Ala. 478, holding it no error to admit charter granted subordinate society, although name of the granting society was different from that appearing in acts of incorporation; Board of Education v. Greenebaum, 39 Ill. 609, holding name of corporation in contract as "the State Board of Education of Illinois," when its corporate name was "The Board of Education of State of Illinois," not material variance; Pierce v. Somersworth, 10 N. H. 369, holding the misnomer of corporation known as the "Proprietors of Dover Turnpike Road in New Hampshire" as Dover Turnpike corporation not material variance; Smith v. Tallassee Branch Central Pl. Road Co. 30 Ala. 650, on effect of misnomer of corporation on proceedings by it; Altoona Gas Co. v. Gas Co. 17 Pa. Co. Ct. 662, 5 Pa. Dist. R. 299, on necessity of corporation having a name sufficient to distinguish it from others of a similar kind; St. Luke's Home v. Association for Indigent Females, 52 N. Y. 191, 11 A. R. 697, on effect of misnomer of corporation.

— Naming trustees instead of corporation.

Cited in Keith v. Bingham, 97 Mo. 196, 10 S. W. 32, holding that conveyance made to trustees of corporation without naming them vested the title in the corporation named in the deed; McDonald v. Schneider, 27 Mo. 405, holding lease not invalidated because executed in name of trustees of town instead of "inhabitants" thereof; New York Inst. v. How, 10 N. Y. 84, holding bequest to trustees of an institution bequest to the institution itself.

Who should sue on note referring to payee by description.

Cited in reference note in 55 A. D. 391, on suit in individual name on note in which payee is referred to by description.

Parol evidence as to who was intended as payee.

Cited in reference notes in 63 A. D. 611, on right of person suing on note payable to another to show that he was intended payee; 43 A. D. 98, on parol evidence to show who were intended as payees by description in note; 47 A. D. 148, on parol evidence showing who are payees in promissory note.

34 AM. DEC. 146, BURLEY v. RUSSELL, 10 N. H. 184.

Estoppel of minor from avoiding contract.

Cited in Conrad v. Lane, 26 Minn. 389, 37 A. R. 412, 4 N. W. 695; Whitcomb v. Joslyn, 51 Vt. 79, 31 A. R. 678; Merriam v. Cunningham, 11 Cush. 40,—holding defendant not estopped from setting up infancy as a defense to a contract by fraudulent representations that he was of full age; Wieland v. Kobick, 110 Ill. 16, 51 A. R. 676, holding infant not estopped, when becoming of age, from avoiding a deed by representation in deed that she was unmarried and of age; Fetrow v. Wiseman, 40 Ind. 148; Ferguson v. Bobo, 54 Miss. 121; Watson v.

Ruderman, 79 Conn. 687, 66 Atl. 515,—on false representations as to age
grounds of estopping infant from avoiding contract.

Cited in reference note in 57 A. D. 786, on estoppel *in pais* as applied
infants.

Cited in notes in 57 L.R.A. 684, on estoppel by fraud to plead infancy
contract; 37 A. R. 413, 414, on estoppel of infant to plead infancy by rep
sentation that he was of age; 18 A. S. R. 634, on infant's concealment or m
representation of age affecting contracts.

Liability of infant on contracts.

Cited in reference note in 39 A. D. 236, on infant's liability on contracts.

Cited in note in 18 A. S. R. 611, on infants' bills and notes.

Liability of minor for torts.

Cited in Eckstein v. Frank, 1 Daly, 334, holding minor obtaining prope
upon representing that he was of full age liable in action of tort for dam
or a return of the property.

Cited in reference notes in 42 A. D. 521; 56 A. D. 88,—on infant's liabili
for torts growing out of or connected with contracts.

Cited in notes in 18 A. S. R. 720, on torts of infants connected with contract
57 L.R.A. 677, 678, on liability of infant for torts in inducing contract by fra
ulent representations.

Distinguished in Gilson v. Spear, 38 Vt. 311, 88 A. D. 659, holding that acti
on the case for deceit in sale of a horse could not be maintained against
infant; Nash v. Jewett, 61 Vt. 501, 15 A. S. R. 931, 4 L.R.A. 561, 18 Atl.
holding infancy a good plea to an action *ex delicto* for falsely representing tl
defendant was of full age whereby plaintiff was induced to contract with hi

Infancy as a defense.

Cited in Wallace v. Leroy, 57 W. Va. 263, 110 A. S. R. 777, 50 S. E. 2
holding that infant might set up infancy as a defense in action for purchi
price of goods without returning or offering to return them; Hughes v. Galla
10 Phila. 618, 31 Phila. Leg. Int. 349, 2 Leg. Chron. 247, 3 Luzerne Leg. R
199, holding that no recovery could be had for services rendered an infant
his refusal to pay for them.

Liability of married woman as surety of husband.

Cited in Farmington Nat. Bank v. Buzzell, 60 N. H. 189, holding married wom
signing note as surety for husband not liable, although payee supposed s
signed as principal.

34 AM. DEC. 148, HOIT v. UNDERHILL, 10 N. H. 220.

Ratification necessary to bind infant on contract.

Cited in Fetrow v. Wiseman, 40 Ind. 148, on ratification necessary to b'
infant on contract.

Cited in reference note in 72 A. D. 194, on ratification of infant's contr
made to undisclosed agent or uninterested third person.

Cited in note in 18 A. S. R. 711, on ratification of contracts, executory
infant's part, by new promises or acknowledgments.

Effect of ratification of contract by party after reaching majority.

Cited in Heady v. Boden, 4 Ind. App. 475, 30 N. E. 1119, holding that plaint
might recover from defendant on promissory note executed during infancy, wh
he had ratified it on reaching majority; Stark v. Stinson, 23 N. H. 259,
promise to pay debt contracted during infancy as binding.

Cited in reference notes in 57 A. D. 354, on removal of bar of infancy by promise after majority to pay note; 57 A. D. 310, on removal of bar of infancy by promise to pay after attaining majority.

34 AM. DEC. 150, WOOD v. GALE, 10 N. H. 247.

Right to protect property.

Cited in Aldrich v. Wright, 53 N. H. 398, 16 A. R. 339, holding party not liable for killing wild animals, under statute prohibiting such destruction. when the same was done in the exercise of the right of protecting property; Walker v. Wetherbee, 65 N. H. 656, 23 Atl. 621, on right of party to impound animals in protection of property.

Relevancy of evidence.

Cited in Darling v. Westmoreland, 52 N. H. 401, 13 A. R. 55, holding evidence admissible, on question of whether pile of lumber was likely to frighten horses, to show that horses passing were or were not frightened.

34 AM. DEC. 152, JENNESS v. BEAN, 10 N. H. 266.

Rights as against note taken after maturity.

Cited in reference note in 39 A. D. 710, on defenses to which indorsee of overdue note is subject.

Cited in note in 46 L.R.A. 759, on rights acquired by transfer of negotiable paper after maturity.

— Right of set-off.

Cited in Ordiorne v. Woodman, 39 N. H. 541, allowing maker to set off, as against indorsee, a claim against payee, indorsee having failed to show that he took the note bona fide for a valuable consideration; Leavitt v. Peabody, 62 N. H. 185, holding indorsee in good faith for value of an overdue note not subject to set-off of debts due to maker from payee; Fitch v. Gates, 39 Conn. 366, on right of maker to set off a claim against payee against holder taking after maturity.

Cited in notes in 23 L.R.A. 327, on set-off against assignee of commercial paper transferred after maturity; 46 L.R.A. 794, on rights of holder of negotiable paper transferred after maturity under statutes as to set-off of mutual claims.

Rights of parties to note indorsed as collateral security.

Cited in Smith v. Babcock, 2 Woodb. & M. 246, Fed. Cas. No. 13,009; Williams v. Little, 11 N. H. 66; Bramhall v. Beckett, 31 Me. 205,—holding party taking negotiable not as security for pre-existing debt not regarded as a holder for value; Baker v. Burkett, 75 Miss. 89, 21 So. 970, holding that pledgeor of negotiable note might proceed in equity against maker and pledgee as codefendants for its collection and application of proceeds; Bank of Woodstock v. Kent, 15 N. H. 579; Bowman v. Van Kuren, 29 Wis. 209, 9 A. R. 554; Clement v. Leverett, 12 N. H. 317,—on rights of holder of negotiable instrument given as collateral security for a debt; Rock Springs Nat. Bank v. Luman, 6 Wyo. 123, 42 Pac. 874 (dissenting opinion); Austin v. Curtis, 31 Vt. 64,—on whether holder of negotiable paper transferred as collateral security for pre-existing debt is holder for value.

Cited in reference note in 59 A. S. R. 498, on equities of holders of negotiable instruments as collateral security.

Cited in note in 32 A. S. R. 712, on title of holder of collateral securities.

Distinguished in Tucker v. New Hampshire Sav. Bank, 58 N. H. 83, 42 A. I 580, holding owner of municipal bonds indorsed in blank, who transferred the to third party for safe-keeping and who in violation of trust pledged the to defendant as collateral security for a debt, could not recover them.

Right of indorsee of bill or note taken in payment of pre-existing debt.

Cited in Roxborough v. Messick, 6 Ohio St. 448, 67 A. D. 346 (reversing Handy [Ohio] 348), holding indorsee of promissory note received in good fait before due as collateral security for existing debt not bona fide holder fo value.

Cited in reference note in 33 A. R. 47, on rights of one taking promissory no before maturity as payment or security for antecedent debt.

Distinguished in Blanchard v. Stevens, 3 Cush. 162, 50 A. D. 723, holdin that indorsee of negotiable promissory note, .transferred as satisfaction of pre existing debt by maker, might maintain suit against indorser regardless o equities between original parties.

34 AM. DEC. 155, STEVENSON v. MUDGETT, 10 N. H. 338.

Amendments to pleadings.

Cited in Nickerson v. Bradbury, 88 Me. 593, 34 Atl. 521, refusing amendment o a complaint for conversion of certain horse by seeking to recover for a differen horse; Strang v. Branch Circuit Judge, 108 Mich. 229, 65 N. W. 969, holding tha in suit for breach of contract an allegation that defendant had no title to paten sold might be amended by alleging that the patent sold did not cover th articles represented by defendant; Lawrence v. Langley, 14 N. H. 70, holding i error to allow declaration in action on indorsement of a note to be amende by charging defendant on a count of property sold; Pillsbury v. Springfield, 1 N. H. 565, holding that, in action on judgment of court of certain county, plain tiff could not amend to declare on a judgment of court of different county a different term; Davis v. Hill, 41 N. H. 329, holding writ alleging damage b reason of defective highway amendable by charging damage to want of railin to protect travelers from ^ustructions in highway; Cahill v. Terrio, 55 N. H. 57 holding that declaration .n trespass for assault and battery might be amend so as to include allegation of unlawful detention; Daley v. Gates, 65 Vt. 59: 27 Atl. 193, holding cause of action in declaration charging defendant wit enticing away husband of plaintiff *per quod consortium amisit* not changed b new count charging criminal conversation; Page v. Danforth, 53 Me. 174; Merri v. Russell, 12 N. H. 74; McQuesten v. Young, 19 N. H. 307; Patrick v. Cowles 45 N. H. 553; Porter v. Raymond, 53 N. H. 519; Hurd v. Chesley, 55 N. H. 21; Anthony v. Savage, 3 Utah, 277, 3 Pac. 546; Snyder v. Harper, 24 W. Va. 206 Kuhn v. Brownfield, 34 W. Va. 252, 11 L.R.A. 700, 12 S. E. 519; Thomas v United States, 15 Ct. Cl. 335 (dissenting opinion),—on right to amend pleading

Cited in reference notes in 65 A. D. 73; 98 A. D. 308; 69 A. S. R. 63; 84 A. R. 61,—on amendment of pleadings; 9 A. S. R. 173, on amendment'of complaint 18 A. S. R. 404, on right of amendment; 47 A. D. 743; 91 A. D. 403,—on wha amendments are allowable; 49 A. D. 747; 83 A. D. 450,—on allowance of amend ments to pleadings; 69 A. D. 85, on general doctrine relative to amendments 45 A. D. 307, as to when amendments to defective bill are proper; 64 A. 355, on allowance of amendments being within discretion of court; 56 A. 350, on allowance of amendments generally at common law and under Code

45 A. D. 382, on amendments in equitable suits; 112 A. S. R. 213, on effect
amendment of declaration to arrest statute of limitations.

Cited in note in 51 A. S. R. 429, on admissibility of amendment of pleadin
as to land involved.

— Correction of descriptions or place.

Cited in Haverhill Ins. Co. v. Prescott, 42 N. H. 547, 80 A. D. 123; Dra
v. Found Treasure Min. Co. 53 Fed. 474,—allowing amendment of complaint f
purpose of correcting erroneous description of note, the original cause of acti
not being changed thereby; Alabama G. S. R. Co. v. Thomas, 89 Ala. 294, 18 A.
R. 119, 7 So. 762, holding same to correct a misdescription of contract declar
on; Dodge v. Haskell, 69 Me. 429, holding same when amendment was of t
date of a note described in declaration; Chicago City R. Co. v. McMeen, 2
Ill. 108, 68 N. E. 1093, holding same when amendment to declaration alleged
injury occurring in different street than that stated in original declaratio
Gilman v. Cate, 56 N. H. 160, holding same in action of trespass to corre
mistake in the description of land; Prater v. Snead, 12 Kan. 447, holding it
error on part of court to allow plaintiff to amend his petition by changing o
of facts which entered into description of his cause of action; Newell v. Ho
47 N. H. 329, holding that, on action of tort connected with a contract, plaint
was allowed to amend declaration by selling out the contract clearly and i
relation to the wrong of defendant.

— Supplying deficient allegations or counts.

Cited in Burleigh v. Merrill, 49 N. H. 35, holding insertion of amount of plai
tiff's claim, when the sum was left originally blank, was proper; Pierce v. Woo
23 N. H. 519, holding it proper, when to a count for amount of three notes w
added a count for the balance on a note which had been given for the oth
three; Bailey v. Smith, 43 N. H. 409, holding same by adding to a count f
goods bargained and sold a special count for not accepting and paying for t
goods; Jenness v. Wendell, 51 N. H. 63, 12 A. R. 48, holding same by adding
count for goods sold and delivered a count for goods bargained and sol
Connell v. Putnam, 58 N. H. 335, holding same by adding to count for wrongful
keeping vicious horse which injured plaintiff count for negligence in permitti
horse to roam at large without keeper; Taylor v. Dustin, 43 N. H. 493, holdi
that declaration for obstructing water course by means of a dam might
amended by inserting two dams; Libbey v. Pierce, 47 N. H. 309, holding th
in declaration against indorsers on promissory note, a count for money had a
received might be amended by a count for money paid; Stearns v. Wright,
N. H. 293, holding that, in assumpsit by administrator counting upon pre
ises made to him personally, amendment might be permitted alleging premises
have been made to him as administrator; Chase v. Jefts, 58 N. H. 43, holding th
declaration in assumpsit to recover fees might be amended by a special count
same cause stating facts necessary to sustain action.

Distinguished in Smart v. Tetherly, 58 N. H. 310, holding that declaration f
goods sold and delivered could not be amended by adding special count
acceptance by defendant of order given plaintiff by creditor of defendant.

— Changing form or nature of action.

Cited in Brown v. Leavitt, 52 N. H. 619; Little v. Morgan, 31 N. H. 499,
refusing to allow party to amend complaint in action on a sealed instrument
changing the count from assumpsit to one in debt.

Cited in reference notes in 64 A D. 250, on allowance of amendments changi

form of action; 39 A. D. 68, on amendments varying cause or form of actio
64 A. D. 64; 79 A. D. 482; 86 A. S. R. 413; 123 A. S. R. 689,—on amendments
pleadings which change cause of action; 67 A. D. 204, on amendments changi
cause of action or parties; 80 A. D. 126, on how far amendments varying
altering cause of action allowable; 51 A. S. R. 419, on amendment of declarati
in assumpsit changing cause of action.

Cited in notes in 51 A. S. R. 424, on admissibility of amendments changi
form of action; 51 A. S. R. 414, on inadmissibility of amendments to pleadin
because changing cause of action; 34 A. D. 159, on how far amendments varyi
or altering cause of action are allowable; 51 A. S. R. 432, 433, on admissibili
of amendment changing from tort to assumpsit; 51 A. S. R. 421, on admissibili
of amendment changing action from contract to tort.

Criticized in Stebbins v. Lancashire Ins. Co. 59 N. H. 143, holding that by r
son of later statute form of action might be changed.

— Time of amendment.

Cited in Pouls v. Valcour, 58 N. H. 347, holding that brief statement und
which ordinance was admitted erroneously on trial might after verdict be
corrected as to properly admit the evidence; Hoit v. Russell, 56 N. H. 559,
right to allow amendments to be passed on by court after verdict; Wiggin
Veasey, 43 N. H. 313, allowing record of a judgment of lower court to
amended by entering up judgment as of mortgage with condition of payment d
instead of the same sum as damages alone as originally recorded.

Cited in reference notes in 36 A. D. 608; 84 A. D. 52,—on amendment
pleadings at or after trial; 53 A. D. 669, on right to amend after submission
verdict or judgment; 38 A. S. R. 671, on power to amend pleadings after ju
ment; 39 A. D. 733, on amendment of declaration after verdict or judgmen
85 A. D. 230, on amendments after appeal.

Competency of witness interested in suit.

Cited in Sanborn v. Cole, 63 Vt. 590, 14 L.R.A. 208, 22 Atl. 716, holding th
defendant in action on note, payee of which was dead, could not testify that h
wife was his agent in all business transacted with payee.

Cited in reference notes in 44 A. D. 83, on incompetency of witness on accou
of interest; 58 A. D. 305, on interest as disqualification of witness; 43 A.
718, on what constitutes interest disqualifying witness; 49 A. D. 233, 790, (
release of interest to qualify witness to testify; 67 A. D. 258, on effect
release by witness appearing to be real party plaintiff of all interest to atto
ney of plaintiff; 49 A. D. 233, on admissibility of witness's own testimony o
question of his competency to testify.

. Right to make proof after verdict.

Cited in Janvrin v. Fogg, 49 N. H. 340, holding amendments might be made i
the testimony relating to the competency of records used in evidence, aft
verdict, being of a character not to affect findings of the jury; Hutchins v. Ge
rish, 52 N. H. 205, 13 A. R. 19, holding that verdict would not be set asi
because of the admission of a record not properly authenticated as eviden
if after verdict proper evidence of authentication be furnished.

34 AM. DEC. 162, STATE v. KEAN, 10 N. H. 347.

Evidence admissible to show fact of marriage.

Cited in State v. Clark. 54 N. H. 456, holding testimony of persons who we
present admissible; Dunbarton v. Franklin, 19 N. H. 257, holding cohabitati

prima facie evidence of marriage; Bird v. Com. 21 Gratt. 800, holding testimo
of the clergyman that marriage in another state was duly performed by h
sufficient; State v. Winkley, 14 N. H. 480, on proof necessary to establish f
of marriage.

Cited in reference notes in 36 A. D. 166, on proof and validity of forei
marriage; 67 A. S. R. 802, on sufficiency of proof of foreign marriage; 2 A. S.
117, on presumptions and evidence sufficient to establish marriage.

Cited in notes in 36 A. D. 750, on proof of marriage in criminal cases; 93
D. 254, on proof of marriage in prosecution for bigamy.

Presumption of validity of foreign marriage.

Cited in Cartwright v. McGown, 121 Ill. 388, 2 A. S. R. 105, 12 N. E. 7
on when validity of marriage presumed.

Cited in reference note in 58 A. D. 761, on presumption of validity of marria
solemnized by authorized person.

Cited in note in 14 L.R.A. 540, on presumptions flowing from marria
ceremony.

Materiality of variance from name in indictment.

Cited in Moynahan v. People, 3 Colo. 367, holding indictment for the mur
of Patrick Fitz Patrick where the true name was Patrick Fitzpatrick fata
defective; Patterson v. People, 12 Hun, 137, holding variance between averm
that defendant was doing business under the name of "George Washington Bar
and proof that it was under name of "Geo. Washington Bartk" not materi
Stockton v. State, 25 Tex. 772, holding that mistake in the initial letter insert
between the Christian and the surname of assaulted party as alleged in indi
ment might be disregarded.

Cited in reference note in 58 A. D. 729, on abbreviations of proper names
persons described in indictment being allowable.

Cited in note in 39 A. D. 458, on effect of misnomer in indictment.

Sufficiency of conclusion of indictment.

Cited in State v. Schloss, 93 Mo. 361, 6 S. W. 244; State v. Waters, 1 Mo. A
7,—holding indictment concluding "against the peace and dignity of the st
and contrary to form of statutes in such case made and provided" instead
"against the peace and dignity of state" not bad; Cox v. State, 8 Tex. A
254, 34 A. R. 746, holding indictment concluding "against the peace and digni
of the statute" instead of "against the peace and dignity of the state" invalid

Cited in reference note in 71 A. S. R. 275, on conclusion of indictment.

Cited in note in 3 A. S. R. 283, on sufficiency of concluding words in indictme
for murder.

34 AM. DEC. 165, CLARK v. CLARK, 10 N. H. 380.

Retrospective operation of statute.

Cited in McCraney v. McCraney, 5 Iowa, 232, 68 A. D. 702, upholding rig
to divorce for desertion, beginning before enactment of statute, and continui
statutory period after passage; Greenlaw v. Greenlaw, 12 N. H. 200, denyi
retroactive application of statute granting divorce upon conviction of and i
prisonment for felony; Rairden v. Holden, 15 Ohio St. 207, sustaining ret
active operation of act giving administrator *de bonis non* right of action
bond of administrator dying before enactment.

— Affecting vested rights.

Cited in Denver, S. P. & P. R. Co. v. Woodward, 4 Colo. 162, holding repe of act giving right of action for wrongful death not applicable to case on appeal at time of passage; Evans v. Denver, 26 Colo. 193, 57 Pac. 696, denying validity of amended city charter providing for reassessment of cost of sewer illegally constructed; Day v. Madden, 9 Colo. App. 464, 48 Pac. 1053, holding lien of attachment not affected by repeal of statute under which writ issued; Gilman v. Cutts, 23 N. H. 376, holding that statute of limitations barred action commenced after passage on note made before; Kennett's Petition, 24 N. H. 139, denying application of statute, prescribing new conditions in notice, to petition for new highway offered before passage; Willard v. Harvey, 24 N. H. 344, sustaining statute limiting action on judgment to twenty years as to action commenced nine years after passage on judgment rendered twelve years before; Loveren v. Lamprey, 22 N. H. 434, sustaining statute, allowing testamentary devisee to take property acquired subsequent to execution of will, as to prior will of testator dying after passage; Lakeman v. Moon, 32 N. H. 410, holding repeal of statute allowing penalty for irregular marriages, but giving same penalty, limited in operation, because of saving clause, as to previous marriage; Rich v. Flanders, 39 N. H. 304, upholding statute removing disqualification, as witnesses, of parties to action, as to causes accrued; Pembroke v. Epsom, 44 N. H. 113, denying application of statute abolishing pauper settlements, but excepting pending suits to action subsequently begun, on claim and notice prior to passage; Rockport v. Walden, 54 N. H. 167, 20 A. R. 131, denying application of statute reviving expired claims against decedent's estates, to previous estates; Tufts v. Tufts, 8 Utah, 142, 16 L.R.A. 482, 30 Pac. 309, holding right to divorce not lost by repeal of statute, where new act provides substantially same ground for divorce; Thornburg v. Thornburg, 18 W. Va. 522, holding statute debarring from dower wife who has separated from husband, applies where separation began before passage, and continued until husband's death.

Cited in reference notes in 36 A. D. 704; 47 A. D. 408; 40 A. S. R. 659,—on validity of retrospective statute; 60 A. D. 726, on what are retroactive laws and when they may be constitutionally enacted; 38 A. D. 183, on validity of law authorizing divorce for causes arising subsequent to its passage.

Cited in notes in 14 A. D. 393, on validity of retrospective statutes; 41 L. ed. U. S. 97, on retroactive laws and laws impairing vested rights; 52 L.R.A. 938, on constitutionality of retroactive statute creating right of action or of set-off on account of divorce.

— Affecting remedy.
Cited in Sturges v. Carter, 114 U. S. 511, 29 L. ed. 240, 5 Sup. Ct. Rep. 1014, sustaining statute authorizing auditors to extend inquiries into returns of taxable property over preceding period of four years; New Orleans v. New Orleans & C. R. Co. 35 La. Ann. 679, sustaining statute authorizing assessment of property omitted from rolls of previous years; De Cordova v. Galveston, 4 Tex. 470, holding statute of limitations applicable to action, commenced after passage, on note previously made; Mellinger v. Houston, 68 Tex. 37, 3 S. W. 249, holding statute depriving delinquent taxpayer of defense of limitation, not operative against one in whose favor limitation had run before passage; Pleasants v. Rohrer, 17 Wis. 578, sustaining statute extending time for bringing action for recovery of land sold for taxes, where action not already barred.

— Curative act.

Cited in State v. Squires, 26 Iowa, 340, sustaining statute legalizing school district defectively organized under general law.

Legislative divorces.

Cited in notes in 48 A. D. 438, on constitutionality of legislative divorces; 18 L.R.A. 96, on construction of particular constitutions relative to right of legislature to grant divorces.

Control of marriage rights.

Cited in reference note in 90 A. D. 327, as to how far marriage rights may be controlled.

Equality of rights and privileges.

Cited in State v. Pennoyer, 65 N. H. 113, 5 L.R.A. 709, 18 Atl. 878, holding statute excepting certain resident and foreign physicians from prescribed qualifications for practice of medicine invalid, because of unjust discrimination.

Validity of separation agreement. •

Cited in Foote v. Nickerson, 70 N. H. 496, 54 L.R.A. 554, 48 Atl. 1088, denying validity of voluntary agreement for· separation between husband and wife.

Grounds for divorce.

Cited in Chapline v. Stone, 77 Mo. App. 523, allowing divorce from wife insane at time of marriage and continuing so; True v. Ranney, 21 N. H. 52, 53 A. D. 164, granting divorce to resident incompetent woman legally married in another state.

Cited in reference note in 88 A. D. 501, on desertion as ground for divorce.

Desertion as defense to action for divorce.

Cited in reference note in 70 A. D. 724, on plaintiff's desertion as defense to action for divorce for adultery.

Remarriage of divorced person.

Cited in Roberts v. Ogdensburgh & L. C. R. Co. 34 Hun, 324, upholding validity of remarriage of guilty party to divorce in state permitting it, although prohibited in state where divorce decreed.

34 AM. DEC. 174, BATCHELDER v. KELLY, 10 N. H. 436.

Liability for statutory trespass on timber lands.

Cited in notes in 1 A. S. R. 496, on statutory penalties for cutting down, injuring, destroying, or carrying away timber; 41 L.R.A. 657, on criminal and penal liability for trespass of copartner or · agent in wilfully cutting trees.

— Wilfulness as essential.

Cited in Russell v. Irby, 13 Ala. 131, holding party not liable for statutory penalty when through mistake he cuts timber on land of another; Cohn v. Neeves, 40 Wis. 393; Whitecraft v. Vandever, 12 Ill. 235,—holding it necessary that party committing trespass in cutting trees on land of another do it knowingly or wilfully, in order to render him liable for statutory penalty; Postal Teleg. Cable Co. v. Lenoir, 107 Ala. 640, 18 So. 266, holding that defendants, in action to recover statutory penalty for wilfully and knowingly cutting timber, might show that the trees were cut under the impresssion that they were on land on which they had a license to cut timber; State v.

Shevlin-Carpenter Co. 102 Minn. 470, 113 N. W. 634, reducing the amount of damages to be recovered from defendants trespassing on state lands and removing timber, the evidence showing it was not wilful but under belief of right; Lane v. Ruhl, 103 Mich. 38, 61 N. W. 347, on liability for penalty for unintentional trespass; Barnes v. Jones, 51 Cal. 303, holding averment that it was wilful, knowing, or malicious, necessary; Morrison v. Bedell, 22 N. H. 234, on necessity of proving trespass was wilful and malicious to recover under statute imposing a penalty; Whiting v. Adams, 66 Vt. 679, 44 A. S. R. 875. 25 L.R.A. 598, 30 Atl. 32, on damages recoverable for wilful trespass in cutting timber.

Distinguished in Gebhart v. Adams, 23 Ill. 397, 76 A. D. 702, holding it not necessary to aver that it was wilfully or knowingly cut, when cause of action was alleged in words of statute.

Measure of damages for trespass.

Cited in reference notes in 48 A. D. 530, on measure of damages in action for trespass; 80 A. D. 153, as to when exemplary damages recoverable in trespass.

Construction of penal statute.

Cited in Thurn v. Alta Teleg. Co. 15 Cal. 472, on necessity of penal statutes being strictly construed.

34 AM. DEC. 176, HALE v. WOODS, 10 N. H. 470.

Deed by agent as act of principal.

Cited in Nobleboro v. Clark, 68 Me. 87, 28 A. R. 22, holding deed by the inhabitants of a town by the land of duly authorized agent acknowledging it to be act of inhabitants of town valid deed of the inhabitants; Donovan v. Welch, 11 N. D. 113, 90 N. W. 262, holding deed under power of attorney describing grantor as attorney in fact for principal, and signed and acknowledged in same manner, valid deed of principal; McClure v. Herring, 70 Mo. 18, 35 A. R. 404, as to when principal is bound by deed executed under power of attorney; Tenney v. East Warren Lumber Co. 43 N. H. 343, on necessity of instrument being executed in name of principal; Shuetze v. Bailey, 40 Mo. 69, on how purport of instrument importing to be deed of principal by agent determined.

Cited in reference notes in 56 A. D. 142, as to when deed made by attorney will bind principal; 55 A. D. 344, on form of execution of deed or contract by agent to bind principal; 50 A. D. 114, on execution of deed by attorney in name and as act of principal; 48 A. D. 671; 54 A. D. 298,—on necessity that deed by attorney be executed in name, and as act, of principal.

Cited in notes in 81 A. D. 778, on construction and execution of power of attorney; 54 A. D. 720, on sufficiency of agent's contract to bind principal; 8 E. R. C. 640, on duty of agent to execute instrument in name of principal.

Liability of agent on contract executed by him.

Cited in reference note in 70 A. D. 610, on agent's liability on sealed instrument made in his name.

34 AM. DEC. 178, PEASLEE v. BREED, 10 N. H. 489.

Right of contribution.

Cited in Shoemaker v. Wood, 9 Kulp, 436, applying principle that equality of right requires equality of burden, to liability of joint maker to contribute share of note paid by comaker.

Cited in reference notes in 61 A. D. 294, on contribution among joint principals; 63 A. D. 708, on contribution between joint obligors; 52 A. D. 641, on right of contribution between makers of note in favor of one paying entire amount.

Cited in notes in 115 A. S. R. 87, on right of surety paying debt; 10 A. S. R. 641, on right of surety to contribution from cosurety when principal is insolvent.

— Against one discharged from direct liability.

Cited in Preslar v. Stallworth, 37 Ala. 402, holding that where joint maker of note continues liable, liability of comaker for contribution remains, notwithstanding discharge from direct liability under statute of limitations; Godfrey v. Rice, 59 Me. 308, upholding assumpsit by indorser paying note, against maker discharged from direct liability by statute of limitations; Boardman v. Paige, 11 N. H. 431, holding joint maker compelled to pay note, entitled to contribution from comaker, notwithstanding latter's discharge from direct liability; Martin v. Frantz, 127 Pa. 389, 14 A. S. R. 859, 18 Atl. 20, 46 Phila. Leg. Int. 456 (affirming 24 W. N. C. 325), holding that running of statute of limitations in favor of surety will not release him from liability for contribution to cosurety paying note; Glasscock v. Hamilton, 62 Tex. 143, holding that surety's payment of judgment when limitation on bond would have been complete if judgment not recovered, will not defeat right of contribution; Willis v. Chowning, 90 Tex. 617, 59 A. S. R. 842, 40 S. W. 395, holding that running of limitation in favor of principal, will not discharge surety, since latter upon paying bond may recover of principal; Aldrich v. Aldrich, 56 Vt. 324, 48 A. R. 791, holding surety on outlawed note, going without fraudulent intent, to foreign state · where judgment recovered against him, entitled to contribution.

Cited in note in 98 A. S. R. 44, on right to contribution for payment of debt barred by limitation.

Competency of witnesses.

Cited in Odell v. Dana, 33 Me. 182, holding principal, as to whom note is barred, not competent witness in action against surety, because of liability for contribution; Whipple v. Stevens, 19 N. H. 150, holding joint maker as to whom note is barred, but who may be liable for contribution, is incompetent as interested witness in action against comaker.

Limitation of actions.

Cited in Hirst v. Brooks, 50 Barb. 334, holding action begun after six years from date of demand note barred by statute of limitation.

Cited in note in 60 A. S. R. 208, on effect of bar of limitations when some of the parties to mortgage are protected by it.

— For contribution.

Cited in Comins v. Culver, 35 N. J. Eq. 94, upholding recovery by creditor and surety of partnership against deceased partner's heirs, where surviving partner has right of contribution against deceased partner's estate.

Distinguished in Walker v. Cheever, 39 N. H. 420, holding suit for contribution against executor of comaker of note barred by statute of limitations governing actions against administrators; Faires v. Cockerell, 88 Tex. 428, 28 L.R.A. 528, 31 S. W. 190, holding right of action to compel contribution from

joint maker of written contract arises upon implied promise and is barred
after two years.

34 AM. DEC. 182, OBART v. LETSON, 17 N. J. L. 78.

Presumption of payment from receipt.

Cited in 1 Elliott, Ev. § 119, to point that a receipt is evidence of payment,
and raises presumption that specific debt named, or if in full, that all existing indebtedness has been paid.

34 AM. DEC. 184, SINNICKSON v. JOHNSON, 17 N. J. L. 129.

Powers of legislature.

Cited in reference note in 42 A. D. 315, on legislative control over navigation on public rivers.

Cited in note in 17 L.R.A. 840, on implied restrictions on power of legislatures.

Liability for act done under legislative authority.

Cited in Bohan v. Port Jervis Gaslight Co. 122 N. Y. 18, 9 L.R.A. 711, 25
N. E. 246, holding corporation authorized to carry on quasi-public business
liable to suit of individual for damages for special inconvenience or discom-
fort; Costigan v. Pennsylvania R. Co. 54 N. J. L. 233, 23 Atl. 810, holding
railroad authorized to construct its road liable for private wrong committed
upon lands of adjoining owner; Baltimore & P. R. Co. v. Fifth Baptist Church,
108 U. S. 317, 27 L. ed. 739, 2 Sup. Ct. Rep. 719, 56 A. R. 11 note, holding
railroad liable for damages caused adjoining owners for erection and operation
of engine house and repair ship; Tinsman v. Belvidere Delaware R. Co. 26
N. J. L. 148, 69 A. D. 565, holding private corporation authorized to construct
public highway, liable in tort for direct injury in its execution; Bordentown
& S. A. Turnp. Road v. Camden & A. R. & Transp. Co. 17 N. J. L. 314, holding
private corporation so authorized, liable for negligence in performance of
work; Delaware & R. Canal Co. v. Lee, 22 N. J. L. 243, holding private corporation authorized to construct canal, liable in exercise of power for injuries
caused adjoining owners; Trenton Water Power Co. v. Raff, 36 N. J. L. 335,
holding private corporation, liable for injuries, although work be incidentally
of benefit to public; Haggart v. Stehlin, 137 Ind. 43, 22 L.R.A. 577, 35 N. E.
997, holding owner of saloon, under license, liable for damage caused by
its operation to adjoining owner; Burch v. Dowling, 5 Cranch, C. C. 646,
Fed. Cas. No. 12,139, on taking private property by private corporation without compensation in execution of public work.

Cited in notes in 59 L.R.A. 823, on legislative authority to dam back water
of stream; 16 E. R. C. 585, on liability of individual maintaining dam under
statutory authority; 70 L.R.A. 597, on presumption as to statutory authority
of individuals to commit nuisance.

Compensation as part of eminent domain.

Cited in Monongahela Nav. Co. v. United States, 148 U. S. 312, 37 L. ed.
463, 13 Sup. Ct. Rep. 622, holding right to compensation an inseparable part
of exercise of eminent domain; Chicago, B. & Q. R. Co. v. Chicago, 166 U. S.
226, 41 L. ed. 979, 17 Sup. Ct. Rep. 581, holding that judgment of state court,
under authority of statute, taking private property for public use without
compensation is within prohibition of 14th Amendment; Opinion of Justices. 66 N.
H. 629, 33 Atl. 1076, holding that state cannot, even in absence of provision

in Constitution forbidding it, take private property without paying its value; Orr v. Quimby, 54 N. H. 590 (dissenting opinion), on taking private property for public use without compensation; State, Winans, Prosecutor, v. Crane, 36 N. J. L. 394, on exercise of right of eminent domain as attribute of sovereignty.

Taking without due process of law.

Cited in Coster v. Tide Water Co. 18 N. J. Eq. 54, holding that legislature cannot give property of one individual to another, with or without compensation; Kansas v. Walruff, 26 Fed. 178, holding adoption of constitutional amendment depriving owner of use of property acquired before its adoption, without compensation, void; Chicago, B. & Q. R. Co. v. Illinois, 200 U. S. 561, 50 L. ed. 596, 26 Sup. Ct. Rep. 341, 4 A. & E. Ann. Cas. 1175 (dissenting opinion), on requiring owner of bridge to rebuild it, in improving navigation by state, at his own expense, as constituting a taking.

Cited in note in 4 L.R.A. 786, on abuse of right of eminent domain.

Flowage of lands as a taking.

Cited in Weaver v. Mississippi & R. River Boom Co. 28 Minn. 534, 11 N. W. 114, holding construction of a boom which caused overflow of lands by backwater, a taking of lands for public use, for which compensation must first be made; Pumpelly v. Green Bay & M. Canal Co. 13 Wall. 166, 20 L. ed. 557, holding overflowing of lands under statute authorizing improvement of stream for public benefit, a "taking" within Constitution requiring compensation; Eaton v. Boston, C. & M. R. Co. 51 N. H. 504, 12 A. R. 147, holding flooding of lands caused in construction of railroad, a taking of land requiring compensation; United States v. Lynah, 188 U. S. 445, 47 L. ed. 539, 23 Sup. Ct. Rep. 349, holding overflowing and destruction of land by government in improving navigation, a taking requiring compensation; Hollingsworth v. Texas Parish, 4 Woods, 280, 17 Fed. 109, holding destruction of land by the state in constructing levee, a taking for which compensation must be paid.

Corporate franchise as giving riparian rights.

Cited in note in 3 L.R.A. 611, on rule that corporate franchises do not confer riparian rights.

Liability of individual for injuries in performance of public duty.

Cited in American Print Works v. Lawrence, 23 N. J. L. 590, 57 A. D. 420 (affirming 21 N. J. L. 248, 1 N. Y. Code Rep. 14), holding person in discharge of public duty, while acting with due care and caution in performance thereof, not liable for injury unwittingly caused another.

84 AM. DEC. 195, GARWOOD v. ELDRIDGE, 2 N. J. EQ. 145, Judgment on exceptions to decision of master in 2 N. J. Eq. 290.

Relief from mistake of law.

Cited in Freichnecht v. Meyer, 39 N. J. Eq. 551, holding that, where mistake is mutual, equity will afford redress to party jeopardized, if it will not work substantial injustice to other party; Stastny v. Pease, 124 Iowa, 587, 100 N. W. 482, holding that purchasers of property have constructive notice of judgment of record, although through fault of abstracter they have no actual notice.

Cited in reference note in 51 A. D. 428, on ignorance of law as ground of relief in equity.

Cited in notes in 6 L.R.A. 836, on mistake of law as ground for relief; 5 A. S. R. 703, on remedy in equity where mortgage is canceled by fraud, accident, or mistake.

Disapproved in Culbreath v. Culbreath, 7 Ga. 64, 50 A. D. 375, holding that money paid under mistake of law may be recovered in action for money had and received.

Discharge or release of mortgage.

Cited in reference notes in 82 A. D. 58, on discharge or release of mortgage; 96 A. D. 403; 2 A. S. R. 600,—on effect of release of mortgage; 76 A. D. 521, on payment of money due on mortgage operating as discharge.

Reinstatement of mortgage satisfied by mistake.

Cited in Bentley v. Whittemore, 18 N. J. Eq. 366, holding that purchaser of equity of redemption who pays mortgage and cancels it in fact and of record, under misapprehension of title, cannot, on failure of title, have mortgage declared in force; Guy v. DuUprey, 16 Cal. 195, 76 A. D. 518, holding that stranger who voluntarily pays and satisfies mortgage of record, but fails to take assignment, cannot, in absence of fraud, accident, or mistake in equity, be subrogated to rights of mortgagee or have mortgage reinstated; Mueller v. Renkes, 31 Mont. 100, 77 Pac. 512, on reinstatement of mortgage canceled of record without consideration; Campbell v. Carter, 14 Ill. 286, holding mortgagee who cancels mortgage in consideration of conveyance to him of premises, in ignorance of existence of judgment, not entitled to have mortgage reinstated; Young v. Hill, 31 N. J. Eq. 429, holding mortgagee who cancels mortgage in ignorance of collusive judgment fraudulently concealed by mortgagor, entitled to have cancelation set aside and lien reimposed.

Cited in notes in 58 L.R.A. 806, on right to reinstatement of mortgage released or discharged under, mistake of law; 58 L.R.A. 796, on right to reinstatement of mortgage released or discharged in ignorance of intervening judgments and attachments.

Criticized in Swedesboro Loan & Bldg. Asso. v. Gans, 65 N. J. Eq. 132, 55 Atl. 82, holding mortgagee who, through mistake of law, takes deed from certain heirs and, without consideration, cancels mortgage, entitled against other heirs to have mortgage reinstated.

Right to subrogation.

Cited in Deavitt v. Ring, 76 Vt. 216, 56 Atl. 978, holding purchaser who, through mistake of law, does not obtain property to extent he believed, not entitled to be subrogated to rights of mortgagee to whom purchase price was paid in satisfaction of indebtedness.

Cited in notes in 99 A. S. R. 482, on laches and negligence as affecting and controlling right to subrogation; 16 L.R.A.(N.S.) 473, on revival of, or subrogation to, discharged mortgage in favor of assignee of equity of redemption, who pays it, as against junior lien.

Criticized in Hyde v. Tanner, 1 Barb. 75, holding that holder of antecedent equity, who relinquishes legal right under circumstances raising inference of mistake of fact, will, as against other equitable claimants, be afforded relief.

34 AM. DEC. 200, SEAMAN v. RIGGINS, 2 N. J. EQ. 214.

Relief from fraudulent judicial sale.

Cited in National Bank v. Sprague, 21 N. J. Eq. 458, holding that equity had power to set aside sale affected by fraud or mistake; Stephenson v. Kilpatrick

166 Mo. 262, 65 S. W. 773, holding that equity will grant relief, where failure to raise redemption money in proper time is caused by fraud of party to whom due; Vanernan v. Cooper, 4 Clark (Pa.) 371, holding adjournment of sale by purchaser on his own bid and purchase at lower figure at next bidding, ground for setting aside sale.

Cited in reference notes in 69 A. D. 604, as to when equity will interfere in sheriffs' sales; 83 A. D. 112, on circumstances under which chancery will set aside execution sales.

Avoidance of judicial sale for accident or mistake.

Cited in Dunn v. McCoy, 150 Mo. 548, 52 S. W. 21, holding sale after continued postponement by creditor at request of debtor, under promise to get money, and no attempt by latter to obtain it, would not be set aside for accident and surprise; Howell v. Hester, 4 N. J. Eq. 266, holding failure to attend sale caused by misapprehension as to time, ground for setting sale aside; Woodward v. Bullock, 27 N. J. Eq. 507, holding that sale will be set aside for surprise or misapprehension caused by conduct of purchaser or of officer; Hayes v. Stiger, 29 N. J. Eq. 196, holding that equity will not grant relief by setting aside sale for mistake of law.

Inadequacy of price as ground for avoiding judicial sale.

Cited in Morrisse v. Inglis, 46 N. J. Eq. 306, 19 Atl. 16, holding that judicial sale, unaffected by fraud, accident, or mistake, will not be set aside for inadequacy of price; Graffam v. Burgess, 117 U. S. 180, 29 L. ed. 839, 6 Sup. Ct. Rep. 686, holding that gross inadequacy of price, accompanied by circumstances of unfairness or surprise, renders sale void; Lawyers' Co-op. Pub. Co. v. Bennett, 34 Fla. 302, 16 So. 185, holding gross inadequacy resulting from mistake or misunderstanding of officer making sale, sufficient.

Cited in note in 40 L. ed. U. S. 721, on setting aside judicial sale for fraud, irregularity, accident, mistake, or inadequacy of price.

— Inadequacy with nonattendance at sale.

Cited in Wetzler v. Schaumann, 24 N. J. Eq. 60, holding gross inadequacy, with failure to attend by person injuriously affected, through mistake, sufficient; Aldrich v. Wilcox, 10 R. I. 405, holding inadequacy because of ignorance and failure to bid because of misapprehension, sufficient; Kauffman v. Morriss, 60 Tex. 119, holding gross inadequacy, and failure to attend because of ignorance and mistake, and circumstances of unfairness in sale, sufficient; Rogers & B. Hardware Co. v. Cleveland Bldg. Co. 132 Mo. 442, 53 A. S. R. 494, 31 L.R.A. 335, 34 S. W. 57, holding that circumstances showing accident or mistake, or that debtor was misled, with inadequacy of price, will invalidate sale; Davis v. Chicago Dock Co. 129 Ill. 180, 21 N. E. 830, holding same of levy without previous demand on debtor, and no actual notice to him, and sale at grossly inadequate price; Magann v. Segal, 34 C. C. A. 323, 92 Fed. 252, holding inadequacy of price together with failure to bid because of accidental failure to make required deposit, sufficient; Kloepping v. Stellmacher, 21 N. J. Eq. 328, holding same in case of gross inadequacy with failure to attend sale under mistake or misapprehension; Holdsworth v. Shannon, 113 Mo. 508, 35 A. S. R. 719, 21 S. W. 85, holding same of sale at premature hour preventing debtor from attending, with inadequacy of price; Marlatt v. Warwick, 18 N. J. Eq. 108, holding inadequacy and failure to bid under mistake as to intention of purchaser, sufficient.

34 AM. DEC. 204, READ v. CRAMER, 2 N. J. EQ. 277.

Alteration of Instruments.

Cited in reference notes in 48 A. D. 415, on alteration of instruments; 61 A. D. 204, on interlineations, erasures, or alterations in deeds as affecting their validity.

Relief from error in description in deed.

Cited in Gough v. Williamson, 62 N. J. Eq. 526, 50 Atl. 323, holding that purchaser who purchases by general description may have conveyance of portion not included in particular description in deed.

Cited in note in 4 L.R.A. 425, on descriptions in deeds.

Equitable relief from mistake in contract.

Cited in note in 12 L.R.A. 273, on equity jurisdiction to correct mistakes in contracts.

Distinguished in McCobb v. Richardson, 24 Me. 82, 41 A. D. 374, holding that where parties act on equal information, and vendor acts in entire good faith, vendee cannot recover on ground of mistake because lands do not prove as valuable as anticipated.

Conformity of decree to prayer.

Cited in Berryman v. Graham, 21 N. J. Eq. 370 (affirming 19 N. J. Eq. 29), holding mistake in estimate of value of goods in contract induced by fraud, ground for equitable relief under prayer based on fraud; Pensacola & G. R. Co. v. Spratt, 12 Fla. 26, 91 A. D. 747, holding that under general prayer for relief court could not grant relief if particular prayer was properly grantable.

34 AM. DEC. 209, RE GALLOWAY, 21 WEND. 32.

Liability of administrator for rents payable by deceased.

Cited in Traylor v. Cabanne, 8 Mo. App. 131, holding him liable under lease with covenant to pay rent, accrued after death of testator; Miller v. Knox, 48 N. Y. 232, holding that landlord may collect rents accruing after death of tenant from administrator personally to extent of rents received by him, or from estate.

Cited in reference note in 61 A. D. 542, on liability of administrator on covenants in deeds of intestate.

Cited in note in 68 A. D. 759, on liability of representative upon decedent's covenant in lease.

Entering into possession of land by administrator.

Cited in Miller v. Knox, 48 N. Y. 232, holding collection of rents by administrator of deceased tenant equivalent to entering into possession.

Lessee's covenant to pay taxes.

Cited in note in 51 A. D. 305, on construction and effect of lessee's covenant to pay taxes.

Liabilities of assignee of lease.

Cited in Jermain v. Pattison, 46 Barb. 9, holding, where trustee of lessee enters into possession, estate not liable to lessor for use and occupation, where there are no assets in estate; Gordon v. George, 12 Ind. 408, holding that assignee of lease who goes into possession becomes liable to performance of stipulations therein; Michenfelder v. Gunther, 66 How. Pr. 464, holding that widow who remains in possession after death of tenant, in adsence of administration, holds prima facie as assignee of term, and is liable as such; Dennistoun v.

Hubbell, 10 Bosw. 155, holding that collection of rent from subtenant assignee of trust property, in ignorance of its true character, does not make h liable for subsequently accruing rent.

Attachment against nonresident administrator.

Cited in note in 47 L.R.A. 357, on application to executor and administrat of statutes as to attachment of absent, concealed, and absconding debtors.

Foreign judgment against personal representative.

Cited in note in 27 L.R.A. 113, 116, on judgments of another state or count rendered against executor or administrator.

34 AM. DEC. 211, SWART v. SERVICE, 21 WEND. 36.

Deed as mortgage.

Cited in reference notes in 46 A. D. 301, on deed absolute on face given secure debt as mortgage; 79 A. D. 373, on deed absolute on face as mortga when intended to secure existing debt; 71 A. D. 438, as to when deed absolu will be construed as a mortgage.

Mortgage as mere security.

Cited in note in 22 A. D. 668, on mortgage as mere security.

Right of mortgagee to bring ejectment.

Cited in reference notes in 38 A. D. 693, on right of mortgagee to bring eje ment after forfeiture; 38 A. D. 57, on right of mortgagee to recover in ejectme in New York; 79 A. D. 361, on rule of some states that mortgagee may n maintain ejectment or writ of entry against mortgagor.

Parol evidence to rebut apparent character of writing.

Cited in Fuller v. Parrish, 3 Mich. 211, holding it admissible in law to sh bill of sale, absolute on its face, a mortgage.

Disapproved in Egleston v. Knickerbacker, 6 Barb. 458, holding such eviden inadmissible to show absolute receipt to be on condition.

— To show deed a mortgage.

Cited in Griswold v. Fowler, 6 Abb. Pr. 113, holding such evidence admissi in case of fraud, accident, or mistake, to show deed a mortgage; Jackson Lodge, 36 Cal. 28, holding such evidence admissible to show deed a mortgag Webb v. Rice, 6 Hill, 219; Carr v. Carr, 4 Lans. 314; dissenting opinion in We v. Rice, 1 Hill, 606,—on admissibility of parol evidence to show deed to mortgage; Russell v. Kinney, 1 Sandf. Ch. 34, holding parol evidence inadmissi to show bond and mortgage were not to be paid until the performance of co temporaneous agreement.

Cited in reference notes in 36 A. D. 242; 54 A. D. 489; 62 A. D. 506; A. D. 668; 90 A. D. 708,—on parol evidence to show that deed absolute mortgage; 65 A. D. 496, on parol evidence to show that bill of sale was i tended as a mortgage; 47 A. S. R. 627, on parol evidence to show that absolu instrument was intended as collateral security.

Criticized in Brainerd v. Brainerd, 15 Conn. 575, holding parol evidence admi sible to prove that contract of mortgage has been fraudulently converted in an absolute conveyance.

Disapproved in Fairchild v. Rasdall, 9 Wis. 379, holding such evidence inadmi sible to show deed absolute on its face to be a trust deed; Cook v. Eaton, Barb. 439; Abbott v. Hanson, 24 N. J. L. 493; Hogel v. Lindell, 10 Mo. 483, holding it inadmissible to show deed a mortgage.

Parol evidence in equity to show character of instrument.

Cited in Lee v. Evans, 8 Cal. 424, holding it inadmissible to show deed a mortgage except in cases of fraud, accident, or mistake; Cook v. Eaton, 16 Barb. 439, holding it inadmissible to show deed a mortgage except in cases of fraud, accident, or mistake; Griswold v. Fowler, 6 Abb. Pr. 113, on time of execution of instrument sought to be declared of different character.

Disapproved in Russell v. Kinney, 2 N. Y. Leg. Obs. 233, holding it inadmissible to show mortgage, absolute on its face, was upon condition of fulfilment of contemporaneous contract.

Contemporaneous parol agreement.

Cited in Bank of Albion v. Smith, 27 Barb. 489, holding that legal effect of indorsement in blank of promissory note cannot be varied by parol contemporaneous agreement.

Possession of grantor, when adverse.

Cited in Smith v. Jackson, 76 Ill. 254, holding possession of grantor, after absolute conveyance, not adverse without sufficient disclaimer of grantee's title.

Presumption of payment of mortgage.

Cited in reference notes in 34 A. D. 359, on presumption of payment of mortgage from lapse of time; 66 A. D. 615, on presumption of payment of mortgage debt from uninterrupted possession by mortgagor for twenty years.

34 AM. DEC. 213, SMITH v. CLARK, 21 WEND. 83, Reversed in unreported opinion on grounds not affecting doctrine of case, See 2 Barb. 523.

When contract a bailment or a sale.

Cited in reference notes in 59 A. D. 630; 74 A. D. 209,—on distinction between sale and bailment; 37 A. D. 400, on what constitutes bailment; 11 A. S. R. 179, as to whether contract is bailment or sale.

Cited in note in 94 A. S. R. 216, on distinction between absolute sales and bailment.

—Deposit of goods for manufacture or return.

Cited in Pierce v. Schenck, 3 Hill, 28, holding that delivery of logs to be manufactured into boards within specified time, on shares, constituted bailment; Austin v. Seligman, 21 Blatchf. 506, 18 Fed. 519, 66 How. Pr. 87, holding delivery of jewelry sweepings on option that refined product was to be returned or value accounted for, a sale; Bradley v. Mirick, 25 Hun, 272, holding delivery of goods on promise to return same quantity and quality, a sale; Reed v. Abbey, 2 Thomp. & C. 381, holding delivery of sheep under agreement to return same number in equal condition and age, a sale; Moore v. Holland, 39 Me. 307, on delivery of article to be returned in altered form, as constituting bailment.

Distinguished in Wescott v. Tilton, 1 Duer, 53, 10 N. Y. Leg. Obs. 278, holding sale of ale in barrels with agreement to return barrels and stipulation as to their value if return impracticable, a bailment of barrels; Arnold v. Hatch, 177 U. S. 276, 44 L. ed. 769, 20 Sup. Ct. Rep. 625, holding agreement of indefinite duration to assume management of farm, keep up same, and retain profits, without fixing of purchase price, and on demand to return same with same personalty or its equivalent in value not a sale.

—Deposits of grain.

Cited with special approval in Baker v. Woodruff, 2 Barb. 520, holding that

delivery of wheat to be returned in an agreed quantity of flour of a certain gra
was sale.

Cited in Johnston v. Browne, 37 Iowa, 200, holding delivery of grain
warehouseman on agreement to return same quantity and same quality of gr
or highest market price, a sale; Norton v. Woodruff, 2 N. Y. 153, holding tl
agreement to take wheat and give in payment flour, in absence of agreem(
that latter shall be made from former, constitutes sale; Chase v. Washbu
1 Ohio St. 244, 59 A. D. 623, holding deposit of wheat with warehouseman un
agreement to return it or other wheat of same quality and value, or pay high
market price, a sale; O'Neal v. Stone, 79 Mo. App. 279, holding delivery
wheat to be returned the same or of equal value, or to be paid for in money,
sale.

Cited in reference notes in 53 A. D. 435, on nature and effect of contract
deliver wheat to be paid for in flour; 57 A. D. 534; 94 A. S. R. 209,—on delive
of wheat to miller to be paid for in flour.

Cited in note in 94 A. S. R. 222, on distinction between absolute sale a
bailment of cereals in warehouse.

Distinguished in Sexton v. Graham, 53 Iowa, 181, 4 N. W. 1090, holdi
deposit of grain with warehouseman under agreement that it may be mix
with common mass, a bailment, notwithstanding warehouseman mixes his o
grain with common mass; Mallory v. Willis, 4 N. Y. 76, holding that delive
of wheat to be manufactured into flour, furnishing of barrels therefor, rece
of residue after manufacture, and payment of price for manufacture on one si
and agreement to deliver flour of certain grade on other, constituted bailme

Loss on bailment for hire.

Cited in Clark v. United States, 1 Ct. Cl. 246 (dissenting opinion), on risk
loss upon delivery of article to be manufactured.

Sale by bailee.

Cited in reference note in 48 A. D. 651, on title acquired by bona fide purchas
on unauthorized sale by bailee.

Cited in note in 66 A. D. 758, on power of bailees to make absolute sale
property bailed.

Liability of bailee.

Cited in note in 10 A. D. 491, on liability of bailee.

When replevin lies.

Cited in note in 19 A. D. 468, as to when replevin lies.

Parties in replevin suit.

Cited in note in 80 A. S. R. 752, on parties defendant in replevin or cla'
and delivery.

34 AM. DEC. 216, HANNA v. MILLS, 21 WEND. 90.

When assumpsit lies.

Cited in reference note in 71 A. D. 578, on assumpsit for money had a
received.

Evidence admissible under general issue.

Cited in reference notes in 43 A. D. 750; 60 A. D. 381; 68 A. D. 623,
admissibility of evidence of payment under general issue.

Cited in note in 61 A. D. 60, on proof of payment under general issue a
under general denial.

Right of action on sale on credit.

Cited in Landis v. Morrissey, 69 Cal. 83, 10 Pac. 258, holding that in sale on credit, action cannot be maintained before expiration of credit.

— Under agreement to give security.

Cited in Cooke v. Cook, 110 Ala. 567, 20 So. 64, holding that vendor may sue immediately on failure to give security; Barron v. Mullin, 21 Minn. 374, holding that vendor may sue at once on breach; Kelly v. Pierce, 16 N. D. 234, 12 L.R.A.(N.S.) 180, 112 N. W. 995; Young v. Dalton, 83 Tex. 497, 18 S. W. 819; Stephenson v. Repp, 47 Ohio St. 551, 10 L.R.A. 620, 25 N. E. 803,—holding that seller of goods on agreement to give promissory note payable at future date, may, on refusal to give note, sue at once on agreement; Turner v. Morgan, 4 Tex. Civ. App. 192, 23 S. W. 284; Carnahan v. Hughes, 108 Ind. 225, 9 N. E. 79,—holding that on refusal to give note vendor may maintain action at once, and recover full price of goods sold; Manton v. Gammon, 7 Ill. App. 201; Orr v. Leathers, 27 Ind. App. 572, 61 N. E. 941,—holding that vendor may sue at once on breach of such agreement, without waiting for expiration of term of credit; Gibson v. Stevens, 3 McLean, 551, Fed. Cas. No. 5,401, on right to sue immediately on breach of special agreement to give security on sale; Cook v. Stevenson, 30 Mich. 242, holding defense that reasonable time was to be extended for payment is unavailing to buyer who, on receipt of goods, failed to immediately give securities as agreed; Wheeler v. Harrah, 14 Or. 325, 12 Pac. 500, holding that, on breach of condition to obtain acceptable surety on note, vendor may sue for price before expiration of credit; Brown v. Van Winkle Gin & Mach. Works, 141 Ala. 580, 6 L.R.A.(N.S.) 585, 39 So. 243, holding that on breach of agreement to deliver securities action may be begun at once; Aultman v. Daggs, 50 Mo. App. 280, holding that vendor can, on suit on breach of agreement, recover amount of note agreed to be given.

Cited in reference note in 6 A. S. R. 121, on vendor's recovery for nonpayment of goods when he agreed to take note payable in futuro, which was not given.

Cited in note in 12 L.R.A.(N.S.) 180, 182, on effect of refusal to execute purchase-money notes to give vendor an immediate right of action.

Immediate action on breach of future agreement.

Cited in Lee v. Decker, 2 N. Y. Trans. App. 248, 43 How. Pr. 479, 3 Abb. App. Dec. 53, 6 Abb. Pr. N. S. 392, holding that repudiation of contingent agreement gives immediate cause of action.

— On breach of agreement to give security.

Cited in Stoddard v. Mix, 14 Conn. 12, holding that party who compromises and dismisses action on promise of other to execute note may sue at once on breach; O'Connor v. Dingley, 26 Cal. 11, holding that party who has performed may sue at once upon failure to give security as agreed by other.

Variance.

Cited in Ronge v. Dawson, 9 Wis. 246, holding verdict on one of two material pleas erroneous as not disposing all issues raised; Rogers-Ruger Co. v. McCord, 115 Wis. 261, 91 N. W. 685, holding that, in action on contract to enforce payment of money, plaintiff must prove facts establishing duty to pay; Van-Steenburgh v. Hoffman, 6 How. Pr. 492, on duty of referee to state all material facts in issue and his findings thereon.

34 AM. DEC. 219, NEWCOMB v. RAYNOR, 21 WEND. 108.

Discharge of party secondarily liable on negotiable instrument.

Cited in Farmers' Bank v. Blair, 44 Barb. 641; Homestead Bank v. Hollister, 7 Misc. 422, 27 N. Y. Supp. 1015,—holding indorser released by discharge of maker; Jones v. Bacon, 72 Hun, 506, 25 N. Y. Supp. 212, holding promisor in contract of indemnity to indorser released by discharge of maker by indorser; Ross v. Jones, 22 Wall. 576, 22 L. ed. 730, holding that delay in enforcing payment against maker does not, after presentment, demand, and notice of dishonor, relieve indorser.

Cited in reference note in 59 A. D. 104, on duty of creditor to do nothing to impair rights and remedy of surety.

Cited in note in 115 A. S. R. 102, on effect on creditor's right against surety where lien in favor of creditor is lost by operation of law.

Distinguished in Deck v. Works, 18 Hun, 266, 57 How. Pr. 292, holding guarantor not released by failure to give notice of nonpayment to prior indorser, in absence of such provision in guaranty; Phelps v. Borland, 30 Hun, 362, holding that discharge in bankruptcy of drawee without assent of holder did not relieve drawer who is indorser.

34 AM. DEC. 220, HERKIMER COUNTY BANK v. COX, 21 WEND. 119.

Protest of paper by officer of bank.

Cited in note in 43 A. D. 217, on proper person to protest foreign draft.

Distinguished in Nelson v. First Nat. Bank, 16 C. C. A. 425, 32 U. S. App. 554, 69 Fed. 798, holding that, rule of disqualification of witness for interest being abrogated in circuit courts of United States, cashier of bank may legally protest paper; Moreland v Citizens' Sav. Bank, 97 Ky. 211, 30 S. W. 637, holding, under statute, protest by notary, who is cashier, valid.

34 AM. DEC. 220, UTICA & S. R. CO. v. BRINCKERHOFF, 21 WEND. 139.

When mutual promises binding.

Cited in Walker v. Gilbert, 2 Daly, 80, holding agreement, concurrent in point of time, that tenant should send goods to auction and that damages sustained, being difference between such price and invoice, should be paid by landlord, binding; Walker v. Gilbert, 2 Robt. 214, holding promise by landlord to pay difference between price obtained at auction and invoice price, tenant not agreeing so to dispose, not binding by subsequently selling at auction; Morrow v. Southern Exp. Co. 101 Ga. 810, 28 S. E. 998, holding promise to carry such goods as another might offer for shipment, without undertaking by such other to make such shipments, not binding; Boyce v. Brown, 7 Barb. 80, holding agreement to grant use of road in consideration of other's building thereon, without concurring obligation so to build, not binding by subsequent compliance with offer; Coe v Tough, 116 N. Y. 273, 22 N. E. 550, holding offer of debtor to sell goods to his creditor in payment of debt, founded on no new consideration, not rendered a valid contract of sale by subsequent acceptance; McConnell v. Brillhart, 17 Ill. 354, 65 A. D. 661, holding general offer to sell and acceptance thereof, founded on sufficient consideration, binding; Hoffman v. Maffioli, 104 Wis. 630, 47 L.R.A. 427, 80 N. W. 1032, holding that offer to sell another such goods as he desired and unqualified acceptance did not create a binding contract; Marietta Paper Mfg. Co. v. Bussey, 104 Ga. 477, 31 S. E. 415 (dissenting opinion), on necessity of concurrence of obligation in mutual promises to make them binding.

Cited in note in 18 E. R. C. 614, on independent and dependent covenants.

Distinguished in Burrell v. Root, 40 N. Y. 496, holding agreement under seal to buy back property at future date, executed simultaneously with deed, not void for want of consideration.

Liability on subscription agreement.

Cited in Troy & B. R. Co. v. Tibbits, 18 Barb. 297, holding that signer of preliminary subscription prior to organization of corporation, agreeing to take and pay for stock, does not thereby become stockholder and liable for calls; Powers v. Rude, 14 Okla. 381, 79 Pac. 89, holding that subscription contract, to be binding, must be accepted within time specified or within reasonable time if none is specified; Land Grant R. & Trust Co. v. Davis County, 6 Kan. 256, holding voting by county to issue bonds and to subscribe for railway stock on condition of railroad being built, not a contract, and not binding by performance of condition; Crawford County v. Louisville, N. A. & St. L. Air Line R. Co. 39 Ind. 192, holding that railroad could not, under statute authorizing municipality to subscribe to stock, compel such subscription, the road not being bound to furnish stock on offer to subscribe; Broadbent v. Johnson, 2 Idaho, 325, 13 Pac. 83, holding that gratuitous subscription is mere offer which, until accepted in express terms or by performance of condition stipulated therein, is *nudum pactum;* Macedon & B. Pl. Road Co. v. Snediker, 18 Barb. 317, holding subscription on condition of performance of certain act without agreement of other so to perform, void for want of consideration and mutuality; Barnes v. Perine. 15 Barb. 249 (dissenting opinion), on liability of subscriber on agreement which is not presently obligatory on all.

Disapproved in Taggart v. Western Maryland R. Co. 24 Md. 563, 89 A. D. 760, holding that conditional subscription to stock is continuing offer, and when accepted becomes absolute and binding.

— Contract of employment.

Cited in Wilkinson v. Heavenrich, 58 Mich. 574, 55 A. R. 708, 26 N. W. 139. holding contract for services for three years signed by employer only, not binding upon him for want of mutuality.

Necessity for consideration.

Cited in reference note in 21 A. S. R. 889, on effect of want of consideration.

Cited in note in 6 E. R. C. 8, on necessity of consideration to support action on contract not under seal.

34 AM. DEC. 223, DOWNING v. RUGAR, 21 WEND. 178.

Exercise of joint or common authority for public purpose.

Cited in People ex rel. Mygatt v. Chenango County, 11 N. Y. 563, holding where statute provides that assessment shall be made by board, assessment by one assessor invalid; Jennings v. Jenkins, 9 Ala. 285, holding that sale of land by commissioners acting under order of court need not be with as strict compliance to authority granted as that of individual power; Oakley v. Aspinwall, 3 N. Y. 547 (dissenting opinion), on exercise of public duty by all to whom it is delegated, in absence of provision for its exercise by less number.

Cited in reference notes in 34 A. D. 235; 52 A. D. 463,—on how authority delegated to several is exercised.

Cited in note in 1 A. D. 201, on necessity of all arbitrators acting.

— Power of majority when legally convoked.

Cited in Burke v. Burpo, 75 Hun, 568, 27 N. Y. Supp. 684, holding that authority conferred on two or more persons of same class can only be exercised
when all have been duly convened and act as board; People ex rel. Haws v.
Walker, 2 Abb. Pr. 421, 23 Barb. 304, holding, in absence of words as to what
shall constitute quorum in act creating board, action of majority after notice
of meeting to all, binding; People ex rel. Crawford v. Lothrop County, 3 Colo.
428, holding action of majority of board, which is organic part of government,
binding where all have been notified of meeting; Colgin v. State Bank, 11 Ala.
222, holding bank commissioners public officers, and exercise of authority by
majority, binding; School Dist v. Bennett, 52 Ark. 511, 13 S. W. 132, holding
contract made by two commissioners at meeting attended by third binding;
Re Fourth Ave. 11 Abb. Pr. 189, holding report of two commissioners appointed
to appraise land for public purpose, binding, where third member has met and
concurred, but dissents from report; Cowan v. Murch, 97 Tenn. 590, 34 L.R.A.
538, 37 S. W. 393, holding that two members of court of chancery may hear,
consider, and decide causes, where other member is absent, although act creating
court does not provide number which shall constitute quorum.

Cited in reference notes in 73 A. D. 723, as to when act of majority will not
bind minority; 66 A. D. 501, on power of majority of corporators to act.

— Necessity of attendance of, or notice to, all.

Cited in Stewart v. Wallis, 30 Barb. 344, holding order signed by two commissioners without showing that third met and deliberated, or was notified and
failed to attend, void; Schuyler v. Marsh, 37 Barb. 350, holding balloting in
presence of two commissioners, in absence of third, void under statute requiring
balloting to be in presence of the commissioners; Re Thirty-fourth Street, 31
How. Pr. 42, holding confirmation of assessment by majority of board, where all
have not met together for purpose of acting, invalid; Harris v. Whitney, 6 How.
Pr. 175, holding order signed by majority of judges of court, where all have not
met and conferred on matter, defective; Keeler v. Frost, 22 Barb. 400, holding
apportionment of taxes made by two trustees without consultation with third,
void; Pike County v. Rowland, 94 Pa. 238, 9 W. N. C. 241; Paola & F. River
R. Co. v. Anderson County, 16 Kan. 302,—holding action of majority of board
at special meeting of which no notice was sent to all members, invalid; Hamilton v. State, 3 Ind. 452, holding action of board at which one member is absent,
invalid; Kavanaugh v. Wausau, 120 Wis. 611, 98 N. W. 550, holding that public body charged with judicial duty can act by majority only where all members are present, or have been notified and given opportunity to be present;
Stephenson v. Hall, 14 Barb. 222, holding action of two trustees without notice
to third, invalid.

Distinguished in Parrott v. Knickerbocker Ice Co. 38 How. Pr. 508, 8 Abb.
Pr. N. S. 234, 1 Sweeny, 533, holding that statute requiring action of public
officers by majority to be upon meeting of all did not apply to distinctly judicial officers, and decision of two judges without consultation with third, binding; Johnson v. Dodd, 56 N. Y. 76, holding, under statute, exercise of authority
by majority, irrespective of and without consultation with minority, binding.

—Authority vested in two persons.

Cited in Perry v. Tynen, 22 Barb. 137, holding that public authority delegated
to two cannot be performed by one without consent of other; Snodgrass v.
Wetzel County Ct. 44 W. Va. 56, 29 S. E. 1035, holding that ministerial act

to be performed by two may be performed by one in presence of other, and by his authority, in name of both; Powell v. Tuttle, 3 N. Y. 396, holding sale by one commissioner under statute authorizing sale by two, irregular and void.

Criticized in Williamsburg v. Jackson, 11 Ohio, 37, holding act of one official where authority is conferred on two, void.

— In case of vacancy or refusal to act.

Cited in People ex rel. Kingsland v. Palmer, 52 N. Y. 83, holding execution of instrument by three commissioners, others of board having ceased to hold office, valid and presumed to be by concurrence of all; North Platte v. North Platte Waterworks Co. 56 Neb. 403, 76 N. W. 906, holding action of four members present and voting, out of body of six of whom one had resigned, binding under statute authorizing action by three fourths of total number of body; Rushville Gas Co. v. Rushville, 121 Ind. 206, 16 A. S. R. 388, 6 L.R.A. 315, 23 N. E. 72, holding vote of majority of quorum present, although number of those who refuse to vote equals number who do, effective; First Nat. Bank v. Mt. Tabor, 52 Vt. 87, 36 A. R. 734, holding execution of certificate under statutory authority by two commissioners, the third sharing and participating in deliberations but refusing to sign, conclusive.

Presumption of regularity.

Cited in Brick's Estate, 15 Abb. Pr. 12, holding appointment of guardian by court having jurisdiction, presumed to be according to its established practice.

— In performance of official duty.

Cited in Reynolds v. Schweinefus, 27 Ohio St. 311 (reversing 1 Cin. Sup. Ct. Rep. 215), holding that presumption exists that city council passed ordinance upon recommendation of proper board according to charter; Re New York, 95 App. Div. 533, 88 N. Y. Supp. 769, holding that, where map is filed in proper office in pursuance of statute, presumption exists that preliminary legal steps were duly taken.

Cited in reference note in 27 A. D. 126, on presumption of performance of official duty.

— Of regular call and meeting of public board.

Cited in Hill v. Peekskill Sav. Bank, 46 Hun, 180, holding that presumption is that action by majority of board was upon meeting and conference with all; Keeler v. Frost, 22 Barb. 400, holding action by majority of board presumed to be upon meeting and consultation of all; Tucker v. Rankin, 15 Barb. 471, holding that order signed by two members of board will, in absence of contrary proof, be presumed to have been upon meeting and consultation with third; Jackson v. Hampden, 20 Me. 37, holding certificate of majority of board prima facie evidence of proper performance of duty; Board of Excise v. Doherty, 16 How. Pr. 46, holding action of majority of commissioners presumed to have been on meeting and conference of all; West Jersey Traction Co. v. Camden Horse R. Co. 52 N. J. Eq. 452, 29 Atl. 333, holding that presumption of joint deliberation arises in execution of public duty requiring concurrence of officials.

— Of consent to act of co-officer or cotrustee.

Cited in Perry v. Tynen, 22 Barb. 137, holding that consent of one of two public officers to performance of exclusively ministerial act in name of both may be presumed, but not where act is not beneficial to body for whom officers are acting; Wells v. Gates, 18 Barb. 554, holding performance of ministerial act by two managers of private trust presumed to be by consent of third; Scott v.

Detroit Young Men's Soc. 1 Dougl. (Mich.) 119, holding that, where performance of public duty is enjoined on two or more, presumption arises that
act performed was by concurrence of all; Board of Excise v. Sackrider, 35
N. Y. 154, holding approval by one member of board of institution of suit not
sufficient to sustain presumption of concurrence by other members.

Distinguished in Mark v. West Troy, 69 Hun, 442, 23 N. Y. Supp. 422, holding
that making of contract by one city official personally cannot be presumed to be
by authority of board empowered to make contract, there being no evidence
that they ever acted or assumed to act in the matter.

Presumption as to authority and duty.

Cited in Tuthill v. Wheeler, 6 Barb. 362, holding duty imposed by law upon
public officer, presumed to be performed by him; Kluwicki v. Munro, 95 Mich.
28, 54 N. W. 703, holding acts of member of board authorized by board, under
statute, to do certain work, presumed within his authority; Huey v. Van Wie,
23 Wis. 613, holding that, under statute declaring tax deed shall not be invalidated for error in conveyance, signing of such deed by deputy will, in
absence of showing of disability, be presumed to be by authority of clerk;
Miller v. Lewis, 4 N. Y. 554 (dissenting opinion), on presumption of authority
to execute certificate by deputy clerk.

Effect of official return or certificate.

Cited in Albany County Sav. Bank v. McCarty, 149 N. Y. 71, 43 N. E. 427,
holding certificate of acknowledgment by commissioner of deeds, prima facie
evidence of facts certified therein.

Estoppel to deny concurrence of associate.

Distinguished in Doughty v. Hope, 3 Denio, 594 (reversing 3 Denio, 249),
holding official who acted, competent witness to prove that one who did not
was not consulted.

Conclusiveness of findings of law and fact.

Cited in Wakeman v. Wilbur, 147 N. Y. 657, 42 N. E. 341, holding findings
by jury or referee, based on questions of law and fact, not erroneous as matter
of law.

34 AM. DEC. 228, CROCKER v. CRANE, 21 WEND. 211.

Certificate of notary as evidence.

Cited in reference note in 82 A. D. 108, on effect of certificate of notary as
evidence.

Cited in note in 96 A. D. 606, on presumptions in favor of protest and what
statements therein are evidence.

Proof of sending notice by mail.

Cited in reference note in 36 A. D. 126, on sufficiency of proof of sending
notice by mail.

Construction of statutes.

Cited in People v. Hill, 3 Utah, 334, 3 Pac. 75, holding that intention of
legislature if manifest will be carried into effect, although apt words are not
used; Maynard v. Johnson, 2 Nev. 25, holding that statute should be construed
to give it effect, and not to allow it to be eluded; People v. Deming, 13 How. Pr.
441, 1 Hilt. 271, holding that intention of legislature should be followed, although in apparent contrariety to letter of statute; Marion Twp. Union Drain
Co. v. Norris, 37 Ind. 424, on construction of statute to effect intention of

legislature; Pettit v. Fretz, 33 Pa. 118; Jersey Co. v. Davison, 29 N. J. L. 415, —holding that court will interpret doubtful statute consonant with equity.

Execution of joint powers in concert.

Cited in Keeler v. Frost, 22 Barb. 400, holding assessment made by two trustees without notice to and meeting with third, void; Birge v. People, 5 Park. Crim. Rep. 9, holding performance of duty requiring judgment and discretion, by one judge in absence of others, invalid; Perry v. Tynen, 22 Barb. 137, holding that, where two officers have begun suit, one cannot discontinue suit without consent or concurrence of other; Doughty v. Hope, 3 Denio, 249, holding assessment by one assessor without meeting and consultation with others of board, invalid; Oakley v. Aspinwall, 3 N. Y. 547 (dissenting opinion), on rendering of decision by less than entire number of court in absence of provision in regard thereto.

Cited in reference note in 34 A. D. 227, on mode of exercising authority delegated to several for public or private purposes.

Cited in note in 1 A. D. 201, on necessity of all arbitrators acting.

Distinguished in Parrott v. Knickerbocker Ice Co. 38 How. Pr. 508, 1 Sweeny, 533, 8 Abb. Pr. N. S. 234, holding that statute requiring concurrence did not apply to distinctly judicial officers, and decision may be rendered by two judges who heard cause without consultation with third.

— Power of majority.

Cited in Schwanbeck v. People, 15 Colo. 64, 24 Pac. 575, holding in absence of express authority so to do, act by majority of board, in absence of other members, void; Carroll v. Alsup, 107 Tenn. 257, 64 S. W. 193, holding that where statute creates board of three, and provides majority shall constitute quorum, presence and concurrence of two members at regular meeting renders action binding; Townsend v. Hazard, 9 R. I. 436, holding report by majority of commissioners appointed by court, valid, where minority has met and conferred with majority; Tucker v. Rankin, 15 Barb. 471, holding execution of instrument by two commissioners effective, as presumption exists that third commissioner met and consulted with them; Cowan v. Murch, 97 Tenn. 590, 34 L.R.A. 538, 37 S. W. 393, holding that, in absence of one member of court, because of disability, two remaining members may hear, consider, and decide causes, although no provision is made for action by majority in act creating court; First Nat. Bank v. Mt. Tabor, 52 Vt. 87, 36 A. R. 734, holding execution of certificate by majority of commissioners, where all have met and deliberated but part refuse to execute, conclusive; Re State Treasurer's Settlement (Bartley v. Meserve), 51 Neb. 116, 36 L.R.A. 746, 70 N. W. 532, holding execution of instrument by majority, where all members of commission have met and considered, effective; People v. Coghill, 47 Cal. 361, holding, where statute creating board has failed to provide for quorum, action by two where third has not met and consulted, void; People ex rel. Henry v. Nostrand, 46 N. Y. 375, holding, where power is expressly devolved on three, exercise of authority by two commissioners, the third having resigned, invalid; Schenck v. Peay, Woolw. 175, Fed. Cas. No. 12,450, holding, where statute requires act to be performed by three commissioners, action by two where third never qualified nor entered office, void; Gibbons v. Mobile & G. N. R. Co. 36 Ala. 410, on validity of subscription authorized by city council some of whose members are stockholders in corporation.

—Power of minority.

Cited in State ex rel. Whedon v. Smith, 57 Neb. 41, 77 N. W. 384, holding nominations by minority of political committee invalid, where all members were not notified of time and place of meeting.

Nature of act of taking subscriptions.

Cited in reference note in 89 A. D. 772, on the taking of subscriptions by commissioners under statute being ministerial act.

Cited in note in 81 A. D. 397, on what agents can receive subscriptions.

Defense to action on stock subscription.

Cited in reference note in 63 A. D. 526, on insufficiency of organization or forfeiture of charter as defense to action on stock subscription.

Release of subscriber for stock.

Cited in note in 81 A. D. 401, on withdrawal or release of subscriber.

Necessity of cash payment on stock subscription.

Cited in Beach v. Smith, 28 Barb. 254, holding payment in money *eo nomine* at time of subscription not necessary to its validity, and subsequent payment will operate as waiver of condition; State Ins. Co. v. Redmond, 1 McCrary, 308, 3 Fed. 764, holding that, where charter and by-laws require certain percentage of subscription to be paid in cash at time of subscribing, corporation cannot enforce payment of subscription, where such payment was not made; Ogdensburgh, C. & R. R. Co. v. Wolley, 1 Keyes, 118 (dissenting opinion), on invalidity of subscription on which no cash payment was made as required by charter.

Distinguished in Minneapolis & St. L. R. Co. v. Bassett, 20 Minn. 535, Gil. 478, 18 A. R. 376, holding subscription after incorporation on which nothing is paid as required by charter, binding.

Disapproved in Pittsburgh, W. & K. R. Co. v. Applegate, 21 W. Va. 172, holding subscription not invalid where no payment was made at time of subscribing as required by charter.

Sufficiency of payment on subscriptions for corporate stock.

Cited in McDougald v. Lane, 18 Ga. 444, holding stockholder liable to innocent creditor although organization detective for failure to pay required portion of stock in specie; Kirksey v. Florida & G. P. R. Co. 7 Fla. 23, 68 A. D. 426 (dissenting opinion), on invalidity of subscription where amount of capital and number and value of shares are not included in charter.

—Payment in checks or paper.

Cited in Syracuse, P. & O. R. Co. v. Gere, 4 Hun, 392, 6 Thomp. & C. 636, holding payment by check equivalent to cash although given under agreement with agent that check would never be presented for payment, such agent having no authority to bind corporation; Hayne v. Beauchamp, 5 Smedes & M. 515, holding that where charter provides certain percentage shall be paid at time of subscribing, a payment by note does not render subscriber stockholder, and subscription is void; Napier v. Poe, 12 Ga. 170, holding, where charter provides payments on subscription shall be in specie, organization where payments are made by draft a nullity; Thorp v. Woodhull, 1 Sandf. Ch. 411, holding that taking, in single instance, of check of subscriber on funds in bank, secured by bond and mortgage, did not as against subscriber render subscription void.

Cited in reference notes in 64 A. D. 296, on checks as payment; 55 A. D. 710, on invalidity of note or check taken for first instalment on stock subscription.

Distinguished in Clark v. Farrington, 11 Wis. 306, holding taking of note and mortgage in payment of stock after incorporation valid and binding.

Legal subscriptions as precedent to corporate existence.

Cited in Franklin F. Ins. Co. v. Hart, 31 Md. 59, holding subscription to stock, condition precedent to organization, and corporation not liable for services engaged before completion of subscriptions.

Distinguished in Union Water Co. v. Kean, 52 N. J. Eq. 111, 27 Atl. 1015, holding, under statute, opening of subscription books and receiving of subscriptions not a condition precedent to corporate existence.

Compelling exercise of discretionary powers.

Cited in note in 8 L.R.A. 176, as to whether equity will interfere with exercise of discretionary powers.

34 AM. DEC. 236, MORRIS v. SCOTT, 21 WEND. 281.

Form of action in malicious prosecution.

Cited in Hays v. Younglove, 7 B. Mon. 545, holding, either trespass or case proper, where court had no jurisdiction, and proceeding was malicious and without foundation; Mack v. Rawls, 57 Miss. 270, holding trespass on case proper where proceedings were on false charge and malicious, although affidavit on which prosecution was based fails to charge criminal offense; Apgar v. Woolston, 43 N. J. L. 57, holding trespass on the case maintainable, where malice and want of probable cause are gravamen of charge, where court was without jurisdiction; Platt v. Niles, 1 Edm. Sel. Cas. 230, holding where gravamen of action is not malice and want of probable cause, case not maintainable where arrest was caused on warrant void for want of jurisdiction; Shipman v. Fletcher, 9 Mackey, 245, holding where malice and falsehood of charge are gravamen, case maintainable where court had no jurisdiction.

Fatally defective or void malicious prosecution.

Cited in Castro v. Uriarte, 2 N. Y. Civ. Proc. Rep. (McCarty) 199, 2 N. Y. Civ. Proc. Rep. 210, holding irregularity and want of jurisdiction in proceedings, where subject-matter, person, and offense are within jurisdiction of magistrate, not a defense; Stubbs v. Mulholland, 168 Mo. 47, 67 S. W. 650, holding invalidity of warrant and want of jurisdiction of court where proceedings were had, not a defense; Stocking v. Howard, 73 Mo. 25, holding failure of affidavit on which prosecution was based to state crime, not a defense; Stancliff v. Palmeter, 18 Ind. 321, holding, where prosecution is with malice and without probable cause, failure of complaint to state criminal offense not a defense; Long v. Rogers, 17 Ala. 540, holding fact that charge on which arrest was made was not a statutory or common law crime, not a defense; Chapman v. Dodd, 10 Minn. 350, Gil. 277, holding failure to subscribe complaint on which warrant, regular on its face, issues, not a defense; Dennis v. Ryan, 65 N. Y. 385, 22 A. R. 635 (affirming 5 Lans. 350), holding false accusation alleging facts not constituting crime charged in indictment, not a defense; Ward v. Sutor, 70 Tex. 343, 8 A. S. R. 606, 8 S. W. 51, holding irregularity of proceedings in court having jurisdiction in which acquittal was had, not a defense; Potter v. Gjertsen, 37 Minn. 386, 34 N. W. 746; Minneapolis Threshing Mach. Co. v. Regier, 51 Neb. 402, 70 N. W. 934,— holding insufficiency of complaint on which arrest was had, not a defense in malicious prosecution; Ailstock v. Moore Lime Co. 104 Va. 565, 113 A. S. R. 1060, 2 L.R.A.(N.S.) 1100, 52 S. E. 213, 7 A. & E. Ann. Cas. 545, holding want of jurisdiction in malicious attachment, not a defense; Sweet v. Negus, 30

Mich. 406, holding want of jurisdiction, not apparent on face of warrant, not defense; Shaul v. Brown, 28 Iowa, 37, 4 A. R. 151, holding defect in indictme not a defense.

Cited in notes in 61 A. D. 444, as to whether action lies for malicious prosec tion before court having no jurisdiction; 26 A. S. R. 130; 2 L.R.A.(N.S.) 1101 on effect of lack of jurisdiction of court in which malicious prosecution is be upon right to maintain action therefor.

Pleadings in action for malicious prosecution.

Cited in note in 26 A. S. R. 152, on plaintiff's pleadings in malicious prosec tion.

Liability of complaining witness.

Cited in Dennis v. Ryan, 65 N. Y. 385, 22 A. R. 635 (dissenting opinio on liability to suit for malicious prosecution of witness, stating facts not co stituting criminal offense, on whose testimony indictment is returned.

Remedy for false imprisonment on void process.

Cited in Rice v. Platt, 3 Denio, 81, holding want of jurisdiction a defense action on case for false arrest and imprisonment.

34 AM. DEC. 238, HOWARD v. THOMPSON, 21 WEND. 319.

Privileged communications.

Cited in Hannens v. Nelson, 36 N. Y. S. R. 905, 13 N. Y. Supp. 175, on privile of communication on a subject-matter in reference to which the party co municating has a duty; Byam v. Collins, 111 N. Y. 143, 7 A. S. R. 726, 2 L.R. 129, 19 N. E. 75 (dissenting opinion), on defense of privilege of communicatio Words v. Wiman, 47 Hun, 362, holding a publication in a pamphlet delivered a governor, favoring a certain bill before him, to be privileged; Smith v. Ke 1 Edm. Sel. Cas. 190, holding same as to words spoken to a police officer whi were material for the detection of a robber; Streety v. Wood, 15 Barb. 1 holding communications addressed to a public officer to prevent an appointme of an individual to office, privileged.

Cited in reference notes in 66 A. D. 486, on what are privileged communi tions; 38 A. D. 143, on privilege attaching to communications made in cou of judicial proceedings; 76 A. D. 282, as to when publications concerning pub officers are libelous.

Cited in notes in 27 A. D. 158, on privileged communications; 15 A. D. 2 on privileged nature of communication addressed to body or individual to p cure redress; 28 L. ed. U. S. 159, on privileged communications to magistr or grand jury charging a crime.

Distinguished in Hosmer v. Loveland, 19 Barb. 111, holding that an affida in support of a petition to a governor to do an act which he has no authori to do is not privileged.

—Letters to public officer making charges against subordinate.

Referred to as a leading case in Henry v. Moberly, 6 Ind. App. 490, 33 N. 981, holding that a written protest to a board of trustees objecting to plainti employment as a teacher is privileged.

Cited in Larkin v. Noonan, 19 Wis. 83, holding statements made in a petiti to the governor for the removal of a sheriff from office privileged; Halstead Nelson, 24 Hun, 395 (later appeal in 36 Hun, 149), holding that a commuı cation made to a board of trustees of a public institution, affecting the charact of a teacher therein, is privileged unless shown to have been made witho probable cause and in bad faith; O'Donaghue v. M'Govern, 23 Wend. 26, holding that a communication to a bishop and ecclesiastical authorities of the diocese to which the plaintiff, a priest, was amenable, in respect to character and conduct of priest, if made in good faith is privileged otherwise is false and maliciously made.

— **Burden of proof as to malice and want of probable cause.**

Cited in Van Wyck v. Aspinwall, 17 N. Y. 190, holding that fact that a communication is privileged repels the inference of malice which would otherwise be drawn; Lathrop v. Hyde, 25 Wend. 448, holding that where express malice is shown that a privileged communication may be slanderous; Briggs v. Garrett, 111 Pa. 404, 56 A. R. 274, 17 W. N. C. 129, 2 Atl. 513, 43 Phila. Leg. Int. 99; Chapman v. Calder, 14 Pa. 365,—holding that issue in such case is, had the defendant probable cause for statement complained off; Klinck v. Colby, 46 N. Y. 427, 7 A. R. 360, holding that in such case plaintiff must prove malice in fact, and that defendant was actuated by motives of spite or ill will independent of the circumstances in which the communication was privileged; Ormsby v. Douglass, 37 N. Y. 477, holding that in such case plaintiff must show that defendant was influenced by some other motive than the mere discharge of a duty, and that communication was not made solely for privileged purposes; Decker v. Gaylord, 35 Hun, 584, holding that a communication to a school commission by a resident of a district, charging a woman then teaching with being unchaste, will be presumed to be made in good faith; Newfield v. Copperman, 10 Jones & S. 302; Viele v. Gray, 18 How Pr. 550, 10 Abb. Pr. 1,—holding that proof of want of probable cause is essential in such case.

Abuse of privileged communication as slander or libel.

Cited in Rall v. Donnelly, 56 Ill. App. 425, holding that, to hold a person liable for statements made in an affidavit in opposition to a motion for alimony, plaintiff must show express malice and want of probable cause; Smith v. Howard, 28 Iowa, 51, holding statement of a witness making impertinent answer and not bona fide but for purpose of defaming plaintiff 'is not privileged; Miller v. Nuckolls, 77 Ark. 64, 113 A. S. R. 122, 4 L.R.A.(N.S.) 149, 91 S. W. 759, 7 A. & E. Ann. Cas. 110; holding that a communication to a peace officer to aid in detection of crime is privileged only when made in good faith, and not when made to gratify personal malice.

Distinguished in Cranfill v. Hayden, 97 Tex. 544, 80 S. W. 609, holding that one who makes charges against the character of an officer of the Baptist General Convention at such convention is liable if not only impelled by a sense of duty, but also with a desire to injure the character of plaintiff.

Sending letter as publication.

Cited in reference note in 52 A. D. 770, as to whether sending libelous letter to another is publication or not.

Construction of words complained of in slander and libel.

Cited in Greenwood v. Cobbey, 26 Neb. 449, 42 N. W. 413, holding that a court cannot extend the meaning of words beyond their plain import to make them slanderous.

Parol evidence to show contents of a privileged communication.

Cited in Worthington v. Scribner, 109 Mass. 487, 12 A. R. 736, holding that, in an action for libel for statements made to the treasury department, defendant could not be compelled to answer interrogatories inquiring whether he gave certain information to department.

Questions of law as to libel.

Cited in reference note in 24 A. S. R. 722, on privilege of publication as qu
tion of law.

Cited in note in 5 L.R.A. 645, on province of jury in libel.

Mitigation of damages for libel.

Cited in notes in 15 A. S. R. 340, on elements increasing or mitigating damag
for newspaper libel; 21 A. D. 114, on truth as justification and in mitigati

34 AM. DEC. 250, BLANCHARD v. ELY, 21 WEND. 342.

Assignment of chose in action.

Cited in reference notes in 63 A. D. 130, on effect of assignment of chose
action; 44 A. D. 585, on assignment of choses in action as transfer of assigno
legal interest; 57 A. D. 310, on title acquired by assignee of non-negotia
chose in action.

Cited in note in 64 A. D. 429, on pledges of mortgages and negotiable instr
ments and sale thereof.

Parties to action.

Cited in Beach v. Fairbanks, 52 Conn. 167, holding that, in determini
questions that arise with regard to the parties to actions at law, the court loo
at the parties on the record.

Damages allowable by way of recoupment.

Cited in Rogers v. Humphrey, 39 Me. 382, holding that, where a contract
not fully performed, damages suffered by reason thereof may be deducted
suit on contract; Hatchett v. Gibson, 13 Ala. 587, holding that, in an action
a contract for storage of cotton to recover advances made, bailor could reco
damage sustained by destruction of cotton; Allaire Works v. Guion, 10 Ba
55, holding that damage cannot be allowed by way of recoupment on account
the malice with which the wrongful acts were done.

Cited in reference note in 100 A. S. R. 721, on what may be subject of set-o

Cited in notes in 40 A. D. 327, on measure of damages in recoupment;
A. D. 332, on recoupments in contracts for work and labor.

Loss of profits as an element of damage.

Cited in Choctaw, O. & G. R. Co. v. Jacobs, 15 Okla. 493, 82 Pac. 502; Cowe
Falls Mfg. Co. v. Rogers, 19 Ga. 416, 65 A. D. 602; Howard v. Stillwell & B. Mf
Co. 139 U. S. 199, 35 L. ed. 147, 11 Sup. Ct. Rep. 500,—holding that in certa
anticipated profits, lost by breach of a contract, are not recoverable as damage
Jones v. Judd, 4 N. Y. 411, holding that profits expected under a contract cann
be recouped; Howe Mach. Co. v. Bryson, 44 Iowa, 159, 24 A. R. 735, holdi
remote and contingent damages based upon profits purely speculative in chara
ter not recoverable as damages for breach of contract; Bell v. Reynolds, 78 A?
511, 56 A. R. 52, holding loss of profits not allowable as damages for failu
to deliver goods; Devlin v. New York, 63 N. Y. 8, 50 How. Pr. 1, holding adva
tages and benefits of subcontracts not to be considered in estimating damag
to original contractor; Griffin v. Colver, 16 N. Y. 489, 69 A. D. 718 (affirmi
22 Barb. 587), holding, in an action for the recovery of purchase price of a stea
engine, that loss of gains and profits which would have arisen from use of engi
had it been delivered at time agreed, cannot be recouped; Finch v. Heerma
5 Luzerne Leg. Reg. 125, holding profits which might have been made by u
of mill but for delay in construction not available in action for contract pri

of construction; New York Academy of Music v. Hackett, 2 Hilt. 217, holding
that profits anticipated from a future public performance of a vocalist cannot
be recovered; Krom v. Levy, 48 N. Y. 679, holding, in an action for breach of
contract to furnish a plate to print the backs of cards, that damage for loss
of business by being deprived of plate should not be allowed; Wehle v. Haviland,
69 N. Y. 448, holding, in an action for conversion of a stock of goods, that loss
of speculative profits is not allowable as damages; Draper v. Sweet, 66 Barb.
145, holding that where warranted steel was defective, and defect was found
as soon as vendee began to use it, he has no right to go on using steel on
expectation of recovering expenses and loss of profits; Brauer v. Oceanic Steam
Nav. Co. 34 Misc. 127, 69 N. Y. Supp. 465, holding loss of commissions by
reason of failure of defendant to deliver cattle, not recoverable; Western Gravel
Road Co. v. Cox, 39 Ind. 260, holding loss of tolls not allowable as damages for
failure to complete road at time specified; Ripley v. Mosely, 57 Me. 76, holding
where a stock of goods was wrongfully held under an attachment, that probable
profits lost could not be recovered; Western U. Teleg. Co. v. Graham, 1 Colo.
230, 9 A. R. 136, holding, in an action against a telegraph company to recover
damages for the nondelivery of a telegram, that plaintiff cannot recover profits
which he might have made by transaction; Merschiem v. Musical Mut. Protective
Union, 24 Abb. N. C. 252, 18 N. Y. Supp. 702, holding, in an action for damages
for an unlawful expulsion from a labor association, that proof of how much
his earnings were diminished and his inability to obtain continuous employment
after expulsion was admissible.

Cited in reference notes in 78 A. D. 387, on recovery of loss of profits as
damages; 56 A. D. 318, on allowance of damages for remote and speculative loss
of profits; 30 A. S. R. 471, on profits as element of damages for breach of
contract; 52 A. D. 199; 61 A. D. 761,—as to when future or probable profits
may be considered in estimating damages.

Cited in notes in 60 A. R. 494, on loss of profits as damages; 53 L.R.A. 52,
on loss of profits as element of damages for breach of contract to construct or
repair buildings, vessels, etc.; 53 L. R. A. 39, on effect of speculativeness or contingency on right to recover profits lost by breach of contract.

Distinguished in Taylor v. Bradley, 4 Abb. App. Dec. 363, holding that profits
which would certainly have been realized but for breach of contract are recoverable; Davis v. Talcott, 14 Barb. 611, holding, under agreement by seller to
pay vendees all damages, losses, injury, and expenses they might incur by reason
of the insufficiency of machinery, that loss of profits arising from defects of
machinery could be recovered; Hinckley v. Beckwith, 13 Wis. 31, holding, in
an action for breach of contract to repair mill, that profits of cutting logs
which were hauled to mill was a proper element of damages; St. John v. New
York, 13 How. Pr. 527, 6 Duer, 315, holding, in an action for damages because
of a nuisance maintained on and about a sidewalk, injuring plaintiffs' business,
that loss of custom is a proper ground of recovery; Howe Machine Co. v. Bryson,
44 Iowa, 159, 24 A. R. 735 (dissenting opinion); Lattin v. Davis, Hill & D. Supp.
9 (dissenting opinion),—on loss of profit as a measure of damages.

Questioned in Albert v. Bleecker Street & C. R. Co. 2 Daly, 389, holding,
where plaintiff's business as an expressman was wholly suspended by reason
of a fatal injury of his horse caused by defendant's negligence, that loss of
profits during a reasonable time in which plaintiff was selecting another horse
was recoverable.

Consequential damages.

Cited in Gerson v. Slemons, 30 Ark. 50; Wibert v. New York & E. R. Co. 19 Barb. 36,—holding that damages must be the natural and proximate consequences of the act complained of; Freeman v. Clute, 3 Barb. 424, holding that where there is a breach of warranty of personal property sold, vendee can only recover of vendor the difference in value between the property as it was in fact and as it was represented to be; Walrath v. Redfield, 11 Barb. 368, holding that, in an action for damages to a sawmill, occasioned by the construction of a dam below, deterioration in value of logs, or their depression in market price is not allowable; Sledge v. Reid, 73 N. C. 440, holding that, in an action for conversion of a mule, recovery for loss of a part of crop because of loss of mule cannot be had; Sharon v. Mosher, 17 Barb. 518, holding, where vendor of a horse made fraudulent representations as to its nature, that damages by reason of a broken leg due to vicious propensity of horse could be recovered; Woodbury v. Jones, 44 N. H. 206, holding cost of removal of property recoverable for breach of agreement that if one would go to a place he would be given a contract there; Evans v. Root, 4 Abb. App. Dec. 160, holding that the fall in the market is the measure or damages in an action against a factor for omitting to sell goods consigned according to instructions; Page v. Ford, 12 Ind. 46, on what consequential damages are recoverable; Mott v. Hudson River R. Co. 1 Robt. 585, holding that damages caused by the spreading of a fire because of defendant negligently injuring a hose actually in use in extinguishing fire and cutting off only access to water not recoverable; Rich v. Smith, 34 Hun, 136, holding that injuries resulting from a collision with another vehicle while running away cannot be recovered in an action for breach of a general warranty of a horse; Porter v. Woods, 3 Humph. 56, 39 A. D. 152, holding that in action for breach of contract to deliver casting, damages for delay in business cannot be recovered.

Cited in reference notes in 48 A. D. 392, on remoteness of damages; 41 A. D. 767, on consequential damages; 61 A. D. 209, on extent of consequential damages allowed for breach of contract or deceit in sale of chattels.

Cited in note in 45 A. D. 484, on consequential damages for breach of contract.

Distinguished in Manville v. Western U. Teleg. Co. 37 Iowa, 214, 18 A. R. 8, holding measure of damages for failure to deliver telegram to "ship logs at once" was the difference between the market values; True v. International Teleg. Co. 60 Me. 9, 11 A. R. 156, holding damage for failure to deliver telegram for an order of corn was difference between price named and that which would have to be paid for an order at same place.

— For breach depriving of use of property.

Cited in Green v. Mann, 11 Ill. 613, holding that, for failure to furnish certain machinery for a mill, measure of damages was the value of the use of that portion of machinery; Cassidy v. Le Fevre, 45 N. Y. 562, holding rent or hire during loss of time, measure of damage for breach of warranty by vendor of an engine; Washington & G. R. Co. v. American Car Co. 5 App. D. C. 524, holding that reasonable rental value less interest on contract price during delay is measure of damages for failure to deliver cars on time.

Cited in note in 19 L.R.A.(N.S.) 157, on measure of damages for breach of contract preventing operation of industrial business in contemplation, but not established or in actual operation.

Distinguished in Fisk v. Tank, 12 Wis. 276, 78 A. D. 737, holding, where there is a delay in delivery of machinery under contract, that wages and board of workingman kept idle could be recovered.

— **For loss of use of boat.**

Cited in Brownell v. Chapman, 84 Iowa, 504, 35 A. S. R. 326, 51 N. W. 249, holding rental value of boat measure of damages in case of breach of contract to supply her boiler and machinery; The Rhode Island, 2 Blatchf. 113, Fed. Cas. No. 11,744 (affirming Abb. Adm. 100, Fed. Cas. No. 11,740a), holding a libellant in admiralty not entitled to damages, in case of collision, for the delay and loss of trips while his vessel is undergoing necessary repairs; De Ford v. Maryland Steel Co. 51 C. C. A. 59, 113 Fed. 72, holding breach of contract to complete and deliver ship at specified time not ground for recovery of lost profits; Rogers v. Beard, 36 Barb. 31, holding that measure of damages for neglect to repair a vessel within a reasonable time is rent of vessel and not loss of profits; Mitchell v. Cornell, 12 Jones & S. 401, holding that, for breach of a charter of a vessel to be used in an excursion, profits expected from trip cannot be recovered; Taylor v. Maguire, 12 Mo. 313, holding, in an action for stipulated price for building a hull, that profits failed to be realized because delay after time specified for delivery of boat could not be recouped.

— **Interest on idle investment as damages.**

Cited in American Bridge Co. v. Camden Interstate R. Co. 68 C. C. A. 131, 135 Fed. 323, holding that interest on money expended on extension could be assessed as damages in an action for delay in constructing a bridge which was to join an extension, which fact was known to contractor at time the contract was made; Myerle v. United States, 31 Ct. Cl. 105, 33 Ct. Cl. 1, holding that a contractor cannot recover interest which he paid upon loans necessitated by suspension of work on the contract.

Measure of damages for breach of contract.

Cited in Deming v. Grand Trunk R. Co. 48 N. H. 455, 2 A. R. 267, holding difference between contract price and value when goods were delivered proper measure against carrier which failed to deliver as agreed in time to make the sale; Hargous v. Ablon, 3 Denio, 406 (affirming 5 Hill, 472; 45 A. D. 481), holding that when goods sold are by mistake deficient in quality, the vendee is entitled to recover for deficiency at rate they were purchased; Lattin v. Davis, Hill & D. Supp. 9, holding that, for breach of warranty, measure of damages is difference in value between a sound and unsound article at the place of delivery.

Cited in notes in 34 A. D. 266; 12 A. S. R. 303; 21 A. S. R. 922; 3 L.R.A. 587; 6 E. R. C. 623,—on measure of damages recoverable on breach of a contract; 42 A. D. 48, on damages for breach of executory contract, loss of profits etc.; 20 A. D. 632, on measure of damages for breach of covenant to convey or eviction after conveyance.

— **For breach of covenant to repair.**

Cited in Middlekauff v. Smith, 1 Md. 329, holding measure of damages for failure to keep a mill in repair to be cost to tenant to repair, circumstances permitting the repair; De Freest v. Bloomingdale, 5 Denio, 304, holding that damages for nonperformance of covenant to repair by landlord is cost to make repair, and not detriment by reason of nonrepair; Brooklyn v. Brooklyn City R. Co. 47 N. Y. 475, 7 A. R. 469, on measure of damages for breach of covenant to repair.

Nature and amount of demurrage.

Cited in note in 41 L. ed. U. S. 941, on nature and amount of demurrage.

Fraudulent violation of a contract as an element of damage.

Distinguished in Flynn v. Hatton, 43 How. Pr. 333, holding that a wil
refusal or neglect on part of landlord to repair is no ground for additio
damages for nonperformance.

Right of violator of law to recover for injury.

Cited in note in 36 A. S. R. 818, on right of one violating law to recover
negligent injury.

Opinions of witnesses as to damages.

Cited in Harger v. Edmonds, 4 Barb. 256, holding opinion of witness as
amount of damages tenant has sustained by reason of breach of covenant
repair inadmissible; Giles v. O'Toole, 4 Barb. 201, holding same in an action
a lessee to recover damages for refusal of lessor to give possession of demis
premises.

Erroneous rule of damages as ground for new trial.

Cited in Vanderslice v. Newton, 4 N. Y. 130, on new trial where ruling
respect to damages allowable is erroneous.

34 AM. DEC. 258, CITY FIRE INS. CO. v. CORLIES, 21 WEND. 36

What constitutes a loss by fire under an insurance clause.

Cited in Babcock v. Montgomery County Mut. Ins. Co. 6 Barb. 637, holdi
actual burning not necessary where loss is the immediate consequence of fir
Singleton v. Phenix Ins. Co. 132 N. Y. 298, 30 N. E. 839 (affirming 32 N.
S. R. 494; 11 N. Y. Supp. 141), holding sinking of boat discovered to be on
through the slacking of lime to prevent a total destruction a loss by fire; N
York & B. Despatch Exp. Co. v. Traders & M. Ins. Co. 132 Mass. 377, 42 A.
440, holding same where a fire broke out on a steamboat which sank before goo
insured were touched by fire; Case v. Hartford F. Ins. Co. 13 Ill. 676, holdi
same as to a loss sustained to goods in consequence of a removal from fir
White v. Republic F. Ins. Co. 57 Me. 91, 2 A. R. 22, holding same as to a l
occasioned by removing insured goods from apparent imminent destruction
fire, although building was not in fact burned; Tilton v. Hamilton F. Ins.
1 Bosw. 367; Witherell v. Maine Ins. Co. 49 Me. 200,—holding same as to a l
by theft by reason of fire.

Cited in reference notes in 40 A. D. 193, as to what is loss by fire; 57 A.
120, on what is deemed loss by fire under insurance policy.

Cited in note in 14 E. R. C. 24, on rules of construction of contracts of
surance.

Distinguished in Merchants' & M. Transp. Co. v. Baltimore Associated Fi
men's Ins. Co. 53 Md. 448, 36 A. R. 428, holding that, under an insurance agai
fire on a steamer which was sunk to prevent a total destruction by fire, ins
ance company was liable for damage to ship but not for the general average l
upon the cargo.

— Loss by explosion.

Cited in Scripture v. Lowell Mut. F. Ins. Co. 64 Mass. 356, 57 A. D. 1
holding that loss arising in part from explosion and in part from combusti
of gunpowder on the premises was by fire; Renshaw v. Missouri State Mut.
& M. Ins. Co. 103 Mo. 595, 23 A. S. R. 904, 15 S. W. 945, holding same whe

destruction was caused by an explosion of gasoline caused by a fire in buildin American Steam Boiler Ins. Co. v. Chicago Sugar Ref. Co. 21 L.R.A. 572, 6 C. A. 336, 9 U. S. App. 186, 57 Fed. 294, holding that a loss by an explosi caused by a fire is a loss by fire, and is not covered by a policy insuring aga' explosion.

Cited in notes in 45 A. D. 659, as to whether loss by explosion is covered insurance against fire; 36 A. S. R. 858, on fire accompanied by explosion proximate cause of loss of insured property.

Distinguished in Heuer v. North Western Nat. Ins. Co. 144 Ill. 393, 19 L.R 594, 33 N. E. 411, holding where a lighted match caused an explosion which stroyed building, that loss was within an exception of loss by explosion.

Destruction of property in case of fire.

Cited in reference notes in 58 A. D. 388, on destruction of property in case fire; 50 A. D. 403, on power of municipal corporations to destroy private pro erty to stop spread of fire.

Articles prohibited by insurance policy.

Cited in note in 24 A. R. 152, on effect of condition in policy against kee ing certain articles on insured premises.

What is a "storing" of gunpowder.

Cited in reference notes in 38 A. D. 530, on placing gunpowder in a buildi as a "storing;" 48 A. D. 521, on placing of gunpowder within building f purpose of blowing it up as storing within prohibition of policy.

Insurance on building destroyed to check fire.

Cited in Pentz v. Ætna F. Ins. Co. 9 Paige, 568 (reversing 3 Edw. Ch. 341 holding that where premises were destroyed by gunpowder by city authorities stop fire, owner, after obtaining a verdict against city for amount less th absolute loss and for less than insurer's liability, could resort to insurance co pany for balance.

Risks assumed under a policy of insurance.

Cited in Franklin Ins. Co. v. Humphrey, 65 Ind. 549, 32 A. R. 78, hol under a policy assuming risks of seas, lakes, rivers, canals, fires, jettisoi rovers, and assailing thieves, that a loss by ice was covered.

— Loss due to necessary act.

Cited in Klopf v. Bernville Live Stock Ins. Co. 1 Woodw. Dec. 445, holdi that an owner of a horse was entitled to recover insurance for death of an sured animal at his own hand, if act was necessary and done in good faith.

Cited in note in 36 A. S. R. 859, on acts done to save insured goods as proj mate cause of loss.

What constitutes a "usurped power" under a provision of an insuran policy.

Cited in Boon v. Ætna Ins. Co. 40 Conn. 575, 12 Blatchf. 24, Fed. Cas. N 1,639, holding that "usurped power" has application to force illegally employ and adverse to the government; Portsmouth Ins. Co. v. Reynolds, 32 Gratt. 61 holding that burning of Navy yards by Federal officers on eve of secession w not an "usurped power" as to neighboring building to which fire spread.

34 AM. DEC. 262, SHANNON v. COMSTOCK, 21 WEND. 457.

Conclusiveness of affidavit for arrest before justice of the peace.

Cited in Johnson v. Florence, 32 How. Pr. 230, sustaining right of a justi to discharge an arrest on counter affidavits if sufficient on face.

Pleading over after objection as a waiver.

Cited in Randall v. Crandall, 6 Hill, 342, holding that by pleading in bar without objection a party waives his privilege from arrest; Converse v. Warren, 4 Iowa, 158, holding that objections to process taken in proper time and manner are not waived by pleading over; Broadhead v. McConnell, 3 Barb. 175, holding bond to prevent imprisonment no estoppel to deny jurisdiction, obligor having objected to process and answered to merits after objection was overruled; Dewey v. Greene, 4 Denio, 93, holding same where an objection is taken to an affidavit for an attachment before pleading to general issue; Horton v. Fancher, 14 Hun, 172; Coatsworth v. Thompson, 5 N. Y. S. R. 809,—holding that, where an objection to a proceeding is overruled by justice, party may plead over and not waive question raised.

Parties to a dilatory plea.

Cited in Hurley v. Second Bldg. Asso. 15 Abb. Pr. 206, holding that a dilatory plea to be good must be common to all defendants and pleaded by all.

Measure of general damages.

Cited in Hicks v. Foster, 13 Barb. 663, holding that damages must be the natural and proximate consequences of the act complained of; Rhoads v. Detwiler, 3 W. N. C. 327, holding that in trover the measure of damages is the value of the property at the time of conversion.

Cited in note in 40 A. D. 327, on measure of damages in recoupment.

— For breach of contract.

Cited in Jones v. Van Patten, 3 Ind. 107, holding that actual injury is measure of damages for breach of a simple contract; Pinkston v. Huie, 9 Ala. 252; Hertzog v. Hertzog, 34 Pa. 418; Richards v. Edick, 17 Barb. 260; Bechrich v. North Tonawanda, 171 N. Y. 292, 64 N. E. 6; Garrard v. Dollar, 49 N. C. (4 Jones, L.) 175, 67 A. D. 271,—holding that measure of damages against a vendee for refusing to perform his contract to purchase land, the vendor having offered to perform, is the purchase money with interest; Dayton, W. Valley & X. Turnp. Co. v. Coy, 13 Ohio St. 84, to same point; Durkee v. Mott, 8 Barb. 423, holding that measure for breach of contract to raft logs at a specified price is profit party could have made by fulfilment of contract and loss in preparing to perform; Billings v. Vanderbeck, 23 Barb. 546, holding that measure for refusal to accept goods sold is difference between contract and market price at time fixed for delivery; Kehoe v. Rutherford, 56 N. J. L. 23, 27 Atl. 912, holding that, in respect to work not done, measure of damages is such profits as would arise by performing work; M'Clowry v. Croghan, 1 Grant, Cas. 307, holding that measure for breach of a contract to lease, is consideration paid with interest; Bagley v. Smith, 10 N. Y. 489, 61 A. D. 756, 19 How. Pr. 1, holding measure for an unauthorized dissolution of a partnership is the profits which would have accrued had the partnership continued; Masterton v. Brooklyn, 7 Hill, 61, 42 A D. 38, holding that, for breach of contract to manufacture marble blocks, the manufacturer was entitled to the difference between what performance would have cost and contract price, as damages; George v. Cahawba & M. R. Co. 8 Ala. 234, holding that profits which he would have made is measure of damages recoverable by contractor prevented by other party from completing work; Oldham v. Kerchner, 79 N. C. 106, 28 A. R. 302 (dissenting opinion), on measure of damages for breach of contract to furnish corn for grinding; Evans v. Root, 4 Abb. App. Dec. 157, holding that the fall in the market is the measure of damages in an action against a factor for omitting to sell goods consigned according to instructions.

Cited in reference notes in 43 A. D. 672, on measure of damages for breach of executory contracts; 91 A. D. 450, on measure of damages for carrier's delay in delivery of freight.

Cited in notes in 42 A. D. 48, on damages for breach of executory contract, loss of profits, etc.; 20 A. D. 632, on measure of damages for breach of covenant to convey or eviction after conveyance; 3 L.R.A. 588, on loss of profits as element of damages for breach of contract.

Distinguished in Beth Elohim v. Central Presby. Church, 10 Abb. Pr. N. S. 484, holding that, in an executory contract for the sale of real property, the seller cannot recover of purchaser in default the contract price, except in an action for specific performance.

— For failure to give agreed employment.

Cited in Pritchard v. Martin, 27 Miss. 305, holding that on breach of contract by an employer, damages which employee may receive in consequence of breach may be immediately recovered; Hale v. Trout, 35 Cal. 229, holding same where there was a breach of a contract to make merchantable lumber for another.

Cited in note in 43 A. D. 211, on measure of damages for wrongful discharge of servant before expiration of contract.

Remedies of discharged employee.

Cited in note in 5 L.R.A. 760, on remedies of servant wrongfully discharged.

Duty to minimize damages.

Cited in Vicksburg & M. R. Co. v. Ragsdale, 46 Miss. 458; Hamilton v. McPherson, 28 N. Y. 72, 84 A. D. 330,—holding that law imposes upon a party subjected to injury by a breach of contract the active duty of making reasonable exertions to render injury as light as possible; Wilson v. Martin, 1 Denio, 602, holding, where there was a breach of contract to rent rooms, that plaintiff could not refuse rooms to other lodgers, leaving them idle, and then recover for use and occupation; Oldham v. Kerchner, 81 N. C. 430, holding that burden is on defendant to show all matters in diminution of damages.

— On breach of contract of affreightment.

Cited in Heckscher v. McCrea, 24 Wend. 304, holding that where a party agrees to ship a given amount of tons and falls short, and a third person offers to ship an amount, sufficient to make up deficiency, earnings which would accrue thereby should be deducted; Pregenzer v. Burleigh, 6 Misc. 140, holding that damages for delay in furnishing a cargo are to be reduced by excess profit, where profit on cargo furnished exceeds that which would have been made on one promised; Murrell v. Whiting, 32 Ala. 54; Bailey v. Damon, 3 Gray, 92; Medbery v. Sweet, 3 Pinney (Wis.) 210, 3 Chand. (Wis.) 233,—holding that, in breach of a contract to furnish freight, damages may be mitigated by showing that other freight was or might have been procured.

Distinguished in Sullivan v. McMillan, 37 Fla. 134, 53 A. S. R. 239, 19 So. 340, holding that rule as to mitigation of damages by subsequent earning and profits does not apply where contract is not one for personal service and does not require personal attention.

— On breach of contract of employment.

Cited in Costigan v. Mohawk & H. R. R. Co. 2 Denio, 609, 43 A. D. 758, holding that it may be shown that plaintiff was offered same kind of employment and refused, in reduction of damage; Strauss v. Meertief, 64 Ala. 299, 38 A. R. 8, holding, in such case, if person discharged has an offer or an opportunity of similar employment by another person during the term, it is his duty to accept it; Utter v. Chapman, 38 Cal. 659; Williams v. Anderson, 9 Minn. 50, Gil. 39; Huntington v. Ogdensburgh & L. C. R. Co. 33 How. Pr. 416; Hendrickson v. Anderson, 50 N. C. (5 Jones & L.) 246,—holding that it may be shown that discharged employee had engaged· in other lucrative business during time; Walworth v. Pool, 9 Ark. 394, holding that, in such case, defendant may show that plaintiff found other employment for balance of time; Wilkinson v. Black, 80 Ala. 329, holding that, in such case, recovery may be reduced by showing party discharged obtained or might have obtained other employment by exercise of reasonable diligence; Jones v. Jones, 2 Swan, 605, holding that, in such case, recovery will be reduced by amount he receives in second employment; Polsley v. Anderson, 7 W. Va. 202, 23 A. R. 613; Dorr v. Stewart, 3 Tex. 479,— holding that, in such case, compensation for injury, and not amount agreed to be paid, is measure of damages; Gillis v. Space, 63 Barb. 177, holding that a breach of contract for employment casts burden on defendant to show that, by reasonable exertion, like employment could have been obtained in same vicinity; Fuchs v. Koerner, 20 Jones & S. 77, holding that a discharged employee is only bound to accept suitable employment similar in kind; Polk v. Daly, 14 Abb. Pr. N. S. 156, 4 Daly, 411, holding where one wrongfully discharged, instead of holding himself in readiness to perform, left town for purposes of his own that no recovery could be had; Perry v. Dickerson, 7 Abb. N. C. 466, sustaining right of one wrongfully discharged to wait until end of term.

Damages for fraudulent breach of contract.

Cited in Malaun v. Ammon, 1 Grant, Cas. 123, on measure of damages for breach of contract in cases of fraud.

Tender as payment.

Cited in note in 77 A. D. 488, on effect of tender as payment and discharge.

34 AM. DEC. 267, GRIFFITH v. REED, 21 WEND. 502.

Acceptor's presumptive possession of funds to pay bill.

Cited in Clement v. Leverett, 12 N. H. 317, holding that the acceptance of a bill is an admission that acceptor has funds of drawer or is indebted to him for that amount; Phœnix Bank v. Bank of America, 1 N. Y. Leg. Obs. 26; Lee Bank v. Satterlee, 17 Abb. Pr. 6,—holding that such acceptance raises presumption of funds in hands of acceptor; Hidden v. Waldo, 55 N. Y. 294, holding that, as between the parties, the presumption that acceptor has funds of the drawer may be rebutted.

Cited in reference notes in 85 A. D. 308, on acceptance of bill as presumptive evidence that acceptor has effects of drawer in his hands; 1 A. S. R. 134, on rebuttability of presumption from acceptance of bill that acceptor has funds of drawer in his hands.

Parol evidence of true relation of parties to bills and notes.

Cited in Barry v. Ransom, 12 N. Y. 462, holding that relation between parties to a written obligation as between themselves may be shown by parol; Easterly v. Barber, 3 Thomp. & C. 421, holding that the presumption which the law attaches to the position of the parties to a negotiable instrument may be rebutted by parol evidence; Rouse v. Whited, 25 N. Y. 170, 82 A. D. 337, holding that, as between parties, it may be shown that makers made note for accommodation of indorser; Port v. Robbins, 35 Iowa, 208; Mansfield v. Edwards, 136 Mass. 15, 49 A. R. 1,—holding that parol evidence is admissible to show true relations of the parties, no matter in what form their obligation is expressed; Morgan v. Thompson, 72 N. J. L. 244, 62 Atl. 410; Whitehouse v. Hanson, 42 N. H. 9,—holding that as between the parties and one who takes note with knowledge of their true relation such relation may be shown.

Cited in reference note in 35 A. D. 690, on parol evidence to vary effect of indorsement.

— **To show suretyship of one of obligors of writing.**

Cited in Easterly v. Barber, 66 N. Y. 433, holding evidence that all indorsers were accommodation indorsers and as between themselves cosureties, admissible in an action between indorsers; Artcher v. Douglass, 5 Denio, 509, holding that where two persons signed an indemnity bond to sheriff, it may be shown that they executed bond as sureties, and that plaintiff had released principal.

Rights of an acceptor paying bill for drawer's accommodation.

Cited in Pomeroy v. Tanner, 70 N. Y. 547; Suydam v. Westfall, 2 Denio, 205,—holding that an accommodation acceptor of a bill must sue upon the implied undertaking of the drawer to refund the money paid for his use; Thurman v. Van Brunt, 19 Barb. 409, holding that an implied promise to indemnify does not arise, where bill is accepted under an express agreement with acceptor; Israel v. Ayer, 2 S. C. 344, holding that an accommodation acceptor of a bill is liable as debtor on bill though facts are known to payee; Wright v. Garlinghouse, 26 N. Y. 539 (dissenting opinion), on rights of an accommodation acceptor.

Undertaking of surety.

Cited in reference note in 55 A. D. 481, on nature of surety's undertaking.

Liability of surety on note or bill to parties having notice.

Cited in Dunham v. Countryman, 66 Barb. 268, holding that, where holder of a note has notice that a party thereto was a surety, the principles applicable to liability of a surety apply.

— **Liability of drawer's surety to drawee.**

Cited in Wright v. Garlinghouse, 26 N. Y. 539 (reversing 27 Barb. 474), holding, where drawee of a bill accepts without funds under a pre-existing agreement, that surety thereon was liable only to payee; Suydam v. Westfall, 4 Hill, 211, holding that where an acceptance is made with knowledge that one of drawers signed as surety, he will not be liable as acceptor; Wing v. Terry, 5 Hill, 160, holding that where drawee pays bill without having funds of drawer and there is a surety on bill, law will raise an implied promise by principal and not by surety to refund amount advanced.

Disapproved in Nelson v. Richardson, 4 Sneed, 307, holding a surety drawer liable as principal; Swilley v. Lyon, 18 Ala. 552, holding a surety drawer of a bill liable to an accommodation acceptor.

Rights of accommodation indorsers, etc.

Cited in Van Patten v. Ulrich, 37 N. Y. S. R. 348, 13 N. Y. Supp. 940. holding an accommodation indorser entitled to rights of a surety as respects all having notice of facts; Pitts v. Congdon, 2 N. Y. 352, 51 A. D. 299, holding that when an individual becomes a party to a note or bill at request and for benefit of another, the relation of principal and surety exists and is to be so regarded by all affected with notice.

Cited in note in 51 A. D. 303, on rights and liabilities of accommodation
dorsers, acceptors, and makers.

Action on accommodation note.

Cited in note in 1 L.R.A. 817, on actions on accommodation note.

Right of a co-obligor or surety to reimbursement.

Cited in Lazarus v. Rosenberg, 70 App. Div. 105, 75 N. Y. Supp. 11, holdi
that an accommodation indorser of a note who pays note must sue debtor
assumpsit; Faires v. Cockerell, 88 Tex. 428, 28 L.R.A. 528, 31 S. W. 190, ho
ing that, where a co-obligor or surety pays debt, he has a right of action agai
others for reimbursement on an implied promise.

Causes discharging surety.

Cited in La Farge v. Herter, 11 Barb. 159, holding that what will discha
the surety in equity will discharge him in a court of law.

Distinction between an indorser and a surety.

Cited in Bradford v. Corey, 5 Barb. 461, 4 How. Pr. 161, holding that an
dorser, although in the nature of a surety, is not for all purposes entitled
privileges of that character.

Effect of payment of bill.

Cited in Byrd v. Bertrand, 7 Ark. 321, holding that when a bill is paid
taken up by the drawee, it ceases to be an obligation upon any of the parties

34 AM. DEC. 273, HARTFIELD v. ROPER, 21 WEND. 615.

Action for injury to child.

Cited in Patterson v. Thompson, 24 Ark. 55, holding that to recover for
injury to a child the action must be in the name of the child.

Cited in reference note in 88 A. S. R. 45, on minor child's right of action
injury.

Cited in note in 48 A. D. 623, on action for injuries to children.

Right of parent to recover for injury to child.

Cited in Hennessey v. Bavarian Brewing Co. 63 Mo. App. 111, holding t
parent has no remedy for injury to a child by wrongful act of another, wh
child cannot be treated in law as servant.

Cited in note in 49 A. S. R. 408, on negligence of parent seeking to recover
injury to child.

Contributory negligence.

Cited in Hull v. Richmond, 2 Woodb. & M. 337, Fed. Cas. No. 6,861; Schi
v. Sliter, 64 Hun, 463, 19 N. Y. Supp. 644; Brown v. Maxwell, 6 Hill, 592, 41
D. 771,—holding that, to enable one to recover for an injury occasioned
another's negligence, he must himself be free from negligence; Perkins
Eastern R. Co. 29 Me. 307, 50 A. D. 589; Moore v. Central R. Co. 24 N. J.
268,—holding that want of ordinary care or prudence contributing to injury
bar recovery for injury; Jacobs v. Duke, 1 E. D. Smith, 271, holding that
want of ordinary care on part of party injured concurs with that of defenda
no recovery can be had; Kennard v. Burton, 25 Me. 39, 43 A. D. 249, holdi
same, otherwise where want of such care does not contribute to produce the
jury; Galena & C. U. R. Co. v. Jacobs, 20 Ill. 478, holding that there must
no want of ordinary care o npart of plaintiff; New Jersey Exp. Co. v. Nich
33 N. J. L. 434, 97 A. D. 722, holding comparative negligence of parties i
material; Haring v. New York & E. R. Co. 13 Barb. 9; Barker v. Savage,

N. Y. 191, 6 A. R. 60; Brand v. Schenectady & T. R. Co. 8 Barb. 368,—denying recovery where plaintiff's own negligence and imprudence contributed to the injury; Clark v. Syracuse & U. R. Co. 11 Barb. 112, holding same where injury was the result of want of ordinary care; Button v. Hudson River Co. 18 N. Y. 248, holding that negligence of defendant and ordinary care by plaintiff are necessary to sustain an action for injury; Chamberlain v. Milwaukee & M. R. Co. 7 Wis. 425, holding that one injured while in a perilous position must show that his own negligence in no way contributed to produce the injury; Ginnon v. New York & H. R. Co. 3 Robt. 25, holding that the neglect of driver of a street railway car to stop car will not justify passenger in descending from car while in rapid motion; Eckert v. Long Island R. Co. 43 N. Y. 502, 3 A. R. 721 (dissenting opinion), on contributory negligence as bar to an action for injury.

Cited in reference notes in 36 A. D. 659, on contributory negligence; 68 A. D. 559, on burden of proof as to contributory negligence; 36 A. D. 236, on contributory negligence defeating recovery; 43 A. D. 255, on contributory negligence as affecting right to recover for injury; 46 A. D. 671; 55 A. D. 65,—as to when contributory negligence will defeat recovery for injuries; 35 A. D. 104, on contributory negligence as defense in case of gross negligence.

Cited in notes in 54 A. D. 469, on contributory negligence as affecting right to recover for injury; 53 A. D. 388, on effect of contributory negligence of party injured on his right of action; 43 A. D. 364, on passenger's contributory negligence as affecting his right to recover for injury.

Questioned in . Center v. Finney, 17 Barb. 94, holding that one exercising reasonable diligence to prevent damage cannot be considered author of wrong.

— **Persons on highways or the like.**

Cited in Spencer v. Utica & S. R. Co. 5 Barb. 337, denying action for injury occasioned by being struck by train at railroad crossing, where plaintiff was not free from negligence; Brooks v. Buffalo & N. F. R. Co. 25 Barb. 600, holding same as where a person crosses a railroad in ignorance of the approach of a train, which could easily be seen by looking for it; New Orleans, J. & G. N. R. Co. v. Harrison, 48 Miss. 112, 12 A. R. 356, holding applying rule to one volunteering service of uncoupling cars; Gonzales v. New York & H. R. Co. 1 Sweeny, 506, holding it negligence for a person bereft of sight or hearing to go upon a railroad track without aid or assistance.

Distinguished in Wiel v. Wright, 29 N. Y. S. R. 763, 8 N. Y. Supp. 776, holding that a person walking on a highway is not bound to look back or listen for the coming of another; Gonzales v. New York & H. R. Co. 39 How. Pr. 407, holding that it i sduty of the railroad company to take proper precaution to prevent passengers from exposing themselves to danger; Davenport v. Ruckman, 16 Abb. Pr. 341, 5 Bosw. 20, holding that one who has sufficient sight to go with reasonable assurance on the street may recover for an injury by reason of an excavation which a person of good sight might have avoided.

— **Animals suffered to be at large.**

Cited in Bowman v. Troy & B. R. Co. 37 Barb. 516, holding party guilty of negligence in suffering a cow to be at large and astray upon a railroad track; Munger v. Tonawanda R. Co. 4 N. Y. 349, 53 A. D. 384, holding railroad company not liable where plaintiff's cattle escaped his inclosure and strayed upon the track of the railroad; Morris v. Phelps, 2 Hilt. 38,—holding that one negligently leaving horse near edge of a dock cannot recover, where horse was struck and thrown into river.

— Wrongdoers.

Cited in Norris v. Litchfield, 35 N. H. 271, 69 A. D. 546, holding that where plaintiff himself is a wrongdoer, he can maintain no action, however prudent he might have been.

Gross negligence toward person not exercising due care.

Cited in Williams v. Michigan C. R. Co. 2 Mich. 259, 55 A. D. 59; Brownell v. Flagler, 5 Hill, 282,—holding that no action can be maintained for an injury resulting from the negligence of both parties, without an intentional wrong on part of either; Bouwmeester v. Grand Rapids & I. R. Co. 63 Mich. 557, 30 N. W. 337, holding that contributory negligence is no defense, where action of defendant is wanton or wilful and injury ensues; McCool v. Galena & C. Union R. Co. 17 Iowa, 461, holding a railroad company liable for gross negligence in killing stock unlawfully running at large; Union P. R. Co. v. Rollins, 5 Kan. 167, holding a railroad not liable for injury to cattle on track, unless guilty of gross negligence; McGrath v. Hudson River R. Co. 19 How. Pr. 211, 32 Barb. 144, on right of one guilty of slight negligence to recover from one guilty of gross negligence.

Cited in noote in 13 L.R.A. 765, on trespass and unwarrantable interference in its relation to negligence.

Contributory negligence of infant.

Cited in Honegsberger v. Second Ave. R. Co. 33 How. Pr. 193, 2 Abb. App. Dec. 378, 1 Keyes, 570, 24 Phila. Leg. Int. 333, holding a child six or seven years of age barred from recovery by contributory negligence; McCarthy v. New York C. & H. R. R. Co. 37 App. Div. 187, 55 N. Y. Supp. 1013, holding a girl seven years of age *sui juris* and liable for contributory negligence; Albert v. New York, 75 App. Div. 553, 78 N. Y. Supp. 355, holding a boy twelve years old standing on a dangerous place and attempting to throw a sling shot guilty of contributory negligence.

Cited in Flynn v. Erie Preserving Co. 12 N. Y. S. R. 88, on allowance for imperfect discretion of an infant in determining question of contributory negligence.

Cited in note in 49 A. S. R. 411, on infant's contributory negligence as question for jury.

Distinguished in Mowrey v. Central City R. Co. 66 Barb. 43, holding, in an action for an injury to an infant eighteen years of age, that his age of infant is to be considered in determining what would be due diligence for him.

Disapproved in Duffy v. Missouri P. R. Co. 19 Mo. App. 380; Boland v. Missouri R. Co. 36 Mo. 484,—holding that an infant must exercise such care and prudence only as is equal to his capacity; Pennsylvania R. Co. v. Kelly, 31 Pa. 372, holding a boy nine years of age not bound to same degree of care in avoiding injury from neglect of others as that required of an adult; Edgington v. Burlington, C. R. & N. R. Co. 116 Iowa, 410, 57 L.R.A. 561, 90 N. W. 95, holding that a child seven years old cannot be held to be negligent, as a matter of law, in playing on an unfastened turntable.

— Children on street or railroad tracks.

Cited in Wendell v. New York C. & H. R. R. Co. 91 N. Y. 420, denying recovery where an infant seven years of age was struck by a train while crossing a track, by reason of his own negligence; Kunz v. Troy, 36 Hun, 615, holding boy five or six years old intermeddling with a bar counter on a sidewalk guilty of such negligence as to bar recovery for his injury.

Distinguished in Holmes v. Missouri P. R. Co. 190 Mo. 198, 88 S. W. 623, holding that a child which has reached the age of discretion will be required to exercise no higher degree of care than is usually exercised by persons of similar age; Indianapolis P. & C. R. Co. v. Pitzer, 109 Ind. 179, 58 A. R. 387, 10 N. E. 70, holding trainmen bound to greater care toward young child seen on tracks than they owe towards adult.

Disapproved in Rauch v. Lloyd, 31 Pa. 358, 72 A. D. 747, holding a child not guilty of negligence for attempting to pass under a car left standing across a street.

Negligence of an infant non sui juris.

Cited in Louisville & P. Canal Co. v. Murphy, 9 Bush, 522, holding that the negligence of a child *non sui juris* must be regarded as the negligence of the parents, and not that of the infant; Kunz v. Troy, 104 N. Y. 344, 58 A. R. 508, 10 N. E. 442, holding where infant is *non sui juris*, that contributory negligence on part of child will not bar action unless there is concurring negligence on the part of parent or guardian.

Cited in note in 12 L.R.A. 217, on contributory negligence of infant of tender age.

Doctrine of imputable negligence.

Referred to as leading case in Mangam v. Brooklyn City R. Co. 36 Barb. 230; Thurber v. Harlem Bridge, M. & F. R. Co. 60 N. Y. 326,—on doctrine of imputable negligence.

Cited in Willetts v. Buffalo & R. R. Co. 14 Barb. 585, holding that negligence of father having charge of a lunatic is imputable to lunatic who is injured thereby.

Cited in reference notes in 44 A. D. 212, on liability of lessor for injury caused by lessee's negligence; 34 A. S. R. 317, on imputing lessee's negligence in driving team to owner while latter is riding in carriage.

Cited in note in 8 L.R.A.(N.S.) 664, 666, 667, 668, on imputing driver's negligence to infants of tender years riding with him.

— Of parent or custodian of child non sui juris.

Cited in Pittsburgh, Ft. W. & C. R. Co. v. Vining, 27 Ind. 513, 92 A. D. 269; Wright v. Malden & M. R. Co. 4 Allen, 283; Fitzgerald v. St. Paul, M. & M. R. Co. 29 Minn. 336, 43 A. R. 212, 13 N. W. 168; Ihl v. Forty-Second Street & G. Street Ferry R. Co. 47 N. Y. 317, 7 A. R. 450,—holding that the negligence of parents or custodians of infants not *sui juris* will preclude a recovery by infant or representatives; Chicago & M. R. Co. v. Patchin, 16 Ill. 198, 61 A. D. 05; Aurora Branch R. Co. v. Grimes, 13 Ill. 585,—on same point; Dudley v. Westcott, 44 N. Y. S. R. 882, 18 N. Y. Supp. 130, holding that the negligence of a mother in sending a child three and one half years old on the street unattended is imputed to the child; Juskowitz v. Dry Dock, E. B. & B. R. Co. 25 Misc. 64, 53 N. Y. Supp. 992, holding same as to a child three and one half years old allowed to play on street unattended; Kreig v. Wells, 1 E. D. Smith, 74, holding same of child seventeen months of age allowed to be on a street without an attendant; Lehman v. Brooklyn, 29 Barb. 234, holding that negligence of parent in allowing a child to stray into danger is imputable to child; McLain v. Van Zandt, 7 Jones & S. 347, holding that negligence of father in sending a *non sui juris* child where an exercise of a discretion was required will prevent a recovery for injury to child; Metcalfe v. Rochester R. Co. 12 App. Div. 147, 42 N. Y. Supp. 661, holding that the negligence of a driver of a vehicle with whom a child *non sui juris* is permitted by its mother to ride is imputable to the child; Bamberger v. Citizens' Street R. Co. 95 Tenn. 18, 49 A. S. R. 909, 28 L.R.A. 486, 31 S. W. 163, holding that negligence of a parent contributing to the death of his infant child will defeat a recovery by him as administrator of child, when he is sole beneficiary of action; Edgington v. Burlington, C. R. & N. R. Co. 116 Iowa, 410, 57 L.R.A. 561, 90 N. W. 95, on imputing negligence of person having charge of infant to infant.

Cited in reference notes in 68 A. D. 420; 98 A. D. 185,—on imputability of parent's negligence to child; 69 A. D. 230, as to whether negligence of parent can be imputed to child; 1 A. S. R. 442, on effect of parents' permitting child to be in street on right to recover for injury.

Cited in notes in 43 A. R. 216; 57 A. R. 474; 9 A. S. R. 880,—on imputing parent's negligence to child; 5 A. R. 148, on negligence of parent or guardian as defense to action by infant; 110 A. S. R. 283, on imputing parent's negligence to child in action for latter's benefit; 6 L.R.A. 545, on imputing to child the contributory negligence of parent or guardian; 4 L.R.A. 126, on doctrine of imputed negligence in case of negligence resulting in injury or death of child; 16 L.R.A.(N.S.) 396, on unexplained presence of unattended child *non sui juris* in place of danger as prima facie evidence of negligence on part of parents; 18 L.R.A.(N.S.) 320, on contributory negligence of parent or custodian of child as bar to action by child for negligent injuries; 55 A. D. 677, on parent's negligence in permitting child to be at large in the streets or upon railroad track as defense against action for personal injury; 21 L.R.A. 77, 79, 80, on contributory negligence of parent or custodian in permitting child to stray into danger as bar to action by child for negligent injuries.

Distinguished in Birkett v. Knickerbocker Ice Co. 10 N. Y. Civ. Proc. Rep. 52, 41 Hun, 404, holding that to permit a child four and one-half years old to go upon street with its brother six years old was not, as a matter of law, negligence; McGarry v. Loomis, 63 N. Y. 104, 20 A. R. 510, holding that when a child has done no negligent act, the conduct of the parents is immaterial; Hennessey v. Brooklyn City R. Co. 6 App. Div. 206, 39 N. Y. Supp. 805; Lannen v. Albany Gaslight Co. 46 Barb. 264,—holding that when infant himself is free from negligence, the negligence of a parent will not be imputed to him where, if he were an adult, he would escape it; Barry v. Second Ave. R. Co. 41 N. Y. S. R. 342, 16 N. Y. Supp. 518; Mangam v. Brooklyn R. Co. 38 N. Y. 455, 98 A. D. 60 (reversing 36 Barb. 288), holding where parents are not negligent, that a child three or four years old is incapable of forfeiting a remedy for injury by his own negligence; Finkelstein v. Crane, 2 Misc. 545, 22 N. Y. Supp. 399, denying a motion to dismiss case on ground that a child six years old was on highway unattended; St. Paul v. Kuby, 8 Minn. 154, Gil. 125, holding that no presumption of negligence arises from the fact that a child, without the knowledge of its parents, wanders into street, and falls into an excavation because of a defective sidewalk; Burke v. Broadway & S. Ave. R. Co. 49 Barb. 529 (dissenting opinion), on when negligence of parent is imputable to infant.

Questioned in Elze v. Baumann, 2 Misc. 72, 21 N. Y. Supp. 782, holding where a boy six years old is injured while crossing a street at a crossing, that the question of negligence should go to the jury; Atlanta & C. Air-Line R. Co. v. Gravitt, 93 Ga. 369, 44 A. S. R. 145, 26 L.R.A. 553, 20 S. E. 550, on when negligence of parent will bar recovery for injury to child.

Disapproved in Chicago G. W. R. Co. v. Kowalski, 34 C. C. A. 1, 92 Fed. 310;

Berry v. Lake Erie & W. R. Co. 70 Fed. 679; Chicago City R. Co. v. Wilcox, 138 Ill. 370, 21 L.R.A. 76, 27 N. E. 899 (affirming (Ill.) 8 L.R.A. 494, 24 N. E. 419); Evansville v. Senhenn, 151 Ind. 42, 68 A. S. R. 218, 41 L.R.A. 728, 47 N. E. 634; Wymore v. Mahaska County, 78 Iowa, 396, 16 A. S. R. 449, 6 L.R.A. 545, 43 N. W. 264; Westerfield v. Levis, 43 La. Ann. 63, 9 So. 52; Schindler v. Milwaukee, L. S. & W. R. Co. 87 Mich. 400, 49 N. W. 670; Mattson v. Minnesota & N. W. R. Co. 95 Minn. 477, 111 A. S. R. 483, 70 L.R.A. 503, 104 N. W. 443, 5 A. & E. Ann. Cas. 498; Newman v. Phillipsburg Horse Car R. Co. 52 N. J. L. 446, 8 L.R.A. 842, 19 Atl. 1102; Bottoms v. Seaboard & R. R. Co. 114 N. C. 699, 41 A. S. R. 199, 25 L.R.A. 784, 19 S E. 730; Bellefontaine & I. R. Co. v. Snyder, 18 Ohio St. 399, 98 A. D. 175; Atchison, T. & S. F. R. Co. v. Calhoun, 18 Okla. 75, 89 Pac. 207, 11 A. & E. Ann. Cas. 681; Macdonald v. O'Reilly, 45 Or. 589, 78 Pac. 753; Norfolk & P. R. Co. v. Ormsby, 27 Gratt. 455; Smith v. O'Connor, 48 Pa. 218, 86 A. D. 582, 22 Phila. Leg. Int. 28; Watson v. Southern R. Co. 66 S. C. 47, 44 S. E. 375; Whirley v. Whiteman, 1 Head, 610; Nashville R. Co. v. Howard, 112 Tenn. 107, 64 L.R.A. 437, 78 S. W. 1098; Galveston, H. & H. R. Co. v. Moore, 59 Tex. 64, 46 A. R. 265; Norfolk & W. R. Co. v. Groseclose, 88 Va. 267, 29 A. S. R. 718, 13 S. E. 454; Warren v. Manchester Street R. Co. 70 N. H. 352, 47 Atl. 735,—holding that the negligence of a parent or custodian, in permitting an irresponsible infant to be exposed to danger, is not imputable to infant; Jacksonville Electric Co. v. Adams, 50 Fla. 429, 39 So. 183, 7 A. & E. Ann. Cas. 241, holding same in an action by child for injury received by him; Gunn v. Ohio River R. Co. 42 W. Va. 676, 36 L.R.A. 575, 26 S. E. 546, holding same where the child is living and suing; Battishill v. Humphreys, 64 Mich. 494, 31 N. W. 894, on same point; Ploof v. Burlington Traction Co. 70 Vt. 509, 43 L.R.A. 108, 41 Atl. 1017; Robinson v. Cone, 22 Vt. 213, 54 A. D. 67,—holding defendant liable for an injury to a child in the highway, though the child was of tender years and was in the highway by fault of its parents; Davis v. Seaboard Air Line R. Co. 136 N. C. 115, 48 S. E. 591, 1 A. & E. Ann. Cas. 214, holding where action is by parent or the parent is real beneficiary, that contributory negligence of parent may be shown in bar to action; Winters v. Kansas City Cable R. Co. 99 Mo. 509, 17 A. S. R. 591, 6 L.R.A. 536, 12 S. W. 652, holding negligence of mother in allowing a child on a public street not imputable to child; Mahoney v. Railroad Co. 6 Phila. 242, 24 Phila. Leg. Int. 253, holding negligence of one having charge of a child of tender years, without authority from parents, not imputable to child.

Maxim, respondeat superior, as applied to torts.

Cited in State v. Pittsburgh, C. C. & St. L. R. Co. 135 Ind. 578, 35 N. E. 700, holding a lessor of a railroad not within a statute relating to the conduct and management of passenger trains.

Action for wrongful interference with a member of family.

Cited in Pegram v. Stortz, 31 W. Va. 220, 6 S. E. 485, on actionable wrong to member of family.

Tort liability of infant or persons non sui juris.

Cited in Bannon v. Baltimore & O. R. Co. 24 Md. 108, holding that duties of persons cannot vary according to the years or degree of intellect of natural persons; Huchting v. Engel, 17 Wis. 230, 84 A. D. 741, holding that an infant, though under seven years of age, is liable in an action for a trespass, for compensatory damages; Pegram v. Stortz, 31 W. Va. 220, 6 S. E. 485, on liability of an infant for a tort; Williams v. Hays, 143 N. Y. 442, 42 A. S. R. 743, 26

L.R.A. 153, 38 N. E. 449, holding that insanity constitutes no defense to a tort action.

Cited in note in 19 A. D. 568, on infants' liability for torts.

Distinguished in Crozier v. People, 1 Park. Crim. Rep. 453, on the incapability of a lunatic or idiot of entertaining a criminal intent.

Binding instructions where facts are undisputably established.

Cited in Fay v. Grimsteed, 10 Barb. 321, granting new trial where court failed to instruct jury to find for plaintiff, where defense of usury was pleaded but no evidence given to sustain defense; Dascomb v. Buffalo & S. L. R. Co. 27 Barb. 221, holding that where the fact in issue is established by undisputed evidence, and such fact is decisive of the cause, a question of law arises which the court must decide; Steves v. Oswego & S. R. Co. 18 N. Y. 422, holding that where, conceding all the effect that can reasonably be claimed for plaintiff's testimony, it will not warrant a verdict for plaintiff, a nonsuit should be granted; Hopkins v. Nashville, C. & St. L. R. Co. 96 Tenn. 409, 32 L.R.A. 354, 34 S. W. 1029, on allowance of motion for nonsuit where no liability is established against defendant.

Malice as an element of a tort.

Cited in Cady v. Brooklyn Union Pub. Co. 23 Misc. 409, 51 N. Y. Supp. 198, holding motive or malice not an essential element of a tort.

— Unavoidable accident as tort.

Cited in Sanford v. Chicago & L. S. R. Co. 2 Mich. N. P. 133, holding that no one is responsible for an injury caused purely by unavoidable accident while he is engaged in a lawful business, even though the injury was direct consequence of his own act.

Mode of objection to defect in pleading.

Cited in reference note in 39 A. D. 368, on mode of objecting to defect in declaration.

34 AM. DEC. 281, BANK OF UTICA v. BENDER, 21 WEND. 643.

Reasonableness of demand and notice as law question.

Cited in Rhett v. Poe, 2 How. 457, 11 L. ed. 338; Belden v. Lamb, 17 Conn. 441; Strawbridge v. Robinson, 10 Ill. 470, 50 A. D. 420; Bell v. Hagerstown Bank, 7 Gill, 216; Dole v. Gold, 5 Barb. 490, 7 N. Y. Leg. Obs. 247; Walker v. Stetson, 14 Ohio St. 89, 84 A. D. 362; Spencer v. Bank of Salina, 3 Hill, 250,— holding that where the facts upon which the question of due diligence depends are known, it becomes purely a question of law.

Cited in reference notes in 39 A. D. 115, on due diligence as to demand and notice a question for court; 50 A. D. 422, on reasonableness of demand and notice as mixed question of law and fact.

Cited in note in 34 A. D. 284, on what is a reasonable demand and notice as question of law.

Notice of dishonor of note.

Cited in reference notes in 54 A. D. 648, on nature of question of reasonableness of demand and notice of dishonor of bill or note; 98 A. D. 426, on sufficiency of notice of dishonor served at indorser's place of business.

Cited in notes in 39 A. D. 553; 43 A. D. 226,—on sufficiency of notice of protest by mail.

— Where residence is not known.

Cited in Marshall v. Shafter, 33 Cal. 176; Wood v. Corl, 4 Met. 203; Burk v. Shreve, 39 N. J. L. 214; Beale v. Parrish, 20 N. Y. 407, 75 A. D. 414; Ramson v. Mack, 2 Hill, 587, 38 A. D. 602,—holding that where holder uses due diligence to ascertain the residence of the indorser, and from information so received sends the notice to the wrong postoffice, it is nevertheless sufficient; McVeigh v. Bank of Old Dominion, 26 Gratt. 785, on same point; Branch Bank v. Peirce, 3 Ala. 321; Gawtry v. Doane, 51 N. Y. 84; Carroll v. Upton, 2 Sandf. 171; Wilson v. Senier, 14 Wis. 380; Requa v. Collins, 51 N. Y. 144,—holding that where indorser's residence is not actually known by holder, notice may be addressed to the place where, after diligent inquiry, he is informed and believes he resides; Kleekamp v. Meyer, 5 Mo. App. 444, holding that a notice of protest left at the usual place of business of an indorser will bind him though it is never received; Hunt v. Maybee, 7 N. Y. 266, holding that where the indorser has no residence which the reasonable diligence of the holder can enable him to discover, the law dispenses with giving regular notice.

— Inquiry to ascertain residence.

Cited in Lawrence v. Miller, 16 N. Y. 235, holding that inquiry may and should be made of the maker if the information cannot be otherwise obtained; Greenwich Bank v. De Groot, 7 Hun, 210; Whitridge v. Rider, 22 Md. 548,— holding that such diligence should be used as business men usually employ when their interest depends upon obtaining accurate information; Saco Nat. Bank v. Sanborn,. 63 Me. 340, 18 A. R. 224, holding that inquiry must be pursued until all sources of information are exhausted, unless satisfactory information is sooner received; Brighton Market Bank v. Philbrick, 40 N. H. 506, holding that where the holder of a dishonored note applies to a man worthy of belief for information, and is answered distinctly that indorser resides at a particular place, he is not bound to push inquiry further.

Cited in reference notes in 36 A. D. 127, on diligence required in ascertaining indorser's residence; 35 A. D. 628, on due diligence in ascertaining indorser's place of residence for the purpose of giving him notice.

Distinction between question of law and one of fact.

Cited in Minor v. Edwards, 12 Mo. 137, 49 A. D. 121, holding that what acts or what declarations amount to a waiver is a question of law; Adams v. Boyd, 33 Ark. 33, holding that, the facts of the case being ascertained, it is the duty of the court to declare the law to the jury, who have a corresponding duty to receive and carry out the law as declared by the court.

34 AM. DEC. 285, NELLIS v. LATHROP, 22 WEND. 121.

Title by relation.

Cited in Fuller v. Van Geesen, 4 Hill, 171, holding that confirmation of foreclosure sale relates back to delivery of deed; Cheney v. Woodruff, 45 N. Y. 98, on limitation of doctrine of relation.

Cited in reference notes in 50 A. D. 528, on relation of sheriff's deeds; 44 A. D. 707, on relation of sheriff's deed to time when party is entitled thereto.

Cited in notes in 58 A. D. 58, on relation of sheriff's deeds; 15 A. D. 250, on application of doctrine of relation to execution sales.

Right of tenant to set up outstanding title or to purchase title against landlord.

Cited in Tilyou v. Reynolds, 108 N. Y. 558, 15 N. E 534, holding that while relation of landlord and tenant continues, the tenant is estopped from denying landlord's title; Stout v. Merrill, 35 Iowa, 47; Hetzel v. Barber, 69 N. Y. 1; Randolph v. Carlton, 8 Ala. 606,—holding that tenant may show that title of landlord has expired or has been extinguished by operation of law; Moore v. Smead, 89 Wis. 558, 62 N. W. 426, on right of tenant to show landlord's title had expired; Chase v. Dearborn, 21 Wis. 58, holding that, in ejectment against tenant for holding over, he may depend on the ground that the title has passed from plaintiff since the commencement of his term; Pickett v. Ferguson, 45 Ark. 177, 55 A. R. 545, holding that tenant cannot extinguish his landlord's title by purchasing a title adverse to landlord, but he may do so and terminate lease by purchasing his landlord's title at voluntary or forced sale; Reed v. Munn, 80 C. C. A. 215, 148 Fed. 737, holding that lessee has right to purchase landlord's title at execution sale, or to acquire by deed through landlord in fee, and thereby put an end to relation of landlord and tenant; Tilghman v. Little, 13 Ill. 239, holding that tenant may show that his landlord's title has terminated, and that his relation as tenant has changed; or if he becomes a purchaser under a judgment, he may set up his title in bar of an action brought against him by his landlord; Higgins v. Turner, 61 Mo. 249; Sharpe v. Kelley, 5 Denio, 431; Senior v. Marcinkowiski, 1 How. Pr. N. S. 331,—holding that tenant may acquire tax title as against his landlord; Hadley v. Musselman, 104 Ind. 459, 3 N. E. 122, holding that when bailee is under no contract or duty to pay taxes on property bailed, he may buy same at sale for taxes; Ten Eyck v. Craig, 62 N. Y. 406, holding by analogy mortgagee in possession may purchase and hold adversely to mortgagor; Roe v. Doe, 48 Ga. 165, 15 A. R. 656, holding that vendee in possession under contract of purchase may, if vendor parts with title or if it is sold under execution against him, attorn to purchaser, and, in action of ejectment by vendor against vendee, the latter may show such sale and attornment as defense to action.

Cited in reference note in 56 A. D. 584, on tenant's acquiring lessor's title by purchase on execution.

Cited in notes in 11 E. R. C. 77, on estoppel of tenant to deny landlord's title; 89 A. S. R. 82, on acquisition of landlord's title by tenant; 15 E. R. C. 305, on right of tenant to purchase landlord's property sold on execution; 53 L.R.A. 938, on right of tenant to acquire title derived from judicial sale during tenancy.

Distinguished in O'Donnell v. McIntyre, 37 Hun, 623, holding that while relationship of landlord and tenant exists, tenant cannot set up title hostile to landlord.

— As defense to action for rent.

Cited in Moffat v. Strong, 9 Bosw. 57, holding eviction under paramount title defense to action for rent; Smith v. Scanlan, 106 Ky. 572, 51 S. W. 152, holding that purchase by tenant of leased property under execution does not inure to landlord's benefit, and landlord is not entitled to rent from time of such purchase.

Effect of judicial sale of lessor's estate.

Cited in Apley v. Eubanks, 11 Ill. App. 272, holding it has same effect as if lessor had conveyed.

Apportionment of rent.

Cited in Van Rensselaer v. Jones, 2 Barb. 643, holding rents apportionable when demised premises are aliened in part; Church v. Seeley, 39 Hun, 269, on question of apportionment of rent when landlord releases part of land; Williams v. Morris, 95 U. S. 444, 24 L. ed. 360, on question of necessity of such apportionment; Van Rensselaer v. Chadwick, 24 Barb. 333, on question of what constitutes apportionment of rent by contract; Van Rensselaer v. Gallup, 5 Denio, 454 (dissenting opinion), as to when doctrine of apportionment has been applied.

Cited in reference notes in 35 A. D. 604; 40 A. D. 592; 88 A. D. 332,—on apportionment of rent.

Cited in notes in 39 A. D. 724, on apportionment in general; 45 A. D. 456, as to when apportionment of rent is made; 15 E. R. C. 637, on right of assignee to rent.

34 AM. DEC. 289, ALLEN v. MERCHANTS' BANK, 22 WEND. 215.

Indorsing paper for collection.

Cited in reference notes in 81 A. S. R. 641, on indorsement of commercia paper for collection; 96 A. D. 360, on indorsements for collection; 71 A. S. R. 614, on vesting of title by indorsement "for collection."

Liability of bank receiving paper for collection.

Cited in First Nat. Bank v. Reno County Bank, 1 McCrary, 491, 3 Fed. 257 (dissenting opinion), on right of bank owning paper which it restrictively indorsed for collection to recover proceeds from last indorsee bank which collected and retained same; Naser v. First Nat. Bank, 116 N. Y. 492, 22 N. E. 1077, holding that bank which receives draft for collection alone is liable to owner for proceeds collected through subagent; Smith v. Essex County Bank, 22 Barb. 627, denying collecting bank's liability to maker who paid note, for neglect to account for proceeds.

Cited in reference notes in 46 A. S. R. 677, on negligence of collecting bank; 38 A. D. 141; 83 A. D. 339,—on liability of bank receiving note for collection; 45 A. D. 76; 65 A. S. R. 754; 74 A. S. R. 536; 77 A. S. R. 613,—on liability of bank as agent for collection; 35 A. D. 206, on duty of bank holding note for collection as to demand and notice; 38 A. S. R. 775, on liability of bank for acts of its immediate officers in making collections; 117 A. S. R. 45, on duty and liability of banks in forwarding paper for collection; 79 A. D. 330, on liability of bank taking note or bill payable at distance.

Cited in notes in 77 A. S. R. 616, on duty of collecting banks as to presentment; 77 A. S. R. 618, on duty of collecting banks as to demand and protest; 38 A. S. R. 775; 77 A. S. R. 615,—on duty of bank acting as collection agent; 61 A. S. R. 553; 77 A. S. R. 620, 621,—on duty of collecting banks as to notice of dishonor; 1 L.R.A.(N.S.) 249, on damages for negligence as to collection of check; 8 L.R.A. 43, on collecting bank as agent of owner where paper is indorsed for collection.

Distinguished in City Bank v. Weiss, 67 Tex. 331, 60 A. R. 27, 3 S. W. 299, holding bank which restrictively indorsed draft to another for collection entitled to recover proceeds from latter's correspondent who applied them on debt due from his immediate restrictive indorser.

Disapproved in Merchants' Nat. Bank v. Goodman, 109 Pa. 422, 58 A. R. 728, 2 Atl. 687, 43 Phila. Leg. Int. 28 (affirming 14 W. N. C. 531), holding bank which received check for collection liable for loss through insolvency of drawee to which directly transmitted for collection.

—For misconduct or neglect of notary.

Cited in Britton v. Nicolls, 104 U. S. 757, 26 L. ed. 917, holding bank which received notes for collection not liable for notary's failure to make presentation for payment when properly intrusted with notes; May v. Jones, 88 Ga. 308, 30 A. S. R. 154, 15 L.R.A. 637, 14 S. E. 552, holding bank which received paper for collection not liable for wrongful protest by notary who was also its agent and employee; First Nat. Bank v. German Bank, 107 Iowa, 543, 70 A. S. R. 216, 44 L.R.A. 133, 78 N. W. 195, holding bank not liable for failure of notary, also its assistant cashier, to properly notify indorser of dishonor of inland draft received for collection; Bank of Lindsborg v. Ober, 31 Kan. 599, 3 Pac. 324, holding bank which received paper from correspondent originally intrusted there- with liable to owner for failure of its notary to make proper demand and give due notice; Gerhardt v. Boatman's Sav. Inst. 38 Mo. 60, 90 A. D. 407, holding bank which received paper for collection liable for failure of notary, employed for a year under bond, to notify indorser of dishoner; Ayrault v. Pacific Bank, 47 N. Y. 570, 7 A. R. 489, affirming 6 Robt. 337, holding bank which received note for collection liable for failure of its notary to properly present note for payment.

Cited in reference notes in 36 A. D. 624; 40 A. D. 85; 90 A. D. 412; 30 A. S. R. 159,—on liability of bank for negligence of notaries; 70 A. S. R. 219, 220, on liability for negligence of notary protesting negotiable paper; 63 A. D. 717, on liability of bank of collection for notary's failure to give notice of protest; 13 A. S. R. 253, on liability of bank in making collections for acts of notary public; 33 A. D. 50, on liability of bank for omissions or mistakes of notary employed by it.

Cited in notes in 38 A. S. R. 776, on liability of bank making collection for acts of notary; 77 A. S. R. 627, on liability of collecting banks for their own negligence and that of their notaries, correspondents, and other agents.

— For default of correspondents and subagents.

Cited in Exchange Nat. Bank v. Third Nat. Bank, 112 U. S. 276, 28 L. ed. 722, 5 Sup. Ct. Rep. 141, holding bank which received paper for collection entitled to recover against correspondent for failure of subagent to procure proper ac- ceptance; Power v. First Nat. Bank, 6 Mont. 251, 12 Pac. 597; Streissguth v. National German American Bank, 43 Minn. 50, 19 A. S. R. 213, 7 L.R.A. 363, 44 N. W. 797; Kent v. Dawson Bank, 13 Blatchf. 237, Fed. Cas. No. 7,714,— holding bank which received draft for collection liable for loss through failure of its correspondent to remit proceeds before becoming insolvent; Bailie v. Augusta Sav. Bank, 95 Ga. 277, 51 A. S. R. 74, 21 S. E. 717, holding bank which receives check for collection liable for subagent's failure to promptly collect and remit proceeds; Irwin v. Reeves Pulley Co. 20 Ind. App. 101, 48 N. E. 601, holding bank which received draft for collection not liable for loss through subsequent insolvency of correspondent selected with due care; Simpson v. Wald- by, 63 Mich. 439, 30 N. W. 199, holding bank which received draft for collection liable for loss from insolvency of correspondent before collection of draft re- mitted for proceeds; Daly v. Butchers' & D. Bank, 56 Mo. 94, 17 A. R. 663, hold- ing bank which received paper for collection not liable for loss through insol- vency of reputable correspondent to which draft forwarded with proper in- structions; St. Nicholas Bank v. State Nat. Bank, 128 N. Y. 26, 13 L.R.A. 241, 27 N. E. 849, holding bank which received check for collection liable for loss through dishonor of draft remitted by correspondent which collected and re- tained proceeds; Reeves v. State Bank, 8 Ohio St. 465, holding bank which re- ceives draft for collection liable for proceeds credited to it by correspondent who

collected same; Young v. Noble, 2 Disney (Ohio) 485, holding bank which re
ceived bill of exchange for collection liable for loss resulting from correspondent'
failure before proceeds remitted.

Cited in reference notes in 62 A. S. R. 873, on liability of bank for negli
gence of collecting agent; 13 A. S. R. 253; 19 A. S. R. 215,—on liability o
collecting bank for negligence of correspondents; 33 A. S. R. 649, on bank'
liability for bills transmitted to agent for collection; 24 A. S. R. 625, on bank'
liability for notes transmitted to agent for collection; 98 A. S. R. 443,
liability of bank as to collection of paper forwarded to another bank.

Cited in notes in 38 A. S. R. 777, on liability of bank for its correspondent
and other subagents; 3 E. R. C. 777, 778, on liability of bank for negligence o
its correspondent bank in making collections at distant place.

Denied in Waterloo Mill Co. v. Kuenster, 158 Ill. 259, 49 A. S. R. 156, 2
L.R.A. 794, 41 N. E. 906, holding bank which received paper for collection no
liable for loss through insolvency of supposedly reliable correspondent to whic
instrument promptly forwarded with proper instructions.

Disapproved in Harrington v. Merchants' Nat. Bank, 17 Phila. 38, 41 Phi
Leg. Int. 272; First Nat. Bank v. Sprague, 34 Neb. 318, 33 A. S. R. 644, 1
L.R.A. 498, 51 N. W. 846,—denying liability of transmitting bank for default o
correspondent bank chosen with due care.

— For correspondent's failure to make demand or protest.

Cited in Guelich v. National State Bank, 56 Iowa, 434, 47 A. R. 110, 9 N.
328, holding bank which received paper for collection not liable for failure o
correspondent to duly present paper for payment and to protest for dishonor
Third Nat. Bank v. Vicksburg Bank, 61 Miss. 112, 48 A. R. 78 (dissentin
opinion), on liability of bank which received draft for collection for loss throug
failure of carefully selected subagent to protest paper for nonpayment; Titt
v. Mechanics' Nat. Bank, 35 N. J. L. 588, holding bank which received pape
for collection liable for failure of correspondent to make proper presentmen
and protest; Montgomery County Bank v. Albany City Bank, 7 N. Y. 45
(reversing 8 Barb. 396), holding bank which received paper for collection alon
answerable for correspondent's neglect to present for payment or notify indors
of dishonor; Commercial Bank v. Union Bank, 11 N. Y. 203 (affirming 19 Bar
391), holding bank which received paper on account entitled to recover again
bank to which forwarded for collection, for failure of latter's correspondent
make demand and protest; Commercial Bank v. Red River Valley Nat. Ban
8 N. D. 382, 79 N. W. 859, holding bank which received paper for collecti
entitled to recover against correspondent for negligent delay in giving notice
dishonor.

Denied in Ætna Ins. Co. v. Alton City Bank, 25 Ill. 243, 79 A. D. 328, holdi
bank which received paper for collection not liable for failure of competent co
spondent to protest for nonpayment, when paper promptly forwarded with prop
instructions; Bank of Louisville v. First Nat. Bank, 8 Baxt. 101, 35 A. R. 69
denying right of recovery by bank which received paper for collection again
correspondent for failure to protest for nonpayment; Stacy v. Dane County Ban
12 Wis. 629, holding bank which received note for collection not liable for negl
gence of reliable correspondent in making demand and protest before maturit

— Mitigation of damages.

Cited in Borup v. Nininger, 5 Minn. 523, Gil. 417, sustaining bank's right show any fact which will lessen actual loss resulting from failure to fix indorser's liability upon paper received for collection.

Lien of correspondent bank on paper transmitted.

Cited in reference note in 44 A. D. 699, on lien of correspondent bank on paper transmitted for collection.

Liability of person receiving claim for collection.

Cited in American Exp. Co. v. Haire, 21 Ind. 4, 83 A. D. 334, holding express company which received paper for collection liable for negligence of its notary in making demand and protest before maturity; Dyas v. Hanson, 14 Mo. App. 363, holding merchant who receives draft for collection liable for failure of bank, with which deposited for collection, to promptly present for payment; Hoard v. Garner, 3 Sandf. 179 (affirmed in 10 N. Y. 261), holding party who covenants "to take proper means" for collection of bond and mortgage liable for solicitor's unreasonable delay to prosecute foreclosure; Peck v. Taylor, 4 N. Y. Leg. Obs. 141, holding broker who received note for collection liable for proceeds collected and retained by his correspondent.

Cited in notes in 50 A. S. R. 117, on liability of collection agencies for default of their attorneys; 32 A. D. 569, on duty of agent intrusted with collection of bill; 7 L.R.A. 856, on right to appoint subagent to collect commercial paper.

Agency of correspondent of bank.

Cited in Corn Exchange Bank v. Farmers' Nat. Bank, 118 N. Y. 443, 7 L.R.A. 559, 23 N. E. 923, holding bank which originally received paper for collection owner's agent, while correspondents resorted to by it are its agents only; Wheatland v. Pryor, 133 N. Y. 97, 30 N. E. 652, holding bank intrusted with collection of draft by bank which originally received it for collection latter's agent.

Cited in reference note in 41 A. S. R. 799, on relation between bank transmitting paper for collection and bank receiving same.

Cited in note in 50 A. S. R. 123, on correspondent of collecting bank as its agent.

Agency of attorney employed by collection agency.

Cited in Hoover v. Wise, 91 U. S. 308, 23 L. ed. 392, holding attorney engaged by collection agency agent of such agency, not of creditors; Dale v. Hepburn, 11 Misc. 286, 32 N. Y. Supp. 269, holding attorney employed by collection agency intrusted with collection of debt agent of such company, not of creditor.

Principal's rights under agent's contracts.

Cited in Oelricks v. Ford, 23 How. 49, 16 L. ed. 534, sustaining foreign principal's right of action upon contract of sale in state where effected by agent, when agency and principal's name and residence revealed in memorandum.

Distinguished in Le Marchant v. Moore, 150 N. Y. 209, 44 N. E. 770, holding that title to stock purchased by broker through correspondent, for undisclosed principal, passes to latter when agent notifies him of purchase.

Banking customs.

Cited in reference notes in 96 A. D. 764, on validity of banking usages; 54 A. D. 217, on what is necessary to bind indorser of promissory note.

Cited in note in 21 L.R.A. 440, on banking customs.

Proof of custom or usage.

Cited in Warren Bank v. Suffolk Bank, 10 Cush. 582, holding evidence of known custom of handing paper to notary admissible to show nonresponsibility for latter's negligence in demanding payment; Commercial Bank v. Varnum, 3 Lans. 86, holding proof of custom inadmissible to excuse notary's statutory and well-defined duty as to demand and protest; Dalton v. Daniels, 2 Hilt. 472, holding custom of estimating quantity of liquor by measuring one barrel in ten admissible to establish amount delivered; Bowen v. Newell, 2 Duer, 584, holding proof that usage of all banks in Connecticut is not to allow days of grace upon checks on time, and that, by laws of that state, the allowance of grace is governed by usage, admissible; Commercial Bank v. Kortright, 22 Wend. 348, 34 A. D. 317, holding proof of customary mode of transferring stock admissible to explain meaning and intent of transfer by blank power of attorney; Fabbri v. Mercantile Mut. Ins. Co. 6 Lans. 446, 64 Barb. 85, holding evidence of custom of accepting application for indefinite sums admissible in explanation of contract of insurance.

— How established.

Cited in Cleveland, C. C. & St. L. R. Co. v. Jenkins, 174 Ill. 398, 66 A. S. R. 296, 62 L.R.A. 922, 51 N. E. 811, holding usage not established by proof of isolated instances; Gallup v. Lederer, 3 Thomp. & C. 710, holding judgment or conclusion of witness inadmissible to prove existence of mercantile custom or usage.

Conflict of laws as to bills and notes.

Cited in Huse v. Hamblin, 29 Iowa, 501, 4 A. R. 244; Short v. Trabue, 4 Met. (Ky.) 299; Hunt v. Standart, 15 Ind. 33, 77 A. D. 79,—holding rights and liability of indorser governed by law of place where indorsement made; Spies v. National City Bank, 174 N. Y. 222, 61 L.R.A. 193, 66 N. E. 736, holding contract of indorsement governed by law of state where made, though note executed and payable elsewhere; Amsinck v. Rogers, 189 N. Y. 252, 121 A. S. R. 858, 12 L.R.A. (N.S.) 875, 82 N. E. 134 (affirming 103 App. Div. 428, 93 N. Y. Supp. 87), holding rights and liabilities as to foreign bills of exchange governed by law of place where bill is drawn; Nichol v. Porter, 2 W. Va. 13, 94 A. D. 501, holding contract of assignment of note governed by law of place where assignment made.

Cited in reference notes in 77 A. D. 87, as to what law governs inland bills; 77 A. D. 87, as to what law governs contract of indorsement; 50 A. D. 422, on law governing necessity and sufficiency of protest and notice of dishonor.

Cited in notes in 121 A. S. R. 870, on law governing bill drawn in one state and payable in another; 121 A. S. R. 878, on law governing notice of dishonor of foreign bill; 121 A. S. R. 872, on law governing demand, protest, and notice of dishonor of bill of exchange; 61 L.R.A. 217, on conflict of laws as to necessity of notice of dishonor of negotiable paper.

Demand, notice, and protest generally.

Cited in Minier v. Second Nat. Bank, 13 N. Y. S. R. 222, holding bank which receives paper for collection bound to protest same for nonpayment and to notify indorsers; State Bank v. Bank of the Capitol, 27 How. Pr. 57, 41 Barb. 343, 17 Abb. Pr. 364, holding that bank which receives paper from correspondent for collection discharges duty by giving seasonable notice of nonpayment to its principal in absence of agreement or usage to contrary.

Cited in reference notes in 43 A. D. 170, on necessity for presentment of draft for acceptance; 52 A. D. 594, on necessity of demand and notice to indorser or drawer to charge him; 90 A. D. 121, on demand upon note payable at designated place; 65 A. D. 98, on necessity of due diligence in making demand and notice in order to charge drawees or indorsees.

Cited in note in 38 A. D. 610, on who are parties residing in same place purposes of notice of dishonor of bills and notes.

— **Sufficiency of notice.**

Cited in Big Sandy Nat. Bank v. Chilton, 40 W. Va. 491, 21 S. E. 774, holdi indorser, residing where indorsee for collection located, sufficiently notified wh latter gives timely notice to principal who duly mails notice to indorser.

Liability of notary or his sureties.

Cited in Williams v. Parks, 63 Neb. 747, 56 L.R.A. 759, 89 N. W. 395, holdi sureties on official bond of, notary liable for his failure to give notice of dishon of paper; Commercial Bank v. Varnum, 3 Lans. 90 note, sustaining right of ba .which owns draft to recover, by statute, against correspondent's notary for fective presentation and protest; Henderson v. Smith, 26 W. Va. 829, 53 A. 139, holding notary not liable for defective execution of certificate of ackno edgment of married woman, without notice or improper motive.

Collateral security.

Cited in Clinton Nat. Bank v. National Park Bank, 37 App. Div. 601, 56 N. Supp. 244, as to whether receipt of bonds by one bank at request of another, collateral to loan made by latter, is mere gratuitous act; Clinton Nat. Bank National Park Bank, 37 App. Div. 601, 56 N. Y. Supp. 244, holding bank whi received collateral as security for loan by another bank bound only to give th examination customary among bankers.

Disapproved in Mt. Vernon Bridge Co. v. Knox County Sav. Bank, 46 Ohio 224, 20 N. E. 339, holding bank which received note as collateral not liable f loss through sending it to bank where payable for collection.

Right of bank to recover money paid by mistake.

Explained in Bank of Orleans v. Smith, 3 Hill, 560, holding bank which ceived note from correspondent for collection entitled to recover directly agai owner for money paid through mistake of fact.

Right of bank to issue time paper.

Cited in Curtis v. Leavitt, 15 N. Y. 9, sustaining banking association's right issue time paper, prior to act of June 3, 1840, when not intended to circulate money.

Right of owner to maintain trover for chattel.

Cited in Dudley v. Hawley, 40 Barb. 397, sustaining owner's right to mai tain trover against jeweler who innocently received and gratuitously negotia sale of converted property.

34 AM. DEC. 317, COMMERCIAL BANK v. KORTRIGHT, 22 WEN 348.

Liability of principal for acts of agent.

Cited in Emmons v. Dowe, 2 Wis. 322, holding that acts of agent, to co clude principal, must be within scope of his authority; Schneider v. Evans, Wis. 241, 3 A. R. 56, on liability of principal for acts of agent who has be enabled to hold himself out as possessing certain authority.

Cited in reference notes in 45 A. D. 405, on liability of corporation for ac of its agents; 85 A. D. 316, on liability of bank receiving bill or note f collection; 11 A. S. R. 679, on binding effect upon principal of agent's a within general scope of authority; 33 A. S. R. 720, on corporation's liabili for wrongs of agents or officers.

—Effect of private instructions.

Cited in reference notes in 65 A. D. 556, on right to limit agent's authority by secret instructions; 45 A. D. 98; 57 A. D. 606; 65 A. D. 308,—on power to limit authority of general agent by private instructions; 49 A. D. 152, on limitation by private instructions of general agent's authority to bind principal; 10 A. S. R. 587, on liability of princepal for acts of agent done contrary to private instructions.

Cited in note in 2 L.R.A. 824, on effect upon third persons of private restrictions on agent's authority.

—Agents furnished with indicia of ownership.

Cited in Walker v. Detroit Transit R. Co. 47 Mich. 338, 11 N. W. 187; Clement v. Leverett, 12 N. H. 317; Tucker v. New Hampshire Sav. Bank, 58 N. H. 83, 42 A. R. 580; Mallory v. Burrett, 1 E. D. Smith, 234; Moore v. Metropolitan Nat. Bank, 55 N. Y. 41, 14 A. R. 173; Passumpsic Bank v. Goss, 31 Vt. 315; Strause v. Josephthal, 8 Daly, 417; Creighton v. Black, 2 Mont. 354,—holding principal not bound by agent's unauthorized disposition of nonnegotiable vouchers to one who acquires them in good faith and without notice; McCramer v. Thompson, 21 Iowa, 244, on liability of principal.

—Holders of stock of principal.

Cited in Brewster v. Sime, 42 Cal. 139, holding that mere fact that a person holding the legal title to stock, and apparently having the right of disposition, is styled "trustee" raises no implication that he has no authority to sell or hypothecate it in the usual course of business.

Fraudulent sale by possessor of title papers.

Cited in Simson v. Bank of Commerce, 43 Hun, 156, as to when grantor is estopped from questioning title of purchaser in good faith from grantee who has fraudulently obtained possession of deed delivered in escrow.

Distinguished in Muller v. Pondir, 55 N. Y. 325, 14 A. R. 259, holding that one who purchases from one claiming to have right to disposal, but who has not the evidences of title, cannot claim to be bona fide holder for value.

Assignability of corporate stock.

Cited in reference notes in 44 A. D. 477; 81 A. D. 169; 3 A. S. R. 594,—on assignability of shares of stock; 71 A. S. R. 67, on assignment of corporate stock; 26 A. S. R. 179, on right of stockholder to transfer stock.

Cited in notes in 14 A. D. 530, on transfer of stock; 12 L.R.A. 781, on right of holder of stock certificate to pledge same; 5 E. R. C. 183, on validity of transfer of stock certificate signed in blank.

Title to stock transferred without entry upon books of corporation.

Cited in Bridgens v. Dollar Sav. Bank, 66 Fed. 9; International Bank v. German Bank, 71 Mo. 183, 36 A. R. 468; Leitch v. Wells, 48 N. Y. 585; Leggett v. Bank of Sing Sing, 24 N. Y. 283; Smith v. American Coal Co. 7 Lans. 317; Mount Holly, L. & M. Turnp. Co. v. Ferree, 17 N. J. Eq. 117; Broadway Bank v. McElrath, 13 N. J. Eq. 24; McNeil v. Tenth Nat. Bank, 46 N. Y. 325, 7 A. R. 341; De Comeau v. Guild Farm Oil Co. 3 Daly, 218; Black v. Zacharie, 3 How. 483, 11 L. ed. 690,—holding transfer sufficient to pass title between vendor and vendee; Johnston v. Laflin, 103 U. S. 800, 26 L. ed. 532 (affirming Fed. Cas. No. 7,393, 5 Dill. 65, 25 Pittsb. L. J. 119), holding that title passes where owner delivers his stock to purchaser, with authority to him or anyone whom he may name to transfer them on the books of the company; Nicollet Nat. Bank v. City Bank, 38 Minn. 85, 8 A. S. R. 643, 35 N. W. 577; Orr v. Bigelow, 14 N. Y. 556; Conant v. Reed, 1 Ohio St. 298; Strange v. Houston & T. C. R. Co. 53 Tex. 162; Bruce v. Smith, 44 Ind. 1,— holding that delivery of certificate of stock without transfer on books vests equitable title in vendee; Merchant's Nat. Bank v. Richards, 6 Mo. App. 454, holding that in absence of statute restricting transfer of stock to any particular mode, the transfer is complete on delivery of the certificate with power to transfer, and payment of the purchase money, not only between vendor and vendee, but when the corporation has unjustifiably refused to make transfer on its books, against a creditor of vendor without notice; People ex rel. Probert v. Robinson, 64 Cal. 373, 1 Pac. 156, holding that, until stock is transferred upon the books or demanded to be transferred, the person in whose name it is entered upon books of the company is, between himself and the company, the owner to all intents and purposes, and particularly for purpose of election; Mann v. Currie, 2 Barb. 294, holding subscriber whose assignee had not made transfer on corporate books, liable for unpaid subscription, whatever his equities towards real stockholder; Johnson v. Underhill, 52 N. Y. 203, holding that, until transfer upon the books is in fact made, the vendor is the nominal owner, and is to be treated as trustee of the stock for his vendee; Fisher v. Essex Bank, 5 Gray, 373, holding that shares in bank whose charter provides that they shall "be transferable only at its banking house and on its books" cannot be effectually transferred as against a creditor of vendor who attaches them without notice of transfer by delivery of certificates thereof; Boatmen's Ins. & T. Co. v. Able, 48 Mo. 136, holding that, although the purchaser may insist as a condition precedent to purchase of stock that the certificate be surrendered to the company for cancelation, yet where no such condition was insisted on, and the transfer was in fact made on the books, such assignment would be sufficient without surrender of certificate; State ex rel. Rankin v. Leete, 16 Nev. 242 (dissenting opinion); Mechanics' Bank v. New York & N. H. R. Co. 13 N. Y. 599, 4 Duer, 480; Vansands v. Middlesex County Bank, 26 Conn. 144,—on validity of transfer of stock not entered upon books of corporation; Isham v. Buckingham, 49 N. Y. 216, on question of title passed by transfer of stock not on books of corporation; Downer v. South Royalton Bank, 39 Vt. 25; Summers v. Hutson, 48 Ind. 228,—on relative equities of those who record their stock and those who do not; Hoppin v. Buffum, 9 R. I. 513, 11 A. R. 291, on object of requiring transfers of stock to be registered; Thorp v. Woodhull, 1 Sandf. Ch. 411, on question of transfer of stock on books of company; Delafield v. Illinois, 26 Wend. 192, on rights of bona fide holders of stock not transferred on books of corporation; Burrall v. Bushwick R. Co. 75 N. Y. 211, on title acquired by transfer of stock when nothing is required by corporation to give transfer validity.

Cited in reference note in 63 A. D. 120, on effect, as between vendor and vendee, of corporate stock of failure to make transfer on books.

Cited in note in 67 L.R.A. 607, on validity as against attachments, executions, or subsequent transfers of pledge or other transfer of corporate stock not made in books of company under statutory provisions that stock should be transferred only on books.

Disapproved in State Ins. Co. v. Sax, 2 Tenn. Ch. 507, holding title of assignee to stock in a corporation not complete as against creditors of assignor until notice to the corporation.

Right to have stock transfer made on books.

Cited in Simpson v. Jersey City Contracting Co. 165 N. Y. 193, 55 L.R.
796, 58 N. E. 896, 31 N. Y. Civ. Proc. Rep. 286, holding that managing age
of corporation have no discretionary power to refuse to register proposed tra
fer of stock; Driscoll v. West Bradley & C. Mfg. Co. 59 N. Y. 96, as to wh
corporation may refuse to transfer stock; Thompson v. Hudgins, 116 Ala.
22 So. 632, on right of owner to have stock transferred on the boo
Mechanics' Bkg. Asso. v. Maripósa Co. 3 Robt. 395 (dissenting opinion),
the right of holders of stock to have same transferred upon books of the cor
ration; Johnson v. Laflin, 5 Dill, 65, Fed. Cas. No. 7,393, 25 Pittsb. L. J. 1
holding that national bank must make transfer on books unless good reas
exists for refusal.

Cited in reference notes in 30 A. S. R. 668, on action for refusing to tra
fer corporate stock; 82 A. D. 703, on liability of corporation for wrong
refusal to transfer stock.

Cited in note in 51 A. R. 800, 801, on mandamus to compel transfer of
porate stock to purchaser.

Distinguished in Dunn v. Commercial Bank, 11 Barb. 580, holding nak
possession of certificates and blank assignments and powers of attorney
such evidences of title as to render bank liable for refusal to transfer stock
books.

Effect of transfer on stock books.

Cited in note in 51 A. D. 313, on transfer of stock on corporation's books
bona fide purchaser as passing title.

Implied authority of officers of corporations.

Cited in Mitchell v. Vermont Copper Min. Co. 67 N. Y. 280, holding th
president of corporation has implied authority to accept payment of asse
ment; Smith v. Lansing, 22 N. Y. 520, on implied authority of president
corporation.

—Authority of corporate officer to allow stock transfer.

Cited in Hayes v. Shoemaker, 39 Fed. 319; Case v. Citizens' Bank, 100 U.
446, 25 L. ed. 695,—holding that the cashier has implied authority to transi
stock on books of bank.

Cited in note in 77 A. D. 763, on power of bank cashier to transfer b
stock.

Authority to fill in writings executed in blank.

Cited in South Berwick v. Huntress, 53 Me. 89, 87 A. D. 535, holding t
party executing instrument and delivering same to another, knowing th
there are blanks in it to be filled necessary to make it a perfect instrume
must be considered as agreeing that the blanks may be thus filled after he h
executed it; International Bank v. German Bank, 71 Mo. 183, 36 A. R. 4
holding that a blank indorsement of a non-negotiable certificate of deposit
payee thereof, accompanied by delivery, will enable holder to make a val
pledge of the certificate to innocent party; White v. New York State .
Soc. 45 Hun, 580, upholding presumption that name of proxy was written
blank by authority of maker; Simms v. Hervey, 19 Iowa, 273, on question
power to fill blank under a parol authority; Chauncey v. Arnold, 24 N.
330, on question as to whether a mortgage with name of mortgagee left bla
could be made effectual by parol authority from mortgagor to insert lende
name as mortgagee; Richmond Mfg. Co. v. Davis, 7 Blackf. 412; Bartlett

Board of Education, 59 Ill. 364,—on validity of bonds signed in blank and filled up.

Cited in notes in 5 E. R. C. 182, on authority to fill up blank in deed after delivery; 8 E. R. C. 632, on sufficiency of parol authorization, to fill blanks in deeds; 13 A. D. 671, on effect of filling up blanks left in written instruments.

— Authority to fill up transfer of stock in blank.

Cited in Matthews v. Massachusetts Nat. Bank, Holmes, 396, Fed. Cas. No. 9,286, 6 Legal Gaz. 308, holding that it is within the general authority of a bank to sign, in its behalf, a blank transfer upon a certificate of stock in name of bank held by it as a collateral security for a loan, and deliver certificate to pledgeor on payment of the loan; Leavitt v. Fisher, 4 Duer, 1, holding that holder of a certificate of shares of stock, accompanied by an irrevocable power of attorney to transfer them, is the apparent owner, although the power may be in blank for the name of the attorney, and when he is the holder for value, without notice, his title cannot be impeached; Holbrook v. New Jersey Zinc Co. 57 N. Y. 616, holding that holder of stock may fill up blanks in power of attorney.

Evidence of custom.

Cited in Bower v. Newell, 12 N. Y. Leg. Obs. 231, holding it admissible to show practice of banks in regard to days of grace; Bowen v. Newell, 2 Duer. 584, holding proof of usage of all banks in state not to allow days of grace on checks on time, and that by laws of the state allowance of grace is governed by usage, admissible.

Measure of damages for refusal to transfer stock on books of corporation.

Cited in Dow v. Humbert, 91 U. S. 294, 23 L. ed. 368, as to measure of such damages being depreciation of the stock; Wilson v. Little, 1 Sandf. 351; Van Allen v. Illinois C. R. Co. 7 Bosw. 515,—as to measure of damages for refusal to transfer stock on books of corporation.

Measure of damages in conversion.

Cited in Romaine v. Van Allen, 26 N. Y. 309; Wilson v. Mathews, 24 Barb. 295,—holding that it is highest value of the property at any time between act of conversion and day of trial; Scott v. Rogers, 4 Abb. App. Dec. 163, note; Hamer v. Hathaway, 33 Cal. 117,—as to proper measures of damages; Wilson v. Little. 2 N. Y. 443, 51 A. D. 307; Ainsworth v. Bowen, 9 Wis. 348,—as to when damages for conversion of certificates would be the value of same at time of conversion; Smith v. Dunlap, 12 Ill. 184, on measure of damages for conversion of stocks.

Distinguished in Baker v. Drake, 53 N. Y. 211, 13 A. R. 507, holding that a fixed, unqualified rule, giving the plaintiff in all cases of conversion of property the highest market price from the time of the conversion to the time of trial, cannot be upheld.

Measure of damages for failure to perform duty.

Cited in Clark v. Miller, 54 N. Y. 528, holding that it is the whole amount which plaintiff has been unable to obtain by reason of defendant's refusal to perform his duty.

Remedy for refusal to transfer stock.

Cited in Dooley v. Gladiator Consol. Gold Mines & Mill. Co. 134 Iowa, 468, 109 N. W. 864, holding that it amounts to a conversion; Purchase v New York

Exch. Bank, 3 Robt. 164, as to when it constitutes conversion; Bank v. Manufacturers' & T. Bank, 20 N. Y. 501 (dissenting opinion), as to remedy for failure of corporation to transfer stock on books; Smith v. Poor, 40 Me. 415, 63 A. D. 672, holding on corporation's being liable in assumpsit for·refusal to permit transfer of stock on books of company; Ex parte Fireman's Ins. Co. 6 Hill, 243; People ex rel. Jenkins v. Parker Vein Coal Co. 1 Abb. Pr. 128, 10 How. Pr. 543; Baker v. Marshall, 15 Minn. 177, Gil. 136; State, Galbraith, Prosecutor, v. People's Bldg. & L. Asso. 43 N. J. L. 389; Townes v. Nichols, 73 Me. 515,—holding that mandamus will not lie to compel issuance or transfer of stock by corporation; People ex rel. Krohn v. Miller, 39 Hun, 557, 9 N. Y. Civ. Proc. Rep. 149, holding that mandamus would not lie to compel corporation to issue certificate of membership to plaintiff; Cushman v. Thayer Mfg. Jewelry Co. 7 Daly, 330; Cushman v. Thayer Mfg. Jewelry Co. 76 N. Y. 365, 32 A. R. 315 (affirming 7 Daly, 330, which affirmed 53 How. Pr. 60), holding that an equitable action will lie to compel a transfer of stock upon books of corporation; Condouris v. Imperial Turkish Tobacco & Cigarette Co. 3 Misc. 66, 22 N. Y. Supp. 695, holding it no defense to action of assumpsit against corporation for refusal to transfer its stock that a judgment against it will not vest title to stock in corporation; Ramsey v. Erie R. Co. 7 Abb. Pr. N. S. 156, 38 How. Pr. 193, on question of remedies of holder of stock when corporation refuses to transfer same on books.

Liability of corporation for permitting wrongful transfer of stock.

Cited in New York & N. H. R. Co. v. Schuyler, 38 Barb. 534, holding it liable in damages; New York & N. H. R. Co. v. Schuyler, 34 N. Y. 30, holding that corporation having constructive notice of outstanding certificates of stock is liable to holders of such certificates for permitting the stock to which they were entitled to be transferred to another.

Parol evidence as to prior action of board of directors or stockholders.

Cited in Allis v. Jones, 45 Fed. 148, holding it admissible when the record fails.

Liability of corporation for acts of agent.

Cited in Bank of Lyons v. Demmon, Hill & D. Supp. 398, holding that it may affirm the acts of an assumed agent, and be bound by them the same as an individual; Bank of Vergenness v. Warren, 7 Hill, 91, holding that authority of cashier to accept payment of money due bank will be presumed unless contrary expressly appears; Hooker v. Eagle Bank, 30 N. Y. 83, 86 A. D. 351, holding that officers and agents of a corporation may employ persons to perform services for it, and such employment, being within the scope of the agent or officer's duty, binds the corporation; Moss v. Averell, 10 N. Y. 449, on acts of corporate agents with acquiescence, as evidence of authority; Clark v. Miller, 47 Barb. 38, on when corporation is liable for acts of its officers and agents.

Assumpsit as remedy.

Cited in Manuscript opinion, 2 Hill, 46, note, holding assumpsit proper to recover salary earned from municipality.

—As remedy for neglect of corporate duty.

Cited in People ex rel. Lynch v. New York, 25 Wend. 680, on question of action of assumpsit lying for such neglect.

Irregular or incomplete transfers of property.

Cited in Perry Mfg. Co. v. Brown, 2 Woodb. & M. 449, Fed. Cas. No. 11,015, on defects in sale available to creditor of seller.

34 AM. DEC. 330, HASTINGS v. LUSK, 22 WEND. 410.
Privileged communications.

Cited in Sunley v. Metropolitan L. Ins. Co. 132 Iowa, 123, 12 L.R.A.(N.S.) 91, 109 N. W. 463, holding statements of an employer made to a surety of an employee concerning his defalcation not privileged, if maliciously made; Larkin v. Noonan, 19 Wis. 83, holding statements made in petition to governor for removal of sheriff from office privileged; Streety v. Wood, 15 Barb. 105, preferring charges to a lodge by one member against another charging violation of rules of order, if made in good faith, privileged; Perkins v. Mitchell, 31 Barb. 461, holding that, to constitute a statement by a physician privileged, he must utter it as a medical man, and in the discharge of his duty; Nichols v. Eaton, 110 Iowa, 509, 80 A. S. R. 319, 47 L.R.A. 483, 81 N. W. 792, holding that communication by life insurance company to its soliciting agent, with relation to an alleged forgery by an examining physician of the signature to an application for insurance, is privileged; Neuskey v. Mundt, 4 Legal Gaz. 230, holding that one mistaken for notorious criminal and excluded from place of popular amusement on that ground cannot recover without showing express malice; Klinck v. Colby, 46 N. Y. 427, 7 A. R. 360, holding that where defendants had been defrauded by reason of false representations; and having probable cause to believe that plaintiff was a party to the fraud signed a paper in which they stated that they had been "robbed and swindled" by plaintiff and others, and agreed to share expense of prosecution, the paper was privileged; Byam v. Collins, 111 N. Y. 143, 7 A. S. R. 726, 2 L.R.A 129, 19 N. E. 75 (dissenting opinion), as to what constitutes privileged communication; Hemmens v. Nelson, 138 N. Y. 517, 20 L.R.A. 440, 34 N. E. 342, on what communications are privileged; Kinyon v. Palmer, 18 Iowa, 377, on question of proof of malice in privileged communications.

Cited in reference note in 69 A. D. 65, on privileged communications i slander.

— Statements in course of judicial proceedings.

Cited in Johnson v. Brown, 13 W. Va. 71; Burdette v. Argile, 94 Ill. App 171,—holding that words spoken or written in a judicial proceeding privilege if material and pertinent; Hoar v. Wood, 3 Met. 193; Youmans v. Smith, 153 N Y. 214, 47 N. E. 265; Suydam v. Moffat, 1 Sandf. 459; Marsh v. Elsworth, Sweeny, 52, 36 How. Pr. 532; Sickles v. Kling, 60 App. Div. 515, 69 N. Y. Supp 944; Shelfer v. Gooding, 47 N. C. (2 Jones, L.) 175; Jennings v. Paine, 4 Wis 358; Maulsby v. Reifsnider, 69 Md. 143, 14 Atl. 505,—holding that word written or spoken by counsel in a judicial proceeding, if relevant to inquiry are not actionable, although they may be false and malicious; Perzel v. Tousey 20 Jones & S. 79, holding allegations in bill of particulars privileged; Mc Laughlin v. Charles, 60 Hun, 239, 14 N. Y. Supp. 608; McDavitt v. Boyer, 16 Ill. 475, 48 N. E. 317,—holding that words spoken by witnesses in judicial proceeding, if relevant, are privileged; Harlow v. Carroll, 6 App. D. C. 128, holding false and scandalous matter contained in answer not privileged if irrelevant Lawson v. Hicks, 38 Ala. 279, 81 A. D. 49, holding that words spoken or written in course of judicial proceeding, if relevant or believed to be relevant by speaker or writer, are privileged; Carpenter v. Ashley, 148 Cal. 422, 83 Pac. 444, 7 A & E. Ann. Cas. 601, holding words spoken by one counsel charging opposing counsel with perjury and subornation of perjury not privileged; Dada v Piper, 41 Hun, 254, holding that presumption is that a complaint drawn and signed by an attorney is a privileged communication; Maulsby v. Reifsnider, 6

Md. 143, 14 Atl. 505, on question as to where matter spoken by counsel is relevant or not being question for court or jury; Miller v. Nuckolls, 77 Ark. 64, 113 A. S. R. 122, 4 L.R.A.(N.S.) 149, 91 S. W. 759, 7 A. & E. Ann. Cas. 110, holding written statement made by defendant to peace officer, informing him of rumor connecting plaintiff with commission of a crime, privileged if made in good faith, but otherwise if made maliciously; Warden v. Whalen, 8 Pa. Co. Ct. 660, holding affidavit for search warrant privileged; Hosmer v. Loveland, 19 Barb. 111, holding that as governor has no power to revoke or recall a warrant issued for fugitive from justice, an affidavit made and used in support of such an application is not privileged; Moore v. Manufacturers' Natt. Bank, 123 N. Y. 420, 11 L.R.A. 753, 25 N. E. 1048 (reversing 51 Hun, 472, 4 N. Y. Supp. 378); Clemmons v. Danforth, 67 Vt. 617, 48 A. S. R. 836, 32 Atl. 626; Gilbert v. People, 1 Denio, 41, 43 A. D. 646,—holding that words spoken or written in a judicial proceeding to be privileged must be material or pertinent; Link v. Moore, 84 Hun, 118, 32 N. Y. Supp. 461, holding allegations in pleading privileged if relevant and material; Warner v. Paine, 2 Sandf. 195, holding that where, in an affidavit to oppose a motion, the defendant alleged that plaintiff had been guilty of perjury in his affidavit in support of the motion, the statement was privileged; Lanning v. Christy, 30 Ohio St. 115, 27 A. R. 431, holding that an action will not lie for statements contained in an answer, if such statements were honestly made, without malice, and if they were relevant, believed by defendant to be true, and were made upon probable cause, and under advice of counsel; Marsh v. Ellsworth, 50 N. Y. 309, holding that objections filed by attorney to discharge of bankrupt, charging bankrupt with procuring plaintiff to testify falsely as to who were partners in the firm were material and pertinent and therefore privileged; Hollis v. Meux, 69 Cal. 625, 58 A. R. 574, 11 Pac. 248, holding specifications filed by an attorney in course of his employment, in opposition to discharge of an insolvent, alleging that insolvent had made fraudulent entries in his books with intent to defraud creditors, absolutely privileged; Wilkins v. Hyde, 142 Ind. 260, 41 N. E. 536, holding petition under statute authorizing board of children's guardians to file a petition whenever they have cause to believe that parents are guilty of "low and gross debauchery," privileged; Nissen v. Cramer, 104 N. C. 574, 6 L.R.A. 780, 10 S. E. 676, holding that person who files sworn information before judicial officer, charging another with having committed a crime, is absolutely protected as to all relevant statements.

Cited in reference notes in 20 A. D. 649, on liability for words spoken in judicial proceedings; 51 A. D. 135, on words privileged because spoken in judicial proceedings; 38 A. D. 143, on privilege attaching to communications made in course of judicial proceedings; 80 A. D. 741, as to when words are privileged because spoken in judicial proceedings; 123 A. S. R. 648, on protection of attorney and counsel in respect to libel or slander in course of judicial proceedings; 81 A. D. 56, on council's liability for words spoken in judicial proceeding, if not pertinent to case; 123 A. S. R. 636, on liability for irrelevancy as libel or slander in course of judicial proceedings; 81 A. D. 56, on words spoken by counsel in conducting case not being slanderous, though spoken maliciously, if pertinent to case.

Cited in notes in 2 A. D. 433, on statements before judicial bodies as privileged; 17 A. D. 195, on liability of counsel for words spoken at trial; 7 E. R. C. 729, on liability of counsel for defamatory words published in course of judicial proceeding; 3 L.R.A. 418, on rule that privilege in judicial proceedings extends to both attorney and client; 22 L.R.A. 836, on privilege of witness as to defamatory testimony.

— Malice as jury question.

Cited in Bacon v. Michigan C. R. Co. 66 Mich. 166, 33 N. W. 181, holding that jury may find existence of actual malice from language of alleged libelous communication as well as from extrinsic evidence; Fowles v. Bowen, 30 N. Y. 20, holding that, in cases of privileged communications, slight evidence of malice may be left to jury.

Pleading privilege.

Cited in Donahoe v. Star Pub. Co. 3 Penn. (Del.) 545, 53 Atl. 1028, holding that privilege need not be pleaded specially; Barrows v. Carpenter, 1 Cliff. 204, Fed. Cas. No. 1,058, on question of admissibility of facts showing privilege under general issue; Johnson v. Brown, 13 W. Va. 71, on question of admissibility of privilege under general issue; Byam v. Collins, 111 N. Y. 143, 7 A. S. R. 726, 2 L.R.A. 129, 19 N. E. 75 (dissenting opinion), as to necessity of specially pleading privilege.

Liability of attorneys at law for acts done in exercise of their proper functions.

Cited in Campbell v. Brown, 2 Woods, 349, Fed. Cas. No. 2,355, holding them not liable when acts are performed in good faith.

34 AM. DEC. 340, GARDNER v. GARDNER, 22 WEND. 526.

Followed without discussion in Bradley v. Mirick, 26 Hun, 242.

Power of married woman over separate estate.

Cited in Radford v. Carwile, 13 W. Va. 572; Wylly v. Collins, 9 Ga. 223,— holding that married woman is a *feme sole* as to her separate estate, unless controlled by settlement; Strong v. Skinner, 4 Barb. 546, holding that *feme covert* with respect to her separate property is considered in equity a *feme sole;* Todd v. Lee, 15 Wis. 366, holding that contracts of a *feme covert,* when necessary or convenient to proper use and enjoyment of ·her separate estate, under statute, are binding at law; Selover v. American Russian Commercial Co. 7 Cal. 266, on power of wife to dispose of separate estate; Cartwright v. Hollis, 5 Tex. 152, on power of wife over separate property in New York; Howland v. Ft. Edward Paper Mill Co. 8 How. Pr. 505, on question of separate property of wife at common law.

Cited in reference note in 42 A. D. 168, on wife's power to charge her separate estate.

Cited in note in 30 A. D. 239, on power of *feme covert* over separate estate in absence of statutory regulation.

— Power to charge or encumber.

Cited in Cheever v. Wilson, 9 Wall. 100, 19 L. ed. 604, 2 Legal Gaz. 244, holding that she has power to encumber the rents; Miller v. Newton, 23 Cal. 554, holding that married woman may charge her separate estate with her debts, if it may fairly be inferred that such was her intention; Bruner v. Wheaton, 46 Mo. 363, holding contracts of married woman valid in equity, when made on credit or for benefit of her separate estate; Yale v. Dederer, 18 N. Y. 265, 72 A. D. 503, 17 How. Pr. 165 (reversing 21 Barb. 291), holding that equity recognizes a married woman's debt, and charges it upon her separate estate;

Chapman v. Lemon, 11 How. Pr. 235, holding that judgment against married women can be charged in equity as a lien against her separate estate; Puryear v. Beard, 14 Ala. 121, holding that right of wife to charge and dispose of her separate estate is only recognized and enforced in equity; Heath v. Van Cott, 9 Wis. 516, holding that married woman may charge her separate property with the payment of an indebtedness, and a court of equity will enforce such a contract by proceedings *in rem* against the property charged; Colvin v. Currier, 22 Barb. 371, holding wife's separate estate chargeable with labor and materials furnished therefor; Cobine v. St. John, 12 How. Pr. 333, on question whether payment of a note or bond, executed by married woman as surety, can be enforced against her separate estate; Bank of Louisiana v. Williams, 46 Miss. 618, 12 A. R. 319, holding under statute separate estate of married woman liable for her debts; Vanderheyden v. Mallory, 1 N. Y. 452 (reversing 3 Barb. Ch. 9), holding that separate estate of married woman is not. liable at common law for her debts contracted before marriage, and the only ground on which it can be reached in equity is by some act after marriage indicating an intention to charge the property.

— **Charges to or for husband.**

Cited in Bradford v. Greenway, 17 Ala. 797, 52 A. D. 203, holding that wife may charge her separate estate for payment of her husband's debts; Selph v. Howland, 23 Miss. 264, holding that she has no power to contract, either separately or jointly with her husband, for the labor of a mechanic, to be performed in, or for materials furnished for, building or repairing upon her separate estate; Berry v. Bland, 7 Smedes & M. 77, holding the fact that debt of married woman has been contracted during coverture, either as a principal or as a surety for her husband, or jointly with him, prima facie evidence to charge her separate estate, without any proof of a positive agreement or intention to do so; Hoard v. Garner, 3 Sandf. 79, on power of wife to charge separate estate with husband's debt.

— **Evidence as to intent to charge.**

Cited in Kimm v. Weippert, 46 Mo. 532, 2 A. R. 541, holding that note by married woman, to create a charge on her separate estate, must show an intent to charge it, and the intent must be gathered from contract itself; Henry v. Blackburn, 32 Ark. 445, holding that where married woman contracts for the improvement and preservation of her separate estate, it will be implied that she contracts upon the faith of the estate, and intends to create a charge upon it; Oakley v. Pound, 14 N. J. Eq. 178, holding that an agreement that debt shall be paid out of the separate property is a charge upon the separate estate; Coon v. Brook, 21 Barb. 546, holding that where a married woman has a separate estate, her obligation incurred on the faith of it, or for its benefit, is enforced when capable of being enforced, as a charge, and never as a personal liability; Goelet v. Gori, 31 Barb. 314, holding that, in case of a joint lease to husband and wife, the wife will not be deemed to have intended to charge her separate estate, by the covenant for payment of rent.

Capacity of married woman to contract.

Cited in Bruner v. Wheaton, 46 Mo. 363, upholding capacity of married woman to contract for purchase of real property on her private account.

Gifts inter vivos and causa mortis.

Cited in Doty v. Wilson, 5 Lans. 7, holding that, to render gift effectual, there must be delivery of the thing which is subject of the gift.

Cited in reference note in 47 A. D. 505, on what constitutes gift.

Cited in note in 9 E. R. C. 864, on note as subject of gift *causa mortis*.

— Gift of debt to debtor.

Cited in Denunzio v. Scholtz, 117 Ky. 182, 77 S. W. 715, 4 A. & E. Ann. Cas. 529, holding that where donor declared his intention to make gift, and delivered the thing of value, and destroyed the evidence of the debt which encumbered the thing given, it amounted to valid gift; Brinkerhoff v. Lawrence, 2 Sandf. Ch. 400, distinguishing between donations unaccompanied by delivery, where the object is to forgive a debt, and those in which the donor's apparent intent is to transfer property, either in his possession or by means of his own note or bond.

Power of chancery to award an issue.

Cited in Beverly v. Walden, 20 Gratt. 147, holding whether a court of equity will direct an issue to be tried by a jury is a question of discretion, but it is a sound discretion, and if improperly exercised, an appellate court will correct it; Patterson v. Gaines, 6 How. 550, 12 L. ed. 553, holding that practice of granting issues is limited to cases in which the court, in the fair exercise of its discreation, considers that justice will be best obtained by that course; Wise v. Lamb, 9 Gratt. 294, on discretion of court to direct an issue; O'Brien v. Bowes, 10 Abb. Pr. 106, 4 Bosw. 661; Brinkley v. Brinkley, 2 Thomp. & C. 501,—on power of court of chancery to award an issue.

Presumption of sanity.

Cited in Coffey v. Home Ins. Co. 44 How. Pr. 481, 35 N. Y. Sup. Ct. 322, holding that law presumes every person sane.

Capacity of drunkard.

Cited in Van Wyck v. Brasher, 81 N. Y. 260; Wright v. Fisher, 65 Mich. 275, 8 A. S. R. 886, 32 N. W. 605,—holding that drunkard is incompetent upon proof that, at the time of the act, his understanding was clouded, or his reason dethroned by actual intoxication.

Cited in reference notes in 49 A. D. 68; 59 A. D. 501,—on contracts of intoxicated persons; 76 A. D. 105; on intoxication as ground for avoidance of contract; 33 A. S. R. 738, on effect of intoxication of one party to contract.

Cited in note in 39 L.R.A. 221, on habits of intoxication as affecting testamentary capacity.

— Testamentary capacity.

Cited in Re Reed, 2 Connoly, 403, 20 N. Y. Supp. 91, holding that a drunkard may make a valid will if he comprehends the nature, extent, and disposition of his estate, his relations to those who have or might have a claim on his bounty, and is free from undue influence, fraud, or coercion; Re Lee, 46 N. J. Eq. 193, 18 Atl. 525, holding that where habitual intoxication is shown, there will be no presumption that there was incapacitating drunkenness at time will was made; Gross's Estate, 7 N. Y. S. R. 739, holding that occasional use of intoxicants did not deprive decedent of testamentary capacity; Re Sutherland, 28 Misc. 424, 59 N. Y. Supp. 989, holding that, to invalidate will of drunkard, it must be shown that when will was executed her understanding was clouded or her reason dethroned; Higgins v. Carlton, 28 Md. 115, 92 A. D. 666, on question of capacity to make will.

Cited in reference note in 84 A. D. 240, on competency of habitual drunkard to make will.

Cited in note in 39 L.R.A. 226, on presumption and burden of proof as drunkenness affecting testamentary capacity.

Distinguished in Re Ely, 16 Misc. 228, 39 N. Y. Supp. 177, 1 Gibbons S Rep. 587, holding one suffering from general insanity as result of excessive dulgence in drink incompetent to make a will.

Presumption of continuance of alcoholism.

Cited in note in 35 L.R.A. 122, 123, on presumption of continuance of alcoholi and alcoholic insanity.

Undue influence.

Cited in Davis v. Culver, 13 How. Pr. 62; Barnes v. Barnes, 66 Me. 286, holding that, to avoid will, the influence must amount either to deception else to force and coercion, in either case destroying free agency; Re Johns 7 Misc. 220, 27 N. Y. Supp. 649; Re Johnson, 7 Misc. 220, 27 N. Y. Supp. 6 57 N. Y. S. R. 846, 1 Power, 579,—holding that, in order to warrant a findi that undue influence had been exercised over a drunkard to procure the e cution of a will in favor of a member of his family, it must be shown that the were threats made, or force or coercion employed, which destroyed the free agen of the testator; Butler v. Benson, 1 Barb. 526, holding that old age alone in testator is not a sufficient ground for presuming imposition upon him.

Cited in reference notes in 49 A. D. 633; 96 A. D. 705; 45 A. S. R. 514, what is undue influence; 51 A. D. 413, 653, on what undue influence is necessa to vitiate acts.

Cited in notes in 16 A. D. 260, on destruction of free agency as essential undue influence; 31 A. S. R. 674, on necessity that undue influence destroy fr agency to invalidate will.

— Influence of wife on husband.

Cited in Clarke v. Davis, 1 Redf. 249, holding that natural influence of a wi arising from her relations with the testator, without proof of any specific ac will not amount to undue influence.

Agreements between husband and wife.

Cited in Hendricks v. Isaacs, 117 N. Y. 411, 15 A. S. R. 524, 6 L.R.A. 55 22 N. E. 1029, holding that courts of equity will not enforce a mere volunta agreement not founded upon any consideration, in favor of either one or t other.

Actions between husband and wife.

Cited in Higgins v. Higgins, 14 Abb. N. C. 15, holding that husband ma bring action against wife to establish a trust and require an accounting respect to his property held by her.

Obligation of equity to follow law.

Cited in Logan v. Hall, 19 Iowa, 491, holding that chancery would decree cording to evidence.

Jurisdiction of surrogate to reach equitable assets.

Cited in Re Potter, 32 Hun, 599, as reversing 7 Paige, 112, but not on th point of surrogate's jurisdiction to charge a conveyance as assets.

34 AM. DEC. 355, HEYER v. PRUYN, 7 PAIGE, 465.

Rights of purchaser from mortgagor.

Cited in Lovelace v. Webb. 62 Ala. 271, holding that purchaser takes ject to all the rights and disabilities of mortgagor.

— Acts of mortgagor arresting bar of limitation as against his privies.

Cited in Blackburn University v. Weer, 21 Ill. App. 29, holding that all claiming under mortgagor and chargeable with notice are bound by his payment to stop running of limitation; Harrington v. Slade, 22 Barb. 161; Palmer v. Butler, 30 Iowa, 576,—holding purchaser bound by prior admission of mortgagor removing bar of limitation; Carson v. Cochran, 52 Minn. 67, 53 N. W. 1130, holding same as to prior payment removing bar of limitation; Jordan v. Sayre, 24 Fla. 1, 3 So. 329, holdng grantee under warranty deed from mortgagor subject to same period of limitation as to enforcement of foreclosure suit; Johnston v. Lasker Real Estate Asso. 2 Tex. Civ. App. 494, 21 S. W. 961, holding junior encumbrancer bound by subsequent agreement for extension between mortgagor and holder of a senior lien.

Distinguished in Cook v. Union Trust Co. (Cook v. Bramel) 106 Ky. 803, 45 L.R.A. 212, 51 S. W. 600, holding that payments on notes, secured by vendor's lien, after execution of mortgage by debtor, do not extend time as against mortgagee.

— Payments rebutting presumption of payment.

Cited in Kendall v. Tracy, 64 Vt. 522, 24 Atl. 1118, holding purchaser bound by subsequent payment nullifying presumption from lapse of time; New York L. Ins. Co. v. Covert, 6 Abb. Pr. N. S. 154, 3 Abb. App. Dec. 350 (reversing 29 Barb. 435), holding same provided there was actual or constructive notice; Whittington v. Flint, 43 Ark. 504, 51 A. R. 572, on effect on purchaser of a subsequent payment by mortgagor.

Land as primary fund for payment of mortgage debt.

Cited in notes in 34 A. D. 359; 5 L.R.A. 281,—on land as primary fund for payment of mortgage debt.

Bar of debt as affecting lien.

Cited in Jones v. Merchants' Bank, 4 Robt. 221, holding that it does not bar action for conversion of property pledged; Chapman v. Lee, 64 Ala. 483, holding it no defense to suit to foreclose a vendor's lien; Plett v. Willson, 50 Hun, 60, 4 N. Y. Supp. 507, holding it does not bar action to enforce unsealed contract for sale of realty.

Cited in reference notes in 50 A. D. 810; 66 A. D. 615,—on continuance of mortgage lien although debt secured is barred by limitations.

Cited in notes in 31 A. R. 41, on effect on lien of running of statute of limitations on debt; 55 L.R.A. 680, on extension of lien of mortgage as against subsequent encumbrancers or grantees by renewal of secured debt.

— As affecting mortgage.

Cited in Princeton Sav. Bank v. Martin, 53 N. J. Eq. 463, 33 Atl. 45, holding that lien of mortgage may subsist after debt barred; Almy v. Wilbur, 2 Woodb. & M. 371, Fed. Cas. No. 256, holding that it does not affect debt if mortgage is not barred; Hulbert v. Clark, 128 N. Y. 295, 14 L.R.A. 59, 28 N. E. 638; Pratt v. Huggins, 29 Barb. 277; Gillette v. Smith, 18 Hun, 10; Capehart v. Dettrick, 91 N. C. 344; Harris v. Vaughn, 2 Tenn. Ch. 483; Hayes v. Frey, 54 Wis. 503, 11 N. W. 695; Browne v. Browne, 17 Fla. 607, 35 A. R. 96,—holding that it does not bar suit to foreclose; Gillett v. Hill, 32 Iowa, 220, on same point; Ohio Life Ins. & T. Co. v. Winn, 4 Md. Ch. 253, holding it does not affect legal advantage under the mortgage.

Cited in reference note in 62 A. D. 539, as to whether bar of statute of limitations of debt is bar of remedy on mortgage.

Cited in notes in 95 A. S. R. 664, on effect of bar of debt on right to enforce mortgage; 21 L.R.A. 552, on effect of statutory bar of principal debt on right to foreclose mortgage or deed of trust securing same.

Distinguished in Borst v. Corey, 15 N. Y. 505, holding that it bars action to enforce equitable lien for purchase money of land; Blackwell v. Barnett, 52 Tex. 326, holding that it bars remedy on mortgage; Schmucker v. Sibert, 18 Kan. 104, 26 A. R. 765, holding that revivor of a barred note will revive mortgage as against mortgagor, though otherwise as against a previous grantee; Fowler v. Wood, 78 Hun, 304, 28 N. Y. Supp. 976, holding that limitations may run against cause of action on mortgage though bond may remain enforceable; Meredith Bridge Sav. Bank v. Ladd, 40 N. H. 459, holding that statute allowing action on note during life of mortgage applies only to persons signing both note and mortgage.

Primary liability for mortgage debt after sale of equity of redemption.

Cited in Hanger v. State, 27 Ark. 667; Fletcher v. Chamberlin, 61 N. H. 438; Clift v. White, 12 N. Y. 519 (reversing 15 Barb. 70); Weaver v. Toogood, 1 Barb. 238; Gilbert v. Averill, 15 Barb. 20; Vanderkemp v. Shelton, 11 Page, 28,— holding land a primary fund as against purchaser of the equity of redemption; Kinney v. M'Cullough, 1 Sandf. Ch. 370, holding conversely, that a winding-up partner was bound to pay a debt which he had assumed in exoneration of lands secretly mortgaged to secure it and sold to his partner; Parkey v. Veatch, 68 Mo. App. 67, holding that purchaser of equity of redemption in one of two mortgaged tracts cannot buy mortgage and enforce it solely against remaining tract.

Cited in note in 8 L.R.A. 317, on test of personal obligation of grantee of property conveyed subject to mortgage.

Distinguished in Woods v. Spalding, 45 Barb. 602, holding rule that land is a fund for payment unavailable to defeat equitable priority between various purchasers under different executions against the mortgagor.

Acknowledgment to remove bar of limitations.

Cited in Carll v. Hart, 15 Barb. 565, holding it sufficient prior to statute, if by parol; Moore v. Clark, 40 N. J. Eq. 152, holding recital in deed that title was taken subject to a mortgage, sufficient; Phelan v. Fitzpatrick, 84 Wis. 240, 54 N. W. 614, holding certain letters written by mortgagor to attorneys of mortgagee insufficient.

Cited in reference notes in 50 A. D. 681, on acknowledgment of debt barred by limitations; 52 A. D. 221, on acknowledgment to remove bar of limitations; 49 A. D. 742, on sufficiency of acknowledgment of debt to remove bar of statute of limitations; 23 A. S. R. 286, on confession of judgment as acknowledgment taking case out of statute of limitations.

Cited in note in 102 A. S. R. 761, on effect of admissions in affidavits or pleadings or at the trial to suspend the running or remove bar of limitations.

Absence from state as renewing secured debt.

Cited in note in 55 L.R.A. 686, on absence from state as operating to renew secured debt.

Last payment on mortgage as date from which limitation runs.

Cited in note in 11 L.R.A.(N.S.) 745, as to whether last payment on past-due debt secured by mortgage, which debt subsequently becomes barred, fixes the period from which limitation applicable to the mortgage is to be computed.

Presumption of payment of mortgage by lapse of time.

Cited in New York v. Colgate, 12 N. Y. 140; Fisher v. New York, 6 Thomp. & C. 100,—holding that it does not arise until after lapse of twenty years; Tripe v. Marcy, 39 N. H. 439, holding that it arises after continued possession for twenty years without rebutting circumstances; Gould v. Holland Purchase Ins. Co. 16 Hun, 538, holding circumstances insufficient to justify the presumption; Hughes v. Thomas, 131 Wis. 315, 11 L.R.A.(N.S.) 744, 111 N. W. 474, 11 A. & E. Ann. Cas. 673, holding that cause of action for enforcement continues twenty years from date of last payment of interest.

Cited in reference note in 66 A. D. 615, on presumption of payment of mortgage debt from uninterrupted possession by mortgagor for twenty years.

Rebutting presumption of payment arising from lapse of time.

Cited in Morey v. Farmers' Loan & T. Co. 18 Barb. 401, holding that statute requires presumption arising from lapse of twenty years to be rebutted by proof of part payment or written acknowledgment.

Limitation of lien of assessment.

Cited in Fisher v. New York, 3 Hun, 648, holding lien of assessment similar to mortgage and subject to no law of limitation, except presumption of pay· ment after twenty years.

Registry of mortgage as notice.

Cited in Tripe v. Marcy, 39 N. H. 439, holding that it operates as constructive notice.

34 AM. DEC. 360, MILLSPAUGH v. McBRIDE, 7 PAIGE, 509.

Merger of mortgage in fee.

Cited in Platt v. Brick, 35 Hun, 121, holding that it occurs on purchase of mortgage by owner of equity of redemption, except as protection against intervening charges is needed; Day v. Mooney, 4 Hun, 134, holding it does not occur on conveyance from mortgagor to mortgagee contrary to their intention; Badger v. Sutton, 30 App. Div. 294, 52 N. Y: Supp. 16, holding same when it would be contrary to either intention or interest; Miller v. Finn, 1 Neb. 254, holding that right acquired must be precisely coextensive with subsisting right, must be held in same condition without intervention of any other claim in order to effect a merger; Schermerhorn v. Merrill, 1 Barb. 511, holding that no merger occurs on sheriff's sale of equity of redemption to mortgagee followed by an assignment of the mortgage and a conveyance of the land; Hanlon v. Doherty, 109 Ind. 37, 9 N. E. 782; Day v. Mooney, 6 Thomp. & C. 382,—holding that it does not occur where a junior claim would be let in; McMahon v. Russell, 17 Fla. 698, holding same when it would let in dower; Lumber Exch. Bank v. Miller, 18 Misc. 127, 40 N. Y. Supp. 1073, holding that prior mortgagee canceling and taking new mortgage under erroneous belief that all parties in interest had consented does not let in unknown rights; Moses v. Philadelphia Mortg. & T. Co. 149 Ala. 88, 42 So. 868, holding that owner of equity of redemption may keep senior encumbrance, purchased by him, alive as a protection against a junior lien; Brendt v. Brendt, 25 Misc. 359, 53 N. Y. Supp. 1026, holding that mortgage purchased by owner by descent of undivided portion of land does not merge so as to let in intervening lien; Barnes v. Camack, 1 Barb. 392, holding senior mortgagee, executing satisfaction and taking new mortgage, not postponed to an intervening mortgage unknown to him; Knickerbocker v. Boutwell, 2 Sandf. Ch. 319, holding that purchase of mortgage on one's own and another's land merges so much of it as was chargeable on the purchaser's land; Casey v. Buttolph, 12 Barb. 637, holding mortgage purchased by one of two sons of mortgagor, each of whom received a quitclaim from their father, does not merge as to other brother's land; Warner v. Blakeman, 36 Barb. 501, holding that mortgagee in possession, purchasing and canceling mortgage debt as part of consideration, will be protected against judgment creditors; Payne v. Wilson, 74 N. Y. 348, holding that equitable mortgage does not merge on taking of a legal mortgage so as to be postponed to an intervening mechanics' lien; Sheldon v. Edwards, 35 N. Y. 279, holding rights under a chattel mortgage of machinery in mill not extinguished on purchase of equity of redemption in realty mortgage; Clift v. White, 12 N. Y. 519, on intention as determinative of merger on purchase at sale under junior lien by executor of senior mortgagee; Glenn v. Rudd, 68 S. C. 102, 102 A. S. R. 659, 46 S. E. 555, on whether conveyance from mortgagor to mortgagee will be presumed not to merge in absence of evidence of intention.

Cited in reference notes in 63 A. D. 298, on equitable disfavor as to doctrine of merger of estates; 30 A. S. R. 245, as to when doctrine of merger does not apply; 77 A. D. 353, as to when mortgage and equity of redemption merge; 85 A. D. 538, as to when merger occurs by mortgagee becoming owner of equity of redemption.

Cited in note in 15 A. D. 83, on merger of estates in realty.

Distinguished in Townsend v. Provident Realty Co. 110 App. Div. 226, 96 N. Y. Supp. 1091, holding that taking of title by senior mortgagee for purpose of giving a junior mortgage precedence creates a merger; Sherow v. Livingston, 22 App. Div. 530, 48 N. Y. Supp. 269, holding that mortgagor cannot take assignments to himself of mortgages, and, by assigning them, give priority over a subsequent mortgage prior to the assignment; Thompson v. Van Vechten, 27 N. Y. 568 (modifying 6 Bosw. 373, which reversed 5 Abb. Pr. 458), holding chattel mortgage extinguished by payment with debtor's money by purchaser at sale, to whom it was fraudulently assigned.

Equitable assignees of mortgage.

Cited in note in 5 L.R.A. 293, on who are equitable assignees of mortgagor.

Right to open decree or judgment.

Cited in Lilly v. Shaw, 59 Ill. 72, holding it not permissible to open decree as a general rule except by a bill of review, after close of term; Herbert v. Rowles, 30 Md. 271, refusing to vacate enrolment where case was submitted on the merits; Brinkerhoff v. Franklin, 21 N. J. Eq. 334, holding that enrolment may be vacated as to interests not heard provided there was no laches on part of applicant; Tripp v. Vincent, 8 Paige, 176, holding that enrolled default on irregular service of process will be opened to let in meritorious defense where there was no laches; Embury v. Bergamini, 24 N. J. Eq. 227, upholding power to open default after enrolment, where meritorious defense was not heard through want of knowledge; Rogan v. Walker, 1 Wis. 631, refusing to relieve against a default attributable to applicant's own negligence or laches; Hall v. Lamb, 28 Vt. 85, holding that opening of default after enrolment to let in defense on merits rests in discretion; Low v. Mills, 61 Mich. 35, 27 N. W. 877, holding circumstances insufficient to authorize judicial discretion in setting aside default; Keenan v. Strange, 12 Ala. 290, holding that reversal with directions as to particular course to be pursued does not prevent setting aside of a default so as to let in defense on merits; Bishop's Appeal, 26 Pa. 470, holding that final decree of orphans' court may be corrected on petition for rehearing setting forth grounds of application verified by oath; Hazard v. Durant, 12 R. I. 99, vacating default on motion with affidavits of defense by respondent in contempt for violation of injunction and unable to purge himself; Thompson v. Maxwell, 16 Fla. 773, on power to open decree not correctable by a rehearing or bill of review; Ferguson v. Bruckman, 18 App. Div. 358, 46 N. Y. Supp. 23, upholding power to open judgment in partnership accounting, already paid, so as to let in proof inadvertently omitted; Nash v. Wetmore, 33 Barb. 155, upholding motion to vacate a judgment already entered and appealed, where only a partial defense was made because facts were unknown until after the taking of the appeal.

Cited in reference notes in 23 A. S. R. 286, on reopening of judgment; 73 A. D. 693; 36 A. S. R. 574,—as to when judgment of foreclosure will be opened to let in defenses.

Cited in notes in 19 A. D. 605, on power of equity to relieve against judgment at law; 60 A. S. R. 640, as to time to move for vacation of judgments and decrees.

Distinguished in Thompson v. Goulding, 5 Allen, 81, holding that enrolment precludes rehearing in absence of exceptional circumstances.

Criticized in Stribling v. Hart, 20 Fla. 235, holding that simple showing of merits without proof of due diligence will not justify opening of default.

— Decree suffered by negligence of counsel or representative.

Cited in Day v. Allaire, 31 N. J. Eq. 303, upholding right to open default where failure to defend was caused by negligence of counsel; Curtis v. Ballagh, 4 Edw. Ch. 635, holding that infant coming of age may open enrolled decree to let in defense not interposed by guardian *ad litem;* Babcock v. Perry, 4 Wis. 31, holding right to open default for negligence of counsel dependent on party's proving a defense and want of laches on his own part; English v. Aldrich, 132 Ind. 500, 32 A. S. R. 270, 31 N. E. 456, holding right to annulment of decree for mistake or fraud dependent on diligence and application within a reasonable time; Volland v. Wilcox, 17 Neb. 46, 22 N. W. 71, holding that county court may vacate its own judgments during term at which rendered for sufficient cause; Searles v. Christensen, 5 S. D. 650, 60 N. W. 29, upholding power to open judgments for negligence of counsel.

Distinguished in McDowell v. Perrine, 36 N. J. Eq. 632, holding that mistake or error of counsel is no ground for a rehearing.

Power of chancery as to taking of further proof.

Cited in Greenwich Bank v. Loomis, 2 Sandf. Ch. 70, holding that purchaser *pendente lite* cannot make himself a party by supplemental bill after decree except in an extreme case.

Power of equity to relieve against mistakes in judicial proceedings.

Cited in Beard v. Green, 51 Miss. 856, holding it error not to grant motion to remand for further proof before entry of decree, though necessity arose from negligence; Barthell v. Roderick, 34 Iowa, 517, holding error as to amount of judgment in action on note, due to mistake of attorney, correctable; Knobloch v. Mueller, 123 Ill. 554, 17 N. E. 696, on power to relieve on same rules as govern the setting aside of contracts.

34 AM. DEC. 363, NODINE v. GREENFIELD, 7 PAIGE, 544.

Title to land pending sale by executors.

Cited in reference notes in 45 A. D. 783, on vesting of fee in heirs until sale by executors; 47 A. S. R. 895, on title to property pending sale under power vested in executor.

Contingent or vested future devises.

Cited in Parker v. Ross, 69 N. H. 213, 45 Atl. 576, holding remainder to children of certain deceased sisters after a life estate, and, if no children are then living, to certain other devisees, vested; Leggett v. Hunter, 19 N. Y. 445, holding that trust for use, of life tenants with limitation over to their issue creates vested remainder in living children subject to let in those subsequently born; Williamson v. Field, 2 Sandf. Ch. 533; Wood v. Mather, 38 Barb. 473,—holding vested equitable remainder of same nature created where there was trust for life tenant and to convey to her surviving children; Yeaton v. Roberts, 28 N. H. 459, holding vested legal remainder of same kind created under devise to life tenant with remainder to children of certain persons and such other children as they may thereafter have; Jones v. Knappen, 63 Vt. 391, 14 L.R.A. 293, 22 Atl. 630, holding that remaindermen take vested interest at testator's death under will giving widow life estate and bequeathing specific sums to certain persons with residue to next of kin.

Cited in reference note in 47 A. D. 527, as to when devisee takes vested remainder in fee.

Cited in note in 10 E. R. C. 820, on vested remainders.

Distinguished in Byrnes v. Stilwell, 103 N. Y. 453, 57 A. R. 760, 9 N. E. 241 (modifying 38 Hun, 523), holding, on a devise to daughter for life and after her death to her lawful child or children or their children, that children living at death of testator but who died during life of mother without issue took a vested remainder capable of alienation; Tarocque v. Clark (Saxton's Estate), 1 Redf. 469, 1 Tucker, 32, holding that legacies of personalty payable in future vest from death of testator, and are not devested by death of legatee.

Parties to a foreclosure suit.

Cited in Daly v. Burchell, 13 Abb. Pr. N. S. 264, holding that neither a mortgagor, who assigned his interest, nor his heirs in case of his death, need be joined; Goebel v. Iffla, 48 Hun, 21, holding same of children born after foreclosure of mortgage on land devised, who could have no interest except through their parents representable by them; Williamson v. Field, 2 Sandf. Ch. 533, holding that persons having vested equitable remainder in equity of redemption as well as trustee vested with legal title must be joined; New York Secur. & T. Co. v. Schoenberg, 87 App. Div. 262, 84 N. Supp. 359, holding that statute requires contingent remainderman to be joined in action to revive and be subrogated to satisfied mortgages and to foreclose them.

Cited in note in 27 A. D. 224, as to when persons not represented before court are bound by its proceedings.

Distinguished in Lockman v. Reilly, 95 N. Y. 64, holding executrix, buying property at sale under second mortgage belonging to estate, and not beneficiaries under will, required to be joined in foreclosure of a senior mortgage.

Representation and devestiture of persons not in being.

Cited in notes in 8 L.R.A.(N.S.) 58, on who represent the unborn in judicial proceedings; 8 L.R.A.(N.S.) 50, on devestiture of estates of persons not in being;

8 L.R.A.(N.S.) 71, on devestiture of estates of persons not in being by fore-closure of mortgages.

Particular owner as representative of contingent estates in land.

Cited in Ruggles v. Tyson, 104 Wis. 500, 48 L.R.A. 809, 79 N. W. 766, holding, as a general rule, that owners in being of realty stand not only for themselves but for all that come after; Gragg v. Gragg, 40 Misc. 197, 94 N. Y. Supp. 53, holding that payment on a legacy by devisee, operating to remove bar of limi-tation, binds contingent interests claiming in same right; Kent v. Church of St. Michael, 136 N. Y. 10, 32 A. S. R. 693, 18 L.R.A. 331, 32 N. E. 704, holding children born after judgment establishing existence of lost conveyance, who could have no interest except through persons in whom estate was then vested, representable by them; Fox v. Fee, 24 App. Div. 314, 49 N. Y. Supp. 292, holding children born after an action of partition of land devised, who can have no interest except through their father, representable by him; Gray v. Smith, 76 Fed. 525, holding that widow, disclaiming under will, bars contingent interests of after-born children by joining the devisee of present inheritance in bill to quiet title; Sohier v. Williams, 1 Curt. C. C. 479, Fed. Cas. No. 13,159, holding that life tenant and contingent remainderman in fee may represent in-heritance in bill for specific performance, though their interests are equitable, provided issue of remainderman take in case he does not; Brevoort v. Brevoort, 70 N. Y. 136; Mead v. Mitchell, 17 N. Y. 210, 72 A. D. 455,—holding that statute makes sale under judgment of partition bar future contingent interests of persons not *in esse* without publication of notice to unknown parties, though such owners may take as purchasers; Chaffin v. Hull, 49 Fed. 524, holding interest of contingent remainderman not barred where no one was before court except a trustee of an executed trust and a life tenant whose estate was to be made a fee by the decree.

Distinguished in Irving v. Campbell, 24 Jones & S. 224, 4 N. Y. Supp. 103, on inapplicability of rule requiring only persons *in esse* having first estate of in-heritance to come before court in actions to reform deed conferring on persons *in esse* contingent rights; Brevoort v. Grace, 53 N. Y. 245, where question was as to power of legislature to extinguish vested or contingent interest of adults without their consent.

Right to specific performance as affected by delay.

Cited in Parsons v. Gilbert, 45 Iowa, 33, denying right to vendor, unable to convey until four months after stipulated time, where purchaser sustained damage.

Distinguished in Liddell v. Sims, 9 Smedes & M. 596, holding right to rescis-sion dependent on proof of fraud or a plain and palpable mistake.

"Issue" as meaning children.

Cited in Cochrane v. Schell, 140 N. Y. 516, 35 N. E. 971, holding that gift to grandchildren named and in case of death of any over to "issue" left by such one was gift over to children as purchasers.

34 AM. DEC. 366, REED v. WHEATON, 7 PAIGE, 663.

Exhaustion of legal remedies as precedent to creditor's suit.

Cited in Webster v. Clark, 25 Me. 313, holding averment of existence of judg-ment, issuance of execution, and its return unsatisfied, essential; Wales v. Lawrence, 36 N. J. Eq. 207, refusing to set aside a fraudulent conveyance where satisfaction was obtainable under a levy; Voorhees v. Howard, 4 Abb. App. Dec.

503, 4 Keyes, 371, holding that issuance of execution against all defendants liable on debt, and return unsatisfied, must be shown by bill under the statute; Fenton v. Flagg, 24 How. Pr. 499, holding that due issuance of execution and return unsatisfied will sustain appointment of receiver.

Cited in reference notes in 39 A. S. R. 888, on what creditors' bill must show to entitle him to relief; 90 A. D. 288, on necessity of creditor's exhausting remedy at law before filing creditors' bill; 44 A. D. 722, on necessity of creditor having judgment and execution unsatisfied to maintain bill to reach debtor's equitable assets or property fraudulently transferred.

— **Exhaustion of process in county of debtor's residence.**

Cited in Payne v. Sheldon, 63 Barb. 169; Wilbur v. Collier, Clarke Ch. 315; Smith v. Fitch, Clarke Ch. 265,—holding averment that execution issued to county where defendant then resided, essential; Merchants' & M. Bank v. Griffith, 10 Paige, 519; Wheeler v. Heermans, 3 Sandf. Ch. 597, 4 N. Y. Leg. Obs. 382; Durand v. Gray, 129 Ill. 9, 21 N. E. 610,—holding same provided there was no sufficient excuse and execution could issue in any county; Stark v. Cheathem, 2 Tenn. Ch. 300, holding proof of issuance of execution of county of residence, and return unsatisfied, sufficient without proof that execution issued in county where judgment was rendered; Brown v. Bates, 10 Ala. 432, holding issuance of execution to county where defendant resides at time, essential, though burden is on defendant to prove issuance to wrong county; Salt Lake Hardware Co. v. Tintic Mill Co. 13 Utah, 423, 45 Pac. 200, holding that return, unsatisfied, of an execution in county other than where defendant corporation resides or has property will not sustain equity action against shareholders; Minkler v. United States Sheep Co. 4 N. D. 507, 33 L.R.A. 546, 62 N. W. 594, holding right of judgment creditor to appointment of receiver dependent on issuance of execution in county of defendant's residence.

Distinguished in Sayre v. Thompson, 18 Neb. 33, 24 N. W. 383, holding return, unsatisfied, of an execution in original county, and averment that defendant had no property whatever subject to execution, sufficient; Noon v. Finnegan, 32 Minn. 81, 19 N. W. 391, holding action to set aside fraudulent conveyance of legal title maintainable upon proof of judgment and its docketing at location of land.

34 AM. DEC. 368, BRANDRETH v. LANCE, 8 PAIGE, 24.

Injunction against threatened torts or crimes.

Cited in Montgomery & W. P. R. Co. v. Walton, 14 Ala. 207, holding threat to commit personal trespass not enjoinable; Burnett v. Craig, 30 Ala. 135, 68 A. D. 115, holding quasi-criminal proceedings for violation of city ordinance not enjoinable; State ex rel. Circuit Attorney v. Uhrig, 14 Mo. App. 413, holding keeping of unlicensed dramshop, though amounting to a nuisance, not enjoinable; Carleton v. Rugg, 149 Mass. 550, 14 A. S. R. 446, 5 L.R.A. 193, 22 N. E. 55, holding use of building for illegal purposes enjoinable in discretion of court if respondents admit truth of petition; Reynolds v. Everett, 67 Hun, 294, 22 N. Y. Supp. 306, on impropriety of enjoining combination formed to entice employees from service in absence of special facts.

Cited in reference note in 18 A. S. R. 564, on equity jurisdiction to issue injunction.

Cited in notes in 89 A. S. R. 852, on injunction against right of privacy; 32 L.R.A. 832, on prevention of speech or publication as interference with constitutional freedom of speech and of the press; 37 L.R.A. 786, as to whether a court of equity can protect personal rights relating to the intellectual, emotional, and moral life.

— Scandalous or libelous publications.

Cited in Dailey v. Superior Court, 112 Cal. 94, 53 A. S. R. 160, 32 L.R.A. 273, 44 Pac. 458, holding theatrical presentation of facts in criminal case, not enjoinable; New York Juvenile Guardian Soc. v. Roosevelt, 7 Daly, 188, holding libel charging mismanagement of a juvenile society, not enjoinable.

Cited in reference note in 25 A. S. R. 628, on right to enjoin libel.

—Against publications injurious to trade or business.

Cited in Montgomery v. South Dakota Retail Merchants' & Hardware Dealers' Asso. 150 Fed. 413, holding publication of retailer's action against catalogue houses, not enjoinable; De Wick v. Dobson, 18 App. Div. 399, 46 N. Y. Supp. 390, holding same of libelous advertisement; Marlin Fire Arms Co. v. Shields, 171 N. Y. 384, 59 L.R.A. 310, 64 N. E. 163 (reversing 68 App. Div. 88, 74 N. Y. Supp. 84), holding libel relating to manufactured article, not enjoinable; Kidd v. Horry, 28 Fed. 773, 18 W. N. C. 287; Allegretti Chocolate Cream Co. v. Rubel, 83 Ill. App. 558; Life Asso. of America v. Boogher, 3 Mo. App. 173,—holding libel on business, not enjoinable; Flint v. Hutchinson Smoke Burner Co. 110 Mo. 492, 33 A. S. R. 476, 16 L.R.A. 243, 19 S. W. 804, holding mere slander of title, not enjoinable; Reyes v. Middleton, 36 Fla. 99, 51 A. S. R. 17, 29 L.R.A. 66, 17 So. 937, holding libel and slander of title, not enjoinable where no breach of contract is involved; Covell v. Chadwick, 153 Mass. 263, 25 A. S. R. 625, 26 N. E. 856, holding libels, amounting to mere false representations as to character of property, not enjoinable.

—Against publications of private nature.

Cited in Corliss v. E. W. Walker Co. 31 L.R.A. 283, 57 Fed. 434, 30 Abb. N. C. 372, holding publication of life of an inventor, not enjoinable as an invasion of right of privacy; Atkinson v. Doherty, 121 Mich. 372, 80 A. S. R. 507, 46 L.R.A. 219, 80 N. W. 285, holding use of private name and likeness of deceased person as cigar label, not amounting to libel, not enjoinable; Murray v. Gast Lithographic & Engraving Co. 8 Misc. 36, 28 N. Y. Supp. 271, 31 Abb. N. C. 266, holding publication of portrait of infant child, not enjoinable by a parent; Owen v. Partridge, 40 Misc. 415, 82 N. Y. Supp. 248, holding exhibition or publication of photograph and measurements of suspected criminal, not enjoinable; Wetmore v. Scovill, 3 Edw. Ch. 515, holding publication of private letters of business without literary or pecuniary value, not enjoinable; Wookey v. Judd, 4 Duer, 596 (dissenting opinion), on same point.

34 AM. DEC. 371, BELL v. LOCKE, 8 PAIGE, 75.

Relief against appropriation of name or trademark.

Cited in Coffeen v. Brunton, 4 McLean, 516, Fed. Cas. No. 2,946, holding fraudulent simulation of trademark, enjoinable; Ex parte Walker, 1 Tenn. Ch. 97; Newby v. Oregon C. R. Co. Deady, 609, Fed. Cas. No. 10,144,—holding appropriation of corporate name, enjoinable; Taylor v. Carpenter, 11 Paige, 292, 2 Sandf. Ch. 601, 42 A. D. 114, holding coloring and labeling of thread as near like rivals, as possible, enjoinable; Tallcot v. Moore, 6 Hun, 106, holding use of similar labels and advertisements, not ordinarily misleading, not enjoinable; Radam v. Microbe Destroyer Co. 81 Tex. 122, 26 A. S. R. 783, 16 S. W. 990, holding use of similar labels and packages not calculated to deceive an ordinary purchaser, not enjoinable; Colton v. Thomas, 7 Phila. 257, 26 Phila. Leg. Int. 5, 2 Brewst. (Pa.) 308, holding use by former employee of a simulated card and sign calculated to deceive by difference in size of letters, enjoinable; Farmers' Loan & T. Co. v. Farmers' Loan & T. Co. 21 Abb. N. C. 104, 1 N. Y. Supp. 44, holding that "F. L. & T. Co. of Kansas" will be enjoined from advertising without word "Kansas" at suit of "F. L. & T. Co.;" Corwin v. Daly, 7 Bosw. 222, holding that "Club House" proprietor cannot enjoin use of name, "London Club House," where labels and color of boxes were different; Bloss v. Bloomer, 23 Barb. 604, on enjoinment of unauthorized use of an author's or inventor's trademark; Tyack v. Bromley, 4 Edw. Ch. 258, 1 Barb. Ch. 519, on whether port wardens, without exclusive right, can enjoin assimilation of their business and calling, operating to mislead the public; Howe v. Searing, 6 Bosw. 354, 19 How. Pr. 14, 10 Abb. Pr. 264 (dissenting opinion), on enjoinment of fraudulent use of another's name in business; Smith v. Gibbs, 44 N. H. 335, on protection from rivals, fraudulently holding themselves out as conducting an established business; Taylor v. Carpenter, 2 Woodb. & M. 1, Fed. Cas. No. 13,785, holding that alien, whose marks on goods are used by others and sold as his, may recover damages; Marsh v. Billings, 7 Cush. 322, 54 A. D. 723, holding that carriage proprietor, authorized to use name of hotel, can maintain case against others using the name for soliciting of business.

Distinguished in Appollinaris Co. v. Scherer, 23 Blatchf. 459, 27 Fed. 18, holding that owner of contract for exclusive sale of mineral water in certain countries cannot enjoin sales of same product rightfully purchased abroad and shipped to this country; Gilman v. Hunnewell, 122 Mass. 139, holding certain alleged similarity in labels and packages of patent medicines, insufficient to warrant inference of fraud.

Cited in notes in 47 A. D. 287, on what trademark may be applied to and protection of same; 5 L.R.A. 130, on violation of trademarks; 9 L.R.A. 150, on protection of right to sole use of trademark; 1 L.R.A. 46, on right to restrain unauthorized use of trademark as fraud; 17 L.R.A. 131, on refusal of courts to protect a trademark which contains a fraud.

—Appropriation of name of publication.

Cited in Potter v. McPherson, 21 Hun, 559, holding that owners of book "National System of Penmanship" can enjoin use of name "Independent National System of Penmanship;" Munro v. Tousey, 129 N. Y. 38, 14 L.R.A. 245, 29 N. E. 9, holding that use of name "Old Sleuth" to designate serial publications does not give right to injunction against use of word "Sleuth" in similar stories; American Grocer Pub. Asso. v. Grocer Pub. Co. 25 Hun, 398, holding that "American Grocer" can enjoin use of name "Grocer" by paper of like character; Matsell v. Flanagan, 2 Abb. Pr. N. S. 459, holding that "National Police Gazette" can enjoin use of name "United States Police Gazette," actually printed so as to deceive the public; Commercial Advertiser Asso. v. Haynes, 26 App. Div. 279, 49 N. Y. Supp. 938, holding that "Commercial Advertiser" cannot enjoin use of name "New York Commercial" by different kind of a paper; Gannett v. Ruppert, 119 Fed. 221, holding that periodical "Comfort" circulating in rural district cannot enjoin use of name "Home Comfort" by juvenile paper.

Cited in reference note in 42 A. D. 117, on right to injunction against publishing newspaper of same name.

Cited in note in 33 A. R. 336, on right to enjoin fraudulent imitation of name of a publication.

Good will as recognizable in equity.

Cited in Moorehead v. Hyde, 38 Iowa, 382, holding contract for sale of go will, capable of specific performance; Perkins v. Currier, 3 Woodb. & M. Fed. Cas. No. 10,985, on recognition of good will by equity.

Cited in note in 3 L.R.A. 769, on good will in business as property.

34 AM. DEC. 374, McMORINE v. STOREY, 20 N. C. 329 (4 DEV. & L.) 189.

Who is an executor de son tort.

Cited in reference notes in 85 A. D. 423, on definition of executor de son tor 45 A. D. 778, as to how executor de son tort is constituted and liability of.

Cited in notes in 85 A. D. 424, on what acts constitute person executor son tort; 17 A. D. 561, on one intermeddling with decedent's estate under col able right as executor de son tort; 98 A. S. R. 198, on intermeddlers after lette testamentary or of administration have issued as executors de son tort.

— Fraudulent grantee as.

Cited in McLean v. Weeks, 61 Me. 277 (dissenting opinion), on the liabili of a fraudulent donee as an executor de son tort.

Cited in reference notes in 38 A. D. 583, on liability of fraudulent donee creditors of donor; 44 A. D. 49, on liability to creditor as executor de son to of donee under deed fraudulent as to creditors.

Liability of personal representative.

Cited in notes in 55 A. D. 439, on power, title, and liability of executor son tort; 85 A. D. 427, on liability of executor or administrator for his o acts before qualifying.

Right of administrator to property fraudulently assigned.

Cited in Burton v. Farinholt, 86 N. C. 260, denying right to recover procee of insurance fraudulently assigned by intestate.

Admissibility of former testimony of deceased witness.

Cited in Smith v. Hawley, 8 S. D. 363, 66 N. W. 942; Bryan v. Malloy, N. C. 508,—holding it incompetent unless the parties and issues are the same.

Cited in reference notes in 49 A. D. 282; 64 A. D. 592,—on evidence of d ceased witness's testimony given in another suit.

Cited in notes in 63 A. D. 633, on admissibility of evidence of witness's test mony on former trial; 91 A. S. R. 199, on admissibility of evidence given o former trial, in other action or proceeding.

34 AM. DEC. 376, ANDERS v. MEREDITH, 20 N. C. 339 (4 DEV. & L.) 199.

Actionable injury by cotenant.

Cited in Moody v. Buck, 1 Sandf. 304, holding negligence by one cotenant i exclusive possession not actionable by another; Arthur v. Gayle, 38 Ala. 25 holding sale of slaves by owner of particular estate actionable by remainde man.

Form of action against cotenant.

Cited in Bond v. Hilton, 44 N. C. (Busbee, L.) 308, 59 A. D. 552, holdin case maintainable for partial injury while total destruction will sustain trespas or trover; Alderson v. Schulze, 64 Wis. 460, 24 N. W. 492, holding total d struction or its equivalent necessary to sustain trover; Grim v. Wicker, 80

C. 343, holding destruction, carrying beyond state, or sale so as to prevent recovery, when perishable, essential to sustain trover.

Cited in reference notes in 58 A. D. 385, on forcible entry and unlawful detainer between cotenants; 82 A. D. 496, on trespass by one contenant against another.·

Cited in note in 10 L.R.A.(N.S.) 214, on trespass *quare clausum fregit* by tenant in common of realty against cotenant.

Discretion as to amendments.

Cited in State v. Swepson, 84 N. C. 827, holding amendment so as to show absence of prisoner at trial, discretionary; State v. Swepson, 83 N. C. 584, on same point.

34 AM. DEC. 378, HORAH v. LONG, 20 N. C. 416 (4 DEV. & B. L.)
   274, Collection of judgment enjoined in 36 N. C. (1 Ired. Eq.) 358,
   36 A. D. 48.

Right of suit on note taken by one for another.

Cited in McGuffin v. Coyle, 16 Okla. 648, 6 L.R.A.(N.S.) 524, 86 Pac. 962 (dissenting opinion), on right of director to recover on note taken in his own name for railroad; White v. Griffin, 47 N. C. (2 Jones, L.) 3, holding administrator of deceased person indebted to him on bills payable to former "as cashier," entitled to retain against creditors.

Cited in reference notes in 53 A. S. R. 311, on words of description in negotiable instrument; 49 A. D. 314, on necessity for plaintiff suing on bill of exchange to show title.

Cited in notes in 35 A. D. 113; 42 A. D. 378,—on who may sue on note payable to cashier; 12 A. D. 715, on principal's right to sue on notes to cashiers of banks and to agents of other corporations.

Disapproved in Lookout Bank v. Aull, 93 Tenn. 645, 42 A. S. R. 934, 27 S. W. 1014, holding that bank, discounting note payable to cashier, can maintain suit in its own name.

34 AM. DEC. 379, LEWIS v. MOBLEY, 20 N. C. 467 (4 DEV. & B. L.)
   323.

Presumption of death from absence.

Cited in reference notes in 53 A. D. 402, on presumption of death from absence; 68 A. D. 303; 83 A. D. 526,—on presumption of death after seven years' absence.

Cited in note in 92 A. D. 705, on presumption of death.

Right of remainderman on sale of slave by owner of particular estate.

Cited in Isler v. Isler, 88 N. C. 576, upholding right to proceeds with interest from death of life tenant; Haughton v. Benbury, 55 N. C. (2 Jones, Eq.) 337, holding that fraudulent disposal by life tenant creates right to proceeds in equity notwithstanding death of slave.

Cited in reference note in 47 A. D. 527, on remedies of reversioner or remainderman for injury to freehold.

Cited in note in 14 A. S. R. 629, on mode of determining rights and remedies of reversioners and remaindermen.

—**Right to maintain trover.**

Cited in Philips v. Martiney, 10 Gratt. 333, holding trover not maintainable against one purchasing slave during continuation of life estate; Cole v. Robinson, 23 N. C. (1 Ired. L.) 541, holding trover not maintainable against a co-remainderman, purchasing life estate and removing slave during its continuance; Harvey v. Epes, 12 Gratt. 153, on whether a sale renders hirer of slaves for a year liable in trover; Green v. Fagan, 15 Ala. 335, on whether sale of slaves creates a liability for conversion where there was an outstanding life interest.

When trover maintainable generally.

Cited in reference note in 32 A. S. R. 487, as to when trover is maintainable.

—Right of property and possession necessary to sustain trover.

Cited in Lapp v. Pinover, 27 Ill. App. 169; Robison v. Hardy, 22 Ill. App. 512,—holding right to immediate possession at time of conversion, essential; Brazier v. Ansley, 33 N. C. (11 Ired. L.) 12, 51 A. D. 408, holding right of property and of possession at time of conversion, essential; Jones v. Baird, 52 N. C. (7 Jones, L.) 152, holding by analogy that right to waive conversion and sue in assumpsit is exerciseable only where there was a right to money at conversion.

Cited in reference notes in 38 A. D. 511, on property necessary to maintenance of trover; 97 A. S. R. 623, on title and possession sufficient to maintain trover; 69 A. D. 772, as to what possession and title are necessary to maintain trover; 48 A. D. 76, on necessity of plaintiff in trover showing title in himself and possession at the time of conversion.

Conversion of commercial paper.

Cited in note in 2 L.R.A. 449, on conversion of commercial paper.

Burden of proof on remainderman.

Cited in Ladd v. Byrd, 113 N. C. 466, 18 S. E. 666, holding that owner of remainder after a homestead estate must prove death of homesteader and arrival at full age of youngest child.

34 AM. DEC. 382, THROWER v. McINTIRE, 20 N. C. 493 (4 DEV. & B. L.) 359.

Right of action on real covenant on death of covenantee.

Cited in Mills v. Abrams, 41 N. C. (6 Ired. Eq.) 456, holding that right to rescind deed for want of title is in heirs and not in executor; Rutherford v. Green, 37 N. C. (2 Ired. Eq.) 121, on whether administrator of obligee can sue on bond for a conveyance.

34 AM. DEC. 383, STATE v. HOOVER, 20 N. C. 500 (4 DEV. & B. L.) 365.

What constitutes murder.

Cited in reference notes in 52 A. D. 736, on distinguishing between murder and manslaughter; 34 A. D. 401, on what constitutes murder in the first degree; 42 A. D. 153, on what constitutes murder.

Cited in notes in 38 A. S. R. 80, on causing death by act calculated to produce fatal results as murder or manslaughter; 3 L.R.A. 646, on liability to indictment for negligently causing death.

—Homicide by excessive chastisement.

Cited in State v. Shaw, 64 S. C. 566, 92 A. S. R. 817, 60 L.R.A. 801, 43 S. E. 14, holding death of child from moderate punishment by parent, manslaughter, though jury may infer intent to murder; State v. Robbins, 48 N

C. (3 Jones, L.) 249, holding that death of slave from wanton and excessi
punishment does not reduce crime to manslaughter.

Cited in reference note in 92 A. S. R. 820, on unintentional homicide
servant.

Cited in note in 60 L.R.A. 804, on homicide of servant, slave, or apprenti
by excessive or. improper chastisement.

Intent to kill as element in murder.

Cited in State v. Shirley, 64 N. C. 610, holding intent to kill or do gre
bodily harm, essential.

Proof of other crime to show intent.

Cited in reference note in 21 A. S. R. 399, on proof of other crime to sh
intent to commit murder.

34 AM. DEC. 387, STATE v. POOR, 20 N. C. 519 (4 DEV. & B. L.) 38

What constitutes a levy.

Cited in Long v. Hall, 97 N. C. 286, 2 S. E. 229, holding actual or co
structive seizure, essential.

Cited in reference notes in 36 A. D. 717, on what is a sufficient levy of
tachment; 9 A. S. R. 504, on what is necessary to constitute a valid le\
48 A. D. 449, on necessity of actual seizure to levy of personalty; 73 A.
615, on incompleteness of levy of attachment without actual seizure or so
other equivalent act of notoriety; 38 A. D. 397, on levy of attachment
growing crops.

Cited in note in 16 L.R.A.(N.S.) 1049, on proper mode of levying on gro
ing crop.

Priority under writ as determined by levy.

Cited in Penland v. Leatherwood, 101 N. C. 509, 9 A. S. R. 38, 8 S. E. 2
holding that levy and not the judgment determines right to lien on personalt
though otherwise if realty is involved.

**34 AM. DEC. 388, DEAVER v. RICE, 20 N. C. 567 (4 DEV. & B. L
431.**

Rights of property in rent reserved in products.

Cited in Gordon v. Armstrong, 27 N. C. (5 Ired. L.) 409, holding th
execution cannot be levied on lessor's unallotted share of crop reserved
rent; Haywood v. Rogers, 73 N. C. 320; Ross v. Swaringer, 31 N. C. (9 Ir
L.) 481,—denying lessor's right to take possession of crop under like agr
ment; Harrison v. Ricks, 71 N. C. 7, holding that lessee can sell crop und
like agreement; Howland v. Forlaw, 108 N. C. 567, 13 S. E. 173, holding th
statute does not give lessor a lien on product reserved as rent, except in leas
of agricultural land.

Cited in reference note in 35 A. D. 124, on ownership of crop where land
let on shares.

Cited in notes in 51 A. D. 278, on rent payable in produce or services;
L.R.A. 261, on crops of landlord and tenant as personal property for p
pose of levy and sale; 51 A. D. 411, on inchoate interest of croppers not
ing subject to execution.

Distinguished in Kornegay v. Collier, 65 N. C. 69, holding that execut\
sale of lessor's interest in lease for years passes rent reserved but not
due.

Relation of lessor to third persons in regard to leased property.

Cited in Biggs v. Ferrell, 34 N. C. (12 Ired. L.) 1, holding lessor of ferry not liable to third person for damage from mismanagement by lessee.

Relation of landlord and tenant on shares.

Cited in Neal v. Brandon, 70 Ark. 79, 66 S. W. 200, holding it exists where exclusive possession was in occupant, and the owner was to receive a part of crop as rent.

Cited in note in 37 A. D. 319, on agreement to work land on shares as making occupier, tenant and owner of crops.

Passing to purchaser of land of rent due in future.

Cited in reference note in 61 A. D. 370, on passing of rent reserved on lease for years not yet due with reversion to purchaser of lessor's interest at execution sale.

34 AM. DEC. 390, HAFNER v. IRWIN, 20 N. C. 570 (4 DEV. & B. L.) 433.

Conflict between clauses in deed.

Cited in Wilkins v. Norman, 139 N. C. 40, 111 A. S. R. 767, 51 S. E. 797; Blackwell v. Blackwell, 124 N. C. 269, 32 S. E. 676,—holding that first clause will prevail.

—Between habendum and granting clause.

Cited in Berridge v. Glassey, 16 W. N. C. 255, 42 Phila. Leg. Int. 256; Smith v. Smith, 71 Mich. 633, 40 N. W. 21,—holding that habendum is void in such a case; Wilson v. Terry, 130 Mich. 73, 89 N. W. 566, holding that habendum will prevail if such appears to be the intention from the entire instrument; Utter v. Sidman, 170 Mo. 284, 70 S. W. 702, holding that habendum may be looked to for the intention unless necessarily repugnant; Kirtland v. Purdy University, 7 Lea, 243, holding that habendum cannot abridge estate given in the premises; Beecher v. Hicks, 7 Lea, 207, holding that modern tendency is to look for intention regardless of formal parts.

Cited in reference notes in 53 A. D. 228; 94 A. D. 369,—on effect of repugnancy between premises and habendum clause in deed; 69 A. D. 110, on validity of habendum clause repugnant to premises of deed; 45 A. D. 214, on validity of reservation in habendum of deed repugnant to estate granted; 55 A. D. 407, on invalidity of habendum of deed which is repugnant to estate in premises.

Cited in note in 56 A. R. 328, on conflict between habendum and granting clauses of deed.

Proper contents of habendum.

Cited in Midgett v. Brooks, 34 N. C. (12 Ired. L.) 145, 55 A. D. 405, holding that covenant may appear for first time in the habendum.

Distinguished in McLeod v. Tarrant, 39 S. C. 271, 20 L.R.A. 846, 17 S. E. 773 (dissenting opinion), on inability of grantee first appearing in habendum to take under the deed.

Necessity of habendum clause.

Cited in note in 14 E. R. C. 788, on necessity of habendum clause in deed of conveyance and right to resort to habendum to ascertain intention of grantor.

34 AM. DEC. 392, JONES v. JUDKINS, 20 N. C. 591 (4 DEV. & B. L.) 454.

Priority under writ as determined by levy.

Cited in Burnham v. Dickson, 5 Okla. 112, 47 Pac. 1059, holding that junior attachment, first levied, prevails over senior execution; Phillips v. Johnston, 77 N. C. 227, holding that prior purchaser under junior judgment gets title, prior to Code, against subsequent one under a senior judgment; Isler v. Moore, 67 N. C. 74, holding that prior purchaser gets title against a subsequent one under an execution of equal teste; Alexander v. Springs, 27 N. C. (5 Ired. L.) 475, holding that levy and not teste of execution determines rights as against purchaser under deed; Watt v. Johnson, 49 N. C. (4 Jones, L.) 190, holding that sheriff may return *nulla bona* to execution, tested before, but not coming into his hands until after, debtor's assignment; Penland v. Leatherwood, 101 N. C. 509, 9 A. S. R. 38, 8 S. E. 234, holding that judgment creates lien on personalty from time of levy, though otherwise as to realty; Field v. Milburn, 9 Mo. 492, holding that executions take priority from levy, and not from time of delivery to officer; Grant v. Hughes, 82 N. C. 216, holding personalty allotted to widow as her year's support subject to execution against husband, tested before death but issued afterwards; Dobson v. Prather, 41 N. C. (6 Ired. Eq.) 31, on right of purchaser under junior execution first levied to property exempt from lien of senior execution regardless of notice; McDaniel v. Nethercut, 53 N. C. (8 Jones, L.) 97, on superiority of first levy as between two officers with writs of execution.

Cited in reference note in 70 A. D. 675, on senior judgment lien being lost by sale of premises under junior judgment and execution.

Cited in note in 12 A. D. 595, on sale under junior writ.

Conclusiveness of record.

Cited in Doe ex dem. Burke v. Elliott, 26 N. C. (4 Ired. L.) 355, 42 A. D. 142, holding proceedings in county court on return of levy including rendition of judgment and issuance of execution, not subject to collateral attack; Spillman v. Williams, 91 N. C. 483, holding justice's judgment in attachment, not subject to collateral attack for insufficiency of affidavit.

Cited in reference notes in 69 A. D. 381, on right to impeach record by evidence *aliunde;* 74 A. D. 138, on contradiction of record by parol; 11 A. S. R. 748, on judicial record as evidence of matters therein contained; 42 A. D. 155, on collateral impeachment of truth of facts certified in record.

Effect of execution lien on debtor's estate.

Cited in Horton v. McCall, 66 N. C. 159, holding that it does not devest title, but amounts only to a charge.

Cited in note in 11 A. D. 772, 773, on time from which execution binds property.

Lien of judgment.

Cited in Alsop v. Moseley, 104 N. C. 60, 10 S. E. 124, holding that statute does not make simple rendition of judgment, without docketing at location of land, operate as a lien.

34 AM. DEC. 395, TYLER v. MORRIS, 20 N. C. 625 (4 DEV. & B. L.) 487.

Writ of error coram nobis to correct error in fact.

Cited in Howard v. State, 58 Ark. 229, 24 S. W. 8, holding that it does not lie, after expiration of time for obtaining new trial, on ground of new evidence.

Cited in notes in 18 L.R.A. 841, on right to writ *coram nobis;* 18 L.R.A. 8
on procedure as to writ *coram nobis;* 46 A. D. 260, 261, on practice under w
of error *coram nobis.*

Writ of error coram nobis as a matter of discretion.

Cited in State v. Wallace, 209 Mo. 358, 108 S. W. 542, holding that its gra
or refusal is a matter of discretion; Milam County v. Robertson, 47 Tex. 22
Lynn v. Lowe, 88 N. C. 478 (dissenting opinion),—on same point.

Cited in reference note in 79 A. D. 686, on issuance of writ of error *coram no*
as in discretion of court.

Cited in note in 97 A. S. R. 365, as to whether writs of error *coram nobis*
writs of error *coram vobis* are writs of right.

Effect of appeal.

Cited in reference notes in 59 A. D. 572, on effect of appeal on proceedings
lower court; 49 A. D. 595, on effect of appeal or error as supersedeas.

34 AM. DEC. 396, STATE v. HILL, 20 N. C. 629 (4 DEV. & B. L.) 49

Right to kill in self-defense.

Cited in State v. Kennedy, 91 N. C. 572, holding it not justifiable unless slay
was closely pressed and retreated in good faith as far as possible and convenien
State v. Chavis, 80 N. C. 353, holding it not excusable without proof of retreat
prevention by fierceness of the fight, or that killing was necessary to save on
own life; People v. Shorter, 4 Barb. 460 (dissenting opinion), on necessity
killing as an element in a justifiable homicide; State v. Whitson, 111 N. C. 6
16 S. E. 332, holding it not self-defense where evidence shows shooting of decea
while endeavoring to escape; McNeezer v. State, 63 Ala. 169, holding char
properly refused, where evidence showed unnecessary killing in a quarrel m
tually entered upon; State v. Lilliston, 141 N. C. 857, 115 A. S. R. 705,
S. E. 427, holding shooting at assailant, fleeing after end of affray, not jus
fiable.

Cited in reference notes in 47 A. D. 268, on extent of right of self-defense
assault and battery; 72 A. D. 201, as to whether using dangerous weapon
return blow with naked hand is justifiable.

Cited in notes in 51 A. D. 293, as to when homicide is deemed justifiable
ground of self-defense; 6 L.R.A. 425, on force permissible in self-defense;
L.R.A.(N.S.) 65, on increased or undiminished risk as affecting duty to r
treat.

—Right of self-defense by assailant.

Cited in State v. Partlow, 90 Mo. 608, 59 A. R. 31, 4 S. W. 14, holding o
fense not murder whatever the outcome provided assailant did not commen
the affray maliciously; State v. Culler, 82 Mo. 623; Hash v. Com. 88 Va. 17
13 S. E. 398,—holding right of self-defense available to assailant, provided
did not commence affray maliciously; Watkins v. United States, 1 Ind. Te
364, 41 S. W. 1044, holding instruction "that a party cannot himself provo
a difficulty and then slay his adversary upon ground of self-defense" erroneo
under the facts; Cartwright v. State, 14 Tex. App. 486, holding charge "th
whenever a party has produced by his own acts any necessity to take human li
in order to preserve his own life, he cannot be excused or justified" error; Sta
v. Hensley, 94 N. C. 1021, holding assailant bringing on combat with inte
to kill in case of resistance, guilty of murder, though he encountered gr
peril from deceased.

Cited in notes in 45 L.R.A. 692, on self-defense set up by accused who began conflict; 51 A. D. 293, on effect of resistance to assault disproportionate to violence of attack; 45 L.R.A. 696, on what amounts to provoking or bringing on difficulty or producing occasion preventing one's relying on self-defense.

— Necessity of withdawal by aggressor.

Cited in State v. Rogers, 18 Kan. 78, 26 A. R. 754, holding assailant without intent to kill, not justified in defending his own life, where there was no attempt to withdraw at the retreat of assailed; Hittner v. State, 19 Ind. 48, holding that assailant must have attempted to withdraw in good faith, in order to justify slaying; State v. Talmage, 107 Mo. 543, 17 S. W. 990, holding killing justified in self-defense of provoker of quarrel by language, after his attempting in good faith to withdraw; State v. Medlin, 126 N. C. 1127, 36 S. E. 344, holding circumstances insufficient to show withdrawal from conflict so as to make right of self-defense available; Hull v. State, 6 Lea. 249, holding attempt to escape with all possible ability essential to reduce degree of killing with a deadly weapon after voluntary provocation of a fight.

Distinction between murder and manslaughter.

Cited in Noble v. State, 75 Ark. 246, 87 S. W. 120,—holding that violence by party assaulted beyond what is proportionate to the assault, which was not intended to kill, renders killing by original assailant without time for cooling, manslaughter only; State v. Gentry, 47 N. C. (2 Jones, L.) 406, holding killing in quarrel resulting from heat of passion excited by a violent assault, manslaughter; State v. Hunt, 134 N. C. 684, 47 S. E. 49, holding that killing in a brutal and ferocious manner amounts to murder though there was some provocation; State v. Reed, 154 Mo. 122, 55 S. W. 278, holding killing with pick in hot blood produced by provocation, manslaughter provided there was no malice; State v. Horn, 116 N. C. 1037, 21 S. E. 694, holding killing found to have been done under recent provocation rather than under malice followed by reconciliation, manslaughter; United States v. Barnaby, 51 Fed. 20, on possibility of an unlawful and intentional killing not amounting to murder.

Cited in reference notes in 42 A. D. 153, on what constitutes murder; 51 A. D. 464, on what is manslaughter; 37 A. D. 642; 52 A. D. 736,—distinguishing between murder and manslaughter.

— Passion sufficient to reduce below murder.

Cited with special approval in Beasley v. State, 64 Miss. 518, 8 So. 234, holding instruction that "instant" and "deliberate" shooting of an assailant who had shot and missed, would be murder, error.

Cited in Maher v. People, 10 Mich. 212, 81 A. D. 871, holding it sufficient if such as might render an ordinary man liable to act rashly; State v. Davis, 50 S. C. 405, 62 A. S. R. 837, 27 S. E. 905, holding it need not dethrone reason or shut out volition, though it must be such as to naturally render mind incapable of cool reflection; Johnson v. State, 129 Wis. 146, 5 L.R.A. (N. S.) 809, 108 N. W. 55, 9 A. & E. Ann. Cas. 923, holding required heat of passion not inconsistent with intelligent action or consciousness of situation; Smith v. State, 83 Ala. 26, 3 So. 551, holding provocation causing transport of passion, suspending exercise of judgment, but not entirely dethroning reason, sufficient; State v. Ellis, 74 Mo. 207, holding term "reasonable" properly used in instruction defining the necessary kind of passion; State v. Henderson, 24 Or. 100, 32 Pac. 1030, holding that design to kill, formed when reason is obscured by passion, does not make homicide murder in first degree, though slayer knew he was about to take a life; State v. Cooper, 112 La. 281, 104 A. S. R. 447, 36 So. 350, holding offer to prove that prisoner's daughter communicated fact of an assault on her person thirty minutes prior to homicide, competent.

Cited in note in 5 L.R.A.(N.S.) 818, on sufficiency of passion to mitigate or reduce degree of homicide.

— **Prior malice and recent provocation.**

Cited in Karr v. State, 106 Ala. 1, 17 So. 328, holding that proof of more immediate cause raises presumption that killing was not based on former grudges and threats; People v. Hyndman, 99 Cal. 1, 33 Pac. 782; State v. Barnwell, 80 N. C. 466,—holding that proof of recent provocation raises presumption that killing was not based on prior malice followed by a reconciliation; State v. Clark, 51 W. Va. 457, 41 S. E. 204, holding that it is for jury to determine whether killing was induced by' previous grudge or new provocation.

Cited in reference notes in 43 A. D. 395, on malice as essential element of murder; 81 A. D. 791, on what provocation reduces intentional killing to manslaughter; 52 A. D. 737, on provocation mitigating homicide from murder to manslaughter; 71 A. D. 168, on lapse of time between provocation and killing as determining crime to be murder or manslaughter.

Cited in notes in 5 L.R.A.(N.S.) 812, on necessity of heat of passion to mitigate or reduce degree of homicide; 5 L.R.A.(N.S.) 814, on malice or intent to kill as affecting mitigation or reduction of degree of homicide because of heat of passion.

— **Words of insult or offense as provocation.**

Cited in State v. Carter, 76 N. C. 20, holding words insufficient provocation for such passion, though otherwise as to blows; People v. Olsen, 4 Utah, 413, 11 Pac. 577, holding mere words of reproach insufficient, when killing was committed with a deadly weapon.

Cited in reference note in 52 A. D. 737, on insufficiency of words only as provocation to mitigate homicide to manslaughter.

Cited in note in 4 L.R.A.(N.S.) 157, on insulting words or conduct as provocation to homicide where mutual combat results.

34 AM. DEC. 402, MUNNERLIN v. BIRMINGHAM, 22 N. C. (2 DEV. & B. EQ.) 358.

Absolute transfer as a mortgage in equity.

Cited in M'Laurin v. Wright, 37 N. C. (2 Ired. Eq.) 94, holding that fair price and possession taken and no covenant to repay do not show a mortgage in absence of other evidence.

Cited in reference notes in 90 A. D. 350; 32 A. S. R. 741,—on distinction between conditional sales and mortgages; 90 A. D. 351, on agreement to resell as conditional sale; 34 A. D. 420, on agreement for resale as a mortgage; 90 A. D. 351, on intention to secure indebtedness by conveyance or bill of sale as criterion of mortgage; 59 A. D. 188, on effect of vendee's or vendor's noncompliance with conditions to make conditional sale absolute.

Cited in note in 50 A. D. 196, on considering transaction as mortgage instead of conditional sale in case of doubt.

34 AM. DEC. 403, HOUGH v. MARTIN, 22 N. C. (2 DEV. & B. E 379.

Suit for construction of will.

Cited in Cozart v. Lyon, 91 N. .C. 282, holding it not maintainable whe devisees claim a mere legal estate and no trusts are involved.

Cited in reference note in 41 A. D. 740, on jurisdiction of equity to const will.

Jurisdiction over boundary disputes.

Cited in reference note in 67 A. D. 621, on jurisdiction of equity over bo ary disputes.

Cited in note in 119 A. S. R. 70, on grounds for assuming jurisdiction suits to declare and ascertain boundaries.

Suit to enjoin waste.

Cited in Law v. Wilgees, 5 Biss. 13, Fed. Cas. No. 8,132, holding proof good title and right to possession essential.

Right to discovery.

Cited in reference notes in 57 A. D. 380, on requisites of bill for discove of deeds; 42 A. D. 175, on right to discovery where leading circumstan rest in defendant's knowledge.

34 AM. DEC. 407, TALLY v. TALLY, 22 N. C. (2 DEV. & B. EQ.) 38

Liability of lunatic on contracts.

Cited in reference notes in 83 A. D. 523, on validity of contracts of ins persons; 55 A. D. 431, on liability of insane persons on contracts.

— For necessaries.

Cited in Richardson v. Strong, 35 N. C. (13 Ired. L.) 106, 55 A. D. 4 holding fair contract for necessaries suitable to condition in life, valid; parte Northington, 37 Ala. 496, 79 A. D. 67, holding adult lunatic, without guardian, liable to suit on implied contract for necessaries.

Cited in note in 15 A. D. 368, on liability of lunatic for necessaries.

Setting apart fund for maintenance of lunatic as against creditors.

Cited in Patton v. Thompson, 55 N. C. (2 Jones, Eq.) 411, 67 A. D. holding guardian not entitled to credit for expenditures exceeding annual come, if made without consent of court; Re Latham, 39 N. C. (4 Ired. Eq 231, holding that claims of creditors and for previous support do not p vent equity from setting aside fund for maintenance of lunatic and his f ily; Smith v. Pipkin, 79 N. C. 569, on same point.

Limited in Lemly v. Ellis, 146 N. C. 221, 59 S. E. 683, holding rights creditors not denied, where care and support of lunatic and his family a otherwise provided for.

Jurisdiction of equity to determine lunacy.

Cited in Dowell v. Jacks, 58 N. C. (5 Jones, Eq.) 417, holding court cf equi without jurisdiction to inquire whether person is an idiot or lunatic or not.

34 AM. DEC. 410, POLK v. GALLANT, 22 N. C. (2 DEV. & B. EQ.) 39

When purchaser is protected against prior equities.

Cited in Todd v. Outlaw, 79 N. C. 235, holding mortgagee of legal ti without actual or constructive notice; protected; Durant v. Crowell, 97 N. 367, 2 S. E. 541, holding that the inadequacy of price was notice.

Cited in reference notes in 40 A. D. 628, on priority of mere equities; 72 A. D. 68, on assignee of chose in action taking subject to equities; 31 A. S. R. 914, on applicability of doctrine of bona fides to purchaser of legal title only.

— As to purchasers of equities.

Cited in People v. Mahoney, 77 Cal. 529, 20 Pac. 73, holding assignee of a certificate of purchase not protected; Re Reynolds, 16 Nat. Bankr. Reg. 158, Fed. Cas. No. 11,724, holding neither assignee nor judgment creditor of obligee in bond for title, protected; Winborn v. Gorrell, 38 N. C. (3 Ired. Eq.) 117, 140 A. D. 456, holding assignee from purchaser entitled to a conveyance on payment of purchase money, not protected; Durant v. Crowell, 97 N. C. 367, 2 S. E. 541, holding purchaser of equity of redemption at judicial sale, not protected.

Cited in reference notes in 53 A. D. 507, on maxim that "priority in time among mere equities gives priority of right;" 67 A. D. 609, on liability of purchaser of equity to prior equity; 55 A. D. 478, on purchaser of mere equity taking subject to equities against vendor.

Cited in note in 97 A. D. 434, as to whether and when purchaser of equitable title is entitled to protection as purchaser in good faith without notice.

— Rights and equities of or against purchaser at execution sale.

Cited in Vannoy v. Martin, 41 N. C. (6 Ired. Eq.) 169, 51 A. D. 418; Walke v. Moody, 65 N. C. 599; Hicks v. Skinner, 71 N. C. 539, 17 A. R. 16; Ross v. Henderson, 77 N. C. 170; Carr v. Fearington, 63 N. C. 560,—holding such a purchaser not protected though he had no notice; Parker v. Pierce, 16 Iowa, 227; State v. Brim, 57 N. C. (4 Jones, Eq.) 300,—on same point.

Cited in reference notes in 54 A. D. 462, on rights of purchaser at execution sale; 56 A. D. 761; 90 A. D. 546,—as to title acquired by purchaser of land at execution sale; 84 A. D. 162, on rule that execution purchaser acquires only such land as debtor had; 82 A. D. 613, on title acquired by bona fide purchaser at execution sale without notice of prior equities; 61 A. D. 194, as to whether purchaser at execution sale is affected by prior equity of which he had no notice; 39 A. D. 46, on effect of secret trust on purchaser at execution.

Cited in notes in 89 A. D. 587; 21 L.R.A. 45,—on title acquired by purchaser at execution or judicial sale; 28 L.R.A. 174, on position of purchaser of partnership real estate under execution against partner.

Distinguished in Hall v. Livingston, 3 Del. Ch. 348, as not being an authority as to sufficiency of notice.

Right of surety to indemnity or exoneration from primary security.

Cited in Edgerton v. Alley, 41 N. C. (6 Ired. Eq.) 188, holding sureties for insolvent purchaser entitled, either before paying money or afterwards, to a sale of land retained by vendor as security; Barnes v. Morris, 39 N. C. (4 Ired. Eq.) 22; Shoffner v. Fogleman, 60 N. C. (Winst. Eq.) 12,—holding same as against a bona fide purchaser without notice from principal; Smith v. Smith, 40 N. C. (5 Ired. Eq.) 34, holding that surety for price of land, entitled to exoneration or indemnity, may file bill to prevent conveyance by vendor to purchaser; Morgan v. Tillet, 55 N. C. (2 Jones, Eq.) 39, holding that surety for vendor compelled to repay purchase money may follow land in hands of purchaser at sale under execution against vendor; Barbour v. National Exch. Bank, 45 Ohio St. 133, 12 N. E. 5, holding that statute allows surety on overdue indebtedness of an insolvent to require payment in assets on hand; Uptmoor v. Young, 57 Ark. 528, 22 S. W. 169, holding that statute allowing action at law for indemnity does not bar suit to compel exoneration from debt not due.

Cited in reference notes in 54 A. D. 598, on right of surety paying debt to recover from principal; 45 A. D. 584, on right of surety to proceed against principal as soon as judgment has been rendered against him.

Cited in note in 117 A. S. R. 38, on effect of insolvency of principal or surety on right of surety to compel principal to discharge obligation.

Distinguished in Miller v. Miller, 62 N. C. (Phill. Eq.) 85, holding right of surety to pursue land as indemnity against his liability, for purchase money, inapplicable where title is not retained.

When assignor must be joined as a party in equity.

Cited in Mullins v. McCandless, 57 N. C. (4 Jones, Eq.) 425, holding that he need not be made a party if bill and answer show a transfer of entire interest; Robinson v. Springfield Co. 21 Fla. 203, holding that he need not be joined, if assignment is absolutely without retention of interest; Clark v. Edney, 28 N. C. (6 Ired. L.) 50, holding that he must be joined where alleged instrument of assignment does not purport to be such on its face.

34 AM. DEC. 415, ST. CLAIR v. MORRIS, 9 OHIO, 15.

Mortgage as bar of wife's dower right.

Cited in Duval v. Febiger, 1 Cin. Sup. Ct. Rep. 268, holding that where wife joins in mortgage and subsequently husband alone conveys his equity of redemption, her right of dower is barred; Carter v. Goodin, 3 Ohio St. 75, holding that where purchaser, as part of price of land, pays a mortgage thereon given by vendor and wife, the dower estate of vendor's wife is not barred thereby; Ryan v. Fergusson, 3 Wash. 356, 28 Pac. 910, holding that community property mortgaged by husband and wife may be sold by administrator of husband under order of court to pay mortgage debt, and wife's interest therein passes.

Cited in reference notes in 61 A. S. R. 830, on release of dower by mortgage; 37 A. D. 392, on effect, as to dower, of wife's joining in mortgage of husband's land.

Distinguished in Taylor v. Fowler, 18 Ohio, 567, 51 A. D. 469, holding that where wife joins in mortgage, and the land is subsequently sold under judgment of stranger, her right of dower is not barred though part of proceeds of sale are used to pay mortgage; Ketchum v. Shaw, 28 Ohio St. 503, holding that where wife joins in mortgage, and subsequently the lands are sold under insolvency proceedings at price greatly in excess of mortgage debt which is paid, her dower right is not barred.

Right of assignee of debt to benefit of security.

Cited in Swartz v. Hurd, 2 Ohio Dec. Reprint, 134, holding that assignee of note secured by mortgage acquires equitable title to mortgage security.

34 AM. DEC. 418, STRATTON v. SABIN, 9 OHIO, 28.

What constitutes a mortgage.

Cited in reference notes in 90 A. D. 351, on agreement to resell as conditional sale; 34 A. D. 403, on intention of parties as determining whether instrument is mortgage or conditional sale.

Cited in note in 18 E. R. C. 15, as to test whether transaction is mortga or conditional sale.

Distinguished in Liskey v. Snyder, 56 W. Va. 610, 49 S. E. 515, holdi that purchase at execution sale by stranger, and resale to debtor by executo contract at advance in pursuance of prior verbal contract, is a loan on the la as security.

34 AM. DEC. 420, FOOTE v. CINCINNATI, 9 OHIO, 31.

Action of tort against corporation.

Cited in Ward v. Toledo, N. & C. R. Co. 1 Ohio Dec. Reprint, 553, holdi corporation not liable to an action of trespass *quare clausum fregit*.

Cited in reference notes in 64 A. D. 86, on trespass *quare clausum fre* against corporation aggregate; 75 A. D. 728, on right to maintain tres *quare clausum fregit* against private corporation.

Cited in note in 13 A. D. 596, on liability of corporation for torts.

Disapproved in Fenton v. Wilson Sewing Mach. Co. 9 Phila. 189, 31 Phi Leg. Int. 132, holding that action for malicious prosecution will lie against corporation aggregate.

34 AM. DEC. 422, LEBANON v. WARREN COUNTY, 9 OHIO, 80.

Dedication of lands to public use.

Cited in Lamar Co. v. Clements, 49 Tex. 347, holding that where plat sho lands dedicated to public use, and lots are sold with reference thereto, t owner is estopped to use those parts for purpose inconsistent with such de cation; Parrish v, Stephens, 1 Or. 59, holding that the erection of tempora buildings on disputed grounds are not evidence of private property agai clear proofs of dedication.

Cited in reference notes in 40 A. D. 217, on dedication to public use; 48 D. 514, on mode of establishing dedication of land to public use; 41 A. 661, on dedication of land without deed; 60 A. D. 422, on dedication by s utory method of acknowledging and recording town plat.

Cited in note in 40 A. D. 492, as to what constitutes dedication.

— Of public square.

Cited in Huber v. Gazley, 18 Ohio, 18, holding that land designated in corded plat as public square is thereby dedicated to the public, and no sub quent disposition of it by the original owner can affect such use; Evans Blankenship, 4 Ariz. 307, 39 Pac. 812, holding that declarations as to a purpc for which a square was dedicated, made subsequent to its dedication as "pub grounds," cannot control its use.

34 AM. DEC. 424, HALL v. ASHBY, 9 OHIO, 96.

Effect of quitclaim deed.

Cited in Skerrett v. First Presby. Soc. 41 Ohio St. 606; Davidson v. Coo 125 Ind. 497, 9 L.R.A. 584, 25 N. E. 601,—holding that title passes by qu claim deed as effectually as by any other; Bagley v. Fletcher, 44 Ark. 18 holding that quitclaim deed conveys all the interest of grantor, though gran has neither prior possession nor any interest in lands conveyed; Cutler James, 64 Wis. 173, 54 A. R. 603, 24 N. W. 874, holding that a recorded qu claim deed conveys title as against prior unrecorded warranty deed.

Cited in reference note in 38 A. D. 130, on deed of release as conveyance.

Cited in notes in 53 A. R. 749, on interest conveyed by quitclaim deed; 1 A. S. R. 856, on effect of quitclaim deeds given for purpose of transmitti grantor's estate or title.

Conveyance of lands held adversely.

Cited in Michigan C. R. Co. v. McNaughton, 45 Mich. 87, 7 N. W. 7 holding that conveyance of lands held adversely by another is valid; Borl v. Marshall, 2 Ohio St. 308, holding that husband may have tenancy by cu in lands of wife, though they were in adverse possession of another duri coverture.

Cited in reference notes in 36 A. D. 242, on conveyance by grantor out possession; 45 A. D. 571; 70 A. D. 478,—as to when conveyance of land adverse possession by another is void.

Cited in note in 55 A. D. 414, on deed of property of which grantor is d seised.

Criticized in Cresinger v. Welch, 15 Ohio, 156, 45 A. D. 565, holding su conveyance valid.

Relation of probate to title under will.

Cited in Goodman v. Winter, 64 Ala. 410, 38 A. R. 13, holding that whe registration or probate of will is necessary under statute, such registrati relates back and title vests from death of testator; Jones v. Robinson, 17 Oh St. 171, on the same point; McArthur v. Scott, 113 U. S. 340, 28 L. ed. 101 5 Sup. Ct. Rep. 652, holding that where will is duly probated in one count the recording and probate of the will in another county in which land devis is located is for evidence only and not to make the probate effective; Broo v. McComb, 38 Fed. 317, holding that where statute requires foreign will to recorded before becoming effectual to pass title, the recording of a will relat back so as to validate a conveyance made prior to such recording.

Distinguished in Douglass v. Miller, 3 Ohio N. P. 220, holding that title devisee is not acquired until probate of the will under statute.

Jurisdiction to establish will.

Cited in Morning Star v. Selby, 15 Ohio, 345, 45 A. D. 579, holding t court of chancery has no jurisdiction to establish a lost or destroyed will.

Effect of probate decrees.

Cited in Mayhugh v. Rosenthal, 1 Cin. Sup. Ct. 492 (dissenting opinion), conclusiveness of decree of court granting letters of administration.

Cited in reference note in 48 L.R.A. 151, on effect of probate of will another state.

Cited in notes in 48 L.R.A. 141, on conclusiveness of probate of will fro another state; 113 A. S. R. 216, on conclusiveness and effect of foreign proba where real estate is involved.

Effect of assignment of lease upon right of re-entry.

Cited in Countee v. Armstrong, 10 Ohio L. J. 339, 10 Ohio Dec. Reprint, 6 holding lessor's right of re-entry for nonpayment of rent not extinguished assignment of lease.

34 AM. DEC. 427, PILLSBURY v. DUGAN, 9 OHIO, 117.

Application of doctrine of idem sonans.

Cited in Rowe v. Palmer, 29 Kan. 337, holding that judgment by defau upon service by publication is valid under doctrine of *idem sonans* tho

name was slightly misspelled; Schlacks v. Johnson, 13 Colo. App. 130, 56 P
673, holding that a slight variance between spelling of name in summons a
in return thereon will not invalidate the service of the summons; M'Claskey
Barr, 47 Fed. 154, on error in name not being fatal where identity of pers
intended is established.

Cited in note in 100 A. S. R. 349, on alphabetical list of names held to
idem sonans.

Mistake as ground for relief in equity.

Cited in notes in 37 A. D. 76; 12 L.R.A. 275,—on mistake in drawing
strument as ground for equitable relief.

Parol evidence of mistake.

Cited in reference note in 57 A. D. 606, on parol evidence to show mistake
written instruments.

Judgments in rem.

Cited in Good v. Norley, 28 Iowa, 188 (dissenting opinion), on probate p
ceedings for sale of lands being proceedings *in rem.*

Nature of partition suit.

Cited in reference note in 41 A. D. 165, on nature of partition procee
ings.

Parties to partition suit.

Cited in reference note in 75 A. D. 172, on all persons interested as nec
sary parties in partition suit.

Effect and conclusiveness of judgment in partition.

Cited in reference notes in 79 A. D. 452, on effect of judgment in partitio
78 A. D. 686, on conclusiveness of judgments in partition; 72 A. D. 461, on
cree in partition binding cotenant who is beyond jurisdiction of court.

Cited in note in 101 A. S. R. 866, on effect of compulsory partition on h
bands or wives of parties to the suit.

Collateral attack on judgments or judicial sales.

Cited in Cadwallader v. Evans, 1 Disney (Ohio) 585, holding that decr
of court, having jurisdiction, in proceedings for sale of lands by administrat
cannot be attacked collaterally; Adams v. Jeffries, 12 Ohio, 253, 40 A.
477, on the same point; Maxsom v. Sawyer, 12 Ohio, 195, holding that whe
court has ratified a guardian's sale, it will be presumed that the necessary p
liminaries have been properly done; Adams v. Jeffries, 12 Ohio, 253, 40 A.
477, holding that administrator's sale under order of court, without showi
that heirs were parties to the proceedings, is void under statute; Smith
Pratt, 13 Ohio, 548, on presumptions being in favor of the validity of partiti
proceedings.

Cited in note in 21 L.R.A. 854, on collateral attack on judgment obtain
on unauthorized appearance by attorney.

Validity of judgment upon unauthorized appearance of attorney.

Cited in Watson v. Hopkins, 27 Tex. 637, holding that domestic judgme
cannot be attacked collaterally for failure to show authority of attorney
appear for defendant therein; Martin v. Judd, 60 Ill. 78, holding that jud
ment, where appearance of defendant is entered by unauthorized attorney,
voidable only and may be ratified; Prince v. Griffin, 16 Iowa, 552, holding th
service of notice upon attorneys is not void because their authority does n
appear upon face of the record; Harshey v. Blackmarr, 20 Iowa, 161, 89 A.

520, holding judgment and sale under fraudulent appearance by unauthorized attorney void.

Cited in note in 21 L.R.A. 848, on effect of judgment obtained on unauthorized appearance by attorney.

Attorney's unauthorized acts.

Cited in Wade v. Pettibone, 11 Ohio, 57, 37 A. D. 408, holding creditor in an execution entitled to benefit of purchase made by his attorney, if claimed within a reasonable time.

Suit by cotenant as preventing bar of statute.

Cited in Barr v. Chapman, 30 Ohio L. J. 264, 11 Ohio Dec. Reprint, 867, holding that institution of partition suit by one claimant before statute of limitations has run does not save the rights of all claimants.

34 AM. DEC. 429, DENNISON v. FOSTER, 9 OHIO, 126.

Rights under sale by tenant in common.

Cited in Worthington v. Staunton, 16 W. Va. 208; Lamb v. Wakefield, 1 Sawy. 251, Fed. Cas. No. 8,024,—holding that deed of tenant in common for part of premises held in common is good against the grantor but void as against his cotenant's right to partition; Kenoye v. Brown, 82 Miss. 607, 100 A. S. R. 645, 35 So. 163, holding that, under conveyance by cotenant of described part of lands held in common, purchaser takes title thereto by estoppel if that part is set off to grantor upon partition; Burt & B. Lumber Co. v. Clay City Lumber Co. 111 Ky. 725, 64 S. W. 652, holding that a tenant in common cannot sell the right to cut logs on lands held in common so as to pass legal title to purchaser; Jolliffe v. Maxwell, 3 Neb. (Unof.) 244, 91 N. W. 563, holding that where a cotenant mortgages his undivided interest in lands held in common, such mortgage becomes a lien only upon the part set off to the mortgagor upon partition; Holbrook v. Bowman, 62 N. H. 313, on how far deed of cotenant conveying described part of lands held in common is valid against his cotenants.

Cited in reference notes in 30 A. S. R. 541, on conveyance by one tenant in common; 75 A. D. 171, on conveyance of his interest by tenant in common; 41 A. D. 406; 63 A. D. 651,—on right of cotenant to convey part of common property by metes and bounds.

Cited in notes in 11 L.R.A. 278, on conveyance by tenant in common by metes and bounds; 100 A. S. R. 652, on what interest passes by conveyance by one cotenant of specific part of common property; 100 A. S. R. 651, on estoppel as against grantor of conveyance by one cotenant of specific part of common property.

— Equities of elder and junior purchaser.

Distinguished in Arnold v. Cauble, 49 Tex. 527, holding that elder purchaser should have preference over a later one with notice, in proceedings for partition.

Purchase by one cotenant inuring to cotenant.

Cited in reference note in 41 A. D. 166, as to whether outstanding title purchased by tenant in common inures to benefit of cotenant.

Voluntary partition.

Cited in Farmers' & M. Nat. Bank v. Wallace, 45 Ohio St. 152, 12 N. E. 439, holding that mutual quitclaims upon voluntary partition are based upon good consideration.

Distinguished in Dawson v. Lawrence, 13 Ohio, 543, 42 A. R. 210, holding that purchasers of separate parts from tenants under a void partition have such interest as will be protected in equity as far as consistent with rights of cotenants to valid partition.

Necessity of grantor's being party to operative part of deed.

Cited in Berrigan v. Fleming, 2 Lea, 271, holding that grantor must be party to the operative part of a conveyance in order to pass his title; Hoge v. Hollister, 2 Tenn. Ch. 606, holding the same with special reference to deed signed by married woman.

34 AM. DEC. 432, BRIGHT v. CARPENTER, 9 OHIO, 139.

Liability of irregular indorser of note.

Cited in Salisbury v. First Nat. Bank, 37 Neb. 872, 40 A. S. R. 527, 56 N. W. 727; Wetherwax v. Paine, 2 Mich. 555,—holding that indorser in blank of note before delivery is a joint promisor with the maker; Fischer v. Penterman, 8 Ohio Dec. Reprint, 540, 8 Ohio L. J. 306, holding that one signing his name upon back of note before it is given is an original promisor or surety; Gale v. Van Arman, 18 Ohio, 336, holding that where stranger to note payable in clocks writes and signs a guaranty of fulfilment of the contract, he becomes liable jointly thereon; Castle v. Rickly, 44 Ohio St. 490, 58 A. R. 839, 9 N. E. 136, holding that stranger indorsing note after delivery, but before maturity, becomes an unconditional guarantor of its payment; Stage v. Olds, 12 Ohio, 158, holding that where bond is executed by several persons at the same time and upon the same considerations, but some as principals and others as sureties, they may be sued as joint obligors, regardless of where their signatures appear.

Cited in reference notes in 49 A. D. 790, on liability of indorser as original promisor; 56 A. D. 359, on irregular indorser as original promisor or maker; 37 A. D. 138, on effect of indorsement of note at time of execution; 38 A. D. 467; 33 A. S. R. 526,—on liability on indosement not by payee; 38 A. D. 99, on effect of blank indorsement by one not a holder or payee; 75 A. D. 330, on effect of indorsement of negotiable note by stranger before delivery to payee; 39 A. D. 132, on one writing name on note not being holder or payee, being treated as maker or original promisor.

Cited in note in 72 A. S. R. 679, on effect of indorsement by stranger before delivery.

Distinguished in Deming v. Ohio Agri. & Mechanical College, 31 Ohio St. 41; Mowery v. Mast, 9 Neb. 445, 4 N. W. 69,—holding that one who places a guaranty on note and signs it before delivery is not liable as joint maker.

Indorsement of firm name upon partner's individual note.

Cited in Benninger v. Fuchs, 7 Ohio Dec. Reprint, 613, 4 Ohio L. J. 270, holding that indorsement of firm name by partner upon his individual note makes firm joint makers with rights of sureties.

Parol explanation of indorsement.

Cited in Hoffman v. Levy, 2 Cin. Sup. Ct. Rep. 224; Seymour v. Mickey, 15 Ohio St. 515; Oldham v. Broom, 28 Ohio St. 41; Ewan v. Brooks-Waterfield Co. 55 Ohio St. 596, 60 A. S. R. 719, 35 L.R.A. 786, 45 N. E. 1094; Cook v. Southwick, 9 Tex. 615, 60 A. D. 181; Atkinson v. Bennet, 103 Ga. 508, 30 S. E. 599,—holding that third person placing his name on back of note before delivery to payee may show by parol what relation to the note he assumed thereby.

Cited in reference notes in 66 A. D. 477, on parol evidence affecting indorsement; 43 A. D. 289; 60 A. D. 185,—on parol evidence to vary effect of indorsement; 79 A. D. 571, on admissibility of evidence to vary effect of indorsement; 59 A. D. 292, on extrinsic evidence to limit apparent liability of party to note.

Distinguished in Dibble v. Duncan, 2 McLean, 553, Fed. Cas. No. 3,880, holding that parol evidence is admissible to explain an indorsement only where the intent of it is doubtful on its face.

34 AM. DEC. 434, PENDLETON v. GALLOWAY, 9 OHIO, 178.

Relief from judgment.

Cited in reference notes in 51 A. D. 394, on setting aside judgment; 41 A. D. 628, on relief in equity against judgment at law; 70 A. D. 313, on impeachment of judgment for fraud after lapse of time.

Specifications in bill for relief for fraud.

Cited in Davis v. Landcraft, 10 W. Va. 718; Conway v. Ellison, 14 Ark. 360,—holding that bill for relief for fraud must specify distinctly the facts and circumstances constituting the fraud.

Cited in reference note in 41 A. D. 743, on necessity of specifically setting out fraud in obtaining judgment, in suit to obtain relief therefrom.

Laches as bar to relief.

Cited in Clark v. Potter, 32 Ohio St. 49, holding that equity of redemption is barred by twenty-one years' adverse possession though decree of foreclosure was void; Bridenbaugh v. King, 42 Ohio St. 410, holding that holder of a certificate entitling him to deed from state cannot set up his right as against subsequent purchaser in possession, where he has delayed for forty years.

34 AM. DEC. 436, McINTIRE POOR SCHOOL v. ZANESVILLE CANAL & MFG. CO. 9 OHIO, 203.

Gifts and devises for public, charitable purposes.

Cited in O'Neal v. Caulfield, 5 Ohio N. P. 149, 8 Ohio S. & C. P. Dec. 248, holding that bequests to charity should be liberally construed.

Cited in reference note in 59 A. D. 619, on validity of bequests to charitable uses.

— To unincorporated society.

Cited in reference notes in 40 A. D. 554, on bequests to unincorporated societies; 67 A. D. 185, on devises and bequests to unincorporated societies for charitable uses.

Cited in note in 14 L.R.A. 411, on effect of subsequent incorporation to make valid a gift to an unincorporated association.

— Necessity of trustee or donee.

Cited in Clayton v. Hallett, 30 Colo. 231, 97 A. S. R. 117, 59 L.R.A. 407, 70 Pac. 429, holding that a gift for charitable purposes will not fail for want of a trustee; Johnson v. Mayne, 4 Iowa, 180; St. John v. Andrews Institute, 191 N. Y. 254, 83 N. E. 981; Ould v. Washington Hospital, 95 U. S. 303, 24 L. ed. 450,—sustaining devise for charitable purposes to corporation to be created; Miller v. Chittenden, 2 Iowa, 315, holding that devise for charitable purpose will be sustained, though trustee is not *in esse* at time of devise; Re John, 30 Or. 494, 36 L.R.A. 242, 47 Pac. 341, holding charitable devise valid though trustees were to be appointed in the future; Cruse v. Axtell, 50 Ind. 49, holding that devise to lodge of Masons for building is for charitable use and valid, though the lodge was not a corporation *de jure;* Vincennes University v. Indiana, 14 How. 268, 14 L. ed. 416, holding that grant to a seminary of learning by Congress will vest in such a corporation when organized, though no grantee existed at the time.

— Certainty as to beneficiaries or purpose.

Cited in Mannix v. Purcell, 46 Ohio St. 102, 2 L.R.A. 753, 19 N. E. 572, holding that devise for religious purposes is for charitable use, and valid; Landis v. Wooden, 1 Ohio St. 160, 59 A. D. 615, holding that bequest to "such poor as are not able to support themselves" is valid and beneficiaries are sufficiently designated; Cincinnati v. McMicken, 6 Ohio C. C. 188, 3 Ohio C. Dec. 409, holding that devise to a city for college to be erected on a certain site does not restrict it to that place if it becomes unsuitable; Wyandotte County v. First Presby. Church, 30 Kan. 620, 1 Pac. 109, holding that dedication of lots for church purposes will be enforced as gift for charitable purpose.

Cited in note in 106 A. S. R. 507, on necessity of precatory words to be certain as to both subject and object of intended trusts.

Statute of uses.

Cited in note in 36 A. S. R. 254, on statute of uses.

Chancery jurisdiction over trusts and charities.

Cited in Jones v. Henderson, 149 Ind. 458, 49 N. E. 443, holding that chancery has jurisdiction over trusts until fully executed; Re Philadelphia, 2 Brewst. (Pa.) 462, holding that where all testator's directions cannot be complied with, court may apply *cy prés* doctrine to part so as to support the trust; Perin v. Carey, 24 How. 465, 16 L. ed. 701, holding that courts of chancery will sustain gifts and devises to public charitable uses, where not contrary to positive rule of law.

Cited in note in 14 L.R.A.(N.S.) 97, on enforcement of general bequest for educational and literary purposes.

How corporation created.

Cited in note in 7 E. R. C. 259, on necessity of express words to create corporation.

Subsequent recognition of corporate existence.

Cited in reference note in 41 A. D. 120, on subsequent recognition of corporate existence.

Dissolution of corporation.

Cited in People v. College of California, 38 Cal. 166, holding that private corporation may dissolve itself by surrender of its franchise; Merchants & Planters Line v. Wagner, 71 Ala. 581, holding that where by-law of private corporation, adopted at time of organization, provides for dissolution on certain day, the corporation ends on day designated; Goebel v. Herancourt Brewing Co. 7 Ohio N. P. 230, holding that receiver cannot be appointed for corporation except where it has been dissolved or wound up, or as preliminary to such winding up.

Cited in reference notes in 41 A. D. 694, on what will work forfeiture of corporate franchise and mode of enforcing same; 96 A. D. 754, as to how corporations may be dissolved at common law and under present law; 41 A. D. 120, on dissolving of corporation by suffering act destructive of object of incorporation.

Cited in note in 8 A. S. R. 179, on forfeiture of corporate franchises.

34 AM. DEC. 442, HANNAH v. SWARNER, 8 WATTS, 9.

Delivery of deed.

Cited in reference notes in 51 A. D. 674, on what constitutes delivery of deed; 40 A. R. 218, on sufficiency of delivery of deed; 44 A. D. 707, on necessity and sufficiency of delivery of deed; 52 A. D. 744, on nondelivery of deed to one of two grantees.

— To third person.

Cited in Webb v. Webb, 130 Iowa, 457, 104 N. W. 438, holding that delivery of deed to one grantee with knowledge and consent of the others is valid delivery to all; Jones v. Swayze, 42 N. J. L. 279, holding that delivery of deed to third party for use of grantee, where grantor parts with all control over it, is good delivery to grantee.

Cited in notes in 54 L.R.A. 871, on requisites on part of grantor on delivery of deed to third person; 54 L.R.A. 869, on delivery of deed to third person not previously authorized or designated by grantee.

Delivery of deed as jury question.

Cited in Hibberd v. Smith, 67 Cal. 547, 56 A. R. 726, 8 Pac. 46; Jones v. Swayze, 42 N. J. L. 279; Hastings v. Vaughn, 5 Cal. 315,—holding that delivery of deed is a question of fact for the jury.

Cited in reference note in 51 A. D. 674, on delivery being question of fact for jury.

34 AM. DEC. 445, COM. USE OF HAHN v. McCOY, 8 WATTS, 153.

Liability on sheriffs' bond.

Cited in Com. use of Anthony v. Steigerwalt, 18 Lanc. L. Rev. 301; Smith v. Com. 59 Pa. 320,—holding that sureties are liable upon sheriff's bond for a breach of its conditions, without prior suit against sheriff.

— Necessity of damage to plaintiff.

Cited in Wright v. Darlington, 108 Pa. 372, 16 W. N. C. 173, 42 Phila. Leg. Int. 130; Com. ex rel. Irwin v. Contner, 21 Pa. 266,—holding that in civil suit on sheriffs bound plaintiff cannot recover unless he has been actually damaged; Com. v. Lelar, 5 Clark (Pa.) 167, 1 Phila. 333, 9 Phila. Leg. Int. 50; Taylor v. Johnson, 17 Ga. 521,—holding that civil liability of sheriff on his bond is limited to damages actually sustained by the plaintiff; Com. v. Osler, 34 Pa. Super. Ct. 138, holding sheriff liable to sureties on liquor dealers' bond for failure to make levy against principal upon execution against him, whereby the sureties were damaged.

Indorsement on writ as justification of officer.

Cited in Griffith v. Lyle, 7 Phila. 244, 26 Phila. Leg. Int. 228, holding that where amount named in writ and that indorsed on back thereof vary, the sheriff must obey the latter, and may rely on that as justification.

Distinguished in Schock v. Waidelich, 27 Pa. Super. Ct. 215, holding that indorsement calling sheriff's attention to waiver of exemptions is not valid justification if sheriff seizes property to which waiver does not apply.

Liability of sheriff for neglect to levy and sell.

Cited in Pardee v. Robertson, 6 Hill, 550, on no action on the case being maintainable against sheriff at common law for not having money at return day of writ.

Procedure in proceeding against sheriff for neglect.

Cited in Houston's Appeal, 11 Pittsb. L. J. N. S. 412; Borlin's Appeal, Phila. Leg. Int. 293,—holding that, in summary proceedings against sher for neglect, he should first be ruled to make his return.

Cited in notes in 25 A. D. 572, as to how officer may be compelled to make turn to execution; 3 L.R.A.(N.S.) 423, on burden of proof in action to recov for failure to execute final process.

Taxing judgment fee for attorney.

Cited in McCulla v. Opple, 1 Pearson (Pa.)150, holding that judgment f for attorney cannot be taxed on an award of arbitration that is appealed fro

34 AM. DEC. 449, MILLER v. GETTYSBURG BANK, 8 WATTS, 192.

Duty of pledgee of notes as collateral.

Cited in reference note in 50 A. D. 177, on duties and liabilities of pledgee negotiable paper.

Cited in notes in 32 A. S. R. 719, 720, on duties of holder of collateral curity; 49 A. D. 738, or rights and liabilities of parties to pledge of negotiab instrument; 64 A. D. 429, on pledges of mortgages and negotiable instrumen and sale thereof.

— To collect.

Cited in Hanna v. Holton, 78 Pa. 334, 21 A. R. 20, 1 Legal Chron. 335, Legal Gaz. 179, 3 Phila. Leg. Int. 233; Hawley Bros. Hardware Co. v. Bro stone, 123 Cal. 643, 46 Pac. 468,—holding that creditor holding notes as lateral security is liable for loss thereon caused by his negligence, also citi annotation on this point; Mt. Vernon Bridge Co. v. Knox County Sav. Ban 46 Ohio St. 224, 20 N. E. 339; Scott v. First Nat. Bank, 5 Ind. Terr. 292, L.R.A. 488, 82 S. W. 751,—holding that creditor holding note as collateral curity is required to exercise ordinary diligence only, also citing annotation this point; Semplé & B. Mfg. Co. v. Detwiler, 30 Kan. 386, 2 Pac. 511, holdi that where bank takes notes as collateral security with instructions to colle them, simple demand of payment is not sufficient diligence.

Cited in reference notes in 34 A. S. R. 744; 35 A. S. R. 317,—on diligence collecting collateral security; 100 A. D. 194, on right and duty of pledgee collect collateral security; 27 A. S. R. 539, on necessity to realize upon collater security; 90 A. D. 310, on obligation of pledgee of negotiable paper to diligen

Liability of collecting bank.

Cited in reference notes in 38 A. D. 141, on liability of bank taking note f collection; 13 A. S. R. 253, on liability of banks in making collections for the own negligence.

Collaterals in hands of third person.

Cited in Dean v. Church, 3 Lack. Leg. News, 234, holding creditor not a countable for collaterals placed by debtor in hands of third person and ov which he has no control.

34 AM. DEC. 453, HAY v. MAYER, 8 WATTS, 203.

Deed as conveyance of personal interest or as appointment under powe

Cited in Phillips v. Brown, 16 R. I. 279, 15 Atl. 90; Owen v. Switzer, 51 M 322,—holding that where grantor has an interest in land and also a power sell, a deed without reference to the power conveys only the personal interest the grantor; Heiss v. McCauley, 20 Lanc. L. Rev. 409, holding conveyance by one having power to sell and an interest in land, not deemed an execution of the power unless such intention be shown; Scott v. Bryan, 29 Pittsb. L. J. N. S. 340, holding that conveyance by life tenant with power to sell conveys only her interest in absence of some reference to power; McCreary v. Homberger, 151 Pa. 323, 31 A. S. R. 760, 24 Atl. 1066, 31 W. N. C. 41; McCauley v. Heise, 20 Lanc. L. Rev. 313,—holding that deed executed by person given power of sale under will will be presumed an execution of the power; Robeno v. Marlatt, 46 Phila. Leg. Int. 36, 6 Pa. Co. Ct. 251, holding that where will grants power to sell, a conveyance showing intent to convey under the power, though not so expressly stated in the deed, will be referred to the power; Jones v. Wood, 16 Pa. 25, holding that where grantee of power has no personal interest in the lands, a conveyance thereof will be deemed an execution of the power, though not so expressed in the deed.

Subordination of power to curtesy or dower.

Distinguished in Gast v. Porter, 13 Pa. 533, holding conveyance under power to sell land at the death of widow, valid though widow was living, where she joins in the deed.

Powers of sale.

Cited in Alabama Conference v. Price, 42 Ala. 39, holding that power of sale conferred by a will, will not support a sale made under order of the court without reference to the power; Southern Cotton Oil Co. v. Henshaw, 89 Ala. 448, 7 So. 760, holding that power to sell lands is not included in power to settle up and divide an estate.

Cited in reference notes in 55 A. D. 506, on power to be executed on contingency; 39 A. D. 601, on construction of power of attorney.

Cited in note in 27 L.R.A. 351, on right of heirs of deceased partner in partnership real estate as against surviving partner.

— Conveyance of lands subject to.

Cited in Costen's Appeal, 13 Pa. 292, holding that where land is devised with absolute direction to sell for purpose of distribution, a conveyance by a devisee of his part of the land passes only the right to his share of the proceeds; Dutton's Appeal, 181 Pa. 426, 37 Atl. 582, holding that mortgage of interest in a recognizance in partition is an equitable assignment thereof; Campbell's Estate, 13 Pa. Co. Ct. 35, 2 Pa. Dist. R. 665, holding that a mortgage of a legacy payable out of proceeds of real estate is a valid, equitable assignment thereof; Horner's Appeal, 56 Pa. 405; Wells v. Sloyer, 1 Clark (Pa.) 516,—holding that a direction in will to sell lands vests the legal estate in the executor, and a purchaser of such lands from a legatee takes only his right to share in the proceeds.

Authority of agent.

Cited in reference note in 54 A. D. 299, on agent's implied authority to bind principal by note.

Executory devises.

Cited in reference note in 42 A. D. 122, on executory devises.

34 AM. DEC. 460, SHERBAN v. COM. 8 WATTS, 212.

Certainty required in indictments.

Cited in Com. v. Keenan, 67 Pa. 203; Com. v. Howells, 18 Pa. Super. Ct. 323;

Com. v. White, 24 Pa. Super. Ct. 178; Com. v. Swallow, 8 Pa. Super. Ct. 539,—holding indictment good where it states the charge sufficiently to inform defendant what he is called upon to answer, and so that court may know how to render proper judgment; Com. v. Farrell, 12 Luzerne Leg. Reg. 348, 10 North. Co. Rep. 57, 31 Pa. Co. Ct. 118, holding indictment for larceny for stealing three ducks sufficient without any further description of the ducks; Com. v. Christy, 26 Pa. Co. Ct. 121, 11 Pa. Dist. R. 221, holding indictment for fornication and bastardy good, though it failed to state the sex of the bastard; Com. v. Wickert, 6 Pa. Dist. R. 387, holding that indictment under statute containing a proviso need not negative the proviso; Sikes v. State, 67 Ala. 77, holding indictment defective where averments of necessary attending facts relate to time of finding of the indictment, and not to time the alleged offense was committed.

Cited in reference notes in 54 A. D. 378, on sufficiency of indictment; 58 A. D. 696, on description of offenses in indictment; 36 A. D. 264, on degree of certainty required in indictments; 37 A. D. 84, on form of indictment charging statutory offense; 65 A. S. R. 251, on negativing exceptions in information.

— Indictment for betting on election.

Distinguished in Com. v. Leak, 116 Ky. 540, 76 .S. W. 368, holding that warrant for betting on an election is fatally defective, where it charges the offense being committed after the election without specifically alleging that the result was not known.

Certainty as to common intent in pleading generally.

Cited in Com. v. Commercial Bank, 28 Pa. 391, holding certainty as to a common intent sufficient in information in quo warranto proceedings; Election Cases (Re Contested Elections), 65 Pa. 20, 2 Brewst. (Pa.) 1, 2 Legal Gaz. 57, holding certainty as to a common intent sufficient in petition contesting an election.

34 AM. DEC. 461, CRONISTER v. WEISE, 8 WATTS, 215.

Effect of sale under mortgage.

Cited in Clarke v. Stanley, 10 Pa. 472, holding that sale under mortgage devests the mortgage and all subsequent liens; Moyer v. Garrett, 96 Pa. 376, on sale under judgment for instalment due on mortgage debt discharging the mortgage; Taylor v. Young, 71 Pa. 81, 4 Legal Gaz. 218, 29 Phila. Leg. Int. 220; Mendenhall v. West Chester & P. R. Co. 36 Pa. 145 note,—on sale under judgment on one of bonds secured by mortgage discharging the mortgage.

Cited in reference note in 42 A. D. 323, on extent to which judicial sale devests lien.

Estoppel in pais.

Cited in reference note in 49 A. D. 238, on estoppel *in pais.*

34 AM. DEC. 465, FORSYTHE v. PRICE, 8 WATTS, 282.

Rights in growing crops.

Cited in Reilly v. Ringland, 39 Iowa, 106, holding that one lawfully in possession of land as tenant at will is entitled to enter, after termination of tenancy, and harvest his outgoing crops; Myers v. Elmer, 24 Lanc. L. Rev. 347, holding tenant receiving crop growing on land when he took possession not entitled to way-going crop; Backentoss v. Stahler, 33 Pa. 251, 75 A. D. 592, holding that where administrator had right to cut and remove a growing crop, he could

maintain trover for its recovery if wrongfully removed; Loose v. Scharff, 6
Super. Ct. 153, on liability to seizure for debt of landlord's interest in growi
crop.

Cited in reference notes in 6 A. D. 417; 70 A. D. 159,— on tenant's right
way-going crop.

Cited in notes in 64 A. D. 369, on right of tenant for life to emblements;
A. D. 515, on right of tenant to emblements, etc., after expiration of his term.

—Effect of custom.

Cited in notes in 50 A. D. 102, on customs of landlord and tenant and th
validity; 15 E. R. C. 556, on effect of custom between landlord and tenant as
crops after expiration of term.

Liability for trespass by animals.

Cited in reference notes in 72 A. D. 335; 49 A. S. R. 745,—on liability
owner of animals for their trespasses.

Cited in note in 49 A. D. 249, on common-law rule as to liability for tr
passes of animals.

34 AM. DEC. 469, GILCHRIST v. BALE, 8 WATTS, 355.

Right of action for alienation of wife's affections.

Cited in reference notes in 51 A. D. 408, on action for enticing away wif
82 A. D. 434, on husband's right of action for enticing away his wife.

Cited in notes in 44 A. S. R. 845, on action for alienation of wife's affection
48 A. D. 620, on action for injury to wife not resulting in death.

**Evidence of ill treatment of wife in suits for seduction and alienation
affections.**

Cited in Palmer v. Crook, 7 Gray, 418; Coleman v. White, 43 Ind. 429,—ho
ing that evidence of wife's ill treatment by her husband prior to the alleg
seduction is admissible in mitigation of damages in action by the husband
her seduction; Kilburn v. Mullen, 22 Iowa, 498, on same point; Perry v. Lo
joy, 49 Mich. 529, 14 N. W. 485, holding same in an action for enticing aw
plaintiff's wife.

Cited in note in 44 A. S. R. 849, on evidence in action for alienation of wif
affections.

—Ill feeling between wife and husband.

Cited in Horner v. Yance, 93 Wis. 352, 67 N. W. 720; Rudd v. Rounds,
Vt. 432, 25 Atl. 438,—holding that evidence of wife's feelings toward her h
band, and declarations thereof made at time of, and prior to, leaving him
admissible in suit for alienation of her affections.

Declarations as res gestæ.

Cited in State v. Howard, 32 Vt. 380; Asbury L. Ins. Co. v. Warren, 66 ?
523, 22 A. R. 590,—holding declarations as to nature, symptoms, and effects
sickness under which a person is suffering, admissible where bodily health
at issue; Swift v. Massachusetts Mut. L. Ins. Co. 63 N. Y. 186, 20 A. R. 5
holding applicant's declarations to other parties as to state of his health, ma
about the time of his examination for insurance, admissible on question of tru
of statements made at examination; Stein v. Railway Co. 10 Phila. 440,
Phila. Leg. Int. 256, 1 W. N. C. 531, 7 Legal Gaz. 223, holding declarations
son immediately after accident, admissible in suit by father for injury to
son; Cook v. State, 22 Tex. App. 511, 3 S. W. 749, holding declarations of w
at time of commission of a murder by the husband admissible as *res gestæ.*

Cited in notes in 39 L. ed. U. S. 977, as to when declarations of party are competent evidence in his own favor; 95 A. D. 60, on necessity that acts and declarations be contemporaneous with principal transaction to be admissible as part of *res gestæ;* 95 A. D. 68, on admissibility of declarations to show motive and purpose of act, as part of *res gestæ;* 95 A. D. 66, on admissibility of exclamations of pain and declarations respecting injuries.

— Of wife or husband as evincing feelings toward each other.

Cited in Roesner v. Darrah, 65 Kan. 599, 70 Pac. 597, holding declarations of wife prior to the alleged seduction, admissible in action for seduction, when they tend to show the state of her feelings toward husband and toward the alleged seducer; Billings v. Allbright, 66 App. Div. 239, 73 N. Y. Supp. 22, holding that declarations of wife to husband are admissible in mitigation of damages in suit for criminal conversation, where they indicate the state of wife's feelings toward her husband; Pollock v. Pollock, 9 Misc. 82, 29 N. Y. Supp. 37, holding declarations of husband or wife prior to abandonment, admissible only to show the existing relation between them.

Cited in reference note in 80 A. D. 332, on competency of wife's declarations against husband.

Distinguished in Higham v. Vanosdol, 101 Ind. 160, holding that, in action for enticing wife away, her declarations made to a third party on day of leaving are not admissible, where they do not impute to the husband violence or ill treatment.

Evidence admissible under general issue.

Cited in Scott v. Kittanning Coal Co. 89 Pa. 231, 33 A. R. 753, 7 W. N. C. 289, 36 Phila. Leg. Int. 236, holding that, under plea of nonassumpsit, defendant may give in evidence anything which shows that plaintiff had no right to recover.

Cited in reference notes in 43 A. D. 62, on admissibility under general issue of evidence of former recovery; 46 A. D. 154, on former recovery admissible in evidence under general issue; 41 A. D. 682, on admissibility and effect of former judgment as plea in bar or as evidence under general issue in subsequent action.

Former recovery as a bar.

Cited in Lacey v. Pennsylvania & N. Y. Canal & R. Co. 10 Luzerne Leg. Reg. 97, holding plea of former recovery sustainable in cases of either actual or presumptive former recovery.

Cited in reference notes in 38 A. D. 697, on conclusiveness of judgment; 44 A. D. 763, on conclusiveness of former recovery in tort; 49 A. D. 120; 52 A. D. 540,—on former recovery as bar to another action; 79 A. D. 707, on former recovery as bar to action for same injury.

Cited in note in 44 A. S. R. 852, on bar to action for alienation of wife's affections.

Discharge in bankruptcy as bar.

Cited in Kames v. Fox, 14 Phila. 208, 37 Phila. Leg. Int. 282, holding that discharge in bankruptcy bars suit for funds embezzled as to which judgment in assumpsit had been recovered and proved in the bankruptcy proceedings.

Pleadings in action for alienating affections.

Cited in note in 44 A. S. R. 847, on pleadings in action for alienation of wife's affections.

34 AM. DEC. 474, PATTERSON v. MARTZ, 8 WATTS, 374.

Specific performance of contract.

Cited in reference notes in 37 A. D. 633, on specific performance of contracts; 95 A. D. 445, as to when specific performance will not be decreed.

Defense to specific performance.

Cited in Finley v. Aiken, 1 Grant, Cas. 83 (dissenting opinion), on fraud as defeating right to specific performance; Rhine v. Robinson, 27 Pa. 30, on claim in violation of mere verbal contract or moral obligation not being enforceable in equity.

Cited in reference notes in 58 A. D. 144, on specific performance not maintainable when facts show abandonment of contract; 66 A. D. 405, on refusal of specific performance in case of fraud or mistake or inequitable conditions.

— Laches as defense.

Cited in Russell v. Baughman, 94 Pa. 400, 9 W. N. C. 284; Lowther Oil Co. v. Miller-Sibley Oil Co. 53 W. Va. 501, 97 A. S. R. 1027, 44 S. E. 433; Shisler's Estate, 13 Pa. Co. Ct. 513, 2 Pa. Dist. R. 588,—holding that specific performance will not be decreed where vendee unreasonably delays his demands until circumstances have materially changed.

Cited in reference notes in 48 A. D. 172, on lapse of time as bar to specific performance; 33 A. S. R. 261, on effect of laches in suit for specific performance; 39 A. D. 246, on delay and default of one party to contract as bar to specific performance; 63 A. D. 486, on effect of failure to perform on part of party seeking specific performance; 59 A. D. 684, on unexplained delay and great increase of value of land as bar to specific performance; 65 A. D. 308, on refusal of specific performance for laches where material change in value of property has taken place; 63 A. D. 486, as to when laches may be imputed to party seeking specific performance; 43 A. D. 58, as to when time is of essence of contract in equity and when not.

Abandonment of contract.

Cited in McGrew v. Foster, 113 Pa. 642, 6 Atl. 346, 18 W. N. C. 487, 44 Phila Leg. Int. 82, 17 Pittsb. L. J. N. S. 493, holding that vendee, under unrecorded contract, who has paid part of purchase money and then for nearly thirty years has made no payment and asserted no right of possession, cannot maintain trespass against one holding title by recorded deed.

34 AM. DEC. 477, EVANS v. COM. 8 WATTS, 398.

Judgment against principal as evidence against his sureties.

Cited in McMicken v. Com. 58 Pa. 213, 25 Phila. Leg. Int. 340; State use of Hannibal & St. J. R. Co. v. Shacklett, 37 Mo. 280,—holding that judgment against sheriff for official misconduct is conclusive evidence in suit against him and his sureties; Tracy v. Goodwin, 5 Allen, 409, holding same of judgment against constable for official misconduct; State use of Story v. Jennings, 14 Ohio St. 73, holding that such judgment is prima facie evidence only where sureties had no notice of the suit against the constable; Lloyd v. Barr, 11 Pa. 41, on same point; Com. v. Smith, 4 Phila. 51, 17 Phila. Leg. Int. 125, holding judgment against trustee conclusive against sureties on his bond; Hicks v. McBride, 3 Phila. 377, 16 Phila. Leg. Int. 147, holding that judgment against defendant is conclusive on sureties on property bond in replevin; Stephens v. Shafer, 48 Wis. 54, 33 A. R. 793, 3 N. W. 835; Ihrig v. Scott, 13 Wash. 559, 43 Pac. 633,—

holding that judgment against principal on statutory bond is prima facie e
dence against his sureties; Braiden v. Mercer, 44 Ohio St. 339, 7 N. E. 1
holding that final settlement of guardian's account in probate court is conclus
evidence in suit against his sureties; Garber v. Com. 7 Pa. 265; Com. ex 1
Whiteside v. Wood, 22 Lanc. L. Rev. 245, 14 Pa. Dist. R. 509,—holding same
to administrator's account; Spencer v. Dearth, 43 Vt. 98, on judgment agai
principal being conclusive on sureties.

Cited in reference notes in 43 A. D. 440, on judgment against constable as ϵ
dence against sureties; 73 A. D. 651, on conclusiveness of judgment in s
against constable on liability of sureties.

Cited in notes in 17 A. D. 676, on conclusiveness on sureties of judgmϵ
against principal; 83 A. D. 383, on conclusiveness of judgment against sheri
and constables on their sureties; 52 L.R.A. 172, 174, as to when judgment
covered in action against officer is prima facie evidence against surety on offic
bond; 52 L.R.A. 176, 179, as to when judgment recovered in action agai
officer is conclusive evidence against surety on official bond.

Distinguished in Snapp v. Com. 2 Pa. St. 49, holding that, to hold suret
liable, the officer must be sued in his official capacity.

34 AM. DEC. 480, NERHOOTH v. ALTHOUSE, 8 WATTS, 427.

Right to set up adverse title to land held under contract.

Cited in Hersey v. Turbett, 27 Pa. 418, on general rule that one who obtai
possession under contract to purchase, cannot set up an adverse title, but m
pay the price or restore possession; Erwin v. Myers, 20 Phila. Leg. Int. 3
holding that vendee of land must either pay purchase money or restore p
session.

Cited in note in 89 A. S. R. 66, on necessity of tenant admitting title to be
landlord.

34 AM. DEC. 483, BIRD v. SMITH, 8 WATTS, 434.

Prescriptive right to easement.

Cited in note in 10 E. R. C. 94, on acquisition of easement by prescription.

— Franchise for ferry.

Cited in Johnson's Appeal, 6 W. N. C. 33, on nonpresumption of ferry gra
from mere length of time.

Cited in note in 59 L.R.A. 516, on prescriptive ferry privileges.

— Right to use ferry landing.

Cited in reference notes in 40 A. D. 751, on prescriptive right to use fe
landing; 44 A. D. 92, on presumption of exclusive right to land ferry at cert
point from long exercise of right.

Right to landings on river generally.

Cited in Buford v. Smith, 2 Tex. Civ. App. 178, 21 S. W. 168; Prosser
Wapello County, 18 Iowa, 327,—holding that a ferry license does not give hol
thereof the right to use the termini of a public highway for a ferry landing wi
out the consent of the owner of the fee; Stoops's Estate, 14 Pittsb. L. J. N.
34, holding use of ferry, subject to control of owner of fee of landing; Braddϵ
Ferry Co.'s Appeal, 3 Pennyp. 32, on right of riparian owner to control embar
tion and landing.

Cited in reference notes in 47 A. D. 550; 72 A. D. 368,—on right of owners
shores of navigable rivers to control embarkation and landing.

Cited in notes in 81 A. D. 588, on navigator's right to land or deposit goods on private property; 59 L.R.A. 537, on acquisition by ferries of right to use landings.

Exclusiveness of easement.

Cited in Campbell v. Kuhlmann, 39 Mo. App. 628, holding that under grant of easement of way, not exclusive in its terms, grantor has right of user in common with grantee; Thompson v. Germania L. Ins. Co. 97 Minn. 89, 106 N. W. 102, holding that the character of an easement as to exclusiveness depends upon the use shown and upon the agreement creating it.

Title of riparian owner on navigable waters.

Cited in Philadelphia & R. R. Co. v. Morris, 7 Phila. 286, 26 Phila. Leg. Int. 252, holding that riparian owner on navigable water owns to low-water mark and the commonwealth owns beyond; Clement v. Burns, 43 N. H. 609, holding that owner of land upon navigable water may maintain trespass for entry and removal of soil from shore between high and low water mark; Gould v. Hudson River R. Co. 6 N. Y. 522 (dissenting opinion), on right of riparian owner on navigable stream to shore between high and low water mark; People ex rel. Loomis v. Canal Appraisers, 33 N. Y. 461, on test of actual navigability.

Cited in reference note in 36 A. D. 145, on riparian owner's rights to shore on navigable stream.

Cited in note in 10 A. D. 385, on navigable river as boundary.

What are navigable waters.

Cited in reference note in 59 A. D. 220, on what are navigable waters.

Cited in note, in 41 L. ed. U. S. 998, on navigable waters and right therein.

Declarations of one in possession of lands as evidence.

Cited in Cunningham v. Fuller, 35 Neb. 58, 52 N. W. 836, holding that declarations of one in possession of land, as to his title, are admissible in evidence against him and his assigns.

Cited in reference notes in 67 A. D. 270, on admissibility of declarations of former owner against those claiming under him; 61 A. D. 318, as to when declarations of grantor as to fraudulent conveyance are admissible.

Cited in notes in 42 A. D. 632, as to when declarations of vendor are evidence against vendee to show fraud; 40 A. D. 241; 45 A. D. 381,—on admissibility of admissions of grantor of land while he owned it against one claiming under him.

Estoppel by silence.

Cited in note in 19 A. D. 626, on estoppel by silence.

---

34 AM. DEC. 489, HOOD v. FAHNESTOCK, 8 WATTS, 489.

Notice to agent as constructive notice to principal.

Cited in Lightcap v. Nicola, 34 Pa. Super. Ct. 189; Houseman v. Girard Mut. Bldg. & L. Asso. 81 Pa. 256, 2 W. N. C. 573, 33 Phila. Leg. Int. 108; Gilkeson v. Thompson, 210 Pa. 355, 59 Atl. 1114; Chester v. Schaffer, 9 Del. Co. Rep. 66, 24 Pa. Super. Ct. 162; Mutual Bldg. & L. Asso. v. Ambrose, 7 Pa. Dist. R. 526, 19 Pa. Co. Ct. 504; Bracken v. Miller, 4 Watts & S. 102; Sullivan v. Brown, 8 Wash. 347, 36 Pac. 273; Dunning v. Reese, 7 Kulp, 201,—holding that, to charge principal with constructive notice, the knowledge of the agent must have been obtained in the course of the same transaction in which he is employed by the principal; Meehan v. Williams, 48 Pa. 238, 22 Phila. Leg. Int. 164; Langenheim v. Anshutz-Bradberry Co. 38 W. N. C. 505, 2 Pa. Super. Ct. 285,—on same point.

Cited in notes in 32 L.R.A. 62, on knowledge of or notice to agent as sufficient to put purchaser on inquiry as to vendor's fraudulent intent; 39 A. R. 325, on effect of knowledge by agent of unrecorded deed as notice to corporation.

— Knowledge acquired outside of agency or in other agency.

Cited in Martin v. Jackson, 27 Pa. 504, 67 A. D. 489; Melms v. Pabst Brewing Co. 93 Wis. 153, 57 A. S. R. 899, 66 N. W. 518; McCormick v. Wheeler, 36 Ill. 114, 85 A. D. 388,—holding that knowledge obtained as attorney for one party is not notice to him as attorney for another party; Snyder v. Partridge, 138 Ill. 173, 32 A. S. R. 130, 29 N. E. 851, holding that knowledge obtained by agent before commencement of his agency is not constructive notice to his principal; Dight v. Chapman, 44 Or. 265, 65 L.R.A. 793, 75 Pac. 585, holding that knowledge of agent is notice to his principal, unless knowledge is obtained in confidential relation to a third party; Re Bryan, 4 Phila. 228, 17 Phila. Leg. Int. 157, holding creditors and heirs of decedent not charged with notice given to a person prior to his becoming trustee of the estate; Red River Valley Land & Invest. Co. v. Smith, 7 N. D. 236, 74 N. W. 194, holding that, to charge corporation with notice from knowledge of an officer, it must be shown that he obtained the knowledge in his official capacity, or that such knowledge was in his mind at the time.

Cited in reference note in 67 A. D. 495, on knowledge acquired by attorney before relation began as notice to client.

Cited in notes in 24 A. S. R. 232, on notice to agent previous to employment as notice to principal; 57 A. S. R. 916, on information acquired by attorney in other transactions as notice to client,

Validity of title obtained from party to fraudulent transfer.

Cited in Very v. Russell, 65 N. H. 646, 23 Atl. 522; Boyer v. Weimer, 204 Pa. 295, 54 Atl. 21; Colquitt v. Thomas, 8 Ga. 258,—holding that bona fide purchaser from fraudulent grantee obtains good title; Heath v. Page, 63 Pa. 108, 3 A. R. 533, 27 Phila. Leg. Int. 252, on same point; Gilliland v. Fenn, 90 Ala. 230, 9 L.R.A. 413, 8 So. 15, holding title of subsequent purchaser from grantor good as against title of heirs of grantee in a fraudulent conveyance; Massey v. Noon, 37 W. N. C. 523, holding that bona fide purchaser without notice obtains title free from any equities against grantor; Hood v. Fahnestock, 1 Pa. St. 470, 44 A. D. 147, holding that retaining possession by grantor is notice to purchaser from grantee under fraudulent conveyance; Apple v. Fetter, 18 Lanc. L. Rev. 337, on validity of title of bona fide purchaser from fraudulent grantor or grantee.

Cited in reference notes in 37 A. D. 145, 381; 49 A. D. 131; 50 A. D. 469,—on protection of bona fide purchaser from fraudulent grantor or grantee; 72 A. D. 568, on protection of title of bona fide purchaser for valuable consideration without notice.

Cited in notes in 32 L.R.A. 69, on purchase from fraudulent grantees; 39 A. D. 716; 67 L.R.A. 898,—on title of bona fide purchaser from fraudulent grantee; 10 E. R. C. 544, on protection of bona fide purchaser against equities.

34 AM. DEC. 492, ABBOTT v. COM. 8 WATTS, 517.

Repeal of statute by implication.

Cited in reference notes in 74 A. D. 317, on repeal of statute by implication; 42 A. D. 680, as to when enactment of subsequent statute operates as repeal of former one.

Effect of repeal of statute on proceedings begun under it.

Cited in Re Extension of North Street, 1 Pearson (Pa.) 199, holding that proceedings for laying out a street begun under a law which is repealed are thereby terminated.

Cited in reference notes in 36 A. D. 186; 81 A. D. 193,—on effect on pending actions of repeal of statute.

Distinguished in The Hickory Tree Road, 43 Pa. 139, holding that where proceedings for laying out a road have been begun, and the road laws are changed so as to change the remedies, but not take away the jurisdiction, the proceedings may continue under the new law.

— Repeal of criminal statute.

Cited in Butler v. Palmer, 1 Hill, 324; Com. v. Shubel, 4 Pa. Co. Ct. 12; United States v. Hague, 22 Fed. 706,—holding that repeal of statute, with no saving clause in the repealing act, terminates a prosecution begun under it; Com. v. Shopp, 1 Woodw. Dec. 123; State v. Showers, 34 Kan. 269, 8 Pac. 474,—on same point.

Cited in reference note in 71 A. D. 599, on effect on pending appeal of repeal of statute under which conviction was had in inferior court.

Cited in note in 94 A. D. 218, on effect of repeal of criminal statute.

Interpretation of statute by common law.

Cited in Com. v. Bank of Commerce, 2 Pittsb. 248, 8 Pittsb. L. J. 382, holding that statutes are to be interpreted and administered as near as may be according to principles of common law.

34 AM. DEC. 494, ALTEMAS v. CAMPBELL, 9 WATTS, 28.

Entry as terminating adverse possession.

Cited in Hinman v. Cranmer, 9 Pa. 40, holding that an entry by the actual owner suspends the running of the statute of limitations; Douglass v. Lucas, 63 Pa. 9, on same point; Elliott v. Powell, 10 Watts, 453, 56 A. D. 200, holding that an entry by the owner puts him for the time in actual possession; Hood v. Hood, 25 Pa. 417; Ingersoll v. Lewis, 11 Pa. 212, 51 A. D. 536,—holding that entry by agent of owner, with avowed object of asserting ownership, terminates an adverse possession; Hale v. Rittenhouse, 19 Pa. 305; Smith v. Steele, 17 Pa. 30,—holding that entry by stranger, though under color of title, does not affect an adverse possession; Pella v. Scholte, 24 Iowa, 283, 95 A. D. 729, on entry as equivalent to an action to interrupt the running of the statute of limitations.

Cited in reference notes in 62 A. D. 334, on entry by owner as tolling statute of limitations; 61 A. D. 304, on avoidance of operation of statute of limitations by entry on lands.

Cited in note in 51 A. D. 539, on effect of entry by true owner to avoid statute of limitations running in favor of disseisor.

— Sufficiency of entry.

Cited in Stettnische v. Lamb, 18 Neb. 619, 26 N. W. 314, holding actual entry and ouster necessary for beginning of adverse possession; Batchelder v. Robbins, 93 Me. 579, 45 Atl. 837, holding that entry by record owner, such as to give adverse holder notice of intention to assert his title, is sufficient to revest possession; Byers v. Danley, 27 Ark. 77, holding that an entry to devest possession must show unequivocal intent to claim the land; New Shoreham v. Ball, 14 R. I. 566; Murphy v. Com. 187 Mass. 361, 73 N. E. 524,—holding that entry to interrupt adverse possession must show affirmatively intention to resume possession; McCombs v. Rowan, 59 Pa. 414, holding that making a survey of land without asserting title is not a sufficient entry; Hoopes v. Garver, 15 Pa. 517, holding that sufficiency of acts to constitute an entry should be submitted to the jury; Bradley v. West, 60 Mo. 33, holding that entry to interrupt adverse possession must be made before expiration of statutory period.

Cited in note in 16 E. R. C. 341, on sufficiency of entry to stop running of prescription.

Declarations of one in possession as evidence.

Cited in St. Clair v. Shale, 9 Pa. 252, holding declarations of party in possession admissible to show that his possession was not adverse.

Presumptive abandonment of suit.

Cited in Hillside Coal & Iron Co. v. Pitt, 4 Lack. L. News, 335, holding that ejectment suit will not be presumed to have been abandoned until after twenty-one years.

34 AM. DEC. 497, McFARLAND v. NEWMAN, 9 WATTS, 55.

Implied warranty on sale of chattels.

Cited in Boyd v. Wilson, 83 Pa. 319, 24 A. R. 176, 3 W. N. C. 523, 34 Phila. Leg. Int. 106, holding that sale by sample is not an implied warranty of the goods unless it was understood that sample should be standard of quality; Cleveland Linseed Oil Co. v. A. F. Buchanan & Sons, 57 C. C. A. 498, 120 Fed. 906, on hopelessness of arriving at satisfactory conclusions from the decisions as to warranty in sale of chattels.

Cited in reference note in 39 A. D. 500, on implied warranty in sale of chattels.

Cited in notes in 6 A. D. 114, on implied warranties; 6 E. R. C. 502, as to what will constitute a warranty in sense of condition on failure of which party may repudiate contract *in toto*.

—Representations as warranty.

Cited in Matlock v. Meyers, 64 Mo. 531; McAllister v. Morgan, 29 Pa. Super. Ct. 476; Weimer v. Clement, 37 Pa. 147, 78 A. D. 411; Whitaker v. Eastwick, 75 Pa. 229, 2 Legal Chron. 166, 6 Legal Gaz. 221, 31 Phila. Leg. Int. 165; Shisler v. Baxter, 109 Pa. 443, 58 A R. 738, 42 Phila. Leg. Int. 405; Holmes v. Tyson, 147 Pa. 305, 15 L.R.A. 209, 23 Atl. 564; Mahaffey v. Ferguson, 156 Pa. 156, 27 Atl. 21, 32 W. N. C. 549; Weilson v. Wetherill, 1 Phila. 207, 8 Phila. Leg. Int. 112; Benhead v. Scott, 1 Phila. 84, 7 Phila. Leg. Int. 150; Herman v. Brinker, 17 Pa. Super. Ct. 177; Welles v. Oakley, 10 Luzerne Leg. Reg. 204; Lindsay v. Davis, 30 Mo. 406,—holding that simple affirmation as to chattels sold does not constitute a warranty unless so intended and understood; McNeal v. Banks, 6 Kulp, 371; Matthews v. Hartson, 3 Pittsb. 86; Ives v. Ellis, 50 App. Div. 399, 64 N. Y. Supp. 147,—holding that no warranty is implied from statements made at sale of chattel. not amounting to express warranty or fraud; Phipps v. Buckman, 30 Pa. 401, holding that false statement of an opinion on a point where knowledge is equally accessible to both parties will not invalidate a contract.

Cited in reference notes in 59 A. D. 743, on representations as warranties; 64 A. D. 83, on representations as to quality of goods as warranty.

Fraudulent representations as defense.

Cited in Price v. Lewis, 17 Pa. 51, 55 A. D. 536, holding that claim of fraudulent representation is admissible as an equitable defense in suit upon contract of sale; Dushane v. Benedict, 120 U. S. 630, 30 L. ed. 810, 7 Sup. Ct. Rep. 696, holding that claim for fraudulent representation cannot be set off in suit upon contract under Pennsylvania statute; Sceak v. Wright, 5 Kulp, 246, holding that rule as to fraudulent representations in sales does not apply where purchaser can inspect the article and the defect is obvious; Smith v. Smith, 21 Pa. 367, 60 A. D. 51, holding that vendee's insolvency and his intent not to pay, uncommunicated to vendor at time of sale, is not such fraud as will avoid the sale.

Distinguished in Cassel v. Herron, 5 Clark (Pa.) 250, holding that concealment of latent disease not observable by vendee of horse avoids a contract for its sale.

Construction of oral declarations and contracts as jury function.

Cited in Speers v. Knarr, 4 Pa. Super. Ct. 80, 40 W. N. C. 85; Kaufman v. Abeles, 11 Pa. Super. Ct. 616; Pessano v. Eyre, 13 Pa. Super. Ct. 157; Lavelle v. Melley, 27 Pa. Super. Ct. 69; Henderson v. Sonneborn, 30 Pa. Super. Ct. 182; Brubaker v. Okeson, 36 Pa. 519, 7 Luzerne Leg. Reg. 184; Maynes v. Atwater, 88 Pa. 496, 6 W. N. C. 535, 36 Phila. Leg. Int. 321; Holmes v. Chartiers Oil Co. 138 Pa. 546, 21 A. S. R. 919, 21 Atl. 231, 27 W. N. C. 150, 21 Pittsb. L. J. N. S. 387; Hawn v. Stoler, 22 Pa. Super. Ct. 307,—holding that meaning of oral declarations is for the jury to determine; Philadelphia v. Stewart, 201 Pa. 526, 51 Atl. 348, holding that where, parol agreement forms part of a contract, the whole contract is for the jury.

Cited in note in 21 A. D. 394, on construction of words of witness as question for jury.

Distinguished in Camden Wood Turning Co. v. Malcolm, 190 Pa. 62, 42 Atl. 458, holding that where there was no contradictory evidence as to a contract, the court properly directed a verdict.

34 AM. DEC. 503, ATWOOD v. RELIANCE TRANSP. CO. 9 WATTS, 87.

Liability of carrier.

Cited in reference notes in 39 A. D. 508, on common carrier's liability; 37 A. D. 438, on carrier's liability for loss of goods.

Right of carriers to limit their liability.

Cited in Earnest v. Southern Exp. Co. 1 Woods, 573, Fed. Cas. No. 4,248; Pennsylvania R. Co. v. Raiordon, 119 Pa. 577, 4 A. S. R. 670, 13 Atl. 324, 21 W. N. C. 283, 45 Phila. Leg. Int. 276; Allam v. Pennsylvania R. Co. 183 Pa. 174, 39 L.R.A. 535, 38 Atl. 709, 41 W. N. C. 205; Crary v. Lehigh Valley R. Co. 203 Pa. 525, 93 A. S. R. 778, 59 L.R.A. 815, 53 Atl. 363; Bingham v. Rogers, 6 Watts & S. 495, 40 A. D. 581; York Mfg. Co. v. Illinois C. R. Co. 3 Wall. 107, 18 L. ed. 170,—holding that common carrier may by special contract limit his common-law liability.

Cited in reference note in 39 A. D. 406, on power of common carrier to limit liability.

— By notice or special agreement.

Cited in Mercantile Mut. Ins. Co. v. Chase, 1 E. D. Smith, 115; Hartwell v. Northern Pacific Exp. Co. 5 Dak. 463, 3 L.R.A. 342, 41 N. W. 732,—holding that bill of lading not signed by consignor is not a special contract by which common carrier may limit his liability; Gould v. Hill, 2 Hill, 623, holding that common carriers cannot limit their liability by special acceptance of the goods or by express agreement; Fish v. Chapman, 2 Ga. 349, 46 A. D. 393, holding that common carrier cannot limit his liabililty by a notice or by special acceptance; Laing v. Colder, 8 Pa. 479, 49 A. D. 533, holding that common carrier may limit his liability by notice to passengers that baggage is at their own risk.

Cited in reference notes in 43 A. D. 202, on power of carrier to limit liability by notice; 40 A. D. 585; 16 A. S. R. 726,—on carrier's right to limit liability by special contract; 56 A. D. 84, on common carrier's power to limit liability by express agreement.

Cited in notes in 5 E. R. C. 343, 345, on right of carrier to limit his liability by notice; 5 A. S. R. 722, on limitation of the common-law liability of carrier of goods by general notice; 42 A. D. 498, on carrier's power to limit liability by notice or special contract; 6 L.R.A. 850, on power of carrier to limit his liability by express contract; 85 A. D. 226, on receipt for goods by carrier accepted by shipper as contract restricting carrier's liability by its conditions.

— Construction of such agreements.

Cited in Steele v. Townsend, 37 Ala. 247, 79 A. D. 49; Louisville & N. R. Co. v. Touart, 97 Ala. 514, 11 So. 756; Hooper v. Wells, F. & Co. 27 Cal. 11, 85 A. D. 211; Levering v. Union Transp. & Ins. Co. 42 Mo. 88, 97 A. D. 320; The Queen of the Pacific, 61 Fed. 213,—holding that exceptions to carriers' common-law liability should be strictly construed against the carrier; Leonard v. Hendrickson, 18 Pa. 40, 55 A. D. 587, on same point; New Jersey Steam Nav. Co. v. Merchants' Bank, 6 How. 344, 12 L. ed. 465, on contract limiting liability not exonerating from actual misbehavior.

What are "perils of the sea," etc.

Cited in reference note in 9 A. S. R. 187, on perils of the sea within policy of marine insurance.

Cited in note in 41 A. D. 282, on meaning of term "perils of the sea" and similar terms.

What risks covered by marine policy.

Cited in reference note in 86 A. D. 500, as to what losses are or are not within marine policy of insurance.

When usage will bind parties.

Cited in reference notes in 39 A. D. 614, as to how far and when usages become part of contract; 66 A. D. 427, on right to receive usage to control operation of law; 55 A. D. 171; 58 A. D. 638,—on usage contrary to common law being of no effect; 55 A. D. 329, on custom or usage in derogation of rules of law or contrary to terms of contract or intention of parties.

Cited in note in 11 A. S. R. 632, on proof of custom or usage to contravene rule of law or to alter or contradict terms of unambiguous contract.

Meaning of unavoidable accident.

Cited in Hays v. Kennedy, 41 Pa. 378, 80 A. D. 627, 20 Phila. Leg. Int. 116 (dissenting opinion in 3 Grant Cas. 351), on construction of phrase "unavoidable accidents."

34 AM. DEC. 507, BELL v. McCLINTOCK, 9 WATTS, 119.

Liability for injury by dam or other obstruction of stream.

Cited in reference note in 35 A. S. R. 413, on injury caused by diversion of stream.

Cited in notes in 85 A. S. R. 711, on right to diminish or impede flow of stream by dam; 57 A. D. 691, on care and skill required in constructing and maintaining dam; 59 L.R.A. 871, on drift and *débris* causing damming back of water of stream; 41 L.R.A. 749, on right as between upper and lower proprietors to throw back flow of stream.

— In case of freshet.

Cited in McCoy v. Danley, 20 Pa. 85, 57 A. D. 680; Casebeer v. Mowry, 55 Pa. 419, 93 A. D. 766; Humphrey v. Irvin, 18 W. N. C. 449, 6 Atl. 479, 3 Sadler (Pa.) 272, 43 Phila. Leg. Int. 236; Dorman v. Ames, 12 Minn. 451,— holding that owner of dam is liable for damage arising from usual and ordinary freshets; Thatcher v. Baker, 2 Del. Co. Rep. 297, holding owner of dam not bound to provide outlet for unusual floods; Central Trust Co. v. Wabash, St. L. & P. R. Co. 57 Fed. 441, holding owner of embankment on water course, not liable for damage caused by extraordinary floods; Illinois C. R. Co. v. Bethel, 11 Ill. App. 17, holding the same as to owner of bridges and culverts over stream; Proctor v. Jennings, 6 Nev. 83, 3 A. R. 240, holding proprietor of dam not liable for damages caused by circumstances arising from other causes, unforeseen at time of its erection, acting in connection with the dam; Hannaher v. St. Paul, M. & M. R. Co. 5 Dak. 1, 37 N. W. 717; Ritchie v. Pittsburg & L. E. R. Co. 14 Pittsb. L. J. N. S. 424,—holding railroad erecting embankment not liable for damage due to water being thrown back on adjacent lands in time of flood; State v. Ousatonic Water Co. 51 Conn. 137, holding company chartered to erect dam bound to protect road against damage from ordinary freshets, but not against extraordinary conditions; Borchardt v. Wausau Boom Co. 54 Wis. 107, 11 N. W. 472, holding boom company not liable for damages caused by extraordinary freshet; Thatcher v. Baker, 109 Pa. 22, 42 Phila. Leg. Int. 374, holding owner of dam not bound to provide against extraordinary floods; Knoll v. Light, 76 Pa. 268, 31 Phila. Leg. Int. 348, holding owner of dam not liable for flood caused by grass naturally growing in stream, where the dam was not the cause; Miller v. Shenandoah Pulp Co. 38 W. Va. 558, 18 S. E. 740, holding that owner of dam may swell the water in the stream only to the line of his adjoining owner above.

Cited in reference note in 47 A. D. 478, on liability of riparian owner for injury occasioned by dam in case of high water.

Meaning of ordinary flood.

Cited in Meister v. Lang, 28 Ill. App. 624, holding that ordinary rains are such as may be expected in certain seasons annually; Decorah Woolen Mills Co. v. Greer, 58 Iowa, 86, 12 N. W. 128, holding that ordinary stage of water is such as results from rises to be expected in ordinary seasons.

34 AM. DEC. 509, DAY v. SHARP, 4 WHART. 339.

Admitting evidence which may subsequently become competent.

Cited in reference note in 56 A. D. 190, on admission of evidence which may be made competent by subsequent testimony as error.

Voidability of executions.

Cited in McClelland v. Devilbiss, 1 Pa. Co. Ct. 613, on irregularity in iss of execution making it voidable.

Cited in reference notes in 37 A. D. 170; 39 A. D. 497,—as to when exec tions are voidable only; 50 A. D. 132, on voidability of execution issued aft plaintiff's death.

— Executions issued after death of plaintiff.

Cited in Banta v. School Dist. No. 3, 39 N. J. Eq. 123, holding that iss of execution ofter plaintiff's death without revivor is erroneous but not voi Webb v. Mallard, 27 Tex. 80, on same point; Moore v. Bell, 13 Ala. 469, hol ing that execution sued out on a judgment after death of plaintiff, in h name, is irregular and may be quashed on motion; Finch v. Burr, 79 Con 682, 10 L.R.A.(N.S.) 1049, 66 Atl. 504, holding administrator not liable trespass for causing issue of execution in good faith though judgment credit was dead; New Orleans, J. & G. M. R. Co. v. Rollins, 36 Miss. 384, holding th writ of error will lie against administrator to revise judgment secured by plai tiff, who has since died, without revivor in administrator's name.

Cited in note in 61 L.R.A. 393, on effect of death of one of the parties aft judgment upon remedy by execution.

Disapproved in Graham v. Chandler, 15 Ala. 342; Dunham v. Bentley, 1 Iowa, 136, 72 N. W. 437; Stewart v. Nuckols, 15 Ala. 225, 50 A. D. 127, holding that execution issued on a judgment after death of plaintiff, is void.

Revival of judgment.

Cited in reference note in 68 A. S. R. 382, on revival of judgment.

— On death of party before execution issues.

Cited in reference note in 68 A. D. 186, on necessity for revival of judgme after death of party and before issuance of execution.

Cited in notes in 61 L.R.A. 355, on necessity of revivor on death of so judgment creditor before issuance of execution; 61 L.R.A. 358, on reviv otherwise than by scire facias on death of sole judgment creditor before issuan of execution.

Process or judgment as justification for acts done.

Cited in Breckwoldt v. Morris, 149 Pa. 291, 24 Atl. 300, holding that pu chaser and constable under execution, regular on its face though based voidable judgment, may justify under it.

Cited in reference notes in 44 A. D. 77; 50 A. D. 143,—on voidable process justification for acts of officer thereunder; 43 A. D. 765, on process regular face as justification of acts of officer under it; 66 A. D. 462, on party whose instance magistrate has acted, as trespasser with respect to all ac done in the execution of process issued by such magistrate in excess of autho ity.

Cited in notes in 61 A. D. 409, as to when process is justification for ac done under it; 43 A. D. 52, on sufficiency of process to justify acts under i 64 A. D. 52, on liability of judicial officers.

Distinguished in Cassel v. Seibert, 1 Dauph. Co. Rep. 16, holding that voi judgment affords no protection to a judicial officer.

Necessity of quashal of voidable execution to fix liability.

Cited in Cogburn v. Spence, 15 Ala. 549, 50 A. D. 140, holding that aft voidable process has been set aside, the party who caused its issue is liable f injury resulting therefrom.

Right of surety paying debt without taking assignment of it.

Cited in Lloyd v. Barr, 11 Pa. 41, holding that surety paying judgment against principal is entitled to be subrogated without actual assignment of the judgment.

34 AM. DEC. 514, MEECH v. ROBINSON, 4 WHART. 360.

Sacrifice for general average.

Cited in Slater v. Hayward Rubber Co. 26 Conn. 128, on right of general average where a vessel in danger voluntarily sacrifices part of cargo for safety of the remainder.

Cited in notes in 14 A. D. 613, 614, on necessity of voluntary sacrifice to general average; 14 E. R. C. 383, on loss incurred by extraordinary circumstances as general average loss.

34 AM. DEC. 517, VAN AMRINGE v. MORTON, 4 WHART. 382.

Necessity and sufficiency of delivery of deed, etc.

Cited in Garrett v. Goff, 61 W. Va. 221, 56 S. E. 351, holding deed not delivered of no effect.

Cited in reference notes in 37 A. D. 566, on delivery of deed; 67 A. D. 270, on delivery giving effect to deed; 39 A. S. R. 73, on necessity for delivery of deed; 51 A. D. 674, on delivery of deed being essential to its validity; 44 A. D. 707, on necessity and sufficiency of delivery of deed; 44 A. D. 688, on necessity of delivery to validity of bond.

Cited in notes in 53 A. S. R. 537, on delivery of deed; 55 A. D. 413, on invalidity of deed for want of delivery; 53 A. S. R. 550, on illustrations of insufficient delivery of deed; 53 A. S. R. 539, on persons by and to whom deed may be delivered.

Estoppel to deny delivery.

Cited in Simms v. Hervey, 19 Iowa, 273, on estoppel to deny delivery of deed.

Cited in reference note in 35 A. D. 425, on ratification after filling blank left in bond for insertion of amount.

Cited in note in 9 L.R.A.(N.S.) 950, on validation of undelivered deed by ratification or estoppel of grantor.

Bona fide purchasers from holder of void deed.

Cited in Smith v. South Royalton Bank, 32 Vt. 341, 76 A. D. 179, holding that innocent purchaser from one who holds under void deed obtains no title; Pry v. Pry, 109 Ill. 466, holding that innocent purchasers from one who holds title under forged deed obtain no title; Reck v. Clapp, 98 Pa. 581, 1 Pennyp. 339, 12 Pittsb. L. J. N. S. 156, 39 Phila. Leg. Int. 219, on same point; Luther v. Clay, 100 Ga. 236, 39 L.R.A. 95, 28 S. E. 46, holding that purchaser of mortgaged premises, where a satisfaction of the mortgage has been forged and recorded, takes title subject to the mortgage, though he had no notice; Arrison v. Harmstead, 2 Pa. St. 191, holding that innocent purchaser from one who alters deed after delivery obtains no better title than his grantor; Pace v. Yost, 10 Kulp, 538, holding that deed in escrow, altered by custodian thereof by substituting another grantee, conveys no title to the substituted grantee.

Cited in note in 28 A. D. 688, on title acquired by bona fide purchaser from fraudulent purchaser.

Distinguished in Blight v. Schenck, 10 Pa. 285, 51 A. D. 478, holding that innocent purchaser from grantee in voidable deed obtains good title.

— Under deed not delivered.

Cited in Stone v. French, 37 Kan. 145, 1 A. S. R. 237, 14 Pac. 530; Kay v. Gray, 24 Pa. Super. Ct. 536; Steffian v. Milmo Nat. Bank, 69 Tex. 513, 6 S. W. 823; Henry v. Carson, 96 Ind. 412,—holding that innocent purchasers from grantee in deed not delivered obtain no title; Cameron v. Gray, 202 Pa. 566, 25 Atl. 132, on same point; Nolan v. King, 4 Pa. Dist. R. 156, holding that mortgaged not delivered by maker, but put in circulation without his consent, is void.

Cited in reference note in 1 A. S. R. 243, on title acquired by bona fide holder of undelivered and not fully executed deed stolen from grantor.

Possession as notice.

Cited in reference notes in 38 A. D. 131, on possession as notice of title; 68 A. D. 521, on stranger's possession as putting purchaser on inquiry.

Cited in note in 13 L.R.A.(N.S.) 83, on requisites and sufficiency of possession of land based on right as notice of title.

34 AM. DEC. 521, WATKINSON v. BANK OF PENNSYLVANIA, 4 WHART. 482.

Notice of dissolution of partnership.

Cited in Brown v. Clark, 14 Pa. 469; Clark v. Fletcher, 96 Pa. 416, 11 Pittsb. L. J. N. S. 329, 38 Phila. Leg. Int. 241; New York Nat. Exch. Bank v. Crowell, 177 Pa. 313, 35 Atl. 613, 39 W. N. C. 228; Mellor v. Negley, 1 Pittsb. 110,—holding notice of dissolution necessary in order to affect parties dealing on the strength thereof.

Cited in reference notes in 58 A. D. 414, on necessity for actual notice of dissolution of firm to person dealing with firm; 58 A. D. 174, on actual notice of dissolution of partnership required as to customers in order to exonerate retiring partner.

Cited in, notes in 40 A. S. R. 573, on notice to terminate liability after dissolution of firm; 23 L. ed. U. S. 852, on what notice of dissolution of firm is sufficient to avoid liability.

— Sufficiency of notice by advertisement.

Cited in Solomon v. Kirkwood, 55 Mich. 256, 21 N. W. 336, holding that sufficiency of notice of dissolution of partnership is for the jury; Kenney v. Altvater, 77 Pa. 34, 7 Legal Gaz. 30, 31 Phila. Leg. Int. 412; Ahlborn Bros. v. Slowitzsky, 6 Kulp, 321, 9 Lanc. L. Rev. 48; Devin v. Harris, 3 G. Greene, 186,—holding actual notice of change in partnership necessary to affect customers of the firm; Burnet v. Howell, 8 Phila. 531, 28 Phila. Leg. Int. 214, on same point; Robinson v. Floyd, 159 Pa. 165, 28 Atl. 258, 24 Pittsb. L. J. N. S. 427, 33 W. N. C. 413; Forepaugh v. Baker, 10 Sadler (Pa.) 97, 13 Atl. 465, 21 W. N. C. 299, 45 Phila. Leg. Int. 322,—holding that customers are entitled to actual notice of dissolution, and as to third parties notice by publication is sufficient; Farrar v. Babb, 4 Pa. Co. Ct. 407, on same point; Page v. Brant, 18 Ill. 37, on the necessity of actual notice to customers of change in partnership.

Cited in reference notes in 84 A. D. 356, on sufficiency of newspaper notice of dissolution of partnership; 36 A. D. 257, on sufficiency of publication of dissolution of partnership in newspapers; 58 A. D. 174, on publication of notice of dissolution of partnership sufficient as to strangers.

Cited in note in 62 A. D. 321, 322, on inference of notice arising from ne
paper articles or publication not required or authorized by law.

34 AM. DEC. 523, PEARCE v. AUSTIN, 4 WHART. 489.

Right to sue for use of another.

Cited in Newton v. Nutt, 58 N. H. 599, holding that guardian cannot
in his own name on an account for the labor of his ward.

Right of legal holder to sue on note in own name for use of another.

Cited in First Nat. Bank v. Mann, 94 Tenn. 17, 27 L.R.A. 568, 27 S. W. 10
Logan v. Cassell, 88 Pa. 288, 32 A. R. 453, 6 W. N. C. 444, 36 Phila. Leg.
365,—holding that indorsee of note taken as collateral security may main
suit thereon against the maker, unless maker is thereby deprived of an equita
defense against payee.

Cited in reference notes in 1 A. S. R. 807, on rights of indorsee; 51 A.
188, as to when agent may sue in his own name; 39 A. D. 658; 44 A. D. 540,
on right of agent to sue in his own name on note indorsed in blank; 61 A.
751, on right of agent or treasurer of private association to sue on note
to him by name with addition of agency or office.

Cited in note in 46 A. D. 97, on right of party having no interest in bill to
thereon.

Sufficiency of answer denying plaintiff's ownership.

Cited in note in 66 L.R.A. 518, on sufficiency of answers denying owners
of plaintiff in actions by third parties on negotiable instruments.

34 AM. DEC. 525, KNOWLES v. LORD, 4 WHART. 500.

Conclusiveness of an officer's return.

Cited in Rickard v. Major, 34 Pa. Super. Ct. 107; Michels v. Stork,
Mich. 260, 17 N. W. 833,—holding that officer's return is conclusive upon
parties to a suit in any collateral proceeding; Sauser v. Werntz, 1 Leg. Chr
249, on parol evidence of matters consistent with officer's return being
missible.

Cited in reference notes in 53 A. D. 517; 74 A. D. 133, 427; 97 A. D. 280
on conclusiveness of sheriff's return; 80 A. D. 432, on conclusiveness of
ficer's return when collaterally called into question; 52 A. D. 645, on
ficer's return as evidence of what has been done by him under writ; 34 A.
549, on nature of evidence afforded by sheriff's return; 73 A. D. 789, on co
clusiveness of return of process on parties to record when collaterally called
question; 58 A. D. 370, on parol evidence to correct sheriff's return.

Cited in note in 43 A. D. 531, on sheriff's return of process as evidence
tween parties.

Distinguished in Jordan v. Minster, 3 Clark (Pa.) 457, holding parol e
dence admissible to show facts consistent with, but not appearing on, office
return; Susquehanna Boom Co. v. Finney, 58 Pa. 200, holding that where w
of replevin and return called for a certain number of feet of logs, more
less, parol evidence of actual quantity is admissible; Gibbs v. Bartlett,
Watts & S. 29, holding that value given in writ of replevin is prima fa
evidence of the value of the property, subject to parol evidence of act
value.

Effect of bond for return of property.

Cited in reference note in 78 A. S. R. 798, on effect of giving bond for return of replevied property.

Rights of vendor in case of fraud or insolvency of purchaser.

Cited in reference note in 97 A. D. 592, on vendor's right to avoid sale induced by fraud.

Cited in notes in 43 A. D. 654, on right of vendor to rescind sale for fraud; 2 L.R.A. 154, on title acquired by fraudulent purchaser of goods; 23 L. ed. U. S. 994, on validity of sale of goods on credit to insolvent vendee; 10 L.R.A. 235, on effect of conditional delivery of goods to purchaser with reservation of title in seller; 17 L.R.A.(N.S.) 1033, on seller's right to reclaim goods as against assignee for creditors or trustee in bankruptcy of buyer, who procured them by false representations.

Title of assignee under voluntary assignment.

Cited in Maas v. Goodman, 2 Hilt. 275; Schieffelin v. Hawkins, 1 Daly, 289, 14 Abb. Pr. 118; Ludwig v. Highley, 5 Pa. 132; Foulke v. Harding, 13 Pa. 242; Williams's Appeal, 101 Pa. 474, 13 W. N. C. 217, 14 Pittsb. L. J. N. S. 61, 40 Phila. Leg. Int. 310; Roberts v. Corbin, 26 Iowa, 315, 96 A. D. 146,—holding that assignee in voluntary assignment takes the property subject to all equities existing against the assignor; Bell v. Moss, 5 Whart. 189, holding that assignees under voluntary assignment are not purchasers for valuable consideration; Pierson v. Manning, 2 Mich. 445; Fulton's Estate, 51 Pa. 204, 23 Phila. Leg. Int. 108; Dobbins v. Walton, 37 Ga. 614, 95 A. D. 37,—holding that assignee or creditors whom he represents under voluntary assignment are not purchasers for value, as against prior liens; Gardner v. Commercial Nat. Bank, 13 R. I. 155, on subsequent assignment conveying only property obtained after a prior assignment; Griffith's Estate, 1 Chester Co. Rep. 39, holding assignee for benefit of creditors entitled to rents of assigned realty.

Cited in note in 37 A. D. 327, on rights of assignee for creditors of fraudulent vendee.

Fraudulent preferential assignments.

Cited in Fechheimer v. Hollander, 21 D. C. 76, holding that assignment preferring certain creditors, but with intent to defraud others, is void as to them, though preferred creditors were not parties to the fraud.

34 AM. DEC. 530, SMITH v. PLUMMER, 5 WHART. 89.

Right of third party to maintain suit on a contract.

Cited in Bell v. Moss, 5 Whart. 189, on right of third party from whom consideration moved to maintain suit on the contract.

Cited in reference notes in 77 A. D. 172. on right of third person to sue on contract made for his benefit; 93 A. D. 57, on rights and liabilities of undisclosed principal; 95 A. D. 236, as to when undisclosed principal may sue on contract made by agent; 38 A. D. 620, on liability of undisclosed principal on contracts of agent; 52 A. D. 551, on right of one selling goods to agent to sue either agent or undiscovered principal; 41 A. D. 436, on right to sue undisclosed principal when discovered.

Cited in note in 2 E. R. C. 483, on right of vendor to hold undisclosed principal.

Ratification of agent's contract.

Cited in Shoninger v. Peabody, 57 Conn. 42, holding that suit by princi on agent's unauthorized contract ratifies the entire contract.

34 AM. DEC. 533, ROMIG v. ERDMAN, 5 WHART. 112.

Administrator's claim against an estate.

Cited in Lazarus's Estate, 6 Kulp, 53, holding that statute of limitati as to claims against estate will not bar a private claim of the administrat

Presumption as to payment by trustee of his own compensation.

Cited in Re Semple, 16 Pittsb. L. J. N. S. 267, presuming that trustee ing funds in his possession retained compensation for services as fast earned.

34 AM. DEC. 535, YARDLEY v. RAUB, 5 WHART. 117.

Wife's separate estate.

Cited in reference notes in 40 A. D. 622, on trusts in favor of wife; 40 D. 444, as to what is wife's separate property.

— Liability for husband's debts.

Cited in reference notes in 64 A. D. 587, on separate estate of wife as s ject to execution sale for husband's debts; 72 A. D. 577, as to when wif property is subject to execution for husband's debts.

34 AM. DEC. 537, BROTZMAN v. BUNNELL, 5 WHART. 128.

Apprenticeship of infant.

Cited in reference notes in 42 A. D. 696; 84 A. D. 781,—on infant's power make binding contract of apprenticeship.

Cited in notes in 18 A. S. R. 627, on apprenticeship of infants; 18 A. S. 626, on infants' contracts for services; 18 A. S. R. 626, on apprenticeship infants.

34 AM. DEC. 539, AGNEW v. DORR, 5 WHART. 131.

Stipulations and conditions in assignments for benefit of creditors.

Cited in Re Bank of United States, 2 Pars. Sel. Eq. Cas. 110, holding t condition in assignment that creditors must present their claims within specified time in order to share in distribution is valid.

Cited in reference notes in 42 A. D. 592, as to when assignment for c ors is void; 77 A. D. 515, on validity of conditional assignment for benefit creditors.

— For "full release."

Cited in Tyson v. Dorr, 6 Whart. 256, holding that where assignment sti lated for full release from creditors, a release containing a condition will held to be release in full and the condition void.

Cited in reference note in 77 A. D. 515, on effect of stipulation for release creditors in assignment for benefit of creditors.

34 AM. DEC. 542, HINDS'S ESTATE, 5 WHART. 138.

Effect of reduction of wife's choses or property to possession.

Cited in Timbers v. Katz, 6 Watts & S. 290; Vreeland v. Schoonmaker, N. J. Eq. 512,—holding that the effect of reduction into possession by h band of wife's choses in action depends upon his intention thereby; McDowell v. Potter, 8 Pa. 189, 49 A. D. 503; Miller v. Blackburn, 14 Ind. 62 (dissenting opinion),—on same point; Young v. Wilkinson, Thomp. Tenn. Cas. 161, on wife's choses in action reduced to possession of husband, thereby becoming his property.

Cited in reference notes in 67 A. D. 579, on circumstances under which husband's marital rights attach; 73 A. D. 302, on what acts of husband will amount to appropriation by him of wife's choses in action.

Cited in note in 37 A. D. 578, on reducing wife's choses in action to possession.

Right of husband to possess wife's personalty.

Cited in Andrews v. Jones, 10 Ala. 400, holding that husband's right to reduce wife's choses in action into possession is optional with him; Goodyear v. Rumbaugh, 13 Pa. 480, on same point; Smethurst v. Thurston, Brightly, (Pa.) 127, holding that creditors of husband cannot compel him to reduce wife's choses in action into possession so as to make them liable for his debts; Coale v. Smith, 4 Pa. 376, on right of husband to reduce wife's chose in action to possession, thereby becoming the owner.

— Evidence of conversion to husband's use.

Cited in Nolen's Appeal, 23 Pa. 37 (affirming 1 Phila. 298, 9 Phila. Leg. Int. 31); Moyer's Appeal, 77 Pa. 482, 1 W. N. C. 527, 2 Legal Gaz. 212, 32 Phila. Leg. Int. 320; Messner v. Messner, 1 Pearson (Pa.) 222,—holding that possession by husband of wife's choses in action is prima facie evidence of conversion to his own use, which may be rebutted by proof; Little v. Birdwell, 21 Tex. 597, 73 A. D. 242, on same point; Re Gray, 1 Pa. St. 327, holding that husband's disclaimer of conversion to his own use may be established by his subsequent admissions if clear and positive; Boose's Appeal, 18 Pa. 392, holding that where husband was to pay interest of proceeds of sale to wife annually, a failure so to do was a conversion thereof to his own use; Keil v. Wolf, 7 Pa. 424, holding that judgment confessed to husband and wife for separate use of the wife is prima facie evidence that the debt was due to the wife.

Wife's separate property.

Cited in Jeanes v. Davis, 3 Clark (Pa.) 60, holding that damages recovered in suit by husband and wife for injury to wife are hers, and cannot be attached for husband's debt.

Contracts between husband and wife.

Cited in Johnston v. Johnston, 31 Pa. 450, 1 Grant's Cases, 468, holding contract between husband and wife void for want of parties, as law recognizes no separate will as between husband and wife; McCampbell v. McCampbell, 2 Lea, 661, 31 A. R. 623, holding that note given by husband to wife during coverture for money collected on chose in action due her will be enforced in equity, where no rights of creditors are affected; Fowle v. Torrey, 135 Mass. 87 (dissenting opinion), on equitable enforcement of contract between husband and wife against husband's estate.

What are fixtures and right to remove same.

Cited in reference notes in 42 A. D. 601, on what are fixtures; 37 A. D. 494, on what erections by life tenant are fixtures; 64 A. D. 76, on tenant's right to chattels and articles of furniture after surrender of possession under lease; 66 A. D. 426, on application of same rule with respect to fixtures between mortgagor and mortgagee, vendor and vendee, debtor and execution creditor as between heir and executor.

Cited in note in 69 A. D. 515, on tenant's right to remove fixtures after expiration of his term.

34 AM. DEC. 546, MENTZ v. HAMMAN, 5 WHART. 150.

Effect of execution without intent to have levy and sale.

Cited in Wunsch v. McGraw, 4 Wash. 72, 29 Pac. 832, holding that execution placed in officer's hands with instructions not to levy is postponed to levy under a subsequent judgment; Miller v. Getz, 135 Pa. 558, 20 A. J. R. 887, 19 Atl. 955; Burleigh v. Piper, 51 Iowa, 649, 2 N. W. 520,—holding that levy upon growing crop so early as to make sale thereunder improbable during life of the writ is not valid as against subsequent liens.

Cited in reference note in 49 A. D. 63, on effect of stay of execution as to subsequent execution during stay.

Cited in note in 27 L.R.A. 380, on loss of priority of execution by creditor's indefinite postponement of sale.

Conclusiveness of officer's return.

Cited in Lowber v. Richardson, 1 Clark (Pa.) 263; Rickard v. Major, 34 Pa. Super. Ct. 107; Hill v. Robertson, 2 Pittsb. 103,—holding that sheriff's return to writ is conclusive as between the parties to an action; Schwartz v. Gabler, 42 W. N. C. 485; Stranghellan v. Ward, 13 W. N. C. 111,—on same point; Ruth's Appeal, 45 Phila. Leg. Int. 16, on conclusiveness of sheriff's return of sale of property under writ; Anonymous, 4 How. Pr. 112, holding that sheriff's return cannot be impeached collaterally; Smith's Estate, 13 Pa. Dist. R. 80; Philadelphia Sav. Fund Soc. v. Purcell, 24 Pa. Super. Ct. 205; Flick v. Troxsell, 7 Watts & S. 65,—holding parol evidence inadmissible to vary sheriff's return; French v. Pennsylvania & N. Y. Canal & R. Co. 1 Legal Chron. 67, holding that officer's return of service upon agent of railroad company is conclusive that person served was such agent as might be served; Com. v. Catawissa, W. & E. R. Co. 1 Pearson (Pa.) 341, holding that sheriff's return of service of summons on an officer of a certain corporation is conclusive as to existence of the corporation and official position of person served.

Cited in reference notes in 53 A. D. 517; 28 A. S. R. 368,—on conclusiveness of officer's return; 34 A. D. 530, on conclusiveness of sheriff's return on parties to suit; 49 A. D. 63, on conclusiveness of sheriff's return as to record parties; 73 A. D. 789, on conclusiveness of return of process on parties to record when collaterally called in question; 58 A. D. 370, on parol evidence to correct sheriff's return.

Cited in notes in 43 A. D. 531, on sheriff's return of process as evidence between parties; 15 A. D. 581, on conclusiveness of sheriff's return as between the parties.

—Against the officer.

Cited in Governor v. Bancroft, 16 Ala. 605, holding that evidence of incorrectness of sheriff's return on writ is not admissible in suit against sheriff and his sureties; Sauser v. Werntz, 1 Legal Chron. 249, 1 Foster, 227, on sheriff's return as evidence in suit against him.

Recitals of hearsay information in return.

Cited in Kleckner v. Lehigh County, 6 Whart. 66, holding that sheriff's re-

turn of service on parties "said to be commissioners" is valid return of se
ice on commissioners, "said to be" being surplusage.

Alteration of officer's return.

Cited in Washington Mill Co. v. Kinnear, 1 Wash. Terr. 99, holding th
court cannot compel officer to alter a return regular on its face; Flynn
Kalamazoo Circuit Judge, 138 Mich. 126, 101 N. W. 222, 4 A. & E. Ann. C
1167, holding that amendment to sheriff's return as to a matter of fact c
only be made by the voluntary act of the sheriffs; Garner's Appeal, 1 Wa
(Pa.) 438, on same point; Dixon v. White Sewing Mach. Co. 128 Pa. 397,
A. S. R. 683, 5 L.R.A. 659, 18 Atl. 502, 24 W. N. C. 433, 46 Phila. Leg. Int. 5
holding that writ is in control of sheriff until return filed, and he may chan
his return on the writ at any time prior to its filing.

Liability for act of deputy.

Cited in Bennethum v. Bowers, 133 Pa. 332, 19 Atl. 361, 21 Pittsb. L. J.
S. 79, 47 Phila. Leg. Int. 311, holding that adoption by sheriff of act of dépu
in serving process is sufficient to show his authority without adding depu
sheriff to return.

34 AM. DEC. 549, ROBERTS v. WILLIAMS, 5 WHART. 170.

Effect of judicial sale of mortgaged premises.

Cited in reference notes in 42 A. D. 323, on extent to which judicial s
devests lien; 53 A. D. 450, on extinguishment of mortgage by sale of la
under order of orphans' court.

Cited in notes in 51 A. D. 550, as to when judicial sale devests mortga
liens in Pennsylvania; 88 A. S. R. 359, on rights and remedies of mortgag
where mortgaged property is disposed of by judicial sale.

Validity of sale under mortgage without service of writ upon mortgag

Distinguished in Taylor v. Beekley, 211 Pa. 606, 61 Atl. 79 (reversing
Pa. Dist. R. 452), holding that where mortgagor conveyed property subject
mortgage, the purchaser at sheriff's sale under the mortgage obtains tit
though writ was not served on mortgagor.

Right to set up general defense as special plea.

Cited in Johns v. Bolton, 12 Pa. 339; South Easton v. Norton, 2 Pa. Co.
187, 2 Lehigh Valley L. Rep. 309,—holding that party may set up matter
defense as special plea though the matter might be proved under the gener
issue.

34 AM. DEC. 554, SHARP v. EMMET, 5 WHART. 288.

Liability of agent on indorsement to principal.

Cited in Byers v. Harris, 9 Heisk. 652, holding that agent remitting b
with his indorsement to his principal is not liable to him thereon in t
absence of other facts creating liability: Henbach Bros. v. Rother, 2 Duer, 2
on effect of indorsement by agent of bill remitted to principal in his bu
ness.

Cited in note in 58 A. D. 171, on *del credere* factors.

Agency as defense to bills and notes.

Cited in Roberts v. Austin, 5 Whart. 313, holding that, in suit by pay
against drawer of bill, it is good defense to show that bill was given and
cepted in payment for goods for the drawee as principal; Markley v. Qua

8 W. N. C. 145, 14 Phila. 164, 37 Phila. Leg. Int. 14, holding that, in suit payee against maker of check, a defense that check was drawn as chairman committee for debt due from them is admissible.

Impeaching witness by proof of contradictory statements.

Cited in Kay v. Fredrigal, 3 Pa. St. 221; McKee v. Jones, 6 Pa. 425; Rot rock v. Gallaher, 91 Pa. 108; Cronkrite v. Trexler, 20 Pa. Co. Ct. 469, 7 Dist. R. 64,—holding that admission of evidence of contradictory statemen by witness without first examining him as to them rests in discretion of t trial court; Stearns v. Merchants' Bank, 53 Pa. 490, on same point.

Cited in reference notes in 38 A. D. 706, on impeachment of witness; 56 D. 342, on impeaching witness by evidence of contradictory statements.

Cited in notes in 39 A. D. 656; 82 A. S. R. 42,—on impeachment of w ness by proof of prior contradictory statements; 73 A. D. 764, on layi foundation for introducing evidence of prior contradictory statements by recting mind of witness to time, place, and circumstances involved in suppo contradiction.

34 AM. DEC. 558, FREVALL v. FITCH, 5 WHART. 325.

Effect of indorsement of non-negotiable instrument.

Cited in Jossey v. Rushin, 109 Ga. 319, 77 A. S. R. 377, 34 S. E. 558, holdi that payee of non-negotiable paper assumes no liability by mere indorseme thereof, but proof of assumption of liability is admissible; Patterson v. Poi dexter, 6 Watts & S. 227, 40 A. D. 554, holding that indorsement of no negotiable instrument is an assignment thereof without recourse to the signor; Gillespie v. Mather, 10 Pa. 28, holding that indorsement of n negotiable order does not vest in the holder a right to sue upon it in his o name.

Cited in note in 97 A. S. R. 988, on liability of payee indorsing non-nego able instrument.

Effect of seal of corporation on instrument negotiable in form.

Cited in Hopkins v. Cumberland Valley R. Co. 3 Watts & S. 410, holdi that instrument in form of negotiable promissory note of a company, attes by corporate seal,' is a specialty.

Cited in reference notes in 41 A. D. 433, on liability created by indo ment of sealed instrument; 40 A. D. 560, on liability of indorser of seal instrument in the form of a promissory note.

Cited in notes in 11 L.R.A. 833, on effect of seal attached to commerci paper; 35 L.R.A. 607, on effect of seal on negotiability of corporate note.

Cited as overruled in Mason v. Frick, 105 Pa. 162, 51 A. D. 191, 15 N. C. 369, 42 Phila. Leg. Int. 90, holding that corporate bonds payable to bea er are negotiable instruments though attested by corporate seal; Stevens Philadelphia Ball Club, 142 Pa. 52, 11 L.R.A. 860, 21 Atl. 797, 28 W. N. 37, on same point.

Contract based upon mistaken facts.

Cited in Fink v. Smith, 170 Pa. 124, 50 A. S. R. 750, 32 Atl. 566, 37 W. C. 46, holding that contract based upon facts assumed by both parties, b afterwards found not to exist, is inoperative; Riddle v. Hall, 99 Pa. 116, Pittsb. L. J. N. S. 199, 39 Phila. Leg. Int. 33, holding that mortgage sign to cover another's defalcation on the mistaken representation that no prosec tion would be begun was voidable.

Cited in reference notes in 29 A. S. R. 869, as to when mistake of law will be relieved against; 39 A. D. 639, on effect of agreement made under mistake of law.

34 AM. DEC. 561, BENSELL v. CHANCELLOR, 5 WHART. 371.

Parol evidence of lack of capacity in grantor.

Cited in note in 11 E. R. C. 231, on parol evidence to show lack of capacity in grantor.

Effect of contract of person of unsound mind.

Cited in Rogers v. Walker, 6 Pa. 371, 47 A. D. 470, holding that lunatic's conveyance is void; Philadelphia Trust Co. v. Kneedler, 12 Phila. 421, 35 Phila. Leg. Int. 234, on same point; Dexter v. Hall, 15 Wall. 9, 21 L. ed. 268, holding that power of attorney executed by person of unsound mind is void; Cook v. Parker, 4 Phila. 265, 18 Phila. Leg. Int. 53, holding that mortgage executed by lunatic is voidable; Clifton v. Davis, 1 Pars. Sel. Eq. Cas. 31, holding that equity will set aside a deed on application of grantor on ground of drunkenness to such extent as to render him incapable of contracting; Crawford v. Scovell, 94 Pa. 48, 39 A. R. 766, 8 W. N. C. 364, 37 Phila. Leg. Int. 323, holding that grantor may avoid his deed by showing his unsoundness of mind at time of its execution; Freeman's Appeal, 22 W. N. C. 173, on same point; Allen v. Berryhill, 27 Iowa, 534, 1 A. R. 309 (dissenting opinion), on right of lunatic to set up lunacy as defense to his alleged contract.

Cited in reference notes in 55 A. D. 431, on liability of insane persons on contracts; 66 A. D. 421, on voidability of deed of insane person; 45 A. D. 700, as to whether deeds of lunatics are void or voidable; 66 A. D. 267, on insanity of grantor as affecting validity of deed; 83 A. D. 523, on avoidance of deed by lunatic; 47 A. D. 474, on validity of, and who may avoid, deeds of lunatics; 36 A. D. 580, on right of grantor or heirs or representatives to avoid deed on ground of insanity.

Cited in notes in 15 A. D. 361, on liability of insane persons on contracts; 16 E. R. C. 739, on avoidance of contract of alleged insane person; 71 A. S. R. 431; 19 L.R.A. 480,—on validity of a deed made by an insane person.

Mode of pleading defense of lunacy.

Cited in Gibson v. Western N. Y. & P. R. Co. 164 Pa. 142, 44 A. S. R. 586, 30 Atl. 308, 35 W. N. C. 381, holding that lunacy can be proven under plea of *non est factum*.

Limitations as to person under disability.

Cited in Henry v. Carson, 59 Pa. 297, holding that person under disability has only ten years after disability ceases, if that makes total of twenty years since right accrued, to bring action to recover real property.

Cited in reference notes in 44 A. D. 329, on necessity that disability to prevent running of limitations exist at time cause of action accrues; 1 A. S. R. 789, on continuance of statute of limitations after it has commenced to run; 44 A. D. 159, on continuance of running of statutes of limitations notwithstanding intervening disability; 43 A. D. 320, on effect of disability occurring after statute of limitation commences to run.

Cited in notes in 16 E. R. C. 153, on disability to sue as affecting running of statute of limitations; 11 A. S. R. 342; 25 L. ed. U. S. 318,—on effect of disability occurring after statute of limitations begins to run; 10 A. D. 457, on successive disabilities.

34 AM. DEC. 565, CHAPMAN v. COM. 5 WHART. 427.

Necessity of using term "wilfully" in indictment.

Doubted in State v. Abbott, 31 N. H. 434, holding use of term "wilfully" in indictment for unlawful sale of liquor unnecessary where statute does not use such term.

Malicious mischief.

Cited in note in 32 A. D. 666, on malicious mischief under statutory regulations.

Conclusion of indictment charging statutory offense.

Cited in reference notes in 37 A. D. 84, on form of indictment charging statutory offense; 54 A. D. 378, on requisities of conclusion of indictment for statutory offense; 44 A. D. 116; 53 A. D. 279,—on necessity that statutory offense conclude *contra formam statute;* 94 A. D. 253, as to when indictment for statutory offense must conclude "against form of statute."

Burning of barn as offense.

Cited in State v. Smith, 28 Iowa, 565, on burning of barn being an offense, regardless of its contents.

Cited in note in 81 A. D. 68, 74, as to what constitutes arson.

34 AM. DEC. 566, HEIDLEBERG v. LYNN, 5 WHART. 430.

Settlement of pauper.

Cited in Bradford Twp. v. Huston Twp. 15 Pa. Co. Ct. 323, holding that a laborer must work continuously for hire for a year within the district; Huntington v. Fairmount, 12 Luzerne Leg. Reg. 275, holding that poor person rendering valuable services for series of years under contract of hiring gains settlement; Northampton County v. Stroudsburg Poor Dist. 9 Pa. Dist. R. 614, 7 North Co. Rep. 314, holding that emancipated minor gains settlement by living and doing service for hire for more than a year in the district; Re Overseers of the Poor, 1 Legal Gaz. 42, holding that unmarried person may gain settlement by rendering services in township for a year under contract of hiring; Turbett Twp. v. Port Royal, 33 Pa. Super. Ct. 520, holding that widow whose children are of age may gain settlement by more than a year's service, under law as to unmarried person not having a child; Butler v. Sugarloaf, 6 Pa. 262, on payment of rent of premises by surety as sufficient to gain settlement by tenant.

—Sufficiency of contract for hire under statute.

Cited in Lewiston v. Granville, 5 Pa. 283, holding that in order to constitute service for hire there must be a contract express or implied; Buffalo Twp. Poor Dist. v. Mifflinburg Borough Poor Dist. 168 Pa. 445, 32 Atl. 28; Fayette Twp. v. Fermanagh Twp. 1 Pa. Dist. R. 795, 11 Pa. Co. Ct. 70; Shickshinny Poor Dist. v. Montour Poor Dist. 6 Kulp, 173,—holding that service for a year may be under one or under several contracts; Schuylkill County v. Northampton County, 10 North. Co. Rep. 401, holding that one rendering services in a township for more than a year under contracts of hiring gains settlement; Moreland Twp. v. Davidson Twp. 71 Pa. 371; Hemlock Twp. v. Shickshinny, 6 Kulp, 169,—holding that contract for hire will be presumed from service for more than a year by one not a relative nor an object of charity; Plum Creek v. South Bend, 1 Pennyp. 408, on necessity of contract of hire being such as could be enforced at law.

34 AM. DEC. 569, STEM'S APPEAL, 5 WHART. 472.

Duty of guardian to realize on unsecured debts due ward.

Cited in Neff's Appeal, 57 Pa. 91, 25 Phila. Leg. Int. 92, holding that ecutor is not bound to sue at once on debt, unless he is aware of danger delay.

Liability of guardian as to care of funds.

Cited in Redfield's Estate, 31 Pa. Co. Ct. 621, holding that guardian is quired to use only common skill, prudence, and caution in caring for fun Worrell's Estate, 14 Phila. 311, 38 Phila. Leg. Int. 270, holding guardian liable for loss from investment made in good faith under belief that it safe and judicious.

Cited in reference note in 49 A. D. 722, on liability of guardian for loss trust funds by unsafe investment.

Cited in notes in 75 A. D. 448, on personal liability of guardians; 21 A. 381, on liability of gurdians and executors.

— Loans on unsecured paper.

Distinguished in Dietterich v. Heft, 5 Pa. 87, holding guardian liable loss of money loaned on personal note of one in equivocal circumstances.

34 AM. DEC. 571, MILLER v. BANK OF NEW ORLEANS, 5 WH 503.

Necessity and sufficiency of tender.

Cited in reference notes in 86 A. D. 521, on duty of debtor to seek credi and make tender of amount due; 51 A. D. 192, on deposit of funds in bank meet payment as tender.

Cited in note in 77 A. D. 472, giving illustrations of sufficient tender.

— Deposit as tender to prevent interest accruing on debt.

Cited in Emlen v. Lehigh Coal & Nav. Co. 47 Pa. 76, 86 A. D. 518, holdi that where loan to corporation is payable at fixed time and place, inter thereon ceases from time due, if money was on hand at all times to pay though not separated from other funds.

Interest as depending on demand.

Cited in note in 6 A. D. 194, as to when recovery of interest depends demand.

34 AM. DEC. 572, EX PARTE ELLIOTT, 5 WHART. 524.

Power given executors to sell.

Cited in reference note in 49 A. D. 458, as to when executors take an inter in land intrusted to them to sell.

Cited in note in 87 A. D 216, as to when executors and other trustees are implication vested with power to sell.

34 AM. DEC. 574, DAVIS'S ESTATE, 5 WHART. 530.

Note as payment of antecedent debt.

Cited in Kendig v. Kendig, 2 Pearson (Pa.) 89; Patterson's Estate, 3 L Chron. 47,—holding that giving note for antecedent debt is not payment unl so agreed; Bantz v. Basnett, 12 W. Va. 772, on same point.

Cited in reference notes in 28 A. S. R. 136, on note as extinguishment pre-existing debt; 42 A. D. 383, on effect of accepting note for pre-existi debt; 36 A. D. 718, on taking note for pre-existing debt; 36 A. D. 126, as to when note given for pre-existing debt is deemed payment; 64 A. D. 296, on necessity of agreement that promissory note shall be payment.

Renewal note as continuing original debt.

Cited in Nightingale v. Chafee, 11 R. I. 609, 23 A. R. 531, holding that note given after dissolution in renewal of firm note does not release retiring partner; Hayward v. Burke, 151 Ill. 121, 37 N. E. 846, holding that indorsement of payment of interest and extension of time of payment of firm debt after death of one partner does not release his estate from liability.

Effect of taking individual obligation or payment for joint debt.

Cited in Bantz v. Basnett, 12 W. Va. 772, on acceptance by creditor of note of one joint debtor as discharging other joint debtors; Mason v. Wickersham, 4 Watts & S. 100, holding that note given by one partner after dissolution for a firm debt does not discharge the other partners from liability; Kauffman v. Fisher, 3 Grant Cas. 302, holding that confession of judgment by one partner for partnership debt does not release the other partners; First Nat. Bank v. Cody, 93 Ga. 127, 19 S. E. 831, holding that note given by one partner after dissolution of firm by death of a partner, in renewal of firm note, releases the other partners personally, but does not release partnership assets; Kimberly's Appeal, 3 Sadler (Pa.) 528, 7 Atl. 75, on separate note for joint debt not being payment unless so agreed; Coleman v. Fobes, 22 Pa. 156, 60 A. D. 75, holding that payment on note by one of two joint debtors, not partners at the time, will not avoid the statute of limitations as to the other; Campbell v. Floyd, 153 Pa. 84, 25 Atl. 1033, 23 Pittsb. L. J. N. S. 304, holding that payment of interest on firm debt by liquidating partner would prevent the running of the statute of limitations in favor of the firm; Houser v. Irvine, 3 Watts & S. 345, 38 A. D. 768, holding that payment by partner, after dissolution, on contract debt of firm suspends running of statute of limitations against the debt.

Cited in reference note in 80 A. D. 640, on effect of payment by one joint debtor by note or otherwise.

· Cited in note in 15 L.R.A.(N.S.) 1020, on note or other commercial paper of individual partner as payment of firm debt which he had not previously assumed.

Power of partner after dissolution as to firm business.

Cited in Whitehead v. Bank of Pittsburgh, 2 Watts & S. 172, holding that, after dissolution, one partner cannot bind the others by using the firm name unless so agreed in winding up the business; Ward v. Tyler, 24 Phila. Leg. Int. 4, on authority of partner to sign firm name after dissolution, while business remains unsettled; Kauffman v. Fisher, 3 Grant Cas. 302, holding that payment of interest on firm debt by liquidating partner keeps debt alive.

Cited in reference note in 38 A. D. 771, on power of partner to bind firm after dissolution.

Cited in notes in 40 A. S. R. 572, on powers, rights, and liabilities of liquidating partner; 40 A. S. R. 568, on partner's right to borrow money after dissolution.

— As to notes in firm name.

Cited in Robinson v. Taylor, 4 Pa. 242; McCowin v. Cubbison, 72 Pa. 358; Kemp v. Coffin, 3 G. Greene, 190,—holding that liquidating partner after dissolution may give note for firm debt, which binds the partners: Beatty v. Wray, 19 Pa. 516, on the same point; Seigfried v. Ludwig, 102 Pa. 547, holding that liquidating partner may bind partnership by note for money borrowed and applied to payment of firm debt; People's Nat. Bank v. Wilcox, 136 Mich. 567, 100 N. W. 24, 4 A. & E. Ann. Cas. 465, holding that mortgage given by surviving partner to secure a firm debt takes precedence over subsequent judgment against firm assets by a creditor; Brown v. Clark, 14 Pa. 469; Dundass v. Gallagher, 4 Pa. 205,—holding that surviving partner has implied right to renew a firm note; Schoneman v. Fegley, 7 Pa. 433, holding that promise of partner after dissolution to pay note indorsed by firm, of which no notice of dishonor has been given, does not bind the other partners; Durant v. Pierson, 124 N. Y. 444, 21 A. S. R. 686, 12 L.R.A. 146, 26 N. E. 1095, holding that assets of firm will be bound for payment of note given by partner after dissolution for debt due from the firm.

Disapproved in Palmer v. Dodge, 4 Ohio St. 21, holding partners not bound by note given by one partner after dissolution in renewal of firm note; Haven v. Goodell, 1 Disney (Ohio) 26, holding partners not liable on note given by one partner after dissolution, signed in firm name without knowledge of the other partners, even though proceeds were used to pay firm debts.

Presumptions as to firm or individual obligation.

Cited in Tams v. Hitner, 9 Pa. 441, holding that where note is signed by some members of firm only, but for firm business, burden of proof is on them to show nonliability of the firm; Denton v. Merrill, 43 Hun, 224, on presumption of firm liability for money borrowed by partner and used in partnership business.

Liability for firm debts on dissolution.

Cited in Wadhams v. Page, 1 Wash. 420, 25 Pac. 462, holding that agreement between partners upon dissolution that one of them shall pay firm debts is not binding on the creditors.

Dissolution of partnership by sale.

Cited in Wilson v. Waugh, 101 Pa. 233, 13 Pittsb. L. J. N. S. 176, 40 Phila. Leg. Int. 242, on dissolution of partnership by sale by one partner of his interest.

34 AM. DEC. 581, SIMS v. DAVIS, CHEVES, L. 1.

Right of way by prescription.

Cited in Hogg v. Gill, 1 McMull, L. 329, holding that party using the way must use it as though he was exercising a right of property in himself uncontrollable by owner of soil over which it runs; Pearce v. McClenaghan, 5 Rich. L. 178, 55 A. D. 710; Shuman v. Heldman, 63 S. C. 494, 41 S. E. 765,— holding that a public way may be shown by twenty years' mere use, but to have a private way the use for the twenty years must be adverse; McBryde v. Sayre, 86 Ala. 458, 3 L.R.A. 861, 5 So. 791, on right of way by prescription.

Cited in reference notes in 47 A. D. 162, on right of way by prescription; 37 A. D. 89; 40 A. D. 165,—on presumption of grant of easement; 82 A. D. 498, as to what must be shown to establish presumption of right of way.

Distinguished in Hankinson v. Charlotte, C. & A. R. Co. 41 S. C. 1, 19 S. E. 206, holding where land is inclosed, and where use is adverse, that a right of way over lands may be acquired by prescription.

— Use of uninclosed lands.

Cited in Gibson v. Durham, 3 Rich. L. 85, holding that use of uninclosed lands of another as a private way will not of itself give a title by prescription; Hutto v. Tindall, 6 Rich. L. 396, holding that right of way by use over un-inclosed woodland must be by use continued for twenty years and adverse; Watt v. Trapp, 2 Rich. L. 136; Nash v. Peden, 1 Speers, L. 17,—holding that in such case mere use, unaccompanied by acts indicating a claim of use by right, cannot give a right of way; State v. Tyler, 54 S. C. 294, 32 S. E. 422, holding that, though land is uninclosed, a highway arises by prescription from continuous, uninterrupted, adverse use thereof by the public under a claim of right for twenty years.

Cited in reference note in 39 A. D. 757, on right of way over uninclosed lands.

34 AM. DEC. 584, DAVIS v. RUFF, CHEVES, L. 17.

What is actionable slander.

Cited in Smith v. Bradstreet Co. 63 S. C. 525, 41 S. E. 763, holding that a false and malicious statement of the credit of a merchant is a libel *per se;* Sanderson v. Caldwell, 45 N. Y. 398, 6 A. R. 105, holding that words spoken in relation to the profession or occupation of plaintiff that directly tend to injury in respect to it, or to impair confidence in his character, are actionable though not applied to his profession; Darling v. Clement, 69 Vt. 292, 37 Atl 779, holding that words charging plaintiff with habitual intemperance have a natural tendency to injure him in his business of keeping and teaching boys.

Cited in reference notes in 36 A. D. 254, on words impugning solvency and impairing credit; 58 A. D. 708, on implication of damages from utterance of words actionable *per se;* 44 A. D. 111, on actionability of words affecting one's business or profession.

Cited in note in 4 L.R.A.(N.S.) 975, on oral charge of insolvency against merchant as slander.

Measure of damages for slander.

Cited in reference note in 43 A. S. R. 596, on exemplary damages as question for jury in action for slander.

Cited in note in 72 A. D. 431, on actual loss and injury as element of damages in slander or libel.

Excessive damages as ground for a new trial.

Cited in Bodie v. Charleston & W. C. R. Co. 66 S. C. 302, 44 S. E. 943 (dissenting opinion), on excessive damages as a ground for a new trial.

Cited in reference note in 36 A. D. 569, on excessive damages as ground for new trial in slander.

Cited in note in 8 E. R. C. 460, on excessive damages as ground for new trial.

34 AM. DEC. 586, THOMAS v. ERVIN, CHEVES, L. 22.

Time when statutes of limitations begin to run.

Cited in Rosborough v. Albright, 4 Rich. L. 39, holding that statute of limitations begins to run from time of committing the misconduct; Cohrs v. Fraser, 5 S. C. 351, holding that where goods held for safe-keeping are destroyed, the statute begins to run at latest from time of notice of loss and not from time of demand; Hemming v. Zimmerschitte, 4 Tex. 159, holding that statute begins to run from time party indicates his intention to refuse compliance with obligation of contract; Estes v. Stokes, 2 Rich. L. 133, holding that statute will run in favor of a private agent to collect and pay over money from the time he collects it.

— **Action for negligence.**

Cited in Sinclair v. Bank of South Carolina, 2 Strobh. L. 344, holding th statute begins to run from time of negligence, and not from the time of t loss thereby occasioned.

Cited in reference note in 29 A. S. R. 120, on limitation of actions for neg gence or tort.

Cited in note in 12 L.R.A.(N.S.) 1006, as to when limitations commence run against action for negligence or misconduct of attorney in performance professional duties.

34 AM. DEC. 590, STUCKY v. CLYBURN, CHEVES, L. 186.

Warranty against patent defects.

Cited in Butz v. Manwiller, 2 Woodw. Dec. 260, holding that, under a gener warranty that a mare is sound, jury should ascertain manifest defects whi must not have been contemplated by parties.

Cited in reference notes in 35 A. S. R. 490, on liability on express warrant 41 A. D. 217, on express warranty as covering open defects known to purchase 52 A. D. 343; 75 A. D. 743,—on purchaser's knowledge of existence of defe as exempting seller from liability on express warranty of soundness.

Cited in note in 12 L.R.A.(N.S.) 84, as to whether warranty extends obvious defects in animal or slave.

Parol evidence as to terms of written agreement.

Cited in note in 19 L.R.A.(N.S.) 1194, on right to show parol warranty connection with contract of sale of personalty.

Distinguished in Rapley v. Klugh, 40 S. C. 134, 18 S. E. 680, holding agr ment expressed in short and incomplete terms explainable by parol eviden consistent with it.

34 AM. DEC. 593, STATE v. CHAMBLYSS, CHEVES, L. 220.

Meaning of "tavern."

Cited in Re Schneider, 11 Or. 288, holding that terms "barroom" and "drin ing shop" mean a house licensed to sell liquors in small quantities to be dru on the spot.

Cited in note in 35 A. D. 137, on what is a tavern.

34 AM. DEC. 599, BENTHAM v. SMITH, CHEVES, EQ. 33.

Quantum of estate for life with power of appointment annexed.

Cited in Wilson v. Gaines, 9 Rich. Eq. 420, holding that a conveyance slaves to a trustee for the sole use of a married woman during her natur life, and subject to her disposal at death, conveys a life estate to such marri woman with power of appointment; McCullough v. Anderson, 90 Ky. 126, L.R.A. 836, 13 S. W. 353, holding that where an estate is given to a pers for life and annexes a power of disposal, an estate in fee is not thereby co veyed.

Cited in notes in 41 A. D. 704, on interest of donee in power of appointmen 41 A. D. 705, on interest vested in donee by unexecuted power of appointment.

Power to appoint by will.

Distinguished in Manning v. Screven, 56 S. C. 78, 34 S. E. 22, holding th the power to appoint to uses conferred by trust deed may be executed in mortgage.

Execution of power of appointment.

Cited in Andrews v. Roye, 12 Rich. L. 536, holding that a power to alien i particular mode must be pursued strictly; Bilderback v. Boyce, 14 S. C. 5 holding a devise of "all the rest and residue of my estate wherever and wh ever" no execution of a power; Humphrey v. Campbell, 59 S. C. 39, 37 S. 20, holding same as to an instruction to an executor to pay certain debts.

Cited in reference note in 25 A. S. R. 901, on exercise of power of appoi ment in will.

Cited in notes in 64 L.R.A. 909, on validity of attempt to exercise by d power of appointment limited to will; 21 E. R. C. 396, on equitable aid in spect to defectively executed powers.

34 AM. DEC. 602, PALMER v. MILLER, CHEVES, EQ. 62.

Allowance for improvements made by an administrator or executor.

Cited in Trimmier v. Darden, 61 S. C. 220, 39 S. E. 373, holding neces improvements and repairs made in good judgment and which benefited estate of remainderman allowable to administratrix.

34 AM. DEC. 605, DUNCAN v. TOBIN, CHEVES, EQ. 143.

Liability of executor or administrator for interest.

Cited in reference notes in 60 A. D. 478, on liability for interest; 39 A. 493; 60 A. D. 181,—as to when executor is chargeable with interest.

Computation of interest chargeable to administrator.

Cited in Pettus v. Clawson, 4 Rich. Eq. 92, holding that all funds received the current year should be regarded as unproductive until the close of it, and the expenditures in the course of the year should be regarded as made bef balance is struck, to bear interest.

Verification of account by administrator.

Cited in Buerhaus v. De Saussure, 41 S. C. 457, 19 S. E. 926, holding t all accounts must be verified by affidavit as to their accuracy, and must con the details of the account.

Burden of proof on accounting party.

Distinguished in Devereux v. McCrady, 53 S. C. 382, 31 S. E. 294, hold that, in an accounting between debtor and creditor, it is the duty of the credi to state and prove his claims, and of debtor to state and prove payments, counts, and counterclaims.

34 AM. DEC. 608, PRICE v. PRICE, CHEVES, EQ. 167.

Implied agreement to pay for services of relative.

Cited in reference notes in 72 A. D. 347, on value of son's services recovera from father's estate; 67 A. D. 432, on presumption of promise to pay services between members of same families.

Cited in notes in 53 A. D. 306, as to when services are deemed gratuitio and no promise implied to pay therefor; 11 L.R.A.(N.S.) 892, on rebuttal of p sumption as to gratuitous character of services by relative or member household by proof of agreement to remunerate them.

Limitations against contingent contract.

Cited in Callum v. Rice, 35 S. C. 551, 15 S. E. 268, holding that where o makes a binding contract to do a certain thing upon a future contingent ev limitation does not run until the event happens; Cann v. Cann, 40 W. Va. 138, 20 S. E. 910, holding that where a right of action on a contract does not run until death of promisor, statute does not commence to run until that time.

Cited in note in 6 L.R.A.(N.S.) 703, on right to recover for services rendered beyond statutory period of limitation on breach of parol contract to make provision by will.

34 AM. DEC. 613, CROSTHWAIT v. ROSS, 1 HUMPH. 23.

Authority of partner to bind firm.

Cited in Venable v. Levick, 2 Head, 351, holding that contract must be incident to or appropriate to the partnership business; Gavin v. Walker, 14 Lea, 643, holding that a partner can bind his copartner in a matter which, according to the usual course of dealing, has reference to the business transacted by the firm; Pooley v. Whitmore, 10 Heisk. 629, 27 A. R. 733, holding that firm note must have been given within scope of business, or usage of trade, or dealing of the particular firm; Ferguson v. Shepherd, 1 Sneed, 254, holding note not binding if given by one partner in the name of the firm in a transaction unconnected with its business, if that fact is known by party taking it; Third Nat. Bank v. Snyder, 10 Mo. App. 211, denying right of one member of a firm of coffee brokers to bind firm by a note; Lee v. First Nat. Bank, 45 Kan. 8, 11 L.R.A. 238, 25 Pac. 196, holding same as to a member of a copartnership formed for the purpose of carrying on a real estate, loan, and insurance business.

Cited in reference notes in 52 A. D. 570; 72 A. D. 323,—on power to bind copartner; 99 A. D. 521, on power to bind copartners by contract; 65 A. S. R. 572, on power of one partner to bind firm.

Cited in notes in 19 E. R. C. 438, on authority of partner to bind partnership; 13 A. D. 117, on partner's power to bind firm on note negotiated for its benefit.

— Nontrading firms.

Cited in Horn v. Newton City Bank, 32 Kan. 518, 4 Pac. 1022; Pease v. Cole, 53 Conn. 53, 55 A. R. 53, 22 Atl. 681,—holding that, in case of a nontrading partnership, there is no implied authority in a partner to bind partnership by a note; National State Capital Bank v. Noyes, 62 N. H. 35, holding that the burden is upon the holder of a note given by a member of a nontrading partnership to prove authority, necessity, or usage; Alley v. Bowen-Merrill Co. 76 Ark. 4, 113 A. S. R. 73, 88 S. W. 838, 6 A. & E. Ann. Cas. 127, sustaining the authority of one member of a partnership for the practice of law to purchase such law books in firm name as are reasonably necessary in the firm's business; Anderson v. Binford, 2 Baxt. 310, on authority of nontrading partners as to notes in firm name.

Cited in note in 48 A. S. R. 441, 442, as to when nontrading partnership is bound by loan effected by one member.

Distinguished in Smith v. Sloan, 37 Wis. 285, 19 A. R. 757, holding that one partner in a nontrading partnership cannot bind his copartner by a note in firm name.

Interest of partners in partnership effects.

Cited in reference note in 65 A. D. 798, on interest of partners in partnership effects.

Form of plea to deny that note is a firm obligation.

Cited in Johl v. Fernberger, 10 Heisk. 37, holding that a plea of *non est*

factum is a proper plea where the defendant intends to deny he is a memb
of the firm in whose name a contract is executed.

34 AM. DEC. 616, ELLEDGE v. TODD, 1 HUMPH. 43.

Grounds for setting aside verdict.

Cited in reference note in 39 A. D. 180, on vacation of verdicts for irregula
ties on part of jury.

Cited in note in 35 A. D. 260, on misconduct of jurors in mode of arrivi
at verdict as ground for new trial.

— Average or chance verdicts.

Cited in Manix v. Malony, 7 Iowa, 81; Wright v. Mississippi & I. Teleg.
20 Iowa, 195; Parham v. Harney, 6 Smedes & M. 55,—holding that agreem
that each juror should put down a sum, and that this sum divided by twe
should be the amount, avoided the verdict; Barton v. Holmes, 16 Iowa, 2
holding same where there is an agreement to be bound by the results; Harv
v. Jones, 3 Humph. 157, holding use of a gambling device as an experiment
ascertain the amount, which, if satisfactory, may be returned as a verdict, val.

Cited in reference notes in 63 A. D. 80, on validity of verdicts reached
average or chance; 31 A. S. R. 432, on invalidity of compromise verdict.

Cited in note in 11 L.R.A. 706, on validity of chance verdicts.

Distinguished in Johnson v. Perry, 2 Humph. 569, holding average arrived
by quotient and used as basis for agreement, valid.

Affidavit of jurors to impeach verdict.

Cited in Harris v. State, 24 Neb. 803, 40 N. W. 317; Joyce v. State, 7 B
273; Norris v. State, 3 Humph. 333, 39 A. D. 175,—holding that, upon a moti
for a new trial, it is competent to produce affidavits of jurors to prove fa
which will vitiate their verdict; McBean v. State, 83 Wis. 206, 53 N. W. 4
holding same to show jury agreed to verdict only after receiving assurance
trial judge that clemency of court would be made to defendant; Perry v. Bail
12 Kan. 539, holding affidavits admissible to show one of jurors was dru
during deliberation; Moses v. Central Park & E. R. Co. 3 Misc. 322, 23 N.
Supp. 23, holding that a quotient verdict involves misconduct on the part of t
juror, and therefore the affidavits are inadmissible to impeach the verdict.

Cited in reference notes in 37 A. D. 600, on right of jurors to impea
verdict; 24 A. D. 475; 34 A. D. 657; 36 A. D. 534; 63 A. D. 80; 37 A. S.
833,—on impeachment of verdict by affidavit of juror; 40 A. D. 169, on a
davits of jurors to impeach or sustain their verdict.

Disapproved in Bishop v. State, 9 Ga. 121, holding that the affidavit of
juror will not be admitted to impeach his verdict.

34 AM. DEC. 618, WILKS v. FITZPATRICK, 1 HUMPH. 54.

Wife's equity of settlement.

Cited in Scobey v. Waters, 10 Lea, 551, holding that, before chancery w
order the estate of the wife paid to the husband, a suitable provision will
made for her unless she waives such right on an examination under directi
of that court; Jennings v. Jennings, 2 Heisk. 283, holding where money of w
is obtained by the husband by a privy examination of the wife during infan
and she permits it to remain with husband after she comes of age and to be u
by him, that she cannot complain.

Cited in reference note in 56 A. D. 736, on wife's equity of settlement.

Assignment of an equitable right of a feme covert.

Cited in Coppedge v. Threadgill, 3 Sneed, 577, holding that equitable right of a married woman in property before it has been reduced to possession by husband can be assigned only on her private examination; Farnsworth v. Lemons, 11 Humph. 140, holding that wife, by joining with her husband in an alienation of a legacy, without having been previously examined privately as to her consent, does not prejudice her rights; Palmer v. Cross, 1 Smedes & M. 48, holding that a conveyance of wife's separate property by husband, she remaining silent, does not devest her interest; Drake v. Glover, 30 Ala. 382, holding that unless silence of wife is fraudulent, the wife is not bound to interpose against her husband when, in her presence, he sells her property.

Distinguished in Bugg v. Franklin, 4 Sneed, 129, holding that a fair and equitable adjustment between the husbands of two married women, joined in by wives, of a contingent interest of both, and possession given and taken accordingly and acquiesced in, is binding.

34 AM. DEC. 619, PARKER v. SWAN, 1 HUMPH. 80.

Certainty in justice's judgment.

Cited in Cowan v. Lowry, 7 Lea, 620; Anderson v. Kimbrough, 5 Coldw. 260,—holding that every intendment by the Code is to be made in favor of proceedings before justices of the peace; Clay v. Clay, 7 Tex. 250, holding that a reasonable certainty and intelligibility only is required in proceeding of such tribunals; Fowler v. Thomsen, 68 Neb. 578, 94 N. W. 810, holding that a marginal entry of taxation of costs shows an intention of justice to enter judgment for costs.

Cited in reference note in 53 A. D. 574, on finality of judgment of justice whose intention to give final judgment is apparent.

Description of land in levy, sheriff's deed, etc.

Cited in Gibbs v. Thompson, 7 Humph. 179, holding that description must be such as to prevent one piece of land being sold and another conveyed; Lente v. Clarke, 22 Fla. 515, 1 So. 149, holding that where description will apply with equal exactness to any one of an indefinite number of tracts, parol evidence is not admissible to designate tract intended; Trotter v. Nelson, 1 Swan, 7, holding valid a levy which is uncertain merely because same person may have other lands, in same district containing same quantity of acres; Wolf v. Plunkett, 1 Flipp. 427, Fed. Cas. No. 17,926, holding same where uncertainty depended on fact of party owning two northwest quarter sections in strip between the old and new state line of Tennessee, each containing 159 acres; Brown v. Dickson, 2 Humph. 395, 37 A. D. 500, holding a levy in the following words, "Levied on lot No. — in the town of Greenville with its improvements," void for uncertainty; Brigance v. Erwin, 1 Swan, 375, 57 A. D. 779, holding void a levy in following words, "Levied 20th August, 1825, on 1,950 acres of land in Henderson county, part of tract of 2,500 acres located by Daniel Gilchrist."

Cited in reference notes in 70 A. D. 318, on sufficiency of description in levy; 38 A. D. 712, on description of property levied upon under execution; 37 A. D. 561, on sufficiency of sheriff's return of execution; 27 A. D. 524, on certainty of description in sheriff's levy, return, or deed; 50 A. D. 705, on sufficiency of description of land in levy or return of execution or in sheriff's deed; 50 A. D. 545, on sufficiency of description of property sold under execution; 41 A. D. 661, on necessity of describing land with reasonable certainty in sheriff's deed.

Distinguished in Riley v. Frost, 2 Shannon Cas. 333, holding a descripti
"100 acres of land the property of R. and F. adjoining lands of J. in fifth
trict," insufficient.

— **How insufficient description cured.**
Distinguished in Helms v. Alexander, 10 Humph. 44, holding that where t
description in a deed is inconsistent and repugnant to the description in lev
it does not cure the defective description in the levy.

Lien of execution.
Cited in Lattimore v. Cowan, 2 Tenn. Ch. App. 459, holding execution issu
by justice of the peace not a lien until levy is made.
Cited in note in 11 E. R. C. 628, as to when lien of writ of execution attach

Title under execution sale by relation to levy.
Cited in Knight v. Ogden, 2 Tenn. Ch. 473, holding that a chattel purcha
under a levy takes title as of date of levy.
Cited in reference note in 44 A. D. 707, 784, on relation of sale to time wh
lien of writ attached.
Cited in notes in 58 A. D. 57, on relation of sheriff's deeds; 15 A. D. 249,
application of doctrine of relation to execution sales.

Record entry of grant of appeal.
Cited in Teasdale v. Manchester Produce Co. 104 Tenn. 267, 56 S. W. 8
holding that an appeal must be granted as well as prayed, and that fact m
appear by a minute entry in the record.

34 AM. DEC. 622, TURBEVILLE v. RYAN, 1 HUMPH. 113.
Authority to bind another by sealed instrument.
Cited in Garrett v. Belmont Land Co. 94 Tenn. 459, 29 S. W. 726, holdi
that a person cannot bind another by seal unless authorized by seal; Kerr
Billingsly, 1 Thomp. Tenn. Cas. 23, 1 Shannon, Cas. 7, holding that authori
to fill in a blank in a sealed instrument can be shown only by deed; Cain
Heard, 1 Coldw. 163; Smith v. Dickinson, 6 Humph. 261, 44 A. D. 306,—holdi
that no parol assent or subsequent adoption will bind party unless the inst
ment be acknowledged and redelivered.
Cited in reference note in 40 A. D. 409, as to how authority to execute d
must be given.
Cited in notes in 2 E. R. C. 280, on necessity of sealed writing to authori
agent to execute deed; 8 E. R. C. 630, on necessity that power of attorney
execute deed be under seal.

— **As between partners.**
Cited in McNutt v. McMahan, 1 Head, 98; Mosby v. Arkansas, 4 Sneed, 32
Napier v. Catron, 2 Humph. 534,—holding that one partner has no power to bi
his copartner by deed unless he be expressly so authorized by deed.
Cited in reference notes in 48 A. S. R. 74, on sale and conveyance of realty
one partner; 40 A. D. 551, on right of partner to bind firm by instrument und
seal; 55 A. D. 343, on power of partner to bind copartner by deed; 52 A. D. 5:
on necessity of authority under seal to enable one copartner to bind others
note; 60 A. D. 310, on partner's power to bind copartners by instrument und
seal if they assent thereto before execution or ratify it afterwards; 38 A.
735, on effect of acceptance of bond of one partner for simple contract debt
firm as release of other partners.

— Delegation of power to municipality.

Cited in reference notes in 33 A. S. R. 846, on delegation of police power municipalities; 90 A. D. 283; 53 A. S. R. 331,—on delegation of legislati powers to municipal corporations; 21 A. S. R. 374, on power of legislature delegate authority to municipal corporations.

Cited in notes in 81 A. D. 671, on legislature's right to delegate to muni palities, power to enact ordinances; 74 A. D. 593, on delegation of taxi power to municipal and public corporations.

Validity of a privilege tax.

Cited in Pullman Southern Car Co. v. Nolan, 22 Fed. 276, holding that t legislature may tax any occupation or business which it may prohibit all gether.

Cited in reference notes in 33 A. S. R. 821, on validity of license taxes; A. S. R. 305, on imposition of license fee on business or occupation; 27 A. R. 445; 31 A. S. R. 773,—on municipal power to tax occupations; 52 A. S. 246, on imposition of license tax on street car companies by municipal corp rations.

Cited in note in 2 L.R.A. 284, on municipal taxation of occupations.

Mode of exercise of a municipal power.

Cited in Jacksonville v. Ledwith, 26 Fla. 163, 23 A. S. R. 558, 9 L.R.A. 7 So. 885, on power of a city council to act by resolution, citing annotation al to this point.

Annotation cited in McGavock v. Omaha, 40 Neb. 64, 58 N. W. 543, holdi that where a city is invested with power to regulate certain matters and mo of exercise of such power is not prescribed, the council may act by resolutio Crawfordsville v. Braden, 130 Ind. 149, 30 A. S. R. 214, 14 L.R.A. 268, 28 E. 849, holding where city council is given power to act but manner is n prescribed, it may act either by resolution or ordinance.

By-laws of private corporations.

Cited in notes in 85 A. D. 618, on what by-laws private corporation ag gate may adopt; 7 E. R. C. 288, on reasonableness or validity of by-laws ma by private corporation.

34 AM. DEC. 644, LAWRENCE v. STATE, 1 HUMPH. 228.

Possession and taking in larceny.

Cited in Pritchett v. State, 2 Sneed, 285, 62 A. D. 468, holding that, to co stitute larceny, the goods at the time of taking must be in the actual or co structive possession of some one.

Cited in reference notes in 38 A. D. 250, on allegation of property in indi ment for larceny; 96 A. D. 769, on possession of owner as element of larcen 43 A. D. 650, on larceny by taking goods from constructive possession owner.

Cited in notes in 88 A. S. R. 592, on larceny of lost property; 57 A. D. 2 on larceny by finders of lost goods or estrays; 88 A. S. R. 567, on trespass case of lost goods as element of larceny.

Distinguished in Griggs v. State, 58 Ala. 425, 29 A. R. 762, holding one w carried away a sack of coffee found in a public road, and who knew when took it who owner was, guilty of larceny.

What is lost property.

Cited in Sovern v. Yoran, 16 Or. 269, 8 A. S. R. 293, 20 Pac. 100, holdi

that money hidden in the earth for safe-keeping is not lost; Ferguson v.
44 Or. 557, 102 A. S. R. 648, 1 L.R.A.(N.S.) 477, 77 Pac. 600, 1 A. & E. /
Cas. 1, holding same as to a quartz rock bearing gold found embedded in
ground unconnected with any natural mineral deposit, though rock had ap
ently been in a cloth sack; Livermore v. White, 74 Me. 452, 43 A. R.
holding hides which owner failed to remove from vat not lost; Deaderick
Oulds, 86 Tenn. 14, 6 A. S. R. 812, 5 S. W. 487, holding that unmarked 1
which floated away from owner's land two years before was lost.

Cited in reference note in 93 A. D. 143, on property put in particular pla
but forgotten by owner as lost property.

Cited in note in 37 L.R.A. 121, on what property is lost within rule as
rights and liabilities of finder.

Distinguished in Durfee v. Jones, 11 R. I. 588, 23 A. R. 528, holding th
property having slipped from the place where deposited without knowledge
true owner is lost.

Rights in lost property.

Cited in Loucks v. Gallogly, 1 Misc. 22, 23 N. Y. Supp. 126, holding th
money left on a desk of a bank is not lost, so as to give finder thereof right
same as against the bank; Gleason v. Sanitary Milk Supply Co. 11 Alle
544, holding that a stranger who first discovered a pocketbook accidental
left on a table in a barber shop is not entitled to hold the same as again
shopkeeper; Hoagland v. Forest Park Highlands Amusement Co. 170 Mo. 3
94 A. S. R. 740, 70 S. W. 878, holding that finder of a pocketbook found
the ground under a table at an open-air place of amusement and refreshme
is entitled to it against all persons except the real owner.

Cited in reference note in 87 A. D. 735, on right to possession of proper
accidentally laid down at store or house and uncalled for.

Distinguished in Kuykendall v. Fisher, 61 W. Va. 87, 8 L.R.A.(N.S.) 94,
S. E. 48, 11 A. & E. Ann. Cas. 700, holding that the finder of treasure-tro
is entitled to possession thereof as against all the world but the true owner.

Replevin as a possessory action.

Cited in note in 11 L.R.A. 172, on replevin as a possessory action.

34 AM. DEC. 646, COLUMBIA v. BEASLEY, 1 HUMPH. 232.

Unreasonable ordinances and regulations.

Cited in Smith v. Knoxville, 3 Head, 245, holding that a city ordinance m
be reasonable and not oppressive; Bennett v. Pulaski (Tenn.) 47 L.R.A. 2
52 S. W. 913, holding that an ordinance making it a misdemeanor to let
person in or out of a saloon during hours when saloon is required to be clo
is unreasonable.

Cited in reference note in 90 A. D. 283, as to valid exercise of police pow
by municipal corporations.

Cited in notes in 41 L. ed. U. S. 520, on reasonableness of municipal or
nances; 2 L.R.A. 723, on necessity that municipal ordinances be reasonab!
34 A. D. 634, on invalidity of unreasonable municipal ordinances; 35 A.
703, on validity of ordinances regulating business; 30 L.R.A. 436, on what i
positions of license fees of municipalities are reasonable; 7 E. R. C. 2
on reasonableness or validity of by-law made by private corporation.

Mode of assessing municipal privilege tax.

Cited in Adams v. Somerville, 2 Head, 363, holding that where mayor a

alderman are authorized by charter "to license, tax, and regulate" negro tr
ers, the mode of state taxation need not necessarily be followed; Nashvi
v. Althrop, 5 Coldw. 554, holding same as to a tax upon the mercantile pri
lege, where such is authorized by charter.

Validity of a privilege tax.

Cited in Pullman Southern Car Co. v. Nolan, 22 Fed. 276, holding that t
legislature may tax any occupation or business which it may prohibit al
gether; State v. Harrington, 68 Vt. 622, 34 L.R.A. 100, 35 Atl. 515, s
taining a statute imposing a license tax on itinerant vendors.

Cited in notes in 30 L.R.A. 415, on power to fix license fees; 30 L.R.A.
on right of municipal corporations to discriminate as to license fees.

Statutory proceedings.

Cited in Moore v. Lynch, 4 Baxt. 287, holding that there is no presumpti
in favor of a new and special jurisdiction.

34 AM. DEC. 648, JENKINS v. ATKINS, 1 HUMPH. 294.

Personal liability of agent acting without authority.

Cited in note in 48 A. S. R. 916, on personal liability to third persons
agent assuming without authority to make contract for corporation.

Revocation of agency by death of principal.

Cited in Vance v. Anderson, 39 Iowa, 426, holding that acts of agent do
after death of principal, though in ignorance of it and in good faith, are voi
Long v. Thayer, 150 U. S. 520, 37 L. ed. 1167, 14 Sup. Ct. Rep. 189, holdi
payments made to agent after death of principal, and in ignorance of th
fact, not sufficient to discharge obligation to estate of principal.

Cited in reference notes in 12 A. S. R. 29, on revocation of agency
death; 37 A. D. 196, on principal's death as revoking agent's authority.

Cited in notes in 23 L.R.A. 710, on effect on contract of agency of death
party thereto; 39 A. D. 88, on validity of agent's act where parties a
ignorant of principal's death.

Distinguished in Ish v. Crane, 13 Ohio St. 574; Ish v. Crane, 8 Ohio St. 520,
holding heirs estopped where possession of land is given by attorney in fa
and part of purchase money paid in ignorance of principal's death, and resid
of purchase money is paid heirs on demand.

Mutuality in contracts.

Cited in Wilkinson v. Harwell, 13 Ala. 660, holding that a court of equi
will not specifically enforce a contract unless it is mutually binding.

34 AM. DEC. 650, TUCKER v. ATKINSON, 1 HUMPH. 300.

Execution, or attachment on money held by an officer.

Cited in Russell v. Millett, 20 Wash. 212, 55 Pac. 44, holding that whe
case is settled, and a receiver has no further duty other than to turn over t
money and property held by him to parties entitled thereto, the property
his hands is liable to execution.

Cited in reference notes in 42 A. D. 362, on right to attach money
sheriff's hands; 69 A. D. 768, on right to attach or garnish money in t
custody of the law.

Cited in note in 55 A. D. 264, as to whether money in officer's hands is su
ject to attachment.

— **On surplus money in hands of sheriff.**

Cited in Wheeler v. Smith, 11 Barb. 345; Mays v. Frazer, 3 Tenn. Ch. 413, holding that surplus funds in hands of sheriff, which he is bound to pay to d fendant in execution, may be attached.

Cited in reference note in 85 A. D. 296, on attachment or garnishment surplus money in sheriff's hands after satisfaction of execution.

Distinguished in Drane v. McGavock, 7 Humph. 131, holding clerk of court not liable to garnishment for money in his hands, which he holds su ject to order of court; Lightner v. Steinagel, 33 Ill. 510, 85 A. D. 292, hol ing that redemption money in hands of sheriff is not subject to execution.

34 AM. DEC. 652, PIPKIN v. JAMES, 1 HUMPH. 325.

Sufficiency of memorandum of sale of real estate.

Cited in Munk v. Weidner, 9 Tex. Civ. App. 491, 29 S. W. 409, holdin that if what parties assented to can be gathered from the writing it is su ficient; McCarty v. Kyle, 4 Coldw. 348, holding that the terms of the contrac must appear; McConnell v. Brillhart, 17 Ill. 354, 65 A. D. 661; Sheid Stamps, 2 Sneed, 172,—holding that the sale, its terms, the designation the parties, and the land sold must be stated with reasonable certainty.

Cited in reference notes in 66 A. D. 549; 67 A. D. 505,—on sufficiency memorandum under statute of frauds; 58 A. D. 213, on sufficiency of mem randum of contract for sale of land under statute of frauds; 65 A. D. 668, o general requisites of memorandum required by statute of frauds.

Cited in note in 11 L.R.A. 97, on essentials of memorandum of agreemen to authorize specific performance.

— **Description of land.**

Cited in Gudger v. Barnes, 4 Heisk. 570, holding that contract must descri lands so as to distinguish them from other lands; Johnson v. Kellogg, Heisk. 262, holding that description must enable court to determine wit reasonable certainty what property is embraced; Seifreid v. People's Bank, Tenn. Ch. 17, holding an assignment for benefit of creditors conveying "all th lands and tenements, etc., of every nature and description" not sufficient.

Recovery of money paid on parol executory contract to convey land.

Cited in Sheid v. Stamps, 2 Sneed, 172, holding that money paid on a con tract void under the statute of frauds may be recovered in assumpsit; Vaugh v. Vaughn, 100 Tenn. 282, holding that, on repudiation of a voidable sale o real property, vendee may recover purchase money paid with interest.

Distinguished in Hurst v. Means, 2 Swan, 594, holding that an action fo money had and received will not lie by vendee against vendor to recover pur chase money paid, where vendor has broken a valid contract to convey.

Right of rescission for want of title in vendor.

Cited in McClure v. Harris, 7 Heisk. 379; Nichol v. Nichol, 4 Baxt. 145, holding that purchaser is not bound to proceed to execute an executory con tract, where, by reason of defects not previously disclosed, the vendor cannot mak a title free from doubt; Topp v. White, 12 Heisk. 165, holding that where vendo at time of sale has no title, either legal or equitable, which fact he conceals, th vendee may have a rescission though afterwards vendor acquires title which offers to convey; Hurley v. Brown, 98 Mass. 545, 96 A. D. 671, holding that i such case specific performance will not be granted in favor of vendor.

Distinguished in Dresel v. Jordan, 104 Mass. 407, holding that if vendor i

able in season to comply with requirements of contract to make good t
title which he has undertaken to convey, it is sufficient.

Recovery of price paid to vendor of land without title.

Cited in reference note in 47 A. D. 732, on assumpsit for money paid
executory contract to convey lands where title defective.

Cited in note in 52 A. D. 760, on recovery on count for money had and
ceived of money paid on consideration which has failed.

Disapproved in Getchell v. Chase, 37 N. H. 106, holding that, in the abser
of fraud, money paid as consideration for a quitclaim deed cannot be
covered.

Parol contract for sale of land.

Cited in note in 39 A. D. 762, on statute of frauds.

Questioned in Citty v. Southern Queen Mfg. Co. 93 Tenn. 276, 42 A. S.
919, 24 S. W. 121; Brakefield v. Anderson, 87 Tenn. 206, 10 S. W. 360,—ho
ing a parol contract for the sale of land is voidable only.

Effect of payment of money on parol sale of land.

Cited in Jennings v. Bishop, 3 Shannon Cas. 138, holding payment of p
chase money not sufficient to take contract out of statute.

34 AM. DEC. 655, BENNETT v. BAKER, 1 HUMPH. 399.

Quotient or average verdicts.

Cited in Joyce v. State, 7 Baxt. 273, holding quotient verdict ground for n
trial; Columbus v. Ogletree, 102 Ga. 293, 29 S. E. 749, holding the mere fa
that papers found in jury room tend to show that they had figured for a quotie
verdict, not sufficient evidence on which to grant a new trial; Moses v. Centr
Park & E. R. Co. 3 Misc. 322, holding that if a proposed verdict is found by taki
one twelfth of the aggregate amount, and this is afterwards assented to, t
verdict is good.

Cited in reference note in 63 A. D. 80, on validity of verdicts reached
average or chance.

Affidavit of juror to impeach verdict.

Cited in Norris v. State, 3 Humph. 333, 39 A. D. 175, holding that t
affidavit of a juror that he misunderstood the charge of the judge cannot
received and heard on motion for a new trial.

Cited in reference notes in 37 A. D. 600, on right of jurors to impeach v
dict; 34 A. D. 617; 36 A. D. 534; 63 A. D. 80,—on affidavits of jurors to i
peach verdict.

Cited in note in 24 A. D. 475, on affidavits of jurors to impeach their v
dict.

Distinguished in Rumford Chemical Works v. Finnie, 2 Flipp. 459, Fe
Cas. No. 12,130, holding affidavits of jurors inadmissible to show mode
computation adopted by jury.

34 AM. DEC. 657, HUMES v. KNOXVILLE, 1 HUMPH. 403.

Duties and liabilities of a municipality as to streets.

Cited in McHarge v. Newcomer, 117 Tenn. 595, 9 L.R.A.(N.S.) 298, 100
W. 700; Smith v. East End Street R. Co. 87 Tenn. 26, 11 S. W. 709,—holdi
that municipal authorities hold the streets in trust for the public; Nashvil
v. Brown, 9 Heisk. 1, 24 A. R. 289, holding that a municipal corporation

proprietor of the streets; State v. Taylor, 107 Tenn. 455, 64 S. W. 766, holding that fee to land covered by streets remains in original owner and his vendees; Simmons v. Camden, 26 Ark. 276, 7 A. R. 620; Iron Mountain R. Co. v. Bingham, 87 Tenn. 522, 11 S. W. 705,—holding that municipal corporation incurs no liability to abutting lot owners, where corporation in a lawful and prudent manner exercises the power of improving its streets.

Cited in reference notes in 36 A. D. 210, on power of municipal corporation over streets; 96 A. D. 252, on right of municipal corporations to control their streets; 52 A. D. 487, on right of municipality to authorize obstruction of streets.

—Injuries in grading and improving streets.

Cited in Chattanooga v. Neely, 97 Tenn. 527, 37 S. W. 281, on same point; Nashville v. Sutherland, 92 Tenn. 335, 36 A. S. R. 88, 19 L.R.A. 619, 21 S. W. 674, holding that a city in constructing a sewer is liable only for want of reasonable care and skill in execution of work; Smith v. St. Louis Mut. L. Ins. Co. 3 Tenn. Ch. 631, holding that damage to property by reason of elevation or depression of a street is *damnum absque injuria;* Pontiac v. Carter, 32 Mich. 164; Creal v. Keokuk, 4 G. Greene, 47,—holding city not liable for damages growing out of a proper exercise of power to grade streets; Memphis v. Lasser, 9 Humph. 757, holding municipality liable for the negligent maintenance of its streets; Burton v. Chattanooga, 7 Lea, 739, holding municipal corporation liable where it cut ditches and canals for conveyance of water in such a manner as to flood private property; Vanderlip v. Grand Rapids, 73 Mich. 522, 16 A. S. R. 597, 3 L.R.A. 247, 41 N. W. 672, holding city liable for damages where earth from graded street slid onto adjoining property; Smith v. Alexandria, 33 Gratt. 208, 36 A. R. 788, holding municipal corporation liable for damage done by water thrown back by filling up a street, where by proper care and means the damage might have been prevented.

Cited in reference notes in 55 A. D. 90, on power of municipality to grade or regrade street; 51 A. D. 458, as to when municipality is liable for injuries resulting from grading streets; 12 A. S. R. 362, on municipal liability for damages arising from changes to, improvements in, or grading of, streets.

Cited in notes in 23 L.R.A. 658, on damage to abutting owner by first grading and improvement of street; 14 L.R.A. 371, on injury to abutter's easements by changing grade of street; 26 A. R. 457, on right to enjoin municipality from changing street grade when adjacent land is injured thereby; 30 A S. R. 392, on municipal liability for interference with surface waters by grading streets; 53 A. D. 366, on right to recover for consequential injuries through street improvement authorized by law; 66 A. D. 438, on municipal liability for consequential damages resulting from act done under authority of valid statute or charter.

Distinguished in Hamilton County v. Rape, 101 Tenn. 222, 47 S. W. 416, holding that, where title of abutting owner extends to center of street, he may recover compensation for the impairment of the right of egress and ingress to his lot, occasioned by changing grade of street or road.

Presumptive assent of lot owner to change of grade.

Cited in Montgomery v. Townsend, 84 Ala. 478, 4 So. 780, holding purchaser of property fronting on street conclusively presumed to assent to necessary changes in grade and surface.

Charter as protection for acts of corporation.

Cited in Tennessee & A. R. Co. v. Adams, 3 Head, 596, holding that corpo
tion doing no more than warranted by charter is not a wrongdoer.

Distinguished in Eaton v. Boston, C. & M. R. Co. 51 N. H, 504, 12 A. R. 1
holding a railroad corporation liable where, in cutting away a ridge, it
lowed water during freshets to flood and damage plaintiff's land.

Liability of a corporation for tort or crime.

Cited in Wheless v. Second Nat. Bank, 1 .Baxt. 469, 25 A. R. 783, holding
corporation liable for maliciously suing out an attachment; State v. Bal
more & O. R. Co. 15 W. Va. 362, 36 A. R. 803, holding a corporation lia
for "Sabbath breaking" under the statute.

Distinguished in Pesterfield v. Vickers, 3 Coldw. 205, holding munici
corporation not liable for wrongful acts of its officers.

Liability for abuse of privilege.

Cited in Crawford v. Maxwell, 3 Humph. 476, holding that one who mis
haves while at an inn is liable in trespass.

Cited in note in 8 L.R.A. 809, on right to use of one's own property.

34 AM. DEC. 659, WALLACE v. HANNUM, 1 HUMPH. 443.

Effect of adverse possession to create title.

Cited in Hopkins v. Calloway, 7 Coldw. 37, Thomp. Tenn. Cas. 282, holdi
that statute barring action, bars the remedy only, but does not confer a ti
on the adverse holder; McLain v. Ferrell, 1 Swan, 48, holding that a stat
protecting a party in possession after a certain period of possession vests ti
in adverse possessor; Earnest v. Little River Land & Lumber Co. 109 Te
427, 75 S. W. 1122, holding that adverse occupant takes a perfect title und
statute; Norris v. Ellis, 7 Humph. 463, holding that seven years' possessi
of land under a bond for title does not vest such a title in the purchaser
can be taken in execution; Coal Creek Consol. Coal Co. v. East Tennessee Ir
& Coal Co. 105 Tenn. 563, 59 S. W. 634, holding that, where three grants
different dates have a common interlap, adverse holding under the young
grant will extinguish elder grant of land within common interlap; Sanders
Everett, 3 Tenn. Ch. 520, holding that possession under a parol sale for mo
than seven years will protect possessor in amount of land inclosed.

Cited in reference note in 61 A. D. 305, on necessity of existence of adver
possession for prescribed period to toll owner's right of entry.

Cited in note in 34 A. D. 664, on title acquired by seven years' possessi
under bonds for title.

— Sufficiency of possession.

Cited in reference note in 53 A. D. 726, on sufficiency of possession requir
by statute of limitations to bar action.

— Necessity of color of title.

Cited in notes in 14 A. D. 765, as to necessity of color of title to obtain tit
by adverse possession; 15 L.R.A.(N.S.) 1183, 1260, on necessity of color of tit
when not expressly made a condition by statute to found title by adverse po
session.

— Break in possession.

Cited in reference note in 62 A. D. 296, on right of grantee or heir of one pr
tected by statute of limitations to same protection.

Cited in note in 15 L.R.A.(N.S.) 1204, on unbroken continuity as essenti
element in adverse possession.

— **Tacking adverse possessions.**

Cited in Erck v.. Church, 87 Tenn. 575, 4 L.R.A. 641, 11 S. W. 794, holdi
that where there is no privity of estate or privity of contract conveying su
possessory right, possessions cannot be tacked.

Distinguished in Marr v. Gilliam, 1 Coldw. 488, holding that where pos
sion of party is adverse, he may transfer his right by deed to one who m
continue to hold adversely for unexpired part of seven years and bar action.

34 AM. DEC. 664, SMITHEAL v. GRAY, 1 HUMPH. 491.

Resulting trust from payment of purchase money.

Cited in Brown v. Bigley, 3 Tenn. Ch. 618, on resulting trust arising fro
the payment of the purchase money.

Cited in reference notes in 52 A. D. 144, as to when resulting trusts ari
36 A. D. 166, on trust resulting in favor of party paying consideration;
A. D. 46, on resulting trust in favor of party furnishing consideration for la
conveyed; 65 A. D. 501, on resulting trust in favor of one paying considerati
where conveyance is taken in name of another; 67 A. D. 630, on presumpti
of advancement in purchase by parent in child's name; 43 A. D. 288, on s
ficiency of declaration of trust.

Distinguished in Lockhard v. Brodie, 1 Tenn. Ch. 384, holding that the p
sumption of a resulting trust which arises from payment of purchase mon
may be rebutted.

— **Establishment of by parol.**

Cited in reference notes in 47 A. D. 532; 50 A. D. 624; 63 A. D. 423,
right to prove resulting trust by parol; 57 A. D. 618, on parol evidence
show resulting trust from purchase of land.

Cited in notes in 34 L. ed. U. S. 1095, on proof of resulting trust by paro
11 E. R. C. 232, on parol evidence to engraft resulting trust.

Execution against resulting trust.

Cited in Hershy v. Latham, 42 Ark. 305; Turley v. Massengill, 7 Lea, 35
State v. Miller, 11 Lea, 620; Butler v. Rutledge, 2 Coldw. 4,—holding that a
sulting trust is subject to sale and execution at law; Thomas v. Walker,
Humph. 93, holding that a resulting trust is subject to execution, and is t
affected by judgments against holder of legal title; Martin v. Lincoln, 4
334, holding that in such a case a judgment against the beneficiary is a li
on the land; Gaugh v. Henderson, 2 Head, 628, on execution against an equ
table interest in property.

Cited in reference note in 24 A. D. 436, on resulting trust as subject of lev
and sale.

Cited in note in 97 A. D. 308, on interest of beneficiary under resulting tru
being subject to execution.

Equities of creditors of trustee of resulting trust.

Cited in Gass v. Gass, 1 Heisk, 613, holding that the right of a beneficia
in a resulting trust arising because of payments of purchase price with mon
of another is preferred to that of creditors of trustee.

Cited in note in 67 L.R.A. 887, on effect as to creditors on legal title of co
veyance of land purchased and paid for by debtor, but conveyed to anoth
in fraud of creditors.

Defense of innocent purchaser.

Cited in Newman v. Schwerin, 48 C. C. A. 742, 100 Fed. 942, holding th the defense of innocent purchaser for value in good faith must be explici made by plea or answer; Livingston v. Noe, 1 Lea, 55, holding that defer cannot be had where purchase money has not actually been paid; Reeves Hager, 101 Tenn. 712, 50 S. W. 760, holding that where the equities betwe an innocent purchaser and heirs are equal, the purchaser must support equity with a legal title.

Cited in reference notes in 62 A. D. 647, on rights of purchaser of trust pr erty; 52 A. D. 384, on allegation necessary to protect one as an innocent p chaser of trust property.

Cited in note in 97 A. D. 435, as to whether and when purchaser of equita title is entitled to protection as purchaser in good faith without notice.

34 AM. DEC. 668, HUMPHREY v. DOUGLASS, 11 VT. 22.

Injury to trespassing animals set at large.

Cited in reference note in 30 A. S. R. 427, on rights and liability of l owner as to trespassing animals.

Cited in note in 49 A. D. 259, on liability for injury to trespassing anim while removing them.

Distinguished in Russell v. Hanley, 20 Iowa, 219, 89 A. D. 535, holding th one who wilfully leaves open a gate through which cattle pass upon a railro track is liable for injury to cattle.

Effect of bad motive.

Cited in notes in 62 L.R.A. 604, on effect of bad motive to make actiona an injury to property which otherwise would not be; 62 L.R.A. 676, on eff of bad motive to make actionable acts in exercise of rights without interf ence with legal rights of others.

34 AM. DEC. 669, NIMS v. ROOD, 11 VT. 96.

What subject to set-off.

Cited in reference note in 45 A. D. 137, 667, as to what demands are subje to set-off.

Cited in note in 47 A. S. R. 588, on set-off against insolvent estate of decede

— Equitable set-off.

Cited in Smith v. Wainwright, 24 Vt. 97, holding that sureties on note pa able to estate by insolvents may have it set off against a bond running from cedent to the principals.

Cited in reference note in 43 A. D. 160, on set-off in equity.

— Unliquidated claim as set-off.

Cited in Boyer v. Clark, 3 Neb. 161, holding that a claim sounding merely damages, the recovery of which is still uncertain, cannot be set off.

Cited in reference note in 64 A. D. 234, on unliquidated damages as subje of set-off.

34 AM. DEC. 71, MILTON v. STORY, 11 VT. 101.

Right of third person to enforce contract.

Cited in note in 71 A. S. R. 179, on third person's right to enforce contra for his benefit.

34 AM. DEC. 682, HOUGH v. BIRGE, 11 VT. 190.

Action for use and occupation.

Cited in Watson v. Brainard, 33 Vt. 88; Chamberlin v. Donahue, 44 Vt. 57,— holding that the relation of landlord and tenant must have existed between the parties evidenced by a contract either express or implied; Clark v. Clark, 58 Vt. 527, 3 Atl. 508, holding that father who occupied lands devised to his children during settlement of estate is not liable.

Cited in reference notes in 64 A. D. 113, on action for use and occupation against one holding under contract to purchase, which fell through by no fault of his; 62 A. D. 665, on duty of vendor to account for rents and profits upon rescission of the sale.

Cited in note in 89 A. D. 428, on assumpsit not being proper action to try title.

— Liability of purchaser in possession.

Cited in Way v. Raymond, 16 Vt. 371, holding that one who enters possession under a parol contract to purchase the land is not liable for rent, where vendor fails to procure title he agreed to convey; Kaar's Estate, 2 Pa. Co. Ct 55; Bardsley's Appeal, 20 W. N. C. 90,—holding that where contract has failed through fault of vendor, action will not lie against vendee for use of land preceding default; McNair v. Schwartz, 16 Ill. 24, holding that one who acquires possession of land under a contract for sale, and refuses to perform contract, is not liable; Dwight v. Cutler, 3 Mich. 566, 64 A. D. 105, holding same as to possession by one pending his negotiations for purchase of premises.

34 AM. DEC. 684, STRONG v. BARNES, 11 VT. 221.

Reviewableness of findings of fact.

Cited in Bowman v. Sanborn, 25 N. H. 87, holding finding of trial court without a jury on proper occasion not reviewable.

Cited in reference note in 59 A. D. 320, on finality of trial court's decision on facts.

Implied warranty of title in sale of personal property.

Cited in Shepherd v. Jenkins, 73 Mo. 510, holding that a sale and transfer of an invention and the right to enjoy it "to full end of term of patent" implied that a patent has been issued in due form.

Cited in reference note in 87 A. D. 482, on action for breach of warranty of title to personal property.

Construction of related instruments.

Cited in Rogers v. Bancroft, 20 Vt. 250, holding that partition deeds executed at the same time, and relating to the same subject-matter, are to be construed as one instrument; Wing v. Cooper, 37 Vt. 169, holding same as to a deed and a bond so executed; Weston v. Estey, 22 Colo. 334, 45 Pac. 367, holding same as to a deed to land and a contract in respect to land executed under like circumstances.

Cited in reference notes in 62 A. D. 511, as to when different writings are taken as one instrument; 47 A. D. 337, on different writings on same subject, executed at same time as one instrument.

Distinguished in Doe ex dem. Holman v. Crane, 16 Ala. 570, holding that where subject-matter of each instrument is different, that they will not be construed together.

34 AM. DEC. 685, MOUNTHOLLY v. ANDOVER, 11 VT. 226.

Marriage as a civil contract.

Cited in reference note in 58 A. D. 63, on marriage being civil contract.

Validity of marriage.

Cited in reference note in 16 A. S. R. 572, on necessity of consent to va
marriage.

Cited in notes in 44 A. D. 54, on definition of void marriage; 124 A. S.
111, on consent of parties to common-law marriage; 79 A. S. R. 370, on val
ity of marriage without consent or obtained by force or duress.

Collateral impeachment of a marriage.

Cited in Manchester v. Springfield, 15 Vt. 385, holding that third per
in interest may impeach the validity of a void marriage.

Distinguished in Wiser v. Lockwood, 42 Vt. 720, holding that, the fact of
marriage of a deceased person being established, a probate court must distrib
his property accordingly, though marriage might have been declared void
ground that one of parties was insane.

Annulment of marriage.

Cited in Clark v. Field, 13 Vt. 460, sustaining power of equity to annul
marriage ceremony performed by a justice of the peace, where consent w
not voluntarily given.

Cited in reference note in 58 A. D. 63, on third person's having no right
institute proceedings to annul marriage.

34 AM. DEC. 688, STATE v. BENEDICT, 11 VT. 236.

Breach of the peace under statute.

Cited in State v. Riggs, 22 Vt. 321, holding that breach of peace under t
statute is assault and battery or other kindred acts calculated to put one
fear of bodily harm and disturbing the quiet, repose, rest, and comfort of soci
life; State v. Barrows, 57 Vt. 576, holding that a criminal complaint ch
ging an assault and battery with force and arms is a charge of breach of t
peace; State v. Coffin, 64 Vt. 25, 23 Atl. 632, holding same as to a charge
firing guns, blowing horns, and beating tin pans, and other unnecessary and
fensive noise, though committed in daytime; Neola v. Reichart, 131 Iowa, 4
109 N. W. 5, holding that any riotous or forcible conduct, or the utterance
blasphemous language in a public place, is a breach of the peace; State
Matthews, 42 Vt. 542, holding that several acts mentioned in statute cons
tute modes of committing one offense, that of breach of peace.

Cited in note in 90 A. S. R. 800, on security against breach of peace.

What constitutes a criminal assault.

Cited in Balkum v. State, 40 Ala. 671, holding that to compel one to gi
up his gun through fear of bodily harm, reasonably excited in his mind
conduct of prisoner, is an assault; State v. Shepard, 10 Iowa, 126, holding th
pointing a gun which is not loaded in a threatening manner at another cons
tutes an assault, when party at whom it is pointed does not know and has
reason to believe it is not loaded.

Disapproved in Chapman v. State, 78 Ala. 463, 56 A. R. 42, holding th
presenting and aiming an unloaded gun at a person within shooting distan
in such a manner as to terrify him, he not knowing that the gun was n
loaded, does not constitute a criminal assault.

Threats of bodily harm as a crime.

Cited in State v. Herron, 12 Mont. 230, 33 A. S. R. 576, 29 Pac. 819, holding that, in a trial for an attempt to commit an assault with a deadly weapon, proof of pointing a gun at complainant in a threatening manner is sufficient without showing gun was loaded.

34 AM. DEC. 690, THOMAS v. DIKE, 11 VT. 273.

Suits by infants under guardianship.

Cited in Robson v. Osborn, 13 Tex. 298, holding that an infant may sue by his next friend notwithstanding he may have a guardian, if the guardian does not dissent; Stewart v. Sims, 112 Tenn. 296, 79 S. W. 385, holding that a ward may sue in his own name through his guardian as next friend; Lanier v. Chappell, 2 Fla. 621, sustaining right of an infant to sue by a next friend; Williams v. Cleaveland, 76 Conn. 426, 56 Atl. 850, allowing an appeal by a minor from a probate decree where taken by his next friend, where general guardian refused to appeal; Carlton v. Miller, 2 Tex. Civ. App. 619, 21 S. W. 697, holding that a writ of error may be prosecuted by a next friend, though a guardian *ad litem* was appointed; it appearing that such guardian had neglected to prosecute writ, but had no objection to its prosecution; Grant v. Anderson, 1 Tex. App. Civ. Cas. (White & W.) 76, holding that a minor may sue on a note made payable to guardian after arriving at majority, the guardian not objecting.

Cited in reference notes in 40 A. D. 593, on infant suing by *prochein ami;* 65 A. D. 65, on necessity of persons under legal disabilities suing by *prochein ami.*

In whose name suit by infant should be brought.

Cited in Baltimore & P. R. Co. v. Taylor, 6 App. D. C. 259, holding that action for injury to property of an infant should be brought in name of infant by next friend or guardian.

Right of infant who has avoided his contract for labor.

Cited in Lufkin v. Mayall, 25 N. H. 82, holding that an infant who has avoided his contract for labor on the ground of infancy may recover compensation for his services performed under it; Hoxie v. Lincoln, 25 Vt. 206; Patrick v. Putnam, 27 Vt. 759; Meeker v. Hurd, 31 Vt. 639,—holding that an infant may recover on a *quantum meruit* the value of services performed by him under a contract of service which he afterwards avoids, deducting any loss the employer may have sustained by the infant's failure to fully perform; Medbury v. Watrous, 7 Hill, 110, holding same where infant performed labor as part payment for the purchase of property; Forsyth v. Hastings, 27 Vt. 646, on same point; Danville v. Amoskeag Mfg. Co. 62 N. H. 133, holding that a stipulation for a forfeiture in a contract by an infant for services, in case infant did not give two weeks' notice before quitting, could not be enforced.

Cited in notes in 18 A. S. R. 621, on infants' contracts for services; 15 L.R.A. 214, on right of infant to repudiate contract for services and sue on *quantum meruit;* 40 A. D. 334, on right to recoupment on action for goods or services as dependent on whether contract is entire or not; 24 L.R.A. 233, on forfeiture of wages on part performance of contract.

Distinguished in Shurtleff v. Millard, 12 R. I. 272, 34 A. R. 640, holding that expense of resale could not be recouped against infant, who defaulted and sued to recover purchase money paid.

Liability of infant on executory contract.

Cited in Mauldin v. Southern Shorthand & B. University, 3 Ga. App. 8 60 S. E. 358, holding that an infant cannot bind himself by an executory co tract for necessaries.

Right of an infant to disaffirm a contract.

Cited in Robinson v. Weeks, 56 Me. 102, holding that, to enable him to cover back money paid under a voidable contract, a rescinding minor need n offer to return mere receipts taken therefor.

34 AM. DEC. 693, SWIFT v. DEAN, 11 VT. 323.

Levy of execution on equity of redemption.

Cited in Tudor v. Taylor, 26 Vt. 444, holding that an execution levied metes and bounds on a portion of mortgaged premises is void.

Estoppel to deny title of landlord.

Cited in Stedman v. Gassett, 18 Vt. 346, holding that where, after conditi broken, mortgagee gives notice to the tenant of mortgagor and demands re paid to him, and tenant remains in possession, the tenant is not liable to mo gagor for rent.

Cited in reference notes in 43 A. D. 269, on estoppel of tenant to deny l lord's title; 53 A. D. 421, as to when tenant is not estopped to deny title lessor.

Cited in notes in 21 L. ed. U. S. 780, on right of tenant to dispute lar lord's title; 1 L.R.A.(N.S.) 1182, on right of tenant who was in possession taking lease to dispute lessor's title; 15 E. R. C. 306, on estoppel of tenant question landlord's title where he was in possession at execution of lease; A. D. 69, on acceptance of lease by one in possession from one claiming title creating estoppel to deny claimant's title.

Distinguished in Franklin v. Merida, 35 Cal. 558, 95 A. D. 129, holding th tenant is not estopped where he was in possession when he took lease; Con gational Soc. v. Walker, 18 Vt. 600, holding that a tenant from a religio society in a town is not at liberty to question title of society.

—Acknowledgment of title or attornment by mistake.

Cited in Lakin v. Dolly, 53 Fed. 333, holding that where parties have act under a mistake as to the law in regard to the title, tenant is not estopped deny it; Pearce v. Nix, 34 Ala. 183, holding same 'as to an acknowledgme made under a misapprehension and mistake by one in possession under own equitable title; McDevitt v. Sullivan, 8 Cal. 592, holding that tena may show that an attornment was made under a mistake of fact; De Wolf Martin, 12 R. I. 533, holding that where landlord has conveyed his interest the premises, the tenant may show transfer was invalid, though he h acknowledged title of claimant, if such was made under a misapprehensio Tewksbury v. Magraff, 33 Cal. 237 (dissenting opinion), on exceptions to ri precluding tenant from impeaching title of landlord.

Cited in reference note in 60 A. D. 712, on tenant's right to dispute landlor title when attornment was made under misapprehension.

Cited in note in 89 A. S. R. 103, on validity of attornment to stranger.

Distinguished in Derrick v. Luddy, 64 Vt. 462, 24 Atl. 1050, holding th burden is on tenant to show that acknowledgment of landlord's title was indu by fraud.

Notice of conditional signature.

Cited in Baker County v. Huntington, 46 Or. 275, 79 Pac. 187, holding pa
put on inquiry as to real conditions of bond where total amount written af
names of sureties was only $7,000, while $10,000 was required by statute and t
sureties did not justify; State v. Peck, 53 Me. 284, holding that where bond
on its face complete and perfect, an agreement for the procurement of a cosur
before delivery cannot be shown; McCramer v. Thompson, 21 Iowa, 244, hold
that the erasure of the name of a surety who had first signed a note without c
sent of sureties signing, while his name was on the note, released the sureties,
condition of the note showing the erasure.

Validity of a bond not signed by all the parties required or named there

Cited in Hall v. Smith, 14 Bush, 604; Butte v. Cook, 29 Mont. 88, 74 Pac.
Middleboro Nat. Bank v. Richards, 55 Neb. 682, 76 N. W. 528; Ward v. Chu
18 Gratt. 801, 98 A. D. 749,—holding that where a bond on its face indica
that others are to sign it, it may be shown that bond was delivered on condit
that they sign; State v. Churchill, 48 Ark. 426, 3 S. W. 352, holding tha
surety signing a bond on the express condition that all named in the body s
sign is released if one of them does not sign; Allen v. Marney, 65 Ind. 398,
A. R. 73, holding fact that principal had erased name of a surety named
body of bond before delivery did not alter case; Pepper v. State, 22 Ind. 399,
A. D. 430; Sacramento v. Dunlap, 14 Cal. 421,—holding that where one execu
a bond, it is presumed to be upon the understanding that the others named
obligors will also execute it; Clarke v. Williams, 61 Minn. 12, 62 N. W. 11
holding sureties not liable where bond is delivered before execution by all
obligors; Cutler v. Roberts, 7 Neb. 4, 29 A. R. 371, holding that, under stat
requiring two sureties to a certain bond signed by but one surety, the sur
signing is not liable; Conegys v. Eversol, 1 Handy (Ohio) 24, holding that wh
statute requires two sureties to a bond, the presumption is that party first si
ing delivered instrument conditioned on procurement of another party.

Cited in reference notes in 40 A. S. R. 52, on liability on bonds not execu
by some of the parties; 79 A. D. 597; 85 A. D. 444,—on validity of bond
signed by all parties named therein; 50 A. D. 328, on effect of bond or note
livered in escrow to procure additional sureties.

Cited in notes in 82 A. D. 763, on effect of unfilled blanks in official bon
45 L. R. A. 345, on failure to perform condition as to procuring other signers
negotiable instrument as defense; 45 L. R. A. 336, on conditional execution
bonds of sheriffs, deputies, constables, etc., under parol agreement not to t
effect until signed by others; 28 A. D. 679, on validity of bond not signed by
who are expected to sign, of which fact obligee has notice.

Distinguished in Davis v. O'Bryant, 23 Ind. App. 376, 55 N. E. 261, hold
that the fact that a part of obligors whose names appear in body of an ap
bond did not sign is no ground for demurrer; King County v. Ferry, 5 W
536, 34 A. S. R. 880, 19 L.R.A. 500, 32 Pac. 538, holding that the erasure of
name of a surety and the substitution of another one will not release sure
who have signed bond, where bond when delivered was regular on its face,
obligee had no notice of change; Johnson v. Weatherwax, 9 Kan. 75, holding t
where the names of two sureties appear in body of bond, and one signs and
livers bond to obligee without restricting his liability, he is liable though ot
surety did not sign; O'Hanlon v. Scott, 89 Hun, 44, 35 N. Y. Supp. 31, hold
a bond of a tax collector of a school district not void because not signed
collector.

—Bond not signed by principal.

Cited in Weir v. Mead, 101 Cal. 125, 40 A. S. R. 46, 35 Pac. 567; People v. Hartley, 21 Cal. 585, 82 A. D. 758,—holding signature of principal essential to liability of sureties; Schiek v. Trustees of Schools, 16 Ill. App. 49; Board of Education v. Sweeney, 1 S. D. 642, 36 A. S. R. 767, 48 N. W. 302,—holding that a bond not executed by party who appears as principal is prima facie void; Ney v. Orr, 2 Mont. 559, holding sureties on an appeal bond from the judgment of the probate court, not signed by the principal who is named in bond, are not liable on bond; Novak v. Pittick, 120 Iowa, 286, 98 A. S. R. 360, 94 N. W. 916, holding that an incomplete bond unsigned by the principal can not be enforced against a surety unless a consent to such delivery is shown; State v. Hill, 47 Neb. 456, 66 N. W. 541, on necessity of principal signing a bond.

Parol evidence as to bond.

Cited in note in 11 E. R. C. 234, on parol evidence to contradict or explain bonds.

Burden of proving conditional signature.

Cited in Mullen v. Morris, 43 Neb. 596, 62 N. W. 74; Gay v. Murphy, 134 Mo. 98, 56 A. S. R. 496, 34 S. W. 1091,—holding that where a bond is not signed by one of the sureties named in the bond, if those who sign it would avoid responsibility thereon, they must show that it was delivered on condition that all should sign.

34 AM. DEC. 700, GILMAN v. HALL, 11 VT. 510.

Recovery on quantum meruit for part performance of a contract for labor or service.

Cited in Jordan v. Fitz, 63 N. H. 227, holding that, in contracts where the consideration is not entire or may be reasonably apportioned, recovery may be had for part performance, deducting the damages for failure to complete; Bedow v. Tonkin, 5 S. D. 432, 59 N. W. 222; Swift v. Harriman, 30 Vt. 607; Booth v. Tyson, 15 Vt. 515,—allowing recovery unless entire performance is made a condition precedent under the contract to do labor at a stipulated price; Kelly v. Bradford, 33 Vt. 35, holding same where there has been a substantial performance and not a wilful departure from contract; Viles v. Barre & M. Traction & Power Co. 79 Vt. 311, 65 Atl. 104, holding same under a contract to furnish electric power, where party has endeavored to perform in good faith; Merrow v. Huntoon, 25 Vt. 8, holding that on contract for labor not strictly performed according to stipulations of contract, laborer may recover stipulated price less the damage to other party by reason of nonperformance; Bast v. Byrne, 51 Wis. 531, 37 A. R. 841, 8 N. W. 494, holding that one who contracts to labor for a term certain cannot be required, after the expiration of the term, to make up for days lost during the term; Wilson v. Freedley, 129 Fed. 835, holding that the value of work done under a contract partially performed is with reference to contract price; Carpenter v. Gay, 12 R. I. 306, holding that before a recovery of *quantum meruit may* be had there must have been an honest intention to conform to contract.

Cited in reference notes in 81 A. D. 291, on recovery on *quantum meruit;* 43 A. D. 46, on recovery on *quantum meruit* where contract is partly performed; 56 A. D. 98, on recovery for services where work is beneficial to defendant; 43 A. D. 672, on measure of damages for rescission or prevention of performance of executory contract.

Cited in notes in 58 A. D. 622, on apportionment of contracts and recovery f
part performance thereof; 54 A. D. 479, on recovery for work and materials wh
not furnished in time or manner required by special contract.

34 AM. DEC. 702, GILMAN v. PECK, 11 VT. 516.

Effect of payment in notes of an insolvent bank.

Cited in Townsends v. Bank of Racine, 7 Wis. 185, holding that payment ma
in the bills of a bank which had failed is no payment; Pickett v. Pearsons,
Vt. 470, on same point.

Cited in reference notes in 34 A. D. 711; 75 A. D. 511,—on effect of payment
bills of insolvent bank.

Cited in notes in 37 A. D. 449; 10 L.R.A.(N.S.) 532, 533,—on effect of tran
fer without indorsement of worthless circulating bank notes.

— In worthless negotiable paper.

Cited in Torrey v. Baxter, 13 Vt. 452, holding that a debt is not released
the giving of a firm note executed by a member of firm after dissolution; Goc
rich v. Tracy, 43 Vt. 314, 5 A. R. 281, holding that the taking of a forged prom
sory vote is not payment.

Cited in reference notes in 75 A. D. 757, on payment in badly depreciated ba
bills as payment; 38 A. D. 290, on effect of payment in worthless or depreciat
bank bills; 81 A. D. 287, on payment in worthless bank bills not being valid pa
ment; 10 A. S. R. 619, on receipt of forged note as payment of debt or note whi
it renews.

Distinguished in Farr v. Stevens, 26 Vt. 299, holding that where vendee
property accepts the note of a third party as payment the debt is extinguishe
State v. Wilson, 71 Tex. 291, 9 S. W. 155, holding that the holder of state wa
rants, who sells them at a discount because of a delay in payment of the
cannot recover from the state his loss thereby sustained.

— Recourse on original debt.

Cited in Loomis v. Wainwright, 21 Vt. 520, holding that seller induced to ta
worthless thing in payment might pursue remedy as if no payment had be
made.

Implied warranty in sale of commercial paper.

Cited in Thrall v. Newell, 19 Vt. 202, 47 A. D. 682, holding that the assignee
a note vouches for its genuineness.

When action of book account appropriate.

Distinguished in Hall v. Eaton, 12 Vt. 510, holding that action of book accou
is not the appropriate remedy of husband to recover money paid by a marri
woman after marriage out of her own separate property, on a debt contracted
her while *sole.*

34 AM. DEC. 704, MOWER v. WATSON, 11 VT. 536.

Privileged communications.

Cited in reference notes in 69 A. D. 65, on privileged communications
slander; 32 A. S. R. 87, as to when slanderous words are privileged.

— Statements made in judicial proceedings generally.

Cited in Dunham v. Powers, 42 Vt. 1, holding that words spoken by petit juro
in discharge of their duty are privileged; Schultz v. Strauss, 127 Wis. 325, 1
N. W. 1066, 7 A. & E. Ann. Cas. 528, holding same as to words spoken durin

judicial proceedings of a grand jury; Cooper v. Phipps, 24 Or. 357, 22 L.R.A. 83
33 Pac. 985, holding same as to statements of a witness unless impertinent
the issue and false, malicious, and not responsive; Lauder v. Jones, 13 N. D. 5⁹
101 N. W. 907, holding same as to testimony of a witness which is pertinent
the issue; Clemmons v. Danforth, 67 Vt. 617, 48 A. S. R. 836, 32 Atl. 626, hol
ing one liable for words spoken in course of judicial proceedings, where he e
ceeds his privilege; Lawson v. Hicks, 38 Ala. 279, 81 A. D. 49, holding a reasc
able and probable cause to believe them true sufficient, where words are spok
in a judicial proceeding.

Cited in reference notes in 51 A. D. 135; 80 A. D. 741,—as to when wor
are privileged because spoken in judicial proceedings; 38 A. D. 143, on privile
attaching to communications made in course of judicial proceedings; 123 A. S.
635, on privileged nature of relevant statements in course of judicial proceedin
123 A. S. R. 636, on liability for irrelevancy as libel or slander in course
judicial proceedings.

Cited in notes in 3 L.R.A. 418, on privilege of written and spoken matter
judicial proceedings; 6 A. S. R. 826, on actions for slander consisting of sta
ments made on witness stand.

— **Words of parties or counsel.**

Cited in Johnson v. Brown, 13 W. Va. 71, holding that counsel or client
protected from liability for what he may pertinently say or write in a caus
Maulsby v. Reifsnider, 69 Md. 143, 14 Atl. 505, holding that slanderous wor
spoken by counsel having no relation to any subject-matter involved in caus?
trial are actionable; Hoar v. Wood, 3 Met. 193, holding that party or couns
shall not gratify private malice by uttering slanderous expressions which ha
no relation to cause or subject-matter of inquiry.

Cited in reference note in 81 A. D. 56, on words spoken by counsel in conducti
case not being slanderous, though spoken maliciously, if pertinent to case.

Cited in notes in 17 A. D. 195, on liability of counsel for words spoken at tria
7 E. R. C. 730, on liability of counsel for defamatory words published in cour
of judicial proceedings.

— **Burden of proof.**

Cited in Hartung v. Shaw, 130 Mich. 177, 89 N. W. 701, holding that, as
words in declaration prima facie privileged, it must be shown that they we
impertinent and in bad faith.

34 AM. DEC. 707, WAINWRIGHT v. WEBSTER, 11 VT. 576.

Worthless bank paper as payment.

Cited in Westfall v. Braley, 10 Ohio St. 188, 75 A. D. 509, holding that whe
payment is made in bills of a bank which has stopped payment, the loss falls
party making payment; Dille v. White, 132 Iowa, 327, 10 L.R.A.(N.S.) 51
109 N. W. 909, holding that loss falls on assignor of a worthless cashier's chec
Catlin v. Munn, 37 Hun, 23, holding that where payment for services is m
in certificates, there is an implied warranty that certificates are valid i
collectible.

Cited in reference notes in 42 A. D. 563, on effect of payment in bank no
38 A. D. 290; 75 A. D. 511,—on effect of payment in bills of insolvent bai
75 A. D. 757, on bona fide payment in notes of bank that has failed as discha
of debt.

Cited in notes in 27 A. D. 188, on payment in bills of insolvent bank; 37 A.

449, on effect of payment of obligation in bills of insolvent bank; 10 L.R.A. (N.S.) 531, on effect of transfer without indorsement of worthless circulating bank notes.

Distinguished in Cadens v. Teasdale, 53 Vt. 469, 38 A. R. 697, holding that one taking a note of a third person in satisfaction of a debt thereby assumes the risk of the maker's solvency; State v. Wilson, 71 Tex. 291, 9 S. W. 155, holding that the holder of state warrants, who sells them at a discount because of a delay in payment of them, cannot recover from the state his loss thereby sustained. .

34 AM. DEC. 711, EDWARDS v. EDWARDS, 11 VT. 587.

When trespass maintainable.

Cited in reference note in 76 A. D. 316, on owner's right to maintain trespass against sheriff and plaintiff in attachment.

— Possession sufficient to support action.

Cited in Thomas v. Ramsey, 47 Mo. App. 84, holding that plaintiff at time of trespass must have had the actual or constructive possession of the goods.

Cited in reference notes in 60 A. D. 390, on sufficiency of possession in trespass for taking chattel against mere wrongdoer; 69 A. D. 90, on title and possession of chattels necessary to maintain trespass and replevin.   -

34 AM. DEC. 712, WOODRUFF v. HINMAN, 11 VT. 592.

Contracts partaking of illegal consideration.

Cited in Cobb v. Cowdery, 40 Vt. 25, 94 A. D. 370, holding that if any part of the consideration is illegal, it vitiates the whole contract; Cotten v. McKenzie, 57 Miss. 418; Widoe v. Webb, 29 Ohio St. 431, 5 A. R. 664; Storer v. Haskell, 50 Vt. 341,—holding a note void where part of consideration was intoxicating liquors sold in violation of the law; Korman v. Henry, 32 Kan. 343, 4 Pac. 262, denying validity of mortgage of intoxicating liquors as conditional sale in violation of prohibitory liquor law; Dow v. Taylor, 71 Vt. 337, 76 A. S. R. 775, 45 Atl. 220, holding note void where part of consideration given was in contravention of the statute against fraudulent conveyances; Edwards County v. Jennings, 89 Tex. 618, 35 S. W. 1053, holding same as to a contract, part of the consideration of which was the creation of a monopoly; Hazelton v. Sheckells, 202 U. S. 71, 50 L. ed. 939, 26 Sup. Ct. Rep. 567, 6 A. & E. Ann. Cas. 217, holding same where part of consideration of contract is to procure certain legislation of Congress for a certain purchase of property.

Cited in reference notes in 40 A. D. 524, on contracts deemed void as against public policy; 73 A. S. R. 586, on validity of contracts interfering with enforcement of law; 31 A. D. 633; 60 A. S. R. 950,—on validity of contract in consideration of suppression of criminal prosecution.

Cited in notes in 31 A. 'D. 601, on contracts whose consideration is agreement to compound or stifle criminal prosecution; 117 A. S. R. 523, on enforceability of contracts compounding criminal prosecutions.

Distinguished in Shaw v. Carpenter, 54 Vt. 155, 41 A. R. 837, holding that where part of a stock of goods sold was intoxicating liquors the sale of which was illegal, a mortgage given to secure the price could be foreclosed for the amount of legal sales.

Questioned in Hynds v. Hays, 25 Ind. 31, holding that where illegal consideration can be separated from legal part, recovery may be had to the extent of the legal consideration; Pollak v. Gregory, 9 Bosw. 116, holding that test is wheth-

er plaintiff requires aid from the illegal part to secure his right to the legal,
not recovery may be had on such part.

Partial invalidity of consideration.

Cited in King v. King, 63 Ohio St. 363, 81 A. S. R. 635, 52 L.R.A. 157, 5
N. E. 111, holding that if one of two considerations for a contract is void merel
for insufficiency, and not for illegality, the other will support the contrac

Cited in reference note in 47 A. D. 424, on invalidity of entire contract whe
founded on indivisible consideration party illegal.

Cited in notes in 51 A. D. 344, on contracts partly illegal or void; 4 L.R.
157, on divisibility of contracts partly valid and partly invalid; 117 A. S. R. 49
on distinction between illegality and partial failure of consideration.

34 AM. DEC. 713, FOSTER v. McGREGOR, 11 VT. 595.

Sales valid without change of possession.

Cited in Daniels v. Nelson, 41 Vt. 161, 98 A. D. 577, holding that ru
requiring change of possession does not apply in favor of a state or town levyi
a tax.

Cited in reference notes in 42 A. D. 734, as to when retention of possessi
by vendor is fraudulent; 67 A. D. 560, on effect of retention of chattels l
debtor after their sale on execution; 39 A. D. 623, as to when retention
possession by vendor is fraudulent as to creditors.

Validity as against creditors of sale of exempt property.

Cited in Gilbert v. Decker, 53 Conn. 401, 4 Atl. 685; Leavitt v. Jones,
Vt. 423, 41 A. R. 849; George v. Bassett, 54 Vt. 217,—holding that sale
personal property exempt from execution is valid as against creditors of t
vendor without change in the possession; Jewitt v. Guyer, 38 Vt. 209, holdi
that, on sale of exempt property, no change of possession is necessary to prot
it from attachment by creditors of vendor.

Cited in reference notes in 35 A. S. R. 289, on fraudulent conveyance of pro
erty not subject to execution; 20 A. R. 150, on right of creditors to char
fraudulent conveyance of exempt property.

Cited in note in 87 A. D. 274, on sale of homestead under execution.

Fraud without injury.

Cited in Fellows v. Lewis, 65 Ala. 343, 39 A. R. 1, holding that fraud witho
an injury will not support an action; Kennedy v. First Nat. Bank, 107 A
170, 36 L. R. A. 308, 18 So. 396, holding that a claim of a homestead exempti
may be asserted in property which was conveyed to defraud creditors af
such conveyance has been set aside at the suit of a creditor and land declar
subject to his judgment.

34 AM. DEC. 714, GILMAN v. THOMPSON, 11 VT. 643.

Acquisition of jurisdiction generally

Cited in reference notes in 79 A. D. 443, on how courts obtain jurisdictio
95 A. D. 461, on acquisition of jurisdiction of person; 54 A. D. 243, on acquiri
jurisdiction of persons by their voluntary appearance or by constructive servi
of process.

Necessity of notice to personal jurisdiction of defendant generally.

Cited in Morse v. Presby, 25 N. H. 299, holding that, in the absence of noti
to defendant as required by law, a judgment will be voidable.

Jurisdiction over property.

Cited in reference note in 48 A. D. 320, on jurisdiction of court over prope within state.

— By seizure generally.

Distinguished in Schneider v. McFarland, 2 N. Y. 459, holding that, in proc ings for the sale of real estate, the surrogate must have jurisdiction of the per in manner provided by statute.

— By attachment of property generally.

Cited in Hodson v. Tibbetts, 16 Iowa, 97, holding that where jurisdict attaches by levy and seizure of property, subsequent irregularities will ren judgment voidable only.

Cited in reference note in 89 A. D. 658, as to when court acquires jurisdict in attachment.

Cited in note in 76 A. S. R. 805, on judgments depending for validity attachment of property.

— Effect of failure to give notice to attachment defendant.

Cited in Spaulding v. Swift, 18 Vt. 214, holding that a judgment obtained attachment is not a nullity, though no notice is given to defendant; Kittre v. Emerson, 15 N. H. 227, holding that the delivery of the summons is no p of the attachment which is made before the summons is served. ·

Cited in reference note in 82 A. S. R. 501, on necessity of notice of attachm on land.

Collateral attack on jurisdiction.

Cited in Kittredge v. Emerson, 15 N. H. 227, holding that where a court jurisdiction, its judgment is binding until reversed for error; Kittredge v. E son, 15 N. H. 227, sustaining the right of the state court to inquire into jurisdiction of the district courts of the United States to stay proceeding in st courts.

Forfeiture of an estate held by an alien.

Cited in Lenehan v. Spaulding, 57 Vt. 115, holding that state alone can enf a forfeiture of the estate of an alien.

Description of land in levy, return, or sheriff's deed.

Cited in Barnard v. Russell, 19 Vt. 334, holding that where starting point stated to be on a certain highway and at the northwest corner of a cert house, and the southwest corner was the only point that joined the road, co would correct the clerical error and substitute "southwest" for "northwest."

Cited in reference notes in 70 A. D. 318, on sufficiency of description in le 71 A. D. 308, as to when levy on land is void for uncertainty of description; A. D. 656, on sufficiency of description in return of execution; 38 A. D. on description of property levied upon under execution; 50 A. D. 545, on su ciency of description of property sold under execution; 50 A. D. 705, on sufficie of description of land in levy or return of execution or in sheriff's deed.

— By reference.

Cited in Childs v. Vallon, 5 R. I. 537, holding that description uncertain exc by reference to a deed as on record which is not in fact on record makes l void; Cutting v. Pike, 21 N. H. 347, on description in a levy by reference possession described by clear and definite limits.

Cited in reference note in 77 A. S. R. 410, on reference to record for descript of land.

Cited in note in 73 A. S. R. 165, 168, on conclusiveness against beneficiar of judgment against trustees.

Bar of limitations in cases of trusts.

Cited in reference notes in 54 A. D. 45, on applicability of statute of limitati to implied trusts; 51 A. D. 505, as to when statute of limitations runs agai trustees and *cestuis que trust;* 65 A. D. 413, on bar by limitation *cestui que trust* where trustee is barred; 36 A. D. 60, on effects on *ces que trust* produced by running of limitations against trustee in favor of th person.

Proof of gift inter vivos.

Cited in Jones v. Falls, 101 Mo. App. 526, 73 S. W. 903, holding that it m be established by clear and convincing testimony.

Cited in reference notes in 43 A. D. 320, on sufficiency of evidence to show pa gift; 67 A. D. 432; 32 A. S. R. 599,—on evidence to establish parol gift of la by parent to child.

Disapproved in Betts v. Francis, 30 N. J. L. 152, holding that transfer possession of household goods to son and furnishing his house presumes a gi

34 AM. DEC. 725, POWNAL v. TAYLOR, 10 LEIGH, 172.

Construction of deeds as to covenants or conditions.

Cited in Detroit Union R. Depot & Station Co. v. Fort Street Union Depot 128 Mich. 184, 87 N. W. 214, construing provision in lease as covenant, and condition.

Cited in notes in 44 A. D. 759, on validity of conditions subsequent; L.R.A. 667, on creation or declaration of trusts.

— Provision for support of grantor.

Cited in Helms v. Helms, 135 N. C. 164, 47 S. E. 415, holding that conveya in consideration of support to be furnished grantor does not create a conditi Lowman v. Crawford, 99 Va. 688, 40 S. E. 17, holding provision for care i support covenant and not condition subsequent; Campau v. Chene, 1 Mich. 4 holding deed providing for support of grantor, not stating that property deeded upon condition that grantee should support grantor, not deed up condition.

Cited in reference note in 58 A. D. 746, on effect of condition by grantee deed to support grantor.

Charge on land for maintenance.

Cited in Bates v. Swiger, 40 W. Va. 420, 21 S. E. 874, holding it valid thou no amount fixed.

Jurisdiction of equity to cancel deed for breach of covenants.

Cited in Fluharty v. Fluharty, 54 W. Va. 407, 46 S. E. 199, holding it has su jurisdiction; Carney v. Barnes, 56 W. Va. 581, 49 S. E. 423, on question jurisdiction of equity to cancel deed for mere failure to perform its covenan when there is no clause of forfeiture for such failure.

What constitutes breach of condition for support.

Cited in reference note in 75 A. D. 172, on what constitutes breach of conditi to support grantor or to pay his debts.

When instrument deemed recorded.

Cited in reference note in 94 A. D. 439, as to when instrument is consider recorded.

Adverse possession.

Cited in Bissing v. Smith, 85 Hun, 564, 33 N. Y. Supp. 123, as to nature of such possession.

Cited in reference notes in 47 A. D. 465, on evidence of adverse holding; 2 A. S. R. 744, on presumption of adverse possession; 36 A. D. 575, on presumption of adverse possession against one residing on land; 54 A. D. 395, on operation of statute of limitations against executor, guardian, or trustee of minor.

Distinguished in Layne v. Norris, 16 Gratt. 236, holding possession bound to be in defendant by special verdict in detinue presumed to be adverse, in absence of finding to contrary.

Title acquired by purchaser from trustee.

Cited in Sulphur Mines Co. v. Thompson, 93 Va. 293, 25 S. E. 232, holding that he acquires an absolute legal title; Wasserman v. Metzger, 105 Va. 744, 7 L.R.A.(N.S.) 1019, 54 S. E. 893, on invalidity of sale by trustee to himself and in violation of terms of trust.

34 AM. DEC. 731, MOSS v. GREEN, 10 LEIGH, 251.

Mortgage or conditional sale.

Cited in Robinson v. Farrelly, 16 Ala. 472, holding that, if the parties to an instrument, at the time of its execution intend it as a security, whatever may be its form, equity will consider it a mortgage; West v. Hendrix, 28 Ala. 226, holding that inadequacy of consideration, of itself, is not sufficient to convert an absolute conveyance into security for the repayment of money; Earp v. Boothe, 24 Gratt. 368, holding that, if object of transaction is loan of money, and security is given for payment, the transaction is a mortgage; Hollingsworth v. Handcock, 7 Fla. 338, distinguishing between mortgage and conditional bill of sale.

Cited in reference notes in 68 A. D. 370, on distinction between conditional sale and mortgage; 90 A. D. 351, on agreement to resell as conditional sale; 44 A. D. 124, on what amounts to and effect of conditional sale.

Cited in note in 50 A. D. 196, on considering transaction as mortgage instead of conditional sale in case of doubt.

34 AM. DEC. 737, TAYLOR v. COOPER, 10 LEIGH, 317.

Necessity and effect of confirmation of judicial sale.

Cited in Daniel v. Leitch, 13 Gratt. 195; Kable v. Mitchell, 9 W. Va. 492; Childs v. Hurd, 25 W. Va. 530; Coche v. Gilpin, 1 Rob. (Va.) 20,—holding it is necessary; Childers v. Loudin, 51 W. Va. 559, 42 S. E. 637, on title of purchaser before confirmation.

Cited in reference notes in 24 A. S. R. 276; 66 A. S. R. 706,—on necessity for confirmation of execution sale; 73 A. D. 134, on effect of confirmation of chancery sale.

Cited in note in 51 A. D. 554, on necessity and effect of confirmation of probate sale.

Relation back of confirmation of judicial sales.

Cited in Jashenosky v. Volrath, 59 Ohio St. 540, 69 A. S. R. 786, 53 N. E. 46; Edwards v. Gill, 5 Tex. Civ. App. 203, 23 S. W. 742; Houston & T. C. R. Co. v. Bath, 17 Tex. Civ. App. 697, 44 S. W. 595; Lathrop v. Nelson, 4 Dill. 194, Fed. Cas. No. 8,111,—holding that as a general rule it relates back to time of sale;

Donahue v. Fackler, 21 W. Va. 124, on question of relation back of confirmati
of sale.

Cited in reference note in 69 A. S. R. 787, on title to rents after judicial sa
Cited in note in 29 A. S. R. 497, on relation back of confirmation to day
judicial sale.

Discretion to confirm or set aside judicial sale.

Cited in Berlin v. Melhorn, 75 Va. 639; Terry v. Coles, 80 Va. 695; Todd
Gallego Mills Mfg. Co. 84 Va. 586, 5 S. E. 676; Carr v. Carr, 88 Va. 735, 14 S.
368; Brock v. Rice, 27 Gratt. 812,—holding that court does not exercise
arbitrary but a sound legal discretion in view of all the circumstances; Stout
Philippi Mfg. & Mercantile Co. 41 W. Va. 339, 56 A. S. R. 843, 23 S. E. 7
on power of court to release purchaser at judicial sale or grant an abateme
in price; Hyman v. Smith, 13 W. Va. 744, on question as to when court w
confirm or grant resale.

Cited in reference note in 73 A. D. 134, on setting aside chancery sale on off
of advance in price bid.

34 AM. DEC. 739, McCLUNG v. BEIRNE, 10 LEIGH, 394.

Right of surety to subrogation.

Cited in Zook v. Clemmer, 44 Ind. 15 (dissenting opinion); Nuzum v. Morr
25 W. Va. 559,—on right of surety to be subrogated to security of creditor.

Cited in reference notes in 37 A. D. 458, on surety's right of subrogation;
A. D. 592, on surety's right to subrogation after paying debt.

Cited in note in 41 L. ed. U. S. 414, on subrogation of sureties.

— Surety for payment of judgment.

Cited in Johnson v. Young, 20 W. Va. 614; Buchanan v. Clark, 10 Gratt. 164,
holding surety entitled to be subrogated to lien of judgment creditor; Peirce
Higgins, 101 Ind. 178, holding that surety on an appeal bond has a right
be subrogated to the lien of the judgment appealed from and paid by him.

Cited in notes in 99 A. S. R. 508, on subrogation of surety on appeal bon
68 L.R.A. 536, on subrogation of sureties paying judgments against principals
rights and remedies; 68 L.R.A. 530, on subrogation of sureties paying judgme
against principals to collateral securities; 16 L.R.A. 117, on right of sure
who has paid judgment to enforce it for his own benefit in equity; 68 L.R.
564, on extinction of judgments against principals by payment by sureties whe
suretyship is created by separate contract.

Scope of lien of judgment.

Cited in Barron v. Thompson, 54 Tex. 235, holding that it operates upon aft
acquired land; Michaux v. Brown, 10 Gratt. 612, holding that damages
dissolution of an injunction against a judgment become as to the party obta
ing it a part of the judgment, and are embraced in the lien of the judgmen
McCance v. Taylor, 10 Gratt. 580, holding that it includes costs in court of
peals.

Cited in reference notes in 38 A. D. 455; 81 A. D. 281,—on extent of judgme
lien; 47 A. D. 319, on nature and extent of judgment lien; 81 A. D. 462, on li
of judgment against owner of equity of redemption; 95 A. D. 349, on attachme
of judgment lien to whole of debtor's estate at time of docketing.

Cited in notes in 39 A. D. 162, on nature of judgment lien at common la
93 A. D. 357, on applicability of judgment lien to after-acquired lands.

Remedy of judgment creditor when debtor has fraudulently conveyed land.

Cited in Taylor v. Spindle, 2 Gratt. 44, holding that he may maintain suit in equity for relief; M'New v. Smith, 5 Gratt. 84, holding that, upon setting aside a conveyance of real estate as fraudulent, at suit of a judgment creditor, the court can decree a sale of only one moiety of land to satisfy the judgment.

Subjection of property to liens in inverse order of alienation.

Cited in Harman v. Oberdorfer, 33 Gratt. 497; Whitten v. Saunders, 75 Va. 563; Brengle v. Richardson, 78 Va. 406; Miller v. Holland, 84 Va. 652, 5 S. E. 701; Sturm v. Parish, 1 W. Va. 125; Gracey v. Myers, 15 W. Va. 194; Henkle v. Allstadt, 4 Gratt. 284,—holding that parcels are liable to the satisfaction of the lien in the inverse order of alienation; Jones v. Phelan, 20 Gratt. 229; McClintic v. Wise, 25 Gratt. 448, 18 A. R. 694,—on right of contribution between several purchasers of several parcels of land covered by lien; Buchanan v. Clark, 10 Gratt. 164, holding that lands remaining in a debtor should be first applied to relief of subsequent alienees and encumbrances; Payne v. Webb, 23 W. Va. 558, on same point.

Cited in reference notes in 47 A. D. 93, on order of alienation of land subject to judgment lien; 47 A. D. 717, on order of application of lands subject to judgment lien.

Cited in note in 5 L.R.A. 284, on equitable rights of first purchaser of part of mortgaged premises.

Distinguished in Alley v. Rogers, 19 Gratt. 366, holding that rule did not apply in this case as the several purchasers purchased the land on same day.

Necessity of resorting to rents and profits of land before decree of sale.

Cited in Ewart v. Saunders, 25 Gratt. 203, holding it not necessary when none of the parties ask it; Newlon v. Wade, 43 W. Va. 283, 27 S. E. 244, holding that, under statute, a judgment debtor's real estate cannot be decreed for sale to pay the judgment liens thereon until such real estate has been properly ascertained, and it appears to the court that the rents and profits thereof will not satisfy such liens within five years; Rose v. Brown, 11 W. Va. 122, holding that court ought not to enforce judgment lien by sale of the land if the rents and profits of the land will satisfy the liens charged upon it in a reasonable time, unless consent to such sale be made; Cromie v. Hart, 18 Gratt. 739, on application of statute requiring inquiry as to sufficiency of rents and profits to pay judgment before court can decree sale of land; Werdenbaugh v. Reid, 20 W. Va. 588, on question of equity selling land of judgment debtor, when rents and profits would not pay debts in reasonable time; Horton v. Bond, 28 Gratt. 815, on necessity and mode of proving insufficiency of rents and profits when resort thereto is demanded.

Relation of appeal to original suit.

Cited in Bailey v. McCormick, 22 W. Va. 95, on whether an appeal is a continuation of original suit.

Damages on dissolution of injunction.

Cited in Jeter v. Langhorne, 5 Gratt. 193 (dissenting opinion), on right to recover damages allowed on dissolution of injunction for period during which appeal from order was pending.

34 AM. DEC. 745, HAXALL v. SHIPPEN, 10 LEIGH, 536.

Application of insurance money between life tenant and reversioner.

Cited in Culbertson v. Cox, 29 Minn. 309, 43 A. R. 204, 13 N. W. 177, holding that widow holding life estate in property was entitled to use for life of insurance money; Green v. Green, 50 S. C. 514, 62 A. S. R. 846, 27 S. E. 952, holding that insurance money collected by life tenant on a total loss by fire should be used in rebuilding, or should go to the remainderman, reserving the interest for life of life tenant for him; Bennett v. Featherstone, 110 Tenn. 27, 71 S. W. 589; Clyburn v. Reynolds, 31 S. C. 91, 9 S. E. 973,—holding that insurance money passes to remainderman, life tenant taking the interest thereon during his lifetime; Stevens v. Melcher, 152 N. Y. 551, 46 N. E. 965, on interest of tenant for life in insurance money; Brough v. Higgins, 2 Gratt. 408, holding, on partial destruction of insured building, either tenant for life or reversioner entitled to have insurance money applied to repairs.

Relation of policies of insurance to the realty.

Cited in Wyman v. Prosser, 36 Barb. 368, holding that they are not attached to the realty, nor in any manner go with the same as incident thereto by any conveyance or assignment.

Construction of policy payable to heirs.

Distinguished in Georgia Home Ins. Co. v. Kinnier, 28 Gratt. 88, where policy ran to "legal representatives."

34 AM. DEC. 755, HERBERT v. HUIE, 1 ALA. 18.

Liability of signer or indorser of blank bill or note.

Cited in Huntington v. Branch Bank, 3 Ala. 186; Robertson v. Smith, 18 Ala. 220; Decatur Bank v. Spence, 9 Ala. 800,—holding party who signs his name to a note in blank with the understanding that it shall be filled up with a particular amount, or used in a particular manner, is liable to bona fide holder who receives it in ignorance of the agreement; Bertrand v. Barkman, 13 Ark. 150, on question of rights of bona fide holder of paper fraudulently put in circulation.

Cited in note in 40 A. D. 87, on liability of person signing and delivering note in blank.

Distinguished in Nance v. Lary, 5 Ala. 370, holding one who signed his name on blank paper not liable as maker on a note written above it by a person who took the paper without right; Manning v. Norwood, 1 Ala. 429, holding that proof that person signed piece of blank paper and handed it to another to be filled up for sum of money, does not authorize the implication of an authority to seal and deliver it as the bond of signer.

Failure to charge jury as error.

Cited in Knox v. Rives, 14 Ala. 249, 48 A. D. 97; Williams v. State, 147 Ala. 10, 41 So. 992; Leigh v. Lightfoot, 11 Ala. 935,—holding that omission to instruct jury upon all legal questions suggested by the proof is not a ground for reversal.

Cited in reference notes in 52 A. D. 685, on neglect to charge jury on point on which no instructions were asked; 64 A. D. 393, on failure to give instruction not asked as ground of exception; 64 A. D. 87, on absence of instructions not specifically prayed as error; 49 A. D. 421, on effect of neglect to charge on point not requested.

Cited in notes in 99 A. D. 130, on erroneous instructions as ground for reversal

69, as to whether surety is discharged by creditor surrendering security or li
on principal's property.

Cited in notes in 51 A. D. 303, on holder's surrender of collateral security
discharge of surety; 115 A. S. R. 95, on effect upon creditor's rights agaii
surety, of creditor releasing securities or funds in his possession.

Effect of payment of note by surety upon securities.

Cited in Murray v. Catlett, 4 G. Greene, 108, holding that payment of note
surety did not discharge mortgage lien.

Sale of equity of redemption.

Cited in Powell v. Williams, 14 Ala. 476, 48 A. D. 105, on question of liabili
of equity of redemption to be sold on execution; Colby v. Cato, 47 Ala. 247, ho
ing that grant for security with power of sale left nothing in grantor which
might sell but equity of redemption and possession till law day; Gresham
Ware, 79 Ala. 192, holding rights of surety unaffected by mortgagee's purchase
equity of redemption under agreement that purchase shall not discharge mortga

Discharge or merger of mortgage.

Cited in reference note in 66 A. S. R. 92, on discharge of mortgage.

Cited in note in 99 A. S. R. 165, on merger of mortgage by purchase of equi
of redemption.

34 AM. DEC. 762, BOYD v. BARCLAY, 1 ALA. 34.

Illegal contract and rights of parties to same.

Cited in McGehee v. Lindsay, 6 Ala. 16; Corprew v. Arthur, 15 Ala. 525; H
v. Freeman, 73 Ala. 200, 49 A. R. 48; Overshiner v. Wisehart, 59 Ind. 135; N
Ewen v. Shannon, 64 Vt. 583, 25 Atl. 661; Morris v. Hall, 41 Ala. 510,—holdi
that neither can maintain an action on the contract.

Cited in reference notes in 36 A. D. 613; 53 A. D. 770,—on rights of parti
to illegal or fraudulent transactions; 30 A. S. R. 630, on rights of parties
fraudulent conveyances; 35 A. D. 39, on noninterference in favor of either par
to illegal contract which has been executed; 50 A. D. 261, on right of recove
by party who has to rely on illegal contract or transaction; 86 A. D. 339,
right of one to avoid his contract for fraud in which he participated; 44 A.
723, on right of party *in pari delicto* to enforce illegal or fraudulent contrac
42 A. D. 169; 67 A. D. 401,—on validity between the parties of sale in fra
of creditors; 62 A. D. 505, on validity of conveyances to defraud creditors
subsequent purchasers; 98 A. D. 791, on invalidity of contracts founded up
illegal consideration; 38 A. D. 583, on effect of conveyance in fraud of creditor
40 A. D. 117, on enforceability of illegal contracts; 56 A. D. 603; 50 A. S.
708,—on enforcement of illegal contracts; 46 A. D. 423, on unenforceability
contracts in violation of law; 86 A. D. 340, on fraud in obtaining note as defen
in action thereon; 56 A. D. 603, on recovery of money paid under illegal co
tract; 79 A. S. R. 729, on right to recover from third person money paid for on
use under illegal contract; 33 A. S. R. 837, as to when specific performance w
be refused; 49 A. S. R. 842, on specific performance of contracts fraudulent
to creditors; 39 A. D. 599, on who may impeach conveyance on ground of frau

Cited in notes in 82 A. D. 428, as to whether one can avoid his contract f
fraud in which he participated; 7 A. S. R. 587, on relief of grantor from co
veyance made to evade law or accomplish unlawful purpose; 3 A. S. R. 739,
grantee's right to lay claim to property on ground that conveyance to him w
in fraud of creditors; 99 A. D. 61, on defense against recovery of money c

lected on ground that it was collected on unlawful contract or for illegal purpose.

— **Contracts to defraud public.**

Cited in McGehee v. Powell, 8 Ala. 827, on rights of parties to contract to defraud the public.

Cited in reference notes in 34 A. S. R. 613, on invalidity of contract to procure legislation; 80 A. D. 680, as to when agreements to influence legislation are void; 61 A. D. 350, on illegality of contract whose consideration is to compound or to stifle criminal prosecution.

Cited in note in 66 A. D. 507, on invalidity of lobbying contracts.

34 AM. DEC. 768, WINSTON v. EWING, 1 ALA. 129.

Liability of interest of partner to individual or partnership debts.

Cited in Hopkinson v. Shelton, 37 Ala. 306; Wilson v. Strobach, 59 Ala. 488,— holding that interest of partner may be sold to pay his individual indebtedness; Andrews v. Keith, 34 Ala. 722, holding that sheriff having in his hands an execution against one member of a partnership may levy it upon that partner's undivided interest in partnership effects; McIntosh v. Walker, 17 Ala. 20, holding by analogy that interest of one of several joint proprietors in a chattel may be levied upon by execution; Monroe v. Hamilton, 60 Ala. 226, on liability of partner's interest for individual debts; Wiley v. Sledge, 8 Ga. 532, on question of attachment of interest of nonresident partner.

Cited in reference notes in 74 A. D. 291, on liability to execution, of partner's interest in firm property; 47 A. D. 319, on liability of partner's share to payment of individual debt, when firm creditors paid; 85 A. D. 642, on interest in partnership property liable to satisfaction of separate debts of partners; 59 A. D. 364, on respective rights of creditors of partnership and creditors of individual partners.

Cited in note in 46 L.R.A. 485, on what may be sold under levy on partnership property for debt of partner.

— **Garnishment of firm by partner's creditor.**

Cited in Moore v. Sample, 3 Ala. 319; Trickett v. Moore, 34 Kan. 755, 10 Pac. 147,—holding that what is due a partnership cannot be subjected to garnishment as a credit due one of the firm; Barry v. Fisher, 8 Abb. Pr. N. S. 369, 39 How. Pr. 521, holding that credits or balances of account due from third persons to a copartnership cannot be seized on an attachment against the property of a copartner for his individual debt; Seaton v. Brooking, 1 Tex. App. Civ. Cas. (White & W.) 585, on question whether interest of individual partner in partnership credits may be reached by garnishment; Conklin v. Harris, 5 Ala. 213, on question of debt due partnership being attached to pay debt of partner.

Cited in notes in 59 L.R.A. 378, on garnishment of partnership claims on contract; 57 A. S. R. 442, on garnishment of interest of one partner in debt due partnership.

— **Necessity of previous settlement of firm rights.**

Cited in Berry v. Harris, 22 Md. 30, 85 A. D. 639, holding that separate creditor of an individual surviving partner may attach, by way of execution, a debt due the partnership of which that individual partner was a member, for the separate debt of such surviving partner without showing the state of accounts between him and his deceased partner; Hoaglin v. Henderson, 119 Iowa, 720, 97 A. S. R. 335, 61 L.R.A. 756, 94 N. W. 247,—holding that individual interest of a partner in a firm debt cannot be reached by garnishment in a court having power to acquire jurisdiction of the partnership or determine the interests of t partners; Peoples' Bank v. Shryock, 48 Md. 427, 30 A. R. 476, holding that de due to a copartnership is not liable to an attachment at a suit of a creditor one of the partners, where the partnership is a continuing one, and where th has been no adjustment of partnership affairs.

Right of partner to sell undivided interest in firm.

Cited in Scruggs v. Burruss, 25 W. Va. 670, holding that one member of fi may execute a deed of trust on personal property to secure the creditors genera of the partnership.

Interest of partner in firm property.

Cited in Roberts v. Hein, 27 Ala. 678, on incapacity of one partner alone recover specific chattels from firm.

Interest taken by execution purchaser of partner's share.

Cited in Daniel v. Owens, 70 Ala. 297, holding that purchaser at sale partnership goods under execution against one partner acquires only the in vidual interest of the partner, subject to all the liens, encumbrances, and char which rested on it in favor of the partnership, its creditors, or other partne Dunklin v. Kimball, 50 Ala. 251 (dissenting opinion), on the interest acquired purchaser under execution levied upon partner's interest in firm.

34 AM. DEC. 771, FUQUA v. HUNT, 1 ALA. 197.

Suit by guardian in own name for benefit of ward.

Cited in reference note in 76 A. D. 306, on guardian's right to sue in his o name for ward's use.

Cited in note in 38 L. ed. U. S. 530, on appointment of guardians and th powers and duties as to personal and real property of their wards.

Distinguished in Newton v. Nutt, 58 N. H. 599, holding that guardian can bring suit in his own name on an account for the labor of his ward, it not bei a purely possessory action.

34 AM. DEC. 772, RHEA v. HUGHES, 1 ALA. 219.

Entryman's right on public lands.

Cited in McTyer v. McDowell, 36 Ala. 39, on question of nature of right.

Cited in reference notes in 44 A. D. 730, on possessory claims and improveme of settlers on public lands; 39 A. D. 460, on sale of improvements erected public land as consideration for note for their price.

Cited in note in 70 L.R.A. 801, on right of one who buys, or makes lawful en on public land, to improvements placed thereon by another.

Estates liable to sale on execution.

Cited in Doe ex dem. Cook v. Webb, 18 Ala. 810, holding that statute authorizi widow to retain possession of the dwelling house in which her husband dwelt n before his death, until dower is assigned her, does not invest her with such a le title therein as can be sold under execution at law; Elmore v. Harris, 13 Ala. 36 Lang v. Waring, 17 Ala. 145,—holding, under statute, equitable title not subj to sale on execution; Doe ex dem. Davis v. McKinney, 5 Ala. 719, holding th under statute, a title in lands which is merely equitable can only be sold for t payment of debts by suit in chancery.

Distinguished in Doe v. Mitchell, 6 Ala. 70, holding that where one has been in possession of land for several years, and made improvements thereon, the inference is that his occupation is legal, and he has such an interest as may be sold under execution; Land v. Hopkins, 7 Ala. 115, holding that inchoate legal title to lands may be levied on and sold under a fieri facias.

— **Pre-emption or settlement rights on public lands.**

Cited in Johnson v. Collins, 12 Ala. 322, on question of settlement and improvement on public lands, being subject to levy and sale under execution.

34 AM. DEC. 773, PRINCE v. COMMERCIAL BANK, 1 ALA. 241.

Necessity of proving incorporation of plaintiff.

Cited in Montgomery R. Co. v. Hurst, 9 Ala. 513; Walker v. Mobile Marine Dock & Mut. Ins. Co. 31 Ala. 529; Washington v. Finley, 10 Ark. 423, 52 A. D. 244; Meyerson v. First Nat. Bank, 30 Fla. 398, 18 So. 786; McIntire v. Preston, 10 Ill. 48, 48 A. D. 321,—holding that when defendant pleads general issue, it is unnecessary; Liberian Exodus Joint Stock S. S. Co. v. Rodgers, 21 S. C. 27, holding that where plaintiff corporation alleged its corporate existence, and defendant answered by denial on information and belief, the plaintiff's corporate existence is not in issue.

Cited in reference notes in 36 A. S. R. 103, as to when capacity of corporation must be proved; 40 A. D. 475, as to whether corporation must prove its corporate existence under general issue; 37 A. D. 505; 43 A. D. 465,—on necessity that plaintiff corporation show due incorporation under plea of general issue; 69 A. D. 83, on admission of existence of corporation by pleading general issue.

34 AM. DEC. 777, McRAE v. KENNON, 1 ALA. 295.

Acknowledgment of indebtedness as removal of bar of statute of limitations.

Cited in Jordan v. Hubbard, 26 Ala. 433, holding that an acknowledgment of an indebtedness and present willingness or liability to pay is all that is required.

Distinguished in Cunkle v. Heald, 6 Mackay, 485, holding that acknowledgment of a debt barred by limitations, casually made by debtor to a third person, and not communicated or intended to be communicated to creditor, is not sufficient to revive the debt.

Lightning Source UK Ltd.
Milton Keynes UK
UKHW020753261118
332983UK00013B/1465/P